A HISTORY OF MODERN DRAMA

A HISTORY OF MODERN DRAMA

EDITED BY

BARRETT H. CLARK

Author of *A Study of the Modern Drama, An Hour of American Drama, European Theories of the Drama, Eugene O'Neill, the Man and his Plays*, and editor of *America's Lost Plays* Series

AND

GEORGE FREEDLEY

Author of *Theatrical Designs from the Baroque through Neo-Classicism;* co-author of *Theatre Collections in Libraries and Museums* and *A History of the Theatre*

CONTRIBUTORS

MILDRED ADAMS · BARRETT H. CLARK
SAMUEL J. CITRON · ARTHUR P. COLEMAN
MARION MOORE COLEMAN · H. W. L. DANA
GEORGE FREEDLEY · JAN GRESHOFF
ALRIK GUSTAFSON · FRANZ RAPP
S. A. RHODES · HENRY SCHNITZLER
DOMENICO VITTORINI

A HISTORY OF
MODERN DRAMA

Edited by

BARRETT H. CLARK and GEORGE FREEDLEY

APPLETON-CENTURY-CROFTS, INC.
NEW YORK

COPYRIGHT, 1947, BY
D. APPLETON-CENTURY COMPANY, INC.

All rights reserved. This book, or parts thereof, must not be reproduced in any form without permission of the publisher.

6113-5

PRINTED IN THE UNITED STATES OF AMERICA
E-19413

FOR
EUGENE O'NEILL

Preface

A History of Modern Drama is the first attempt to outline on a broad basis the origin and development of what we have, it is hoped not too arbitrarily, termed the modern drama. Our objective covers those countries and language groups (wherever they may be) that have been influenced by the history and traditions of European civilization. As for the period treated, we look upon Henrik Ibsen as the symbol of the awakening of the modern spirit so far as it affected the dramatic products of those parts of the world which lie within the framework we have chosen to treat: the beginnings of the epoch date back in some cases a century, to the time when Ibsen was beginning his career.

Our field is too broad to permit any one person to treat it as we are convinced it should be treated, that is, by those familiar at first hand with the plays they write about and the conditions in the theater surrounding presentation of them. The mass of plays that any critic should see and read, and the critical and expository material on them, has become so voluminous that no one person could conceivably find time in a life's span even to acquire a superficial knowledge of them. It is for this reason that we have invited a small corps of specialists to join us in providing a far more accurate and illuminating picture of the subject than would otherwise have been possible.

Limitations of various kinds were necessary, even in an outline which, like the present one, runs to over seven hundred pages. First, our subject is drama, not acting, direction, production, or lighting; so far as possible we have all deliberately omitted consideration of matters which, in practice, are necessary parts of the many processes by which a play is brought to its particular form of life before the public. We believe that in view of the many works now available on such matters, there would be real danger, if we included them here, of losing sight of the plays themselves—after all, this book is a history of the drama of the time, not the processes whereby it is interpreted and set forth on the stage. The narrative that follows will therefore be concerned with only so much in the field of *theatrical* presentation as may be necessary to explain the plays themselves. It should be clear, for example, that the plays of Soviet Russia cannot be satisfactorily explained apart from the political and esthetic philosophies of such directors as Stanislavsky and Meyerhold. Except in particular cases, no attempt has been made to trace the ideas that have to a greater or less extent affected the thought and action of the entire world, and therefore its dramatic products.

To detach any function of mankind from its accompanying background in order to describe and analyze it, leads one inevitably to do violence to the facts of history as a whole; yet we plead that to study and describe any part of the history of man, to segregate it even to the extent of turning one's thought that way—let alone record it in black and white—is to do violence to the entire picture. Yet to record anything at all that must be separated from the context it is necessary to distort and therefore to mislead. We have, however, in this book, tried to report rather than to interpret; to expose and not to editorialize.

So far as possible we have sought to avoid bias of idea, of philosophy, of esthetic theory; and what is more difficult with a subject that so often reflects contemporary thought, to give a clear picture.

Although every writer who has contributed to this book has his own critical standards, and of necessity has made use of them, we have all tried to regard the phenomena in our fields as part of a vast picture of human endeavor, and to allow posterity to classify them according to such esthetic standards as may in the future come into being. To each writer has been left the decision when the "old" drama came to an end and when and under what conditions the "new" began. Broadly speaking, we have brought our record up to the date (end of 1945) when the manuscript was completed, though in some cases it was not possible, because of the war, to consult the records beyond 1940.

A History of Modern Drama is not intended, of course, to serve as basic source material for research students, though we call attention to the fact that a great deal of material is here set down for the first time: it is not a dissertation, but a record and guide for the general reader interested in the subject; a work for students, critics, and playgoers, and a reference book which, it is hoped, will serve as a basis for further study and enjoyment.

B.H.C.
G.F.

Contents

	PAGE
PREFACE	vii

CHAPTER

I. THE SCANDINAVIAN COUNTRIES	*Alrik Gustafson*	1
II. GERMANY	*Franz Rapp*	76
III. AUSTRIA	*Henry Schnitzler*	124
IV. ENGLAND AND IRELAND	*George Freedley*	160
V. FRANCE AND BELGIUM	*S. A. Rhodes*	233
VI. ITALY	*Domenico Vittorini*	318
VII. RUSSIA	*H. W. L. Dana*	370
VIII. THE DRAMA OF EUROPE'S MIDDLE ZONE		
edited by *Arthur P.* and *Marion Moore Coleman*		482

DRAMA OF THE BALTIC REGION 482
    Finnish Drama . . . . *John B. Olli* 482
    Estonian Drama . . . . . . *Elizabeth Judas* 485
    Lettish (Latvian) Drama . . . .
        Alfred Senn and *Marion Moore Coleman* 487
    Lithuanian Drama . . . .
        Alfred Senn and *Marion Moore Coleman* 490

THE DRAMA OF THE WESTERN SLAVS 492
    Polish Drama . . . . . . *Marion Moore Coleman* 493
    Lusatian (Wendish) Drama . . *Clarence A. Manning* 502
    Czech (Bohemian) Drama . . . *Marion Moore Coleman* 504
    Slovak Drama . . . . *Cyril J. Potoček* 513
    Hungarian Drama . . . .
        Edmund Vasvary and *Marion Moore Coleman* 515
    Rumanian Drama . . . . . *Marion Moore Coleman* 527

THE DRAMA OF THE SOUTHERN SLAVS 530
    Croatian Drama . . . . . . *Wayne S. Vucinich* 531
    Serbian Drama . . . . . . *Wayne S. Vucinich* 535
    Slovenian Drama . . . . . . *Wayne S. Vucinich* 538

TABLE		PAGE
Bulgarian Drama	*Victor Sharenkoff*	541
MODERN GREEK DRAMA	*Emanuel Athanas*	544
ALBANIAN DRAMA	*Nelo Drizari*	548
IX. THE NETHERLANDS	*Jan Greshoff*	550
X. SPAIN AND SPANISH AMERICA	*Mildred Adams*	558
XI. PORTUGAL AND BRAZIL	*Mildred Adams*	593
XII. YIDDISH AND HEBREW DRAMA	*Samuel J. Citron*	601
XIII. THE UNITED STATES	*Barrett H. Clark*	639
READING LISTS		741
INDEX	*Elizabeth P. Barrett*	761

CONTRIBUTORS TO THIS VOLUME

GUSTAFSON, ALRIK

Professor, University of Minnesota; author of *Six Scandinavian Novelists*, editor of two volumes of *Scandinavian Plays of the Twentieth Century*.

RAPP, FRANZ

Former Curator of the Clara Ziegler Theatermuseum in Munich; Member of the Art Faculty of Howard University; organizer of the German Theatrical Exhibition, Magdeburg, 1927.

SCHNITZLER, HENRY

In charge of Dramatic Art at the University of California; one of the founders of the Theatre Collection at the Nationalbibliothek, Vienna; collaborated in editing the first volumes of *Monumenta Scaenica*; former stage director in Europe and United States; son of the distinguished Austrian playwright, Arthur Schnitzler.

FREEDLEY, GEORGE

In charge of Theatre Collection, New York Public Library; drama critic for the *Morning Telegraph* of New York; author or co-author of *Theatre Collections in Libraries and Museums*, *Theatrical Designs from the Baroque Through Neo-Classicism*, and *A History of the Theatre*.

RHODES, S. A.

Professor of Romance Languages at the College of the City of New York; author of *The Contemporary French Theatre*.

VITTORINI, DOMENICO

Professor in the Department of Romance Languages, University of Pennsylvania; author of *The Drama of Luigi Pirandello*.

DANA, H. W. L.

For many years a university professor and at present connected with Harvard and other educational institutions; for years a close student of the modern Russian theatre and for long a resident of Russia; author of *A Handbook of Soviet Drama*; translator and editor of various modern Russian plays.

COLEMAN, ARTHUR P.

Assistant Professor of East European Languages, Columbia University; associate editor *American Slavic Review*.

COLEMAN, MRS. MARION MOORE

Editor of the *Bulletin of the American Association of Teachers of Slavonic and East European Languages*.

Both Professor and Mrs. Coleman have long been active both in academic and government work, have contributed a great amount of material to magazines and encyclopedias and have familiarized themselves particularly with the countries of Middle Europe.

OLLI, JOHN B.

Professor of Philology and expert on Finnish language and culture, College of the City of New York and Columbia University.

JUDAS, ELIZABETH

Ph.D. Columbia University; author of *Russian Influences on Estonian Literature*.

SENN, ALFRED

Professor of Philology, University of Pennsylvania, formerly at University of Kansas; author of many articles on Lithuanian and Latvian language and culture, and a Lithuanian-German grammar. Chairman of the Slavonic

Group, Modern Language Association of America.

MANNING, CLARENCE A.

Assistant Professor of East European Languages, Columbia University; author of many articles on Slavic and East European literature and culture, and of the book, *Ukranian Literature, A Study of Leading Figures*.

POTOČEK, CYRIL J.

Expert on Slovak origins and literature; author of *Saints Cyril and Methodius, Apostles of the Slavs*.

VASVARY, EDMUND

Auditor of the Hungarian Reformed Federation of America, Washington, D.C.; expert on Hungarian matters.

VUCINICH, WAYNE S.

Editor and publisher of *Slavia;* formerly in the service of the United States government in the Mediterranean area.

SHARENKOFF, VICTOR

Expert on Bulgarian matters, New York Public Library. Author of articles on Bulgarian literature; Editor *National Will*, of Detroit.

ATHANAS, EMANUEL

Member of Department of East European Languages, Columbia University, Teacher of Modern Greek.

DRIZARI, NELO

Teacher of Albanian, Columbia University; author of the only Albanian-English Dictionary.

GRESHOFF, JAN

Editor of *Harvest in the Lowlands*, anthology of Dutch literature in English; formerly in charge of cultural activities of the Netherlands Information Bureau, New York.

CITRON, SAMUEL J.

Director, School Dramatics Department, Jewish Education Committee of New York; formerly associated with Bureau of Jewish Education, the Hebrew Theather Alil, Central Jewish Institute, etc.; author of many Anglo-Jewish plays.

ADAMS, MILDRED

Associated with *New York Times Magazine* and Columbia Broadcasting System; author of many articles on Spanish and Portuguese drama; co-editor of *Lope de Vega* issue of *Theatre Arts*.

CLARK, BARRETT H.

Author of *A Study of Modern Drama, An Hour of American Drama, European Theories of the Drama, Eugene O'Neill, The Man and his Plays*, and editor *America's Lost Plays* Series.

BARRETT, ELIZABETH P.

First Assistant, Theatre Collection New York Public Library, advisor to the Library of the Players, and editorial assistant on Sobel's *Theatre Handbook and Digest of Plays*.

A HISTORY OF MODERN DRAMA

I

The Scandinavian Countries

Norway, Sweden, Denmark, Iceland, and the Swedish Language Drama of Finland

ALRIK GUSTAFSON

We have become accustomed to thinking of the Scandinavian drama in terms of its immediate and vital relationship to what we loosely call "modernity": its frequent preoccupation with social problems; its subtle, penetrating handling of character in terms of the most modern of psychological points of view; and its bold technical experimentation, basically realistic in its earliest manifestations, but later imaginatively employing symbolistic and expressionistic devices of various kinds. And no doubt it is in terms of some such concepts that the Scandinavian drama has made its most remarkable contributions to the modern drama in Europe and America. Ibsen and Strindberg, the two chief figures in the Scandinavian drama, are primarily significant in the history of the modern drama as bold and vigorous innovators, as dramatists who accomplished so successfully a revolution in the history of the drama that the whole of the European drama since their day has in one way or another felt the impact of their modernity. And yet, paradoxically, the modern Scandinavian drama had its origins in an essentially Romantic tradition. Both Ibsen and Björnson in Norway, as well as Strindberg in Sweden, began their creative careers in the theatre by composing an essentially imitative historical drama, which went back to the early nineteenth century, to such a romantic-historical dramatist as the Dane Oehlenschläger, for its materials and its primary inspiration. It is true that Ibsen came to modify the more purely Scandinavian Romantic tradition in the drama in terms of the critical pronouncements of Hermann Hettner's *Das moderne Drama,* and Strindberg's first important historical drama, *Master Olof* (composed 1872), broke with many of the traditions of the romantic historical drama; but the fact remains that both Ibsen and Strindberg began in the historical genre so dear to the Romantic tradition, and Björnson's early work was nearly all done under the sign of the current Norwegian National Romanticism.

The immediate reason for this apparently curious point of departure for the modern Scandinavian drama is that Romanticism as a literary program lingered rather long in the North, particularly in Norway, where it was intimately tied up with her national political aspirations, and in Sweden, where the brilliant tradition of her Romantic poets towered for many decades menacingly over any who might dare to challenge their literary eminence. It was not until the great Danish critic Georg Brandes made, in the early 1870's, his direct frontal attack upon a reactionary Romanticism (particularly in his provocative *Main Currents in Nineteenth Century European Literature*) that the pale, imitative epigon Romanticism of the mid-century was dealt a final death-blow in the Scandinavian countries. And by this time Ibsen was more than forty years of age, Björnson only four years younger, and both of them had been active on the literary scene for some two decades. Strindberg was still in his early twenties; but even his first work for the theatre was historical in its outward garment, though in its revolutionary inner spirit it was in most respects essentially modern. Both Ibsen and Björnson had, indeed, experimented in the late 1860's somewhat hesitantly with modern themes and modern techniques, Ibsen in *Love's Comedy* (1862) and *The League of Youth* (1869) and Björnson in *The Newly-Weds* (1865); but it was not until Brandes threw down the gauntlet to the Romantic tradition with his famous formula "literature must put problems into debate" and suggested that the Scandinavian countries, too long intellectually isolated, must open their windows toward the modern ferment of Continental ideas that Scandinavian literature broke definitely and finally with an imitative traditional Romanticism. The Scandinavian literatures of the seventies and eighties became in consequence a modern literature, alert and sensitive to every wind of modern doctrine, incorporating rapidly into its thought all of the most recent scientific ideas and philosophical speculations, and adapting its techniques in general to the more advanced realistic and naturalistic criteria of art.

Why it was that the Scandinavian countries rather than some other country of Europe should be the birthplace of the modern drama cannot be entered upon here. One can but call attention to the fact that, though there were some tentative leads toward a modern drama before the Scandinavians in both Germany (particularly in a play or two by Hebbel) and France (in some of the not very successful naturalistic experiments of Zola and his followers), it was not until the vigorous creative geniuses of Ibsen, Björnson, and Strindberg appeared in the North that a large enough body of significant plays was provided to give an overpowering impetus to the development of what we know as the modern European drama. Of the three Scandinavians most important in this development, Ibsen was the first to make his influence felt in a significant way on the Continent, and his influence has on the whole been more pervasive than that of any other Scandinavian, especially in the early phases of development in the modern drama of Europe. Strindberg's influence has been more apparent in the twentieth century, particularly since the First World War.

Henrik Ibsen (1828-1906) was born in the small harbor town of Skien, on the southeastern coast of Norway. His family was counted among the more prominent of the middle-class citizenry of the town; but when Henrik was only eight years of age his father was forced into bankruptcy and the sensitive boy, who even before this family misfortune had been not a little shy and retiring, withdrew still more into himself. Instead of taking part in the usual out-of-doors activities of the normal child, he pored for hours on end over old illustrated books that he found in the attic of his home, and he mixed with other children apparently little, except when he enlisted their occasional interest in a crude kind of doll theatre that he had created. Inasmuch as the circumstances of his family could not permit an education much beyond the rudiments, he was apprenticed, at sixteen, to an apothecary at Grimstad, a harbor village a short distance to the south of Skien. During the first of the six Grimstad years he continued to live much to himself, but later he came to mix with some of the young people of the town and even join in their social life. He was, during these years, however, in a constant state of revolt against the narrow bourgeois spirit of the town, and not infrequently this revolt found expression in poems and sketches which caricatured with little mercy some of the "solid citizens" of Grimstad. This spirit of revolt found also a broader, and less immediately personal, expression during the last Grimstad year in Ibsen's first play *Cataline* (published 1850), in which the young Norwegian apothecary's apprentice gave indirect but unmistakable vent to certain very real though only vaguely defined feelings aroused in him by events on the Continent in the revolutionary year 1848.

Though *Cataline* revealed little more of literary promise than an undeniable facility at writing rather rhetorical and bombastic verse and an interesting concentration upon the psychological problem posed in the character of the Roman hero of the play, it served as a means of bringing to a focus the young Ibsen's incipient literary ambitions; and in 1850 he found himself in Christiania, determined to seek a university education and prepare himself for a possible literary career in the future. His efforts to prepare himself for university entrance were only partially successful, and he never was actually enrolled in the University; but he identified himself with the student life of the day, and he wrote for student publications as well as for two liberal papers of the day, *Arbeider-Foreningernes Blad* and *Andhrimner,* the former a radical labor journal, the latter a liberal critical journal interested more broadly in general cultural trends and animated by an ironic, skeptical spirit in the manner of Holberg and Heine. In his contacts with the labor agitation represented in *Arbeider-Foreningernes Blad* Ibsen just missed arrest in July, 1850, when the leaders of the labor movement, Abildgaard and Thrane, were imprisoned. In the midst of these miscellaneous journalistic activities, however, Ibsen did not lose sight of his more serious literary plans. Though his play *Cataline* aroused no general interest among the Norwegian reading public, it received reasonably favorable attention at the hands of two of the important literary critics of the capital; and Ibsen was further encouraged when the Christiania Theatre performed in September, 1850, his one-act play *The Warrior's Barrow*. Unfortunately, however, none of these journalistic and literary activities brought him anything like an income, and had it not been for the financial assistance of Ole Schulerud, a former Grimstad friend with whom Ibsen occupied quarters in Christiania, he would no doubt have starved. As it was he was living on the very verge of starvation during the early months in Christiania. It was therefore that he accepted with alacrity an opening on the staff of the new Norwegian National Theatre at Bergen when it was offered him by Ole Bull during the summer of 1851.

Ibsen's duties at this provincial theatre were not from the outset very clearly defined, except that he was expected, according to the terms of the contract, to write an original play for the Bergen theatre each year, to be performed on January 2, the date of the founding of the theatre. Inasmuch as the theatre already had a kind of "director," the new member of the staff was apparently expected in a general way to assist him; and as time went on Ibsen took over most of the specific detail work connected with the actual production of the plays included in the repertoire. He carried out these duties conscientiously, if with little imagination; his diffident, very reserved temperament seldom permitted him to manage his relationship with the actors in an outspoken, positive manner. This reserved manner is certainly not to be interpreted, however, as apathy toward his work. The young stage-manager's mouth may have been tightly closed, but his eyes were open and his mind active; and he doubtless learned a great deal about problems of staging and the general mechanics of the theatre while he was in Bergen, knowledge which was to stand him in good stead in his later career as a dramatist. Perhaps the only two seriously unfortunate things about his theatrical apprenticeship at Bergen were: first, that the limitations of repertoire necessary to the work of a still half-amateur theatre introduced Ibsen a bit dangerously to plays of mere intrigue, such as those of the then very popular Scribe; and secondly, that the Bergen institution, being a theatre with a strong Norwegian National Romantic emphasis, necessitated Ibsen's almost exclusive creative pre-occupation with Romantic national themes in the plays he was to write for the annual Founders' Day performances.

It is true that Ibsen came to write two plays for the Bergen theatre—*Lady Inger of Östråt* (composed 1854, published 1857) and *The Vikings at Helgeland* (1857)—which reveal more than occasional flashes of real dramatic genius; but on the whole the six plays that he wrote while at Bergen represent but Ibsen's more or less brilliant contribution to the final hectic afterglow of a dying Norwegian Romanticism rather than the vigorous promise of a new, significant modern drama. And it is significant to note that even in the genre of the historical drama, a form so dear to the whole Romantic tradition in the North, Ibsen did not create his one undeniable masterpiece, *The Pretenders,* until 1864, a full seven years after he had shaken off the immediate influence of the local National Romantic tradition of the Bergen days.

Something of the difficulties with which Ibsen was struggling as a young dramatist in Bergen is suggested by the fact that the most sentimentally romantic of all the plays he wrote during these years, *The Feast at Solhaug* (1856), was his only real public success in Bergen. *Lady Inger of Östråt,* which despite its over-complicated intrigue rose to real tragic heights in its handling of character, fell flat with Ibsen's provincial audience in 1855, the audience that a year later was to indulge in an orgy of sentimental national enthusiasm over the empty but colorful pageantry and the facile lyricism of the ballad play *The Feast at Solhaug.* Such a lack of discrimination on the part of his local audience scarcely provided the restraints necessary to intellectual and artistic discipline for an aspiring young dramatist. Ibsen was not so flattered by the reception of such a dramatic bagatelle as *The Feast of Solhaug,* however, that he continued for long in the same manner. *Olaf Liljekrans,* in 1857, is the last play in which he uses ballad material. In *The Vikings at Helgeland,* appearing in the same year as *Olaf Liljekrans,* Ibsen turns for his inspiration and his story to the sternly tragic materials of the ancient family sagas and to the tale of the Nibelungs, instead of to the colorful pageantry of Romantic balladry.

If the good people of Bergen could not offer the critical atmosphere necessary to Ibsen's development as a serious dramatist, his own native instinct provided him even in these early years with a kind of vague inner discipline, and his reading of Hermann Hettner's discriminating and provocative *Das moderne Drama* during the first Bergen years suggested ideals for the writing of historical drama that served to maintain in him a healthy suspicion for the pitfalls of the traditional Romantic drama and the play of mere intrigue, even while he was partially indulging in the sins native to these traditions in the theatre of the day. Hettner's insistence that great historical tragedy must concern itself primarily with character rather than with mere intrigue had borne fruit even in these early Bergen years in Ibsen's creation of Lady Inger and of Hiördis (the latter in *The Vikings at Helgeland*), two characters of permanent dramatic significance in the galaxy of Ibsen's famous feminine rôles. Otherwise, however, not much that Ibsen wrote during these years has undeniable permanent importance for the theatre. Though they were productive enough years, they have provided us with no single entirely satisfactory drama, and most of the six plays written during this period represent at best only partially successful gropings toward really vital dramatic forms.

If the Bergen years were relatively happy and productive, but significant largely in the sense that they provided early apprenticeship experience in the theatre, the Christiania years that followed (from 1857 to 1864) were years of struggle and hardship and self-doubting years that found Ibsen for long periods of time quite incapable of regular dramatic creation. He had left Bergen for the capital in the late summer of 1857 because he felt that the larger conditions in Christiania would provide a better milieu in which to develop his creative powers; but he found himself instead becoming involved, in the years immediately following, in such a constantly increasing web of complicating circumstances that his inner life became sour and embittered and his creative urge became for a number of years seriously atrophied. He had come to Christiania with plans for a number of new plays; but these plans came gradually to be set aside while he indulged a rather curious penchant for sterile occasional verse and became hopelessly involved in some embittered journalistic controversy on theatrical subjects. Ibsen was apparently heading for a break-up. Finally, however, he pulled himself together, completing in 1862 *The Comedy of Love* and in 1863 *The Pretenders*. Both of these plays reveal a much more mature Ibsen than we have known before; and the first of them, in its vigorous satire on one aspect of contemporary life, may be said to provide the original point of departure for Ibsen's series of attacks on various social institutions which came to be the central strain in his work at least down through *An Enemy of the People* in 1882. In dramatic structure as well as in its central theme and its handling of character *The Pretenders* stands in a class by itself among Ibsen's historical plays. No longer does he follow the lead of Scribe in providing an intricate mechanical web of dramatic intrigue. The characters themselves provide the necessary motivation for an entirely natural complication of action; and the central idea of the play—the so-called King's Thought, "Norway has been a Kingdom; it shall become a People"— comes gradually to dominate the action of the play and provide at the last the necessary solution to the various conflicting dramatic elements. Though the play was written in prose, as was the case in *The Vikings at Helgeland,* Ibsen has freed himself completely in *The Pretenders* from the awkward archaisms of *The Vikings* with no loss of purely historical effectiveness.

In *The Comedy of Love* Ibsen handles the large abstract problem (frequently recurrent in later Scandinavian plays, particularly around 1890) of the relation between love and creative work, and the more concrete problem of the relation between love and the institution of marriage. In the first of these problems he was treading in the footprints of Romantic tradition, so far from the immediate practical modern scene that a conservative bourgeois society should have been little disturbed at the possible immediate implications of his thought; but when he broached the more concrete problem, the relation between love and marriage, and suggested by a none too delicate inference that marriage as conceived by society actually destroys love, then he was treading on dangerous ground. And his unhesitating, clearly indignant application of these ideas to a *contemporary Norwegian* society did not make the implications of his thought any more acceptable to the conservative Christiania citizenry of his day. The attack on *The Comedy of Love* was instantaneous, and almost unbelievably severe; never before had such a controversy been stirred up around Ibsen's name, and even that small group of "advanced spirits" on whom Ibsen felt he might depend for support defended the play only hesitantly and with numerous qualifications. The attack even took on a personal form, sinister gossip being circulated in Christiania that Ibsen was drinking heavily and that his own marriage was drifting toward the rocks. These attacks and insinuations infuriated Ibsen and left their mark on him for years afterwards. He was determined to leave Norway as soon as possible, but his condition of indebtedness forbade this for some time, and he remained in Christiania for a couple of years more. Meanwhile the success of *The Pretenders* in 1863 only partially placated him.

In April of 1864, he at last found himself in a position to leave Norway, not to return to make his residence there again until twenty-seven years later. The bitterness toward his countrymen that developed particularly as an aftermath of the publication of *The Comedy of Love* was intensified in the months immediately following Ibsen's departure from Norway by what he considered Norwegian (and Swedish) cowardice in not going to little Denmark's assistance in her hopeless struggle with Prussia and Austria for Schleswig-Holstein. This combination of circumstances was the immediate background of the two new dramas of indignation that Ibsen composed during his first years abroad. Two years after his departure from Norway he had completed the epic-lyric play *Brand,* a burning general indictment of the spirit of weakness and compromise which Ibsen at this time felt was so frequently the real content behind an outwardly boastful Norwegian national temper; and the following year appeared the dramatic fantasia *Peer Gynt,* a rollicking, expansive accumulation of satiric thrusts aimed primarily, as *Brand* had been, at the weaknesses of Norwegian national character, but including, in its intoxicating, capricious medley of satire, some telling incidental thrusts at other national types, those of Sweden, England, and Germany, and even France and America. Though neither *Brand* nor *Peer Gynt* was written for the theatre, they have on occasion been staged, *Brand* as early as 1876 by the Swedish theatre director Ludwig Josephson at the Christiania Theatre. Neither the difficulty of adapting them to the stage nor the unrestrained vehemence of their satiric outbursts seems, however, to have been a serious deterrent to their general popularity as reading dramas to Ibsen's Norwegian countrymen. *Brand* was an instantaneous success as a publishing venture, four printings appearing in the year of its publication. Never before had an Ibsen play enjoyed anything like this success. And *Peer Gynt,* also highly successful upon its original publication, has become with the years the great national poem of Norway.

Ibsen began writing *Brand* in narrative verse, but in this form composition moved slowly. It was not until he had dropped this form in favor of a loose epic-dramatic manner (apparently under the spell of the free, dynamic, highly personal manner of some of Michelangelo's work in St. Peter's at Rome) that his work went on apace. This was the ideal form for the severe Judgment Sermon which *Brand* was to be. It was the moral rigorism of Ibsen's indictment that provided such a profound challenge to the Norwegian people of the day. Here was a Jeremiad conceived in a massive heroic mould and expressed with such lyric variety and fervor that it affected all literate Norwegians of the day with a peculiar fascination and power. No Norwegian had ever spoken with such fervent and eloquent *directness* to the whole people; and none had elicited such a response as Ibsen was to get. Björnson, who had previously on the whole been very sympathetic to Ibsen's work, recoiled at first from *Brand,* insisting that the hero-priest's moral rigorism was unhealthy and spiritually dangerous in its uncompromising other-worldliness of spirit; and few, if any, Norwegians were prepared to follow Brand literally in his uncompromising "claim of the ideal." And yet the play, with all its ethical paradoxes, served at once as a moral purgative and a moral tonic for the Scandinavian peoples of the day, providing a rallying point for a newly aroused sense of ethical values which became the distinguishing mark of nearly all Scandinavian literature—Swedish and Danish as well as Norwegian—during the immediately ensuing decades. Though the rollicking, full-throated satirical laughter of *Peer Gynt* makes it a more acceptable play today than is the grim satire and the narrow though heroic fanaticism of *Brand,* the latter play left a much more profound impression on the literary conscience of the generation when the two plays first appeared. For better or for worse the spirit of Brand stalked solemnly down through most of the Scandinavian "problem literature" of the seventies and eighties. It may be said, I think, that Ibsen himself did not shake off the spirit of *Brand* until he wrote *The Wild Duck* in 1884, and this was about the time that the influence of *Brand* was reaching its height in Sweden. Even Strindberg, most violent and consistent of Ibsen opponents through much of his career, read *Brand* with avidity in the earliest days of his authorship and was undoubtedly influenced by it for a time.

The League of Youth (1869), the first play that Ibsen wrote after *Brand* and *Peer Gynt,* is outwardly as different from the two plays that preceded it as any piece of literature can well be; and yet the shafts of Ibsen's satire in this new prose play on modern politics are animated by the same immediate desire on the part of the author to judge in terms of a severe moral standard as is the satire of *Brand* and *Peer Gynt*. Its hero, Stensgaard, has been aptly called by one critic "Peer Gynt in politics," because of his adeptness in the art of moral self-delusion, particularly when under the influence of his own easy flow of rhetoric. Aimed rather directly at Norwegian political conditions of the day, the play aroused a flurry of indignation among some of Ibsen's countrymen, including his old friend Björnson, who felt, perhaps not without reason, that Stensgaard was meant as a partial caricature of himself. In Ibsen's general dramatic development the play is of little importance, except that it points the way toward the contemporary social reform drama in prose that Ibsen is later to develop so effectively.

Though Ibsen came to insist in later years that he was a creative artist rather than a moralist or social critic, one must certainly accept this distinction with some reservations. On the basis of the actual record of his work it would be more accurate to say that he was a creative artist *and* a moralist social critic. It is true that in the later phases of his work, beginning with *The Wild Duck* in 1884, he became progressively less the moralist and conversely more the objective student of human behavior, particularly in certain of its unusual, in some cases perverse manifestations; but nothing can be clearer than that Ibsen's work from *Brand* and *Peer Gynt* down through *An Enemy of the People,* a period of nearly two decades of crucial importance in his dramatic development, reveals a dramatist who is constantly concerned with ethical problems and usually prepared to state or imply an ethical judgment. In *Brand* and *Peer Gynt* the dramatist's moral indignation finds its outlet in a broad, general satire of society, particularly the Norwegian society of the day. In the so-called "social problem plays" that follow, the dramatist focuses more narrowly, in each case, upon some *one particular social problem*—in the case of *The League of Youth* on politics, in *Pillars of Society* on social falsehoods, in *A Doll's House* and *Ghosts* on individual morality versus social convention, and in *An Enemy of the People* on the practical evils resulting inevitably from the abuse of majority rule.

Ibsen came in these plays to be the great master of the social-problem play; and yet the first of these plays that attracted fairly widespread attention, *Pillars of Society* (1877), was antedated by at least two plays of the same general type by Björnson. *The League of Youth* had, indeed, preceded these Björnson plays by some years; but instead of immediately following up the lead of *The League of Youth,* Ibsen turned in the years after 1869 to a couple of quite different literary tasks, a collected edition of his poems, which appeared in 1871, and the composition of his massive ten-act ethico-philosophical drama *Emperor and Galilean,* published late in 1873. When he turned again to the contemporary social-problem play with *Pillars of Society* in 1877, he was prepared to continue with this type through the four purely social-problem plays which brought him a European reputation. Perhaps Björnson's success with this type of play encouraged Ibsen to take it up again and perfect it.

Though each of Ibsen's social-problem plays deals with a different immediate problem, they are all related to each other in more ways than in their common ethical origins. First of all, each of them deals with the general problem, so characteristic of late nineteenth-century thought, of the relation between the individual and society; and in them Ibsen invariably champions the right of the individual as over against what he considers certain outmoded social traditions and mores. Secondly, each of these plays is organically tied up to the play that immediately precedes it, usually in the sense that its central theme grows more or less directly out of some secondary theme of the preceding play. In *Ghosts,* for instance, Ibsen wishes to demonstrate what happens when Mrs. Alving *does* submit to social convention in contrast to Nora's refusal to submit in *A Doll's House.*

It is perhaps in the matter of dramatic technique, however, that Ibsen makes his greatest contribution to the development of the modern European drama in these plays. Having determined to use modern social problems as the materials of his plays, he saw, with Björnson and others of the day, the necessity of using everyday, idiomatic prose as the appropriate form of his dialogue. He had, indeed, experimented with prose before this, even in two of the early historical dramas; but the three so-called "dramas of indignation" which preceded the social-reform plays proper were all written in poetic form. But after *Peer Gynt* Ibsen employs prose only in his plays. The greatest technical advance, however, in the new social-problem plays is certainly to be found in Ibsen's perfecting of what critics have variously called "the play of ripe circumstance" or "the drama of retrospective analysis," that is, Ibsen's regular practice (from *Pillars of Society* on) of beginning the action of the play in the midst of a crisis, which invariably resolves itself with swift dramatic power, meanwhile revealing naturally in the course of the dialogue the whole web of circumstance leading up to and determining the nature of the crisis. Besides permitting the dramatist, as he gains complete mastery of his technique, to dispense with all of the old theatrical tricks of the "well-made play" (such as the monologue, the aside, the stage whisper, and the raisonneur), the drama of retrospective analysis provided the possibility of a firm, tightly knit construction which increases tremendously the dramatic intensity of the play.

Though these plays were "problem plays," concerned in the last analysis with ideas in their practical application to situations in life, they never descended to the level of mere pamphleteering. Ibsen always succeeded in vivifying his ideas by means of a marvelously skilful embodiment of these ideas in characters almost invariably vital and alive. An examination of the material in the volume of Archer's translations entitled *From Ibsen's Workshop* suggests how Ibsen managed to do this so effectively. These materials reveal that the point of creative inception of an Ibsen play was almost invariably an idea, usually an ethical formula of some kind. With this in mind Ibsen made a choice of characters and sketched a "plot," whereupon he wrote rather rapidly a first draft of the play. Frequently, however, the manuscript finally submitted for publication (usually a third draft) differed rather markedly from the first draft, though not so much in the central idea as in the conception of character finally arrived at. His characters became with successive new drafts and revisions more complex, more alive, less rigidly the mouthpiece of an idea the farther Ibsen's creative processes receded from the ethical formula which formed the original basis of the play. This explains why, not infrequently, what seems to be the central idea in an Ibsen play is not always entirely consistent with the actual characters who are apparently intended to represent the idea. Nora, for instance, in *A Doll's House,* with her petty, all-too-human weaknesses, her childish vanity and her tendency to play a bit loosely with facts, is not always consistent with the high ethical program that she comes to preach in the course of the play.

The play *Pillars of Society,* which introduced in 1877 the series of social-problem plays, is in most respects typical in both theme and technical innovations, of these plays, though one notes not infrequently in it artificial elements of intrigue in the manner of Scribe, and the "happy ending" is scarcely suitable to modern taste nor entirely consistent with what seems to be the satiric intent of the author. *A Doll's House,* on the other hand, is thoroughly typical of this group of plays. It is the classical literary expression of the theme of "women's rights," so characteristic of the advanced thought of the day; and its ending, unlike that of *Pillars of Society,* carries the central theme of the play to its inevitable logical conclusion. A morality based quite frankly upon individual rights as opposed to social convention triumphs in the end. The dialogue is reasonably spontaneous and natural, the characters alive and on the whole convincing. The few touches of mechanical intrigue which may be discerned by the discriminating reader are not apt to disturb one seriously, and certainly they have not interfered with the success of the play on the stage. The bits of melodrama scattered through the play and the somewhat stilted closing scene are more disturbing, and have led to a number of ingenious interpretations partly designed to make them more palatable to modern taste. Considerations of space unfortunately forbid us to take up these interpretations here. It should perhaps be recorded as one of the curiosities of literary history that the ending of *A Doll's House,* with Nora deliberately leaving her husband and children, shocked Ibsen's contemporaries not a little, even though the play fascinated them to the extent that it was immediately upon publication performed (sometimes with a ridiculously garbled ending) on nearly all of the major stages of the day, in Germany as well as in all of the Scandinavian countries. It was Ibsen's first great European success.

If *A Doll's House* shocked Ibsen's contemporaries and provoked endless discussion, *Ghosts,* which followed, both horrified and infuriated them, and led to almost universal condemnation of the author. The reason for this condemnation lay perhaps primarily in what seems to have been a faulty interpretation of the play. Ibsen's contemporaries almost without exception considered Oswald, rather than Mrs. Alving, his mother, the central character of the play, and accused Ibsen, therefore, of indulging primarily in a grossly indelicate physiological-clinical study in degenerate heredity. Later critics have come to see, however, that Oswald is in reality incidental to the purposes of the dramatist, and that Mrs. Alving, with her fearfully baffling *ethical* problem, is the central tragic figure of the play. It may be admitted that Ibsen indulges in this play in what some call "indelicacies," that he has more than enough commerce with the gruesome and with a strain of grimly grotesque humor, that the ending comes dangerously close to sheer melodrama; but all of this is incidental rather than central—the scenes in which Mrs. Alving appears are by and large invested with the note of high tragedy in the old Greek sense and arouse our sympathy in a manner consistent with the greatest traditions of pure tragedy, even though Ibsen's play may employ a modern scientific form of Nemesis. It is in the double symbolism of the play, expressed so clearly by Mrs. Alving, that we find its profoundly tragic meaning:

Ghosts! When I heard Regina and Oswald in there, it was just like seeing ghosts before my eyes. I am half inclined to think we are all ghosts, Mr. Manders. It is not only what we have inherited from our fathers and mothers that exists again in us, but all sorts of old dead ideas, and all kinds of old dead beliefs and things of that kind. They are not actually alive in us; but they are dormant, all the same, and we can never be rid of them. Whenever I take up a newspaper and read it, I fancy I see ghosts creeping between the lines. There must be ghosts all over the world. They must be countless as the grains of the sands, it seems to me. And we are so miserably afraid of the light, all of us.

These words of Mrs. Alving's provide an attack upon society the implications of which are worlds removed from a mere study in degenerate heredity. They lift the play above a mere consideration of the operations of natural law up to the whole superstructure of ethical concepts and human society with reference to such concepts. Too often, Ibsen suggests in this play, society's formulation of these concepts is but a lifeless, meaningless form, causing untold suffering and much human tragedy. It is clear from the play that society is directly responsible for the tragedy of Mrs. Alving. Ibsen's "individualism," so uncompromisingly expressed in the earlier *A Doll's House,* has been applied with even more devastating effect in *Ghosts*. It seems in this new play to have in it the final disruptive elements of anarchism. No wonder even some of the more liberal, democratic groups in the society of the day were dismayed.

Not since the unhappy reception of *A Comedy of Love* had Ibsen been so aroused as he was by the torrent of criticism heaped upon *Ghosts;* and he replied to his critics, within a year, with another play, *An Enemy of the People*. This play is certainly not to be considered among Ibsen's best. Its satire, broad, at times even burlesque in manner, is directed at rather obvious targets; and its characters—with the single remarkable exception of Dr. Stockmann—are either wooden or superficially sketched. The theme of the play—"the strongest man in the world is he who stands most alone"—

is an interesting enough paradox in the challenge that it lays down to the claims of majority rule; and yet it is perhaps not entirely convincing because of the at least partial fatuity of the boyishly lovable Dr. Stockmann who gives expression to it. The good doctor is in himself, however, one of Ibsen's undeniable triumphs in humorous characterization; he ranks as such with the young Peer Gynt, the Peer we know from the first three acts of *Peer Gynt,* before the tarnishing exigencies of foreign residence and shady business activities had tempered the utterly irrepressible buoyancy of his youthful spirit.

That Dr. Stockmann's motives are on the whole noble, no one can deny; and that he is prepared to sacrifice all for the ideal is equally undeniable. In these respects he certainly differs from the young Peer Gynt. And yet the boyish ebullience of spirit with which Stockmann goes to the attack against society in *An Enemy of the People* is definitely reminiscent of the youthful Peer Gynt in admittedly less responsible circumstances. For a man of Stockmann's responsible official position, indeed, the good doctor brings his weapons into the fray with a nobly half-blind impulsiveness that delights our purely comic sense even while it causes us to make pause in coming to a final judgment on his adequacy as a vehicle for the expression of what seems to be the clear-cut theme of the play. In Ibsen's day, when the theme may have had a more immediate and obvious application than it does today, this disparity between character and theme may have been a more serious technical flaw in the play than it seems to us today. At any rate, as modern readers we are apt to be so delighted with the overflowing vitality of Dr. Stockmann, together with his impish love of battle and his numerous little human irrationalities, that we gladly forgive Ibsen a mere *technical* flaw in the construction of the play. *An Enemy of the People* is a rousing comedy; but this very quality suggests its limitations. Ibsen is not probing deeply here; he is simply giving vent to a boisterous flow of satiric laughter at the expense of certain obvious shortcomings in a society that had made a rather paltry fetish of the concept of majority rule.

In his next play, *The Wild Duck,* Ibsen plunges more deeply into the analysis of the human comedy, finding in it elements of profound pathos, if not actual tragedy, which had completely escaped his range of vision in *An Enemy of the People* and the plays immediately preceding it. "The spirits of Truth and Freedom—*these* are the Pillars of Society," Lona Hessel had reminded the penitent Consul Bernick at the close of *Pillars of Society,* the play which had introduced the series of social-problem dramas that come to a close with *An Enemy of the People.* And Ibsen had apparently proceeded in this series of plays on the assumption that truth and freedom were fixed moral entities, ethical absolutes incapable of compromise, always equally applicable in the solution of the whole series of ethical categories involving man in his relation to his fellows.

But suppose this is not so? Suppose that truth may be relative rather than absolute, that even a lie may at times be a necessary condition for satisfactory human existence? It is such questions as these that Ibsen's alert and probing genius begins to raise at the juncture in his creative development represented in *The Wild Duck;* and as Ibsen raises such questions the center of gravity in his thinking may be said gradually to shift from purely social and ethical preoccupations to a new, essentially objective *psychological* approach to the problem of human fate. He becomes increasingly interested from now on in a study of human behavior for its own sake rather than in human behavior as experimental material suitable for the application of a final moral judgment. And this shift in the essential content of his dramas is accompanied, quite naturally, by new technical developments in the form of his plays, particularly in terms of a constantly increasing use of symbolistic devices of various kinds. Studies in the intricate, fluid ways of human consciousness have a way of escaping the vocabulary and logical formulas suitable to the expression of normal ethical concepts, and so Ibsen is forced to employ symbols which may suggest by indirection certain thought contents where words and logical formulas frequently fail. *The Wild Duck* and *Rosmersholm,* perhaps the greatest of Ibsen's plays (with the possible exception of *Peer Gynt*), are saturated with fascinatingly provocative symbolic elements; and they owe much of their subtle power to this symbolism. In later plays Ibsen continues to employ symbolical techniques, though scarcely with the same consistent power, partly, no doubt, because old age was approaching (he was nearly sixty when he completed *Rosmersholm*) and he found it difficult to maintain the fine intensity of focus upon the human scene that he managed in *The Wild Duck* and *Rosmersholm.* The only later play comparable in power to these two is *John Gabriel Borkman.*

In stepping out of the clear, bracing atmosphere of *An Enemy of the People* into the dim half-vapors which float ominously here and there over the action of *The Wild Duck,* we seem to be stepping into another world, a world partly real and partly phantasmagoric. There lies over this play something of the eerie quality that haunts the scene of Maeterlinck and the Strindberg after 1900, though Ibsen never permits the eerie element really to dominate. We are definitely in a world of reality in *The Wild Duck,* and yet this world of reality projects itself at least partly into the world of make-believe. The characters, in their pathetic way, are certainly real enough, and they are clearly bounded by physical and economic laws operative in all normal human life. It is the very severity of these outward limitations, in fact, that provokes in most of the central characters in the play that half-satisfactory kind of day-dreaming that enables them to live relatively happily within these limitations. They have managed to create a kind of "life illusion" which permits them to ignore life's tragic implications. The "life illusion" that all of the Ekdals, with the exception of the practical-minded Gina, live by finds its central symbol in the play in a winged wild duck which Old Ekdal, father of Hjalmar, the head of the family, had housed in an empty attic room in the apartment in which the Ekdals reside. The wild thing, we are told, had adapted itself satisfactorily to the new environment, had forgotten its natural habitat, was in fact growing fat under these new circumstances! So it was with the Ekdals; they had also found at least relative happiness in a curiously circumscribed existence.

But this happiness, we come to know through Gregers Werle, is based on a lie. The Hjalmar Ekdal home manages to hold itself together economically because of the mysterious assistance of a "benefactor," who, it turns out presently, is the probable father of little Hedvig. Gregers Werle, the son of the "benefactor," feels called upon in the play to reveal to Hjalmar Ekdal the ignominy of his position in a home based on such a lie and to get Hjalmar to revolt openly against this false position. Unfortunately, the Ekdal ménage, and particularly its head, the egotistical sentimentalist Hjalmar, is scarcely capable of responding adequately to the heroic claim of "the ideal." They cannot live except in the illusion, paltry as it may be; and Gregers Werle, suffering, we are told, from "an acute attack of integrity," brings only tragedy into the Ekdal home by his misplaced, meddling truth-telling. Relling, the down-at-the-heel physician who serves as a kind of raisonneur in the play, points the moral of the final tragedy in these words: "Oh, life would be quite tolerable, after all, if only we could be rid of the confounded duns that keep on pestering us, in our poverty, with the claim of the ideal." These words suggest something of how far Ibsen has traveled in his analysis of the human scene since he created the character of Brand. That truth is not always a necessary, or even a desirable, condition of human existence is a conclusion which seems distinctly novel to the student of Ibsen's earlier plays. The human scene has now become to Ibsen somewhat more complicated than it was in the days when the relatively simple outline of an ethical formula suggested in the last analysis the limits of a dramatic action.

In *The Wild Duck* Ibsen had experimented, not unsuccessfully, with a rather daring combination of broad comedy and deeply moving tragedy. Though Hjalmar Ekdal ranks with Ibsen's great comic creations, the play as a whole contains a strong tragic undercurrent, which rises finally to the surface in the suicide of little Hedvig at the close. In *Rosmersholm* Ibsen has written a pure tragedy—the tragedy which occurs in human life when man's will is unequal to his vision. The two chief characters in the new play, Johannes Rosmer and Rebecca West, are people of marked distinction, in sharp contrast to the leading figures in *The Wild Duck*. Rosmer, middle-aged, son of an aristocratic old family, is a man of mellow culture and genuine refinement. Though Rebecca can lay claim neither to Rosmer's distinguished ancestry nor to his broad, sensitive cultural attainments, she is in her way a person of marked distinction and strength of will. It is her almost hypnotic power of will that has led Rosmer, by the time the play opens, to the decision to break with his conservative past and identify himself with the new liberal social and political currents that are finally gaining force in the society of the day. But Rebecca's will had also, by subtle, perhaps only half-conscious indirection, been the apparent cause of the suicide of Rosmer's wife, Beata. Of this latter fact Rosmer becomes only gradually aware as the action of the play progresses; but when he does so, his will to take an active part in man's struggle for liberty receives its death-blow, and with this the final tragic outcome of the play is inevitable— Rosmer and Rebecca together meet their death in the whirlpool in which Beata had earlier plunged. The play, in its broad ethical implications, represents the struggle between ancient moral tradition and modern intellectual emancipation, between the sensitive, overrefined, essentially Christian culture of Rosmer and the wild, instinctive pagan strength of Rebecca. Neither of these forces triumphs in the end; both Rebecca and Rosmer are destroyed because, in their cases at least, the forces at work in life are stronger than the human vessels that seek in their weakness to control them.

Ibsen had originally intended to call the play *White Horses* in order to bring into sharp relief the central symbolism of the play; but on second thought he eliminated this too obvious symbolism from the title, retaining it, however, as a central dramatic device in the body of the play. The White Horses symbolize that unconscious power which the Rosmer tradition exercises over all whom this tradition touches, first Johannes Rosmer himself, the immediate spiritual heir of the tradition, and later even Rebecca, who, while vaguely fearing the power of this tradition, manages at first to rise above it in splendid pagan revolt, only to become gradually affected and overwhelmed by it in the end. Never has Ibsen plunged more deeply into the secret recesses of human consciousness than in this play; not conscious will, but the slow, inexorable workings of subconscious and unconscious motivations determine final action in the working out of the tragic fate of Rosmer and Rebecca. The symbolism of the White Horses (and only to a lesser extent the symbolism of great natural forces, such as those of the Sea) is, in its irrationality, the appropriate artistic vehicle for the expression of the subtle, intricate interplay of psychological motivation that is the pattern of this subdued but powerful tragedy. Ibsen's symbolism has undergone a remarkable process of refinement since the crude allegory of *A Doll's House*.

After *Rosmersholm* Ibsen continues his dramatic studies of the hidden, mysterious ways of human consciousness, though scarcely with the same uncanny imaginative power as in *The Wild Duck* and *Rosmersholm*. Though certain individual characters and some details of plot and symbolism in Ibsen's later plays suggest something of the dramatic power of *The Wild Duck* and *Rosmersholm,* these later plays as a whole, perhaps with the single exception of *John Gabriel Borkman,* do not entirely satisfy. *The Lady from the Sea* (which followed *Rosmersholm*) is too abstract, too far removed from the plane of reality, and its symbolism, lacking focus, is on the whole too vague and dispersed. *Little Eyolf* (1894) is scarcely more satisfactory; its central male character, who is apparently meant to impress, leaves us cold, and his unctuous prating about "the law of change" is hardly convincing. An underplot not closely interlocked with the main plot adds to our sense of dramatic inadequacy in this play. The dramatic epilogue *When We Dead Awaken* (from 1898, the last of Ibsen's plays) arouses our interest chiefly as a more or less fascinating autobiographical document rather than as a living, vital drama.

Hedda Gabler, published in 1890, and *The Master Builder,* published two years later, are more important, though they can scarcely be said to represent the great Ibsen. *Hedda Gabler* has in it most of the elements of "good theatre," but we may be permitted just therefore to raise the question as to whether it is great drama. Nearly every great actress of the last half century has been attracted to the rôle of Hedda, but so have they also been to Sudermann's Magda, certainly not a character creation of first importance in the history of the drama. Theatre audiences are attracted to Hedda almost as much as are "the first ladies of the theatre"—and perhaps not *merely* because the average theatre-goer is interested in the great actresses in themselves. Ibsen has, it is obvious, created in Hedda a character so repulsive in her cold, clammy spiritual sterility that we are attracted to the phenomenon as we are to a poisonous snake—in spite of ourselves. Like the Rebecca West that we meet in the early scenes of *Rosmersholm* Hedda Gabler is a woman of no scruples; but, unlike Rebecca, Hedda is quite incapable of any spiritual growth—she is as inwardly empty and limited as she assumes her whole environment to be. Her reaction to life is entirely negative; she can be moved by no single noble motive. Ibsen may be said to have encroached in his creation of Hedda Gabler upon Strindberg's favorite ground, the creation of the thoroughly emancipated vampire woman; and he has, in his way, created a character quite worthy of the curious gallery of female half-men that is one of Strindberg's unique contributions to the theatre.

Among those late plays of Ibsen in which the dramatist becomes involved in certain broad autobiographical preoccupations, *The Master Builder* is together with *John Gabriel Borkman,* the most important, chiefly because Ibsen is less completely concerned with general ethical abstractions here than in such plays as *Little Eyolf* and *When We Dead Awaken.* It can scarcely be denied that Solness, the hero of *The Master Builder,* is deeply concerned with the moral consequences of certain acts in his past life, especially those originally motivated by the overwhelming desire which he had had at one time to succeed in his life work. But the modern reader of Ibsen's drama is perhaps less concerned with this ethical problem than he is with the purely psychological *results* of the unequal moral struggle going on in the brooding consciousness of Solness. Ibsen has in Solness created a definitely pathological character, hovering dangerously on the verge of a serious mental disorder. His half-perverse indulgence in practices of "salutary self-torture," his belief in certain forms of mental clairvoyance, in the evil power of mental suggestion, and his ready submission to the curious directives of the young, strangely fascinating Hilda Wangel—all this suggests a mental condition of a distinctly abnormal kind. The studies in strange ways of the human mind that Ibsen had begun in *The Wild Duck* are here given a new dramatic prominence. Critics have at times been disturbed, not without some reason, by what they consider superficial theatrical effects in the play, particularly the dénouement, in which Solness, against his own will, climbs to the top of the tower at the behest of Hilda, and falls to his death. But it is possibly not too far-fetched to find this scene quite understandable in the light of the pathological condition of Solness. And it is to be kept in mind that Hilda Wangel herself, as Weigand has suggested, is a remarkable case of arrested development quite capable of making such fantastic demands as the play depicts upon her chosen "hero." As to the rather dispersed symbolism of *The Master Builder,* it may be said that Ibsen has, by design or otherwise, left the symbolical elements in such partly ambiguous form that they have naturally been subjected by critics to a wide range of ingenious interpretations, most of which are plausible if not probable. Ibsen no doubt enjoyed the mystification.

The only Ibsen play from the 1890's that satisfies in almost every respect the most discriminating dramatic taste is *John Gabriel Borkman*. It is a drama of bitter, unyielding hatred, in which Ibsen attains a sustained intensity of dramatic action realized in none of his other plays, not even in *Ghosts*. The three central characters, Borkman, his wife, and Ella Rentheim, sister of Mrs. Borkman and the former fiancée of Borkman, are each driven to speak and act with an intense, consuming hatred. This hatred has its origins in events of the past. Borkman's career has followed something of the pattern of that of Solness in *The Master Builder*: he is a strong-willed man who has never hesitated to adopt any means, no matter how morally culpable, in order to gain his end. As a young man he had deliberately given up his first love, Ella Rentheim, and married her sister for money with which to establish himself. Later, at the height of his economic power, he had embezzled funds, for which he was apprehended and imprisoned. This has not, however, broken him. He has no pangs of conscience, as had Solness. In the massive self-sufficiency of his egotism he refuses to admit wrong-doing, he disdains bowing in submission to a society which he deems inferior to his own superior moral understanding. When we first meet Borkman in the play he is marching nervously up and down in the faded munificence of the great gallery in the ancient Rentheim mansion—waiting for society to come to *him*. For he is certain that the society which had "wronged" him during eight long years of preliminary detention and imprisonment, the society which later had ignored him for the eight following years, this society would eventually need him again, and then it would come and seek his help in its own helplessness. It is the colossal proportions of Borkman's egotism, the magnificent integrity of his delusion that impresses one. In the solemn intensity of dramatic progression in the play this delusion is piece by piece destroyed; and when it is destroyed Borkman's mind completely disintegrates, and he marches out into a bitter winter landscape to meet his death, meanwhile in a passionately lyric outburst of delirium giving a final tragically hopeless utterance to his dream of serving a society which could not understand either the terms or the sweep of vision that his service entailed. Only over his dead body do the two sisters, who down through the years had hated each other with such consuming hatred, find a kind of final reconciliation—"two shadows—over the dead man." The elevated lyricism of both concept and utterance in this closing scene is peculiarly appropriate to a drama so steeped otherwise in a subtle variety of deeply personal lyrical adjuncts which step by step prepare our minds for the final catastrophe. Not since *Peer Gynt* had Ibsen combined poetry and great drama with the success he has here. The general technique of *John Gabriel Borkman* is in sharp contrast to *Peer Gynt,* however, in its tight, closely knit, highly concentrated dramatic form. In the construction of the play Ibsen has managed with astonishing success to make the time of the action represented exactly correspond with the time employed in the actual stage presentation. The unity of time has never been more rigidly observed. Though both the haunting, recurrent lyricism of the play and its highly concentrated structure add much to our sense of dramatic intensity, it is Ibsen's intent focus upon the three central characters, with their deep-seated, consuming hatreds, that accounts primarily for the final tragic power of the drama. Motivation is not precariously *dispersed* here into a number of only partly related areas of the subconscious and the unconscious: one motive, that of hatred, is dominant, imperious, and it never permits itself to be checked by secondary considerations, by the less immediate interplay of only half-felt motivations. In this respect Ibsen's play reminds one definitely of the Strindberg of *The Father* and *The Dance of Death.*

Ibsen calls his last play, *When We Dead Awaken* (1899), quite appropriately "a dramatic epilogue." The play is of interest chiefly as a piece of dramatic autobiography, the last of that group of plays, beginning with *The Master Builder* and continuing with *Little Eyolf* and *John Gabriel Borkman,* in which the aging dramatist is drawing up accounts with himself. The central problem running through these plays, as a recent Norwegian critic, Francis Bull, has pointed out, is Ibsen's "anxious questioning whether he had chosen wrongly that time when he in the poem from the sixties 'On the Fells' renounced life's realities and sought rather the world of art." In *When We Dead Awaken* this problem is taken up more directly, however, than it had been in the other plays; and the symbolism of the play becomes therefore more tangible, more obvious, less vague and mystifying than it is in other dramas by Ibsen.

Though Ibsen may in the last years of his life have been increasingly concerned with whether he had chosen rightly when he turned away from life and decided to dedicate his powers to the single service of art, those who find in the theatre a fundamental manifestation of man's creative strivings are not apt to share Ibsen's doubt as to the value of his work as expressed in *When We Dead Awaken*. Many have contributed to the creation of the modern drama, but it is to Ibsen that must go the credit for first having seen new possibilities for the drama in a really significant, fruitful way. It was he who first among modern dramatists made of the drama a really effective vehicle for the expression of modern ideas, and it was he who developed and perfected a highly concentrated dramatic technique that dispensed with many of the artificialities of the older drama. Ibsen is significant also because he was constantly searching for still newer contents and techniques: after he had perfected the so-called "social-problem play," with its ethical emphasis and its natural prose dialogue, he moved on to a new type of psychological play, in which his probing genius, working with a subtly modulated half-symbolical art, has employed for dramatic purposes elements of the subconscious and the unconscious. It should perhaps be stressed, however, that even though Ibsen was constantly experimenting with new or only partly tried dramatic forms he was never an extreme revolutionary in the drama. As a dramatist he advanced gradually, step by step, only by degrees freeing himself from older dramatic traditions, and never breaking entirely with them.

In marked contrast to Ibsen in this respect was his Swedish contemporary Strindberg, a born revolutionary in life and in art, whose eruptive, violently volcanic temperament gave to the naturalistic drama in the late 1880's a new life and form and created in the closing years of the century a religious expressionistic drama which broke entirely with current dramatic traditions. August Strindberg (1849-1912) was born in what the Swedes call "the City within the Bridges," that is, that part of Stockholm which comprised the original medieval city built on the island now known as Riddarholmen. He just missed illegitimacy, his mother being married to his father shortly before his birth. He was only one among a constantly increasing brood of brothers and sisters—eleven in all. When he was thirteen his mother died, and shortly thereafter his father's former housekeeper became August's stepmother. One should accept with some reservations Strindberg's later depiction of the early horrors of his childhood existence, but there can be no doubt that he was a hyper-sensitive, abnormally nervous child, and that he found it all but impossible to adjust himself satisfactorily to his early environment. His father was a shipping merchant of a somewhat heavy temperament made more melancholy than he was perhaps by nature by some early business reverses and by his isolation from contact with near relatives who felt that he had married beneath his station in life. Both August's mother and his stepmother came originally from the lower classes and had marked pietistic leanings. The father not infrequently had serious disciplinary difficulties with the boy, while both mother and stepmother, given to favoring certain of the other children, failed completely to understand the boy, who yearned above all else for mother-love. When in later years Strindberg came to write of the first memories of childhood, he entitles the opening chapter of his autobiography (*The Son of a Servant*) "Fear and Hunger." Highly nervous from the very earliest years, he feared almost everything, above all the heavy hand of parental discipline; and his otherwise healthy growing body never seemed to get sufficient nourishment from a rather limited family table which had to provide some kind of dietary satisfaction for a very large family. In school the boy was more than acceptable in the subjects he enjoyed (history and natural science), although he was just short of hopeless in other subjects (mathematics and ancient languages); and for reasons primarily concerned with his inability to adjust himself to certain environments he attended three different lower schools before his university education began. The severe forms of physical punishment common as a disciplinary measure in most of the lower schools of the day, hard enough on ordinary boys, were a source of absolute terror to a boy of Strindberg's nervous constitution. Only the summers of his late boyhood seem to have been relatively happy, for these he, together with his brothers, was permitted to spend largely in a healthy out-of-doors life on farms in the neighborhood of Stockholm. But even then, paradoxically, he would frequently become homesick and long for a mother's presence.

If his childhood years at home and at school were unhappy, the years that followed were not much more satisfactory, though they provided a partial escape from the objectionable domination of his father. These years of late youth and early manhood (from 1867 to 1874) were spent partly as a student at Upsala University, partly at Stockholm in a hectic miscellany of activities, as private tutor and public and private school teacher, as a medical assistant, as a journalist and a member of a bohemian artist coterie of extremist radical intellectual leanings. Even the theatre was given a fling, when the young Strindberg, anxious to become an actor, was permitted to act in some very insignificant rôles at the Dramatic Theatre in Stockholm.

It was during this short period of an abortive apprenticeship in the theatre in the spring of 1869 that he came by reason of a curious accident to discover his gift as a dramatist. One day, during rehearsal, he was assigned a somewhat more important rôle than was customary in his case—and he made a fiasco of it. Driven to desperation by this he attempted suicide by taking opium, but the dose, instead of being fatal, left him merely in a highly fevered condition. As he lay the following day tossing on his cot with his head in a whirl of confused ideas and images, he became aware, gradually, of a curious process taking place in his mind—a little story from Topelius which he had recently read began to take on dramatic form, characters attaching themselves almost automatically to a central dramatic theme, the scene laying itself out clearly in all its detail, dialogue as if by itself finding its seemingly appointed place. Startled at the vividness of the unexpected phenomenon, and recognizing with only partly suppressed jubilation that this was dramatic *creation* that he was experiencing, he leaped to his feet and began putting down the material as it lay ready at hand and apparently in complete dramatic form in his mind. He had it all transferred to paper within four hours, read it later to some admiring friends, and finally submitted it to the Dramatic Theatre. This first play by Strindberg was not accepted for performance at the time, and no copy of it has survived; but the young Strindberg knew now that he wanted to be a dramatist, and he turned much of his energies during the immediately succeeding period to dramatic composition. Within the next three years (the fiasco at rehearsal had occurred in the spring of 1869) he wrote five plays, four of which (*Hermione, In Rome, The Freethinker*, and *The Outlaw*) were slight but reasonably promising dramatic sketches, the fifth, the prose version of *Master Olof,* composed in the summer of 1872, being the first really great play in the history of the Swedish theatre, though contemporary criticism was blind to its real merit.

Of the four plays preceding his first masterpiece *Master Olof*, two (*Hermione* and *In Rome*) were in poetic form, the other two in prose. Their chief interest lies now in the way in which certain themes tend to recur in them, the conflict between parent and child (usually father and son) and the conflict between opposed religious beliefs. Both of these themes grew directly out of the young Strindberg's own immediate experience of life. The last of the four plays, *The Outlaw,* is the only one that is still read today for its own sake. It was written in the fall of 1871, toward the close of Strindberg's second, and last, period of residence at Upsala University. He never found himself at home in this university environment, he was constantly in revolt against it. He despised most of his teachers and refused to adjust himself to what he considered petty and meaningless university regulations, with the result that he read intensively in the subjects that appealed to him and never took a degree. He apparently took little part in the general student life of the day; but he was one of the organizers during the early 1870's of a literary organization at the University called The Runa Society, which affected an interest in ancient Scandinavian life and encouraged its members to literary activity concerned with ancient Nordic themes. Strindberg soon came to be recognized as the only really gifted pen in this group, and it was in consequence of the encouragement of his fellow members of Runa that Strindberg set himself the task of writing a drama on an Old Norse theme, partly, no doubt, in imitation of Ibsen and Björnson, who during the fifties and early sixties had cultivated such material in the drama. The dialogue in *The Outlaw* affects not unsuccessfully the abrupt, laconic manner of Ibsen's *Vikings at Helgeland;* and the theme, the conflict between paganism and Christianity, is the same as that of Ibsen's early play *The Warrior's Barrow,* though the conflict in Strindberg's little one-act play is developed with greater dramatic tenseness than is the case in the more essentially Romantic lyrical play from Ibsen's youth. Strindberg's *The Outlaw* is undeniably, however, the work of a beginner.

One wonders if ever in the history of the theatre a dramatist has made such a sudden *leap* into creative maturity as the twenty-three-year old Strindberg did, not many months after the completion of *The Outlaw,* when he wrote the prose version of *Master Olof* in the course of "two quiet months of a regular, healthy existence" on the island of Kymmendö outside Stockholm in the Baltic during the summer of 1872. For the difference in essential dramatic quality between *The Outlaw* and *Master Olof* is nothing short of startling. *Master Olof,* like *The Outlaw,* is at core an idea drama; but in his new drama Strindberg has managed something far more than a skillful finger exercise in dramatic dialogue—he has created a complicated symphonic pattern, warm and rich in coloring, alive and natural in its episodic sequence, pulsing and diversified as is life itself. Strindberg himself has told us that he wrote *Master Olof* directly under the spell of Shakespeare's *Julius Caesar* and Goethe's youthful *Götz von Berlichingen;* and this undoubtedly accounts for certain of the technical qualities of the play— its looseness in general structure, its numerous, rapidly changing scenes, its multitude of characters, its not infrequent historical anachronisms. But the young Strindberg's reading of Shakespeare and Goethe does not account for either the basic idea of the play or for the concept of its central characters, Master Olof and Gert the Printer. Strindberg has chosen as the subject of his play the Swedish Reformation, with its sharp religious conflict between the Catholic Church and the new Lutheran doctrine; but he has superimposed on these historical materials certain revolutionary political ideas of a later, essentially nineteenth-century vintage. The historical anachronism involved in such a procedure has not, however, destroyed the effectiveness of the play. It has, on the contrary, added materially to its dramatic intensity.

In Strindberg's first sketches of the drama (composed at Upsala in the fall of 1871) he had conceived Olof as a character formed on the pattern of Ibsen's Brand—severe, forceful, uncompromising, and finally meeting his fate, as did Brand, because he was unwilling to adjust himself to the practical exigencies of the life about him. In the completed manuscript dating from the summer of 1872, however, Olof does yield to practical pressure; his tragedy is to be found in the fact that he at the last sacrifices his earlier ideals, submits to outward authority, becoming a traitor to the program of reform which he had earlier sworn to realize or die in the attempt. It is Gert the Printer, rather than Olof, who remains true to the uncompromising revolutionary ideal; and it is Gert who pronounces the final judgment— "Renegade!"—as Olof sinks down wearily at the foot of the pillory in the closing scene.

It is clear that Olof's final disloyalty to an earlier idealistic program of religious reformation derives from two sources: first, a fundamental, native weakness in his character, a constant vacillating between courageous determination and hesitating reflection; and secondly, a tendency to think in relativistic rather than in absolute terms. Olof's vacillating, overreflective character can be explained by the fact that Strindberg (by his own admission) has in Olof drawn a picture of himself at this time. The relativistic bias of Olof's thinking is to be explained, on the other hand, in the circumstance that Strindberg had been reading during the months between the first sketch of *Master Olof* and the final version Buckle's *History of Civilization in England,* which just at this time appeared in a Swedish translation. Buckle's suggestion that truth, and particularly religious truth, changes from generation to generation, that it derives from natural rather than supernatural sources, and that it therefore is relative rather than absolute, had profoundly affected the young Strindberg. In the play these ideas are given sharp expression in the dialogue between Olof, the young Lutheran reformer, and his mother, who had remained faithful to the Roman faith—

Mother. Perhaps I and my forbears have lived and worshipped and died in a lie?
Olof. It wasn't a lie, but it has become one. When you were young, mother, you were right, and when I grow old—well, perhaps I may find myself in the wrong. One cannot keep apace with the times.

It is scarcely to be wondered at that the Olof who expresses such a conception of truth finds at least an *intellectual* excuse for his late apostasy toward his earlier belief in the absolute rightness of his work of reform.

Though Olof, the religious revolutionary, finds reason to desert his early ideals, Gert, the fanatical political revolutionary, remains true to his original program of reform. If Olof was what Strindberg knew himself to be, Gert, Strindberg tells us, was what he was "in moments of strong, passionate feeling." This intimate identification of the author with his characters, together with the blending of older with more modern ideas, has given to *Master Olof* a note of warm, vital reality almost invariably lacking in the stiff rhetorical manner of the traditional historical drama of the day. Strindberg's contemporaries, however, found this an unpardonable departure from the elevated tradition of the historical drama when he submitted it to the Royal Theatre at Stockholm. He was advised to rewrite it in poetic form, eliminating its more frankly realistic passages and being more considerate of the prevailing historical tradition in his conception of the central characters. Seriously disturbed by this indifferent reaction to his play, and convinced that this judgment was narrow and prejudiced, Strindberg nevertheless attempted in the course of the following years to revise it at least partly in accordance with the advice that he had received from the management of the Royal Theatre. A poetic version of it was in consequence finally published in 1878, and in 1881 it was for the first time performed.

Strindberg's suggestion that Olof's hesitation in the presence of the challenge of his life-work was a picture of himself at the time is borne out by an examination of his activities during the six or seven years following the composition of *Master Olof*. At the beginning his spirit of revolt was nurtured strongly by the bohemian company which he affected among the younger artists and intellectuals in Stockholm; but in 1874 he had made a definite preliminary overture to society in successfully seeking an appointment at the Royal Library, and his marriage a few years later further forced him to make certain practical adjustments to life in order to provide a reasonably sound economic foundation for the establishment of a home. In consequence his innermost desire to revolt against society only gradually and hesitantly revealed itself. It was not until he wrote *The Red Room* in 1879 that his half-quiescent radicalism broke out in the full fury of revolutionary satire. Meantime he tried his hand at miscellaneous journalism, became for a brief time a scholar of sorts (which enabled him to live, as he tells us, in "a state of healthy idiocy"), and published in 1877 a volume of lightly satirical tales and sketches chiefly concerned with memories of his student days at Upsala. None of this work attracted any general attention; and even the final publication of the poetic version of *Master Olof* in 1878 went by largely in silence.

When his next book, the novel *The Red Room,* appeared in the following year Strindberg was determined to be ignored no longer, as is evident from the book's provocative title-page motto taken from Voltaire: "Rien n'est si désagréable que d'être pendu obscurément." He was not ignored. Overnight he became the most talked-of literary man in the country. Nothing like this brilliantly slashing satire on well-nigh all phases of contemporary life had ever appeared in Sweden. The success of *The Red Room* was followed in the next few years by a phenomenally prolific literary production, including two volumes of Swedish cultural history, a series of fascinating historical tales, a volume of verse, a volume of prose satire even more violent and personal than *The Red Room,* and three plays. This amazing literary productivity was naturally of unequal quality, and some of it, especially the more ambitious phases of his work as a cultural historian, involved Strindberg in some vitriolic and protracted controversy which embittered him so deeply that he was determined early in the 1880's to leave Sweden as soon as it was economically possible. This he did finally in the fall of 1883.

None of the three plays from the early eighties is of permanent importance. They were written in part to provide rôles for Strindberg's wife, who had theatrical ambitions; and their interest today lies perhaps chiefly in the fact that they reflect certain attitudes and ideas with which Strindberg was concerned at the time, particularly "the woman question," later to become so fatefully central in nearly all of Strindberg's work. It is in

Herr Bengt's Wife (1882) that the woman question first comes into the focus of Strindberg's dramatic imagination. The play is clearly an effort on the part of Strindberg to deal with the problem of the emancipated woman as it had been posed three years earlier in Ibsen's *A Doll's House*; and in the play we find a solution of what might be called "the Nora problem" in strong contrast to that of Ibsen. In the first acts of the play Herr Bengt and his wife (Margit) are involved in a conflict broadly parallel to that of Torvald Helmer and Nora in *A Doll's House*; but in the last act Margit and Herr Bengt become reconciled because love, an irrational natural power, triumphs over purely theoretical ethical considerations. Herr Bengt says in the closing scene,

> You did not want to love me, Margit, because your pride forbade it; but you love me anyway. You love me in spite of the fact that I lifted my hand against you, even though I was shamefully weak when misfortune came. I wanted to hate you, because you left me; I wished to kill you because you wanted to sacrifice your child—but still I love you. Do you not believe that love has final power over our evil wills?

To which Margit answers: "I believe! ..."

Strindberg has placed the action of this play in an early historical period, but the historical framework deceives no one as to the essentially modern, nineteenth-century theme. The play is clearly Strindberg's first contribution to the literature of feminine emancipation, and it is prophetic of what is to come that he takes a position opposite Ibsen. The other two plays from the early eighties—*The Secret of the Guild* and *Lucky Pehr*—similarly employ historical backgrounds in which are inserted thoroughly modern themes, though neither of them is concerned so centrally with the woman question. The former reflects certain autobiographical elements of little interest to the general student of the modern European drama, whereas the latter is an interesting experiment in an only half-satirical fairy-tale drama influenced by Hans Christian Andersen and Dickens. It was not until the late 1880's that Strindberg came to write a series of plays which attracted European attention to him as a literary figure.

Upon first coming to the Continent in the early 1880's (at first to France, later to Switzerland), Strindberg had determined to turn away from belles-lettres to journalism and to broad social, economic, and political criticism. In a volume of poems entitled *Somnambulist Nights in Broad Daylight,* the first composition from his self-imposed exile, Strindberg attempts a critical analysis of his position with reference to the social and political organization and the characteristic thought trends of the day. He arrives finally at a set of conclusions which reflect a kind of half-disillusioned utilitarian social philosophy, with a strong admixture of Rousseauism. The Rousseauistic suspicion of modern industry becomes even more marked in the succession of volumes in prose that immediately follows—two volumes of essays entitled *This and That,* a collection of modern utopian tales called *Utopias in Reality,* and the first two volumes of *The Son of a Servant.*

Strindberg's preoccupation with broad social and economic problems became, however, gradually pushed aside after the middle of the 1880's by concerns of a more immediate and personal kind. His marriage, which had shown some signs of disintegration the last year or two in Sweden, headed rapidly for a break-up during the early years of his residence on the Continent. His wife apparently wanted to return to Sweden and once again take up her work in the theatre. Strindberg was determined to oppose such a move. The clash of temperaments and wills which ensued, with its utterly demoralizing effect on Strindberg's peace of mind, has been depicted in *The Confession of a Fool* (written 1887-1888, first published in 1893), one of the most brutal documents in the history of confessional literature. And simultaneously with this profoundly disturbing development in his private life, Strindberg had to stand trial in Stockholm on the charge of blasphemy as an aftermath of the publication of the first volume of *Married* (1884), a collection of short stories dealing in a semidisillusioned manner with the institution of marriage in modern life. The double burden of his disintegrating married life and a serious lawsuit that might have resulted in imprisonment at hard labor (he was in fact acquitted) brought on a severe mental crisis. The second volume of *Married,* composed in 1885, is obviously written by a man suffering under very serious mental disturbances. He has by this time arrived at the conclusion that all of womenkind—especially the modern "emancipated" women—are banded in a league against him; and he implies, in words of violently unrestrained bitterness, that his own marriage is heading toward the rocks in direct consequence of the machinations of his enemies. He developed, in short, a dangerous case of what modern psychology calls the persecution complex. Realizing the danger of a permanent mental ailment, he traveled to Denmark and unsuccessfully sought entrance into a private asylum where he might live under proper observation.

It is in the light of this immediate personal crisis that nearly all of Strindberg's dramatic work of the late eighties and early nineties (the period of his so-called "naturalistic dramas") must be considered. Between 1886 and 1893 he wrote, in all, fourteen plays, five of which are of first importance not only in Strindberg's work as such but in the general history of the European drama. Zola and others had attempted with only indifferent success in the seventies and early eighties to create a drama which would satisfy all the demands of the current naturalistic program in literature. Ibsen's *Ghosts* had been perhaps the most successful of these attempts, but Ibsen did not follow up with any plays in a similar vein. It remained for Strindberg to perfect the type. Strindberg did not, however, deliberately set out with the intention of writing a series of dramas in accordance with a clearly defined naturalistic program. His first two plays in this manner,

Comrades (1886) and *The Father* (1887), are only in part naturalistic in theme and in technique. It was not until Zola (in December, 1887) had written to Strindberg highly praising *The Father* that the Swedish dramatist set himself to the task of writing a play (*Miss Julia*) which was deliberately conceived and executed in terms of a naturalistic program.

Of the two plays immediately preceding *Miss Julia, Comrades* is definitely the less important, though it has enjoyed considerable success in the theatre, chiefly perhaps because of its rather obvious satire and its clever handling of dramatic situation. Conceived originally as a light comic satire on the emancipated woman, it came in its final form to include elements of bitterness and brutality at least somewhat suggestive of the naturalistic tone and manner. *The Father,* in marked contrast to *Comrades,* is pure tragedy. A slight touch of the comic in its opening scene is soon buried forever in the rapidly developing, intensely tragic central action of the play. Here for the first time Strindberg develops a motif which is to become central in his later plays: the head-on, savage collision of two wills, usually those of a man and a woman, each seeking absolute mastery over the other, neither willing to yield, and with the weaker though finer will being finally crushed by the stronger, less scrupulous will. In *The Father* the Captain, a passionate and self-willed but highly intelligent and essentially good man, is gradually driven to insanity by his wife, Laura, because she is more thick-skinned, less intelligent, less punctilious in matters of honor in the struggle that is being waged. The weapon she employs with a deliberate, satanic skill to gain her end is that of mental suggestion. Strindberg had been immersing himself at the time he wrote *The Father* in that group of pseudo-scientific psychologists of the day (Liébeault, Bernheim, and others) who had been investigating such phenomena as hypnotism, mesmerism, and some of the more inclusive aspects of mental suggestion; and his play from one point of view is but a brilliant dramatic exposition of some of the psychological theories that he had come upon in this reading. *The Father* gains its terrifying tragic reality, its intense actuality, however, from the fact that Strindberg is here telling the story of his own marital life. Strindberg himself is the Captain, breaking inexorably bit by bit under the insistently horrible pressure of a stronger will. The best commentary on *The Father* is, in consequence, the autobiographical volume *The Confession of a Fool,* written shortly after *The Father* and containing all of the psychological motifs employed by Strindberg in the drama.

Though one need not search beyond the purely personal materials of this crisis in Strindberg's life to explain the tragic theme in *The Father,* it should be apparent that in certain technical elements in this play Strindberg has felt the impact of earlier traditions in the drama. One finds echoes of both Shakespeare and the Greek theatre in Strindberg's otherwise so-modern play. Shakespeare's Iago has certainly contributed to Strindberg's use of the power of suggestion in *The Father*; and the final act of Strindberg's play, with its constantly shifting moods and its bold blending of the brutal and the sentimental, reminds one definitely of Shakespeare. *Lear* has perhaps also contributed. That Strindberg had the Greek drama in mind seems apparent from his use of sharply concentrated action, his employment of a very small number of dramatis personae, and his observation of the unities of time and place. The Omphale motif is an even more striking illustration of the influence of a Greek tradition on Strindberg in this play. It should be stressed, however, that these traces of an earlier dramatic tradition are on the whole incidental rather than basic in *The Father*. They have been so thoroughly assimilated by Strindberg that they seem in no way artificial adjuncts to a play otherwise so undeniably Strindbergian in every essential respect. Strindberg's temperament, with its restive, nervously brooding, half-pathological qualities, lends itself with a sure and masterful dramatic instinct to the passionate intensities, the precipitate action, and the brutally unyielding give-and-take of dialogue which characterize such a play as *The Father*. Strindberg managed, in consequence, to break through the heavy superstructure of quite static outward detail which had made the usual type of naturalistic play so essentially undramatic. He uses, indeed, what the naturalists called "a slice of life" as the basis of his drama; but he does not follow orthodox dramatic naturalism in permitting the action to flow entirely haphazard. Strindberg is too much the born dramatist to become a merely doctrinaire naturalist, much as he was impressed at this stage in his development by the possibilities of the naturalistic view of human life as applied particularly to the conception of dramatic character.

Zola's favorable reaction to *The Father* encouraged Strindberg to continue with the composition of plays in roughly the same manner, though *Miss Julia* and *The Creditors,* particularly the former, move somewhat more sharply than had *The Father* in the direction of the traditional naturalistic drama. Strindberg himself recognized this when in a letter to his publisher Bonnier in 1888 he refers to *Miss Julia* as "the Swedish drama's first naturalistic tragedy." And he added, with considerable self-assurance: *"Ceci datera*—this piece will be noted in the annals." Bonnier did not dare to publish the play (as was the case with *The Father*) because of the prevailing conservative reaction in Sweden against provocative works by the author of *Married*; but Strindberg found another publisher, and his words to Bonnier on the significance of *Miss Julia* have certainly not proved to be a vain prophecy. *Miss Julia* is probably the best frankly naturalistic play ever written, and it certainly stood in a class by itself in its day. The tragic story of the half-decadent daughter of a Count, who in the course of a Midsummer's night offers herself to her father's lackey and before the break of dawn commits suicide when she comes to realize the unworthiness of the man to whom she had yielded in a moment of passion, is based at least in part upon an actual contemporary episode of which Strindberg had heard. Thus the play fulfills the naturalist's demand that literature should deal with documented, observed reality. In matters of staging Strindberg comes even closer to the naturalistic ideal in the theatre: all of the action takes place in the kitchen of the Count's home, and this action is continuous, broken by no sharp artificial divisions into acts. In the interest of greater realism Strindberg also suggests (in his detailed preface to the play) that footlights be abandoned in favor of strong side-lights, that make-up be reduced to a minimum, that dialogue be more natural than is the case usually in the theatre, and that in general all dramatic machinery should be simplified so that the dramatic conflict may stand out in more sharp, bare, starkly effective contours. The significance of these ideas for the development of the modern theatre can hardly be overemphasized, though it was many years before theatrical managers dared to introduce many of them. Most of the early performances of *Miss Julia,* in fact, employed only sparingly Strindberg's suggestions for staging the play. That really forward-looking theatrical managers were impressed by Strindberg's revolutionary Preface, however, is attested by the fact that Antoine went to the trouble of having it translated and distributed to the Parisian audience which witnessed the first French performance of *Miss Julia* at the Théâtre Libre in January 1893.

If these suggestions represent certain naturalistic departures from traditional dramatic ideals, however, Strindberg's conception of character in *Miss Julia* is even more sharply naturalistic. True to the doctrinaire naturalist's conception of character as a product of heredity and environment, Strindberg has his central characters, Miss Julia and the lackey Jean, reveal bit by bit in the course of the dialogue the particular elements in their heredity and in their environmental backgrounds which determine their every action. In this manner of characterization Jean provides the simpler, more elementary problem: a healthy, at times brutal *Streber* type, seeking instinctively to climb in life; something of a blusterer, at base a weak, servile individual. Miss Julia follows a less simple pattern. Born in a marriage resulting from a mésalliance, and brought up under a kind of dual education, in part directed by a sentimental, neurotic mother, in part by a severe, aristocratic father, she is a clear-cut case of the split personality with strongly marked neurotic leanings. Little wonder is it then that under the hauntingly sensuous circumstances of a Midsummer night on the Scandinavian countryside, with a provocatively healthy animalism abroad, she should carry on a momentary flirtation with her father's lackey and ultimately yield to him physically. After the seduction Jean tries, not without some preliminary success, to play the superman, attempting to bend Miss Julia to his purposes; but she gradually comes to see through his empty bluster, realizes the shame of her position, and finds her only possible way out in suicide. In none of Strindberg's other plays dealing with the conflict between man and woman has he been more objective, less inclined to side with one party or the other in the course of the dramatic conflict. In this respect also *Miss Julia* satisfies the naturalistic concept of the drama. Instead of showing, as Strindberg almost invariably does, a marked sympathy for the man in such a struggle, the dramatist through most of this play reveals no perceptible tendency toward taking sides, and in the closing scene one feels that Strindberg's sympathies lean a bit toward Miss Julia.

In *The Father* Strindberg had employed the motif of mental suggestion as the means used by Laura in breaking down the will of the Captain. In *Miss Julia* this motif is again used, though less centrally and in a somewhat different form. At the close of *Miss Julia* the heroine seems to proceed to her act of suicide only half-consciously, in a kind of trance engendered by the hypnotic suggestion of Jean's superior will. The element of hypnosis is employed even more strikingly in Strindberg's next play, *The Creditors* (written 1888, published 1890), where it dominates the entire action of the play. In this new play Strindberg has concentrated completely on the purely psychological aspect of the conflict of wills, ignoring for the moment the material, largely physiological side of human motivation which had loomed so large in *Miss Julia*. The entire action of *The Creditors* consists merely of a series of precariously balanced psychic interrelations among the three characters, in which each character is bent on imposing pain upon the other two, and in which finally Gustaf, the strongest will, wreaks a terrible vengeance, first on Tekla, his former wife, and then on Adolf, Tekla's present husband. In the highly charged dramatic scenes of *The Creditors* hatred lurks everywhere, ready to spring into devastating explosive action; the dialogue is handled with uncanny virtuosity; never has a play been written with a more concentrated, tightly knit construction. Though all of this gives to the play something of an artificial, schematic quality not at all characteristic of *The Father* and only at times present in *Miss Julia, The Creditors* was the first play by Strindberg successfully performed on the Continent (Berlin in 1893), and it has remained to our day among the most frequently played of Strindberg's dramas both in Europe and America.

The fascination which abnormal psychological phenomena held for Strindberg in his full-length naturalistic plays from just after the middle of the 1880's carried over into a number of less important plays—the three one-act plays, *Pariah, The Stronger,* and *Simoon*—which he wrote in order to provide a repertoire for the experimental theatre which he attempted unsuccessfully to establish in Copenhagen in the late 1880's. Two circumstances at this time had moved Strindberg to try his hand at the shorter type of play, Antoine's experiments with such plays at the Théâtre Libre in Paris and the limited resources and personnel of the company that the Swedish dramatist tried at the time to organize. It was at this time that Strindberg first came to read Edgar Allan Poe, whose horror themes and intricate detective pattern intrigues fascinated him and left their mark clearly upon both *Pariah* and *Simoon*. The most important of these two plays is *Pariah,* Strindberg's re-working for the theatre of a short story by his countryman

Ola Hansson. This little play is Strindberg's only effort in the genre of the criminal tale, but he handles the type with such consummate mastery of dialogue and intrigue that one wishes he had attempted a few more plays of the kind.

In the spring of 1889 Strindberg, together with his family, left Denmark for Stockholm, the first time that he had set foot on Swedish soil since the fateful trial on the charge of blasphemy in the late fall of 1884. Almost immediately after arriving at Stockholm the family moved for the summer out to the archipelago lying just outside Stockholm in the Baltic—a natural environment which Strindberg loved more than anything else in the world. But his relations with his wife, which had undergone so many serious crises during the period of residence in Denmark, continued to deteriorate, and finally reached a permanent impasse. His wife was granted a divorce in 1891. Meantime Strindberg was living a restless, roving existence, partly on the islands of the archipelago, partly in the mainland environs of Stockholm, the while engaging in scientific reading and research (especially in botany and geology) and writing in a variety of genres, a number of short stories, a novel of primarily autobiographical significance, *By the Open Sea,* and a number (seven in all) of plays. Only one of these dramas, *The Link,* is of permanent importance. Many of the central motifs in these plays were drawn from Strindberg's own marital experience, but it seems that he had finally exhausted the possibilities of such materials for dramatic purposes. The opening scene of one of the plays, *The Keys of the Kingdom,* reveals Strindberg at his best in the poetry of deep personal pathos; but after this promising beginning the play rapidly deteriorates into a succession of rather pointless, and only slightly coördinated, satiric episodes. *The Link,* on the other hand, is among Strindberg's more important naturalistic dramas. It is a case of "court reporting," a re-telling in dramatic form of Strindberg's own divorce case; and as such it fulfils most of the thematic and technical demands of the naturalistic theatre. In attempting to establish personal responsibility for the divorce, Strindberg lays more blame on the woman than on the man in the course of the action; but the closing scene distributes justice rather more evenly, in that both man and woman are found in the last analysis to be victims of forces beyond their control. Though *The Link* has never been popular on the Swedish stage, in part certainly because Swedes are too immediately aware of the real story that lies behind it, the play has been performed very successfully in other countries, notably in Germany and in Russia.

After his divorce Strindberg was a broken man. Particularly hard did he take the loss of the children, who had been surrendered to the mother as a part of the divorce judgment. His finances, always precarious, now became hopeless. Publishers hesitated to handle his books. Never had his fortunes seemed at a lower ebb. At this critical juncture, however, some friends in Berlin, particularly Ola Hansson and Hansson's German-born wife Laura

Marholm, came to his rescue by sending him a sum of money sufficient to permit him to depart for the Continent once again. He settled for the time being in Berlin, becoming the central figure in a brilliant group of artists and intellectuals from the Scandinavian countries as well as from Germany and Poland who gathered nightly in a saloon-restaurant called Zum schwarzen Ferkel, where some six hundred varieties of alcoholic liquors were to be had. Wild as this night-life seems to have been, Strindberg's never-resting mind was busily engaged during most of the daylight hours, though with scientific rather than literary subjects. Here in Berlin also he had a new love-affair, this time with a young Viennese journalist named Frieda Uhl. The affair resulted in marriage in the spring of 1893; but Strindberg deserted his wife on the honeymoon, and despite a number of later reconciliations the marriage was dissolved not long afterward. Meantime he immersed himself more and more in scientific investigations by which he proposed nothing less than to overthrow the whole foundation upon which modern chemistry was based.

In 1894 he came to Paris in order to continue his scientific research in the laboratories at the Sorbonne. He was determined to produce gold from other chemical elements, and thereby prove the transmutability of elements. He worked with the feverish intensity of the medieval alchemist—and with no more success. From this hapless chemical research he shifted by degrees over into theosophical and occult speculations of the most fantastic kind. Meantime he was suffering from various delusions; the persecution complex, which ten years earlier had brought on a severe mental crisis, returned now in new and even more acute forms. It seemed to him that his enemies were seeking to destroy him by magic formulas, and in desperation he practiced in turn "black magic" against these enemies. After a time, however, he came to attribute the persecution to which he was being subjected to certain supernatural beings ("the Powers"), some evil, some good, whose function seemed in some not clearly defined way to be to chasten him. Meantime he had come to read his countryman Swedenborg, eighteenth-century scientist turned mystic; and in Swedenborg's books he found at last what seemed to him a satisfactory explanation of his condition and his destiny. This led—only gradually, and by somewhat devious paths, it must be admitted—to Strindberg's so-called "conversion."

Strindberg has told the story of his crisis and the resultant conversion in *The Inferno* (1897), certainly one of the most amazing autobiographical documents ever written. However critical one might be with regard to the general validity of the religious ideas expressed in this strangely fascinating book, the importance of these ideas in Strindberg's own experience can scarcely be overestimated. Not only did the conclusions to which he finally came save Strindberg from a complete mental breakdown; they came to have the utmost importance in his whole later literary development. In general these conclusions represent a complete shift in his philosophy of life, from his atheistic naturalism of the late eighties and early nineties to the non-dogmatic form of Christianity of his later years, from (as Strindberg himself puts it) his "former fatalism ... to providentialism," with a strong accent on the conception of a personal God. And this shift in his philosophy of life had the most profound effect on both the themes and the techniques of that long list of plays which came from his pen after the Inferno experience.

Though Strindberg composed prolifically in a number of different genres in the fifteen years between *The Inferno* and his death in 1912, his favorite form was the drama (he wrote thirty plays in all during this period), and it was in the drama that the impact of his conversion became most apparent. Some of these plays deal directly with his conversion experience, others reflect this experience no less definitely though in somewhat veiled forms, while still others (particularly the long list of historical dramas) contain a strong religious and ethical undercurrent that derives ultimately from the view of life to which he had come in consequence of the Inferno experience.

On the eighth of March, 1898, Strindberg sent to Gustaf af Geijerstam (at the time editor for the publisher Gernandt in Stockholm) the manuscript of a new play, accompanied by a short note: "Herewith a play, of whose value I haven't the faintest idea. If you find it good, throw it in to the theatre. If you find it impossible, hide it in Gernand't safe. But the manuscript remains my possession. It is my only savings-bank." Geijerstam agreed to publish the play, entitled *To Damascus,* strange as he found both its content and its form. The play was Strindberg's first attempt to give dramatic form to his Inferno experience, and it had, therefore, as Geijerstam expressed it, "a terrifying half-reality behind it." But if the content was strange, haunting, only half-real, the technique of the drama was if possible more strange. In seeking a form which would give adequate expression to the eerie phantasmagoria of his Inferno experience, with its bizarre interplay of the actual and the imagined, the natural and the supernatural, Strindberg had found none of the customary dramatic forms suitable; and in consequence *To Damascus* is utterly revolutionary in form, breaking completely with traditional dramatic techniques. It was Strindberg's first experiment with what has since come to be called "the expressionistic drama," a form of the drama which has had since Strindberg's day a very great, if not always salutary, importance in the modern theatre.

To Damascus, Part I, has three main characters, The Unknown One (Strindberg himself), The Lady (his second wife), and The Unseen One (God, the Almighty). At the beginning of the play The Unknown One is proud, in revolt against his fate, prepared to defy God; but the Powers persecute him in various petty, irritating ways (just as in *The Inferno*), and he is thereby gradually forced to walk in paths of meekness and repentance, and comes finally to realize that The Unseen One is pursuing him in this way in order to guide him to salvation. At the close of the play The Unknown One arrives at the portals of a Church; but whether he shall find a final haven here is doubtful. "Perhaps!" is the last word of the play. *To Damascus,* Part II (written immediately after Part I), covers much the same ground, and can be considered largely as a more violent and brutal variant version of Part I. It closes on the same half-hesitant note as Part I, when The Unknown One, upon finally arriving with a Priest companion at a Cloister which he has decided to enter in order to escape sin and the world, says, somewhat impatiently, "Come, Priest, before I change my mind." This outline of what may be called "the plot" of the play gives but the barest idea of the haunting power of Strindberg's creation, a power which perhaps emanates substantially more from the form in which the play is written than from the story in itself. This form is revolutionary in every respect. Turning away entirely from the severe, concentrated construction of his naturalistic dramas, Strindberg here composes simply a series of tableaux, related to each other by what may be called poetic moods rather than by any sharply defined outward action. The play differs from Strindberg's earlier naturalistic dramas also in that the fundamental dramatic struggle involves a conflict between man and God rather than a struggle between two human wills; and God (The Unseen One) never appears in the play, though he directs and controls the action. Strindberg's most daring technical departure in this play lies, however, in his curious blending of reality and fantasy, a blending as in the materials and the processes of a dream. This is what gives the drama its remarkable, purely Strindbergian quality; for Strindberg himself during the Inferno period, and not infrequently thereafter, found it at times difficult to distinguish between reality and fantasy, life and the dream. It was this that gave to *To Damascus* that "terrifying half-reality" to which Geijerstam referred. This weird, only half earthly manner is to stalk again and again in Strindberg's plays, most successfully, as we shall see, in *Easter* (1901) and *The Dream Play* (1902) and finally in the series of Chamber Plays from 1907.

Shortly after completing the second part of *To Damascus* Strindberg had written two other plays, *Advent* and *There Are Crimes and Crimes.* The former of these is related to *To Damascus* in both theme and form, while the latter, though not employing the visionary techniques of *To Damascus,* concerns itself primarily with problems of sin and penitence. *Advent* is scarcely as successful an experiment in the new manner as *To Damascus* had been, chiefly because its moods are too various, ranging with startling incongruity from grotesque scenes of pure terror to scenes of blue-eyed, childish innocence reminiscent of Hans Christian Andersen and the Dickens of the Christmas Books. *There Are Crimes and Crimes* is more satisfactory, though hardly one of Strindberg's more important dramas. Based upon an episode from the Inferno period, it tells a not uninteresting story from the artist world of Paris. The play as a whole scarcely grips one, but there are individual episodes of remarkable dramatic power. It is interesting to note in passing that the motif of mental suggestion, so successfully employed in Strindberg's naturalistic dramas, finds a central place again in this religious drama on the theme of sin and penance.

During the period December, 1896, to the spring of 1899 Strindberg had lived alternately in Paris and in Lund, the university city in the south of Sweden. In the early summer of 1899 he moved to Stockholm, where he was now to spend the remainder of his life. The striking outward details of the thirteen years which elapsed before his death are neither so numerous nor so significant for his general literary development as had been the crucial experiences of the roving, crisis-filled years of the preceding two decades. For the most part he lived a kind of hermit-like existence quietly and alone, pre-occupied almost exclusively with his literary work and with certain esoteric scientific and philological studies. This quiet existence was broken only occasionally by any contact with the outside world. Love flared up tentatively on a couple of occasions, the first, in 1901, resulting in his third marriage—this time to Harriet Bosse, a promising young actress of Norwegian birth who had first attracted the attention of Strindberg in 1900 when she played the rôle of The Lady in *To Damascus*. This marriage, like Strindberg's previous one, was soon dissolved, but the principals in it remained friends. During his last years only two other episodes drew Strindberg out of his self-imposed isolation: first, the active part that he took in the establishment of a Strindberg theatre (called The Intimate Theatre) under the direction of August Falck from 1907 to 1910; and secondly, the violent controversy that he conducted in 1910 in newspaper columns and pamphlet form against old and new enemies in a final vigorous flare-up of the old Strindbergian spirit of rebellion.

Astonishing as had been Strindberg's literary productivity in the decade and a half before the Inferno crisis, he became around the turn of the century if possible even more productive. One work after another flowed during these years from his never-resting pen—more than a score of plays and two satiric novels, short stories in large numbers and gently moralizing fairy-tales, essays and poems and autobiographical sketches. Some of this is definitely inferior work, more of it falls just short of Strindberg's best work; but much of it is of such importance that the last period in Strindberg's life is certainly to be counted as one of the two most significant periods in his literary career. It is interesting to note in passing that some of the very best of this late work is contained in a collection of lyric poems. But it was into the drama that Strindberg poured most of his best creative energies at this time—first into the historical drama, which he had not exploited since the early eighties, and then only with limited success. The fact that Strindberg, unlike Ibsen, was drawn again in the years of his artistic maturity to try his hand at historical drama suggests something of the permanent attraction that historical personages and historical events had always held for the Swedish dramatist.

The immediate occasion for his decision to write historical plays again seems to have been the success that *Master Olof* (the play of Strindberg's youth) had been having on the Swedish stage in the last years of the century. Encouraged by this tardy but now enthusiastic recognition of his dramatic skill with historical subject matter, Strindberg wrote in rapid succession in 1899-1900 four full-length historical plays, *The Saga of the Folkungs, Gustaf Vasa, Erik XIV,* and *Gustaf Adolf.* These were followed at intervals in later years by eight more historical dramas, *Engelbrekt* and *Karl XII,* both in 1901, *Kristina* and *Gustaf III,* in 1903, *The Nightingale of Wittenberg,* 1904, and finally *The Last Knight, The Regent,* and *The Jarl of Bjälbo,* in 1908 and 1909. Of these plays the first three are the most important, though several of the others, notably *Karl XII* and *Gustaf III,* and parts of *Gustaf Adolf,* fall just short of the three plays of 1899 in vivid dramatic re-creation of earlier historical periods and historical personages. Were it possible for non-Scandinavian students of the drama to identify themselves intimately enough with Scandinavian history to be in position to respond adequately to these historical dramas, Strindberg would certainly be recognized everywhere among those very few dramatists who rank close to Shakespeare in the historical drama. As it is, Strindberg's eminence in the naturalistic and expressionistic drama is universally recognized while his historical plays remain the precious possession of Strindberg's own nation alone.

There are a number of qualities that distinguish Strindberg's historical dramas. Like Shakespeare —whom he was rereading with great enthusiasm at the time he wrote these plays—Strindberg shows no slavish regard for mere historical accuracy. He rearranges historical chronology quite freely to fit his immediate dramatic purposes; he uses as his chief sources certain romantic pseudo-historians rather than the reputable historians of his day; and not infrequently he introduces essentially modern ideas into historical contexts where they certainly had no real historical place. Particularly persistent is he in the plays written in 1899 and thereafter in interpreting individual historical destinies in terms of the religious and ethical concepts originating in his own Inferno experiences, a practice which frequently resulted in gross historical inaccuracies, and yet a practice which lent an undeniable dramatic power to these plays. The innocent and well-meaning King Magnus Erickson, the central character in *The Saga of the Folkungs,* is forced, for instance, to endure all manner of evil and bear a heavy cross of shame and penitence because of the sins of his ancestors, the bloody Folkung line of early Swedish kings. Strindberg's primary concern in these plays is with character rather than with episode or mere complications of plot. In the matter of dramatic structure these plays (with the striking exception of *Gustaf Vasa*) depart almost as completely from the firm, tight construction of Strindberg's naturalistic plays as did *To Damascus*. Professor Martin Lamm likens the general form in these historical plays to a complex symphonic score (*symfonisk mångstämmighet*), and the comparison is especially apropos. Strindberg himself justifies this form of dramatic pattern by referring to Shakespeare. He compares *Hamlet* to "a symphony, developed in a polyphonic manner with independent motifs, which are woven beautifully together." Similarly the structural pattern of Strindberg's own historical plays is on the whole curiously fluid, suggestive of moods in a tragic vein rather than of clear-cut dramatic conflicts; and the dramatist does not hesitate to employ in the course of the solemn progress of action in these plays a variety of subtly meaningful lyric adjuncts to give greater richness, body, and direction to the plays. The opening dialogue of the closing act of *The Saga of the Folkungs* is illustrative:

Magnus. It is autumn!— Outside and in! (*Listens.*)
Blanche. What do you hear, dear?
Magnus. I am listening to the singing of the wind in the door-crack over there. It sounds like the moaning of sick men, or the crying of children over their lost toys—have you noticed the strange way they cry then?— And why does the wind complain in the autumn only? Isn't the air the same that blows in summer? (*Listens.*) Listen!— I should like to put words to its tones of lament.
Blanche. What does it sing of—that melancholy north wind?
Magnus. It sings of youth and vanished love; sings so that I can see it—see the blue lake, with the white castle amid oaks and lindens, suspended over roses and lilies. I see the wedding folk, cheering my youth's bride, to whom I gave my first love.... And one day, a long time after, she comes and lays in my arms a little creature dressed in white; and I feel as though an angel had come down from heaven; for when I gaze into his eyes I become changed from an ordinary sinful mortal to a very good one—or so it seems to me. Yet it was only my son, Erik!— Those were the days of happiness, of rejoicing. And then came the end!—He had me bound with cords....
Blanche. Magnus, how often must I tell you that Erik was not to blame? He was enticed into an action and the use of words which he did not understand.
Magnus. I am not angry with him, but I grieve.... He had me bound with cords:— And I loved him more than my own soul; I gave him the crown while he was still a child, so that he might not fall into the temptation of the Folkungs. But it seems to have been ordained that *that* crime *should* be accomplished. And if you say it took place against his will, then there must have been some one else who wanted it to take place. Brother against brother—that has been the story of our race all the way; but father against son—never till now. It wanted only that final deed for us to make way for new claimants to the throne. Who can comprehend the ways of Providence?— Blanche, you come from a foreign land, and perhaps you do not know the full saga of our race?

And then the King, in quiet, measured phrases, tells to the Queen the grim, blood-stained tale of the rise to power of the ancient Folkung dynasty. Throughout the scene the haunting melodies of poetry and of music provide the appropriate emotional mood for the imminent tragic dénouement.

Gustaf Vasa, looked upon by many as the greatest of Strindberg's historical dramas, is less musical in manner than are *The Saga of the Folkungs* and *Erik XIV*. In general structure it is sharp and clear, almost architectural in its lines; its central character, King Gustaf Vasa, is drawn in bold, striking outline; and the dramatic conflict is presented in clearly perceived ethical terms. But even this play does not lack its poetry, particularly in the first two acts, where the King does not himself appear and yet his person dominates everything, casting its giant shadow over action and dialogue and determining with a strong master hand the destinies of his subjects. It is by a series of massive indirections that we first become aware of the King's presence and his power. Not until the third act does he actually appear on the stage. Seldom has Strindberg been so imaginative in handling the element of dramatic suspense.

Though Strindberg continued at intervals his series of historical dramas in the early years of the new century, he did so with less success. Meantime he published a number of plays of a different kind, the most important of which are *Easter* and *The Dance of Death,* in 1901, and *The Bridal Crown* and *The Dream Play,* in 1902. Three of these plays are gently tragic in general tone, interpreting human fate as a thing of infinite sadness, but in any case endurable if approached in the spirit of humility and penitence. The fourth, *The Dance of Death,* is the most hopelessly pessimistic picture of human life that Strindberg ever penned. It is, of course, another domestic tragedy—in the category of *Comrades, The Father,* and *Creditors.* Even the most violent of these earlier plays, *The Father,* cannot, however, compare with *The Dance of Death* in sheer brutality of tragic representation. "*The Father* is wilder but shorter," as one Swedish critic puts it. And then he adds: "The terrifying thing about *The Dance of Death* is that the conflict here is endless, and yet never lets the reader go, never lets him tire or turn his mind away from the horror. It depicts not only an endless quarrel, it pictures an endless loathing, an eternal tedium." For five and twenty years Edgar, Captain in the Artillery, and Alice, his wife, a former actress, have lived together—on the basis of hatred born apparently of love. They have hated each other so long that the emotion of hatred has become a fixed complex, a thing that is loathesome to them and yet a thing without which they cannot exist. And so they go on living together in order to gain what perverse half-pleasures they can out of inflicting pain upon each other. Quite isolated from the outside world—their conduct has caused all former friends to break with them, and even servants leave them almost as soon as hired— they have only each other upon whom to exercise their spite. The arrival of Curt, cousin to Alice, shortly after the opening of the play permits an occasion for a momentary escape from their ennui and mutual hatred, but merely because each of them hopes to win Curt to his side. Alice carries on a flirtation with Curt in order to spite the Captain, but this flirtation leads to consequences that are nauseating to Curt and that lead nowhere for Alice. No one gets anywhere in this play; life to Alice and the Captain continues to be, as it had been for more than two decades, simply an aimless round of pettiness and hatred and loathing. Though the play is packed throughout with the most grotesque of brutalities, never is the sense of bitter, unyielding hatred more starkly expressed than in the quiet hammer-blow dialogue of the opening scene. The voices are subdued, too weary to break out in violent exchanges of spite; but just therefore does the measured staccato of words cut the more deeply, lacerating without seeming effort what may be left of feeling in the two contending parties. It is worthy of note that in this domestic tragedy Strindberg finds both man and woman equally guilty, which would seem to suggest that he has finally arrived at the conclusion that woman in herself is not the beginning of evil. Life itself is evil.

The gentle, religious play *Easter* was composed, curiously enough, just before *The Dance of Death*. One could scarcely conceive of two works more different in manner and tone, despite the fact that neither depicts life optimistically. *The Dance of Death* is of the same brutal vintage as the naturalistic plays of the eighties. *Easter,* on the other hand, is the most delicately beautiful of all of Strindberg's works. Only *Swanwhite* can be compared with it; but this little play, written during the period of courtship with Harriet Bosse and sent to her as a suitor's gift, is in the last analysis a rather wooden imitation of Maeterlinck, maintaining little of the exquisite unity of effect that emanates so subtly from every scene of *Easter*. None of Strindberg's plays is more free of harsh, strong effects than *Easter*. The dialogue is curiously subdued, and the characters seem only half real. In the immediate background lies a harsh enough reality, it is true: the father of the Heyst family has been imprisoned for embezzlement, and Lindquist, the creditor, is apparently ready to descend upon the hapless mother and her children. But Lindquist does not arrive when expected: one merely hears his boots on the cobblestones outside; one sees his shadow on the curtains. And when he does arrive, at the last, he comes as a forgiving judge rather than as an instrument of torture. The play is everywhere saturated with the quiet symbolism of Good Friday and the day before Easter; and into this symbolism is fitted with beautiful appropriateness the gentle figure of Eleonora, weak-minded, but a religious visionary who bears the burden of the sin of others because of her telepathic sensitiveness to their pain. In suffering for others Eleonora becomes in the play both the symbol of the religious concept of *satisfactio vicaria* and an example in penitence which her whole family must finally follow in order to find the salvation come to man in the Easter season.

In *The Bridal Crown* Strindberg develops further such Christian concepts, now, however, in the form of a folk (peasant) tragedy. His letters reveal that he had originally intended to write a picturesque, colorful folk comedy—"I see it so fair and beautiful... the Swedish landscape with red cottages, white birch, and green fir trees." When Strindberg had finished the play, however, the landscape and the peasants were left, but the scene was not fair and beautiful and the romantic red cottages were no longer in evidence. The picturesque element remained, but it became a heavy and foreboding picturesqueness, with a background of darksome folk superstitions in keeping with the tragic religious note of the play as it was finally written. The story is a kind of Swedish peasant variant of the Romeo and Juliet motif. The lovers, Kersti and Mats, must carry on their courtship surreptitiously because their families have been traditional enemies for generations. The two families finally grudgingly agree to a marriage between the two lovers, but in order to wear the Bridal Crown and thus triumph over the pride of Mats' family, Kersti kills the child born out of wedlock. Her own pride is broken, however, on the discovery of her deed of child murder; and she must offer her own life, thereby bringing about a reconciliation of the two families. This play is perhaps the most romantic (in the traditional sense of Romanticism) that Strindberg has ever written, alternating scenes of pure fantasy with the real episodes of the drama, and employing legendary elements from both Christian and Pagan folk superstitions. Christian legend is represented particularly in the strange appearances of The Child in White (the Jesus child), while Pagan superstition is employed in the use of The Neck (Man of the Waterfall), with his melancholy song, and the half-legendary Midwife. With its simple tragic story and its rich play of fantasy, it is not strange that Ture Rangström, a Swedish composer, has used the text of this play unchanged as a libretto for a folk opera. The play lends itself marvelously to musical composition.

The Dream Play was written at about the same time as *Easter* and *The Bridal Crown,* and it is invested with the same general mood of melancholy that characterizes these two plays. But the note of sadness with which Strindberg looks upon life in *Easter* and *The Bridal Crown* is on the whole more heavy, more unrelieved in *The Dream Play*. In both *Easter* and *The Bridal Crown* resignation and penitence lead finally to salvation in the religious sense, though in the latter play the conflict otherwise results in tragedy. But in *The Dream Play* the pervading note is one of all but utter hopelessness, and the dramatist (in the person of the daughter of Indra) can but have an infinite compassion for the sad and heavy lot of mankind upon the earth. The play, in consequence, finally resolves itself into a religiously colored note of pessimism rather obviously inspired by Nirvana-like Buddhistic speculations on the subject of evil in human life. The theme of the play is, however, less interesting than its form. Here also it somewhat resembles *Easter* and *The Bridal Crown,* for these plays had experimented liberally with what might be called the poetry of symbolism. But *The Dream Play* carries these techniques much farther, adopting techniques that are more closely related to the revolutionary dramatic form of *To Damascus*. Baffling as *The Dream Play* is upon a first reading, it is unquestionably Strindberg's most successful experiment in the new type of drama that he had introduced in the earlier autobiographical play *To Damascus*. The earlier expressionistic play was not, however, quite so revolutionary in form as is *The Dream Play*. Strange as is the weird procession of eerie tableaux in *To Damascus,* the drama is held together by an at least vaguely outlined "story" as well as by its subtly integrated play of moods and ideas. In *The Dream Play,* on the other hand, Strindberg has eliminated entirely any succession of episodes forming a pattern or a story. The "action" of the play is wholly phantasmagoric, entirely irrational, ignoring both time and space relationships, and following the lawless vagaries of the pure dream world. Never had a dramatist indulged in a more capricious play of fantasy. The only thing that holds the play together at all is its mood, which finds periodic expression down through the drama in the daughter's plaintive lamentation: "Life is evil! Men are to be pitied!" Strindberg himself has given perhaps the best short analysis of his play in the following words:

As he did in his previous dream play [*To Damascus*], so in this one the author has tried to imitate the disconnected but seemingly logical form of the dream. Anything may happen; everything is possible and probable. Time and space do not exist. On an insignificant background of reality, imagination designs and embroiders novel patterns: a medley of memories, experiences, free fancies, absurdities, and improvisations.

The characters split, double, multiply, vanish, solidify, blur, clarify. But one consciousness reigns above them all—that of the dreamer; and before it there are no secrets, no incongruities, no scruples, no laws. There is neither judgment nor exoneration, but merely narration. And as the dream is mostly painful, rarely pleasant, a note of melancholy and of pity with all living things runs right through the wobbly tale. Sleep, the liberator, plays often a dismal part, but when the pain is at its worst, the awakening comes and reconciles the sufferer to reality, which, however distressing it may be, nevertheless seems happy in comparison with the torments of the dream.

The Dream Play and *The Spook Sonata,* with their revolutionary expressionistic techniques and their preoccupation with man's fate as such rather than with individual human fates, are the two Strindberg plays that have most strongly attracted dramatic experimenters since Strindberg's day, first in Germany (where the Expressionism of Wedekind, Kaiser, Toller, Werfel, and many others was derived more or less directly from Strindberg), and later in America, particularly in the plays of Eugene O'Neill. The debt that O'Neill owes to Strindberg has been freely admitted by the American dramatist on numerous occasions, most strikingly perhaps on the occasion of the Provincetown Players' performances of *The Spook*

Sonata in 1924 and *The Dream Play* in 1926. Writing in the Provincetown Playbill when *The Spook Sonata* was performed in New York, O'Neill said:

> Strindberg was the precursor of all modernity in our present theatre just as Ibsen, a lesser man as he himself surmised, was the father of the modernity of twenty years or so ago.... All that is enduring in what we loosely call "Expressionism"—all that is artistically valid and sound theatre—can be clearly traced back through Wedekind to Strindberg's *The Dream Play, There Are Crimes and Crimes, The Spook Sonata,* etc.

It was in 1907, five years after the publication of *The Dream Play*, that Strindberg wrote *The Spook Sonata* as one of that series of four "Chamber Plays" written for the Intimate Theatre at Stockholm. This little theatre, seating only one hundred seventy-five persons, was founded jointly by Strindberg and a young director, August Falck, for the purpose of performing plays by Strindberg. Besides writing plays specifically for this theatre, Strindberg engaged actively in the new theatrical venture by providing a considerable part of its capital, by writing a series of open "Letters" for the guidance of its actors, and by occasionally appearing as author-critic at rehearsals. The Intimate Theatre, though reasonably successful for some time, was forced to disband in 1910 when Strindberg, disagreeing in certain matters of policy with Falck, withdrew his support from the venture. Falck remained for many years, however, the most enthusiastic and successful actor-producer of Strindberg plays in the Scandinavian countries. The four Chamber Plays written for this theatre in 1907 are of interest both because they provide a remarkable impression of Strindberg's state of mind at one point in the beginning of his old age and because they reveal further developments in the dramatic experiments begun in *To Damascus* and *The Dream Play*. As Strindberg approached old age, isolated, living almost completely within himself, his imagination never ceased working in the most original of manners on the material of life that drifted into his ken. Each of the four Chamber Plays illustrates this, but none more startlingly than *The Spook Sonata*. Never has Strindberg been more bizarre: the stage is not only peopled with ghost-like living human beings, mummies appear in the action, dead men suddenly come to life and walk, living persons turn suddenly into mummies. The characters are caricatured, distorted, twisted into horribly grotesque forms. Though the point of departure for his play is a real-enough situation, Strindberg develops a world of wraiths and monsters in order to give adequate expression to the monomaniac view of human life that possessed him at the time. The Stranger in another of the Chamber Plays (*After the Fire*) expresses a view of life that could be placed as a motto over *The Spook Sonata:* "I tell you, my dear sister-in-law, that when you happen to be born without a film over your eyes, then you see life and your fellow creatures as they are—and you have to be a pig to feel at home in such a mess." Professor Lamm—in pointing out that *The Spook Sonata* provides us with the most fearful expression of Strindberg's scorn for mankind which we know—compares the Strindberg of this play with Swift:

> It is with something of the ageing Swift's lack of pity that he depicts these curious tatters of mankind, on whom all is loosely hung, from the wig and teeth to the beautiful attributes with which they invest themselves. There is something of Swift's acerbity in the view of existence as a marsh where every living being feeds on others, where all try to give pain to others, and where there is no escape except in death.... There is something of the ageing Swift's greatness in *The Spook Sonata*, and at the same time something of his taste for the nauseating and the abnormal, something of his inability to moderate the blows of the whip.

Though the view of life expressed in *The Spook Sonata* is substantially the same as that of *The Dream Play*, the former drama is borne by no note of pity, no infinitely sad compassion toward mankind. In *The Spook Sonata* life is not only sad, it is evil to the very core, worthy only of annihilation. Given this view of human life and Strindberg's fantastic imaginative capacities, it is little wonder that *The Spook Sonata* attains the ultimate in bizarre stage effects. One type of expressionistic drama could be carried no farther.

After the Chamber Plays Strindberg wrote six pieces for the theatre, two of them (*Abu Casem's Slippers* and *The Black Glove*) mere dramatic bagatelles, three of them historical plays of little importance, and one, his last play, *The Great Highway*, a magnificently conceived, but only in part well executed, autobiographical drama in the manner of *To Damascus*. The play is Strindbergian to the core, reflecting his faults as well as his virtues, giving expression to the petty as well as to the noble strain in his restless, always-searching spirit. In certain of its central monologues *The Great Highway* reaches poetic heights never surpassed, and seldom equalled, in Strindberg's earlier plays; but the drama as a whole reveals a Strindberg in decline, tired and resigned to the dissolution which was creeping in upon him. Three years after the publication of *The Great Highway* he died, though in the meantime he had indulged in one final outburst of controversy with certain of his contemporaries in Sweden which found almost every Swede of consequence at the time taking sides for or against him. It is perhaps fitting that Strindberg was thus an eruptive controversial figure up to the very verge of the grave. The penitential robes of the Inferno experience fitted rather precariously over his storm-filled spirit.

Björnstjerne Björnson (1832-1910), the figure who next to Ibsen and Strindberg is most responsible for the rise to world eminence of the Scandinavian drama in the last half of the nineteenth century, had a career studded with as many bitter controversies as had Strindberg, but otherwise it is difficult to conceive of a character and an artistic temperament more different from Strindberg. Björnson was an open, hearty nature, sure of his powers, loving nothing better than an open battle, but having none of those heavy, half-pathological strains that are the peculiar mark of Strindberg's darkly eruptive genius. It is clear that Björnson also had his inner struggles, that life did not always present itself to him in a naïvely simple formula; but his inner struggles were certainly less violent than those of Strindberg, and his work reflects a much greater serenity and moral balance—with an undeniable tendency, however, toward superficiality and an optimism scarcely in keeping with implications implicit in much of modern thought. Björnson was more of a dynamic folk leader than a profound thinker or an original artist. His widely ranging energies and his artistic vitality were, however, nothing short of amazing; and he managed in the course of a very active life as journalist and pamphleteer, theatrical manager and popular lecturer and folk leader, to produce an astonishing number of short stories and novels, lyric and narrative poems, essays and dramas. This body of work makes him next to Ibsen the strongest literary force of his day in Norway. It is as a lyric poet and as a teller of peasant tales that he is most apt to live for future generations of Norwegians; but in the drama he has also written a few plays of permanent importance, certain of his plays being in their day of crucial significance in the development of the modern Scandinavian drama. To Björnson, for instance, must be given the credit for writing in 1874 the first "social-reform play" that really succeeded in the theatre (*A Bankruptcy*), a play which apparently encouraged Ibsen to continue with a type of drama with which he had experimented only half-heartedly before.

Björnson's literary career began, as had Ibsen's, in the tradition of National Romanticism current in Norway at the middle of the nineteenth century. His earliest literary effort, *Between the Battles* (written 1857, published 1858), was a short poem in dramatic form going back for its subject-matter to the medieval past. This slight effort attracted little attention, however. His first work of any real consequence was the immensely successful series of short novels beginning with *Synnöve Solbakken* (1857) and continuing with *Arne* (1858) and *A Happy Boy* (1860). These were peasant tales, somewhat idealized, but maintaining on the whole a healthy, balanced attitude toward the peasant and written in a clear, simple, spontaneous prose that fascinated Björnson's contemporaries even as it has attracted Norwegians down to our day. Two saga plays, *Lame Hulda* and *King Sverre*, dating from 1858 and 1861 respectively, were little noticed by a public entranced by the peasant tales; and the critics were rather severe in their notices of the two plays. In 1857 Björnson had accepted a position at the Bergen theatre as the successor to Ibsen, who had moved to the capital in the same year. During the two years that Björnson remained in Bergen he displayed characteristic energy by editing a newspaper and taking an active part in local politics in addition to carrying out his duties at the theatre. In 1862 his dramatic trilogy *Sigurd the Bastard* found numerous admirers, among them Hans Christian Andersen in Denmark, and Ibsen; and its success was the immediate occasion for the Norwegian parliament's awarding Björnson a "poet's pension" in the amount of 400 specie-dollars (about 400 dollars in American money) a year, which enabled him to devote all of his energies in the next few years to the writing of creative literature.

Though *Sigurd the Bastard* is entirely too lengthy to succeed as a popular acting drama, it has on occasion been staged. It has frequently been compared with Ibsen's *Pretenders,* particularly because of certain similarities in characterization and in the ultimate fates of the central characters in the two dramas. Sigurd, like Earl Skule in Ibsen's drama, is a pretender to the throne, and one who strives to attain his ends even though his claim to the throne is at best questionable. Like Earl Skule, Sigurd also fails in his efforts, and his death clears the way for a just determination of who shall finally occupy the throne. Ibsen's *The Pretenders* reveals, however, a much more profound understanding of psychological motivations, though *Sigurd the Bastard* reflects a finer sense of general historical perspective. In certain individual scenes also Björnson's drama has great power, particularly in the second part of the trilogy. Both Shakespeare and Schiller had left obvious imprints on *Sigurd the Bastard,* and when Björnson wrote his next play, *Mary Stuart of Scotland* (1864), he tried his hand, not unsuccessfully, with an historical character whom Schiller also had handled. This play about Mary Stuart is, next to *Sigurd the Bastard,* Björnson's best historical drama; but it has nevertheless numerous rather glaring defects, the closing act being on the whole unsatisfactory, and the characters being too much concerned with "explaining themselves" in rather tiresome rounds of dialogue. The characters in themselves are interesting enough, however, especially the sensitive and will-less but deeply loyal Darnley, and Knox, the man whom even the Queen comes to admire despite her distaste for all that his forbidding Puritan idealism stands for.

The year after *Mary Stuart* Björnson published a play, *The Newly-Weds,* which is the first prose play on a contemporary theme in the modern Norwegian drama. Despite the instant success of this little piece (it was immediately accepted for performance in all of the capitals of the North, Copenhagen, Christiania, and Stockholm, something unheard of for the day), Björnson did not follow up this success with other plays on modern themes until a decade later. Contemporary accounts reveal that *The Newly-Weds* aroused almost as much discussion and controversy in the middle of the sixties as did Ibsen's *A Doll's House* fourteen years later. This suggests something of conditions in the Scandinavian theatre of the time, for Björnson's little play certainly did not challenge modern society in any fundamental respect, as did *A Doll's House,* and its ending, a happy one, might be said to satisfy even a good bourgeois taste. The play was, however, a distinct novelty at the time, departing as it did from traditional historical themes and dealing in a forthright natural prose with a modern domestic problem.

After the success of *The Newly-Weds* Björnson was active in a number of ways, with further literary efforts in a variety of forms, most happily in lyric and narrative poetry, with journalism and political controversy, and with general cultural studies of various kinds. Particularly significant for his later dramas are the political controversies and the cultural studies, for these led him in the early 1870's toward a set of conclusions that were to effect a radical change in his whole philosophy of life. Having identified himself during the late fifties with a worship of the past and of the peasant, the twin enthusiasms of Norwegian National Romanticism, Björnson found it quite natural in the sixties to feel a strong kinship to the Grundtvigian synthesis of Christianity and nationalism which found its chief positive expression in the program of the folk high-school movement originating in Denmark but spreading soon to Norway. In the early seventies, however, in consequence particularly of his growing acquaintance with modern science and philosophy (Darwin, Mill, Spencer, and others), Björnson became more critical of traditional social institutions, less inclined to worship the past with all that it represented. This did not lead to a complete break with the Grundtvigian social and cultural program, but it did lead to Björnson's challenging some parts of the program (particularly its extreme nationalism and its uncritical admiration for the peasant as the bearer of all fundamental cultural values) and, more significantly, it led to a break with the Established Church and with all forms of a supernatural Christianity. In his creative literature this break finds partial expression as early as 1877 in the drama entitled *The King*, but it is not until 1883, in *Beyond Human Power I*, that a natural as opposed to a supernatural religion becomes the central theme in a Björnson drama.

Meantime Björnson wrote "problem plays" of a somewhat different kind, though each of these plays in its way reveals that he was now prepared to face modern problems in an essentially critical manner. *A Bankruptcy* (1874) is a domestic drama, dealing with certain aspects of financial speculation. *The Editor*, dating from the same year, is an attack upon the evils of powerful and unscrupulous journalism. *The King* (1877) is a political play, the central idea of which is that the traditional concept of royalty must gradually be modified in terms of a growing republican spirit. *Leonarda* (1879) and *A Gauntlet* (1883) treat certain aspects of morality and marriage. *The New System* (1879) attacks social hypocrisy and the worship of traditional authority in a manner not unlike Ibsen's *An Enemy of the People*. Though none of these plays is of permanent importance, each originates in a vital idea, and each served in its day to "put problems into debate" in the same manner as Ibsen's social-reform plays. Two of them, *The Bankruptcy* and *The Editor*, antedated by some years Ibsen's plays in the same genre.

The Editor did not have the early success on the stage that Björnson had expected. It created, indeed, something of a purely local sensation in Norway when it appeared on a Christiania stage the year after its publication, but chiefly because it was looked upon primarily as a political pamphlet aimed at a particular individual in the Christiania of the day rather than because of its qualities as a new and challenging form of dramatic literature. And in both Sweden and Germany where the play was performed at about the same time it aroused little interest. *A Bankruptcy*, on the other hand, immediately enjoyed a phenomenal success in the theatres of all three of the Scandinavian countries as well as in Germany. Its clearly delineated characters and lively dialogue, together with its happy ending, made it very acceptable theatrical fare for the general run of audience which could scarcely distinguish its dramatic inadequacies. Both *The Editor* and *A Bankruptcy*, however, served a vital purpose in breaking down the historical tradition in the Scandinavian drama of the day and in pointing a way toward new dramatic themes. "They were the signal rockets," wrote Strindberg in the 1880's, "which rose toward the heavens and broke out into salvos whose echoes we have not yet forgotten." Both Ibsen and Strindberg were to go much farther than did Björnson in the creation of a new modern drama, but it remains an historical fact that Björnson provided the original impetus toward these new forms when in 1874 he published *A Bankruptcy* and *The Editor*.

Perhaps the two most interesting of Björnson's early group of social-reform plays are *The King* and *Leonarda*, both because they deal somewhat more boldly than was usual in Björnson with what at the time were really delicate problems, and because in each of these plays the central character is conceived with a depth and understanding not always characteristic of Björnson. Spontaneity of dialogue and rapid sweep of dramatic movement are more apt to be the qualities found in Björnson's dramas than psychological profundities. But in the sensitive, solitary character of the King and in the nobly passionate struggle of Leonarda to find a place for herself in life, Björnson has succeeded in creating figures not unworthy of his countryman Ibsen. Both of these characters are conceived as victims of social conditions, though in the case of Leonarda some elements in society seem at the end of the play to be prepared to make what restitution they can for the wrongs they have perpetrated in the name of truth and morality.

In *Leonarda* it is noteworthy that a churchman is the personage who at the end of the drama admits that society and the Church have been unfair in judging Leonarda as they did. Björnson's satire on the Established Church as the instrument of a narrow dogmatic morality is thus somewhat unexpectedly tempered at the end of the play. In *Beyond Human Power I,* Björnson writes a purely religious play, and one which in the scope of its thought, the depth of its feeling, and the noble pathos of its tragedy ranks as one of the very few really great Scandinavian plays on a religious theme.

Beyond Human Power I, is not concerned primarily with religious practices or religious dogmas as they may find expression in any particular society or community; it is concerned rather with a much more profound and universal aspect of religious experience and practice—the tendency on the part of certain religions, particularly perhaps Protestant Christianity, to stress the supernatural to the point where human life is frequently distorted and ideal values are destroyed. Pastor Sang, the central character in the drama, is an essentially tragic figure. With something of both Ibsen's Brand and Rosmer in his character, Sang is sensitive and self-sacrificing, pure and strong and idealistic; but his fanatical belief in the miracle, in the direct interposition of the hand of God in human affairs leads to destruction and to final tragedy. Björnson wishes in this play to illustrate that an idealism which postulates that which is impossible of attainment leads inevitably to evil rather than to good. *Beyond Human Power I* rises above its thesis, however, developing with a dramatic power and a sustained poetic feeling that Björnson attains in none of his other dramas. In construction it is firm, balanced, thoroughly classical both in line and in form. Though its moods shift from moment to moment in the course of its rapidly developing action, over the whole rests a serenity, a quiet self-contained majesty such as is found only in the greatest works of classical art. Even such Ibsen admirers and Björnson skeptics as Georg Brandes and Gunnar Heiberg were entirely satisfied with *Beyond Human Power I*. Heiberg was, in fact, lyrical in his praise of the drama; and Brandes wrote of it: "Björnson has never written a better play—nor Ibsen either."

If in *Beyond Human Power I* Björnson had created a work of great and timeless art, raised far above the concerns of immediate contemporary "problems," in another play, *A Gauntlet,* also published in 1883, he descends again into the hurly-burly of the market-place, mounts the rostrum, and proceeds to preach—this time more vehemently than ever before in his plays. *A Gauntlet* is nothing more nor less than a sermon, in thinly disguised dramatic form, on the subject of a single standard of morality; and when it appeared a storm of protest and ridicule descended upon the author, this time, however, from the camp of liberal bohemians rather than from the conservatives of the day. Undismayed by the reaction that the little play aroused in some quarters, Björnson demonstrated how seriously he took its subject by traveling far and wide through the Scandinavian countries delivering an impassioned lay-sermon entitled "Monogamy and Polygamy." And because the original form of the play did not with sufficient finality push home the message intended, Björnson later revised the last act, making of the drama even more of a moral pamphlet than it had been in its original form.

Unimportant as *A Gauntlet* is from a purely dramatic point of view, its subject may be said to provide a kind of general point of departure for most of Björnson's later plays. Though the play might on first reading seem to be concerned exclusively with a question of private morality, it is clear from Björnson's statements at the time that he was primarily concerned with a larger question, the preservation of the family as the basic unit in the development of the nation and the race. And it is therefore that Björnson comes more and more in his later plays to focus on problems concerned more or less directly with love and marriage and life within the home. In *Love and Geography* (1885) he writes an ingratiating but pointed comedy on the relation between a man and his wife and child. In *Laboremus* (1901) and *At Storhove* (1904) he contributes a couple of dramatic studies in the fatal effect which the completely emancipated woman can exercise on marriage relationships. And in *Dayland* (1904) and *When the Vineyards Are in Blossom* (1909) he deals with the subject of the proper adjustment between parents and children. In only two of the plays that Björnson composed between the middle of the 1880's and his death in 1910 can it be said that the family is not at the focus of his attention. These plays are *Beyond Human Power II,* dealing with the relationship between labor and capital, and *Paul Lange and Tora Parsberg,* concerned primarily with a political problem.

Beyond Human Power II, is a reasonably successful play, though one tends to be critical toward it because its title invites comparison with Björnson's great play, *Beyond Human Power I.* In the second play under the common title Björnson deals with the fanatical martyr complex inherent in a modern labor movement just as previously he had dealt with fanatical idealism in religion; and he wishes to suggest how futile it is to apply fanatical, absolute concepts to a solution of the conflict between labor and capital. In its general construction and the pointing of its central idea, *Beyond Human Power II* is certainly a satisfying play, but its handling of character tends to be schematic and abstract. In *Paul Lange and Tora Parsberg,* however, Björnson is occupied much more profoundly with character than with ideas and dramatic patterns; and he succeeds in giving us a wholly convincing picture of the way in which politics distorts fine individual values and finally destroys them altogether. Paul Lange has much in common with Ibsen's Johannes Rosmer, though unlike Rosmer he has had a political career when we meet him in the drama. Like Rosmer he is sensitive, idealistic, but with a strain of weakness in his character. It is this weakness that causes him to hesitate at a moment of crisis in his political career, with the result that an insensitive public, including some of his best friends and former political associates, misunderstand his motives and accuse him of disloyalty to his earlier political program. This leads to his suicide—a victim of political badgering of the most unfeeling and vicious kind. "It is my fault!" his old friend Arne Kraft cries out at the end. To which Tora Parsberg, who realizes that all, rather than any one single person, have wronged Paul Lange, replies: "And mine!...Or not our fault. It lies deeper. Oh, why should it be so, that those who are good often become martyrs? Will we never come so far that they will become our leaders?" Björnson had not infrequently in earlier plays been concerned with political problems, most markedly in *The Editor* and *The King;* but only in *Paul Lange and Tora Parsberg* has he managed to write a political play of first importance. The chief reason for his success in this instance is perhaps that he has come to see more deeply than before the personal problem in politics, and the relation of this personal problem to the whole question of human progress. How clearly he has seen these two aspects of the problem is revealed in his words about Paul Lange:

> ...that the noble, the good nature, the finest instinct as a rule is associated with something weak.... Society must not be permitted to destroy that which is fine together with that which is weak.... Almost all future-looking, reforming individuals are nervous, easily influenced, therefore also what we call "weak"; but among these are to be found the world's greatest spirits.

Aside from Ibsen, Björnson, and Strindberg, the only dramatist of commanding importance to appear in the Scandinavian countries well before the end of the nineteenth century was Gunnar Heiberg (1857-1929). In Norway Gabriel Finne (1866-1899) showed some dramatic promise in *The Owl* (1893), a naturalistic psychological study in the manner of the Strindberg of the 1880's; and two distinguished Norwegian novelists, Jonas Lie (1883-1908) and Alexander Kielland (1849-1906), tried their hands at an occasional play, neither very successfully, though Kielland's airy comedies *Three Couples* (1886) and *Betty's Guardian* (1887) provided some relief in the theatre from the heavy-footed manner in which questions of feminine emancipation, politics, and related subjects were wont to be treated in contemporary Scandinavian novels and plays. In Denmark Edvard Brandes (1847-1931) and Peter Nansen (1861-1918) turned out a large number of light, sophisticated plays dealing with artistic as well as bourgeois circles in the Copenhagen of the day. And in Sweden Gustaf af Geijerstam (1858-1909) turned his hand occasionally to popular peasant comedies as well as fairy-tale plays and wrote one folk tragedy, *Criminals* (1894; produced at the Théâtre de l'Oeuvre in Paris), which attempted to exploit the horror theme in crude imitation of the Russians. Only the Norwegian Gunnar Heiberg, among these authors, however, produced a considerable body of really significant dramas. He wrote fifteen plays in all, at least a half dozen of which are of first importance, and the others are, with one or two exceptions, thoroughly competent dramatic compositions. Besides being one of the more distinguished dramatists around the turn of the century, Heiberg is known as a scintillating essayist and one of the most penetrating of Scandinavian theatrical critics. For a short time in the eighties he was a theatrical director at Bergen, during which time he produced with great enthusiasm and success Ibsen's *The Wild Duck* and *Rosmersholm,* and included even in his repertoire, not without some opposition from those who were responsible for the theatre's finances, Zola's *Thérèse Raquin*.

Though Heiberg's literary origins were in the Scandinavian 1880's, with their realism and emphasis on social problems, his work on the whole represents the most complete break with the eighties that is to be found in the Scandinavian drama of the late nineteenth century outside Strindberg's revolutionary experiments in the expressionistic drama. Heiberg's first play, *Tante Ulrikke* (1883), was a realistic "problem play," for the most part clearly in the tradition of the day, though already in this drama one notes an interest in character on its purely psychological side that suggests a healthy, though perhaps only half-conscious reaction against the central ethical concerns of so much of the literature then current. In *King Midas* (1890) Heiberg's opposition to all that the literature of the eighties stood for becomes much more apparent; for this play is a direct attack upon Björnson, one of the authors who had been most instrumental in creating the literature of the preceding decade. Heiberg's satire in this play is loosed without mercy on the person of Johannes Ramseth (Björnson), who as an egotistical, self-satisfied journalist-reformer seeks to dominate other individuals to the point of distorting their personalities and destroying certain fine individual human values. Over against the vainglorious egotism of Ramseth the dramatist places two characters, Finn Hals and the artist Gerhard Hielm, who ultimately succeed in breaking the ugly spell that Ramseth had maintained for years over Fru Anna Hielm, a woman of an essentially fine and noble character. Both Finn Hals and Gerhard Hielm serve a double purpose in the drama: they determine the course of the action and they serve as a pair of clever satiric raisonneurs, pointing the shafts of their wit at those people who are constantly engaged in a busybody activity of loud-mouthed preaching and reform and who in their blind preoccupation with problems and programs and what-not forget that life itself in all of its manifold spontaneous and natural manifestations is to be treasured and preserved. As Hielm puts it at one point:

Before we know it life is completely gone, flown away, far away, or dead; and so we stand there, first we and then our descendants after us, and they demand it of us, and curse us because we were so busy improving the world and forgetting the very joy of existing.

Despite the attack in *King Midas* on the spirit of the eighties as personified by Björnson, the play yields no evidence that Heiberg was prepared to dispense with the realistic techniques current in the drama at the time. It was in another play of 1890, the little half-lyric piece *Night Scenes,* that Heiberg breaks completely with the eighties. This play is followed, three and four years later respectively, by *Artists* and *Gert's Garden,* two dramas which are more significant experiments in Heiberg's new dramatic form than *Night Scenes* had been; and these three plays together point the way unmistakably to a new kind of play that Heiberg was to develop, with necessary variations in terms of varying subject-matter, down through his whole later career as a dramatist. These plays have no "problems" in the old sense, and they dispense entirely with the carefully worked out intrigue (plot) which formed the structural basis of the plays of the eighties. Heiberg substitutes for the dramatist's preoccupation with problems and a carefully constructed logical intrigue an almost total preoccupation with character, and structurally he concentrates upon a number of basic scenes in which a highly charged, essentially lyric dialogue focuses our attention and throws a probing, finely penetrating light upon the central characters in the play. At times this form of drama became in Heiberg's hands somewhat schematic, a bit stylized, but in most of his best plays he manages it with remarkable skill and power, most successfully perhaps in *The Tragedy of Love,* which appeared in 1904, eleven years after Heiberg's first experiments with this form of drama.

The Tragedy of Love is Heiberg's most successful treatment of a theme central in his work—the conflict between love and man's striving toward larger cultural ideals. The theme first appears sharply in *The Balcony* (1894), though in this play it is developed in a somewhat schematic way, the lines of conflict being rather too obviously drawn and the characters being reduced to types, almost to abstractions, rather than people of flesh and blood and clearly perceived individual traits. *The Balcony* is concerned with a central character, Julie, and her relations with three men, her husband Ressman and two lovers, Abel and Antonio. Ressman is a satanic embodiment of gross, sensual love for whom Julie can feel nothing but the deepest loathing. Abel, in the sharpest possible contrast to Ressman, is a fine, sensitive, idealistic individual reminiscent of Johannes Rosmer; and to him love has little finally to do with passion—he wishes to transform passion into tenderness and altruism and to make of it a fine civilizing agency. Ready as Julie had been to desert Ressman and turn to Abel as the play opens, she cannot with the best of intentions understand Abel's desire to transform the essentially individual, natural force of love as passion into a pale, largely abstract program of altruism. In consequence she finally rejects Abel and turns instead to Antonio, a healthy, open-minded animal type, who admires Abel in a way but submits without much hesitation to the domineering passion of Julie. "Do you have sympathy with the spirits?" Julie cries out at the end of the play in bitter scorn of Antonio's momentary attraction to Abel's conception of love. "Do you agree with him? Are you going to capitulate—then go! Go, go, go!" These closing words are not a little hysterical, though not incongruous with the general tone of the play or with Julie's character as one comes to know it in earlier scenes of the drama.

In *The Tragedy of Love* the concept of individual love as a natural force in unyielding conflict with civilization, with man's ideal strivings, is developed much more satisfactorily than in *The Balcony*. Karen and Erling Kruse in this drama carry on the same conflict as do Julie and Abel in *The Balcony*, and they are no more able to solve the problem that faces two people who love and yet who have entirely different conceptions of the nature and the function of love. But Karen and Erling, unlike Julie and Abel, are not dramatic abstractions; they reveal themselves to us as concrete, living persons, creatures of flesh and blood and a warmly pulsing life. And in *The Tragedy of Love* individual passion is elevated by the dramatist to a plane of noble religious seriousness. In the experience of love man and woman find the most significant fact in human experience: "Be proud, Erling Kruse. Place a cross upon your door. A bloody cross. For love has visited your house." To Karen love is everything—not a means but the very end of existence. And when, therefore, Karen finally comes to see that Erling cannot understand this conception of love, when she knows that he will subordinate his love to his work, then she finds existence meaningless and ends her own life. Early in the play Hartvig Hadeln, the poet, had said: "He who loves most deeply always loses, for he loses the one whom he loves." This is the tragedy of love. Though the physical had a central place in Karen's conception of love, passion was not to her an end in itself. In this respect Heiberg's *The Tragedy of Love* is worlds removed from Wedekind's dramas of sex. Wedekind looked upon all expressions of love except the purely sensual as mere hypocrisy. To Heiberg sex was merely one of the contents in a conception of love that in essence was a consuming spirit. It was because Karen lost control of Erling's soul that she found life ultimately meaningless, essentially tragic. The noble, elevated tone which Heiberg manages to infuse into his great tragedy may be said to issue almost as much from the lyric intensity of the dialogue and the magnificent natural setting of the play as it does from the beautifully conceived dramatic conflict. Heiberg's plays are as a rule lyric in the intimate sense, employing interiors or only suggestive touches of natural background in order to develop the appropriate mood. In a play with the imaginative sweep and the religious fervor of *The Tragedy of Love*, however, Heiberg has the action appropriately taking place against the vast, bare primitive sweep of the Norwegian fjeld country. One is reminded inevitably of Ibsen's *Brand* and Björnson's *Beyond Human Power I*. Despite Heiberg's strong reaction against Björnson and most of his work, he never failed to express the deepest enthusiasm for *Beyond Human Power I*. Björnson's play has obviously left its mark upon Heiberg's *The Tragedy of Love*.

Though Heiberg had reacted so strongly in the early nineties against the typical social-problem play of the previous decade, it may be said that many of the plays that he wrote in the late nineties and the first dozen years of the new century were problem plays also in their own way, plays in which he takes up, usually with satiric intent, certain characteristic manifestations of the life of his day. It should be emphasized, however, that his thinking in these plays is always strongly individualistic, in sharp contrast to the ethico-social emphasis of most of the literature of the eighties, and that the new dramatic techniques that he had experimented with so successfully in the early nineties are applied consistently in all of his later dramas. These dramas deal with a wide variety of contemporary problems—with politics in *The Council of the People* (1897) and *I Will Defend My Country* (1912), with problems connected with the rise of an industrial proletariat class in *The Grand Prize* (1895), with the demoralization of modern journalism in *Harald Svan's Mother* (1899), and with certain forms of hypocritical idealism in *Love Your Neighbor* (1902). Though some of these plays, technically speaking, are broad comedies, with occasional even farcical elements, they were all written with a burning moral pathos that is always the central mark of Heiberg's work. *I Will Defend My Country* is perhaps the most remarkable of all of these plays; but its brilliant development of Heiberg's ideas on individualism and nationalism, particularly with reference to Norway's break with Sweden in 1905, is of interest chiefly to the Norwegian people. In *The Parade Bed* (1913), the last and the most notorious of Heiberg's plays, the dramatist's moral indignation descends with explosive and devastating violence upon certain of Björnson's descendants who had employed the last hours of the dying poet and the funeral ceremonies for purposes of publicity and direct economic gain. Never had Heiberg's satire been more grim, more witheringly brilliant; but the general Norwegian feeling seems to be that he has in this play overstepped the bounds of the permissible, that he has here shown little more of a sense of reverence for the dead than had those who aroused his fury by using the occasion of death for their own selfish purposes. Even as late as 1924, when the play was performed for the first time in Oslo, it aroused a strong current of public protest.

The first two decades of the twentieth century witnessed no continuation of the great tradition in the drama that was the chief glory of Scandinavian literature in the last quarter of the nineteenth century. Strindberg, Björnson, and Heiberg continued to produce significant plays in the first years of the new century; but much of their work had its origins in an earlier generation, and though the later work of Strindberg and the plays of Heiberg pointed new ways for the generation of dramatists after 1900, the younger generation of dramatists were in the main scarcely prepared to follow the leads suggested. It was not until after World War I, and particularly in the 1930's, that the Scandinavian drama came to exploit successfully the new dramatic techniques of Strindberg and Heiberg. No new dramatist of commanding stature appeared in the first two decades of the twentieth century, though the production of plays can hardly be said to have decreased markedly. A couple of reasons may be given for the falling off in quality of dramatic composition in the years immediately after 1900:

first, the mighty shadows of Ibsen and Strindberg hung fatefully over any one who attempted to produce in dramatic form, inviting comparisons not happy for lesser dramatic talents; and secondly, the neo-romantic trends becoming dominant in Scandinavian literature after 1890 found lyric poetry and prose narrative more to its purposes than the drama. The great literary figures who appeared in the nineties were either lyric poets (Gustaf Fröding, Erik Axel Karlfeldt, Johannes Jörgenson, and Sigbjörn Obstfelder) or novelists (Knut Hamsun and Selma Lagerlöf) or poet-novelists (Verner von Heidenstam). The ability of Strindberg and Heiberg in the late nineties and after to combine lyric and dramatic forms in an essentially new type of drama, and thus assimilate into the drama some of the characteristic features of the art and thought of the nineties, was not typical of other literary figures of the day, though there was in the first two decades of the twentieth century a considerable vogue for poetic closet dramas reminiscent of the romantic drama of a century earlier.

Into this latter category may be said to fall the scarcely successful plays of the Norwegian novelist Knut Hamsun (1859-   ) and many of the verse dramas of the Swedes Per Hallström (1866-   ) and Tor Hedberg (1862-1931), though Hallström and Hedberg have also written plays conceived definitely with the modern stage in mind. Both Hallström and Hedberg wrote, besides plays, lyric poems, essays, and narrative fiction, Hallström being especially distinguished as a short-story writer. As a theatrical critic and as the director of the Royal Theatre at Stockholm (from 1910 to 1922) Hedberg revealed a remarkably catholic taste in the drama, being one of the few distinguished Swedish critics in the early twentieth century who reveals a discriminating sympathy for Strindberg's late dramatic work. As a dramatist Hedberg wrote some twenty plays, all of which are competent pieces, but these plays, with one or two exceptions, are not to be counted among Scandinavian dramas of the very first importance. Hedberg, like Gunnar Heiberg, is interested primarily in character, in careful dramatic studies of human psychology. But unlike Heiberg his plays frequently lack many of those qualities that make for effective theatre. They are as a rule a bit heavy, perhaps all too solidly built, frequently wanting in spontaneity and vividness of dialogue and in sharply defined dramatic conflicts. Among his more successful plays are *Gold and Green Forests* (1895), a rollicking bit of satire on contemporary life, *Borga Estate* (1915), a quietly penetrating treatment of life on a modern Swedish estate, and *Johan Ulvstjerna* (1907), the one undeniable masterpiece among Hedberg's long list of dramas. *Johan Ulvstjerna* is a political play, a free dramatic retelling of the fate of a Finnish poet who meets a noble martyr's death as the champion of an oppressed people in a period of this people's deepest political shame. The characters in this play are drawn with a fine, warmly sensitive touch; the action moves rapidly, the central dramatic conflict being managed with a controlled intensity rare in the Scandinavian drama; and over the whole play rests a quiet, natural lyricism of conception and utterance that leaves nothing to be desired. Particularly effective is Hedberg in his handling of the central character. Johan Ulvstjerna is no ordinary martyr type, moved to his actions in consequence of a fanatical martyr complex. He is at the opening of the play, in fact, a somewhat pathetic figure: a once-famous poet now gone to seed, living a flaccid, comfortable existence because he had capitulated to the oppressor, and having lost all real contact with the youth of his nation who longed above all else to give positive expression to their hatred of the oppressor and their dream of freedom. Johan Ulvstjerna's son, Helge, is one of a number of young university students who have sworn to assassinate the terrorist foreign governor of their country, now simply a helpless Grand Duchy of a great foreign power. When Johan Ulvstjerna discovers that Helge is among the conspirators and that his son had been chosen to commit the actual deed of murdering the governor, he commits the deed himself, not with the grand gesture of a fanatical martyr but simply because he feels that in this way he can regain his own soul and save a younger generation for a long life of more substantial service to the country than he, the representative of an old, decrepit generation, can hope now to accomplish. "Father!" cries out Helge at the close. "What have you done? This I should have done!" To which Johan Ulvstjerna replies in a calm low voice, just as the gendarmes arrive to arrest him, "Quiet! Quiet! Don't you see that I must die so that you may live."

None of Per Hallström's dozen plays can be said to measure up to the standard of Hedberg's *Johan Ulvstjerna,* though his two historical dramas of 1918, *Charles XI* and *Gustaf III,* are, after Strindberg, among the more significant efforts in Sweden to employ historical materials for dramatic purposes. Hallström's greatest service to the Swedish theatre is, however, the magnificent translation of Shakespeare upon which he worked intensively for some ten years beginning in the early 1920's. Like Hedberg, Hallström wrote plays on a large variety of themes; but he differs from the sober, undemonstrative Hedberg in that his plays reflect a richness of color and an imaginative complexity that draws on the Renaissance for its primary inspiration. His master was Shakespeare, not Ibsen. His taste for Renaissance warmth and color is reflected even in the dramatic motifs employed in his early plays, among which may be mentioned *Bianca Capello* (1900), a heavy tragedy of blood and passion, and *A Venetian Comedy* (1901), a light and airy comedy in Shakespeare's most playful manner. Though Hallström occasionally turns to modern life for his dramatic themes, he does not seem to find himself entirely at home in these materials. In *Erotikon* (1908) he has written a fairly clever satire on the superficialities and the irresponsibility of the contemporary cult of eroticism, and in *The Mantle of Nessus* (1919) he has vilified with considerable success modern political charlatanism.

In Denmark Gustaf Wied (1858-1914) and Hjalmar Bergström (1868-

1914) were perhaps the two most important dramatists between the turn of the century and World War I. Wied is the more prolific of the two, and by far the more original; but his eccentric fancy lacks the inner discipline necessary to great creative production, and his clever cynicism had in it the seed of intellectual sterility. He reminds one of Strindberg in a number of ways, though his genius lacked the artistic range and the startling dramatic intensity of Strindberg. He was, however, enormously productive, turning out short stories and novels and plays with amazing rapidity. In his prose fiction he is a master of vividly conceived individual scenes, although he is very careless in matters of general construction. The same may be said to be true of his plays, though occasionally, as in the sophisticated comedy $2 \times 2 = 5$ (1906) he manages both episode and plot in a thoroughly satisfactory manner. Wied was in general a restless experimenter in dramatic forms of various kinds, but these experiments are for the most part of no importance in the history of the drama, chiefly because they represent on the whole merely the work of a brilliant dramatic dilettante. He was gifted with a sense of the comic not frequently found among Scandinavian dramatists, but he never developed his gift into the really great comic strain of which he seems to have been capable. His forte is the small genre picture, full of oddities in characterization and dialogue, and reinforced by scenic adjuncts which provide the exactly appropriate atmosphere for such episodic drama. His most original dramatic experimentation is to be found in his so-called Satyr Plays, a name that he gave to a group of satiric comedies (the most important of which are *Nobility, Clergy, Citizen, and Peasant,* 1897; *The Weaker Sex,* 1900; and *The Dancing Mice,* 1905), in which the stage is very small, a kind of doll theatre, with revolving scenes and an open horizon at the rear, and in which the "director" not only prompts the actors but also the spectators with lengthy stage directions and subtle comments on the significance of the action taking place before us. The satire here is frequently indirect but none the less devastating in its implications, and one follows these plays better by reading them than by witnessing them. Their utterly disillusioned view of human life as well as the originality of their dramatic conception reminds us inevitably of the Strindberg of the Chamber Plays. That Wied was on occasion capable of comic portraiture in a more traditional dramatic form is apparent in his very popular $2 \times 2 = 5$. In this play Wied's disillusionment and cynicism is given an inimitably light, Puck-like expression, which made it palatable even to a conservative middle-class taste. It is so airily entertaining that only the hopeless cynic would insist upon exposing its deeper implications.

Hjalmar Bergström, in marked contrast to his brilliantly eccentric countryman Wied, is a solid journeyman artist, who sees clearly what he wants to do in a given play and proceeds to do it with intelligence and an eye for the practical limitations of the theatre. His plays lack fire and imaginative sweep, but they are honest and usually effective representations of characteristic social problems of the day in Denmark. His master is obviously Ibsen, particularly the Ibsen of the social-problem plays. After having tried his hand with little success at prose fiction, Bergström turned to the drama, composing between 1901 and his death in 1914 nine plays, the most important of which are *Lynggaard and Company, Karen Bornemann,* and the slight but interesting piece *Ladies' Tea.* In the last of these plays Bergström indulges fairly successfully in a type of light dramatic sketch frequently exploited by Danish dramatists. There is no "conflict" in the play: the action consists merely in some miscellaneous social chitchat carried on by a number of quite ordinary unmarried females who, at an afternoon tea, become more confidential with each other than usual, explaining anecdotally and with a minimum of feminine indirection why they have not married. The topic provides opportunity for much comedy and a dash of pathos. *Lynggaard and Company* and *Karen Bornemann* are more ambitious plays, the former an only partly successful study in modern industrial conditions, the latter a rather daring treatment of the contemporary "emancipated woman." Both of these plays are well constructed, and they employ enough characters to give one a realistic sense of the ramifications of the problems involved; but the characters strike us for the most part as types rather than living embodiments of the ideas they represent. This is particularly true of *Lynggaard and Company,* in which the struggle between capital and labor is not sharply enough conceived, with the result that the play seems to get nowhere in particular. In *Karen Bornemann,* on the other hand, the dramatic conflict is very sharply drawn, one is tempted to say almost too sharply. Karen Bornemann, the daughter of a theological professor in Copenhagen, has had before the play opens two serious love-affairs outside the bonds of marriage, one with a young Danish novelist who died, the other with a promising young sculptor in Paris. The latter she has left because he had not been faithful to her. At the opening of the play she is living with her parents in Copenhagen. Presently a suitor appears in the person of a successful young physician of liberal intellectual leanings. When he finally proposes marriage, Karen tells him that she has formerly loved and been loved, whereupon the young physician's "liberalism" evaporates and he breaks off contact with Karen. This arouses the suspicions of the theologian father, to whom in turn Karen, with no apologies, confesses her "past." Horrified at this confession, the father, consistent with his oft-expressed "Christian principles," insists that Karen marry the sculptor, who has conveniently arrived in Copenhagen from Paris and desires nothing more than that Karen return to him. This Karen refuses to do, for she now feels nothing but loathing for him. At the end of the play she gives a quite honest expression to her conception of love, a free, untrammeled relation between man and woman which is not necessarily dependent upon the "blessings" of the church or a traditional code of Christian morality. She has at the end but pity for her father, who breaks down under the burden of Karen's earlier confession and the final expression of her conception of love. "I pity you, father," Karen says quietly at the close. "But how can I help it that I am a child of a time you don't understand? We have never wanted to hurt each other, of course, but I suppose it is the law of life that nothing new can come into the world without pain." In its central dramatic conflict between a traditional parental conception of "honor" and a young woman's insistence upon solving the problem of love in a manner consistent with a more modern view of the sexual relationship, this play may be compared with Sudermann's *Magda* and Stanley Houghton's *Hindle Wakes*. In its general dramatic technique *Karen Bornemann* follows Ibsen closely, with the materials of the past necessary to our understanding of the motivation of the characters being gradually revealed in the course of the dialogue. The central problem of the play may also be said to have some general parallels with *A Doll's House,* but Bergström's Karen is concerned far less with ethical abstractions in seeking to live her own individual life than is Ibsen's Nora. Karen is a creature of passion, in very marked contrast to Ibsen's almost "philosophical" Nora; and despite the unfortunate issue of her former experiences of love, Karen is quite frankly prepared at the end of the play to respond again to the call of passion in case a man whom she could consider worthy of her love should appear at some time in the future. Ibsen probably never dreamed of the length to which later dramatists were to carry what they might consider some of the implications of his Nora-doctrine!

Though neither Finland nor Iceland have been especially productive in dramatic literature, both of these countries have since 1900 made contributions in the drama of some significance. Among the dramatists writing in Swedish in Finland,[1] Mikael Dybeck (1864-1925) is unquestionably the most important, while a number of other authors, of whom may in particular be mentioned Arvid Mörne (1876-   ) and Runar Schildt (1888-1925), have written an occasional play that has attracted some attention. Mörne has written three plays, the most important of which is perhaps *Our Heritage* (1918), which deals with an episode connected with the Russian military command in his native district of Nyland on Finland's southern coast. Schildt showed considerable dramatic promise in three plays late in his literary career, *The Gallows Man* (1922), *The Great Rôle* (1923), and *The Knight-errant* (1924); but his early death provided no opportunity for further development as a dramatist. In his three plays, however, Schildt experiments interestingly with a variety of dramatic techniques, realistic and symbolical, though all of his plays deal in one way or another with the same theme, the saving power of feminine love. Both Mörne and Schildt as well as Dybeck write preferably in genres other than the drama. Dybeck, however, has written in dramatic form with more frequency than any of his Finno-Swedish contemporaries, six plays having come from his pen. His

[1] The drama of Finland written in Finnish is dealt with in another section of this volume.

dramas reveal a strong Ibsen influence, especially in their careful workmanship and in their stern moral pathos. Two of them, *The Lizard* (1908) and *Dean Bomander* (1923), concern themselves with ethical and religious questions, *The Lizard* reminding one strongly in both characters and ideas of Ibsen's *Rosmersholm* and *Hedda Gabler*. Two others, *The Dynasty Peterberg* (1913) and *The Red André* (1917), are political plays, giving somewhat indirect but unmistakable expression to the dramatist's Finnish nationalist ideas. *The Dynasty Peterberg* has, of all of Dybeck's plays, been most successful on the stage, partly perhaps because of the actuality of its theme, partly no doubt because of its clean logical structure and its strong ethical idealism. The characterization of Chamberlain André Peterberg, with his smirking manner and his antics as a political-climber type of Czarist Russia's diplomatic careerist, is a masterpiece of icy satiric scorn. It is, however, in *Brother and Sister* (1915) that Dybeck has written his most artistically satisfying play. If in *The Dynasty Peterberg* the dramatist had expressed a nauseating disgust of human nature in its lowest form, he finds in Per Ennius, the central male figure in *Brother and Sister,* occasion to immortalize all that which is fine and noble in man. Over this quiet little play, in which each phrase, each word breathes a blessing on man's fate, Dybeck's sensitive lyric spirit hovers with a warm and jealous care. Few Scandinavian plays are so unobtrusively impressive as *Brother and Sister*.

Quite unlike Dybeck's Finnish plays are the dramas of the two Icelanders Jóhann Sigurjónsson (1880-1919) and Gudmundur Kamban (1888-   ). It may be said, indeed, that no modern Scandinavian dramas are quite like the plays of these two Icelanders. They have struck an essentially *new* note in the Scandinavian drama of the last half century—a fresh, vigorous, fiercely primitive note, in which the most violent of feelings are permitted quite uninhibited expression, and in which the dramatic conflict is usually conceived as a life-and-death struggle. These dramas have no finesses, no subtleties, no carefully conscious art. At times they spill over into mere rhetoric, but they manage on the whole to maintain reasonably proper bounds for the eager lyricism of their expression. The literary origins of both Sigurjónsson and Kamban are to be found in the spacious and vigorous world of the Icelandic saga, with its dark violences and its primitive backgrounds, rather than in a more civilized modern literary tradition, though occasionally one seems to note an echo of Ibsen or of Strindberg. In modern Icelandic literature only Indridi Einarsson (1851-1939) and Matthías Jochumsson (1835-1920) wrote an occasional play before Sigurjónsson and Kamban appeared on the scene, but the work of neither of these men is significant for the drama of their two important successors. Of these two really significant Icelandic dramatists, Sigurjónsson's work is more rounded and complete, giving expression to a more consistent dramatic temperament. Kamban is a more restless, explosive, essentially dramatic genius, in whom it is very difficult as yet, however, to discern any regular line of development.

Sigurjónsson appeared first—in the opening decade of the century. His earliest play, *Dr. Rung* (1905), deals with a tragic series of experiments carried on by a young scientist in Copenhagen. It contains a few scenes of some dramatic power, but it is on the whole scarcely more than an awkward imitation of Ibsen. In his next two plays, *The Hraun Farm* (1908) and *Eyvind of the Hills* (1911), Sigurjónsson returns to Iceland for dramatic motifs, with strikingly successful results, particularly in the latter of these plays. *The Hraun Farm* suffers somewhat because the dramatic conflict is not drawn sharply enough; but as a detailed and realistic dramatic sketch it provides a remarkably convincing picture of life and customs on a large Icelandic farm. In *Eyvind of the Hills* Sigurjónsson reveals a much more adequate control of the elements of dramatic conflict. The drama is based upon a real story from Icelandic tradition, the tragic fate of the outlaw Eyvind and the woman Halla who gave up a peaceful and prosperous farm life and followed Eyvind in the desolate, uninhabited hill country when the law sought him. Here the two live under great difficulties, constantly pursued by the law and harassed by the severity of the seasons. Both of their children perish, one at the hands of its mother in order to facilitate flight when the authorities are hot upon the trail of the pair. Driven at last without food into the most wild and remote part of the mountain country, Eyvind and his woman perish in a howling snow-storm. The last act—with its note of elevated, triumphant passion dominating an undercurrent of hopeless, partly bitter dialogue—is among the most impressive in modern Scandinavian literature. Of Sigurjónsson's last two plays, *The Wish* (1915) and *The Liar* (1917), the former is the more important. In *The Liar* the dramatist has taken his materials directly from Njal's Saga, but he does not succeed in making living drama of this material. *The Wish* is based on an early eighteenth-century tale of black magic, in which a young student, Loftur, becomes involved with two young women, one (Steinunn) whom he has loved surreptitiously in the flower of early youth, the other (Disa, daughter of the Bishop of Holar) whom he wishes to marry. In a moment of desperation Loftur employs a formula of black magic in order to destroy Steinunn, who stands in the way of his proposed later union with Disa. Steinunn's death by suicide drives Loftur to madness, and then to death by a stroke when he seeks to sell his soul to the Devil in return for earthly power. The Faust theme, only sparingly used in the early acts of the play, emerges with an intense dramatic effect in the last act, the action of which takes place in the dimly lighted, shadow-filled Cathedral in the deep of night. The poet in Sigurjónsson brings such an intense imaginative focus on this final scene that it manages to avoid the purely melodramatic effects which it may well have stumbled into.

Though Sigurjónsson restricted himself almost entirely to the dramatic form, Kamban has written successfully both novels and plays. His novels are in fact to date perhaps the most mature part of his work, but his plays with all of their fairly obvious faults reveal an instinctive feeling of dramatic incident and dramatic conflict which is not common in the contemporary Scandinavian drama. In his first two dramas, *Hadda Padda* (1914) and *The Royal Wrestling* (1915), Kamban exploits quite unabashedly the most explosive of primitive passions, and the dramatic conflict in these plays can in consequence be resolved only by violent deaths. "I do not *think*," cries Hekla, the central character in *The Royal Wrestling*. "I *fight* to save myself. As one who is shipwrecked does. I cling fast to the swimmer, as one does when drowning. Perhaps we may both be saved, perhaps we will both go under." In neither of Kamban's first plays does he show much sense for the niceties of dramatic structure, but the reader is nevertheless impressed by the rich dramatic expressiveness of language and idea and character in these plays. They are saturated with the spirit of youth, brutally impatient of controls, fiercely fighting for ideals whose exact contents are not always very clearly conceived. In his later plays, *Marble* (1918) and *We Murderers* (1920), Kamban has taken up more mature subjects but with little if any loss of the fierce dramatic intensity central in his earlier plays. *We Murderers,* Kamban's best drama to date, is a powerful study in the mutual demands of two married people upon each other. Though it seems on first reading to be simply a startling resurrection of the central problem of Strindberg's naturalistic plays from the 1880's, Kamban has succeeded in giving to the problem an essentially original treatment without any loss of the volcanic emotional intensities characteristic of Strindberg. One feels that Kamban may in the future develop into a dramatist of really commanding stature, once he has mastered more solidly the disciplines of firm dramatic structure.

Among the more productive of Scandinavian dramatists whose work spans both the pre-World War I and the post-World War I generations may be mentioned the Dane Einar Christiansen (1861-1939), the Norwegian Peter Egge (1869-   ), and the Swedes Ernst Didring (1868-1931) and Hjalmar Söderberg (1869-1941). Except for Söderberg their output has been prolific, and their plays, often well conceived and skilfully executed, have been seen frequently on the Scandinavian stage. But they have attracted little attention outside their own countries, and their work scarcely warrants any serious attention here. Christiansen has tried his hand with only fair success in some twenty plays at a number of dramatic forms—fairy-tale plays, drawing-room sketches, and social-reform dramas. Egge, besides cultivating the novel somewhat extensively, has written more than a dozen plays, having had a good deal of success with distinctive popular comedies such as *Jacob and Christopher* (1900), *Love and Friendship* (1904), and *Wilhelmina's Bureau* (1915), as well as with serious problem dramas in the vein of Ibsen such as *The Idyl* (1910), *The Rift* (1914), and *The Fool* (1917). Didring, more productive than either Christiansen or Egge, leans primarily toward the problem drama, his most successful play being *High*

Stakes (1909), an arresting dramatic study in jealousy. Söderberg, who is primarily significant in Swedish literature as its one indubitable master of the short story, has written only three plays, one of which, *Gertrud* (1906), a sharply delineated treatment of the disillusioning vagaries of love between the sexes, has aroused some attention even outside of Sweden.

Two other authors of this generation, the Dane Helge Rode (1870-1937) and the Norwegian Hans E. Kinck (1865-1926), would seem to be definitely more important, though neither of them moves as successfully in the dramatic form as he does in other literary genres. Both of these men may be said to be chiefly significant in a general cultural rather than in a narrow literary sense, though Rode is one of the ranking lyric poets of his age in Denmark, and Kinck is a master of the extended essay as well as of a variety of narrative prose forms. Rode's general cultural contribution lies in his sensitive and intelligent reaction against the critical ideas of Georg Brandes, whereas Kinck is one of the most profound Norwegian students of ideational and racial phenomena in their broad historical manifestations. Though both Rode and Kinck not infrequently employed the dramatic form to give expression to their ideas, when they did so their plays tended to suffer from a too-great admixture of the philosophical element. Among the more successful dramas in which Rode indulges in an analysis of general cultural phenomena are *Count Peasant and His House* (1912) and *A Man Went Down from Jerusalem* (1920), the former an effort to come to some conclusions on the significance of Tolstoi and his work, the latter an attack upon Brandes as an interpreter, particularly for Denmark, of certain broad modern cultural values. Kinck, a more forceful original genius than Rode, wrote plays that are as a rule somewhat more impressive on the stage than are Rode's. Kinck's profound interest in the Italian Renaissance produced two distinctive dramas, *The Last Guest* (1910), a subtle tragedy based on the life of Pietro Aretino, and *Toward Carnival Time* (1916), a penetrating psychological study of Machiavelli. *On Erkre Estate* (1913) is, on the other hand, a play dealing with the modern class struggle in Norway. It suggests, with considerable originality of approach, a solution of the modern conflict between capital and labor along national historical lines. Kinck's most original plays, however, are *The Cattle Driver* (1908) and its late sequel *At Rindal Camp* (1925). These two plays inevitably remind one of Ibsen's *Peer Gynt* in a number of respects, particularly in their loose epic structure, their fascinating lyric quality, and their whimsical play of fantasy. To some extent also Vraal, the hero of Kinck's two dramas, reminds one of Peer in Ibsen's play. Both Vraal and Peer are pure individualists, men of almost preternatural imaginative powers who refuse to identify themselves closely with the normal patterns of man's social existence. But Vraal, in the most marked of possible contrasts with Peer, uses his imagination constructively, as an instrument of truth, as a means of discovering life's deepest values. Vraal becomes therefore in Kinck's two plays the figure in whom the dramatist gives expression to his positive ideas rather than, as in *Peer Gynt*, the character on whom the dramatist is intent upon passing a final negative moral judgment.

In the last couple of decades, particularly since 1930, the Scandinavian drama has been experiencing a kind of renaissance which promises well for the Scandinavian theatre of the future. At least a dozen dramatists of more than ordinary ability have appeared in the Scandinavian countries within the last twenty years, and the most important of the Scandinavian theatres have been ready to produce important native plays with both enthusiasm and imagination. The list of authors who have made their mark during the last couple of decades (all born in the 1890's or shortly thereafter) includes Sigurd Christiansen, Ronald Fangen, Finn Halvorsen, Johan Borgen, Helge Krog, and Nordahl Grieg in Norway, Herbert Grevenius, Rudolf Värnlund, Ragnar Josephson, Vilhelm Moberg, and Pär Lagerkvist in Sweden, and Kjeld Abell, Leck Fischer, Svend Borberg, and Kaj Munk in Denmark. In addition to these the Norwegian Oscar Braaten and the two Swedes Hjalmar Bergman and Sigfrid Siwertz, all of whom had written for the stage well before the 1920's, became significant in the theatre only in more recent years after having built up solid literary reputations in the genre of prose fiction.

Of these Hjalmar Bergman (1883-1931) is incomparably the most significant both as novelist and dramatist. Though he composed prolifically in both dramatic and prose narrative forms in the earlier years of his authorship (his first published work was an unsuccessful drama, *Mary, Mother of Jesus*, 1905), he had great difficulty in finding a sympathetic public for his work because of the dark, sinister undercurrents of pessimism which it contained and because of the eerie *fantasterie* of its form. He did not succeed in gaining a large reading public until 1919, with the fabulously popular tale of life in the Swedish Bergslagen district entitled *Markurells i Wadköping* (translated into English under the title *God's Orchid*, 1924). Though Bergman's earliest plays reveal some evidences of an influence from Ibsen, he came soon to be much more deeply attracted to the characteristic moods and attitudes toward life of Maeterlinck and Strindberg— to the obscure and ominous fatalism of the former, to the brutal, primitive, only half-religious "providentialism" which finds expression in certain late plays of the latter. Strindberg's impact on Bergman was more diffuse than that of Maeterlinck, but not therefore less profound. Maeterlinck's influence is perhaps more demonstrable, particularly in the group of Bergman plays entitled collectively "Marionette Plays" from 1917, which includes *Death's Harlequin, A Shadow,* and *Mr. Sleeman Is Coming*. Though each of these plays is a separate dramatic unit in itself, and though in both subject-matter and technique each is clearly distinguishable from the others, all three of the plays are similar in their subtle evocation of brooding fatalistic moods and in their view of human destiny as being determined by irrational, darkly evil forces incapable of being either controlled or understood by man.

Though Bergman composed a dozen plays in the first two decades of his authorship, he did not succeed in breaking through in the theatre until 1925, and then with the phenomenally successful *Swedenhielms* (produced in America in 1932 under the title *The Nobel Prize*). From the middle of the 1920's to his death in 1931 Bergman maintained the closest of contacts with all institutions concerned with present-day dramatic expression—with the legitimate theatre, with the film industry, and even with the purely theatrical side of radio broadcasting. In the legitimate theatre his triumph with *Swedenhielms* was followed, in 1928, by the almost equally successful play *The Rabble,* with the famous Swedish actor Gösta Ekman in the title rôle; and in the last year of his life Bergman adapted for the stage, with instant success, two of his most famous novels, *His Grace's Last Testament* and *God's Orchid,* the title rôle in the latter providing the vehicle for one of the greatest theatrical triumphs of Anders de Wahl in more than a half century of distinguished service on the Scandinavian stage. The living vitality of Hjalmar Bergman's theatre is attested by the fact that his popularity is growing rapidly and solidly on the Swedish stage now more than a decade and a half after his death.

Though it is difficult to determine even the relative importance of the younger group of authors of the present generation, it would seem that the most significant figures of our day in the Scandinavian drama are Pär Lagerkvist, Helge Krog, Nordahl Grieg, and Kaj Munk. Others have written individual plays of importance, but they are scarcely to be considered, as yet at least, central formative figures in the present-day Scandinavian drama.

Perhaps the most striking feature of the Scandinavian drama of the last two decades is the boldness and originality with which it comes to grips with certain characteristic phases of modern life, particularly those economic and political developments in the life of our day which have had such a revolutionary effect upon individuals as well as upon nations. In order to understand the Scandinavian drama of our day one must constantly keep in mind that this drama is a between-the-wars drama, created primarily by a literary generation which has felt the impact of conditions of war and the between-the-wars chaos of the modern world. The fact that none of the Scandinavian countries was an active participant in World War I in no way released the literary conscience of these nations from a preoccupation with the political and moral problems which the war posed. Only two Scandinavian plays dealing specifically with certain aspects of the war itself are apt to live—the Dane Svend Borberg's *No One* (1920) and the Norwegian Nordahl Grieg's *Our Honor and Our Power* (1935). But many of the most important plays of the last two decades reflect more or less directly certain phases of after-war psychology and contemporary economic and political circumstances conditioned by the war. Fascism and Nazism and related political phenomena are treated in such plays as Halvorsen's *Dictator* (1933), Munk's *Victory* (1936), and Lagerkvist's *The Hangman* (dramatized from a short novel in 1934), while other important dramas give only less direct expression to developments in European politics of our day. The economic and political struggles of the laboring classes find extensive and sympathetic interpretation in such distinctive proletariat authors as Braaten, Grevenius, and Värnlund, and other dramatists such as Sigurd Christiansen (particularly in *Edmund Jahr,* 1926) and Helge Krog (in *The Big We,* 1919, and *The House of the Jarl,* 1923) find occasion at times to deal with the problem of capital and labor from a more inclusive standpoint. Still other dramatists, recognizing the deeper psychological and moral implications of the struggles for class domination and political power, have faced the problems of a chaotic modern world from a more purely ethical and religious point of view. This is the case with Lagerkvist and Munk as well as with some lesser figures such as Fangen and Halvorsen. Though important plays dealing with the modern Scandinavian peasant are not numerous in the Scandinavian literatures of the last two decades, Moberg's *The Wife* (1929) is certainly to be counted among the more powerful peasant dramas in the repertoire of the Scandinavian theatre. One of the contemporary Scandinavian plays which grapples most boldly with the fundamental philosophical concepts of good and evil in human conduct is the powerfully conceived but somewhat obscure blank-verse drama with an ominous medieval setting by Karl Ragnar Gierow entitled *The Werewolf* (1941).

Among the more important of the Scandinavian dramatists of our generation—Lagerkvist, Krog, Grieg, and Munk—Pär Lagerkvist (1891-   ) is the most significant figure both as an artist and a thinker. Esthetically he derives primarily from the modern French painters and from the expressionistic dramatic techniques of Strindberg; intellectually he finds his point of departure in the spirit of skepticism and defiance characteristic of the post-World War I generation, though a profoundly probing metaphysical and religious bent in his temperament leads him finally, after a severe and prolonged spiritual crisis, to a firm belief in the ultimate trumph of good over evil, "however terrifying life in this world may seem to be." His first book, entitled *Word Art and Graphic Art* (1913), consisted of prose criticism in a controversial vein and revealed clearly Lagerkvist's early leanings toward expressionism, cubism, and naïvism in modern painting; and his first volume of poems, *Motifs* (1914), applies these modern-art theories to poetic composition. In these poems, as a recent Swedish critic has pointed out, Cézanne's gentle idyllicism and Van Gogh's strenuous, muscular hyperemotionalism join with Picasso's half-fascinated, half-terrified response to a crudely powerful primitive sculpture—the combination forming an often startlingly violent and yet a strangely haunting total poetic result.

And the view of life that one comes upon in these poems, as a thing of brutal struggle, of terror, and of hopelessness, only occasionally relieved by a moment of calm and relative peace, is thoroughly consistent with the poetic medium which Lagerkvist employs. In the succeeding years four more volumes of poems, several collections of short stories, and a couple of very significant autobiographical fragments came from Lagerkvist's pen. Meantime he turned also to the drama, which gradually became the form that he most frequently, and perhaps by preference, employs. Since 1917, when *The Last Man,* his first play, appeared, he has written six dramas in addition to a group of three experimental one-act sketches and a dramatized form of his short novel *The Hangman.*

In his plays as in his poetry and his prose fiction Lagerkvist is primarily concerned with ultimate metaphysical problems, with the soul and its relation to outward reality and to the eternal forces; and he therefore dispenses quite boldly, in the manner of the later Strindberg, with practically all realistic and naturalistic techniques in the drama. In an introductory critical essay to a volume entitled *Theatre* (1917), Lagerkvist reacts sharply against the old realistic traditions in the theatre as represented particularly by Ibsen's "one-wall-away-drama" with "silent treading on carpets through five long acts with words, words, words." The dramatist of today can without danger ignore Ibsen, he insists, but not Strindberg, who "stands in the middle of the way, and one cannot slip past him except by first understanding him." Though Lagerkvist's first plays revealed a dramatist of fascinating visionary powers and great depth of feeling, he was not infrequently obscure, chiefly perhaps because his symbolism could be followed only by the initiated, and also probably because his thought had not as yet clarified itself sufficiently in his own mind. The most successful of his early plays is *The Secret of Heaven* (1919), in which the dramatist conjures up a ghastly vision of life, with a pitiable assemblage of mankind, broken in body and in spirit, crawling aimlessly over a vast globe representing the earth, with an old-man-God helplessly observing the phenomena from a great distance in the heavens. A single clear note of love breaks the horrible progression of the scene for one fleeting moment, only to be drowned again in the ghastly cacophony of moans and shrieks and lamentations that emanate from the assemblage of the damned. Evil and agony and hatred are the fate of man upon the earth, Lagerkvist would suggest. Goodness and love make only the most transitory of visitations to the household of man, as if perhaps to mock him in his otherwise complete and ultimate misery. The philosophical implications of a deterministic science, emphasized most brutally in the flaming holocaust of World War I, had led the speculative brooding genius of Lagerkvist inevitably to such a view of life.

In Lagerkvist's immediately following dramas this pessimism comes by degrees, however, to be displaced by an essentially positive view of life, in which the dramatist gives expression to his final faith in the human spirit's ability to rise above evil and to conquer the shackles placed upon it by the limitations of the material world. And at the same time that his view of life changes, Lagerkvist's plays undergo a gradual technical change, away from the purely visionary, somewhat obscure manner of the early plays and toward a more immediate, simple, and tangible form, which may perhaps best be described as a kind of expressionistic naïvism. Symbols and expressionistic devices are employed more sparingly, and the episodic element is simplified by permitting the action to take place in a world of immediate recognizable actuality. But the dramatist's primary preoccupation remains man's *soul,* in the metaphysical and religious senses of the term; he is still concerned centrally with the problem of good and evil. The first play that reveals a partial shift in dramatic form is *He Who Lived His Life Over Again* (1928), the action of which takes place in a shoemaker's shop, with the dramatist employing only two bits of visionary technique, both of which could be eliminated with no fundamental loss in dramatic effect. It is with a subtle, quietly unassuming art that Lagerkvist in this play manages to give universal human significance to the struggle between good and evil that goes on in the shoemaker's soul. By careful self-discipline the shoemaker controls the evil within himself, but when in an unguarded moment he criticizes his son, he brings about the young man's self-destruction. The point seems to be that goodness and evil are infinitely pervasive forces, maintained in the most delicate and precarious balance in the human soul and in all human relationships; one man may destroy another even as he saves his own soul.

In the 1930's Lagerkvist's art and thought undergo a process of further maturing in the directions suggested by the play *He Who Lived His Life Over Again.* His concern with the problem of good and evil finds expression now, however, with reference particularly to contemporary political developments in the modern world. In four plays, *The King* (1932), *The Hangman* (1934), *The Man Without a Soul* (1936), and *Victory in the Dark* (1939), Lagerkvist turns the probing light of his mind on the political scene, particularly the totalitarian phase of contemporary political development in Europe. Among these plays *The Hangman* is the most sensational, in both the highly experimental form in which it is cast and the fiercely uncompromising spirit in which the brutal violences of totalitarian rule are attacked. The central figure of the play is The Hangman—ghastly symbol of the idea, born of medieval superstition, that good may come of evil, that violence, brutality, and bloodshed are in some mysterious way the most effective instruments of progress. The play consists of two striking scenes, with no pause between them: the first scene, a dimly lighted medieval tavern, the second, a sharply lighted, garishly decorated modern jazz restaurant-dance hall. In the first scene ignorant beer-guzzling workmen react half in fascination, half in horror to the sinister figure of The Hangman, sitting alone in one corner of the tavern; in the second, men and women dressed in evening apparel, with a scattering of gray field military uniforms, work themselves up into a frenzy of admiration for The Hangman, who symbolizes for them the essence of the modern political spirit. The application to Hitler-dominated Nazi Germany is unmistakable. The play gains much of its terrifying power of utterance by the skilful use of modern cinematic devices and startling lighting effects as well as by the focal use of The Hangman, a huge hulk of a man, silent, brooding, massively portentous in his blood-red cloak and sepulchral features. *The Man Without a Soul* and *Victory in the Dark* deal with contemporary political trends in a far less sensational manner than does *The Hangman*; but these later plays, particularly *Victory in the Dark*, reveal Lagerkvist's art as a dramatist in its most finished and satisfying form. *The Man Without a Soul* is a quiet dramatic study in the conversion to purely humanitarian ideals of a young political agitator who had at one time considered heartless violence and the spirit of revenge as the only driving forces of the human spirit. *Victory in the Dark* is a more broadly inclusive study of two political philosophies, the one, democratic humanitarian idealism, the other, cold-blooded, calculating demogoguery. Outwardly the humanitarian idealist fails, for he cannot gain the complete confidence of the masses, and he loses his life in the political struggle. Inwardly he saves his own soul and regains the love and respect of his wife. The demagogue, on the other hand, wins an outward victory; but he finds himself finally helpless in the whirlpool of forces that he has set loose around him. His appeal to passion and prejudice rather than to love and reason create conditions that will ultimately destroy the pretentious political edifice which he has succeeded in building.

The dramas of Nordahl Grieg (who was born in 1902 and who died in a bombing expedition over Germany in December, 1943), resemble those of Lagerkvist more than any other present-day Scandinavian plays, though there is no evidence that Lagerkvist has directly influenced his Norwegian contemporary. Grieg seems to have learned more from the Russians than from any one else, especially in his use of mass effects, and he employs rapid changes of scene and other cinematic effects in common with Lagerkvist and other contemporary dramatists; but on the whole his plays are definitely independent compositions, revealing a marked individual genius for the theatre. In addition to the six plays which came from his pen, he wrote some poetry, a couple of novels, and a number of critical essays on certain English poets, the most interesting of which is the one on Keats. His formal education was largely Norwegian, with a short period at Oxford and Cambridge. His experience of life otherwise included a year at sea as an ordinary seaman, activities as a newspaper correspondent in revolutionary China and the Spain of the Civil War, and a fairly extended residence in Russia for the purpose of studying the Soviet economic and political experiment. Though he was accused before the present war by reactionary groups in Norway of being a Communist, he never joined "the party," preferring to remain an objective student of modern social and political phenomena and to retain thereby his intellectual and artistic integrity. There can be little question, however, that he had a deep sympathy for the struggle of the masses and that he was by instinct or otherwise sharply critical of certain phases of modern capitalism. Had the war not intervened and brought about a thoroughly united Norway it is probable that Grieg's literary talents would have been employed more and more in the cause of those social and political trends which are given such sharp expression in his later dramas. The war transformed him instead into a Norwegian national poet whose every energy was employed in opposing the Nazification of his homeland and of Europe.

Grieg's six plays—*A Young Man's Love* and *Barrabas*, both 1927, *The Atlantic* (1932), *Our Honor and Our Power* (1935), *But Tomororw*—(1936), and *The Defeat* (1937)—reveal in the main a dramatist of a stern, uncompromising social conscience, intent upon heaping wrathful satire upon social, economic, and political abuses in the modern world. *Our Honor and Our Power* and *The Defeat* are the most significant of these dramas. The former is a satire in the spirit and something in the manner of Lagerkvist's *The Hangman* on the murderous speculation of Norwegian ship-owners during World War I. The play is ultra-modern in form, consisting of fifteen loosely related scenes tied together by symbolical elements and by appropriate incidental music. The "characters" in the play are groups rather than individuals: the avaricious ship-owner group on the one hand, and the seamen who sacrifice their lives for little more than a pittance on the other. The lash of satire falls mercilessly on the former group, big-mouthed sentimentalists, self-styled patriots, who speculate freely in human lives while they protest their own moral innocence and their undying domestic and social virtues. So sensational were the charges made by the dramatist against one of the dominant classes in Norway that the play nearly failed to appear on the Norwegian stage. When it did, in 1935, it was one of the events of the theatrical season. *The Defeat,* is a long, four-act drama dealing with the uprising of the Commune in Paris in 1871. Here even more markedly than in *Our Honor and Our Power* the group is the dramatist's primary concern—the motley company of the Paris Commune, men and women and children, working-men and artists, materialists and idealists being the collective hero of the play. Fifty reasonably identifiable individuals appear in the course of the action, besides masses of unidentified working-men, officers, soldiers, and women. Most of the action takes place in the streets and behind the barricades; but we catch also occasional glimpses of interiors—the office of the leaders of the insurrection, the director's room of the Bank of France, and a room at the headquarters of Thiers. The progress of the action is maintained with all of the sense of movement and direction possible in a drama of mass motives and mass effects, though occasionally the introduction of political theorizing into the dialogue gives to the play a not entirely happy static quality. On the whole, however, the vast panorama of political and military action of the Commune uprising and its final collapse is handled with imaginative power and reasonable dramatic sharpness and clarity.

Helge Krog (1889-   ), the other Norwegian of our day who has made the most important contribution to the Scandinavian drama, has in some respects a more natural gift for the theatre than any of his Scandinavian contemporaries. Beginning his dramatic career as early as 1915, he has produced steadily since, at present having written eleven plays, almost all of which have been successfully staged, and some of which are dramas of first significance. Krog has turned his hand to various kinds of plays: problem dramas dealing with social and political themes (*The Great We*, 1915; *The House of the Jarl*, 1923; and *On the Way*, 1931), modern psychological studies (*Break-Up*, 1936), and clever, refreshing comedies (*On the Sunny Side*, 1927). His problem dramas are perhaps the least successful of his plays; but he is the one master in modern Scandinavian of the light comic vein in the theatre, and his psychological plays are in many ways the most interesting in Norwegian literature since Gunnar Heiberg, one of them, *Break-Up*, being among the most distinguished Scandinavian dramas of the last couple of decades. Krog is not an extreme experimenter with new dramatic forms, as are his contemporaries Lagerkvist and Nordahl Grieg; but he usually handles problems of dramatic construction with remarkable skill and economy, and his dialogue is almost invariably sure, natural, and alive. Krog's master is Gunnar Heiberg, whose concentrated form and scintillating irony he has taken over, especially in his later more serious plays. In the light, airy comedies Krog seems more purely himself, though these plays are not without a touch of the Heiberg of such a play as *Gert's Garden*.

Both Krog's *On the Sunny Side* and Heiberg's much earlier *Gert's Garden* are comedies dealing with harmless love-affairs of relatively young people during a summer holiday; and in skill of dialogue and a rare comic sense of the ironic in situation and character both plays have much in common. Krog's play is the lighter, the more irresponsible of the two, however, and as such it represents an attitude toward love typical of the post-World War I generation of the twenties in contrast to the more serious turn-of-the-century conception of love which Heiberg permitted to form a subtle undercurrent in his otherwise light-hearted *Gert's Garden*. In *Break-Up*, Krog's most important play to date, the psychology of love is subjected to a more serious, keenly probing analysis, somewhat in the manner of Heiberg's *The Balcony* and *The Tragedy of Love*. But Krog, more modern and sophisticated than Heiberg, never permits the seriousness of his dramatic intentions in *Break-Up* to elevate love between the sexes to a passionate spiritual ceremony with all the appropriate romantic trappings in the manner of Heiberg. Seriously as Krog takes the crisis that arises in the curious triangle that develops in *Break-Up,* he faces the implications of the problem at all times with a sober analytic mind, in which the complications of passion are permitted purely dramatic outlets rather than the lyric-dramatic expression that characterizes the crucial scenes in *The Balcony* and *The Tragedy of Love.* Krog's recent leanings toward the serious psychological drama promise well for his development in the future. His sharp critical intelligence, combined with a remarkable talent for dialogue and an instinctive sense for dramatic form, marks him as a dramatist of very real distinction.

The Dane Kaj Munk (1898-1944), the fourth of the Scandinavian dramatists of our generation with whom we are concerned here, is a literary phenomenon of a wholly different kind than Helge Krog. His literary career at almost every point is marked by a series of sensational failures or sensational successes; and though there can be little doubt that some of his work will live for a long time in the theatre, discriminating critics may well wince at many of the means which he employs in order to gain his indubitably strong dramatic effects. Munk, a clergyman from the Danish provinces with astonishing literary energies, first came to the attention of the Danish theatre public in 1928 with a play about Herod entitled, curiously enough, *An Idealist*. The play was a failure on the stage, but this initial failure in no way discouraged Munk in his desire to write for the theatre. He composed a much more important play, *In the Breakers,* within the year after the fiasco with *An Idealist*; and in the 1930's he found time at the side of his regular pastoral duties to write in rapid succession five full-length plays, in addition to a couple of volumes of poetry, a travel book, a sheaf of vigorous hunting letters, and a large collection of journalistic verse, short stories, sketches, and essays. After the German invasion of Denmark in April, 1940 Munk became both in his pulpit and, insofar as censorship permitted, in print one of the most outspoken critics of the Nazi political philosophy and its occupation policy in Denmark. He paid for this opposition with his life early in January, 1944, at the hands of a band of Nazi assassins, but not before he had written another play, *Niels Ebbesen,* in which he gave a final dramatic expression to his scorn for German aggression and all that it stood for.

The amount and variety of Munk's literary work precludes the possibility of a uniformly high quality, and yet this work, particularly the plays, make him without question the most arresting literary phenomenon in the Denmark of our generation even before the immediate political consequences of the Nazi invasion of his country made him first a popular national hero and finally a national martyr. In his literary work Munk quite frankly despised an overcareful, highly conscious artistic workmanship, which all too frequently, he insisted, lacked artistic vitality and vigor. He himself wrote always in a fury of activity, each of his plays having been composed in a single, only modestly extended period of creative inspiration, and his other literary work seems to have been tossed off at odd moments when occasion demanded.

In the drama Munk's program was to resurrect a theatre in the grand manner, employing vigorous and not infrequently brutal realistic elements to bring the theatre into direct contact with all the pulsing forces of human life past and present. He has summed up this program in the following provocative, if somewhat bombastic, words:

It seems impossible that we here in Denmark should fail to respond to the new artistic ideas awakening all over the world. A young generation has grown up which does not go to the theatre in order to sit prettily and politely looking at pretty and polite things: its appetite for life is too lusty to be fed with crackers and tea and have its mouth wiped with whispering pieces, the authors of which must have been full of nervous dread lest by chance anything should happen on the stage. Their eyes have seen too much of the red mist of reality to be held by hour-long soul dissections. They prefer the film; there at least something happens, people fight and run away, are cheated and forgiven, kiss and murder; there a life is mirrored which has not been carefully thought out in a bloodless poet's weary brain, but has sprung from the flaming contradictions of purpose as revealed by God Himself: life from that world in which this younger generation has grown up, where people rose up against people with existence at stake, where necessity broke all laws, and good and evil no more existed because every one thought only of himself and was a God unto himself, while heads fell and limbs were crushed and brains burst, and peace came with labor troubles and deadened senses and poverty and pestilence. This youth will demand that art must stand right out in the struggle of the world if they are not to yawn and turn away from it. If art will not do this—if it wants to remain refined and stay within its well-known tastefully furnished living-room, with the windows closed and the doors locked, and the man and wife and the friend each sitting in a chair—well, then it will have to stay there and die of its own narrowness, forgotten and forsaken. But art has only one answer: an affirmation of life. It must plunge in, no matter how terrifying.

Because of Munk's strong predilection for violent physical action, for the passionate and the brutal as fundamental manifestations of life, he turns by preference in his dramas to historical figures whose hands are bloody with the mark of evil deeds—to Herod in *An Idealist,* to Henry VIII in *Cant,* to Mussolini in *The Victory,* and to Vitinghofen (a fourteenth-century German oppressor of the Danish peasantry) in *Niels Ebbesen*. These are plays with huge canvases, variegated in pattern, colorful, restive with bloody action and the final judgment of God. But these are not Munk's best plays, though *Niels Ebbesen* certainly is among the better of the historical plays which have appeared in the Scandinavian countries. Munk's religious drama *The Word* is unquestionably his one really great play, while two others, *In the Breakers,* dealing with Georg Brandes as a cultural personality, and *He Sits by the Melting-Pot,* which treats of a quiet, fussy old German scholar who has the moral courage not to bow to the Nazi yoke, are only less effective drama than *The Word*. Munk has in *The Word* said almost all that he has to say and said it well. There is a fine poetic quality over the play, and there are at times dramatic effects that flirt dangerously with mere melodrama; but on the whole the alternately satiric and sympathetic treatment of a narrow religious group who did not have the courage of their convictions in a moment of crisis and who had to be shown "the way" by a half-demented boy is a deeply gripping piece of theatre. "It is charged with eternal life," as one Danish critic has observed—"and with well-tested theatrical effects." It is doubtful whether Munk would ever have written many plays of the quality of *The Word* had he lived longer than he has. His work in general reveals little sense of self-discipline, and one wonders therefore whether his dramatic art had in it the possibilities of really significant dramatic development despite the undeniable flair for dramatic action which he possessed in a measure not common to Scandinavian dramatists. His work, arresting as it nearly always is, reflects few evidences of a *maturing* art; it is only sporadically gripping and powerful in spite of its highly serious pretensions.

Both dramatic composition and theatrical production in present-day Scandinavia are on the whole, however, definitely more mature and artistically self-disciplined than in the plays of Munk. In the drama of Pär Lagerkvist and Nordahl Grieg and Helge Krog, as well as in that of a dozen other only less significant figures, the Scandinavian countries have in the last two decades produced a body of dramatic literature which in variety and power is neither inferior to that of the European drama in general today nor unworthy of the great tradition in the Scandinavian drama of the late nineteenth century—the tradition of Ibsen and Strindberg, Björnson and Gunnar Heiberg.[1]

[1] For a somewhat more detailed account of some phases of the contemporary Scandinavian drama than space permits in the present work see my Introductions to *Scandinavian Plays of the Twentieth Century:* First and Second Series (Princeton and New York, 1944).

II

Germany

FRANZ RAPP

"In tyrannos" had been the motto of *Die Raeuber,* the drama which earned its author, Friedrich Schiller, honorary citizenship in Revolutionary France. Revolt against absolutism, the revolutionary comparison between oppressed citizens and unscrupulous nobility, form the basic motive of *Kabale und Liebe,* in which the same author fought for the liberation of the lower classes from despotism and social subordination. The position of a generation of writers whose political hopes had been betrayed after the so-called wars of liberation (1813-1815) and the fall of Napoleon I form a close parallel to the state of mind of the Storm and Stress (Sturm und Drang) period which found its classical expression in this drama by the young Schiller. At the beginning there had been merely the demands for the national unity of divided Germany and democratic rights for its citizens, but these were augmented by the new and powerful interest in social conditions, originating in France, as presented in the writings of Count Claude Henry de St. Simon. Questions concerning the position of woman, the sanctity of marriage, the significance of the sciences, and the equally important ethical-religious problems were discussed and interpreted. But the claims of this new Sturm und Drang remained purely theoretical until a new and decidedly political form of literature was brought into being by the French Revolution of July 1830, accompanied by the threat of persecution by Metternich's police.

The writers and poets who gave expression to the new political ideals are comprehensively grouped under the designation Das Junge Deutschland (Young Germany). The greatest poetical talent of this movement was Heinrich Heine (1797-1856), its most forceful dramatist Karl Gutzkow (1811-1876), who agitated against the evils in civic life and for the liberal demands of the time. His *Uriel Acosta* (1846), directed against dogmatic coercion and religious intolerance, has still a certain timely reality and, because of its gallant title rôle, attracts even today the talented character actors. *Der Koenigsleutnant* (1849), showing dramatic episodes from Goethe's youth, was written on the occasion of the poet's hundredth birthday; in time, it has become a sort of festival piece which is being performed, now and then, on Goethe celebrations. Besides Gutzkow, Heinrich Laube (1806-

1884) must also be mentioned. In his *Struensee* (1845) he created the figure of a martyr of liberal politics, and his effective *Graf Essex* (1856) has been performed as late as this century. His principal importance for the German drama lies in his writings on the dramatic arts and in his activities as a theatrical director in Vienna and Leipzig. An admirer and translator of the French, he introduced the plays of Augier, Dumas fils, Sardou, and Scribe on the German stage and thus inspired that particular group of realistic plays and dramas which formed the pattern for the fertile and successful activity of Paul Lindau (1839-1919); today none of these plays would arouse any interest.

The victorious war against France (1870-1871) brought the unification of the Reich, of which Young Germany had been dreaming. The economic and technical progress which had put Germany into the ranks of the industrial countries as far back as 1850, now soared to undreamed-of heights. It led to the almost unlimited power of capitalism and, simultaneously, to the consolidation of the masses of wage-earners in the social-democratic proletariat. Literature was concerned with this contrast at an early date. Friedrich Spielhagen (1829-1911) published his novel *In Reih und Glied* in 1866; it portrays a social-democratic leader after the image of Ferdinand Lasalle; and, in 1869, the same Spielhagen, in his *Hammer und Amboss*, confronted the liberal idea of a free work-community with the socialistic theory of the class war. However, Ferdinand Freiligrath's (1810-1876) and Heinrich Heine's poems had made the Germans conscious of proletarian misery and pride twenty-five years previously. Now that the contrasts had been brought out into the open, the opposing parties confronted each other. But not alone in Germany, since all over Europe the same economic development was in process. The rise of capitalism was accompanied by the constant growth of the large cities, the cities with their contrasts of rich and poor and crass social differences. Above all this, there spread a philosophy which based its principles upon the natural sciences and the general tendency to renounce investigation of deep-seated metaphyical associations, and to insist on concrete, material evidence. What Stuart Mill's *System of Logic* (1843) and Spencer's *Progress, Its Law and Cause* (1857) had been to England that was in Germany Ludwig Feuerbach's positivistic philosophy which, in the last analysis, considered all organic-spiritual aspects as concomitant phenomena of material processes. This materialistic conception of life was set against a background of pessimism which, in this world of transitoriness, makes every life story a story of suffering. This pessimism which now expanded with Arthur Schopenhauer's philosophy found new, lasting sustenance in Darwin's theory of the struggle for existence and his law of heredity. Furthermore, Hippolyte Adolphe Taine's thesis, that the character and fate of a human being are less the result of his personality and will than the product of his environment, had far-reaching effect. These views which, in a way, were the continuation of the problems that had occupied Young Germany met with resistance from a generation of recognized poets who idealized mythology as well as history, to the great satisfaction of a wide and grateful public; and where they had to touch pressing problems of the present they did it very carefully, and optimistically befogged the shadowy side of life and social injustice by the introduction of improbable noble and kind characters—for instance Gustav Freitag (1816-1895); Heinrich Riehl (1823-1897); Victor von Scheffel (1826-1886); Georg Ebers (1837-1898); Emanuel Geibel (1815-1884); Paul Heyse (1830-1914). A new Sturm und Drang was in the making.

German literature, including the drama, had so long taken the French as model that it is not surprising when now the decisive impetus came again from France. It was especially Emile Zola whose social novels and theoretical writings (*Roman expérimental*, 1880) furnished examples and theories for a dispassionate and complete description of reality, as the natural sciences taught them. Beside France, it was Russia that attracted attention and exerted an influence in Germany with the melancholy milieu descriptions, so dear to naturalistic sensibilities, in the works of Tolstoi and the deeply affecting psychological observations in the novels of Dostoevski. A third, and the strongest influence upon the drama made itself felt from Scandinavia; at that time, it was especially Henrik Ibsen, with his socio-critical works, *The Pillars of Society* (performed 1878 in Berlin), exposing their egotism; *A Doll's House* (performed as *Nora* in 1880 in Berlin) pleading for emancipation; and *Ghosts* (first Berlin performance in 1887) bringing disaster and death in the form of social prejudices and heredity.

From such basic influences a new artistic movement started in Germany which crystallized in two principal centers: Berlin and Munich. In Berlin the two Hart brothers, Heinrich (1855-1906) and Julius (1859-1930), launched the first violent attacks against the fashionable, saccharine literature and the lukewarm society dramas after French patterns in their *Kritische Waffengaenge* (1882-1884); simultaneously they demanded for the younger generation truth, life, realism, and nature. In Munich, it was Michael Georg Conrad (1846-1927) who made a similar attack against the tyranny of the recognized authors and, in the magazine *Die Gesellschaft*, declared Zola to be the ideal writer. Critics and theatrical people soon joined the Berlin group; in 1889 they formed the Freie Buehne, a society for performing dramatic plays in the manner of André Antoine's Théâtre Libre in Paris. Free from police censorship and uninfluenced by mercenary consideration, the works of the Moderne—the collective name given the new art which covered a wide scope of activities—were to be offered there. The leader of the Freie Buehne was Otto Brahm (1856-1912); on September 20, 1889, he presented Ibsen's *Ghosts,* and on October 20 of the same year, Gerhart Hauptmann's *Vor Sonnenaufgang*. The performance of the latter did two things: it brought the new German drama to the stage, and it revealed its most important playwright.

It is significant that Gerhart Hauptmann dedicated this play to two likeminded friends "for important inspirations"; they were Arno Holz (1863-1929) and Johannes Schlaf (1862-   ) who had just published, jointly, a volume of short novels (*Papa Hamlet*, 1889) in the new naturalistic manner. They also collaborated in the writing of a drama, *Die Familie Selicke*, which was performed by the Freie Buehne in April, 1890. Finally, they formulated and defended the fundamental program of naturalism in *Die Kunst, ihr Wesen und ihre Gesetze* (1890-1892). They established the principle that art must become nature again. To achieve this goal one must be consistent in the exact reproduction of nature. This demand was met by the exact observation of nature in every single, and even unimportant detail. For instance, since in ordinary life connected speech was unknown, it must also be avoided on the stage. The use of dialect was recommended for achieving the right atmospheric color. Monologues and asides had already been done away with by Ibsen.

Gerhart Hauptmann (1862-1946) followed these instructions very conscientiously in his first play, *Vor Sonnenaufgang*. The whole scope of naturalism is covered in this drama, the new political ideas as well as the new social ones. A young socialist comes into a village in a coal-mining district to study the conditions among the mine workers. The peasants upon whose property the black treasure has been discovered have suddenly become rich, and their wealth has brought misery to the whole family, the central characters of the play. They have all become drunkards and are utterly degraded, physically and morally. The only exception is a daughter from the peasant's first marriage who can hardly escape the wily attentions of the local males. She puts great hope in the young socialist with his ideals, principles, and world-improving plans. But when he learns from the doctor that this girl, too, is unable to bring healthy children into the world because she has not escaped the hereditary evil, he breaks off their tender love-affair and leaves. The abandoned girl stabs herself. The title of the play is symbolical: *Vor Sonnenaufgang* means before daybreak, when the right road can already be recognized. In Hauptmann's next play (1890), with the ironic title *Ein Friedensfest*, human stubbornness, developing into violence and resulting in physical conflict, brings catastrophe into the life of a family. The evil influence of alcohol also plays a part in it. The tragedy *Einsame Menschen* (1891), however, is composed entirely of descriptions and psychological observations. The hero represents the middle-class son of that period who leaves the secure ground of his profession to become an apostle of the new scientific life. This move estranges him from his family and his friends, but he finds understanding and love with a friend of his wife, a university student who symbolizes the emancipated woman of that time. But he is not strong enough to break away from his conventional connections and follow his ideals, and he sees voluntary death as the only way out. Henrik Ibsen's *Rosmersholm* has obviously exerted its influence upon Hauptmann in this case; in Ibsen's play, family spirit and conventions also break the will and strength of an all-too weak human being. *Einsame Menschen* touched the problems of the whole young generation of that day, far beyond the borders of Germany. It brought the author to the attention of all Europe. Hauptmann leaves the field of individual tragedy to write the drama of a whole social stratum in *Die Weber* (1892) produced in the United States and England as *The Weavers*. The revolt of the weavers in the Silesian mountains in the summer of 1844, which had already inspired Heine and Freiligrath to write poems about it, furnished him the material for a great naturalistic drama about social misery. Despite an abundance of sharply etched individualized characters, the hero of this drama is the whole group of weavers who are left powerless when the revolt collapses before the shots of the soldiers. Crampton, in the play *Kollege Crampton* (1892), is a painter of talent and renown; but as teacher in an art academy among colleagues, none of whom is an artist, he feels degraded, takes to drink, and would have gone cheerfully to the dogs if understanding people had not at last led him back to free creative activity. In the thieves' comedy *Der Biberpelz* (1893) we meet the narrow-minded representative of an arrogant bureaucracy who considers democrats as enemies of the state, but is unable to discover the rascals who make themselves at home in his own house.

Whereas *Der Biberpelz* retained, in a Germany ruled by bureaucrats, an unmistakable odor of insubordination, and *Die Weber* was regarded by many as inciting to revolution (even during the period after the First World War when Germany had gone through a social revolution) *Hanneles Himmelfahrt* (1893) produced in English as *Hannele,* immediately gained the lasting affection of all classes of play-goers. This dream play was first performed in the Koenigliche Schauspielhaus in Berlin—a notable fact in the history of the new art and its reception. Hannele, fourteen, is about to drown herself because, maltreated by her drunkard of a father, she wants to follow her mother to the grave. She is saved, but in her feverish dreams fairy-tales and biblical stories combine to form glorious, fantastic pictures which console and inspire her. Although Hauptmann leaves here the field of naturalistic description, he also mixes beautifully sounding verse with the prose of the Silesian dialect.

Even greater popularity was achieved by *Die versunkene Glocke* (1896), produced in English as *The Sunken Bell,* a fairy-tale all in verse. Hauptmann's theme is here the man between two women, the principal subject in *Einsame Menschen,* linked with the tragedy of an artist who feels oppressed by the narrowness of his home and environment. A pious bell-founder is surprised by a goblin who throws a bell meant for the mountain chapel into the lake and lures the man away from wife and child onto the airy heights and into the company of an amiable water-nymph. With her assistance the bell-founder wants to construct the complete chimes for a heathen temple. But his creative powers abandon him; conscience-driven, he returns home exhausted, and dies.

In *Florian Geyer* (1896) the poet's approach to naturalism is again more pronounced; he tries to give us not only an historically and culturally exact picture of the time of the Peasants' Rebellion of 1525, but also to reproduce the ancient speech of the sixteenth century. This drama deals again with a social group, the peasant serfs who, in the grip of the ideals of freedom of the Reformation period, fought for their human rights. But their victories turn into defeat because dissension, selfishness, and distrust take the impetus out of the revolution. They sink back into serfdom, and Knight Geyer, who had led them in their fight because he approved of their just cause, is betrayed and assassinated.

Fuhrmann Henschel (1898) is again pure naturalism so far as description of the social sphere and close, realistic character-creation are concerned. Henschel has committed a sin by breaking the promise he gave to his dying wife: he married his servant and is being ruined by the latter's infamy and faithlessness. Two years earlier, Hauptmann had used the same dramatic theme in his dream play *Elga* (1896, performed 1905), based on Franz Grillparzer's novel *Das Kloster bei Sendomir.*

In *Schluck und Jau* (1900) he used the story-within-a-story form, similar to Shakespeare's *The Taming of the Shrew* and Holberg's *Jeppe paa Bjerget,* for demonstrating that although a change of environment cannot alter character, it can develop it. Jau, the discontented vagabond, becomes a real tyrant when princely powers are bestowed upon him, while humorous Schluck squanders himself from pure goodness of heart.

Gerhart Hauptmann's special gift of arousing sympathy for oppressed humanity and revealing aspects of human greatness become evident in *Michael Kramer* (1900). Again it is an artist who is disappointed in fate, this time in the son whom the father had hoped to be an overpowering genius, but who turns out to be an unhappy, crippled lad who comes to a miserable end. A continuation of *Der Biberpelz* is *Der Rote Hahn* (1901) in which the characters are kept consistently in their original rôles in the first play.

In *Der Arme Heinrich* (1902) Hauptmann has dramatized Hartmann von der Aue's epic of the Middle Ages. Heinrich, a mighty and heroic knight, has become lonely and dejected because he suffers from leprosy. The love of a girl, willing to sacrifice herself, saves him. The author had long since overcome naturalism as a form, and with this verse play he has already taken a completely new direction, a direction for which he laid the ground in *Hannele* and *Die versunkenet Glocke.* This new form of expression is called new romanticism. Content and form of naturalism was the reproduction of reality with a decided tendency for ugly and oppressing spectacles of life; the new romanticism, similar to the romanticism of a hundred years before, makes use of fairy-tales and legends of days long gone, and distant civilizations into which are poured modern conflicts of the soul and the senses. Nietzsche's philosophical theories, from which the naturalists had picked primarily the negations of traditional moral and religious conceptions, had a positive effect with the new romanticists, who glorified aristocratic civilizations and justified deep passions by the mere fact of their existence.

From then on many different forms of dramatic creations exist side by side in Gerhart Hauptmann's work, for as a genuine poet he cannot permit himself to be limited in any way, nor be captured by any doctrine. The uniform quality of all his work; however, is "the ability to demonstrate human greatness, not through action and victory, but through suffering and failure." By this expression of deep sympathy with the creature that is delivered up to fate, Gerhart Hauptmann has presented naturalism with a quality which the theoreticians of the movement had certainly never put on its program.

There follows, in chronological order the next drama *Rose Bernd* (1903), showing a naturalistic trend in the use of dialect and in the magnificent shaping of the milieu. The old theme of the good girl who is not equal to the changing conditions of life and falls into sin and misery is treated with harrowing realism and deep understanding. The fairy-tale of the glassworks, *Und Pippa tanzt* (1906), is a poetic romance with symbolical meaning. Pippa, the daughter of an Italian glass-blower, embodies the beauty that every one is seeking. But she is conquered by the brutal force of Huhn, another glass-blower, who crushes her with his coarse hands as if she were glass. The comedy *Die Jungfern vom Bischofsberg* (1907), in which some of Hauptmann's memories of youth are revived, is rich in lyrical beauty, but also filled with burlesque elements; *Kaiser Karls Geisel* (1908) shows the conflict between duty and love, and the problem of an aging man who loves a young woman is solved by a deed of renunciation.

Griselda (1909), tells of the charcoal-burner's daughter who, in the old legend, had to prove her innocence under severe temptations. In Hauptmann's comedy she becomes a proud peasant girl; the margrave pursues her with violent love. He makes her his wife and out of jealousy takes her child away from her, for he does not want to share his love for her with the baby. Griselda, however, remains untouched in the dignity of her womanhood. *Die Ratten* (1911) introduces us to Berlin's slum quarters; its theme is the love and struggle of two women for the same child, the characters a group of sharply outlined, big-city people. *Gabriel Schillings Flucht* (written in 1906, performed and published in 1912) brings a morally weak man between two women, a situation recalling that of *Einsame Menschen*. The worried middle-class wife and the fascinating mistress contend for Gabriel Schilling, a painter, whose nerves cannot withstand the tension. The catastrophic climax happens on an island in the Baltic. Death in the sea is his way out of the dilemma.

Festspiel in deutschen Reimen (1913), written to celebrate the centenary of the wars of liberation, with world-historical characters as marionettes, achieved so little of the patriotic pathos desired for the festival that it was frowned upon by government authorities and rejected by them.

A journey to Greece in 1907 moved Hauptmann deeply and seemed to give him a true natural understanding of her myths. *Der Bogen des Odysseus* (1914) is based upon these impressions. Ulysses returns, disguised as a beggar; but while pretending to be a beggar, he is tortured by the divergence which his miserable appearance and his suppressed claim to power create in him. This Ulysses is filled with the despair of a King Lear and the doubts of a Hamlet, and only slowly does he regain enough inner strength and self-reliance to commit the bloody deed and become again Ulysses, the ruler.

Selma Lagerloef's novel *Herr Arne's Hoard* furnished Hauptmann with the fable for his *Winterballade* (1917), in which he demonstrates how a man who is capable of the most horrible, murderous deeds is condemned and destroyed by his own conscience, though he has escaped all physical pursuit. In *Der Weisse Heiland* (1920) Hauptmann describes the unmerited ruin of a man and a whole civilization. Montezuma, King of the Aztecs, sees in Hernando Cortez the white savior, promised by legend. The Spaniards' greed for gold and blood make him doubt his belief that salvation will come from these white men, and when he gives expression to his disappointment he is insulted and hit, and finally dies, sacrificing himself for his enemies. Contrasted with the noble human qualities of this martyr, the representatives of Christendom appear to be brutal, greedy, and dominating barbarians. Also written in verse, like *Der Weisse Heiland,* is *Indipohdi* (1920) first performed in 1922 in Dresden under the title *Das Opfer*. The exotic background is something else these two plays have in common. On an ocean island there reigns Prospero, an exiled king and powerful sorcerer, similar to his namesake in Shakespeare's *The Tempest*. Under his influence the inhabitants of the island have abandoned the cult of sacrificing human beings to reconcile the demons of the volcano. When the mountain begins to erupt again, the subjects revolt. Prospero's son, who once before had dethroned his father and has now landed on the island, shipwrecked, is to be the victim. But the father decides that he himself must be sacrificed; he frees the son and climbs to the volcano's crater.

This drama of sacrifice is followed by the tragicomedy *Peter Brauer* (1921), a play again built around the life of an artist. This painter is a miserable bungler who is finally ruined by his laziness and inebriety. In *Veland* (1925) human passions are given supernatural qualities; it is the story of the artistic smith who takes horrible revenge on his torturers and then flies away on wings he constructed himself. With *Dorothea Angermann* (1926) Hauptmann once again entered the field of naturalism. Dorothea, the daughter of a rather worldly preacher, cannot resist the attentions of Mario, a cook, and when she is with child by him her father forces her to marry and emigrate. She sinks into immorality and ends by suicide. In the one-act play *Die Schwarze Maske,* which appeared together with *Hexenritt* under the title *Spuk* (1930), Hauptmann treats a similar theme. In the latter he shows his interest in semi-psychological and occult matters and gives them amusing expression. *Die Schwarze Maske* shows us again woman in her irresolute submission to the brutal laws of the body and as a powerless slave of her inborn desires.

In the year that marked his seventieth birthday, Hauptmann, forty-three years after his first drama, describes in *Vor Sonnenuntergang* (1932) the love of a man of seventy, recovering from a severe illness, for the twenty-year-old niece of his gardener. He wants to marry her, but his children fear for their inheritance and want to have him declared irresponsible and put under a guardian. He puts his relatives out, frees himself of all former connections, and wants to be a bachelor again. His unlimited fury turns against the portrait of his late wife who has given birth to all these stupid people. He slashes the picture with a knife and dies of a heart attack.

This action-filled and effective play was followed by *Die goldene Harfe* (1933), a dramatic poem completely immersed in music, with special music written even for the intervals between the acts. Two brothers, deeply attached to each other in inseparable friendship, fall in love with the same girl, a being of rare charm. Passion destroys the spiritual unity of the brothers. The girl is inclined to favor the physically stronger of the two but decides for the more delicate one and he proves to be strongest after all by going voluntarily to his death.

Profound studies had led Gerhart Hauptmann to write a new version of Shakespeare's *Hamlet* (1927); later he felt the urge to present the famous Danish prince during his student days. *Hamlet in Wittenberg* (1935) shows the wild life of the students, interwoven with the inescapable approach of the dark, threatening fate to which Shakespeare gave final form.

The story of *Die Tochter der Kathedrale* (1940) was taken from an old French legend. Deadly enmity and everlasting war reigned between the two princely houses of Andorra and Foix, because the Duke of Andorra's wife had presented him with twins, and the Duchess of Foix had remarked that twins were a sign of marital infidelity. When she gives birth to twin girls herself, she keeps one of them secret, afraid of the consequences of her own words. This child is abandoned on the altar of the cathedral of Andorra; the sacristan and his wife adopt her, she grows up as the "daughter of the cathedral," and becomes a maid of great beauty. Peter, one of the twin princes of Andorra, falls in love with her and marries her against the wishes of his family. His brother Paul encounters the other sister while hunting; she is a beautiful amazon. In a contest he gets the better of her and falls in love. The double wedding restores peace to the two families.

Iphigenie in Delphi (1941), Gerhart Hauptmann's latest drama, was inspired by a remark of Goethe who recognized fertile dramatic soil in the return of Orestes and Iphigenia, in their unforeseen meeting, and in the contrast between Iphigenia's saintly calm and Electra's earthly passion. Hauptmann treated his theme with that deep affection for Greek antiquity which inspired him in *Griechischer Fruehling* (1908), a prose travel book, and *Der Bogen des Odysseus*, and with that pure feeling of humanity which is the outstanding mark of all his works, whether they treat of problems of the social order naturalistically, or follow the development and progress of spiritual problems.

Having surveyed Gerhart Hauptmann's many-sided activities in the creative field of the drama, we now return to the early days of naturalism. We mentioned *Familie Selicke* (1890) by Arno Holz and Johannes Schlaf as an example of "consistent naturalism," for it contains exclusively descriptive situations. Selicke, a bookkeeper, is a drunkard. That is the reason for the wretchedness of the whole family: the youngest child dies under the treatment of a quack, the son is going to become a procurer, and the eldest daughter finally renounces a marriage to a young preacher in order to prevent the family from going entirely to ruin. From such misery there is no escape, no salvation, not even through death. This conclusion is in contrast with that of Hauptmann who showed such a road even in *Das Friedensfest*. Later, Johannes Schlaf alone showed in *Meister Oelze* (1892; performed 1901) the horrible fear of a man who committed murder for the sake of an inheritance but avoided making a confession with tenacious energy, even on his death-bed. Much later, Holz, in collaboration with Oscar Jerschke, wrote *Traumulus* (1904), a drama of school life, in which the efforts of a school director with new pedagogical ideas come to naught because his pupils abuse his kindness with undisciplined excesses. Although *Traumulus* was a great stage success, his artist drama *Sonnenfinsternis* (1907) on the Cenci theme, his comedy *Buexel* (1911), and the uncouth *Ignorabimus* (1912), while opening new poetical territory, left no lasting impression.

The most successful dramatist of naturalism was Hermann Sudermann (1857-1928); he took just enough from naturalism to appear realistic and modern, and kept just enough of the old tried-and-true methods, all of which he mixed with masterly dramatic technique and thus created from the very start an atmosphere of understanding between the audience and the stage. His old proven material was modeled upon the plays by Augier, Sardou, and Lindau, with their polished dialogue; the new parts presented themselves in well-observed scenes from the lower strata of society, where feelings were mostly expressed in dialect. Sudermann's first play, *Die Ehre* (1889), was an immediate, gigantic success. Front-house and rear-house (divided by a paved court) are contrasted, furnishing scenery as well as atmosphere. The play demonstrates that there are two kinds of honor, depending on whether one lives in an apartment in the front-house with the well-to-do middle-class, or in a tenement in the rear-house with the proletariat. A girl from the rear-house has been seduced by a boy from the front. The parents of the boy dispose of the affair by paying a huge sum of money. The son from the rear, however, has acquired the views of a higher social class, having been abroad on business. He cannot agree with his own family nor with the conscienceless people in the front. His friend, a noble, wise, and rich *deus ex machina,* gives him the money to repay the ill-gotten gain and also offers him the high position which will enable him to marry a girl in the front-house he has fallen in love with, making him a social equal in the eyes of her family. In *Sodoms Ende* (1891) Sudermann shows us the decayed world of Berlin's parvenus, stock-speculators, and epicures; it is ripe for collapse. His world-wide success, however, was *Heimat (Magda,* 1893), the story of an army officer's daughter who, turned out by her father previously, returns to her home town as a celebrated singer. She heeds the requests of her family to marry the father of her child, who has become a respectable official in the town. But he declines the proposition on the grounds that it would compromise his position and reputation. She breaks the relationship and angers her father to such an extent that he takes a pistol and is about to shoot her when he suffers a stroke. The effective rôle of the prima donna has attracted actresses of all nationalities: Sarah Bernhardt, Helena Modjeska, Eleonora Duse have portrayed and carried her into all the world. With *Schmetterlingsschlacht* (1895) Sudermann had little success, perhaps because he formulated his indictments of society with somewhat less obvious means than in *Sodoms Ende*. He laid more stress upon poetic atmosphere than dramatic effectiveness in *Das Glueck im Winkel* (1896). A poor daughter of the nobility marries a widower. She becomes an attentive mother to her three step-children, and thanks to her farsightedness and diligence the financial situation of the family improves. This happy circle is entered by a man who is accustomed to conquer women. She succumbs, too, and decides to pay for her guilt with her life. Her husband, who has observed everything, steps in her path as she is about to drown herself in the river. In a conversation, with understanding on both sides, they regain their love and mutual confidence. The influence of Ibsen's *The Lady from the Sea* is unmistakable. One of Sudermann's most accomplished plays technically is *Fritzchen,* especially effective because of the terseness of its characterization and the form of expression used. It belongs to the cycle of one-act plays known as *Morituri* (1896) and shows the fate of a young officer who is the victim of heredity and the rigid conventions of his caste. The tragedy *Johannes* (1896), produced in English as *John the Baptist,* transfers the tragedy of *Sodoms Ende* to antiquity. Herodias, the evil one, and the sensuous Salome, are the center of a world of abnormal horrors and general degeneration. The loud and palpable effects of the Salome affair unfortunately throw into the background the more valuable part of the play, the depiction of Johannes as a predecessor of Christ, ruined by Christ's moral superiority. After these historical themes,

Sudermann, in *Die drei Reiherfedern* (1899), chose the romantic one of the dreamer who chases luck, not knowing that he holds it in his own hands; in his hour of death he recognizes how deceptive all his striving has been. The situation of the man between two women is treated by Sudermann in *Johannesfeuer* (1900), produced in English as *The Fires of St. John*. A boy loves his adopted sister, but he finds it more to his interest to become engaged to his well-to-do cousin. During the intoxication of a midsummer night the boy and the girl he really loves give in to their physical passion, yet the boy finally decides to follow conservative convention and lets the adopted sister go her way. Sudermann continued with a veritable stream of dramas to contribute to the theatre until his death. He varied the themes which were successful; with his *Strandkinder* (1909), *Der Bettler von Syrakus* (1912), and *Die Lobgesaenge des Claudian* (1914) he entered without effort the ranks of the Schiller imitators. A few years after Sudermann's death, his publishers surprised the theatre world with a posthumous work. *Die Entscheidung der Lissa Hart* (1932), which deals with the men who returned home from war-imprisonment, a subject of timely interest after the First World War. The heroine decides in favor of her lover, in preference to her fiancé. This work was praised by the critics and accepted by many leading theatres which had lost interest in Sudermann long ago. In the deceased playwright, qualities were discovered which had been overlooked while he was alive; and again he was elevated to the front rank among modern dramatists. Nobody apparently noticed that the book had been available ten years before, under the title *Wie die Traeumenden;* as such it had passed unnoticed.

Hermann Sudermann and Gerhart Hauptmann were for quite a while considered to be the representative playwrights of the naturalistic drama, just as Schiller and Goethe used to be put on the same shelf as the representatives of German classical literature. Taking Sudermann as the exponent of masterly technique and Hauptmann as the master of true, creative poetry, they represent, perhaps, the characteristics of an epoch in which the ideas of the time were expressed dramatically by a number of other writers, too. Among them were Max Halbe, Otto Erich Hartleben, Georg Hirschfeld, Ernst Rosmer, Max Dreyer, and Otto Ernst. In a certain sense, Ernst von Wildenbruch and Ludwig Fulda belong with this group; but both have their roots in the old-style realism and pay tribute to naturalism, at the same time drifting along in the direction of new romanticism, for a while.

Mar Halbe's (1865-1944) first success remained his most important play. This love drama, *Jugend* (1893), takes place at a Catholic vicarage in West Prussia where a niece of the priest and her demented half-brother grow up together. The girl is an illegitimate child, and the chaplain urges her to enter a convent and so save her mother from purgatory. But a young cousin arrives; he is on his way from high school to college, and now the two fall deeply in love with each other. The frenzied love-affair might still have ended harmoniously had not the weak-minded brother shot at the cousin in an attack of jealousy, thus killing the girl who had thrown herself in front of her lover. In *Mutter Erde* (1898) Halbe shows a pair of lovers who seem destined to pass each through an unfortunate marriage before they can become united. But since the exterior obstacles seem to be insurmountable, they chose to go back to *Mutter Erde*—that is, Mother Earth— by dying together. *Der Strom* (1904) shows strong effects reminiscent of Sudermann's theatrical genius. Three brothers love the same woman. She marries the second who, by a swindle, has become sole possessor of the family estate. But she loves the eldest brother who has become wealthy and respected abroad. The youngest, a boy of seventeen, who is treated by his brother like a hired hand and who hates him, has fallen madly in love with the beautiful woman. When the truly loved one returns unexpectedly, the old passion flames up again and is returned. The swindle of the owner is discovered. Furious, and insanely jealous, the youngest brother plans revenge. He tries to destroy the dam in a nearby river releasing the high waters so that all may perish. The master of the place tears the tool used for that purpose out of his hand; they fight and fall into the flooding waters, leaving behind the two lovers who are meant for each other.

In the drama *Schloss Zeitvorbei* (1917) and, later, in *Die Traumgesichte des Adam Thor* (1929), the former naturalist makes room for the mystic who is no longer interested in matters as they are, but rather in what goes on behind them. No mere human beings of everyday life carry on the show but figures of romantic creation. *Die Traumgesichte des Adam Thor* is based upon a certain theory of the recurrence of events and matters, and consists of nightmarish fantasies in which a former private teacher repeats incidents of his experience with his erstwhile pupil. The continuity of these melancholy dramas, which no stage could ever have endowed with life, was relieved, now and then, by some comedies in which the humorless author, with peevish witticism, tries to make fun of his time which does not understand him any longer.

George Hirschfeld (1873-194-?) has always passed for Gerhart Hauptmann's real disciple. His one-act play *Zu Hause* (1893) is a milieu-piece of dreariest objectivity, not unlike *Familie Selicke*. *Die Muetter* (1896) touches for the first time the conflict between father and son which later became a favorite subject with the Expressionists. A young musician, misunderstood and suppressed by his father, has left his home and lives with his mistress, a proletarian girl of great warmth and sympathy. When the father dies, he is drawn back to his old home and to his mother, and the girl lets him go without bitterness for she recognizes where his happiness lies; she consoles herself with her own pleasure which consists of becoming the mother of his child. In *Agnes Jordan* (1898) Hirschfeld brings us the life of his heroine in five tableaux, from the time of her engagement to the wedding of the eldest of her sons. Simultaneously, by contrasting esthetic and artistic tendencies with egocentric and materialistic interests, he presents a broad view of Jewish family life. With *Mieze und Maria* (1907) Hirschfeld's efficacy on the stage came to an end. Mieze, a healthy proletarian child, is adopted under the name of Maria by a highly civilized couple who can have no children of their own. But Mieze cannot stand the high-toned atmosphere and returns to her real mother and her swarm of bothers and sisters. In none of the many plays Hirschfeld wrote later did he ever recover the unencumbered naturalness of the products of his youth. One of his later novels, however, deserves special mention: in *Die Frau mit den hundert Masken* (1931) he describes the life of a great actress, basing the fascinating and gripping story on the wealth of his experience.

Otto Erich Hartleben (1864-1905) became famous through his *Rosenmontag* (Rose Monday, the day before Shrove Tuesday) (1900), a tragedy about two young people, an officer and his sweetheart from the lower classes, who are ruined by the prejudices of society and the various conceptions of honor. The play, whose theme recalls Sudermann's *Fritzchen* and its structure *Die Ehre,* has documentary value as a description of the German officers' caste of 1900. Of much greater artistic value is *Hanna Jagert* (1892). Hanna is a young, intelligent, self-reliant working girl who, with the help of three men, creates her own sphere of activity where she learns to enjoy spiritual values and the full flavor of life.

In *Daemmerung* (1894) Ernst Rosmer (Elsa Porges-Bernstein, 1866-   ) gives expression to her strong and understanding humanity. This play portrays the growing of a delicate, demure love of a highly educated woman for a childlike, happy old man; the raging jealousy of the man's daughter, who is growing blind, requires a sacrifice. Inspired by Hauptmann's *Versunkene Glocke,* the same authoress created the fairy-play *Koenigskinder* (1895), which became the libretto for Engelbert Humperdinck (1894-1921) and survived most dramatic works of that period.

Max Dreyer (1862-   ) who, with his drama *Winterschlaf* (1895) created a play close to nature and filled with clear observations, following Ibsen, later wrote the purposeful *Der Probekandidat* (1899), making use of naturalism in a rugged and successful manner. It is the story of a young teacher whose manner of teaching arouses doubt; he is ordered to prove before the pious and conservative school board that orthodox religion ranks above natural science. But he declares himself in favor of what he considers to be the truth, though as a result he loses his position as well as the girl he loves. In his comedy *Das Tal des Lebens* (1902) an impotent margrave is presented with an heir through the efforts of a soldier who has found favor with the margravine. Though the play was suppressed in Prussia it was widely successful in the other states of Germany. His *Die Pfarrerstochter von Strehladorf* (1909) was a variation of Sudermann's *Magda,* and *Die*

Siebzehnjaehrigen (1920) one of the many plays strongly influenced by Wedekind's *Fruehlings Erwachen*.

Otto Ernst (Otto Ernst Schmidt, 1862-1926) went to work in a very superficial manner when, in *Jugend von Heute* (1900), he criticized his time and made Nietzsche responsible for the moral breakdown of the young generation, which he showed on the stage as caricatures. In *Flachsmann als Erzieher* (1902) he portrayed a false and scheming schoolmaster, a type as distorted as it was popular.

Naturalism of the purest conception, as far as bitterness in the description of humanity and violence of social criticism are concerned, is to be found in Fritz Stavenhagen (1876-1906), who wrote in the dialect of Germany's low countries, and in the two Bavarian writers Josef Ruederer (1861-1915) and Ludwig Thoma (1867-1920).

Stavenhagen's *Mudder Mews* (*Mother Mews,* 1903, performed 1905) shows one of those efficient, self-righteous persons who make life a hell on earth for their fellowmen by their hard unkindness. His comedy *De ruge Hoff* (*The Tough Farm,* performed 1905, printed 1906) has, in its description of the moral decay of the peasantry, a certain similarity with Ruederer's *Fahnenweihe* (1895) in which the corruption of farmers and city dwellers is exposed with uncompromising severity. Ruederer's other comedy *Morgenroete* (1904), shows the Munich riots of 1848, with Lola Montez as principal figure; it demonstrates that Munich's beergarden politicians think more of a full stein than any revolution. Among Ludwig Thoma's comedies, *Moral* (1908), produced in the United States under its original title, is a bitter mockery of narrow-minded hypocrisy, and *Lokalbahn* (1902) an effective satire of the Bavarian philistines. Both authors intensify naturalistic observation to the point of brutal grotesqueness.

When Ernst von Wildenbruch (1845-1909) had gained a secure position in the German theatre, first with *Die Karolinger* (1881), and later with his great success *Die Quitzows* (1888), there was talk of a brilliant new period for German dramatic literature. Although his patriotic dramas, constructed with firm ability, certainly won the literary interest of a great part of the public that looked to the theatre for entertainment only, his uncomplicated characters took little account of the contemporary desire for psychological depth. One of his peculiar traits was that he rejected the influence of foreign dramatic patterns. However, impressed by the plays of the naturalists he wrote *Die Haubenlerche* (*The Crested Lark,* 1890) which is concerned with proletarian destiny. A workman's daughter, an early riser —hence the nickname "crested lark"—is courted by her two employers. One promises to marry her, the other wants to make her his mistress. But she does not feel equal to entering society, nor does she feel helpless in the face of temptation. She decides for the factory worker, who loves her sincerely. Similar as this play is to some of Sudermann's, we find here that social-political ideas form the basis of abundant conversations, but the developments are mostly rhetorical and have little connection with actual life. In *Meister Balzer* (1893) Wildenbruch takes up the desperate battle of the artisan against the modern factory, but the success of this play was also due primarily to the dramatic technique of the traditional middle-class drama, and not so much to its naturalistic milieu and characters. Wildenbruch's last and very great success was *Die Rabensteinerin* (1907), a sturdy, historical play about the passionate love of a young Augsburg patrician for the beautiful daughter of a robber baron, trained in the use of weapons. He liberates her from the hangman and takes her away to the newly discovered Indian lands, where new struggles await them.

The last of this group is Ludwig Fulda (1862-1939). He derives his sound stage technique from Kotzebue (1761-1819) and the French. He was a great admirer of Ibsen, and performed a valuable service for the German theatre by translating Molière and Rostand. Paying his respects to naturalism, he wrote *Jugendfreunde (Friends of Youth,* 1898) and *Die Sklavin* (1891); later he mastered the drama in all its forms and styles. His great success was *Der Talisman* (1892) and his principal literary merit is the introduction of the fairy play, which arrived just in time to liberate the mind of the theatre-going public from the nightmare of the proletarian atmosphere after a flood of naturalism, and to escort it to exotic lands and fantastic adventures. The *Talisman* is a play in verse, inspired by Hans Christian Andersen's tale of the *Emperor's New Clothes,* in which the tyrannical prince is forced to differentiate between truth and appearance and becomes a wise ruler.

We have seen in Gerhart Hauptmann's *Hannele* how fairy dreams and transcendental figures grew out of a naturalistic atmosphere, and in *Die versunkene Glocke* we found a symbolical, poetic fairy-tale. And as naturalism halts before the inevitability of fate, so the fairy-tale stops short of solving the riddles of reality. Both have in common the awareness of man's enigmatic dependency on destiny, and because these two methods found expression during the same period, poets have readily been able to proceed from one to the other. Maurice Maeterlinck, the Belgian, has exerted great inspirational influence upon the symbolical drama. The noblest works of this kind in the German language were created by Hugo von Hofmannsthal, the Austrian poet; their perfect form and verbal beauty have become the ideal of a whole generation. In Germany, we find Karl Gustav Vollmoeller (1875-   ) as an early follower of Hofmannsthal. *Katharina, Graefin von Armagnac und ihre beiden Liebhaber* (1903) stems from Balzac's *Contes drôlatiques.* Katharina lures her admirer to her castle and to death, then dies herself, after having emitted a stream of ringing verse. After a series of bloody love tragedies in Oriental, Italian, and other historical costumes, Vollmoeller became world-famous as the author of the libretto for the pantomime *Das Mirakel* (1912) which is based on Gottfried Keller's (1800-1881) *Sieben Legenden,* and on Maeterlinck's *Soeur Béatrice;* under

Max Reinhardt's direction it became a tremendous success. It was successfully produced in London in 1911 and in New York in 1924 as *The Miracle*.

Eduard Stucken (1865-   ), an extraordinary connoisseur of the old civilizations and a poet of great originality, wrote between 1902 and 1916 a scenic cycle, *Der Gral,* composed of eight plays about the Arthurian legends. In the first, *Gawân* (1902), for which Jessie Weston's version of the Middle-English poem *The Green Knight* served as source, the knight Gawân passes through physical and spiritual temptations, suffering, guilt, and atonement, to ultimate deliverance. In *Lanvâl* (1903, performed 1911), based on the old Celtic Melusine legend as described in the old English fairy-tale *Sir Lanfel,* the hero is ruined by his love for two women. *Lancelot* (1909), the real hero of the Grail drama, is also a victim of the same dualism. Stucken treated more realistic material in his psychological drama of family life, *Myrrha* (1908), in the manner of Ibsen; in it a young girl goes to her death because of the adultery of her father. In his *Die Gesellschaft des Abbé Chateauneuf* (1908, performed 1912) he treats the story of Ninon de l'Enclos. Here, Ninon becomes the mistress of her son, who kills himself when he learns of the true relationship between them.

Ernst Hardt (1876-   ) begins his dramatic writing with *Tote Zeit* (1898), an everyday play with little action, following Ibsen and Maeterlinck. *Der Kampf ums Rosenrote* (1903) shows the conflict between a daughter who falls in love with a socialist and a son who wants to go on the stage, and their well-to-do, middle-class parents. But after that, Hardt came entirely under the influence of Hofmannsthal's poetry. His verse drama, *Tantris der Narr* (1908) derives from an episode of the French poem about Tristan in which the hero, disguised as a buffoon, dares to enter King Mark's court a second time, but is not recognized by Isolde. There is also an exciting scene in which Mark, in raging jealousy, delivers Isolde, nude, to the lepers. All this and much more was presented in five acts rich in atmosphere but poor in action; the success was enormous. On the other hand, *Gudrun* (1912) found less acclaim, for the meaning of the songs of loyalty of the Middle Ages had been transformed into the opposite, and the heroes of old were but ill adapted for presentation as persons of modern sensibilities. In *Schirin und Gertraude* (1913) Ernst Hardt finally wrote a travesty of the legend of the Count von Gleichen, a crusader who was saved by a Turkish girl; the Pope permitted her to be his second wife. In this play he brings her secretly to his house, disguised as a boy. But the women find so much pleasure in one another's company that they have no longer any time for the count.

Of more passionate temperament, richer in imagination, and, above all, gifted with a sense of humor is Herbert Eulenberg (1876-   ). In his early work we find him attracted again and again by what is really one and the same theme: the depiction of a full-blooded, exuberant, intractable man who collides with a foolish world and is destroyed. In *Anna Walewska* (1899) we find him as a Polish count who is ruined by his unrestrained love for his own daughter. The same type of man appears in the humble, death-bound tragedy *Leidenschaft* (1901). *Ritter Blaubart* (1904), murderer of women, is a remarkable man, pursued by a dark fate. The most fascinating character of them all is probably *Ulrich, Fuerst von Waldeck* (1906) who wants to act like a human being on the throne but, despairing of the servility and cabals at court, he escapes into the woods where he lives with the animals. Finally, there is *Simson* (1909) who, in raging desire for a prostitute, leaves wife and child, home and country. In the midst of all these plays of violence stands *Cassandra* (1903), the prophetess who understands the meaning of every human life; the background of this play is the fall of Troy, presented in the obscure and dreamy language of Hofmannsthal.

With *Der natuerliche Vater* (1907) Eulenberg begins a series of romantic, middle-class comedies and tragicomedies. *Alles um Liebe* (1910) shows delicate and sentimental people of the Biedermeier period (about 1840), whirling through joy and grief, anxiety and laughter, in the manner of Shakespeare's comedies. *Belinde* (1912) is the drama of a woman loved by two men. The one she married goes abroad to earn riches for her; he is so certain of their mutual love that he never writes. But she craves affection and attaches herself to a young man. On the eve of their marriage the husband returns; officially he had been reported as dead. The two men make possession of the woman dependent on the outcome of drawing lots. The younger one loses and must kill himself. Belinde, however, torn between love for her dead sweetheart and the reawakening affection for her husband, finds it impossible to keep on living. A play of pure fantasy is *Die Insel* (1917), in which Eulenberg frees himself of all overwriting by using verse. In his devotion to fantasy Eulenberg loses the sense of inner necessity and for the organic structure of the drama. His plays become amiable, moralizing fairy-tales as in *Der himmlische Handelsmann* (1929), or sentimental irrelevancy as in *Der Kuckuck und sein Kind* (1930) who, in the rôle of "wastral poet," acclaims the "daughter of the vegetable woman" as his own and sings her praises after she has become famous and fabulously rich as a film star. In *Industrie* (1930) Eulenberg finally tried to paint the soulless world of the machine age. Here the mixture of horror and grotesqueness, so attractive in his earlier works, proves to be stale and dull.

The problem of the man with two women, which Ernst Hardt tried to solve in a comedy, was treated in tragic fashion by Wilhelm Schmidtbonn (1876-). In *Der Graf von Gleichen,* the Count, who believes himself all-powerful, is convinced that he can master a double marriage. But the Countess, his most Christian wife, feels that her honor has been deeply offended; furthermore, she does not want to share her man with any one else. She murders the Saracen rival. But her happiness does not return, and she retires to live as a hermit, while the Count goes alone into a foreign land. Schmidtbonn's first success had been *Mutter Landstrasse* (1904), in which a son, miserable and hungry, wants to return home but is repulsed by his father who insists that his own good standing as a citizen should not be endangered. In *Der Zorn des Achilles* (1909) the hero seeks voluntary death on the battlefield to expiate his excesses. *Hilfe! Ein Kind ist vom Himmel gefallen* (1910) is a tragicomedy in which a burglar takes the daughter of the house in preference to the money he has come for. Sincere love develops, and after the man has also received a dowry through sheer effrontery, the couple are on the road to an orderly existence. After the historical drama called *Die Stadt der Besessenen* (1915) which was written on the subject of anabaptists, and a comedy of considerable poetic beauty, *Die Schauspieler* (1921), there follows a play of deep psychological content, *Der Geschlagene* (1920). An aviator, having crashed, comes home blind. He is filled with distrust against the seeing world, his wife, and his brother, but is reconciled to his fate by the all-surpassing love of the woman. *Die Fahrt nach Orplid* (1922), a drama laid among emigrants, contrasts the dreamer and the enthusiast; the one wants to flee from the world in his disappointment, the other is a man of action who sees his task in tackling the world as it is. Finally, Schmidtbonn has created a comedy of great beauty in *Maruff, der tolle Luegner* (1924), based upon a tale in the *Thousand and One Nights*. Maruff is not a swindler but a poet, and the good spirits present him with those things he has imagined and given to others in his imagination.

To the circle of new romanticism much rather than to the naturalists belongs Carl Hauptmann (1858-1921), the elder brother of Gerhart Hauptmann. In his early plays, *Marianne* (1894), *Waldleute* (1895), and the Silesian dialect piece *Ephraims Breite* (*Brigitte*, 1898), he stands close to Ludwig Anzengruber, the Austrian writer. A fairy-like quality enters his dramas with *Die lange Jule* (*Lanky Julia*, 1912, performed 1913), and becomes a dominant factor in *Die armseligen Besenbinder* (1913). In his Bonaparte plays, *Buerger Napoleon* (1910) and *Kaiser Napoleon* (1911), he shows the great emperor as the man who realized the ideals of the Revolution and created France's true democratic constitution, but who perished as soon as he sought selfishly for personal power and greatness. In *Krieg* (1913) Carl Hauptmann becomes a creative visionary and shows, before the beginning of the First World War, all the horrors of devastation. The trilogy *Die goldenen Strassen* (1916-1920) brings us *Tobias Bundschuh,* the tragedy of a physically misshapen man who, despite riches and brilliant intellect, cannot gain the selfless love of a girl. *Gaukler, Tod und Juwelier* deals with the end of an epicure, and *Musik* reveals the happiness of the creative artist. These works bring Carl Hauptmann into the domain of Expressionism which he helped to prepare and which now, in *Der Abtruen-*

nige Zar (1914, performed 1921), takes all his attention. In this play words give way to expressive action, and action must give its utmost.

Maximilian Dauthendey (1867-1918), one of the most prolific and delicate of lyricists, has written a considerable number of dramas which range all the way from naturalism (*Das Kind,* 1895) through impressionism of the Austrian kind (*Glueck,* 1895, *Ein Schatten fiel ueber den Tisch,* 1907) to the realistic historical drama. Of all these only *Die Spielereien einer Kaiserin* (1910), which depicts events from the life of Catherine I of Russia, has remained on the stage, for it offers extraordinary chances to experienced actresses as a costume and character piece.

Quite isolated among all these playwrights for the theatre we find Alfred Mombert (1877-1942) who, with his *Aeon* trilogy (1907-1941), tries to portray the battle between chaos and form as a dramatic symphony. Mombert writes metaphysical dramas that surpass the limits of what can be shown on the stage, and probably represent the richest flowering of new-romantic imagination. In his drama *Aiglas Herabkunft* (1929) Mombert aspires to a neoclassical style.

Directed against the naturalism of misery and poverty on the one hand, and the new romanticism that lived in beauty and legendary words on the other, were the new classicists whose leader was Paul Ernst (1866-1933). Here we must devote a few words to the real originator of this movement who had died more than a generation before and had neither pupils nor immediate followers: Friedrich Hebbel (1813-1863). The most mature of his dramas, *Gyges und sein Ring* (1855), was not performed until 1898. At this time, a Hebbel renaissance came into being and as interest in Ibsen's social criticism declined, Hebbel's star rose. There is *Judith* (1840), who slays Holofernes because he has insulted her dignity as a human being. In *Herodes und Marianne* (1849, performed 1850) and in *Gyges,* woman's right to self-determination is the center of the tragic conflicts. *Die Nibelungen* (1861, printed in 1862) is a tragic trilogy about hurt pride, whereas in *Maria Magdalena* (1844, performed 1846) timebound middle-class morality is shown to be the basis of the catastrophe. Tragic guilt in Hebbel's plays is always caused by the clash of the will of the individual with that of the community; it is a guilt which, unlike the naturalistic and kindred schools, does not lead fatefully and inevitably to catastrophe, but has its origin in the will and is atoned for by death.

Paul Ernst, who took up this thread, had gone through naturalism (*Lumpenbagasch,* 1898; *Im Chambre Séparée,* 1898, performed 1899) and new romanticism (*Wenn die Blaetter fallen,* 1900, performed 1899; and *Der Tod,* 1900). In Italy he learned to love the classical form; his comedies *Eine Nacht in Florenz* (1905), *Ritter Lanval* (1905, performed 1914), *Der Hulla* (1906, performed 1911) are in the manner of Latin comedies, and the characters are caricatured types of romance conventionality. In his theoretical paper *Der Weg zur Form* (1906) he develops his ideas for a new classical style. It was mainly the example of Sophocles and the teachings of Hebbel which returned tragic necessity to its leading position in the drama that deals with the conflict of the individual with the community; the principal characters break a confirmed moral law and perish thereby. In *Demetrios* (1905, performed 1910) this principle has not yet been fully worked out; it is the tragedy of a ruler who, because he is an illegitimate child, stands undecided between two parties. But in *Canossa* (1908, performed 1918), the struggle between Pope Gregory VII, God's servant, and the worldly ruler becomes a passionate expression of two contrasting philosophies and leads to the political victory of the emperor. A typical example of the neo-classical drama may be seen in *Brunhilde* (1909, performed 1911), where the good principle is contrasted in Brunhilde and Siegfried with the evil one in Gunther and Krimhild, and perishes, for Siegfried has had dealings with evil. And thus *Ninon de l'Enclos* (1910, performed 1911) means no more to Ernst than just a wanton woman who is condemned for her dubious moral ideas; *Ariadne* (1912, performed 1914) must carry her tragic burden and thus becomes her father's murderess; and *Der heilige Crispin* (1913, performed 1927), who has stolen leather to make shoes for the poor, must go to the gallows, because in his Christian humility he declines to accept the salvation an emperor offers. Fanatical devotion to duty to which every human trait is sacrificed is the basic motive in the drama *Preussengeist* (1915) in which the loyal Katte gives his life that Crown Prince Friedrich may be converted to the idea of royalty. Almost at the end of Paul Ernst's long list of works we find his comedy *Pantalon und seine Soehne* (1916, performed 1933). Here the characters of the Italian *commedia dell' arte* exchange light, polished observations among themselves and with the public, which the intellectual audience receives with appropriate understanding. Thus what was essentially natural humor, the original idea behind the improvised comedy, is turned into the exact opposite. As the theoretician always prevails over the artist in Paul Ernst, his characters become types, the structures of his dramas mathematical constructions. No wonder that these plays never exerted any vital effect. Only after National-Socialistic ideology had identified Paul Ernst's absolutism as Aryan virtue, and his lack of popularity as democratic lack of understanding, were his plays put again on the stage, by order of the authorities. But that didn't help; they never made a hit.

Samuel Lublinski (1868-1910), who took a theoretical position against naturalism in his *Der Ausgang der Moderne* (1909), wrote historical plays (*Hannibal,* 1902; *Peter von Russland,* 1906) in which the heroes attempt to shape their own destinies. In *Gunther and Brunhild* (1908) and *Kaiser und Kanzler* (1910) he is completely under the influence of Paul Ernst.

From his opposition to materialistic thinking, Albert Steffen (1884-   ) derives his purely spiritual, moral values. He found the pattern for his form of expression in Paul Ernst's classical methods; thus his dramas *Auszug aus Aegypten* (1916) and *Die Manichäer* (1916) are constructions of the intellect rather than vital creative poetry. He joined the Anthroposophic movement and tried to explain the teachings of this religious sect in his *Das Viergetier* (1924) and *Hieram and Salomo* (1927).

Wilhelm von Scholz (1874-   ) is another writer who never used "superficial reality" as an immediate base for his plays. To him imagination is the essence and source of all art. His drama *Der Jude von Konstanz* (1905) is laid in the Middle Ages. Its hero is a Jewish physician who has become a Christian in order to do good without any interference. Now Jewry as well as great masses of intolerant Christians are against him. When a pogrom starts he returns to the Jewish faith and dies a martyr to humanity. *Meroe* (1906), a mythical tragedy based on the son-father conflict, is still new romanticism in its content, but neoclassical in form. But Scholz soon freed himself from oppressive formulas, and in *Vertauschte Seelen* (1910) he succeeds in creating the beautiful atmosphere of a fairy-tale in which, after a fable by Tirso da Molina (1571-1648), the beggar is shown as a king, and the king as a beggar. In *Der Wettlauf mit dem Schatten* (1921) a poet encounters in person one of the characters of his own novel, a part of himself; he becomes a rival with whom the author wages an exciting struggle for his own wife. Dramatized psychoanalysis, showing the double life of a woman in her consciousness and subconsciousness, is presented in *Die glaeserne Frau* (1924). The heroine subconsciously loves a doctor, but must die because she tries to free herself from the sphere of his suggestive powers.

Walter Harlan (1867-1931) in *Schule des Lustspiels* (1903) attempts to reveal the laws of dramaturgy. He stands thus in close proximity to Otto Ernst. Harlan wrote comedies only, but the heartfelt humor of his plays separates his works from the polished cleverness of the neoclassicists. "To be God means to work"; this expression of the philosopher Eduard von Hartmann (1842-1906) occurs in Harlan's *Der Jahrmarkt zu Pulsnitz* (1904, performed 1905); the proof of it is demonstrated by means of the example of a hat manufacturer who has retired from business at an early age, and whose aim in life is to astonish his fellowmen in the Dionysian manner. His inheritance-hungry relatives make his whim an excuse to make life miserable for him until he realizes that he can be master of his own fate only if he returns to active life. Work as a means of deliverance from all need and for attaining ultimate success is also the underlying sense of *Das Nuernbergisch Ei* (1913). Martin Behaim (1459-1506), the geographer, inspires Peter Henlein, locksmith and mechanic, to invent the pocket watch. While working on his invention he suffers an attack of cancer, but he prefers the certainty of death to an operation with uncertain outcome in order that he may finish his invention quickly and successfully. *Die Braeute von Bamberg* (1927, performed 1928) takes us back to the period of Pope Gregory VII, when celibacy became obligatory for the Catholic clergy.

The greatest talent of the neoclassical school, however, is Hans Frank

(1879-   ); he believed in its theory and he overcame it. *Der Herzog von Reichstadt* (1909) is still written in Paul Ernst's style. The son of Napoleon, who has inherited his father's obligation but not the necessary strength for the ruling profession, is ruined between the powers of the Revolution and those of law and order. *Herzog Heinrichs Heimkehr* (1910) brings a son into conflict with a father who, after thirty years of pilgrimage and imprisonment, demands reinstatement from his son, a wise ruler who has made the country prosperous; but finally he desists and dies. *Godiva* (1917) is based on the legend of that name; Frank turns it into a dramatic struggle between the male and the female ideas of purity. *Freie Knechte* (1918) deals with German peasants of the lowlands during World War I. Two sons have fallen already, and the mother, with simple natural feeling, now battles for the third with the father who regards it as his duty to sacrifice even the most cherished one. In *Geschlagen* (1923) Frederick the Great and his brother Prince Wilhelm oppose one another when the conflict between war's necessity and the desire for peace must be decided. *Kanzler und Koenig* (1926) gives a forceful and original interpretation of Struensee's fate. *Klaus Michel* (1925) is a play about a peasant boy who has become a successful surgeon and believes himself capable of mastering life by daring, rationalistic methods. But his mania for power ruins him and, to make amends, he seeks death on the battlefield. The title of the play is in itself a clue to its symbolic meaning: it is the tragedy of the Germans who went through an epoch of mania for power to ultimate catastrophe. In *Kleist* (1933) we see the dramatist as political agitator against Napoleon; with this play Frank left the field of idealistically conceived dramatization and entered that of chauvinistic ideologies.

Ernst Bacmeister (1874-   ), in his essays about the drama, also urged that tragedy be set apart from everyday life. His plays usually concern themselves with the contrasts of unselfishness and noble sentiments, on one side, and lack of understanding and enmity on the other. *Andreas und die Koenigin* (performed 1913, 1922) treats of the often dramatized Joanna of-Naples. There is important material in *Maheli wider Moses* (1932); Moses is contrasted with his brother who leaves the world rather than agree to the misrepresentation of truth in the interest of the state.

A much greater elementary effect upon the further development of the German drama than that of the academic program of the neoclassicists was exerted by Frank Wedekind (1864-1918). Even in one of his earliest comedies, *Die junge Welt* (1890), he makes fun of the naturalists who, he held, could do no better than copy life. With *Fruehlings Erwachen* (1891, performed 1905) it became evident that nothing he offered had anything in common with mere observation of nature, but was imagination—so intensified as to appear unreal, even improbable and spectral—used to give most forcible expression to his moral demands. Thus Wedekind entered the ranks of the "tendency" dramatists, but he also indicated the road to

Expressionism. *Fruehlings Erwachen* is a tragedy about children who are left by narrow-minded and dull methods of education to find their own way through the exigencies of puberty, get lost, and end in bewilderment and ruin. Boy and girl are seized by stupefying desire and experience great happiness, but the new young life must not flourish, for middle-class morality disapproves. The girl dies of the abortive medicines of a quack; the boy is put into a reformatory. Another boy, shy and afraid, escapes from the heartless school and the torments of his own body by shooting himself. Finally there is the fantastic scene in which the young suicide and the boy who has run away from the reformatory meet at the grave of the girl and discuss the stupidity of middle-class morality and order. The theme of the play is the unnaturalness of this morality which destroys nature and shatters life itself.

Not only was the theme unusual and the tendency quite new, but the very form of this play was peculiarly its own: it consists of short scenes only. These scenes are no longer mere parts of an act, they are independently constructed and have their own functions. This dramatic technique of individual pictures had already been used during the Sturm und Drang period in the eighteenth century; Hebbel's *Judith* was constructed in this manner. But the real inspiration of Wedekind, of the dramatists of Expressionism after him, and of their further developments had been the plays of Georg Buechner (1813-1837). Georg Buechner, who also represented the political side of Young Germany as a democratic agitator, was discovered as an important dramatist only in the present century. *Dantons Tod* (1835, performed in 1916) presents man's tragic subjection to fate, even in heroic men of action, whereas *Woyzeck* (1836, performed 1913), with gripping realism and deep sympathy for the tortured man's fate, shows the decline of a poor creature of instincts.

Frank Wedekind took over Buechner's theories of construction and regarded his intensity as congenial to his own temperament. His *Erdgeist* (1895) shows Lulu, the archtype of woman, "the wild, beautiful animal," as central character; she destroys every one with whom she comes in contact. The same Lulu, in the play *Die Buechse der Pandora* (1903), after killing one of her men and fleeing from the penitentiary, lives later in Paris among roués, confidence men, and procurers; finally she is murdered in London by Jack the Ripper, the male beast. *Der Kammersaenger* (1899), to whom women cling as persistently as men do to Lulu, uses his brutal intelligence to make his way as an artist.

Der Marquis von Keith (1900) is the first in a series of plays in which Wedekind has drawn parts of a self-portrait. The Marquis is an adventurer who chases happiness; he tumbles from the height he has gained and starts anew; for "life is like a toboggan slide." The title character in *Karl Hetman, der Zwerg-Riese* (retitled *Hidalla*, 1904) is the founder of an international organization for breeding beautiful human beings who shall save the world with a new morality; its highest command is beauty. But the undertaking is ruined by the resistance and ignorance of the world. In *So ist das Leben* (*Koenig Nicolo,* 1902) a king is driven from his throne and lands among a group of actors; but he is given no rôle in serious tragedy, only that of the court fool to the usurper. It is the lament of the poet who realizes that he is not taken seriously. In *Tod und Teufel* (originally called *Totentanz,* 1906) the white-slaver Casti Piani, one of the characters in *Die Buechse der Pandora,* is an enthusiastic idealist of sensual enjoyment, but the vulgar reality of earthly existence ruins him. *Zensur* (1907) is the explicit justification of the poet and his misunderstood work. There follows *Musik* (1907), in which he again makes war against middle-class morality, as in *Fruehlings Erwachen,* and there are similarly thrilling scenes. The trilogy *Schloss Wetterstein* (1910) continues the Lulu problem with the women Leonore and Effie. In *Simson* (*Samson,* 1914) Delilah is once again the great destroyer. *Franziska* (1911), a sort of female Faust, makes a pact with her Mephisto, Veit Kunz, which secures for her two years of male life with all sensual enjoyments and freedom of movement. She passes through a period of hybrid existence and finally lands in middle-class marriage. *Herakles* (1917) is the drama of a superman who is burdened with a curse. Between the two last dramas we find *Bismarck* (1916), a play without relation to anything, written in sober, factual, biographical style. Heinrich Lautensack (1881-1919) was a close personal friend of Wedekind's and designated himself as his pupil. His comedy *Hahnenkampf* (1908) is about a girl who resembles Lulu. But the sturdy Bavarian peasant atmosphere and the human warmth of the play's philosophy are evidently related to naturalism; the same applies to his *Pfarrhauskomoedie* (1911).

Hermann Essig (1878-1918) in *Ihr stilles Glueck* (1912) shows the pure, true love of a girl who suffocates in human vulgarity. From this naturalistic basis of his art, Essig enlarges his characters to fantastic proportions and accelerates his powerful dramatic language to a rapid pace. Thus, the comedies *Die Weiber von Weinsberg* (1909) and *Die Glueckskuh* (1910) become grinning caricatures. His drama *Mariae Heimsuchung* (1909) is a veritable snakes' nest of insanity, incest, envy, and hatred. *Ueberteufel* (1912, performed 1923), concerned with the themes of patricide and incestuous love, attains Wedekind's demoniacal powers and the explosive vehemence of Expressionism.

In the transitional period between epochs we find Heinrich Mann (1871-   ). His *Schauspielerin* (1911) is the psychological analysis of an actress in a position to choose between two men; but she loses both, for stage routine has made true feeling impossible for her. *Madame Legros* (1917) frees an innocent man from the Bastille and thus helps to kindle the French Revolution of which, however, she wants no part, having done her share for the rights of humanity. *Der Weg zur Macht* (1919, performed 1920) is expressionistic in form and shows General Bonaparte as an adventurer on a large scale who regards the Revolution as a means to an end. *Das gastliche Haus* (1924, performed 1927) is a comedy about confidence men and shows contemporary figures in all walks of life. *Bibi, Jugend 1928* (1928) is a topical play with music, and concerns itself with the troubles and doubtful morals of the young generation; it is neither complaint nor accusation; it shows the understanding wisdom of a man who knows that these things are temporary.

Whereas Wedekind writes against narrow middle-class morality, especially the lies of sex morality, Carl Sternheim (1878-1943) turns irony and hatred against viciousness, hypocrisy, and obsequiousness. He started as a romanticist with the dramatic poem *Ulrich und Brigitte* (1908, performed 1916). His resonant *Don Juan* (1910, performed 1912) was a failure on the stage, but with his first comedy of middle-class life, *Die Hose* (1911), he had already laid a foundation for the successes he was to achieve in the next fifteen years. The wife of an official loses an intimate piece of lingerie right in the street, and she and her spouse fear that the gossip about this incident may put him in difficulties with his superiors and somehow sully their civic honor. But the opposite comes to pass: the event results in an increased income and makes a higher standard of life possible for them. The name of the hero of this piece is Theobald Maske, and from now on we meet the dynasty of the Maskes in a number of comedies and plays to which Sternheim has given the collective title *Aus dem buergerlichen Heldenleben. Die Kassette* (performed 1911, 1912) is about a chest which contains the riches of a wealthy aunt, and discloses the greed for money and the base sentiments of the impatient inheritors.

In *Buerger Schippel* (1912) a proletarian attains success through his beautiful tenor voice and by fighting a duel in which, in fear and trembling, he manages to acquit himself creditably. He is happy when he is acclaimed a good citizen. *Der Snob* (1913) is Christian Maske, Theobald's son, who has risen in the world and become a great captain of industry. Now he can marry a real countess and he does not hesitate to invent an extramarital affair between his mother and a viscount to give himself the nimbus of aristocratic descent. In *1913* (1915, performed 1919) Christian Maske is seventy; he is now His Excellency the Baron. War is in the air, immense profits can be realized through army contracts. For business reasons Maske changes his religious faith. Schippel, too, returns; in *Tabula rasa* (1916, performed 1919) he has become the director of a glass factory and succeeds in converting the representatives of organized labor to middle-class self-complacency. *Perleberg* (1917) is a satire on the greed for profit of well-to-do citizens. The leading character in *Das Fossil* (performed 1923, 1925) is a Prussian general whose family belonged to the old nobility when "the Hohenzollerns were still crawling on trees." He kills his daughter because she is in love with an aristocratic bolshevist. Diderot's novel about the revenge of a great lady who caused her lover to be married to a prostitute has been dramatized by Sternheim in *Die Marquise von Arcis* (1919). In *Manon Lescaut* (1921), based on the novel by the Abbé Prévost, the Chevalier allies himself with the girl of the people against the mob. In *Oscar Wilde* (1923, performed 1925) he has honored the memory of the great European writer. Then, with *Die Schule von Uznach* (1926), he followed the path of Wedekind by contrasting the old-fashioned educational methods with the new culture of the body that leads to consciousness of beauty.

An abundant talent of extraordinary scope is that of Georg Kaiser (1878-1945), who has written about forty Expressionistic plays of the most precise intellectual type. *Grossbuerger Moeller* (performed 1915, retitled *David und Goliath,* 1921), a comedy with a happy ending, showed a surprisingly sure grasp of stage effects. *Die Sorina* (1917) combines the comics of Gogol's *The Inspector General* with the sultriness of Wedekind's eroticism. *Der Fall des Schuelers Vegesack* (1914) and *Rektor Kleist* (1918) derive from Wedekind's *Fruehlings Erwachen* and continue discusions of school life as did Holz and Jerschke in *Traumulus,* Ernst in *Flachsmann als Erzieher,* and Dreyer in *Probekandidat.* Here we can recognize Sternheim's high stylistic standard as a model. *Der Zentaur* (1916), in complete conformity with Sternheim's satires, shows a pedant who prepares himself for his future marital duties and thus earns the reputation of being a libertine; and *Die Versuchung* (1917) is a drama about marriage in the Ibsen manner. During the same period, and to some extent even before then, he wrote plays that were stylistically quite his own. *Die juedische Witwe* (1911) strips the Judith legend of its religious symbolism and heroic greatness and turns Judith into a man-mad wench who kills Holofernes only because she wants to get Nebuchadnezzar. She saves the city—quite unintentionally—is consecrated as the untouchable priestess, and would thus have been cheated of all earthly joys were it not for the virile high priest. *Koenig Hahnrei* (1913) is a travesty on the Tristan and Isolde theme. But a great and daring play, completely free of sexual problems, is *Die Buerger von Calais* (1914): France has been defeated; the King of England consents to spare Calais, but only if six citizens volunteer to die as a sacrifice. Eustache de Saint-Pierre is the first to come forward; six others follow him; thus, there are seven. The one who presents himself last in the market-place the next morning shall be free. Eustache is missing; he has chosen voluntary death to bind the other six to their decision. The English king, softened by the birth of his son, pardons the six. The idea of immaculate self-sacrifice is imposingly expressed in this play.

Europa (1915), a dance play, has a solemnity of language that recalls Maeterlinck, yet is rich in humor and wit. The playmates of the king's daughter follow the rough warriors of Cadmus, while she is only too willing to have herself abducted by the wild bull to the country that received her name. *Von Morgens bis Mitternacht* (1916), produced by the Theatre

Guild as *From Morn to Midnight,* covers a period of fourteen hours during which a bank employee, fascinated by a beautiful woman, embezzles a large sum of money and races through all possible excitements of a metropolis and all capitalistic feelings of power until his money-madness is exhausted. *Die Koralle* (1917) is thematically connected with *Gas I* (1918) and *Gas II* (1920). Here Kaiser comes to grips with the problem of capitalistic society. The coral is an ornament on the watch chain of a secretary; this is the only external difference between the secretary and his employer, a multimillionaire whose complete double he is. What really sets them apart from each other, however, is their memories of youth. This precipitates the crisis. The millionaire has come from an environment of abject social misery, the secretary comes from a happy and untroubled youth. The millionaire does not want to hear about misery; he leaves it to the secretary to ease misfortune through benevolent deeds. He lives far from his business interests and does everything to keep his children away from the crude realities of life. Then his son discovers the social injustice inherent in the capitalistic system; he wants to open the father's eyes. The latter is only too well acquainted with the facts. Envy of those who are happy causes him to kill his secretary; then he waits stoically for his execution which seems to open to him the road to paradise. In *Gas I* the son has introduced socialism into the plant. His profit-sharing plan for all his workers results in products of the highest quality. A newly invented gas opens undreamed-of possibilities for technical progress. Suddenly an explosion destroys the plant. The millionaire's son wants to liberate the masses from industrial slavery and lead them to a peaceful life in settlements in the country. But they refuse. The plant is rebuilt. *Gas II* is an ecstatic vision of war and mass strikes, poison-gas, and chaos. Three one-act plays, *Claudius, Friedrich und Anna,* and *Juana* (1918), and the full-length plays *Brand im Opernhaus* (1919) and *Frauenopfer* (1920), are erotic works of great precision and theatrical effectiveness. *Hoelle, Weg und Erde* (1919) touches again on the problem of capitalism. *Der gerettete Alkibiades* (1920) is a cleverly reversed picture of Plato's Socrates. *Kanzlist Krehler* (1922) is a tragicomedy about a repressed creature who gets a view of the universe and loses his head over it. *Noli me tangere* (1922) is the dramatic justification for a clash between poet and the middle-class conception of private property. A master in the construction of dramatic action and the entangling of dramatic events, Georg Kaiser, in *Gilles und Jeanne* (1923), brings Gilles de Rais, monstrous murderer, together with Jeanne d'Arc; the man's testimony sends Jeanne to the stake. In *Nebeneinander* (1923) Kaiser treats ironically the hopeless loneliness of city dwellers and the uselessness of their occasional attacks of sentimentality. In a similar artistic and surprising manner, he uses the sentimental theme of a cheap novel in *Kolportage* (1924) to produce an amusing entertainment. The revue *Zwei Krawatten* (1930) shows masterly construction and the precision of a good machine. Purely theoretical in form as well as in content is *Gats* (1925) in which social problems find a solution in the prevention of overpopulation. A technically clever play of ideas is *Die Lederkoepfe* (1928); the Leatherheads mentioned in the title are symbolic for the destruction of all human values through the war, a cry of revolt against absolutism. Another drama of ideas is *Mississippi* (1931), in which religious communism fights against materialism; it is based upon an actual event which threatened the river valley in 1928. In *Oktobertag* (1928), which tells of a dream of love that became reality, and *Hellseherei* (1930), an entertaining detective story, Kaiser enters the field of the occult sciences. Finally, in *Silbersee* (1933), he tells the fairy-tale of the folly of being rich and the happiness that comes from freedom from want. Kurt Weill wrote the music for this play; Kaiser also furnished Weill with the librettos *Der Protagonist* (1926) and *Der Zar laesst sich photographieren* (1928).

Formal Expressionism, which originated in Wedekind's passion for abstractions and is responsible for the marionnette-like characters in Sternheim's dramas, has found complete interpretation in Kaiser's cubistic constructions. Beside it a dynamic Expressionism comes into being. This becomes the language of the young generation which, during World War I, learned to disbelieve in the simplicity of human destiny, as naturalism saw it and as new romanticism painted it. Now the drama is to become the expression of all spiritual powers, and the dramatis personae are no longer mere characters but super-realistic, ecstatic figures, the intensified expression of human nature. August Strindberg exerted a profound influence upon the young generation with his later works *A Dream Play* and *To Damascus*.

At the beginning we find Reinhard Sorge (1892-1916) with *Der Bettler* (1912, performed 1917). This piece includes characters some of which are real, and others merely symbolical. It contains quite new technical instructions for the stage by which groups of characters can suddenly be made to appear or disappear through the use of spotlights. The beggar mentioned in the title of *Der Bettler* is a poet who is looking for a theatre to produce his play; he tries to convince people of the importance of his dramatic mission. In between, a drama of family life of intense power is interwoven. Sorge, who started with Nietzsche's ideas, later embraced Catholicism and wrote a number of mystical dramas: *Guntwar, Schule eines Propheten* (1914); *Metanoite* (1915), a trilogy of mysteries; and *Koenig David* (1916), who is God's administrator on earth and a forerunner of Christ.

But the Expressionistic drama that was first performed on the stage was Walter Hasenclever's (1890-1940) *Der Sohn* (1914, performed 1916). The revolutionary conduct of the generation is nowhere more clearly expressed than in this theme: son against father. It appeared in Hauptmann's *Michael Kramer* and flamed up again in Georg Kaiser's *Koralle*. Now we meet with it constantly. Hasenclever gives it the most rebellious and pathetic form.

The son runs away from school and his strict father; he organizes a league of youth against the world, has his first love-affair, and is returned to the father by the police. The father threatens the boy with his riding whip, but suffers a timely stroke and dies when the son aims a revolver at him. This occurrence was offered in simple form and very modern language; it made the play popular and, simultaneously, the prototype of the modern Expressionistic drama. *Der Retter* (1915), written during the war, was an appeal of the pacifist author for humanity, fraternity, and love. His version of Sophocles' *Antigone* (1917, performed 1919) for Max Reinhardt's production in the circus was again an expression of a desperate longing for justice, love, and reconciliation. *Menschen* (1918) uses a theme by August Stramm (1874-1915) which contrasts voluntary martyrdom with low selfishness. *Jenseits (Beyond,* 1920), produced in New York by the Provincetown Players in 1925, connects life with the occult existence of the dead. After a dramatization of Balzac's *Gobseck* (1922) and the drama *Mord* (1926), Hasenclever abandoned the pathetic manner of Expressionism and turned to comedy. *Ein besserer Herr* (1927) shows the successful career of a matrimonial swindler. In *Ehen werden im Himmel geschlossen* (1929) three suicides—a woman and two men—at the instance of Mary Magdalen, are twice returned to earthly existence to give them new chances in life. But the result is always the same, for the fate of the individual is a matter of predestination and inevitable. *Napoleon greift ein (Napoleon Enters,* 1930) was a political satire of the present time with the clever effectiveness of a musical comedy. Hasenclever's return to reality is best documented in his comedy *Kommt ein Vogel geflogen* (1931), in which we see again a man between two women or, to be more precise, between a mother and a daughter who share the man without serious difficulties.

Beside Hasenclever, Reinhard Goering (1887-1936) gained recognition as an exponent of Expressionism with his *Seeschlacht* (1918). Quite unnaturalistic, rhythmic language gives a lifelike picture of what is in the minds of seven sailors in the battle-tower of a warship during the Battle of Jutland: the sense of loneliness in the vast ocean, dreamy memories of adventures ashore, a premonition of the coming disaster, fear and courage during the battle, thoughts of mutiny, fore-warnings of death. *Scapa Flow* (1919) was like an epilogue to the previous drama, a moving lament for the surrendered German fleet. *Der Erste* (1918) shows in the hasty continuity of short scenes the tragedy of a priest who tries to free himself from an entangling affair with a woman. *Der Zweite* (1919) was the tragedy of two married couples, hopelessly ensnared. *Die Retter* (1919) is a tragic affirmation of life, *Die Suedpolarexpedition des Kapitaen Scott* (1929) a eulogy of courage, bravery, comradeship, and patriotism.

Fritz von Unruh (1885-   ) has created his own style within the domain of Expressionism. His first drama, *Offiziere* (1912), is an atmosphere piece with impressive, realistic outlines showing the conflict between military obedience and personal responsibility. *Louis Ferdinand, Prinz von Preussen* (1913, performed 1921) is also a drama about duty. The prince, an especially amiable and artistically inclined person, is to be put on the throne to replace the king who lacks decision and energy. But he prefers death in battle to violating his loyalty to the king. With his dramatic poem *Vor der Entscheidung* (1914) it became evident that the author, who was at that time an officer in the field, had become a pacifist. Confronted with the horrors of war, he demands to know the meaning of the unspeakable suffering and murder, and finds that life's most valuable asset is love. The tragedy *Ein Geschlecht* (1918) is an allegorical hymn in which three sons and a daughter, represented in outline as mere types, rebelliously confront their mother for having brought them into the world during these times of horror. *Platz* (1920) continues this theme and shows us a better future, in which woman becomes the savior of the world. The revised early play *Stuerme* (1923) is a drama of revolt with intensified motives. *Heinrich von Andernach* (1925), written especially for the thousandth anniversary festival of the Rhineland, is dedicated entirely to the idea of peace. *Bonaparte* (1927) concerns itself with the theme of rebellion. This time it is the Duke d'Enghien who has not enough strength to overthrow the Corsican and therefore must die before the former can proclaim himself dictator. With *Phaea* (1930) and *Zero* (1932) Unruh has gone over to comedy. The sound-film concern Phaea is anxious to serve the public what it is denied by real life. Thus the sultry atmosphere of a night club, the constantly changing life of the entertainment world, and the breath-taking sensational event of a political murder are photographed in all details. The author of a scenario pleads in vain with the producers for the realization of his artistic ideas. *Zero* is the lucky number in a roulette game in Monte Carlo. But zero is also the symbol of a world in decline and the beginning of a new world of higher ethics.

The importance of August Stramm (1874-1915) and Lothar Schreyer (1886-   ) lies above all else in their language which has become the ideal model of Expressionism for the younger members of the generation. August Stramm who started with naturalistic sketches (*Bauern,* performed 1929), later wrote theatrical products (*Kraefte,* 1915, performed 1921) that were pantomimes with disconnected words interspersed. Lothar Schreyer's dramas (*Jungfrau,* 1917; *Nacht,* 1919) pile up crying shouts into cubist pictures which have no relation to conceptions but only express indistinct feeling.

Strong, creative powers, however, are displayed in the dramas of Ernst Barlach (1870-1938), the sculptor, although the visible world and the non-visible are interwoven in them into a sort of modern myth. *Der tote Tag* (1912) uses the fairy-tale form to tell of a mother who does not want to see her son go through the experiences of this world, and destroys him and herself. *Der arme Vetter* (1918) embodies the spiritual person in his fight against the well-fed, busy, unsensitive philistine. *Die echten Sedemunds*

(1920) of the title are represented by an old, criminal, wild father contrasted with a son, swollen with nobility and world-reforming ideas. *Der Findling* (1922) is an allegorical pageant of horror and nausea, meanness and ugliness which, nevertheless, leads to world-liberating love. In *Die Suendflut* (1924), pious Noah is being saved while the wicked Calan sees himself as God even in his hour of ruin. *Der blaue Boll* (1926) is concerned with Faustian problems with a good deal of humor. *Die gute Zeit* (1930) shows an insurance company which issues policies against every difficulty life might present.

Between the extremes of irresistible, physical passions and strict asceticism we find the plays of Alfred Brust (1891-1934). *Der ewige Mensch* (1919) proclaims the curative faculty of eternal love. *Der singende Fisch* (1920, performed 1921) concerns a pious legend of the Baltic regions which attains dramatic reality in an atmosphere of local forests and Slavic ecstacy. The three one-act plays which are combined under the title *Tolkening* (1921-1924), express symbolically the extremes of sexual passion and the conquest of them. *Die Woelfe* symbolizes the most gruesome form of masochism, *Die Wuermer* the goal of sadistic passion, and finally *Phoenix* represents the struggle against the principle of evil and the victory over and contempt for all sensual things. After several comedies (*Das Nachthorn,* 1929; *Der unaussprechliche Hirt,* 1929; *Schmoff,* 1930) Alfred Brust, a few months after the principle of evil in the person of Adolf Hitler came to political power, attempted to demonstrate in his *Kaufmann Christleit* (1933) that there exists something higher than human love, and that is human kindness, which smooths the road for all men and matters, and brings heaven's blessings.

Physical passions and perversities comprise the main themes of the plays of Hans Henry Jahnn (1894-   ). His *Pastor Ephraim Magnus* (1919) utterly exhausts the antithetic themes of sovereignty over and submission to the body. *Die Kroenung Koenig Richards III* (1921) makes use of the historical fable to unleash a number of complicated sexual murders. *Medea* (1925, performed 1927) is a mixture of bestiality and demoniac superman behavior.

Julius Maria Becker (1887-   ), who also roots in Expressionism, sees the road to true humanity in the conquest of selfishness. His first play, *Das letzte Gericht* (1919), a passion play in the style of Strindberg's mysteries, treats the theme of self-conquest against a background of war. *Der Schaecher zur Linken* (1923) touches the profoundest problem of Christianity, the question as to whether some one else might do penance for our sins. In *Der Brueckengeist* (1929) Becker finds a style of his own in which his romantic and poetic nature is now able to express itself; this is a delicate play about the departed spirits of two lovers who while alive were prevented from joining each other.

A poet, a general, and a multi-millionaire are among those rescued after a catastrophic train collision; they become aware that they owe the world more and higher things than they have so far given. In the shadow of death and at the very place where the accident happened, an everyday miracle comes to pass: in a nearby supply shed, a poor emigrant woman gives birth to a boy. All three of them go there in *Die Nacht der Koenige* (1931) and become the child's godfathers. In *Mann Nummer Soundsoviel* (1931) we have the story of a common soldier who, after being wounded and shell-shocked, suffers from amnesia. Two women claim him; the play is filled with tense situations. *Mata Hari* (1932), a play in verse, makes a martyr of love of the now already legendary figure of the famous spy; she and her beloved are united in death. In *Ludwig II* (1932) Julius Maria Becker has dramatized the tragic destiny of the insane King of Bavaria, and in *Auge um Auge* (1937) he demonstrates through the story of Alboin and Rosamund the conflict between a woman's love for her father and that for her husband.

A poet of the Catholic faith is Leo Weismantel (1888-   ). War and revolution were described in his three one-act plays under the combined title of *Die Reiter der Apokalypse* (1919). Germany's collapse became the fable of *Der Waechter am Galgen* (1920), in which the characters are merely symbolical of various epochs in Germany's history. *Totentanz* (1921) was modeled after a religious play of the Middle Ages. *Das Spiel vom Blute Luzifers* (1921) is an extremely vivid dramatization of the legend about the bishop who sallied forth to find the poorest person in the world; but he finally realizes that spiritual wealth, that is faith, means more than riches in physical things. The festival play *Der Kurfuerst* (1925) is an avowal of faith in Christian politics and a warning to the temporal powers to act with justice, love, and faith. Finally, *Das Pest—und Passionsgeluebde von Anno 1633 zu Oberammergau* (1933) gave dramatic form to the legend of the founding of that famous passion play.

Rolf Lauckner (1887-   ), step-son of Hermann Sudermann, is an Expressionist primarily in the matter of form. It is his aim to arouse our feeling for the fates of individuals and to reveal their meanings for humanity. *Der Sturz des Apostels Paulus* (1918) shows a benefactor of humanity who rises in the world as a faith healer but ends in failure; yet even in his complete loneliness he still has faith in his calling. *Christa, die Tante* (1919) is a play about an old maid who falls in love with a young man; all she gets out of it is ridicule and disappointment. *Predigt in Litauen* (1918) shows the father-son problem in an orthodox, secluded preacher who refuses burial to a suicide and drives his own son to his death. The useless struggle of an enthusiastic but weak man with the social chaos of the revolution is demonstrated in *Wahnschaffe* (1920). *Die Reise gegen Gott* (1923) concerns the fate of a painter (Paul Gauguin) who loses his creative powers as he loses touch with his native land. An effective theatrical piece was *Die Entkleidung des Antonio Carossa* (1925), a comedy about swindlers. *Matumbo* (1924) deals with the problem of the Negro in Europe.

In *Krisis* (1928) we have again a man between two women, both of whom finally turn against him, similar to the action in Ernst Hardt's *Schirin und Gertraude*. *Bernhard von Weimar* (1933) marked Lauckner's return to the historical drama; it deals with a fighter for the liberation and unification of Germany at the time of the Thirty Years' War.

Klabund (Alfred Henschke, 1891-1928) is known as a lyrical poet, translator and adaptor of oriental poetry, and as novelist. As a dramatist he started with a typical monologue drama in the expressionistic manner, *Die Nachtwandler* (1920); his play *Brennende Erde* (1926) calls upon the sin and blood encumbered world to seek salvation. He created a new version of the old folk play about Wagner the sorcerer, and called it *Der Teufelspakt* (1925). With this play, but especially with *Der Kreidekreis* (1923), performed in New York as *The Circle of Chalk*, he has gone completely over to the Romanticists. *Kreidekreis*, a play from the Chinese, concerns a poor, good girl who must go through suffering and persecution, but finally becomes the wife of the just emperor.

Otto Brues (1897-   ), in *Heilandsflur* (1921), shows a group of soldiers who want to escape the chaos of revolution and settle down to a peaceful country life; but military orders put them back into the political strife. *Der Prophet von Lochau* (1923) is the story of an ecstatic priest who prophesies the coming of Judgment Day, causing fear and panic in his community. His other dramatic productions were done for special occasions. In 1936, he added *Papa Wrangel*, a patriotic comedy.

Arnold Zweig (1887-   ) dramatized the biblical story of *Abigail und Nabal* (1912); in *Ritualmord in Ungarn* (1915, retitled *Die Sendung Semaels*, 1920) he gives a passionate description of human misery in the form of a religious play. *Die Umkehr des Abtruennigen* (1925, performed 1929) shows Johannes von Brixen, Lord-Bishop, feared for his brutal pogroms against the Jews; he is of Jewish descent and is finally ruined by the spiritual schism. *Der Streit um den Sergeanten Grischa* (1930) is the dramatization of the author's own famous novel of the same title; the miserable fate of an escaped war prisoner who is suspected of espionage becomes a magnificent indictment against war.

The inner conflict of an Alsatian frontier dweller during the war is shown by René Schickele (1883-1940) in his *Hans im Schnakenloch* (1916). Schnakenloch (Gnat's Hole) is the name of an estate near Strasbourg, and Hans is the owner. His heart belongs to his wife, but he deceives her with a clever and racy Frenchwoman. When the war comes he decides to enter the French army, after he has saved the life of his brother, a German officer. This play is in style still almost naturalistic as far as the description of spiritual occurrences and the milieu are concerned. *Am Glockenturm* (1920), however, and *Die neuen Kerle* (1921) are criticisms of the time in expressionistic form.

The most forceful of the Expressionistic writers of drama is Ernst Toller

(1893-1939), who wrote a number of tendencious dramas with ardent, social understanding. *Wandlung, das Ringen eines Menschen* (1918) shows, in thirteen scenes, actual happenings together with dream pictures. A young Jew believes he must earn the privilege of belonging to his community by volunteering his services for the war. But the horrors of war and the brutalities of the people in power turn him into a revolutionary, after he has struggled to attain for himself a true philosophy based on humanity. *Masse Mensch* (1919, performed 1921 and played in the United States as *Man and the Masses*) also leads us into the miseries of war, shows revolution, street fighting, prison; the principal character is a woman who tries in vain to convert the raging masses to the principle of peaceful humanitarianism. In *Die Maschinenstuermer* (1922) the leader of the revolting weavers is slain by the thoughtless mob which refuses to see that nothing can be accomplished by the destruction of machinery, and that machines should rather be used as helpers of humanity. The material for this drama, which challenges comparison with Hauptmann's *Die Weber,* was taken by Toller from the revolt of the English Chartists, Nothingham, 1811; in his prologue he translates Lord Byron's maiden speech in the House of Lords in defense of the rioters. *Hinkemann* (1923), produced in England in 1926 as *Broken-Brow,* and in America at Cleveland in the 1930-1931 season, is the horrifying, gripping tragedy of the returning soldier who lost his manhood in the war; it is, perhaps, a crass symbol of Germany grown powerless. *Hoppla, wir leben* (1927), produced in England as *Hopplal,* is the story of a revolutionary who has been condemned to death, then pardoned and discharged after eight years in an insane asylum; out in the world he cannot find his way any longer. Produced by Erwin Piscator, the play became a sensation. In his historical play *Feuer aus den Kesseln* (1930), Toller tells the story of the revolt of the German navy, using official documents. Personal experiences form the basis for *Die blinde Goettin* (1932), Justitia, who imprisons innocent people as well as guilty, and lets no one leave her jails without being damaged for life. Another late play of Toller's *Nie wieder Friede,* was produced by the Federal Theatre under the title *No More Peace* in the late thirties. His last play was *Pastor Hall* (1939), a drama of a German clergyman who defies the Nazi storm-troopers.

Alfons Paquet (1881-   ), who more than any other German of his day based his philosophy on Walt Whitman, gave his *Sturmflut* (1926) the full realism of the Russian Revolution; interwoven are the revolt of the German sailors and the sinking of the fleet at Scapa Flow. It was the first play in which Erwin Piscator, the director, illustrated by means of a film the actor's speech on the stage. *Fahnen* (1923, performed 1924) shows the struggle and failure of the great strike in Chicago, 1886, with simple and honest sentiments. *Eleonora Duse* (1929) and *William Penn* (1929) are biographies in dialogue form. *Stinchen von der Krone* (1932) shows the fate of a woman deeply in love who, feeling herself insulted, seeks revenge in the strife among political parties and is driven to her death; it is a costume play of the Middle Ages.

A revolutionary drama of the purest form and spotless purity of intentions is Johannes R. Becher's (1891-   ) *Arbeiter, Bauern, Soldaten* (1921); Becher tried here to create a new kind of theatre technique in which actors and audience combine to form a united mass of ecstatic, enthusiastic people.

Hanns Johst (1890-   ) produced his first dramatic piece with *Die Stunde des Sterbenden* (1914); in the night, on the battlefield, doubt and desperation lead to revolution. His amusing comedy *Stroh* (1915) comes close to naturalism; it deals brutally and vividly with betrayed betrayers in business during the war. *Der junge Mensch* (1915), however, was an "ecstatic scenario," the designation given to this continuity of pictures, a form of dramatic Expressionism. The play is directed against the wrong kind of education given by parents and teachers; it is based on Wedekind as well as on Strindberg and Sorge. In his next drama, *Der Einsame* (1917), he makes Christian Dietrich Grabbe's grief for the loss of a beautiful, delicate, beloved girl the foundation for the tragedy of that dramatic genius; here, as well as in his *Thomas Paine* (1927), he arbitrarily bends his biographical material to suit his own purposes. *Der Koenig* (1920), in form a typically expressionistic drama, shows Johst's political position: the king is a martyr of his devotion to duty; he is ruined because he wants the best for his people. In *Propheten* (1923) he puts Martin Luther on the stage as the representative of German faith. *Wechsler und Haendler* (1923) are swindlers of the post-war inflation period who are contrasted with an aristocratic refugee as the representative of moral principles. With this play Johst leaves Expressionism; in his *Wissen und Gewissen* (1924) he explains his theories on drama. The tragedy *Die froehliche Stadt* (1925) turns to the question of the existence of God. *Komoedie am Klavier* (1929) confronts realism and idealism in everyday philistine life.

Johst advanced these theses: "the German drama must be born of the blood and essence of Germanism," and "the theatre is the last pedagogical possibility to save the people from the complete materialism of a purely realistic world." He was an early follower of the National Socialist (Nazi) movement. His drama *Schlageter* (1933) shows and idealizes the resistance against French occupation of the Rhineland. It was written "for Adolf Hitler, in affectionate veneration and unchanging loyalty." This passage occurs in it: "When I hear 'Kultur' I loosen the safety catch on my revolver."

Paul Zech (1881-   ), a lyric poet, erected in his *Das trunkene Schiff* (1925) a literary memorial to Arthur Rimbaud, the great French poet and inspirer of the young generation of poets. With great dramatic energy, he recreated the eventful life of this man, who wanted to turn poetry into action. Herman Kasack (1896-   ) has written the drama of a spiritually lonesome man in *Vincent* (1924) in which the painters, metaphysical Vincent van Gogh and realist Paul Gauguin, are contrasted. The Swiss writer

Robert Faesi (1883-) started with a delicate comedy in the manner of Arthur Schnitzler, *Die offenen Tueren* (1911). In *Odysseus und Nausikaa* (1911) he used a classical style similar to Paul Ernst's. In *Opferspiel* (1925) he wrote an intensified dramatic version of the story of the burghers of Calais for a church festival. Finally, in *Leerlauf* (1931) he made fun of the pompous activities of his contemporaries.

Ernst Lissauer (1882-1938), another German follower of Walt Whitman, shows us in *Eckermann* (1921) the figure of Goethe as the ideal giver, and his amanuensis, Eckermann, as the ideal receiver. *Luther und Thomas Muenzer* (1929) puts the religious reformer, who wants to enforce God's kingdom through His word, in opposition to Muenzer, the leader of the revolting peasants, who wants to enforce it through violence; the play shows the tragical fate of the revolutionary reformer, whose good intentions, however, bring evil results. The biblical story from Judges about the captain who must sacrifice his daughter to keep a vow becomes the struggle of a mother against her husband in *Das Weib des Jephta* (1928, performed 1929). With *Aufruhr des Goldes* (1931), a play concerned with economic and political crises, Lissauer entered the realm of present-day problems.

Hermann Burte (H. Strube, 1879-) wrote *Herzog Utz* (1913), a romantic play in which a prince of the Middle Ages finds his way back to duty after many erroneous experiments with love. In *Katte* (1914, performed 1918) we see how the conflict between the Prussian king and father, Friedrich Wilhelm I, and his son, Crown Prince Friedrich, later Frederick the Great, is resolved by the sacrifice of Lieutenant Katte. *Simson* (that is, Samson) (1917) gains self-confidence after he has been blinded, and triumphs over his enemies. After *Der letzte Zeuge* (1921), a melodrama using expressionistic techniques, Burte puts the biblical story of the trial of Jesus on the stage in *Krist vor Gericht* (1930); the trial is conducted in the modern manner, with witnesses and experts. *Prometheus* (1932, performed 1933) contrasts in classical verse the rebellious superman with the servile Epimetheus, and leads up to an interpretation of the myth that was current during the Middle Ages, which considered Prometheus to be the forerunner of Christ's message of salvation. In *Mensch mit uns* (1936) we find Siegfried, the old Germanic hero, and the laws of unity and race, which were needed by the National Socialist theatre. Burte had used these ideas in an earlier novel, by the way; it was *Wiltfeber, der ewige Deutsche* (1912).

Bruno Frank (1887-1945) wrote the historical play *Zwoelftausend* (1927) while Expressionism was on the decline. The theme is that of Schiller's *Kabale und Liebe* (1783). To raise money for his private amusements an autocratic duke makes a profitable deal by which his subjects must serve as soldiers for England in her war against America, the land they yearn for "where man stands on his own, on his inherent right, an equal among equals, and free." Previously Frank had made a social accusation in *Das Weib auf dem Tiere* (1921). In *Perlenkomoedie* (1929) he wrote a witty and graceful comedy, full of the knowledge of human nature. *Sturm im Wasserglas* (1930), produced in New York as *Storm Over Patsy*, was a satire on bureaucracy. *Nina* (1931), with the rôles of the film star and her double played by the same actress, was written especially for charming Fritzi Massary. *Der General und das Gold* (1932) is the dramatized story of John Sutter, whose California paradise was ruined by the gold-diggers, and who for thirty years sued in vain for his rights.

Kurt Heynicke (1891-   ) who started with radical Expressionism and also wrote delicate lyrical poetry, created *Ehe* (1923), a drama in Ibsen's manner, and *Das Meer* (1925), a play about sea-going men, in terse scenes. Between the comedies *Wer gewinnt Lisette?* (1928) and *Frau ins Haus* (1937) stands his *Neurode* (1934), a play with mass choirs for the assembly places of the Third Reich; it glorifies the community spirit of the crew of a coal mine which is being kept at work to avoid unemployment, although constant new catastrophes demand that the work cease.

To almost all dramatic writers, Expressionism was merely a transitory stage. We observed in the careers of Alfons Paquet, Bruno Frank, Hanns Johst, and others how, after the ecstasy of Expressionism, a striving for objectivity asserts itself. The writers search for unbiased lucidity, reminiscent of the keen scrutiny of naturalism and, for a while at least, turn away from expressions of sympathy and the sentimentality of their naturalistic and new-romantic predecessors. It is remarkable how large a space is allotted to dramas about historical events for explaining the conflicts of the present, in addition to plays which deal directly with the problems of the present. These different phases might be demonstrated with the example of just one author, Hans José Rehfisch (1891-   ). *Die goldenen Waffen* (1912) was a new-romantic variation of the *Ajax* of Sophocles; *Erziehung durch Kolibri* (performed 1921; 1922) was a satire on the money-greedy, moralizing philistines written in the manner of Carl Sternheim. *Wer weint um Juckenack?* (1924), the story of a subaltern official who wants to be sure that his heirs shall be moved to tears, was a successful play in Georg Kaiser's style. *Duell am Lido* (1926), a comedy about confidence men and a wise mixture of sentimentality and cynicism, became a success of the expressionistic theatre when Leopold Jessner put it on the stage in grand style. Under the pen-name of René Kestner, Rehfisch, in collaboration with Wilhelm Herzog, then dramatized *Die Affaire Dreyfus* (1929); he used official documents, and made Emile Zola a central character with his gripping appeal to protect the Republic against the autocracy of the military caste. Finally, in *Brest-Litowsk* (1931), Rehfisch made use of Lev Trotski's memoirs for staging an historical continuity of tableaux of striking objectivity.

Dramatic history in the manner of *Die Affaire Dreyfus* and accounts of historical events, either recent or older, as *Brest-Litowsk*, were produced on the stage in great numbers, before and after 1930. All these plays have in common the aim of exerting some sort of political influence through historical example. We shall examine this type of drama shortly.

The model for the drama of the new objectivity is Georg Buechner, to whom Frank Wedekind had turned to find a pattern for the structure of his plays. Rapidly changing scenes, packed with a sort of electric atmosphere, are the external characteristics of this new style, too. Such plays as Wolfgang Goetz's *Gneisenau,* Alfred Neumann's *Der Patriot,* Bernard Blume's *Bonaparte,* were all created under the influence of *Dantons Tod* which, since the beginning of this century, had been staged with constantly increasing success.

Wolfgang Goetz (1885-   ) achieved in his *Gneisenau* (1925) the portrayal of a Prussian general, an important and peculiar person, a superior spirit, delicately and profoundly civilized, who was deeply hurt because neither the king nor the field-marshal understood him; he encountered resistance for his proposed reforms with people of his own class; he met with hatred from the soldiers from whom he had expected great things, and from the people whom he had to burden with heavy taxes. This picture of a leader has helped point out the road to chauvinism and the demands of the nationalists. After the representation of such a hero, *Robert Emmet* (1928) was somewhat disappointing; the Irish fighter for liberty is shown as a man torn between love for his country and love for a woman; he succumbs to the latter. The drama *Der feurige Ofen* (1924) is concerned entirely with love. The comedy *Cavaliere* (1930) is written with bluntness and is full of cheap humor; in it Lola Montez, expelled from Munich, falls into the company of sundry gentlemen. *Kuckuckseier* (1934) is a comedy about Shakespeare's actors, with happy and serious love intrigues, which point to *The Merry Wives of Windsor* and *Othello.*

A powerful creator of impressive plays about human destinies is Alfred Neumann (1895-   ). In *Der Patriot* (1926) he shows us the Russian Governor Peter von der Pahlen who shoulders the responsibility for the revolution and the removal of the insane Czar Paul I, and leads the country back to sound conditions. *Koenigsmaske* (1928) introduces us to France after the July revolution and the struggle the legitimists waged against King Louis Philippe; the pretender, a man too weak to be a ruler, is vanquished because he has neither the strength nor the will-power to assert himself. *Frauenschuh* (1929) is concerned with the conflict between duty and love; the man, loyal to his duty, dies and there is a song of great love in a grotesque epilogue.

Bernard Blume (1901-   ), after his exciting *Fahrt nach der Suedsee* (1924, performed 1925) in which political prisoners seize a ship but do not know how to steer it, created in *Bonaparte* (1926) a series of scenes in very impressive language; this play shows Napoleon in the period before his exile to Elba, driven by the demon of power, in scenes that change with violent speed and are packed with tension. *Treibjagd* (1928) shows the fate of persecuted human beings in scenes from the Bolshevist Revolution. In his drama *Im Namen des Volkes* (1929, performed 1930) Blume, as so many of his contemporaries, criticizes that administration of justice which adheres to the cold letter of the law; with this play he enters the ranks of the topical dramatists. Hermann Kesten (1898-   ) who, together with Ernst Toller, dramatized the life of the founder of Christian Science in *Wunder in Amerika (Mary Baker Eddy,* 1931) gave us in *Admet* (1929) a new version of the Alcestis legend. Whereas Euripides showed us Alcestis sacrificing herself for her husband whom she loves more than life itself, the new Alcestis goes to her death in deep loathing for her inferior husband who is quite willing to barter for his miserable life at any price.

Ernst Penzold (1892-   ), a follower of Buechner with a romantic-lyrical talent, wrote a fantastic drama about the *Portugalesische Schlacht* (1930) in which he confirms, with irony, the immortality of the desire to have a king. The king, greedy for glory, fights a meaningless battle and needlessly loses his life. The people cannot be without a hero and get a double. The enemy does away with him, too, but a substitute is found immediately. In *Sand* (1931) Penzold strips the aura of martyrdom for democratic liberty from the student Karl Ludwig Sand, murderer of Kotzebue, while Sigmund Graff (1899-   ) in *Die einsame Tat* (1931) makes him a fanatic of an *idée fixe.*

A full-blooded, forceful dramatist with kindness and a sense of humor is Carl Zuckmayer (1896-   ). His earliest play *Der Kreuzweg* (1920) was about knights, peasants, and troubadours in costumes of the Middle Ages but was written in expressionistic language. But in *Pankraz und die Hinterwaeldler* (1925), in which noble Indians and treacherous farmers are shown, he has already returned to nature. Then came *Der froehliche Weinberg* (1925), a popular play placed in the environment of a small town on the Rhine, full of life, genuine humor, and sound satire, and written with immediate knowledge of the milieu. *Schinderhannes* (1927), the notorious bandit who, as friend and helper of the poor, was a kind of Robin Hood, and took it upon himself to solve the social question in his own peculiar way, and the magnificently created character of the woman who loves him, gain our full sympathy in this play which contains scenes of finest creative beauty. Refreshingly straightforward and simple, if a bit sentimental, is the story of *Katharina Knie* (1929) who declines to follow the demands of her heart to insure the continued existence of a celebrated troupe of tight-rope walkers. Under the régime of Wilhelm II, a discharged jailbird acquired an officer's uniform and, with a handful of soldiers, marched into the city hall of a small German town, confiscated the cash box, and escaped without interference; and the world laughed at this wonderful satire on the Prussian spirit of subordination and the all-powerful military set. Zuckmayer has used this incident in his comedy *Der Hauptmann von Koepenick* (1930), another humorous parallel to Gogol's *The Inspector General.* His new version of the old legendary material about *Der Schelm von Bergen* (1934), the outlawed hangman who assists the childless empress in getting an heir to the throne, constitutes his last dramatic work up to the present time.

Together with Zuckmayer, Hans Mueller-Schloesser (1884-   ) must be mentioned for he showed humor and temperament in his comedy *Schneider Wibbel* (1914, performed 1913). In the sequel to this piece, *Schnieder Wibbels Auferstehung* (1929), he entertained us mainly through his clever technique and blunt buffoonery. Finally, in *Die Laus im Pelze* (1933) he transformed the problematic theme of the reportedly lost and unexpectedly returning soldier-husband into a drastic burlesque.

Another follower of Zuckmayer is Alois Johannes Lippl (1903-   ) who shows in amusing scenes in his Bavarian-dialect comedy *Die Pfingstorgel* (1933) how poor itinerant musicians present an organ to the Church of Misers' Village.

The tragic side of native dramatic literature is represented by Friedrich Griese (1890-   ); in *Godam (Mensch aus Erde gemacht,* 1923) he presents the struggle of two peasants for a woman in which the whole severity of the North-German temperament is brought to the fore. He also wrote several peasant comedies which combined strong realism with many amusing situations; *Die Schafschur* (1934), for example. Finally, he fell under the sway of the blood-and-soil ideology.

Hans Christoph Kaergel (1889-   ) belongs to the category of native writers; in *Volk ohne Heimat* (1927, performed 1931) he dramatizes the struggle of the foundry workers in Upper Silesia with Polish insurgents and uses these dramatic events to incite discussion and to proclaim militant nationalism. With his *Andreas Hollmann* (1933) and *Hockewanzel* (1934) Kaergel did his share to stir up German hatred against the Czechs.

Hans Kyser (1882-   ), an eclectic talent who tried his hand at a number of interesting dramatic themes before the First World War, joined the ranks of the writers of political pieces with *Es brennt an der Grenze* (1931); it concerns the fixing of the Polish-German border line and its unhappy consequences and takes the form of a factual report. In *Schicksal um Yorck* (1933) and *Schillers deutscher Traum* (1934) he agitates for nationalistic ideas and opposes those of democracy.

Political propaganda on the Right was balanced by violent demonstration on the Left. Wilhelm Herzog (1884-   ) made his *Panama* (1931) a symbol for the battle between democrats and monarchists and entrusts the administration of the decaying republic to the socialism of disciplined labor. Eberhard Wolfgang Moeller (1906-   ) exploited the same theme in the same year under the title *Panamaskandal* (1931) in an anti-republican, demagogical sense, and continued to be active in that direction.

Peter Martin Lampel (1894-   ) put the secret armament maneuvers and their political consequences and dangers under the spotlight of the theatre (*Putsch,* 1930; *Giftgas ueber Berlin,* 1929). With *Revolte im Erziehungs-*

haus (1928) he exposes in a quite naturalistic manner the usual conditions and evils in reformatories and criticizes society for allowing them to exist. He met as much opposition as he found approval for *Wir sind Kameraden* (1931), in which he tried to conciliate nationalistic and communistic youth groups. Curt Corrinth (1894-   ) has tried to reproduce the atmosphere in secret political organizations which sought to attain their ends through acts of terrorism and the effect of the political phrase in his *Sektion Rahnstaetten* (1930). In *Trojaner* (1929) he produced a tragedy about students, in which he attempted to plead for justice and kindness in the midst of political and racial agitation, using the most outworn methods of naturalism, however. But Robert L. Stemmle (1903-   ) in his *Kampf um Kitsch* (1931), with painstaking fidelity to facts, lets us look into the inner workings of a democratically conducted school and poses the question whether it would not be better to educate youth after the principles of liberty rather than turn out mere cannon-fodder.

The keenest fighter on the Left was Friedrich Wolf (1888-   ). But while it is astonishing how speedily most of these writers of dramatic pieces seize topical themes and how cleverly they handle the theatrical technique, it must be admitted of Friedrich Wolf that his poetic passion is at least as strong as his political ardor. He began in the expressionistic tradition with *Das bist Du* (1919), a love tragedy; determined revolutionism is back of *Der Unbedingte* (1919) in which individual characters merge. *Der arme Konrad* (1924), however, treats the revolt of the peasants of Wuerttemberg, in 1514, already in the naturalistic manner and with that deep human sympathy which is a quality of true naturalism. *Kolonne Hund* (1929), a drama of swamp settlers, recalled Hauptmann's *Die Weber*. In *Cyankali-Paragraph 218* (1931) Wolf took up one of the burning questions of the time and exposed conditions which needed immediate improvement. The proletariat fights against capitalism in *Tai Yang erwacht* (1931), a play laid in Shanghai. *Die Jungen von Mons* (1931) is concerned with the disintegrating and aggressive methods of fascist politicians. Collective methods, after the Russian pattern, are introduced in *Bauer Baetz* (1932) as a cure for the misery of indebted peasants. *Floridsdorf* (1935) permits the reader to witness the battles of the Vienna workers against reaction and fascism. *Dr. Mamlocks Ausweg* (1935), performed in New York as *Professor Mamlock*, in 1937, the story of the Jewish surgeon who, slandered, maltreated, and driven from his operating table, puts an end to his life, gives a faithful picture of the national-socialistic terror and the pogroms under Hitler's régime. This tragedy was internationally acclaimed when produced as a film under the title *Professor Mamlock* (1938). *Die Matrosen von Cattaro* (1931), staged in New York by the Theatre Union as *Sailors of Cattaro*, 1934, shows the revolt of the Austrian navy at the end of the First World War, the impotent collapse of the movement, and the manly end of its leaders. Symbolic of the eternal struggle for freedom and humanity, it is

Wolf's most impressive drama because its creative artistry endows it with lasting value.

Hermann Kesser (1880-   ), in *Rotation* (1931), called an international congress for the examination of the deeper causes of unemployment and indicated means for solving this problem. The economic difficulties of the farmers which, on one side, caused indebtedness, clash with the bureaucratic revenue authorities. Severe legal measures on their part and ill-considered, criminal acts on the part of the farmers are treated, simultaneously, with some of Friedrich Wolf's plays by Hans Christoph Kaergel in his own, upsetting manner in his drama *Bauer unterm Hammer* (1932). August Hinrichs (1879-   ) has used this material for a laugh-provoking comedy entitled *Krach um Jolanthe* (*Scandal about Jolanthe,* 1930) which was performed in many theatres and also became a film. Gerhard Menzel (1894-   ) shows in the character of the landowner *Bork* (*Die Steuerfaust,* performed 1930, published 1931) an important tragic figure in conflict with the state; he is finally defeated. The same author contrasts European activity with Asiatic passivity in *Fern-Ost* (1929). A revolt in China against the imperialistic invasion of the whites, similar to the action in Tretyakov's *Roar China!,* is used as a symbol for the battle between philosophies.

Much space in the discussion of theatrical matters is given plays which seek to bring about judicial reform and the amendment or abrogation of certain criminal laws. Max Alsberg (1877-1933), a respected lawyer, in his *Konflikt* (1933) raised the question whether a defense lawyer should be permitted to ask for an acquittal when he is convinced of his client's guilt. Together with Otto Ernst Hesse, who wrote a play about a revolutionary of 1848 called *Robert Blum,* Alsberg directed searching criticism against the methods of preliminary examination in court procedure in his *Voruntersuchung* (1930).

The realization that society, too, is, to a certain extent responsible for the offense of a criminal was worded thus: "Not the murderer, but the murdered person is guilty." Leonhard Frank, using psychoanalytical arguments, had told in his novel *Die Ursache* (1913) how a boy who had been treated harshly and unjustly by a teacher retained resentment even as a man of thirty. He decides to see the teacher, talk to him, and become reconciled. He arrives at the very moment when the teacher is maltreating a boy and is so enraged by the sight that he kills the teacher. In 1929, Frank dramatized this novel; the description of the bare facts, the chilly brutality of law enforcement, the insane fear of death that grips the offender before his execution, made the performance of this play a strong argument against capital punishment. At about the same time, Willi Schaeferfdick (1903-   ) in *Moerder fuer uns* (1927) vindicated the desperate, unemployed culprits of an attack upon a train. Alfred Wolfenstein, who adapted versions of the old Spanish novel *La Celestina* and Shelley's *Cenci* for the German stage, strongly supported the campaign against capital punishment with his play

Die Nacht vor dem Beil (1929) in which a young fellow tries to save a condemned man by attempting to delay the execution. Klaus Mann (1906-   ) who, in *Anja und Esther* (1925) concerned himself with several erotic problems, tried in *Die Geschwister* (1931), a drama based on Jean Cocteau's *Les Enfants terribles,* to give an authentic account of a tragic love-affair between brother and sister. But the most forceful arguments were directed from the stage against that particular paragraph in Germany's law books which concerns the arbitrary interruption of pregnancy. *Der Frauenarzt* (1927), by Hans José Rehfisch; *Paragraph 218* (1930), *Justizkrise* (1931), and *Aerzte im Kampf* (1933), by Carl Credé; *Mary und Lisa* (1931), by Sigmund Graff; *Schwarzmann und die Magd* (1933), by Walter Erich Schaefer; and particularly Alfred Doeblin's *Ehe* (1931) and Friedrich Wolf's already-mentioned *Cyankali-Paragraph 218,* all took up this problem and exposed frightful conditions of social misery which often drive human beings to take so desperate a step.

The war of 1914-1918 was mirrored and explained through the drama ten years after it had come to an end. Just as Erich Maria Remarque's novel *Im Westen nichts Neues* (1928) started an avalanche of war books in all languages, so R. C. Sheriff's *Journey's End* (1928) became the model for the most successful war play on the German stage, *Die endlose Strasse* (1929, performed 1930), by Sigmund Graff (1898-   ) and Ernst Hintze (-   ). It shows the fate of a company of soldiers who are relieved from fighting in the front lines to enjoy a short rest; then they return to the horrors of war. The everyday existence of average war life is portrayed faithfully from experience, without pathos, without heroic deeds. Later, Georg Wilhelm Mueller (1881-   ) in his *1914* (1930) has concentrated the documentary evidence of that fateful year in a powerful play of unpoetical objectivity. Paul Joseph Cremers (1879-   ) in *Die Marneschlacht* (1932, performed 1933) gives a description of the battle in strict accordance with reliable sources and makes the failure of the high command the comprehensible reason for the German defeat. The French General Nivelle is the hero of Maxim Ziese's drama *Der Tag J* (1931), in which realism is mixed with expressionistic vision. The German offensive of March 1918 has been presented by Fritz von Zwehl (1883-   ) in *Unternehmen Michael* (1934) with many colorful descriptions, military-technical episodes, and a romantic hero. War as the experience and fate of the individual, the chaotic mixture of energy and insufficiency, has been created by Gerhard Menzel in the character of his *Hauptmann Tobbogan* (1927) who resists death in vain.

Beside these heroic and historical plays stand the dramas about the return and fate of war prisoners and those allegedly dead. Hermann Sudermann was obviously much too early with his *Die Entscheidung der Lissa Hart* (1922). The play did not find its way into the theatre until ten years later. In Sudermann's piece the story concerned a girl who gave up her fiancé to marry his friend; war and imprisonment were merely the background. In Leonhard Frank's *Karl und Anna* (1928) the woman accepts the returned friend who succeeds in making her believe that he is her husband; and she clings to him and goes with him into a new future when the real spouse eventually returns. This drama was staged in New York by the Theatre Guild in 1929. In Siegmund Graff's *Die Heimkehr des Matthias Bruck* (1933) the hero, who was reported dead long ago, finds his wife married to an efficient farmer who takes as good care of the property as he himself had done, and is a good father to the child. Rather than disturb this peaceful life he quietly does away with himself.

Lion Feuchtwanger's (1884-   ) success as a novelist overshadows his effectiveness as a dramatist. No theatre dared to produce his *Die Kriegsgefangenen* (1919) in which a young Frenchman is lucky in love with several German girls but is wrecked by his jealousy. Of greater importance is his drama *Thomas Wendt* (Neunzehnhundertachtzehn, 1920): the hero—reversing the action in Toller's *Wandlung*—turns into a revolutionary ruler after having been a lamenting, revolutionary poet. Finally, sobered by disagreeable and brutal realities, he abdicates. Feuchtwanger calls this piece a "dramatic novel," which is to say that he has slowed down the action of the play with certain epical additions, designed to explain the causative and psychological relations more clearly than is usual in plays for the theatre.

Kalkutta, 4. Mai (1928) is an effective play in which Feuchtwanger shows Warren Hastings, who conquered India for England, in his struggle against bureaucratic narrow-mindedness and world ignorance. *Der hollaendische Kaufmann* (1923, performed 1928) is a person of genius who, through endurance and forceful action, knows how to reach his goal despite all opposition. *Die Petroleuminseln* (1927) presents a woman of extreme ugliness; she makes up for it by will-power and energetic activity. Feuchtwanger has also prepared versions of the Indian *Vasantasena*, by Shudraka, *The Persians*, by Æschylus, and *The Peace*, by Aristophanes, for the German stage. Together with Berthold Brecht he has rewritten Christopher Marlowe's *Eduard II* (1924); by adding new vivid incidents, the external action has been made even more breath taking.

Berthold Brecht (1898-   ) took over the dramatic form of Feuchtwanger's *Thomas Wendt*, developed it independently, and gave it a theoretical basis. He attracted attention first with his drama *Trommeln in der Nacht* (1923), another play about a soldier believed to be dead, who surprises his fiancé in the act of marrying a man who has profited by the revolution. But he gets the girl back and frees himself from the sentimentalities of his revolutionary surroundings, then takes his fate into his own hands. Expressionistic in form, and grotesque in some of its exaggerations, its language was clear and the lyrical parts had the simplicity of folk songs; as a whole it indicated that the author was a real poet. *Im Dickicht der Staedte* (performed 1922, printed 1923) leads us into the stony wilderness of a large city and shows the struggle of two men, symbolical of the senselessness of some human ambitions.

Mann ist Mann (1927) is a grotesque play which demonstrates that any man can fill without difficulty the place of another. *Aufstieg und Fall der Stadt Mahagony* (1927), with music by Kurt Weill, was Brecht's first attempt to turn the opera which, in its traditional form is a matter of sensory enjoyment, to instructive purposes. He explained his intentions in detail in his paper *Ueber die Oper* (1932). The libretto consists of one great ballad about the paradise-city Mahagony, where only those may live who have money. For money means more than honor and honesty, money is stronger than morality and right. The collaboration of Brecht and Weill also produced *Die Dreigroschenoper* (1928), based upon John Gay's *The Beggar's Opera*. The Brecht music-drama was adapted into English as *The Three-Penny Opera* (1933) by Gifford Cochran and Jerrold Krimsky. The great success of this play was achieved through Brecht's biting irony and the songs which quickly became popular. The "school operas" *Der Jasager* und *Der Neinsager* (1931) are written again for educational purposes, and are based on English versions of Japanese plays; the music for the first one was composed by Weill. *Die Massnahme* (1931), with music by Hans Eisler, presents an attempt to educate the audience, by means of an instructive play, to form its own judgment. The theatre is arranged like a court room where the characters must give an account of themselves in a case involving a political murder; the judges are sitting in the audience, and every spectator instinctively becomes a judge. Brecht gives his own explanation of this kind of drama and of the underlying intention:[1] "I do not like plays to contain pathetic overtones, they must be convincing like court pleas. The main thing is to teach the spectator to reach a verdict. This trains the mind. Any fool knows how to feel sad and share suffering...."

His version of Maxim Gorki's *Mutter* (1932) is based upon these principles; the whole play is adapted to German conditions, of course; only the names remained Russian. The development of this instructive type of play is based upon Brecht's idea that art is a branch of education and its task, therefore, is to teach. His dramas become constantly and plainly more instructive. He calls this "Epic Theatre"; it is his principal aim and quite different from the traditional theatre which he designates as "Aristotelian Theatre." Whereas the traditional theatre seeks to get the spectator's attention through his emotions, the "Epic Theatre" appeals to his intellect. The suggestive effect of the "Aristotelian Theatre" is here replaced by sober evidence. "Objectivity," the distinguishing mark of Germany's youngest phase of dramatic writing, has here found its purest expression, indeed.

However, Brecht has also written Aristotelian drama when it was necessary to influence a large audience which could only be approached by

[1] Quoted by S. M. Tretyakov in "Bert Brecht," *International Literature*, Moscow (May, 1937), pp. 60-70.

traditional means. In this category belong *Die Gewehre der Frau Carrar* (*Señora Carrar's Rifles,* 1937) a play about the Spanish Civil War, written for a group of actors in France; and *Furcht und Elend des Dritten Reiches* (*The Private Life of the Master Race,* 1939), a series of one-act plays which show with uncanny accuracy the atmosphere of uncertainty and horror in Hitler Germany.

Belonging neither to the "Epic" nor the "Aristotelian" theatre is *Die Rundkoepfe und die Spitzkoepfe* (*Round Heads, Peak Heads;* or, *Rich and Rich Make Good Company,* 1935, performed in Copenhagen, 1937) since "it was conceived as a variation of Shakespeare's *Measure for Measure,*" but "any illusion of reality was carefully avoided and the writing was deliberately unrealistic." The action takes place in a country whose inhabitants belong to two different races. As long as there are mutual economic interests, the difference in race is of no importance. But when, as a consequence of an economic crisis, a revolution threatens to break out, the ruler segregates the two races and incites one against the other. The connection with the immediate present puts this play into the category of "topical theatre"; its artistic form merits the additional epithet "romantic." Here, the political trend is quite obvious. Literary and political opponents of Brecht have maintained that many of his plays are nihilistic: the underlying ideas are not always easily recognized, or, as in *Aufstieg und Fall der Stadt Mahagony,* they form a single indictment of the world where everything is evil. However, it is not Brecht's intention at all to bring about an immediate catharsis of the spectator while he is in the theatre, but rather to effect through the play an influence of longer duration than the performance. His philosophy is obviously contained in these verses from his *Die heilige Johanna der Schlachthoefe* (1922), a caustic parody of Schiller's *Jungfrau von Orleans:*

> Make it not your goal
> That in the hour of death
> You yourself be better.
> Let it be your goal
> That in the hour of death
> You leave a bettered world.[1]

This survey of the dramatic literature of Germany during the last sixty years is framed by two personalities: Gerhart Hauptmann, representative of naturalism not less than of symbolism and classicism, has never lost his intention and aim toward, and his sympathy for, suffering man. Bert Brecht, at the end of the list, Expressionist and creator of a form of dramatic reality, ardently strives for the establishment of a better world. Between these two extremes we find a multitude of aims which have, however, one persistent note: a continual struggle for individual freedom,

---

[1] From S. M. Tretyakov's paper referred to above.

so emphatically expressed by Schiller's *In Tyrannos* and so persistently sounded throughout the succeeding years.

The last decade of the period, unfortunately, has obscured the clarity of the preceding years, because the Nazi ideology has been imposed upon the drama as a means of propaganda. Dictatorship forced all literary expression into the service of a narrow-minded conception of race superiority.

Not until this war, precipitated by a class of upstart tyrants, has been ultimately won on behalf of the democratic idea, and not until the conception of a rightful peace has become rooted in Germany, will it be possible to determine the future of German drama.

III

Austria

HENRY SCHNITZLER

Austria-Hungary, the Empire of the Hapsburgs, comprised within her far-flung boundaries many and widely different nations and races which frequently developed their own literatures in their respective languages. However, speaking of Austrian literature, we have in mind only works written in German. The term "Austrian drama," therefore, denotes plays in the German language by dramatists born within the realm of the Hapsburg monarchy. Included also, of course, are such plays as were created after the dissolution of the old Empire, until the temporary annexation of Austria by Hitler's Germany in 1938.

Ever since the sixteenth century, when the Counter Reformation brought about an intellectual separation between Catholic Austria and Protestant Germany, Austrian literature has been going through its own peculiar evolution. In the seventeenth century, Austrian Baroque culture, combining Catholic tendencies with the classical heritage of Humanism, manifested itself in outstanding musical and architectural works. Moreover, although no significant dramatist appeared during that period, it was a heyday of the stage and its arts and crafts. Three distinct features characterize the Austrian baroque theatre: the heroic-mythological court opera; the religious drama of the Jesuits; and the folk theatre. Although Spanish and Italian influences prevailed in these works, such influences were absorbed by the popular spirit and resulted in that original dramatic genre, the Viennese folk comedy. Abundant imagination, combined with the satirical and humorous talents of the people, gave birth to a unique creation, the Viennese fairy-tale play. A classic work representing this dramatic form is the libretto of Mozart's *The Magic Flute* (1791). The era of enlightenment brought to the fore German as well as French influences. Yet, their dramatic results were either weak and bloodless tragedies, or insignificant comedies. Now as before, the popular theatre, antagonistic to all rationalistic tendencies, remained the center of dramatic life in the capital. In the nineteenth century, it reached its culmination in its two undisputed masters: the poetic and imaginative Ferdinand Raimund (1790-1836), and the witty and cynical Johann Nestroy (1806-1862). Now arose also Austria's first tragic dramatic writer: Franz Grillparzer (1791-1872), whose towering work might be called a synthesis of the Austrian baroque tradition and the classical spirit of Weimar. For Goethe and Schiller exerted as much influence upon him as did the old fairy-tale plays of the popular theatre and the Spanish tradition of the Hapsburg Empire. His insight into the subconscious and his uncanny ability to analyze the human soul, foreshadowed later developments which were to become typical in Viennese literature. The rise of a sophisticated society brought about the first genuine master of high comedy in Eduard Bauernfeld (1802-1890). His plays combine highly polished and cultivated dialogue with elements of political and social satire. At the same time, the classical verse drama deteriorated in the works of formally accomplished but empty craftsmen, while the traditional folk play, in the hands of Raimund's and Nestroy's successors, became a matter of shallow routine.

Modern trends, although still hidden behind an entirely conventional technique, entered into Austrian drama with Ludwig Anzengruber (1839-1889). He represented the liberal attitude of the seventies and eighties. In his peasant plays he attacked the influence of the Catholic Church, accusing it of thwarting all natural emotions and instincts. In his plays of Viennese manners he became the pioneer of a new ethical and social code and the relentless assailant of false conventions. His masterpiece of this genre, *Das vierte Gebot* (*The Fourth Commandment*, 1877) demonstrates with pitiless realism the depravity of a group of middle-class characters. This frank depiction of the reverse-side of "gay Vienna" may be called the first modern Austrian play.

In order to understand the intellectual and political atmosphere in which the modern Austrian drama developed, it is imperative to remember that the final flowering of Austrian literature coincided with the slow deterioration and eventual dissolution of the old Empire. The presentiment of impending catastrophe created in a great number of people an attitude of uneasiness or even apathy. However, the hackneyed notion of "gay Vienna" was still justified to a certain degree. Until 1914, the capital was to remain the center of cultural life, concealing under its proverbial "Gemuetlichkeit" the unmistakable signs of disintegration. During the First World War, the last effort to unite the many nations and races which formed the Hapsburg monarchy failed and the ultimate disaster left the country in a hopeless condition. The two following decades were years of desperate struggle for economic and political survival. After 1933, the continuous threat of National Socialist Germany split the population into violently opposed camps. Political disunity, combined with economic misery, eventually made the impoverished country an easy prey for the propaganda methods of the Nazi régime. Vienna rapidly lost her gaiety, and only the outside world, encouraged by flimsy movies and idiotic operettas, stubbornly clung to the conviction that the essence of Viennese life was waltzing, drinking, and flirting.

At the beginning of the nineties, when Vienna still was radiant with life, a group of young writers gathered in the Café Griensteidl of literary fame. What united them was not a critical dogma of any kind but the desire to revitalize Austrian art. This group, sometimes called "Young Vienna," looked for inspiration to the West rather than to the North. Contemporary French trends appealed more to their creative temperament than did the "consistent naturalism" proclaimed by the literary circles of the German capital. "Nervenkunst"—art of the nerves—became one of the catchwords of the group, whose members, impressed by French Symbolism, were interested rather in the exploration of the soul and its ever-changing moods than in a photographically true reproduction of external reality, or in the discussion of social and economic questions.

The man who made himself the spokesman for these young writers was Hermann Bahr (1863-1934). During numerous travels abroad he had become thoroughly familiar with the most recent intellectual tendencies. Now he endeavored not only to introduce "Modernism" into his homeland, but also to impel his fellow-countrymen to help in the creation of an original modern Austrian art. Bahr's life work includes novels, short stories, essays, dramatic criticism, plays, and finally diaries which mirror an entire epoch of Europe's cultural history. His most striking merit lies in his unusual flair for recognizing every new trend and in his readiness to become the enthusiastic prophet of every significant movement. Yet, here also lies his main weakness. Bahr experimented with all forms, all styles, and all ideologies, to such an extent that it is sometimes hard to detect his own convictions. Nevertheless, it is possible to find one basic tendency in his work: he invariably took sides with life, with organic growth, with naturalness, as against everything artificial, untrue, conventional. He emphatically loved life with all its inconsistencies—including his own—and declined to be identified with any particular philosophy. Although his many plays are uneven in quality, some of them have been highly successful and all of them are stimulating as manifestations of an alert and brilliant mind. Of these only the most characteristic can be mentioned here.

Bahr's first play, *Die neuen Menschen* (*The New Men,* 1887), proclaims the conviction that a new and better humanity, based upon inner liberty and mutual love, will come into being only if its apostles reject cold reason and dead theories and rely solely on their instinctive feelings. *Die Mutter* (*The Mother,* 1891), shocked the public by a relentless and ridiculously exaggerated presentation of sexual perversions. This was Bahr's tribute to the "decadent" movement of the day. His first comedy success was *Josephine* (1898), a highly amusing play written around the young Napoleon. Bahr's intention was to show that even the great hero, with his little joys and pleasures, is a human being like you or me. The fun in the play is provided by the attitude of Napoleon who is not in the least interested in winning battles and becoming a famous general, but solely in making love to his young wife. *Der Star* (1898), contrasts the world of the stage and the bourgeois world, emphasizing that there can be no bridge between them.

One of Bahr's most genuinely felt plays is *Der Franzl* (1900), dealing with the life story of the Austrian dialect poet Franz Stelzhamer (1802-1874). The comedy *Wienerinnen* (*Viennese Women,* 1900), pokes fun at certain society people who lose themselves in artificiality and sham intellectualism. *Der Apostel* (*The Apostle,* 1901) is the tragicomedy of an idealist and reformer who, in his capacity as politician, becomes sadly aware of the fact that men are not mature enough to grasp his lofty ideals. *Der Meister* (*The Master,* 1903), one of Bahr's most successful plays, revolves around a doctor who aims to be master not only over the life of others but also over his own. With cold reason he tries to subdue every emotion, with logic he opposes the senseless conventions of society. He remains victorious but has to pay dearly for his triumph: horrified at the inhumanity of this "superman," his wife leaves him, in order to form a less complex but more spontaneous union. *Sanna* (1905) paints in delicate colors the portrait of a girl who perishes because of the narrow-mindedness and the lack of imagination in a small provincial town of the early nineteenth century. *Die Andere* (*The Other Woman,* 1906), deals with the problem of the split personality, demonstrated in the case of a brilliant girl who becomes the victim of destructive, animal forces which suddenly break through the surface of her gentle nature.

Ringelspiel (*Merry-Go-Round,* 1907), is an extreme expression of Bahr's philosophy of life. The men and women in this play do not recognize any moral or ethical laws. They merely drift along, incapable of mastering their lives, led by the incomprehensible force which sets in motion the merry-go-round of our lives. *Die gelbe Nachtigall* (*The Yellow Nightingale,* 1907), reveals with amusing irony the theatre as a world of deception, and compares it to the theatre of our life. *Das Konzert* (*The Concert,* 1909), an international success, attempts a humorously new solution of the problem of adultery: the best way to win back the unfaithful partner is to release him (or her). In this manner not only the marriage of the celebrated piano virtuoso Heink is saved, but also that of the clever Dr. Jura, whose pretty wife Heink had wanted to include in his vast collection of companions in similar adventures. *Die Kinder* (*The Children,* 1911), is designed to prove that the power of blood-instincts is merely a legend. Although the two children in this comedy are not really children of their supposed fathers, their filial love is none the less sincere. *Das Taenzchen* (*The Little Dance,* 1911) is a satire against political and social conditions within the Prussian Junker class in the Germany of Wilhelm II. To be sure, the "revolutionary" who attacks the Junkers turns out to be just as corrupt and devoid of all ethics as his opponents.

The comedy *Das Prinzip* (*The Principle,* 1912), is particularly characteristic of Bahr's attitude. Its central character is a reformer who has built up for himself and his family a very definite philosophy. Yet, he learns that the incalculability of life dooms even the most elaborate system. This bitter experience, however, does not discourage him in the least; on the contrary, it immediately becomes the basis for a new principle. Thus Bahr wishes to prove that constant transformation must be the basis of our existence. *Das Phantom* (1913), is a new variation of the theme already treated in *The Concert:* the husband, realizing that his wife is in danger of succumbing to the spell of another man, manages to show her the other one in his true light, whereupon the "great passion" vanishes like a phantom. In the farce *Der muntere Seifensieder (The Merry Soap-Boiler,* 1914), Bahr had the courage, immediately after the outbreak of the war, to debunk the exalted raptures of war fever and to satirize the superpatriots and their empty phrases. *Der Querulant (The Complainer,* 1914), juxtaposes the natural ethics of a primitive peasant with our supposedly reasonable and logical law practices and sheds doubt on their expediency. *Die Stimme (The Voice,* 1916), is the theatrical document of Bahr's ultimate conversion to Catholicism. A sceptic, after having experienced a deep shock in his personal life, learns to believe in a miracle and thus returns within the pale of the Church. After this emphatic manifestation of his religious awakening, Bahr wrote a number of farcical comedies whose main feature is a frivolity utterly incompatible with his newly acquired attitude. Insignificant, or even bad, as these last plays are, they at least prove that their author was consistent in one respect: in his inconsistency.

Bahr's untiring efforts were soon to be rewarded with the appearance in the early nineties of the two writers who stand out as the most notable members of the "Young Vienna" group: Hugo von Hofmannsthal and Arthur Schnitzler.

Hugo von Hofmannsthal (1874-1929), fused into his life work the entire cultural tradition of Austria. For years, misunderstanding and superficial interpretation has tried to define him as a mere "esthete," and therefore "decadent"; but since his death, a more profound recognition of his significance has set in. At the age of seventeen he baffled and enchanted his contemporaries with poems of matchless beauty, depth, and formal perfection. During the first decade of his literary activity, his writing was predominantly lyrical. Even the first works he wrote for the stage were called by himself "Lyrische Dramen." As a matter of fact, they can hardly be called plays in the usual sense of the term. They are without exception short dramatic compositions, written in verses of great distinction and in a highly personal idiom. Although it is impossible to find a common denominator for their emotional and spiritual complexity, one may say that they all focus on one basic problem: the relation of the poet to life. This relation is utterly problematical, revealing a supersensitive being whose emotional receptivity enables him to experience sensations of an almost mystic nature. Life appears mysterious, cruel, inexplicable, and distant, yet alluring and fascinating in its fullness and richness. The poet stands aloof from life, at the same time realizing that this aloofness will necessarily be fruitless or even destructive. Thus these early plays express not only the attitude of the esthete who looks at life with the detached and disillusioned eyes of a tired spectator, but also the criticism of this attitude. The desperate attempt to take hold of reality leads to tragic inner conflicts.

Hofmannsthal's first lyric drama, *Gestern* (*Yesterday*, 1891), shows such a conflict. The hero, Andrea, wants to master life by clinging to the lure of the moment, ignoring past and future. Yet he learns that any such attempt is doomed to fail. "Yesterday" casts its shadow over "today," affecting and changing it. *Der Tod des Tizian* (*The Death of Titian*, 1892), contrasts the world of pure art and beauty with the world of unbeautiful reality. The artist lives secluded, untouched by the problems of our everyday life, devoted solely to the perfection of his work. *Der Tor und der Tod* (*Death and the Fool*, 1893) formulates conclusively the problem of man's estrangement from life and demonstrates the tragic futility of an aloof attitude. The Fool is the dilettante of life, never able to grasp the reality of things, and wandering around on this world like a poor actor in a play. In the hour of his death he belatedly recognizes his error and now becomes aware that he actually has not lived at all.

These short plays, as well as the lyric dramas, *Das kleine Welttheater* (*The Little Theatre of the World*, 1897); *Der Kaiser und die Hexe* (*The Emperor and the Witch*, 1897); *Der weise Faecher* (*The White Fan*, 1897); *Die Frau im Fenster* (*The Lady at the Window*, 1897), are not concerned with plot or action but solely with the exploration of the human soul and its various attitudes. However, Hofmannsthal's succeeding dramatic works conform more and more to the exigencies of the stage. The characters gradually lose their shadowy and evanescent quality and become consistent and plastic human material. *Der Abenteurer und die Saengerin* (*The Adventurer and the Singer*, 1899), has as its background eighteenth-century Venice. The worshipper of the moment, rootless and irresponsible, yet utterly fascinating, demonstrated in the figure of the adventurer Casanova, is juxtaposed with the inherently constant woman. Her moral superiority triumphs over her former lover when she meets him after an interval of many years and he neither remembers her nor recognizes their son. In *Die Hochzeit der Sobeide* (*Sobeide's Wedding*, 1899), the central character is an innocent girl who by her passionate desire for life is plunged into a series of shattering experiences. After having learned in one night all the fearfulness and cruelty of life, there is only one way left to her: self-destruction.

Das Bergwerk zu Falun (*The Mine at Falun*, 1899), Hofmannsthal's first full-length play, symbolizes in an extreme way the struggle between life and the dark powers which try to alienate man from this earth and its positive tasks. Although here man succumbs to the lure of mystical forces, the play marked a turning point in Hofmannsthal's spiritual evolution. He had overcome the dangerous conflicts of his earlier years and now turned toward life with growing strength and tenacity. One of his chief aims from then on was to appeal to his contemporaries through the medium of the stage. The fact that many of his plays are based upon the great dramatic heritage of the past does not mean that he was, as some have contended, a mere eclectic. For his adaptations, like Shakespeare's *Hamlet* and Goethe's *Faust,* are adaptations only in the sense that they are based upon works of the past. Actually the material has been rewoven into an utterly new texture. Even his translations are recreations, thoroughly imbued with the spirit of the modern dramatist. At first Hofmannsthal turned to the Greeks. As early as 1894 he had made a free translation of Euripides' tragedy *Alcestis*. Then he adapted Sophocles' *Electra* (1903). Hofmannsthal's conception of antiquity, however, changed the very soul of the ancient tragedy, and resulted in a completely new work which took from the original only the story. Familiar with the conception of Greece as embodied in the writings of Friedrich Nietzsche, the philosopher, and Jakob Burckhardt, the historian, Hofmannsthal tore the mask from the ancient characters and revealed their human faces; still more, he, the contemporary and compatriot of Freud, laid bare their very nerves. Hofmannsthal's Greeks are "modern" human beings, oversensitive, high-strung, hysterical. Wrapped in an atmosphere of terror, haunted by a horrid and incomprehensible fate, driven by violent passions of love and hatred, they often resemble neurotics of our own day. Harmony and poise is replaced by chaotic disintegration. Moreover, the classic form of Greek drama is destroyed; the measured flow of the verses is substituted by volcanic rhythms; and the choral parts are distributed among individual voices.

Out of Hofmannsthal's study of the Elizabethans and later English dramatists originated *Das gerettete Venedig* (*Venice Preserved,* 1905), a recreation of Thomas Otway's drama of the same title. Here too the characters are transformed into modern human beings, whose actions the playwright has motivated with the methods of penetrating psychology. His preoccupation with the Greek myths led to the tragedy *Œdipus und die Sphinx* (*Œdipus and the Sphinx,* 1906), dramatizing the events which precede the Sophoclean tragedy *Œdipus Rex,* and interpreting them in accordance with Hofmannsthal's conception of antiquity. Stimulating in all these efforts was the close collaboration with Max Reinhardt, whose impressionistic stagecraft provided the ideal medium for the representation of Hofmannsthal's plays. *Cristinas Heimreise* (*Cristina's Journey Home,* 1908; new version 1910), Hofmannsthal's first comedy, tells, in an eighteenth-century Venice setting, the story of a country girl. On her first trip to the city she meets the irresponsible yet irresistible adventurer Florindo, but her natural and innocent instincts lead her out of a dangerous emotional confusion into marriage with a straightforward and sincere man. To be sure, no brief indication of the plot, the basis of which was taken from an episode in Casanova's *Memoirs,* can convey the inimitable charm and delicate humor of the play.

When, in 1909, *Electra* was set to music by Richard Strauss, this event marked the beginning of a collaboration between poet and composer which was to become decisive for the evolution of modern opera.[1] The librettos which Hofmannsthal subsequently wrote for Strauss, were to lift opera to an intellectual level rarely achieved in the history of musical drama. For a production directed by Max Reinhardt, Hofmannsthal wrote *Koenig Œdipus (Oedipus Rex,* 1910), an inspired translation of the Sophoclean tragedy. *Ariadne auf Naxos (Ariadne at Naxos,* 1910) was the second libretto written for Strauss. At first intended to be the afterpiece to Molière's *Le Bourgeois Gentilhomme,* it was later issued as an independent work with an original dramatic prologue (1916). Here two main elements of the baroque theatre, Heroic Opera and *Commedia dell' Arte,* are united in a most provocative manner. Tragic and comic action are blended into one artistic whole, contrasting at the same time the virtuous Ariadne and the fickle Zerbinetta. In *Jedermann (Everyman,* 1911), the old English morality play was completely renewed and rewritten. The abstract and somewhat diadactic quality of the original is subdued and the resulting work is an excitingly modern drama. The collaboration with Richard Strauss triumphed in a work which has won world fame: *Der Rosenkavalier* (1911). In the setting of eighteenth-century Vienna, a delightfully amusing comedy of love, intrigue, and disguise, takes place. Also for Strauss was written *Die Frau ohne Schatten (The Woman Without a Shadow,* 1919), a fairy-tale opera in an oriental setting, whose theme was used for the story of the same title (1919). The shadow symbolizes maternity, and thus the opera turns into a panegyric of the highest ethical duties of woman. In 1920 the Salzburg Festivals were opened with a performance of *Jedermann,* staged by Max Reinhardt before the portals of the Salzburg cathedral. Hofmannsthal had been instrumental in organizing the Festivals whose sensational success gave impetus to similar institutions in other countries. Every year the old morality play in its modernized version moved deeply thousands of spectators who had come from all corners of the globe, especially from the United States. The effect went still further: the Salzburg poet Franz Loeser (1889-   ) wrote a dialect version of the play and wandered with a company of peasant players into the remotest valleys of the Austrian Alps in order to present it before peasant audiences.

During the First World War and especially after the downfall of the Hapsburg Empire, Hofmannsthal, in a number of masterly essays, turned his attention more and more to the problems of his fatherland and its European mission. The comedy *Der Schwierige (The Unmanageable,* 1921),

---

[1] The significance and extent of this collaboration may be studied in the two men's highly revealing correspondence *Richard Strauss' Briefwechsel mit Hugo von Hofmannsthal* (Vienna, 1926; English translation by Paul England, New York, 1927).

is, to use a phrase of Hermann Bahr, a "farewell to Austria." Its characters represent the typically Austrian aristocratic society and its own carefree and highly cultivated form of life. The "unmanageable" Count Kari von Buehl, kindly, oversensitive, and intensely humane, is the personification of the very best qualities of this society. It is of symbolical significance that his shyness and restraint are misunderstood by every one, especially by a North German aristocrat, the man of action and energy who tactlessly expresses his contempt for this "absolute no-account" as well as for a conception of life whose values he is unable to grasp. At this time Hofmannsthal received new inspiration from the greatest dramatist of the Spanish Baroque. In 1920 he had published a new translation of Calderon de la Barca's comedy *La dama duende,* under the title *Dame Kobold (The Elfin Lady).* Now he readapted one of Calderon's "autos sacramentales," the religious festival play *El gran teatro del mundo,* under the title *Das grosse Salzburger Welttheater (The Salzburg Great Theatre of the World,* 1922). Here King, Wisdom, Beauty, The Rich Man, The Peasant, and The Beggar, are called before God in order to perform the play of Man's life. The Beggar, who symbolizes the social misery and disorder of the post-war years, receives God's highest praise because he has withstood the urge toward force and rebellion and attained the true inner liberty of the soul.

Hofmannsthal's last drama, the culmination of his life work, is based upon Calderon's *La vida es sueño (Life Is a Dream).* It is *Der Turm (The Tower,* 1925; revised stage version, 1927). The central character is Prince Sigismund, the ideal ruler, who opposes violence and anarchy. A Christian hero in the true baroque tradition, he sacrifices his own life, proclaiming to his last breath the ideal of non-violence and love. Opposite him stands the soldier Olivier, a symbol of brute force, who makes himself the leader of the rebels, terrorizing the country under the sign of the blood-banner. The vision of a better future is conjured up in the concluding episode of the Child King who, in an atmosphere of cruelty and savagery, sets up the kingdom of the innocent children. After this political confession, Hofmannsthal wrote two more librettos for Richard Strauss. *Die aegyptische Helena (The Egyptian Helen,* 1928), based upon a Greek legend, deals with the events during the return of Menelaus and Helen after the destruction of Troy, and turns into a eulogy of the sanctity and indestructibility of marriage. *Arabella* (posthumously published in 1933) deals with the triumph of a high-minded girl over various comedy intrigues and confusions, the action taking place in the Vienna of 1860.

Arthur Schnitzler (1862-1931) was a practising physician before he turned entirely to literature, dividing his interests equally between narrative and dramatic works. To one of his characters Schnitzler, illuminating at the same time his own outlook and dominant interest, has given the line: "The soul is a vast domain." For one may say that his entire work was devoted to the exploration of that domain to its most obscure regions. In this "vast domain," as Schnitzler found it, the most contradictory impulses and emotions exist side by side and thus create a state of chaos. "To be sure, we try to get some order into ourselves, as much as is possible, but this order is merely artificial...." With his ability to trace the most complex psychological phenomena, Schnitzler combined a high degree of craftsmanship and an unusual gift for dramatic dialogue. Despite the profusion of his problems certain basic questions haunted him throughout his life. He probed them again and again, to be sure, each time in a different and, as the years proceeded, more and more searching manner. One of these basic problems was the relation of the sexes, and the fateful part it plays in man's life. There is scarcely a form of the relation between man and woman, from the purest and loftiest down to the basest and most primitive, which has not been treated in one of Schnitzler's works. Rarely is the relation a happy one; it is invariably overshadowed to some extent by a depressing awareness of its transience and futility. More than once it is rendered tragic by the utter impossibility of one individual's ever understanding the other. The hopelessness of this situation results in pathological jealousy which poisons or destroys the relation. Closely connected with such conflicts is the problem of truth and falsehood. Where is the border line between the two? How is it possible to perceive it, since words are used not so much to reveal as to hide the true condition of the human soul? This again results in a profound uncertainty in all human relations, and thus for many of Schnitzler's figures life assumes the quality of an illusion, a dream, as unreal as if it were fiction, or a stage play. "We are constantly play-acting; he who knows it, is wise," says another of his characters. Moreover, the border line between "Schein und Sein," between reality and appearance, is blurred, sometimes almost unrecognizable, like the one between truth and falsehood. This stage play of our existence is directed by a mysterious power. Whether we call it God, or Fate, it is a power we do not know, one whose intentions we cannot grasp.

Schnitzler presents his ever-changing modulations and variations of these problems with the detached attitude of a physician who uses his scalpel to dissect the inner life of his characters. It is certainly no accident that at the same time another Viennese started to dissect the human soul in a manner which has revolutionized our way of thinking: Sigmund Freud, the founder of Psychoanalysis. Schnitzler anticipated many of Freud's conclusions and more than once the findings of both men, who were fellow students and friends, run along parallel lines. Although Schnitzler was interested in the individual rather than in a whole class, the vast assembly of his characters furnishes a complete picture of Viennese society during the last decades of Austria. The melancholy of a declining culture permeates even some of his comedies. Behind his men and women stands Death, threatening or sometimes luring them. In the midst of love and merriment they are aware of their doom. The evanescence of happiness is ever present in their minds and therefore they cling to the moment, glorifying its joys as the only secure possession they have.

Schnitzler's first full-length play, *Das Maerchen* (*The Fairy-Tale*, 1891) criticizes society for its inhuman attitude toward the so-called "fallen woman." Opposed to the "double standard" in sexual ethics, Schnitzler here defends woman's equal right to live her life fully. *Anatol* (1893) is a series of one-act plays written around the figure of the melancholy philanderer who has given his name to this work. In each of the seven scenes the "hero" is confronted with a different woman, yet he remains the same. Although he is deceived and disappointed again and again, he clings to the belief that he can gain happiness by flying from one affair to the other. Anatol is the perfect impressionist who lives solely for the sake of the moment and its joys, yet is hampered by his ever-awake consciousness of its evanescence. Thus he is always unhappy, always the victim of ever-changing moods which he himself analyses with wit and irony. That Schnitzler himself did not take his hero too seriously became apparent when among his posthumous papers the one-act play *Anatol's Groessenwahn* (*Anatol's Megalomania*) was found (produced 1932, not published), in which the aged philanderer is depicted and ridiculed as an old fool.

Although *Anatol,* because of its charm, its humor, and its sparkling dialogue, has become (in Harley Granville-Barker's superb adaptation) the most popular of Schnitzler's plays in the English-speaking countries, it is by no means typical of his entire work. His next play proved that he saw beyond the frivolous and charming side of Vienna's society. *Liebelei* (*Light-o'-Love,* 1895) is the story of a girl of the people who learns that her lover, a young man from the upper classes, has died in a duel fought for another woman. Realizing now that she had been a mere plaything to him, she kills herself. The social connotations of the play, whose first draft bore the title *The Poor Girl,* are obvious. After having paid homage to the typically Viennese character of the "suesse Maedel" in some much-quoted lines in *Anatol,* Schnitzler had now made that "sweet young girl" the tragic heroine of a deeply moving and poignantly absorbing folk drama. Its unusual dramatic qualities have made it the most enduringly popular of Schnitzler's plays in his own homeland. It is significant that *Liebelei* has been the first play banned by the Nazis to be revived all over Austria after the country's liberation in 1945.

Freiwild (*Free Game,* 1896) openly and courageously attacked two social evils of the day: the custom of dueling for some fantastic point of honor, and the helpless condition of young actresses who were regarded as free game by everybody. *Reigen* (*Hands Around,* 1897) has rightfully been called a "death dance of love." It is a series of ten dialogues, each between a man and a woman, in which representatives of all social classes are united in such a way that one partner in each dialogue becomes one of the partners in the next, until the circle is closed at the end. The external circumstances are always the same: the situation preceding and following the physical consummation of love. With cruel and pitiless wit, Schnitzler implies the emptiness of merely sexual love, at the same time demonstrating that the animal urge wipes out all social distinctions.

Das Vermaechtnis (The Legacy, 1898) attacks the conventional morality of society which in its narrowness and lack of human understanding destroys the life of a woman. The one-act play *Parazelsus* (1898) bears traces of Schnitzler's own hypnotic experiments as a doctor. The great physician of the sixteenth century plunges the wife of a self-righteous philistine into hypnotic sleep and reveals the hidden desires and dreams which slumber under the surface of her consciousness. In the one-act play *Die Gefaehrtin (The Mate,* 1899), the husband learns, after the death of his wife, that she, his life-long companion, has actually been a stranger to him and that he has never known anything about her inner being. *Der gruene Kakadu* (1899), also a one-act play, takes place in Paris, in a tavern called The Green Cockatoo, on the night of the storming of the Bastille in 1789. The star of a company of comedians, impersonating before his fashionable audience a jealous husband, learns that the fiction of his play is reality and stabs the aristocratic lover of his wife. At the same time, the acted revolution of the comedians turns into the grim reality of the French Revolution. The transition from illusion to truth is handled in a most exciting and effective manner. The verse play, *Der Schleier der Beatrice (The Veil of Beatrice,* 1900) is set against the colorful background of the Italian Renaissance. In a single night, the fate of a young girl is fulfilled. Haunted by her dark instincts, she drives two men to their death and then perishes herself. The central problem is the mysterious and incalculable nature of woman. The four one-act plays, united under the title *Lebendige Stunden (Living Hours,* 1902), include *Lebendige Stunden; Die Frau mit dem Dolche (The Woman With the Dagger); Die letzten Masken (The Last Masks); Literatur.* They are variations on the theme of art versus life. The artist who uses his personal experience as material for his work is discussed in various ways, tragic and comic. The last play, *Literature,* is a mordant literary satire. Here Schnitzler mercilessly castigates those literati who become shameless exhibitionists for the sake of their second-rate achievements.

Der einsame Weg (The Lonely Way, 1904) may be called Schnitzler's most characteristic and beautiful play. The lonely way is the way of the selfish, who have lived only for the sake of the moment and must face the utter solitude of old age. Unable to give themselves up to another being, they have destroyed others' happiness as well as their own. The autumnal atmosphere of the play is enhanced by its subdued mood and by the melancholy rhythm of its language. *Zwischenspiel (Intermezzo,* 1905) deals with the problem of marriage, exemplified in two artists who fail in the attempt to solve honestly and openly their marital difficulties. Three one-act plays are united under the title *Marionetten (Marionettes,* 1906): *Der Puppenspieler*

(*The Puppet-Player*); *Der tapfere Cassian* (*The Gallant Cassian*); *Zum Grossen Wurstel* (*The Great Puppet Show*). Their basic idea is that we are all puppets in the hands of a superior power, even though we believe that we handle the strings ourselves. The last play, *The Great Puppet Show,* is a self-parody of the playwright who acknowledges that he himself is merely a marionette led by an unknown force.

Der Ruf des Lebens (*The Call of Life,* 1906) takes place in nineteenth-century Vienna. Two girls respond to the call of life, each in her own way. One, radiating vitality, plunges into crime and sin until she shudders at the terrifying possibilities within herself; the other, consumptive and certain of her near end, staggers through passion and madness to her death. *Komtesse Mizzi* (*Countess Mizzi,* 1908), a one-act comedy, satirizes amusingly the moral standards of Austrian aristocrats. *Der junge Medardus* (*The Young Medardus,* 1910) conjures up the year 1809, when Napoleon occupied Vienna. Medardus, who wants to become the savior of his fatherland by murdering the French Emperor, is a problematical hero. His inner weakness and the emotional conflicts in which he becomes involved, turn the intended deed into a burlesque: instead of killing Napoleon, he unwittingly saves the Emperor's life. Fate has made a fool of him; yet he proves to be a true hero when he unflinchingly faces the firing squad. Numerous crowd scenes give a vivid interpretation of the Viennese folk character. *Das weite Land* (*The Vast Domain,* 1911) centers around a philanderer more complex and dangerous than his rather harmless predecessor Anatol. The manufacturer Hofreiter, brutal and incalculable, proves by all his actions that the soul is a vast domain indeed, in whose realm the most contrary emotions may exist at the same time. He and the superficial crowd around him, who are devoted only to idle flirtation, are indignantly denounced by the only morally stable character in the play, a doctor. *Professor Bernhardi* (1912) deals with the Jewish question, and, in a broader sense, with the theme of science versus religion. Bernhardi, a distinguished physician and a Jew, prevents a Catholic priest from entering the ward of a dying girl, because he does not want to disturb her last hours. The consequence of this incident is a political scandal of the first order. Bernhardi is condemned for having offended the religious feelings of the population. The plotting of the various parties provides a cross-section of political life in old Austria. The climax of the play is a conversation between Bernhardi and the priest, a noble and honest man, concluding with an appeal for mutual respect, since there seems to be no hope for mutual understanding.

Three one-act plays under the title *Komoedie der Worte* (*Comedies of Words,* 1915) include: *Stunde des Erkennens* (*The Hour of Recognition*); *Grosse Szene* (*Big Scene*); *Das Bacchusfest* (*The Feast of Bacchus*); they are united by the thought that man is constantly play-acting, using words merely to conceal his true self. The comedy *Fink und Fliederbusch* (1917) is a satire on a type of irresponsible journalist, embodied in the impudent

Fliederbusch who, under his own name and under the name Fink, simultaneously writes for two opposing newspapers until he is finally confronted with the embarrassing necessity of fighting a duel with himself. *Die Schwestern, oder Casanova in Spa* (*The Sisters, or Casanova in Spa*, 1919), a verse comedy, tells a freely invented episode from the life of the famed adventurer. Behind the apparently frivolous action, however, there is a meaningful consideration of the problem of fidelity. To be faithful, so contends Schnitzler, means to return, even after many wanderings. *Komoedie der Verfuehrung* (*Comedy of Seduction*, 1924) is set against the background of the last weeks before the outbreak of the First World War. The involved plot combines the tragic story of a young girl and her three suitors, with that of a charming philanderer and his more or less innocent victims, representing at the same time a sort of death dance of the Austrian pre-war society which Schnitzler had depicted so often. The pensive verse play *Der Gang zum Weiher* (*The Walk to the Pond*, 1926) is concerned not so much with plot as with an analysis of several complex individuals. Although the setting is eighteenth-century Austria, the numerous political discussions have obvious timely connotations. *Im Spiel der Sommerluefte* (*Light as the Summer's Air*, 1929) shows a group of characters in a country-house near nineteenth-century Vienna. Slight tragedies and comedies pass through their lives without leaving a trace, like a thunderstorm on a summer's day.

Closely connected with the "Young Vienna" group was Richard Beer-Hofmann (1866-1945). After having published a few short stories and a much anthologized poem, *Schlaflied fuer Mirjam* (*Cradle Song for Mirjam*), he turned to the stage with an adaptation of the seventeenth-century English play *The Fatal Dowry*, by Massinger and Field, renaming it *Der Graf von Charolais* (*The Count of Charolais*, 1904). Like Hofmannsthal in his adaptations, Beer-Hofmann retained the story but imbued it with his own poetic spirit and with the psychological insight of a modern age. His tendency was to explain the strange events of the old drama in terms of a tragedy of fate, by having his characters appear as mere tools in the hands of an incomprehensible and terrible power. Massinger's and Field's forceful directness is replaced by impressionistic portraiture of the human soul and its varying moods. After a long pause Beer-Hofmann published the biblical verse drama *Jaakobs Traum* (*Jacob's Dream*, 1918), the prologue to a trilogy to be called *Die Historie vom Koenig David* (*The History of King David*). Beer-Hofmann had now become the conscious poet of his Jewish race, whose historical figures are conceived as symbols of the Jewish fate. Thus *Jaakobs Traum* becomes the panegyric of Judaism, prophesying the mission as well as the trials of the Jewish people. Only the first part of the trilogy was published, *Der junge David* (*The Young David*, 1933), which, in seven scenes, retells the story of Saul's fall and David's rise. Both plays excel not only in their highly poetical language but also in their author's unusual ability to bring to dramatic life the traditional characters and to recreate the biblical atmosphere in a moving and theatrically effective manner.

To the circle of "Young Vienna" belonged many other writers who devoted at least part of their literary production to the theatre. Felix Doermann (pseudonym of Felix Biedermann, 1870-1928) was much talked about when he published morbid and decadent poetry. In his first plays he turned to the sordid aspects of Viennese society. His comedies, *Ledige Leute* (*Unmarried People,* 1897), and *Zimmerherren* (*Lodgers,* 1900), depict the complete rottenness and amorality in certain bourgeois circles. His frankness, especially in sexual matters, shocked his contemporaries and brought him into conflicts with the Imperial censorship. Later he became a highly successful provider of librettos for Viennese operettas, as for instance for the world-famous *Ein Walzertraum* (*A Waltz Dream,* 1907; music by Oscar Straus).

Felix Salten (pseudonym of Siegmund Salzmann, 1869-1945) founded his fame upon his remarkable work as a story-teller and journalist, especially upon his enchanting animal tales such, for instance, as *Bambi* (1923). However, he too was repeatedly attracted to the stage. Influenced by the naturalistic tendencies of the nineties he wrote his drama *Der Gemeine* (*The Private,* 1901). The tragedy of a soldier torn between his love for a Viennese girl and his military duties, contains some anti-militaristic elements but cautiously avoids any openly revolutionary attitude. Later he wrote a number of one-act plays, published under the titles *Vom andern Ufer* (*From the Other Shore,* 1908) and *Kinder der Freude* (*Children of Joy,* 1917), in which original and often witty situations reveal his talent as a short-story writer. Less fortunate was his attempt to dramatize a famous court scandal of the early twentieth century, in *Luise von Koburg* (1932).

Aside from being a distinguished story-teller and dramatic critic, Raoul Auernheimer (1876-   ) continued in the best Viennese comedy tradition of Bauernfeld by writing a number of amusing comedies of manners. *Die grosse Leidenschaft* (*The Great Passion,* 1905) and *Das Paar nach der Mode* (*The Fashionable Couple,* 1913), poke fun at "modern" marriage. He ventured into the historical field in *Die verbuendeten Maechte* (*The Allied Powers,* 1915), a comedy of love and politics, set against the colorful background of the Vienna Congress of 1815; and in *Casanova in Wien* (*Casanova in Vienna,* 1924), he was attracted—like Hofmannsthal and Schnitzler—by the figure of the great adventurer.

Siegfried Trebitsch (1868-   ) deserves to be mentioned here mainly as the authorized translator of G. B. Shaw's works, to whose enormous popularity in the German-speaking world he has contributed greatly. His own plays include *Frau Gittas Suehne* (1920), dealing with the harrowing conflict into which an adulterous woman is plunged after her lover's sudden death. Out of gratitude for the man who had done so much for his works, G. B. Shaw adapted this play under the title *Jitta's Atonement,* and published it in his *Translations and Tomfooleries* (1926). However, not even Shaw's generous collaboration was able to improve the rather weak original, although he provided a comedy ending more in keeping with the artificial story than Trebitsch's unconvincing last act.

Among the numerous writers of light and merely entertaining plays may be mentioned the versatile Rudolph Lothar (pseudonym of Spitzer, 1865-   ), whose *Koenig Harlekin* (*King Harlequin,* 1900) was an instant success and whose erotically tinged comedies amused audiences all over the world.

Aloof from the "Young Vienna" group and connected with it only by the withering attacks he hurled against some of its members, stood Karl Kraus (1874-1936), the last great satirist of Austria. In his magazine *Die Fackel* (*The Torch,* 1899-1936) he waged a relentless war against corruption, sham, and hypocrisy in public and literary life. Kraus has been rightly called "the good conscience of Austria." The experience of the war shocked him deeply. The contrast between the heroism and suffering in the trenches, and the hollow oratory and unblushing complacency evinced by so many of his compatriots on the home front, lashed him into wild fury. In 1918, he published his first drama, *Die letzten Tage der Menschheit* (*The Last Days of Mankind*), a flaming indictment against the brutalization of man. This unique play—the printed edition fills 792 pages, and the performance would, according to Kraus' own words, take ten nights—is one gigantic nightmare. Aside from the scenes in which he himself poured out his wrath and compassion, he used all the documentary evidence he could gather, such as newspaper reports, letters, and interviews. Documents turn into dramatic characters; historical figures reënact episodes from their own lives. Kraus used here for the first time a technique which was later adopted by the type of drama called the Living Newspaper. However, in the poetic epilogue, *Die letzte Nacht* (*The Last Night*), appears an apocalyptic vision of the general destruction of all human and spiritual values by the frenzy of war, a hellish image of horror and despair, and an engrossing appeal to the conscience of mankind. Kraus' other plays are either devoted to the expression of his personal beliefs—*Traumstueck* (*Dream Play,* 1923); *Traumtheater* (*Dream Theatre,* 1924)—or to devastating attacks upon certain literary and political trends—*Literatur* (*Literature,* 1921); *Wolkenkuckucksheim* (*Cloud-Cuckoo-Home,* 1923), based on *The Birds,* by Aristophanes; *Die Unueberwindlichen* (*The Invincibles,* 1928). Kraus' enormous influence, especially upon a considerbale part of Viennese youth, was enhanced through his incomparable lecture recitals. Here he opposed his own "Theater der Dichtung" (Theatre of Poetry) to the commercialized theatre of the day, bringing to life in an unforgettable manner the great works of the world's dramatic literature. He has rediscovered for his generation Offenbach and Nestroy, with whose spiritual attitude he had much in common. His tribute to the greatest dramatist of all times was to be a new translation of Shakespeare's plays, the first volume of which was published in 1934, containing *King Lear, The Taming of the Shrew,* and *The Winter's Tale.*

The fact that Austria has never produced any play concerned with the conditions of the masses, reveals one of the most striking differences between her modern drama and Germany's. Even when Austrian dramatists dealt with social themes, they seemed to be interested rather in the individual and his inner conflicts than in the group. A typical example is Philipp Langmann (1862-1931) whose tragedy *Bartel Turaser* (1897), shows the misery of a poor factory worker who through his desperate economic situation is driven to perjury. Although the play develops against the background of a strike, it presents the story of an individual conflict rather than that of mass conditions. The technique of the powerful play, which even resorts to apparitions, is indeed a far cry from North German naturalism. Franz Adamus (pseudonym of Ferdinand Bronner, 1867-) wrote a social drama which has been called the Austrian counterpart of Hauptmann's *The Weavers;* this was *Familie Wawroch (The Wawroch Family,* 1899). Yet, here too, the story of young Wawroch who, as a soldier called with his regiment to quell a strike in the mining region of Bohemia, shoots his own father, a drunkard and agitator, gives rather the account of an individual tragedy than the description of an entire class. Another play of the author, *Schmelz, der Nibelunge (Schmelz, the Nibelung,* 1905), deals with the beginnings of anti-Semitism in Austria. It revolves around the character of a Jewish student who, in his desire to escape the mounting persecution of his race, denies his faith and wants to enter the ranks of a nationalistic and anti-Semitic students' association whose members may be called forerunners of the Nazis. In this connection it ought to be mentioned that Theodor Herzl (1860-1904), the founder of the Zionist movement, also wrote a play dealing with the Jewish question: *Das neue Ghetto (The New Ghetto,* 1897) shows the desperate struggle of emancipated Viennese Jews to escape prejudice and persecution, a struggle which at that time Herzl thought hopeless.

The attempt to rejuvenate Austrian literature as a whole also brought about an attempt to reinvigorate the Viennese folk play. Its most successful reformer was C. Karlweis (pseudonym of Karl Weiss, 1850-1901), who waged an amusing and never too serious comedy-war against certain customs and follies of the Viennese bourgeoisie, especially in his plays *Das grobe Hemd (The Rough Shirt,* 1897) and *Onkel Toni (Uncle Toni,* 1899). *Der kleine Mann (The Man in the Street,* 1899), satirized the political agitation of contemporary anti-Semitic circles.

Not only the Viennese folk play but, in the wake of Anzengruber's pioneering achievements, also the peasant play was to be rejuvenated. The Austrian Tyrol with her long-standing theatrical tradition produced a powerful and original dramatist in Franz Kranewitter (1860-). He tried to present episodes of Tyrolean history in a modern manner, devoid of melodramatics and theatrical heroism. *Michel Gaissmayr* (1899) focuses on the peasant who in 1525 led his fellow-countrymen in their desperate struggle against suppression and clericalism, while in *Andre Hofer* (1902), he attempted to show the celebrated hero of the Tyrol's struggle against Napoleon, not as a conventional stage character but as a human being. Between 1905 and 1925, Kranewitter published a series of one-act plays under the title *Die sieben Todsünden* (*The Seven Deadly Sins*) which in terse and most impressive scenes depict the various human passions.

From the Tyrol also came one of Austria's outstanding modern dramatists, Karl Schoenherr (1869-1943). He discovered the peasant for the modern stage and, inspired solely by the desire to be true, depicted him as he really is. With this quality of stark realism, Schoenherr combined a superior knowledge of dramatic technique. If his plays are effective, they are so not for the sake of theatrical tricks but always out of an inner and psychologically motivated necessity. His language is terse, simple, unadorned. His peasants are hard, unsentimental, driven by primitive urges of sex and greed, yet imbued with genuine and often deeply moving love for the soil and sincere piety which dictates their natural rules of ethical behavior. This characterization, however, applies only to one part of Schoenherr's dramatic production, the one dealing with the world of the peasant. The other part, concerned with the misery of the middle class after the First World War and with the struggles within the medical profession—Schoenherr, like Schnitzler, was a doctor in his early years—is amazingly weak. Here Schoenherr seemed not to move with perfect sureness although he chose such themes prompted by sincere compassion. Never satisfied with his own plays, he rewrote some of them again and again. This accounts for the fact that very often one and the same theme is treated in works bearing different titles.

His first success was a one-act play, *Die Bildschnitzer* (*The Woodcarvers*, 1900). The action of this forceful peasant tragedy shows the misery of simple people as well as their natural honesty and decency. The drama *Sonnwendtag* (*Solstice Day*, in different versions 1902, 1905, and 1912) depicts the struggles of the conservative peasantry against the irruption of modern liberal ideas. The central character is a bigoted peasant woman who tries to atone for the sins of her own youth by forcing her children into a mode of life they no longer understand. Schoenherr tried to treat the same subject in the form of a comedy when he wrote *Die Trenkwalder* (*The Trenkwalders*, 1913). The one-act play *Karrnerleut'* (*Vagrants*, 1904), is the touching tragedy of a child. The comedy *Erde* (*Earth*, 1907) has as its basic theme the close relationship of the peasant with the soil which gives him almost superhuman strength. This is demonstrated in the superb figure of Old Grutz, the seventy-year-old peasant whose urge to live helps him to cheat death. At the end of the play, we see Grutz, whose death had been eagerly awaited by his greedy heirs, smashing his own coffin with an axe: a symbol of the earth's power and of the peasant's close kinship with it.

Schoenherr's first attempt to venture into a field other than that of peasant life, was the drama *Ueber die Bruecke* (*Across the Bridge,* 1909). Its theme is the irreconcilable conflict between the world of the theatre and the bourgeois world, shown in the tragicomedy of an actor for whom every emotion becomes merely material to be used for his next performance. Other versions of the same play are *Der Komoediant* (*The Comedian,* 1924) and *Lorbeer* (*Laurel,* 1927). Schoenherr's greatest success was the tragedy *Glaube und Heimat* (*Faith and Fatherland,* 1910) which shows the desperate fight of Protestant peasants against the Counter Reformation. The men and women who prefer to suffer and die for their chosen faith rather than to betray their own conscience are driven from their land with ruthless brutality. In *Der Weibsteufel* (*The She-Devil,* 1914) Schoenherr has succeeded in writing five acts full of suspense despite his use of only three characters. The She-Devil is a young peasant woman who, urged by a primitive impulse to destroy, recklessly uses her sexual power over men and thus dooms her husband as well as her would-be lover.

Volk in Not (*Ordeal of a People,* 1915) shows the heroic struggle for liberation of the Tyroleans in 1809, under their peasant leader Andreas Hofer. *Frau Suitner* (1916), written with the utmost simplicity and with an unusual feeling for mood and atmosphere, is the tragedy of an aging woman who is unable to bear children. She finally kills herself so that her husband may form another union with a young girl who will be able to satisfy his desire for an heir. *Narrenspiel des Lebens* (*Life is a Fool's Jest,* 1918) presents a gloomy and hopeless picture of a famous doctor whom disillusionment and disgust drive to suicide. *Kindertragoedie* (*The Children's Tragedy,* 1919) deals with the suffering of three children who find out that their mother is unfaithful to their father. Schoenherr shows how the sin of the mother utterly destroys the souls of the children. A number of plays are devoted to the misery of the medical profession: *Vivat Academia* (1922); *Der Kampf* (*The Struggle,* 1920); *Der Spurius* (*The Hunch,* 1927); *Herr Doktor, haben Sie zu essen?* (*Doctor, Have You Anything to Eat?,* 1930). The doctors starve while quacks are thriving, thanks to the gullibility of people whose minds, unbalanced by the shock of the World War, are easy prey to all kinds of superstition. The drama *Es* (*It,* 1922) uses only two characters for its five acts, the theme of which reveals the author's familiarity with medical questions. It is the tragedy of a doctor who fights against the procreation of tubercular men and who learns, after his wife has told him that she is pregnant, that he himself has tuberculosis. All his attempts, however, to apply his principles to his own case, prove futile: the power of life is stronger than all theories. The misery of the Austrian middle class after the starvation period of the last war years is the subject of the plays

Hungerblockade (*Hunger Blockade,* 1925); *Der Armendoktor* (*The Doctor of the Poor,* 1926); *Der Nothelfer* (*The Helper,* 1926); and *Blockade* (1938). *Der Judas von Tirol* (*The Judas of the Tyrol,* 1927), a new adaptation of Schoenherr's very first play, which had been a failure in 1897, has a favorite theme of the Austrian drama: acting in a play turns into grim seriousness. The peasant performer of Judas in a passion play given in a Tyrolean village in 1810, becomes the Judas to the country's savior, Andreas Hofer. Finally Schoenherr also tried to dramatize the story of Christ in his *Passionsspiel* (*Passion Play,* 1933) which contains elements of the folk play, and tries to motivate Judas' deed psychologically.

Although Schoenherr lived in Vienna, his work developed in complete independence of the Viennese writers of his generation. However, a number of younger dramatists, though widely different from each other, stood more or less under the influence of "Young Vienna."

Thaddaeus Rittner (1873-1921) was the dramatist of subtle, restrained moods, and of an often tragically tinged humor. With an ironical smile he described tragedies and comedies of everyday life and everyday people, never resorting to more robust theatrical devices. *Das kleine Heim* (*The Little Home,* 1908) is a provincial tragedy, telling the story of a doctor's wife who succumbs to the advances of a worthless seducer. The doctor shoots her and is acquitted, yet, unable to overcome the loss of the beloved and the feeling of his own guilt, he finally kills himself. *Unterwegs* (*On the Way,* 1909) is a Don Juan drama in modern dress. The Baron, who seduces one woman after the other, eventually is killed by his own secretary whose wife he had tried to make his mistress. *Sommer* (*Summer,* 1912) is an amusing comedy involving the various guests in a middle-class summer resort. *Woelfe in der Nacht* (*Wolves in the Night,* 1916) pokes fun at a philistine pedant, whose security is being disturbed by his own past. A considerable success was also scored by the fairy-tale comedy *Der Garten der Jugend* (*The Garden of Youth,* 1917).

Less subtle is Hans Mueller (1882-   ) whose numerous and highly successful plays furnished the stars of countless theatres with effective parts. He has touched on problems of all kinds and experimented in the most divergent dramatic styles, always a skilful craftsman of the stage whose craving for actuality and for effectiveness, however, sometimes hampered the artistic quality of his work. *Koenige* (*Kings,* 1915) originated in the patriotic fervor of the First World War and, in historical disguise, hailed the alliance between Austria and Germany. *Der Schoepfer* (*The Creator,* 1918) tells the story of a great doctor who tries to save the life of his wife's lover, while *Die Sterne* (*The Stars,* 1919) dramatizes the figure of Galileo Galilei. Sensationally successful was *Flamme* (*Flame,* 1920), the story of a Viennese prostitute whose frantic desire to find her way back into society ends with her suicide. *Veronika* (1926) tells of the emotional conflict within a nurse torn between her duties and her womanly longing for a child.

Internationally appreciated was *Im weissen Roessl* (*The White Horse Inn*, 1930), a musical comedy based on an old (1898) farce by Oskar Blumenthal and Gustav Kadelburg (music by Ralph Benatzky).

Devoting himself to the rejuvenation of medieval forms, Max Mell (1882-   ), has gained acclaim as a writer of high distinction. In the simple verses of his dramatized legends he has told edifying stories with the aim of infusing the principles of Christian love and charity into minds which had lost their faith during the post-war years. *Das Wiener Kripperl von 1919* (*The Viennese Manger of 1919*, 1921) is a miracle play, written under the impression of Vienna's saddening post-war conditions. Despair, demoralization, and starvation can only be fought, so the play tells us, if the people again turn to faith and to a social order based upon Christian morals. *Das Schutzengelspiel* (*The Play of the Guardian Angel*, 1923) shows how a young girl is led from arrogance to humility, and points out that only he who shows himself humble in the face of adversity will be rewarded by God. *Das Apostelspiel* (*The Apostle Play*, 1924), the most moving of Mell's works, is the story of a simple peasant girl whose genuine piety converts two callous rakes who have entered her miserable hut. They leave, deeply touched by the purity and naïveté they have encountered, and changed by the message of love. In *Das Nachfolge Christi Spiel* (*The Play of the Imitation of Christ*, 1927) a kind nobleman, attacked by a gang of robbers during the Turkish wars of the seventeenth century, sets an example of true faith by sacrificing his own life so that the scoundrels may be saved. *Die Sieben gegen Theben* (*The Seven Against Thebes*, 1931) retells the story of Œdipus and Antigone in a modernized version, interpreting Antigone's fate as a sacrificial death in the Christian sense. *Das Spiel von den deutschen Ahnen* (*The Play of the German Ancestors*, 1933) is, like Mell's legend plays, a warning to his contemporaries. An old family in the Alps is about to sell its farm, disillusioned and discouraged by the trials of the post-war years. As a result of the appearance of two ancestors, clad in their eighteenth-century clothes, the family is reminded of its responsibilities toward the inherited soil and determines to hold out, even in the face of difficulties. The play, written in prose, has a striking similarity to Elmer Rice's play *American Landscape* (1939).

Stefan Zweig (1881-1942) is known chiefly as an essayist, biographer, and novelist. Yet he too wrote several works for the stage, though he was less successful in this field than in his other literary achievements. In the verse tragedy *Tersites* (1907) he wanted to prove the spiritual superiority of the physically inferior. *Das Haus am Meer* (*The House by the Sea*, 1912), also a verse tragedy, presents the grim picture of an old family whose dignity and righteousness are slowly undermined by the evil influence of a woman. The one-act play *Der verwandelte Komoediant* (*The Transformed Comedian*, 1913) deals with a favorite theme of the Austrian theatre: the power of an actor over others and his proud awareness of his transforming abilities.

Legende eines Lebens (*Legend of a Life*, 1919) wants to prove that the true story of a great man has more vitality than the elaborate legend his family wants to build around him after his death, even if the truth should imply human weaknesses and errors. Of considerably more interest than these earlier efforts is *Jeremias* (*Jeremiah*, 1917). Written during the First World War, the play is a forceful indictment of war and violence in every form. The figure of the Jewish prophet grows into a living protest against the irresponsibility of the war-mongers of all times. Finally Zweig prophesies the fate of the Jewish people; despite everlasting persecution, their spirit and faith will prove stronger than brute force. *Das Lamm des Armen* (*The One Ewe Lamb,* 1929) is the tragicomedy of a Napoleonic officer whose marital happiness is destroyed because the Emperor, for a mere whim, seduces his wife. The timely message of the play is the utter helplessness of the individual under a dictatorship. Highly successful was Zweig's adaptation of Ben Jonson's *Volpone* (1926). Also from Ben Jonson was taken the libretto for Richard Strauss' opera *Die schweigsame Frau* (*The Silent Woman,* 1933).

The men so far discussed were rooted spiritually in the pre-war world of the old Hapsburg Empire; but in the meantime a younger generation grew up, independent of the tendencies which had determined the "Young Vienna" group and its followers. These new men began to write either during the war and under its overpowering impression, or after the downfall of the monarchy. In some the old Austrian heritage is unmistakable; others broke away from it, reflecting in their works an utterly changed world and the impact of new literary and political ideas.

The writers of Bohemia, which after the war was to become independent Czechoslovakia, formed two distinct groups. One, comprising men of Sudeten-German descent, was attracted by those tendencies which later developed into the National Socialist ideology. The other, mainly centering in Prague, identified itself, at least in part, with the expressionist wave of post-war Germany.

The outstanding representative of the first group is Erwin Guido Kolbenheyer (1878-   ). Although mainly known through his highly popular novels and his philosophical writings, he has contributed to the stage a number of interesting plays, combining the manifestation of his ideas with theatrical effectiveness. *Heroische Leidenschaften* (*Heroic Passions,* 1928; an earlier version under the title *Giordano Bruno,* 1903) interprets the struggle of the sixteenth-century philosopher against the Catholic Church and its dogmatic views, in terms of the contrast between the Nordic race and the Roman world of the popery. Giordano, as the son of a German mother, tries to break Rome's supremacy over the German spirit. *Die Bruecke* (*The Bridge,* 1929) deals with the problem of the generations. The future can be secure only if the young generation comes to an appreciation of what their elders have achieved, if a spiritual bridge is erected between the old and the new. *Jagt ihn—ein Mensch!* (*Hunt Him—He Is a Man!* 1930) expressed the belief that social problems can be solved neither by capital nor by labor since these two groups work only for their own selfish interests. No material progress can better the condition of society unless men realize that every one has equal rights and equal duties in the great commonwealth of mankind. *Das Gesetz in dir* (*The Law Within You*, 1931) shows a man who, regardless of the mandates of human law, driven merely by the ethical law within himself, assumes guilt for a deed he has not committed. Not only in his plays but also in his other writings, Kolbenheyer had repeatedly expressed views closely related to the ideology of the National Socialists, and so it was not astonishing that he hailed their rise to power. The first dramatic proof of his enthusiasm was a collection of speaking choruses under the title *Deutsches Bekenntnis* (*German Confession*, 1933). The drama *Gregor und Heinrich* (1934), dedicated "To the resurgent German spirit," deals with the struggle of Henry VI against Pope Gregory VII. Even when Henry, after having been banished by the Pope, stands in front of his adversary in the famed meeting at Canossa, in order to atone for his sins, he insists on his idea of the "Reich" and of the irreconcilability of worldly and papal power. In view of the attitude of the National Socialists toward the Catholic Church, the timely implications are obvious.

The most notable among the writers who came from Prague was Franz Werfel (1890-1945). Although his world fame rests mainly upon his novels and poems, some of his dramatic efforts belong to the most characteristic achievements of modern European drama. As early as 1913, he recreated Euripides' *Die Troerinnen* (*The Trojan Women*). He prophetically felt that the world had arrived at a point similar to that in which this staggering indictment of war was written. After the war he wrote the "magic trilogy" *Spiegelmensch* (*Mirror Man*, 1920), a drama of redemption in the form of a fantasy. Its hero, Thamal, is drawn into guilt and sin by the Mirror Man, the personification of his evil instincts. Eventually his conscience triumphs over the allurements of the fiendish spirit and liberates him from the mephistophelian spell. At length Thamal is purified and ready to enter the realm of the highest perfection. The scenes in which he succumbs to the Mirror Man's influence gave Werfel an opportunity to lash out at certain distressing features of the post-war years. *Bocksgesang* (*Goat Song*, 1921), although more real in its conception, uses fantastic elements to deliver a message foreshadowing our own day. The monstrous goat, miraculously born as the offspring of two peasants at the end of the eighteenth century, breaks loose from the wretched hut where his parents have tried to hide him. The beast is worshipped like a godly being and sets up a reign of terror and anarchy. Although he is finally killed, he is not banned from the earth, for a peasant girl bears his child. The goat is a portentous symbol of the pagan instincts slumbering under the surface of our Christian civilization, eternally present and ready to break out at any moment. The tragedy *Schweiger* (1922) tells the story of a man who, years ago, in a sudden outbreak of insanity, has fired several shots at a group of school children, killing some of them. After a period of amnesia, he learns what he did and frantically tries to atone for his crime. Yet he becomes involved in the political struggles of post-war Austria. Communists as well as forerunners of the Nazis try to use Schweiger for their respective purposes. Finally, under the impact of the desperate struggle to free himself from his own past as well as from all political influences, he breaks down again and commits suicide. The attempt to cram too many divergent motives into one play has hampered the effectiveness of this otherwise most interesting work.

Whereas these plays show in their style and also in some ideas the influence of Expressionism, Werfel now turned to an interpretation of history in terms of what might be called a sublimated realism. *Juarez und Maximilian* (1924) tells the story of the Austrian Archduke Maximilian who in 1864 was made Emperor of Mexico and was executed by a firing squad three years later. Maximilian is drawn as the apostle of non-violence and humanitarianism, a pure idealist, unable to comprehend the realities of politics. His dreams are ruthlessly shattered by his opponent Juarez who, however, never appears on the stage. Maximilian dies almost cheerfully, true only to his innermost beliefs and not willing to make any concessions to the revolutionary forces which to him symbolize chaos. *Paulus unter den Juden* (*Paul Among the Jews*, 1925) tries to evoke one of the most decisive periods in history, the moment when Christendom detached itself from its roots, the world of Judaism. Mainly a drama of ideas, it does not come to life on the stage, despite some passages of great beauty and a number of superbly conceived characters. *Das Reich Gottes in Boehmen* (*God's Kingdom in Bohemia*, 1930) leads us to the period of the Hussites, a religious sect of the fifteenth century which, under the guidance of Prokop, aimed at setting up a social order based on communist principles. Yet, as soon as the masses attain some power, they spoil the pure ideals of their leader and the result is brutality and chaos. At the end of the play, Prokop is an utterly disillusioned and disgusted man, compelled to resort to the methods he had previously despised. *Der Weg der Verheissung* (*The Eternal Road*, 1935), written under the impression of Hitler's persecution of the Jews, is a spectacular pageant, retelling the story of the Jewish people and their sufferings throughout the ages. The remembrance of the past is intended to lend strength and resisting power to the victims of another age of persecution. *In einer Nacht* (*In One Night*, 1937) is a rather unconvincing excursion into the supernatural. The "Seelengestalt"—the materialization of the soul—of one of the characters who is believed to have been killed, appears on the stage, trying to communicate with the world of the living and to influence their actions.

Also from Prague came Paul Kornfeld (1889-1944), whose first two plays may be regarded as standard works of expressionist drama. *Die Verfuehrung (The Seduction,* 1913) has as its central character the unhappy Bitterlich whose sensitive and confused soul suffers from an inability to cope with life. Out of his hatred against the philistine society which surrounds him, he kills a completely innocent man who, in his eyes, represents philistinism at its worst. Gladly he lets himself be put in jail, until a girl comes to rescue him. He heeds her seductive appeal to return to life, proclaiming in ecstatic speeches his love for mankind. The girl's brother succeeds in poisoning Bitterlich but is persuaded by his own victim to shoot himself. Eventually, the girl takes poison too. This melodramatic story is told with the unscrupulous use of the most hackneyed theatrical effects and without the slightest consideration for motivation or consistency. All the characters indulge in endless speeches, rhetorically pouring out their exalted emotions. Yet there can be no doubt of Kornfeld's genuine sincerity. This quality became even more apparent in *Himmel und Hoelle (Heaven and Hell,* 1919). The men and women in this tragedy traverse the depths of guilt and crime until they are eventually able to rescue themselves through understanding and all-embracing love. A deeply felt sympathy with mankind pervades this drama of redemption, which is written partly in an overheated and relentlessly moving prose, partly in ecstatic verses. There are scenes of great power and poignancy, revealing Kornfeld's poetic talent as well as his honesty. His later works, however, are disappointing. *Der ewige Traum (The Eternal Dream,* 1922) is a rather bitter comedy, castigating those pseudo-intellectuals who spoil every genuine feeling, and again proclaiming the supremacy of love. *Palme, oder der Gekraenkte (Palme, or The Touchy,* 1924) is a character comedy about an oversensitive man who suffers from persecution mania. *Kilian, oder die gelbe Rose (Kilian, or The Yellow Rose,* 1926) pokes fun at certain circles of society who in their indiscriminate craving for intellectual excitement have lost the capacity for simple emotions.

One of the most promising talents, Hermann Ungar (1893-1929), came from Moravia. His comedy *Die Gartenlaube (The Garden Pavilion,* 1929) is distinguished not so much by its story as by a number of superbly drawn characters and devastating wit. The servant Modlizki is contrasted with a provincial philistine family whose members indulge in middle-class sentimentalism and stock emotions. Modlizki hates everything they believe in and systematically sets out to destroy their ideals of beauty, love, and art. He rapes the daughter of the family in order to impair her "value" according to bourgeois standards, declaring this to be an act of social revolution. The sober, spiteful, yet intensely humorous character of the proletarian who, out of hatred and resentment, deliberately attempts to wreck the conventions of bourgeois society, is a remarkable manifestation of Ungar's creative ability.

Whereas German post-war literature was largely influenced by Expressionism, the new artistic creed touched Viennese writers only temporarily and without leaving noticeable traces. Only a few may be called Expressionists in the exact sense of the term, and even these soon turned their backs upon the frenzies and outbursts of the expressionist school. Yet, strangely enough, it was an Austrian, the painter Oskar Kokoschka (1886-   ) who wrote the earliest Expressionist work for the stage: *Moerder, Hoffnung der Frauen* (*Murderer, Hope of Women*, 1907). This one-act play, however, can hardly be called a drama. It is a nightmarish vision of the eternal battle between the sexes, written in an ecstatic and sometimes almost incomprehensible language. Similar is *Der brennende Dornbusch* (*The Burning Bush*, 1911), which sees in the lack of kindness the cause of all tragedies between man and woman. *Hiob* (*Job*, 1917) is an Expressionist farce, demonstrating with the help of grotesque exaggerations that women are the very embodiment of evil. *Orpheus and Eurydike* (1918) presents the Greek legend, using, like the author's first play, the form of a nightmare. Here again, the central problem is the conflict between the sexes and again the language is so obscure that it is at times hard to grasp the meaning of the lines. Kokoschka's plays are interesting as examples of a consistent application of expressionist style in its most extreme form.

Completely under the spell of Expressionism was also Hans Kaltneker (1895-1919) who wrote a "trilogy of redemption" (1919). The first play, *Das Bergwerk* (*The Mine*) preaches love for mankind as the only way to solve social problems and opposes any revolutionary movement based upon force. The second play, *Die Opferung* (*The Offering*) portrays a man who has to go through sin and crime in order to realize that only humility and love may redeem the world; he dies cheerfully, offering his own life for the sake of humanity. The last play, *Die Schwester* (*The Sister*), attempts to convey the same message, this time purposely using an extreme case to drive home its point. A lesbian descends to the depths of vice and depravity before she becomes an apostle of Christian love. However, Kaltneker's unquestionable sincerity is somewhat impaired by the overheated and overstrained atmosphere which pervades his plays.

Franz Theodor Csokor (1885-   ) started out as a follower of Expressionism. His *Die rote Strasse* (*The Red Road*, 1918) uses the most spectacular features of the expressionist theatre. It presents a fantastic vision of the conflict between the sexes and points out the catastrophic influence of social conditions in general and money in particular. Thoroughly expressionistic is also *Ballade von der Stadt* (*Ballad of the City*, 1924). Modern civilization, most clearly symbolized by the city, is denounced as the curse of mankind. In the renunciation of material progress and in the return to a simple life, Csokor sees the vision of a new and better world. Although his later plays sometimes show some traces of Expressionism, especially in their terse and stylized language, Csokor turned his back upon abstract conceptions and concentrated his interest mainly on the interpretation of social and political forces in history. *Gesellschaft der Menschenrechte* (*The Society of Human Rights*, 1929) deals with the figure of the German dramatist Georg Buechner (1813-1837) who in many respects may be called a forerunner of Expressionism. *Besetztes Gebiet* (*Occupied Zone*, 1930) provides a revealing picture of Germany before the advent of Hitler, showing the clash between the various political ideologies in a small town at the time of the Rhineland occupation. A group of National Socialists sets out to terrorize the inhabitants in the most brutal fashion. The figure of their leader is a most fascinating study of Nazi psychology with all its immediate and horrifying implications, which gives the play considerable documentary value.

Gewesene Menschen (*Faded Men*, 1932) shows the tragedy of Russian émigrés. A group of men of inner nobility is confronted with a brutal and common world whose representatives hunt down their powerless victims. *Dritter November 1918* (*November Third, 1918*, 1936), Csokor's most mature and beautiful play, recalls the moment when the Hapsburg Empire broke apart. A group of officers of the Imperial Army represent the different races and nations which composed the old monarchy. In realistic scenes which, however, are full of symbolical meaning, Csokor shows how the various members of the group leave the doomed Empire without realizing that they are about to destroy a political organism whose maintenance might have been essential for the peace of Europe. Csokor makes it clear that in his opinion the disappearance of Austria-Hungary as a political and economical entity would have catastrophic consequences and that in this very part of the continent new conflagrations would be likely to start—a view which recent events have proved to be correct.

Although the work of Anton Wildgans (1881-1932) shows certain features of Expressionism, he can hardly be called an adherent of their artistic creed. His verse is soft and lyrical, widely different from the strain and stress of expressionist writers. He differs also in being more interested in human beings and their personal predicament than in abstract conceptions, to say nothing of political problems. Wildgans was the tragic poet of the Viennese middle class whose emotional conflicts and miserable economic conditions moved his compassionate heart. His first success was a one-act play, *In Ewigkeit Amen!* (*For Ever and Ever, Amen*, 1913), a completely realistic picture of judicial life. A sadistic judge is confronted with an old and helpless man who is unjustly accused of a petty crime and who, despite his physical inferiority, proves to be spiritually superior. Wildgans' most popular play is *Armut* (*Poverty*, 1913). The story is more than simple: it describes the slow dying of an old government official who, after a miserable life, succumbs to weakness and undernourishment, leaving his family in a most pitiable situation. In the ecstatic speeches of the son sitting at his father's bed, the play lifts itself to the heights of moving poetry. It ends with a warning to men to understand the sufferings of their fellows and thus to ripen into human beings imbued with the spirit of love. The tragedy *Liebe* (*Love*, 1916) deals with the problem of marriage. Realizing that deep conflicts between husband and wife are inevitable because of the dwindling of sexual attraction, Wildgans recommends as the only possible solution the complete suppression of all fleshly instincts. Moreover, he proclaims that the urge of sex is merely a delusion, obstructing the only union that matters: that of two souls. *Dies Irae* (1918) is the tragedy of the unwanted child who, not conceived in the spirit of love, perishes in the atmosphere of hate which pervades the home of his parents. After four acts of engrossing and pitiless realism, the play ends, in its completely unrealistic fifth act, with a flaming accusation against parents who bestow upon their children neither understanding nor love. A mystical chorus of the unborn reminds the parents of the grave responsibility they take upon themselves when they beget children. Turning away from his middle-class tragedies, Wildgans started to write a biblical trilogy *Cain, Moses,* and *Christ*. Yet he was able to complete only the first play, the tragedy *Kain* (1920), which he called a "mythical poem." Abel becomes the symbol of all positive and imaginative forces of man, whereas Cain, tortured by his own ugliness, is the manifestation of greed, materialism, and sex. The biblical fratricide is interpreted as a foreshadowing of the fate of humanity: again and again Cain will arise to kill Abel.

Arnolt Bronnen (pseudonym of Bronner, 1895-   ) was born in Vienna, the son of Ferdinand Bronner who, under the pseudonym Franz Adamus, had published *The Wawroch Family,* already mentioned. The younger Bronner moved to Berlin very soon and identified himself completely with the spiritual and literary tendencies of the German capital. He immediately plunged into the tidal wave of Expressionism and took sides with those authors who, like Walter Hasenclever in his *Der Sohn* (*The Son*), made the conflict between succeeding generations their central problem. As early as 1914, he wrote the fantastic play *Die Geburt der Jugend* (*The Birth of Youth*). In ecstatically overcharged scenes, the young generation is called to revolt against parents and teachers as well as against law and authority. The most interesting character is the leader of youth, Karl, who proclaims his hatred for everything and everybody and pours forth inflammatory speeches, hardly surpassable in brutality, against the "old ones."

In 1915, Bronnen wrote *Vatermord* (*Parricide*), the most consistent and ruthless manifestation of the expressionist attitude toward the problem of the generations. Aside from summoning the young to fight their parents and teachers, the play might be called a dramatization of Freud's "Œdipus complex": the son not only butchers his father with a kitchen knife but also makes love to his mother. If Bronnen's first plays may be regarded as characteristic documents of an epoch, his later production makes increasing use of melodramatic devices, excelling in orgies of sex and brutality. *Die*

Exzesse (*The Excesses,* 1923) is a farce around a group of sex-ridden young men and women. The language of the play is almost incredibly coarse. *Katalaunische Schlacht* (*Katalaunian Battle,* 1924) shows a woman chased by several rather shady characters, the story being set against the background of a demoralized and rotten post-war atmosphere. *Anarchie in Sillian* (*Anarchy at Sillian,* 1924) takes place in a power-station in the Tyrolean Alps. The gist of the story is the brutal struggle of two men for a woman, in which the engineer Carrel, a superman, vanquishes anarchy in two ways: he kills his competitor, a political radical, and throws out the seductive woman who had been endangering his work by her exciting presence. *Rheinische Rebellen* (*Rhenish Rebels,* 1925) uses the machinations of the Separatist Party in the Rhineland during the post-war years as background for a brutal melodrama of sexual greed. The "villain" is the unscrupulous adventurer Occc—this is the way he spells his name—while the "heroine" is the pure Teutonic maiden who fights against the advances of the villain and lives only for the greatness of the German Nation. Bronnen's early transformation into an ardent supporter of National Socialism is foreshadowed in this play as well as in the comedy *Reparationen* (*Reparations,* 1926), an allegory of Germany suffering under the consequences of the Versailles Treaty. "Mark" and "Pfennig," who symbolize the suffering Germans, finally outwit the scoundrels "Franc" and "Pound" and liberate themselves from their tyranny. Interesting from a technical viewpoint is the drama *Ostpolzug* (*Quest for the East Pole,* 1926) which employs only a single actor, supposed to represent alternately Alexander the Great and a modern Alexander. If it is possible to find any meaning in this confused and pretentious concoction, it might be said that it symbolizes mankind's eternal longing for the unattainable.

Another Viennese dramatist who left his homeland and moved to Berlin is Ferdinand Bruckner (pseudonym of Theodor Tagger, 1891-   ). He first created a sensation when he wrote *Krankheit der Jugend* (*Sickness of Youth,* 1928), a play which today is more interesting as a cultural document than as a work of art. It shows, in the setting of a Berlin boardinghouse, a group of young men and women who, faithless and unstable, drift through perverted erotic experiences. Although some of them are conscious of their forlorn and wretched condition, they all lack strength to gain a positive attitude towards life. More interesting is *Die Verbrecher* (*The Criminals,* 1929), a most impressive cross-section of post-war Germany. Every one of the many vividly and arrestingly drawn characters is a criminal in some way, yet the manner in which each is either punished or escapes punishment also shows the questionable aspects of judicial practice. At the end Bruckner appeals to conscience as the only legitimate judge, the prosecutor within ourselves. In 1939, Bruckner, then an exile, wrote a new version of this play, emphasizing the infiltration of Nazism into German life before 1933. Equally successful was *Elisabeth von England* (1930), a psychoanalytical interpretation of the Virgin Queen. Elizabeth's attitude toward Philip of Spain as well as her relation to Essex is interpreted as an ambiguous mixture of love and hatred. As the play ends after Essex' execution and Philip's death, Elizabeth remains a lonely, old, and disillusioned woman. Through the skilful use of a divided stage Bruckner was able to evoke in a most impressive manner the two contrasting worlds of Protestant England and Catholic Spain. Less convincing is the drama *Kreatur* (*Creature*, 1930), dealing with the marital crises and sexual conflicts of a neurotic couple. In long-drawn conversations, the characters indulge in torturing dissections of their own emotions. The tragedy *Timon* (1932), following approximately the story of Shakespeare's play, attempts to motivate through the use of modern idioms and modern psychology the figure of the Athenian misanthrope. *Die Marquise von O.* (*The Marquise of O.*, 1933), based on a masterful short story by Heinrich von Kleist (1777-1811), is a psychoanalytical interpretation of the original. Bruckner showed himself again at the height of his talent when he wrote *Die Rassen* (*Races*, 1933). This was the first anti-Nazi play, and it is still one of the best. In a series of deeply moving scenes Bruckner depicts the catastrophic consequences of Hitler's racial theory. He further shows how Germany's youth is affected by the Nazi revolution: those who subscribe to the new creed are mentally destroyed, while those who try to resist it are brutally disposed of. In the drama *Napoleon* (1936) Bruckner concerned himself not solely with the political career of the Emperor but rather with the tragic conflict between his love for Josephine and his irrepressible urge for power.

Especially after the war, many dramatists turned to subjects taken from Austrian history. Some glorified the old Empire in a more or less sentimental manner, others tried to find out the reasons for its downfall.

Friedrich Schreyvogl (1899-   ), in *Habsburgerlegende* (*Hapsburg Legend*, 1933), the best of his numerous plays, told the story of the Archduke Johann Nepomuk Salvator who in 1889 renounced all his titles, called himself Johann Orth, and fled the narrowness of the Viennese court. After marrying a girl of the people, he boarded the ship *Santa Margherita*, started out on a trip around the world, and vanished without leaving a trace. He was declared dead in 1911. In Schreyvogl's play, however, the story continues in a different way. Under the name of John Another, he lives for thirty years, unknown and unrecognized, as a farmer near Santiago, Chile. As his life draws to a close, he returns to Vienna where, after the World War, he faces his own image in an exhibition of waxworks. Although every one believes him dead, he lives in the legend of the romantic dreamer who rebelled against the policies of the old Emperor Franz Joseph. Hans Sassmann (1882-   ), endowed with the skill of a theatrical craftsman, contrived numerous effective but superficial pseudo-historical plays, dealing with episodes from the Austrian past. Richard Duschinsky (1897-   ) scored a sensational success with his *Kaiser Franz Joseph I. von Oesterreich*

(1931), in a series of colorful scenes calling up the almost legendary figure of the Emperor. Georg Rendl (1903-   ) applied the same technique to the equally legendary figure of the Empress, in his drama *Elisabeth, Kaiserin von Oesterreich* (1937); Hans Naderer, in his *Lueger* (1934), paid tribute to the popular Mayor of Vienna, who had introduced anti-Semitism into Austrian political life and whom Adolf Hitler later acknowledged as one of his teachers in the art of demagogy. Joseph Wenter (1880-   ) turned entirely to historical subjects. In rather conventionally composed but technically accomplished plays, he retold episodes from the history of his home province, the Austrian Tyrol: *Der Kanzler von Tirol* (*The Chancellor of the Tyrol*, 1936), and *Die schoene Welserin* (*The Lovely Philippine Welser*, 1938). Other works, however, he devoted to the history of medieval Germany. The old German dream of the "Reich" and the struggle between Emperors and Popes comes to life in *Der deutsche Heinrich* (*The German Heinrich*, 1938); and *Der sechste Heinrich* (*Henry VI*, 1938). *Die Landgraefin von Thueringen* (*The Landgravine of Thuringia*, 1936) tells the story of Saint Elizabeth (1207-1231), the Hungarian Princess, who renounced all worldly riches and spent her life among the sick and poor.

Austrian feeling was emphasized also in plays of a lighter vein. Stephan Kamare (pseudonym of Cokorac von Kamare, 1885-   ) based his comedy *Der junge Baron Neuhaus* (*Young Baron Neuhaus*, 1933) on an idea which had been used before in Heinrich von Kleist's famous *Der zerbrochene Krug* (*The Broken Jug*, 1808): through a chain of odd circumstances, the culprit becomes the judge at his own trial. The background of eighteenth-century Vienna and the atmosphere of the Viennese Rococo is delightfully reproduced to the minutest detail of language, customs, and mannerisms. Kamare's comedy *Leinen aus Irland* (*Linen from Ireland*, 1933) also takes place in old Austria. The typical pre-war milieu of government officials furnishes the background for an amusing love story. The figure of an impudent swindler and parvenu, portrayed with malicious wit, contributed greatly to the stage success of this play. The tradition of light and entertaining comedies which did not search into any deeper problems but were distinguished by clever dialogue, was continued in a great number of plays, some of which have been performed on the stages of the English-speaking world. Particularly successful were *Mit der Liebe spielen* (*Playing with Love*, 1920, produced in English under the title *Caprice*), by Sil-Vara (pseudonym of Geza Silberer, 1876-1938); and *Kleine Komoedie* (*Little Comedy*, 1927, produced in English under the title *Candle-Light*), by Siegfried Geyer.

Still to be considered is the youngest generation of Austrian dramatists, among whom are some writers of distinction and promise.

Alexander Lernet-Holenia (1897-   ) started out with a historical subject which had tempted such dramatists as Schiller and Hebbel: *Demetrius* (1926). In six passionate, ballad-like scenes, it depicts in an atmosphere of crime, vice, and horror the rise and fall of the ill-famed Polish pretender who was murdered in 1606. After that, Lernet-Holenia turned entirely to what might be called comedies of bad manners. *Ollapotrida* (*Hotchpotch*, 1926) revolves around an actor and his mistress who, acting in a farce, find themselves confronted with a stage situation which parallels one in their own lives. The solution, however, is as farcical as the play in which they have appeared. Of considerably more interest is *Oesterreichische Komoedie* (*Austrian Comedy*, 1927). The theme is the social and moral decay of the old aristocracy after the First World War. The only character who still maintains the standards of nobility is an old servant. A member of the bourgeoisie is called upon to rescue the family from an impending scandal brought about by their utter depravity. This bitter comedy is of real value as a document of the period. However, Lernet-Holenia's later plays became more and more farcical, employing without hesitation all the time-honored tricks of the comic theatre. Invariably the turbulent adventures, confusions, and love-affairs involve members of the old aristocracy, mostly former officers of the Imperial Army. Although Lernet-Holenia possesses considerable original wit, his most remarkable quality is a boundless cynicism. All moral and ethical values and standards are impudently brushed aside, marriage as well as love, honor as well as honesty. Adultery is a matter of course, while faithfulness becomes the ridiculed exception. Moreover, all these love-affairs do not spring from any passion, they are merely the sport of a class of idlers, cheats, and rogues. Lernet-Holenia's comedies reveal, under their farcical and amusing surface, the bitter and sometimes shocking spectacle of the general decomposition of a once-esteemed class and the breakdown of all values and standards after the First World War.

Wholly influenced by the shattering impression of the post-war years was Hans Chlumberg (pseudonym of Hans Bardach Edler von Chlumberg, 1897-1930), when he wrote his fantasy *Wunder um Verdun* (*Miracle at Verdun*, 1930). Dead soldiers of the great war leave their common grave and return to the world in order to find out whether they have suffered and died in vain. They find themselves among people who have forgotten their sacrifice, who have learned nothing, who fight each other, and whose countries are preparing for the next war. Now they know that their death was futile, and they return to the grave. Chlumberg's play is one of the most stirring documents of the post-war years. His death, resulting from an accident, deprived Austria of one of her most promising young dramatists.

An accident also claimed the life of another highly promising playwright and novelist, Oedoen von Horvath (1901-1938). He combined an unusual sense of humor with a keen awareness of the political and social conditions which foreshadowed the rise of National Socialism. His folk play *Italienische Nacht* (*Italian Night*, 1930) is a satire on the political situation in a small town in southern Germany. Around a garden-party, given by the Republicans under the device "Italian Night," revolve the amusing scenes of this comedy. Yet, beneath the facetious surface, one can feel the impending danger of Nazism, although the "fascists" in the play are merely funny characters, drawn with sparkling wit and pungent observation. When Horvath wrote another folk play, *Geschichten aus dem Wiener Wald* (*Tales from the Vienna Woods,* 1931), he chose the title of the famous Strauss waltz not in order to glorify or to sentimentalize "gay Vienna" but to sketch a grim picture of a city completely changed after the war. The Viennese in this play are neither "charming" nor "gemuetlich" but torn by political and economic depravity, brutality, and greed, and a weird image of disintegration appears on the stage.

From Upper Austria came Hermann Heinz Ortner (1895-   ) who started with Catholic legend plays. *Tobias Wunderlich* (1929) is the name of a simple and believing shoemaker whose piety is rewarded by a miracle. When an old, carved wooden altar is about to be sold to an American, Tobias vainly protests. Thereupon the St. Barbara of the altar comes to life and approaches Tobias. Under the impression of this miracle, he turns into a preacher against post-war materialism and superficiality. *Sebastianlegende* (*The Legend of Sebastian,* 1929) also tells the story of a miracle. A religious maid-servant in a little village experiences the miracle of stigmatization and her naïve purity has a transforming effect upon the whole community, as well as upon the tramp Sebastian, whom she loves. *Wer will unter die Soldaten?* (*Who Wants to Join the Army?,* 1930) is a bitter depiction of the post-war years in Austria. In a number of forceful scenes, Ortner shows the demoralization, the political unrest, and the human misery of that period, with an outspoken anti-militaristic tendency, and ends with an admonition to love and kindness. *Schuster Anton Hitt* (*Shoemaker Anton Hitt,* 1932) is a village tragedy. Its message is that a crime committed in thought cries out for the same atonement as a crime which has actually been committed. *Isabella von Spanien* (*Isabella of Spain,* 1938) shows the Queen as a national heroine solely concerned with the greatness of her country. She loves Sanchez de Carera, the competitor of Columbus for the journey to the unknown West, because of his pure enthusiasm for the national ideal. On the other hand Columbus—who does not appear in the play—is described as an unscrupulous adventurer who is only interested in material gains. Eventually the Queen sacrifices her love for Sanchez to the welfare of the country, while the King, who has become completely alienated from her, decides in favor of Columbus.

Also from Upper Austria, Richard Billinger (1890-   ), is the most interesting, powerful, and original dramatist of the youngest generation. He is preoccupied with the figure of the peasant. Yet his peasants are widely different from those depicted by Schoenherr and other Austrian writers. Billinger wishes to show the peasant's soul as a battle-ground of two conflicting forces: Catholicism on the one hand, and the remnants of a pagan past on the other. The pagan forces, again and again breaking through the surface of Christianity, lead to violent and tragic collisions. The heritage of paganism is today, in the age of progress and civilization, just as vividly alive in the peasant as the Catholic belief in saints and miracles. The customs and festivities of peasant life reflect both these worlds. Often the pagan forces come to life in the form of demons and ghosts, just as the saints and angels of the Catholic Church take active part as visible beings in the peasant's existence. The close kinship of peasant and nature is symbolized in Billinger's work in the demonic manifestations of the elemental powers which fight, haunt, or tease him, while he tries to escape their tribulations by appealing to the protection of the Christian saints and angels. Contrasted with the peasant's world is that of the city as a hostile force which is regarded by the country folk as alien or even dangerous. In the eyes of the peasants, the man from the city is the rationalized being of the technical age who has lost all connection with the mystic forces of the soil.

Billinger's most striking achievement lies in his remarkable ability to bring to life this whole complex atmosphere of the country world, and his extraordinary creative power. A host of vividly and compellingly drawn characters populate his plays, which are permeated with the almost perceptible air of village and farm. In addition to that, he is endowed with a most original and often grotesque kind of humor, which sometimes expresses itself in a strange proclivity to odd or ludicrous figures, to cripples, decrepit old people, possessed and deranged characters. Most of his peasants, however, are exuberant with health and a reckless vitality, driven above all by their sexual instincts in a manner which often leads them to crime and madness. *Das Perchtenspiel* (*The Perchten Play*, 1928) shows the struggle between a peasant and the "Perchten," pagan nature demons. The peasant Peter has fallen in love with a young Perchten but tries to get back to his wife. Thereupon the "bad" Perchten sets fire to Peter's farm and his wife is burnt to death, while Peter is slain by his irate ancestor. Only the illegitimate child which Peter has had by a maid-servant is saved. At the end appear the fourteen "Nothelfer" (helpers in need) as the forces of the Catholic Church, ready to protect the peasants from being further troubled by the pagan demons. Billinger's most powerful play is the drama *Rauhnacht* (1931). The "Rauhnacht" is the night of December twenty-third. According to old traditions, all pagan spirits are let loose during this night in order to plunge the country-folk into turmoil and misfortune. The peasant Simon Kreuzlechner has just returned from Africa where he had intended to become a missionary. Among the savages he had encountered the same pagan forces which slumber within the peasants of his homeland, there, to be sure, uninhibited by Christian influence. He lures a young girl into his house, dons an African dance mask and starts, accompanied by the horrifying sound of an African drum, to perform a magic dance before the spellbound girl. After that, he rapes and kills her in a sort of blood-frenzy. Against the background of the pagan customs of the "Rauhnacht," the irruption of anti-Christian elements into the peaceful pre-Christmas calm of the Alpine village, is depicted with compelling force.

The drama *Rosse* (*Horses*, 1931) tells the story of a farmhand who has to take care of the horses, which he loves in an almost mystic way. When he sees his beloved animals threatened by a salesman who has come from the city in order to sell motorized farm machines, he murders this representative of civilization and hangs himself in the stable, close to "his" horses. The comedy, *Lob des Landes* (*Praise of the Country*, 1932) points out the impossibility of bridging the gulf between peasants and townspeople and sketches a number of most amusing characters who are drawn with a queer and often gruesome humor. *Das Verloebnis* (*The Engagement*, 1933) has as its central figures a man and a woman, both peasants, whom sexual obsession and the frantic desire to be united drive to double murder. The comedy *Stille Gaeste* (*Silent Guests*, 1934) shows the contrast between town and country. The "silent guests" are spirits of the deceased who appear only before people still capable of true love. The enlightened and civilized townspeople are no longer able to experience genuine emotions, but the couple from the country see the "silent guests," even in our modern time. *Die Hexe von Passau* (*The Witch of Passau*, 1935), Billinger's first venture into a past age, is set against the background of a peasant revolt of the seventeenth century. The "Witch" is an actress in a company of strolling players. The Count who has come to subdue the peasants is so deeply moved by her performance in a religious play that he not only pardons the rebels but becomes their leader. *Der Gigant* (*The Giant*, 1937) endeavors to prove that the city is an evil force, a giant who recklessly destroys everything genuine and vital.

Billinger's work has symbolical implications. The irruption of pagan forces into Christian civilization, which is the leitmotiv of his plays, was to become also that of our century. Moreover, his homeland was to be the first victim of these forces. When Hitler's legions marched into Austria in 1938, they immediately began to obliterate the very traditions of her culture. Not even her name, changed to Ostmark, was left to remind the world of her identity. Vienna became an insignificant provincial town, ruled by Prussian officials and Nazi Stormtroopers. Austria had temporarily ceased to exist.

Had Austrian culture ceased to exist, too? Certainly not. Her music lived on in the works of Haydn, Mozart, Schubert, Bruckner, Wolf, and Mahler; and her literature continued to be appreciated wherever there had been no burning of books.

A great number of Austrian writers left their country voluntarily, or were forced into exile. They have carried on their work, often in the face of the greatest intellectual and material difficulties and, as far as the playwrights among them are concerned, with hardly a chance to see their plays performed. Yet, they worked—and they waited.

In the spring of 1945 the Allied armies liberated Austria. At the time of this writing, the country is once more free and independent. Its cultural life has again started in the midst of the spiritual and physical destruction caused by seven years of Nazi occupation.

No complete record is as yet available of the plays written in Austria during that period. However, the theatres have resumed their activities everywhere in the country, performing some of the plays which had been banned by the Nazi régime.

If one considers Austria's illustrious theatrical past, one can hardly doubt that its tradition will be taken up by a new generation of dramatists. It may be well to remember at this moment, when Austria is about to emerge from the nightmare of the most shameful episode in her history, that the writers who have embodied her spiritual tradition in its purest form, men such as Franz Grillparzer, Adalbert Stifter, Ludwig Anzengruber, Arthur Schnitzler, Hugo von Hofmannsthal, Karl Kraus, Franz Werfel—to mention only a few—invariably stood for the ideals of humanitarianism, tolerance, and mutual understanding; and that they fought for human dignity and freedom. It is to be hoped that future Austrian writers will carry on in this lofty tradition. Then, and only then, it will be possible to speak of an Austria reborn.

IV

England and Ireland

GEORGE FREEDLEY

The morale of the British theatre was considerably enlivened by the Act of 1842 which freed the stage from the artificial restrictions of the supposed monopoly which the Theatres Royal, Drury Lane, Covent Garden, and the Haymarket had maintained for a century. It is characteristic of Anglo-Saxons that we prefer to violate laws rather than to repeal them. The vociferous minority acts as a check on the sluggish, not-caring majority. Eventually, however, this mass was leavened and it became apparent just how ridiculous it was to have a statute on the books which was violated every night by the existence of such playhouses as the Adelphi, the Lyceum, St. James's, and a score or more of others. The immediate result of the repeal of the monopoly was to force the Drury Lane, for instance, to rival openly the theatres which it had long been doing secretly. Pantomimes, vaudevilles, foreign stars in foreign-language drama, melodramas of a lurid nature were introduced into the bills in order to attract the public. There were a few sound dramatists who still looked back to the eighteenth century conventions or who riveted their attention upon the library to provide serious plays for the enormous middle class which was growing rich with Britain's vast international trade; such men as Bulwer-Lytton, Douglas Jerrold, Robert Browning, Alfred Lord Tennyson, Algernon Charles Swinburne. These Victorian writers lacked dramatic passion, sincere curiosity as to people's motives, and conscious application to the psychology of man's actions. They were not the men to bring about a revival of the drama; they could only keep the stage warm until a new great crop of dramatists was born.

Perhaps the first playwright who could really lay claim to belonging to the realistic school was Thomas William Robertson (1829-1871) for he had examined life about him and had reported it to his audiences at the Prince of Wales' Theatre where Squire Bancroft (Sir to be) and the lovely and accomplished comédienne, Marie Wilton (later Lady Bancroft) held sway. Not that Robertson *was* a realist, for he only examined the surface of life and at best described amusingly its foibles and eccentricities. Its crotchets, its subterfuges, its humorous display of impecuniousness, its fashions and its follies are treated to a dramatic performance which depended largely on the skill and known characteristics of its actors for success. In an obscure little playhouse in muddy Tottenham Court Road, center of the French émigrés of dubious standards and standing, the grandiloquently named Queen's Theatre was hired by Marie Wilton. The neighbors most accurately referred to it as the "dust hole," which proved that they had experienced the dubious joys of its theatrical attractions. Equipped with H. J. Byron's burlesques (which were not so funny as they were recently thought to have been) the little soubrette had refurbished the playhouse. She had engaged an excellent company of comedians which included the down-on-his-luck gentleman, Squire Bancroft, whom the little actress fancied as much as a man as an actor.

The playwrights' vein of writing had run out and the whole venture was in danger of failing when into its midst came Tom Robertson, an unsuccessful actor, son of a struggling suburban manager, grandson and great-grandson of traveling players. Nothing but failure had dogged his steps as both writer and as actor; his *A Night's Adventure* had failed financially with William Farren at the Olympic (1851) as well as *A Cantab* (1861) at the Haymarket; drabness, unhappiness, and bitterness had been his lot since then. He was a hack translator from the French who sold his pieces to various booksellers for a few shillings to keep alive. While he was doing this, however, he was absorbing some of the liveliness of melodrama which soon would serve to revive British drama. Turning to look about him at the Bohemia in which he lived, he was moved to compose a genre picture in which his impecunious artistic friends were contrasted with the great social world whose women he never knew, but whose men he encountered at clubs and informal dinners. The result of this was *Society* (1865), which had been written while he was supported by the small profits of *David Garrick* (1864), an improbable and unrealistic adaptation from the French which the elder Sothern played at the Haymarket. The new comedy, however, was turned down and Robertson was in despair again. It was then that he and *Society* and Marie Wilton came together and the result was a profitable and successful career for author and actress up to his death, and beyond, because the Bancrofts (she had married her handsome gentleman-actor) continued to play these "cup-and-saucer" comedies for twenty years.

The Robertson pieces had just enough reflection of life in them to attract a public which was curious about comment on itself. At the same time, the author contrived his situations to allow a happy ending which pleased the sentimental. He studied the Bancrofts' comedy and cut his cloth to fit their talents and he succeeded most marvelously as a dramatic tailor for actors and actresses. *Ours* followed in 1866 and a year later it was *Caste* which titillated London drawing-rooms. *Play* was produced the next year and in 1869 there were two new Robertsonian creations: *School*, constructed from Roderich Benedix's *Aschenbroedel,* and *Home,* an anglicization (with due regard for the middle-class British taste) of Augier's *L'Aventuriere*. *M.P.* was his last work and a year later Tom Robertson was dead and gone. His last few years were happy and successful and so made up, in part, for his long hopeless drudgery. At least he tasted, more than tasted, the sweets of success. The Bancrofts savored them even longer for it was not until 1885 that they retired from the stage to lead the life of the well-to-do, the happy, the proud and respectable.

Though not precisely "modern" as we today understand the word, Robertson was the first nineteenth-century playwright in England to think in terms of the life around him. It was two years after his death before *The Fortnightly Review* published Sir Edmund Gosse's critique on the importance of Ibsen as a playwright. But the first bubbles had worked their way through the yeasty dough and the bread had begun to rise. It would be twenty years before it reached those recognizable loaves that we can call modern plays, but the leaven was working.

However, before Shaw was to arise in 1891 as the first modernist, there were a few men who, though they wore the Victorian mantle, in some instances successfully cast it off. These were Pinero, Wilde, Henry Arthur Jones, and Sydney Grundy. The first and third of these were to continue almost to our day, though their writing was much more likely to have come out of the stage's fly galleries than from honest observation of life translated into theatrical terms.

Perhaps before we turn to the above-mentioned gentlemen we should cast a quick and appraising eye on the Victorian fooling of Sir William Schwenk Gilbert (1835-1911). There is certainly no real conception of the trend of modern drama to be found in this devastatingly witty writer, though his satiric treatment of British shibboleths is just as funny today as it was in the seventies, eighties, and nineties. Because Gilbert's ideas (with or without Sullivan's enchanting melodies) remain so timely it is difficult for us to think of him as anything but "modern." His plays without music, such as *Pygmalion and Galatea* (1871) or *Engaged* (1877), are much more definitely, traditionally conventional, pretty, contrived, and artificial than his musical pieces. When he and Sullivan combined (despite their personal jealousies and quarrels) to contrive *H. M. S. Pinafore; or, The Lass That Loved a Sailor* (1878); or their delightful play on Wilde's esthetic extravagances, *Patience; or Bunthorne's Bride* (1881); or *The Pirates of Penzance; or The Slave to Duty* (1879); or the completely fascinating *Iolanthe; or The Peer and the Peri* (1882); or that perennial favorite, *The Mikado; or The Town of Titipu* (1885) then their work took on a timelessness that is completely timely. They were gadflies; together they were England's ninetenth-century Thersites. Their plays are a witty comment on living and thinking even if they were composed in purely conventional patterns.

Certainly no one would call Oscar Wilde (1856-1900) a modernist despite his ever-present desire to shock. He made a fine art of *épater le bourgeois*.

If he were interested in Ibsen or in the awakening of dramatic forces, it never showed in his own writings. It was his desire to be as witty, as scintillating, as perverse as his brilliant and somewhat superficial mind would permit. At the same time he certainly cannot be ignored for his comedies were so enormously popular that they reflected London taste of the time. Nevertheless, we do not expect our Shaftesbury Avenue playwrights to copy Ibsen or Strindberg or Chekhov or even to think like them that life and man's soul must be revealed in dramatic writing. Wilde wrote to please himself, shock his friends and enemies, amuse his public, and make money. He did all of these things. Had he not also carried the secret of his destruction within himself, he might have continued as London's favorite comic-writing talent up to his dying day. That his sexual aberrations, which seem to have been heightened by folly and extravagances, finally exposed him to the scorn of his enemies and the penalties of England's harsh legal system is regrettable and made all this impossible. None of his plays, which were once so admired, stands up today save his last, *The Importance of Being Earnest* (1895). Called the wittiest comedy in the English language in the more than a century since Sheridan's *The Rivals* (1777), it is more accurately to be termed a farce. Witty it is, for it has withstood innumerable revivals. The most recent successful one is John Gielgud's in London in 1943.

Certainly the false heroics of that problem piece, *Lady Windermere's Fan* (1892), despite its clever lines, do not stand up today as drama worth reviving. Students still do (and should) read its lines as an example of English drama in the last quarter of the last century. *A Woman of No Importance* (1893) and *An Ideal Husband* (1895) do not fare even as well as the drama of the naughty Mrs. Erlynne and her proper, but stupid daughter, though the latter was successfully revived with a superlative cast by Robert Donat in 1944. Wilde's only other dramatic offering of merit belongs to the poetic school and ranks high there, despite its intended decadence. Written in French for Sarah Bernhardt, *Salomé* (1892) was long to go unproduced in England. Though the great Lugné-Poe braved criticism to show it in France, it was not until 1905 that the Lord Chamberlain would permit it to be acted in England.

While Wilde was writing brilliant, mannered, and literary pieces, there was an actor who wrote one farce for which he will always be remembered out of a number of supremely unimportant plays. Brandon Thomas (1856-1914) was responsible for *Charley's Aunt* (1892) which had a hysterical success at the time both in England and America and was widely translated. This piece concerning an Oxford undergraduate's impersonation of a friend's unknown aunt (from Brazil "where the nuts come from") has been performed literally *somewhere* in the world ever since its première up to the outbreak of World War II. Its most successful revival in recent years in New York came as late as the 1940-1941 season.

A contemporary and, in a sense, a rival of Wilde's was Sir Arthur Pinero (1855-1934). Really a Victorian at heart, he wrote his first plays at a time when Ibsenism began its assault upon Albion. His later and more noted problem pieces represent an incomplete understanding of realism mated to a fine sense of construction. Scribe, Augier, Sardou were the French technicians whom he emulated. His ability to construct plays was extraordinately fine; his main difficulty lay in an insufficient ability to observe life and humanity and reveal what he saw. Once he outgrew his early comedies which brought him fame and much money, he plunged into thesis plays which were successful in their day, but which seem childishly unresolved today. This, despite the fact that it was said at the time that no English dramatist of this era has ever surpassed his amazing comprehension of play construction. Yet he had little or no realization of the world and those who populate it. It was George Bernard Shaw who said of Pinero that he who "has never written a line from which it could be guessed that he is a contemporary of Ibsen, Tolstoi, Meredith or Sarah Grand, finds himself at the dawn of the twentieth [century] hailed as a man of new ideas, of daring originality, of supreme literary distinction, and even—which is perhaps oddest—of consummate stage craft."[1] The truth of it is that his thinking and the construction of his plays passed muster at a time when all but a few of the public and nearly every critic were blind to the changes in dramatic thinking and structure which had come about. Only Shaw, Gosse, Archer, and a handful of others comprehended the magnitude of the revolution in the theatre which Ibsen had initiated.

The Second Mrs. Tanqueray (1893) is the play most likely to be remembered of Pinero's work despite the fact that he was writing (and being played and published) steadily from 1877 to 1932, a matter of fifty-five years. Only Shaw has a longer record in English drama. Pinero began with one-acters which in those days had a real market as curtain-raisers. The pit and the gallery went to the theatre early, but occupants of the stalls dined later, so that something was needed to occupy the time of the small-pursed public while their financial betters ate their dessert or savory. Present-day play-goers who are addicted to arriving on time as a courtesy to the actors and others, as well as because they like to hear the play, might find the curtain-raiser habit a good one. At least we might be entertained while the dinner-party public is drinking itself to the point of making a good noisy entrance between nine and nine-thirty. What a shock they would get if they arrived at the theatre and found a brief intermission and the main play only about to begin.

It was this practice which set Pinero's hand and gave him the experience at comedy writing which enabled him to turn out *The Magistrate* (1885), *The School Mistress* (1886), and the sentimental *Sweet Lavender* (1888).

---

[1] G. B. Shaw, *Dramatic Opinions and Essays* (New York, Brentano's Inc., 1906), Vol. I, pp. 36-37.

The following year he turned serious in *The Profligate* which he topped in his piece about Paula Tanqueray's shame. The public and critics (except Shaw) went mad over the piece. No actress in London would touch the part of a woman with a past until Mrs. Patrick Campbell was found. Apparently it was her gloriously passionate performance which blinded the eyes of all to the deficiencies of Pinero's writing. He aimed at tragedy, but never achieved it because his serious plays were mundane affairs which never purged their audiences. *The Notorious Mrs. Ebbsmith* (1896), *Iris* (1903), and *Midchannel* (1909) were in similar vein. They had commercial success, as, indeed, did most of this playwright's work until the outbreak of the First World War and a new crop of modern playwrights finally belatedly opened audiences' eyes to the Victorianism of his plays. *Trelawney of the Wells* (1898) and *The Gay Lord Quex* the same year were two popular starring vehicles; the first has known a number of famous revivals on both sides of the ocean. Despite the period of time which Pinero lived and wrote, his work was never a part of our modern life.

Though a lesser light even in his own day, we'll turn now to Sydney Grundy (1848-1915) before touching on Henry Arthur Jones who came closest of his group to being a modern dramatist. Grundy's principal contribution to British drama lay in his translation and adaptation of certain French playwrights such as Labiche, Delacour, Feuillet, Meilhac, Halévy, and Mirabeau and the German, von Moser. These French and German playwrights were scarcely the best in their own country, but in their time they represented something of an advance over what Britain had to offer. Grundy, in his heavy-handed way, tried to relate play writing to life, but his vision was so limited that he saw only certain of the most obvious facets of living. Having helped in even so small a way to advance the drama, he soon lost all touch with it and was horrified and disgusted by the turn it took.

Several of his works for the stage, all of which smell of mothballs, include *Mammon* (1866), which he fashioned from Feuillet's *Montjoye; In Honour Bound* (1880), which Grundy modestly stated was "suggested" by Scribe's *Une Chaine; A Pair of Spectacles* (1883), perhaps the best of the lot, which he took from Labiche's and Delacourt's *Les Petits Oiseaux; A Bunch of Violets* (1894), another rendering of Feuillet's drama; and the highly successful *Business Is Business* (1905), from Octave Mirabeau's competently fashioned *Les Affaires Sont les Affaires*. This is hardly a respectable showing for a man who was touted by his fellows as the superior, along with Pinero, of such wild Irishmen as Bernard Shaw and any others who were taken in by this Ibsen nonsense.

Not altogether happy is a rereading of the plays of Henry Arthur Jones (1851-1929), but at least most of his faults lie on the side of the angels. His was a forthright mind which surprisingly enough tended at moments toward mysticism. This is the more amazing because his first great success in the theatre came in melodrama. *The Silver King* (1882) was popular for a generation. Today we are inclined to wonder why, but London and provincial audiences, to say nothing of America, and Australia and the other British dominions, took this piece of good acting claptrap to their uncritical bosoms. Henry Herman collaborated in the writing, while Wilson Barrett did even more to further its success by his acting. Jones, however, was alive to what was going on around him—in which he differed sharply from Pinero. He was most conscious of Ibsen and his one-man revival of drama in Scandinavia. So conscious was he of this movement that he undertook an adaptation of *A Doll's House* with Henry Herman which was seen in 1884. *Breaking a Butterfly* was such a misstatement of Ibsen's dramatic purpose that Jones, in later years, preferred to forget it. Unfortunately it frequently rose to plague him.

The same year came his *Saints and Sinners* and five years later the better-known *The Middleman*. This latter, along with *Wealth* (1889), represent in a sense Jones's effort to use the drama as a means of social reform. These plays and this line of thinking were uppermost in his mind when he wrote *The Renascence of the English Drama* (1895). He was in despair of Pinerotic superficiality of thinking, though he felt that dramatists of late nineteenth-century England had encompassed enormous advances in play structure and the turning of ideas into play form.

He considered the mystical and somewhat confused *Michael and His Lost Angel* (1896) his best play though West End London audiences would have little of it. Shaw, certainly no push-over as a critic, considered it his finest work, and championed it among the Philistines. Among his comedies, two of his best came just about this time, *The Masqueraders* (1894) and *The Liars* (1897). There was some depth in his comedy, but its surface implications were quite sufficient for his audiences for a good long time. The public, and some of the critics, who rejected his chef-d'œuvre, cottoned to *Mrs. Dane's Defense* (1900), which was expressed in much more conventionally theatrical tones and which lent itself to the very smooth acting current in London and New York at the turn of the century. This was a "problem play" and the intellectuals (self-styled) as well as the plainer but no less outspoken play-goers liked a bit of meat to chew on when they went to the theatre. You can't live on a diet of soufflés or cream puffs always, they opined.

The Jones plays that followed are of so little importance that a list of their titles is not needed here. His place in the theatre is measured best by his recognition of Ibsen, by his honesty in writing, by the need to raise standards, by the importance of his forthrightness, rather than by his plays themselves. You have to like this old codger whose background was so evangelical he never saw a play until he was eighteen. He triumphed over background, environment, and fin-de-siècle surroundings and friends.

The decks are cleared. We can now begin a consideration of modern

English drama. This was largely due to the persons of Shaw, William Archer, Gosse, J. T. Grein, Elizabeth Robbins, Janet Achurch, and Florence Foss, and was primarily a personal homage to Ibsen and an understanding of his teachings. The first two were, of course, critic-playwrights; Gosse was pure critic, Grein a manager, and the ladies were all actresses. Of the lot only one was American-born, Elizabeth Robbins; her correspondence with Henry James, ex-patriate dramatist-novelist, has not secured so wide a public as the Shaw-Terry letters but is fully as significant. The ladies were concerned with getting Ibsen done, because quite aside from his ideas, which seemed rather revolutionary even to them, the dramatist knew how to provide meaty acting parts. This is not intended to suggest that their financial sacrifices in producing Ibsen were to be minimized, but that they saw that here was a great writing talent whose work should be displayed to as wide a public as possible.

The year of 1879 had electrified the thinking world by Gosse's illuminating article on Ibsen. Special matinées were arranged of his plays as rapidly as they could be translated. In 1884 Jones and Herman gave birth to their misunderstood version of *A Doll's House*. This Ibsenism was in the air. The Independent Theatre was organized by J. T. Grein in 1891 to provide an outlet for the new English drama as well as translations from the Continent. The Hollander had been responsible for *Ghosts,* which caused the English critics, notably Clement Scott of the *Daily Telegraph,* to get out their nastiest and most putrid adjectives.

Though devotees of the Irish drama may beat their breasts and tear their hair, the compiler of these two sections of drama in the English language is going to rob them of their greatest talent and present it to Britain. The reason for this is a good one. If Shaw himself had seen any possibility of developing along his chosen literary lines on his native heath, he would have done so. Instead he chose to emigrate to England and there to domicile himself permanently. He never returned to Ireland to remain any length of time and he never dedicated his work to any existing Irish theatre except once in his vast literary life. This exception, in the case of *John Bull's Other Island,* is discussed at its chronological point in the story. It was his peculiar pleasure to bait the English but he chose to write about them and to live among them.[1] Modern English drama without Shaw would be as complete as the Elizabethan without Shakespeare. The white-bearded bard can take a well-justified bow. Therefore it was not surprising that

[1] Shaw is so truly a British rather than an Irish or English playwright that this chronicler once contemplated wedding the drama of all sections of the British Commonwealth of Nations into one component whole. His co-editor, Barrett H. Clark, however, persuaded him that the Irish would be so horrified that this would be inadvisable. He might, however, have remained adamant to such admonitions of clear-headed caution if he had not attempted the wedding at least of the English and Irish sections. As a result he nearly lost his life swimming the Irish Sea and decided that perhaps the elder editor was as wise as he was cautious. At any rate Ireland is granted its own section but Shaw has been presented to England—let the Irish confetti fall where it may.

when Grein sought the most likely person around London to give him a full-length English play, his choice fell on the then red-headed Irishman, George Bernard Shaw (1856-   ), whose trumpeting on all subjects were noticeable to the intelligentsia even without ear trumpets. His lively mind had embraced so many subjects that it was natural for a manager to think of him as a likely playwright. Brought up on poverty and hard knocks, and of high tastes and thinking, Shaw is today still a controversial person because his asceticism has always been maintained and his scorn of the fleshpots was and is proverbial. So many biographers have "done" Shaw. Of these the best are Archibald Henderson, Hesketh Pearson (who obviously depended a great deal on his predecessor), and Maurice Colbourne, who was more concerned with winnowing the playwright's millions of words to find out what Shaw thought than to delve into personal biography. So much is known and not known of the man that we are clearly informed on all his opinions whether we agree with them or not, but of his personal life and motivations of being we are still lamentably unserved. If Shaw has the autobiography up his sleeve to come after his death, which he has frequently hinted, then we apparently must be content to wait.

In 1885, William Archer, the critic, who fancied himself more or less correctly an expert at play construction (at least he wrote a book about it which still brings in royalties) and Shaw, who was convinced he could write devilishly good dialogue, agreed to collaborate. Borrowing from one of Augier's plots, Archer provided Shaw with what he considered a perfect scenario. Shaw wrote two long acts which put his collaborator to sleep and that was the end of that. However, when Grein came knocking at his door six years or so later, the manuscript was dug out of a pile of discarded work and a third act was added. Presumably the play was pruned because the audience stayed awake. That, of course, may have been because the author's left-wing friends applauded *Widowers' Houses* (1892) vigorously while the pretty-pretty party hissed. It was Shaw's ideas about landlords and tenements that upset the critics, not his play construction. They damned his drama with a vengeance. Shaw throve on the clamor.

Thus began a career as dramatic author which has offered plays up to and including 1939. The man is still alive and unpredictable so that it is entirely possible there may still be more plays for us to consider before the curtain falls. He followed his première a year later with *The Philanderer*, which the Independent Theatre was unable to cast since Charles Wyndham, who might have played the lead, could not be interested in it. In this "unpleasant play" Shaw was partly autobiographical and partly satirized his friends the Ibsenites. It is typical of him that he should jest at his own friends and supporters for had he not written *The Quintessence of Ibsenism* in 1891, a critical study which still stands today more than half a century later? At any rate production of this piece, which annoyed William Archer as a piece of disloyalty, was abandoned.

The same year brought *Mrs. Warren's Profession* which restored Archer to the Shavian ranks but caused consternation everywhere else. As Shaw hinted—no, stated—that prostitution of women was an inevitable result of the capitalism under which we still live, no manager would touch it and the Lord Chamberlain denied it a license. The ban was lifted in 1924. (Why then? Perhaps a labor government.) But in 1902 the Stage Society produced it for private performances for its own members as these could not be touched by the law. Arnold Daly, against the author's admonitions, produced the piece in New York in 1905. Every one thought it an indecent play so they clamored for tickets and stormed the doors. The police arrested the entire cast and the case was taken to trial and the defendants were acquitted. Shaw's own pertinent comments on the matter were expressed before a committee of Parliament which in 1909 was considering the whole question of the censorship of the stage. The reader is directed to the minutes of the meetings or to the various biographies of G. B. S. for further enlightenment.

After these frightening and unprofitable ventures with the theatre, Shaw began the composition of what he termed "pleasant plays" as opposed to the three preceding them. Here for the first time we perceive his famous wit, his amazing sense of the stage, his conscious juxtaposition of events and expressions which appeared both shocking and delightful. From then on the Shavian star began to rise over Shaftesbury Avenue despite the comparative failure of *Arms and the Man* (1894) with Florence Farr. On opening night the actors played seriously and were extremely funny. After that, having realized it was a comedy they were playing, they changed their style so only one *real* performance of the play was given in its eleven-weeks' run. Later, in this country, it received the success which it deserved and subsequently London learned to like it.

Candida (1897) was certainly the best of Shaw's early plays and has remained an enormous favorite ever since. Almost every actress of note on both sides of the water has attempted the part, but apparently it was not until 1942 that the perfect *cast* was assembled, for Morell and Marchbanks are infinitely more difficult parts to do than the title rôle. Janet Achurch was the first Candida and (to point of writing) Katharine Cornell was the last. It is peculiarly her part. Though she played it three times over fifteen years, it was not until Raymond Massey undertook Morell and, especially, Burgess Meredith became Marchbanks that the play came completely into focus. This play of a woman between two men whose struggle is in reality the important point in the piece won a real public for Shaw despite the usual conservative reactions of its natal day. So enthusiastic were its initial admirers that he characteristically dubbed them "Candidamaniacs," which group, to this day, many genuinely astute critics have been proud to claim as their own.

In 1897, Shaw wrote *The Man of Destiny,* a short play about Napoleon, which he admittedly patterned on Richard Mansfield whose acting he much admired and who had much to do with the initial success of Shaw's plays in America. Mansfield apparently felt that the portrait of himself as Napoleon did not measure up to his own high regard for himself so he rejected the comedy. Ellen Terry (for whom *Candida* had been intended, even though the author had promised it to Janet Achurch) was Shaw's candidate for the Strange Lady. She was, however, so irrevocably wed professionally to Sir Henry Irving, who disliked G. B. S. as cordially as our irascible friend did him, that nothing came of that. Finally Murray Carson produced it at the Grand Theatre in Croydon on July first.

Then came *You Never Can Tell* which he wrote in 1895-1896 with the idea of composing a comedy for the current taste. Cyril Maude took it for performance at the Haymarket, but the play so baffled the cast, who couldn't get the hang of it or understand what the author meant, that he withdrew it after two weeks of rehearsal. All of this fussing and bother annoyed Shaw who quickly grew bored with his own work, though he published the comedy in 1898. The Stage Society performed it the following year and in 1900 it ran for two weeks of matinées at the Strand Theatre and eventually became a great popular draw for the Granville-Barker-Vedrenne management in their days at the Court Theatre in 1907.

Not content with one experience with an actor-manager, our Irish friend decided to write a piece for William Terriss, then a handsome idol in Adelphi melodramas. This was *The Devil's Disciple* (1897) and it would have been produced but for the fact that Terriss was assassinated. Terriss's decision to do it had been influenced by reports of Mansfield's huge success as Dick Dudgeon in America. Then this "melodrama" fell into the hands of Sir Johnston Forbes-Robertson and the playwright was invited to direct it. Evidently tales of Shaw's bad temper and bad manners, which he utilized to get his own way, had reached the ears of the actor-manager. By inviting active participation, he forestalled the famous "silent treatment" to which Maude had been subjected. This fine piece of acting-drama was performed in a suburban theatre (the Coronet at Notting Hill) in September 1900, and then was taken on a provincial tour. This play between England and America brought substantial financial returns to the dramatist. It was the United States which first welcomed Shaw to its bosom despite his calculated insults of "Amurricans." Perhaps our critics and audiences were surer of themselves and what was good than were their British contemporaries....

The next play to come is one of Shaw's most important. *Cæsar and Cleopatra* is undoubtedly the finest drama of his first decade as a playwright. An enormous amount of thought and energy went into the writing of this play which sought to restore to Cæsar the importance and dignity of which Shaw felt Shakespeare had robbed him. He based his objections on the ground that Plutarch influenced the Bard of Avon, while Mommsen and Goethe would have blessed the Bard of Bloomsbury. While he was recovering from an injured foot, he wrote this play mainly on the Isle of Wight where he was honeymooning in 1898. He had intended it for Forbes-Robertson and Mrs. Patrick Campbell who were then playing together. However, they had parted company by the time it was staged in 1907 and Cleopatra was created by Gertrude Elliott (Lady Forbes-Robertson).

This drama has had a considerable influence on modern writing because since then there has developed a marked tendency to treat historical personages and subjects with levity or humorous affection. Any one of you can name a dozen modern plays which probably would never have been written (well, perhaps) if *Cæsar and Cleopatra* had never been played or published. Of course, if we are to take the work of Ferrari (and why shouldn't we, for he is an Italian authority on the subject) Shakespeare's Cæsar is a more realistic and more accurate portrait than Shaw's. Let us let it rest at that.

Shaw's next play comes as a play of idealism opposed to imperialism, which may have been why it was a failure at a time when the British Lion roared intolerantly. *Captain Brassbound's Conversion* was intended for Ellen Terry (how he wooed that lovely lady with words), but she, ever-encumbered with Irving, had to decline to be the first Lady Cicely. Ada Rehan, similarly short-sighted, would have none of it for America, when the Stage Society came along and offered Shaw a production. It was put on in 1900 with Janet Achurch in the part, but she was unable to play the high lady with sufficient distinction and the author was unsatisfied. Finally in the spring of 1907, he got what he wanted once Irving was dead; Ellen Terry *did* play Lady Cicely at the Court Theatre under the Vedrenne-Barker management. Eighty-nine performances were all they could manage and the play was a comparative failure. She took to the road and eventually to America, where as usual with *his* plays and *her* acting, it was a real success.

Then came one of Shaw's super-length pieces, *Man and Superman* which was published in 1903 and staged in 1905. Usually he kept more strictly to the requirements of conventional stage usage. In this he positively cut loose because he was riding his economic theories hard. Nothing can restrain an enthusiast when he has mounted his hobby except a rigorous artistic sense. This Shaw frequently lacks because he is unable, or unwilling, to control his eloquence or garrulousness (depending on how *you* feel about his opinions and his way of expressing them). However, eventually, *Man and Superman* achieved almost an official "cut" version. Esmé Percy seems to have been almost the only actor willing to risk everything on uncut Shaw and this was not until twenty years later. However, Percy has not done badly by his faith or purism because he built up quite a following for his Shavian interpretations. The third act, called *Don Juan in Hell,* is Shaw rewriting the Bible, but it is certainly worth reading and even seeing if the orchestra chairs are well-cushioned and there is enough knee-room, the chronic complaint of the professional play-goer.

This play of creative evolution was published in 1903 and the critics were much impressed with Shaw's thinking and his basic philosophy. The author wrote Sir Johnston Forbes-Robertson,[1] "My last book has turned the tables on the people who will not admit that I am serious: they used to laugh when I was serious; but now the fashion has changed: they take off their hats when I joke, which is still more trying." The play was staged by the Stage Society on May 21, 1905; Harley Granville-Barker was Jack Tanner and boasted a make-up modeled on the author. Two days later it was produced at the famous Court Theatre in Sloan Square. Lillah McCarthy, the first Mrs. Granville-Barker, was Ann and was really wonderful in the part. The play had a very real success in repertory at the Court. When Robert Loraine read the published piece, he fell in love with it and nothing would make him happy until he played Tanner. This he did at the Hudson Theatre in New York on September 5, 1905 for a nine-month's run and a comfortable tour. In 1907 he acted Don Juan Tenorio in the third act when it was performed at the Court. Shaw had now become an established and respected dramatist after fifteen years of trial and error.

William Butler Yeats for some time had been begging Shaw to do his duty to his native country by writing a play for the Irish Literary Theatre. He answered with *John Bull's Other Island* (1903) which proved much too difficult for the Dublin group to produce at that time and was certainly not in keeping with the spirit and style which characterized the Irish literary movement. Its first performance was given at the Court Theatre where it proved successful largely because Shaw's satiric portraits of the Englishman as a prosperous sentimentalist and the Irishman as what Londoners took to be a failure pleased the British public because it set down in theatrical terms what they at that time believed. That Shaw was pulling his leg never struck the average play-goer.

How He Lied to Her Husband (1904) was a one-acter, a kind of mate to *Candida,* which he wrote at Arnold Daly's request to fill out the evening when the latter was acting *The Man of Destiny* in America. *Major Barbara* (1905) was reputed to have been written to please Mrs. Shaw, for in this he dealt with the crime of poverty while considering the Salvation Army as a weapon of moral uplift. Munition makers and those who profit from wars fell under Shavian scrutiny. Andrew Undershaft, the armament manufacturer, is one of his best-drawn characters. The first two acts captivated the audiences, but the last, which is sheer talk even if very good, bewildered them. The enthusiast and reformer won out again over the skilled dramatist.

The various aspects of socialized medicine and medical morality were dissected in *The Doctor's Dilemma* (1906). His opinions are still considered so revolutionary even by those who are *not* members of the American

---

[1] As quoted by Hesketh Pearson in *G. B. S.: A Full Length Portrait* (New York, Harper & Bros., 1942), p. 200.

Medical Association that there was fresh discussion of them a few years ago (1941) on the occasion of the play's most recent revival in New York. In 1943, this ethical drama was running in a London which had been brought by a war-revised economy to very nearly complete sympathy with the author's views.

Getting Married (1908) is an intermissionless play which has never very much attracted audiences or critics, though it has known several revivals on both sides of the Atlantic. The curtain was dropped, for it is a long piece, for the physical relief of the audience, but Shaw maintained his conception of the Aristotelian unities. The same demonstration was given in *Misalliance* (1910) but neither of the pieces seem particularly important now nor did they when they were produced, though the first, when staged, had more real success than the latter. *Press Cuttings* (1909) and *The Shewing Up of Blanco Posnet,* the same year, were next. The latter, a religious tract if there ever was one, was intended for the considerably inflated Sir Herbert Beerbohm Tree, who would have none of it. The Lord Chamberlain, for some unknown reason, considered it irreligious and banned it, so perspicacious was he. It looked as though that might be the end of it for a time when Lady Gregory came to the rescue. A Shaw play finally received its première at the Abbey Theatre and during Horse Show Week too. It is difficult now to discover what all the shooting was about.

In *Fanny's First Play* (1911) Shaw had some fun with his former fellow critics whom he caricatured to their discomfiture (or so it was said at the time) and to the unmixed delight of some of the play's more prescient spectators. It is certainly not out of the author's top drawer, which may explain something of its instantaneous success. Housed in a small theatre with a not-too-expensive cast headed by Lillah McCarthy, always a favorite of Shaw for whom she played many parts, the play ran for six hundred performances. Needless to say, Miss McCarthy had a higher opinion of the piece than any one else though Shaw was never really willing to admit publicly that this was a distinctly lesser opus. Which author is?

In 1912, he got quite definitely into his stride with his religious comedy, *Androcles and the Lion.* This study of early Christianity in ancient Rome should have a salutary effect on the stuffier members of certain *respectable* sects, but I doubt if even the quicker-witted among them take unto themselves these barbs of wisdom. It is, however, a favorite of the average audience as witness the success of the Federal Theatre Project's Negro revival of the piece in the 1938-1939 season.[1] What might have been merely a stunt proved the universality of the dramatist's message regardless of race, color, or previous condition of servitude. Cæsar was treated with humanity and respect and its original production was graced with Granville-Barker's direction and the cast was decorated by Lillah McCarthy, Hesketh Pearson (Shaw's most recent biographer and witty, too), Leon Quartermaine, Ben

---

[1] Seen in revival 1946-1947 by The American Repertory Theatre.

Webster (a fine actor, but more generally referred to as the father of Margaret Webster and the husband of Dame May Whitty), and O. P. Heggie. In New York it adorned the last season of the famous old Wallack's Theatre on Broadway at Thirtieth Street in which Granville-Barker productions did much to revolutionize theatrical art and staging in this country.

Then came the wise and witty *Pygmalion* (1913) which boasted the services of Mrs. Patrick Campbell as Liza Doolittle, the gutter-snipe cockney, who provided the contrast to the brilliance and inhumanity of Henry Higgins, a phoneticist, who was acted by none other than Tree, typecasting of the rankest kind. The story of the rehearsals is unbelievable only to those who have never worked back stage with actors. This dramatic study of the English language and the difficulty of those who, born to it, find it impossible to speak correctly, is both good drama and good theatre. Lynn Fontanne was unforgettable in the Theatre Guild's New York revival in 1926, while in 1940 Gabriel Pascal made a film of it for which Shaw contributed one fine new scene. The garden-party was transformed into a ball which the cinema is well adapted to show. It was a triumph for Wendy Hiller and the costumer Ladislas Czettel.

A series of one-acters produced between 1910 and 1918 failed to advance Shaw as a dramatist. Only *The Dark Lady of the Sonnets* (1910) and *Overruled* (1912) have any merit at all. Before World War I broke out he had been thinking about European civilization along the lines both of Chekhov's reasoning, and dramatic approach. Over a period of years *Heartbreak House* (1920) came to be written while Shaw was fighting for an honest, unsentimental appraisal of the war for which he was hysterically accused of being pro-German and a first-class traitor. Some of the despair which is for the first time to be found in a Shavian drama must have come from his unenviable watching of his fellow-countrymen, his fellow dramatists (like Henry Arthur Jones) go stark, staring mad like frothy-mouthed dogs. Certainly the profundity of his thinking and the darkness of its expression is un-Shavian. Many of his followers reject the play because of this.

He resisted demands that *Heartbreak House* be given a public reading in 1916 and felt that in production it would be swallowed up in the silly froth of the war theatre which was building high in London between 1915 and 1918. It was America and the Theatre Guild which gave it its first presentation and thus began a long association between that group and the author. St. John Ervine affected the introduction and Shaw said that he doubted if in New York there could be a producing organization "bold enough and clever enough to know the alternative to pleasing an audience for two hours is to put the utmost strain upon their attention for three; and send them home exhausted but impressed." [1]

The Guild realized the importance of advancing their prestige by giving

---

[1] As quoted by Walter Prichard Eaton in *The Theatre Guild: The First Ten Years* (New York, Brentano's, 1929), p. 49.

the "world première" to a Shaw play and announced it for October production in a presidential-election year. The canny Irishman, knowing American preoccupation with political affairs at a time like that, stated [1] "better to produce *Heartbreak House* with the first cast you could pick out of the gutter on November fifteenth; than to produce it on October fifteenth with Sarah Bernhardt, the two Guitrys, Edwin Booth, John Drew, Maude Adams, Mary Pickford, and Charlie Chaplin." The Guild's cast was not this one, but it certainly was distinguished and included Elizabeth Risdon, Helen Westley, Albert Perry, Lucile Watson, Effie Shannon, Erskin Sanford, Fred Eric, Dudley Digges, Ralph Roeder, and Henry Travers. It played 129 performances. It was not until 1921 that London saw it first. Orson Welles gave the play a distinguished revival with a superlative cast in the late spring of 1938 in New York.

Next came Shaw's magnum opus of vast length, *Back to Methuslah* (1922), which no one in Britain would have thought of producing, but in those days the Theatre Guild rushed in where angels feared to tread. As a result they lost a $20,000 shirt, but the prestige and satisfaction of doing it was worth the agony, travail, and financial loss. The author wanted it performed at successive evening and matinée performances, certainly the best way, but the Guild subscription list couldn't stand for it as many were not free to attend matinées (the working professional and white-collar class were the mainstay of the list). They compromised by dividing this five-part play of creative evolution transpiring over thousands of years into three sections and performed each for a week (nights only). The budget had to be kept down so Lee Simonson made liberal use of projections in his designs and actors willing to learn several vast sets of sides were engaged to play at least three parts apiece. Irene Lewisohn and Agnes Morgan of the Neighborhood Playhouse staged Parts I and II with George Gaul, Ernita Lascelles, Margaret Wycherly, Dennis King, Albert Bruning, A. P. Kaye, and Claude King. Frank Reicher handled the next two and Philip Moeller directed the finale which was played in the third week. Twenty-five performances of the whole play were given.

When the play was produced by Sir Barry Jackson at the Birmingham Repertory Theatre in October, 1923, it was performed in the sequence Shaw wanted, but these five showings only got through the play once. The following February saw it staged at the Court in London. Interestingly enough Shaw's burlesque of Asquith and Lloyd George as Lubin and Joyce Burge, was as successfully received in New York as it was in England. Shaw's appeal for the lengthening of human life and the general improvement of conditions under which perforce we must live contains some of his best as well as some of his most long-winded writing. It bored many, but stimulated vastly many more.

Now we come to what is probably (I'd say certainly) his best play. *St.*

---

[1] As quoted by Eaton, *op. cit.*, p. 50.

Joan (1923) was long in his mind before he sat down to write it. It was his intention to make a dramatic study of religious belief; the fact that he chose Jeanne D'Arc rather than Mohammed was due to his fear of the effect his daring would have on the Moslem faithful who might consider it their duty to see that he was assassinated for sacrilege.

He intended Joan for Dame Sybil Thorndike but it was Winifred Lenihan who played it first (in New York on December 29, 1923). The revised version did not arrive in time and the play ran endlessly and the critics complained, but the public was taken with it and it ran into the summer and toured (with Julia Arthur) the next season. London saw it with Dame Sybil in March. In 1934, Shaw staged it at the Old Vic with Mary Newcomb as the Maid and Maurice Evans as the Dauphin. In 1937 Katharine Cornell offered New York a successful revival with Mr. Evans in her own production staged by Guthrie McClintic.

The epilogue has been violently attacked as anti-climactic, but Shaw insisted upon it because it was his opportunity to comment upon the influence of Joan upon the world. The rest he insists is straight dramatizing of the records. Those of you who have sat through the trial scene know that it is one of the theatre's most magnificent experiences. Because of this the foolery of the epilogue, which shatters the mood, irritates many. Only after reading and seeing the play many times has this reviewer been able to accept it in the sense which Shaw intended.

After *St. Joan,* he turned his attention to other writing, wore himself out, had a breakdown and a seventieth birthday, and then recovered to write a new piece to inaugurate Sir Barry Jackson's initial Malvern Festival in the Summer of 1929. *The Apple Cart* is not top-flight Shaw, but it contains some of his best writing and most ingenious horseplay. Nothing he has written since has been any better except *On the Rocks* (1933) which had its first showing in Ireland, while *Village Wooing* was seen first in Dallas, Texas in 1934. *Too True to Be Good* (1932) saw the light of day at Malvern. In this Shaw introduced a recognizable portrait of the famous Lawrence of Arabia as Private Meek. America circused the performance by providing a cast which included Beatrice Lillie—a revue artiste and a great one—and Hope Williams, a boyish tomgirl who had created an acting reputation by an amusing walk, clipped speech, and like haircut. *The Simpleton of the Unexpected Isles* (1935) was played first by Nazimova for the Guild and subsequently at Malvern. *The Six of Calais* (1934) was performed in Regents Park in London whereas *The Millionairess* (1936) was first seen in Vienna, subsequently at Malvern. *Geneva* (1938), which satirized Hitler and Mussolini, was performed there and in a revised version later in Canada and New York (1940). The last play of all up to now—Shaw is only ninety now so one can still expect, or at least hope for more—was *In Good King Charles's Golden Days* (1939). This extremely talky but witty piece was reasonably well received in England and at the last Malvern Festival before the outbreak of World War II. It hasn't been seen in America and isn't likely to be unless some public-spirited organization, such as the Pasadena Playhouse, undertakes it, as its acting requirements are demanding and it must be superlatively and expensively produced professionally if it is to pay its own way. In other words it is too great a risk for a commercial manager. Concerned with manners, morals, and ideas of the Restoration period, Shaw brought Charles II and his bigoted brother James, Fox the Quaker, Nell Gwynn, and various of Charles' bawdy duchesses together at Sir Isaac Newton's house. Shavian enthusiasts will revel in it. Here the bearded Irishman is at ninety, and still going strong as far as public pronouncements and letters to the press in his ninety-first year (1947). His is the one giant dramatic talent of England since the Elizabethan period. His is the light that led the dramatic revival in England. He has survived all his confrères and is still the greatest of them all.

There are, one hears, bitter-ender Scottish gentlemen who claim at least as much autonomy for Scotland as the warlike-minded brothers of the neighboring isle claim for themselves. In a history of English drama, however, no such claim for a pure Scottish culture, as opposed to the English, can be put forward as in the case of Ireland. For this reason, then, it is in this section that we are within our rights when we deal with Barrie. If there was ever a writer who was the antithesis of Shaw it was Sir James Matthew Barrie (1860-1937). The tiny Scotsman was as great an egoist as his Irish contemporary, they both made literature, and they both had a great charm, but there the resemblance ends. Sentimentalist to the core, even to saccharinity, devoted to children, a snob to his fingertips, an uncomfortable (if delightful) friend to possess, writing with great effort sometimes as though it was out of his own marrow; this was Barrie. He loved frequently, chivvied his friends into performing impossible and foolish tasks because he wanted them to do it regardless of how much they disliked it, yet was unbearably harsh to them if they crossed him. Much of his personal life was exceptionally unhappy and it was only with children that he was at his best, perhaps because he *really was* Peter Pan, the boy who wouldn't grow up. He told them fascinating stories, tales as delightful to them as Oscar Wilde's amazing stories are to adults.

However, it is Barrie the dramatist with whom we are concerned. He anticipated Shaw by beginning his stage career in 1891. This venture was *Richard Savage,* a collaboration with H. B. Marriott Watson, a four-act drama which was given an afternoon performance at the author's expense. Sir Bernard Partridge (then Bernard Gould), Cyril Maude, and Phyllis Broughton were among those in the cast. The critics damned it justly, but the virus of the theatre was in Barrie's blood and there was no holding him back. He had come to know a lot of actors and managers including Sir Charles Wyndham, Sir Henry Irving, and J. L. Toole, the veteran English low comedian. There were all sorts of opportunities. Ibsen was represented in London, in one way or another, by *A Doll's House, Hedda Gabler,* and *Ghosts,* which inspired Barrie to do a one-act burlesque, then a very popular type, called *Ibsen's Ghost; or, Toole Up to Date,* which Toole (made up like Papa Ibsen), George Shelton, and Irene Vanbrugh acted to the hilt. The audience roared its delight and Barrie was on his way. Then came *Walker, London* (1892) which idea of a houseboat comedy had been in his mind for a long time. Toole, Irene Vanbrugh, Sir Seymour Hicks (then a youngster), and Mary Ansell, an attractive ingénue whom Barrie insisted upon having in the company (and who later became his wife), headed the cast. It was a light and charming, if flimsy comedy, but audiences liked it and it ran over five hundred performances at Toole's Theatre. In 1893 Barrie combined with Sir Arthur Conan Doyle to do an operetta, *Jane Annie; or The Good Conduct Prize,* which was a dud.

The Professor's Love Story (1892) was a somewhat tenuous piece which was rejected by Irving, Alexander, Hare, and Toole. It eventually went (with American rights disposed of for a fifty-pound song) to E. S. Willard who kept it in his repertory to the end of his acting life. It was he who gave this play its London première in 1894 where his performance was admired as well as the play. It was not so successful as *Walker, London* but it paid dividends and displayed that quiet charm which was the first requirement of the Barrie enthusiasts and made them self-constituted drum-beaters for the plays and books of the diminutive Scotsman.

It was inevitable that his popular novel, *The Little Minister,* should be turned into a play (1897), which he was persuaded to do when in New York because Charles Frohman was seeking a vehicle for his fragile, wistful young actress, Maude Adams. The first adaptation was not acceptable because the male rôle overshadowed Lady Babbie, but after the author had left America a new version was accepted by the manager who wished to turn his featured player into a star. It was unveiled at the Empire after a discouraging Washington tryout and was a hit indeed. News of this reached the Haymarket where Cyril Maude and his wife Winifred Emery were rehearsing this story of Scotland at the time of the weavers' riots. The play was a resounding hit, audience *and* critical, and delighted spectators jammed the spacious playhouse from November until mid-July. The legend of Barrie was now really established.

Barrie had to have *his* try at the problem play (the little man must do everything) and it was called, finally, *The Wedding Guest* (1900). Its Scottish beginning was cordially received as being unusual, but the play as a whole was not very well liked. The critics felt that he had yet to master the dramatic form and audibly moaned for more of his novels rather than plays. This despite the success of its predecessor. H. B. Irving, Irene Vanbrugh, and Dorothea Baird appeared in the leads.

The gossamer *Quality Street* (1902) was next and, despite its third-act faults, did more than anything so far to bolster his dramatic reputation. It was Maude Adams who created the lead for Frohman in America, she having liked the success she had with *The Little Minister*. Duplicating her rôle in London was Ellaline Terriss. Her husband, Seymour Hicks, and Marion Terry also headed the cast. This charming tale of a small town of long ago was loved for years and today still radiates the somewhat faded "charrrm" which was the prerogative of the author and his proudest possession.

Once on the highroad of dramatic success, Barrie, who was always stagestruck, pursued his muse with *The Admirable Crichton* (1903), which is one of his most enduring plays. Every extravagance of production was provided by Frohman as manager and Dion (Dot) Boucicault as director. A play with a butler as a hero was unheard of, but it was Barriesque. It was fortunate in possessing more plot and more ideas than usual, which won it rather high critical regard and the public chuckled and laughed over the wittiness of his lines. It was an unmixed pleasure for all concerned with the management of the handsome Duke of York's Theatre. The author enjoyed all the fuss and to-do which go into a play's production. He liked dropping in on rehearsals, making suggestions as to direction, changing situations, ordering the alteration of the settings and even of the lines, in that mystic period which goes into making a perfect first night. He liked children, toys, pretending, games of his own invention, pleasant foolishness. Because of this it is easy to see why those facets of his plays which we admire are the tiny, the perfect, the charming whereas we suspect much of his sentimentality and call it saccharine. However, in *The Admirable Crichton*, Barrie reached his furthest point of development as a dramatist; after that it was always a repetition of small perfect things, and charm, charrm, charrrm.

Next comes the play for which he will always be remembered and which introduced a new phrase into our language which we welcomed, *Peter Pan; or, the Boy Who Never Grew Up* (1904). This piece grew out of his delicious games with children of his friends (he had none of his own) in which he invented a Never-Never Land. Peter came partly from Peter Davies (who eventually became his co-literary executor with Lady Cynthia Asquith), grandson of George du Maurier. Frohman fell in love with this fantastic story of Peter and Wendy as have audiences for forty years. Call it sentimental, call it anything you like, its appeal is still very large. English children and adults (Shaw is supposed to have said it was the grown-ups who really liked it, not the children) saw it at the Christmas holidays every season until the war came along to close the theatres. When the British government recovered from its fright the stages were made available again and *Peter Pan* has reappeared.

The play is one which called for handsome mounting and it got it to the hilt, hang the expense. William Nicholson designed most of the costumes and Henry Ford did Peter's himself. All of the animal masks were carefully done; the lighting was as perfect as could be. Dot Boucicault assembled a magnificent cast which included his sister Nina as Peter, Gerald du Maurier as Mr. Darling and Captain Hook, Dorothea Baird as Mrs. Darling, Hilda Trevelyan as Wendy, Arthur Lupino as Nana the dog, and George Shelton as Smee. This play, by the way, grew through the years so that new scenes and new characters were inserted. The play's influence on children was enormous. Naturally more in England (for it was intended for British children) than in America though Maude Adams found in it one of her most successful rôles. It was last seen in a New York opening with Miss Eva Le Gallienne as a very undressed and attractive Peter at her old Civic Repertory Theatre in the 1928-1929 season.

Then came the one-act, two-scened *Pantaloon* (1905) as a curtain-raiser to *Alice-Sit-by-the-Fire*, which was a short three-act burlesque of the conventional triangle play in which Ellen Terry acted her one and only Barrie rôle. Though it had a small success and Barrie and Frohman were as usual in love with it, the public was rather cold. A three-act spoof is too long. It has, however, several endearing qualities even if Dame Ellen was later to complain the part didn't fit her and she felt as if she were bursting the seams.

What Every Woman Knows (1908) reveals nothing new in Barrie, only a reworking of the old, but his study of a woman who makes a successful man out of her asinine husband is still valid theatre. In London in September Hilda Trevelyan was Maggie Wylie and Gerald du Maurier was John Shand. Lillah McCarthy, Edmund Gwenn, and Lady Tree were in the cast. In America it was inevitably Miss Adams as Maggie, with Richard Bennett playing Shand. It was a resounding success on both sides of the Atlantic, of course. Never having been exposed to the tremendous charm which was Maude Adams' and which did such extraordinary things to her auditors, I can only say that the rôle is a perfect one for the stage[1] after observing Miss Helen Hayes in 1926 and again in 1938 (a very much improved performance) as Maggie.

Then came a succession of one-acters, *Old Friends* (1910) which was hardly worth producing; *The Twelve-Pound Look* (1910) a really masterly piece of technique superbly played by Edmund Gwenn and Lena Ashwell in Charles Frohman's failure of a repertory scheme at Duke of York's, which has been played steadily by amateurs and professionals (notably Ethel Barrymore) ever since; *A Slice of Life* (1910), a burlesque of stage conventions, was also included; and *Rosalind* (1912), an acting vehicle for an actress, in the first case Irene Vanbrugh, it has been played everywhere by everybody ever since.

The Will (1913) had enough plot and basic idea for a full-length piece, but Barrie's writing was becoming more and more compressed. This was offered as a curtain-raiser to *The Adored One, A Legend of the Old Bailey*,

[1] Acted by June Duprez for The American Repertory Theatre, 1946-1947.

which is known in America as *The Legend of Leonora,* a better title. Mrs. Patrick Campbell was Leonora in a play about a woman who was so charming, so delightful, so devastating, that she could murder her husband and be acquitted. Barrie was anticipating some of America's famous murder trials of the 1920's, but a London audience was shocked by it and didn't like it. The gallery booed it on opening night. The author revised it, made the second and third acts a dream, introduced a new scene to explain them, and gave the piece a conventional happy ending. Even that failed to save it. The damage was done. London was *not* amused. Maude Adams played it with success in the United States and Grace George revived it to pleasant returns a dozen years later. It was always better understood and liked in this country.

Half an Hour (1913), a short melodrama, was played at the Hippodrome, a music hall, with considerable popular acclaim among the variety acts. This was the period in which Barrie was intrigued with winning a new audience in this field of the theatre. *Der Tag; or the Tragic Man* (1914) was another in the same company; this one was his contribution to the war effort and rather abortive too. *The New World* (1915) was a curtain-raiser to his musical comedy, *Rosy Rapture, the Pride of the Beauty Chorus,* which failed as a wartime revue. There were other bits and pieces not worth mentioning, so we won't.

A Kiss for Cinderella (1916) was a return to the old Barrie, with all its faults and virtues. Fantasy, sentimentality, charm, they were all there in this story of a London waif in wartime, who populates her world as she would have it. Hilda Trevelyan, closely associated with the author in the public's mind, was Miss Thing and Gerald du Maurier (now a manager-producer) acted the Policeman. In America, Maude Adams, of course, was the little slavey.

The Old Lady Shows Her Medals (1917), with Jean Cadell in London and Beryl Mercer in New York, won real success and appreciation despite the fact that it was another one-acter. This little war play is perfect in its way. Then came *Dear Brutus* (1917), a full-length play and a hit, with Gerald du Maurier as Will Dearth, Arthur Hathaway as Lob (a character not unlike the author), and Faith Celli as the dream-daughter, Margaret (Helen Hayes played her to William Gillette's Dearth in New York). This dream piece caught the English fancy in wartime, but some minor short plays came next, *Barbara's Wedding* and *A Well Remembered Voice,* both in 1918. Then came *Mary Rose* (1920) which packed the Haymarket for 399 performances, and the Barrie enthusiasts loved it. It is as dream-like, as sentimental and, to this writer, as incomprehensible as anything Barrie ever wrote. It had been intended for Maude Adams, but it was Ruth Chatterton who acted it. Then came, in 1921, the first act of a mystery play which in his fifteen remaining years of life he was never able to complete, *Shall We Join the Ladies?* It was given its initial performance as a benefit for the Royal

Academy of Dramatic Art (Tree's old school) with a cast made up of ex-academicians. The cast was a tribute to Barrie as well as to the school. Dion (Dot) Boucicault, Fay Compton, Charles Hawtrey, Dame Sybil Thorndike, Cyril Maude, Lady Tree, Leon Quartermaine, Lillah McCarthy, Nelson Keys, Madge Titheradge, Sir Johnston Forbes-Robertson, Irene Vanbrugh, Marie Lohr, Norman Forbes, Hilda Trevelyan, and Sir Gerald du Maurier composed the company. The play was regularly produced in London the following year with a group of actors more nearly in keeping with the slight if delightful proportions of his single act. In America in January 1925, Margaret Lawrence, Leslie Howard, and Ilka Chase were seen in it at the Empire as an afterpiece.

We are now come to Barrie's last play, a retelling of the Biblical story which the elfin personality of Elisabeth Bergner inspired, *The Boy David* (1936). Some passages of the play have the old charm, but for the most part it is longwinded and deeply involved. Neither critics nor public were very appreciative and the author was too ill to do the rewriting necessary. He was very nearly dying and did not long survive his last play. Barrie was the sentimental balance to Shaw's witty vivisection. His was the best representation of fantasy, whimsy, and quiet imaginativeness to be found in recent English drama.

The next of the great Old Guard for us to consider is John Galsworthy (1867-1933) who was introduced to the stage by Harley Granville-Barker in 1906 at the Court. His career as a successful novelist already established, Galsworthy represented the results of a pioneering manager's efforts to induce first-rate writing talents to contribute to the theatre. *The Silver Box* dealt with the special problems of the servant class and its relations to its employers. Always concerned with social problems, at least in so far as drama is concerned, Galsworthy made a fetish of being fair to both sides. This honorable characteristic weakened the dramatic qualities of most of his plays because audiences really like to identify themselves passionately with one side or the other. For this reason many persons, then and now, find the cool, balanced fairness of this dramatist *too* untheatrical for their tastes. However, this same characteristic has made such plays as *Strife* (1909) and *Justice* (1910) notable and credible portrayals of problems of labor-management and legal justice in a fashion that a more hysterical approach could never equal. It is in the latter piece that Galsworthy really gets under the skin of his audience.

Joy (1907), *The Little Dream* (1911), and *The Eldest Son* (1912) are sound, if rather unexciting writing. In *The Pigeon* (1912) the creative artist in himself was expressed in his plea for recognition of the humanity of the artist in a world organized for Philistines. Then came *The Fugitive* (1913) which was a study of a woman's personal problems and her effort to maintain herself in society. In *The Mob* (1914), he was concerned with the injury done an individual man in wartime. We find it difficult to accept some of his special pleading in his assignment of causes for the mental anguish and final death of Stephen More.

A somewhat similar character, Michael Strangway, appears in *A Bit O'Love* (1915), which is a curious, if pleasant combination of high-mindedness and rustic wit, which latter he handles very well indeed. *The Foundations* (1917) was almost straight comedy, his nearest approach to that type of writing. He gave it up in *The Skin Game* (1920) in which he turned to the brittle rivalry of the established, aristocratic Hillcrists and the crude, nouveau-riche qualities of Hornblower. This was a life and death struggle which probably seemed much more important in 1920 than it did when both parties to the quarrel are on the same side in the mighty effort of England to survive Hitler's damnedest and conquer with us all.

Windows (1922) shows Galsworthy tackling the problem of what happens in a family when they are divided by idealism and practicality and come up against a concrete problem in their midst. Rather ineffective writing and thinking, but in *Loyalties* (the same year) he composed one of his finest plays. He boldly tackled the question of anti-Semitism in upper-class England and set it in such broadly dramatic terms as to render it a popular as well as a critical success. *The Forest* (1924) is a lesser piece of writing, but in *Old English* (1924) he wrote his best acting part for the stage, which was superbly interpreted by George Arliss. This is entirely a character comedy whereas in *Escape* (1926) he modified the film chase to permit Galsworthian comment on the merits of the man who is endeavoring to escape the ill effects of an innocent action. It should be compared with *Cynara* in its somewhat different treatment of a similar problem. Neither *The Roof* (1929) nor *Exiled* (1929) have much to say to us. Of his short pieces, *The Little Man* (1915) is by far the best and the most performed. Galsworthy represents the enlightened upper-middle-class point of view in England. He was class conscious in a way not intended by the present-day followers of Karl Marx. Snob he was not, but he recognized an England of class privileges and differences and so recorded them. His thinking seems out of place at the present time of writing. Perhaps this war will teach us nothing (he showed that he understood that of the last struggle) and his ideas will again become apropos, or at least analogous. His fairness, pity, and irony are his strength and weakness as a dramatist.

Harley Granville-Barker (1877-1946) couldn't always find the plays to produce and act that he wanted so he wrote them as well. His initial venture by himself was *The Marrying of Ann Leete* (1901) which is realistic in concept and treatment, yet is concerned with the mystery of life, as is *Man and Superman,* and has been compared with *Heartbreak House* and Chekhov's *The Cherry Orchard* for its symbolism and mystery. He turned from this to fantasy of a gentle and comic mold in *Brunella* (1904) which he wrote with Laurence Housman. Then the next year he returned to his accepted style in *The Voysey Inheritance*. That is, he is realistic in a natural way, seeking to fit his dialogue to his characters in a fashion that Shaw never attempted and Barrie but rarely. This is true of *Waste* (1907), which the Lord Chamberlain banned from the stage because Granville-Barker had returned to the idea of life continuing through sexual connection which was implicit in *The Marrying of Ann Leete,* as well as in *The Madras House* (1910), his best play. In *The Madras House* he discovers, through the ministrations of Mrs. Huxtable, the tyranny of convention and its destruction of human rights and values. He wrote this for its broad theatrical effect at a time when such examples were rare but not unknown. Now they all may be said to have disappeared, but we have only to search our own memories or to look around us in our families and friends to see lesser examples of the same thing.

These plays represent Granville-Barker's most important contribution to English drama. Several others have borne his name. He arranged Thomas Hardy's mighty pageant, *The Dynasts* (1904-1907), for production in 1914. His translation of Schnitzler's *Anatol* and Jules Romains' *Dr. Knock* are matched by a dozen translations from the Spanish of Martinez-Sierra with his second wife, Helen Granville-Barker. His force in the theatre, as an actor, a producer, and a stage director *par excellence* have perhaps surpassed his writings. It is certainly true that in recent years we have been tempted to think of his management of the Court Theatre, his superb productions in the last season of Wallack's Theatre on Broadway at Thirtieth Street, rather than of his composition of plays. Nonetheless, along with Galsworthy, he is responsible for much of the firmness of the base of modern English drama.

St. John Hankin (1860-1909) lies between Shaw and Granville-Barker in so far as realism is concerned. His work is witty, urbane, mildly cynical, carefully constructed. These plays are not very well known in America and a reading of them is recommended so as to understand the way in which he eluded Victorianism and made progress toward the unspectacular method of improving dramatic standards which is characteristic of him and of other middle-of-the-roaders. *The Two Mr. Weatherbys* (1903) was his first play and *The Last of the De Mullins* (1908) was the last. His best known full-length drama is *The Cassilis Engagement* (1907) in which he shows the workings of a clever woman to defeat an unfortunate and unhappy marriage for her son. That she succeeds and that Hankin understands the clarity of motive and methods of his lady, is a tribute to them both. His last drama seems to indicate that it was his intention finally to emerge into the kind of realism which was Granville-Barker's and more particularly Stanley Houghton's. A comparison of *The Last of the De Mullins* is invited with *Hindle Wakes*.

In the large industrial city of Manchester there was a great lady of the theatre who did as much to enlarge the horizon of the English stage as any other single one of the giants and more than some. Miss A. E. F. Horniman was responsible for the financial backing which permitted some of the early experimental productions in London, notably Florence Foss's at the Avenue Theatre. She aided the great Abbey Theatre of Dublin, but it is because of her fine work at the Gaiety Theatre in Manchester that we remember her especially. Not only did she develop fine actors, but she gave impetus to native writing. Her encouragement of authors in the so-called Manchester school of playwrights was of demonstrable value.

Stanley Houghton (1881-1914) wrote several one-acters and a long play or two, but it is for his *Hindle Wakes* (1912) that he is likely to be remembered. This drama honestly considers the mental state of an enlightened young woman who knows her own mind. It is unlikely that Houghton would have ever created Fanny Hawthorn without the stimulus which Ibsen brought to modern drama. Fanny spends a week-end with a young man, Alan Jeffcote, and when the news of this escapade comes out, does not want him to marry her despite the pressure both families bring on them. She had entered into the affair as light-heartedly as a man would have done and had no intention of being married to a man whom she did not respect even if she *had* momentarily desired him. The piece created a stir in England which is still remembered. Whether Houghton could have advanced as a writer is unknown because he died too soon after to allow for more than one or two more one-acters.

Another one-play author (to all intents and purposes) is Elizabeth Baker whose first piece, *Chains* (1909), made her reputation. She has never come near equaling it since, though she continued play writing for another twenty years. She dealt with the dreary little suburbs of London as Houghton had written of Manchester. It is the story of two families, with a free spirit in each who chafes at the bonds. It is not love but a passionate desire for release from boredom which motivates Charley and Maggie. Maggie escapes her further entanglements, but Charley is anchored forever by the announcement that his self-satisfied wife Lily, is presenting him with a baby which will effectually hold him no matter how high his spirit may soar. For *The Price of Thomas Scott* (1913) Miss Baker found a producer in Miss Horniman at Manchester. This play concerns itself with the struggle of a puritan between comfort and self-imposed duty in which the latter wins after a heavy and bitter battle.

George Calderon (1868-1915) participated in the same movement, but his work was confined to the one-act play form. C. Hadden Chambers (1860-1921) moved in more conventional fields being a champion of the "well-made play." His two best-known examples were *The Tyranny of Tears* (1899) and *Tante* (1913). Harold Chapin (1886-1916) was much more of an original with his *Augustus in Search of a Father* (1911), *It's the Poor That Helps the Poor* (1915), and *The New Morality* (1916). Guy Du Maurier (who died in 1916) wrote one play, *An Englishman's House* (1909), which created a stir as it depicted an England invaded and outraged.

Hubert Henry Davies (1871-1916) was a polished and conventional writer of the period who delighted his audiences. Beginning with *Cousin Kate* (1903), a pleasing study of a young woman, he passed on to the brittle improprieties of *Mrs. Corringe's Necklace* (1903) and the more serious *The Mollusc* (1907). *Outcast* (1914) dealt with the double standard of marriage and a high-grade courtesan and was probably his most successful piece of writing commercially, though *Cousin Kate* and *The Mollusc* were much better dramatically.

Alfred Sutro (1863-1933) was a serious writer of the well-made play who moved from drama to light comedy with that expert efficiency which is the hallmark of the second- or third-rate talent. In his more than thirty years of play writing he was one of the most popular dramatists of his day. His first great success was *The Walls of Jerricho* (1904), though the short piece *Carrots* (1900), which treated one of his favorite topics, that of money, had been well liked. In this a man wrings happiness out of life and saves his soul despite his fortune. In contrast *John Glayde's Honor* (1907) dramatizes the story of a man who loses all in life because of his devotion to money. *The Fascinating Mr. Vanderveldt* (1906) was delightful, scintillating, but completely artificial. *The Perplexed Husband* (1911) wavered between serious drama and broad burlesque in its treatment of the feminist movement. Of *The Laughing Lady* (1922), Thomas H. Dickinson said that Sutro "handles clichés so expertly as to give the illusion of life." He was a stylist of the well-made tradition and as such occupied an honored position in the commercial theatre though it is rather unlikely that his plays will ever be revived.

Israel Zangwill (1864-1926) was a distinguished Jewish dramatist who selected certain subjects close to his heart, or to that of his race, for consideration. *Children of the Ghetto* (1899) was a semirealistic attempt to evaluate several Jewish problems where as *Merely Mary Ann* (1903) was primarily a somewhat sentimental character study. *The Melting Pot* (1908) endeavored to dramatize the problem of racial amalgamation. *The War God* (1911) asserted its theme in its title. *We Moderns* (1926) was an honest attempt to evaluate post-war society. Zangwill's dramatic contribution was not outstanding but his plays were sufficiently notable for him to achieve a kind of fare which was quite outside that usually accorded to more conventional, less socially-minded playwrights.

Another provincial dramatist was Harold Brighouse (1882-   ) whose work is closely identified with the northern industrial city, being the second of the Manchester School of Playwrights. He wrote many one-act pieces which have been widely played, such as *Lonesome-Like* (1911); *The Hillary's* (1915), with Stanley Houghton; *Maid of France* (1917); and *Followers* (1915). He is known for his Lancashire comedy, having a pleasing facility in this medium. Of his long plays, *Hobson's Choice* (1916) has had wide success on both sides of the Atlantic. Another of the Manchester School is Allan Monkhouse (1858-1936) who alternated between light comedies and minor tragedies. His was a small talent and his two plays most likely to be remembered for a certain perfection of their kind are *The Grand Cham's Diamond* (1918), a one-acter; *The Conquering Hero* (1923), which was a psychological drama of war's effect on a sensitive man; and *The Education of Mr. Surrage* (1912), an entertaining light comedy with dialogue which is quite as good as St. John Hankin. While this group was bridging the gap from pre-war to post-war England there were certain men who wrote for the theatre whose output was of no particularly high calibre, but whose work had sufficient success on the stage to merit at least some mention in a work of this kind. The novelist George Moore blossomed early with *The Strike at Arlingford* (1893), *The Bending of the Bough* (1900), and especially *Esther Waters* (1911), a dramatization of his famous novel. His heart was never really in it as he was principally a fictionist who could not adapt his literary abilities to the compulsion and compactness of the play form. Greta Sowerby contributed in *Rutherford and Son* (1912) a grim and somber drama of industrialism which was much admired at the time and it is still regarded as an honest piece of writing.

Arnold Bennett (1867-1931) tried more often and cared more about it, though he had conspicuous success only once, and then he collaborated with a trained, if uninspired playwright, Edward Knoblock (American-born though domiciled in London) on *Milestones* (1912). This saga of the rise of an English industrial family carried with it some of the cumulative savor of his novels. *The Great Adventure* (1913) was a social comedy of some merit. Another commercially successful playwright whose work has covered a vast number of years and a vast number of plays is Louis Napoleon Parker (1852-1944). He is, however, likely to be remembered best for a star's acting vehicle, *Disraeli* (1911), which raised George Arliss to international fame through his various tours and the two film versions of the play. The script will not bear too close inspection, but as an acting venture, it is extremely effective. The following year Parker obliged again with a bit of Victorian and whimsical charm, *Pomander Walk,* which was later turned into an attractive musical piece, *Marjolaine*. Of his long list of plays, the one-acter, *The Monkey's Paw* (1905) dramatized from the story by W. W. Jacobs was (and is) deservedly successful. Graham Moffat (1866-   ) obliged with a bit of Scotch quaintness, which tugged both at the audience's heart and purse strings to good effect, *Bunty Pulls the Strings* (1911).

There were countless other writers in this period who contributed one or more works to popularity. Our concern must be for the principal dramatists who influenced the course of the stage and its performed works and who thus determined the conditions under which the lesser lights worked then and now.

Though their poetry was never indigenous to the soil as was that of their Irish confrères, there were in the early part of the century certain English writers who wove that phase of literary art into their plays. Certainly the leading person to attempt to restore poetry to drama at this time was Stephen Phillips (1868-1915). His talent was certainly no match for his Irish brothers in the theatre, but in a respectable conventional sort of way he set out to match them. He was rated rather too high in his own time and then distinctly too low later. Now it can easily be seen that his position was at the top of the third or very low in the second rank of poetic dramatists. For his own time in England he was very nearly unique. Not really conscious of what was happening across the Irish Sea, his eyes were fixed on Greece, but naturally enough he was most successful when he adhered to the Elizabethan tradition as he did in *Paolo and Francesca* (1901). This had come about because of the contemporary demand for literary drama, which cry the actor-manager, Sir George Alexander, had headed in commissioning Phillips to do a play after reading his published verse. *Herod, A Tragedy* (1900), however, was performed first as Beerbohm Tree marched in while Alexander dallied. As his titles indicate, Phillips was in love with the remote past; the last three pieces were *Ulysses* (1902), *The Sin of David* (1904, acted 1914), and *Nero* (1906), but it is for this first play that he is likely to be remembered—if at all.

Another lyric writer who was attracted to the theatre was John Masefield (1875-   ) who became Poet Laureate in 1930. Of his poetic dramas, none had so much power as *The Tragedy of Nan* (1908) which he wrought out of the folk ways of England. This is a high tragedy of considerable merit which he was never able to equal. *The Campden Wonder* (1907) in prose and the psychological piece, *The Witch* (1910) from the Norwegian of H. Wiers-Jensen, are two others works which deserve mention. *Pompey the Great* (1910), however, fails because its last act is not strong enough. This, too, was written in prose, but nonetheless has high lyric quality and his characterization of the great Roman leader is finely done. In *Philip the King* (1914) Masefield turns to rhyme to show the tortured, superstitious mind of the monarch who launched the Spanish Armada against England. *The Faithful* (1915) was a prose tragedy of the Japanese fanatic mind interspersed with lyric passages, and in *Melloney Holtspur* (1923) he went into spiritualism and drew some of his characters from beyond the grave. Christ's passion is the subject of *Good Friday* (1917) and *The Trial of Jesus* (1916) which are more pious than dramatically successful plays. Jezebel is the leading character of *A King's Daughter* (1928) and Masefield, too, had recourse to famous legend in his *Tristan and Isolt* (1927); in 1937 he adapted a French Miracle play under the title of *The Empress of Rome*. He did much to advance poetic drama beyond the standard set by Stephen Phillips. His lyric passages are uplifting even if his dramatic structure never matched his poetry except in his sorrowful story of Nan, his greatest play and a high-water mark in English poetic composition for the stage.

Perhaps this is as good a place as any to consider John Drinkwater (1882-1937) who was a poetic as well as a historical playwright. Though he belongs primarily to the post-war writers he is allied to Phillips, Masefield, and Flecker, and so, perhaps, should be discussed out of turn. His first play came in the first year of World War I in *Rebellion,* which was a protest in prose against what Victorianism stands for. In 1917 he published *Four Poetic Plays,* the best of which was a pæan to peace, *X—O; A Night of the Trojan War,* which borrowed from the great Euripides. His best play, *Abraham Lincoln* (1919), had a deserved success both in England and America. This play was popular because Lincoln's story is essentially dramatic, rising to a high climax. For this very reason, *Oliver Cromwell* (1920, published 1921, acted 1922) and *Robert E. Lee* (1923) were failures as dramas. *Mary Stuart* does not completely succeed either, but it is subtly written and has sections of fine poetry and high drama. Drinkwater had a great hit in *Bird in Hand* (1927), a pleasant little comedy of small people which shows a family relationship with *The Farmer's Wife* (1916, but acted 1924) by Eden Phillpotts (1862-   ) which too, had a great success as did *Yellow Sands* (1926) by Eden and Adelaide Phillpotts. Of Drinkwater's later plays, the most important was *A Man's House* (1934) which treats of Jesus in the familiar indirect fashion in which the impact of the Messiah is reflected in the events in one Jewish household. With the important exceptions of *Abraham Lincoln* and *Bird in Hand,* Drinkwater's plays make better reading than playing as you can easily test for yourself.

Another poet in England in this period wrote for the stage. He was James Elroy Flecker (1884-1915) who composed *Don Juan* (written 1911, published 1925) which Shaw admired publicly, but above all, *Hassan* (published 1922). This Oriental piece shows somewhat his similarity of interest with Dunsany. Some critics felt it pretentious and rated it on a par with Edward Knoblock's *Kismet* (1912) and the wartime musical extravaganza of phenomenal run, Oscar Ashe's *Chu-Chin-Chow* (1916). However, careful reading shows it to be full of sensuous beauty and poetic concept. It had a good run in London in 1923-1924 in somewhat abridged form with ballets by Fokine and music by Delius. Flecker never saw either of his plays published or produced. Had he been granted more encouragement, what might he not have done?

Stephen Phillips was the writer who restored poetry to the English stage as the dramatic work of the Victorian writers was almost wholly confined to the library. He was certainly not without his influence though Dunsany belongs rather to the Irish school despite his residence in London. For this reason, it fell on Laurence Binyon (1869-   ), Phillips' cousin, to carry on his relative's rather pompous style. *Paris and Oenone* (1906) attracted little attention, but *Attila* (1907) was resounding enough to be acclaimed for its "poetic dignity" and "splendid effect." This blank-verse drama was well received by critics and public alike. *Sakuntala* (1919) was an adaptation from *The Kalidasa* whereas in *Arthur* (1923), written in collaboration with the actor Sir John Martin-Harvey, and in *Boadicea* (1925) he explored early

British history without conspicuous success. His real position in the literary-artistic world came rather more from his post as Keeper of Prints and Drawings at the British Museum than as a writer. Years later, by coincidence, a similar post came to be occupied by James Laver, whose contributions to the theatre were *Nymph Errant* (1933) a phantasmagoric, satirical, musical comedy by Romney Brent from Laver's novel of the same name, *The House That Went to Sea* (1936), and a literary drama of Shelley's life, *The Heart Was Not Burned* (1938). Laver is at the Victoria and Albert Museum.

Gordon Bottomley (1874-   ), though born East of the Irish Sea, was more than a little influenced by the poetry writers of Erin. It has been said of him, that though he set many of his plays in Scotland, that his folklore was Irish. He began with *The Crier by Night* (1902), though it was *King Lear's Wife* (1915) which won him fame in Sir Barry Jackson's Birmingham Repertory Theatre production. *Gruach* (1921) was well received and won the Femina-Vie Heureuse Prize in Paris in 1923.

Lascelles Abercrombie (1881-1938) was perhaps better known as a poet and lecturer on the drama than as a playwright. Of his six plays from *The Adder* (1913) to *Phoenix* (1923), the best known and the best-liked was *Deborah* (1913). In this he showed he was a poet of unusual force, originality, and power to excite, amongst other emotions, terror. He was a psychological poet-dramatist and so is the logical bridge to the Eliot modern school which presently occupies England's stage. But of that group we will speak when we reach them in our chronology.

The 1914-1918 cataclysm had a profound effect on the drama of the British Isles. Most of its younger writers were in the armed services and contributed little or nothing to the stage. The elder dramatists such as Shaw, Barrie, and Galsworthy wrote little that was important and the theatre was largely given over to that which was completely trivial. Anglo-Saxons apparently cared little for that which was intellectually stirring in World War I. This time, people took what they were fighting for more seriously and occasionally want it to find outlet on the stage. This is more true of London and the provincial English cities than of America which seeks complete escapism. The actual bombing of England brought a keen interest in the forces which go to make up war.

The last war provoked enormous disillusion among the young men and women because they saw their agony and travail go for naught as the politicians dissipated what they had fought for so bravely. They saw the old rivalries rise anew and the same stupidities return to plague us all and so to build a new war and a more horrible one. This time we cannot fail the peace.

Loosening of marriage bonds, sexual promiscuity, brutality and the horrors of modern war were reflected in the writing of those who survived World War I or who grew to adolescence in its devastating life. The stage was filled with pieces of extreme bitterness, of vast cynicism and sardonic contemplation of the ruins of decent living. These conditions affected the elder dramatists less because their philosophies and habits of thinking had been formed in the generation before the war. But in the writing and thinking of England's "lost generation" we find reflection of all these things.

Even a man such as William Somerset Maugham (1874-   ) whose stage career had begun in a quieter period with comparatively trivial comedies was shaken by this experience to the extent that his plays took on a brilliant bitterness which elevated him as a dramatist. After a beginning with *Schiff Bruchig* (1901) in German in Berlin, he followed with *A Man of Honour* (1903) and the scintillant, if scarcely profound, style in *Lady Frederick* (1907). It was not, however, until his serious comedy, *Our Betters* (1917), that Maugham could be counted of any real theatrical importance. Unproduced in England until after the war, this mordant piece is one of the best expositions of Anglo-American manners and tastes among those of the wealthy who have little nationalism in their make-up. There seems little international solidarity of a point of view except in those who live below the subsistence level and in those who flourish extravagantly far above it in what is known accurately enough as "the international set" or "that Riviera crowd."

The Circle (1921) is his other comedy which deserves high rank today. This comedy of manners has frequently been compared with the best work of Congreve, Wycherley, Sheridan, and Wilde. Maugham does not come off too badly in the comparison. Unfortunately, he has pandered to tawdry taste for most of his theatrical career with such popular pieces of tripe which have been saved by superior acting as *East of Suez* (1922), *The Sacred Flame* (1925), or *The Letter* (1927). Then just to prove that he can turn in a bit of first-class comic writing he offered us the witty and moderately wise, *The Constant Wife* (1927). His best piece of serious drama is *For Services Rendered* (1932) which is an appallingly realistic study of the effect of modern war on a typical middle-class English family. Maugham's contribution to twentieth-century English drama lies in his realistic depiction of the manners and morals of his time.

One of the reasons that the survey of dramatic writing is so completely fascinating is the very considerable range allowed to its contributors. Living and writing at approximately the same time as the worldly Maugham is that compounder of whimsy, fancy, and treacle, Alan Alexander Milne (1882-   ) who shares some of Barrie's most endearing and most exasperating qualities. He, like many of the most successful British dramatists of the present day, is inordinately fond of thin, but brilliant situations, dramatic fluff blown up by the polite laughter which London audiences prefer. His plays, like those of Coward, van Druten, or Munro, abound in quiet humor that crosses the Atlantic more nearly intact in book form than on the stage.

Milne began his stage-writing career with an amusing piece cut down from three acts (about too little) to one, which was just right for the comic idea of *Wurzel-Flummery* (1917). *Belinda* came along the following year and was full length, but the subject was too slight for serious consideration. *The Lucky One* (1919) came to the stage several years later and was somewhat more serious in tone, being a character study of two brothers, one brilliant, one dull; of course, the tortoise won the race for the hand of the girl they both wanted in typically Æsopish fashion.

His first play of popular importance was *Mr. Pim Passes By* (1919), a gently satiric and sentimental piece which scored a tremendous success in both London and New York. Irene Vanbrugh and Laura Hope Crews, respectively, were the charming Mrs. Marden who married twice. *The Romantic Age* (1920) had more sentiment than satire, but in *The Truth About Blayds* (1921) Milne tells the story of a great literateur who, having long tyrannized his adoring family circle, horrifies them by his death-bed confession that he had stolen the work of another and palmed it off as his own. After the flurry is past it becomes evident to the family that it would be financially and socially more beneficial to them to disregard the confession as an old man's fancy and say nothing of it to the world—which they do. This is probably Milne's best play.

The Dover Road (1922) is frankly a contrived, if amusing, comedy which failed to advance him as a dramatist though it has long pleased English and American audiences. His situation is that of a farce, but his development of his characters is in the comedy tradition. In *The Ivory Door* (1927), *The Perfect Alibi* (1928), and *Michael and Mary* (1929) he marched deeper and deeper into sentiment, but he had found a large and quiescent audience which reveled in it. There was always enough saltiness mixed in with the sweet to keep it from cloying the popular taste of a decade ago. For the past few years, Milne has lost touch with this audience and so has written for the reading rather than the seeing public. *The Ivory Door* was a romantic fantasy about appearances which was a tremendous hit in Charles Hopkins' tiny New York Playhouse. For a few years, while the stars of the producer-director and playwright were in the ascendant, people were saying that here was another Frohman and Barrie combination. The illusion is gone now, but it was pleasant while it lasted. *The Perfect Alibi* was that anomaly on the stage, a literate detective-comedy and as such had deserved success, though it certainly added little to Milne's not very towering stature as a playwright. *Michael and Mary* had more quality than any of his later plays, sentimental it was, but it came at a time when the wide public was rather fed up with the noisy, so-called sophistication which came in the years before the depression and so it won many hearts by its quiet charm and that neat felicity of phrase which brought Milne into prominence in several fields of literary expression.

C. K. Munro (1899-   ) is next in line for consideration. His talent for the theatre is definitely special and is not as general as that of Milne. His appeal to the British public has certainly been much more considerable than in the United States. It cannot be reiterated sufficiently that we cannot properly evaluate English dramatists if we overlook the reaction of American audiences. Perhaps Albion's reaction to the playwrights on this side of the Atlantic is less important because it took the emotionalism (and, we trust, the clear thinking) of World War II to make Britishers conscious that there is an American literature whether dramatic or not and that it is liable to appreciation on, at least, equal terms.

It is certainly not intended by this generalization to make a point that Munro has been embraced by the land of his adoption (he is a native of North Ireland) for he has been chastised by his critics even oftener than he has won real popular approval. This success came mainly for his *At Mrs. Beam's* (1921) which is an enlivening and satiric portrayal of a London boarding-house, invaded by an attractive, unscrupulous, and romping pair of crooks. Its companion piece is *Coronation at Mrs. Beam's* which is explained by the connotations of its title. In contrast to these we have several plays which were severely criticized because of Munro's wordiness. *The Rumour* (1922) might equally have been subject to attack because he chose to castigate imperialism and the breakdown of democratic principles. *Storm* (1924) and *The Mountain; or the Story of Captain Yevan* (1926) were similarly criticized because of Munro's loquacity. Like Shaw, when he mounts his hobby, he tosses aside his blue pencil.

If the average man on the street in London, Johannesburg, Sydney, Montreal, Auckland, Edinburgh, or New York were queried as to the playwright he thought most representative and most outstanding of post-war Britain, it is reasonably sure that the answer would be Noel Coward (1899-   ). This exceptionably versatile young man (author, dramatist, actor, producer, director, scenarist, cinema director, composer) has about run the gamut of theatrical expression in the nearly quarter of a century since his first play was staged. He has attempted farce, comedy, drama, satire, historical drama, and literary documentary film with equal facility. He was said to have been lacking in genuine emotion and any of his work on that side was called thin until he came along with the sentimental *Cavalcade* (1931) which was even more popular as a film, and the stirring *In Which We Serve* (1942) a semi-documentary cinema.

After mild and casual beginnings, Coward burst into theatrical prominence with his writing (and acting) of *The Vortex* (1924). In this he deals with the distinctly "unpleasant" situation of a mother who is heartbroken over the loss of her young lover to the sweetheart of her son who is a drug addict and a neurotic. Their scene of mutual recrimination and finally of reconciliation was the highlight of a play the sensationalism of which won considerable popular and critical support. Noel Coward and Lillian Braithwaite's acting played no small part in the success of the piece, which ended at the very point that it became genuinely enthralling. *Fallen Angels* (1925) lays its principal claim to fame on an extremely funny drunken scene in which two young married women break down and tell all while they await the arrival of an all-important young man. *Hay Fever* (1925) is popularly supposed to have been inspired by a week-end the author spent with the family of a well-known American actress. Certainly this is a brilliant comedy about a worthless lot of people. *Easy Virtue* (1925) is a kind of *The Second Mrs. Tanqueray* in reverse, as in this instance it is a bourgeois society which is castigated because of its lack of tolerance toward a lady who has loved widely and well. In his satirical treatment of a well-born County family, Coward is at his best.

Neither *This Was a Man* nor the jazzed-up Ruritanian comedy *The Queen was in the Parlour* nor the delicate but unimportant *The Marquise* (all 1927), added a thing to his reputation. These plays did, however, reveal the fact that he was writing too fast and was forcing a talent that is at its best only when it has allowed an idea to mature before setting it down on paper. Financial pressure in the beginning and then a desire to capitalize on "all of this wonderful new publicity and success" betrayed him.

Then came *Home Chat* (1927), *Sirocco* (the same year), his highly successful musical revue, *This Year of Grace* (1928) in which he co-starred with Beatrice Lillie, and then his nostalgic, sentimental, and delightful operetta, *Bitter Sweet* (1929). Coward alternates between sentimentality and cynicism in all of this period and basically neither have entirely left him, nor is it likely that they will; they are too ingrained by now.

Private Lives (1930) was his first fully rounded piece of comic writing. That it was still being played in America on tour as these lines were written gives some idea of its popularity, for most modern plays have a shorter life. Producers force them to the utmost to make every penny out of them before the inevitable film version is released. *Private Lives* represents an economical use of the essential characters in a study of marital relations and cloaks the carefulness of its psychology in the language of high comedy. The result was so good that Coward's writing has leaned in this direction ever since.

Cavalcade (1931) is said to have been written because a large production was needed to populate the vast stage of Drury Lane, but it turned out to be a stirring drama of England from the Boer War to Armistice Night in World War I. This was transformed into one of the most effective films the studios have yet turned out for the public. In *Design for Living,* two years later, Coward turned to an entertaining, if highly unusual, love triangle which offered two men and a woman in every possible combination. This had a tremendous "smart" success though the homosexuality involved probably kept it from attaining broad acceptance. Coward, Alfred Lunt, and Lynn Fontanne starred in its original production which took place in New York.

Conversation Piece (1934) was a tour de force in that it was written in both French and English. It was a mannered comedy of sentiment about personages at the then-fashionable Brighton of 1811. This was succeeded by a tempestuous, theatrically effective melodrama, *Point Valaine* (1934) which he wrote for the Lunts. Perhaps just to prove that the one-act form was still commercially valuable in the modern professional theatre, when every one said that was no longer true, Noel Coward wrote nine short plays which were produced in 1935 under the collective title of *Tonight at 8:30*. The author wrote these pieces primarily for himself and Gertrude Lawrence as stars, probably with no strong conviction that they would have wide public use. If he thought that, then he was pleasantly proved wrong because such plays as *We Were Dancing, The Astonished Heart, Red Peppers, Hands Across the Sea, Fumed Oak, Shadow Play, Family Album, Ways and Means,* and *Still Life* have filled the bills of summer and little theatres everywhere, particularly in the United States. *Operette* (1938) is an unusually literate operetta which was not followed until the war was two years old, this time with *Blithe Spirit* (1941), which delighted two countries and enjoyed in New York the longest run a Coward play has ever had anywhere. This is a fantastic comedy about a man who marries a second time, is plagued by the ghost of his first wife, and only achieves peace after his second wife's death requires his exorcization. Two of Coward's plays which were written earlier, but not produced until 1943 and not yet published, are *This Happy Breed* and *Present Laughter*.[1] The former has recently been filmed in England. During 1942 he wrote, directed, acted, and produced one of the outstanding films of the war, *In Which We Serve,* a semi-documentary story of a British destroyer and the men who manned her together with their wives and children ashore. Coward, still in his forties, is capable of even better work than he has yet given us so that it is too early to give any final verdict on his contribution to British drama.

Although Frederick Lonsdale (1881-   ) began his career as a playwright some years before World War I, 1908 to be exact, it was not until he wrote *Aren't We All?*, a pleasantly brittle comedy, in 1923 that he can be said to have advanced sufficiently to come into the proper orbit of English drama. Though principally concerned with writing witty lines about naughty people for excellent actors to act, Lonsdale at one time knew a good deal about the construction of a play. *The Last of Mrs. Cheyney* (1923) was enormously successful as was *The High Road* (1927) whereas *On Approval,* the same year, was a four-character comedy with bright talk and not a great deal of action; cast to the hilt, however, it managed to secure a run. In addition to the books for innumerable and entirely unimportant musical comedies, he offered a thin piece entitled *Canaries Sometimes Sing* (1930), *The Foreigners* (1932), which was even thinner, and *Once is Enough* (1938) which approached some of the brilliance and wit of his comedies of the 1920's, but Ina Claire had a good deal to do with that, so scintillating was her acting. His was a peacetime style which was very attractive in its day, but which has not proved particularly enduring. *Another*

---

[1] Produced in New York, 1946-1947 season.

Love Story (1944) was proof of this. On the other hand audiences in the horrible rocket-bomb blitz of London in the summer of 1944 found *The Last of Mrs. Cheyney,* which was well revived, of vast entertainment value. The familiar is usually popular in the British capital.

Among the writers of comedy are such dissimilar people of such varying standards that it is extremely difficult to fit them into the pattern of English drama of the last twenty years. There is no unity of style, save perhaps a surface brilliance; there is no unity of subject-matter; there is only their nationality to hold them together. John van Druten, H. M. Harwood, and F. Tennyson Jesse, James Bridie, Ashley Dukes, Ivor Novello, Dodie Smith, Benn W. Levy, Merton Hodge, Terence Rattigan, Ian Hay, Margaret Kennedy, and Gerald Savory are among the leading dramatists. There is a group of lesser writers who have had success with a play or two, regardless of how many they have had produced in one theatre or another, whose plays would be mentioned in a work of greater extent than the present volume, though in all fairness there can be no individual discussion here of their merits as playwrights. In this group are to be found such names as Ronald Jeans; Gilbert Edward Wakefield; Henry M. Wallbrook; Gertrude Jennings; Helen Jerome (whose *Pride and Prejudice* is a better-than-average adaptation of a period novel); Harry Wall; Henry Francis Maltby; Cicely Hamilton; Basil Hastings; Philip Johnson; Sydney Blow; Michael Egan; Walter W. Ellis; E. E. Hemmerde and Francis Neilson, who wrote *A Butterfly on the Wheel* (1911); James Bernard Fagan (who is remembered for his charming tale of Samuel Pepys and his wife, *And So To Bed,* 1926, though some years before he adapted Robert Hichens' novel *Bella Donna,* 1911, these being his major dramatic achievements out of a not inconsiderable list); Eleanor Herbert and Joseph Jefferson Farjeon (grandchildren of the great acting Joe Jefferson, and particularly addicted to amusing, intimate revues); Neil Grant; Anthony P. Wharton, well known for *Irene Wycherly* (1907) and *The O'Cuddy* (1943); Leslie Howard; Miles Malleson (for his *The Fanatics,* 1927, among a host of adaptations); and Robert Morley (an actor, chiefly known for his uncanny performances in the title rôle of *Oscar Wilde*) who wrote *Short Story* (1937) and *Goodness, How Sad* (1937), two light comedies of no considerable importance. Noel Langley (1911-   ) is a young South African actor whose avocation is play writing. *Farm of Three Echoes* (1935) was a melodrama of his native land which provided an interesting character study of an aged woman of uncanny liveliness which served Dame May Whitty in London and Ethel Barrymore in New York reasonably well. His light comedy *The Walrus and the Carpenter* (1941), sometimes known as *The Mulberry Bush,* failed to live up to the promise of his earlier play. The Canadian Mazo de la Roche in 1936 was responsible for *Whiteoaks,* a study of a centenarian, which was acted by Nancy Price in London, and with great relish and success by Ethel Barrymore in America.

Playwrights who are also best known by single plays are Ronald Mackenzie (1903-1932) with his Chekhovian echo, *Musical Chairs* (1931), though *The Maitlands* (1934), a psychological comedy, had style; Rafael Sabatini for *The Tyrant* (1925), a swashbuckling affair; G. B. Stern (1890-   ), best known as a popular novelist, for her family study, *The Matriarch* (1929); J. H. Turner (1892-   ) for his high comedy, *The Lilies of the Field* (1923); and Lesley Storm (1903-   ) for her comedy of wartime London, *Heart of a City* (1942). W. J. Turner is remembered best for his fantastic comedy, *The Man Who Ate the Popomack* (1922). Aimee (1891-   ) and Philip Stuart (1887-1936) wrote an all-woman drama of life in a department store in *Nine 'til Six* (1930) and a delicate study of Lesbianism in *Love of Women* (1935). Dorothy Massingham (1889-1933) won great success with *The Lake* (1933), an effective study of a young woman in love with a man she has just met; the play, however, owed much of its popular following to a bawdily comic scene of a county wedding which takes place under a marquee in the drenching rains of her native land. Charles Morgan (1894-   ), drama critic of *The Times* of London, proved the truism in *The Flashing Stream* that the analytical is not usually the creative mind. Though John van Druten has never written dramatic criticism, his brilliant analysis of play construction, proven by his stage direction, is an example of the obverse side of the medal. Mrs. Morgan (Hilda Vaughan) is also known for one play, *She, Too, Was Young* (1938), a Victorian comedy-drama of the mother-daughter relationship.

But let us turn our attention to that distinguished writer of comedy, John van Druten (1901-   ), who is now an American citizen and in very recent years has turned to American subjects. Since the larger portion of his writing career was spent in England, however, we can still consider him a British playwright, though undoubtedly this is the last book dealing with the drama which will. His first success was *Young Woodley* (1925), a tender comedy of adolescence which was immediately popular in America while the Lord Chamberlain declined to license its performance in London, a ban which was later lifted, as it usually is. Showing the enlivening effect of a youngster in school when he falls head over heels for the headmaster's wife, van Druten's comedy reveals a touching reticence and a nice feeling for character. *Diversion* (1928) was a not unsuccessful tragedy of modern sophisticates and their search for pleasure and death. In *The Return of the Soldier* the same year he kept close to the line of Rebecca West's novel. *After All* is concerned with the struggle between generations. Perhaps to show that the generalizations are wrong, the daughter turns one way and the son the other in their relations to their parents. *London Wall* (1931) is a minor comedy of English office life which shows a pretty knowledge of such affairs without materially advancing the author's pretensions toward being a first-rate writer of gentle comedy which is his forte. The same year brought an adaptation of Marcel Pagnol's *Marius* which van Druten and

Auriol Lee (better known as a director and an actress) turned into *Sea Fever*.

In 1931 the nimble-penned writer turned out his highly felicitous four-character comedy, *There's Always Juliet,* which is one of the five successful attempts to portray an American in the whole field of modern English drama. Perhaps the fact that the author is half Dutch explains his ability to get away from the stuffy conventionalism which encloses most English playwrights when they endeavor to picture the mental processes of one who speaks their language without sharing their native land. Canadians, Australians and other subjects of the British dominions are similarly unfortunately depicted.

Van Druten owes much of his success in the theatre to his ability to understand and use actors felicitously and his remarkable comprehension of feminine psychology. Even women have been known to declare that this is *one* dramatist who understands how they function. This was most evident in his drawing of Leonora in *There's Always Juliet* in which he etched her character deftly while keeping aloft his gossamer lines. This tendency toward airy writing is one which may eventually lead him into a mere thinness which most English comic writers share.

Hollywood Holiday (1931) was a collaboration with Benn W. Levy in which they spoofed film personalities in an abortive comedy which failed to come off, and *Somebody Knows* (1932) is a tense psychological study of murder and its implications. His characterization of Lance, the exhibitionistic young man who may or may not have committed the crime, is carefully observed and brilliantly executed. His next major piece was *The Distaff Side* (1933) which established him as a writer who knew how to portray women three dimensionally, to reveal their inner meaning. *Flowers of the Forest* (1934) was a serious attempt to explain the strange struggle between an emotional woman and a sensitive man who are drawn together in the cataclysm of the First World War. *Most of the Game* (1935) was a mild and trivial comedy about writers and their vanities and *Gertie Maude* (1937) dealt with a chorus girl who fell in love with her protector; when he marries some one in his own class, she kills herself. Careful as to detail, it lacks the centrifugal force of a vitalizing idea.

In *Leave Her to Heaven* (1940) van Druten again returned to the fascination of a study of a murderer, this time a beautiful woman. *Old Acquaintance* (1940) is one of his most successful comedies. In this he stresses the friendship which is possible, but not usual, between completely unlike women—both writers again. As a playwright he is familiar and enormously interested in the problems of those who earn their living with the typewriter and an eraser.

Solitaire (1942) was the dramatization of an improbable novel by Edmund Goulding (English-born novelist-playwright now domiciled in the United States) which was concerned with the relationship between a little girl and a tramp. What was touching, if sentimental, in the novel became (without fault on van Druten's part) merely cloying yet embarrassingly terrible in the play. *The Damask Cheek* (1942) was his collaboration with Lloyd Morris who supplied the background and atmosphere of New York in 1909 although the writing was van Druten's. This gentle and mannered comedy was concerned with an ugly duckling who grows up and gets her man without turning into a swan. *The Voice of the Turtle* (1943) proved a sheer delight both in writing and in playing. A tour de force employing only three characters, this comedy of love in the spring in Manhattan was the smash dramatic hit of New York's 1943-1944 season. Van Druten's deftness in character depiction was never more apparent. He enlarged the two principals to the point that they were on the stage for an hour and a half without the audience's becoming bored. They would have resented the intrusion of other characters. Margaret Sullavan and, especially, Elliott Nugent, played the actress and the soldier to the hilt. Many of van Druten's plays have been American in background. With his home established here we have found him in the 1944-1945 season becoming more and more American in thought and feeling as well as content. This is certainly proved true in his adaptation of Kathryn Forbes' stories, *Mama's Bank Account,* as *I Remember Mama* (1944). This is a nostalgic, beautifully textured, deftly fashioned, honestly sentimental comedy-drama. Should this volume be revised ten years hence, this able playwright of high and character comedy may very well find himself transferred by his own volition from Britain to the United States.

James Bridie (1888-   ), born Osborne Henry Mavor, is a Scottish physician who has amazingly amusing ideas for the theatre but who seems to be extremely lazy when it comes to working his plays into a form satisfactory to the stage. His first play was *The Sunlight Sonata* (1928), but it was in *The Switchback* (1929), a serious drama of medicine, that he first attracted critical attention. Two years later *The Anatomist,* his macabre drama of a man who is wed to the science of anatomy until he discovers the seamy side of scientific experiment, brought him fame. This was vigorous treatment of the murders of Burke and Hare. In 1932 one of his charming comedies was produced in London in *Tobias and the Angel.* His whimsical regard for character has fascinated as well as exasperated his audiences and critics, because he leaves so many of his plays completely at loose ends. The very titles of his pieces, such as *The Girl Who Did Not Want to Go to Kuala* (1930), frequently reveal the essential whimsy of his nature. The Bible of Tobias was again a subject when he turned to *Jonah and the Whale* (1932). This piece has a style which lies halfway between a moral fairy-tale and symbolic satire. Being Scottish, the church and religion naturally were of interest to him whether he upholds them or pokes fun at them. This held true in *The Amazed Evangelist* (1932) and *A Sleeping Clergyman* the next year. The latter suffered sea change when it was imported to

America as did *The Anatomist.* None of Bridie's plays has had any commercial success in this country.

Then came *Marriage Is No Joke* (1934) and *Colonel Witherspoon* the same year as he continued to turn out plays too rapidly ever to polish them sufficiently, always offering an interesting and amusing character or two, a sprightly or measured or gruesome situation. Later in 1934 he brought forth *Mary Read,* with the collaborative assistance of Claude Gurney; this is the tale of Britain's famous woman pirate and starred Flora Robson, who had made a great hit in *The Anatomist,* and Robert Donat who later won wide popularity in the films. Then came that bright piece of fooling, which undoubtedly owes something to Barrie whether either Scotsman would care to admit it, *The Black Eye* (1935). *Susannah and the Elders* (1937) was a throwback to an earlier technique whereas *The King of Nowhere* (1938), dealing with an actor's meglomania, partook of allegory as does his latest play, *The Devil and Mr. Bolfry* (1943) which treats engagingly of the devil in a contemporary setting. *The Last Trump* (1938) has four themes woven into one. It is original, stimulating, rich, and amusing. In *Let Them Say* (1939) he snaps his fingers at respectability in what is really a farce. Bridie is a first-rate depicter of character, who has a dry sense of humor but too little sense of form and dramatic progression to attain the heights of which at first glance he seemed capable.

Man and wife, H. M. Harwood (1874-   ) and F(ryniwyd) Tennyson Jesse (granddaughter of England's poet laureate) have been united on many occasions to compose comedies and occasionally dramas of character. *The Pelican* (1924), which details the struggle of parents for their own happiness as opposed to the needs and demands of their children, and the comedy-drama of the last war, *Billeted* (1917), are typical. Harwood wrote a really good comedy of manners in *The Man in Possession* (1930) and in *Cynara,* the same year, an involved, but exciting character melodrama about a man trapped by his own decency and good impulses. This latter was written with R. Gore-Browne as was his light comedy, *King, Queen, Knave* (1932). A prolific writer, a collaborator with Gabrielle Enthoven and Laurence Kirk as well, Harwood represents the healthy, prosperous playwright, who supplies entertainment if no great distinction to the stage.

Ashley Dukes is perhaps better known as a manager (the tiny experimental Mercury Theatre in the Nottinghill Gate section of London), a critic (English editor of *Theatre Arts*), and translator and adapter of Continental drama than he is a playwright per se. He adapted *From Morn till Midnight* (1920), *The Machine Wreckers* (1923), *The Patriot* (1928), *Elizabeth of England* (1931), and *Vintage Wine* (1934) from the German and *The Man Who Married a Dumb Wife* (1914) and *Mozart* (1926) from the French. Only in his romantic comedy *The Man with a Load of Mischief* (1924) has Dukes written a play of his own which merits mention.

In contrast the actor-playwright Ivor Novello (1893-   ) has devoted himself to native writing, but always with his own rôle in mind. This forethought provided him with a glamorous and lucrative career as an actor, a splendid income, and the acclaim of his audiences. His plays are thin and brittle whether comedy or melodrama. The best of them are *The Truth Game* (1928), *A Symphony in Two Flats* (1929), *Fresh Fields* (1933), and *Comedienne* (1938), as well as a series of elaborate musical comedies. The son of a distinguished singer, Clara Novello, he has always had a wholesome respect of music's rôle in creating dramatic effect. The best of his plays were "brilliant," brittle, and loosely constructed.

Dodie Smith (Dorothy Gladys Smith, 1896-   ) in contrast, has written for others without thought of herself and has been extremely successful in light as well as domestic comedy. Like Rose Franken in America she has the personal-identification touch which makes millions like her plays because they can visualize themselves in similar situations. Her first hit was that Alpine idyl, *Autumn Crocus* (1931), which celebrated the sentimental affair between a young guide and an English school-teacher. Francis Lederer, a personable Czech actor, established his reputation first on the London and then the New York stage in this play. *Service* (1932) failed to advance Miss Smith (originally known by the pseudonym C. L. Anthony) dramatically, but in 1934 came *Touchwood,* the first two acts of which are brilliant domestic comedy. The theme of husband, wife, and challenging young girl was repeated with a variation in *Lovers and Friends*. In the earlier comedy, however, the young interruption to homely felicity was sympathetically treated.

Call It a Day (1935), however, was amply possessed of all the kindly English virtues and their family life with all its ups and downs. The dramatic device of forcing all the action into one day (hence the punning title) made the play a neat success with the public despite the enforced telescoping of character development which this technique demanded. This play almost equalled its English popularity with that accorded it in America. *Bonnet over the Windmill* (1937) came next. It was a theatre piece which described a young girl's first bitter taste of passion. The first two acts were, perhaps, her best writing up to that time, but it was not until *Dear Octopus* (1938) that the author again hit the financial jack-pot. Family life, that dear octopus, again held her attention and that of the public. Then came silence until 1943 which brought *Lovers and Friends* which to date has only been seen in America (where Dodie Smith is now living), but doubtless London will have the chance later. Katharine Cornell, Raymond Massey, and Henry Daniell headed a distinguished cast in this reflective comedy of marital fidelity and infidelity. This play is rather too pat in its writing and thinking; the wife is all beauty, charm, and nobility and "the other woman" is shallow, hard, and unyielding. This lack of balance robs the play of the dramatic conflict necessary to keep it alive though its characterization has much to attract admiration. Miss Smith in all her plays has felicity of expression and an aptness which has won her a public on both sides of the Atlantic. She writes with sureness and honesty, two extremely worth-while qualities.

Among the lesser writers of comedy aside from Terence Rattigan, who is considered elsewhere, are Gerald Savory (1909-   ) whose very slight but deft *George and Margaret* (1937) had an enormous English success; and Ian Hay (1876-   ) who began having plays produced in 1918, but hit the commercial success with two middling comedies, *The Middle Watch* (1929, with Stephen King-Hall) and the frolicsome *Housemaster* (1936, known in America as *Bachelor Born*).

Then there is Benn W. Levy (1900-   ) who has spent so much time in America that he is often thought of as a native of our country. He began with an amusing comedy, *This Woman Business* (1925), turned to horror in the dramatization of Sir Hugh Walpole's story *The Man With Red Hair* (1928), and then to extreme sentimentality in *Mrs. Moonlight* (1929), which was a considerable success. *Art and Mrs. Bottle* (1929) was a shade less coy and commanded a respectable following. Certainly his best piece of comic writing has been *Springtime for Henry* (1931) which despite its farcical implications, was sound in its humor. This has proved his most popular play in America and has been widely performed. For his *Hollywood Holiday* (1931), comments will be found in the section on John van Druten, his collaborator. *The Devil Passes* (1932), sometimes known as *The Devil,* was a modern morality play of no great importance. *Young Madam Conti* (1936) was a melodrama fashioned from Bruno Frank's German with the assistance of Hubert Griffith. His adaptation of Gaston Baty's *Madame Bovary* (1937) was only partially successful but revealed a sound dramatic technique. Paul Hervey Fox joined him to fashion *If I Were You* (1938), a tasteless farce about the reversal of sex externals by a young married couple, which was a quick and deserved failure. *The Jealous God* (1939) was a dramatization of the struggle between God and Mammon, showing the destructiveness of the impact of war which possessed a brilliant but verbose and divided mind.

Esther McCracken caught the popular fancy with her pleasant, formless, and innocuous comedies *Quiet Wedding* (1938) and *Quiet Weekend* (1942), at a time when the English public definitely felt the need of that reassurance which comes from emphasizing the normal, everyday habits of living, or the variants from the norm which come in peacetime.

Margaret Kennedy (1896-   ), the novelist, dramatized with Basil Dean her highly successful novel, *The Constant Nymph* (1926), which has been twice filmed. This romantic drama of love among the artists was highly popular as was the sequel *Escape Me Never* (1933) in which the German star, Elisabeth Bergner, made an enormous splash in her English-speaking début and repeated that sensation in America.

Clemence Dane (the pseudonym for Winifred Ashton) is a brilliant woman and, at times, a playwright of very considerable power. She frequently dissipates her theatrical talents in footling ways but in the end one must respect her contribution to the English drama. Her first plays are really her best and so one is unable to tell whether she will ever develop as a playwright or not—the presumption, regrettably, is no. She has frequently occupied herself with novel- and story-writing in which she has attained a high rank so that it may well be that any future success will lie in these fields.

Miss Dane began with a moving drama about the implications of the last war, *A Bill of Divorcement* (1921), which was concerned with the impact of a man's return from the asylum when he is thought hopelessly deranged because of shell shock. He arrives on the eve of his wife's remarriage (she has divorced him) and it is through the sacrifice of his daughter that it is possible for him to remain and for his wife to find happiness for herself. In England, Meggie Albanesi played the daughter, Sydney; in America Katharine Cornell established herself as an actress through her performance; In the films it was the making of Katherine Hepburn.

The same year brought *Will Shakespeare* (1921), which was a brave attempt to explain the man's power, genius, and fascination. Although not entirely satisfactory as drama, it has a quality which won it some adherents when it was first produced and still others in the more than twenty years that have elapsed since. It is a brilliant literary drama. *The Way Things Happen* (1924) was a sympathetic drama of a woman's sacrifice of her honor to save the man she loves only to learn that some gifts are too great to be accepted. Miss Dane weakened her play by giving it a happy ending which wrenched belief. *Naboth's Vineyard* (1925) was the straightforward retelling of Jezebel and her love for Jehu and the murder of Naboth. *Granite* (1926) and *Mariners* (1927) are alike in their devotion to the sea and its influence on the people who live by it or near it. *Adam's Opera* (1928), a social satire in the form of a fairy-tale with music by Richard Addinsell, was an attempt to combine words and music properly in the theatre. *Gooseberry Fool* (1930), written with Helen Simpson, however, failed to advance Miss Dane's status as a playwright. *Wild Decembers* (1932) was an interpretation of the lives of the turbulent Brontë sisters which was intermittently effective as drama. Although the critical reception of *Come of Age* (1934), a play of words and music (composed by Richard Addinsell), was distinctly mixed, it seemed to this writer to be a moving experience in the theatre. Taking the tragic story of Thomas Chatterton, Clemence Dane has translated it into modern terms and has chosen a kind of poetic doggerel to realize the triviality and tragedy inherent in the theme. The late Stephen Haggard and Judith Anderson made theatre history with its New York première. It was subsequently given an experimental performance or two in London.

It was the same year that *Moonlight is Silver* was staged and proved a rather trivial comedy of no depth though considerable pretentiousness. Since that time there have been only her adaptation of *L'Aiglon,* Max Beerbohm's *The Happy Hypocrite* and Hebbel's *Herod and Mariamne* and the short radio dramas published under the collective title of *The Saviours* (1942), which is trenchant, religious stuff. As far as the theatre is concerned, Miss Dane had made most of her contribution in her youth. Whether there is more to come is not clearly indicated. If she were to work further with the words and music patterns of *Adam's Opera* and *Come of Age,* she would find a relatively empty field which aches to be productive.

J. B. Priestley (1894-   ) has made for himself a deservedly high place in English letters as a dramatist, novelist, essayist, and political and economic reporter. This last phase has come about with World War II. He had returned from Arizona, which he had made his home, to his native England to do even more than offer his services. Since then he has done much to heighten the morale of his people through his writings and his broadcasts over BBC. He began his theatrical career with a dramatization which he and Edward Knoblock made of his novel, *The Good Companions* (1931), which was rollicking, good-humored, and picturesque. His first play alone, *The Roundabout* (1932), was a minor effort, but in the same year he achieved real success with a psychological melodrama, *Dangerous Corner,* which titillated the nerves and bordered on the sensational, a fact that had much to do with its popularity. The dramatic device of having the play return to the point at which it began was definitely appealing to the audience. The following year he wrote a folksy comedy of lower middle-class English suburban life in *Laburnum Grove,* which showed a very considerable rise in his ability to depict character. The respectable counterfeiter as impersonated by Edmund Gwenn was delightful. *Eden End* (1934) was not nearly so effective in its effort to recapture the frowzy atmosphere of the stage of thirty years ago and its impact on the characters of those who followed it and their relationship with the commonplace families they had left behind.

Neither *Duet in Floodlight* (1935) nor *Cornelius* (in the same year) did much to advance Priestley as a playwright though his central character in the latter piece has a definite interest for those who study dramatic technique. *Bees on the Boatdeck* (1936) combines fantasy, comedy, and a little searching thinking about capital and labor. However, in recent years his name has been associated with a preoccupation with matters of time and space. Donne and Ouspensky and the others have found a ready disciple in Priestley as is proved by his trilogy on the subject, *Time and the Conways, I Have Been Here Before,* and *I'm a Stranger Here* (all in 1937). His partisans insist that the playwright has put profound thinking into dramatic form while his opponents assert that he has wed confused theorizing to a limping theatre style which advances neither. Despite an admiration for Priestley's novelistic ability to depict character, I am rather inclined to agree with the dissenters rather than with the eulogists. It must be emphasized, however, that is for stage purposes only. Their appeal for the reading public is enormous.

People at Sea (1937) was a rewrite and renaming of *I'm a Stranger Here,* while *Music at Night* is a sincere effort to show the liberating effect of music on people's minds and emotions which does not completely come off though it is undoubtedly a major move in the direction of wedding drama to music.

In *When We Are Married* (1938) Priestley descended into mere horseplay made bearable in the theatre by the cheap if occasionally effective trick of dressing his people in the mode of another period which always seems vaguely ridiculous to his audience and is a frequently successful device in comedy. In *Johnson over Jordan* (1939) the impact of the disintegration of European civilization seems finally to have caught up with him and in desperation he turns to fantasy, expressionistic at that. The play is only moderately well done, but it represents a spiritual advance over his earlier well-made pieces. In *The Long Mirror* (1940) his fascination with otherworldliness led him to the subject of an extra-sensory or second-sight relationship between a girl and a man. As acted by Jean Forbes-Robertson at Oxford the play came alive, though in its present form it is perhaps not for the general public. Nonetheless, it is thoughtful, honest, and restrained, and in many ways his most penetrating play. *Goodnight Children* (1942) was a dullish satire on the British Broadcasting Corporation, always fair game for clowning, but in *They Came to a City* (1943) he has definitely faced up to present-day realities of thinking and acting and has preached the need for immediate recognition of our responsibilities for a future decent world. *Desert Highway* (1943) is his attempt to set down at this time the impact of the war on a group of soldiers. Critical reactions have been mixed, though the majority were favorable in tone owing to the admirable fashion in which he captured the language, thought, and spirit of the British soldiers.

Priestley is a first-rate writer whose plays are not sufficiently gauged to the specific limitations of the proscenium arch nor to the broad implications which the stage's cyclorama can give. It is only in his definitely lesser pieces that he seems to have recognized this. He is still too young to say that he may not yet achieve a distinction which is as yet not his in dramatic literature. He is, however, in the front rank of those who seek a higher type of drama than has been functioning in England for a generation. He is trying to create an audience which will demand the best even if he has not always been able to supply it himself. He is an articulate advocate for the new non-realistic theatre.

There is a group of dramatists, most of whom belong to the post-war coterie of writers, who have dealt largely with matters pertaining to history and to World War I. Some of these men began their literary careers in the years before 1914 though their principal work lies in the period after the war. Some of them have been mentioned before but must be considered again briefly in their places in that flowering of drama which always follows a major conflict. The very subtraction of the distractions of war seems to cause men and women to turn to creation to repair the damages done to their spirits and bodies and minds. Some of the writers are gone, dead, hospitalized, or their peace of mind wrecked by the anguish of the conflict. England was no exception to this as has been noted in introducing such writers as Coward, Milne, Munro, and others.

The play which best recorded the war was undoubtedly *Journey's End* (1928) which was written by an insurance clerk named Robert Cedric Sheriff (1896-   ). This drama told of a group of British officers and men under fire. In its very restraint, in its lack of heroism, and in its lack of hate, it caught much of the feeling of the men themselves. It was for this reason that the play of the British in the dugouts of France was played successfully all over the world. This popularity was not restricted to the cities of the late allies, for Germany took it to heart and the Berlin production received as much acclaim as did the New York presentation. A whole group of young actors came to fame in their portrayals of those men near to their ways of thinking even if not necessarily to their own nationalities.

Sheriff's next two plays were negligible, but in 1936 he combined with Jeanne de Casalis (1897-   ) to compose one of the best modern historical dramas, *St. Helena,* which tells the tale of Napoleon in his last years of exile on the barren South Atlantic island. These English authors have wonderfully caught the spirit and mind of the caged French warrior and their picture of the pitiful quarrelling society of his last friends and the minor persecution forced on the Emperor by the British government is both accurate and dramatically compelling.

Laurence Housman (1867-   ), who collaborated with Harley Granville-Barker and who has specialized in the one-act form such as the *Little Plays of St. Francis,* outdid himself in his Victorian cycle, a portion of which was produced as *Victoria Regina* (1935). These carefully etched vignettes of the astute yet stupid and bigoted woman who so long occupied the British throne make a compelling stage picture. Pamela Stanley created the part in private English performances but it remained for Helen Hayes to make the rôle so peculiarly her own that it is not possible to recall her name without thinking of the perky, charming, and almost magnificent queen which she created. Housman's skill as a dramatist is considerable though his impress on the popular stage is likely to rest on this one play, which was also most successfully filmed.

Turning from historical to literary figures, a noteworthy drama of recent years is *The Barretts of Wimpole Street* (1930) by Rudolph Besier (1878-1942) who made a pre-war reputation with such appealing if unimportant dramas, as *Don* (1909), *Lady Patricia* (1911), and *Kipps* (1912), the last with H. G. Wells. His sentimental *Secrets* (1922) with May Edginton was a popular and actresses' favorite. Besier knew very well how to write good acting parts as his portraits of Elizabeth Barrett, Robert Browning, and the

Barretts amply demonstrate. Gwen Ffrangcon Davies created the tubercular poetess, and in America Katharine Cornell made it her best-loved part which she has revived more than once. During the war she toured the battle areas of Europe in this drama

Clifford Bax (1886-   ) is a playwright who has been much admired for his neat style, his precision of story-telling and his pointed delineation of character. His best-liked characterization was that of Henry VIII in *The Rose Without a Thorn* (1932) which Frank Vosper created to such good effect. With H. F. Rubenstein (1891-   ) he wrote an interesting if unstirring *Shakespeare* (1921); he told the charming tale of Samuel Pepys in a ballad opera, *Mr. Pepys* (1926). In *The Venetian* (1930) and *The House of Borgia* (1935) Bax turned to northern Italy, but without much success. He returned to England and reality in *The King and Mistress Shore* (1936) which characters had been the subject of the famous *Jane Shore* of Nicholas Rowe in the first years of the eighteenth century. Rubinstein's two best-known plays are *Exodus* (1923), written with Halcott Glover, and *Churchill* (1925), with A. J. Talbot. These are, however, minor writers at best though they suggest the rich and varied qualities of English drama.

Maurice Browne (1881-   ), actor and director, is, perhaps, best known for his enormously interesting and provocative collaboration with Robert Nichols to create *Wings over Europe* (1928). This scientific pacifist play of modern European politics set in 10 Downing Street commanded critical respect and some popular support. William Percy Lipscomb (1887-   ) attracted attention with iconoclastic *Clive of India* (1934, with R. J. Minney), a play which was typical of the debunking period between the wars. He found Samuel Pepys much more to his liking when he read Arthur Bryant's biography which he turned into a moderately successful play known both as *Thank You, Mr. Pepys* (1937) and *Ninety-Sail.*

Norman Ginsbury (1903-   ) contributed another historical portrait in *Viceroy Sarah* (1934), which told of the intrigues of the Duke and Duchess of Marlborough and of Queen Anne. This was produced in America as *Anne of England* (1941) in a revised form by Mary Casa Canfield and Ethel Borden. In their effort to give the play "contemporary" analogies they buried what was at best a mild little comedy carried to success in England by Barbara Everest's acting of the Queen.

Elizabeth Mackintosh who employs the pen-name of Gordon Daviot has added at least two historical or literary dramas to this same school. Her greatest popular success was, of course, *Richard of Bourdeaux* (1932) which is a sentimentalized but facile retelling of the tale of Richard II. John Gielgud's romantic playing of the part undoubtedly contributed largely to its run of over a year at the New Theatre. *Queen of Scots* (1932) was a not too satisfactory tale of the celebrated Mary Stuart.

Moved like Sheriff with the need to set down the problems of war, other men had turned to its dramatic treatment. The most satisfactory of these pieces were *Prisoners of War* (1925) by J. R. Ackerly which dealt with British prisoners in a psychopathic fashion, and the highly dramatic *Tunnel Trench* (1925) by Hubert Griffith, sometime dramatic critic. Griffith (1896-   ) was also author of *The Tragic Muse* (1928) made from Henry James' mannered story and *Red Sunday* (1929). He also adapted *Youth at the Helm* (1934) from the German of Paul Vulpius and with Benn W. Levy he fashioned the melodrama, *Young Madame Conti* (1936), also from the German. In 1937 he was responsible for the adaptation of Alexander Afinogenov's *Distant Point*. It is, however, as an adapter and critic that Griffith has the most to offer the theatre.

Other notable plays in this group include *The Lady with a Lamp* (1929) by Reginald Berkeley in which Edith Evans impersonated Florence Nightingale in a pageant-like drama; and *She Passed through Lorraine* (1932) by Lionel Hale which presented the young Joan of Arc in moving fashion. Leslie and Sewell Stokes found an absorbing topic in the last years of the brilliant and witty Wilde which they celebrated in the successful *Oscar Wilde* (1936) which was made notable by the superb performance of Robert Morley. James Parrish caught the likeness of an epoch in the Great Plague of London in 1666 in his *Cheapside* (1938). Native character and/or understanding of human nature was the chief contribution of D. H. Lawrence to the theatre in his *The Widowing of Mrs. Holdroyd* (1914), *Touch and Go* (1920), and *David* (1926), though he was certainly not truly post-war in his ideology. Joan Temple, an actress, turned her hand to many plays of no particular importance; the best of these dealt with the literary Lambs, *Charles and Mary* (1930). George Arliss (1868-1946)—who did so much to popularize *Disraeli, The Green Goddess,* and *Old English,* which have been previously considered—treated the career of a great statesman in his *Hamilton* (1917) which he wrote in collaboration with Mrs. Arliss. James R. Gregson turned to *Robert Owen* (1937). Alfred Sangster (1880-   ) contributed two not particularly brilliant biographical dramas in *The Brontës* (1933) and *Napoleon* (1934), while *Ned Kean of Old Drury* (1923) by Arthur Shirley (1853-1925) definitely belonged to the old-fashioned romantic type of historical play. On the other hand Hugh Ross Williamson (1901-   ) held to the realistic tradition in his study of one of England's great parliamentarians and prime ministers in *Mr. Gladstone* (1937) while Anthony Gibbs was responsible for *The Aunt of England* (1935) along with Cosmo Hamilton. Naomi Reyde-Smith, the novelist, is also the author of several pieces of closet drama, notably *Mrs. Siddons* (1933) which great actress also served her as subject for a biography.

There is one great field in which modern English writers have excelled over all competitors, the mystery and horror genre. Patrick Hamilton (1904-   ) is, perhaps, the best known and certainly the most successful of the lot. *Rope* (1929, known in America as *Rope's End*) is a brilliant study of perversity where it enters the field of the so-called "thrill murder."

The relentless tracing down of the pair by the sadistic Oxford Don was enormously effective in the theatre. Though he has tried his hand with other forms, it is in the melodrama that he is most at home. His *Gaslight* (1938) achieved even greater success in New York as *Angel Street* (1941) where it ran for over three years. This is a taut and absorbing study of a woman whose husband is deliberately setting out to destroy her by driving her mad. *The Duke in Darkness* (1942) is literate but dull. His suspense is the best part of it, but his effort to comment on the modern world through the utilization of the French religious wars of the sixteenth century is ineffectual.

Arnold Ridley (1896-   ), though the author of a dozen plays, is principally known for his chiller *The Ghost Train* (1925) which is still seen in stock and amateur performances on both sides of the Atlantic. Another playwright who is known primarily for a single piece is Anthony Armstrong (1897-   ), whose *Ten-Minute Alibi* (1933) was an ingenious affair involving an alibi which the audience watched being set with awe and then enjoyed seeing it inexorably destroyed by the detective. A similar episode carried *Interference* (1927), by Harold Dearden and Roland Pertwee, to popular aclaim. This tried-and-true method of arousing spectator interest was recently successful in *The Two Mrs. Carrolls* by Martin Vale (Mrs. Bayard Veiller), an American piece first shown in London.

The shocker method was the favorite device of Edgar Wallace (1875-1932). Perhaps *On the Spot* (1930), in which Anna May Wong made a true hit on either side of the ocean, was his best-known piece. It was a candid bit of hokum which popularized American gangster plays in London. *The Squeaker* (1928) was known as *The Sign of the Leopard* in New York, and *The Case of the Frightened Lady* (1931) as *Criminal at Large,* but his efforts were of the commercial variety and of no permanent value. None the less Wallace had a very considerable interest in the field of detective fiction and, to a lesser extent, in current melodrama.

With somewhat more psychological approach than Wallace, definitely more literary, but still with an eye well cocked toward the box office is Max Catto (1907-   ) whose mysterious *Green Waters* (1936) and *They Walk Alone* (1938), sadistic and slightly disgusting, titillated English imaginations but failed to attract American audiences; it is essential to capture readers and listeners in both empires before greatness can honestly be said to have been achieved.

Then of course there is Barré Lyndon (1896-   ) who shot into fame with his reasonably literate melodrama, *The Amazing Dr. Clitterhouse* (1936), which told of illegal London doings with theatrical highlights which brought it international fame. The success of this drama was nearly equalled by *The Man in Half-Moon Street* (1939).

The straight melodramas were well represented by such playwrights as Leon Gordon (1884-   ) who came into enormous success with *White*

Cargo (1923), a torrid piece of no real importance with intimate revelations of the doings of white men with African natives; Jeffrey Dell (1899-   ) who wrote *Payment Deferred* (1931), a completely demoralizing story of a murderer unmasked; and finally Reginald Denham (1894-   ) who, in collaboration with Edward Percy, composed *Suspect* (1937), a not entirely apt study of murder, which owed such success as it had to a horrifying third-act curtain. Denham then followed with *Ladies in Retirement* (1939, also with Percy), a brilliant study of feminine psychology in the environment of murder, in which Edith Evans starred in London and Flora Robson in New York; the piece won considerable success for the collaborators, and particularly for Denham, the director.

There were also those that dealt with unusual problems such as Sutton Sutton-Vane (1888-   ) who, in *Outward Bound* (1923) wrote the brilliant and always nostalgic study of souls after death and in that indeterminate stage sometimes known as purgatory; Mordaunt Shairp (1887-1939) who both startled and delighted a sophisticated audience with his sensitive portrayal of homosexuality in *The Green Bay Tree* (1932); and Robins Millar (1889-   ) who offered the macabre post-war drama, *Thunder in the Air* (1928). Norman Macowan (1877-   ), who had been responsible for *The Infinite Shoeblack* (1929), a dreary drama of moral regeneration and death, produced the anti-Nazi *Glorious Morning* (1938).

Ronald Mackenzie (1903-1932), a brilliant writer whose death stopped him before he could write more than one significant drama, was strongly influenced by Chekhov in his outwardly formless *Musical Chairs* (1931) which John Gielgud, Frank Vosper, Carol Goodner, and Margaret Webster acted to good advantage both at the Arts and the Criterion theatres. He followed this with a weak but not uninteresting family study in *The Maitlands* (1934). Mackenzie is occasionally compared with Rodney Ackland (1908-   ) whose *Strange Orchestra* (1932) was a dramatic cacophony much admired in London for its portrayal of a gallery of characters but hooted off the stage after a single performance in New York. Ackland's *The Old Ladies* (1935) was a brilliant adaptation of Sir Hugh Walpole's novel, which though concerned with three aged gentlefolk, was actually a tour de force. In *After October* (1936) and *Remembrance of Things Past* (1938) he explored the Chekhovian field for himself with results which interested the few rather than the many, but which make uncommonly good listening and reading.

Just as Ireland won her independence and Scotland did not, Wales has long been agitating for separate culture and autonomy. Some writing has been done in Welsh but it is to the English language that her writers turn when they would reach a really wide public. The drama has only recently been a concern of theirs and it is in Emlyn Williams (1905-   ) that they have found their principal playwright. He began his theatrical career as an actor which may or may not have something to do with the structural weakness of his plays and a certain superficiality in his thinking. A smartish melodrama, *A Murder Has Been Arranged* (1930), was his first play to attract notice while his adaptation of René Fauchois' entertaining comedy of artists and avarice, *Guardez à la peinture* which he laid in Wales, was a huge success. His Elizabethan comedy, *Spring 1600* (1934) was a failure, but *Night Must Fall* (1935) ran a year in London and then was transplanted (less successfully) to America. The films, summer, and little theatres have counted it a stand-by.

Despite John Gielgud's efforts, Williams' drama *He Was Born Gay* (1937)—the story of Louis XVII, the lost Dauphin of France—was a failure. The next year he wrote his most successful and best play, *The Corn is Green*, a tender comedy about a Welsh schoolmistress and a tough young collier who encounters education and masters it despite all handicaps. Dame Sybil Thorndike in England and Ethel Barrymore in America brilliantly realized the character of Miss Moffat though the famous American actress made the teacher more nearly herself than the part called for, as is the wont with most actors of great reputation in New York. *The Light of Heart* (1940) was a London hit and, as *Yesterday's Magic*, a New York failure. It was concerned with an alcoholic actor and a self-sacrificing daughter who attempts to rehabilitate him. *The Morning Star* (1941) succeeded in London as a portrayal of the resistance of the English to the German blitz although it seemed shallow, obvious, and ineffectual to a New York remote from actual danger. Lesley Storm (1903-   ) found this out in her *Heart of a City* (1942) which portrayed the Windmill Theatre and its heroic actresses under bombing conditions and Terence Rattigan (1912-   ) discovered the same thing in *Flare Path* (1942), a story of English air pilots and the folk they leave behind. *Flare Path* was an enormous hit in London where the people found the characters' problems their own, and a flop in New York where it all seemed tame and trivial (bad casting of the leading parts contributed to its failure, however). The author's smashing farce comedy *French Without Tears* (1936), was a subsequent pushover in America despite its obvious comic merits. *While the Sun Shines* (1944) was a wartime hit in London and was brought to Broadway in the 1944-1945 season. Slight but charming was the verdict.

Emlyn Williams has, however, returned to Wales with a vengeance in *The Druids' Rest* (1944) in which he employs his native language for so great a part of the first act as to render much of it nearly unintelligible to an English-speaking audience. Competent critics have admired his characterizations in this work if not his play structure.

Keith Winter (1906-   ) has had a certain success in the theatre without ever coming completely alive as a dramatist. He has a strong interest in melodrama which he is inclined to regard as straight drama and so to treat it. *The Shining Hour* (1934) is definitely his best play to date and was successful in New York before London saw it. He writes lines and situations which are good for actors. His comic invention is weak as evidenced by *Worse Things Happen at Sea* (1935).

Merton Hodge (1904-   ) rocketed to fame with his gentle comedy of medical students in an Edinburgh boarding-house, *The Wind and the Rain* (1933). It had a nostalgic quality which provoked its thousand-and-one performance run in London and a respectable figure in New York. *Grief Goes Over* (1935) failed to realize any definite audience response. Since then Hodge has done two adaptations, *The Orchard Walls* (1937) from Laszlo Fodor's Hungarian, and *The Story of an African Farm* (1938) from Olive Schreiner's great book. Neither translation achieved much success, either critically or popularly.

Ronald Gow (1897-   ) composed a moving historical drama of John Brown's life in *Gallows Glorious* (1933) but his most noteworthy play is *Love on the Dole* (1935) which he dramatized with Walter Greenwood from the latter's novel of the same name. This study of the British depression of the 1930's was singularly human, touching, and found some popular support.

An earlier playwright who has been largely overlooked is Herman Ould (1886-   ) none of whose plays achieved any prominence on the stage, but who has written several sensitive and serious dramas, the best of which are *Between Sunset and Dawn* (1913), *Christmas Eve* (1919), and *The Black Virgin* (1922). This last was a careful, articulated study of an unhappy homosexual relation in early post-war Germany. Coupled with the confusion and unhappiness of a defeated people, it was mingled with a religiosity older and much more powerful than any of the persons involved.

Michael Arlen (1895-   ), a Bulgarian-born Armenian who was educated in England, was once an extremely popular writer whose novel, *The Green Hat,* sold into the millions of copies in the British Empire and the United States. His was a pseudo-brilliant world of "smart" people and for a decade he was acclaimed and then very nearly forgotten. *Dear Father* (1924) was an adaptation of his *These Charming People*. The next year he dramatized *The Green Hat* which Tallulah Bankhead in London and Katharine Cornell in New York played to the hilt and several reputations, including the author's, were rapidly enhanced. His straight plays, *The Zoo* (1927) with Winchell Smith, and *Good Losers* (1931) with Walter Hackett, both Americans, were of no importance whatsoever.

Coming along at the same time and appealing likewise to a superficial, bad-mannered crowd was Beverly Nichols (1898-   ) who aspired somewhat higher than Arlen, but who has yet to achieve wide popularity because his writing has a hollow ring to it. *Evensong* (1932), with Edward Knoblock, is his most successful work, and that largely because Edith Evans really suggested Dame Nellie Melba, the opera singer on whose life and character the drama was reputedly patterned. *Mesmer* (1935) and *Floodlight* (1937) were even less close to the main stream of English drama. But to

.eturn to pure melodrama, Frank Vosper (1899-1937) wrote one of the best in *Love from a Stranger* (1936) which he adapted from a story by Agatha Christie. In this he dramatized the terror of a woman who has married a man of whose background she is completely ignorant, and whom she finds to be a murderer. Frank Vosper acted the husband to the nines. Another writer in this field is Jack Celestin (1894-   ) who wrote mystery thrillers of the Edgar Wallace variety, *The Silent Witness* (1930) with Jack de Leon being his best known play. Charles Bennett (1899-   ) is well known as a melodramatist, though his skill is more superficial than deep-seated, particularly for his *Blackmail* (1928).

De Leon was also responsible for *The House of Danger* (1930) and *Crime on the Hill* (1932). Terence De Marney (1909-   ), better known as a romantic actor, combined with Percy Robinson to compose two melodramas, *Whispering Gallery* (1928) and *Wanted for Murder* (1937). Robinson (1899-   ) alone wrote *To What Red Hell?* (1928), a psychological study of an unwitting victim of circumstantial evidence. Ronald Jeans (1887-   ), who wrote mostly minor farces and the books for musicals, was also the author of a mystery drama of distinctly minor value called *Ghost for Sale* (1938). Though Michael Morton (1854?-1931) wrote many plays, including an adaptation of Tolstoy's *Resurrection* (1903), his dramatization of Agatha Christie's detective novel as *Alibi* (1928) was his only first-rate piece of stock-theatre writing.

Agatha Christie herself, turned her successful novel *And Then There Were None* into a fascinating mystery melodrama known in England as *Ten Little Niggers* (1944) and in America as *Ten Little Indians*.

Probably no one country has contributed as much to the drama of criminal psychology as has England. Occasionally these plays have been lacking in depth but they have been expertly constructed and shrewdly adapted to the theatre. Hamilton, Ridley, Williams, Wallace, Denham, Percy, Armstrong are definitely masters of their art, minor as it may be in the full stream of English drama.

The English have been quite successful in their handling of the revue and musical comedy field though fewer of these wares travel across the waters. Perhaps this is because American taste has changed in this instance whereas English humor has remained in the same tradition. Some of the best-known librettists and lyricists are Noel Coward, Marriott Edgar, Frank Eyton, Frank and Eleanor Farjean, Douglas Furber, Harry Graham, Harry Grattan, Percy Greenbank, Clifford Grey, Charles Henry, Sir Edward Seymour Hicks, Jack Hulbert, Ronald Jeans, Graham John, Bert Lee, Rowland Leigh, Frederick Lonsdale, Robert MacDermot, Arthur Macrae, Eric Maschwitz, Austin Melford, Archie Menzies, Diana Morgan, Robert Nesbitt, Greatex Newman, Beverly Nichols, Ivor Novello, Cecil Raleigh, Arthur Rigby, W. Graham Robertson, Sax Rohmer, Paul Rubens, Harold Simpson, Paul Gerard Smith, Fred Thompson (notable for the celebrated wartime show, *The Bing Boys Are Here,* 1916, with George Grossmith), Con West, Robert P. Weston, Arthur Wimperis, P. G. Wodehouse, Hugh E. Wright, Sir Alan Herbert, and Lauri Wylie. Their attack has varied from the subtleties of the Charlot revues to the broadest of musical farces.

The unmusical version of this type of writing has had much greater success in England than in America. The broad, characterless lines have a local humor which is appealing to popular audiences. Those are the situations, habits, characteristics which amuse a relatively unthinking public. This requires extremely expert writing of a commercial kind which is highly lucrative to the authors. Many of these men are actors as well, and occasionally managers. They are keenly attuned to popular taste and are well equipped to serve it. A few of the best known and most successful are Firth Shephard, Archie Menzies, Ben Travers, Vernon Sylvaine, and, of course, the previously mentioned Brandon Thomas of *Charley's Aunt* fame and reputation.

If there be any real hope for the development of new great, powerful English drama in the fruitful period which will follow World War II, then it must come, aside from J. B. Priestley, from the poets in the theatre. There are several of these who may be counted on to try for this revival. Of these the most important by far seems to be Eliot.

T. S. Eliot (1888-   ) is an American-born writer who has become so much a part of the English scene that he is only thought of as an American when critics on our side of the ocean wish to claim him as a poet, or more recently as a dramatist. He is probably the finest writer of poetic drama which the twentieth-century English language possesses. His development, so far as the theatre goes, is his own. He has no ties with the older poetic school headed by Stephen Phillips nor does he seem to relate to Lascelles Abercrombie or Lawrence Binyon, or Gordon Bottomly, or James Elroy Flecker. His kinship lies with those writers younger than himself who are attuned to intellectual poetry. His plays, however, cannot truly be said to have influenced Auden, Isherwood, or Hassall, but his poems may very readily have done so as they have had their effect on minds in all fields in the literary high places. Eliot's first play came in 1934 in his collaboration with E. Martin Browne on *The Rock,* which was a puzzling piece though sufficiently provocative to attract attention. A year later came a drama of first-rate importance written for production at Canterbury and first performed here. *Murder in the Cathedral* caught the imagination of all English-speaking peoples. The simple faith of the Archbishop triumphing over himself as well as over his external enemies came at a time of world-wide financial depression and so, perhaps, took on new meanings. Ashley Duke's production at his tiny Mercury Theatre in London ran for over a year and was later seen in New York, though with considerably less success. This failure in all probability came about because the Federal Theatre had already staged it to both popular and critical acclaim two years before. The American production had emphasized the spectacular and broadly religious aspects of the drama rather than the poetry and exquisite diction of the play's chorus. *Sweeney Agonistes* (1933) and *The Family Reunion* (1939) were more definitely appealing to the smaller public which is interested in experimentation in all literary genres. In the former, Eliot attempts to comment in humorous fashion on the Greek form while in the latter he uses that particular technique of writing to express his indictment of modern society. It has been called the greatest English tragedy since the Elizabethans. This would seem to be rather an overstatement but certainly some of Eliot's finest writing is in the piece though as a whole it does not equal *Murder in the Cathedral*. In *The Family Reunion* he tries to force a modern English domestic tragedy into the Greek mold without doing real justice to either. There are many passages of beautiful writing and some scenes which are effective on the stage, but the play as a whole does not come off very well. Only in *Murder in the Cathedral* has Eliot made that broad contact with humanity which is essential to success in the popular theatre.

The energetic poet-dramatist, W. H. Auden (born Wysten Hugh Auden, 1907), is probably the best of the younger men working in his genre. Nothing he has written so far for the theatre reaches Eliot's chef d'œuvre, but his plays are sufficiently theatrical to attract the play-goer and have sufficient literary import to titillate the critic. *Paid on Both Sides* (1930) is a somewhat confused short drama which is merely a beginner's prelude to what follows. His first long piece, *The Dance of Death* (1933), is a satiric drama of capitalism and its stultifying effects on the world. He makes good use of color, music, and dance to make his play palatable. In 1935 came the first of the collaborations with Christopher Isherwood, the much-admired, poetic *The Dog Beneath the Skin*. Here satire again combines with genuine poetry of the disillusioned Eliot school to make a drama of real importance. The play had more than a *succès d'estime* when Ashley Dukes produced it in his Mercury Theatre, because the criticism of capitalism, fascism, and sheer materialism attracted a wider audience than its poetic language and unusual dramatic form might have naturally commanded. Isherwood had a sounder knowledge of the theatre than did Auden and the construction, which was part of his contribution, when wed to Auden's undoubted poetic merits produced three plays of considerable importance. The following year brought their *Ascent of F6* which was a brilliant and cruel indictment of imperialism and opportunism in modern society. The exploration of the numbered mountain gave the authors an opportunity to use their rapiers on the press, the government, and the sentimentality of the lower middle class. *On the Frontier* (1937) is a warning against the futility of war when no high principles are involved. It is more serious in tone and less theatrically effective. Auden alone is responsible for *Paul Bunyan,* a choral operetta (1941), which continues his established style without advancing his position as a playwright.

Christopher Hassall (1912-   ) began as an actor but soon turned to poetic writing and belongs definitely to the Eliot school. His *Devil's Dyke* (1936) and *Christ's Comet* the following year make a definite commentary on living though set in terms seemingly removed from the contemporary surroundings. Stephen Spender (1909-   ) who is known almost wholly as a poet has made at least one contribution to the theatre. *Trial of a Judge* (1938) has both reading and playing values. It is somewhat attenuated and is not likely to survive in the hurly-burly of commercial producing. These men have had and have a real opportunity to restore English drama to its former high estate. Eliot, Auden, and Isherwood are the white hopes in the poetic field. What they can do after the war is a moot point.

There are certain writers who have made their success in a genre remote from playwriting and yet have displayed a dramatic flair which has perhaps surprised no one more than themselves. Dorothy L. Sayers (1893-   ) is certainly an example, for she has been long established in the field of detective fiction where her careful confections concerning Lord Peter Wimsey have been relished by peer and peasant. Her first venture into the drama, in fact, was a pleasant, if rather mild, melodrama, *Busman's Honeymoon* (1936), in which she portrayed her favorite hero with the collaborative efforts of M. St. Clare Byrne. A year later she revealed her true interest in the stage in her composition of *The Zeal of Thy House,* a poetic and religious drama written for production at Canterbury. This has high quality, sensitiveness of expression, and dramatic sweep. The same may be extended to *The Devil to Pay* (1939), which for this reason causes Miss Sayers to be grouped with the younger poetic dramatists.

And so we bring to a conclusion this brief survey of the great and near-great in modern drama in the larger half of the British Isles. From Robertson to Dorothy Sayers, we have essayed to touch on their importance dramatically and, to a lesser extent, theatrically, as well as to deal with their relations to each other and to their native land. It is all too true that in many instances, we are perhaps too close to the plays themselves to evaluate them historically. Perhaps some writers are overrated while others have been scamped. However, we have set down as impartially as we could those trends, those currents and eddies which go to make up the whole stream of modern dramatic literature in England.

IRISH DRAMA

There is no country in the modern world which ranks higher in poetic drama than the Emerald Isle. Torn by wars, external and internal, disunited by irreconcilable political, religious, and economic differences, divided into North Ireland and Eire, this island has, nevertheless, managed to offer to the world something of very considerable importance. This theatrical awakening has come about largely in the last half century, for before that dramatic writing in Ireland was entirely derivative and imitative. Its theatre was a provincial outpost for English stars and touring companies, just as were Scotland and Wales. Not that Ireland has been backward in providing leading actors for the London stage and, in the case of the Sheridans, playwrights as well. However, it was not until the nineties that Irish writers caught up with their actors and in the new nationalistic sense turned their energies toward creating a National Drama.

What makes the Irish Literary Movement peculiar is the fact that it was essentially poetic. Not since the great Elizabethan age had there been an important poetic revival in the literature of Britain and Ireland. The work of these men and women compares favorably with all save the greatest (Shakespeare) of the sixteenth-seventeenth century period. Had Synge lived long enough, there is no telling what heights he might have attained. O'Casey has superbly high moments as did Yeats.

Probably in the popular mind no one man is better known for his pioneer work in Ireland than William Butler Yeats (1865-1939). Along with Edward Martin, George Moore, and, above all, Lady Gregory, Yeats managed to get the Irish Literary Theatre launched on May 8, 1899 in Dublin at the Ancient Concert Rooms in Great Brunswick Street. However, his writing career antedated this for *The Countess Cathleen,* which was on the first bill, had been written as far back as 1892. This beautiful piece partakes of those characteristics which mark all of his work. It is sheer poetry; the language is glorious and the ideals are high. The struggle between material and spiritual things is the theme of this play and one that constantly recurs in all his work.

Before this drama was acted, Yeats' charming one-acter, *The Land of Heart's Desire,* was offered at the Avenue Theatre in London in 1894 with Florence Farr for whom the piece was written. It was played on the same bill with Shaw's *Arms and the Man.* Yeats was enchanted by her glorious voice which sang his verse so magnificently. He sent her *The Shadowy Waters* (1900) to read before a London Theosophical conference so that he might know how to shape it as a play. It was revised in 1904 and again in 1906. The spiritual world is indeed a reality in this as absolute beauty is in his other plays. The portrayal of Ireland's great heroic traditions was also inherent in his writing. This characteristic was present in *Diarmuid and Grania* (1901) which he composed with George Moore. The next year he brought forth another poem to old Ireland in *Cathleen ni Houlihan.* The aged woman is the spirit of revolt and independence who wins the youth from his bride to fight again against England's hordes in order that Ireland may be free.

Yeats' nearest approach to comedy and compact dramatic writing came in his short piece, *The Pot of Broth,* the same year. He was primarily a lyric poet and no characterizer at all. For this reason, though many of his lines are glowingly beautiful, most of his long plays are obscure. The mythology and legends which people them are not too well known even to his own countrymen. In 1903 he composed the prose morality play, *The Hour Glass,* which is great writing. In 1912 he turned it into his favorite verse. After *The King's Threshold* (1903), *Where There is Nothing* (rewritten as *The Unicorn from the Stars* with Lady Gregory, produced 1907) and the meandering *On Balie's Strand* followed the next year. He revised the latter the same year he wrote *Deirdre* (1906); based on Ireland's national heroes—again there is little action until his thrilling climax.

His passion was writing, revising, rewriting, twisting, turning his dramas until he had wrung all from them that he possibly could. Almost all of his plays appear in several forms and under several titles. In his later years he fell under the influence of the Nō plays of Japan and composed his series of plays for dancers which emphasize the purely formal and abstract aspects of the theatre. Most play-goers lost track of what he was doing. His last play was a free translation of Sophocles' *Oedipus Rex* (1933) which the Abbey Theatre Players gave for one weird performance in New York.[1]

Collaborating with Yeats on the establishment of a theatre native to Ireland was Edward Martyn (1859-1923), as stout a Catholic as Lady Gregory was a Protestant. His own dramas cannot now be considered important. They loomed larger than life size at a time when an Irish dramatic theatre was being launched. Strongly under the influence of Ibsen and, like all the rest, in love with Irish nationalism, he wrote under the impetus of these twin fires. It was the poetic rather than the realistic Ibsen who inspired him, particularly the dramatist of *Rosmersholm* and *Lady from the Sea.* Of his plays the best were *The Heather Field* (1899), *Maeve* (1900), *An Enchanted Sea* (1902), *and Grangecolman* (1912). His early pieces were highly poetic, really imaginative pageants which bogged down in stilted dialogue which he was never able entirely to master. The idealism of his early work turned into drabness and to a certain kind of realism which shows Chekhovian influence. In his career as a dramatist Martyn was susceptible to both influences but was at his best when he drew straight from the heart of old Erin where lay his own heart and soul.

The last of the triumvirate was Lady Augusta Gregory (1859-1932) who expressed the drama of Ireland even better in her living than in her plays. She cannot rank nearly so high as Synge; her plays lack the lyricism of Yeats; but what is most important, she did have a strong feeling for the everyday personal problems of the Irish people. These are best reflected in her one-act pieces. She was, however, a propagandist so that if the character of the persons who existed in her plays would not fit the twist of the plot which would carry her point, she did not hesitate to distort the character to suit her ends. It is for this reason that she failed to reach as high a rank as her other many talents would have given her. Her poetic feeling for the Western Isles and the hidden places of her native land is strong and almost always moving. Her faerie quality is easy to accept because the audience

---

[1] Brilliantly performed by the Old Vic Theatre Company, 1945.

knows from experience that the seeming naïveté is chosen, not inflicted by an inadequate command of dramatic technique.

Spreading the News (1904) is a charming as well as hilarious one-act piece about gossip in a small Irish town. *Hyacinth Halvey* (1907) is concerned with a young man who has a good reputation thrust upon him and nothing he can do to rid himself of it. In complete contrast to these rollicking comedies is the tragic *The Gaol Gate* (1906), which is frequently paired with *Riders to the Sea* for dramatic intensity. A man's wife and his mother have come to the jail where they believe he is held because he has saved his own life by betraying a friend. To their sorrow and joy they learn that he gave his own because of a deep sense of loyalty to that friend.

In *The Rising of the Moon* (1907), to give the proper happy ending to her play, and, at the same time perhaps, to work for better understanding between the nations, she perverts the character of the British policeman so as to allow for the escape of the Irishman. It is good theatre if not sure drama. In contrast, *The Workhouse Ward* (1907) is a carefully constructed and well integrated piece which develops naturally out of the characters of the two protagonists. Two old men have carried a lifelong quarrel into the workhouse; when the niece of one of them would reclaim him from public charity, he refuses because it would separate him from his cherished antagonist. *The Image,* which she wrote in 1909, produced in 1921, and published the following year, is an example of the weakness of Lady Gregory's work when she tries to expand her subjects and methods into the three-act form. She is excellent in her chosen field and was most effective when she remained in it. Many persons feel that she reached her highwater mark as a playwright with *Grania* (1912), which is a folk tragedy but little understood except in Ireland where it is admired extravagantly. She is remembered as a warm-hearted woman with a flair for the one-act play form as well as being a born organizer who did much to establish the Irish drama and to place the Abbey Theatre on so firm a footing that it has survived two world wars with their attendant economic disruption.

Probably, in fact undoubtedly, the greatest Irish dramatist who has ever lived is John Millington Synge (1871-1909) for Shaw is certainly to be considered non-Irish as far as drama movements are concerned. Few playwrights have made more earnest or devoted preparation for writing than did Synge. At Yeats' wise suggestion, and we are indebted to him for additional beauty in Synge's lines, he spent several years in the Aran Islands and elsewhere in rural Ireland, studying the people with great care. Their habits of thinking and doing, their variants of vocabulary, their manner of living, were all the subject of thoughtful consideration. When he came to write his plays and show them to the world in the six short years which remained of his life, he could write surely and freely because he was sure of his subject-matter and background.

Ireland being the kind of country that it is, it is natural that when his first play, *The Shadow of the Glen* (1903) was offered it was considered a vicious libel against all the women of Eire and hostile demonstrations were organized and directed in opposition to its production by the Irish Literary Theatre. In this play he is concerned with a kind of Irish Nora who has tired of her husband, plays him false, and finally runs away with the Tramp. In this instance we have learned of her unfaithfulness whilst she sits by the open coffin of her supposedly dead husband. Death falsely reported is a favorite device of Synge's.

Close on this comedy came the short and perfect tragedy, *Riders to the Sea* (1904), which rightly has been held up as an example of the modern application of the tragic impulse. There is catharsis here which most present-day writers lack when they compose the dirges which they *call* tragedies. The character of the mother, Maurya, is beautifully developed. In this play there is the endless struggle between Nature as expressed by the sea and Humanity as represented in the persons of the poor fisherfolk. Maurya has lost her husband, her father-in-law, and four sons previously to the sea. The fifth son, Michael, has just been recovered drowned. The last boy, Bartley, has gone to the horse fair over on the mainland. His dripping body is carried in as Maurya is describing to her women friends the deaths of his older brothers. Her resignation to Fate and the realization that now that the last is dead there is nothing that can hurt her any more raises this drama to great heights.

The Well of the Saints (1905) shows Synge in a characteristically sardonic and playful mood. In this a blind old couple are beautifully happy because every one has told them how beautiful they are. The Saint restores their sight and they see each other in all their ugliness; then the billingsgate which flows from their lips is something wonderful to hear. They separate and in the course of time lose their sight again. By chance they meet and memory is dulled so that they half forget past bitterness in a rekindling of their own imaginations. At this moment the Saint reënters and announces that he will restore their sight which they have so sadly lost again. They are in despair; their happy blindness is to be taken from them and they can do nothing about it. In desperation the husband dashes the vessel containing the holy water from the Saint's hands. Thus their blessed state of blindness is permitted them evermore. The irony and intent of Synge is plainly apparent. His desire to satirize his fellow-countrymen is boundless, though his comedy is almost always goodhumored.

He wrote one of the great plays of modern drama in *The Playboy of the Western World* (1907) which so satirizes the ignorance, stupidity, blindness, and cruelty of the Irish that a riot took place when it was first performed at the Abbey. The uproar had not died down four years later when the play was offered on the Abbey Players' first American tour. An outbreak occurred in Maxine Elliott's Theatre by Americans of Irish descent, always more Irish than the Irish. Another demonstration was attempted in Boston, but with the assistance of several of his students (including Barrett H. Clark), George Pierce Baker stopped that affair. Powerful voices were raised in behalf of the play both in America and in Ireland and the play is now accepted as a masterpiece everywhere. The circumstances of its première are not unlike those which accompanied the opening of Conal O'Riordan's *The Piper* (1908) in Dublin. Shameful circumstances both!

In Synge's piece Christy Mahon has been admired in the pothouses of Ireland for his boasted parricide and Pegeen throws over Shawn, her fiancé, to take up with this wondrous young man. Unhappily for Christy, his "murdered" parent arrives on the scene and dashes down the house of cards. Pegeen throws him over and Christy's world is ruined. Infuriated by the fact that his old man has followed him and so destroyed his great legend, he attacks his father in dead earnest and leaves him again murdered, or so he thinks. It is again reported that he is a parricide, but this time it happened too close at hand and there is no legend attached to it, so every one, including Pegeen, is horrified. She turns him over to the authorities and he is bound awaiting transfer to jail when his twice-murdered father walks in. This is too much for the guards, who flee. Mahon unties his son and they escape together, leaving behind a legend which is as bright as the first Christy perpetrated. This splendid, ironic comedy has won enthusiastic support from such unalike individuals as Maxim Gorki and Theodore Roosevelt.

The next play in point of production was *The Tinker's Wedding* (1909) though it had been written probably in 1902. It is a crude, Hans Sachs kind of farce which is broadly and coarsely humorous without being finished in any sense of the word. It was a trial piece which he might have reworked had he lived (he died at thirty-eight). His final play was never finished either but this was entirely a different piece of writing. Even in its present state, it is a distinguished work of art and might have been his greatest play. *Deirdre of the Sorrows,* a beautiful retelling of the Deirdre legend, is a magnificent piece of poetry in the Greek or pagan meaning of the word. This was staged after his death at the Abbey Theatre on January 13, 1910. There is both power and beauty in this simple tale of the great Irish of a bygone day. There is a peacefulness and calm which is lacking in his other work (except for *Riders to the Sea*), which hints at a full new style which would have raised his work even higher had he lived. Even yet, Synge's name outranks that of any other Irish dramatist though at moments Sean O'Casey crowds him and may yet surpass him.

Among the "greats" of Irish drama is to be found such a distinguished literary name as Æ., a pseudonym used by George W. Russell (1867-1935) when he composed his *Deirdre* (1902) which was more literary than dramatic. He had a definite interest and importance to the Irish stage because of his encouragement of Yeats, the brothers Fay, Frank and William, and the highly significant Abbey Theatre.

One cannot say more of the dramatists of Ireland without a word of commendation for the Abbey which grew out of the Irish Literary Theatre and so made possible a powerful organ of expression for the playwrights. Actors had to be imported from London at first, which fact must have made Irish faces burn, and English tongues twisting over Irish vowel sounds must have done damage to both. At any rate that practical patron saint of the repertory theatre, Miss A. E. F. Horniman offered to train a company of young Irish hopefuls. This she did and the famous and still enduring Abbey Theatre was born. This troupe has never been interested in décor or spectacular stage effect nor, to judge from the performances given in New York, in direction either. It is acting pure and simple which has absorbed its attention, acting and giving tongue to some of the most fluent writing talents in modern drama. Despite defections in the last two decades to the West End of London, Broadway, or Hollywood, there is always the nucleus of a fine company. This upholds the inner spirit of the theatre and provides impetus to the new members as they are added from time to time. Among the names which have always been associated with the Abbey—in addition to Yeats, Gregory, and Synge—are Sara Allgood, Maire O'Neill, Dudley Digges, Barry Fitzgerald, F. J. McCormick, Arthur Shields, Eileen Crowne, Una O'Connor, Dennis O'Dea to name a few of their many fine players.

At this same time we find Dunsany's early work being performed in Ireland though he was later to transfer his work to England so as almost to be taken for an English playwright. In America his plays were seized upon by amateurs and experimenters in the drama so that his name is widely known in off-Broadway circles. Nevertheless Lord Dunsany (Edward John Moreton Plunkett, 1878-   ) was born in Ireland and it was there that his genius, if so it can be called, stemmed. His one-acter, *The Glittering Gate* (1909), perhaps his best as well as his first piece, had its première at the Abbey Theatre. The dramatic irony of this play has made it singularly popular among amateurs. Dunsany has been as fond of the Orient as James Elroy Flecker, so nearly all of his plays are laid in the East. His poetic Irish heart took refuge in the lore of Egypt, Persia, and India. However, except in that excellent short melodrama, *A Night at an Inn* (1916), he has never made any real contact with the professional stage or with the average playgoer. The latter has found his plays arty, self-conscious, and incomprehensible. *The Gods of the Mountain* (1914), *The Queen's Enemies* (1916), and *If* (1921) are probably the best of his full-length plays. Dunsany reads well but is inclined to seem very thin indeed on the stage and to require almost superlative acting to keep the plays from sounding ridiculous.

Next we turn to the North of Ireland to a playwright who was born there, though he was conspicuously identified with Dublin, and for the past thirty years with London where he remains. St. John Ervine (1883-   ) is Ulster born, but there was a time when he was closely associated with the Abbey as author and producer. The fact that he was an astute director had nothing to do with the success of his early plays for it was not until 1915 that he came to the Abbey. Ulster Irish by birth and tradition, his thinking and writing has mostly been pure English, but with occasional excursions into the North of Ireland. He is a serious dramatist (or was), concerned primarily with the various problems that beset us in life. In recent years he has written only plays designed for commercial success.

Ervine began his writing career with a harsh and bitter piece about religious hypocrisy called *The Magnanimous Lover* (1912) which was not produced until after *Mixed Marriage* (1911) though it was written several years earlier. The first is of little importance, but the second established him as a playwright of distinction in this study of Protestants and Catholics in Belfast. John Rainey's is the consistently drawn character of a stubborn realist, whereas his wife is movingly tender, generous, and humorous. The agony of conflict which seems peculiarly virulent in Ireland is admirably expressed in this drama. If the play ends in a tragic impasse it is because no solution has yet been found, and even now in the midst of a bitter ideological war in the whole world, the Irish are still unable to resolve their difficulties.

Annoyed at the newspaper reception of *The Magnanimous Lover*, at the Abbey, Ervine retaliated by satirizing the gentry of the press in *The Critics* (1913). This slight but entertaining piece did little to improve the situation when he was called to the Abbey as producer in 1915. Following *The Critics* came another well regarded drama, *Jane Clegg* (1913), which was entirely English in feeling and subject-matter. This study of the indomitable woman in sordid surroundings fighting for the education and freedom of her children is lifted out of humdrum reality by the nobility, perseverance, and extraordinary patience of Jane Clegg.

His next important work, and by far his best, was *John Ferguson* (1915) in which he created another powerful, noble character in the upstanding father who clings to his religious faith in the midst of adversity. Ervine weakens most of his serious plays by piling horror on horror. In this he is positively Elizabethan. The rape of Hannah in this play, the death of Nora in *Mixed Marriage,* are not entirely convincing. These things may very well have happened, but there is no dramatic conviction on the part of an audience that they must happen at the particular time that they did. Friends of the Theatre Guild wax sentimental over *John Ferguson* as its popular success saved that budding organization when it was on the rocks in 1920.

The same accidental happening, as in *Mixed Marriage,* crops up in the death of the son at sea which provides the dénouement of *The Ship* (1922). *Mary, Mary, Quite Contrary* is a thin and only faintly amusing comedy about the playful, amorous antics of a London actress. *The Lady of Belmont* (1927) is a reworking of *The Merchant of Venice. The First Mrs.*

Fraser (1928) is a smooth, polished, slick comedy for Shaftesbury Avenue and Broadway. It plays well; it is (or was) faintly shocking, just enough to titillate the senses. It was nicely calculated to win the large success it had, but it is unlikely that it would stand revival. *Anthony and Anna* (1927) and *Robert's Wife* (1937) are fitted with middle-class English morality and humor and have had a good deal of popular success though the writing is rather stodgy. Probably Ervine has written out all the good that is in him. Violent he was, occasionally improbable, but certainly the man had real power in his three early plays, two of Ulster and one of England.

Let us turn to Ireland pure and simple and South of Ireland this time, in Lennox Robinson (1886-   ) who began writing slightly earlier than Ervine. *The Clancy Name,* a one-acter, was performed in 1908, revised and represented the following year. It is a grim tragedy of Irish pride which does not quite come off though it is provided with an ironic ending. Robinson was no more successful with *The Cross Roads* the same year in which he lost his balance completely. *Harvest* (1910) shows some improvement though his basic thesis seems wrong. Granted that formal education may be more suited to urban rather than rural living, all the horrors that befall the Hurley family do not rightly stem from education. *Patriots* (1912) displays a fine contempt for the lack of spirit in Ireland just prior to World War I. In *The Dreamers* (1915), Robinson writes of Robert Emmett's attempted rebellion of 1803 and in this historical piece he finds himself as a dramatist.

The Whiteheaded Boy (1916) is one of the best Irish comedies—curiously enough there have been few good ones to come out of a people whose sense of humor is notoriously fine. This is full, warm, human writing. Robinson enjoys himself in this play poking fun at his Irish friends just as he does in *Drama at Inish* (1933, produced in America as *Is Life Worth Living?*). *The Lost Leader* (1918) is one of his most exciting dramas which does not quite come off, evidently because as a dramatist he never made up his mind whether he wanted to make an audience believe that Parnell did not die but was still alive as old Lucius Lenihan, or not. It is nevertheless an arresting play which kindles the imagination.

There is a mixture of satire and sheer charm to his one-act *Crabbed Youth and Age* (1922). Of his later plays, perhaps the most interesting is the nostalgic *The Big House* (1926) which welcomes into being the New Ireland at the same time that it regrets the passing of the great Anglo-Irish families with their culture, charm, and hospitality. *The Far-Off Hills* (1928) has ironic and wry dramatic values, but it is certainly in his comedies that he reaches his highest attainments. Lennox Robinson is closely identified with the Abbey Theatre where most of his plays were first given. He was manager and director from 1909 to 1914 and again from 1919 to 1923, and later on was stage director with Arthur Shields after being relieved of his office and managerial tasks. He is one of the best and most characteristic of the Irish dramatists. Although never reaching the heights of Synge or O'Casey, he has achieved the respectable rank of second-best writer.

T. C. Murray (1873-   ) is one of the leading Irich Catholic dramatists and the one who can best be said to represent enlightened Roman thought in Eire as opposed to the Protestant view of Robinson. He is a realist as *Birthright* (1910), his second play, indicates, but no one who lives in his country can be entirely without poetry or longing as this retelling of the Cain and Abel story shows. *Maurice Harte,* two years later, emphasizes the inherent realism which is characteristic of all Murray's work. He pulls no punches in his condemnation of the barter system and sheer commercialism in Irish marriages which were to be found in the rural areas. He tackled this in his first piece, a one-act drama, *The Wheel of Fortune* (1909) as well. Too often Murray depends on accidental happenings to turn the plot and effect the conclusion he is seeking. The climax then is forced, unnatural, and not always inevitable. His best play certainly is *Autumn Fire* (1924) which treats the same situation that Eugene O'Neill does in *Desire Under the Elms,* that of a widower who is still extremely passionate and marries a young wife whom his son also desires. As a good Catholic, Murray could not see divorce as a solution—or sudden death for that matter—so when the play ends the struggle is still unresolved and the younger pair can only resign themselves to wait for the death of the older man.

Padraic Colum (1881-   ) has been long domiciled in America, but his principal contribution to the drama came in his early years in Ireland so he properly belongs to this section of the book. It now is hard to believe that Colum was once as highly regarded as Synge or Lady Gregory. He was a very young man at the time of the establishment of the Irish Literary Theatre and grew up with the movement. His first pieces were *The Kingdom of Youth* and *The Foleys,* both in 1902, *The Saxon Shillin',* the following year, which propagandized against Irishmen's joining up with English regiments. *Broken Soil* (1903) was rewritten as *The Fiddler's House* four years later and remains Colum's best play, or at least the first two acts of it do. The third is weak and destroys much of the powerful effect of this tale of a man who loves music and wandering, but who has remained at home because of the love, devotion, and sheer force of his two daughters. *The Land* (1905) is a bleak portrayal of the struggle between the older and the younger generations, while in *Thomas Muskerry* (1910) Colum wrote one of the last of his full-length plays. In this he shows clearly the influence of Ibsen and in it is more imitative than interpretative. This latter is what had given his other plays a kinship with the drama of Ireland. In his language, too, is to be found the Irish speech most usually spoken because his poetry lay in his imagination rather than in his dialogue. There were, of course, the rather formless *Mogu, The Wanderer* (1917) and *Balloon,* which has again been rewritten and was performed with some success at Ogunquit, Maine, in 1946. Colum's continued absence from the drama of

Ireland or America is a real loss; perhaps *Balloon* will restore him to the theatre of his adopted if not his native land.

There are at least three other Irish playwrights who should be mentioned, if only briefly. There is a genuinely comic quality about the writing of William Boyle (1853-1923) which has always been popular in his own country, though his plays seem flat and rather uninteresting to a foreigner. The celebrated "House Full" sign went up on the doors of the Abbey Theatre when *The Building Fund* (1905), *The Eloquent Dempsey* (1906), *The Mineral Workers* (1906), *Family Failing* (1912), and *Nic* (1916) were offered. *The Mineral Workers* (1906) was a serious attempt to deal with economics in Boyle's native land, though its solution was a little pat, as though he had seen too many plays by Robertson and Pinero.

George Fitzmaurice has attracted the attention of Irish critics though the public has never taken too kindly to his plays, nor have they attracted a following outside his own country. He is a folk dramatist like Colum, Lady Gregory, and Synge, but a long way removed from them in dramatic force. *The Country Dressmaker* (1907) was a well observed piece of writing and in many ways a remarkable first play. He followed it the next year with an unusual one-acter, *The Pie-Dish,* which offended many of the Abbey Theatre's audience. It was five years before his next piece, *The Magic Glasses* appeared. This one-acter was a fantasy with realistic phrasing and can be linked with *The Dandy Dolls* (1914) another short piece which it closely resembles in style. *The Moonlighter* (1914) is a four-acter which is laid at the time of the agrarian revolution in Ireland and is more nearly conventional than any other work of Fitzmaurice. Just to offer contrast the managers of the Abbey who had encouraged Fitzmaurice, would have nothing to do with Seumas O'Kelly (1881-1918) until after he had won acclaim elsewhere; of course, a good deal of this must have come from his adherence to the Theatre of Ireland, a rival group, which had been set up as a chauvinistic political protest against *The Playboy of the Western World*. It was through that organization that O'Kelly's most considerable play, *The Shuiler's Child,* had its première in 1909, although when the Abbey got around to it late the following year, O'Kelly's name became known to a wider public. It is as a novelist and a short-story writer that he was best known outside of Ireland, but certainly this one social drama at least deserves the largest possible audience. Of other Irish dramatists some account is given in volumes exclusively devoted to the Irish branch of British drama, here let it suffice to mention Joseph Campbell, Seumas O'Brien, Thomas McDonagh, Rutherford Mayne, and Lewis Purcell as men who contributed to the local stage in the decade between 1905 and World War I.

Among Irish dramatists who came to the fore after World War I Sean O'Casey (1884-   ) has no peer. In fact he could acknowledge but one superior, and that is Synge. The stature of his plays is such as to command instantaneous respect. His characterization and his ability to write dialogue have thrust him into the forefront of the truly great modern dramatists of whatever nationality. His background was of the poorest, having been brought up in a slum near Dublin, the story of which he has recounted in two brilliant volumes of autobiography—*I Knock at the Door* and *Pictures in the Hallway*. He worked as a bricklayer in his native city, having taught himself to read through his absorption of Shakespeare when he was fourteen. For a long time no one would give his plays serious attention. Finally at the age of thirty-nine, after years of trying, the doors of the Abbey were opened, where in his youth he had gone night after night to watch the plays of the great and the near-great, and so to learn his technique by observation of the best writing available to him. His first play to be seen was *The Shadow of a Gunman* (1923) which is a brilliant melodrama of cowardice. In this play three of his great gallery of characters were shown to a wildly cheering audience—brave Minnie Powell, cowardly Seumas, who had been thought a gunman, and Donal Davoren, "poet and poltroon, poltroon and poet."

O'Casey's plays are completely lacking in classic form. Like all great innovators in modern drama he wrote of life and the people about him, the people he knew well and loved and pitied and hated and admired. Like Chekhov and Schnitzler and O'Neill, he projected something of his own environment before the footlights, a new rich source of dramatic tales. His sense of plot has always been slight and his abrupt shift from laughter to tears and back again has puzzled the critics but delighted the crowds. In the end the farseeing reviewers were rewarded for their faith in this softspoken Dubliner. In America it was George Jean Nathan who first preached the gospel of O'Casey, but the other critics were not too far behind. Though Nathan could not and would not follow O'Casey into Communism, he has never failed to admire his work and to be his spokesman, after a fashion.

Cathleen Listens In (1923) and *Nannie's Night Out* (1924) are negligible farcical comedies, but the latter year brought one of this century's great dramas, *Juno and the Paycock*. This unforgettable tale of the terror of civil war in Ireland, the depredations of the Black and Tans and the Irish Republican Army, is not likely soon to leave the mind of a single one of its auditors. The tragic and humorous wasters, Captain Boyle, the Paycock, and his irrepressible crony, Joxer, and the great, unhappy, loving Juno who is one of the most magnificent mothers of Irish or any other drama, stand out in memory. The quick shifts from uproarious laughter to bitter despair and unbearable anguish are hard to accept in the theatre, but audience after audience has accepted them and applauded O'Casey.

The Plough and the Stars (1926) produced absolute pandemonium on the occasion of its première. You would have to go back to *The Playboy of the Western World* and O'Riordan's *The Piper* to find another such scene of shame and disorder. It is not quite clear why this play rather than the two major ones which preceded it evoked such violence. O'Casey had himself fought in the Citizen Army in the famous Easter Week rebellion of 1916. He had the utmost respect for the men who fought that mistaken but gallant fight. At the same time he was anti-militarist and he refused to glorify what seemed to him at the time of writing, perhaps, a tragic mistake. He relates the story of that week in the terms of the people of one tenement—Catholic and gossipy Mrs. Gogan; good-for-nothing Fluther; tragic, unhappy, and eventually mad Nora Clitheroe; and her young husband who was torn twixt love and duty. These people pulsate with life in a way that makes your heart go out to them.

However, when it came time for *The Silver Tassie* (1929), the Abbey would have none of it. It was left to a London producer to give it its première at the Apollo Theatre with Charles Laughton (as Harry Heegan, the incapacitated sportsman and warrior), Beatrix Lehman, and Barry Fitzgerald. This play is harsh, cruel, and unbearably honest in its dealings with impotency, horror, and the wrongness of fighting of any kind. This pacificism infuriated O'Casey's Irish enemies and even dampened the enthusiasm of some of his friends. Despite Irish neutrality in the present world conflict, which has some able apologists, the Irish people are hardly to be described as pacificists.

It was not until 1934 and in New York that O'Casey's next play was offered under the sponsorship of George Bushar (Markle) and John Tuerk. *Within the Gates* was both a critical and popular success. This allegory of the modern world with its symbolical Young Whore, The Young Dreamer, The Bishop, and The Old Woman is laid in a Hyde Park of the author's imagination. Some of his richest and most lyrical writing is to be found here. The music of Milton Lusk and Lehman Engel, though a bit too "modern," did much to enrich the production as did the acting of Lillian Gish, Bramwell Fletcher, Moffat Johnson, and Mary Morris. This play showed a change in direction in O'Casey's writing which has recurred in *The Stars Turn Red* and *Red Roses For Me*. *The End of the Beginning* (1939) is merely a forty-minute comic one-acter staged in Paris which has no great significance for this work.

Some of O'Casey's greatest admirers either were baffled or annoyed by the implicit communism in *The Stars Turn Red* (1940). Several readings of the play fail to bring to light any reason for such violent reactions on their part. Laid in Dublin during the 1913 strike, the author has made bold use of symbolism as in *Within the Gates,* but the comic spirit which is always present in O'Casey breaks out in a few spots. It is a fine and moving play which would scarcely seem more than left-liberal in production in the opinion of this writer. *Purple Dust,* published the same year, is an enormously amusing comedy which spoofs the more obvious English types and contrasts them with Irish wit and wiliness. George Jean Nathan has hailed it as a first-rate comedy but it has not yet been played. The reasons which prevented its performance in the year it was published were frankly these: England had just undergone the great blitz, London and Coventry and Dover had been blasted by vandals. Any play satirizing the English would have given aid and comfort to their enemies and strengthened the hands of certain persons in America who wished to place England in the most unfavorable light possible. However, for its reading public, the play is sheer delight, being filled with the rich and biting humor for which O'Casey is famous.

His most recent piece is *Red Roses For Me,* which attracted attention on the occasion of its late spring 1943 première in Dublin. Richard Watts Jr. reported that it is a straightforward drama for the first two acts and then switches to symbolism for the last two. In it, he finds some of the author's best writing, some engaging characters (always an O'Casey trade-mark), and a basically interesting idea. On the debit side he found that in production the symbolism destroys some of the drama's effectiveness.

Of some authors, it is impossible to say whether their work will endure or not, but of O'Casey there can be no doubt. His amazingly fine and true dialogue, his three-dimensional characters, his accurate depiction of a background, and his fine sense of selective realism are major contributions not only to the Irish branch of British drama, but to the whole field of modern play writing.

Next to O'Casey the best-known name in this last decade is certainly that of Paul Vincent Carroll (1900-   ). This Irish-born Glasgow schoolmaster came into prominence at a moment when the older dramatist was preoccupied with theatrical experimentation and autobiography. After a none too auspicious beginning with *The Watched Pot* (1931) he rapidly progressed to *Things That Are Caesar's* (1932, in collaboration with the deaf and dumb playwright, Teresa Deevey, who was alone responsible for the moving *Katie Roche,* 1936) which won the Abbey Theatre Prize and was seen in Dublin and widely on tour in the United States. This was a portrait of the Hardy family showing the struggle between the bigoted mother and the free-thinking father over their daughter's happiness. This hostility to certain aspects of the Church is carried over into *Shadow and Substance* (1934) which contrasted the liberal and illiberal wings of Catholicism in their reaction to a seeming miracle. The idealistic and irreligious schoolmaster is obviously a favorite Carroll character. This play was chosen as the best foreign play of the season 1936-1937 by the New York Drama Critics' Circle. This honor was later accorded to *The White Steed* (1938) in which more than ever Carroll lined up the three opposing educational forces. In this case the rather stupid old-fashioned vicar is infinitely more human and humane than the terrifyingly modern priest. The rebellious schoolteacher and young librarian are caught between two fires and mowed down mercilessly. These plays, despite their themes, contain a rich fund of humor which has done much to make them popular with the average public. His one-act play, *The Coggerers* (1939) deals with the Easter rebellion, a favorite Irish dramatic subject. Carroll's last two plays do not measure up to his first work though much of the thinking and writing of *Kindred* (1939) is as fine as anything he has ever done. The family, art, and the artist are the subjects of some fine introspective and poetic writing which does not quite come off dramatically. The following year brought a combination of Irish dreams and broad horseplay in *The Old Foolishness* which was out of the author's ragbag of unassimilated dramatic ideas.

Dublin took most kindly to the war play, *The Strings, My Lord, Are False* (1942), but the New York verdict was thumbs down. It is a confused play about the place of the Church in modern war. The scene was laid in the crypt and offices of the church itself with the kind-hearted canon of a Scottish flock taking his Christian duties most literally. Carroll obviously wrote the play with his heart rather than with his mind. The scope of his subject-matter, so far, is somewhat limited which has robbed him of some of his natural force. However, in the conflict of the Church and liberalism he has given us at least two fine plays and is still a relatively young man so that the final verdict on Carroll is to be found a long way in the future.

Developing alongside O'Casey and slightly preceding Carroll was Brinsley MacNamara (1890-   ) who is known outside Ireland as a novelist, and also as an actor for he toured America with the Abbey Theatre Players, but who has some considerable reputation in his own country as a playwright. His first play, *The Rebellion in Balleycullen* (1919) was a satire on Irish jingoism which augured well for his development as a dramatist. He followed this with a serious and angry indictment of the men who sponsor land agitation in Ireland and then appropriate the gains for themselves. *The Land for the People* (1920) was several times rewritten and revived. The most successful version came in 1927. In the meantime he turned to light comedy with the popular *The Glorious Uncertainty* (1923) which celebrated in hilarious fashion the doings of race-track followers. MacNamara excels in the details of character drawing, perhaps it is because he has the novelist's approach. The foibles of the self-righteous made up the small-town fun of *Look at the Heffernans* (1926). Both of these plays were great favorites at the Abbey Theatre and have frequently reappeared in their repertoire. In *The Master* (1928), MacNamara returns both in style and in subject-matter to his first play. In them both he was striving to show the political turmoil of the New Ireland as it was settling down to become just what the Old Ireland was. *Margaret Gillan* (1933) does not depart from his normal dramatic approach. In *The Three Thimbles* (1942), a title taken from the old confidence game, the playwright returns to the rollicking mood of *The Glorious Uncertainty*. The play is unnecessarily confused because MacNamara does not take his audience into his confidence until the third act. His characterization is as rich as ever. It is for this facet of dramatic writing that he is likely to be remembered.

George Shiels (1886-   ) is a lively comic writer with a flair for dialogue and for plot. His first play was the one-acter, *Bedmates* (1921) which was succeeded by another mild farce, *Insurance Money,* the same year. *Paul Twyning* (1922) was liked, despite its complicated plot, because of its central figure, an itinerant worker. He is a kind of symbol of a past Ireland and as such provoked the Abbey audiences to laughter. Shiels has become increasingly important to that theatre because of his many contributions to its repertoire. An invalid due to an accident, he has been considerably handicapped by his inability to watch his plays in rehearsal and performance, an invaluable aid to any author no matter how experienced. *Professor Tim* (1925) which is again character comedy, built around the antics of the name part, repeated its Dublin success in London two years later. Of his later plays, easily the best is *The New Gossoon* (1930), which is a lively comedy about a young wastrel son of a respected family. Dennis O'Dea contributed much to the humor of the piece by the deftness of his playing of Luke Cary, the "Gossoon." It is unlikely that Shiels will ever emerge as a first-rate dramatist because of the contrived nature of his plots which is particularly noticeable in *The Jailbird* (1936), *Quin's Secret* (1937), and *Neal Maquade* (1938). Two of Shiel's later plays have, however, enhanced his local reputation by their sparkling characterization of the Tansey family. These sequels are *The Rugged Path* (1940) and *The Summit* (1941) which held Dublin audiences and won approbation from the Irish critics.

Denis Johnston (1901-   ) is a later Irish playwright who has written several plays of interest and at least one of importance, *The Moon in the Yellow River* (1931). This is a fine and uncompromising study of Irish character which is honest and forthright. Hostility to change, resistance to new ideas, dislike of liberalism, so permeate most of the people that even any idea of improvement in their living habits is impossible. If Irish dramatists truthfully reflect Ireland in their plays, and there is abundant evidence that they do, then it is a wonder indeed that *any* plays of merit get written at all. *The Old Lady Says 'No'* (1929) is an expressionist piece which is not unlike the mood which produced Strindberg's *The Dream Play*. *A Bride for the Unicorn* (1933) follows the same tradition and contains some very nearly great poetry which sings and soars and falls. *Storm Song* (1934) is a rather heavy-handed attempt at a satire on the cinema, in this instance, the expeditions which make such documentary films as that fine one, *Man of Aran*. *Blind Man's Buff* (1936) after Ernst Toller, the German dramatist, was a rather abortive attempt to capture the inherent, ironic tragedy of the original *Die Blinde Gottin* (1934). In *The Golden Cuckoo* (1939) Johnston has sought to portray a modern Diogenes. On the whole his work is uneven, but never uninteresting. It is too soon to pigeonhole him.

The Earl of Longford (Edward Arthur Henry Dakenham, 1902-   ) and Lady Longford who joined Dublin Gate Theatre in 1931, an organization designed to be international rather than local in its outlook, also wrote plays. Of these the best known is the historical drama about Dean Swift, which is called *Yahoo* (1933). The play had a very considerable success in Dublin where the irascible eighteenth-century writer was very much at home. However the script fails to carry across the Atlantic. In 1943 there was a popular revival in its own country, a small island surrounded by war.

There are new writers coming along in present-day Ireland, but none of them so far has risen high enough to merit mention. There is a vigorous dramatic tradition inherent in Irish writing which bodes well for the future. After periods of comparative sterility, the bush has always borne blooms again. Despite frequent public indifference to what is good, despite church meddling or downright effort to censor the literary output, despite the insistence of the extreme nationalists on muzzling any drama which seems to suggest that life in Ireland is not perfect, despite the fuzzy sentimentality that turns to rage at any valid, constructive criticism, Irish drama of the twentieth century is healthy and reasonably prolific. More power then to the Irish writers, who, in their own country, receive so little encouragement to write honestly and without impediment.

V

France and Belgium

S. A. RHODES

The French drama is traditional in essence. It rebels against rules and conventions periodically in order to get back to first principles, to its roots and substance. That is why modern dramatic movements and advanced-guard theatres have included in their repertoires classical plays by Molière and Shakespeare. They are like young branches that shoot off the trunk of an old tree. Ultimately they blend with its secular outline; but the flowers and fruits they bear are fresh every season.

The modern French drama can be appreciated best then in the light of its traditions and ideals. These began back in the Middle Ages, when the theatre was liturgical and allegorical in character, on the one hand, reared by the Church for the religious edification of the masses, and comical and satirical, on the other, fostered by the people as an entertaining mirror of their earthly foibles. Both aspects gave rise to significant dramatic genres in later ages, the former to the religious tragedies of Corneille, Racine, and the mystery-dramas of Claudel—than which there are no equivalents in any other literature, save in the sacramental autos of Calderón—and the latter, more popular in vein, and refined through Attic, Roman, and Italian models, to the theatre of Molière and its posterity, the comedy of manners and character. As for the neoclassic tragedy, it was ushered onto the modern stage by the Renaissance at the same time that the miracle play was ushered out by the Reformation. This revival culminated in the art of Corneille and Racine which they converted into appropriate dramatic patterns apt to interpret the heroic and tragic moods of the age, as Molière did of the comedy for its prosaic and poetic daily aspects. Artistic simplicity, intensity, and integrity, technically manifested in the tenets of the three unities of action, time, and place, became their dramatic ideals, as they had been in principle for their Greek models. Thus by the latter half of the seventeenth century, the French drama had come of age. In its tragedy and comedy it had founded traditions of the heroic, the tragic, and the comic on the stage which future dramatic generations were to emulate, to break, or to revert to intermittently, but which they were never to forget at their best.

The age of Voltaire was radical in thought but traditional in form. In the drama it cleaved to the neoclassical line. But its loyalty proved to be superior to its performance. Midway between the tragedy and the comedy there evolved, then, a new genre, the "serious comedy" or "bourgeois drama," which partook of the virtues of both, and which sought to express the newly rising middle-class tempo on the social as well as on the sentimental levels. This was heralded by the subtle, "spiderweb" variations on love of Marivaux (1688-1763), a "Racine in miniature," the threads of which were to be recaptured by a Musset or a Sarment in future generations, or by the "tearful comedy" of Nivelle de la Chaussée (1692-1754), which was destined to have its own posterity of pathetic "tear-jerkers." The new drama found its stoutest champion in Denis Diderot (1713-1784). He sought to focus the limelight not on what is sublime in human passion, which is the domain of tragedy, nor on what is amusing in the spectacle of human frailty, which is that of traditional comedy, but on what makes a true emotional and edifying appeal, be the characters portrayed as noble or humble, involved in personal and domestic difficulties and sorrows, or in moral, social, and philosophical problems. This idea, which he embodied in the play *Le Père de famille* (1758), represented the embryo of the modern drama. Unfortunately, Diderot's creative faculty did not measure up to the originality of his conception. It was to be developed to its fuller potentialities in future years in the dramas of Emile Augier and Alexandre Dumas fils.

The Molièresque comedy of manners and character prospered, on the other hand, thanks to Alain-René Lesage (1668-1747), whose *Turcaret* (1709) became the ancestral model for later portraits of unscrupulous financiers by Balzac or Henri Becque; and thanks to Beaumarchais (1732-1799), a witty, genial, and satirical French Sheridan, whose *Le Mariage de Figaro* (1784), adapted as *The Follies of a Day or The Marriage of Figaro* by the British dramatist Thomas Holcroft, and played in America in 1795, had sounded "the tocsin of the Revolution" not only in the political and social, but in the dramatic fields as well.

The Revolution overthrew everything save the three unities and the pseudo-classic tragedy of the day, out of sentimental loyalty, in part, to what it esteemed to be its ancient Greek and Roman republican antecedents. It seized upon the theatre as an instrument of propaganda, and filled the old bottles with the heady and cloudy wine of the season's vintage. In this, indeed, lay the virtue of the revolutionary drama. Directly or indirectly, it expressed contemporary passions and struggles, and so it laid down a bridge between the stage and the masses, and reëstablished that intimate contact between the two upon which the existence of the theatre depends.

Of the new genres that were attempted, Marie-Joseph Chénier's (1764-1811) historical "national tragedy" proved to be a tempting but empty bubble. A better fate awaited N. Lemercier's (1771-1840) ingenious "historical comedy" *Pinto* (1799), in which the dramatic process of the classical tragedy is inverted, and great passions and events are reduced to the scale of the common man, as befitted an equalitarian age. The genre was to be exploited in after years by Eugène Scribe and his theatrical progeny. The same pull from below caused the bourgeois drama envisaged by Diderot to deviate and deteriorate into melodrama that catered to the growing appetite of the drama-conscious crowd. The latter may be credited, in turn, with introducing and fostering increased action, color, design, and movement on the stage, and with forwarding the nullification of the sacrosanct rules of the unities which was to be completed by the forthcoming romantic drama.

The Empire, like the Revolution, was not very fortunate on the stage. Napoleon favored the classical tragedy, and complained bitterly of the poor stuff that was strutted before the imperial footlights. "I have heard some abominable verses sung at the Opera," he wrote in 1806 from Berlin. "Are they trying to disgrace literature in France? It is ridiculous to order an eclogue like a muslin dress. Since literature is your domain," he told his minister Champany, "make it your business to look after it, for in truth what has been sung at the Opera is much too shameful." But it was easier for him to win campaigns than to inspire beautiful dramatic works. In brief, the pseudo-classic theatre had reached a dead end. The old social, moral, and religious order it had mirrored was disintegrating, and its traditions and dramatic design had become warped and stultified, at last.

In that confined dramatic climate, scarcely relieved by the melodramatic innovations of Guilbert de Pixerécourt's (1773-1844) very popular boulevard theatre—with its elaborate scenery, complicated intrigue, violent action, sympathetic hero and heroine, arch villain, and comic relief (later to be found in the romantic drama), and happy dénouements—the effect of foreign influences—Shakespeare's, Schiller's, Manzoni's, whose works were translated or re-edited in 1821 and 1823—was like an influx of fresh air into a close atmosphere. The appearance of a Shakespearean company of actors, headed by Kemple, Kean, and Miss Smithson (the future Mrs. Hector Berlioz, who starred as Ophelia and Desdemona), stirred the imagination of the rising generation with the spectacle of a drama free from the shackles of the unities of time and place, and rich with an abundance of the color, movement, depth, comedy, and tragedy of life which made the pseudo-classic tragedy look quite pale by contrast. In December of that same year, 1827, Victor Hugo's (1802-1885) preface to his unplayable *Cromwell* gave a ringing expression to those new dramatic stirrings and served as a manifesto for the rising romantic school. In 1829 Alexandre Dumas (1802-1870) inaugurated the historical drama with *Henri III et sa cour,* and the season after, at the première, which turned out to be the battle, of Hugo's *Hernani,* the romantic phalanx pitted itself against the pseudo-classicists who still dominated the stage. The old guard was routed, and for thirteen years after the romantic standards were to wave on the stage.

The romantic drama that ensued was historical in general, drawing its dramatic substance from national and foreign medieval or later epochs, and, in contrast to the pseudo-classic tragedy, priding itself on faithfulness to picturesque detail and local color. It threw off the traditional restraints governing versification and the unities, but distinguished itself from contemporary melodrama by donning a cloak of poetry. To crown all, it is worthy of note that in keeping with the romantic poet's newly assumed social rôle, the drama too claimed to have a novel moral and symbolic mission. In practice it proved to be a complicated pattern of passionate characters, extravagant contradictions, lofty declamations, and unbelievable intrigues that betrayed a chaotic vision of reality rather than a keen insight into the drama of life. Through it, as Jean-Richard Bloch observes, an orgy of moonlighted or stormy scenes, of galloping horses, clashing swords, dark forests and highways, penetrated pell-mell the French creative imagination and stage. Gradually, the type became hackneyed and commercialized. In time the public wearied of its sensationalism. Beginning in 1838, the classical tragedy experienced a triumphant, if short-lived, revival, through the genius of the actress Rachel. Five years later, the failure of Hugo's *Les Burgraves*, coinciding with the success of François Ponsard's (1814-1867) pseudo-classic tragedy *Lucrèce*, signaled the triumph of the School of Common Sense and the end of the romantic period in the drama.

Withal, its concern with the social and moral destiny of the individual had made of it a forerunner of the later social drama. Hugo's *Marion Delorme* (1831) was the ancestress of all future Camilles. Dumas' *Antony* (1831)— a rôle created by the actor Bocage, "tall, dark, and handsome," who became the model of the fatal romantic lover for two generations after—portrayed the destiny of the social outcast caught in the tangles of love, crime, and violence, and foreshadowed the modern drama of domestic struggles and tragedies. Alfred de Vigny's (1797-1863) *Chatterton* (1835), one of the best plays of the period, dramatized the situation of the superior man ill-adapted in society, with characters that stand as symbols—thus betokening the future drama of ideas.

But the outstanding dramatic contribution of the era was made by Alfred de Musset (1810-1857), the most romantic temperamentally, although the least dogmatic esthetically, of the romantic writers. Designed with a perfect blend of reality and fiction, his plays unfold in an exquisitely ordered realm that is situated between the passionate depth of Racine's tragedies and the precious gallantries of Marivaux's comedies, with something in it of Shakespeare's flights of fancy. Their subtle psychological insight into human emotion, their delicacy of tone and lyric expression created a poetic mood which has been echoed repeatedly in succeeding generations on the French stage.

The social order that had sprung from the Revolution, bourgeois, industrial, and agrarian in character, was anything but romantic in its political philosophy. Long before 1843, it had found in the theatre of Eugène Scribe (1791-1861) a pleasing image of its smug design of life. Too refined to satisfy the masses, yet too banal to please people of refinement, his well-made, genteel comedies, some four hundred of them, won and held the suffrage of his middle-class patrons, and not those of his own country alone. The historical drama *Adrienne Lecouvreur* (written with Ernest Legouvé, 1849), whose American première dates from 1853, was still being revived in New York as late as 1908, and the clever *Bataille de dames* (with Legouvé, 1851), first adapted in America in 1867, reappeared here as *There's Many a Slip* in 1902.

"What is the secret of your art?" he asked A. de Musset after a performance of the latter's *Le Chandelier,* in 1850.

"What is yours?" rejoined Musset.

"My secret," said Scribe, "is to amuse the public."

"Mine," replied Musset, "is to amuse myself."

That is the secret of the best in art, but Scribe's was not of the best. Skilful at weaving amusing and striking situations, at arousing curiosity and suspense, at tying and untying impossible knots, he had, in addition, the secret of imparting the illusion of reality to arbitrary intrigues and characters. The latter were sentimental and gay marionettes no less theatrical than the cardboard heroes of the romantic drama, even though Scribe controlled their simulated movements on the stage with more dexterous fingers. His theatre, in brief, was an exhibition of showmanship rather than an expression of life. He formalized and systematized dramatic creativeness, spontaneity, reality, and truth in the theatre. He converted playwriting into a craft which aspiring dramatists studied afterwards, using his well-made plays as textbooks. But though his influence was persistent and widespread, and because of it, it proved to be detrimental to genuine dramatic creation for a legion of followers and descendants who adhered to his system slavishly. Because of it, Emile Zola observed, "the dramatic art was dying of inanity."

A reaction set in against this theatrical "inanity" and against its antithetic romantic extravagance. This resulted in the surge of the realistic movement, and the resurgence of the social drama previewed the century before. The amusing, self-complacent picture of the middle classes exhibited in the puppet-show of Scribe was displaced by a searching, not always amusing, and realistic portrait in the plays of Augier and Dumas fils. Its nascence, or renascence, had been prefigured by Honoré de Balzac's (1799-1850) brave dramatic essays, in particular his *Mercadet* (1851), which d'Ennery had put into final shape, and which portrayed the world of finance and usury. He tried to transplant from the novel to the drama his genius for observation and character study. But the art of the theatre, of creating living dialogue and character on the stage, was beyond his ken.

The School of Common Sense, already referred to, represented a transition stage between expiring romanticism and nascent realism. It was symbolized by the work of its presumed founder, François Ponsard, whose play *Charlotte Corday,* dating from the exact middle of the century, pretends to the picturesqueness of romantic drama and the simplicity of classical tragedy.

That middle of the century saw also a throne tumble down, the birth and death of a republic, the rise of a dictatorship, the growth of positive science, materialism, and industrialism. Romantic fantasy was superseded by reason, not the pure reason of the seventeenth century, which aspired to apprehend what is universal and absolute, but every man's own private reason. These private reasons, the particular modes and passions of life of individual characters, are what the realistic drama was to study, or defend, and not what concerned all men in all times and climes. It was to be social in the restricted sense of a special social class, specifically the middle class. Its most gifted exponents were Augier and Dumas fils.

Emile Augier (1820-1889) began his career as an adept of the school of Common Sense, to whose ideals he remained faithful always on the moral side. His early dramas in verse are typified by his *Gabrielle* (1849) with its celebrated line: "O father of the family, O poet, I love you!" The verse changed to prose in his later plays, but the spirit remained the same, and had as its motif what one may describe as the "defense and illustration" of the bourgeois social and moral codes. His chief themes were the virtues of the family and the dangers that threatened it, from within and without. This he illustrated well with *Le Gendre de M. Poirier* (1854), where he dramatized the conflicts between the moneyed and the blood aristocracies; and with *Le Mariage d'Olympe* (1855), which Clyde Fitch adapted into English as *The Marriage Game* (1901), and in which Augier condemns the courtesan, whom Dumas fils had portrayed in flattering colors shortly before.

He broached other social problems: that of clerical meddling in politics, in *Le Fils de Giboyer* (1862); that of the unscrupulous lawyer and his shady business dealings, in *Maître Guérin* (1864). But his dramas were circumscribed by the virtues and failings of a social perspective which exalted the kind father, the honest man, the sympathetic husband, all of whom, however, mirror their period, its strait-laced morality, prejudices, and worship of money. Awkwardly enough for the dramatist the result is that his worthy and favorite characters appear less interesting and alive on the stage than his rascals and villains.

His art was solid but unimaginative. Withal, it stood above that of Scribe by its vigorous, if limited grasp of vital matters, by his creation of living characters who are confronted with living issues. With him the author got off the stage once the curtain was raised, and the characters were left alone to struggle with their problems according to their own temperaments.

Such, unfortunately, was not the case with Alexandre Dumas fils (1824-1895). The circumstance of his having been "a natural son" brought up by "a prodigal father" made him turn his theatre into a platform against the social and moral conditions that made such things possible. He came into the limelight with *La Dame aux Camélias* (1852), which he had drawn in 1848 from his novel with the same title. He had written it in a few weeks under the emotional compulsion of a great sorrow, the death of a beloved friend, the well-known courtesan Marie Duplessis, a singularity that spiced for the public the genuine merits of the play, as well as afforded it a passionate dramatic experience quite unlike the cheery banalities it had become accustomed to in the Scribian comedies. In essence, the drama was a variation of the old romantic theme of Marion Delorme, of the courtesan regenerated by love. But the transmutation of the declamatory passions of a heroine of melodrama into the genuine sufferings of an intensely living creature launched the drama on a world-wide career. In New York *Camille* made an unpromising début in 1853, but it came into its own in after years, with such stars as Sarah Bernhardt, Réjane, Ethel Barrymore, and Eva Le Gallienne, among many others, to plead the cause of the lady of the camellias on the stage, and Greta Garbo on the silver screen. The play struck the note of the author's later dramatic work. Love was to be its chief motif—not the unbridled, all-forgiving passion of the romanticists, but love that redeems and uplifts the individual and society. That is why he condemned the bad fallen woman, in *La Femme de Claude* (1873), where he argued the husband's right even to kill her, but was merciful toward the gentle lamb who had gone astray, in *Les Idées de Mme Aubray* (1867), where the mother consents in the end to her son's marriage with his penitent mistress. He gave to love the social rôle Augier assigned to the family. "We must revive love in France," he pleaded, love within the law and the bonds of matrimony. He censured conjugal fickleness, the emancipated woman, and the seducer. He pleaded for civil protection for illegitimate children, and for divorce laws to solve conflicting marital relationships. His plays became abstract and didactic disquisitions on social problems of which the solutions were foreshadowed from the start. He converted the well-made play into a thesis play, and the stage into a sounding-board for the moral edification of bourgeois society. "We must inaugurate the 'useful theatre,'" he wrote in the preface to *Un Père prodigue* (1859), "at the risk of challenging the apostles of *l'art pour l'art,* three words utterly devoid of meaning. All literature whose aim is not perfectibility, morality—usefulness, in short—is a rickety and unhealthy, still-born literature." In brief, the reformer in him, the raisonneur, got constantly in the way of the dramatist.

But the thesis play did not kill the well-made Scribian comedy. It enjoyed a revival thanks especially to the genius of Victorien Sardou (1831-1908). On his shoulders fell the tinsel mantle of the old master. He broached all genres with equal facility and success: the comedy of intrigue, as with *Les Pattes de mouche* (1860), played as *A Scrap of Paper,* in America, since 1879; the gay satire of social manners, as in *La Famille Benoîton* (1865); or the political satire with *Rabagas* (1872), in which he painted the demagogue who turns conservative on reaching power. His works include dramas, melodramas, dramatic spectacles, humorous comedies like *Divorçons* (written with Emile de Najac, 1880), in which a wife decides not to leave her husband since the proposed Naquet divorce law took the spice out of adultery; dramas of passion written for Sarah Bernhardt, like *Fedora* (1882); and historical plays of which the best is the brilliant *Madame Sans-Gêne* (1893), an American favorite from its first production here in 1895. All are characterized by sparkling humor, gaiety, and the illusion of reality. He could stir up emotion and pathos, but lacked the depth and social purpose that distinguished his contemporaries Augier and Dumas fils. He excelled in the art of treating lightly serious subjects, and in the craft of pulling the dramatic strings in the best Scribian manner toward happy endings.

The other specialists of the light comedy at this time included the amiable and witty team of Henri Meilhac (1831-1897) and Ludovic Halévy (1834-1908). They wrote farces, comic-opera librettos, gay and light comedies like *La petite Marquise* (1874), and even a sentimental one like *Froufrou* (1869), in which a giddy adulteress repents and dies in the end, a play Agnes Ethel introduced to New York in 1870, and which has been revived as *Frou-Frou* several times since. They are all marked by humorous observation of social frailties and absurdities, and constitute a kaleidoscopic picture of all that was ephemeral, artificial, and mad in the Paris of their day. Another observer of contemporary manners and foibles was Edouard Pailleron (1834-1899), whose charming satire on popular lecturers, literary ladies, and pedants, *Le Monde où l'on s'ennuie* (1881), is a minor masterpiece. The outstanding playwright among them was Eugène Labiche (1815-1888). He was a master of high vaudeville, as with his celebrated *Le Chapeau de paille d'Italie* (1851), which was adapted as *The Wedding March* in New York in 1904, and readapted as *Horse Eats Hat,* by Edwin Denby and Orson Welles, as late as in 1936. On a higher plane were his farces which painted human failings, vices, and moral disorders, but in a jocular vein, and without straining for moral effects. To the latter category belongs *Le Voyage de M. Perrichon* (1860), written in collaboration with Edouard Martin, and freely adapted as *Cousin Billy,* by Clyde Fitch, in 1905. It is an ironical portrait of a bourgeois who prefers for son-in-law the man who is indebted to him to the one he is indebted to for saving his life. Labiche raised the farce to the level of satire, and developed it to the apogee of the genre.

Glancing back at this point, it will be seen that the French stage was held by the thesis play, on the one hand, and the entertaining but often frivolous, light comedy, on the other, with real drama struggling to catch a ray of the spotlight. Salvation for it lay in that dramatic struggle.

The bourgeois drama under the Second Empire developed moral traits and dramatic power, but no ideological perspective or poetic breath. Opposition to its circumscribed view of life and reality, though ineffective at first, gradually gathered momentum. In 1865, the Goncourt Brothers (Edmond, 1822-1896, and Jules de, 1830-1870) ventured a first sketch of a more literary drama that deviated from the well-made and the thesis plays. It represented a transition stage between the realistic and the naturalistic forms, with a curious admixture of morbid and poetic moods in it. *Henriette Maréchal* dramatized the situation then new on the stage of the daughter who falls in love with her mother's lover. The play was the victim of a cabal organized in the belief that it had been patronized by Princess Mathilde at the Comédie Française. It failed, and the authors who thought they had written an epoch-making masterpiece were quite bitter at the experience.

After them Villiers de l'Isle-Adam (1838-1889) raised the voice of rebellion with his little gem, *La Révolte,* produced in 1870 thanks to the sponsorship of Dumas fils himself, and staged as *The Revolt,* in New York, in 1905. The play anticipated Ibsen's *Doll's House* by nine years. It portrays a more realistic Nora who must return to her husband with her empty jewel box of dreams. Unlike Ibsen's drama, which sets forth a conflict between different temperaments and argues for the social emancipation of women, Villiers' opposes two contrary conceptions of life. Elisabeth represents the soul thirsting for the ideal, her husband the positivist mentality, and the twain could never meet. They speak different languages, and only the audience becomes aware of the abyss that divides them; the husband never does. It is a satire on modern materialism, which was suppressed after the fifth performance as dangerous to public morality. One critic observed that its heroine was not a "sympathetic" character because she had no lover; and others of his colleagues were no more understanding. "The theatre in France, which had been left in a good condition by Poquelin de Molière and Pierre Corneille, has become the opprobrium of modern art," retorted the exasperated author.

Another to try to save the stage, and to share the same fate, was Alphonse Daudet (1840-1897), with *L'Arlésienne* (1872), now a perennial favorite with the music of Bizet. The great Flaubert (1821-1880) was no more fortunate with his dramatic essays. Like Balzac he put all his drama in his novels. "The dramatic style is beginning to get on my nerves," he complained in connection with his play *Le Candidat,* which proved to be a failure in 1874. Discouraged and disgruntled, these novelists then gave up the drama as a hopeless genre in modern times. But there was at least one who proved to be more tenacious in his determination to save the theatre from itself, even though he himself did not possess the secret of the art any better than his colleagues did. He was Emile Zola (1840-1902). His first and best drama, *Thérèse Raquin* (1873), is an intense study of life in the lower depths, of two lovers who drown the unwanted husband and who seek in vain to live down their crime, under the accusing eyes of the dumb and paralyzed mother, and their own unremitting remorse, which leads them to suicide. The play deserved better than failure, witness the wide influence it has had over European drama. Zola's other dramatic works did not throw the pack of critics off his tracks. He supplemented his stage experiments with a sensational series of articles which he later collected in *Le Naturalisme au théâtre* and *Nos auteurs dramatiques,* and in which he championed with vigor and telling effect his naturalistic conception of dramatic art.

Unlike the classical ideal which held life to be rational and well-ordered, the naturalistic doctrine held it to be adrift in an eddy of blind instincts, of hereditary and social evils, of which art could take revealing snapshots. These are the "fragments of existence" Zola spoke of, the feelings, ideas, virtues, and vices he would study objectively, physiologically, and functionally in the theatre, just as sugar and vitriol are analyzed in the laboratory. He condemned the well-constructed drama in which the characters are predetermined along conventional patterns; he fought the rhetorical thesis play which argues from the surface of society about the decay going on within, instead of making a field exploration into its inner depths.

I am absolutely convinced [he wrote], that the naturalistic movement will soon assert itself in the theatre and will bring to it the power of reality, the new life of modern art. The experimental and scientific spirit of the century will spread to the theatre, and therein lies the only possibility of revival for our stage.

His prediction seemed to be borne out by the success of the dramatized version of *L'Assommoir* (1879) made by William Busnach and Gastineau, which Charles Reade adapted as *Drink* for the New York stage in 1903. Nevertheless, it may be doubted whether the drama called for would have materialized but for the appearance of a born dramatist who transformed the theories of the naturalistic school into the active ferment of a living drama. His name was Henri Becque.

Henri Becque (1837-1899) is the Flaubert of the theatre. He stands equally distant from the thesis play and the simon-pure naturalistic drama. "I have never had a great liking for assassins, hysterical and alcoholic characters, or for those martyrs of heredity and victims of evolution," he wrote. The play which established his reputation—after earlier hesitating essays like the still semimelodramatic *Michel Pauper* (1870)—and which inaugurated the modern French drama, was *Les Corbeaux*. Rejected by seven directors, it was produced finally at the Comédie Française, in 1882. It had three performances—three battles reminiscent of those of *Hernani*. It is the drama of a middle-class family well described by the servant Rosalie who says: "When a man dies and the creditors knock at the door, we can very well say: 'Here come the ravens, they leave only what they cannot carry off.'" The motif in the play might be different today; its treatment would be about the same. No technical frills, no thesis upholds or mars the dramatic action, which arises from an inevitable clash of circumstances and temperaments. Before the play is finished, the destiny of every character in it has been profoundly affected, but each according to his nature. And there is no spectacular conclusion to it, save the sad one that life is like that.

Becque's next play, *La Parisienne,* was likewise refused by a number of theatres before it was given at the Renaissance, in 1885, and has survived the censure with which it was greeted by most of the contemporary critics. It is a keen satire that owes its comic effects not to the intrigue, which is slight, but to the portrait of the volatile yet strait-laced nature of the heroine who orders her adulterous life with the strictest regard for external proprieties as well as the utmost consideration for the comfort and welfare of her husband. It is the ancestor of the modern triangle comedy, of the *ménage à trois* type, just as *Les Corbeaux* engendered a long line of modern social dramas.

The naturalistic drama and that of Becque were clear indications of a change in the theatrical tempo. Nevertheless, the Paris bill-boards in the year 1887 still announced such plays as Scribe's *Valérie* (1822) and Dumas' double-standard thesis play *Francillon* (1887). That same year the Théâtre Libre was born. It seemed like the fulfilment of August Strindberg's prayer for "a free theatre where there is room for everything but incompetence, hypocrisy, and stupidity"; and it sprang up not on the professional stage, but from an unexpected amateur quarter. André Antoine (1858-1943), its founder, was a self-educated, obscure employee of the Paris Gas Company. His passion for the stage had led him to join a little-theatre group called Le Cercle Gaulois. Tiring of its sentimental and traditional repertory, however, he planned to modify it in line with his own sympathies for the naturalistic drama. But the sedate Cercle Gaulois demurred at the boldness of presenting original plays with the name of Zola on its bill-board. Antoine organized then his own company of semiprofessionals, secured the rear of a cabaret for rehearsals, enlisted miraculously the collaboration of the newspapers which published his announcements, and, with a wardrobe borrowed from his mother, the rental for the hall paid out of the salary he had received from the gas company that very day, he initiated his new theatrical venture on the evening of March 30, 1887. The first two one-act plays left the select audience indifferent; but *Jacques Damour,* a sort of Enoch Arden drama which Léon Hennique had drawn from Zola's work, saved the night.

Encouraged by this first reception, Antoine organized a second program, including Emile Bergerat's *Nuit bergamasque,* a comedy in verse taken outside the naturalistic school and *En Famille,* a "slice of life" by Oscar Méténier. The production on May 30 of the same year proved to be a tremendous success. The Théâtre Libre came into existence that night. Antoine then gave up his prosaic job in order to prepare his next season. To secure sufficient patronage he conceived the idea of soliciting subscription memberships, seconding his prospectus with personally written appeals which he delivered himself, in order to save postage. The immediate response was not encouraging. Only a score of subscriptions were obtained after weeks of campaigning, but not long after he opened his season he had thousands of requests for seats, although the playhouse he had moved into, in the out of the way Rue de la Gaîté, in Montmartre, could accommodate only eight hundred. Then began for the Théâtre Libre its heroic period, from October 11, 1887, to June 12, 1893, five seasons, the first of seven, and the others of eight productions each, which revealed to the public new authors and new plays, both French and foreign, and which transformed the character of the French theatre. Among the former were Georges de Porto-Riche's *La Chance de Françoise,* François de Curel's *L'Envers d'une sainte* and *Les Fossiles,* Eugène Brieux's *Blanchette,* and Georges Courteline's *Boubouroche.* The latter included Tolstoi's *The Power of Darkness,* forbidden in Russia, and decried by Augier and Dumas before its performance, but one of the dramatic peaks in the Théâtre Libre repertoire. Ibsen was represented by *Ghosts,* which was found to be dull and incomprehensible by some critics, though it was recognized as a masterpiece by others; and by *The Wild Duck,* in connection with which Antoine remarked: "Just as I was the first to open my doors wide to the naturalistic drama, so shall I open them wide also to symbolistic drama, provided it is drama," but to the failure of which may be attributed his rejection of Maeterlinck's symbolistic plays. His other foreign works included Hauptmann's *The Weavers* and the *Assumption of Hannele Mattern.*

Esthetically, the Théâtre Libre reflected the virtues and failings of Zola's doctrines. Realism in subject-matter, simplicity, naturalness, and verisimilitude in the expression of the passions, in staging and acting, became its guiding tenets. Antoine inveighed against the oratorical, stilted tradition of speaking and acting taught at the Conservatoire, then in vogue in French theatres. He gave much thought to the problem of group action on the stage. The romanticists, and Sardou after them, had shown crowds before the footlights, but it was as background, and to add atmosphere. Antoine understood the principle of mass psychology and mob scenes, of the integration of their emotions into the movement of the drama and the destiny of its protagonists, and he applied it after the manner of the Meiningen players, whom he had seen in Brussels in 1888.

He criticized the star-actor system which caused both the author and the public to favor the interpreter to the detriment of the play, and objected to the tradition of actresses buying their own dresses, the moral issue involved being complicated by an artistic one, for one often saw the spectacle of chambermaids dressed like duchesses on the stage. He was against the excessive elegance of French staging and its inevitable thwarting of the necessary scenic illusion, and advocated naturalness and simplicity instead, a thing he carried often to the point of a subservient imitation of reality.

On the whole, the Théâtre Libre became a faithful mirror for the "slices of life" the naturalists were carving out of reality. "Plays in which life is the source of action begin to replace those in which action is the source of life," observed Adolphe Thalasso, its historiographer. Complicated plots gave way to simple ones; the characters became plausible, if not always normal; superficial idealism and optimism were shunned; declamation and pathos were frowned upon; the traditional raisonneur, or author's mouthpiece, was banished. The morality of the play was drawn from the contemplation of a life which was not always edifying, however. For the reality it depicted was primarily that of the lower middle and working classes which up to that time had not been truly represented on the stage. This portrayal of the lower classes in the theatre coincided with their rising social and political struggles against the upper bourgeoisie depicted in the dramas of Augier and Dumas fils. As Jean-Richard Bloch observes: "Antoine belonged through his popular origin to the social classes which were to start the Dreyfus offensive nine years later. The Théâtre Libre is the Dreyfus Affair of the theatre," an observation that becomes all the more significant when it is recalled that its patron saint, Zola, became the greatest hero of that affair. All classes of society had been mirrored on the stage before, and painted, mostly, in rosy colors—all save the lower classes, where the colors of life are usually dull or dark. The task of representing them before the footlights fell to the lot of the naturalistic writers, who set out to paint them as they saw them in their daily, unhappy, and bitter aspects.

Ultimately, the Théâtre Libre suffered from the abuse of what had been its virtues. Its "slices of life" became too spicy even for strong natures to stomach. It splashed on the stage the crude, forbidding horrors of the lower depths, of the animal in man, and overlooked, or slighted, the flickering light of the spirit within. Something of the mire it sought to reflect before the footlights tarnished the mirror itself. The dramatic purgation to which reality must be subjected often miscarried, and the play left then a feeling of spiritual nausea as its aftermath. The well-made play and the right-thinking play were displaced by two new genres: the *pièce mufle*, or tough play, and the *comédie rosse*, or cynical comedy, of which it was said there were seven kinds, one for each capital sin. Antoine's early eclecticism in the selection of his repertory gradually gave way to his infatuation with dramas based on heredity, the influence of environment, and the instincts, which were the accepted tenets of the naturalistic doctrine. But as early as 1891 the critical poll conducted by Jules Huret in his *Enquête sur l'évolution littéraire* had indicated that public taste was veering in the opposite direction. The positivism of Comte and Taine was faced with rising idealistic and symbolistic trends. Literary men like Paul Bourget were proclaiming the "failure of science." Antoine himself had introduced the enemy into his camp when he produced Tolstoi, Ibsen, and Hauptmann. His most promising authors, his best actors, together with his reforms, innovations, and plays had penetrated the commercial and even the State theatres. The Théâtre Libre had fulfilled its mission of liberalizing the traditions of the French drama, and had entered into a period of decline.

In the spring of 1894 Antoine turned over its direction to the actor Larochelle and started on a tour of the Continent with a company of his actors. October 1894 found him stranded in Rome, however, as poor as when he had begun seven years earlier in Paris, nay poorer, for he had piled up a huge financial deficit on the debit side of his dramatic ledger. But on the credit side he could put down the impetus he had given to the renascence of the drama not only in France, but abroad as well. Free theatres modeled after his own had sprung elsewhere in Europe, notably the Freie Bühne, in Berlin, in 1889, where Hauptmann's work first faced the footlights, and Jacob T. Grein's Independent Theatre, in London, in 1891, which served to launch the career of George Bernard Shaw. When Antoine came back to Paris, the theatre he had founded was in a moribund state. On April 27, 1896, it closed its doors. He became then codirector of the Odéon Theatre, but left it soon after and went on a tour of foreign countries. Upon his return he opened the Théâtre Antoine, on September 1897, where he carried on for the general public the best traditions of the Théâtre Libre, as other Parisian theatres were now doing too. In 1906 he assumed the sole management of the Odéon Theatre. He brought there his dramatic ideals, and, without upsetting its respectable ways, infused it with new life, revealing such writers of the younger generation as Jules Romains and Georges Duhamel. In 1914 he resigned and turned dramatic critic thereafter. His activities reflect a quarter of a century of French dramatic history.

The idealistic movement in the closing years of the century arose in reaction to the prevailing positivist trend of the era and its literary manifestation in the naturalistic school. Esthetically and spiritually it found support in the music-drama of Wagner, then at the apogee of its popularity in Paris, and in the newly propounded philosophical speculations of Bergson. In contrast to the naturalists, its partisans proclaimed their faith in the validity of the suprasensible world, and looked upon reality as but its contingent and deceptive form. First among the moderns, they broached the problem of the soul and of pure ideas as subjects for dramatic treatment, and planted the stage in the domain of the ideal. One of its foremost champions was Villiers de l'Isle-Adam. We have studied his place in the evolution of the realistic drama. That which he occupies in the idealistic theatre is far more important, for if he was a rebel in the former movement, he was regarded as the apostle of the latter. His play *Axël* was the Bible of the idealists. Although it wasn't produced until February 26, 1894 (by Larochelle), it had been published in 1890, and had been written years before. It is the story of Sara and Axël each of whom is in search of a hidden treasure upon which they come simultaneously in the castle of Auërsperg. They fall in love with each other, and in their bliss they agree to relinquish all earthly treasures and promises of happiness, and finally life itself, because nothing on earth could match henceforth the ecstasy of their first adoration, and to live it anew every day would be to tarnish its image and to become the victims of a deceiving illusion. Such idealism lacks the principle of redemption inherent in Wagner's *Tetralogy,* with which the play has certain analogies. Villiers himself recognized its shortcomings, and was preparing a new version ending with a final renunciation at the foot of the cross, when he died. Larochelle produced another play of Villiers, *Elen* (1895), at the Théâtre Libre. It portrays the disillusion of an idealist who discovers that the woman he has endowed with spiritual virtues in his imagination is but a courtesan attached to earthly passions and realities. The rapprochement here is with Wagner's *Tannhäuser*. Villiers' characters are moved by spiritual rather than carnal passions. He expressed an ascetic conception of love of a nature to be reflected in the work of Maeterlinck, who felt greatly his influence. "Everything I have done," the latter has professed, "I owe to Villiers."

Even before the decline of the Théâtre Libre, a number of younger opponents had banded themselves together in opposition to its esthetics. One of its leaders was the young poet Paul Fort. At the age of seventeen, and while he was still at the Lycée, he founded the Théâtre d'Art, in 1890, with the collaboration of Lugné-Poe, a former actor of Antoine, the blessings of symbolists and impressionists, and the assistance of student-actors from the Conservatoire. Despite lack of funds, with simple, symbolistic settings, it gave from November 1890 to March 1892, a series of poetic and dramatic performances that included Shelley's *The Cenci,* Maeterlinck's *L'Intruse* and *Les Aveugles,* Marlowe's *Dr. Faustus,* and Charles Van Lerberghe's *Les Flaireurs.* It has then the honor of having opened the stage doors to the rising symbolistic drama. In 1893, however, wishing to devote himself to writing, Paul Fort withdrew from the direction of his experimental theatre, and entrusted to Lugné-Poe the task of carrying on its ideals. With the collaboration of Maeterlinck, the poet Camille Mauclair, and the painter Edouard Vuillard, Lugné-Poe founded then the Théâtre de l'Œuvre which was triumphantly inaugurated May 17, 1893. Its aim was to fight naturalism and "to make known the great foreign dramatists and the plays of young idealists." Among the latter were plays like Alfred Jarry's fantastic *Ubu Roi;* Rachilde's (Mme Alfred Vallette, 1862-1935) *L'Araignée de cristal* (1894), which studies the growth of an obsessing idea that leads a man to self-destruction; and Maurice de Beaubourg's *L'Image* (1894) and *La Vie muette* (1894), both of which illustrate the tyrannical power of dreams and ideals over human life. Unfortunately, the young writers did not fulfil all Lugné-Poe's high expectations, and he turned more and more to foreign works, to Ibsen's *Rosmersholm* and *Peer Gynt,* or Hauptmann's *The Sunken Bell.* Antoine also had produced these authors, but whereas he stressed the realistic aspects of their plays, Lugné-Poe emphasized their symbolic connotations, and the lyrical and mysterious traits of the characters they portrayed.

The Théâtre de l'Œuvre experienced momentary periods of decline throughout the long years of an existence that has endured to our day. These were redeemed by periods of revival, when it produced such works as Maeterlinck's *Monna Vanna* in 1902, and Claudel's *L'Annonce faite à Marie,* in 1912, after which it entered, in the years following the First

World War, into a new era of glory when it became a potent force in the renascence of the contemporary drama, and produced such young authors as J.-J. Bernard, Raynal, Passeur, and Natanson. It has been the link between the idealist theatre of the nineties, and the post-war avant-garde dramatic schools. It was for many years what Paul Claudel called "the intellectual Holy Land" of the stage where one went of an evening on a "literary pilgrimage, a spiritual crusade." Like the Théâtre Libre, it helped to broaden and deepen the horizons of the French drama.

The realistic theatre was concerned with portraying the material life of man, his habits, passions, and institutions, and neglected his soul and its unknown destiny in the universe. It could visualize and represent realistically man's struggles with the visible and tangible powers of evil in society, the clash of motives in love, honor, duty, greed, but not the spirit's conflict with its mysterious fate. These conflicts are concentrated in the heart and soul, and can be perceived and represented only symbolically and allegorically. Hence the symbolistic drama may be looked upon as a reaction as well as a complementary movement to the naturalistic theatre.

A first sketch of such a drama may be seen in the Belgian poet Charles Van Lerberghe's (1861-1907) *Les Flaireurs,* produced in 1892, but published three years earlier. It portrays the approach of the emissaries of death who come knocking at the door of a dying woman defended only by her terrified daughter. The play had an influence on Maurice Maeterlinck, in whose work is to be found the best expression of the symbolistic drama. Maurice Maeterlinck was born in Ghent, Belgium, August 29, 1862, and was educated at the Jesuit college of the town. The seed the good fathers planted in him brought forth in time spiritual flowers but no fruits of belief. This factor was to influence his career, for the mystic asleep in his Flemish soul was to awaken and to seek throughout life, outside the Church, the certainty it had failed to inculcate in him. Having joined the phalanx of young symbolists in Paris, in 1886, he fell under the spell of Villiers' fantastic idealism, as well as under the transcendentalism of mystics like Ruysbroeck the Admirable, Novalis, and Emerson. Disregarding the materially perceptible but spiritually opaque traditional matter of dramatic art, he undertook to tap new sources of it in what is invisible, in what appears unreal, in the world of dream and the subconscious. "The dramatic poet," he stated, "must bring down into real life, into daily life, the idea he has of the unknown. He must show us in what way, under what form, under what conditions, according to what laws, to what end, the superior powers, the unintelligible influences, the first and last principles which, as a poet, he feels certain fill the universe, work upon our destiny." These mysterious powers which, he came to believe, like a malicious Peter Pan were leading humanity to destruction and death, constitute the invisible dramatis personae of his drama. Obscurely symbolized in his first play, *La Princesse Maleine,* published in 1889, which won the extravagant praise of

Octave Mirbeau—a praise that rendered its author famous overnight—the idea becomes more clearly delineated in his succeeding work, *L'Intruse* (1891), where the grandfather alone, his eyes blind to the world of appearances, sees and feels the approach of Death, because he can penetrate the mysterious universe with the antennae of his soul. The blind men of *Les Aveugles* (1891), on the other hand, because they are both physically and spiritually blind, like humanity itself, are lost in the woods, their guide, the priest—that is the Church—dead at their feet. The symbol Maeterlinck used must have been one of the motives that caused his work to be placed on the *Index Expurgatorius*.

The conflict between these frail human creatures and cruel Fate is more magnificently illustrated in *Pelléas et Mélisande* (1893). The characters are like lost waifs groping through haunted ways. They are assailed by fear of invisible powers hostile to love and life. Yet the souls of the protagonists remain aloof from their earthly destinies, and uncontaminated by their physical passions and actions. They express and symbolize poetic and tragic perceptions and mysteries not readily accessible to our rational sensibilities, and which transcend the limitations of external reality. They make of the play what Maeterlinck wished it to be, "a temple of dream."

So are his immediately succeeding plays. Maeterlinck said he intended them "for creatures indulgent to poetry, and which, for want of a better term, I call Marionettes." Such is *Intérieur* (1895), where Death still shadows the characters filling them with an anguish too keen to bear. But in later plays his pessimism evolved more rapidly toward a tempered optimism, a change that was presaged in his book of essays, *Le Trésor des humbles* (1896). With *Monna Vanna* (1902), he proved he could construct a powerful play with living characters moved by strong passions. In *L'Oiseau bleu* (1908), the most popular of his plays, Tyltyl and Mytyl discover that death does not even exist, but also that happiness can be found nowhere except in the heart of the seeker. Thus in his last plays, which include *Le Bourgmestre de Stilmonde* (1918), a portrait of a heroic spirit resisting brutal force, as well as in his philosophical essays, Maeterlinck asserts his faith that the soul can thwart the force of evil in the universe, for it is spiritual and cannot be stained by the sins of the flesh.

Maeterlinck transferred the stage to the *terra incognita* of the soul. It is from it that ascend the shadows and echoes, faint cries, brief exclamations, silent but eloquent expressions of spiritual struggles otherwise unheard and unseen, and of which his plays are the suggestive and symbolic representations on the stage. Their influence on the modern drama has been subtle but profound, and may be perceived in the works of Henri-René Lenormand, Luigi Pirandello, or Leonid Andreiev.

In America the commercial theatres have not proven to be treasure houses for Maeterlinck. *Pelléas et Mélisande* made two poor showings on Broadway, despite the starring of Mrs. Patrick Campbell, in 1902, and of Jane

Cowl, in 1923. Doubtless the play has now become too intimately associated in the public's mind with the music of Debussy. *The Blue Bird,* on the other hand, turned out to be a good box-office success, in 1910, closely followed by its sequel, *Les Fiançailles (The Betrothal),* in 1918. *Monna Vanna* had only a moderate run, despite the acting of Bertha Kalich as Giovanna, in 1905, and *Le Bourgmestre de Stilmonde (A Burgomaster of Belgium)* fared still less well, in 1919. But the experimental theatres supplemented these commercial offerings with productions like *A Miracle of Saint Anthony* and *Interior* by the Washington Square Players in 1915, and *Aglavaine and Selysette* by the Afternoon Theatre Company in 1922 with Clare Eames and Eva Le Gallienne.

Another symbolist dramatist worth mentioning is Edouard Dujardin (1861-   ) whose trilogy of *Antonia* plays (1891-1893) dramatizes the vanity of impossible dreams and the necessity of resignation and love. Having found little favor in his time, Dujardin did not return to the stage until 1913, when Lugné-Poe produced his *Marthe et Marie.* Like his succeeding plays, it is a drama of spiritual aspirations manifested athwart earthly preoccupations. In *Le Retour éternel* (1932) he portrayed the survival of humanity symbolized in the destiny of a family which undergoes terrible sacrifices at different ages in history, a play in substance like Thornton Wilder's *The Skin of Our Teeth* (1943).

The idealistic movement caused a revival of the drama in verse, too, both in the neoclassic and neoromantic forms. The latter was best embodied in the work of Edmond Rostand (1868-1918). Following the production of his first play, *Les Romanesques* (1894), which is a pleasing parody of *Romeo and Juliet,* he gave *La Princesse lointaine* (1895), which was adapted as *The Lady of Dreams* in New York in 1912. The play is a symbolic interpretation of ideal love and self-renunciation, with the hero Rudel, like Axël, dying when he has beheld the lady of his dreams, so that his ideal will remain unsullied by reality. Nothing in these plays, nor in the next one, *La Samaritaine* (1897), which dramatized the story of the woman of Samaria, had prepared the public for the meteoric triumph of his next one, *Cyrano de Bergerac* (1897), which proved to be his masterpiece. The play was an evocation of one of those minor romantic figures who seem more glamorous through their failures than their successes. Its clever combination of poetic virtuosity, heroic mood, glorification of self-sacrifice, with smart intrigue and satire; its reconstruction of the *précieux* seventeenth-century atmosphere, with its superficialities in manner and speech, its bombast, wigs, ruffs, masked women, and theatrical duels, dazzled a public surfeited with naturalistic dramas of everyday life. The gay, witty, tender, and grotesque passions and frustrations of its hero—a fascinating hybrid between a sentimental Don Quixote and a melancholy Sir John Falstaff—won him more hearts on the stage than his model did in real life. The play proved to be a dramatic success unique in the annals of the French stage. Richard Mansfield created the rôle in 1898 in America, being succeeded by Walter Hampden in 1923, and the popularity of the play had hardly waned at its last revival in New York in 1936.

Rostand never again reached those dramatic heights. *L'Aiglon* (1900), a dramatic evocation of comic-opera heroes, glorious ghosts, and lost illusions, is as ineffective as its protagonist, the pale son of Napoleon, was in real life, although it has many dramatic and poetic passages of great beauty. The play was swept along on the wave of popularity of *Cyrano* and the genius of Maude Adams and Sarah Bernhardt who interpreted the stellar rôle in America the same year, in 1900. *Chantecler* (1910) which followed, and upon which he worked for long years, is a lyrical dramatization of the creative artist's faith in the nobility of his task, however frustrating his worldly experience—symbolized by the cock's belief that his crowing makes the sun rise. It is, besides, a hymn to nature and its humbler creatures, and was regarded by Rostand as the most personal of his creations. "My cock is not a real hero of comedy," he said, "he is a character I created to express my own dreams and to incarnate a little of myself." The author's personal interest in the cock notwithstanding, neither Lucien Guitry nor Maude Adams, who created the part in Paris and New York respectively, were quite themselves under the rooster's feathers. The play did not measure up to the advance build-up it had received for years. His last play, *La dernière Nuit de Don Juan* (1922), published and played posthumously, and adapted by Sidney Howard as *The Last Night of Don Juan* for its New York production in 1925, is likewise a hymn to spiritual love, a condemnation of man's frivolity, and exaltation of woman's noblest virtues.

Rostand's drama was acclaimed with delirious praise as an antidote to revolting naturalism and nebulous idealism, and as a triumph of the Gallic spirit. But time has tarnished much of the tinsel that glittered at first in his poetry. His genuine lyrical virtuosity, his dramatic ingenuity, and his sparkling wit were spoiled by excessive rhetoric, punning, pompous tirades, theatrical superficialities, and romantic claptrap. He neglected those genuinely French virtues which Jacques Copeau described as "taste and measure, sober expression, the art of the nuance, finesse, and psychological penetration." His characters are portraits of conceited failures. Cyrano, the eaglet, the cock are full of impulses which miscarry, of dreams which end in frustration and self-deception. Withal they incarnated the author's as well as human longing for a nobler and more heroic view of life, a gilding and ennobling of its bleak realities through idealism and poetry.

Edmond Rostand was regarded as the renovator of the poetic drama by some, and as a "magnificent anachronism" by others. He hastened the end of the naturalistic drama, but also that of the genre he had created, for the public was quickly satiated with its grandiloquence, and so it fostered indirectly a swing of public taste from naturalism to a saner form of realism.

Besides Rostand, however, there were other talented experts of the romantic art. One of the most gifted was Jean Richepin (1849-1926). His fertile imagination found expression in picaresque romances and lyric melodramas which he peopled with sympathetic rascals who are involved in idyllic or grotesque adventures. The hero of his masterpiece *Le Chemineau* (1897), which was produced as *The Harvester* in New York in 1904, is a lovable itinerant worker who returns fortuitously to the scene of a former adventure, where he settles the social and marital difficulties of Toinette's son, who is suspected of being his illegitimate child—the fruit of a festive night there twenty years before—and then departs once more, unable to resist the call of the road. Lesser lights in the same genre included Catulle Mendès (1843-1909), who evoked on the stage unhappy historical figures like *Scarron* (1905), the unfortunate first husband of Françoise d'Aubigny, later Mme de Maintenon; and *Glatigny* (1906), the bohemian poet-comedian who dreamed of fame and wallowed in poverty and obscurity. Another one was Jacques Richepin (1880-   ), who, like his father, was endowed with fantasy and dramatic verve. After his early romantic plays, such as *La Cavalière* (1901), and *Cadet Roussel* (1904), he turned to more jolly and popular comedies like *Le Minaret* (1913), in which the stake between the two antagonists in the play is the possession of a widowed and merry harem. Finally, a more delicate poetic vein ran through the comedies of Miguel Zamacoïs (1866-   ), author of the quite successful *Les Bouffons* (*The Jesters,* 1907), in which Maude Adams starred in New York in 1908; and also through those of André Rivoire (1872-1930). Besides his well-known prose comedies *Mon ami Teddy* (*My Friend Teddy,* 1910), written in collaboration with Lucien Besnard, and produced here in 1913, and *Pour vivre heureux* (written with Yves Mirande, 1912), which was produced here as *The Temperamental Journey* in 1913, Rivoire wrote charming poetic plays, like *Le bon roi Dagobert* (1908), where the king falls in love and marries in the end the slave girl in lieu of his intended Spanish princess. His *Juliette et Roméo* (1920) was original in the use he made in the fifth act of the *dénouement* as told in Luigi da Porto's story, where Romeo expires after Julie awakes and the two discourse on their unhappy fate.

The revival of the romantic drama was paralleled by that of the classical tragedy. Without the presence of a Rostand in its ranks, however, the works produced never reached the commercial footlights, despite their literary merits. Among its devotees, Joséphin Péladan (1859-1918), fervent disciple of Æschylus and Wagner, fought *Zolisme* with *Wagnérisme,* and aimed to inject the spirit of Christian idealism into the mould of classical tragedy. His plays dramatized always the triumph of love over brutal force, as in his *Babylone* (1893), which Jules Claretie, the director of the Comédie Française, had declared to be either "supra-possible or supra-impossible." His *Prométhéide* aimed to complete the tragedy of Æschylus, and shows Zeus, the god of thunder, turning into a god of goodness, and Prometheus into a precursor of Christ. Its production in 1925 caused A.

Mortier to write: "What a shameful scandal for the morality of French letters that such a work had never found a theatre nor a public for a quarter of a century." The incident bespeaks at least the new catholicity and lyrical trend in the drama of France, as we shall perceive in the postwar era.

The claims of the classical tradition were reaffirmed in the quite successful *Prométhée* (1900) by A.-Ferdinand Hérold and Jean Lorrain; in Jean Moréas' (1856-1910) resplendent *Iphigénie* (1903); in Alfred Poizat's (1863-) *Electre* (1907) or *Antigone* (1911), which interpret ancient themes in a modern mood; in Albert Samain's (1858-1900) exquisitely told story of Polyphemus in love with Galatea, entitled *Polyphème* (1905), to mention only a typical few; and, finally, in Alfred Mortier's (1865-1937) *Penthésilée* (1922) which portrays Achilles and Penthesilea in a modern rivalry of the sexes, a sort of "feminist tragedy." Mortier had begun his career with *La Fille d'Artaban* (1896) at the Théâtre Libre, in what was a kind of symbolistic *pièce mufle*, in which a circus man kills his daughter to prevent her beauty from being defiled by the crowd. He ended it with some veritable triumphs, of which the best was *Le Divin Arétin* (1930), which portrays the life and times of the Renaissance satirist Pietro Aretino.

In a classic spirit also was the "theatre of the soul" of Edouard Schuré (1841-1929), which he wished to extract from the spectacle of stark reality, as with the Greeks, and from a symbolic evocation of humanity through its history and legend—making of it a mirror of a higher life. His drama *Roussalka,* staged by Lugné-Poe in 1903, dramatized the rôle of woman and love in awakening to life the god slumbering in man. It borrowed episodes from the lives of Wilhelmine Schroeder-Devrient and Wagner, as well as motifs from *Tristan and Isolde* and *The Mastersingers.*

Plays of this nature are not for export to the boulevard or the foreign stage; yet they contain something of the essence of the French theatre. The same is true of the religious drama.

One of the brightest manifestations of the idealistic movement was the revival of the religious drama. It found its best expression in the work of Paul Claudel, the former French ambassador to Washington, who is undeniably the greatest Catholic poet and dramatist since Dante, Corneille, and Calderón. Born in 1868, he was sinking "into a state of moral asphyxiation and despair," in the materialistic and naturalistic eighties, when he became converted, after a miraculous religious experience on December 25, 1886. Henceforth his art became a ladder stretching from the earth to the heavens, or, to change the figure of speech, the stage served him as a vestibule to the altar. The first of his plays to be produced, on a memorable evening at the Théâtre de l'Œuvre, was his masterpiece *L'Annonce faite à Marie,* in 1912. It is the greatest modern Christian drama in France, surpassing *Polyeucte* in lyrical and religious splendor, and equaling it in dramatic power. The Vieux Colombier then gave *L'Echange,* a sort of epistle to Americans, in 1914, played as *The Exchange* in London the year after. In

1914 also Lugné-Poe produced *L'Otage,* the first of a trilogy which includes *Le Pain dur* (1917), and *Le Père humilié,* and which is the most successful of Claudel's works from the point of view of the stage. Others that were produced include *Tête d'or* (1924), *Le Partage de Midi* (1921), as well as the less religious and more symbolic drama of dream and desire, *L'Homme et son désir* (1919), played with ballet, and music by Milhaud. Another production indicative of Claudel's attachment to the stage was his *La Femme et son ombre,* a ballet scenario in the Japanese style, with music by Kineya Sakichi, staged in Tokyo in 1923. The only play of his produced in New York was *L'Annonce faite à Marie* which ran for thirty-two performances at the Garrick Theatre in 1923. The last to be produced to date is *Le Soulier de Satin* (1943), an enormous drama compounded of comedy, passion, and mysticism, which resembles in form the dramas of Calderón and Shakespeare, and which represents in spirit a sort of summing up of his other works and the work of his life.

Discussing the handicaps of the religious drama on the stage, André Gide has observed that unlike secular drama its aim is to obliterate rather than to emphasize moral and psychological conflicts. "Every dramatic work must present, besides its profound significance, all sorts of entertainment, be a spectacle, and a beautiful one, not be afraid to speak to the senses," he said, and the religious drama, by implication, cannot do that.[1] Claudel's originality, precisely, lies in his ability to surmount this handicap, for his drama speaks both to the senses and to the spirit. It is close, in this respect, to the form and texture of the Japanese Nō. Like the Japanese Nō, it depicts our struggles with one another and with ourselves in relation to Providence, "the bitter movement of our desire, of our sorrow and our folly ... so that we may comprehend of what eternal attitude each of our poor chance gestures was the unconscious and improvised imitation," [2] Claudel wrote. His plays are then a meeting ground of drama and poetry, of matter and spirit. They cannot be judged by the ordinary criteria of dramatic values. They evolve along a line *sui generis* whose dénouement consists in proclaiming the grace of God from the vantage point of the stage. They are the dramatic stations in the earthly and spiritual journey of a believer. They set forth the Catholic doctrine in relation to political and philosophical speculations on all matters of human interest. The conflicts between their characters, between their worldly loves and desires, on the one hand, and their heavenly aspirations, on the other, bitter and passionate as they are, tend always, however, toward an ultimate spiritual harmony and edification. Hence the drama of Claudel represents a sort of "retreat" from the worldliness that characterizes other aspects of the modern theatre.

Less poetic but more popular than Claudel's, the religious theatre of

---

[1] André Gide, Preface to *Le Roi Candaule* (Paris, Librairie Gallimard, 1930), p. 8.
[2] Quoted by Jean-Richard Bloch in *Destin du théâtre* (Paris, Librairie Gallimard, 1930), p. 191.

Henri Ghéon (1875-   ) aimed to amuse while it proselytized. He had already written secular and social dramas like *Le Pain* (1911), whose protagonist is a socially-conscious baker, and *L'Eau-de-vie* (1914), which deals with Zola's theme in *L'Assommoir,* when he became converted during the First World War. Henceforth he devoted himself to the writing of a repertoire of Catholic plays in the mood of the medieval French theatre. These comprise comedies, mysteries, satires, and miracles which were produced often in the parvis of a cathedral, or in local theatres, by Les Compagnons de Notre-Dame, a theatrical organization he founded in 1925. One of his best plays, *Le Pauvre sous l'escalier,* was performed at the Vieux Colombier in 1921. It dramatizes the life of Saint Alexis who deserted his wife on his wedding night in order to expiate in poverty and suffering the sins of mankind—thus illustrating the Catholic idea of the Communion of the Saints, the sacrifice of self in the spirit of Christ. Typical of his other naïvely religious and commonly artless works are *Les Aventures de Gilles ou le saint malgré lui* (1922), the sacred pastoral *La Bergère au pays des loups* (1922), and *L'Histoire du jeune Bernard de Menthon,* the last being based on the life of the saint in the *Acta Sanctorum,* and given first at the Château de Menthon, near Annecy in 1925. It was translated and produced as *The Marvellous History of St. Bernard* by Sir Barry V. Jackson at the Malvern Festival in 1926—a production that was regarded as "one of the most beautiful things seen on the London stage in our time," according to G. W. Bishop.

Wishing to render accessible to the masses the message and example of the saints, Ghéon sought to humanize them by divesting them of their legendary and canonical halos, bringing them down, even in manner and speech, to the level of his humble public. As a consequence, from the artistic and dramatic points of view, his productions lack the purity and distinction of Claudel's work.

Outstanding among other religious dramas were Edmond Haraucourt's (1857-   ) *La Passion,* banned by the censor in 1890 but produced repeatedly since 1893; Gabriel Trarieux's (1870-   ) *Joseph d'Arimathée* (1898), which exalts the power of faith; Gabrielle d'Annunzio's (1863-1938) magnificent *Le Martyre de Saint Sébastien* (1911), written in beautiful octosyllabic French verses by that Italian virtuoso of the French language, and accompanied by a dazzling score of Debussy; Maurice Maeterlinck's *Marie-Magdeleine* (*Mary Magdalene,* Leipzig and New York, 1910), which is bathed in an atmosphere of admirable religious symbolism; and Paul Demasy's (1884-   ) *Jésus de Nazareth,* a passion play produced by the Odéon Theatre in 1924, and kept in its repertoire since.

Midway between naturalism and idealism in the theatre, part reaction to the one, and part emulation of the other, arose a school that partook of both, that tried to blend action with spirit, reality with poetry. It was baptized *Naturisme* by its chief exponent, Saint-Georges de Bouhélier

(1876-   ). His aim was to interpret reality poetically, to spiritualize the humble and drab aspects of daily existence on the stage. He illustrated his theory with such plays as *Le Carnaval des enfants* (1910). It portrays a widow who is tortured by her puritanic sisters-in-law who have discovered one of her daughters to be illegitimate. The drama occurs in the sordid atmosphere of a laundry shop, and ends with the triumph of love. Another aspect of Bouhélier's work was its resort to heroic and exalted subjects, to the imaginative reconstruction of great historical moments and characters in which the popular legend had its place, in a sort of fusion of Tolstoism with Parsifalism. He attempted this in such plays as *La Tragédie de Tristan et Yseult* (1923), and *Jeanne d'Arc, la pucelle de France* (1934). Despite many magnificent scenes, it cannot be said that his theatre realized fully the high ideal he had traced for it.

Closely analogous to his dramatic scheme was the movement for a people's theatre which was general throughout Europe in the nineties. The Volksbuehne was founded in Germany, in 1889, with the aim of creating a theatre "springing from the people themselves." A Maison du Peuple came into existence in Brussels, in 1892.

In France, one of the most zealous workers in this movement was Maurice Potterchrer (1867-   ) who, in his Théâtre du Peuple at Bussang, in the Vosges, located first in the open air, and later in a vast wooden structure, tried to blend the popular and the bourgeois elements of the drama with the historical and the legendary in comedies and dramas of his own writing. To their type belong his *Le Diable marchand de goutte* (1895), which exposes the evil of drunkenness; *Liberté* (1898), a drama of the Revolution; and *Amys et Amyle* (1913), a dramatic legend of two friends' rivalry for the love of a medieval princess, which was revived at the Odéon in 1928.

Other open-air theatres have prospered throughout France, among them those at Orange, Béziers, Nîmes, Champigny-la-Bataille, where popular spectacles alternated with historical and regional dramas, as well as with classical tragedies. To them, in fact, must be given a share of the credit for the revival of the neoclassical tragedy, for it is in them that works of writers like Péladan and Poizat were first given.

In Paris proper, a Théâtre Civique was organized in 1897, with, among other adherents, Octave Mirbeau, who contributed his play *L'Epidémie,* and even played the rôle of the mayor in it. "We shall," said the founders, "produce verse and prose plays before the people and, to prove clearly our hatred of that corrupting modern thing, money, our performances will be free." Such also was the ideal which inspired, in 1899, the group known as Le Théâtre de la Coopération des Idées, among whose guiding spirits were again Mirbeau—a successful dramatist in his own right—and Romain Rolland. The results achieved fell short of expectations because, Romain Rolland explained, to have a "people's theatre" there must be "a people that has enough freedom of the spirit to enjoy it, . . . that is not crushed by misery and ceaseless toil, a people that is not brutalized by superstitions and fanaticisms from the right or the left, a people that is master of itself." The trouble was also that the movement had radical political motives in it, and suffered from the same proselytizing defects that plagued the religious drama on the stage.

Out of all that, however, has come the theatre of Romain Rolland (1866-1944), his monumental *Tragédies de la Foi* and *Tragédies de la Révolution*, two cycles of stirring historical dramas which include *Les Loups* (1898), produced as *The Wolves* in New York in 1932 (and previously by the Yiddish Art Theatre in 1924), *Danton* (1900), and *Le Jeu de l'amour et de la mort* (1928), staged as *The Game of Love and Death* by the Theatre Guild in 1929. He painted the conflicts of the individual and freedom with social discipline and abnegation, using the storm of the French Revolution as source material, but without partisanship. He depicted its passions, ideas, and characters, its "beasts with a thousand heads, the people, and the beast-tamers," strong, austere souls whom he viewed not in a narrow historical sense, but in a broad psychological spirit. At its best, his drama is both artistic and social, bourgeois and proletarian, and reflects dramatically the political and social struggles of modern times.

The idealistic movement in the theatre proved to be ineffective in swaying the main current of the modern French drama which remained overwhelmingly realistic up to the outbreak of the First World War. The Théâtre Libre, on the other hand, had served as a bridge over which the most gifted of its young dramatists passed from its experimental boards to the larger playhouses. Directly or indirectly, it was conducive to the rise of a brilliant generation of dramatists with diverse dramatic motivations, such as Brieux's social drama, Curel's theatre of ideas, Porto-Riche's drama of passion, most of which are variations of the basic naturalistic drama. These will be studied presently. But first we shall consider rapidly some of the lesser lights, whose careers were either intimately connected with the destiny of the Théâtre Libre, or who reflected closely its dramatic ideals.

Such a one was Georges Ancey (Georges de Curnieu, 1860-   ), master of irony, who wielded the technique of the *comédie rosse* with dexterous art, abusing even its cynical vein, as witness *L'Ecole des veufs* (1889), in which the widower Mirelet consents to share his mistress with his son if only she will promise not to deceive him with anybody else, but she will not swear even to that for, as she explains, she never keeps her word. Best known of his later works was his anticlerical play *Ces Messieurs,* which was suppressed in 1901, and not produced until 1905.

Another dramatist who was second only to Antoine in his defense of the Théâtre Libre dramaturgy was Jean Jullien (1854-1919). He it was who coined the expression "slice of life" for the free, naturalistic play, which, in contrast to the well-made play, he declared must be free from elaborate exposition, dénouement, or sympathetic character. His first play, *La Sérénade*

(1887), embroidered a cynical and amusing intrigue of a daughter and mother who end by becoming respectively the wife and in-law of their common lover. The Théâtre Libre produced also his *Le Maître* (1890), which tells the story of a tramp who comes to an invalid farmer's home; he succeeds in restoring the farmer to health, but is ultimately driven away from the house, though not alone, for the daughter Françoise goes along with him. Jullien widened his dramatic matter subsequently in plays which suggested the social manner of Brieux, as in *L'Ecolière* (1901), and even the symbolical ideology of Curel, in *L'Oasis* (1903)—a drama that begins with the story of a nun married to her Mohammedan captor and ends with her refusal to be liberated from her husband, her child, and the ideal utopia they have set up in a desert oasis.

Among other dramatists in this category reference must be made to Léon Hennique (1851-   ), to the success of whose *Jacques Damour* (1887), at its inauguration, the Théâtre Libre probably owed its existence, and whose *La Mort du Duc d'Enghien* (1888) freed the historical drama from its Scribian strait-jacket; to Henri Céard (1851-1924), author of the much praised *Les Résignés* (1889), who did much in the way of press publicity for the struggling Théâtre Libre; to Rodolphe Darzens (1865-1938), whose *L'Amante du Christ* (1888), a one-act mystery play on the subject of Christ and the harlot, led the way in the revival of the religious drama at this time, and who translated Ibsen's *Ghosts* for Antoine; to Gaston Salandri (1860-   ), whose *La Prose* (1888) set the tone in the beginning for the dramatic atmosphere of the Théâtre Libre, together with the works of Ancey and Jullien; and to Oscar Méténier (1859-1913), who made a specialty of the Grand Guignol type of drama.

The style for the Grand Guignol drama was set by Méténier with his one-act "daring and violent" *En Famille,* a "slice of life" describing the guillotining of a friend of the family, which Antoine put on his second experimental program. It was further elaborated in later plays like *Lui* (1898), in which a street girl discovers to her dismay that the man she had picked up and brought home was a thief and a murderer sought by the police to whom she manages, however, to deliver him in the end. The genre was characterized by brief and violent action, bloodcurdling situation and realistic staging in keeping with it, and unexpected dénouement contrived to arouse intense emotion and terror. It has been referred to as stage *fait divers,* meaning that it was in the mood of the sensational tabloid news item which excites the sensibilities without probing into cause and effect. André de Lorde, one of its protagonists, described it as "the study of physiological and medical cases which hold the public breathless like all introspective problems and conflicts of the spirit." In substance and in practice it was a "slice of life" with ingredients consisting of anguish, madness, torture, alcoholism, pseudo-science, underworld, and revolutionary horrors, revenge, murder, death, all dosed in a manner to leave the excitement-addicted audience in a state bordering on prostration. In fact the management of the Grand Guignol advertised the presence of a nurse in attendance to minister to the weak-hearted. The theatre was founded by Méténier in 1897, in the former studio of the painter Rochegrosse, which had been originally a Jansenist convent. The inaugural performance consisted of seven plays and a prologue, three by Méténier, including his adaptation of Maupassant's *Mademoiselle Fifi,* which has been played some two thousand times, and a one-act play by Courteline, *Un Coup de fusil.* The bill set the standard for the future policy of the theatre, which alternated drama and comedy in order to provoke terror and laughter. Another of its novelties consisted in presenting sometimes the same topic diversely dramatized by different dramatists. Besides Méténier, the genre has been exploited by such adepts as Max Maurey, whose play *Le Navire aveugle* (1927) has as subject a sailing ship all of whose crew are suddenly struck blind in the midst of the vast ocean; and André de Lorde (1871-), author of such hair-raising contraptions as *L'Homme mysterieux* (1910), a drama of insanity and murder, written in collaboration with Alfred Binet; *Les Nuits rouges de la Tchéka* (1926), a spy story with murder and torture, done in collaboration with Henri Bauche; and, illustrating the better type of Guignol play, *Les Bagnes d'enfants* (1910), product of his joint labors with Pierre Chaine. The last is a near-thesis drama that portrays the tyranny of fathers who abandoned wayward children to reformatories, and the greater brutality, cruelty, even sadism of the administrators of such places in the days when such conditions existed. When the young victims in the play make a break, they are hounded and caught one by one, save Georges, the adolescent protagonist, who hangs himself in a farmhouse where he had sought a haven. Despite its melodramatic traits, this ever-popular Parisian theatre drew to its footlights in the better types of drama authors like Mirbeau, Courteline, Lenormand, and Savoir, among many others. In 1923 the Selwyns brought to New York the Grand Guignol Players for a season of seven weeks during which they presented weekly programs alternating horror melodramas with breezy comedies in the original, such as *Au rat mort, cabinet no. 6* (1908), by André de Lorde and Pierre Chaine, which had already been seen on Broadway in 1913 as *A Pair of White Gloves; Une Nuit au bouge* (1919) by Charles Méré, and *Nounouche* (1919) by Henri Duvernois.

One of the dramatists most clearly marked by what the Théâtre Libre came to destroy and what it came to create was Eugène Brieux (1858-1932). The thesis play of Dumas fils, modified by a dramatic infusion of naturalistic social doctrines, gives us the scope of his drama. He has been praised and criticized in superlatives, none of which was fully deserved. His humble origin, which handicapped him in his formal artistic and dramatic training, afforded him, on the other hand, an insight into the life of the people whose problems he espoused in the theatre. Moved by moral and sociological considerations, he undertook to point out with indignation, or to view with alarm, the evils and abuses which he thought were threatening the social structure. His plays became stage pleas for or against something. He argued for good home providers, the economic emancipation of women, protection for the children of divorced parents, for religious education for the masses, and inveighed against adultery, wet-nursing, judicial and political corruption, higher education for the lower classes, organized charity and its subsequent pauperism, the conspiracy of silence over venereal diseases, the abuses of science and medicine, gambling among workers, and other social evils. In none of his plays did he show himself to be a profound thinker; but lacking originality, he had at least the courage to broach subjects heretofore tabooed on the stage. Such was the case with *Les Avariés* (*Damaged Goods,* 1902) which had been suppressed in 1901, not because, it was explained, it dealt with the problem of syphilis, but because the matter was more appropriate to the clinic than to the stage. In fact, the subject of venereal diseases is treated with far more devastating moral and dramatic effect in Ibsen's *Ghosts* than in Brieux's *L'Evasion* (1896). Therein lies the weakness of his "melodramas of ideas" as Jacques Copeau has labeled them. He states his subject-matter inartistically. In that respect, his work leaves much to be desired. Its form and style are inelegant; its construction is loose and banal. Its strength lies in its emotional advocacy of popular causes. Its artistic merit increases in proportion to the universality of the appeal he makes, as may be observed in his best plays, *Blanchette* (1892), *La Robe rouge* (1900)—the latter title suggested by the actress Réjane "because," she said, "people will think it is about some sensational new dress," but well rendered in the American production of the play as *The Letter of the Law* in 1920—or in *Le Bourgeois aux champs* (1914), in which the reformer in him turned gentle satirist. Brieux can create character, depict social manners, produce atmosphere, draw vivid pictures of the lower social strata. He can contrive tense situations and inevitable dénouements. But he usually sacrificed his art on the altar of social reform. He transformed it into what Dumas fils had described as the "useful theatre," and René Doumic called the "lecture theatre." That is why his place in the dramatic hierarchy declined measurably in the post-war world. The transitory problems which had concerned him had ceased to matter, and so did the plays they had caused him to write.

The Pontifical stage cloak Dumas fils had worn fell, however, upon the shoulders of Paul Hervieu (1857-1915) who aimed to create what has been called the modern "bourgeois tragedy," elaborated with what were moral, social, and ideological designs. His main concern, nevertheless, was with the upper-class family, its marital and moral problems and maladjustments. The tragedy in *La Course du flambeau* (1901) arises from the workings of natural instincts—the sacrifice of filial to mother love. But in others of his plays the conflicts issue from the clash of passions and interests that are aggravated by faulty family statutory laws. The crusade of Dumas fils in favor of divorce had resulted in the enactment of the Naquet law which required the consent of both parties, or proof of flagrant crime, for the remarriage of either. The law, moreover, left a ticklish child problem on its trail which Hervieu and other dramatists picked up and brought onto the stage. The child then became the dramatic link that held together, or the magnet that reunited, couples divided by passions and problems that social legislation was impotent to purge or to solve. That is the case in Hervieu's *Les Tenailles* (1895), *La Loi de l'homme* (1897), or *Le Dédale* (1902), of which the last was seen as *The Labyrinth* in New York in 1905. Thus the fallibilities of the civil code—for whose revision he campaigned by implication—replace in his dramatic scheme the immutable Fate of ancient tragedy. He was deeply disturbed by the complexities of marital and social relations of which he stated the dramatic manifestations with the clarity, concreteness, and conciseness of a legal document. But his approach to them was moral rather than psychological. Therein lies the flaw in his dramatic armor. That accounts for the rigidity of his intrigues, the formalism of his ideas, the stiffness of his characters, and, especially, of his style and dialogue, all of which detract from the intensity of his well-constructed dramas. They are man-made, geometrical labyrinths in which the characters stumble in each other's way, until the author leads them out to their proper exits, even to death, when he finds no other avenue out for them. The tragedy seems unavoidable on the stage but not in real life. It is genuine and logical, but not necessary and inevitable.

The Théâtre Libre had created the tool and had given the cue for a new drama, but for the most part the theatre between 1894 and 1914 continued to mirror the life of the French upper bourgeoisie in the manner of Augier and Dumas fils. Few are the plays that reflected the social and economic restlessness of the day. This mood is felt in the dramas of Lucien Descaves (1861-   ), in the social satires he wrote in collaboration with Maurice Donnay, *La Clairière* (1900) and *Oiseaux de passage* (1904). He involved the Théâtre Libre in troubled waters with his antibourgeois play *Les Chapons* (1890), written in collaboration with Georges Darien. In *La Cage* (1898), he drew a somber portrait of a family reduced to suicide through poverty and bitter distress. To the same group of intense and polemical spirits belonged Octave Mirbeau (1848-1917), friend and disciple of Henri Becque, who was endowed with an acid pen, strong convictions, and a sharp-edged temperament which he turned to a caustic satire on the narrow egoisms of the bourgeois social order. His powerful drama *Les mauvais Bergers* (1897), erected on the somber scaffolding of a workers' strike, bears comparison with Curel's *Le Repas du lion,* which takes up the same issue, and was produced the same year. Likewise, his one-act satire on social justice, *Le Portefeuille* (1902), recalls Anatole France's *Crainquebille,* which it preceded by one year. His masterpiece is *Les Affaires sont les affaires* (1903), known as *Business Is Business* on the American stage (1904), in which he made an unforgetable portrait of the financier Isidore Lechat. These plays, as well as *Le Foyer* (1908), a satire of those for whom Sinclair Lewis was to coin the word "philanthrobbers," the professional philanthropists, are among the best examples of the modern social drama in France.

The literary line of Balzac and Becque was represented by another social dramatist of talent in this era, Emile Fabre (1870-   ), for over a score of years the director of the Comédie Française. He delighted in taking apart the creaking mechanism of modern society in order to exhibit its rusty parts. More successful in his portraits of men in public than in private life, and a master of mob scenes and mob psychology on the stage, he satirized the manipulations, intrigues, and deformations of the financial, political, electoral, and colonial worlds with incisiveness and vitality. His plays—*La Vie publique* (1901), *Les Ventres dorés* (1905), *Les Sauterelles* (1911), among others—are powerful and stirring pictures of the problems and complexities of the modern social organism. His play *La Rabouilleuse* (drawn from Balzac, 1903) was a Broadway success as *The Honor of the Family* in 1908, and has been revived since, the last time in 1926.

Finally, the name of Paul Bourget (1852-1935), who turned from the study of charming sinners in his novels to that of social problems in his dramas, takes his place here as spokesman in the theatre for the opposition to the drama with a democratic conception of social problems, and as a defender of the religious, moral, and political traditions of the past. Thus in *La Barricade* (1910), which inevitably calls for comparison with *Les mauvais Bergers,* he sides with the employers and against the striking Syndicalists, without delving into the causes of industrial dissension, as Curel, for instance, did in *Le Repas du lion.* In *Le Tribun* (1911), he aims to prove that family ties are stronger than the doctrinal opposition of its protagonist socialist minister to the institution of the family. The drama's conclusion could have been the same, however, had the minister been a conservative one. In *Un Divorce* (1908), seen in New York in 1909, the subject of divorce is viewed from the Catholic angle. The importance of Bourget's plays as social theses was greater, in any case, than their dramatic significance.

The outstanding dramatist of the realistic theatre in this era was François de Curel (1854-1928). A nobleman by birth, educated in a Jesuit college and at a technological school, his aristocratic, religious, and scientific backgrounds are reflected in the intellectual and moral high tone of his work. He raised the thesis play to the dignity of the philosophical drama. The latter represents, in his case, a fusion of the social play with the prose tragedy and the symbolic comedy. The label "drama of ideas" has been attached to it, but only in the sense that it might be applied to Ibsen or Shaw. Ideas, Curel's mouthpiece observes in *La Comédie du génie* (1921), interest him "much less than the storms they raise in the soul." In the thesis play, the author imposes his ideas on the drama deductively, and pulls the strings of his dramatic conflicts toward dénouements appropriate to them. In the drama of ideas, neither the contending elements nor the conclusion are juggled with arbitrarily to suit a particular point of view. This difference between the two genres was brought out by the advice to study Dumas fils, and especially Scribe, which a reader at the Comédie Française volunteered to Curel when rejecting one of his first plays. But his substance was of a different mettle. His dramatic conflicts arose from the clash of character with religious, sentimental, or intellectual passions, and not from reformist preachings, or technical hocus-pocus. In his earlier works, his problems are primarily sentimental and psychological. Thus in *L'Envers d'une sainte,* the play with which Antoine introduced him to the public in 1892 at the Théâtre Libre, the conflict rages between the passions and spiritual contrition. The dramatic motivation becomes more ideological in the plays of his second manner. It is incited by divergent and perplexing spiritual and social philosophies. These inaugurate dramatic clashes and debates between the social code and the inner law of his characters that result often in tragic dénouements. Thus Albert Donnat, in *La nouvelle Idole* (1899), commits suicide when he loses his faith in science; the futility of her emotional and intellectual experiences in the civilized world drives the heroine of *La Fille sauvage* (1902) back to the bestiality of her native state—a symbol of humanity, for one cannot educate the instincts, the play seems to say; the troubled aristocrat who had espoused the cause of the workers in order to atone for a childhood misdeed, in *Le Repas du lion* (1897), ends by reverting to his own class and natural interests. The last three among these plays, together with *Les Fossiles* (1892), which is a sort of noble valedictory to a dying aristocratic class, rise to the dignity of masterpieces.

In the plays of his third manner, after the First World War, his mood turns somewhat skepical and satirical, as in *L'Ame en folie* (1919), his most resounding, in fact, his only popular, success. If the passions of man can drive the soul insane, salvation, he argues, lies in a stoical attitude for the strong, or in religious escape for the humble in spirit. A third possibility is illustrated in *L'Ivresse du sage* (1922), where Hortense and Hubert de Piolet follow their desires in the way Maia and Ulfheim do in Ibsen's *When We Dead Awaken.* Curel does not advocate one expedient or the other; he merely states the issues, pointing out that humanity is like that. His other plays, like those referred to, represent different moral and emotional labyrinthine designs in which the characters grope for a way out. Weak or strong, they incarnate, in general, Curel's speculative preoccupations, and so their psychological and spiritual dilemmas reflect a philosophical significance intensely dramatic and symbolic in character. This condition overloads the well-constructed and traditional form of his dramas, sometimes, and renders their interpretation difficult on the foreign stage. They brought him, usually, only a *succès d'estime*. But they made of him a writer's playwright.

The influence of Curel's virile and courageous drama was subtle but effective. It can be detected in the concern of Gabriel Trarieux (1870-   ) with issues of a moral nature, as illustrated in *L'Otage* (1907), which portrays the conflict of religious avocation versus political opportunism and free thought, and which ends with tragic consequences. The same interest in problems of conscience and duty, in a world morally and spiritually adrift, is found in the work of Paul-Hyacinthe Loyson (1873-1921). He confronted in his plays religion with reason, faith with unbelief. A skeptic father contends with a devout mother over the education of their daughter in *Les Ames ennemies* (1907), a setup which recalls that in *L'Otage,* and which was produced as *The War of Souls* in New York in 1909. His protagonist in *L'Apôtre* (1911) is a freethinking politician who holds that ethics and reason are sufficient guides for a righteous life; he maintains this view even in the face of his son's transgressions, which he denounces publicly, compelling his own resignation from public office—an attitude which contrasts with the minister's conduct under the same circumstances in Bourget's *Le Tribun*.

Curel's ideological trend is markedly evident in the work of Marie Lenéru (1875-1918) who, as the only woman to have achieved eminence in the theatre in France, deserves special credit. Her dramas are moral conflicts involving characters living, or seeking to live, beyond good and evil. Typical of them is *Les Affranchis* (1910), in which an outwardly respectable but spiritually nihilistic professor and a morally upright ex-novice ultimately sacrifice their love for each other in order to spare the former's wife and the sanctities of the moral law. To the same dramatic line belong the plays of another writer, Edouard Schneider (1800-   ), who analyzed ideological and moral problems of a complex nature, such as that of traditional versus Christian socialism in *Les Mages sans étoiles* (1911), or that of physical versus spiritual passion in *L'Exaltation* (1928). In the latter play a mother's passionate nature, which had driven her into the arms of a lover, becomes transformed into the purest mystic exaltation when transmitted to her daughter. The same dramatic traits characterize the plays of Henry Marx (1882-   ). They are pervaded with ideas and ideals, as witness his *Ariel* (1926), which is sufficiently described by its subtitle: *La Passion de la révolte*. Their high intellectual level, however, did not always mask their rhetorical and dramatic weaknesses. To the same dramatic filiation, finally, belong the morally lofty plays of Gabriel Marcel (1887-   ), which are loaded with ideas that are, in effect, moral conflicts. He wrote a series of powerful dramas of complex conflicts of the heart and spirit, of self-sacrifice and inner desolation, as in *La Chapelle ardente* (1925), which studies the grief that consumes the survivors of a son killed in the war. In the genre of the social drama he presented, in *Le Dard* (1937), the psychological and ideological incompatibilities between creatures of different social extractions, between a Communist teacher and the bourgeois family into which he married. His plays earned him the enviable reputation of being a "new Curel."

The psychological analysis of passion and character has always constituted a basic trait of the best French drama. One of the foremost to resume the tradition of Racine was Georges de Porto-Riche (1849-1930), whose collected plays are published under the significant title of *Théâtre d'Amour*. His first full-length play was a romantic and historical drama, *Un Drame sous Philippe II* (1875). It was not until several years later that he revealed his real vein at the Théâtre Libre with *La Chance de Françoise* (1888), creating a type of psychological comedy that contained in the bud what André Antoine was to describe as "a new sentimental perspective," when the Odéon produced the fully-blossomed flower, *Amoureuse* (1891). Both were produced in New York, the former as *Lover's Luck* in 1916, and the latter, with only moderate success, as *The Tyranny of Love* in 1921. *Amoureuse* is a drama of passion and conjugal incompatibility between a middle-aged man who wearies of the passion he himself arouses, but is too weak to resist, or to bear, and his passionate younger wife whose sway over his senses, his heart, and his mind he seeks to break, at last, in a bitter, heart-searing conflict that ends in tragedy for all. Its analytical baring of the heart and soul was something new in dramatic literature. In its technical aspects, it harked back to the well-made play, but in treatment and substance it recalled *Les Corbeaux* and the "slice of life," though essentially modified in the school of Racine. Love had been used before in modern dramaturgy, but without being dissected and taken apart. Porto-Riche studied its anatomy and physiology and revealed them with undisguised realism. He betrayed its tyranny over the senses, and the wounds and hurts it inflicts. He exhibited on the stage the natural history of love, and one might label it with Racine's apt verse: "C'est Vénus toute entière à sa proie attachée." He converted the stage into a clinic of the heart where the comfortable amenities and morality of the sentimental comedy were discarded once and for all.

He applied the same pattern to his other plays, to *Le Passé* (1897), *Le Vieil homme* (1911), *Le Marchant d'estampes* (1917), cutting through the lustful passions and fickle desires of the men in them, and the all-embracing attachment of the women, with the same stark frankness and incisive insight. In all, however, thanks to the lyric virtues of his style, which acts as a filter for the purification of the turbid passions stirred up, the impression he produces is one of deep sympathy for the sufferings of the characters, especially for the women among them.

It has been said that Georges de Porto-Riche was the father of few plays but the grandfather of many. In his own day, other writers exploited the dramatic vein he had opened. His *théâtre d'amour* transferred from the surgical room to the boudoir, its passions perceptibly moderated, gives the design of that of Maurice Donnay (1859-   ). And the appellation of "Jewish Racine," which has been given him, finds its pendant in that of "boulevard Racine" applied to Donnay. The latter penetrates into the heart with a train of smiling handmaids, bearers of his humor, irony, wit, and sentiment. While he cuts and analyzes its wounds, they soothe and assuage the pain love leaves where it has passed.

Though he prepared to be an engineer, Donnay turned to writing *saynètes,* short dramatic and satirical sketches and verses, for the cabaret *Le Chat Noir,* and made his dramatic bow with *Lysistrata,* in 1892, followed by *Amants,* his masterpiece, in 1895. The play depicts the budding, blossoming, and final withering of a love idyl between two civilized and refined creatures, whose freedom from conventional and emotional shackles keeps the comedy from turning to tragedy. It remains throughout discreetly romantic, and, at its most dramatic point, tinged with a deep and tender melancholy. Donnay broke with the dramatic convention according to which hatred followed love in the heart of former lovers. Here they end with mutual affection and friendship.

The pattern may contain a few more somber threads in others of his comedies, as in *L'Affranchie* (1898), and may even turn entirely tragic, witness *Le Torrent* (1899), where the adulteress throws herself into a torrent. But usually it proves to be engaging and sophisticated. Love is the chief motif always—love outside the bonds of matrimony. "We study adultery because it is after all what divides us least," he observed, meaning that "it was less dangerous to dramatize a sentimental adventure than a conflict between political parties or religious beliefs." The result was that even when he broached moral, social, or racial issues, the drama turned in the end into a problem of love. In *Le Retour de Jérusalem* (1903), which takes the negative side of the question of marriage between Jew and gentile defended by Heijermans in *The Ghetto* (1898), Donnay ascribes the break between the lovers to their racial incompatibility, forgetting that similar emotional conflicts had arisen in others of his plays between characters not so divided. In New York, *The Return from Jerusalem* ran for only fifty-three performances when produced in 1912. Love also enters in his satire on communism, in *La Clairière* (1900), and in that on the petty bourgeoisie and radical ideas, in *Oiseaux de passage* (1904), both written in collaboration with Lucien Descaves. In the comedies of the second half of his career, he widened the scope of his subject-matter without raising their stature. His theatre remained what it was from the beginning, a gentle and amusing chronicle of the urbane sentiments, manners, and speech of a cultured section of his contemporaries. Commenting on the failure of his *L'Assemblée des femmes* (1930), which he had drawn from Aristophanes, Donnay remarked to André Birabeau: "We pre-war authors are played out... the public is no longer gay." Indeed, the mood had changed, but *Amants* will always survive.

Another analyst of sentiment and morals, Jules Lemaître (1853-1914), embraced the theatre after a brilliant career as a critic, and something of the eclectic spirit with which he viewed the stage parade for years reappears in his own dramatic creations. They evoke echoes of dramatic conflicts and techniques which had faced the footlights before. *Le Pardon* (1895), which was seen in a special matinée performance in New York in 1916, portrays a husband and wife who forgive each other's unfaithfulness because they cannot bear to part—calling to mind the dénouement in Porto-Riche's *Amoureuse*. *L'Aînée* (1898) paints the portrait of the eldest of six sisters who sacrifices herself, and is sacrificed by the family to the others, until the author rewards her with a good husband, in happier circumstances than was the case with Becque's eldest daughter in *Les Corbeaux*. He was more original in his full-length study of a corrupted politician, in *Le Député Leveau* (1890), regarded as a take-off on General Boulanger; or in his study of a painter's sacrifice of his budding romance for the sake of his son to whom he abandons his pretty studio assistant, in *La Massière* (1905), which was produced as *Poor Little Thing* in New York in 1915. This is a theme that Porto-Riche turned into a tragedy in *Le Vieil homme*. Lemaître's plays combine the techniques of the thesis play, the "slice of life," and the sentimental comedy. They deal with a wide range of matters: adultery, politics, the family, honor, love, jealousy, in the treatment of which he often displays the psychological subtlety and the charm of style that characterize his other writings.

Closely affiliated with the comedy of sentiment and character is the genre often characterized as the Parisian comedy of manners, in which Henri Lavedan (1859-1940) achieved wide popularity. He presented astute and witty portrayals of the foibles and frailties, the virtues and vices of his epoch without deep feeling or conviction, however, as for instance in his comedy *Le nouveau Jeu* (1898), which turns out to be, in reality, an old one, since it tells the story of an old boulevardier who marries on a bet and lives to regret it. He appears more earnest in the plays on which his fame rests, such as *Le Prince d'Aurec* (1892), which resumes the conflict between the ruined aristocracy and the powerful bourgeoisie which Augier had depicted in *Le Gendre de M. Poirier*. In Lavedan the ungrateful rôle falls on the shoulders of the Jewish banker, Baron de Horn, who becomes henceforth the prototype for the unscrupulous, conventional type of Jewish banker other dramatists will often introduce in their plays. The same struggle between these class adversaries is portrayed in Albert Guinon's (1863-1923) play *Décadence*, which was banned by the censor in 1901, and produced in 1904. Here, however, the irony and satire of the author is directed impartially at the decadent French nobility and the socially ambitious Jewish banker.

Lavedan's other plays include *Le Marquis de Priola* (1902), the portrait of a libertine, which was seen in New York as *The Marquis of Priola* in 1919; and his best work, *Le Duel* (1905), staged as *The Duel* here in 1906. The latter is a sort of comedy of ideas that analyzes the conflict between science and religion, identified in the characters of two brothers who fight one for the body and the other for the soul of a woman. In his later comedies his satire and drama tend toward the artificial and the melodramatic, as in *Sire* (1909) and *Servir* (1913), both of which were staged in New York, the former, a light satirical intrigue, as *Sire* in 1911, and the latter, which debates the question of pacifism, as *Service* in 1918.

To the same category of amiable playwrights belongs Alfred Capus (1858-1922), specialist of Parisian wit, indulgent and amusing observer of boulevard life, master-craftsman of the comedy with a happy ending but not always with a happy point of view. Optimistic in substance but pessimistic in mood, he contrived his successful intrigues to illustrate his comforting if cynical belief that with luck, nerve, and cleverness all conflicts can be adjusted, sufferings avoided, faults forgiven, tragedies averted, and all harassing problems solved happily. He painted a gallery of sympathetic rascals who remain incorrigibly optimistic throughout their difficulties. He pleased his contemporaries with humorous satires of social manners and attitudes in comedies like *Brignolle et sa fille* (1894), *La Veine* (1901), and *Les deux Ecoles* (1902), the last produced in New York as *The Two Schools* in 1902, which are free from the stern moralizing disposition of other dramatists. Thus the trials of a young woman alone in the world that Brieux was to treat as a serious problem in *La Femme seule* (1912), made a delightful story in *La petite Fonctionnaire* (1901). Life is not gay, Capus seems to say, but he made certain that his plays were. When he strayed from this line and attempted serious dramas, like *La Châtelaine* (1902), known here as *The Brighter Side* (1905), or *L'Oiseau blessé* (1908), his public refused to take him seriously, and they were right, for his true vein was in the lighter comedy.

Lacking the humor and dramatic amenity of Capus, but with disabused and incisive psychological penetration, Abel Hermant (1862-   ), better known as a novelist but possessing merit as a dramatist, viewed the corrupt manners and morals of pre-war bourgeois and decadent aristocratic society with cutting frankness and irony. He painted not so much conflicts of violent passions as a dissolute and licentious world rampant with moral and social parasitism, peopled with adulterous and scatter-brained women, with fatuous, venal, and debauched men, with futile and perverse youths, with an unclean and repulsive lot in whose lecherous passions there isn't one spark of genuine emotion. However, Hermant does not moralize. If in some instances he assumes a positive stand, as when he censures the evils of easy divorce laws in *L'Empreinte* (1900) and *Les Jacobines* (1907), in others—*La belle Madame Héber* (1905), *Monsieur de Courpière* (1907)—the moral nihilism they betray stands self-exposed and condemned by his smart and keen satire. But on the whole his plays stand out more for their literary merits than for their dramatic qualities. A play of his, *Starlight,* evidently inspired in part by episodes in the life of Sarah Bernhardt, was adapted and produced in New York in 1925.

The psychological thread found to run through the dramas of passion of Porto-Riche passed also through those of Henry Bataille and Henry Bernstein.

Henry Bataille (1872-1922), the sensitive poet of *La Chambre blanche* (1895), started out in the theatre with the ambition to react against "brutal realism, easy to master, which gives readily to the public the illusion of life," and to elevate the drama to the level of poetry. He ended by creating what has been labelled a *théâtre de la femme,* in which are betrayed a succession of impassioned and emotionally unbalanced characters, most of them women with atrophied will and reason. They are caught in the grip of obsessing desires whose fulfilment is their punishment. They turn the stage into a clinic of morbid and erotic passions that adjoins the boudoir on one side and the morgue on the other. Several among them attempt suicide as the only solution to their torturing physical and moral distress, and some succeed. Their sufferings provide dénouements of dramatic power and terror, but lack unfortunately the purgative quality, the nobility and chastity of the true tragedy. Outstanding among these dramas are *Maman Colibri* (1904), *La Marche nuptiale* (1905), and *La Femme nue* (1908), the latter inspired by the attempted suicide of Rosalie Texier, the deserted wife of Debussy. They are cast in a dramatic pattern that fuses together the lyrical and analytical faculties of the dramatist with his romantic and naturalistic tendencies. They represent an art that some critics have characterized as *littérature brutale.* Several of Bataille's plays have been produced on the Broadway stage, the most successful of them being *Résurrection* (from Tolstoi, 1902), as *Resurrection* in 1903, *La Tendresse* (1921), under the same title, in 1922, and *L'Enfant de l'amour* (1911) as *The Love Child* in 1922.

The epithet *littérature brutale* was applied also to the early work of Henry Bernstein (1876-   ). After his first comedies, typified by *Frère Jacques* (1904), written in collaboration with Pierre Veber, and adapted by Clyde Fitch as *Brother Jacques* for the New York Stage in 1904, and beginning with *La Rafale* (1905), which has been produced as *Baccarat* (1909) and as *The Whirlwind* (1910) in America, his *théâtre d'amour* became a succession of dramatic explosions the central motif of which was lust of the flesh and its concomitant passions. He gave the impression then of dissecting the human heart, as Jean Toulet observed, with a kitchen knife. The drama was drawn from the clash of fortuitous and accidental circumstances that were skilfully contrived to snarl the passions for the *scène à faire,* the inevitable dramatic storm in a following act, with the dénouement or epilogue in the last, often in the form of madness or suicide. This technique enabled him to write some of the most notable successes on the modern stage. *Le Voleur* (1906), as *The Thief,* ran for hundreds of performances on Broadway in 1907. *Samson* (1907) and *Israël* (1908), both produced here under their original titles, the former in 1908 and the latter in 1909, were well received, as was *L'Assaut* (1912) presented as *The Attack* in 1912. The intrigue in all is so well conducted that it holds the audience hanging breathless to the mounting paroxysm of the passions until the final jerking and straining of the nerves.

With *Le Secret* (1913), which was produced as *The Secret* in New York in 1913, and in which he pried into the sadistic and complex nature of a creature who visits misfortune on her friend, his manner changed from the physiological to the psychological. Henceforth he studied the inner mechanisms of the heart and mind that motivate the passions; the conflict of situations was replaced by that of characters; external violence by introspective analysis; exceptional individualities by perplexed and typical representatives of average, middle-class society. He became especially interested in the antagonisms between the older and the younger generations in matters of love and life in the years between the two World Wars. This evolution of his art was, in fact, symbolic of the change in tempo we shall soon observe between the pre-war and the post-war French drama. Representative of this subtler and more lyrical Bernstein are *L'Elévation* (1917) produced under the same title by Grace George in New York in 1917; *La Galerie des glaces* (1924), which makes a searching study of a case of "inferiority complex"; *Mélo* (1929), played on Broadway under the same name in 1931; and, to cite one more play, *Le Cap des tempêtes* (1937), where he analyzes the inner storms of passions with Racinian perspicacity. The list of his works is extensive. Throughout his long career few were the evenings when he did not have one play, and sometimes more than one simultaneously, in the boulevard theatres. In all, Bernstein remained the perfect architect of dramatic situations and intense effects for whom "the play is the thing."

In the work of two other playwrights of this dramatic line, who began their careers at the Théâtre Libre, Pierre Wolff (1865-   ) and Romain Coolus (pseudonym of René Weill, 1868-   ), may be observed the evolution of the *comédie rosse,* showing humanity in cynical colors, into the *comédie rose,* showing it in rosy hues. The former's witty, sentimental, and piquant comedies conceal under trifling or indecorous intrigues a prying insight into the heart and its fallibilities which made him find favor on the American as on the French stage. *Le Secret de Polichinelle* (1903) was produced as *The Secret of Polichinelle* in New York in 1904, and was followed, among others, by *The Lily,* adapted by David Belasco from *Le Lys* (written with Gaston Leroux, 1908) in 1909, and by *The Marionettes,* adapted from *Les Marionettes* (1910) in 1911. Like Wolff, Coolus won the favor of Parisian audiences with his portrayals of the emotional whimsies and ironies of wayward or perverse loves, in light, gay, and amoral comedies like *Les Amants de Sazy* (1901) and *Les Bleus de l'amour* (1911). His *La Sonnette d'alarme* (1922), written in collaboration with Maurice Hannequin, was produced as *The Alarm Clock* in New York in 1923. A finer dramatic vein, finally, provides the substance of another analyst of the passions, Edmond Sée (1875-   ), whose subtle studies of the psychological and sentimental complications, egotisms, and frailties of the heart, in comedies like *La Brebis* (1896), *Les Miettes* (1899), and *L'Indiscret* (1903), are outstanding for their delicacy, pathos, and poetic insight.

Gradually the drama of passion degenerated into melodrama. Georges Polti, author of the idealistic play *Les Cuirs de bœuf* (1918), observed in his book *Les trente-six situations dramatiques* that no matter what the play dealt with, love had become the kernel of the intrigue in most boulevard comedies. A skilful craftsman in this genre was the Belgian-born Henry Kistemaeckers (1872-1938), author of plays in which tears and laughter are mingled adroitly in the best Sardou manner. His *La Rivale* (1907), written in collaboration with Eugène Delard, was produced here with great success by Margaret Anglin as *The Woman of Bronze* in 1920. Two other plays of his, both dealing with spies, had moderate success on the American stage; *La Flambée* (1911) produced as *The Spy* in 1913, and *Un Soir au front* (1918), produced as *Where Poppies Bloom* in 1918. Equally adept at the art was Charles Méré (1883-   ), whose melodramas are often powerful studies of the passions, such as *La Femme masquée* (1922), which was produced on Broadway as *The Masked Woman* in 1922, *Le Lit nuptial* (1926), or *Le Désir* (1933). Other authors who were successful in this genre were Pierre Frondaie (1884-   ) and Fernand Nozière (1874-1931). Frondaie has been clever at adapting novels into plays besides writing on original themes, as with his *Montmartre* (1910), *Aphrodite* (drawn from the novel of Pierre Louys, 1914) and *L'Homme à l'Hispano* (1928). The first two were produced under their original titles on the American stage in 1922 and 1919 respectively. Nozière had a reputation as a writer of *comédies galantes*, like *Les deux Visages* (1909), when he acquired another in the field of melodrama. His play *La Maison de danses* (written with Charles Muller, 1909) was produced in New York as *Café de Danse* and later as *House of Dance* in 1929. Many of these dramatists stood astride the dramatic stream with one foot on the pre-war, and the other on the post-war periods.

The mantle of Thalia fell from the shoulders of Labiche upon those of Georges Courteline (1860-1929) when, on the evening of April 27, 1893, the latter's comedy *Boubouroche* exploded with riotous mirth in the usually somber atmosphere of the Théâtre Libre. As was becoming in such a house, however, the comedy betrayed an undertone of melancholy, a characteristic that was to be observed in Courteline's other plays. He has handled as farce, even as vaudeville, not only what is ridiculous but also what is tragic in life. His comic and satirical veins exhibit a happy blend of humor, sympathy, and good-natured irony that inflicts self-healing wounds. He draws vivid caricatures of human beings, of the railroad clerk, the soldier, the policeman, the magistrate, the shrew, all dreadfully comical and true, in plays like *Les Gaîtés de l'escadron* (1895), *L'Article 330* (1900), and *La Paix chez soi* (1903), the last being produced as *A Private Account* in New York in 1917, followed by *Boubouroche* under its original title in 1921. His analysis of human foibles, stupidities, petty tyrannies, cruelties, and heroisms, relieved by his verve, crackling wit, and lyrical style have made of him the Daumier of the comic stage.

On the same level of excellence stand the sober but subtle comedies of Jules Renard (1864-1910). He is a dry-point artist of the stage, a tight-lipped and poker-faced satirist, whose humor and wit are saturated with deep emotion extracted from a delineation of character and an analysis of the heart and mind that are the perfection of the realistic art. He fused with masterly dramatic art tragic and comic elements in such a little masterpiece as *Poil de Carotte* (1900), which presents the novelty of a child in the principal rôle, played by Ethel Barrymore when the play was produced here as *Carrots* in 1902; and he was able to evoke a sentimental mood in *Monsieur Vernet* (1903) without straining its poetic quality.

The graceful, satirical, and sentimental pictures Robert de Flers (1872-1927) and Gaston-Armand de Caillavet (1869-1915) painted of the society of the Third Republic recall those Meilhac and Halévy had drawn of that under the Second Empire. They were specialists of good-natured fun, of mirth in good taste, of Parisian wit, sparkling dialogue, amusing intrigue, and smiling sentimentality in comedies that can stand the test of reading. Such is the case with *L'Amour veille* (1907), which was produced here as *Love Watches* in 1908, and in which Billie Burke played the part of Jacqueline who tries in vain to render her husband jealous, because "love watches"; and of *L'Ane de Buridan* (1909) in which John Drew starred as the great flirt when the play came to Broadway as *Inconstant George* in 1909. The authors handled with an ever-popular art all types of comedies of love, manner, or character, but they were most successful with those in which naughty but innocuous intrigues served as agreeable vehicles for subtle social and political satire. This may be observed in *Le Roi* (1908), written with Emmanuel Arène, which laughs at democratic and Parisian infatuation with visiting royalty, and which Cohan and Harris produced as *The King* in New York in 1917; in *Le Bois sacré* (1910), where Clémentine's desire for the ribbon of the Legion of Honor becomes the thread of a merry satire and comedy—seen on the New York stage as *Decorating Clementine* in 1910; and in *L'Habit vert* (1912), a take-off on the French Academy, which bore them no grudge but, on the contrary, rewarded one of the authors, de Flers, with election to its select society.

Another comic writer of eminence was Tristan Bernard (1866-   ).

From 1897, and for two generations, he endowed the stage with a brilliant repertoire of farces, satires, sentimental comedies, even melodramas, like *Triplepatte* (written with André Godfernaux, 1905), the story of a shilly-shallier which John Barrymore interpreted when the play was presented in America as *Toddles* in 1908; *Le petit Café* (1911), turned into a musical comedy, *The Little Café*, in New York in 1913; and *La Volonté de l'homme* (1917), which was revived as *Le Sexe fort* in 1930, as a contrast to Edouard Bourdet's *Le Sexe faible*; or *Le Sauvage* (1931). They reveal a gallery of timid souls, of mediocre heroes with petty thoughts who become involved in petty intrigues they know not how nor why, from which the merciful author, with tongue in cheek, extracts them with debonair and nimble-witted skill. His plays are peculiar for their incisive humor, witty observation of human foibles, and keen portrayal of weaknesses and absurdities in which even his skilful caricature of character serves to point out the underlying lesson of his theatre, namely, that success or failure in life depends upon strength or weakness of character.

Finally, in the comic genre aptly described as *théâtre de digestion*—high vaudeville and rollicking satire—amiable, hilarious, and favorable to after-dinner digestion, the name of Georges Feydeau (1862-1921) stands out. Thanks to his amusing intrigues, clever dialogues, wit, and humor he was a favorite of Parisian audiences from 1894 to 1914 with such comedies as *Un Fil à la patte* (1894, *The Lady from Lobster Square,* New York, 1910); *La Dame de chez Maxim* (1899), which has been produced variously as *The Girl from Maxim's* and *The Girl from Montmartre* since 1899 in America; and *Occupe-toi d'Amélie* (1908), known here as *Breakfast in Bed* (1920). Others who competed for public favor included Léon Gandillot (1862-1913) and Alexandre Bisson (1848-1912), the latter well known in America for several plays including *Jalouse* (1897), written with the Belgian Adolphe Leclercq, and produced in New York as *Because She Loved Him So,* in 1899; *Le Contrôleur des wagons-lits* (1898), which has been played as *On and Off* (1901) and as *The Night Boat* (1920); and especially his melodrama *La Femme X* (1908), which has become a fixture in the American repertoire as *Madame X* since 1910. Among the experts of sprightly and fluffy comedy, two other names won the plaudits of the American as of the French theatre public: Pierre Veber (1869-) and Paul Gavault (1867-). Veber is the author of *Les Grands* (1909), a rather original drama of a schoolboy's love for his schoolmaster's wife, written in collaboration with Serge Basset. But he is known here for such successes as *Loute* (1902), which was produced as *The Girl from Rector's* in 1909; *Madame et son filleul* (1916), written with M. Hannequin and Henri de Gorsse, and presented as *The Girl Behind the Gun* in New York in 1918; and, among others, *Le Monsieur de cinq heures* (written with M. Hannequin, 1924), which, as *A Kiss in a Taxi,* starred Claudette Colbert as Ginette, the barmaid, in 1925, and, as *Sunny Days,* had Jeanette Mac-

Donald in the same rôle on Broadway in 1928. Paul Gavault contributed such popular comedies as *Madame Flirt* (written with Georges Berr, 1901), which became known as *The Frisky Mrs. Johnson* here in 1903; *Mlle Josette, ma femme* (written with Robert Charnay, 1906), produced as *My Wife* by Charles Frohman in 1907; and *La petite Chocolatière* (1909), which was staged as *The Richest Girl* in 1909 and as *Tantalizing Tommy* in 1912 in New York. None of these light comedies equaled, however, the stunning New York success of André Picard's (1874-1926) *Kiki* (1918), in 1921. Picard wrote serious works, notably *Le Cuivre* (with Paul Adam, 1895), which satirizes the rapacity and venality of money-makers and corrupt politicians, and *L'Ange gardien* (1910), in which he portrays a puritanic woman who succumbs to love once momentarily only to resume her moral stiffness afterwards. The plays of his which reached Broadway are of lighter stuff, and *Kiki,* which is a mere bubble, ran for 600 performances, a record for a French play in America, and one which, like the welcome usually reserved to other frothy importations, one wishes were accorded also to more weighty plays.

By the year 1914 the French drama had reached a static condition. The vigorous technical innovations, and the new social philosophy which the Théâtre Libre had infused into it had borne fruit; but the dramatic sap was running thin again. The ideals of the naturalistic and idealistic movements had gone to seed. The rebels of yesterday had assimilated the heritage of Augier and Dumas fils, and had in turn become the convention-bound pillars of the thesis and triangle plays. The dramatic range had become narrowed down in form to the ingenious and reliable well-made play, and in substance chiefly to themes on adultery, jealousy, and divorce, with sometimes some pallid excursion into ideological and sociological realms. The general public's partiality to the drama of marital infidelity, and, *mutatus mutendi,* the desire of author, press-agent, and director in quest of success to cater to its taste, conspired to confine the stage in what Emile Faguet described wittily as the domain of "adultocracy," and to bar the doors of the legitimate playhouses to artistic and original creations. This deplorable condition caused Jacques Copeau to sound the alarm in 1913 against what he characterized as the "unbridled industrialization that from day to day more cynically degrades our French stage, and turns away the cultured public." The time had become ripe again for the rise of a new "free theatre," and the coming of a new Antoine to infuse new blood into its arteries. They appeared in the person of Jacques Copeau and his Théâtre du Vieux-Colombier.

Taking Molière as his spiritual guide, Jacques Copeau (1879-   ) started a new heroic venture in the history of the French theatre. He was already a dramatic critic of note, and the co-author with Jean Croué of a drama, *Les Frères Karamazov* (1911, which they had adapted from the Russian novel, and which was produced in New York as *The Brothers Karamazov* in 1927), when, in September, 1913, he published in the *Nouvelle Revue Française,* which he had helped to found with André Gide, in 1908, the now-celebrated manifesto, "Un Essai de rénovation dramatique: Le Théâtre du Vieux-Colombier," calling for the "establishment upon fresh foundations of a new theatre intended to be the rallying point for those who—authors, actors, spectators—are tormented by the need of restoring once more its inherent beauty to the stage." This formula represented the dramatic equivalent of the high literary and poetic ideals which the *Revue* itself embodied. Concurring also seemingly with Eleanora Duse's epigram that "to save the theatre all the actors must first of all be killed off," he took a company of young disciples, including Louis Jouvet and Charles Dullin, to his country place, at Le Limon, near Paris—soon labelled *Chartreuse de comédiens*—and trained them himself for months according to his ideals of the art and craft of the stage. Then with a program consisting of Molière's *L'Amour médecin,* and a translation of Thomas Heywood's play *A Woman Killed with Kindness,* in a little neighborhood playhouse seating some 360 people, he inaugurated his laboratory theatre on the night of October 22, 1913. He wished it to be a naven where authors and their plays would find actors and a public responsive to their ideals. The favor of the "cultured public" was won from the start, and before long the fame of the little theatre had spread beyond the confines of the street of the Vieux Colombier.

Unfortunately, the war came and dispersed the company for a time. It was brought together again under the auspices of the French government, and, on November 27, 1917, it reopened at the Garrick Theatre, in New York, for a stay of two seasons, during which Copeau produced some fifty plays. He was to complain, however, that here he had found again, "with all his heads complete, and more threatening than ever," the dragon he had sallied forth to kill, in 1913. Back in Paris, in 1919, and until May 1924, with a repertoire of classic, modern, and original plays both French and foreign, he sought to foster a purer taste in the public, better acting among the actors, and greater originality among the writers. In spirit and in actuality, the Vieux-Colombier served as the cradle, and then as the spearhead for the renascence of the drama in France in the years between the two World Wars.

The dramatic ideas of Copeau were significant and widely influential. He initiated no theory or doctrine, but labored for a rebirth of the art and science of the old masters. The word *poetry* served him as a password in acting, staging, and writing for the theatre. He looked upon his little playhouse as a sort of temple, or chapel, and upon the actors as priests of a sacred art. He sought "austere nudity" in stage designing, what could speak to the imagination and spirit rather than to the senses; he shunned mechanical and electrical contrivances, and the abuse of scenic theories of even such pioneer designers as Appia, Craig, or Stanislavski, which could end by usurping instead of interpreting the intentions of the author and his play. He aimed at drama that was pure theatre, that fused realistic and idealistic concepts on the literary and architectural plans. He aimed high, but his uncompromising idealism ultimately thwarted his efforts. It caused him to be too exacting toward the dramatists—so that he drove even such contemporary masterpieces as *La Souriante Mme Beudet, Martine, Knock,* and the plays of Pirandello to seek a haven elsewhere. He was equally hard on the fun-seeking public who ended by nicknaming his little temple *Les Folies Calvin,* and stayed away. Besides, the *succès d'estime* only which crowned the fifteen years of labor he put on his own drama, *La Maison natale* (1923), must have certainly capped his disillusion. Worn out in body and spirit, he retired then to a village in Burgundy where until 1930 he played in the countryside with a group of his young actors to whom the appreciative peasants gave the name *Les Copiaux.* Subsequently, he returned to Paris as dramatic critic. In 1936, he was appointed to the Comédie Française as one of its stage directors, and in the winter of 1940 as its administrator.

Long before, however, the example of the Vieux Colombier had extended abroad to such theatres as the New York Theatre Guild; the Théâtre du Marais, in Brussels; The Everyman Theatre, in London; and Il Teatro d'Arte del Convegno, in Milan. In France, the torch Copeau had lighted had been picked up from his wavering hands by his own disciples. One of them, Charles Dullin (1885-   ), who had begun his career by reciting verses at the Lapin Agile café in Paris, and played his first rôle as Smerdiakov in Copeau's *Brothers Karamazov,* founded in 1921 the Atelier, which he dedicated as a workshop not only for actors, but also for young playwrights, something in the spirit of Professor G. P. Baker's workshop English 47. His guiding principle has been that "the play's the thing," that its dramatic quality must be on a footing with, or even superior to, its literary aspects. He has favored what has been termed "pure theatre"—a theatrical spectacle that eschews conventional and servile imitation of reality, and prosaic and even graceful novelties, but which draws its mead from the worlds of poetry, fancy, and even music, in the Wagnerian concept, his pattern thus recalling the idealistic theatre of the late nineties. He veered away in time from his original idea of a drama for the "select few" toward one that was "a living organism having its function in modern society, responsive to the preoccupations, the enthusiasms of every one." He sought to reintegrate in the modern drama the poetic elements of the Greek, the Elizabethan, the Spanish Golden Age, and the French classic ideals, and included in his repertoire plays by Aristophanes, Shakespeare, Calderón de la Barca, besides those of contemporaries like Cocteau, Passeur, Romains, and Pirandello, the last of whom he had the honor of introducing on the French stage.

One of the boldest innovators on the Parisian scene, for whom one would have to modify the old saying to mean "the stage is the thing," was Gaston

Baty (1885-   ). He had been influenced by German and Russian stagecraft, and he aimed to convert the theatre into what the original sense of the Greek radical *theaomai* implied: a spectacle, a thing he was to illustrate in his own plays, like his *Madame Bovary* (1936), which was seen here in 1937, and which are better as theatre than as drama. He regarded the text of a play as its pit, and the staging as the fruit around it. He viewed the footlight boards as the crossroad where all the arts converge to fuse the worlds of make-believe and reality, where the author provides the text, or pretext, for the show, the actors, like marionettes, interpret the spoken words, and the stage manager, new *deus ex machina,* schemes with mechanical, electrical, plastic, and graphic devices in order to express what is unuttered between the lines, the inner emotional content of the drama, on the theory that seeing is believing. He wished to render externally sensible through scenic patterns the language the text speaks, and sometimes does not, thus raising the staging on a par with the writing of a play, with *Sire le Mot*. With a group of distinguished dramatists that included Gantillon, Lenormand, and J.-J. Bernard, he founded the Compagnons de la Chimère, in 1922, and their workshop, La Baraque de la Chimère, the next year. It collapsed soon after, however, and Baty carried his ideals through various Parisian houses, the Odéon, where he staged O'Neill's *The Emperor Jones,* the Studio des Champs-Elysées, where he produced Gantillon's *Maya,* until he settled finally in his own home, the Théâtre-Montparnasse—former happy hunting grounds of the Théâtre Libre and the Théâtre d'Art. As with Copeau, for Baty the theatre was a temple, but one in which his stage-show and its electrical sorcery fulfiled a sort of liturgical function. His theories identified him with the writers of the school of silence, whose works he produced. But he welcomed other young dramatists also, as well as foreign masters, like Shakespeare, Goethe, Shaw, and Pirandello.

Louis Jouvet's (1891-   ) work as actor, director, and designer was always distinguished by perfect artistry and poetic feeling. At the Comédie des Champs-Elysées, where he settled after his days at the Vieux Colombier, and, after 1934, at the Athénée, he created simplified, suggestive settings in which light predominated, and which aimed to be an imaginative, but lucid, even rational interpretation of the author's written expression. Hence he favored dramatists with an intellectual rather than an emotional dramatic disposition, like Romains and Giraudoux, although he produced and interpreted with equal sympathy and understanding romantic dramatists like Sarment and Achard, and others not so romantic, like Vildrac and Passeur.

The edifice where Jouvet's Comédie was located housed a second *scène d'avant-garde,* the Studio des Champs-Elysées, which Baty managed for a time. This was an elegant, *bonbonnière* workshop, seating some two hundred people, but like its next-floor neighbor, it was the scene of many bold and picturesque creations.

Another inspired worker in the renascence of French drama was Georges Pitoëff (1886-1939) who, together with his wife Ludmilla, brought to the Parisian stage the ideals of the Russian and Scandinavian theatres. They were both native Russians whose spiritual heritage was heightened by a thorough French culture. From Switzerland, where he had organized his Compagnie Pitoëff, he was induced to come to Paris by H. R. Lenormand, and he opened his career in the French capital with this author's *Le Temps est un songe,* in 1919. He had no playhouse of his own, and peregrinated from one to another until 1934, when he settled at Les Mathurins. His staging was characterized by simplified and poetic abstractions tending to express the troubled, inner landscape of human passions. He aimed at first to evoke rather than to reproduce the outer shape of things, but he evolved gradually toward a more nuanced pattern of subtle but realistic traits that revealed the inner psychological reality of actions and characters. Sensitive to the troubled temper of the era between the two Wars, he was partial to plays that incarnated the uncertainty and mystery of human destiny, and drew his repertoire from foreign writers like Tolstoi, Chekhov, Ibsen, Shakespeare, Shaw, Pirandello, O'Neill, besides welcoming French contemporaries like Gide, Lenormand, Romains, and Passeur.

Many other professional theatrical agencies did yeoman service for the cause of the drama. One of the most distinguished was the ever-young Lugné-Poe's Théâtre de l'Œuvre, which kept pace with the new generation by producing works by Crommelynck, Sarment, Achard, and other young authors. Another bastion of dramatic art, the Vieux Colombier, reopened its doors in 1931 with the Compagnie des Quinze composed of Copeau's former Copiaux, one of whose members, Michel St.-Denis, later founded the London Theatre Studio. Two years later the Vieux Colombier passed under the management of René Rocher, whose repertoire alternated between contemporary and classic plays. The list of honor includes the name of Firmin Gémier, a worker from the first with André Antoine, and likewise with Gaston Baty, at the Comédie-Gémier, in 1920, where he produced Crommelynck, Claudel, and Lenormand. After 1922, he was director of the Odéon, and tried to swing the respectable state theatre into the current of the modern drama. Another distinguished producer was Rodolphe Darzens, who put the Théâtre des Arts at the disposal of the Société Coopérative des Auteurs Dramatiques, founded in 1919 under the presidency of François de Curel, and who produced several of their works. Finally, mention must be made of dramatic guilds, such as that of Le Canard Sauvage, founded in 1921, with Denys-Amiel, Emile Mazaud, Jean Sarment, and others; and André Lang's Théâtre des Jeunes Auteurs, founded in 1925, which produced distinguished works by member dramatists as well as by non-members.

Besides these professional groups, there were many active associations and workshops that worked on the margin of the regular theatre. Only a few can be referred to here. Outstanding among them was the Cercle des

Escholiers, organized the same day as the Théâtre Libre in 1887. It served as a link between the dramatic generations, producing original works of writers like J.-J. Bernard, André Lang, and Romain Rolland. A younger group, Fernand Bastide's La Grimace, founded in 1911, merged in 1923 with Les Pantins, and in 1929 with Paul Castan's Théâtre Esotérique, which had been producing idealistic plays. Carlos Larronde's pioneer Théâtre Idéaliste, dating from 1912, staged Lady Gregory's *The Gaol Gate* and plays by Maeterlinck and Claudel, and goaded Lugné-Poe to produce the latter's works also. The Société Aide et Protection, established in 1918, produced plays by war veterans and other young writers as well. To these may be added Xavier's de Courville's La Petite Scène, dating from 1920, which specialized in revivals of short, classical works; the group Le Cénacle des Ouvriers; and the Compagnie Art et Action, the latter a workshop with its own little theatre since 1920, which was radical in policies as in art, with a reddish tinge on its stage-curtain. Some of these agencies were short-lived, but all have been active, and many have done more than better-known playhouses for the rebirth of dramatic art in France in the years after the First World War.

Among all these workshops, guilds, and experimental theatres, the four leading organizations of Dullin, Baty, Jouvet, and Pitoëff, which had settled down as regular theatres, ended by forming a Cartel des Quatre, in 1926, with common ideals, even common posters, and reciprocal publicity. Their coöperation ended by breaking the stranglehold the commercial houses had on the French drama. They caused the citadel of tradition, the Comédie Française, to open its doors to the phalanx of rising new dramatists. In 1936, it appointed Copeau, Dullin, Baty, and Jouvet to its hierarchy of stage directors.

In conclusion, and in order to view the French drama in the proper perspective, it is necessary to bear in mind that staging has played, and still plays an honorable but secondary rôle in the French theatre. The stage designer's art made rapid strides, in France, as elsewhere, during this period. Parisian directors adopted foreign scenic innovations—Adolphe Appia's abstract and musical values, Meyerhold's stylized designs with line, color, and volume, or Edward Gordon Craig's graphic abstractions—but they adapted them with eclectic discrimination to their traditional and realistic methods. They shunned the exaggerations of a Meyerhold or a Piscator for whom the play had been a theme around which to weave electrical, musical, or ideological variations. At no time, in France, even with Baty, did staging usurp the privileged position of *Sire le Mot*. The spirit of the classic theatre, for which the stage had been a mere platform for the spoken drama, remained its ideal in fact. Barrett H. Clark spoke in 1915 of the "opposition in France to much that is new in the theatre, that obstinate refusal to learn that the stage is not still an eighteenth-century institution." Although the statement does not fit the theatre after the war, it is nevertheless true in principle. But reversing the indictment, if such it is, one might observe that for a Frenchman the theatre is a place where a play is to be heard primarily. He does not care for spectacles that distract from complete absorption in the drama. "He believes that the great conflicts of the heart are not solved by effects of light and shades... but with words," Jean Giraudoux remarked. For him "the soul can be made to open most naturally, like a safe, with a word, and he resents the German oxyhydrogen blow-pipe method." [1] Mindful of this national trait, French staging has cleaved to the line of the old adage that, to repeat, "the play is the thing," and French drama, for the same reason, has continued to exhibit a literary quality that is as distinctive in the work of the classic Racine and the romantic Musset, as in that of the modern Raynal or Giraudoux.

The pre-war drama, whether it was classic, romantic, or naturalistic, reflected a static and rationalistic conception of life. It voiced man's rebellion against providential laws, or his struggles to free himself from established social, moral, and sentimental bonds. The play dealt with the problem of what was properly right or wrong, and its solution coincided with the dénouement. In the post-war era, right and wrong, truth and reality appeared to be relative, subjective, and mutable. In turn, the drama derived from it became antididactic and antipositive in scope. It was imaginative and inquisitive. With brutal frankness it unmasked man's conscious thoughts from the start, in the first act of the play, and probed from there on his secret and subconscious motives—revealing him not only to the audience, but also to himself. The heart and soul were laid bare, and also what made the characters behave irrationally in what was a reeling and chaotic world. Men were shown to be unlike what they seemed to be to themselves and to others, thus confusing the very notion of personality and reality. As a consequence, the drama sought to determine the inherent nature of that reality; in so doing it would become lost in a maze of disordered human passions, and would often conclude in the lack of any order or law in the scheme of modern life. Some one has remarked that "the eternal sentiments spent a trying quarter of an hour" in the contemporary theatre. That was because nothing seemed eternal in the world after the War of 1914-1918. And the troubled legacy it left behind, the cruelties, disillusions, frivolities, and pessimisms of the hour, the anxieties for the future, became reflected in the drama in multicolored, disturbing, and bewildering ways. Public taste was unreliable and moody. What was booed one season was applauded the next. The fortunes of the theatre ebbed and flowed with the social and spiritual flux of the helter-skelter era.

Unlike the generation of the Théâtre Libre, which had some set dramatic standards, there was no such artistic or spiritual uniformity in the period at hand. The confusion of sentiments, ideas, and interests was reflected in the

---

[1] Giraudoux's Introduction to Claude Cézan, *Louis Jouvet et le Théâtre d'aujourd'hui* (Paris, Emile-Paul Frères, 1938), p. 33.

substance and forms of the drama itself, in the mixture of dramatic genres. Dramatists were solicited by many currents of dramatic theories which ran sometimes counter to each other, or which fused their elements to form singular patterns. They sought to discover new territories with every play, to edge closer to the frontiers of the known and unknown worlds. Many spoke a language that was not understood by all. Yet what looked like a confusing Babel appears in perspective now like a many-colored dome where a lost generation strutted and fretted in the glory and misery of its destiny. It is convenient in order to perceive this bewildering spectacle with profit to set it in order *volens nolens* with the long arm of tradition, and to view it in its characteristic aspects. But it is well to remember that such classification is purely academic and approximative, because authors under one heading could justifiably have been placed under another, and that it is made only for the sake of expediency and simplification.

The psychology of love continued to be exploited as an inexhaustible dramatic bonanza by the dramatists of the post-war period. But their approach to it was original. In the previous era, Porto-Riche and his dramatic progeny had treated love primarily as a thing of the senses. "I love you" meant more "I desire you" than "I cherish you." The *théâtre d'amour* transformed the stage into an antechamber to the boudoir. Then too, beginning with Augier and Dumas fils, the question of love had become complicated with moral and money issues. However, no matter what its other dramatic motives might be, love served always as the guiding motive of an intrigue. This type of play survived the war and was a reliable vehicle for success in the boulevard theatres. It can be studied in the productions of holdover playwrights like Kistemaeckers or Méré, already referred to.

The new psychological comedy, on the other hand, sought to dissociate love from sensuality, and to inquire into its nature and significance, as it did into the personality of man. Money problems and divorce lost their prestige as dramatic conventions because women could work and secure divorce without risking social ostracism. Hence interest shifted from the fallen to the rising woman. The characters of Porto-Riche or Bataille did not stop to consider the consequences of their passionate impulses. Those of Géraldy, J.-J. Bernard, or Giraudoux, on the other hand, are too intelligent and liberated to be led away by conventions or passions. They seek to understand before they act, and if by chance they cannot, the author does for them, delving even into their subconsciousness, when the motives for their actions lie buried beyond the reach of the intelligence—as happens with the protagonist's attempt to understand his many apparently senseless loves in Lenormand's *L'Homme et ses fantômes*. Hélène, in Géraldy's *Aimer,* reasons with her lover, and herself, and does not yield to him, but returns to her husband. "I understood how much I love you," she says. The physical charm of the little peasant girl in J.-J. Bernard's play *Martine* fades in Julian's eyes before the intellectual prestige of his fiancée Jeanne.

Giraudoux's Alcmene can resist even the glamor of a god, and argues him out of his sensuous desire, in *Amphytrion 38*.

Paul Géraldy (1885-   ), the author of the sentimentally delicate poems *Toi et Moi,* took up the problem of love where Porto-Riche left off. He wrote many gentle and agreeable satires on the domestic manners of the day, such as *Les Noces d'argent* (1917), which Grace George adapted as *The Nest* on Broadway in 1922; and *Si je voulais* (written with Robert Spitzer, 1924), the story of a wife who indulges in a little flirtation to test her continued attractiveness to men, which Grace George adapted as *She Had to Know* and in which she starred in 1925. In his outstanding dramas he applied Racine's formula for tragedy which calls for "a simple action, supported by violence of passion, beauty of sentiment, and elegance of expression." They include *Aimer* (1921), which Grace George also adapted and produced under the title *To Love,* and in which she acted in 1922; *Robert et Marianne* (1925); and *Christine* (1932). They approximate the classic pattern by their structural simplicity, their practical resort to the unities, and their economy of characters. The latter face each other across the inner complexities and secret barriers of love without any external intrigue to confuse their deep probing into the ways and the hunger of their hearts—the intermittent budding, flowering, and withering of the passions with all the risks these entail to their mutual happiness. Though deep, however, their passions are not violent. Their exclusive concern with their hearts implies self-absorption into an emotional hothouse which is a sort of escape from the other problems of life. But in their fidelity to Racine's dramatic precept, Géraldy's dramas are in the line of the French classic tradition.

In contrast, the relationship of Stève Passeur (1899-   ) is not so direct, nor so simple. He has woven many threads—classical, romantic, and naturalistic—into his complex pattern, the characteristic mesh of which, however, is psychological, and is intended to serve as a net with which to catch the heart. Conscious of the confusing reality—or irreality—of his time, he turned his theatre into its battleground. Instead of dramatizing situations involving souls stripped of all outer complications, he enmeshed them in a tissue of conflicting actions from which they escape through a violent crisis that betrays their deeply hidden secrets. The situations in which the characters are so placed may be artificial, even improbable, but the passions they feel, and which he depicts, are cruelly real. His dénouements also are psychologically and logically confusing sometimes; that is because his characters do and say what they might in real life if they only dared. He sees them under restraint of convention, family, or their own senses; their attempts to free themselves make them seem frantic and abnormal. They are tortured by their lusts, wild instincts, and hates, like the heroine of *L'Acheteuse* (1930), his best play, who wrings with her gold the affection she cannot win otherwise from the man she loves, so that she ends in suicide when he escapes from her clutches. Passeur can draw more ingratiating pictures too, as in *Je vivrai un grand amour* (1935). But ordinarily his plays are harassing dramas of passion and moral complications which would be harrowing in real life though they are intensely dramatic on the stage.

More lucid, but equally profound, was the art and psychology of Roger Martin du Gard (1881-   ), the novelist, who turned dramatist in his deeply probing pathological study of a brother's passion for his sister, in *Un Taciturne* (1931). The same characteristics apply to the novelist François Mauriac (1885-   ) and his play *Asmodée* (1937), which was produced in Basil Bartlett's translation in London in 1939, and in which he recreated the anguished atmosphere of his novels with the analysis of the turbid influence exerted by a tartuffian character over the life of his hostess, a pretty widow, and her family. Another novelist who proved to be a keen analyst of passion and character in the drama was Martial Piéchaud (1887-   ). His study of an old maid, *Mademoiselle Pascal* (1920)—who must conceal her maternity even in the eyes of her child, a grown-up son—recalls Zoë Akins' later play, *The Old Maid,* which she adapted from Edith Wharton's novel of the same name.

There is a discreet and subtle tone in the psychological comedies of Lucien Besnard, co-author with André Rivoire of *Mon ami Teddy* (1910), the story of an American who manages to win the woman he loves in Paris, which was seen as *My Friend Teddy* in New York in 1913. In his play *Le Cœur partagé* (1926) he studies the case of a young wife who suffers from a father complex. The same delicacy of analysis distinguishes the plays of Belgian-born Léon Ruth who in *L'Homicide* (1930) dramatized a situation analogous to that in Sidney Howard's *The Silver Cord.* Among other minor dramatists who followed the traditional line of the heart, such as Gaston Arthuis, author of *Connaître* (1921), and Henri Jeanson, who wrote *Toi que j'ai tant aimée* (1928), one of the youngest and most promising was Charles Peyret-Chappuis (1912-   ). He made a stunning début in 1938 with *Frénésie,* a study in black and white of the implacable passion of an old maid who holds on to her prey with a crescendo of pathos that becomes frantic.

A gentler, wider, and deeper stream of drama and poetry ran through what was labelled the *école intimiste* or school of silence, perhaps through esthetic analogy with Maurice Maeterlinck's suggestive observation that "true life ... consists of silence." According to it, "the theatre is first and foremost the art of expressing what is unspoken," that is to say, the inaudible but pregnant speech of the heart and soul, what lies inhibited, or buried, in the subconsciousness, what a pretentious rhetoric befogs, or conceals, behind a screen of words. In contrast to the romantic and naturalistic manner, the style of this school, as well as that of the best contemporary drama, is characteristically lyrical, because the lyrical chord alone seems able to render not only the tone of passion, but its undertones and overtones as well. This was the chief virtue of the styles of the Elizabethan and the French classic dramas, and it is that of the school of silence. Its characteristic name notwithstanding, its representatives were among the most eloquent interpreters of the contemporary scene. They included Denys-Amiel, J.-J. Bernard, Charles Vildrac, besides others in whose works one can readily recognize its esthetic traits, like H.-R. Lenormand and J.-V. Pellerin.

Denys Amiel (1884-   ) made a dazzling début with *La Souriante Mme Beudet* (1921), which he wrote in collaboration with André Obey. The play draws the portrait of a provincial heroine unspoiled by sentimental Bovaryism or small-town smugness, who ends by discovering under her husband's philistine skin a loving heart which wins over her own. It was seen here as *The Wife with the Smile* in 1921. Amiel sought to bind in his plays "what is transitory in an epoch with what is permanent." However, most of them deal with the problems of the eternal feminine, and the new situations which the changing world created for the modern woman. They range over a wide field of psychological and emotional conflicts, embracing the aspirations, temptations, and betrayals of love. In *Trois et une* (1932) he dramatized the wish ascribed to a well-known dancer of having children with celebrated men, a sort of collaboration of beauty with genius. Louise Valois, a singer in the play, has realized this fancy, and as a result a complication arises among the three grown-up half-brothers in love with the same woman, which, however turns into a merry modern comedy. The play was adapted by Lewis Galantière and John Houseman and produced as *Three and One* in New York in 1933. What might develop into a somber drama in Bataille, whose secretary Amiel had been for many years, ends instead with sweet reasonableness. Thus too in *La Femme en fleur* (1935) he presented anew the problem of mother and daughter enamored of the same man, but here it is the nineteen-year old, psychologically mature daughter who, realizing their mutual attraction, yields her fiancé to her mother's late-blossoming heart. Amiel's rich dramatic vein penetrated the realm of ideas also, as in *L'Age de fer* (1932), which is a study, and indictment, of our mechanistic and soul-crushing civilization.

One of the school's most representative dramatists was Jean-Jacques Bernard (1888-   ), son of the well-known playwright Tristan Bernard. His dramatic genius was revealed with his first works, especially with *Le Feu qui reprend mal* (1921), which portrays the plight of a war veteran's wife who has fallen in love with the man who lodged in her house during the conflict. Out of pity she decides to abide with her returned husband. The drama portrays the tragedy of love grown cold beneath the ashes of absence and forgetfulness. It was produced as *The Sulky Fire* in London in 1926. J.-J. Bernard's art reached its peak with *Martine* (1922) which tells the simple tale of a peasant girl's romance with a city charmer who, when his cultured fiancée appears on the scene, abandons the innocent country lass to her shattered dream. It was presented here under its original title by the American Laboratory Theatre in 1928. It is a masterly example of pure drama in the sense one speaks of pure poetry, freed from all rhetoric, all ideological and dramatic trappings. The characters in it are transparent; the emotions both genuine and diaphanous. The same qualities pervaded the rest of Bernard's delicately intimate dramas. He has mirrored the illusions and deceptions of life, its pipe-dreams, the rainbows of romance and highways of desire which the imagination builds from the horizons to one's doors, and which reality blows away, or pricks like bubbles. He has painted the tragedies of love, of deep but smothered passion, of lovers divided on earth, and also the dramas of spiritual and social imperfections, and even, as in *A la Recherche des cœurs* (1934), of industrial strife. *L'Invitation au Voyage* (1924), which was adapted under that title by Ernest Boyd and produced by the Civic Repertory Company with Eva Le Gallienne in 1928, portrays a heroine whose country-bred imagination feeds on Baudelaire's nostalgic verses as popularized by Duparc's melodies. She endows a friend of her husband en route for Argentina on business with the glamour of the land of Cockaigne, and fancies herself in love with him. His return in the last act betrays him to her as he is in reality, and brings her down to earth and back to her husband. The frustration is more overwhelming in *L'Ame en peine* (1926), which was produced in London as *The Unquiet Spirit* in a translation by J. L. Frith in 1928. Here the tragedy lies in that the two soulmates meet but fail to recognize each other in their physical, opaque, and earthly forms until, like a blind Tristan, the man comes to die at the threshold of his Isolde, not knowing that his beloved was within. The play is constructed on a spiritual scaffolding, so to speak, perceptible only through the eyes of the soul, a thing which is, of course, a weakness from the point of view of stage dramatics. With J.-J. Bernard poetry catches up with realism and psychology in the theatre. He extracted beauty and pathos from the most fugitive aspects of life—a look, a sigh, a momentary silence. The quality of his analysis, purity of style, and sensitiveness of dramatic climate give to his creations a truly classical ring.

Kindred in spirit was the theatre of Charles Vildrac (1882-   ), whose *Le Paquebot Tenacity* (1920) was one of the highlights of the Vieux Colombier's heroic days. It was produced here as *S. S. "Tenacity"* in an adaptation by Sidney Howard in 1922. The play portrays the shift in the destiny of two friends bound for America, one a dreamer who must leave alone in the end without the girl he had courted and loved, the other, a realist, who marries her instead and settles down to a humdrum existence in France. The scene is a seaport inn; its characters are humble sailors and workmen; but Vildrac excels in lending a poetic tone to the most commonplace aspects of reality. His is an art distinguished by ingenious simplicity and luminous insight into the mysterious byways of the heart and of life in matters of love, friendship, or social ideas. This was confirmed by his next play, *Michel Auclair* (1922), in which, when the good-natured Michel discovers that his sweetheart has jilted him for a worthless fellow, he forgives her and becomes the guardian angel of her married life. The play was adapted under the same title by Sidney Howard and produced by the Provincetown Players in 1925. Vildrac proved also that the psychology of love can be portrayed as deeply and nobly in the atmosphere of a factory as in a palace, for his *Madame Béliard* (1925)—a drama of spiritual kinship but physical incompatibility—is the subject of Racine's *Bérénice* transplanted to a dyeing establishment. Having echoed some of the purer accents of the modern tempo, he gave expression to its harsher tones too in *L'Air du temps* (1938). This is a satire of "our chaotic epoch," a somber portrait of a family's inner discord, villainy, and venality. But it is described *mezzo voce,* without distressing violence, with a purifying candor that acts as a purgative for the sordid passions revealed. Vildrac converted the naturalistic into a psychological and lyrical drama by virtue of the sobriety and poetry of his style, the truth and humanity of his characters, and the integrity of his artistic high-mindedness.

Henri-René Lenormand (1882-   ) is the Eugene O'Neill of the French stage. He made the leap from the psychological to the psychoanalytical stage in the theatre. He fused in his drama the Maeterlinckian probing of the mystery of the soul with the Freudian scrutiny of the mystery of the subconscious life. He did this with the analytical insight of a psychiatrist who is also a poet, for whom the perceptible disturbances in the functioning of the passions are peep holes into the workings of the spirit. He resorted to the psychoanalytic methods sparingly, however, and only in a few of his plays. But all of them "tend towards the elucidation of the mystery of the inner life, towards the deciphering of the enigma that man is to himself. My theatre," he has said, "is a dialogue, a combat between the conscious and the subconscious." That dialogue takes place between tormented characters who are in flight from, or in search of, themselves; who are uncertain of their ways, their past, present, and future. They are shown at grips with natural, social, and moral evils; oppressed by irrational fears and passions they cannot understand nor control; victims of antagonistic instincts, suppressed desires, hereditary taints, and blind fate. Unlike the symbolic and frail waifs of Maeterlinck, or the hypothetical personalities of Pirandello, or the frustrated creatures of J.-J. Bernard, Lenormand's characters are abnormal, but not weaklings. They are confronted with problems of cosmic magnitude, and they succumb fighting. They are involved in conflicts that transcend human reason, as in *Le Temps est un songe* (1919), produced in New York by the Neighborhood Playhouse as *Time Is a Dream* in 1924, in which the past, present, and future are telescoped into a tragic dénouement. They become demoralized by complex and torturing desires in the shadow of evil. *Le Simoun* (1920) depicts the subconscious and incestuous passion of a father for his young daughter, who is the image of his dead wife, under the soul-sapping strain of the African climate, a torment which ends for him only with the death of the innocent girl at the hands of his evil mistress Aïesha. *L'Homme et ses fantômes* (1924) casts a piercing new light into the somber heart of Don Juan, referred to as Man in this play. After a life of dissipation, in the course of which he seeks in women, in physical love, the self-knowledge he dreads to discover in himself, he comes to his end alone, baffled, thwarted, and punished for his self-indulgence by his own ghostly memories, the phantoms of his dead passions which, in the form of Œdipus complexes and psychic superstitions, rise from his subconscious self to haunt and plague him. He dies like a terrified child cuddled against the specter of his mourning mother, with his last breath gasping his wish "to know," the enigma of his life unsolved.

Nearly all of Lenormand's works might have as a collective title that of his play *A l'Ombre du mal* (1924). In nearly all the characters are haunted by superstitions, fear of occult forces, and of death pursuing them into their last fox-holes; or they are tortured by the slow and inexorable disintegration of their moral and spiritual fibers under the adverse blows of hostile destiny, as is best illustrated in the widely-played *Les Ratés* (1920), which the Theatre Guild produced as *The Failures* in New York in 1923, and in which an unsuccessful playwright and his actress-wife are driven to compromise their ideals and the sanctities of life in order to gain temporary respite from their ill-luck, until they succumb in murder and suicide. The plays are like cries of distress uttered and heard in the midst of a chaotic universe. "I am a playwright who has the task of reviving the tragic element on the stage," Lenormand said. "My theatre is, above all, a testimony of the distressing times we are passing through." No other French dramatist could have made such a claim with greater justice. He is one of the most subjective and lyrical among them. An atmosphere of somber poetry and dream bathes his dramas and gives them their peculiar nostalgic accent. They will remain among the most noteworthy dramatic creations of the era.

Complementing the Racinian tradition in the analysis of the passions, there developed in the contemporary drama a lesser parallel current whose doctrine was to emulate the dramatic loftiness and the heroic mood of Corneille's tragedy. Recognizing human imperfections and baser instincts, its sponsors sought nevertheless to give to the drama a high moral tone, so that in the conflict between his moral aspirations and his mortal passions man might discover himself, in the words of Boussac de Saint-Marc, one of its interpreters, "a little bigger, and a little nobler than he is naturally, and living above the level of daily reality." The dramatic dangers which such didactic attitudes invite were obviated, but only in part, thanks to the artistic integrity of the dramatists concerned, and to the chiefly moral, symbolic, and mystic character of their ideas and motifs. They brought to the stage tragic characters who struggle to free themselves from the toils of their evil passions, and noble creatures motivated by soulful aspirations.

Such is the case with André Boussac de Saint-Marc's psychological and mystical drama, *Le Loup de Gubbio* (1921), which portrays a conflict of spiritual regeneration through love and sacrifice. It was received with esteem, as was his *Moloch* (1928), which pictures the tragedy of a man who sacrifices his happiness and that of others on the altar of his creative genius. This was a theme Lenormand had already dealt with in *Les Possédés,* and also in *Une Vie secrète*. The same characteristic high-mindedness is found in the work of René Bruyez. He delves into problems of evil, regret, self-sacrifice, subconscious memory, or moral scruples, the latter well illustrated in *Le Conditionnel passé* (1932), a dramatic study of the brooding of a young woman over the lover, the husband, the child she might have had but for the war, about which she had innocently rejoiced once as a child. The thought of it leads her to commit suicide. The dramas of Philippe Fauré-Frémiet, son and grandson respectively of the composer Fauré and the sculptor Frémiet, are enveloped in a similar rarefied atmosphere. They are tinged with concepts of spiritual redemption, with moral and mystic ideals for "an ever-higher sense of moral decorum." In *Le Souffle du désordre* (1922), he made a profound analysis of a moral crisis in the life of a man who, after he has resisted in youth an engrossing passion for another man's wife, finds at fifty she has become the wife of his brother, and so he must fight desperately to extinguish the fires kindled anew by "the blast of disorder."

Among the dramatists of this class, no one's achievements have measured up as fully to its ideals as those of Paul Raynal (1890-   ), and no other has equalled his high reputation. He began his dramatic career in a dazzling manner with *Le Maître de son cœur* (1920), a drama in which a conflict of love and friendship is treated with a subtlety worthy of Marivaux, the charm of a Musset, and the nobility of Corneille. The play had been written prior to 1913, but before it could be produced the war had intervened, and Raynal joined his regiment. When he returned, he carried in his heart the sufferings and heroisms of all its known and unknown soldiers, and he gave expression to them in *Le Tombeau sous l'Arc de Triomphe* (1924), which was translated as *The Unknown Warrior* by Cecil Lewis and produced in New York in 1928. The play was bitterly assailed and fanatically defended both for its matter and its style. But though oratorical in spots, its style is essentially poetic and exalting. As to its matter, it portrays symbolically the conflict between the desire for peace and its pleasing amenities, on one side, and the tragic call of sacrifice, which is the price for such peace, on the other. It is one of the outstanding war dramas of the generation.

Epic and psychological traits alternated or combined with each other in his other plays; in *La Francerie* (1933), which is a second panel to his war plays; in *Napoléon unique* (1936), which portrays the family prelude to Napoleon's break with Josephine; and in *A souffert sous Ponce Pilate*

(1939), in which he probes the motive for Judas Iscariot's betrayal, and charitably absolves him of evil intention.

The art of Raynal stands out for its sumptuous lyric qualities. It is characterized by psychological insight and moral nobility. It recreated on the contemporary stage the tragic and heroic moods which are distinguishing traits of the French spirit. He is one of those who do most honor to its drama.

The old-fashioned comedy of manner and character aimed to portray and to amuse. Its post-war cousin pointed out also the absurdities and travesties of an era in which it found little to praise. But the characters it depicted were unstable and indefinite. Hence it sought to understand as well as to paint, and it avoided as a mortal sin the moralizing attitude of much of the social drama of pre-war days. It had lost the latter's superb faith in the efficacy of dramatic pleas in favor of lost causes. The war and its troubled legacies had buried under an avalanche of bitterness and sarcasm all pseudo-cures for social ills, and had caused all stage-sponsored panaceas to sound hollow and ridiculous. The change in tempo was well illustrated by the outcome of the competitive prize of 30,000 francs offered by Brieux in 1925 for a play "with social and moralizing" scope. Several hundred manuscripts were examined, but no "social and moralizing" play was discovered, and no prize was awarded. The new social drama did not seek to edify its middle-class patrons, but to observe the vagaries and dislocations of the creaking social mechanism. The sociological and reformist dramas of Brieux or Hervieu were superseded by the imaginative and acid social satires of Romains or Bourdet, and the ironic but optimistic comedies of Donnay or Capus by the bittersweet or sarcastic ones of Deval, Natanson, or Anouilh. In manner and substance they range from the psychological analysis of sentiment to the study of character and social milieu, from the satirical but gay comedy to the serious and ideological drama.

Jules Romains (born Louis Farigoule, 1885-), is the founder of Unanimism in literature, the doctrine which aimed to study the inner psychic kinship that binds together the social and moral aspects of life in a community, and to portray its seemingly unrelated entities not in their solitary attitudes but in their spiritual solidarity and collectivity. This he described as "the organizing idea, the message for the new world and, notably, for dramatic art." Of his plays in verse, *Cromedeyre-le-Vieil* (1920), generally regarded as the finest of all his manifold works, illustrates the point perfectly. Its hero Emmanuel incarnates the spirit, the strength of character, and the love of the community to which he belongs, its collective attachment to its earth, its past, its ideals, and its future. Outstanding among his serious dramas is *Le Dictateur* (1926), a work that portrays the transformation of a representative of the revolutionary masses into a defender of established law and order. It is a study of a future dictator's moral dilemmas rather than an analysis of the problem of dictatorship. Romains is best known for his comedies, however. His comic vein arises from his keen psychological and satirical observation of human foibles and social absurdities, on the one hand, and the mystifying, extravagant nature of his intrigues and situations, which sometimes border on the grotesque, on the other. The best and most popular of them was *Knock ou le Triomphe de la Médecine* (1923), a satire on medical quackery, but also on human credulity, on the imposture and bluff that characterized the era. It was adapted by Harley Granville-Barker and produced as *Doctor Knock* in New York in 1928.

An even more violent indictment of medical malpractices had been made in *Le Caducée,* by André Pascal (pseudonym of Henri de Rothschild), himself a physician. Denounced by the medical profession, the work had to be withdrawn from the the Vaudeville, in 1911, and it was performed first in 1921, at the Renaissance, for the benefit of the group L'Œuvre du Radium. The play portrays the case of a surgeon who, hard pressed for money, performs an unnecessary operation on a rich American, and then commits suicide.

Jules Romains' satirical genius created a particularly amusing character in *Monsieur le Trouhadec saisi par la débauche* (1923), a comedy that was produced in London under the title of *Cupid and the Don,* in 1933. Le Trouhadec is a debauched pedant, a paragon of charlatanry whose fraudulent respectability increases in direct ratio to his social and moral perversity. One of his scientific blunders, a description in his work on geography of a nonexistent city in the center of imaginary gold-fields, is the ridiculous motive, in another of Romains' satires, *Donogoo* (1930), for the formation of a gigantic financial combine that ends by founding and developing the erstwhile imagined city, which raises then a monument to "Scientific Error." His comedies are penetrating and corroding studies of social, moral and spiritual corruption and anarchy, of man's folly, despotism and villainy. Together with the rest of his creative works, they represent a vivid and disturbing pageant of the bewildering tempo of the contemporary life in France.

No less merciless and penetrating in their portrayal of social and moral disarray are the plays of Edouard Bourdet (1887-1945). After such agreeable comedies as *Le Rubicon* (1910), where a bride's marital inhibitions are finally overcome with champagne libations—a play staged on Broadway as *The Rubicon* in 1922—he revealed himself a subtle analyst of the human heart and its secret passions in a drama like *La Prisonnière* (1926), which was produced in New York as *The Captive* in 1926. In this he analyzed the tragedy of a Lesbian woman who is an unhappy prisoner of her own nature, developing a conflict not of characters, but of antagonistic sex instincts, something new in the psychological drama. He studied the male counterpart of it in *La Fleur des pois* (1932), presenting as comedy what he had dealt with previously as tragedy. In *Margot* (1935) the sentimental deviation verges on incest, in the dramatization of the assumed passion for each other, which turns to hate, of Marguerite, wife of Henri of Navarre, and her brother, Henri III. The play draws a picture of social and family disintegration in the historical framework of the Valois court. Bourdet's conflicts of the heart were thus situated often on the borderline of the forbidden, but he managed with consummate art not to overstep the line of dramatic propriety.

He showed himself equally skilful, and a worthy disciple of Beaumarchais and Becque, in his handling of the social satire. With powerful, sardonic, and yet amusing traits he laid bare the decay of morals and manners in the post-war world: the industrialization of literature and the pettiness and cynicism of authors and publishers in *Vient de paraître* (1927)—staged here as *Best Sellers* in 1933; the corruption and perversion in the pre-depression Parisian cosmopolitan world of social parasites, gigolos, and idle foreigners in *Le Sexe faible* (1929), which was acted in America as *The Sex Fable* in 1931; and the ethical immorality, the venality, and hypocrisies of the post-depression bourgeois class in *Les Temps difficiles* (1934), where a family of rich industrialists in trouble marries off an innocent girl to an ugly but rich imbecile in order to make secure its shaky financial status. The play was adapted as *Times Have Changed* by Louis Bromfield and was seen in New York in 1935.

Bourdet proved himself to be a gay moralist and satirist whose social satires were more remarkable for their picturesqueness and irony than for their strictures. He castigated but without pedantry and sermonizing. He painted with a solid but sober art intensely vivid social and dramatic situations and characters which made of him a favorite of the salons as well as of the general public.

Another mordant satirist of the contemporary scene was Marcel Pagnol (1895-   ), whose wit and humor won him a world-wide reputation on the stage before he turned to the movies. He made his first impression with *Les Marchands de gloire* (1925), a tirade against those who crassly capitalize on the heroisms of the men in the trenches; it was written in collaboration with Paul Nivoix, and was produced by the Theatre Guild as *Merchants of Glory* in New York in 1925. After an amusing satire on pedantic scholarship in *Jazz* (1926), he took money and politics for the subject of his immensely successful comedy *Topaze* (1928), which became a hit on Broadway under the same title in 1930. This was a vaudevillesque satire with the acid irony of a Becque or Mirbeau watered, however, with good humor. His popularity was confirmed with *Marius* (1929)—adapted by Sidney Howard as *Marseilles* for the New York stage in 1930—and its sequel *Fanny* (1931), both of which are lively and tender sketches of Marseillaise manners and local color.

In the few satirical plays Georges Duhamel (1884-   ) wrote for the stage he threw into relief the ingratitudes, hypocrisies, and baser motives in the lives of men. His *L'Œuvre des athlètes* (1920), which painted the absurdities and deceits of a writers' club starred by failures and pedants, was a biting satire on literary tartuffism, and was said to portray living authors under fictitious names. But Duhamel protested that he had not sought "to attack individuals, but to describe character."

In some dramatists the analysis of passion, manners, and character was adroitly interwoven with a clever intrigue, a trenchant satire, and a lightsome spirit that dipped sometimes, however, into disillusioned or bitter laughter. To their group belonged Alfred Savoir (born Ponanski, 1883-1934). He wrote before the war, in collaboration with Fernand Nozière, a keen satire on Parisian Jewish society in *Le Baptême* (1907). The authors portrayed a family of social climbers who become baptized, the son joining the Catholic party, the daughter entering a convent, and the father finding the adventure profitable for his business.

A sort of contrast to this critical view of a Jewish family was given by Edmond Fleg (1874-   ) in his play *Le Marchand de Paris* (1929), which New York saw as *Mr. Samuel* in 1930. This merchant is an idealist who determines to turn his factories over to his managers and to grant 50 per cent of the profits to his workers. The family objects, and in the resulting squabble he has a fainting fit which lays him low. Betrayed and threatened with ruin he rises, however, in a burst of supreme energy in time to confound his enemies and to save his fortune, the practical man measuring up to the utopian in him.

After the war Alfred Savoir turned to an acid and farcical portrayal of the social and moral confusion of the topsy-turvy world. He developed an expressionistic technique which enabled him to set forth the personality of his characters athwart the breakdown of conventional forms, thus betraying their inner confusion against a background of disordered external reality. So his theatre has been labelled "symbolistic farce" and "vaudeville of ideas"; it is situated between melodrama and the psychological comedy of manners. Typical of his plays are *La Huitième femme de Barbebleue* (1921), where the wife tames her man before she yields to him, a play produced on Broadway as *Bluebeard's Eighth Wife* with Ina Claire in the lead in 1921; *Banco* (1922), in which the man wins back his wife after losing her, and in which Alfred Lunt starred when it was acted in New York under the same title in 1922; and *La Couturière de Lunéville* (1923), where the heroine's sway over her lover hinges on the clothes she wears—he loves her as a movie star but not when she poses as a seamstress. The same mood prevails in *La Grande Duchesse et le garçon d'étage* (1924), with the expected dénouement taking place between the two protagonists, played in New York by Elsie Ferguson and Basil Rathbone when the comedy was produced here as *The Grand Duchess and the Waiter* in 1925. *Le Dompteur ou l'Anglais tel qu'on le mange* (1925), half farce, half tragedy, is played between half symbolic characters who represent idealism, force, and sensuality. Its protagonist, who loves to free the oppressed from the yoke of their oppressors, follows a circus from town to town in the hope of seeing the lions devour their tamer, and it is he himself who ends by undergoing that fate. The play, as *The Lion Tamer,* had a short run in New York in 1926. In *La Patissière du village* (1932), Savoir told the tragic destiny of a Madelon who inspired love and heroic deeds in soldiers, but who is left alone and abandoned in her village after the war. His plays suffer often from excessively complicated intrigues, faulty psychology, and exaggerated satire. But they are redeemed in part by a certain verve, or by the very grotesqueness of their comical situations.

The art of a greater dramatist, the Belgian-born Fernand Crommelynck (1888-   ) bordered also on the psychological, the satirical, and fanciful comedies. He himself described his tendency somewhat in connection with his play *Tripes d'or* (1925), when he said: "The characters are naturally drawn in a state of crisis, giving rise to exaggerations that approach burlesque but never deformation.... In short, I have wished to make people laugh." This is true also of his other works which recall the expressionistic manner, meaning that the feelings are expressed indirectly, by words and actions devoid of direct sequence, but whose consequence is suggestive or symbolic. After *Le Sculpteur de Masques* (1911), which, somewhat in the suggestive manner of Maeterlinck, tells the story of a man in love with his sister-in-law, by whom he is loved also, to the despair and final suicide of his wife and his own insanity, he produced his masterpiece, *Le Cocu magnifique* (1921). Its hero, Bruno, is so proud of his wife's beauty that he makes her display her bosom to his cousin Petrus, and then, his jealousy aroused by a gleam of desire which he perceives in the latter, and wishing to put her to the test, he ends by driving the poor woman into the arms of Petrus and of every man in the village, until she runs away with a cowherd. It is a Gargantuan satire of a cuckold which can be compared with Emile Mazaud's (1884-   ) magnificent *Dardamelle ou le cocu* (1922). In the latter the deceived husband puts a sign on his door which reads: "Here, Dardamelle, first-class cuckold." This startling publicity inverts the standing of the antagonists, for it renders the wife's position so ridiculous that she begs for mercy and forgiveness.

Among the other plays of Crommelynck, *Carine ou la jeune fille folle de son âme* (1929) is a bizarre admixture of romantic and symbolic characters, well described by its subtitle, for it portrays the reactions of its heroine, the innocent Corinne, to the corruptions of life. A more successful play, *Une Femme qui a le cœur trop petit* (1934), portrays a puritanic wife who shies under her husband's caresses until he breaks her in by dint of blows and kisses. It unfolds within a framework of other intrigues and passions, with pantomime, ballet, and music, and caused critics to speak of Musset, Molière, the *commedia dell' arte,* and so forth in connection with it. This mixture of moods and manners, of passions and motives has been a disconcerting feature of Crommelynck's plays, however, which has puzzled the critics and the public alike, and has caused his fame to remain anchored to his masterpiece *Le Cocu magnifique*.

René Fauchois (1882-) made his reputation at first as an author of plays in verse, like *Beethoven* (1909), which was staged under the same title in New York in 1910, and *Rivoli* (1911). The latter draws a portrait of Napoleon deceived by Josephine with a handsome hussar on the eve of the battle of Rivoli and rising from his quite human resentment to conquer himself and the world. Fauchois put aside then reluctantly a genre which neither the general public nor the producers favored, suggesting as a remedy "a chamber drama, like chamber music, for trios and quartets, to be played upon improvised boards, as in the time of Molière," and turned to comedy. His activity in this field was rewarded with successes like *Le Singe qui parle* (1924), which deals with a love intrigue and a monkey act, and which was staged in New York as *The Monkey Talks* in 1925; and especially with *Prenez garde à la peinture* (1932), which was inspired by the strange destiny of the painter Van Gogh and which satirizes the ways of art dealers who make and break reputations. Adapted by Sidney Howard as *The Late Christopher Bean*, the play proved to be a hit in New York in 1932 with Walter Connolly, and Pauline Lord in the chief rôles. Fauchois drew a sharper and more vaudevillesque picture of corruption of morals and manners in *La Dame aux gants verts* (1934). Here he recreated the far from sympathetic figure of a financier and publicist—Alfred Edwards by name —whose brutal and cynical ways left an unsavory reputation in Parisian annals. Fauchois' plays painted a colorful and amusing though limited panorama of the contemporary scene.

Another variegated fresco, with romantic, sentimental, and imaginative touches is afforded by Jacques Deval (1893-). His comedies are distinguished by clever intrigue, bright dialogue, and rippling humor. Refreshing irony alternates in them with whimsical and often melancholy traits, and the comical borders on the pathetic. In *Une faible Femme* (1920), acted in New York as *A Weak Woman* in 1926, the heroine shows weakness only momentarily; in the end she marries the right man. Likewise in *Dans sa candeur naïve* (1926) Simone hesitates but finally falls in love with the cardboard lover she had hired to keep her from going back to her divorced husband. As *Her Cardboard Lover* the play was a success in New York in 1927. In a more sentimental mood *L'Age de Juliette* (1934) tells the story of a frustrated suicide pact between two adolescent lovers, and the comedy is never very far from tragedy. His best known play, *Tovaritch* (1933), is at once vaudeville, comedy, and drama, and a symbol of the confusion of classes and manners of the times. Adapted by Robert E. Sherwood as *Tovarich*, it won much favor on the stage in New York in 1936. In addition to his comedies, Jacques Deval wrote such dramas as *Etienne* (1930), which was acted as *Another Love* in New York in 1934; and *Mademoiselle* (1932), which Grace George adapted under the same title and in which she starred with Alice Brady when it was produced on Broadway in 1932. Deval revealed himself in them a profound analyst of the heart, probing the passions, joys, and sorrows of adolescence in the former, and drawing in the latter a portrait of an old maid who is consumed by her motherly instinct, so that she adopts and passes as her own her pupil's illegitimate child. In a still more realistic vein he wrote *Prière pour les vivants* (1933) where he paints a distressing picture of contemporary social decadence. This genre was out of his real element, however.

The same sort of evolution, from a lighter toward a more serious mood, is evident in the plays of Jacques Natanson (1901-   ). He was a biographer of the incredible jazz generation, an amusing, ironic, and unsentimental observer of its revelries and cynicism in comedies like *Le Greluchon délicat* (1925), in which he portrays a gutter des Grieux who is not delicate enough not to live with his Manon off the latter's rich and complacent official lover; and *Je t'attendais* (1928), where two young lovers finally desert their older partners for each other. Neither comedy, the first produced as *The Lady of the Orchids* in 1928 and the second as *I Was Waiting for You* in 1933, proved to be successful in New York. Natanson drew later in a serious vein, in *L' Eté* (1934), a broader picture of the social and moral ills from which his generation suffered. The play tells the story of a young couple betrothed on the day peace was signed, in 1919, for whom the promising years of marriage turn into an anxious and troubled interlude between the war that was and the one brewing. It is the drama of the lost "summer" of happiness.

Among other dramatists of talent who contributed kaleidoscopic pictures of contemporary life to the stage, Henry Duvernois (1875-   ) was a holdover from the preceding generation. He was a gentle ironist and a subtle analyst of the heart whose clear and tactful art enabled him to paint with penetrating and tender insight sentiments, manners, and characters. Typical of his plays, many of which are in one act, is *La Dame de bronze et le monsieur de crystal* (1921), in which a henpecked husband pretends insanity in order to escape his wife but is joined by her in the asylum under the same pretext; *Jeanne* (1933), the unborn heroine of which will be missed by her would-be selfish parents in their old age, when it will be too late; *Rouge* (1935), a good-natured satire of pink radicals who live in luxury; and *Après l'amour* (1924), written in collaboration with Pierre Wolff, which was adapted as *Embers* on Broadway in 1926. It deals with the eternal question of switching mistresses, but the situation is complicated here by death and the presence of illegitimate children.

The comedies of a younger dramatist, André Lang (1893-   ), were outstanding for their keen study of sentiment and character and their charming fantasy. In *Le Pauvre homme* (1924) he drew a Molièresque portrait of a family tyrant who ends by becoming in turn the victim of a grasping servant. He was more fanciful in his *Fantaisie amoureuse* (1925), where he shows Cupid as a strolling accordion player playing an old romance.

The satirical vein predominated in the comedies of René Benjamin (1885-), best illustrated by his masterpiece *Il faut que chacun soit à sa place* (1924), which elaborates the idea that in this world nobody is in his right place. Less satirical but not less candid were the plays of Henri Clerc (1881-), who, in addition to fine psychological comedies, brought to the stage civic problems, as in *La Femme de César* (1937), in which he analyzed the parliamentarian and electoral manners of the day, giving a sort of challenge to the old French prejudice against the use of politics on the stage. That challenge was expressed more bitingly by Pierre Chaine (1882-), author of light comedies and Grand Guignol types of plays, in *L' Heure H* (1935), a masterly caricatural satire of politicians who are ever ready to change allegiance to suit circumstances. The "H hour" represented in the play the zero hour for the Communist revolution.

Paul Nivoix, after he collaborated with Marcel Pagnol in the social satire, *Les Marchands de gloire,* previously referred to, turned to comedies that portrayed amusingly the caprices and tyrannies of modern women, such as *Eve toute nue* (1927), in which man is shown to be the weaker of the two in the battle of the sexes. Marcel Espiau (1899-), subtle and ironic student of manners and sentiments, painted in *Le Miroir qui fait rire* (1927) the portrait of an honest but poor dentist who in order to keep his flighty wife turns into a dishonest but successful one. Another young contemporary, Paul Vialar (1898-), tried to express the feelings and frustrations of the postwar generation, and its experiences in the First World War, in plays like *Nous ne sommes pas si forts* (1924), and *Les Hommes* (1931).

Finally, the satiric bow and arrow found an expert wielder in Bernard Zimmer. His comedies were vitriolic satires of morals and manners, like his successful *Le Veau gras* (1924) or *Les Zouaves* (1925), the latter consisting of caustic caricatures of the parasites who trail and prey on soldiers everywhere. In another mood, his *Le Coup du deux décembre* (1928) presented an amusing yet tender study of adolescent love and lost illusions. Zimmer's stage targets were human hypocrisy, greed, vice, and cynicism, but he threw his darts always with great verve and excellent comic effects.

One of the last to come but not least among the younger dramatists of the era was Jean Anouilh (1910-). He directed his sarcastic and humorous satires against the intellectual anarchy, the amoralism, and the hypocritical complacencies of the epoch. From the very first he gave proof of a highly developed dramatic talent. His highly praised *Y'avait un prisonnier* (1935) described a prisoner liberated after fifteen years who, upon returning home, is so disgusted at the moral villainy of his people that he goes off alone in order to save his soul. His equally successful *Le Voyageur sans bagages* (1937) portrays a shell-shocked soldier who, when his memory returns to him after eighteen years, refuses to resume his former selfish nature and mode of life, and will seek to escape from his recovered ego, which is not his better self. It is a sort of Pirandellian drama of a single character in search of himself, and it reiterates the familiar theme of escape from the ugliness of life. Anouilh's plays expressed a vehement antagonism against the spiritual sterility and social injustices of the era; but their inherent pessimism was relieved by his poetic and idealistic instincts.

The light comedy in the tradition of Labiche and Courteline, gay or sentimental, ironic, farcical or vaudevillesque, was kept in vogue by holdover masters like Tristan Bernard, or by younger favorites of the popular stage. Among those whose names were flashed in neon lights on the boulevard theatres, several stood out. Georges Berr (1867-   ), veteran juggler of clever intrigues and humorous dialogues, besides collaborating with Paul Gavault, who has been referred to already, teamed with Marcel Guillemaud in popular comedies like *La Grimpette* (1906), produced as *Oh! Oh! Delphine* in New York in 1912; *Le Satyre* (1907), which became *The Pink Lady* on Broadway in 1911; and *Le Million* (1910), a hit also here as *The Million* in 1911. In 1916 he began with a young admirer and disciple, Louis Verneuil, a collaboration that proved profitable for the box-office and for both authors. Together they produced a score of sure-fire comedies that crackle with gaiety, action, and humor, of the type of *Ma sœur et moi* (1928), staged by the Shuberts as *Meet My Sister* in 1930; and the fanciful *Les Fontaines lumineuses* (1935), in which the charming heroine marries successively a physician, a man of the world, and a young poet, and becomes in turn a reflected image of each, proving that woman has no personality of her own.

Master craftsman in his own right, Louis Verneuil (1893-   ), actor, director, and author of a great many and diverse plays, was son-in-law and spiritual godchild of Georges Feydeau, as well as grandson-in-law of Sarah Bernhardt, whose closing days of acting were lengthened by his youthful plays. Ingenious artificer of smoothly developed comical intrigues, he exploited public taste and had his faithful public, as he had his favorite star interpreters for whom he wrote his unfailing comedy hits. Many were staged on Broadway, among them *Mlle ma mère* (1920) under the title of *Oh Mama* in 1925 and *Boom Boom* in 1929; *Pile ou Face* (1924) adapted by Zoë Akins as *First Love* in 1926; and *Le Mariage de maman* (1925) which Grace George and James Forbes adapted as *Matrimony Pfd.*, and in which the former starred in 1936. These displayed often, in addition to undeniable dramatic dexterity, a keen observation of contemporary manners, as witness also *La Banque Nemo* (1931) which caricatures amusingly the rise of a former newsboy to a position of financial czardom.

André Birabeau was another successful author of witty and whimsical Parisian comedies that verge sometimes upon vaudeville or turn into easy and gay studies of manners and sentiments. He has written conventional but breezy plays like *Déjeuner de soleil* (1925), which became the musical comedy hit *Lovely Lady* on Broadway in 1927; and delicate intrigues like *Dame nature* (1936), which relates the love of two adolescents who have become parents in all innocence, a comedy that Patricia Collinge adapted under the same name for the American stage in 1938. He broached the jovial satire with *Fiston* (1936), a rollicking farce of parliamentarian and ministerial wiles and ways, and handled playfully on the stage a ticklish child problem in *Pamplemousse* (1937), the story of an illegitimate colored boy who is kept under cover by his white father until his unsuspecting wife causes him to be brought to their home, with resulting comical and tragic complications. This play, however, did not find favor in New York when produced as *Little Dark Horse* in 1941.

Francis de Croisset (Frantz Wiener, 1877-1937), besides collaborating with Robert de Flers, wrote also sentimental and clever comedies characterized by humor and gallantry of the type of *La Passerelle* (written with Fred de Gresac, 1902), which became known on the American stage as *The Marriage of Kitty* in 1903 and as *Orange Blossoms,* with music by Victor Herbert, in 1922. Other plays of his which found their way to Broadway were the detective play *Arsène Lupin* (written with Maurice Leblanc, 1908), which was staged under the same name in 1909; *Le Cœur dispose* (1912), in which the private secretary marries in the end the boss's daughter, but marries her because he loves her rather than for her money as he had intended to, and which was adapted here as *The New Secretary* in 1913; and *L'Epervier* (1914), known as *The Hawk* in New York in 1914. His dramatic vein remained equally fertile after as before the First World War, writing comedies like *Pierre ou Jack* (1931), in which he portrayed the traditionally naïve and sentimental young man contrasting him with the modern bold and cynical type in an atmosphere of radio and movie studios.

Among other wielders of the light and ironic fantasy, Léopold Marchand wrote delicate and optimistic comedies on the transitoriness of human emotions and the nostalgia for lost illusions, like *Nous ne sommes plus des enfants* (1927), which shows lovers trying in vain to resume their lost idyl, a comedy which was adapted as *We Are No Longer Children* by Ilka Chase and William B. Murray and staged for a brief run at the Booth Theatre in New York in 1932. A young writer, Claude-André Pujet, anticipated Broadway's wave of interest in plays of adolescence. His comedies in the romantic vein of de Musset are tender and fanciful elaborations of youthful love and the joy of living such as *La Ligne de cœur* (1931) and *Les Jours heureux* (1938). The latter was adapted as *Happy Days* by Zoë Akins and produced in New York in 1941. Pujet adapted also plays of Noel Coward and Robert E. Sherwood for the Parisian stage.

Space is not available to do more than to mention briefly a few other writers among many. Régis Gignoux (1878-1931) is the author of *Le Monde renversé* (1925), a social satire of contemporary corruption, and of comedies such as *Fruit vert* (written with Jacques Théry, 1924), showing the daughter capturing the lover her mother was reserving for herself, which was produced by the Shuberts as *The Madcap* in 1928. Antoine Bibesco wrote amusing comedies in the vein of *Laquelle?* (1927), the story of an amorous adventure at a house party, which was produced on Broadway as *Ladies All* in 1930; and *Mon Héritier* (1930), where the old lord is happy at the infidelity of his wife which has assured him of an heir by proxy. Other names include Michel Duran (*Amitié*, 1932), Roger Ferdinand (*La Foire aux sentiments*, 1928), and Yvan Noé whose comedy *Christian* (1936), produced as *The Man from Cairo* in New York in 1938, tells the story of a petty clerk whose fling once a month to console himself for the mediocrity of his life leads to amusing complications. The best-known and most gifted of these dramatists was Sacha Guitry (1885-   ) whose theatre sums up the virtues and failings of the post-war comedy. He knew the art of pleasing, of dosing with unfailing skill wit and sentiment, gayety and melancholy, realism and fantasy, delicacy and vulgarity, poetry and cynicism. He borrowed from, and adopted, all dramatic genres and techniques with imagination and facility. He broached all subjects, and the list of his successes is long and impressive. His biographical works include *Deburau* (1918), the story of the pantomimist creator of Pierrot and his relations with Marie Duplessis (who was the model for the heroine in Dumas fils's *La Dame aux Camélias*), which was adapted by H. Granville-Barker and produced as *Deburau* with great success in New York in 1920; *Pasteur* (1919) seen here under the same title in 1923; and *Mozart* (1925), which was adapted by Ashley Dukes and staged at the Music Box Theatre in 1926 with music by Reynaldo Hahn. Typical of his light fantasies are *Faisons un rêve* (1916), a sort of comedy of errors and sleeping potions which was produced in New York as *Sleeping Partners* in 1918; and *L'Illusioniste* (1917), the story of a magician and his song-and-dance partner whom he finally prefers to the demimondaine Jacqueline, in which Guitry and Yvonne Printemps starred in New York in 1927 on their American visit. Among others of his comedies, *Le Grand Duc* (1921) was a hit on Broadway as *The Grand Duke* in 1921, but *Le nouveau Testament* (1934), to mention one more, had only an abbreviated run as *Where There's a Will* in 1939. This play is in a more serious vein than is usual with Guitry and shows a wife learning from the will of her supposedly dead husband about his awareness of her infidelity and other bitter truths. Gifted with dramatic virtuosity and verbal facility, juggler with fancy and reality, Guitry has displayed a Molièresque vein that he has exploited often but not always wisely. He has a sense of humor, a power of observation, a technical mastery, and an inexhaustible verve and wit which have lent to his plays dramatic interest, but not depth or universal scope.

    The rediscovery of traditional disciplines in post-war years, and their adaptation to contemporary trends was paralleled by the surge of new dramatic forms that echoed the confusion of ideas prevalent at the time. The latter phenomenon reflected the social disintegration brought about by the war. The war years 1914-1918 had not been fruitful of creative drama. Upon the older school of playwrights they had acted as a blight which withered or stunted their inspiration. The younger generation was in the trenches. When it came out, the dislocated world thwarted the possibility of its reintegration into an orderly social system. So it became in turn morally, psychologically, and artistically dislocated and disintegrated. Whereas the preceding generation, sure of its place in the sun, had been content with painting in the drama the reality of its way of life, the new generation, adrift in the midst of social and moral eddies, tried bravely to understand its chaotic universe, as is manifest in the psychological and social aspects of the drama chronicled in the preceding pages, and, when it could not, its inner and outer moorings broken, it sought escape within itself and without. The drama that mirrored this escape probes the why and wherefore of the sentimental, social, and moral idiosyncracies of life. The characters in it are in a state of uncertainty and perplexity; they are disoriented, befuddled, and incomprehensible to others, as to themselves. They are like the prototypes in Pirandello's dramas which had become the rage in Paris, especially after the production of *Six Characters in Search of an Author*, by Pitoëff, in 1923. Taine had said: "The external personality is a true hallucination." Suppressing the word "true," Pirandello made of hallucination, of the contradictions between life and our consciousness of it, the subject of his drama. He portrayed the aberrations of normalcy, truth, and personality which he had had occasion to observe in real life, and in an intimate manner, in the intermittent insanity of his own wife. Life, he held, does not become fixed in any form, for form is relative, not absolute reality; hence there is no frontier between fictional and external reality. We are different from what we believe we are, or seem to be, and when we finally realize that, it is too late. We have in us the faculty for self-deception. We live borrowed lives, or we seek to escape from the lives we lead. The drama thus becomes one of inner solitude and speculative action.

This sort of dramatic climate saturates the drama of Jean-Victor Pellerin (1885-   ). Author of a book of parodies entitled *The Indiscreet Copyist*, he ridiculed drama and reality with humor and fantasy. His characters live and converse together externally but remain isolated inwardly, their multiple personalities and destinies hovering separately over the joint drama which is dotted with superimposed scenes and interludes. This is depicted in *Intimité* (1922), in which husband and wife in the intimacy of their home pursue their different dreams, which are exteriorized by appropriate staging. It is well illustrated in his extraordinary play *Têtes de rechange* (1926) where the uncle, aghast at seeing a dozen ghosts at his dinner table where he expected to find his nephew, plumps to the ground, whereupon the twelve proclaim him dead, and the lights go out. When they are turned on again, uncle and nephew are seen calmly eating their meal in tête-à-tête. The scene of the ghosts was a fiction, an interlude in the nephew's imagined inner existence, of which the uncle was quite unaware, and in this case even the audience is taken in. Several themes are woven into the play, the contrast between the old, respectable generation and the restless new, the illusions and betrayals of love, the fallacies of bourgeois traditions, the instability of human desires and nature. The logic and cohesion of traditional drama are replaced by an atmosphere of unreality and intermittent becoming, the spirit of which was indicated by the author when he said of another of his plays, *Le plus bel homme de France* (1925): "Not a moment did I ask myself if my characters really existed in life." His dramas were intended to represent instead an escape from reality, from the destructive materialism of the era.

A similar escapist atmosphere pervades the drama of Simon Gantillon (1890-   ). He extracted a poetic and symbolic ideology from what looks like a naturalistic treatment of reality. His first play, *Le Cyclone* (1923), in which a storm at sea is the chief protagonist, attempted to suggest "beyond earthly creatures . . . a little of the mystery of the invisible forces that sway life and death, and to which the sea lends here its thousand forms and voices." *Maya* (1924), his masterpiece, gilds with the colors of poetry a modern "slice of life." It is, on the one hand, an oppressive picture of a prostitute's miserable existence which remains unchanged from beginning to end—a symbol of outcast humanity. It is a social and moral no-man's-land which becomes converted, on the other hand, into a highway of desire or into a realm of illusion for her clients. The prostitute Bella is transformed then into a Bella-Maya, into a Pirandellian heroine in whom every one sees what he wishes her to be, Venus, sweetheart, or mother—vendor of pleasures and purveyor of dreams. The play failed when it was first produced, but revived two years later it proved to be a stunning success. In New York, where it was produced as *Maya,* it was stopped after fifteen performances by order of the District Attorney in 1928.

Thus in Gantillon's drama the traditional bifurcation of life into spirit and matter ceased to have logical or dramatic meaning. Hence his play *Bifur* (1932), based on the doctrine of the transmigration of souls, is situated in a domain that is midway between the two.

This dramatic transformation of reality into its fanciful elements is in line with the grotesque and satirical deformation of it which was early attempted in Alfred Jarry's (1873-1907) pre-war play *Ubu Roi* (1896). This was a monster caricature of a Rabelaisian Macbeth as well as a burlesque of human stupidity. The revival of its spirit was manifested by the formation in 1926 of a Théâtre Alfred Jarry by a group of young dramatists whose manifesto declared:[1]

The spectator who comes to us knows that he comes to submit to a veritable operation in which not only his spirit but his senses and his flesh are at stake.

---

[1] *Nouvelle Revue Française* (November 1, 1926), pp. 643-644.

He will go henceforth to the theatre as he goes to the surgeon or the dentist. In the same state of mind, with evidently the thought that he will not die of it, but that it is a serious matter, and that he will not come out of it intact.

Less threateningly Guillaume Apollinaire's (1880-1918) play *Les Mamelles de Tirésias,* described as a "surrealist drama" by its author, had voiced a similar whimsical and eccentric mood in the midst of war in 1917. Its spirit was reincarnated in the theatre of Jean Cocteau (1892-   ) after the First World War. "Let us give back to the theatre the taste of the miracle," he said. "A train arrives faster when there is an accident than when it comes on time." So his drama and its characters are unshackled by laws of logic or nature. He drags myths and unreality onto the stage by the hair, and reincorporates them with modern thoughts, words, and clothes. He has produced ballets, pantomimes, and parodies of ancient tragedies which re-create reality by caricaturing it in legendary and extravagant ways, often with music by a Milhaud or Honegger, and staging by Picasso or Satie. The intrigue bewilders; phonographs may comment about the action on the stage, flowers speak, chairs move; the women in the choir of his tragedy *Antigone* (1922), which was produced under the same title by the American Laboratory Theatre in 1930, wear white masks, and the men red; a character enters and leaves the stage through a looking-glass, another can stay suspended in mid-air, and a woman, Eurydice, is jealous of the horse who dictates his prophetic words to Orpheus, in *Orphée* (1926). Whether he used ancient, classical tragedy as his stage-horse, as in *La Machine infernale* (1934), which The Play Room Club in New York staged as *The Infernal Machine* in 1937, or as in the plays mentioned above, or modern melodrama, as in his tumultuous and ferocious *Les Parents terribles* (1938), his theatre was an irrational, fanciful creation, a reaction to both old-fashioned romantic and sentimental bourgeois make-believe, something disconcerting, disturbing, and yet poetic. "For me the theatre is a vice, as for others gambling," he said. "One must be ill to like it so much." He was a symbol of the flight from frustrating reality in the era between the two wars.

Another view of fantastic realism on the stage was provided by Armand Salacrou (1900-   ). A former newspaper man, physician, surrealist poet, and movie scenarist, he pictured the contemporary scene as a disorderly, maggoty, yet fascinating spectacle. He proposed to keep the drama boldly abreast of radical esthetic innovations in other arts. "It is claimed nowadays that the drama lags twenty years behind literature. I do not accept this view," he declared, and he proceeded to make good his idea. His plays *Tour à terre* (1925) and *Le Pont de l'Europe* (1927) traced on the stage provoking imaginative trails of ideas, symbols, and adventures that induced Charles Dullin to sign him up for a series of dramatic works. Throughout he wove images of a world in turmoil, characters in flight, physically and emotionally, dreamers, monsters, or Quixotic failures, as in

Atlas-Hôtel (1931), and even, as in *La Terre est ronde* (1938), a caracolling and capricious portrait of the black monk Savonarola, with a love idyl and intrigue that turns, strangely enough, into a satire of political dictatorship and moral and spiritual intolerance. He had summed up his point of view early in his career in the preface to the first two of the plays mentioned above: "Since order is bankrupt," he wrote, "let us try disorder.... It will show the way to discover the great secret, perhaps."

A more traditional form of the theatre of imagination and escape was manifest in the revival of the neoromantic comedy. But unlike the beruffled and belaced ranting extroverts of the 1820's who flaunted their passions and their feathers, as even Rostand's Cyrano was to do in the nineties, their descendants of the 1920's are shy introverts who are bewildered by the confusion in their hearts and minds within, and in the world outside. The rebellious heroes of the 1830's were replaced in 1930 by resigned zeros in quest of their egos. They were victims of the war, and of the peace that followed. When the fireworks of war died down, those who could not step over their dead ideals and go on to worldly success sought escape in their dreams until they stumbled against hard reality. But more intelligent than their grandiloquent ancestors, they were the first to laugh at themselves and at life which seemed trivial, puerile, and tragic. Much as this neoromanticism is colored by Pirandellian motifs, it is nevertheless traditionally intellectual and psychological in character, sentimental with humor, nostalgic with irony, adept at pricking and causing the bubbles of joy, sorrow, and hope to burst, with an art that provokes simultaneously a smile and a tear.

The dramatic domain of Jean Sarment (1897-   ) lay within the frontiers of such reality, poetry, and dream. To him a priest had prognosticated in his boyhood: "You will be a priest or an actor." He became actor and author. His theatre is the epitome of the romantic spirit. His comedies are peopled with creatures who are victims of great expectations and mediocre realizations, of rainbow aspirations and somber disillusions. They are both jaded and sentimental, impetuous and shy, wilful and irresolute. They are inept playthings of their passions, and of life, whose ill fate they accept with comic or tragic resignation. So the hero of *Le Pêcheur d'ombres* (1921) turns insane first, is restored to sanity next, and finally driven to suicide by love. The frail Hamlet of *Le Mariage d'Hamlet* (1922) is killed by a mob when he pretends to live his life according to his real, dreamy nature, and so ends a romantic hero in a naughty world. *Les plus beaux yeux du monde* (1925) are those of the heroine who is blind and cannot see reality. All these characters, moon-struck lovers, abortive Don Juans, sentimental or cynical egotists, dreamers and phantom-heroes, fill a gallery of pitiful failures whose identifying badge could be the title of the play *Je suis trop grand pour moi* (1924): they all outreach themselves. They bespeak the illusions, disenchantments, defeats, and despairs of modern life, but Sarment's lyrical temperament casts over all his creations the glow of his fantasy and poetry.

Another actor, a member of Dullin's Atelier, and at one time Copeau's prompter at the Vieux Colombier, who turned author was Marcel Achard (1899-   ). He converted the stage into a clownish and picturesque moon-lit realm of fancy and sentiment. He dazzled and delighted his contemporaries with his ingenious, frivolous, and often moving intrigues that involve the loves, dreams, despairs, even suicides of actresses, old dukes, hoboes, and adventurers. He paraded in them sentimental and ironical characters, candid, chimerical, and humorous creatures, clowns, lovers, startled and disoriented puppets with real hearts, perpetual children all living through what looked like amusing and often tragic charades, playthings not of destiny but of a capricious whim. Unable to understand the workings of life, they escape on frail rafts of hope and with misty sails of dream to a world ruled over by their own fancies—and seem happier there than does wiser humanity on terra firma. They skirt tragedy and drama and are saved from falling in by the author's dramatic skill and poetic ingenuity. He portrays romantic souls in love with prosaic ones, and fictitious lovers turning into genuine ones, as in *Domino* (1931), which was adapted by Grace George and staged in New York under its original title in 1932. The play recalls Musset's idea in *Le Chandelier,* and Pirandello's in *Il piacere del' onestà,* and also, in the heroine's final choice of a penniless lover, the dénouement in the movie *Tom, Dick, and Harry.* All his characters might be nicknamed after the hero in the play of that name, *Jean de la Lune* (1929), whose blindly romantic loyalty wins finally and reforms also the wicked heart of the one he loves. Achard's fancy spans many dramatic realms with the greatest of ease, as in *Le Corsaire* (1938), in which he portrays the love of Kid Jackson for Evangeline, in 1776, and again in its reincarnated form by the two actors who play the parts for a movie in Hollywood. One might give as a general subtitle to his work the title of one of his plays: *Voulez-vous jouer avec moi* (1923). His is an art that achieves a transposition of reality the better to escape from it, an artistic sleight of hand that seeks to conceal its inner emotional artlessness and instability.

Poetic and imaginative qualities predominated also in the verse drama which, however, became more and more a rarity in this period. It was practiced with dignity and talent by François Porché (1877-   ) in his dramatic evocations of historical subjects. These were distinguished by loftiness of conception, fantasy, and idealism, as illustrated by his *Les Butors et la Finette* (1917), which is an excellent allegorical play portraying the struggle of Finette, France, against the ruffians, the evil hordes which plunge in war and blood her land and culture. The list of his plays includes a fine poetic portrayal of the destiny of Joan of Arc, *La Vierge au grand Cœur* (1925); and *La Race errante,* a dramatic image of the Jewish soul, symbolized in the story of three immigrants in the United States who incarnate its idealistic, realistic, and artistic traits, which was produced in New York as *Sam Abramovitch* in 1927, before its Parisian première in 1932.

The dramatic poem became a favorite also with a poet who had spent a time in the theatre in his youth, Paul Fort (1872-   ), the founder in 1890 of the Théâtre d'Art. Like Shakespeare, he undertook, after 1914, the literary task of depicting in broad dramatic frescos epic moments in the history of his country, using its national chronicles as source material for plays like *Isabeau* (1924), which dramatizes the story of the frivolous Isabeau of Bavaria and her insane king of France, Charles VI; and like his highly successful *Les Compères du Roi Louis* (1926), in all of which the dramatic power rises quite often to the level of their sustained lyrical excellence.

The decline of the drama in verse was ineffectively challenged by a younger author who carried the heritage of the romantic drama in his veins, Maurice Rostand (1891-   ). He collaborated at first with his mother, Rosamonde Gérard (1871-   ), in charming playlets like *Un bon petit Diable* (1911), which as *A Good Little Devil* was a hit on Broadway in 1913, with Mary Pickford in the rôle of the blind little heroine to whom the fairies restore her boy lover and her sight. He wrote then dramas of an exalted romanticism, such as *La Gloire* (1921), which is regarded as his best, and which dramatizes the tragedy and thirst for glory of the untalented son of a great painter—recalling the theme of *L'Aiglon*. Lacking the genius of his father, Maurice Rostand's plays have been marred often by poetic and dramatic failings, or by fanciful and capricious treatment of historical and biographical material, as in *Napoléon IV* (1928), where he ascribes the death of the Imperial Prince in Africa to British-inspired foul play. When he holds his imagination in check, however, as every writer must, he writes works with more dramatic merit, as witness *Le Procès d'Oscar Wilde* (1935), which portrays its protagonist after *The Picture of Dorian Gray*.

Plays in verse were written also by such diverse dramatists as René Fauchois, Sacha Guitry, and Jules Romains who have been referred to previously in this study.

Like the drama in verse, the old-fashioned idealistic and symbolistic plays ceased to be exploited as distinct genres, but both their poetic and symbolic virtues were transfused and diffused into the general current of the drama. This had been the case already in the work of an older author who was, however, forever young, André Gide (1869-   ). His play *Le Roi Candaule* was regarded as a mystification when produced in 1901, because its hero risks and loses both his happiness and life, which he had loved too sincerely. All his dramatic creations are symbolical and ideological approaches to the problem of the ego and quest of self. However, neither his *Saul* (1922), which delves into the moral and sensuous complexity of the Biblical king, nor his philosophical *Œdipe* (1932), with its brilliant variations on the subjects of God, conscience, and fatality, attain as theatre to their eminence on the intellectual level.

Poetic and imaginative qualities distinguish also the drama of disillusion and escape of Jean-Richard Bloch (1884-   ), *Le dernier Empereur* (1926), in which he dramatizes the spiritual and imaginative nature of the individual in conflict with the moral hardness of the multitude. The same thing applies to the symbolic creations of André Obey (1892-   ), co-author with Denys Amiel of the delightful *La Souriante Madame Beudet,* already referred to. He dramatized the legend of Lucrece in *Le Viol de Lucrèce* (1931), taken from Shakespeare's *The Rape of Lucrece;* and the Biblical story of Noah and the Flood in *Noé* (1931). Both works were produced in New York, the former as *Lucrece,* in an adaptation by Thornton Wilder with music by Deems Taylor and with Katharine Cornell in the title rôle in 1932, and the latter as *Noah,* first in 1935 produced by Jerome Mayer in Arthur Wilmurt's adaptation with music by Louis Horst, and again in 1936 as adapted by Carlton Moss with music by Jean Stor and staged by the WPA Negro Theatre Unit. Besides his classical and Biblical sources, Obey has found in modern subjects too the inspiration for lyrical and allegorical plays like *La Bataille de la Marne* (1931), which recalls something of Æschylus' *The Persians,* and which depicts the anguish and hopes of the first weeks of war and invasion during the First World War. It was treated as an oratorio without music, though the march of German troops was suggested by the playing of a Bach Choral at its production at the Vieux Colombier.

Finally, reference must be made to the fantasy and verve that characterize the work of André-Paul Antoine, the son of the founder of the Théâtre Libre. His weird satire *L'Ennemie* (1929) is directed at womankind by the ghosts of the rejected fiancé, husband, and lover who evoke in their cemetery their common fate at the hands of the same woman. It was staged with some success in New York in 1930 as *Love, Honor and Betray,* with a cast that included Alice Brady and Clark Gable. Equally fantastic and mordant is *La Prochaine?* (1932), which involves its Pirandellian characters in a rebellion against the established social and moral order of things and against wars and the tyranny of older over younger generations.

The term *pure drama* is applied advisedly to the work of Jean Giraudoux (1882-1944), for of all twentieth-century French dramatists he comes closest to incarnating the chief features of the renascent French theatre. Master of the impressionistic novel, he came late in life to the stage, and became at once one of its most arresting figures. Combining the lyrical trait we found to be a prime characteristic of the post-war drama with intellectual and philosophical attributes, he accentuated its orientation away from the harshly realistic toward the creatively imaginative. In his case, the theatre ceased to be restrictively psychological, social. moral, of manner, or character, and became a synthetic creation, the distilled essence of all these genres, a fusion of reality, idealism, and poetry in a kind of modern *commedia dell' arte sui generis*. He merged together in his art the elements of realism with those of fancy, legend, and history to give a vivid and absorbing insight into life in a dramatic form that is subtle and stimulating to the spirit. What is whimsical, inventive, and romantic in it verges on what is rational, erudite, and classical. His brilliant array of comedies must be set outside the realm of dramatic *isms*. Their only distant relationship is to those *Drames philosophiques* of Ernest Renan (1823-1892), which the stage of Dumas fils's time was not intelligent enough to produce. But those were near closet-dramas, and Giraudoux's are the epitome of theatrical art. *Siegfried* (1928) combines in one study the themes of race and personality, with, inverting the legendary rôles, a French Eurydice leading her Germanized Orpheus back to his Gallic ego and home. This play was adapted by Philip Carr and produced under its original title by Eva Le Gallienne who played also the rôle of Geneviève in New York in 1930. *Amphitryon 38* (1929), which, with Alfred Lunt and Lynn Fontanne in the rôles of Jupiter and Alcmene, respectively, proved to be a hit on Broadway in 1937 in S. N. Behrman's adaptation under the same title, is likewise a transcendental drama, and also a hymn to conjugal fidelity, with dazzling variations on love and friendship. *La Guerre de Troie n'aura pas lieu* (1935) was a startling prophesy of the then impending catastrophic Second World War, and a despairing diatribe against the folly of men and the indifference of the gods. The tragic *Electre* (1937), the sparkling satire on the critical fraternity, *L'Impromptu de Paris* (1937), and the luminous fairy-tale *Ondine* (1939), are other many-colored facets of his dramatic genius. His art is a perpetual firework of intellectual and verbal virtuosity that ascends to the stratosphere of human thought and sensibility. It exacts an intense concentration from spectator and reader who cannot always, however, escape its airpockets of preciosity. It is an art that converts universal subjects into timely topics, and problems of the day into eternal ones. Like Shaw, he expounds serious ideas lightly, profound problems rationally, and tragic ones humanely; but he surpasses the Irish sage by the elegance of his style and the airiness of his fantasy. He is French by the perfection of his form, and universal by the catholicity of his substance. He represents the culmination of half a century of evolution of the French drama.

The contemporary theatre in France was confronted with a more unstable order of society than was the case with other dramatic eras. The writers of the classic period, in the seventeenth century, believing in the sameness of human nature in all times and climes, painted it in universal traits. They regarded society and life as being providentially ordered and synchronized to an abstract and eternal ideal of values. Whoever, by the force of his passions, contravened what had been preordained, did so with tragic consequences. That was the chief motif of their drama. Its dramatis personae were exceptional creatures in conflict with destiny; they were noblemen, "people of quality," seen and painted in heroic attitudes. The romanticists, rebelling against the concept of a universal and constraining ideal of man, portrayed frantic individuals shadow-boxing with their passions, and tilting against windmill evils in Quixotic postures. The realistic theatre next, neither heroic nor Quixotic, but rather Sancho Panzaic, pot-bellied, and worldly-wise, resorted to making snapshots of stratified social spheres, of conventional emotional attitudes, and of stagey characters sitting often as Eugene O'Neill has observed, in ridiculous poses. Not until contemporary days was the French theatre to mirror men in changing social conditions, or groping alone in the mysterious and subconscious avenues of their egos. Their problems and struggles were not less but more thorny and complex than had been those of their ancestors. But precisely on account of that they were more humble and discreet in their disarray, and the theatre painted them as they were, neither high-mettled nor priggish, but, like humanity at large, alone and adrift in a lawless or confused universe.

The generation between the two world wars was in a state of flux, and so was its profile, and the shadow it cast upon the stage. Reality had become a deception, and realism deceiving. Giraudoux's Siegfried turned out to be Forestier; Gantillon's Bella became a maya; time proved to be a dream in Lenormand's drama, and man the stuff of his phantoms, or, as in Pellerin's play, the creature of his "spare heads" and whims. As the witty Alfred Capus observed once of the men and women of his time, they could not "sit still long enough to be snapped." The remark applies even more aptly to the succeeding generation. Instead of portraying immutable traits, the dramatists pried into, and tried to suggest, the obscure depths in the lives of their contemporaries. This explains the multiplicity of dramatic innovations and movements all trying to keep pace with, and to get closer to, the mutable and elusive core of life. From realistic and photographic, the theatre became impressionistic and interpretative. It extended its frontiers from the domain of what is rational and logical to those of imagination and poetry.

Consequently, the contemporary French drama was converted from a realistic period-piece into a sort of modern lay mystery-play. It ceased to be interested solely in social, moral, and ideological theses, or in conflicts of passion and interests, and turned the spotlight on the clash between reality and dream, between the sensible world and the subconscious and mysterious ones within and at the rim of it. It did not seek so much to express escape from reality as to see it for what it is truly, the realm of the unknown. It sought to rend the opaque curtain in man's social, moral, and sentimental external appearances in order to get at the mysteries of his heart and mind. The rainbow plays of Giraudoux, the lyrical dramas of J.-J. Bernard, the romantic comedies of Sarment or Achard, the fantastic theatre of Gantillon or Salacrou proposed to make of the stage what it was with Aristophanes,

Shakespeare, or Musset, the dressed-up image of man's ever-frustrated dreams. They aimed in fact to lend to the stage the glamour which pertains to the domain of music and poetry.

Hence this drama addressed itself less to the senses than to the intelligence, and less to the intelligence than to the imagination. It does not possess generally the spiritual vigor and faith characteristic of great dramatic eras—although both attributes shine forth in individual authors like Claudel and Raynal. But the heroic mood which it and the epoch it mirrored were shy of, was compensated for by its poetic apprehension of the tragic sense of life, which lent to it a sort of reflected nobility.

In the richness and magnitude of its manifold manifestations, despite inevitable failings and shortcomings, this dramatic renascence fulfilled Jacques Copeau's call, in 1913, for the creation of a new theatre "upon an absolutely intact foundation." The blame the French drama had incurred abroad heretofore of being provincial, custom-ridden, and unimaginative has proven to be no longer applicable. From what precedes, it must be patent that what distinguished it in the period under discussion was—along with much it had retained from its classical and traditional virtues, such as form, order, clarity—precisely its qualities of imagination, fantasy, poetry, and even mysticism. From insular, conventional, and static it became cosmopolitan, adventuresome, and dynamic. As the distinguished dramatic author and critic John Leslie Palmer noted as early as 1927:[1]

> There has been in Paris an extraordinary revival.... From being the most inaccessible to new methods and ideas, it has become as cosmopolitan as Berlin, as enterprising as Moscow, as genially receptive as London, at its best, as acquisitive as New York.... Paris, in fact, has recovered her place as the dramatic capital of Europe.

The Second World War brought to an untimely and tragic close this brilliant era in the French theatre. There are no names in it comparable to Corneille, Molière, or Racine. On the other hand, the general level of its excellence, reflecting somewhat the upsurge of the democratic way of life, is relatively high, and places it historically only second to its forebear, the seventeenth-century French classical era. Unfortunately, what is best in it has not always been made available on the foreign stage, nor did it, in fact, originate on the French commercial stage itself. Much in it reflects the moral and social disequilibrium of an era that deserved better from fate, but a great deal of it is made also of the stuff that survives political and military disasters. At the top, the image it gives is of a France morally and spiritually alert, its social and artistic consciousness geared to a civilized conception of the good life. With the return of peace, the tree that bore such good harvest will bloom again, and bear new flowers for Thespis.

[1] John Leslie Palmer, *Studies in the Contemporary Theatre* (Boston, Little, Brown & Co., 1927), pp. 20, 27.

BELGIAN DRAMA

Though spiritually Belgium constitutes one indivisible nation, it is bilingual in its social and cultural life. One section of its people speaks Flemish, the other French. Reflecting this linguistic condition, its drama, as all its literature, has forked like a tree into two branches, one Flemish, the other French. The former is being considered elsewhere in this volume. The latter alone concerns us here.

The renascence of Belgian-French letters in modern days coincided with the rise of naturalistic and symbolistic trends in literature in the closing years of the nineteenth century. It was initiated by a group of young poets, students at the University of Louvain, who, in 1881, under the leadership of one of their comrades, Max Waller (pseudonym of M. Varlomont, 1860-1889), founded a literary review which became the rallying point of their movement. They called it *La Jeune Belgique,* and adopted as their motto the words: *Soyons-nous*—"Let us be ourselves." Their militant phalanx numbered within its ranks Emile Verhaeren, Ivan Gilkin, Charles Van Lerberghe, Maurice Maeterlinck, Henri Maubel, and Georges Eekhoud. They represented several shades of literary ideas, including naturalistic and symbolistic, although they were predominantly Parnassian in tendency; but their motivating common ideal was to create a new Belgian national literature. In this they had the support and blessings of two older champions of the same cause, Camille Lemonnier (1845-1913) and Edmond Picard (1836-1924). In time the conflicting elements in the group led to the formation of rival literary chapels. Edmond Picard founded the magazine *L'Art moderne.* Georges Eekhoud established *Le Coq rouge.* Withal, despite their rivalries, all remained faithful to their avowed design of creating a new Belgian national literature in the French language.

Thanks to them and the impulse they gave rise to, Belgium ceased to be a land known only for its painters and became a country of poets as well. But it must be recognized that the *Jeune-Belgique* writers scorned the theatre in the beginning. They were poets primarily, and although many turned to the drama afterwards, witness Maeterlinck, their drama remained poetic in essence. Brussels became a literary rather than a theatrical capital. Poetry flourished there, and the novel, too, but its drama often strayed away, lured to the spotlight of the French-speaking world, Paris. As a consequence, the Belgian stage has seemed to be at times in a sort of comparative dimout. In part this is due to the circumstance that Belgium is a small country with a bilingual standard that divides its dramatic potentialities, but in a larger measure to the fact that most of its gifted dramatists inevitably take what is for them the road to success across the French frontier. They become acclimated to the Parisian boulevard or art theatres, which in turn adopt them as their own, and the prodigal sons never, or seldom, return home.

They add their fresh, native springs to the stream of French drama, and are in turn absorbed by it. Such has been the case with writers like Henri Kistemaeckers, Francis de Croisset, Maurice Maeterlinck, and Fernand Crommelynck. With few exceptions, their works were brought to light on the Paris stage, and have become an integral part of the French drama, with which their names are linked in the French section of this history.

Despite this handicap, the Brussels stage kept pace with those of other European capitals. This is illustrated by the number of theatrical laboratories that sprang up there, besides the more celebrated playhouses like the Théâtre de la Monnaie and the Théâtre du Parc which have long histories. They have included La Maison d'Art, 1893-1897, founded by Mouru de Lacotte; Le Groupe Libre, directed by Raymond Rouleau; Le Théâtre Rataillon, organized by Albert Lepage, in 1931; Le Théâtre du Peuple of M. Piette; Le Plateau 33 of Marcel de Beer, founded in 1933; and the Marcel Josz Company. The outstanding one among them was Le Théâtre du Marais, founded in 1921 by Jules Delacre and René Moulaert in the spirit of Copeau's Vieux Colombier. Up to 1926 it gave some fifty productions, including plays by Molière, Ibsen, Maeterlinck, Romains, Achard, and others. In 1930 it was reopened by Aimé Declercq and Raymond Rouleau, who gave a series of modern plays each season, among them works by Shaw, Molnar, and Passeur. The troupe produced Ferdinand Brückner's (pseudonym of Theodor Tagger, 1891-   ) *Krankheit der jugend* (1928) in French as *Le Mal de jeunesse,* in Paris in 1931. The play gives a vivid portrait of the social and moral disarray of German youth after the First World War. The following year it staged there Declercq's *L'Envers vaut l'endroit,* in which is depicted the feverish life backstage in a theatre just before the curtain goes up. It is the third of a trilogy of plays Declercq wrote based on *La Mécanique du théâtre.*

Among the dramatists of the generation of 1880, the most striking figure after Maeterlinck is Emile Verhaeren (1855-1916). He is the Walt Whitman of Belgium, poet of its countryside, its cities, its people, and its soul. He has expressed its complex mysterious forces, its social aspirations, and its spiritual destiny with magnificent lyricism and dramatic power. Both lyricism and power carry over into his dramatic works, the first of which was *Les Aubes* (1898), his most successful play on the stage. It is an epic drama portraying the conflict between city and country, and symbolizing the ultimate triumph of universal brotherhood and social peace. It was followed by *Le Cloître* (1900), which was seen as *The Cloister* in New York in two Sunday performances by the Theatre Guild in 1921. It is a drama in verse and prose that depicts the struggle in a cloister between its patrician monks who have ruled it for centuries, and those of plebeian origin, hard-working, intelligent, and ambitious, who wish to rule in turn. The clash between them breaks out as Dom Balthazar, the favorite to succeed the prior, is induced through remorse to confess a former parricide, and it develops while the monastic order itself is in process of disintegration, a symbol of human society outside its walls. Verhaeren's *Philippe II* (1904) dramatized the domination of a whole epoch and country by a soul-sick king and the Church; his *Hélène de Sparte* (1912), played by Ida Rubinstein with settings by Bakst and music by Déodat de Séverac, paints the tragedy caused by Helen's beauty and the incestuous love inspired in her brother Castor, who slays Menelaus and is slain in turn by Electra.

Next to Maeterlinck and Verhaeren, the outstanding figure in the Belgian literary revival was Georges Rodenbach (1855-1898). He was a poet of the dreamy and languid harmonies of mist-laden Flanders landscapes, and he extracted a poetic drama *Le Mirage* (1901), from his novel *Bruges-la-morte*. He conveys something of the symbolistic mood in *Le Voile* (1894), a one-act play in verse which portrays the longing of Jean to see the hair of a novice who has come to care for his ailing aunt. But when he does he is disillusioned, and his dream vanishes. The play is not important, but Rodenbach owes his reputation to his poetry and his novels rather than to his plays. Charles Van Lerberghe (1861-1907), classmate of Maeterlinck at Ghent, has the merit of having anticipated the latter in the creation of the symbolistic drama of fear, anguish, and mystery, with *Les Flaireurs*, produced in 1892 but published in 1889. In *Pan* (1906), he wrote an ironic satire in the mood of Brueghel or Jordaens, which expresses a deep pantheistic love of nature and life. Other *Jeune-Belgique* authors who wrote for the stage included Georges Eekhoud (1854-1927), translator of plays by John Webster and Marlowe, who drew an interesting historical portrait of a medieval Flemish adventurer in *L'Imposteur magnanime* (1902); and Ivan Gilkin (1858-1924). The latter was a fervent disciple of Baudelaire who, despite his Parnassian sympathies, wrote his tragedy *Prométhée* in free verse, and his historical dramas in prose. In *Les Etudiants russes* (1910) he dramatized a story of love and political struggle featured by the rebellion and cruel repression of students clamoring for liberty and reforms in the capital of the Czars. A similar ideological concept motivates his *Savonarole* (1911). Here he portrayed the moral and spiritual conflict which assails the Dominican prior torn as he is between his religious scruples and political motives, a conflict which ends in his excommunication and burning at the stake.

To the contributors to the poetic theatre must be added the names of Valère Gille (1867-   ), author of *Ce n'était qu'un rêve* (1903), a fairy-comedy in verse; Félix Bodson (1869-   ), who specialized in plays of dream and fancy like his exquisite *La Cour du roi Pétaud* (1909); and Auguste Vierset (1864-   ), who wrote comedies like *Le Coffret* (1912) and *La Gageure* (1920). The same is true of Franz Ansel (pseudonym of Franz Folie, 1874-1937), with his *L'Ecole de Werther* (1925), and of Henri Liebrecht (1884-   ), with *L'Ecole des amants* (1909), as well as of Claude Spaak, who shows his fanciful mood in *A l'Auberge des apparences*.

Two other names, finally, stand out in this dramatic category: Paul Spaak and Albert du Bois. Paul Spaak (1870-1936) reveals his love of his native soil in his poetry and drama. In *Kaatje* (1908), his most successful play, and one of the most successful on the Belgian stage, he portrays a painter who returns after a sojourn in Italy accompanied by his Italian mistress. Nostalgia for her sun-drenched land drives her back home, but his despair is quickly assuaged by a young Dutch girl, Kaatje, who loved him secretly, and who opens his eyes to the beauty of his homeland. The same attachment to the native soil inspires *Baldus et Josina* (1912), but here the story ends more tragically, as it does in *A Damme en Flandre* (1912). The latter play recalls Rodenbach's novel *Bruges-la-morte*. It paints the drama of a prosperous port which is silting up and is being abandoned by all save one of its merchants who remains behind in the place he loved, ruined like it and deserted, besides, by his young wife who cannot resist the call of youth when her lover comes back for her.

The inspiration of Albert du Bois (1875-   ) is more far-flung. He has written a series of dramas in which he aims to evoke the life of humanity at different epochs in its history through portraits of its great figures. Each develops a symbolic concept; so his *Homère* represents the heroic age of the Greek cult of beauty; *Lord Byron* bespeaks romantic egoism, incarnated in the person of the poet who is portrayed vividly but in a rather conventional pattern. He shows originality of conception in such a play as *La dernière Dulcinée,* where we see a sane Don Quixote who is caused to be put in a madhouse by his adulterous wife and who, when he finds out the sad truth, refuses the liberty proffered him, and becomes really insane. The same is true of *Pour l'amour de la Sulamite,* in which he dramatizes the love of Adonijah, the son of King David, for his father's beautiful attendant. Parenthetically, it must be pointed out that notwithstanding the title of the play, the heroine referred to here is not that in the *Song of Songs,* but Abishaj the Shunamite, who ministered to David in his old age. Du Bois has been a prolific writer. His *Cycle des Douze Génies* includes some thirty-six plays, twenty-four of them in verse. Many of them have been produced, and though some may fall short in poetic and dramatic excellence, others have fared well in dramatic production, such as *L'Hérodienne* (1919), and *Notre Déesse* (1935). The latter, known also as *Dea Gallia,* pictures the France of Louis XIII and Richelieu in its struggles against the Papacy, and was placed by the Odéon Theatre in Paris in its regular repertoire.

A fellow-traveler of the *Jeune-Belgique* movement, and a leader in the Belgian literary revival, was Edmond Picard. His best work in the theatre was his *Ambidextre journaliste* (1904). He fought against the influx of frivolous Parisian plays on the Brussels stage, and aimed to create a national drama of ideas. The same ambition was shown by Gustave Vanzype (1869-   ), who has earned the enviable reputation of being the Belgian Curel. Like Curel, he probed the complexities of moral and social problems, the conflicts and debates of the modern spirit, and like Brieux or Hervieu also, he solved them as a moralist, vindicating the ideas of duty and virtue. He had a sound dramatic technique which enabled him to raise his characters drawn from daily life to the level of formal types. The very titles of his plays suggest dramatic theses and ideological developments, witness *La Souveraine* (1899), translated as *Mother Nature;* *L' Aumône* (*Charity*, 1901); and *Les Etapes* (1907), translated as *Progress*. The last deals with a problem of conflicting scientific theories between a father and his son-in-law, leading to their estrangement. Curiously enough, the wife, adopting her father's point of view, leaves the husband she loves despite the fact that she is with child, thus following the dictates of her head rather than those of her heart, a thing most unlikely to happen in a woman in her condition. The situation is more plausible in *Les Liens* (1912), where the case is that of a man who fears hereditary insanity for his son. To deliver him from his anguish, his wife tells him he is not the father of the child. Vanzype looked upon the theatre as a moralizing rather than as an entertaining agency. That may explain why, despite its high-mindedness, his work has not become widely known outside his own country.

Dramas of the inner life preoccupied Henri Maubel (pseudonym of Maurice Belval, 1862-1919), whose best play, *Les Racines* (1902), dramatizes the story of a youth whose wanderlust is checked by the roots he has in his native soil. Ideas also and the influence of Ibsen predominate in the work of Marguerite Duterme (1882-   ). Her plays are the expression of an unquiet spirit in rebellion against conformity and the ugliness of life. Thus in *Vae Victis* (1905) she tells the story of an unhappy husband who offers his daughter to the lover of his wife and who, abetted by the latter, ends by committing suicide. In *La Maison des chimères* (1913) tragedy in an adopted son's love for his benefactor's young wife is averted only when the husband forsakes his lofty ideals and fights for his own happiness, and the play ends with the words: "Be bad, and you will suffer less." An ideological point of view characterizes also the work of Max Deauville (pseudonym of M. Dewez, 1881-   ). He is the sensitive author of the tragicomedy *Rien qu'un homme* (1925), in which he presents a crime from the angle of an indifferent outsider, as a mere scrap of news, showing both its ridiculous and pathetic sides; and of *Tamerlan* (1935), a play that studies the inner loneliness of the conqueror of the steppes in the midst of his vast power.

Reference must be made to Maurice Tumerelle (pseudonym of Maurice Sutton, 1885-   ) whose wit and humor are mixed with delicacy and a tinge of pessimism in a play like *Compagne de mes jours* (1924), which is a comedy of manners, and in *L'Empire de Darius* (1926), which deals only with the dreams of a sailor, its title notwithstanding. Another interesting dramatist is Armand Thibaut, whose play, *La Rivale de l'homme* (1924), characterized by analytical power and vivid dialogue, portrays an original subject, a business woman who is ready to sacrifice the bank she directs in order to save from ruin the man she has fallen in love with for the first time in a life which was otherwise absorbed by her business career.

In addition to the Belgian-born dramatists who have become affiliated with the story of the French drama, and were referred to in connection with it—Maeterlinck, Kistemaeckers, Croisset, and Crommelynck—others have won a reputation on the Paris stage, notably Paul Demasy and Henri Soumagne. The dramas of Paul Demasy (1884-   ) have branched out into the religious, the historical, and the modern social fields. He is the author of the austere passion play, *Jésus de Nazareth* (*Odéon*, 1924); of the historical drama *Dalilah* (Odéon, 1926), in which the traditional antagonism between man and woman is broadened into a symbolic conflict between the spirit and the flesh; and of more modern conflicts, such as that depicted in *La Cavalière Elsa* (Studio des Champs-Elysées, 1925), in which the "monster" Bolshevist revolution is pictured ready to devour peace-trusting France. Demasy has a high concept of his art, dramatic skill, and moral elevation.

The dramatic art of Henri Soumagne (1891-   ) constitutes a mixture of fantasy, extravagance, and philosophical inference. His play *Les Danseurs de gigue* (Œuvre, 1926) shows two music-hall dancers who are modeled after and copy each other to the point where each marries the woman the other should have married; they then end by killing each other. Having portrayed earlier in *L'autre Messie* (1923) a group of Polish Jews in a ghetto bar who discuss the nature of God, Soumagne presented then in *Madame Marie* (Œuvre, 1928) a drama of the Passion in which after stating, from a human point of view, that Jesus was not divine, he ends by proving that he became so in the end.

This spirit of dramatic fantasy is met with in other post-war Belgian writers. Such is the case with Charles Conrardy (1893-   ), who treats as farce subjects of tragedy, as in, for instance, his *Hamlet ou le triomphe de la vertu* (1926), which he labels a *tragédie-farce* for marionettes. One of the most original dramatists in this vein is Michel de Ghelderode (1898-   ). He mingles farce and fantasy with mystery in his theatre. He presents distorted and disordered close-ups of reality that abound in anachronisms of time, place, action, and ideas, but which are expressed, however, with dramatic and lyrical power. His tragic farces, burlesque mysteries, and fantastic pantomimes, typical of which are *La Farce de la Mort qui faillit trépasser* (1925), *Christophe Colomb, Féerie dramatique* (1928), and *Trois acteurs et un drame* (1929), portray athwart their whimsicality an implied faith in the goodness of simple men. They have been translated widely into other languages.

Finally, Odilon-Jean Périer deserves credit for his subtle and original play, *Les Indifférents ou on s'amuse come on peut* (1925), and Herman Closson (1900-   ) for plays like *Godefroi de Bouillon* (1935) and *William ou la Comédie de l'aventure* (1938). In the latter, Closson ventures to study the creative process in Shakespeare, showing the author in search of characters, and seeking in love and adventure what the imagination cannot fancy.

In the genre of the comedy of manners, Horace Van Offel (1876-) displays the influence of Ibsen and, especially, the influence of his own Flemish nature which he conveys with a fantasy that approximates the spirit of Breughel. In *La Victoire* (1909) he pictured the victory of a man over the declining fortunes of his family, and his victory over his own despair when he discovers his wife's infidelity with his own brother, terminating in the suicide of the guilty ones. The play recalls Fabre's *Les Vainqueurs,* where the protagonist's triumph is accompanied by the betrayal of his wife and the death of his son, killed in a duel with his enemy. Another of his plays *Une Nuit de Shakespeare* (1913), weds the twin themes of love and art in a dramatization of a story about Shakespeare supposedly victim of popular indifference and of the coldness of an unapproachable lady. The hero in the play manages to break into her home in the company of a thief, whom he then turns against and drives out, and pleads his own cause so well with the lady that, though the police come in time to arrest him, he wins finally the heart he had come to conquer.

Better known outside of Belgium was the dramatic team of Jean-François Fonson (1870-1924), and Fernand Wicheler (1874-1935), thanks especially to their highly successful comedy *Le Mariage de Mlle Beulemans* (1910), which was seen as *Suzanne* in New York in 1910. The play tells the story of Suzanne, daughter of a Brussels brewer who aspires to the presidency of the brewers' association. To please her father Suzanne must marry his rival's son, but instead she falls in love with a French youth with pleasant manners and speech, and manages to marry him in the end. The play is a satire on the local customs of the Brussels bourgeoisie, its social foibles and speech mannerisms. Their other plays were not quite so successful, including *Le Feu de la Saint-Jean* (1911), in which a Belgian youth is saved from the wiles of a French actress by his father who falls victim to them himself; and *La Demoiselle de magasin* (1913), which was adapted as *Along Came Ruth* by Holman Day and acted in New York in 1914. Fonson alone wrote *La Kommandantür* (1915), the story of a Belgian girl who slays a German police agent to avenge the murder of her fiancé, which was first produced in London in 1915.

Among other writers who deserve to be mentioned, Henri Davignon (1879-) dealt also with Belgian racial and linguistic problems, but in a serious vein, in *Querelle* (1913). In the genre of the light comedy, Ernest Hallo (pseudonym of Eugène Stevens, 1865-) wrote fanciful pieces like *Entre trois feux* (1898), in the mood of Meilhac and Halévy; and another author, Roger Avermaete (1893-), wrote successful farces such as *Maison recommandée* (1930).

Space is lacking to do more than refer by name to a few other writers who have contributed to the theatre, such as Gustave Abel, Sylvain Bonmariage, Charles Desbonnets, Gaston Heux, Robert Merget, François-Charles Morisseaux, Georges Rency, and Romain Sanvic. The list is long of Belgian writers whose literary destiny, like their country, has been ravaged twice by cruel wars. It is to be hoped that with the return of peace the Belgian theatre will rise again to the poetic and dramatic excellence of its Verhaeren and Maeterlinck.

VI

Italy

DOMENICO VITTORINI

The present brief analysis of modern drama in Italy has been written on the assumption that the term "modern" refers especially to the works of playwrights in which our own age can mirror itself. We are aware that the tragedies of Alessandro Manzoni written during the romantic period are not as close to us as are the social plays of Paolo Ferrari and the introspective works of our contemporary, Luigi Pirandello. In content, as well as form, the latter two have given expression to feelings and presented situations in which we can recognize ourselves more readily than in the historical tragedies of the romantic age.

The term "realistic" can be applied to works of the modern age not only in reference to setting but also to the fundamental intuition of the concept of life therein expressed. Modern playwrights have gradually destroyed the traditional way of splitting life into two planes: the real and the ideal. They have constantly veered away from concepts of reality and have focused their attention on the actual aspects of it. Even works strictly imaginative reveal, under their symbolism, their concern with the actual world.

This type of modern realism should not be confused with the realism of the sixteenth-century comedy as represented by Aretino, Lasca, Cecchi, Machiavelli, and the unknown authors of the *Commedia dell' arte*. These playwrights used the social setting of their time in order to reach comic effects with the specific aim of producing laughter through the sordid situations that they portrayed. Modern realists have used the social setting with the clear and avowed purpose of studying it, injecting into the study a dignity, a purposefulness, and a philosophical vein unknown before.

The history of realism is closely associated with the growth of nineteenth-century democracy. As citizens acquired a greater rôle in national and economic life, bringing into being a new type of social organization, dramatic art assumed a new aspect both because it had to address itself to a wider and more practical public and because the playwright felt himself to be a part of the new society. In the fifteenth, sixteenth, and seventeenth centuries, theatres were the privilege of people of the court. Although the Republic of Venice and of a few other cities had public theatres in the eighteenth century, the opening of playhouses to the general public was distinctly a contribution of the nineteenth century. Prizes to encourage dramatic activity were instituted for the first time in 1852 under Cavour, the founder of the liberal state in Italy.

The history of modern drama is here presented first in terms of nineteenth-century realism and then through the study of the works of contemporary authors. The basis of this distinction rests on the change in Italian political history and culture that make of the nineteenth and the twentieth centuries two strikingly distinct epochs. The nineteenth century stressed a more objective study of reality, whereas our own age has granted a wider rôle to imagination. During the nineteenth century science predominated, whereas during the first years of our own century an idealistic reaction claimed first place. This background is substantially accurate provided we do not take it too categorically and picture the nineteenth century as monstrously scientific and the twentieth century as idealistic in a volatile manner. The term "predominance" of one current presupposes and testifies to the presence of the other.

We propose to reconstruct the history of Italian drama in terms of the acclaim or indifference with which contemporaries received the various plays, and then to evaluate them from the observation point of the present when taste and environment have substantially changed. Thus, the history of drama becomes a revision of the reactions of the public of yesterday by the criticism of today.

*
* *

Toward the middle of the nineteenth century the level of the Italian theatre was far from being very high. It was still weighed down by the old division of comedy and tragedy, and examples of the former were as drab as specimens of the latter were stilted and rhetorical. The drama written under the historical tenets of the Romantic School had not produced anything significant. Even the two plays by Alessandro Manzoni, *Il Conte di Carmagnola* (1820) and *Adelchi* (1822) fall short of the height that the author of the *Promessi Sposi* (*The Betrothed,* 1827) attained in his novel. In general, the romantic drama moved the public more because of its political message than by its power of human appeal. Likewise, the tragedy of classical inspiration, rejuvenated by Alfieri in the eighteenth century and continued by Ugo Foscolo and Vincenzo Monti, produced works that today are historical relics and nothing more. But, around 1850, from the traditional comedy, there developed a play with a definite stress on the social element to which we apply the qualification of modern. This type of dramatic art was the outgrowth of the new social order that gradually had been established in Italy.

Two important events influenced Italian life and art in the second half of the nineteenth century: the unification of the country and its gradual passing from an agricultural to an industrial civilization. The unification of Italy culminated with the establishment of Rome as the capital of the new state in 1870. The economic and social life of the country was strongly affected by the opening of the Suez Canal in 1864, whereby Italy was reëstablished in its traditional rôle of link between the East and the West. Economic life was greatly benefited and social conditions were vastly improved. The new direction assumed by Italian life was, on the whole, resisted by the older generation and defended by the younger one. The conservatives presented themselves in the conventional pattern of being Catholic in religion, monarchical in politics, and capitalistic in economics. In art they still adhered to the tenets of pseudo-classicism or to those of the now old romantic school, and viewed with hostility all forms other than the traditional ones. The younger generation, reflecting a more pragmatic point of view, stood courageously for a modern form of progress based on work, on avowed adherence to "facts," and accepted the challenge of modern conditions and problems. The level of the theatre was enormously raised, and dramatic literature was given a new content by the fact that men of high intellect, endowed by a keen sense of observation, assigned to their art the task of studying the society of their time in their search for new situations and effects. These men possessed a well-balanced outlook on life and society, and clung steadfastly to certain basic principles in which they had an absolute faith. They were *galantuomini,* men inherently honest, whose conservatism was alive because it had been reached after a period of doubt and trial. Among such men as these appeared the playwrights in whose works was reflected a social preoccupation which, after 1850, is to be noted with increasing frequency. While Luigi Suñer (1832-1909) and Giuseppe Vollo (1820-1905) are only of minor importance, Vincenzo Martini and Paolo Giacometti deserve greater consideration.

Vincenzo Martini (1803-1862), who held various positions in the government of the Grand Duchy of Tuscany, wrote, among other comedies, three plays that deserve to be mentioned: *Una donna di quarant'anni* (1853), *Il cavaliere d'industria* (1854), and *Il marito e l'amante* (1855). In *Una donna di quarant'anni,* he presents the thesis that it is unwise for an older woman to marry a much younger man. For this reason, when the forty-year-old heroine, Malvina Vercelli, falls in love with the twenty-five-year-old Count of Altavilla, she is discreetly led to give up that love. *Il cavalier d'industria,* written in 1845, but not performed until 1854, is a keen study of the Florentine society of Martini's time that was too prone to open its doors to adventurers of the type of the main character herein presented in Mario Newdork. In *Il marito e l'amante* is depicted with realistic technique the adulterous love of the Duchess Olimpia for a cynical and dishonest nobleman. The woman is made to realize the sad consequences of her romantic attachment. Although the situations herein presented are at times very amusing, the intent of the author goes far beyond humor. Martini was very interested in improving the theatre of his day, and furthered his attempts by writing on dramatic art under the pen-name of Anonimo Fiorentino.

Paolo Giacometti (1816-1882), a professional playwright who earned his living by attaching himself to several dramatic companies and writing for them, deserves special attention, not so much for his *Il poeta e la ballerina* (1841) and *Le metamorfosi politiche* (1849) which, though mediocre from an artistic standpoint, testify to his interest in problems of contemporary society, as for *La morte civile* (1861). In it Giacometti daringly advocates the necessity of divorce in order to safeguard an innocent mother and child from the punishment meted out to the husband who has been sentenced to prison for life for homicide. This play was very well received and it remains even today in the repertoire of good companies. It is a strong play, and Corrado, the main character, is well drawn. The complexity of his psychology lifts the play above the documentary value that the thesis therein presented gives to it.

The outstanding representative of the social play is Paolo Ferrari (1822-1889). Ferrari was a thoughtful man who set forth in his plays his reflections and perplexities before the confused pattern of the society of his time. He often took refuge in the idealism of the past, but more frequently offered his own vision of the dignity of life and of man. He was a staunch patriot and a liberal, a man religious without bigotry, moral without prudishness, who lived a very active life as a journalist, a professor of esthetics at the University of Milan, and as a playwright. He fought the formula of art for art's sake and wanted art to be fired by the desire to correct the social evils of the time. Both historically, in that he dominated the theatre of his day, and esthetically, in that he wrote plays that are still performed and admired, he deserves serious consideration.

In his long and fruitful career he wrote charming comedies of manners, historical dramas, and social plays. His art did not follow the rectilineal development imagined by those who state that Ferrari passed from the comedy of manners to the historical play, and from this to the social play. The chronology of his works disproves this contention. His development, like all true growth, was internal and not external, and was based on his sense of observation and artistic technique that deepened and improved with the passing of the years. His less serious mood expressed itself in humorous comedies like *La medicina d'una ragazza malata* (written 1859, performed 1862) and *Il codicillo dello zio Venanzio* (1865). Among the historical plays, his *Goldoni e le sue sedici commedie nuove* (1851) is noteworthy and is generally recognized as one of the best plays written in Italy during the nineteenth century. It is hardly necessary to say that this reconstruction of Goldoni's life at a critical moment of his career is not significant because of its historical accuracy. Ferrari reflected in it his own aspirations and struggles as a playwright and for this reason Goldoni becomes a new and a live character. Historical, in the same sense, but without achieving the same perfection, is *Parini e la satira* (1856) which places in sharp contrast the noble poetry of Parini and the servile one of his rival, the opportunist Degianni. What animates the play is the passion for true art that moved Ferrari in writing his own plays. Other historical dramas that he wrote do not add greatly to his fame.

What entitles Ferrari to a very important place in the history of drama is a clear strain of social analysis that is found in his plays: *Prosa* (1858), *Il duello* (1868), *Uomini Seri* (1869), *Cause ed effetti* (1871), *Ridicolo* (1872), *Il suicidio* (1875), *Due dame* (1877), and *Roberto Pregalli* (1880). The themes he has developed in these plays testify to his awareness of the social problems of his time. In *Prosa* he suggests that true art is not to be sought in exotic adventures. In *Ridicolo* he holds up to derision the prejudice, then very general, that all actresses are immoral. In *Uomini Seri* he points out the lack of honesty in the political and business life of his time. In *Cause ed effetti* are seen the sad consequences of marriage arranged by parents without the proper consideration of the qualities necessary for the happiness of the children involved. In *Due Dame* the problem of the redemption and nobility of a fallen woman is treated. In *Roberto Pregalli* the author discusses the question whether predisposition to crime is a legitimate cause for acquittal. These problems interested Ferrari in a vital and sincere manner, and his passion communicates dramatic force to the events that unfold in his plays.

What is of greater importance is the fact that Ferrari often reflected in his characters a moment of his own perplexity before the mixture of good and evil that life seemed to him. In a letter to Vincenzo Martini, in reference to his play *Il duello,* he spoke of the "inevitable contradictions between absolute logic and practical logic." This attitude prevents his characters from being categorical imperatives or ethical mannequins, the accusation most frequently addressed against him. It prevents him also from presenting absolute pictures of evil. Critics have repeatedly stated that Ferrari had a bourgeois mentality and justified the ethics and even the prejudices and social conventions of his time. In reality, the idea that he entertained concerning morality was contrary to the general and current one. In *Due dame* he leads Rosalia, a fallen woman, to the pinnacle of womanly perfection. Rather than subscribing to the current prejudice, he argued against those who considered it impossible that a noble heart may still abide in such a woman. If, in the play, she forbids her son to marry Emma, an adventuress not different from what she had been in her youth, this shows Ferrari's sense of measure and lends to the play one of the best scenes in his theatre: the scene where the two women are face to face and Rosalia proves the strength of her moral fibre by confessing her past to her son, yet keeping his esteem, admiration, and love. *Prosa* shows Ferrari taking a stand against the popular idea that a poet has a morality of his own. In *Ridicolo*, he rises against those who believe that an actress is destined to live an immoral life and the man who marries her is certain to become the butt of ridicule. In the play, Federico Braganza, believing himself above this prejudice, marries a celebrated singer. The main concern of the playwright is to show that Federico himself was not capable of rising above that prejudice. Being a man deprived of moral sense, he is the cause of their unhappiness and not the actress who appears in the play as a woman of noble character. In *Il duello* it is shown that there are often situations in life from which we cannot break loose without having recourse to the barbaric practice of dueling.

The importance of Ferrari rests especially upon the creation of his characters. In most of his plays, even in those that are somewhat cumbersome in their structure, are to be found complex and well-drawn characters. Beside Rosalia and Emma, we find Anna in *Cause ed effetti,* Clotilde and Marcella in *Il suicidio,* women endowed with strong will and nobility of soul. Anna reflects Ferrari's critique of the life of the aristocracy when she is made to say to her friend:

You can readily understand whether this life is made for me: to dress and go for a ride, to dress and go paying calls or receiving them, to dress and go to the theatre or to a ball: a crushing toil from morning until night in order to be idle, to hear and see the things that I do not like.... For us women, diversion becomes the chief task and goal of our lives. Don't you wish to understand that we women, too, have in our nerves and in our blood a force, a desire to act, that calls for something better than to dance or engage in social gossip?

She proves in the play the sincerity of her words. She is idealistic, compassionate, and constructive. When she loses her little daughter, she finds solace in adopting the child that the former mistress of her husband had had by Anna's father. Another strongly etched character is Count Sirchi in *Il duello*. First a liberal, then a man who hands his friends to the police of the reactionary Bourbons, Count Sirchi bears traces of deep psychological study. He is not a spy for gain. He uses this weapon to avenge himself for the contempt with which he is treated. Yet he is dissatisfied and tortured by the fact that he has lost the love of his wife and by the remorse of his wrong-doing. He is the embodiment of a fundamentally good person wasted by circumstances. His words ring with the torment of his inability to break the vise-like hold that evil has on him. When, in his diabolical determination to hurt his rival, he challenges the fiancé of the latter's daughter to a duel, he allows himself to be killed by his opponent because he remembers the gentleness with which the girl, whose happiness he is about to destroy, had spoken to him. Thus the duel becomes for him a means of redemption. Sergio in *Uomini Seri* is not the usual romantic adventurer. He is a character possessed of a distorted sense of moral values, who tries to deceive others as well as himself. His reliance on words to mask with decency immoral attitudes and projects lends to him a complexity that places his creator well above the other dramatists of his time.

Italian critics, with the exception of Benedetto Croce, have strenuously tried to reduce Ferrari's art to a mere reflection of the French theatre of Augier and the elder Dumas. No valid foundation for such criticism has been established. Being a painstaking worker, Ferrari read attentively past and contemporary French playwrights. He even translated Augier's *Les Fourchambault* and Pailleron's *Les Faux Ménages*. These contacts with the French theatre helped his dramatic technique, but do not warrant any charge of plagiarism.

However, Ferrari's art as a whole offers some points for legitimate attack. His language is not as limpid and pliable as one would wish. He often introduces fantastic and involved situations that mar the plot. His characters engage at times in long speeches that, although revealing the thought of the author, weigh heavily on the smooth development of the action. Yet in spite of these flaws, Ferrari remains an outstanding personality. Whatever hostile critics may say of him, they cannot deny the fact that he knows how to mold characters and that several of his plays are still very much alive today.

*
* *

Although the cultural background of the second half of the nineteenth century possesses a certain unity, there is a notable difference between the generation that lived before 1870, when Rome became the capital of the kingdom, and the one that lived after that event. The key-note of Italian life was no longer political but social, and the country was called upon to face internal problems: economic development, the right to vote, abolition of taxes which were very hard on the lower classes, public instruction made compulsory and gratuitous. Let us remember that in 1870 the Left Party went to power with Agostino de Pretis as Prime Minister. The struggle between conservatives and liberals became more acute than before, and reflected itself in literature, too. Olindo Guerrini, to quote one of the liberal school, in his *Nova polemica* stated that his opponents did not "understand for what social change the positive school in both science and art stands." The clamor of the young for "truth in art" presupposed a more enlightened view of progress and acceptance of the inevitability of change. The differences that separated the older and the younger generations on political as well as social problems warrant us to establish a distinction between the old liberals and the younger ones, a distinction that, in the field of letters, may be expressed by differentiating between the older realists, as represented by Paolo Ferrari, and the younger ones like Marco Praga, Giuseppe Giacosa, and Roberto Bracco.

In many ways, the generation of the younger realists reduced to a formula the concepts of life and art that in Ferrari existed in a freer and more natural form. They adhered to the esthetic formula that enjoined the representation of life close at hand, painted life in bolder colors than did Ferrari, and were more articulate, passionate, and personal than the old master in denouncing the social evils of their time. Thus they produced a comedy on a narrower canvas, but more impressive in its concentrated pathos. They shunned intrigues and adventures and looked askance at any sentimentality. They were helped in their struggle for a new and better drama by acquainting themselves with the dramatic art of Ibsen and Henri Becque.

Modern critics (Tonelli, Pellizzi, D'Amico) have contemptuously called these playwrights bourgeois and at the same time cynical and unmoral. A moral preoccupation, resting on ethical principles that made them rebel against the morality of the average man who pays lip-service to it and uses moral formulas to excuse his mediocrity, is ever present in their works. Ultimately they react against the false ethical standards of the society of their time; therefore they cannot properly be called bourgeois and unmoral. Fundamentally, they sought dramatic contrasts in the contradiction of the human heart and in the absurdities of social conventions.

The realistic drama of this time has been confused with the naturalistic plays of Giovanni Verga (1840-1922). Naturalism is a more elementary form of art than is realism which is essentially selective. It limits its observation to the world of instinct and it does not possess the intellectual scope of realism. For this reason the realism of playwrights like Praga, Giacosa, and Bracco has very few points of contact with the art of Verga. Naturalism meant for the latter a return to the primitiveness of Sicilian life at the time that he lived in Milan and Florence away from his beloved island. Encouraged by the experiments of the contemporary French theatre (let us remember that the Théâtre Libre was founded in 1887 by Antoine) and by his friend Luigi Capuana, he tried the technique of naturalism in order to rid himself of the rather fulsome style of his early writings. In *Cavalleria rusticanna* (*Rustic Chivalry*, 1889), *La Lupa* (1896), and *La caccia al lupo* (1901), he wrote three dramatic sketches, very vivid in their concentrated pathos, that stand out among the best of our modern theatre. These plays express with elemental force the power of instinct, and render brutal facts soberly and passively. In *Cavalleria rusticanna* Turiddu, in love with Lola, is killed in a duel with Alfio. In *La Lupa* Nenni splits open his mother-in-law's head with a hatchet as she advances, like a hungry she-wolf, to tempt him. In *La caccia al lupo* Mariangela is discovered entertaining her lover; the latter thinks only of how he can escape, which so enrages Mariangela that she shouts from an open window to her husband to kill the fleeing coward. These are the jewels of Italian naturalism that we owe to Verga. In *Portineria* (1895) the story of the unnoticed love of Malia, a girl suffering with tuberculosis, for handsome Carlini, who marries her sister, and in *Dal tuo al mio* (1903) in which a worker who previously had had no compunction in occupying the sulphur mines of his employer, stands ready to defend them with his gun when they become his through his marriage to the owner's daughter, Verga has applied the objectivity of the naturalistic method, but the subject is outside the precincts of strict naturalism.

The naturalistic theatre continued to be represented in the early years of our century by Salvatore di Giacomo (1862-1934), one of the greatest contemporary playwrights. He wrote in Neapolitan dialect *'O voto (The Vow,* 1909), *'O mese mariano (The Month of Mary,* 1909), *Assunta Spina (Assunta Spina,* 1910), unforgettable sublimations of the Neapolitan people. Cristina da Capua, a prostitute in *'O voto,* Assunta Spina in the play that bears her name, and the mother in *'O mese mariano* are characters that in the elemental force of their passions reach the height of real tragedy.

The younger realists we are considering in this chapter, Marco Praga, Camillo Antona-Traversi, his brother Giannino, Girolamo Rovetta, Guiseppe Giacosa, Roberto Bracco, Achille Torelli, and Sabatino Lopez, have a wider range of motifs than had Verga, and their attitude and technique are quite different from those of the Sicilian playwright. Although they focus their attention on passion, they stress the moral aspect of this theme and lend to their characters a more complex psychology. Their activity culminated in the last twenty years of the nineteenth century and extended into our own time. The main centers where this new drama was produced were Milan, Turin, and Naples. In Milan, Praga dominated; in Turin, most of Giacosa's plays were produced; and, in Naples, Bracco lived and wrote his plays.

Milan contributed more than other cities in the development of realistic drama. In that center, worked also Carlo Bertolazzi (1871-1916), Silvio Zambaldi (1870-1932), and Sabatino Lopez, though the latter was born at Livorno. Bertolazzi, among other works, wrote *L'egoista (The Egotist,* 1901), the study of the egotism of Franco Marteno as a child, a husband, and a father, and *La casa del sonno (The House of Slumber,* 1902), the consideration of the moral and economic ruin of Luciano, who left his ancestral home to engage in speculation. Zambaldi is best known for his *La moglie del dottore (A Physician's Wife,* 1908), a psychological study of the reactions of a physician who meets the man who seduced his wife when the latter was a young girl.

The most ardent advocate of the realistic drama in the Milanese group in the nineties was Marco Praga (1862-1929). He was the son of the poet Emilio Praga who, in the sixties, had likewise advocated "truth" as the basis of art. Marco Praga started his career as a bookkeeper in a banking house, but soon dedicated himself to the theatre and lived in and for the theatre till the day he committed suicide. He was president of the Society of Playwrights and dramatic critic of the *Corriere della Sera* of Milan. His reactions to the contemporary theatre are to be found in his eight volumes of *Cronache teatrali* (1921-1928).

Recognition as a dramatist of note was accorded to him when his *Le vergini* (1889) was performed in Milan. This is the most representative of Praga's plays. It epitomizes the material in which the artist is primarily interested and, in presenting the vicissitudes of the characters, reveals his attitude towards the moral problem therein contained. The play deals with a middle-class family where a mother is not unwilling to permit her three daughters to have well-to-do admirers who pay with gifts for the liberties the girls allow. Praga studies pitilessly the attitude of the mother in her concern to keep a mask of decency on her home, balancing herself with perfect ease on the border line of morality and immorality. It is the only means at her disposal of having her daughters go among their friends, well-dressed, displaying fine jewelry, and being happy. This applies, at least, to Ninì and Selene, two of the sisters who play the game with extreme confidence; but not to Paolina, another sister, who is very unhappy in that atmosphere. The drama begins precisely here, carried by Paolina, the individual whose nobility serves the purpose of stressing diversity, creating contrast, and determining the action of the play. When Dario, a spineless student, asks her to be his wife, she is so overjoyed and ennobled that, on the eve of their wedding, she feels it incumbent upon herself to reveal to him that when she was seventeen she was seduced by Vercellini, a friend of her mother's, the same individual who has been chosen to be best man at the wedding. Dario, incapable of perceiving the nobility of this confession, cools in his matrimonial enthusiasm and proposes to her to become his mistress. Paolina refuses with words that echo the indignation of the author and make her tower above Dario's moral obtuseness. The accusation of immorality, so often addressed to Praga, is especially based on this play. From the standpoint of formalistic ethics, the subject may be called immoral, but thoughtful men have never subscribed to such a moral code. Praga advocates here a morality of the soul that can cleanse even the offense rendered to the body. To him immorality lies around Paolina and not in her. She is redeemed by her confession to Dario.

What is said of this play is also applicable to the rest of Praga's dramatic works. He is a grieving sentimentalist moved to expose the pitiful spectacle that society offers him. He does so with great earnestness and with an eye for the dramatic effect that such situations hold for his art. *Il Bell'Apollo* (1894) is developed along the same lines as *Le vergini*. It is a study of masculine profligacy, embodied in Pietro Badia and projected against the real love of Susanna da Ponte, a woman who falls not for vice but because her love has suddenly revealed to her the meaning of her whole existence and has transformed her into a new being. Near her, Praga has placed two other women, Enrichetta, a young shirt-maker, and Dolores Arneiro, wife of a jealous Spaniard, irresponsible beings for whom love is part of their trade, or merely a caprice.

It is evident from what has been said that Praga differentiates between people for whom love is vice and those for whom love is an all-absorbing experience that, when sincerely felt, lifts them to a higher plane. Ninì, Selene, and Pietro Badia were followed, in subsequent plays, by Giulia in *La moglie ideale* (1890) and Alessandro Fara's wife Elisa in *Alleluja* (1892), just as Paolina and Susanna da Ponte were embodied in other characters of the same psychological texture as theirs. Lucia Lovore, in *La morale della favola* (1894-1901), is so fundamentally honest that, upon realizing the enormity of her act in yielding to her lover, Augusto Campese, feels that she cannot return to her husband and children. Conscious of her moral sensitiveness, her uncle, Don Raimondo, a high-minded priest, persuades her to go back to her home and atone for her sin through her consciousness of it. False morality is satirized in the attitude of Augusto Campese, who mentions the sanctity of the home in urging the woman to return to her husband.

Marco Praga has constantly analyzed the love motif as a source of variety in his artistic material. In *La crisi* (1901), the adultery of Nicoletta is studied through the anguish of her husband Pietro Donati, who knows that she betrays him but loves her too much to live without her. Hence his grieving silence. The crisis is brought about by the sudden return of Raimondo, Pietro Donati's brother and an army officer. He senses the truth of the situation and challenges Nicoletta's lover to a duel. The scene in which Pietro Donati openly admits his cowardice is a masterful study of human psychology. Conscious of the irreparable harm that he has unwittingly done to his brother, Raimondo begs Nicoletta to deny her unfaithfulness to Pietro. The play ends with a repentant Nicoletta who returns to the love of her husband.

With the passing of years, Praga searched more and more deeply into the theme of passion and the fruit of his search was *La porta chiusa* (*The Closed Door,* 1913). Eleonora Duse interpreted it and brought out the anguish of the mother who is made to atone for her sin through the loss of her only son, whom she adored.

The seriousness and conservatism underlying Praga's art may be seen in his last play, *Il divorzio* (1915), in which he presents the thesis that divorce "is a grotesque thing when it is not a filthy thing." Emilia, Prince Alessio, her second husband, and Edmondo, her ex-husband, meet by chance at a watering resort. A great emotional conflict arises in Emilia upon seeing again her little son Alfredo, who is now eight years old. Her grief at parting from him is the penalty that Praga, the moralist, has meted out to her.

The artistic creed of Praga was clearly revealed in the words that he addressed to young Italian playwrights in 1919 when he stated that drama is to be found everywhere, in every factory, in every home, and in the conscience of every man. He assigned to playwrights the task not only of reflecting their own time, but also of foreshadowing new states of mind and new events. When so conceived, drama assumed a deeply social and religious character.

Dear friends of Praga were Camillo Antona-Traversi (1857-1934), a professor of Italian literature in a military college, first in Naples, then in Rome, and his brother Giannino. Camillo Antona-Traversi took an active part in journalism and wrote literary criticism. He is especially known for two social plays, *Le Rozeno* (1889) and *I parassiti* (1901). The preface to *Le Rozeno* documents very minutely the hostility with which this play was received by conservative elements, especially in church circles. It informs us also of the warm praise it received from liberal-minded persons.

Le Rozeno bears close resemblance to Praga's *Le vergini*. There is the same background of immorality against which is projected a very sensitive young woman, Lidia Rozeno. There is the same family living on the border line of indecency, frequented by men who pay for the luxuries of the three daughters of Clarissa Rozeno. At the opening of the play, the precarious economic situation of the family is about to be stabilized at the expense of Lidia. An old and wealthy prince, believing the child that Lidia is carrying is his, will leave his money to her and the baby. Lidia, however, refuses to be a part of this sordid game. She knows that her child is the fruit of her love for the student Enrico Valenti. To the playwright, Lidia stands redeemed by the sense of purity that motherhood brings into her life. The play centers about this awakened sense of motherhood that is offended by the cowardliness of Enrico, who offers her the status of mistress.

I parassiti embodies a bitter critique of human dishonesty as studied in Gaudenzi and his family, types of modern parasites. The son Alfredo exploits his wife, Ida, just as Gaudenzi exploits his daughter Lina and the gullible public by forming charity committees whenever there is an earthquake or a flood. Gaudenzi, however, is not presented as a lifeless type. He is studied in his resourcefulness, his genius for intrigue, and his childish optimism. In the opening scenes of the play, we find him in a difficult situation. No great catastrophe has taken place of late and, furthermore, he has too many rivals in organizing charity committees. The sudden news of an earthquake helps him to face his creditors by organizing a new committee. But the committee dissolves because the shock has not been as serious as had been believed. Even now his resourcefulness helps him to overcome his plight, and he goes as manager to a Polish violinist on a tour of South America in which his daughter will be the accompanist.

It is evident that Gaudenzi is not the projection of Antona-Traversi's idea of honesty. The pivot around which the play revolves is the grieving amusement of the author before such phenomena of modern life as are seen in the parasitical Gaudenzi.

Giannino Antona-Traversi (1868-1939) was especially successful with one-act plays in which, with a lighter touch and more subtle irony, but with less dramatic power than Praga or his brother Camillo, he studied the society life of Milan in which he was a conspicuous figure. He seems bent on inquiring what becomes of the noble human passion of love in the heart, or rather, in the cold brain, of society people. In his opinion, flirting and gossiping are their all-absorbing occupations, as he informs us in *La carità mondana* (1906), and deception is the trait that stands out before any one who watches this playing with love. In *Il braccialetto* (1897), *La civetta* (1904), *Per vanità* (1902), and *La prima volta* (1910), we witness various aspects of the empty and pleasure-loving life of society people. Traversi dissects their flirting and finds base intrigues and degrading intentions in their acts.

In these plays the author is definitely ironical, although with a smile that tempers his attitude. More compassionately he treats the characters of *I giorni più lieti* (1903) and *I martiri del lavoro* (1909) in which he develops the theme that the moments of intimacy and happiness that should accompany the days before the wedding or those following it are disturbed and destroyed by the social obligations to which the two fiancés or the two newly-weds are condemned. Although the corruption of society can become conventionalized, Giannino is resourceful enough to produce interesting sketches in the above-mentioned plays, though he definitely fails when he attempts drama on vaster proportions.

La Madre (1909), a drama in four acts, is developed along very conventional lines in presenting the nobility of the old aristocracy and the depravity of a family of the lower class into which has married Fabrizio, the scion of Prince Redona. The mother is the victim of the situation, caught between the unbending principles of her husband and the weakness of her son. She is, however, a cold symbol of perfection rather than a character with strong human traits.

Giannino Antona-Traversi's contribution to the theatre is not of great significance although his plays enjoyed great popularity in the days before the First World War.

To the Milanese group belonged also Girolamo Rovetta (1853-1910). Although he was never very articulate concerning problems of dramatic art, he worked earnestly at his plays and novels. His plays usually have industrial Milan as their background. He was a gentleman of independent means and dedicated his entire life to works of fiction and the theatre. What he thinks of the new Milan with the bustle of its intense economic life can be seen in the plays in which the triumph of dishonesty is portrayed with an insistence that, at times, engenders monotony. *La città di Roma* (1888) informs us that Andrea Borsieri refrains from revealing the adultery of his wife for fear that the latter, an able milliner, may, out of spite, open a shop at the next corner from his own establishment, and ruin his business. The author has reduced the moral sensitivity of the main character to this paltry proportion. We find the same atmosphere in *I Barbarò* (1890) and *La baraonda* (1894), plays that were first written in the form of novels.

Rovetta's best comedy is *La trilogia di Dorina* (1889) woven about the paradoxical stupidity of the Marquis Niccolino who asks an honest and charming girl to become his mistress and then marries her when she has become a famous singer and a corrupted woman. It is a delightful comedy presenting Dorina first as an innocent girl, who refuses Niccolino's advances and pleads with him to marry her if he loves her, and later as a coquette, expert in the use of her guiles. A motley crowd of characters surrounds her: bankers, industrialists, social climbers of all kinds, side by side with the humorous figure of her singing teacher. The simplicity and goodness of the girl stand out as an indictment of society and also of the vulgar temperament of the young Marquis for whom Rovetta reserves the rôle of falling prey to his own sensuality.

I disonesti (1892) and *La realtà* (1895) also reflect a disconsolate outlook on life. In the former play, Rovetta ponders over the case of Carlo Moretti, a paragon of honesty as a treasurer whose moral sense is badly shaken when he discovers that the luxury of his home is being paid for by the head of his firm in return for the favors of his wife. When the death of the employer ends this unsuspected income, he goes to the point of stealing from the firm in order to keep up the impression of prosperity. In *La realtà,* an upright and progressive industrialist commits suicide when, through his wife's perfidy, he faces economic ruin and the destruction of his home. Even the workers, for whose benefit he had introduced coöperatives, abandon him when the financial collapse comes.

In Rovetta's somewhat conventional philosophy, a strain of idealism is clearly visible. In *Papà Eccellenza* (1907), we are permitted to see, better than in other plays, the positive aspect of his idealism, since in it he depicts a character who, behind the occupation and successes of a political life, has as his only reality his love for his daughter.

Rovetta also wrote four historical plays with the clear intent of reducing historical figures to the humble proportions of men seen at close range. It cannot be said that he reached the human element in them. This is true even of *Romanticismo* (1901) which had a distinct success because of its patriotic appeal.

On the whole, Rovetta's attitude is that of a defeatist. He paints with two contrasting colors: the white of honesty and the black of dishonesty, with the black predominating over the white.

Giuseppe Giacosa (1847-1906) was a man endowed with a more positive and constructive mind than his friends of the Milanese group with whom he lived in intimate contact. The picture of the sadness and even tragedy of life is fringed in his work by a halo of faith and hope in man. He studied law, but from his early youth began to write short plays along the lines of the comedy of manners or historical scenes with a romantic turn: *Una partita a scacchi* (1873), *Il marito amante della moglie* (1879), *Il Conte Rosso* (1880).

The success of *Una partita a scacchi* encouraged him to abandon the law and dedicate himself to the theatre. As Giacosa matured, he reflected his deepened sense of experience in *Tristi amori* (1888). This play that has been attributed to French and Scandinavian influences gives the measure of Giacosa's creative power. The author is ever present in it through his perplexity before Emma's action in betraying Giulio, her husband, for a worthless individual like Fabrizio, her husband's assistant in the practice of law. The assistant is the son of a penniless count who is dishonest to the point of forging Giulio's signature on a note. Home life, even in its most prosaic details, is made to loom beautiful and desirable before Emma, tormented by fears and anxiety. Giacosa paints her more as a weak than a vulgar person. Even in her tryst with Fabrizio, she longs for affection, as her own words indicate. When the tryst is discovered through the forged signature of Fabrizio's father, Emma is ready to leave her home, but she is touched by the sight of her child's doll and cannot tear herself away from it. Giulio returns and tells her that he is willing to have her live under his roof for their child's sake, though he will never forgive her. This solution is in keeping with Giulio's sense of right and wrong which, though not extreme, is unbending where decency is concerned. A new drama of broken love and destroyed happiness is envisaged in that solution, a silent drama that Giacosa exquisitely intimates in his restrained technique.

La Contessa di Challant appeared in 1891. Here is to be found the tragedy and complexity of the love theme in an historical setting. The plot is based on one of Bandello's stories, which Giacosa has molded with absolute independence, lending a new soul to the main character. He wrote the play for the great actress Sarah Bernhardt at her request. Bianca of Challant is portrayed as the victim of an unfortunate marriage. She had been thirsty for love and was married to a gouty count. If she passed from one lover to another, she did so because she sought a real love that she never found. She had loved Gaiazzo and had found him stupid. She had loved Ardizzino and found him vulgar. In the end she met real love in a Spanish youth who exposed himself to death for her. A different woman, no longer whimsical and changeable, was revealed in her. She sealed that love by offering her life for her young lover.

The thoughtful strain of Giacosa's mind is even better revealed by *I diritti dell' anima* (1889), the motivation of which is based on the question whether a husband has the right to search into his wife's soul when he knows that she has remained faithful to him. Paolo is shown tormenting Anna with his maddening inquisition concerning her feelings toward a distant relative who had fallen in love with her and, upon being rejected, had committed suicide. Goaded by his incessant questioning, Anna tells him that she loved Luciano and regrets now that she remained faithful to her husband by silencing the voices of her heart. Giacosa daringly brings his theme to a logical conclusion, and Anna leaves Paolo's home. The solution reflects

Giacosa's desire for the new status of woman in the home and bespeaks his open and high mind.

The dramatic success of 1900 was *Come le foglie* that presents to us the sad existence of Giovanni. He has worked "like an ox" all his life, and all his hopes that he had placed in the members of his family have vanished like autumn leaves. His wife, to whom he was devoted, has died. Giulia, his second wife, is superficial and vacuous, interested in studying painting with a Swedish artist who makes love to her. Tommy, his son, spends his youth gambling and flirting; Nennele, his daughter, with her inefficient goodness, withers in the silence of his home. Giovanni is tied to his work, the only tangible but crushing reality of his life. In this gloom and sadness there is a character that brings a positive and healthy note—Massimo, a cousin, healthy of body and of mind, who embodies and expresses Giacosa's constructive views on work, nature, art, and life in general. To him is assigned the task of saving Nennele as well as Giovanni's home. When the girl, unable to stand any longer the burden of her existence, has decided to take her life, Massimo appears and tells her of his love for her.

The social element is quite evident in Giacosa's work, and it plays a paramount part in *Il più forte* (*The Stronger of the Two*, 1904), which depicts the crisis that arises between Cesare Nalli, a banker, and his son Silvio, an artist. The crisis is determined by the clash of two opposite views of honesty. Silvio, the spokesman of Giacosa, feels that his father, one of those bankers who, with the control of huge capital, holds in his hand the destiny of millions, cannot be called honest according to his meaning of the term. It is true that, according to the letter of the law, he is honest, but is it honest to evade the spirit of the law? Cesare Nalli, the man of iron in his business transactions, who loves his family tenderly, is hurt to the quick by the decision of his son to leave his home and earn a living by his art. The artist stands in the play as the stronger of the two.

Giacosa is a significant figure in the history of the modern theatre. He wrote also librettos for Giacomo Puccini's operas *Madame Butterfly, Bohême,* and *Tosca* in collaboration with Luigi Illica. The adverse criticism that he has usually received seems to us totally unjust. His dialogue flows smoothly. His characters are human, complex, and alive. His outlook on life is that of a broad-minded man whose optimism bears traits of having been tested in the school of life.

Roberto Bracco (1861-1943) enlivens his observation of contemporary life with a wide vein of human compassion. The characters that most frequently appear in his plays are victims of society or women who give to love a sincerity that is unknown to men.

This typical attitude of Bracco can be clearly seen in *Pietro Caruso* (1895), the sketch of a shadowy figure of the Neapolitan world, a man without honor in his life of "jack-of-all trades" which includes that of working for political candidates. But he has one redeeming feature: absolute faith in the honesty of his only daughter. When she becomes the mistress of the wealthy man whose political aspirations he serves, Caruso kills himself. A similar drama develops in the poor quarters of Naples in *Sperduti nel buio* (1901). It is the drama of Nunzio and Paolina, a blind boy and a girl, daughter of a prostitute, who meet in a cheap café where Nunzio plays the piano. The short idyl is broken by a man who courts and takes Paolina away from Nunzio. She is, perhaps, the daughter of the Duke of Valenza whose dying moments, embittered by remorse for having abandoned an illegitimate child, are portrayed in the third act. *Nellina* (1908) deals with the same atmosphere of social degradation in which the mother, a prostitute, cannot reveal her identity to Nellina, herself a prostitute. However, in Bracco's mind, society has not been able to wipe out the maternal instinct on which the play is based.

When Bracco relinquished themes set forth by means of local color and sought his material in higher social circles and more complex figures, his attitude did not change. In *Tragedie dell' anima* (1899) and *Maternità* (1903), we find the same faith of Bracco in the fundamental goodness of woman, crushed by the irresponsibility of man to whom love is merely sensuality or a pastime. Psychological treatment and social concern remain the poles around which his drama revolves. In these two plays he has created his drama out of the contrast between the indescructible instinct of motherhood and the sensuous considerations of the two husbands presented in them. The action of the plays assumes a symbolic character that does not jar against the realism that distinguishes it.

The theme of those who live like shadows or are crushed by insensitive persons is also treated in *La piccola fonte* (1905) in which Teresa, in her humility and self-effacement, stands as a sublime figure before the vagaries of her husband who is made to realize what a large part Teresa has played in his success as a poet.

As time went on, the art of Bracco veered constantly towards the psychological. *Fantasmi* (1906) and *Il piccolo santo* (1912) are beautiful examples of the height he reached in his development. *Fantasmi* presents the case of the masculine acquisitive instinct that goes even beyond death. Professor Artunni extorted from his wife Giulia the promise that after his death she would not marry Luciano Marnieri, one of his pupils. From the dark regions of death he was able to continue to stifle the existence of the woman. In *Il piccolo santo* Bracco shows how tragedy passes like a destructive storm over the refuge sought by a young priest, Don Fiorenzo, in the peace of a country parsonage. When Anita, the daughter of a woman he once dearly loved, comes to seek help from him, the old love is rekindled without his realizing it in the interest that he feels in the young girl. Giulio, his brother, returns from America and falls in love with Anita. On the day of their wedding, Barbarello, a half-wit who worships Don Fiorenzo, sensing the hidden tragedy of his master, kills Giulio.

Bracco used, with independence and originality, both the conclusions of the realistic school and his cultural contacts with Ibsen and the French playwrights of his day. Truly great authors, however, have always gone outside the precincts of schools and have not been enslaved by literary contacts. Bracco belongs to this group.

A Neapolitan like Bracco was Achille Torelli (1844-1922). Torelli was librarian of the Royal Library St. Giacomo at Naples, and he wrote extensively while attending to his duties. Benedetto Croce has pointed out that the theme of true love is the main chord in Torelli's dramatic work. His plays are, in fact, variations on this theme. It should be added that the author is led to envisage wider problems through it: art in *La scuola degli artisti* (1885) and *Scrollina* (1885); marriage in *I mariti* (1867) and *La moglie* (1868); women in modern society in *Donne moderne* (1886).

He became famous at the age of twenty-three when *I mariti* was performed at Florence in 1867. This comedy is a sort of modern version of *The Taming of the Shrew,* brilliantly conceived and perfectly worked out. Fabio, the husband, is made to succeed in acquiring, through tact and intellectual superiority, the love of his wife Emma, a daughter of the illustrious Herrera family, who had married him only to obey her parents. The play was enthuiastically received and critics (Ferrini, Capuana, Franchetti) spoke of a new era for the Italian theatre.

The subsequent attempts at drama by this sensitive and penetrating author were, however, coldly received. He was unspeakably hurt and, as a result, condemned himself to a life of retirement, though he continued to write plays that met with increasing indifference. Yet, the plays written after *I mariti* are an exemplification of the fact that Torelli tended toward a more subtle and psychological art in his tormenting study of love and passion. From the observation point of his lonely existence, Torelli was dismayed by the tragic power of passion and expressed his musings through attitudes and conclusions so idealistic and subjective that the public of the time refused to accept them. In *La moglie,* Maria, knowing of the blind passion that Malvina her sister-in-law has conceived for her husband, instead of dramatizing her jealousy and creating a catastrophe, shows to her brother the tryst of her husband with another woman and makes him see the tragedy of her situation that he may find strength to bear his own. She is a sublime victim who offers her shame and grief in sacrifice for the good of those she loves, including the husband whom she forgives. In *L'israelita* (1883) he presents the case of a woman who is goaded into adultery, not by love or passion for her mate, but by her desire to have a child. So genuine is this longing in her and so consistent is the author in bringing his theme to its last conclusions that she refuses to marry the father of her child when her husband dies. The same subjective treatment is accorded to the theme of unfaithfulness in *L'ultimo convegno* (*The Last Meeting,* 1898) in which Patrizio, an invalid who is betrayed by his wife, tells her that he is aware of her infidelity, but begs her to face her guilt and acknowledge it in a spirit of humility that she may find atonement in her remorse. Likewise, in *Triste realtà* (1886), Rio, knowing that he is destined to die in youth, silences the voice of jealousy and the acquisitive instinct to the point of providing that his wife should remarry after his death.

In many ways Torelli, in his tormented individualism, seems to be the forerunner of contemporary playwrights. Thus, while he was close to the generation of Ferrari in *I mariti*, in his later works he went beyond the taste and comprehension of his contemporaries, who were accustomed to the more solid realism that prevailed at that time.

Sabatino Lopez (1867-   ) has lived in Milan during a long career in which he has turned out an impressive number of plays. He was a teacher of Italian literature in the secondary schools of various cities until he relinquished that career to become president of the Italian Society of Playwrights and to dedicate himself to the writing of plays.

His first dramatic sketches were written in 1888: *Oriana* and *Di notte*. In these as well as in other attempts at drama, Lopez was hampered rather than helped by the dictates of naturalism that he followed. In *Di notte*, which received the government prize in 1890, a husband kills his wife because he has seen a man flee from his home at night. The man proves to be the lover of his daughter. The drama ends where it could begin since the consequences of the blunder are left to the imagination of the public.

Quite different in technique and content are *Ninetta* (1895) and *La buona figliuola* (1909) in which the author combined humor with realistic themes. Ninetta, D'Arcole's mistress, proves to be, in her genuine devotion to him, a better woman than the wife for whom he has abandoned her. When his wife betrays him, D'Arcole appreciates Ninetta better and returns to her.

In *La buona figliuola,* Cesarina, a girl who ran away from home and became the mistress of a member of the Italian Parliament, has lost none of her attachment for her family nor any of the qualities of an affectionate daughter. She contributes in every possible way to the well-being of her sister Giulia, to whom she gives as wise advice as a mother would give her daughter. Is this irony? Is it sentiment? It is both, and these two traits are very much in evidence in Lopez' works. This benevolent irony is also found in *La morale che corre* (1904) in which he informs us that Giugiù, a man by no means noted for morality, is very severe upon learning that Giuditta, his housekeeper, though unmarried, is with child, and dismisses her. But later, on meeting her again, as a fashionable harlot, he has no compunction in courting her. Perhaps the best example of the humorous treatment of a realistic theme is found in *La nostra pelle* (1912) which places in sharp contrast the hardships that fall to the lot of Elsa, a modest schoolteacher, when she offers a piece of her skin to be grafted on the body of one of her pupils who has been badly burned, and the good fortune that comes to Fioravanti for having killed a man who terrorized the whole village. Elsa, after her heroic sacrifice, marries the mayor of the town only to become the nurse of his invalid and irascible mother, and the slave of the household. She is also exploited by the father of the child whose life she saved. Her husband sums up well Lopez' point of view: "Some are tied to virtue as others to vice; virtue is an iron ball tied to your feet." *L'ultimo romanzo* (1920), *Fatica* (1920), *La Zia Lu* (1921) are all developments of the author's mood that oscillates between humor and pathos, and they are very effective.

Bufere (1907) shows a different aspect of Lopez' art. It is serious drama. In it he sounds the love of Sabina and Antoniccu, who love each other with the exclusive love of the silent and repressed persons of Sardinia. Their quiet and happy life is broken, however, when Cora Parnell, a circus acrobat, steals Antoniccu's love. Sabina leaves him and returns to her home in Sardinia. The play centers in the conviction of the playwright that Sabina's place is near her husband in his days of trial. (The theme that forgiveness is the only solution in the case of adultery is developed by Lopez in *Il Viluppo,* 1913). But Sabina, true to the ethics of her native island returns, not to forgive, but to kill Cora with a surgical instrument belonging to her husband. Of Lopez' attempts at serious drama, *Bufere* is the best.

Lopez has continued to entertain the Italian public during and after the First World War. Even as late as 1937, he produced a new play, *Luce*. He has remained untouched by the experiments in technique and content that have characterized our epoch, clinging steadfastly to the forms and substance enjoined by the theory of realism that was formulated during his youth.

To have a clear idea of the condition of Italian drama at the end of the past century we should keep in mind that other literary currents coexisted with that represented by the younger realists. The historical play was represented at that time by Felice Cavallotti (1842-1898), a republican member of parliament; Giovanni Bovio (1841-1903); and Pietro Cossa (1830-1881). Cossa is still remembered for his *Nerone* (1871) in which he applied the procedures of the realistic school to historical drama and presented a Nero quite different from the bloodthirsty tyrant of the popular conception of that historical figure. In Cossa's drama Nero is a fickle individual, not deprived of impulses for goodness, suddenly overpowered by cruelty and cowardice. The play is enlivened by the presence of an exquisite Greek dancer, Egloge by name, who gives her love to Nero and dies for it.

To the same generation also belonged Enrico Annibale Butti (1868-1912). He was a solitary man of letters, very much detached from the problems of his age. In his plays, *Vortice* (1893), *La corsa al piacere* (1900), and *Il castello del sogno* (1910), he expressed vaguely mystic and religious aspirations portrayed against the background of the materialism of his age. His plays are brutally realistic when the author looks at modern life, and dreamy and romantic when he reflects his own idealism, to which, however, he was never capable of giving concrete form. He deserves mention for his play

Fiamme nell' ombra (*Flames in the Shadow,* 1905) in which the drama of a young priest is effectively portrayed. The flames are the world, the blood that tingles in his veins, the possibility of advancement in his ecclesiastic career, the moral fall of his sister; the shadow is the life of silence and prayer to which he condemns himself in the hope of redeeming his sister.

In Butti, nerves begin to be in greater evidence than muscle, to use an expression that Benedetto Croce aptly employs in pointing out the difference between the last century and our own.

*
* *

From the first years of our century to the present day, Italian culture has formed a compact though varied zone, dominated by the desire of having Italy not only reënter the current of European history but also to contribute something new to it. In political life, as well as in art, there has been a break with tradition. The hazy ideologies of fascism obliterated the clear-cut pattern of the philosophy of government by the liberals and the social democrats of former days. In art, too, the same departure from tradition was represented by futurism and *La Voce* before the days of the First World War; the former extreme, erratic, irrational, plebeian, and theatrical, the latter very constructive and sane as the expression of the vision of the best minds of the time: Prezzolini, Papini, Salvemini, Amendola, and Borgese. Numerous movements appeared at that time which aimed at directing Italian life toward new goals: in religion, modernism; in politics, nationalism; in art, futurism; in sociology, syndicalism.

During this period, drama assumed a great variety of forms that reflected in a varied measure a harrowing desire for novelty. The descriptive captions of contemporary works bear witness to this trend. Contemporary playwrights have discarded the old terminology of tragedy and comedy and called their works "parables," "grotesque" (used as a noun), "adventures in color." Pirandello even called his *Sei personaggi in cerca d'autore* (*Six Characters in Search of an Author*), "Comedy yet to be made." Nevertheless, whatever technical changes have been introduced, the fundamental qualities of a drama that presents living personalities in situations fraught with tragedy and humor have not been changed, and the works we are to review are to be judged in the light of the effectiveness of the finished product. For clarity's sake, we have divided the copious production of the contemporary drama into several sections: comedy, historical drama, lyrical drama, and the drama of the mind.

Variations of taste and culture are reflected in the drama. The strong anti-bourgeois tendency of the early years of our century was followed by the anarchy that characterized Italian art during and after the First World War. A moment of spiritual reconstruction could be observed around 1925, which was disturbed and eventually destroyed when Mussolini inaugurated his war-like foreign policy and then led Italy to its present tragedy. Gabriele D'Annunzio was the most famous and even notorious playwright in the years preceding 1914. During the war, the authors of the "grottesco" enjoyed great popularity. Luigi Pirandello, together with Dario Niccodemi, dominated the post-war years.

On the whole, dramatic art assumed during this time a greater psychological complexity which led serious authors to fathom nooks of the human heart, unknown to the writers of the previous generation. The art of Luigi Pirandello, Sem Benelli, Luigi Morselli, Cesare Vico Ludovici, and Luigi Chiarelli gained in depth through this analysis. Others produced only ephemeral works in which the study of human personality ended in empty symbolism or in experiments in technique and form.

Among the cultural factors that influenced the contemporary playwrights were Croce's theory of art as a subjective intuition of reality, as well as contacts with foreign authors like Ibsen, Maeterlinck, Rostand, Hauptmann, Gide, Bernstein, and the Russian authors: Tolstoi, Turgenev, Dostoevski, and Chekhov. Theatrical technique, aided by the innovations of Max Reinhardt, became more subtle and effective, just as language was made richer and more flexible in expressing a more complex psychology.

On the whole, the last thirty years have been a period of experimentation with themes and techniques. There have been over two thousand small and large dramatic societies and centers where authors have been allowed to present the results of their efforts.

Under the heading of comedy we are including not only the plays in which, though differently treated, appear themes once dear to the traditional comedy, but also those that reflect a concern for political as well as social problems.

In the early part of our century, the theatre reverberated with the political struggle that was being waged between social democracy and the resurgent nationalism represented by Enrico Corradini (1865-1931). The works of Corradini (*Le vie dell 'oceano*, 1913), Vincenzo Morello (*La flotta degli emigranti*, 1907), and Tomaso Monicelli (*L'esodo*, 1908, *La terra promessa*, 1910) are closely connected with the new concept of nationalism which they sponsored. Questions involving the sanctity of the hearth, emigration, the beauty of agricultural life, the destructive power of commercialism, are no longer envisaged in the light of a humanitarian ideal as in the works of the nineteenth century realist, but in their relationship with the future of the Italian nation.

The question of emigration, for instance, is reflected in the works of these three men, though their plays are developed around events in which emotions have a large part. In *Le vie dell' oceano* by Corradini, we view a clash between an old emigrant to Argentina, who has remained attached to the little Italian village whence he came, and his children who know only the country where they were born and have lived. Likewise, in *La flotta degli emigranti* by Vincenzo Morello (1860-1933), the corruption of a deputy of the old liberal school, Lantosca, is combined with the theme of emigration and his scheme to defraud the shipping companies that carry Italian emigrants to the Americas. It should be noted that in his plays Morello often insisted on the need of an enlightened dictatorship, as in *I condottieri* (1921). *L'esodo* by Monicelli (1884-   ) as well as *La terra promessa* and *Il viandante* (1907) are works that, dictated by political considerations, serve to make us understand the subsequent changes that have intervened in Italian political life.

Such themes, when treated at a later date by younger authors, show a more thoughtful attitude towards international as well as national problems. Thus, in *Il calzolaio di Messina* (1935) by Alessandro de Stefani (1891-   ) are studied the nature and rôle of justice in organized society. A young and well-intentioned man of the lower class, who takes it upon himself to mete out justice, is made to realize that his blunders are different from the possible errors of duly appointed judges, because he is not strengthened by authority vested in him by society. He stands in his own eyes as a murderer and not as a judge, through the remorse that tortures him. A similar motivation is found in *La padrona del mondo* (1934) by Giuseppe Bevilacqua (1891-   ). Our materialistic age is symbolized by a queen who assigns to herself the task of giving happiness to suffering humanity through her discovery of a scientific process whereby she can make gold. The thoughtful and idealistic author concludes in his play that she failed even as our commercial age has failed.

Another trend observed in the best examples of comedy is the psychological trend found in the plays of Lucio D'Ambra, Renato Simoni, and Giuseppe Adami, a trend already noticed in Giacosa, Bracco, and Lopez. Lucio D'Ambra (1887-   ), dramatic critic of the *Tribuna* and *Il Corriere della Sera,* treated various themes, comical, sentimental, historical, and psychological. His best comedy is *Via Basento, Lanterna Rossa, (Basento Street, Red Light,* 1926) in which the psychological element is used to achieve a dramatic effect through the unexpected reaction of a physician who finds in a brothel, where he goes for professional reasons, the peace and tranquillity that he has vainly sought in his home. The author is interested in the elusive play of the character's mind, in a manner dear to Luigi Pirandello.

Renato Simoni (1875-   ), also a dramatic critic, is especially well-known for *La vedova* (1902). It deals with a young woman who, upon the death of her husband, is forced to go to live with her in-laws. She brings into the old and musty home a breath of youth, charm, and beauty that wins the love of her father- and mother-in-law, of their friends, even to the point where they all accept with joy the announcement that she is going to marry again. It is an excellent work of contrast: beauty and widowhood on the one hand and the old home and the spirit of youth on the other.

Close to traditional comedy is the work of Giuseppe Adami (1878-   )

who succeeds best in representing life in minor tones: the joy of a quiet love in *Provincia* (1936), the poetry of old age in *Capelli bianchi* (1915). His main characters are often middle-class and virile women, as in *Felicita Colombo* (1935) and *Nonna Felicita* (1936).

It is interesting to notice what contemporary authors have done with a clever rehandling of old themes. In Aldo de Benedetti's *Lohengrin* (1933), we see a once gay and romantic youth who, after many years, returns to the scene of his gallantries and adventures. Comedy arises especially out of the dismay and amusement of the matured women of the town in seeing again the Don Juan of their youth, now sedate and rotund. A more subtle and psychological treatment is found in the works of Cesare Giulio Viola (1887-   ), who presents in a new fashion the theme of the philandering husband, in *Fine del protagonista* (1930). It shows one such husband in Riccardo who returns home after many years and finds it impossible to remain, when he is received without much ado by his family. The modern playwright stresses the point that the husband finds himself unspeakably humiliated when his return home does not provoke the recriminations that he expected. He is about to resume his odyssey when an old aunt, the stout defender of the home, the clear-headed analyst of his tortuous way of feeling and reasoning, uncovers to him the boundless pride that hides under his false humility. Riccardo remains and reënters the peaceful home life to which he belongs.

The traditional theme of the relationship between parents and children appears centered in the loneliness of children of today, in Stefano Landi's *La casa a due piani* (1923). In this play the author, whose real name is Stefano Pirandello (1895-   ), considers the all-absorbing love of the husband for his wife as the cause of the disintegration of the home and the ruination of the children, one of whom commits suicide. The same theme is given humorous treatment by him in *Un padre ci vuole* (1936). He develops his comedy by reversing the characters of father and son, the former presented as gay and reckless, and the latter sedate and preoccupied. The son assumes the rôle that his father has relinquished.

Those in this field who stood out among their contemporaries during and after the First World War were Dario Niccodemi and Cesare Vico Ludovici. Niccodemi (1875-1934) lived in and for the theatre. He was a dramatic critic in Argentina, secretary of the famous actress Réjane in Paris, and head of a dramatic company that he formed after his return to Italy from France in 1914. He has written plays in Spanish, French, and Italian. In his early plays, written in French, he relied to a great extent on the technique used by Henry Bernstein; sudden and striking contrasts capable of casting a revealing light on a situation and of determining a new direction in the action of the play. This is especially true of *Il rifugio* (1912) which was first written in French. In it he does not go beyond rehandling the old triangle theme by utilizing clever technical means. His interest lies exclusively in the sparkling dialogue in which words are used like polished swords by Gerardo and Saint-Airain for the possession of young Dora.

After his return to Italy, Niccodemi, sobered and saddened by the spectacle of war, produced two plays in which two traits that are fundamental and enduring in his theatre affirm themselves: intimacy and sensitiveness. His characters under a worldly appearance that is used by the playwright for love of contrast, are condemned to a grieving existence. In *L'ombra* (1915), a young wife, an invalid, finds that during her illness her husband has created for himself a new family and that a child has been born to him. What else can she do, according to Niccodemi, but reënter the nook where her existence withers in sadness and loneliness? *Scampolo,* written in the same year and beautifully interpreted by Dina Galli, possesses a romantic vein in the touching and amusing story of a poor girl lost in the noise and confusion of Rome. In her elemental simplicity there abides a distinct personality that is revealed first by her interest in a Bohemian student, whom she happens to meet, and then in her devotion to him. This devotion gradually grows into a love that completely transforms her and rids the student of a profligate woman who had taken hold of him.

That Niccodemi was capable of thoughtful works became more apparent in the plays that followed. They deal with problems arising from the war: *La nemica* (1917), *Il titano* (1917), *Prete nero* (1917), and *La Volata* (1920). *La nemica,* the best of these plays, presents the tragic conflict in the heart of a mother placed by the war in the situation of having to make a choice as to whom she would desire to have die—the legitimate son or the illegitimate. She worships the former and hates the latter, for she sees in him a constant reminder of her guilt. She desires in her heart that the legitimate son be spared. As her eyes are riveted on the prelate who has come to break the news of the death of one of her children, the illegitimate son appears in the doorway.

In *Acidalia* (1922), Niccodemi seems to have abandoned himself to that moment of intellectual bewilderment that was reflected by many authors of the turbulent years that followed the war. The play is a comedy on infidelity seen through the eyes of a pseudo-sociologist who wants to prove that men must be betrayed by their wives in order to attain complete happiness. Yet all his women—a wife, then two mistresses—have apparently been faithful to him, much to his scientific distress. In the end the author, with satirical laughter, shows that all have betrayed him, without happiness as his reward.

A higher tone and a return to a situation heavy with pathos and sacrifice are observable in *La casa segreta* (1923) in which the strange conduct of Claudio Varchi toward youthful Anna is characterized by an extraordinary nobility. It is the drama of Claudio who stifles his love for Anna when he realizes that he is doomed to blindness. He goes to live in a solitary villa where he dictates to his secretary the dreams of his poetic mind.

Niccodemi is a master of dialogue and dramatic technique. His plays and his other efforts on behalf of a dignified theatre in Italy deserve greater praise than has yet been accorded to him.

Cesare Vico Ludovici (1890-   ) is especially well known for *La donna di nessuno* (1919), a work that enjoyed wide and lasting success. Rather than focusing his attention on the daily existence of his characters, he aims at giving expression to emotions and feelings that fringe their lives like a crown of thorns. In his intellectual form of drama, Ludovici considers actual conditions only as the data on which his play is based. Since he is primarily interested in the contrasts and unforeseen situations that beset and torment his characters, actual reality is of secondary importance to him. His art seeks constantly to avoid customary situations. Love for a child had always been a simple means of unraveling a plot. Ludovici, in *La donna di nessuno,* strips the heart of his main character even of this fundamental instinct, making of the woman an automaton. Nevertheless, the effect is truly striking. Viera, in *La buona novella* (1923), finds in herself no moral element that prevents her from experiencing happiness in the fact that she is going to bear an illegitimate child. In *La ruota* (1933), the heroine commits suicide by hurling herself under the wheel of a mill. How exasperating was its constant turning and whirling that marked every moment of her harrowing existence! The life of the woman is soberly presented as an unbearable torment, torn as she is, in the rôle of a wife, between love as a burning passion of the senses and a romantic aspiration toward the purest form of love. Her husband finds it impossible to understand her and she has no other solution than to yield to the voice of the mill wheel. Earlier dramatists, as a rule, have turned to exotic situations to express such a contrast. Ludovici transports it in the ordinary setting of married life, and paints the torment of the woman so powerfully as to make her suicide plausible.

The greatest tribute that can be paid to the art of Ludovici is that, in spite of presenting such tortured and unusual figures, he knows how to hold the attention of large audiences. The truth is that in his plays he touches the fundamental urges of man. The case of Viera in *La buona novella* is particularly illuminating, for in her rebellion against man, she stands as the symbol of motherhood untrammeled by social laws and conventions. Unlike similar heroines in the plays of Praga or Antona-Traversi, she embodies the modern woman who is not so dependent on man as the woman of the past had been.

*
* *

It is customary to single out the theatre of the grotesque and accord to it a separate treatment. The grotesque theatre was an aftergrowth of futurism which had proclaimed in one of its famous "programmi" (1915) the need of the regeneration of the theatre, and in its antagonism to tradition had urged authors to be different at any cost. In reality, if we go beyond the subtleties, forms, and technical experiments of the theatre of the grotesque, we find in it a variety of comedy with a strong leaning towards social satire. Such are the works of Luigi Chiarelli, Luigi Antonelli, and Enrico Cavacchioli, produced during the period of intellectual and artistic chaos of the First World War. They felt the influence of Luigi Pirandello's idea of human personality, but seldom in a positive way.

The genesis of the theatre of the grotesque has been linked to the farcical interpretation that Virgilio Talli gave to *La maschera e il volto* (*The Mask and the Face,* 1916) by Chiarelli, a work said to have been written as serious drama by the author. But this is a legend and nothing more. The grotesque was the sublimation and projection of the mental distress that tormented the generation of Chiarelli, living as it did through the agony, physical and mental, of the First World War. It is interesting to note that the mania for revealing the interplay of reality and dream has been humorously satirized by Arnoldo Fraccaroli (1880-   ) and Luigi Barzini (1874-   ) in their comedy *Quello che non t'aspetti* (1921). The protagonist, in search of escape from the monotony of reality, finds a superreality, created by a troupe of cinema actors, anything but profitable when real thieves ransack and rob his home. This is indicative of the reception that serious-minded people gave to the idiosyncrasies of the theatre of the grotesque. Nevertheless, the effect that this group of young playwrights had on the Italian theatre was highly beneficial and, from their midst, came many comedies of note.

The most distinguished representative of the theatre of the grotesque was Luigi Chiarelli (1886-   ). A depraved and corrupted society forms the warp on which he has woven his comedy, *La maschera e il volto,* the dramatic triumph of 1916. It presents the case of a man who, having said that he would kill his wife if she were unfaithful to him, has not the courage to do so when he finds himself in that predicament. He sends his wife, Savina, abroad, and announces that he has murdered her by drowning her. He is acquitted and becomes a hero to all the ladies of the city, who offer themselves to him. Upon the sudden return of Savina, however, on the day of her planned funeral (the corpse of a woman has been found in the river in a state of putrefaction and all believe it to be that of Savina), Paolo runs the risk of going to prison for having declared himself guilty of a crime he had not committed. Hence his rebellion against the law and society, and the happy dénouement of the play in the reunion of Savina and Paolo. Seldom has the banality of social convention been expressed in grimmer tones. Chiarelli has created truly dramatic situations in making Paolo witness the funeral of a living Savina amidst the insincerity of tears and hollowness of ceremony. He has placed Savina face to face with Luciano Spina, her lover, who had succeeded in having Paolo acquitted by proclaiming the profligacy of his wife. The importance of the play rests on the force of contrasts therein created: the contrast between the reality of Paolo's feelings and the falseness of the mask he wears, between the reality of what has happened and the absurdity of his alleged crime, between Paolo who, when believed guilty of having killed his wife, is freed by the court and lionized by society and Paolo who, innocent, runs the risk of going to prison. This play was staged with great success in London, but failed twice in New York. It is nevertheless intriguing, strong, and impressive drama.

The plays subsequently written by Chiarelli revealed even more clearly, but with infinitely less art, the satirical strain of his temperament. *La scala di seta* (*The Silken Ladder*, 1917) is a satire on political life, viewed through the successful career of Desiré, a dancer, who ends by becoming Prime Minister. *Chimere* (1919) shows how weak moral principles are when selfish interest is at stake. *La morte degli amanti* (1921) is a satire on romantic love, whereas *Fuochi d'artificio* (1923) shows the vacuity of social position in modern society. But *La maschera* is a first-class play. Biting satire is not confined to one aspect only of life. It is directed against life itself, and definite characters move in striking situations.

Another playwright, usually connected with this movement, is Luigi Antonelli (1882-   ). He tried to renew the old comedy by inserting fancy into his plays as a new *deus ex machina*. One usually finds in his works a logical proposition from which he departs into boundless distances, where he leads his characters through extraordinary experiences. In *L'uomo che incontrò se stesso* (1918), the logical proposition from which the author starts is that it is not true that man profits by experience. According to this philosophy, if we could live our lives over again, we would do precisely what we did in our youth. The fantastic adventure in this play is that of unsuspecting Luciano who, after being betrayed by his wife Sonia, goes to a strange island where a magic Dr. Schmidt has the power of transforming the dreams of man into reality. Luciano is thus given the chance of living his life over again. He again falls in love with Sonia, exactly as he had done in his youth. In spite of the abstractness of the motivation, *L'uomo che incontrò se stesso* is an amusing and interesting play.

In *La fiaba dei tre maghi* (1919), Antonelli presents, in each of the three acts of his comedy, three magicians, embodying Truth, Justice, and Poetry. We witness amusing situations through the effects of the exalted virtues of Truth and Justice. In the first act, for instance, through a magic potion, the characters are made to speak the truth with results that can be well imagined. The critique of Justice is not less devastating since we are made to witness the cruelties due this stern force. The only salvation is in poetry, which offers man an escape through illusion. It is evident that the real core of Antonelli's theatre is a satire of man and society. In *Bernardo l'eremita* (1920), Luciano, posing as the fiancé of Nora, whom she has never met, succeeds in making her fall in love with him and in marrying him. In this manner, the "real" fiancé is eliminated by the fictitious one. The author may have meant to embody in the two men actual reality and the fictitious one, but this intellectual motivation is not realized in the play, which remains a weak comedy and nothing more. In *L'isola delle scimmie* (1922), the author projects his idea of the superiority of animal life over human society, in which morality is an aphrodisiac. In one of his latest plays, *Il maestro* (*The Master*, 1934), the author deals with the genuine interest that a famous actor has in the daughter of a woman he once loved. He finds joy in that transference of affection until his quiet dream is shattered by the girl, who falls in love with the actor's youthful son. The everyday reality which in former plays was hidden behind the externals of the grotesque theatre has, with this play, come out in clear evidence.

Another much discussed playwright of this group is Enrico Cavacchioli (1885-   ). Fundamentally, in Cavacchioli there is a typical romantic intuition of man, though carried on the plane of everyday life and exemplified through ordinary mortals. He uses technical contrivances of many kinds: marionettes, wheels that replace human eyes to express their mobility in persons overly excited and under a highly nervous tension, green hair, and the like. But ultimately Cavacchioli looks at man in terms of the split between intellect and the senses. This contrast is expressed by him in *L'uccello del paradiso* (1919) through Lui, a character in the guise of a skeleton dressed in tails and a white tie, who stands as the complementary part of the paltry and negative self of the characters who are swayed by the power of instinct. In the comedy there develops the old contrast between mother and daughter who are in love with the same man, the vacuous Mimotte, lover of the mother. The presence of Lui, who mercilessly dissects their emotions, gives wider range to the play than was encompassed by the old comedy. In *Quella che t'assomiglia* (1919), the place of Lui is taken by marionettes which allow the characters to see in a fixed form the value of their acts in all their vulgarity when stripped of the romantic fringe that they lend to them. The plot is afforded by a war story: a wife who is unfaithful while her husband is at the front. Gabriella is "young, green hair, voluble, sensual, sentimental to the *n*th degree, and finds her humanity only in sentiment." She falls in love with a charlatan, bald and fat, who knows how to use honeyed and beautiful words. The husband returns. He is blind, a wreck of a man. When, sensing the truth of the situation, he tells Gabriella to go with Leonardo if she wishes, the woman, for the first time feels herself bound to him by the heroic unselfishness that he has shown her. He has touched the human being in one who had been only a puppet. The same dualism is found in the ludicrous events of *La danza del ventre* (1921) which presents Pupa, unmoral and irrational, a queer mixture of sensuality and idealism, between Nadir, pure spirit, and Arlecchino, pure sensuality. When Pupa chooses as her lover the servant Arlecchino, Nadir commits suicide; but when love is reduced to pure sensuality, Arlecchino, too, is doomed to be abandoned by Pupa.

That under the dazzling technique of Cavacchioli was hidden a sense of the comical has been proved by his later works. In *L'oasi* (*The Oasis,*

1935), Donatella, placed between the love of an old and celebrated painter and that of a young physician, proves what comedy has always proved: that youth wins over old age.

In spite of many eccentricities, Cavacchioli's works are essentially comedies enlivened by the author's belief that man is split between the little self that obeys the voice of nature and a deeper self that in the past was called conscience.

*
* *

In studying the historical drama, we find ourselves in an atmosphere that is dominated by literary considerations more strongly than is comedy. For the most part, historical dramas are written in verse. Our analysis of such plays can be based only on the consideration of the temperament reflected by each playwright in his interpretation of historical figures and situations.

Gabriele D'Annunzio and Sem Benelli acquired fame in this field before and during the First World War. Less striking personalities have represented the historical play in later years.

Though the fame of Gabriele D'Annunzio (1863-1938) was very great and spread even abroad, it must be said that serious critics and the Italian public in general never accorded them serious recognition. The testimony of Mario Puccini is very illuminating. He informs us that: "As for the stage, the characters of Giacosa and Bracco seemed the exponents, though acceptable, of an art of the third or fourth rank when compared with those of D'Annunzio, who spoke in a winged and hyperbolic language." But he adds: "As for me, the world of D'Annunzio was completely false." The pseudo-intellectual followers of D'Annunzio, as well as D'Annunzio himself, must be looked upon as the product of the industrial civilization that afforded to a large section of the middle class leisure and comforts that previously had been the privilege of the nobility. As was to be expected, these upstarts began to show contempt for their class and to mimic the mannerisms and poses of the aristocracy. D'Annunzio was a classic exemplification of this phenomenon. It is hard to understand the enthusiasm with which such plays as *Gioconda* and *The Dead City* were received in democratic and realistic America.

It is generally conceded that the theatre represents the weakest portion of D'Annunzio's literary activity. He turned to the theatre in 1897 when his fundamental intuition, the reduction of life to pure lust, had become worn out through constant use and fruitless attempts to renew or deepen this inspiration. When a youth in his teens, he had well succeeded in expressing his joyous naturalism through the presentation of peasant men and women observed in the primitive life of his native Abruzzi. His early works in verse and prose are beautiful examples of poetry and story-telling.

But when, in 1881, D'Annunzio went to Rome and came in contact with a complex civilization, he failed to realize that his joyous materialism could only be an artificial over-simplification of life when applied to that environment. His novels, written in subsequent years in the midst of and for the decadent Roman social world, are documents that prove to what complicated pattern he reduced the elementary character of instinct. His dramatic works show the ultimate form that this theme assumed in the man who, in 1892, had said that it was a question "of renewing one's self or of dying." That he had been unable to renew himself is proven by the monotonous repetition of the theme of instinct viewed, both in his novels and in his plays, through the concept of the superman. It is well known that he borrowed that concept from the works of Friedrich Nietzsche. That he did not understand Nietzsche is beside the point. He took from him what he needed in the illusion of reaching the height of tragedy through the exploits of his heroes.

The presence of the superman in D'Annunzio's plays indicated that he had failed to reach, understand, and express the complex and baffling entity called man. The presence of incest, as well as the superman, is indicative also of the effort on the part of the playwright to complicate the theme of instinct upon becoming aware that he had exhausted the artistic presentation of that theme.

An understanding of D'Annunzio's dramatic works becomes clear if we consider them as revolving around the hollow intuition of the superman who is not bound by the laws of average morality. In *La città morta (The Dead City,* 1898), the play centers around Leonardo, an archeologist who goes to Mycenae to excavate the tombs of the Atrides. Written soon after D'Annunzio's trip to Greece, it is projected against the background of Greek civilization viewed in terms of fabulous riches and magnificence. From the tombs of the Atrides there emanates the fatal power that leads the hero to love incestuously his sister Bianca Maria and to kill her when his friend Alessandro, a great poet, falls in love with her. The words of Leonardo, announcing that he has done for her what nobody else would have been able to do, can only be understood if considered as the reflection of an individual not subject to normal passions and ordinary rules of human conduct. In reality, he expresses a hollow concept of man, and his actions are those of a degenerate, even if they are covered with high-sounding phrases. In *Gioconda (Gioconda,* 1899) we have the superman projected through the theme of art. A sculptor, Lucio Settala, needs the adulterous love of Gioconda to create his statues. He sacrifices the devotion of his wife Silvia for her. In *La gloria (Glory,* 1899), the superman is observed in political life. Ruggero Flamma, an imperialist and a nationalist, becomes the lover of an old harlot, Anna Commena, once the mistress of Cesare Bronte, the embodiment of the old liberal party. Tragedy is artificially introduced through the assassination of Flamma by Commena when the former, having established a dictatorship in Rome, realizes his dream of Latin imperialism and of an aristocratic government against which the people rebel. In *Più che l'amore (Beyond Love,* 1906), the superman is embodied in Corrado Branda, an explorer in Italian Africa, who bases his claims to a superhumanity on the fact that he once killed a lioness, and, on another occasion, led a company of native soldiers in an attack against the enemy. Actually, he is a vulgar viveur who in the end cheats at cards after seducing the sister of his best friend. The same concept of morality is applied to Marco Gradico in *La nave (The Ship,* 1908), and to the title character in the tragedy that bears her name, *Fedra (Fedra,* 1909).

The fundamental defect of these plays is that the serious motif that was intended by the author to assert itself is destroyed by lust—destroyed and not opposed. If D'Annunzio had been able to create a clash between the two forces, he would have remained within the boundaries of the human, and a dramatic contrast might have been obtained. By allowing lust to stifle the main theme, D'Annunzio placed himself outside the "boundaries of good and evil" as well as outside the boundaries of true art. *La nave* was meant to glorify the nationalistic aspiration to make the Adriatic an Italian sea, but the love of Marco Gradico for Basiliola occupies the foreground of the play and gradually eliminates the main motif. Love is presented as the supreme justification of the hero's life.

The theme of lust became such an essential and integral part of D'Annunzio's mode of writing as to force its way even into the religious theme dealing with the death of San Sebastian. The play *Le martyre de Saint Sébastien* (1910) was written in French while D'Annunzio lived in France in voluntary exile as a protest against the lack of appreciation of his art on the part of the Italians. It is not difficult to imagine how an artist can mix religion and lust since even the lives of the saints exemplify this combination, though from a different angle. What offends real art is the lack of human feelings that prompts the author to imagine and painstakingly describe the erotic convulsions of the Christian women before the physical beauty of the handsome captain of the imperial guards who was awaiting his death with them.

D'Annunzio's tragedies are static. His characters thunder their greatness from the very beginning, so that there is no possibility of psychological development for them nor any unfolding of the action except toward the climax of a love-affair. His characters speak of "the ego that transforms itself in infinite ways." The spectator waits in vain to see these transformations. The infinite ways in which the ego transforms itself are always reduced to a rhetorical exaltation of the power of lust. The spectator asks in vain why D'Annunzio's characters lay claim to the title of supermen. Their deeds are confined to erotic exploits with the result that their greatness remains a vacuous assumption.

Being subjective to an inordinate degree, D'Annunzio reflects himself constantly in his characters, so that his plays offer little or no variety. His tragedies are gaudy tapestries in which the gifted decorator has immobilized figures that are gigantic in bodily proportions and dwarfed in psychological depth. His characters remind one of Barnini's statues and of the Rococo style.

It has often been said that D'Annunzio wanted to show that man, in the fullness of civilization, remains a prey to instinct as in the days of the caveman. This is precisely what he has failed to do through his literary and academic presentation of instinct. Compare the power of the treatment of this theme in Verga's *La lupa* or Di Giacomo's *Assunta Spina* with the verbose rendering of it in D'Annunzio's plays, and the emptiness of his pompous naturalism will be seen in all its weakness.

There are, however, three plays by D'Annunzio in which he can lay claim to exquisite beauty: *Francesca da Rimini* (*Francesca of Rimini*, 1902), *La figlia di Iorio* (*The Daughter of Iorio*, 1904), and *La fiaccola sotto il moggio* (*The Light under the Bushel*, 1905). *Francesca da Rimini* is a dramatization of the celebrated thirteenth-century love story that Dante presented in the immortal fifth canto of his *Inferno*. The play is important not only because beautiful pages are to be found in it, but also because D'Annunzio has introduced new characters, such as the youthful and fiendish Malatestino and Francesca's exquisite sister. Francesca is endowed in her heroic rôle with a sensitive soul in which love sings with a new voice. The reconstruction of the historical background of the thirteenth century is one of D'Annunzio's literary achievements.

The other two plays possess a note of intimacy in that they are the sublimation of the poet's fond memory of his native Abruzzi. His longing for the place where he spent his youth has taken life in figures and events that are dominated by primitive passions befitting their background. Instinct leads to real tragedy here. D'Annunzio treats his theme lyrically in *La Figlia di Iorio* in presenting Aligi's love, and more realistically in *La fiaccola sotto il moggio* in which we view the decadence of the Sangro family. For lyric beauty, both plays rank among the best that are to be found in Italian literature.

On the whole, D'Annunzio as a dramatist remains a creator of beautiful fragments in an art that is characterized by lack of content. The life that he lived and portrayed made it inevitable that he should be unable to impart to his plays a proper unity though his native talent made it possible for him to write here and there pages of great beauty. He belongs in the company of exquisite decorators, and not in that of the strong creators.

Sem Benelli (1877-   ) also sought in history the basic material of his plays, though he often used realistic themes as a medium of expression. Benelli succeeded best when he reflected himself in characters who are goaded into action by a tormenting consciousness of their own weakness. His first important play was *Tignola* (*The Bookworm*, 1908), a comedy of modern times. The chief character is Giuliano Innocenti, a wan employee in a book-store, who enjoys a short-lived exaltation by presenting himself as a man of the world and full of ideas. For a while he succeeds in his pseudo-heroic rôle and even wins a mistress in a society woman, Adelaide. The husband challenges him to a duel, wounds him, and forces him to reënter the musty air of the book-store to which he is destined. In a vivid scene, the author places face to face Adelaide, who visits the book-store as a dilettante of literature, and the poor bookworm who stands revealed in his pitiful insignificance.

After the success of *Tignola* Benelli tried the historical drama, and to this period we owe three plays that quite properly made him famous: *La maschera di Bruto* (*The Mask of Brutus*, 1908), *La cena delle beffe* (*The Jest*, 1909), and *L'amore dei tre re* (*The Love of the Three Kings*, 1910). The almost subliminal psychology of Giuliano in *Tignola* reflects itself, though in new form, in characters that fundamentally bear the same traits. Lorenzino's de' Medici appears in *La maschera* not in his traditional rôle as a great lover of liberty but as a sly plotter who is tormented by his love for Caterina Ginori. It is for this love that he kills his cousin Alessandro. He is portrayed wandering away from Florence in anguish and despair until the dagger of his assassins, to which he offers himself, brings him liberation from an existence that had become unbearable.

The motif of a tortured mind found a more perfect expression in Giannetto, in *La cena delle beffe* which was twice played with success in New York with distinguished casts that included first the Barrymores and then Basil Sidney. Benelli imagines him as a physically weak youth who has grown up with Neri and Gabriello, the two violent and powerful Chiaramontesi brothers. Giannetto stands out vividly in the humiliations to which he is constantly subjected by them. In the resignation forced on him his mind has become sharp as a sword. With this terrible weapon he engages in a deadly duel with his stronger rivals, planning a jest in the intricate net of which he catches his enemies. He, the weakling, succeeds in taking away from the gigantic Neri his mistress Ginevra, and once his own lady-love. In the diabolic power of his mind he succeeds also in creating a situation in which Neri is driven to kill his brother Gabriello. The madness attributed to Neri in jest becomes madness in reality.

L'amore dei tre re is not, to such an extent as the other plays, mentioned as a drama of striking personalities since in it Benelli wanted to symbolize the effect that Italian civilization had on the medieval barbarians who invaded the beautiful plains of Italy from the north, but were conquered by its more advanced culture. Archibaldo, the old warrior, symbolizes the untamed barbarian who relies only on violence. Manfredo, his son, has, on the contrary, been changed by Christian civilization into a sensitive being, who loves beautiful Flora and marries her. She, however, loves Avito, an Italian prince, for whom she betrays Manfredo. The drama unfolds in a gloomy medieval castle and tragedy stalks into it when Archibaldo strangles unfaithful Flora. Her death is followed by that of her lover, who takes the poison that the old barbarian has placed on her lips, confident that Avito would go to kiss her as she lay in her coffin. Avito dies, but his fate is shared also by Manfredo in the same manner. Although the symbolic motivation of the play transcends that of the action in which the characters engage, the play possesses a rich vein of poetry that flows undisturbed through the love story of Flora and Avito. Its lyrical beauty inspired Montemezzi to write his well-known opera *The Love of the Three Kings*.

This is not the case with the later historical plays in which symbolism assumed a predominant rôle and stifled the meager action that unfolded in them. *Il Mantellaccio* (*The Mantellaccio Society of Poets*, 1911) aimed at presenting the rivalry of various currents of poetry in the sixteenth century: poetry as pure and useless erudition; popular poetry, unadorned and vulgar; and finally poetry as expression of the soul. This esthetic intuition is given expression through the love story of Silvia and Novizio, the latter a member of the Mantellaccio Society. The play wavers between the banal realism of the action and the larger but ineffective meaning that the playwright intended to convey. Like this reconstruction of the sixteenth century, an age to which Benelli was very much attracted, *Rosmunda* (*Rosmunda, Queen of the Lombards*, 1911), *La gorgona* (*The Gorgon*, 1913), *Le nozze dei centauri* (*The Wedding of the Centaurs*, 1915), *Fiorenza* (*Florence*, 1930) and *Caterina Sforza* (*Caterina Sforza*, 1934) do not go beyond an emphatic rendering of historical subjects with a strong stress on the note of patriotism. Although they possess interesting passages, they are ineffectual.

After the First World War, Sem Benelli assumed in his plays the rôle of a self-appointed national poet. He proclaimed the necessity of overcoming materialism and sensuality, and insisted on the peaceful mission of Italy in the world and on the brotherhood of men. In the plays published after six years of silence (1915-1921), Benelli, although keeping his original intuition of a character embodied in an individual torn by the contrast of what he is and what he would like to be, lent to the aspiration of his historical figures a hazy idealism that was not at all consonant with his cynical temperament. Through this orientation, he sank into the rut of the old romantic dualism of spirit and matter, without producing any striking personalities in his work. *Ali* (*Wings*, 1921), *La santa primavera* (*Holy Spring*, 1923), and *L'amorosa tragedia* (*Love and Tragedy*, 1925) are very weak plays in their vaporous idealism. In *Ali*, there is the aspiration toward a life of purity not offended by sensuality, but the drama of Luca and Marta is very blurred. The public found it difficult to understand a play in which Luca claims to need chastity in order to achieve his ideal life, and is killed by the disappointed heroine.

In writing *La santa primavera*, the author stated that he wanted to produce "a vast lyrical poem, freely conceived on a universal theme, not cramped by the narrow limits of acts and scenes." The work is, in fact, a dramatic poem, a hymn to goodness, to the brotherhood of man, to progress, as well as to the greatness of the Italian race.

A didactic purpose is also visible in *L'amorosa tragedia* which had a tremendous success because it was performed in 1925 when Italy was on the verge of a civil war. In it Benelli stressed the need of peace by using a thirteenth-century episode in which figure the feuds between the Black and White factions in the city of Pistoia.

Benelli succeeded better in *L'arzigogolo* (*The Enigma*, 1922), an historical play with a thirteenth-century background. The figure of the jester bears resemblance to Giannetto in *The Jest* in his rôle of conquering beautiful and enigmatic Violante for his master. When Violante awakens his manhood by giving herself to him, Benelli expresses his drama with a force that reminds one of *The Jest*.

At a later date Benelli tried to recast his Giannetto in two characters presented in a realistic environment, but Fabrizio di Poggialto in *Il ragno* (*The Spider*, 1935) and Sergio in *L'elefante* (*The Elephant*, 1937) succeed in being no more than rather distorted character studies.

Sem Benelli, in the essential traits of his intuition of human personality, was the negation of D'Annunzio's superman. D'Annunzio placed on his inwardly weak heroes the mask of the superman; Benelli tears from his characters the mask of grandeur to reveal a pathetically human face that reflects the traits of a pitiful humanity.

Among Benelli's contemporaries who distinguished themselves in the historical drama were Ettore Moschino (1871-   ) and Domenico Tumiati (1874-   ). Moschino, a journalist in his youth who dedicated himself to the theatre, is remembered for his *Cesare Borgia* (1913) in which he presents the tenacious and restless sixteenth-century prince as he meditates over his plans for creating a kingdom for himself in Italy. The play, centering upon the murder of his brother Giovanni, is regarded as a good dramatic poem. Tumiati, well known as an actor, took up the art of playwriting and explored and reconstructed the Risorgimento period. He wrote a cyclical work of vast proportions, preceded by a prologue and followed by five plays that illustrate the Italian struggle for unity through the activities of Mazzini, King Charles Albert, Cavour, and Garibaldi. These plays are better adapted to reading than to production on a stage.

More important is Federico Valerio Ratti (1877-   ). His work is characterized by a symbolic interpretation of the historical events with which he deals. *Il solco quadrato* (*The Square Furrow*) was written in 1911 but was not performed until 1922. Romulus represents in it the collective spirit of social order whereas Remus stands for a romantic individualism that aims at subverting that order. When the latter jumps over the square furrow that Romulus had plowed as the boundary line that was to enclose the future Rome, he is killed because his gesture meant rebellion and chaos. In *Giuda*

(*Judas,* 1923), the betrayer of Christ is ennobled by the author who makes him a sort of Prometheus. In the play Judas does not sell Christ for greed of money. He is after the revelation of the mystery that surrounds life and which, according to him, Christ would reveal to man before his death. Judas is shown inquiring constantly after this mystery that disturbs him. In betraying Christ, he carries out the mission that he has assigned to himself: to lead Christ to death that the veils may be rent and the light of truth may shine on the world. Judas' quest is presented through the reasoning of a passionate dialectician. The play was well received.

Another play that met with success was *Il beffardo* (*The Scoffer* 1919) by Nino Berrini (1879-   ). The scoffer is Cecco Angiolieri, a satirical poet of the time of Dante, who, in his collection of sonnets, related his unhappy life embittered by the unrequited love he bore for a wanton wench by the name of Becchina. The life of Angiolieri was dramatic enough in itself and the task of Berrini was not very difficult in transferring it into his play. The jeering and mocking spirit of the work was well suited to the political and social chaos that prevailed in Italy in 1919.

Criticism of today has justly appraised as negative the work of Gioacchino Forzano (1884-   ) who but yesterday enjoyed a great popularity in fascist Italy. His art bespeaks commercialism to the nth degree. He succeeded in dazzling the paying public through spectacular staging, but he lacks dramatic power. In his career he passed from one style to another, from the historical—*Lorenzino* (*Lorenzino,* 1922), *Ginevra degli Almieri* (*Ginevra of the Almieri,* 1926) to trite comedy—*Un colpo di vento* (*A Gust of Wind,* 1930); from the cyclical presentation of the French Revolution to that of the Italian Risorgimento.

The play in which he has succeeded best is *Gianni Schicchi* (*Gianni Schicchi,* 1918) the plot of which is taken from a well-known episode of Dante's *Inferno.* As is the case with men lacking in inventiveness but gifted in form, Forzano has suceeded well in presenting the roguish character of Gianni Schicchi that tradition offered him already molded.

Several original interpretations of historical characters and myths have appeared in recent years. The myth of Penelope has been cleverly rehandled by Raffaele Calzini (1885-   ) in *La Tela di Penelope* (*Penelope's Weaving,* 1923). Like Gerhardt Hauptmann, the Italian playwright casts a shadow of doubt on the optimism of old father Homer who presented Penelope patiently and faithfully waiting for the return of her wandering husband. In Calzini's version, Penelope is not endowed with any kind of traditional Greek beauty. She appears as a good housewife, plump after twenty years of "widowhood," and greedy for good food. Telemachus is described as a prosaic and ineffectual youth. The royal palace is grimy and nothing remains of the splendid court life of old. Saddened by the contrast between the past grandeur and the present sordidness, Ulysses leaves the island without revealing his identity. After twenty years Penelope forgets for the first time to unravel her web when she contracts a love-affair with Iro, a cheap comedian and one of Ulysses' companions.

The myth of Lucretia is also presented in a new interpretation by Giovanni Cavicchioli (1897-   ). In the traditional version, Sextus, who attacked the noble matron, is placed in a hostile light, cast on him by the many artists who have treated this dramatic episode. In Cavicchioli's *Lucrezia* (*Lucretia*, 1925), the real culprit is her huband, Collatinus, who had proudly boasted of the virtue of his wife, and, in his vanity, had paved the way by his famous test for the rape by Sextus.

Very keen and thoughtful is the psychological interpretation of the resurrection of Lazarus by Giuseppe Antonio Borgese (1882-   ). His *Lazzaro* (*Lazarus,* 1925) presents that Biblical character as a noble youth, greedy for life, who lay for four days in a tomb on the eve of his marriage to beautiful Agar. As Christ calls him back to life, a terrible drama unfolds in him. While his mind and soul urge him to acknowledge the miracle, his natural self rebels at seeing himself as a corpse, a rebellion shared by Agar who shudders at the idea of marrying a man who for four days was a cold cadaver. The climax of the play centers in Lazarus' unconditional acknowledgement of the miracle. As a kneeling multitude witnesses the assumption of Christ to Heaven, Lazarus, who is still struggling within and against himself, is gradually overcome by that vision; and a new resurrection, that of faith in Christ, takes place in him. G. A. Borgese has also written another historical play, *L'Arciduca* (*The Archduke,* 1924) that ascribes the tragedy of Mayerling not to the romantic passion of Rudolph of Austria for Maria Vetsera, but to the struggle which he, an enlightened prince, waged against the reactionary forces of his father's court.

Another interpretation of a traditional theme that attracts our interest is developed by Alberto Spaini (1892-   ), who retold the story of Delilah's betrayal of Samson in *La cattura di Sansone* (1923). Spaini views the betrayal as the effect of Samson's revelation to Delilah of the secret of his strength. By so doing he destroyed the halo of romance that surrounded the hero in the mind of the woman.

From what has been written here it can be seen how large the number of historical plays has been in our time. They also show with what eagerness modern playwrights seek diversity and novelty.

*
* *

We have included in this section plays in which everyday reality loses its clearcut contour, not because of lack of power of expression on the part of the artist, but because the latter aims at giving the value of a symbol to his subject. In such a case, characters whose countenances are intentionally blurred engage in actions that transcend those of the individual.

We find this lyrical afflatus beautifully realized in the works of Ercole

Luigi Morselli (1882-1921). Morselli, who died of tuberculosis, traveled a great deal on the sea in the hope of regaining his health. His plays are variations on the theme of the meaning of life and happiness, questions that poignantly turned over in his mind during his existence as a wanderer. His works give a first impression of pessimism, yet there runs through them a note of faith in the power of the individual imagination. The author went through the hub-bub of the ports of the great markets of the world, among surly men who were too intent on trafficking to look skyward, but he kept his eyes fastened on the high masts of the anchored ships as they gently swayed their tops toward the sky and told him that ultimately only what we dream is true and human material activities avail nothing. This is the message that rings through Morselli's works.

The symbolism and faith of Morselli is revealed in three plays: *Orione* (*Orion*, 1910), *Glauco* (*Glaucus*, 1919), and *Belfagor* (*Belfagor*, published posthumously in 1930). Morselli was a careful and patient artist who loved the pure contours of classical art and the imaginative quality of myths. Both *Orione* and *Glauco* are classical myths recast in modern form. Orione is viewed as a great hunter, an embodiment of instinctive life, gigantic, powerful, happy, given to love and indulging in orgies, who, one day, after being bitten by a small scorpion, suddenly dies. The play seems to be a critique of the vacuity of sensuous life and especially of the age in which we live.

The positive part of Morselli's thought is intimately rendered in *Glauco*. The hero, who seeks adventures far from his native island and becomes unmindful of the great love offered him by Scilla, symbolizes the vain wanderings of the poet when he sought health and peace on the sea and in foreign lands. That peace was not to be reached in the outside world, but closer by, where he could mirror himself in the heart of his Scilla. Glauco returns home after his wanderings and only then discovers how great and beautiful was Scilla's love. But Scilla, an evanescent dream and a diaphanous embodiment of feminine perfection, is dead. The motivation of Glauco was strictly personal: Morselli's wife died while he was on one of his cruises.

Belfagor treats in quite an original manner the motif of the well-known short story by Machiavelli *Belfagor arcidiavolo* (*The Arch-Devil Belfagor*). Departing from Machiavelli, who directed his vitriolic satire against society and marriage, Morselli reinterprets the legend in order to reach a positive and constructive end. The devil comes on earth to experience married life, but the love of Candida for her poor Baldo triumphs over him.

The same thoughtfulness, expressed in a language that at times betrays excessive concern for poetic style, is found in Fausto Maria Martini (1886-1931). Martini lived in intimate communion with a small group of men of letters (Sergio Corrazini, Guido Gozzano, Marino Moretti) who have been qualified by the term *Crepuscolari* (twilight writers). Their art reflected a moment of disillusionment after a life given to sensuality and pleasure.

They sang in minor chords the melancholy and mortification of a humble present. Two of them, Corrazini and Gozzano, died of tuberculosis when very young. Martini was badly maimed in the First World War. The leitmotiv of his art is the idea that in order to reach happiness we must not evade the humble reality of our daily life.

In *Il fioze sotto gli occhi* (*A Flower under One's Very Eyes,* 1921), he presents Silvio, a husband, and his wife Giovanna, who, tired of the monotony of married life, decide to look upon one another as lover and mistress. The reality created by their fancy threatens to overpower Giovanna through the attentions of a suitor, so Silvio takes her away from the worldly atmosphere of Sorrento, and they both return to the modest existence which is theirs. The comedy is not a critique of bourgeois family life, as critics have asserted. On the contrary, it is a critique of the attitude of the two protagonists in their aspiration toward a worldly life. In *L'altra Nanetta* (*The Other Nanetta,* 1923), Martini presents a psychological study of the influence that the dead past can exercise on the living present. After a turbulent youth, Elena has settled down to a peaceful life with her husband Giacomo, a poet. When Giacomo uses her past in a poem, the heroine of which bears the name of Nanetta Elena is so overwhelmed by its reality that she commits suicide. The same theme is continued in *La sera del trenta* (*On the Evening of the Thirtieth,* 1926), called by the author "the drama of what is insignificant." Husband and wife attend a club dance, the last of the season, and are treated in such a way by the snobbish people of the town that their usually peaceful existence is very much embittered. Martini is primarily interested in the psychological effect of the dance on the chief characters, for although the play is developed along realistic lines, the environment does not interest him.

His dreamy mood is revealed in his volume, *Teatro breve* (*Dramatic Sketches,* 1929). In *Un cortile* (*A Courtyard*), the realistic rendering of the background ends in the touching episode of a blind player of a hurdy-gurdy and a blond prostitute, who takes pity on him.

Among the works of Martini there stands out as an anachronism a satirical play, *Ridi, Pagliaccio* (*Laugh, Clown, Laugh,* 1919), staged by Belasco in the United States in the early twenties with great success. It is another document of the tragic conditions that existed in Italy in 1919 as an aftermath of the war. That play marked a momentary eclipse of the positive attitude Martini usually reflected in his works. In Martini, too, the analysis of the human mind constitutes the pivot of his plays.

Ugo Betti (1892-   ) is one of contemporary Italy's best poets. In his poems published under the title of *Re pensieroso* (*The Thoughtful King*), he displays the tenuous grace of fables and legends reinterpreted by his exquisite fancy. His plays give the impression of being the negation of the imaginative world described in his poetry. In them he uses crudely sketched, primitive men of the laboring class, but the main goal of Betti is to dramatize states of mind that assume a tragic and powerful resonance in the elementary consciousness of those men. This is especially true in *Un albergo sul porto* (*An Inn Near the Harbor,* 1934) and *Frana allo scalo nord* (*The Landslide Near the North Wharf,* 1937). The lyrical essence of these plays has been noted by another playwright, Alberto Cecchi, who points out that the dramatic power of *Un albergo sul porto* is not restricted to the lurid atmosphere that is there presented, but to the longing for fatherhood viewed as a cosmic force. Likewise, in *Frana allo scalo nord,* the mob of ragged workers is not used by the author in order to reveal realistic elements in their outward appearance, but to make us aware of a fatal human law, atonement for the wrong we do. It is this feeling that gradually awakens in the consciousness of those men as they wearily walk away from the landslide they have caused. There is a great deal in Betti's plays which is "unexplained and unexpressed," but the absence of these elements is part of the technique consciously used by the poet Betti to render the impalpable atmosphere which surrounds men, their actions, and their emotions.

Alberto Casella (1891-   ) is mentioned here as the author of one of the best plays of the post-war period, *La morte in vacanze* (*Death Takes a Holiday,* 1924). It was performed in that year in Italy and received very coolly. In America, however, it met with an enthusiastic reception. Many Italian critics, including the keen-minded Silvio D'Amico, have looked upon it as if it marked the ultimate degeneration of the grotesque theatre. There is nothing of the grotesque theatre in it. Rather, in its essence, it touches a human note in the old theme of love and death; life and death, so opposed to each other, and yet so near. The motivation of the play rests on the temperament of Grazia, a young girl, ill at ease in the worldly atmosphere of the aristocratic home of the Cattolica family. Grazia is an exquisite creature, who says of herself: "I enjoy everything that gives me a sensation, a vibration, but I enjoy it with melancholy." Melancholy bears within itself the seedling of death in Grazia. She is the only one for whom death under the guise of Prince Sirchi carries no fear. It is natural for her to abandon herself to her love for the stranger who fascinates her. He has revealed to her what the young and featureless Corrado never awoke in her heart. Grazia's love for Prince Sirchi is so strong that she follows him even when he tells her that he is Death.

This fantasy has offered Casella the opportunity of creating beautiful situations: nature, which during the holiday of Death knows no decay; the happiness of life when the black circle that fringes it has been removed; the anguish of Grazia's mother; Sirchi's attachment to life now that Grazia's love has made it so beautiful for him.

Casella has also written other important plays. It is significant that the Russian actress, Tatiana Pavlova, who lived in Italy in the twenties and formed a company of her own, should have noticed the art of Casella, and should have written a play in collaboration with him: *L'imperatrice si diverte* (*The Empress Amuses Herself,* 1934). It is a strong historical and psychological portrayal of Catherine of Russia who, from a humble servant, at last became an empress. The playwright singles out the episode of her love for Mons, chamberlain of Peter the Great, and the efforts of the Czar to discover whether she really loved him. A very dramatic situation is presented when the empress laughs convulsively and dances as Mons is tortured and even when his head is brought before her at the order of the jealous husband.

Rosso di San Secondo (1887-   ) whose real name is Pier Maria Rosso, seems to fit into this section through the central intuition that governs his dramatic output as well as the poetic language with which he describes the stage settings of his plays. For Rosso, humanity lives in exile from a land of purity, and is constantly tormented by memories of it. The closest approximation to this mythical place is found by him in the lands that fringe the Mediterranean and in the people that inhabit them. The negation of it is in the north of Europe with its cold climate and its puritanical inhabitants. This intuition was given to Rosso, in its main traits, by Luigi Pirandello. Rosso elaborated on it through the contrast between the north and the south. From this background, with a logic that is far from flawless, emerge the figures that gave Rosso a great popularity after the First World War. They embody persons who walk on this earth like automatons, restless, unhappy, unmindful of social ties and laws. If they abandon themselves to sensual adventures, they do so only to appease their inner torment.

Marionette, che passione! (*Marionettes of Passion,* 1918) is, in my opinion, the best play Rosso has produced. He has succeeded in projecting into it in living form the exasperation and restlessness of the time in which it was written. There appear in it three main characters that give the play a concentrated development which constitutes one of its chief merits. One afternoon, "the lady with the blue fox fur," "the gentleman in gray," and "the gentleman in mourning" meet in a telegraph office, each with his passion and torment. They cannot resist the urge to speak and confide to each other their anguish. The events that follow are of no importance. Both men feel attracted to the woman and go with her to dine in a restaurant, where the woman's lover appears to take her back to her existence of passion and degradation. The two men remain alone, passive and bewildered. The gentleman in gray slowly puts poison pills in a glass of water, drinks it, leaves the restaurant. The gentleman in black throws himself on the table and breaks into desperate sobs. There are no names given to the characters. They are designated by colors or, for characters that represent ordinary humanity, by their professions: "Guard of the Telegraph Office," "First Worker," "Second Worker," "First Waiter," "Second Waiter." Only a featureless humanity portraying the tormented modern soul, "marionettes who are guided by the thread of passion," as the author states. The power of the play derives from the lyrical motif therein contained. The rest is technique, effective and unforgettable. Here we find the real Rosso, Rosso at his best.

In later plays, such as *La bella addormentata (The Sleeping Beauty,* 1919), he failed to reach the height of *Marionette.* Lyricism is here centered in the title and in the automaton-like existence of the Bella, a prostitute, pastime of the males of the town, who was seduced by a stingy and sordid notary. When she is with child, Il Nero della Zolfara, a sort of daring and violent Robin Hood, forces the notary to marry the Bella whom he has taken under his protection. The play offers many technical contrivances but, in effect, it deals with a theme that had often appeared in the traditional comedy of the sixteenth century and is also found in Luigi Pirandello's *Liolà.* In *La roccia e i monumenti (Stone and Monuments,* 1923), Rosso has no longer relied on exotic technique. This is a serious drama embodying the idea that life is the raw material out of which each person has to fashion himself or herself. This thesis is developed in the study of Brunetto, a hero of the First World War, who finds himself ill at ease in the prose of the daily life to which he has returned. He meets again Isabella, a woman who once loved him but who now is married to a blind man to whom she is devoted. The clash of Brunetto, life in the raw, and Isabella, life constructed into a moral scheme, is inevitable, but the woman resists, as stone monuments resist the storms that lash them.

L'avventura terrestre (Adventure on This Earth, 1924) is also serious drama. The bewilderment of Alessandra, a Russian woman living in Paris, is rendered with vividness and pathos. When she follows Ruggiero to Sicily and finds herself among peasants and miners, though still distressed by the loneliness that oppresses her, she finds relative tranquillity, and in the end decides to cease her wandering life and remain with the philosophical Ruggiero.

In most of Rosso's plays, however, the spectator passes from the intellectual plane to that of the irrational. This is especially true when the dramatist writes more to supply the market with new works than to obey his artistic instinct. In such a case, it is difficult to understand what he means. One remains perplexed before such plays as *Lazzarina fra i coltelli (Lazzarina among Knives,* 1923), *La danza su un piede (Dancing on One Foot,* 1923), *Una cosa di carne (Something Made of Flesh,* 1924), *Il delirio dell' oste Bassà (The Delirium of the Innkeeper Bassà,* 1925), *Tra vestiti che ballano (Among Clothes That Dance,* 1927), and *Canicola (Dog Days,* 1929). We imagine that there must be a poetic nucleus in these plays, but it is evident that the author has failed to express it. Art is primarily an original intuition of reality but it needs also expression and clarity.

Rosso, after the success of *Marionette,* relied too much on technique, so much so that his plays became technical experiments and nothing more.

Where Rosso failed, he produced plays that border on idiocy. In *Marionette,* he created a modern form of tragedy.

*
* *

One of the most truly representative currents of the contemporary theatre has been determined by a consideration of the query: What is reality? The nineteenth century spoke of reality in absolute terms and restricted it, on the whole, to the observable aspects of life close at hand. Many contemporary dramatists have asked whether reality does not also encompass the workings of the intellect and the subconscious self; whether the latter, though more elusive, is not as impelling as the angular reality of the tangible world; whether actual reality may not be influenced by the fantastic one to the point of being changed and molded at will. These are the intellectual positions from which many contemporary authors have looked at life. Psychoanalysis, the cinema with its sudden shifting of backgrounds as well as the quickened tempo of modern life, have influenced this new aspect of dramatic art.

This attitude toward reality is not strictly confined to the playwrights with whom we deal in this chapter. Indeed, it is more or less diffused in the work of most contemporary authors.

In the treatment of characters, this group deviated greatly from the naturalistic tenet of modeling them on actually observed human beings projected on a carefully reconstructed background. The clearcut contour of characters and the detailed rendering of the background are of little concern to the playwright, who is interested in the drama of the mind. In Pirandello, the name of the modern gentleman who, through madness, believes himself to be Henry IV, is not given. Nor does the main character in *Quando si è qualcuno* (*When One Is Somebody,* 1933) bear a name. He is presented as *Qualcuno* (*Somebody*). We have already seen how Rosso di San Secondo and Cavacchioli have resorted to various devices in order to express the impersonal quality of their characters.

In the drama determined by intellectual motivation, the author participates in the action in a more direct manner than did the playwrights of the past. The psychological element in such works plays a much greater rôle than it did in the realistic plays of the nineteenth century. Rather than in material gathered through the observation of matters current and lying near, the contemporary playwright is interested in the modifying influence that reflection exerts on the instinctive impulse to act. His field of observation is to be found in the intellectual and reflective moments of the human mind and imagination.

This type of play was developed to an extraordinary degree during and after the First World War by Luigi Pirandello, who for a long time had been agitating in his novels the problems of human personality conceived as an aggregate of conflicting and shifting selves. We are here considering the treatment of the drama of the mind through his work, not only because he has been the most significant figure of the modern Italian theatre, but also because he exercised a deep and lasting influence on the playwrights of our generation.

The art of Luigi Pirandello (1867-1936) projects itself from a philosophical and religious background, though a vast crowd of characters, tragic and ludicrous at the same time, occupies the foreground of his dramatic work. They gesticulate, shout like persons under great nervous tension; they sneer, but all have a sad story to tell.

For Pirandello life is a cosmic and universal entity that roars, boundless and unfettered, at the fringe of the finite world. Fundamentally, his intuition is not different from the concept that philosophers and religious men have evolved upon looking at the universe and at man. Unlike them, however, Pirandello ponders over what happens to cosmic life when it becomes caught and immobilized in individual forms, be it a tree, an animal, or a man. Ciampa, in *Il berretto a sonagli* (*Cap and Bells,* 1916), informs us that the "divine spirit enters into us and becomes dwarfed into a puppet."

Pirandello has painstakingly dwelt upon the contrast between the cosmic and the individual in life. Man, unlike other beings that crowd the universe, is capable of formulating concepts of his existence and of his very self. Rather than deriving exaltation from this fact, as did the idealists of old, Pirandello reaches bitterly pessimistic conclusions. Through an infernal machine called logic, man reduces himself, his fellowmen, and the whole of reality into an abstract concept, thus losing touch with life. Ciampa declares: "It should be enough to be born puppets through divine will. No, we all add another puppet to that one: the puppet that each of us can be or believes himself to be." This idea is more fully developed in *Il piacere dell' onestà* (*The Pleasure of Honesty,* 1917) in which Baldovino, an outcast of society, is humorously made to serve honesty with the enthusiasm of an old paladin. Baldovino insists on the process that Pirandello calls "costruirsi" ("to build up oneself"), a process thus described by Baldovino as he talks to his rival: "When I enter this house, I present myself to you in a form adapted to the relation that I must assume with you. You, in receiving me, must do the same. But ultimately behind our minds, which are facing each other, behind the Venetian blinds and curtains of hypocrisy, are hidden our most secret thoughts, our most intimate sentiments, all that we really are for ourselves, aside from the relations we wish to establish with one another." What we really are is, for Pirandello, the cosmic that abides in man, painfully imprisoned in the individual self. By his artificial construction of himself, man, instead of obeying the warm flow of life, sees himself live as if from the outside, as if he were another person.

As to our attitudes toward our fellowmen, we crystallize them likewise into cold and unchanging entities. We look at them and say: this man is honest, that one dishonest; this one is serious, that one comical. Here is a poet, here is a husband, here is a teacher. Nothing is more irritating to Pirandello's characters than to be enclosed in these false concepts that destroy in them what they really are. For Pirandello the poet is not only a poet but the aggregate of other aspects of his self. The Father in *Sei Personaggi in cerca d'autore* (*Six Characters in Search of an Author,* 1921) refuses to be branded as immoral, as his step-daughter contemptuously calls him, thus reducing all his self to the image she formed of him when she met him in a house of questionable reputation. Mrs. Morli, in *La signora Morli, una e due* (*Mrs. Morli, One and Two,* 1920), informs us that an individual cannot be categorically said to be serious or light-hearted. Speaking from her own experience, she confides to us that she is joyous and carefree with her former husband Ferrante and serious, silent, and subdued with her lover Lello Carpani. The mother, in *Come prima, megho di prima* (*As Well As Before, Better Than Before,* 1920), resents the fact that, when she left her home because she was disgusted with the sensuality of her husband, the latter told their daughter that her mother had died, picturing her as a saintly woman whom the Lord had called back to Him. When she returns home, this false image prevents her from revealing her identity to her own daughter, who looks upon her as an intruder. Whereupon she leaves home again, but this time takes with her her new-born child who will thus not grow up entertaining any false concept that the husband might nurture in her mind.

The conclusions that Pirandello draws from the contrast between the cosmic and the individual lead him to a destructive critique of man and society. When projected into his characters, this critique constitutes the backbone of his art. Man is pictured as a pitifully carnal being, walking desolately on the bleak road of life. He is unknown to himself, since his consciousness is in a constant state of flux. He is incapable of communicating with others, since words are too inadequate to express his innermost thoughts. In *Come mi vuoi* (*As You Desire Me,* 1930), Pirandello has dwelt on the tragedy of the soul in its inability to find shelter on this earth. Elma, a dancer, is placed by the whim of destiny in the situation of being Cia, the beautiful and lofty wife of Bruno Pieri, who mysteriously disappeared during the First World War. Elma wants to make live again in herself the soul of Cia, but alas! those who surround her are more interested in her physical identity than in her soul. So she returns to her life of torment and passion with Carl Salter, a revolting German whose mistress she is.

Pirandello's vision of society is not very consoling. If man in his intimate nature is cosmic and therefore can live only in absolute freedom, what is the value of organized society with its well-regulated bureaus, its strict laws, unbending codes and conventions? Why so many temples in our cities when the universe is the best place to worship God? Why so many gods, as many at least as there are religions, if the divine personality of God is one?

Pirandello has reflected his political thought in *La nuova colonia* (*The New Colony*, 1928) that hinges precisely on the impossibility of creating a perfect society on this earthly planet. The religious aspect of his inquiry is projected in *Lazzaro* (*Lazarus*, 1929) in which the author, rejecting the idea of the personal survival of the soul, beautifully concludes that through death man reënters the realm of the cosmic.

An interesting conclusion that Pirandello reached in his musing on life is the one relating to art. He saw a violent clash between art, which is life caught in a mold, and actual existence, which is fluid and rebellious against immobility. This motif is diffused in several plays, but is particularly well developed in *Tuda* (*Tuda, a Model*, 1927) and *Trovarsi* (*She Wanted to Find Herself*, 1932). The concept of the mobility of life and the immobility of art is viewed in Tuda in terms of her drama as a model and as a woman who loves Dossi, the artist for whom she poses. The tragic in the play is reached when Giuncano, who represents fluid life, in defense of Tuda strangles Dossi, who stands for static art. The same motif is developed in *Trovarsi* through Donata Genzi who, as an actress, has lost the spontaneity of her emotions, and Elj Nielsen, a youth who symbolizes life in the freest forms. The clash that ensues ends in a positive way in that Donata, being a perfect embodiment of womanhood, succeeds in finding her real self as an artist in Elj's love.

It is natural for the reader to ask himself what attitude toward reality in general Pirandello reached with such a pessimistic view of man and society. Pirandello distinguished between the angular reality of the everyday life that surrounds us and the formalistic reality of our concepts. Both are absurdly limited. But there is another reality which he calls that of the imagination. Through it he refers to the capacity of man to mold the most unbearable situation into one which becomes livable. In this manner he places his faith in the individual efforts directed toward the overcoming of the tragedy of life. This is the most fertile idea that he has exemplified and made living in his plays. *Così è, se vi pare* (*Right You Are, If You Think You Are*, 1917) is a very clear exemplification of this motif. In it the author does not reveal the actual truth concerning the Ponza family that has recently arrived in a small city and has disturbed the peace of its curious and gossiping citizens. The actual truth is of no consequence to him. Reality lies in the pitiful but compassionate deception that Ponza exercises toward Signora Frola, his mother-in-law, and she toward him, concerning the identity of Ponza's wife. The play reaches a climax of touching and exquisite beauty when the latter appears and announces that for Ponza she is the second wife, for Signora Frola she is her daughter, and for herself, no one. In her infinite compassion she has obliterated her very self. The same motif is found in *Il Berretto a sonagli,* though the tone of the play in its humor does not reveal as effectively its intellectual motivation.

Pirandello most often describes individuals who try to escape from the tragedy of their existence. The means which he places at their disposal were perhaps those that he himself used in the unhappy life that he lived with his demented wife while earning a living as a teacher of Italian literature in a college in Rome. Some of his characters try by deceit to find a way out of the situations in which they are placed, as in *Ciascuno a suo modo* (*Each In His Own Way,* 1924). The Father in *Sei personaggi in cerca d'autore* uses voluble words to justify his conduct. Ersilia Drei, in *Vestire gli ignudi* (*Naked,* 1922), tries through a pitiful lie to place a halo of romance around her attempt at suicide. Ciampa resorts to pretending ignorance in order to face the fact that his wife betrays him. Martino Lori, in *Tutto per bene* (*All for the Best,* 1920), carries on through passivity. Henry IV resigns himself to play the rôle of a madman when, after fourteen years of real madness, he finds that he cannot resume his true personality. These artificial but human devices were accorded by Pirandello to his characters, although he saw how painful and imperfect they were.

Deep in Pirandello's heart there was another means of overcoming the tragedy of living: accepting with humility one's human plight. In one of his most tormented plays, *Ciascuno a suo modo,* he writes:

Detach from yourself the little puppet that you create with the fictitious interpretation of your acts and sentiments, and you will immediately see that it has nothing to do with what you are or what you may truly be, with what is in you that you are not conscious of; he is a terrible god, understand, if you oppose him, but he becomes immediately compassionate for every form of guilt if you abandon yourself to him and do not wish to find excuses. . . . Here we teach that you have to build a road on which you walk alone for every step you wish to take, battering down what does not belong to you, because you have not built it yourself, and you have walked on it as a parasite.

In the development of his art Pirandello departed from the elementary naturalism that was prevalent in his youth, and veered more and more toward a psychological art that could adequately express the thought he entrusted to it. Following the precepts of his friends, Luigi Capuana and Giovanni Verga, he first wrote short stories and novels, the settings of many of which are typically naturalistic. He presented in them men and women whom he observed, or had observed, in his native Sicily. In these works there is a sharp contrast between the insignificance of his characters and the intellectual motivation of his stories. This is also true of Pirandello's first attempts at drama around 1915. He recast in dramatic form a great many of his short stories. The humble and elementary characters in whom he enclosed his tragic sentiment of life were not big enough nor possessed of an intellectual stature sufficient to convey his thought. The fullness of Pirandello's art was achieved when he created psychologically complex characters that were capable of carrying in a clear form the weight of his thought and pathos. Then such figures as Henry IV, Elma, the Father, Baldovino, and Donata Genzi appeared to give evidence of the full measure of his art. He had become identified with his characters and merged with them.

Pirandello has received greater recognition abroad than he has in Italy. It was due to a Frenchman, Benjamin Crémieux, and an Irishman, James Joyce, that the international world of letters took cognizance of his art around 1915. Even when fame was accorded to him the Italian public did not share the enthusism of the theatre-going public of France, England, Germany and the United States. He visited this country in 1925 and witnessed the successful staging of *Six Characters in Search of an Author, Henry IV,* and *The Pleasure of Honesty* in the Forty-Fifth Street Theatre in New York. These plays, followed later by *As You Desire Me* with Judith Anderson in the star rôle, created a real stir not only in New York but also in other major cities of the United States. The reception accorded these plays contributed greatly in establishing Pirandello's reputation as a great playwright.

It is strange that Pirandello should have been called an obstruse and cerebral author. Ultimately, there is a strong anti-intellectualistic trend in his thought. His attitudes and conclusions merge with those of thoughtful men who, in the course of centuries, have had the courage to look at life with clear eyes and conclude that human existence is a tragic and short-lived experience.

The basic attitudes that form the nucleus of Pirandello's plays had been expressed by him in 1908, in his *Umorismo (Humor)*. The book attracted little or no attention when it was first published. In subsequent years it has served as a point of reference for a great many contemporary playwrights. We do not claim that Pirandello invented the new psychological form that characterizes the contemporary Italian drama. Its antecedents are to be found not only in Ibsen and in French playwrights, but also in Giacosa and Bracco. But Pirandello developed it and used it more consistently and more successfully than did any other Italian playwright. He firmly established a trend that was felt by his contemporaries both because of his fame and because he founded a company of his own in 1925 that encouraged young playwrights by producing their work. In the plays we have already examined this trend is often visible. It is obvious that it was followed by each author according to his temperament and artistic capacities. At times it was even misused in that it received a mechanical application that hampered rather than helped the artistic effort of the writer. We have seen that the authors of the grotesque theatre often reflected the theory of humor and pathos that Pirandello elucidated in his *Umorismo*. In spirit they are very far from the master.

It is of interest to single out plays and contemporary authors in whom the dramatic forms of Pirandello are very clearly visible. Even an author like Lucio D'Ambra, who had started from an entirely different concept of art, in recent years has veered toward a psychological form that reminds one of

Pirandello. In *Solitudine* (*Solitude*, 1936) a father, having discovered that one of his three children is the fruit of his wife's adultery, keeps his love for the bastard child upon reflecting that for so many years he had looked upon him as his own son. In Pirandello's terms the image of the child obliterates the actual datum of illegitimacy. Likewise, the theme of the reversal of the value of reality through the play of imagination is found in Rosso di San Secondo's *L'illusione dei giorni e delle notti* (*The Illusion of Days and Nights*, 1926), but here it is grotesquely distorted. Rosso imagines that an old man is visited at night by a young woman who gives herself to him because she sees in him an ardent youth, the projection of her dreams.

The author who shows most often, and not in an original form, the influence of Luigi Pirandello is Massimo Bontempelli (1878-   ). Bontempelli appeared as a sort of literary phenomenon in the twenties. He was the originator of the Novecento School through his journal *Novecento,* written first in French and then in Italian, in which he proclaimed with theatrical insistence the value of imagination. He baffled his contemporaries in that, being a man with a thorough classical training, he showed typically futuristic tendencies. In effect, Bontempelli's case can be easily explained through the active part he took in politics and because he carried to absurd extremes the premises of the new psychology. Since unquestionably he has talent, he has succeeded in making an impression on the many, and hence his literary notoriety.

In *Siepe a nordovest* (*High Hedge in the Northwest,* 1923), he has complicated the contrast between the mask and the face by presenting the characters, no longer in the dualism of man and marionette, but in three groups: actors, marionettes, and puppets. He has also reversed the rôle of marionettes, which are supposed to perform for the amusement of men, by having marionettes and actors perform for the enjoyment of puppets. Two actions take place simultaneously on the stage, one carried on by the actors and the other by the marionettes. Both groups move, speak, and act but they are unaware of each other. The Pirandellian idea of the diverse interpretation that can be given to the same act is cynically expressed by making a screen, used by two lovers to cover their tryst, appear to the marionettes as a high hedge to protect a recently built city from the high winds that lash it. The play reduces itself to a banal plot: the love-affair of Carletto and Laura.

In 1925 Bontempelli wrote and published *Nostra Dea* (*Our Goddess*) in which the automaton-like condition of man is exaggerated by making Dea change her personality completely, according to the clothes she wears. When she wears a turtle-gray dress she is gentle and sweet; when she changes to brown with red flowers and a red hat she is voluble, mocking, and masculine. As for herself, she is nothing, by the confession of the author. In substance *Nostra Dea* is an old comedy with the usual ladies, their lovers and jealous husbands, set against the background of an immoral and artificial society.

Likewise, in *Minnie, la candida* (*Minnie, the Pure One,* 1928), we find the current idea of man reduced to an automaton presented in a grotesque form through a woman who fails to distinguish between real men and marionettes.

The only play of Bontempelli that has achieved any degree of significance is *La guardia alla luna* (*Watching for the Moon,* written in 1916 and performed in 1920). The lyrical theme that forms its nucleus is that of a mother who, demented after losing her fifteen-month-old daughter, imagines that the moon has stolen her. After long wanderings among strange people, she goes to the top of a high mountain to kill the moon, but she herself dies of exhaustion and exposure.

Marionettes, which have played such a large part in the Italian theatre, also appear in Ugo Falena's (1875-1931) play, *Il raggio di luna* (*Moonbeam,* 1927), where they are allowed to become animated into real human beings, only to want to become marionettes again. It is evident how far we are from the spirit of Pirandello's sense of the tragedy of man.

The theme of the split personality that so often appears in Pirandello is visible also in the work of Cesare Giulio Viola (1887-   ). In his *Il cuore in due* (*A Heart in Two,* 1926) a girl, who becomes infatuated with the author of a book, is made to discover that the book is the work of two brothers. She succeeds in meeting them and finds them quite different one from the other. Giovanni is a sensitive and almost sickly person whereas Andrea is manly and strong. As might be expected, she chooses Andrea. The conclusion is complicated by Pirandellian considerations of personality that makes heavy reading in this otherwise interesting work. The situation in which Giovanni's peaceful existence with his brother is disturbed by the love of the girl is well presented, yet the mechanical character of the theme is very evident if compared with the deeply human treatment that Pirandello gave to it in *La Signora Morli, una e due.*

A better treatment of the Pirandellian idea of the image that destroys the reality of man is found in the well-received play *La vena d'oro* (*The Vein of Gold,* 1919) by Guglielmo Zorzi (1879-   ). Zorzi presents the reaction of Corrado Usberti upon realizing that his mother has fallen in love with Guido Manfredi, a poet. His reaction is created by the contrast between the image of a mother, through which he had always looked at her, and the sudden apparition of the woman in her. After a long struggle the son is made to accept the situation by the family physician, an old and trusted friend. Even more evident is the influence of Pirandello on Zorzi in his play, *L'immagine* (*The Image,* 1929), in which the love that a woman feels for her adopted son is kindled and kept alive by the image of her real son from whom she was separated when she left her husband. When her real son dies she feels her love for her adopted son die, too.

Orio Vergani (Milan, 1899-   ) has developed in his plays the idea of reality projected on various planes, a concept on which Pirandello strongly insisted and which he beautifully exemplified in his *Sei Personaggi*. Vergani centers his plays on the clash of the actual and the fantastic realities. In *Un vigliacco* (*A Coward,* 1923), he studies the reactions of a sensitive mind as determined by the reading of a novel. The author analyzes subtle states of mind but no action is determined by them. A better play is *Il cammino sulle acque* (*Walking on the Waters,* 1926) in which a husband tries to reconstruct the causes which five years before had brought about his wife's madness. It is really a play within a play, since we witness the past through the reconstruction of it made by the husband as he succeeds in ascertaining that what brought about his wife's tragedy was the discovery that her stepmother had a lover. Unlike Pirandello, who knew how to create drama from the clash of the various planes of reality, Vergani remains static in his plays, since in him the past has no telling influence on the present. These examples, even when not significant, show how persistently contemporary playwrights have sought to treat the themes and forms that Pirandello typified in his art.

Whether in comedy or in lyrical and historical dramas, the outstanding trend in the modern theatre has been characterized by a passionate search into the baffling workings of the human mind. Through it, the theatre of our age has assumed forms that distinguish it from those of the nineteenth century.

VII

Russia

H. W. L. DANA

When we turn from the drama of Western Europe to that of Russia, we are confronted at once with a paradox. For the development of Russian drama presents us with two apparently contradictory features. One is its lateness. The other is its greatness.

The lateness with which drama developed in Russia strikes us the moment we compare it with the other countries of Europe. All through the sixteenth, seventeenth, eighteenth, and early nineteenth centuries, when other great national dramas were at their height, Russian drama lagged far behind. At the time when so many of the greatest authors of other countries—Shakespeare in England, Lope de Vega and Calderón in Spain, Molière and Racine in France, Goethe and Schiller in Germany—were writing their best-known works in dramatic form, most of the great writers in Russia were known primarily as poets or novelists and not as dramatists. One literary historian, Prince Mirski, in his *Encyclopædia Britannica* article on Russian drama, even goes so far as to say: "Old Russia had no theatre and no drama."

The greatness, then, which the Russian theatre ultimately achieved, strikes us as all the more remarkable when we consider the lateness of its beginnings. It is only during the last hundred, or we might say the last fifty years, that the Russian people can be said to have evolved a drama and theatre of their own which can compete with that of other countries. Even in the second half of the nineteenth century, when the Scandinavian countries were exerting a powerful influence on other countries through dramatists such as Ibsen and Strindberg, in Russia it was not so much the dramatists as the novelists—Turgenev, Dostoevski, and Tolstoi—whose influence was felt internationally. With the twentieth century, however, the tide seems at length to have turned in the opposite direction. When, with Chekhov and Gorki, Russian drama at last came to itself and found its voice, it spoke with a terrible sincerity. As the Russian writer Gogol would say: English drama reverberates with a beautiful and wise knowledge of life; French drama glitters and shines and flits away; German drama has a meaning unattainable to any one else; Russian drama, however, is torn from the heart itself.

If we remember that the art of play writing is only one of the many arts of the theatre in Russia and that the director, the actor, the scenic designer there all play an equal part with the dramatist, that in Russia more than anywhere else the theatre is a composite art, we can realize how deep an impression the theatre arts of Russia have at last made upon the rest of the world. If the Russian theatres, like Russian science and Russian industry, long lagged behind the rest of Europe, they have at length caught up. Indeed, one is tempted to say that, if the Russians began behind, they have, at least in some respects, ended ahead. The final greatness of Russian drama has more than made up for its lateness.

What, then, are the reasons for this slowness of Russian drama to develop? One reason that has been given is the remoteness of Russia. Russia did not have in its background, to the same extent as the countries of Western Europe, either the classical traditions of Greek and Roman drama or the medieval traditions of church drama.

It is true that some early sporadic instances can be found in Russia of both secular and religious drama; but they did not have the same dignity or the same continuity that can be found elsewhere in Europe.

In secular drama, for example, there were native bands of strolling jesters and jugglers (*skomorokhi*) which were mentioned as early as 1068 and continued into modern times. Yet these mountebanks and minstrels ranked in the same class with puppet players and dancing bears and their crude secular farces had nothing of the greatness of classical drama. Moreover, they were frowned upon by the Russian Orthodox Church, which retained an exclusive control over cultural life there much longer than the Church did in the West. Even Czar Ivan the Terrible was said to have been rebuked by the clergy for his supposed interest in "God-abhorred comedies."

In religious drama, on the other hand, there were early examples of biblical plays in Russia. These were often acted out by puppets on a sort of three-storied booth (*vertep*): the upper story represented heaven; the central story, earth; and the lower story, hell. Yet this kind of "holy Punch and Judy" had little of the beauty of the best miracle plays and mysteries of England or France. The ritual of the Eastern Church seems to have been rather more narrative and less given to dramatic tropes than the medieval Roman Church. Such miracle plays as came to Russia in the seventeenth century came from Catholic Poland by way of the Ukraine.

Indeed, in all the forms of drama, the chief stimulus in Russia came not so much from native sources as from importations from the West. German, English, French, and Italian actors were invited by the early czars to visit Russia and to act both secular and religious plays at the Imperial Court. Instead, then, of springing up spontaneously from native roots among the common people, Russian drama began at the top, as an importation from abroad, enjoyed by the czars and the courtiers. It was only gradually and only in recent years that it came to reach the masses of the working people.

Russian drama, like Russia itself, was a slumbering giant, slowly waking from a deep sleep. Drama in Russia sprang from a spirit of discontent and rebellion against existing conditions. It gave voice to a series of protests: the protest of the nobles against the Romanovs, the protest of the merchant class against the nobles, the protest of the workers against the merchant class.

The trend of Russian drama—like that of Russian literature in general or indeed that of Russian government—has been a gradual movement "toward the people." It was a movement that gathered both in momentum and magnitude as the centuries went on, passing gradually from the czars and the aristocracy to the merchant classes and the intellectuals, and finally reaching the working classes and the proletariat. In the seventeenth and eighteenth centuries, Russian drama was centered about the czars Peter the Great and Catherine the Great. Throughout the nineteenth century it was still controlled by the nobility and the intelligentsia. It was only in the twentieth century that it came at last into the hands of the common people.

As a background, then, to the later development of Russian drama, let us first glance briefly at the importation of theatres into Russia in the seventeenth century under Peter the Great and the growth of a native Russian drama in the eighteenth century under Catherine the Great.

During the lifetime of Peter the Great (1672-1725), the theatre began to come to life as an important intellectual force in Russia. In 1671, the year before Peter was born, his parents' wedding had been celebrated in Moscow by a church mystery play called *Baba-Yaga*. On October 17, 1672, some four months after Peter's birth, his father, Czar Alexei, invited a German Pastor named Johannes Gottfried Gregory from the Lutheran Colony in Moscow to direct a production in German of a play called *Esther*, based on the familiar Old Testament story. This was performed in the Czar's suburban palace in the Village of the Transfiguration to the east of Moscow. The Court audience sat on wooden benches while the Czar's seat was upholstered in red. The performance is said to have lasted ten hours. As a variety from this and other biblical plays, the pious Czar Alexei enjoyed from time to time dramas on classical subjects; such as one representing Bacchus with his wife, Venus, and his son, Cupid; or *Orpheus and Eurydice,* the first ballet to be staged in Russia.

As a boy of six, Peter had seen some of these plays at his father's court and one of his tutors who had some influence upon him was the Court Poet, Simeon Polotski (1629-1680), a writer and producer of school plays. When, at the age of fifteen, young Peter, already made Czar, traveled abroad and visited Königsberg and Amsterdam, he had a chance to see there plays acted by German and Dutch and English actors. On his return to Moscow, he attempted to open in the Red Square there a building which he called the Comedy House. This was the first regular theatre in Russia, but it was used for visiting actors from foreign lands, rather than for native Russian actors. Peter invited a German troupe and two English actors to come and act there. At the same time, his half-sister, the Princess Sophia, was translating Molière and writing a play of her own on Esther.

In 1705 there was produced in this building in the Red Square an historical play in Russian called *Vladimir*. In this, the triumph of Prince Vladimir over the pagan priests when he introduced Christianity into Russia in the year 988, was dramatized as a prototype of the triumph of Peter the Great over the reactionary elements of his day. Somewhat similarly we shall find long afterwards Peter the Great in turn being used by Soviet dramatists as a prototype of Lenin. This early play on Vladimir had been written by Theophan Prokopovich (1681-1736), who later became the learned clerical advisor and aide of Peter the Great and was made by him Bishop of Novgorod. After Peter's triumph over the invading Swedish army under Charles XII at the Battle of Poltava in 1709, a magnificent dramatic performance was staged in celebration of the victory.

In 1712, the city which Peter the Great had founded and which was named after him, St. Petersburg, became the Imperial Capital; and in the following year, 1713, the Court Theatre was transferred from Moscow to St. Petersburg. Peter's sister, the Grand Duchess Natalie, directed the productions there and wrote some of the plays. One of these was an historical drama in twelve acts called *The Streltsi* and dealt with the musketeers who had attempted to rebel against Peter and had been put to death by him.

In addition to this theatre in St. Petersburg, Peter ordered that plays should be produced at least twice a year in all the schools of the city. Peter the Great had "opened a window upon Europe" and one of the most powerful influences that were to come through that window from the West was European drama which during the seventeenth century had already come to its height in England and Spain and France. It was this influence which was to become more and more important in Russia as the eighteenth century went on and to come into full flower under Catherine the Great.

During the lifetime of Catherine the Great (1729-1796), the Russian theatre and particularly native Russian drama progressed even more rapidly than they had during the life of her grandfather, Peter the Great. Foreign importations were still the vogue. During Catherine's childhood, Italian opera was introduced into Russia and ballets were inserted after every act. The prima ballerina was none other than the mother of the notorious Venetian adventurer Casanova.

More important for the history of Russian drama, however, were the native Russian playwrights and actors such as Sumarokov and Volkov.

Alexander Petrovich Sumarokov (1718-1777) was really the first important Russian playwright and has appropriately been called "the father of Russian drama." He combined the influence of French classical drama with that of Shakespeare. In 1748 he published his *Hamlet*. Here he represents Hamlet as married to Ophelia, which would seem to indicate that he had derived his story through Voltaire's French version rather than directly from Shakespeare. In the following year, 1749, Sumarokov printed and produced at the Academy in St. Petersburg a tragedy of his own called *Khorev*, representing an early prince of Russia as falling in love with his enemy's daughter and finally committing suicide. This historical drama, although it may have been suggested by Shakespeare's chronicle plays, was written not in blank verse but in rhymed Alexandrines and was modeled not so much on the Elizabethan drama of England as on the classical tragedies of France. Voltaire, then, was not far wrong in calling Sumarokov "The Racine of the North." There was sufficient originality in Sumarokov, however, to make his drama a real landmark in the history of the writing of plays in Russia.

If Sumarokov was "the father of Russian drama," it was his friend, Theodore Volkov (1729-1763), who was "the father of the Russian theatre." In 1750 Volkov built in Yaroslavl on the Upper Volga the first regular Russian theatre for native Russian actors. There he directed and acted plays with such success that the local governor carried his fame to the Imperial Court. In 1752 he and his troupe were summoned to St. Petersburg and in 1756, by imperial decree, a Court Theatre was founded there with Sumarokov as director of the theatre and Volkov as stage director and leading actor. Volkov is said to have acted Richard III with what was called a "frenzied temperament."

When Catherine the Great became Empress of Russia in 1762, it is said that she offered to make Volkov a noble and give him a village of seven hundred serfs, but he preferred to remain in the theatre. In honor of her accession to the throne, a magnificent fête was arranged by Sumarokov and Volkov called *The Triumph of Minerva*, in which two hundred gilded chariots were drawn by white oxen. It was through his over-exerting himself in directing this play that Volkov caught a bad cold and died. In his honor the theatre of his native Yaroslavl is today called the Volkov Theatre. The great nineteenth-century Russian actor, Shchepkin, always said of the Russian theatre: "It is to Volkov, Volkov, Volkov, that we are indebted for everything." Even in 1944, in the midst of the German invasion, the Soviet Union paused to celebrate the 215th anniversary of the birth of Volkov.

After Volkov's death, Ivan Dmitrevskoi (1734-1821) became the leading actor and in 1765 traveled abroad to study the French and English theatre and at a dinner in his honor vied with David Garrick in deceiving the guests by his facial expressions. When Catherine founded the first Theatrical School in Russia, it was the actor Dmitrevskoi whom she made the first director.

Catherine the Great, after coming to the throne, took the Russian theatre under her imperial wing, saying: "The theatre is a national school and as such it must be under my control!" At this school the imperial schoolmistress hoped to teach the backward Russians something of the spirit of the enlightenment which she had learned from her friend and correspondent, Monsieur Voltaire, and from the other French philosophers of the period. She was in her way what might have been called later a "parlor pink." In her Hermitage Palace at St. Petersburg, in an auditorium with an amphitheatre of marble seats, she sat in majestic splendor presiding over the plays.

The "Semiramis of the North," as Catherine was called, found time, apart from her educational plans and her diplomacies, her museums and her lovers, to write a number of plays. No one of these has stood the test of time or holds the stage today; but all of them were highly praised then by her favorites who wished to flatter her and even by the great French dramatist, Diderot, who often visited the Russian court and attended the theatre there.

In her comedies she taught lessons as the schoolmistress of the theatre should. In 1772, in her play called *O Tempora!* she castigated the mores of the times. The hypocritical Mrs. Devout (Khanzhakhina) runs to her private chapel—whenever a creditor approaches to collect his bill. The credulous Mrs. Marvel (Chudikhina) asks what good there is in knowing how to read or write. The garrulous Mrs. Prattle (Vestnikova) is given to nothing but superstition and gossip.

In her tragedies, Catherine tried to break away from the prevailing tradition of French classical drama and turned for her subject-matter not to classical antiquity, but to earlier Russian history. In 1786, her historical drama *Oleg* dealt with the legendary Russian conqueror of Kiev in the ninth century. She explained that her tragedies were "modeled on the historical plays of Shakespeare while observing the rules of classical drama." Catherine's plays, however, seemed to attain neither the glory that was Shakespeare nor the grandeur that was Racine.

It was one of her subjects, Denis Ivanovich Fonvizin (1744-1792), whose plays, though few in number, had far more influence on later Russian drama than any of the many plays of Catherine. As a boy of fourteen, he had been taken to the theatre and, as he tells us, "nearly went wild with joy." In 1766, when he was only twenty-two years old, he was asked to read his first play, *The Brigadier General,* before the Empress, who admitted that she was amused. It was a social satire on a general of the old school, who has retired and settled in the country, but continues to translate everything into military language. He tries to rule his son with an iron hand and to force him to marry Sophia, only to discover that his son has already had an affair with Sophia's mother. Sixteen years later, in 1782, came Fonvizin's second play, his masterpiece, and the first Russian play of real, lasting worth. This was called *The Minor* or, as it has also been translated, *The Young Hopeful,* and dealt with the spoiled young heir of a would-be aristocratic family. Mitrofan, as this sixteen-year-old son is called, is a boorish youth who sees no need for a nobleman to be educated. His teachers consist of a former German coachman who tries to teach him science, an ignorant priest who attempts to correct his bad grammar, and an old drunken soldier who seeks to pound arithmetic into him. This pattern gives Fonvizin a chance to satirize the whole educational system of nobles of old Russia. Why should a nobleman learn geography? Let his coachman find out the way. All learning is nonsense. Mitrofan's grandfather was a governor for fifteen years and died illiterate—died of hunger, lying on a chest full of money. His great-uncle, we are told, did not care to know anything, but what a head he had! Riding horseback, very drunk, he struck his head on a stone archway and merely asked if the stone was broken. A learned man, under such circumstances, would have split his head. Why should Mitrofan become as wise as Aristotle? Aristotle was in his grave. When Mitrofan stuffs his stomach with food, he gets a stomach-ache. His head is weaker than his stomach. Why should he stuff his head? He hates his studies and cries impatiently: "I don't want to study; I want to marry." His fond and foolish mother, Mrs. Simpleton (Prostakova), indulges him by letting him neglect his studies and by arranging to have him marry an heiress. She continues to treat him as though he were her "baby," her "Mitrofanushka." The way in which she spoils her overgrown bumpkin of a boy, until finally the ungrateful brute turns and rends her, reminds us of the way in which Mrs. Hardcastle indulges Tony Lumpkin in Goldsmith's *She Stoops to Conquer*. Fonvizin's method of giving his characters symbolic names also suggests the plays which Goldsmith and Sheridan were writing in England within the same decade. As theirs are the only English plays of the eighteenth century which are still commonly acted, so Fonvizin's *Minor* is the one Russian play of the eighteenth century which most consistently holds the stage in Russia. Mitrofan is still such a horrible example of the product of privilege that, whenever a young man in Russia claims a special virtue in being a nobleman, he is reminded: "Mitrofan, also, was a nobleman."

Fonvizin's satire, however, went still farther than merely poking fun at this young booby, and he attacks the whole beastliness of the landed proprietors of the old Russia and the injustice of the serfdom which then prevailed. Mitrofan's uncle, Mr. Beastly (Skotinin), reiterates a passion for pigs. "Only pigs live like swells," he says, and feels that he himself is more akin to hogs than to human beings. He believes in treating his pigs better than his serfs. He urges his sister to "squeeze" her serfs, but she replies: "Since we've taken away everything the peasants have, we can't possibly squeeze anything more out of them." He cries: "Isn't a nobleman at liberty to beat his servant when he feels like it?" It is in vain that Mr. Oldsense (Starodom) pleads: "Nobody is at liberty to tyrannize. It is unlawful for a man to oppress his fellow men with slavery." Already Fonvizin made his plea for the emancipation of the serfs which only came eighty years afterward.

His satire showed the way for later Russian and Soviet drama. Since the Russian Revolution, Fonvizin's *Minor* remained popular as a terrible picture of the old Russia. On the stage of The Theatre of the Revolution, they rubbed in the satire unmercifully, making the home of the country nobles look like a huge pigsty, and the family portraits on the walls look like hogs.

Fonvizin had even dared to criticize the court of Catherine II with its "high society and petty souls." Those who can be useful to the court stay away. Only those go there to whom the court can be useful. Fortunately for Fonvizin, the court favorite, the powerful Prince Potemkin, was hugely amused and cried out: "Bravo, Denis! Either die now or never write again!" —an alternative of which Fonvizin rejected both halves.

Younger contemporaries of Fonvizin, however, who would push their satire still further, were not so immune. The great Catherine was no longer so liberal as she had been. She savagely suppressed the revolt under Pugachev in 1775. When the American Revolution broke out in the same year and General Washington sent a young American envoy, Mr. Francis Dana, to seek recognition, the Russian Empress refused to receive him or to recognize the American Revolution or any people so revolutionary as the Americans. Finally with the coming of the French Revolution, the Imperial Volcano fairly fulminated with fury.

In 1789, the year of the storming of the Bastille, a dramatist named Jacob Borisovich Knyazhnin (1742-1791), the son-in-law of Sumarokov, ventured to write an historical tragedy called *Vadim of Novgorod,* in which the democratic views of the ninth-century Russian hero, Vadim, were made to contrast with the monarchical views of Rurik. This revolutionary spirit of political free-thinking brought down Catherine's wrath on the author's head. All production of the play was forbidden and, even after the dramatist's death when the text was printed, the Empress ordered the book to be burnt by the public executioner.

Again, toward the end of Catherine's reign, a younger dramatist, Vasili Vasilevich Kapnist (1757-1824) made bold to write a play savagely satirizing the corruption, bribery, and extortion of her law courts. Kapnist called his drama *Chicanery* and in one powerful scene had his lawyers and judges and magistrates join together in singing a song with the refrain: "Grab! Grab! Grab!" No wonder Catherine, appalled by this ruthless showing up of judicial injustice in her Empire, ordered the play banned. It was only toward the very end of the eighteenth century, in 1798, two years after Catherine's death, that *Chicanery* was permitted to be acted. Its fame then spread like wild-fire through Russia and prepared the way for the long series of stage attacks on corruption and privilege, extending from the comedies of Griboedov and Gogol in the early nineteenth century down to the Soviet satires of the twentieth.

In the early years of the nineteenth century, the Russians, seeing how the armies of Napoleon were overrunning the rest of Europe, felt that their turn might come next and a number of patriotic plays were produced stirring up the spirit of national defense.

Some of these were based on earlier invasions in Russian history and the heroic defenders of the motherland in the past. For example, on January 14, 1807, Vladislav Alexandrovich Ozerov (1769-1816) produced his play *Dmitri Donskoi* in which, by depicting the defense of Russian by Dmitri on the River Don in 1380 against the invading army of the Tartars under

Mamai, he clearly envisages the defense of Russia under Alexander I from an invasion of Napoleon. The words of Dmitri, "Better an honest death than an ignoble life," helped inspire the Russians to meet the menace that was threatening them.

Only a few months after the production of this play, Michael Kryukovski (1781-1811) produced a play called *Pozharski* on May 22, 1807. In this he represents the defense of Russia against the invading Polish army in 1612 and in the willingness of his heroes to sacrifice their own personal feelings for the sake of their native land, he was clearly warning the Russians against the impending danger of a Napoleonic invasion. It was this play that was produced at the opening of the great Alexandrinski Theatre in St. Petersburg on August 21, 1832, and it was revived again at the centenary of that theatre in 1932.

Just as these plays were written on the eve of Napoleon's invasion of 1812, so similar plays dealing with these same heroes, Dmitri Donskoi and Pozharski and many other earlier defenders of Russia, were acted on the eve of Hitler's attack in 1941.

In 1812, when Napoleon marched on Moscow, a play called *General Levy* by Stefan Ivanovich Viskovatov helped to arouse the populace to the defense of their city; and at the end of the same year, when Napoleon had retreated, *The Cossack Poet* by Prince Alexander Alexandrovich Shakhovski (1777-1811) was performed in celebration of the Russian victory.

Far more important as drama than any of these patriotic plays of the Napoleonic era was a play written a decade later—a play which many have considered the greatest of all in the history of Russian drama. This was written by Alexander Sergeevich Griboedov (1795-1829). He had been a brilliant youth, entering the university of Moscow at the age of eleven, and moving in the revolutionary circles of the young Decembrists. He was only twenty-seven when in 1822 he wrote his masterpiece, *Woe from Wit* (*Gore ot Uma*), which has also been translated variously as *The Misfortune of Being Clever, Intelligence Comes to Grief, To Understand Is to Suffer, Too Thoughtful to be Happy, The Sorrows of the Spirit, Wit Works Woe,* and in several other ways.

The hero of the play, Chatski, like Griboedov himself and to a certain extent like Pushkin and Lermontov, is a young intellectual, whose very brilliance of mind leads him into suffering. He is returning to Moscow from three years' absence abroad, eager to see Sophie whom he loves and feeling that "sweet and pleasant will be the smoke of the fatherland." But the homecoming turns bitter. He finds Sophie throwing herself at a worthless and sneaking sycophant. He finds that in Moscow, "though there may be new houses, there are the same old prejudices." He suffers a "million torments." With withering scorn he tells people just what he thinks of them. They look upon him as a "dangerous dreamer" and lay the blame on his reading of books. Like Shakespeare's Hamlet, the very superiority of his brain makes them think that he has gone out of his mind. Like Molière's Misanthrope, he rails against the society he finds and leaves in disgust.

Instead, however, of using the blank verse of Shakespeare or the Alexandrines of Molière to express these ideas, Griboedov used short, irregular, and intricate rhymed verse such as La Fontaine and Krylov—had used in their satirical fables, so that the epigrams and repartee of his light and lively dialogue fairly sparkled and still continue to sparkle when acted today.

This play circulated during Griboedov's life in thousands of manuscript copies, but the powers that be could not bear to have so devastating a satire of themselves made public. On account of the Czar's censorship and the author's arrest for revolutionary activities, he could never get the play performed or published during his lifetime. When only thirty-four years old, Griboedov was assassinated while on a mission to Teheran in 1829. It was forty years after his death before the complete play was acted, but since then it has become a great favorite. Enthusiastic Soviet audiences at the end of the play cry out from the darkness of the auditorium for "Chatski! Chatski! Chatski!" And when in 1928 Meyerhold risked destroying the masterpiece of Griboedov to create a masterpiece of his own, the whole Russian people entered into furious dispute about the liberties taken with a play that meant so much to them. Many lines from the play have become as familiar as proverbs and at least six Soviet plays have taken as their titles phrases quoted from Griboedov's masterpiece.

Although he never wrote so sparkling a play as Griboedov, Alexander Sergeevich Pushkin (1799-1837) was, in all other respects, an even greater poet—the greatest that Russia has ever known. His most important poetic drama, *Boris Godunov,* of 1825, is the one Russian play which most nearly reaches the tragic grandeur of Shakespeare. Pushkin tells us that he learned English in order to read Shakespeare, whom he felt to be, after God, the greatest creator of living beings. In the preface to this play he said it was Shakespeare who gave him the idea of writing a historical play in blank verse. As Shakespeare had told "sad stories of the deaths of kings," English kings who had lived a hundred years or more before his day, so Pushkin turned back two centuries before his day, to the story of the Russian Czar Boris Godunov. As in the case of some of Shakespeare's kings, this was the solemn chronicle of a monarch who had himself usurped the throne and then lived in terror of some other usurper's taking it from him. In the scenes in which the grim Boris treats his own children with kindness, Pushkin, like Shakespeare, shows the marks of a great dramatist by the tenderness and understanding with which he depicts children. The scenes in which he deals with the common people were, like those of Shakespeare, pitched in a different key from the other scenes; but they went beyond Shakespeare by showing the continuous wail, the ever-growing ground-swell of discontent among the people as a mass, in a way that anticipated the handling of the crowds in the mass scenes of Soviet plays.

Pushkin's play, *Boris Godunov*, became still more familiar, both inside and outside of Russia, in the form of the opera by Musorgski; but it is also still acted in the Soviet Union as a play in the form in which Pushkin wrote it.

The other plays of Pushkin include four short *Dramatic Scenes*, published in 1830. These were also written in blank verse but were rather derivative in their subject-matter. In one of these, *The Stone Guest*, Pushkin adapts the story of Molière's *Don Juan*, but makes his hero fearless and sincere although immoral. In *The Avaricious Knight*, he again differs from Molière's *Avare* by somewhat ennobling the characters both of the old miser and also of the young spendthrift. In *The Feast during the Plague*, his dramatization in verse is a distinct improvement on Christopher North's prose story, *The City of the Plague*. In *Mozart and Salieri*, the most original of these shorter plays, Pushkin analyzes very beautifully the psychology which led the jealous Salieri to poison his more gifted rival.

Two years later, in 1832, Pushkin wrote his uncompleted folk drama, *Rusalka*, about a miller's daughter who is betrayed by a prince, throws herself into the Dnieper River, and becomes a water-nymph (*rusalka*). This play and some of the other shorter plays were later turned into operas, as was Pushkin's great narrative poem, *Eugene Onegin*. Much as he had represented Lenski's death in that poem, Pushkin himself, six years later, was killed in a duel in the snow.

All of Pushkin's narrative poems and tales and his own life and death have furnished an almost inexhaustible reservoir from which later dramatists have drawn the sources for countless plays. In 1937, in the great celebrations in the Soviet Union in commemoration of the centenary of Pushkin's death, fully a hundred plays, operas, ballets, and films, based directly or indirectly on Pushkin were produced. Still more recently, in 1943, Michael Bulgakov's play *The Death of Pushkin*, produced by the Moscow Art Theatre in the midst of the German invasion, proved a really worthy tribute to the greatest of Russian poets.

Like Pushkin, Michael Yurievich Lermontov (1814-1841) was greater as a poet than as a dramatist. He began writing romantic plays at the age of fifteen and produced his most important dramatic work, *The Masquerade*, in 1835 when he was not yet twenty-one years of age. It was written in the irregular rhythm and rhyme of Griboedov's *Woe from Wit;* but whereas Chatski, the hero of that play, in his struggle against hostile forces is a sort of Russian Hamlet, Lermontov's hero, Arbenin, in his jealousy becomes a sort of Russian Othello.

Arbenin is an enlightened and clever man, who has become utterly disillusioned about the external splendor and internal emptiness of society, exemplified by the masked ball to which he takes his wife. His wife, Nina, is the one ideal which he still retains, the one thing he still loves. When a bracelet, which she had let fall, is discovered by him in the hands of a prince, the bracelet takes the place that the handkerchief did in Shakspeare's *Othello*, and Arbenin poisons his wife, trying in vain to force her to confess her guilt. Too late, the prince declares her complete innocence, and Arbenin, overwhelmed with remorse, goes mad.

There is much of the Byronic in Arbenin, as there is in Lermontov; but *The Masquerade* has held the stage longer than most of Byron's plays. Indeed, a brilliant production of it under the direction of Meyerhold—in which the guests at the masked ball, in the magnificent costumes of the old Russian aristocracy, streamed up curving staircases of the orchestra pit on to the stage—was playing its opening night in the great Alexandrinski Theatre in Petrograd on February 26, 1917, the very night when the monarchy was overthrown. When the performance was over, the audience emerging from the theatre into the Nevski Prospect were still so entranced by the romantic poetry of the play that they seemed unable to grasp the reality of the news of the revolution which was then taking place on the streets outside the theatre.

Apart from his plays, many of Lermontov's poems and stories were dramatized as Pushkin's were. The promise of still greater plays and poems was cut short by Lermontov's untimely death. For in 1841, when Lermontov was only twenty-seven years old, he was killed in a duel as Pushkin had been only four years earlier.

In passing from the plays of Pushkin and Lermontov to those of Nicholas Vasilievich Gogol (1809-1852), we pass from poetry to prose, from romanticism to realism. Gogol's great realistic prose play, however, had a far greater influence upon later Russian drama than did their romantic plays in verse.

Gogol was the son of a Ukrainian amateur playwright, and as a boy had acted at school the part of Madame Simpleton (Prostakova) in Fonvizin's *Minor*. He wanted to carry on the use of symbolic names and push the realistic satire still further. Taking a story suggested to him by the poet Pushkin, he developed it into his great play, *The Inspector General (Revizor)*; first produced on April 19, 1836, it had an instant success and has held the stage ever since.

The Inspector General was based on the same formula as Griboedov's *Woe from Wit*—that of a character suddenly introduced from outside, showing up the foibles of the other characters one by one, and then suddenly leaving at the end of the play. In every other respect, however, the plays were entirely different. In place of Griboedov's beautiful verse, Gogol used the realistic prose of actual speech. Instead of making the central character like Griboedov's Chatski, a sincere and honest intellectual scorned by the stupid society around him, Gogol's Khlestakov was an imposter pretending to be the Inspector General and wooed and bribed by all the functionaries of the town from the mayor down. There are no redeeming characters among them. With merciless satire, Gogol shows up the heads of departments one by one: the postmaster who opens other peoples' mail; the school superintendent who smashes the school furniture; the hospital superintendent who lets his patients smoke; the judge who breeds geese in the courthouse. Each one greases the palm of the supposed Inspector General hoping that he would give a favorable report of him in St. Petersburg. The Mayor even hopes to marry his daughter to the imposter.

Suddenly Khlestakov drives off in a carriage drawn by swift horses, taking all the bribes with him. A letter which he had written to a friend elsewhere has been intercepted by the postmaster and is read aloud to all the town functionaries. In this he boasts how easily he has fooled them all into believing him an Inspector General. He declares that the Mayor is a stupid jackass, the postmaster an old soak, the hospital superintendent a pig in a nightcap. As they look at each other, each one sees how true it is of the others, even if it is untrue of himself The Mayor stares at the faces about him—yes, and at the audience too—and cries: "I can see nothing but pigs' snouts in front of me instead of faces."

The Mayor is afraid that some wretched scribbler will put him into a comedy. Gogol did. The Mayor would damn all writers. When the other characters in the play laugh at him, he turns to them and says to them what Gogol says in effect to his audience, what all Russian dramatists have said to their audiences ever since: "What are you laughing at? You are laughing at yourselves!"

At the end of the play, while the characters are all blaming each other for the pickle they are in, a police officer suddenly enters and announces that the real Inspector General from St. Petersburg has arrived. Each gives a look of horror and is transfixed like a wax image in the final tableau. It is the most startling coup de théâtre that is to be found in any play. Indeed the whole plot may be said to be the most ingenious of any in Russian drama.

Naturally there were many objections to the play on the part of those who did not like having their graft laid bare, but it was saved from censorship by its humor. Any one who protested would be accused of lacking a sense of humor. The Czar Nicholas I sanctioned the play by attending the first performance, but he said afterwards: "It hits every one, and me most of all!"

It was indeed the most devastating revelation of the appalling conditions among the Russian provincial bureaucrats. Although it was a comedy and written with a light touch, it gave an almost tragic sense of the terrific problem that the Russian governmental system presented. In spite of that, or perhaps because of that, the play quickly became the most popular of all plays of Russia. The Maly Theatre in Moscow, even since the Russian Revolution, continues to open each theatrical season with it. It has been the most influential of all Russian plays. If it has been said that all later Russian fiction came out of Gogol's *Cloak*, it may be said that all later Russian drama has come out of Gogol's *Inspector General*.

Gogol's other plays are less important. *The Order of St. Vladimir, 3rd Class,* which he started in 1833, was to be a satire on St. Petersburg bureaucracy and the competition for honorary decorations. Gogol soon realized, however, that it would never be permitted on the stage, and he never finished it. It is preserved only in fragments such as *An Official's Morning, Litigation,* and *The Servants' Hall.* In *Marriage,* which had first been called *The Suitors,* a young girl rejects her various suitors in turn—a drunken army officer, a woman-beater named Yaichnitza (Scrambled-Eggs) and an avaricious naval officer—only to accept a timid government clerk. The successful suitor, however, when he finds himself about to be married to her, escapes by jumping out of a window and riding off in a cab. Finally in *The Gamblers* in 1842, Gogol presented a professional card-sharper, who, just when he thinks he has outwitted a gang of gamblers and an apparently innocent young man, finds to his horror that they have got the best of him.

In all these plays, with a ruthless showing up of all sorts and conditions of men and a dénouement that takes away the last hope of finding any one innocent or virtuous, Gogol prepared the way for the coming of Ostrovski and all later Russian comedy.

Most of the great writers of Russia during the first half of the nineteenth century—Pushkin, Lermontov, even Gogol—were primarily poets or novelists and only secondarily dramatists. At most only one or two of their plays were acted. The theatre had not become the chief vehicle for Russian authors, as it had been for English, Spanish, French, and German authors. During the last hundred years, however, beginning with the middle of the nineteenth century, drama has emerged into a far greater importance in Russia.

During the second half of the nineteenth century there was one great writer who was primarily, almost exclusively a dramatist. This was Alexander Nikolaevich Ostrovski (1823-1886). Far from being remembered by a single play, some forty or fifty of his plays continue to hold the stage. All told we have twice as many of his plays as we have of Shakespeare's. Indeed, among all Russian playwrights, Ostrovski looms today as the most important single influence in the history of Russian drama.

He was born and brought up in that part of Moscow which lies on the other side of the Moskva River, a region that had come to be occupied by the newly-rich tradesmen and merchants. They were often the sons of serfs and, having lost the finer qualities of the peasants, retained only the backward and brutal prejudices mingled with the new power that money gave to them. They had not been submitted to the more enlightened influences which Peter the Great and Catherine the Great had brought into St. Petersburg. The environment was one where the head of the family exerted a patriarchal prejudice and became a domineering and stubborn autocrat (*samodur*). The part of Moscow where they lived became one of benighted greed that was described at the time as "The Realm of Darkness." The searchlight which Ostrovski threw upon this region in his drama was called "A Ray of Light in the Realm of Darkness."

Ostrovski's father had been a lawyer for this newly powerful middle class; Ostrovski himself, after being expelled from the University of Moscow, became for eight years a clerk in the so-called "Conscience Court," where tyrannical Moscovite parents brought cases against their own sons and daughters. This gave Ostrovski his marvelous insight into the conflicts between generations that were often so heartrending in that middle-class life. His first book, published in 1847 and his only non-dramatic work, was called *Memoirs of a Trans-Moskva Denizen* and gave his account of his experiences among the merchants who were growing in power by the middle of the nineteenth century.

It was from this same background that Ostrovski drew the human documents which he has analyzed for us so penetratingly in his long series of plays. In a play begun in 1847 as *The Bankrupt* and finished in 1850 with a title taken from a Russian proverb, *It's a Family Affair—We'll Settle It Ourselves,* he deals with the fraudulent bankruptcies so common among these merchants. He shows up his characters as mercilessly as Gogol had those in *The Inspector General,* but there is no ideal of poetic justic introduced at the end threatening to punish the wicked. On the contrary, the villains remain in power and vice is depicted as triumphing unrebuked. It was this that led the play to be called "cynical and dirty." Ostrovski's fierce denunciation of the merchants raised their wrath and the production of the play was, through their influence, prohibited by the censor until 1861. Finally, however, it came to be ranged with *The Minor, Woe from Wit,* and *The Inspector General* as one of the four greatest Russian comedies.

Ostrovski continued in 1852 with *The Poor Bride,* where the heroine, Marya, is forced by a domineering and greedy mother to give up her love for a romantic admirer and give herself instead to a dissolute but financially successful government official. In the fifth act there was a mass scene, in the midst of which the former mistress of the government official was introduced; but the censor would not allow the play to be staged unless this whole last act was omitted. In 1854 in *Poverty Is No Crime,* Ostrovski gives his answer to the all-too-common feeling among the rich merchants that if a man were poor, it was nothing but his own fault. He shows us the true nobility of character in the impoverished and supposedly worthless Lyubim, a rôle beloved by Russian actors ever since. *A Profitable Position* in 1857 showed up the unscrupulous means used to obtain lucrative posts in a corrupt bureaucracy, and met a great success among the common people who recognized the truth of the indictment.

In *The Ward,* which has also been translated as *The Protégée of the Mistress,* the scene was shifted from Moscow to a country estate, where the selfish and self-righteous Mme Ulanbekov is a rich landed proprietor. She will not have her ward married to her son, but to a drunken godson instead. The tyrannical old woman's word is law to her two thousand serfs, who are for her so many cattle. The play was produced in 1859 and was, with Pimenski's *Bitter Fate* of the same year, among the plays that aroused public sentiment to the suffering under serfdom to such an extent that they helped bring about the emancipation of the serfs two years later, in 1861.

Meanwhile in 1860, Ostrovski had taken up again the character of the despotic elder generation, changing the setting to a quiet village on the Volga. This play, *The Thunderstorm,* pushed the theme to the point of tragedy and is considered by many to be his masterpiece. Here Ekaterina is loved by her fond but foolish husband. Their lives, however, are made miserable by the perpetual nagging of his obdurate mother. In her husband's absence, the young wife falls in love with a young man who has been similarly tyrannized by his uncle. In her endeavor to resist this temptation, she starts to throw into the Volga river the key which opens the gate into the garden where a rendezvous with her lover has been arranged. With an almost modern touch, however, she realizes that she will reproach herself in the future for having thrown away this one chance of happiness; so she holds on to the key and unlocks the gate. The husband unexpectedly returns. Then, in the midst of a crashing thunderstorm and flashes of lightning that show up a painting of the Last Judgment on the walls of an old church, she is filled with pangs of remorse, confesses her sins, and throws herself off the cliff into the Volga river. The powerful rôle of Ekaterina has been ever since a favorite of actresses, either when done by Tarasova with the beautiful realism of the Moscow Art Theatre, or by Alice Koonan with the stylized sets of the Kamerny Theatre, or by a great Armenian actress in far-off Erivan.

In *Sin and Sorrow Are Common to All,* written in 1863, Ostrovski again turns to a tragic theme, but this time the characters are very different. A good and loyal husband, a small shopkeeper, has married above his class socially to the pretentious daughter of a government official. She despises him with an insulting scorn which drives him to such fury that he finally murders her. A play called *At the Jolly Spot* (1866) takes it title from the name of a country inn where the somewhat sordid action, laid forty years earlier, takes place.

In *Enough Stupidity in Every Wise Man,* written in 1868 and often regarded as Ostrovski's masterpiece, the central character is the clever and unscrupulous Glumov. It is he who is the wise man—or, if you prefer, the shrewd fellow—who is almost trapped by one bit of stupidity. Like Griboedov's Chatski, he has the intelligence to see the dishonesty of the whole bourgeois society around him, but unlike Chatski he is not going to say so and suffer "the sorrows of the spirit." On the contrary, he shrewdly decides, by flattery and bribery and anonymous letters, to make use of the various dishonesties of the others in order to bring about his own advancement and to gain a lucrative position and the hand of a young heiress. But there is enough stupidity even in the cleverest crook to betray him: Glumov allows the others to steal his secret diary in which he had written down just what he thought of each of them. The scene in which this diary is read aloud by the others in his absence, is the counterpart to the reading of Khlestakov's letter in Gogol's *Inspector General*. In the following scene, however—and here is the novelty—Glumov enters and brazens it out. He points out to them that when he was dishonest and flattered them, they liked him. It is only now, when they have read his diary, the one place where he has really been honest, that they are angry with him. Yet there is nothing there that they do not know it true, nothing that they have not said about each other. They are all just as much hypocrites as he, and now that they are in his power they cannot get along without him. Glumov, then—this Russian equivalent of Molière's Tartuffe—is not discomfited even when he is unmasked, but is still shamelessly triumphant. It is this unexpected ending which offers something new in drama and makes this play of Ostrovski's, in its penetrating analysis of social corruption, anticipate the plays of Chekhov and Gorki and the criticism of bourgeois society to be found in Soviet drama. No wonder the play has continued to be popular after the Russian Revolution, either when acted in the traditional manner at the Maly Theatre in Moscow, or when done with artistic realism at the Moscow Art Theatre with Stanislavski and Kachalov and Moskvin and Olga Knipper Chekhova in the cast, or when produced by Eisenstein as a sort of mad circus at the Proletcult.

The growing power of money in Russia during the second half of the nineteenth century is analyzed by Ostrovski in a long series of powerful plays. In 1869 a comedy called *A Warm Heart* emphasized the vulgarizing effect of wealth upon a suddenly rich contractor, a rôle later made extraordinarily amusing as acted by Moskvin at the Moscow Art Theatre. In 1870, *Mad Money,* which has also been translated as *Fairy Gold,* brought into juxtaposition a decadent aristocratic family who spent money so madly that it seemed to be constantly vanishing, and a new type of hard-working business man—thought at that time to be a kind of "American Russian"—who quietly accumulated what might by contrast be called "wise money." In 1871, a play called *Not a Kopek and Suddenly a Ruble* presented a study of the character of a miser and the devastating effect of the sudden acquisition of even a relatively small amount of money. In 1874, Ostrovski contrasted in *Hard Earned Bread* those who, like a school teacher and a student, bear their poverty gaily, even proudly, with the dull egoism of a rich merchant and the shady scheming of an unscrupulous speculator. The young girl says plaintively: "Is it only money that makes life beautiful? Must one be rich in order to be happy?" It is this play that was revived most effectively by the Moscow Art Theatre in 1940.

In 1875, a play called *Wolves and Sheep* summarized Ostrovski's whole "natural history of society," the society of mid-nineteenth-century Moscow, into two categories: on the one hand the ruthless predatory wolves and on the other stupid gullible sheep, leaving us nothing but the choice of two evils. *Rich Brides* in 1876, *The Last Sacrifice* in 1878, *The Dowerless Girl* in

1079, and *The Bondwomen* in 1881, all continued this contrast of the poor with the rich, but combined with it that other problem which had preoccupied Ostrovski from the start—the subjection of women to the domination of husbands and parents in a society so largely influenced by greed and vulgarity.

In addition to these realistic plays in prose dealing with his own day, Ostrovski wrote also several historical plays in verse dealing with earlier days. For example, in 1865 in *The Voevoda or a Dream on the Volga*, he turned back to the legends of the famous robber brigand of the seventeenth century, Stenka Razin; and in 1873, in *The Snow Maiden* (*Snegurochka*), to still earlier Russian folklore.

One more category of Ostrovski's plays remains to be discussed, his plays about the theatre itself. For some reason there is a great fondness on the part of actors to act actors and on the part of playwrights to write plays about plays. Ostrovski was no exception. His long career as a dramatist through the middle decades of the nineteenth century from 1847 down to his last play in 1885, brought him many contacts with actors and in several of his plays he takes up the cudgels on their behalf. In 1871, in a play called *The Forest,* he introduced two actors in the middle of the journey of their lives meeting in the dark forest. He cleverly contrasted the characters of these two strolling players: one a tall and solemn tragic actor called The Unhappy One (Neschastlivtsev); and the other a short and happy-go-lucky comic actor called The Happy One (Schastlivtsev). They find the ferocity of society even worse than that of the forest from which they have emerged. They succeed in saving from death a maiden who is about to drown herself as Ekaterina had in *The Thunderstorm*. The wealthy landowners refer to them contemptuously as "play-actors" and would throw them out; but they answer proudly:

> Play-actors? No, we are artists, noble artists, and it is you who are the play-actors. If we love, then we love truly; if we hate, we fight; if we help, then we help with our last penny. And you? All your life you merely chatter of love and hate and public welfare. What have you accomplished? Whom have you helped? Whom have you comforted? You have only helped yourselves, comforted yourselves, amused yourselves. You are the comedians, the clowns, and not we. A maiden runs to drown herself. Who drove her into the water? You did. Who rescued her? We did.

Shaking the dust of society from their feet, they go off hand in hand into the dark forest, spouting the words from Schiller's *Robbers:* "You crocodile brood! Your tears are water! Your hearts are steel! Your kisses are daggers! May the wild beasts of the forest devour this whole hellish generation!" When voices are raised in protest against such violent language and threats are made of arresting the actors for such a subversive speech, they take out a copy of Schiller and quote from the title page: "Passed by the Censor! Approved for presentation!" *The Forest* continued to be popular after the

Russian Revolution both when acted realistically and when produced with "bio-mechanics" on a spiral ramp by Meyerhold.

In 1872, in a play called *The Seventeenth-Century Comedian*, Ostrovski turned back in a verse play to depict the life of Russian actors two hundred years earlier. In 1881, in *Talents and their Admirers*, he took up the life of a great actress and her various lovers and admirers. As acted at the Moscow Art Theatre the last scene at the railroad station, where a heart-broken young student is bidding the actress farewell as she leaves on the train with an older and richer man, is one of the most poignant of all drama.

Finally, in 1884, in Ostrovski's last great play, *Guilty without Guilt,* he turned to the life of another great actress, who in her youth had been seduced and abandoned by an official who had stolen her child away and given it to a stranger, pretending it had died. Years later, when the mother has become a famous actress, she returns to her native town (this was nearly twenty years before Sudermann's *Magda*). There she discovers that her own son too has become an actor, playing under another name in the local troupe at the theatre. This play made a great hit both in St. Petersburg and in Moscow with the public who saw in it a passionate appeal for justice and humanity. The Czar's censors, however, objected to the central idea of the play, contained in the very title, *Guilty without Guilt.* If the public were to believe that some one, thought guilty, was really innocent, what would become of imperial justice? Accordingly they made haste to ban the play and it was only after the Russian Revolution that, in the Maly Theatre and later in the Vakhtangov, it came into its own again.

Ostrovski had married an actress and the extraordinary insight which these plays show into the inner workings of an actress's heart were no doubt based on an intimate understanding of his wife's emotions. As time went on, he became more and more sympathetic both with the actors and with his fellow playwrights. He felt that in Russia at that time he and the other dramatists were getting little in return for their long and arduous labors. Popular as he was with the public, he had himself had little financial success. For example, the Director of the Imperial Theatres in 1872 pointed out that during the last nineteen years Ostrovski's plays had netted the theatre managers some two million rubles. Practically none of this, however, reached the playwright, who was indeed in distress for lack of money. A request for a pension for Ostrovski was refused, at the very time when milk was being supplied free for the bath of the visiting French actress, Rachel. Moreover, the Director of the St. Petersburg theatres had declared in 1860 that it was beneath their dignity in the Imperial Capital to act Ostrovski and that they were unwilling to defile their theatres with the stench of the fur coats of the Moscow merchants in Ostrovski's plays.

No wonder, then, that toward the end of his life, in order better to look after his rights and those of other dramatists, Ostrovski organized in 1874 a Society of Dramatic Authors and Operatic Composers. In 1881, when

Alexander III came to the throne, Ostrovski addressed to the new Czar a communication in which he said: "Drama is nearer to the people than any other form of literature. Other literary productions are written for the cultured classes. Drama is written for all the people." He went on in this communication to argue against the star system and in favor of ensemble acting and pleaded for at least a thousand seats in each theatre for the poorer people, to be sold at only 15 kopeks apiece.

Finally, in 1885, Ostrovski himself was appointed director of the Moscow Theatres and hoped to be able, at last, to carry on this plan of his; but he died in the following year before his democratic program could be put into effect.

It was Ostrovski's program, however, which led ultimately to the Soviet stage. Indeed, the Russian Revolution seems to have given Ostrovski a new lease on life in Russia. Lunacharski, the People's Commissar of Education during the first ten years of the Soviet Union, gave as a slogan to the Soviet theatres: "Back to Ostrovski!"

In December, 1917, only a month after the Revolution, Russians began reviving his plays and have gone on ever since. At least forty or fifty of his plays have been acted throughout the Soviet Union. It is doubtful whether in England or America so many plays of any one English or American playwright of the mid-nineteenth century have been revived.

Outside of Russia, Ostrovski had never enjoyed the reputation he deserves. To be sure, at least seven of his plays have been acted in the United States, but much as America might have profited by his attacks on money-grabbing, the plays never seem to have been appreciated here at their true worth. In the Soviet Union, however, they are more popular than ever. Indeed more plays of Ostrovski are acted than of any other dramatist.

The Maly Theatre in Moscow, which was built in 1824, the year after Ostrovski's birth, was the theatre where most of his plays were first acted, and has continued for a century and more to be devoted to Ostrovski's plays. If the Comédie Française in Paris has been called "The House of Molière," the Maly Theatre in Moscow may well be called "The House of Ostrovski." In 1923 the hundredth anniversary of Ostrovski's birth was celebrated throughout the Soviet Union. His plays were produced in the good old-fashioned way at the Maly Theatre on that occasion and in all sorts of expressionist and constructivist ways at other more modernistic theatres. In 1929 the Soviet government erected a bronze statue to his memory, inscribed "To Ostrovski" and representing him seated solidly in an armchair in front of the Maly Theatre and looking out towards the Theatre Square in the very heart of Moscow, a worthy embodiment of the central figure of Russian drama.

Although Ostrovski was the most prolific and versatile dramatist of the period, there were other playwrights of the second half of the nineteenth century who wrote certain plays on certain themes which they pushed to even stronger conclusions than he had. As his work may be divided between realistic plays in prose dealing with his own times and his historical plays in verse so, in dealing with these other dramatists, we may take up first those who wrote social dramas about contemporary life and then turn to the few who continued the tradition of poetic historical plays.

In Ostrovski's plays of social criticism, he had dealt chiefly with the merchant class in the city, and only incidentally took up the peasants of the villages.

There were certain other playwrights, however, who, during the 1850's focused their attention on the evils of Russian serfdom so powerfully that it helped to bring about the emancipation of the serfs in 1861. Count Vladimir Alexandrovich Sollogub (1814-1882) created a sensation in the theatre in 1853 with his play called *The Official*. Here an honest provincial secretary comes in conflict with the selfishness of the landed proprietors and the dishonesty of the government officials and cries out: "Let us shout it out to all Russia that the time has come to tear this evil out by the roots!"

In the following year, 1854, Alexei Antipovich Potekhin (1829-1908) attempted to picture on the stage the real Russian peasants in their own setting, in their own language. His play was called *Man's Judgment Is Not God's* and showed a peasant passing so cruel a judgment on his daughter that she loses her mind and disappears. Later he finds her living as a servant in a country inn and forgives her, realizing that God's judgment may not be the same as that of men. The dramatist followed this play up in the next year, 1855, with a play called *The Property of Another,* in which the son of a peasant inn-keeper plans to rob his father, even if he has to kill him, but is at the end forgiven by the father.

Finally in 1859, on the very eve of the emancipation of the serfs, in the same year when Ostrovski's *The Ward* had taken up cudgels for the oppressed serfs, appeared the most scorching and terrific indictment of the conditions of peasants to be found in any play. This was written by Alexei Feofilaktovich Pisemski (1820-1881) and was called *Bitter Fate,* a play that was later revived in the Moscow Art Theatre. It represents a serf returning home to find that his wife has been seduced by the young landlord and has had a child by him. In his fury, he kills the child and gives himself up to justice, while the landed proprietor gets off free. It was plays such as these, pointing out the inequality of the existing system, which prepared the way for the abolition of serfdom two years later. It anticipates the horror of Tolstoi's *The Power of Darkness,* but Pisemski seems to have caught even better than Tolstoi the sense of impending fate, the emotions of fear and pity of Greek tragedy.

Very different from this series of plays dealing with the tragedies of peasant life in the Russian villages was the famous trilogy dealing with high society in the city written by Alexander Vasilevich Sukhovo-Kobylin (1817-1903); yet here too is the same sense of pessimism and fatalism. The author was a popular Moscow aristocrat and stealer of women's hearts. He had been something of a worthless dandy when suddenly an event occurred as dramatic as any in his plays—an event which changed his whole life. On November 8, 1850, the murdered body of "a woman in a blue mantle" was found thrown out of a carriage in Moscow. It proved to be that of a Frenchwoman, Louise Simon-Dimanche, who had been the mistress of Sukhovo-Kobylin. He was immediately arrested and imprisoned. For seven years this famous trial for murder dragged on. Finally, the Minister of Justice received an imperial order to put an end to an unpleasant business which was "besmirching the prestige of the ruling class." Accordingly, by bribery and torture, the guilt was pinned upon some of the nobleman's serfs and Sukhovo-Kobylin himself was set free and lived on to the good old age of eighty-six in his villa on the Riviera.

While he had been in prison, however, he had written, in 1855, a play called *Krechinski's Wedding*, which was to be the first part of his trilogy. This was written with all the skilful theatrical craftsmanship of a well-made play by Scribe. Krechinski is a nobleman who is unlucky in cards, but lucky in love. As in Sukhovo-Kobylin's own case, women cannot resist him and are ready to sacrifice themselves for his sake. Needing money, he promises marriage to Lidochka, the daughter of a rich landowner and herself the owner of a famous solitaire diamond. During a party on the eve of Krechinski's wedding there is a pounding on the door. It is the police. It transpires that on the strength of her diamond, he has made a large loan from a money-lender, but has fraudulently substituted an imitation diamond. Lidochka, in the kindness of her heart, saves the worthless nobleman by handing over the real diamond and saying that it was her own mistake. Krechinski mutters sardonically something about being saved again by a woman—and disappears.

In the second part of the trilogy, *The Affair*, written in 1862 after Sukhovo-Kobylin's release from prison, we have his terrific indictment of the Russian law courts. Krechinski never appears, but his innocent fiancée, accused of being his accomplice, is caught in the toils of the law. The "affair" drags on for years, as the author's own trial had. Added to "the law's delay" there are the lawyer's exorbitant fees, the extortions of blackmailers, the bribes demanded by the corrupt legal authorities. In all literature there is no such terrible picture of the corruption of law. Lidochka's father, in his desperate efforts to clear his daughter's name, spends all his money, and exhausted by the strain, dies as he pays his last 30,000 rubles. The one honest bailiff, Siderov, gives Lidochka an appalling picture of the Russia of the midnineteenth century:

> There have been three invasions of our country. First it was overrun by the Tartars; then it was invaded by the French; and now it is pillaged by our own government officials. And what is left of our country? She is pitiful to look at: wearied to the bone, rotted through and through, sold in the courts, drunken in

the saloons—she lies on the great plain, unwashed, covered with straw, weak with debauch.

Sukhovo-Kobylin was the Russian translator of Hegel's philosophy; but after the thesis of *Krechinski's Wedding* and the antithesis of *The Affair,* the third part of the trilogy, *Tarelkin's Death* (1869), offered a cynical and sinister synthesis. Now Lidochka has disappeared as well as Krechinski, but the magistrates and lawyers are left like tigers and jackals fighting over the spoils. One of them, Tarelkin, eager to get back at Barrabin, who he thinks has cheated him, even goes so far as to pretend to die, to have a dummy buried in his place, and to continue extorting money from Barrabin. Sukhovo-Kobylin here first treated with grim horror the theme of a man "burying himself," which Tolstoi later treated as tragedy in *The Living Corpse,* and Arnold Bennett as comedy in *The Great Adventure.*

This final picture of legal corruption was so terrific that it was banned by the censor for forty-one years. Since the Russian Revolution, however, the whole trilogy has been revived in all its scorching horror, Meyerhold producing the first and third parts and Michael Chekhov producing the second part at the Second Moscow Art Theatre.

Similarly cynical in its picture of vice going unpunished was a play by Michael Evgrafovich Saltykov-Shchedrin (1826-1889). This was called *The Death of Pazukhin* and was written in 1857, but it was not permitted by the censor to be acted until forty-four years later. In 1914 it was acted by the Moscow Art Theatre in Moscow and in 1924 in New York, with a cast including Moskvin and the widow of Chekhov. In this strange play, old Pazukhin is on his death-bed, and his son, his son-in-law, his daughter-in-law, and his housekeeper are all vying with each other in flattering him and are all intriguing against each other in hopes of inheriting the great wealth stored up in his money chest. There is no poetic justice. On the contrary, it is again those who are most unscrupulous who triumph, and at the end of the play one of the minor characters, turning to the audience, says: "Ladies and gentlemen! Our play is finished! Thus you see how virtue ... fui! [here the actor spits in good Russian fashion to represent his disgust] virtue—I mean vice—is punished. And virtue?—but where is any virtue to be found?"

Where is any virtue to be found? That is the question which this series of devastating pictures of nineteenth-century Russia seems to leave in our minds.

The same is true when we turn to the pictures given of the position of women. Ostrovski had again and again showed up the debasing position of the women in the old Russian society and several others pushed that same theme to still more melodramatic and tragic extremes.

Nicholas Seminovich Leskov (1831-1895), for example, in his famous story of *A Lady Macbeth of the Mtsensk District,* written in 1866 and made into an opera long afterwards by Shostokovich in 1934, depicted in Katerina

Izmailova a peasant woman driven twice into being a murderess. In the absence of her cruel husband, she falls in love with a young clerk, and when her husband's father would betray her love, she puts poison in the mushrooms that the old man is eating. Later, when her husband returns, she, like Lady Macbeth, eggs the clerk on to killing him.

An enormous sensation was created on the stage in 1872 by a play written by Dmitri Vasilevich Averkiev (1836-1905) and called *Old Times of Kashira*. This pictured a poor girl giving up a young man of her own rank in order to follow a prince and finally, disillusioned by both, taking her own life. Again, in 1878, in a play called *The Stewart Vanka,* Luke Mikolaevich Antropov (1843-1884) has his heroine, abandoned by a prince, falling in love with his steward and, when he is hanged by the prince, going out of her mind. Finally, in 1888, Alexei Sergeevich Suvorin (1834-1914), the Director of the Maly Theatre in Moscow, wrote his play called *Tatyana Repina* about the suicide of an actress deserted by the man she loves, a play to which Chekhov wrote a sequel. It was such plays of the fearful fate of unfortunate females that gave Russian drama its reputation for unmitigated gloom and that make even the plays of Chekhov and of Soviet drama seem cheerful by comparison.

Even after Ostrovski's death in 1886, plays similar to his, criticizing social conditions in Russia continued to the end of the century. In the 1890's, however, we find the rich merchants whom Ostrovski had presented in their smelly fur coats and uncultivated manners replaced by slick capitalists in evening clothes, affecting culture and art to give grace to wealth. Thus Prince Alexander Ivanovich Sumbatov (1857-1927), who became the director of Ostrovski's old theatre the Maly, and acted there under the stage name of Yuzhin, wrote towards the end of the century, in 1897, a play about this new type ironically called *The Gentleman.* Again, at the very end of the century, in 1899, he produced his play called *Sunset,* showing both the mental and moral bankruptcy of the old Russian nobility. Thus the social criticism of the ancient régime in Russia was continued down to the very eve of the twentieth century which was to see its dissolution.

Meanwhile, in addition to this long series of nineteenth-century dramatists with their realistic plays of contemporary life, there were a few who, as Ostrovski had occasionally done, turned back to write poetic plays about earlier Russian history. Their favorite period seems to have been that of Ivan the Terrible and the Time of Troubles that followed him. Leo Alexandrovich Mei (1822-1862), for example, in his blank verse play *The Czar's Bride,* first written in 1849, depicted a young girl, torn from the man she loved in order to become the bride of Czar Ivan. In another blank verse play, *The Lady of Pskov,* written in 1860, his heroine, in love with a young revolutionist, discovers to her horror that she is really the daughter of Ivan the Terrible. Both these historical plays by Mei were later turned into operas by Rimsky-Korsakov. A little later Nicholas Alexandrovich Chaev (1824-

1877), who after Ostrovski's death had charge of the repertoire of the Moscow theatres, wrote, among other historical plays, *The False Demetreus* in 1865, and *The Terrible Czar Ivan Vasilevich* in 1869.

The real masterpiece in this genre, however, was the famous trilogy written by Alexei Constantinovich Tolstoi (1817-1875), a cousin of the great Tolstoi. He began with *The Death of Ivan the Terrible,* written in 1866. He next took up the story of the reign of Ivan's well-meaning but weak son, in a play called *Czar Fedor Ivanovich,* written two years later in 1868. He then turned to the usurper who wrested the throne away from him, *Czar Boris,* written again two years later, in 1870. This third part was never very successful because its subject-matter coincided with that of Pushkin's far better known *Boris Godunov.* The second part, because of its scathing criticism of the Russian monarchy, leaving little to choose between wicked czars and weak czars, was banned by the censors for some thirty years. Finally, however, toward the very end of the century, in 1898, it was taken by Stanislavski and Nemirov-Danchenko to be the first play to be staged by their newly organized Moscow Art Theatre. There it achieved a great success, with two of their greatest actors alternating in the part of Czar Fedor: Kachalov bringing out the tragedy and Moskvin the mingled comic and pathetic character of the vacillating monarch. Again, when the Moscow Art Theatre came to New York in 1923, it was with this historical play, rich in the splendid costumes of the old Russia, that they began their series of productions.

Before we turn to discuss the Moscow Art Theatre, however, we must pause to glance at the contributions to drama of the three great Russian novelists: Turgenev, Dostoevski, and Tolstoi.

Looming far larger than any of these nineteenth-century dramatists, both in the general history of Russian literature and also in their fame abroad, are the three great Russian novelists of the nineteenth century: Turgenev, Dostoevski, and Tolstoi. Although all three are famous, of course, primarily as novelists rather than dramatists, each one of them in his way had an important influence on Russian drama.

Ivan Sergeevich Turgenev (1818-1883) wrote at least a dozen plays at the beginning of his career. Indeed, he tells us that he hesitated some time whether to devote himself to drama or to fiction. His plays, although they did not have a great success at the time, have a special significance to us today because Chekhov tells us that it was on these plays of Turgenev, with their subtle analysis of the commonplace events of ordinary life, that he modeled his own technique.

In one of Turgenev's one-act plays, *The Lady from the Provinces,* written in 1851, he gives us a charming picture of a vivacious woman living in the provinces and as eager to get to St. Petersburg as *The Three Sisters* of Chekhov were later to get to Moscow. She plays on the amorous emotions of an elderly count, who had courted her in her youth, in order to get him to give her husband a position in St. Petersburg which will enable them to go and live there. As acted by the Moscow Art Theatre in Moscow in 1912 and in New York in 1923, with Olga Knipper Chekhov as the provincial lady and Stanislavski as the elderly count, it proved what delightfully good theatre Turgenev was after all.

In the meanwhile, in his five-act play *A Month in the Country*, taking the hint from the analysis of an older woman's jealousy for a younger woman revealed in Balzac's *La Marâtre*, Turgenev gave us a remarkable, full-length study of a married woman, bored with her husband and the stuffy, hothouse life that she leads, and envious of the young and healthy love between her little son's tutor and her protégée. Very penetratingly Turgenev shows us the older woman vacillating, eager to dismiss the protégée and retain the young man, and then, when she finds she cannot steal his love, reluctantly dismissing him. With true artistry, however, Turgenev is content with that psychological analysis and does not push the story, as Balzac had, to the suicide of both women. Although Turgenev wrote this play from 1848 to 1850, he had to wait nearly twenty years before it was acted. Discouraged, he felt that his plays were rather to be read than acted, stopped writing plays at the age of thirty-three, and turned to writing novels. It was only after Turgenev's death that Chekhov rediscovered the subtlety of his method, and after Chekhov's death that the Moscow Art Theatre revived the play with great success in 1909, with Chekhov's widow acting the part of the distracted wife. It was still later, in 1930, that Nazimova gave another very poignant interpretation of this Natalia with the Theatre Guild in New York.

Even when he turned exclusively to fiction rather than drama, Turgenev retained enough of the dramatic sense he had acquired in his early playwriting to be the most dramatic of all the Russian novelists. This is why, when his great novel *Fathers and Sons*, written in 1861, was dramatized in the Soviet Union in 1935 under the name of its radical hero, *Eugene Bazarov*, one felt that here is really great drama.

Fedor Mikailovich Dostoevski (1821-1881) had not written plays in his youth as Turgenev had, but after being arrested and imprisoned for conspiracy, after being sentenced to death and undergoing all the sensations of execution, he tells us that he "jokingly began a comedy." This was later turned into his story of *The Village of Stepanchikovo*, published in 1859. Long afterwards, in 1891, it was dramatized with Stanislavski acting the part of the kindly Colonel Rostanov, who falls in love with the governess of his children but plans to marry her to the pretentious writer, Foma. Again, in 1917, on the very eve of the October Revolution, it was revived by the Moscow Art Theatre, with Moskvin acting the part of Foma.

Another story of Dostoevski's, *The Uncle's Dream*, also written in 1859, was dramatized by the Moscow Art Theatre some seventy years later in 1929, with Chekhov's widow acting the part of the ambitious mother who would marry her daughter to a dilapidated old prince with false hair. The daughter for the moment accepts, hoping to get the money which the young man she loves needs for his education. Afterwards they succeed in persuading the befuddled prince into believing that her acceptance was only something which he had imagined in a dream.

It was only after the Russian Revolution that this story was dramatized and the same is true of other novels of Dostoevski. It was natural that the great author who had written of the oppressed under the old Russia—*Poor Folk, The House of the Dead, The Insulted and Injured*—should be appreciated by those who had overthrown that régime and championed the poor people who had been oppressed by it. It is true that some have argued that the Revolution rejected Dostoevski and, using the title of one of his novels, have said that in the Soviet Union Dostoevski himself was "insulted and injured." They could hardly have chosen a more unfortunate allusion, for at that very time, 1932, Dostoevski's *Insulted and Injured* was being acted by the Second Moscow Art Theatre before enthusiastic audiences in the Soviet Union—acted far more beautifully than it had ever been acted before.

The adapters of Dostoevski's novels found they hardly had to change a word in the dialogues, so well had Dostoevski dramatized them. Dostoevski's real contribution to Russian drama comes in his penetrating ability to put himself under the skin of all the unfortunate people he writes about. So much deeper did he probe into the secret places of the human soul than any one had done before, that Russian drama ever since has been dissatisfied with any superficial analysis of characters and has demanded getting down to the deepest psychological roots of men's actions.

It is true that terrible things have been done (elsewhere) to Dostoevski's great masterpiece *Crime and Punishment* (1865): in a moralized British dramatization called *The Humble* written by Sir Henry Irving's son and in French and German film versions of the story of Raskolnikov. *The Idiot* (1868), too, was dramatized in a rather fantastic version in New York. The Russians, on the other hand, treat Dostoevski's text with the greatest respect. *The Possessed* (1871), though the title was changed to the name of the central character, *Nicholas Stavrogin,* and the choice of such a subject at all was severely criticised at the time by Maxim Gorki, was on the whole very faithfully dramatized by the Moscow Art Theatre in 1913. Finally Dostoevski's last great unfinished novel, *The Brothers Karamazov* (1881), although converted into a tightly-knit play in the French manner by Jacques Copeau—acted at the Théâtre des Arts in Paris and by the Theatre Guild in New York—was done in a characteristic Russian way by the Moscow Art Theatre. In this case, unlike the Copeau version, they stuck so close to the actual text of the novel that two narrators, one on either side of the stage, read Dostoevski's narrative word for word, and then, when Dostoevski turned to dialogue, the actors took up the words. During the two seasons of the Moscow Art Theatre in New York, they did three of these scenes in their first season and six in their second season.

Something of the same fidelity to the original novel was shown by the Moscow Art Theatre when it turned to Leo Nikolaevich Tolstoi (1828-1910) and presented his *Resurrection* (1899). In their production in the Soviet Union in 1930, they had their greatest actor Kachalov come out at the beginning in the front of the auditorium of the theatre and recite the actual words with which Tolstoi begins the novel—words describing the coming of spring in a big city. To be sure some of the Americans present, not understanding Russian, were convinced that this must be some Bolshevik giving the audience his interpretation of the relation of Tolstoi to the Five Year Plan. Instead, it was merely one more indication of the devotion of people in the Soviet Union to the very words used by a great writer of the nineteenth century. As the play went on, Kachalov wandered in and out among the actors, from time to time interrupting their dialogue with Tolstoi's own descriptions or philosophical comments on their actions.

When the directors of the Moscow Art Theatre came to dramatize *Anna Karenina* (1877) as recently as 1937, although they did not use this particular device of having a narrator, they showed far greater fidelity to the original novel than most of the other dramatizations and films, there or abroad, had previously shown.

Still more recently, when Russia was invaded by the German armies in 1941, the Russians naturally turned back to the time when they were invaded by the French armies under Napoleon in 1812, and Tolstoi's great historical novel *War and Peace* (1869) was dramatized. Finding it impossible to compress that tremendous novel into one evening's performance, it was arranged to have the performance run on two consecutive days. Here the theme was one that was familiar to all the audience and the spirit of the production was something like that of Greek drama going back to the story of the Trojan War.

In addition to these three great novels of Tolstoi's, innumerable other novels and short stories of his have been dramatized or turned into films. In his case, however, the contribution to drama is by no means merely that of dramatized novels. Tolstoi, like Turgenev, wrote in addition to fiction at least a dozen works in dramatic form. Whereas Turgenev, however, wrote his plays at the beginning of his literary career and finished writing them before he was thirty-three years old, Tolstoi did not turn to writing plays until he was nearly sixty years old and wrote almost all of them during the last twenty-five years of his life. In turning from novels to plays, Tolstoi made an interesting analogy, comparing his work as a novelist to that of a painter and his work as a dramatist to that of a sculptor. Somewhat then as a sculptor might carve a statue out of hard granite, Tolstoi carved out of the life of the peasants about him a tremendous and appalling drama. This was called *The Power of Darkness* (1886) and represented the dark ignorance and superstition and evil that seemed to weigh the peasants down, sapping all humanity out of them. The story has all the grimness of the naturalism of Zola, but the grip of determinism is lifted at the end by a sudden act of free will and sacrifice that enobles even the incredibly base central character. This crude farm-hand Nikita has wronged an orphan girl and killed her. He has then caused a wife to murder her husband in order to marry him and then taken his wife's young stepdaughter as his mistress and forced his wife to act as their servant. The mistress, driven to the barn, gives birth to a child and Nikita, discovering the baby, presses a board over the body till the bones crunch. Later he is haunted by the baby's cries which seem to be still ringing in his ears; he drinks, hoping to drown those cries, and tries to kill himself. At the end, a drunken old soldier Mitrich succeeds in giving Nikita the courage to be himself, to lift himself above his cowardice, and give himself up to justice. It was this last scene of which Bernard Shaw wrote to Tolstoi: "I remember nothing in the whole range of drama that fascinated me more."

The horrible revelation, however, which this play gave of conditions in Russia caused its production to be prohibited there by the Czar's censor. It was then not in Russia but in France, at the newly founded Théâtre Libre of Antoine in Paris, that *The Power of Darkness* was first acted in 1888. At this performance the great French naturalist Zola cried out: "Do not strike out a single scene or a single word!" In the following year, 1889, it was acted at the Freie Bühne, which opened that year in Berlin, and influenced German naturalism. It was only after the death of Czar Alexander III that it was allowed in Russia and finally received worthy treatment in 1902 at the hands of the Moscow Art Theatre with Stanislavski in the rôle of the old soldier.

Two shorter plays by Tolstoi dealt with the evil of drink among the peasants. One of these, *The First Distiller,* written in 1886 in six short "acts" of two or three pages each, told the rather naïve legend of the introduction of liquor into the Russian farms. An Imp, sent by the Chief Devil to get the soul of a peasant, steals his loaf of bread, but the peasant only says good-naturedly: "If some one has taken my bread, may it do him good!" When, however, the peasant has more corn than he can use, the Imp teaches him how to distill it into vodka, and he and his neighbors become drunk, "first like foxes, then like wolves, and finally like swine." The other play, *The Cause of it All,* introduces in two short acts a tramp who preaches against drink as "the cause of it all," and then himself gets drunk and steals from the peasants who have befriended him.

With *The Fruits of Culture,* written in 1889, Tolstoi turned to concoct a satire on the so-called "cultured classes," who for all their pretended enlightenment and happiness are underneath really unhappy. It is, as Bernard Shaw said, "the first of the Heartbreak Houses and the most blighting." Into the midst of these idle rich, Tolstoi introduced with appalling contrast a group of starving peasants asking for bread, thereby bringing in the note of protest.

In *The Living Corpse,* written in 1900, Tolstoi again deals with the upper classes, but the comedy has become tragedy. Fedya, feeling that his wife would be happier if he were dead and she could marry Victor, decides to give out the appearance of having drowned himself and becomes a "living corpse." His existence, however, is discovered, and realizing that his wife will now be imprisoned for bigamy and the only way for him to free her is to become a real corpse, Fedya shoots himself. This great drama of sacrifice was acted by the Moscow Art Theatre in 1911, with Moskvin in the rôle of Fedya and Kachalov as Victor. Other great interpretations of Fedya have been given by Moissi in Germany and by John Barrymore in America, where the play was rechristened *Redemption.*

Finally Tolstoi undertook a great autobiographical drama, which was left unfinished at the time of his death. This was called *The Light Shineth in Darkness* and implied the rest of the biblical quotation "and the darkness comprehendeth it not." It rounded out the cycle begun with *The Power of Darkness,* for Tolstoi now knew that it was not only the peasants who lived in darkness, but even his own circle of family and friends though they appeared on the surface to be enjoying the fruits of enlightenment. Nicholas Ivanovich, who here corresponds to Tolstoi, is troubled that he himself is not really practising the principles of equality which he has been preaching. Accordingly he decides to give—or as he would put it, "give back"—his lands to the peasants, only to have the unhappy result of making his wife feel that thereby he is enslaving his own children. His doctrine of following Christ rather than the Church leads one of his disciples, a priest, into trouble with the Church. Another disciple, the young son of a Princess, is led by the master's teachings of pacifism into refusing military service and is flogged. In despair, Nicholas, like Tolstoi, decides to leave his home. Act V was never written out, but in the rough notes for it there is an indication that at the end Tolstoi planned a dramatic and terrible conclusion: Nicholas is shot by the Princess who feels that his teachings have ruined her son's career.

Bernard Shaw has said: "Tolstoi's masterpiece is his *The Light Shines in Darkness.* In it he turns his deadly touch suicidally on himself." But Tolstoi was not committing suicide. The fault was not that of the light, but that of the power of darkness. The light still shone in the darkness, though the darkness comprehended it not.

The great Russian novelists had thus prepared the ground for great Russian drama with Dostoevski's deep psychology and Tolstoi's broad sociology. All that was now needed was a great theatre for great drama and that was provided at the very end of the nineteenth century by the founding of the Moscow Art Theatre.

Toward the end of the nineteenth century, in 1898, the Moscow Art Theatre was started and served both to give more artistic performances to the plays that had already been written and also to be a stimulus for the writing of more artistic new plays. It was a sort of bridge connecting the nineteenth and the twentieth centuries. In revolting in the name of realism from the artificiality and conventionality of the older theatres, the Moscow Art Theatre treated with equal realism all classes of society. Beginning with a realistic reincarnation of the richness and unhappiness of the old Russian aristocracy in *Czar Fedor Ivanovich*, it turned next to the subtle realistic studies of middle-class futility in the comedies of Chekhov; and then to an unflinchingly realistic presentation of the "lower depths" of society depicted in the plays of Gorki.

The Moscow Art Theatre, then, provided the highest expression for the realism and naturalism of the late nineteenth and early twentieth centuries; and it came later, though few foresaw it, to provide the best stage for the socialist realism of the Soviet Union. After the Russian Revolution of 1917 Lenin said: "If there is any one theatre from the past which we must preserve by all means, it is, of course, the Moscow Art Theatre." Other theatres of more extreme formalism, such as those of Meyerhold or Tairov, had their vogue for a time, but it is the realism of the Moscow Art Theatre which has survived and had its influence on the other theatres. It has itself continued to grow until it has a personnel of over six hundred members. If one takes into account, also, the various studios which have sprung from it and become independent theatres—the First Studio, which became the Second Moscow Art Theatre; the Third Studio, which became the Vakhtangov Theatre; the Fourth Studio, which became the Realistic Theatre; the Hebrew Studio or Habima; the Musical Studio of Nemirovich-Danchenko; the Opera Studio of Stanislavski; the Zavadski Studio; the Khmelev Studio and others—one may well say that the Moscow Art Theatre in all its branches has become the greatest theatre of the twentieth century.

A theatre which has given the most artistic expression both to pre-revolutionary and to post-revolutionary Russian drama, which has survived two Russian Revolutions and two World Wars, and which has emerged stronger than ever, must have had its foundations well laid.

Those foundations were laid in the famous eighteen-hour conversation which took place in the Slavic Bazaar in Moscow on Midsummer Night, June 21, 1897, when two remarkable Russians, each independently seeking such a theatre, met for the first time. Out of that midsummer night's dream of theirs came a masterpiece. It was an ideal combination of two different temperaments which admirably supplemented each other. One—Stanislavski—was an actor and was to take control of what they called the artistic end, the acting and directing. The other—Nemirovich-Danchenko—was a playwright and was to take control of what they called the literary end, the selecting of plays and the arranging of the repertoire. They were to collaborate with each other and with the company in all things, but each was to have the veto power in his particular field. As one entry in the minutes which they kept of their all night meeting put it: "The artistic veto belongs to Stanislavski; the literary veto belongs to Nemirovich-Danchenko."

Constantine Sergeev Stanislavski (1863-1938), or to give him his real family name, Alexeev, had been brought up in a well-to-do family of the merchant class and from early childhood had had an extraordinary passion for acting. His mother was the daughter of a French actress and did everything to encourage Constantine's love for the stage. When a child of only two or three, so he tells us, he made his début in a tableau of the Four Seasons, given in a wing of his father's house. When he was six, he organized and took part in a little home circus, which they called after him "Constanto Alexeev's Circus." He had his puppets and his marionette theatre. When he was fourteen, a new theatre wing was added to the house and there his family group, calling themselves "The Alexeev Circle," acted plays and operas. When he was twenty-two, he adopted the stage name of Stanislavski, which he has since made world famous. He took it from the name of a Dr. Stanislavski who had been fond of amateur theatricals. In that same year, 1885, a German company of actors, the Meiningen Players under the direction of Chronegk and under the patronage of the Duke of Saxo-Meiningen, visited St. Petersburg and Moscow and made a profound impression on the young Stanislavski with their realistic method of acting. Perhaps it would be better to say their acting strengthened the latent instinct in that direction which already existed in the Russian theatre and in Stanislavski.

Three years later, in 1888 when Stanislavski was twenty-five years old, with two other older actors and directors, Alexander Fedotov and Theodore Kommissarzhevski, he founded the Society of Art and Literature. During his ten years' experience with that school of scenic art, and before the Moscow Art Theatre was founded, he had had a chance to act in plays covering a wide range of Russian drama—Pushkin, Gogol, at least ten plays of Ostrovski, plays of Pisemski, Turgenev, and Tolstoi, and some of the youthful one-act plays of Chekhov—not to mention Shakespeare, Racine, Molière, Goldoni, Schiller, Hauptmann, and other non-Russian dramatists.

By the time, then, of his famous meeting with Nemirovich-Danchenko, Stanislavski had already had a large and varied experience in acting and directing and had evolved certain fundamental principles of realism in acting. It was to be a realism of all five senses: the sounds coming from the stage and even the smells were to be realistic as well as the visual impressions. Actors should begin rehearsing in a room not knowing which side of the room was to face the audience. When one side of this three-dimensional stage was decided as the best one to show to the audience, it was to be like the removing of the fourth wall of the room. Some of the chairs, some of the actors would have their backs to the footlights. The actors should not gesticulate. They should not try to "act." That would only make them seem artificial. They must act as if there were no audience there, act toward each other, not toward the audience. "Don't start trying to force your voice. That only makes it seem tricky and pathetic. Learn to make your voice vibrate and be full of resonance without forcing it."

All this external realism, however, was only secondary in importance to the inner realism, the "spiritual" realism, or what might better be called the "psychological" realism. Each actor must feel the part, must live in the part. He must concentrate on what the character is thinking. The right thought will evoke the right emotion and the right emotion will evoke the right action. When in real life an actor is stirred by some strong emotion—love, jealousy, anger—let him analyze what he feels like doing, let him store up that emotion in his "golden box" of imagination, and when the time comes to act that emotion on the stage, let him open the box and let that emotion come out.

These theories, which Stanislavski has explained at length in his great autobiography *My Life in Art,* and which have so often been interpreted and misinterpreted as the Stanislavski Method, constitute not merely a philosophy of art, but also a philosophy of life.

It was in the name, then, of this new realism that he was eager to break away from the old wooden artificiality of the nineteenth century and found a new theatre. All he needed was some collaborator with more experience in play-writing and a greater knowledge of world drama. This need he found admirably filled by Nemirovich-Danchenko.

Vladimir Ivanovich Nemirovich-Danchenko (1858-1943), like Stanislavski, had had a love of the theatre from an early age. In his autobiography, which he modestly called *Out of the Past,* but which has been called in the English translation *My Life in the Theatre,* he tells us how as a little boy of four he used to play "with a toy stage on a broad Russian window sill." At thirteen he began directing plays and proved to be a born teacher. Later, at the Moscow Philharmonic Society, almost all the great Russian actors studied under him. He himself had acted, but in this he was eclipsed by the more dynamic Stanislavski. Moreover he was a successful playwright and a profound dramatic critic and in these respects surpassed Stanislavski, who wrote: "It is seldom that all these qualities are met in one person; but they are met in Nemirovich-Danchenko."

As a playwright and producer, he had already anticipated some of the principles of realism. Way back in 1882, in his earliest play *The Wild Rose,* he first showed us the outside of a two-story house and then, removing the "fourth wall," showed us what was going on inside. Two years later, in 1884 in a play called *The Dark Forest,* he sprinkled the stage with Keller's Essence of Pine to give an added realism through the sense of smell. His plays, with their realistic pictures of the futility of much of middle-class life in the old Russia, were forerunners of the plays of Chekhov and Chekhov gladly paid tribute to him. Because Nemirovich had been married to a baroness, had associated with Prince Sumbatov, and had been presented at court, he was often thought an aristocrat and with his finely shaped head and dignified square beard was sometimes called "The Grand Duke of the Russian Theatre." Yet at heart he was most democratic. In his novel called *A Drama Behind the Scenes,* published in 1896, he sympathized with the struggle of the young actors and playwrights against the intolerance and bigotry of those in power. In his *On the Steppes,* in 1897, he took up the cudgels for the peasants against the landed proprietors so vigorously that the Czar's Censor suppressed nearly half the book. He felt the need of a drastic change and, with the coming of the Russian Revolution in 1917, he wrote: "The Revolution has deepened our conception of art, making it more virile and stronger."

Nemirovich was always quick to recognize the genius of other playwrights. He was the first to urge Chekhov and Gorki to write plays and he helped them. It was his feeling of the need for a better theatre to produce their plays that led him to write to Stanislavski and arrange their meeting at the Slavic Bazaar in 1897. Stanislavski spoke of Nemirovich as "at that time the most popular and talented playwright in Russia." His play *The Value of Life,* dealing with a married couple needlessly estranged, was then having a great success in the theatre and was awarded the Griboedov Prize for the best play of the year. Nemirovich-Danchenko, however, with characteristic modesty, wrote to the Committee: "I cannot accept the prize, for it is merited wholly and indisputably not by my play, but by another play. It is merited by *The Sea-Gull.* Here you have a real diamond, here is a new triumph of Russian playwrighting." *The Sea-Gull* at that time was considered a failure in the theatre, but Nemirovich-Danchenko gladly recognized in its author, Chekhov, a genius in playwriting very far beyond his own.

Anton Pavlovich Chekhov (1860-1904) has become so identified with the Moscow Art Theatre, his subtle artistic realism suiting their acting and their intense psychological realism suiting his plays so well, that we have sometimes come to think of both as having come into existence together. We now know, however, that twenty years before the founding of the Moscow Art Theatre, Chekhov had begun writing plays. Indeed, of his eighteen plays, all but two were written before the Moscow Art Theatre began and without having it at all in mind.

As a boy, so his brother tells us, Anton was "the leading spirit in the theatricals we played at home." He and his brother used to climb up to the gallery of the theatre a couple of hours before the performance to try and get good seats. When he was sixteen years old and his family moved to Moscow, he remained at his native town of Taganrog on the Sea of Azov in the south of Russia. He continued to frequent the theatre there and, when in the seventh form at school, began writing a long serious drama. He also wrote a short amusing vaudeville sketch called *The Scythe Struck a*

Stone, and another called *Not for Nothing Did the Hen Cluck,* which he sent to his brothers in Moscow.

At nineteen, when he joined them in Moscow and attended the Medical School there, he wrote a short farce called *A Clean-Shaven Secretary with a Pistol,* in which a haughty Armenian prince takes a poem to the editor of a poverty-stricken magazine and makes a terrible row when the editor rejects it. He also planned the scenario for another vaudeville sketch to be called *The Power of Hypnotism.*

By this time his medical studies were giving him the power of analysis which he from now on applied to the evils of society. He said: "As a doctor I have tried to diagnose the sicknesses of the soul correctly." In this vein he continued the long play which he had begun while a boy at Taganrog and by the time he was twenty years old, he had developed it into his first important full-length four-act play. It was long thought that the manuscript of this had been destroyed; but in 1923, some six years after the Russian Revolution, the manuscript, in Chekhov's handwriting but without any title, was discovered and published in the Soviet Union under the title *Fatherless.* In 1930 an English translation appeared under the title *That Worthless Fellow Platonov.* The central character in this play, Platonov, is in so many ways a prototype of Chekhov's later heroes and the play contains so many germs of Chekhov's later ideas, that is is worth while examining it in some detail. Platonov is a philosopher who takes whole days discussing labor, suffering, and freedom, but does nothing about them. He cries: "Evil seethes around me ... I sit, look, and am silent ... I see no prospect of change." His is a life that is more death than life. He says: "My soul has long been a skeleton. It is too late to resurrect me." To be sure, he is only twenty-seven years old. There are traces of former beauty in his features, but "on his face are inscribed all the ten plagues of Egypt." He loves all human beings, especially all women. "Without a woman, a man is like an engine without steam." He is devoted to his wife. He worships a brilliant widow. He loves his friend's wife. He has an affair with a girl of the village. He does not know which of these women is the real one. In his philandering, his shamelessness, his lack of conscience, he is a Don Juan. Yet, in his melancholy, his introspection, his wavering, he is a Hamlet. He is a Hamlet with a difference: for whereas Hamlet feared to die, to sleep, to dream, Platonov feared life. His friend, whose wife he has betrayed, tries to stab him in his sleep, but he wakes up just in time. Another "dark character" receives money to wound him with a knife, but tears up the money and disappears. The women that have loved him turn against him. The widow feels that life is like smoking a cigarette: when you come to the end, you throw away the stub. The village girl summons him before the justice of the peace. His wife, feeling herself abandoned, tries to throw herself under a train and tries to take poison. Finally, his friend's wife, Sofya, who had perhaps really loved him most of all, tries to persuade him to go away with her and start life anew, earning bread by the sweat of the brow. When he rejects that plan too and she finds that she also is abandoned by this worthless fellow, she decides to shoot him to death.

In the midst of this terrific indictment of corrupt society, Chekhov shows us constantly the desire that Platonov has that we should rise above all this and, as he puts it, "tear ourselves up by the roots out of this mud. Oh, life! why don't we live as we might live!" Yet he feels that he belongs to a lost generation—a generation that shall die without having lived. They have no solid foundations. They are like poor orphans, illegitimate children, and it is that which suggested the title of the play, *Fatherless*.

In 1885, Chekhov wrote a short play of a somewhat more sympathetic nature. This was called *On the High Road* and was based on his short story called *In the Autumn*. The scene is in a Russian inn on a rainy autumn night. A drunken gentleman enters and orders vodka, but has no money to pay for it, and the other guests ridicule him. To pay for his drinks, he gives the innkeeper a golden locket containing a lady's portrait. It transpires that this is the portrait of his wife who has abandoned him on their wedding day. It is in his endeavor to drown that grief that he has taken to drink. Before long a lady, driving by the inn in the storm, enters seeking some one to repair her carriage. The guests recognize her as the woman whose portrait was in the locket. When she looks at her husband but treats him with scorn and leaves without a word of sympathy, the rough peasants in the inn turn to him with pity and buy him drinks. Among them the most striking is a tramp named Merik, a powerful nature, instinctively sensing the injustice and inducing the innkeeper to return the locket. This sympathetic picture of Merik reminds us, what we are too apt to forget, that Chekhov's own grandfather had been a serf. It was because this character seemed to be treated more sympathetically than the aristocracy that the play was prohibited by the censor. As Chekhov said of Merik, he was "created not for vagabondage nor for a settled life, but for revolution."

In the following year, 1886, Chekhov wrote an amusing stage monologue in one act, representing a hen-pecked husband trying to give a lecture, called *On the Harmfulness of Tobacco*. He also started a dramatization of his short story called *The Night before the Trial*, but this dramatic version was left unfinished.

Far more important was his drama in four acts called *Ivanov*, written in 1887. The director of the Korsh Theatre in Moscow, meeting Chekhov casually in the foyer one night, asked him for a play, expecting some light comedy or farce. Chekhov took this opportunity very seriously and set to work in his dark little study in the Moscow suburb where he lived, and wrote what turned out to be the most grim of all his plays, sending it to Korsh act by act to be submitted to the censor. It was composed in a fortnight of intensive work and produced at the Korsh Theatre November 19,

1887. Theatre-goers said they had never seen such a commotion in a playhouse, such general applause on the one hand and hissing on the other, as occurred at that first performance. In the fight that followed between those who hissed and those who applauded, the chairs in the pit became so moved about and mixed up that the auditors were unable to find their proper seats. Two persons were ejected by the police. Under these circumstances, the actors became more and more nervous and confused. There had been only three rehearsals in place of the ten which had been promised Chekhov. The actors forgot Chekhov's text and began to put in words of their own. Chekhov wrote afterwards: "Every word cut to my spine like a knife ... I failed to recognize my own play." Worst of all, so Chekhov tells us: "A fourth of the lines which I wrote for Ivanov had been wiped out by the censor." Such was what Chekhov had to put up with at the first performance that had been given of any full-length play of his. It was, however, only the first of a series of nights of agony which he had to undergo during the premières of his plays. It was not until seventeen years later, on October 19, 1904, when the Moscow Art Theatre produced *Ivanov* after Chekhov's death, that justice was done to the play. Then Chekhov's widow acted the part of Ivanov's wife and Kachalov acted Ivanov, giving as Chekhov had directed his great soliloquy in Act III "lyrically" and his final soliloquy in Act IV "furiously."

The central character of the play, Ivanov, seems at first sight to be another "worthless fellow" like Platonov in *Fatherless*. Yet he is a Platonov with a difference, and an important difference. He is a Platonov with a conscience. He says: "My conscience aches day and night!" Whereas Platonov drove ahead roughshod over every one without any scruples, Ivanov is always troubled with a feeling of guilt. This, as Chekhov, says, "is a very Russian feeling ... A Russian always feels guilty." He goes on to explain what it is that makes Ivanov in his eyes so characteristically Russian. Russians, Chekhov says, are marked by a sudden excitability, followed by a guilty feeling, and then a complete exhaustion. The French, on the other hand, always maintain their excitability at the same even level and so get used to it; while the Germans never get excited and so are never troubled by a sense of guilt, and never become exhausted.

In the case of Ivanov, the guilty conscience comes from the way he feels he has been treating his sick wife. She is a Jewess who has been most kind and devoted, but Ivanov has become bored with her somehow or other. He feels that his heartlessness has hastened her death. The severe strictures of Dr. Lvov only rub this in. Ivanov feels that he has become "a worthless fellow." He says: "How I despise myself! My God! How I hate my voice, my step, my hands, my clothes, my thoughts ... I cannot endure my contempt for myself." He feels that he is acting a sort of Hamlet, or Byron's Manfred or "a superfluous man" such as Turgenev wrote of. "As soon as the sun goes down, I am overcome by melancholy."

In this plight it is a young girl, Sasha who, like Sofya in *Fatherless,* tries to console him. She proposes that they should run off together to America. "I'll go with you to the ends of the earth ... If you make your way upward, I shall go upward too; if you go down into the pit, I shall go down into the pit too." When he points out that he is a failure, she says: "Any girl would rather love a failure than a man who is a success, because she would like to do something by loving. A man has his work to do, and so for him love is kept in the background; ... but for us love means life. I love you." Ivanov feels that by her willingness to make this sacrifice, she has rejuvenated him: "My youth is awakened within me. My old self is roused!" Yet at the same time he feels he cannot ask her to give her life for him, his old despair returns, and he takes out his revolver and shoots himself.

Unfortunately Chekhov had been so much discouraged by what seemed to him the distorted original performance of *Ivanov* at the Korsh Theatre that it was nearly ten years before he produced again a successful full-length play. In the meanwhile, his chief dramatic efforts consisted of a number of one-act sketches, studies, and "jests."

At the time when Chekhov had been writing about Ivanov's suicide in his play, an event happened in real life—a suicide—which profoundly shook Chekhov. A well-known and beautiful actress named Mlle Kadmin, in whom Chekhov was interested and whose photograph he had, feeling that she was betrayed by her lover, had decided to poison herself. She was to act in the theatre the part of the wife of Ivan the Terrible who was poisoned. Accordingly she arranged to take real poison and died in terrible realistic agony with which the other actors and the audience, including her faithless lover, were deeply impressed until they suddenly realized this was not acting but was reality. Chekhov's friend Suvorin, who had helped him in writing *Ivanov,* now undertook with Chekhov's help to write a play on this subject, which, changing the name of the actress, he called *Tatyana Repina.* It was acted at the Maly Theatre in Moscow by the great actress Ermolova and so agitated the audiences of that day that we are told the ladies went into hysterics. On the whole it was a much greater success than Chekhov's *Ivanov.*

Suvorin's play ended with Tatyana's death and gave no indication as to the effect of this upon her lover or whether he actually went ahead and married the other woman. The idea suddenly occurred to Chekhov to write a one-act sequel, representing the wedding taking place in the Cathedral Church. He has the archpriest, two young priests, a deacon, an acolyte, and a verger carrying out the whole complicated Russian marriage ceremony, interrupting it from time to time by the conversation between the bride and bridegroom and between their relatives and friends in the congregation. Talk turns to the suicide of the abandoned woman, Tatyana Repina. Suddenly, at a critical moment in the ceremony, a "Lady in Black" in the congregation utters a terrible groan. The bridegroom, troubled by a guilty conscience although he thought her safely buried in the graveyard, mutters in a hoarse whisper: "Tatyana Repina is here!"

This play, with what must have seemed a sacrilege of the Orthodox Church service, would never have been permitted by the censor to be performed on the stage. Chekhov merely sent a manuscript copy to his friend, Suvorin, saying: "After reading it, you can say 'Damn!' " Suvorin did not throw the manuscript away but had two copies privately printed, one for himself and one for Chekhov. After the Russian Revolution, Chekhov's copy was found and reprinted.

Chekhov next wrote for the Korsh Theatre some short plays which were more to Korsh's liking. One was a dramatic study in one act called *A Swan-Song* representing an old actor, about to die and left alone with the prompter in the empty theatre, trying to revive the days of his success by reciting passages from Shakespeare's *King Lear* and *Hamlet,* from Pushkin's *Boris Godunov* and Griboedov's *Sorrows of the Spirit.*

This was acted at the Korsh Theatre on February 19, 1888, and was followed on October 28 of the same year by a performance there of a "jest in one act" called *The Bear.* This proved a great success everywhere and was quickly translated into English and acted in America. As Chekhov says: "It was a stupid vaudeville and was successful because it was stupid."

This was followed by two other jests in one act, *The Proposal* in 1888 and *An Unwilling Martyr* in 1889; Chekhov also wrote a "scene in one act" called *The Wedding* in the same year.

Equally disappointed with the hostility to his *Ivanov* and disgusted with the too-facile success of his trivial farces, Chekhov vehemently denounced what he called "the rottenness of the theatre." He wrote: "The modern theatre is a sinful disease of the city. It must be swept away with a broom; it is unwholesome to love it ... The theatre is a serpent that sucks your blood ... It is a scaffold, where playwrights are executed."

To be sure Chekhov tried to show the other side of the picture too and, in his tale called *A Tedious Story,* he has the young girl say: "The theatre is a power uniting in itself all art ... The theatre, even in its present state, is higher than universities, than books, than anything in the world." So she thought before she went on the stage. The old professor in the story, however, knew better. The fact that a part of the public had hissed his *Ivanov* still rankled with Chekhov and he wrote: "I wish that the whole public could be fused into one man and write a play; and that you and I sitting in a box could hiss that play." It was natural, then, that Chekhov should for a time turn back from writing plays to writing stories. He said: "The narrative form is a lawful wife; the dramatic form is a noisy, flashy and insolent mistress."

Many of his short stories were later successfully turned into plays showing how fundamentally dramatic Chekhov was even when writing in the form of fiction. Among the stories so dramatized may be mentioned *The*

Drowning Man, The Thinker, The Witch, A Happy Ending, The Duel, The Ravine.

We know, also, that Chekhov planned some dramas on Biblical and historic subjects. One was to be a play on *Solomon*, of which Solomon's monologue still exists in Chekhov's handwriting. Another one was to be *Judith*, in which Judith was to be represented as falling in love with Holofernes, whom she has gone to kill. He also planned a drama on *Napoleon at Elba* and another drama on *Napoleon III and Empress Eugénie*. There remains the play which Stanislavski tells us Chekhov had in mind, in which two men in love with the same woman go on a polar expedition and see a white vision in the snow which proves to be the soul of the woman who had died in their absence. It appears, however, that none of these plays was ever completed or published or acted.

During this period, in 1888, Chekhov did attempt, with the help of his friend Suvorin, to write another full-length play. This he celled *The Wood-Demon* (*Leshi*), the name of the creature symbolizing the spirit of the woods in Russian folklore—a character whom Ostrovski had introduced into his *Snegurochka*. In Chekhov's case this demon of the woods is a young poet and landscape painter and lover of nature named Korovin. Once while a boy, Korovin had planted a birch tree and when it turned green and the leaves began to rustle in the breeze, his soul was filled with pride: he had caused one more tree to exist in the world. Without trees, life on earth would be unthinkable. He longed to be creative with living organisms, where others were destructive. The Russian forests were going down under the ax. Millions of trees were perishing. The home of wild animals and birds were being laid waste. Rivers were dwindling and drying up. Beautiful scenery was disappearing never to return. Every day the earth was growing poorer and more hideous. Korovin says: "A wood-spirit sits in me." He would preserve the forests, restore the forests, the forests that beautify the country and teach man to understand what is beautiful. "Climate is to some extent in our power. I like to feel that if in a thousand years man is to be happy, I shall have had some small hand in it." In this way, Korovin swings his mind over all Russia and over ten centuries to come.

On December 27, 1889 *The Wood-Demon* was performed at Abramova's Theatre in Moscow, but only ran for six performances. To Chekhov, the opening night was a nightmare. The actors played well, but did not know their parts. The actresses did know their parts, but acted badly. To make matters worse, the part of the young heroine had been given to a rich woman who was a lessee of the theatre, but enormously fat. The small actor who was acting the part of the lover could not reach his arms around her. When the forest fire, the great tragedy to the wood-spirit, came, the devices of the theatre were not sufficient to make it convincing and the audience burst into laughter. Chekhov, discouraged, refused to have the play printed or acted anywhere else.

The play, however, seems to have had a strong influence on Chekhov's later and more successful *Uncle Vanya*. The ideals held by the demon of the woods, Korovin, reappear in those held by Dr. Astrov. The discouraged but hard-working manager of the estate, toiling for the owner his insufferably pompous and gouty brother-in-law, was a rough sketch for Uncle Vanya himself and his brother-in-law. The dramatic scene between the two women at the end of the second act reappeared in the later play. Some have gone so far as to claim that *Uncle Vanya* was merely the last revised version of *The Wood-Demon* with the name changed. Chekhov, however, stoutly insisted that *Uncle Vanya* was a wholly independent play.

With the exception of an unimportant "joke in one act" called *The Anniversary*, written in 1891, it was seven years before Chekhov produced another play.

In the meanwhile, however, a seemingly trifling event in the life of a friend of his had made a strong impression on him. In 1892, while taking a walk in the country with Ilya Levitan, the talented Russian landscape painter, the moody Levitan, who had a hunting gun with him, shot a sea-gull flying over the river. Chekhov, somewhat in the spirit of his wood-demon, said: "Another beautiful living creature is gone, but two stupid men went home to supper." Later Levitan, feeling that he was scorned by the woman he loved, cast the dead bird at her feet and threatened to kill himself. Chekhov, like Trigorin in *The Sea-Gull*, jotted this episode down as "a subject for a little sketch."

In 1895 he began elaborating this relatively insignificant event into his full-length play *The Sea-Gull*. Here it was the emotional young writer, Constantine Treplev, who lays the sea-gull which he has shot at the feet of the young girl whom he loves, Nina, and says: "Soon I shall kill myself in the same way."

The sea-gull becomes a symbol of Nina herself, much as the wild duck had been a symbol of Hedvig in Ibsen's *Wild Duck*. Although he sometimes made fun of him, Chekhov wrote: "You know Ibsen is my favorite writer." Again in Strindberg's *Countess Julie*, the dead canary had been a symbol for Julie. In Knut Hansun's *At the Gates of the Kingdom*, too, a sea-gull was used as a symbol, and from then on symbolic birds became commonplace among the symbolists. Chekhov, however, used symbolism sparingly and half humorously. Nina does not return Constantine's love, being infatuated with a helpless and hopeless love for the older and more successful writer, Trigorin. Like some wild sea-bird she disappears from their midst, only to put in a fleeting appearance before Constantine, toward the end of the play, and then disappear again into the darkness leaving him more despondent than ever. He has wanted to bring "new forms of expression" into literature; but now he realizes that "A man should write without thinking about forms at all, write because thoughts spring freely from his soul." Despairing of ever achieving this, as he is of achieving his love, and mocked by his mother and by the older writer, Trigorin, who has stolen from him both fame and love, he decides to take his own life.

On the fateful night of October 17, 1896, Chekhov's *Sea-Gull* was produced at the great Imperial Theatre in St. Petersburg, the famous Alexandrinski Theatre. In the cast were some of the best actors of the day: Davydov, Varlamov, and Vera Kommissarzhevskaya, whom Chekhov himself admitted was a wonderful artist. At the rehearsals, he tells us, "many people were moved to tears as they looked at her and said that she was the first actress in Russia." At the first performance, however, the audience was not in the right mood for so serious a play. They came expecting to laugh at Chekhov's jokes. Nina's magnificent soliloquy in the play within the play about nature, beginning "men, lions, eagles, partridges, horned-deer, geese, spiders...." was met only with guffaws of laughter. This unnerved the actors and they gave their worst performance. At the end, when Constantine shoots himself off stage and Dr. Dorn, to reassure the mother, says: "It is nothing! My bottle of ether has burst!" the audience again broke into laughter.

For the third time within a decade, poor Chekhov had had to undergo the terrible ordeal of a first-night failure. At *Ivanov* in 1887, there had been those terrible hisses; at *The Wood-Demon* in 1889, there had been that terrible acting; and now, in 1896 at *The Sea-Gull,* there had been, worst of all, this terrible laughing at the wrong places. As Chekhov wrote afterwards: "On the 17 of October it was not my play that failed, but I myself." Again he said: "The play has fallen flat and come down with a crash. ... If I were to live seven hundred years, I shall never again write plays or have them acted."

Chekhov apparently did not mean this very seriously, and took this his third failure, on the whole, more philosophically than he had the first. He wrote: "After the performance, I had supper at Romanov's, which is quite the correct thing. Then I went to bed, slept soundly, and next day went home without uttering a word of complaint.... When I got home I took a dose of castor oil, and had a cold bath, and now I am ready to write another play." Within two months this new play, *Uncle Vanya,* was well under way.

Meanwhile, at the Alexandrinski, the second and third performances were going much better than the first, and before long the play was being acted also in the leading theatre in Kiev. It was not, however, until two years later that a really adequate performance of *The Sea-Gull* was given. This, as all the world now knows, was at the Moscow Art Theatre. They had started on October 14th, 1898 with *Czar Fedor Ivanovich.* Chekhov had gone to see this play and had been enchanted with the actress taking the part of the Czarina. This was Olga Knipper, whom Chekhov later married. He had also become one of the shareholders in the theatre and now on December 17, 1898, only two months after the opening of the theatre, came the memorable first night of *The Sea-Gull* there.

On that occasion the actress Roxanova, in her presentation of the dreamy, mysterious sea-gull girl Nina, gave a marvellous impression of someone "trying not to cry." Stanislavski's wife, Lilina, in sombre black, so tore the hearts of the audience by her final words at the end of the first act that when the curtain fell there was a moment of awful silence, followed by "the roar and thunder of mad ovation." Meyerhold, who was then still acting at the Moscow Art Theatre, gave an emotional performance of the young poet Constantine which Nemirovich-Danchenko described as "tender, touching, and definitely decadent." The part of his mother was acted by the beautiful Olga Knipper. The older writer Trigorin was acted by Stanislavski himself. Chekhov's only criticism was that Stanislavski had made him too well-dressed, and too good-looking. Chekhov said: "The shoes must be torn and the trousers checked and Trigorin must not be handsome. In this lies the salt of the part.... Nina loves him for his fame, not for his clothes or for his looks."

So great was the success of this performance at the Moscow Art Theatre that it became a landmark both in the life of Chekhov and in the history of the theatre. For Chekhov from now on there were no more of those horrible failures, only successes. For the theatre, it was this play, a play by a living author and a play that fitted into all their theories of psychological realism, that marked the real beginning of their new movement. They had helped to make the play famous, and the play in turn helped to make them famous. From now on, on the curtains of the theatre even when they traveled abroad, on their programs, on their letterheads, on the books they published, was this emblem of the Sea-Gull (*Chaika*). The auditorium of the Art Theatre itself became a sort of "moon-lit, sea-gull-haunted place."

Meanwhile, the play upon which Chekhov was already at work, *Uncle Vanya,* was finished and published in 1897. During 1898 it was acted successfully in the provinces and Chekhov was planning to have it acted at the regular Imperial Theatre in Moscow, the Maly Theatre. But they demanded so many changes in his text that he withdrew it and handed it over to the Moscow Art Theatre, where it was finally acted on October 26, 1899. The part of Dr. Astrov, reëmbodying the nature philosophy of *The Wood-Demon,* was acted by Stanislavski. The part of Uncle Vanya himself, acted by Vishnevski, had developed into something far beyond the character of Chekhov's earlier heroes. Like Platonov in *Fatherless* or Ivanov in *Ivanov,* Vanya seems at first sight to be another "worthless fellow," another "superfluous man." Yet there has been a real evolution here. Platonov, way back in 1880, had been the unscrupulous wrecker of women's hearts until he had driven one of them to murder him. Ivanov, in 1887, with more sense of his own guilt, had killed himself, and now, in 1899, Uncle Vanya neither drives others to kill him nor kills himself, though in a moment of distraction he had made a futile effort to kill his infuriating brother-in-law. Moreover Uncle Vanya is no idle waster, but works hard day and night to preserve the estate that had passed into the hands of his brother-in-law. Here again there is a young girl, Sonya, to console him; yet in her too we can mark the evolution from her earlier prototype. Sofya in *Fatherless*, when she could not persuade Platonov to run away with her, had no recourse but to shoot him. Sonya in *Ivanov*, although she could not persuade Ivanov to go with her to America, remained faithful to him till his death. Finally, in *Uncle Vanya*, this new Sonya, far from urging her Uncle Vanya to run away, begs him to stick patiently to his job. At the end, when the others are left and there is only the soft tone of the guitar heard in the background, she says:

We must go on living. . . . We shall work for others, both now and in our old age, and have no rest; and when our time comes we shall die without a murmur, and there beyond the grave . . . we shall rejoice and look back at these troubles of ours with tenderness, with a smile—and we shall rest. I have faith, uncle . . . we shall see all heaven lit with radiance. . . . We shall rest!

Uncle Vanya cannot share her simple faith but there are tears in his eyes as he goes on working. In such a play, the significance lies not so much in what is said as in what is left unsaid. As Chekhov wrote of *Uncle Vanya*: "The whole meaning and drama of man is in internal and not in external phenomena."

The actors of the Moscow Art Theatre and also Chekhov himself were disappointed that he was not able to go to Moscow to see their performance of *Uncle Vanya*. At this time, on account of his increasing tuberculosis, the doctors insisted that he should stay in the warmer climate of the Crimea, in the house that he had there up above Yalta on the beautiful shores of the Black Sea. As Stanislavski put it: "Since Mohammed could not come to the mountain, the mountain would go to Mohammed." Accordingly, during the following month of May, 1900, the spring of the year and the spring of the new century, the entire company of the Moscow Art Theatre made their famous trip to visit Chekhov in Yalta and to act his *Uncle Vanya* there for his special benefit. It was a great occasion attended by musicians such as the young and promising Rakhmaninov, older Russian authors such as Bunin and Kuprin, and, as Stanislavski described him, "the new sensation—Maxim Gorki."

In *Uncle Vanya* the unmitigated gloom which had pervaded Chekhov's earlier full-length plays was brightened at the end by Sonya's vision of a better world; but that was only "beyond the grave." In Chekhov's two remaining plays, the only two written expressly for the Moscow Art Theatre, the evolution was pushed still farther and gives us a glimpse of a possible better life here on earth. As Stanislavski put it about these final plays: "The men and women of Chekhov no longer bathe in their own sorrow. They, like Chekhov himself, seek life, joy, laughter, courage. They want to live and not to die. They are active and surge to overcome the hard and unbearable impasses into which life has plunged them. It is not their fault that Russian life has killed initiative and the best of beginnings and interferes with the free action and life of men and women."

By this time Chekhov was hard at work on a new play to be called *The Three Sisters*. He himself chafed at his exile in Yalta and longed to be in Moscow, where he could be near his friends in the Moscow Art Theatre and above all their greatest actress, Olga Knipper. In his youth at Taganrog, he had longed to get to Moscow and now again he felt the nostalgic longing to be there. It is his voice that we hear ringing through the voices of the three sisters: "Oh, to go to Moscow, to Moscow, to Moscow!" It was this famous passage that the Theatre of the Crooked Looking-Glass parodied when they had the melancholy sisters run through the whole declension of the noun: "Moskva, Moskvy, Moskve, Moskvu, Moskvoyu, o Moskve!"

Chekhov wrote Gorki that *The Three Sisters* was very difficult to write, more difficult than any of his other plays. His problem was to have "three heroines" and to make "each of the three a separate type." Olga, the eldest of the three sisters is a hard-working school teacher, whose life is barren of romance. Masha, the second, is unhappily married to the dull unimaginative Kuligin, but has a romantic attachment to the far more interesting and imaginative Lieutenant-Colonel Vershinin. Irina, the youngest, is engaged to a young Baron who is killed in a duel. As she says: "My soul is like a wonderful piano, only the key with which to unlock it has been lost"—a line intentionally omitted from an important American production of the play.

Chekhov himself said of this play: "Its mood is duller than the dull." A veil of grayness closes down upon the characters. The gloom and doom of the old Russia covers them. The sense of tragedy makes it a painful comedy. Yet, compared to Chekhov's other long plays, we can find a real note of optimism here or, if not of optimism, then at least of meliorism, a sense that if things are not yet all for the best in the best of all possible worlds, at least there is a possibility of things getting better in the future. Instead of saying: "Eat, drink, and be merry; for tomorrow we die!" they seem to be saying: "Work, toil, and be patient; for tomorrow we live!"

The young Baron seems to foresee the coming of a revolution. He says: "The time is at hand, an avalanche is in motion, a mighty clearing storm is coming and will blow the laziness, the indifference, the distaste for work, the rotten boredom out of our society. In another twenty-five or thirty years every one will have to work!" It was not in twenty-five or thirty years, but in sixteen years that there came the revolution in 1917.

Vershinin, a part that was acted by the greatest actors of the Moscow Art Theatre, Kachalov and Stanislavski, places the millennium farther in the future. He says:

In two or three hundred years, perhaps in a thousand years—the time does not matter—a new happy life will come. We may have no share in that life, of course, but we are living for it, we are working for it, yes and suffering for it. We are creating it and that alone is the purpose of our existence—that is our happiness.... Life on earth will be unimaginably beautiful and marvellous.... Oh, what a wonderful life that will be.... People will look at our present manner of life with horror and derision.... People will be born who will be better than we are!

Toward the end of the play, even the brother of the three sisters, unhappily married as he is to a cheap, scolding wife, catches a glimpse of this better way of life. As he wheels the baby carriage, he looks down and sees his son and heir there (the significance of this seems to have been missed in the American production) and says:

The present is hateful, but when I think of the future, I feel light-hearted and free. A new light is dawning. I see liberty coming. I see how my child will be freed from sloth, from kvas, from goose and cabbage, from sleeping after dinner, from mean, parasitic living!

In the closing lines of the play, while the music of the departing regiment fades in the distance and the three sisters are left behind, each in turn echoes this faith in the future. The youngest, Irina, whose fiancé has been killed, says: "A time will come when every one will know what all this suffering is for. Meanwhile, we must live, we must work.... I will give my life to those to whom it may be of use." The second, Masha, whose lover has gone away with his regiment, says: "Oh, how the music plays! They are going away from us.... We are left alone to begin our life over again. We must live!" Finally, the oldest, Olga, putting her arms around the other sisters, says to them: "Our sufferings will pass into joy for those who will live after us. Happiness and peace will be established upon earth and they will remember kindly and bless those who have lived before. Oh, dear sisters, our life is not ended yet. We shall live!... We shall know what we are living for, what we are suffering for. If we only knew—if we only knew!"

The first performance of *The Three Sisters* on January 31, 1901, was a great success. Olga Knipper as Masha, the second of the three sisters, made a particularly deep impression. In May of that same year, she was married to Chekhov and he soon set to work writing his last great play, *The Cherry Orchard,* in which the central character for the first time was to be a woman and was to be acted by his wife. This made an almost perfect combination. The author, like a father, planted the seed. The actress, like a mother, nourished it and brought it to life. The characters which they had thus created together were their children. Rarely in the history of drama has there been so happy a collaboration.

The Cherry Orchard marks the culmination of twenty-five years of Chekhov's dramatic work. He no longer felt the need of violent external dramatic action that he had in his earlier plays. In *Fatherless* of 1880, there had been at least two attempts at suicide, two attempts at manslaughter, and one murder. In *Ivanov* of 1885, there was the final suicide, as there was in *The Sea-Gull* of 1896. In *Uncle Vanya* of 1899 there were two futile attempts at manslaughter; and in *The Three Sisters* of 1901 there was the duel in which the young Baron was killed. In each one of these plays there had been at least one pistol shot. Now, in *The Cherry Orchard,* Chekhov boasted: "There is not a shot in it."

What tragedy there was in it was not the tragedy of blood, murder, and sudden death. It was the tragedy of the commonplace or, as Gorki said, "the tragedy of life's trivialities." As in life itself, there was a poignancy in seemingly trivial matters, almost harder to bear than a heroic death. Chekhov wanted to be true to life. He makes his heroine in *The Cherry Orchard* say: "You should not look at plays, you should look at yourselves." The dramatist is always tempted to manipulate life, so as to make it art. For Chekhov, life was greater than art. Behind the art of other plays, you sometimes do not feel the life. Behind the life of Chekhov's plays you do not feel the art. His was the art to conceal art by making it seem to have all the inconsequentiality of life itself. His was an art of little things, but that art in itself was not a little thing.

In *The Cherry Orchard,* Chekhov steered a middle course between comedy and tragedy. He insisted that it was "not a tragedy, but a comedy, even in part a farce." Yet, in reality, it had elements of both. The tragedy was the disintegration of a decaying world. The element of joy was in the struggle for the beginning of a new world. Yet it is in that tragic element that the comedy lies, and it is the struggle for happiness that seems so nearly tragic. Chekhov had the extraordinary gift to see the faults of his characters and to smile at them; to appreciate their joys and shed a tear. Chekhov did not create heroes or villains. His characters are neither out-and-out saints nor out-and-out sinners. As he said: "To judge between good and bad, between successful and unsuccessful, would need the eye of God." Chekhov's job was not to paint men as they should be, but to depict them as they are. His own unflinching intellectual honesty inspired the same desire in others. Gorki said of him: "In Chekhov's presence every one involuntarily felt the desire to be simpler, more truthful, more himself."

With this point of view in mind, Chekhov wanted in *The Cherry Orchard* to be fair both to the old order that was passing and to the new order which was already beginning to appear on the horizon. From the dawn of the new century in 1900 down to his death in 1904 Chekhov believed that Russia was on the eve of a revolution. Russia *was* on the eve of a revolution, but it was only the unsuccessful revolution of 1905 and not the successful revolution of 1917. Chekhov was already conscious of a growing demand for change. He longed to turn from the old futility and frustration to something full of life and purpose. Vera Kommissarzhevskaya, who had acted the tragic heroine in that tragic first performance of *The Sea-Gull,* wrote asking him about his new play; and he replied saying that it was to be: "Something entirely different, something cheerful and strong. We have outlived the gray dawdle. There is a sharp turn now in public opinion."

Chekhov, then, wanted to find a theme that could symbolize by some simple image the passing of Russia from the hands of the older gentry into those of a new class. This he found in the passing of Mme Ranevskaya's old estate with its house and cherry orchard into the hands of Lopakhin, a self-made man who had been the son of a serf. Chekhov treats with great tenderness the pathos of the situation for the old landowners; but he is not so unsympathetic toward the new order as is sometimes thought. His own father, like Lopakhin, had been the son of a serf. He wanted the part to be acted by Stanislavski himself and wrote to him on October 30, 1903, explaining: "Lopakhin is a very decent person in every sense. He must behave with perfect decorum, like an educated man with no petty ways or tricks of any sort, and it seems to me this part, the central one of the play, would come out brilliantly in your hands." Unfortunately Stanislavski did not act the part, and unfortunately many of the actors who have acted it have not carried out Chekhov's intentions.

The idea of bringing into his play the selling of an estate was not a new one to Chekhov. He had already touched on it in *Fatherless* in 1880 and *Uncle Vanya* in 1897. It was one familiar in American plays of the period, such as Denman Thompson's *The Old Homestead* of 1886 and Herne's *Shore Acres* of 1892. Indeed, the British comedian George Grossmith used to make fun of American drama saying that the essence of it consisted in the phrase: "Don't give up the old farm!"

In the case of the Russian estates of the old families, however, the attachment was one of long tradition and of deep sentiment. When Mme Ranevskaya returns to say good-by to her cherry orchard, she remembers how as a child she had looked out from the nursery windows to see the cherry trees and how happiness waked with her every morning. She remembers how she used to see her mother walking all in white among the trees along the path by the arbor and she seems to see a white tree bending like a woman. She cries: "Oh, my orchard! after the dark gloomy autumn and the cold winter you are young again and full of happiness. The heavenly angels have never left you. All white!—my sweet beautiful cherry orchard! My life, my youth, my happiness, good-by! Good-by!"

For the young student Trofimov—and the part was considered so important by the Moscow Art Theatre that they gave it to their greatest actor, Kachalov—the cherry orchard, on the contrary, was a symbol of all that was terrible in the old Russia: private property, absentee landlordism, serfdom. He says:

Your orchard is a fearful thing and when in the evening or at night one walks about the orchard, the old bark of the trees glimmers dimly in the dusk and the old cherry trees seem to be dreaming of centuries gone by and to be tortured by fearful visions.... From every cherry in the orchard, from every leaf, from every trunk there are human creatures looking at you. You can hear their voices. It is awful!

If for Mme Ranevskaya the past is something beautiful which should be preserved, for Trofimov it is something evil that should be destroyed. He says: "We must expiate our past, we must break with it." The idea of an orchard, a garden, should be something much larger than this private estate. He cries: "All Russia is our orchard. The earth is great and beautiful—there are many beautiful places in it." As the moon is slowly rising and they hear in the distance the sound of a guitar and a breaking harp-string, mournfully dying away, he turns to Mme Ranevskaya's daughter, seventeen-year-old Anya, with whom he is in love, and cries:

To eliminate the petty and transitory which hinders us from being free and happy—that is the aim and meaning of our life. Forward! We go forward irresistably towards the bright star that shines yonder in the distance. Forward!... I have a foreboding of happiness, Anya. I see glimpses of it already. Yes. Here is happiness—here it comes! It is coming nearer and nearer; already I can hear its footsteps. And if we never see it—if we may never know it—what does it matter? Others will see it after us!... I am strong and proud. Humanity is advancing toward the highest truth, the highest happiness, which is possible on earth, and I am in the front ranks. I shall get there. I shall get there or I shall show others the way to get there.

Such was Chekhov's final vision of the coming of a new age—a new age which he unfortunately did not live to see.

The first performance of *The Cherry Orchard* was on Chekhov's birthday, January 17, 1904—his forty-fourth birthday and his last. He was now suffering great pain—such pain, he said, that it made him want to climb the walls of his room. Yet he made every effort to be present for this great occasion. In speaking of the Moscow Art Theatre, he said: "It is the only theatre that I love." When one remembers his frightful experiences at the other theatres, one can well understand this. If the Maly Theatre in Moscow had become the "House of Ostrovski," the Moscow Art Theatre was fast becoming the "House of Chekhov."

During the performance Chekhov stood in the wings to the right of the stage suffering and deadly pale and unable to control his coughing—but happy. It was not only his birthday but also his jubilee, the twenty-fifth anniversary of his literary activity. It was a triple triumph, but as he jested among the presents and flowers that were showered upon him, for those that knew the precarious state of his health, the flowers seemed already to have the smell of a funeral.

The doctors sent him to Badenweiler in the Black Forest in Germany and there, less than six months after the performance of *The Cherry Orchard,* Chekhov died. Up to the last moment, he tried to keep his wife cheerful by making up funny stories with bits of drama. On the night he died, if she failed to leave his sick bed and put in an appearance at supper, it was not because of her grief, but because she had been so entertained by his merriment that she had forgotten about eating. The doctor had ordered champagne and he took the glass, turned to his wife with a smile, saying, "I have not drunk champagne for a long time." He drank the glass to the bottom, lay down peacefully on his left side and presently was silent forever.

When the train brought his body back to Moscow, his friends that went to meet him there noticed, as one of life's little ironies, that the only car which the Germans had found available to carry the body was a green refrigerator car marked: "For the Conveyance of Oysters." Chekhov had been the uncompromising foe of all that was banal; and now, as Gorki said, this seemed to be the "triumphant laugh of banality over its tired enemy."

Meanwhile the Moscow Art Theatre had continued to act his four great plays and later in the year 1904, the year of his death, they revived *Ivanov* and produced dramatizations of three of his short stories: *Surgery, The Malefactor,* and *Non-Commissioned Officer Prischbeev.* In 1906 the Czar's censor forbade *The Cherry Orchard* for popular stages on the ground that: "The play depicts in too clear colors the degeneration of the nobility." Only four performances of it were given that year in the Moscow Art Theatre.

It has sometimes been assumed that the Soviet Union has turned its back on Chekhov. At the time of the Russian Revolution of 1917 there was some uncertainty as to what would be the attitude toward Chekhov's plays of the new audiences, which then flooded the theatres. It happened that at that time the Moscow Art Theatre was acting *The Cherry Orchard*. Stanislavski, Chekhov's widow, and the other actors were impersonating the rôles of the landed proprietors of the old régime—the very class against which the common people were in revolt. Peering through the curtains, the actors nervously scanned this new revolutionary audience and muttered: "Perhaps they will attack us and drive us from the stage." From the auditorium a confusion of excited voices came to their ears. When the curtain rose, the actors waited in fear and trembling for pandemonium to break loose. But the beauty of Chekhov's lyricism, which in this play lights up the dying Russian nobility, that poetry apparently so unfit for the present situation, did not fail to cast its spell upon the audience even then. The new spectators were deeply attentive. The lines of Trofimov about the coming of a new age were more appreciated than they ever had been before. At the end of the performance there was a tremendous ovation. The Moscow Art Theatre felt that the future of Chekhov was in safe hands.

Six years after the Revolution, when the Moscow Art Theatre visited the United States in 1923 and 1924, the influence of Chekhov was more deeply felt in America than it had been before. It left its imprint on the lyric naturalism of the dialogue and the self-torture of the characters depicted by various American playwrights. In America and in England, listening to the original Russian, men heard the "music of the emotions" to an extent hardly possible in translation. As Grenville Barker said, when you turn from the sound of the voices to a reading of the text, it was like turning from an opera to a reading of the libretto: "You miss the sound of the music."

Bernard Shaw is not given to considering his own plays inferior to those of any other dramatist—not even Shakespeare. Yet he said: "Every time I see a play by Chekhov, I want to chuck all my own stuff into the fire."

On January 17, 1944, the Moscow Art Theatre celebrated the fortieth anniversary of their first performance of *The Cherry Orchard* by a production in which there were so many of the original cast that one gets a strange sense of the stability and continuity of Chekhov, unchanged through two Russian Revolutions and two World Wars. One thinks of Russia as having undergone great changes. Yet where else in the world today could you find a theatrical tradition so little changed? Chekhov's widow, for example, was still acting the part of the heroine exactly as she had forty years earlier. From Moscow, on that occasion, she sent a cablegram of friendly greeting to Margaret Webster who was directing a production of *The Cherry Orchard* in New York at the same time. It ended with a tribute to Chekhov's art and that "most delicate instrument of acting—psychological realism."

The fact that the love for Chekhov in the Soviet Union has not merely been maintained, but has actually increased since the Russian Revolution, is borne out by the number of times that *The Cherry Orchard* has been produced each year at the Moscow Art Theatre. In 1905, the year after its first production, it appeared in the repertory twenty-four times; but in 1906 it fell, as we have seen, to only four productions. On the other hand during 1918, the year after the Russian Revolution, it was already given some twenty-eight times, and a dozen years later, in 1930, it had increased to seventy-one performances. If we add to these performances by the Moscow Art Theatre those by other theatres throughout the Soviet Union, we will find that since the Revolution no play has been so popular there as Chekhov's *Cherry Orchard,* with a single exception—Gorki's *Lower Depths.*

When the actors of the Moscow Art Theatre came in the spring of 1900 to make their famous visit to Chekhov's beautiful villa at Yalta overlooking the Black Sea, among the well-dressed and polished intellectuals there was a strange youth dressed in a Russian peasant blouse. In his granite features they could see marks of the suffering and hardships he had already been through, but in his soft blue eyes they could see the great compassion he felt for all who suffered. This was Alexei Maximovich Peshkov, better known by his pen-name, Maxim the Bitter or Maxim Gorki (1869-1936). He had been a shoemaker's apprentice, a poor tailor, a bake-shop worker, a stevedore on the Volga River. He had already been to prison several times for his revolutionary activities. At the age of fifteen he had seen a play by Saltykov-Shchedrin which, he said, "made me feel the terrific force of the theatre." In the summer of 1897 he had organized a theatre among the peasants at Manuylovka in the Ukraine and in the following year had begun to correspond with Chekhov. In February, 1900, he had dedicated his first novel, *Foma Gordeev,* to Chekhov; but so far had not tried his hand at writing a play. Chekhov, however, invited Gorki to come to Yalta in May to meet the actors of the Moscow Art Theatre. With pardonable exaggeration he wrote: "Do come. Study their rehearsals and in five to eight days you will write a play!"

Somewhat hesitatingly Gorki came, but found that they were even more scared of him than he was of them. The leading actress, Olga Knipper, who was to become the wife of Chekhov the following year, said of Gorki's coming: "He shot like a rocket into our quiet intelligentsia life and startled us with his accounts of a world unknown to us." As Gorki himself wrote: "I came from below, from the nethermost ground of life, where was nought but sludge and murk. I was the truthful voice of life, the harsh cry of those who still abode down there and who let me come up to bear witness to their hardship."

Stanislavski wanted for the Moscow Art Theatre a new play expressing "discontent, protest, and the dream of a hero boldly speaking the truth." He was eager to get "the new sensation, Maxim Gorki," as he called him, to write such a play for them. He says: "Once of an evening, sitting on the terrace and listening to the sound of the Crimean waters in the darkness, Gorki told me of his idea of a play he had in mind, which he later called *The Lower Depths."* Gorki had stored up in his memory the lives of the down-and-outs, the submerged populace at the bottom of Russian society. These he wished to bring to the surface. Gorki was, like Dante, a man who had emerged from hell, but he did not come empty-handed. He brought with him the lives and sufferings of those who had been his companions in torment, of those who might yet be his comrades in salvation.

The actors of the Moscow Art Theatre spoke of Gorki's "searching impetuosity turned inwards." They felt "under his calm exterior the storehouse of power in reserve, ready to be hurled forth." Stanislavski tells us how when the company set sail, "Gorki stood on the shore at Yalta watching our steamboat leave, calmly leaning against the bales of baggage and looking thoughtfully into the distance." Gorki then set feverishly to work writing plays. Chekhov bombarded him with letters: "Write! Write! Write!" Yet, instead of the "five to eight days" that Chekhov had optimistically prophesied, Gorki worked for nearly two years on his play, or rather on his two plays. For, in addition to *The Lower Depths,* dealing with the slums, he was also planning to write a play called *The Petty Bourgeois* (also translated as *The Smug Citizen*) dealing with a dull middle-class family.

It is hard to say which of the two is the more devastating picture: that of the seething underworld of *The Lower Depths* in their cellar, or that of the drabness and complacence of *The Smug Citizen* and his family in their comfortable parlor. Both reflected conditions which Gorki wanted to do away with. As Chekhov said: "Gorki is a destroyer who must destroy all that deserves destruction. In this lies his whole strength and it is for this that life has called him."

It was for this very reason that the powers-that-be in Russia were alarmed at the project of either play. They felt, however, that a play dealing with the middle-class might be safer than one dealing with the proletariat. The Moscow Art Theatre was about to move into their new building equipped with all the latest devices for realistic stage settings. This was to be nearer to the heart of Moscow, in the Kamergerski Street which, after the Revolution, was renamed for the Moscow Art Theatre. They decided to open the new theatre with Gorki's *Smug Citizen* first and then to follow it up two months later with his *Lower Depths*.

In the meanwhile, before the new theatre building was opened, *The Smug Citizen* was tried out at a private performance at the Mikhailovski Theatre in St. Petersburg on April 9, 1902. Gorki's election to the Russian Imperial Academy had just been annulled by the authorities on account of his radicalism. Indignation at this spread among the masses. The police feared a demonstration in favor of Gorki and a wave of protest against the authorities. During the rehearsal, the neighborhood of the theatre was accordingly guarded by mounted police. As Stanislavski said, it looked more like the preparation for a general battle than for a general rehearsal.

The Czar's censors, who were present at this dress rehearsal, cut out from the play all passages criticising social conditions in Russia. The head of the bourgeois family, Bessemenov, was not allowed to say: "The times are troubled. Everything is cracking to pieces." On the eve of the Revolution of 1905, this was so near the truth that the authorities could not permit it to be said. Above all, however, the censors were disturbed by one character who was introduced into this play—the grimy and powerful driver of a railroad locomotive, Nil. When he enters, dirty and hungry after a run through the rain and the storm and the cold, the master class would put him as a worker in his place. He turns on them and says: "He who works is the master!" At the end Nil cries: "I and the other honest people who work are commanded now by swine, by fools, by thieves. But they will not be in power forever. The time will come when they will disappear and vanish from our society, just as abscesses disappear from a healthy body."

Such passages sounded like the voice of the coming revolution and in a copy of the text of *The Smug Citizen* which is still preserved in what was the Imperial Library of St. Petersburg, you will find them crossed out by the red pencil of the Czar's censor. It was only, then, in an emasculated form that *The Smug Citizen* could be acted at the opening of the new building of the Moscow Art Theatre on October 25, 1902. It was not until after the Revolution of 1917 that the play could be seen at last in its true form and its true force. In the Red Army Theatre in Moscow in 1935, for example, all these passages were restored and the full significance of the play was brought out

In the meanwhile, even before *The Smug Citizen* opened at the Moscow Art Theatre, rehearsals were under way for another and still greater play of Gorki's, *The Lower Depths*. Gorki had come to Moscow to read to the actors the manuscript of his masterpiece. The opera singer Shaliapin and the dramatist Andreev were also there to listen spellbound to his reading. Kachalov, perhaps the greatest living actor of the day, tells how beautifully Gorki read, and how, when he came to the scene where the pilgrim, Luka, tries to console old Anna on her death-bed, the actors held their breath in stillness and Gorki's own voice trembled and broke as he cried, "The Devil take it!" and wiped away a tear with his finger, ashamed to let them see how much he was being affected by his own play.

The actors became intensely interested in the new types that they were going to depict, these denizens of the lower depths, these "creatures that once were men." They made Gorki take them at night to the Khitrov market in Moscow, where they wandered through the dark and gloomy cellars in a labyrinth of underground dens. Stanislavski gives a terrifying picture of the rows of tired people, men and women, whom they found lying there on boards like corpses. When he told some of them that he was planning to produce a play about people like them, they were so touched that they began to weep. Chekhov's wife was to play the part of the prostitute Nastya, and Gorki naïvely offered to bring a street-walker to stay with her so that the actress would be able to "get a deeper insight into the psychology of an empty soul."

Again, before the play was permitted to be acted, the censors got busy and cut out no less than fifty-four passages. Pepel was not allowed to say: "The barons do not look on us as human beings." That might be taken as a criticism of the aristocracy. The policeman was not allowed to say: "I should know every one in my district, but I don't." He was only allowed to say: "I know every one in my district." Otherwise the policemen might seem not to be on their job. Kvashnaya was not allowed to say: "I prayed to God eight years, and He did not help me." That might imply that God is not on his job. When Pepel asks Luka: "Is there a God?" Luka was not allowed to reply: "If you believe there is, there is. If you believe there isn't, there isn't." That might shake faith in the existence of God. When the dying Anna asks Luka about the world after death he may not answer: "There will be nothing." He must answer: "There will be nothing—to be afraid of."

Even with all these challenging speeches cut out, or changed, there remained enough explosive powder packed away in the play to produce a tremendous effect. When the first performance finally came on the last day of the year 1902, the realistic intensity with which the actors stressed their lines, spoken out of the darkness of "the lower depths," was like hammering on dynamite. Never before or since has the Moscow Art Theatre had such a tremendous triumph. One enthusiast who was present wrote: "The old theatre had ceased to exist. The curtain rose and there appeared a new theatre. Life itself, in all its fullness down to the very dregs, was poured out on the stage."

Among these derelicts of society gathered together in this underground night's lodging, Gorki introduced the old pilgrim, Luka, acted with a marvelous combination of humor and pathos by the great comedian of the Moscow Art Theatre, Moskvin. At first sight it seemed as though Luka were going to convert each one of these wretches by making them into something better. He would turn the prostitute into a virtuous woman; he would console the dying Anna with a belief in Heaven; he would make the "Baron" believe in his aristocracy; he would make the thief into an honest man; he would cure the actor of his alcoholism and enable him to remember his lines. For a time he seemed to restore to them all their faith in themselves. But *The Lower Depths* does not have the facile, sentimental optimism of *The Passing of the Third Floor Back* or *The Servant in the House* or *The Messenger from Mars*. Gorki is too rigid a realist for that. He knows that men cannot be so permanently changed overnight. In the midst of the third act, during the scene in the courtyard outside when the murder takes place, the pilgrim Luka disappears as mysteriously as he had come. In the fourth act, once more in the darkness of the cellar, these characters in the absence of Luka and the temporary illusions which he had created, slump back into what they had been before or something worse, and the actor in despair hangs himself.

In this last act, the group are gathered together once more in their underground den in the brown shadows under the dim light. It is like some great painting of Rembrandt's come to life.

Out of this darkness comes booming the voice of Stanislavski, acting the part of Satin—Satin who had been the counterpart of Luka and, now that the pilgrim has gone, holds the field alone. Satin tells them that Luka lied to them, that weaklings need to be comforted by beautiful lies, that those who exploit them make use of lies; but the man who is strong and free, the man who is his own master, needs no lies. As he puts it:

Lies are the religion of slaves and the master of slaves! Truth is the God of the free man! ... What is the truth? ... Man is the truth! ... All is in man; all is for man! Man alone exists. Everything else is the creation of his hands and his brains. Man! That is something magnificent! What a proud ring the word has! Man! (Che-lo-vek!).... It is good to feel that you are a man. What do we work for? To fill our bellies? No! Man is higher than that! Man is higher than a full belly.... Man is born to conceive a better man.

Such was the voice of the potential power of man arising out of the lower depths. It stirred the audiences in Russia as they had never been stirred before. It reached out beyond the borders of Russia. Max Reinhardt's production in Berlin, under the title *Nachtasyl,* ran for five hundred nights though the German Kaiser refused to see it, not wanting to know how man lived in the lower depths. In America it was produced in German and in Russian long before Arthur Hopkins produced it in English. In *The Lower Depths* one could already hear the onward march of the coming Russian Revolution.

Since the Revolution of 1917, *The Lower Depths* can at last be acted in its unexpurgated text and it has proved the most popular of all plays in the Soviet Theatres. Upon Gorki's return to Moscow in 1928, the Moscow Art Theatre gave in his presence a magnificent performance with almost exactly the same cast that had acted it there when it had been first produced more than a quarter of a century earlier in 1902.

Gorki had been so pleased with those early productions of his first two plays by the Moscow Art Theatre in 1902 that he had written to Chekhov: "Not to love the Art Theatre is impossible; not to work for it is a crime!" He now realized what he had felt at fifteen, "the terrific force of the theatre." Both these plays had been awarded the Griboedov Prize and Gorki was encouraged to go on and write a third play to be called *Summer Folk*. This dealt with still another section of Russian Society—the intelligentsia—the futile intellectuals whom he represents living in idleness in a dacha or summer cottage. A real intellectual, hard working and rebellious, turns on them in a voice that might be Gorki's own and cries:

You are not really intellectuals. You are like summer visitors in your own country, fussy people looking out for your own personal comfort, talking disgustingly much, but doing nothing. You should be forging ahead, blazing a trail for the workers, helping them to find the best way out; but you have lost your own way and the workers now look upon you as their enemies, as parasites who are living from the work that they do.

At the first performance of this play at Vera Kommissarzhevskaya's Theatre in St. Petersburg on November 4, 1904, some of the intelligentsia in the audience hissed this attack on them. Gorki, however, instead of shrinking in the wings as the timid Chekhov might have done, came out before the footlights and vigorously hissed back at them. As he said afterwards: "I certainly out-hissed that bunch of high-brows!"

It was less than two months after this performance that the Revolution of 1905 broke out. Gorki had in a way been the prophet of this revolution, not merely in his plays, but in his famous "Song of the Stormy Petrel." In this he represented the rising of the storm like the rising of a revolution. Other birds begin flying away before the oncoming hurricane, but the stormy petrel flies in the teeth of the gale, crying: "Let the storm come more quickly! Let it break out mightily!"

Gorki himself had been "the stormy petrel of the revolution" and was quickly arrested and imprisoned in the Fortress of St. Peter and St. Paul. His cell in that heroic prison, No. 39 of the Trubetskoi Bastion, is today preserved as a shrine.

There in prison Gorki wrote his next play, the tragicomedy called *The Children of the Sun*. In this play a sympathetic woman Lisa has been present in the Square before the Winter Palace on the "Bloody Sunday" of

January 9, 1905, and has seen "the blood on the snow" when the Czar's officers shot down hundreds of men, women, and children. She finds that her sympathies are all with these victims. Her brother, however, and his snobbish friends feel that she and those with whom she sympathises are the "children of darkness," while he and his friends in their superior intelligence are "children of the sun." In the end their very arrogance provokes the indignant common people to attack them.

The play was produced later in that same year, on October 21, 1905, both by the Art Theatre in Moscow and by Kommissarzhevskaya in St. Petersburg. It was during those tumultuous October days when the first general strike in history was taking place, when there were terrible pogroms at Kiev and Tomsk, and when the Black Hundreds were carrying out a campaign of ruthless repression. In Moscow, a rumor spread that the Black Hundreds looking on Gorki as a dangerous revolutionist, were coming, and were going to attack the theatre during the first performance. In the last act, when the mob rushed on to the stage shooting, some of the audience thought that this was the Black Hundreds and a terrific panic broke out.

Gorki's *Barbarians* was written later in the same year, 1905, but was not produced until 1907 at the so-called Contemporary Theatre. In this play a group of scientists from the city go to live among peasants whom they look down on as "barbarians" although they really prove themselves, with their corruption and degeneracy, to be far more barbarian than the primitive peasants whom they despise.

A far more important play was that written in the following year, 1906, and called *Enemies*. Here Gorki represents the class conflict between the factory owners, sitting in their comfortable gardens, and the factory workers, toiling in the factory on the other side of the fence. The exasperated workers fling their challenge into the face of their oppressors: "We have lived long enough in the darkness—more than enough! But now we have kindled a new light which you will never be able to extinguish. No threats or fears will be able to extinguish it now!" The workers are arrested and led off to prison, but a young girl in the family of the owners cries: "These people will conquer in the end!"

The revolutionary challenge so permeated this whole play that the censor, realizing that it would not be enough to cut out certain passages alone, decided to prohibit the whole play. He wrote:

Because this play stresses sharply the terrible enmity between workers and employers, because it represents the workers as stoical fighters going consciously toward their goal, the abolition of capitalism, while it represents the employers as narrow egotists and enemies of the workers, therefore Gorki's *Enemies* cannot be permitted to be performed.

Accordingly, as long as the Czarist régime lasted, it was impossible to act Gorki's *Enemies* inside Russia. In that same year 1906, however, it was acted at the Kleines Theater in Berlin. It was only after the Russian Revolution that it could be acted in Russia itself, but since then splendid productions of it have been given at the Alexandrinski Theatre in Leningrad and at the Moscow Art Theatre. In the latter production Kachalov acted the manufacturer and Chekhov's widow acted the part of the manufacturer's wife.

In a play called *The Last Ones,* written in 1908, Gorki showed up the brutality and stupidity of the police and of the Black Hundreds during and after the Revolution of 1905. He maintained that only those unfit for any other work, only "the last ones" went into the police force. Again the censor prohibited the play in its entirety, giving as his reason that "It touches the burning question of the relations of the police to civilians. Accordingly I think it necessary to forbid the play." Again it was by Reinhardt in Berlin that the play was first produced and again it is only since the Soviets came into power that it could be acted in Russia.

In this period between the two revolutions, Gorki's freedom of expression was so hampered by the censor that the quality of his plays naturally suffered from it. In *Odd People,* written in 1910 and first acted at the New Dramatic Theatre, he unmasked a group of false characters, all hiding their real selves and pretending to be something else. Through the mouth of the one honest character in their midst, Gorki expresses his opinion of the Russia in that unhappy period, saying: "Russia is a half-destroyed temple and we are pretending to restore it by merely painting it over."

Another play written in 1910 was *Vassa Zheleznova.* This was acted in 1911 at the Nezlobinski Theatre in Moscow and has been revived since the Russian Revolution in the Moscow Trade Union Theatre, the Red Army Theatre, and elsewhere. It gives a terrible picture of a ruthless mother, Vassa Zheleznova, dominating her family by the power of money.

Still another play written in 1910 was a rather unimportant one-act play called *The Meeting* or *The Children.* This represents a group of flatterers meeting a prince at a railroad station in order to buy his forest and calling themselves his "children." In 1912 Gorki wrote a play called *The Zykovs* which was first acted in 1918, the year after the Revolution, at the People's House in Petrograd. It is an unpleasant picture of the Zykov father and son both in love with the same girl.

The False Coin, written in 1913 and produced later by Max Reinhardt in Germany, shows the corrupting influence of counterfeit money upon a poor watch-maker.

At this time Gorki, on account of his health, was living on the island of Capri in Italy. There Lenin while in exile came to see him, and, in spite of some differences in opinion, had a profound influence upon him. When the Revolution of 1917 broke out, Gorki hailed it as "the sunniest and greatest of all revolutions."

After the Revolution, Gorki did all he could at the so-called House of Scientists to look after the needs of the scientists and other scholars, to procure for them, with the help of the Gorki Fund in America, the apparatus, books, and learned periodicals so hard to get at that time in Russia. In 1918 he wrote a play called *The Old Man,* which was acted on January 1, 1919, at the Maly Theatre in Moscow, the first new play to be acted there since the Revolution. It was translated into English and published in 1924 under the title *The Judge.* Here he represents an old man, who has at last been released from prison, hunting down a former prison companion who has become successful and powerful and for whom he accordingly feels jealousy and hatred. Having suffered he cannot bear to see others happy; but, as Gorki says, "truth is not found in suffering." The situation was not dissimilar to that of other revolutionists—Mensheviks or Social Revolutionists or Anarchists—who had often been in the same prisons with the Bolsheviks under the Czar's régime, but were now jealous at seeing them in power and turned against them.

In 1920 Gorki wrote a play called *Slovotekov the Workman,* which was acted in that same year at the Theatre of People's Comedy. By this time, however, Gorki's own health had broken down from the tuberculosis which he had first contracted in Czarist prisons and, at Lenin's advice, he went to recuperate at a sanatorium near Berlin and later at Sorrento in Italy. In 1928 he was welcomed back to Moscow and became very enthusiastic about all that had been accomplished in his absence. With the coming of 1932 at the time of the celebration of the fortieth anniversary of the beginning of his literary career he announced a new trilogy of plays.

The first part of this trilogy was called *Egor Bulychev and Others* and was performed on September 25, 1932, at the Vakhtangov Theatre in Moscow, on the occasion of this anniversary and in the presence of Gorki himself, Henri Barbusse, and other writers who had come there to do him honor. It was also produced on that same day at the Big Dramatic Theatre in Leningrad and later at the Moscow Art Theatre and throughout the Soviet Union. In this play Gorki represented a bourgeois capitalist gradually dying of cancer on the eve of the Russian Revolution, at the very time when the proletarian movement was advancing triumphantly.

The second part of the trilogy, *Dostigaev and Others,* was acted at the Vakhtangov Theatre in the following year 1933, and represented Egor's business partner who hopes to survive the coming of the Revolution and continue to make profits.

The third part of the trilogy *Somov and Others* was still unacted at the time of Gorki's death in 1936. Gorki himself did not take too great stock in these plays of his. He said: "I wrote plays because I had to. That is why they are so bad. But, if I had studied the theory of drama, they would have been much worse!" It must be remembered, however, that in addition to the works written in play form his novels and short stories were dramatized and had an important influence in the theatre. *Mother,* his great novel of the revolution of 1905, was powerfully presented by Okhlopkov at the Realistic Theatre, by Piscator in Berlin, and by others elsewhere. Several scenes from

In the World were beautifully done by the Moscow Art Theatre; and *Chelkash, The Orlov Couple, Malva, Foma Gordeev, Three Men, Kain and Artem,* and other stories were both dramatized on the stage and turned into films.

Taking all these contributions to the theatre together, Gorki's work proves what he himself had earlier called "the terrific force of the theatre." Men who had suffered had a feeling when they saw Gorki's work dramatized that "Gorki knows! Gorki understands!" And somehow, on that account, their own sorrows and hardships seemed easier to bear. Lenin said of him: "Gorki is unquestionably the most significant representative of proletarian art."

Toward the end of his life, in 1931, he received a visit from Bernard Shaw. Both had used drama as a powerful social weapon and they were then perhaps the two greatest living writers of their generation. Yet what a striking difference there was between Shaw, with his full white beard wreathed with genial laughter like a good-natured Santa Claus, and Gorki, restrained and shy with hollow cheeks and only the faint suggestion of a wan smile! What a difference, too, in the methods by which they had tried to bring about a new social order through the use of drama: Shaw's perpetually scintillating satire and Gorki's grim deterministic realism.

In 1932, when the whole Soviet Union was celebrating the fortieth anniversary of the beginning of Gorki's literary career, a great festival was held in the Bolshoi Theatre in Moscow in the presence of Gorki. On that occasion it was announced that the city of Nizhni-Novgorod where Gorki had been born was to be renamed Gorki. The Big Dramatic Theatre in Leningrad which he had founded in 1918 was to be called the Theatre of Gorki and the Moscow Art Theatre was to be called "The Moscow Art Theatre in the name of Gorki." Some jokingly asked whether the emblem of the sea-gull on the curtains of the Moscow Art Theatre would now be changed to that of Gorki's stormy petrel. Poor Gorki, overwhelmed with all these honors, could only shrug his shoulders and put his hands far apart with a gesture indicating his sense of his own unworthiness.

At the time of his death in 1936, however, Gorki stood as a symbol of the latest stage in the development of Russian literature, which in the seventeenth and eighteenth centuries had been centered about the Czars, and in the nineteenth century centered about men of the aristocracy or the middle classes, but had now in the twentieth century come into the hands of the proletariat. Gorki's drama had paved the way for the Soviet drama which followed.

After Chekhov's death in 1904, the psychological realism which he had introduced into his plays seemed to die out in Russian drama. Realism or naturalism of a rather more rugged sort was kept alive by a single solitary and solid personality—that of Gorki. Almost all the other dramatists turned away from realism and escaped into some form of symbolism or mysticism or eroticism. In the year after Chekhov's death came the Revolution of 1905 and with its failure there set in a period of disillusion which took various forms of escapism in the theatre during the dozen years until the Russian Revolution of 1917.

The symbolist movement in drama was already in full swing at the dawn of the twentieth century with Maeterlinck in Belgium, Hofmannsthal in Austria, Yeats in Ireland, and D'Annunzio in Italy. In Chekhov himself there were slight traces of a similar symbolism. He had used the sea-gull as a symbol of a poor girl blown about by the gusts of an unkind fate. He had used the cherry orchard as a symbol of the waning power of landed estates in Russia. Yet Chekhov's sense of realism, his sense of humor if you will, prevented his pushing his symbols or his allegory to extremes. In the period that followed his death, the period between the two revolutions, however, this tendency ran rife uncontrolled. Its influence in drama is to be seen in the mysticism of Andreev, in the symbolism of Alexander Blok, in the estheticism of Sologub, in the eroticism of Artsibashev, and in the theatricality of Evreinov.

Leonid Nikolaevich Andreev (1871-1919) undoubtedly had from his early years a predilection toward the mysterious, the morbid, the gloomy. Three times in his youth he had tried to commit suicide, once attempting to throw himself under a railroad train. In his early stories he had symbolized the sex passion as an abyss or as a fog. He had set great hopes on the Revolution of 1905, but after his imprisonment, was bitterly disillusioned.

In October of that year his friend Gorki's play *The Children of the Sun* had been acted both in the Moscow Art Theatre and in St. Petersburg, and Andreev hoped for a similar success. Gorki had represented a superior scientist holding himself aloof from the Revolution in which the scientist's sister took a part. In the following month, November, 1905, in a play called *To the Stars,* Andreev tried to push the same idea even further. Here an astronomer, in his observatory on a mountain peak, holds himself superior to the turmoil of the revolution going on below him—the revolution in which his own son has been wounded, taken prisoner, and beaten into insanity. The exact opposite of the astronomer is represented in one of the revolutionists, the working man Treich, who like Nil in Gorki's *Smug Citizen* expresses the spirit of defiance and self-reliance. Treich says:

We must go ahead. There has been some talk here about defeat, but there is no such thing. I know only victory. The earth is wax in the hands of men. We must create new forms. If we meet a wall, we must destroy it. If we meet a mountain, we must remove it. If we meet a precipice, we must fly over it. If we have no wings, we must produce wings. We must go ahead as long as the sun is shining.

This was the one and only time that a powerful tone so akin to that of Gorki was heard in Andreev. The authorities forbade his play from production on the stage in Russia. In the following year, 1906, his disillusion had sunk much deeper. In his play called *Savva* he represented a man of fiery temper, impatient with the moderation of all the revolutionists who had failed in 1905—with the Constitutional Democrats, with the Social Revolutionists, with the Mensheviks, with the Bolsheviks, even with the Anarchists. Savva is a Nihilist. Everything must be annihilated. God must be destroyed. At that time in Russia a young man named Ufimtsev had attempted to blow up the Icon of the Virgin of Kursk. Andreev adopted this idea and has Savva plan to blow up a shrine in order to prove that dynamite is stronger than God and that man is the creator of both. The monks, however, remove the Icon just before the explosion and then replace it quietly afterward; so that the fanatical mob, seeing in its preservation the signs of a miracle, turn upon Savva and torture and mangle him to death "for the greater glory of God." The play was actually produced under Meyerhold's direction at Kommissarzhevskaya's Theatre in St. Petersburg; but the authorities soon forbade its production and it was only after the Russian Revolution that it was again acted in Russia at the Moscow Trade Union Theatre in 1922 and 1923.

Later in 1906 Andreev wrote his famous morality play, *The Life of Man,* which was acted both at the Kommissarzhevskaya Theatre and also at the Moscow Art Theatre. As in the English morality play *Everyman,* so here the characters have no individual names, but are called Man, The Wife of Man, and so forth. The play begins and ends in darkness. In the corner of the stage there stands motionless throughout the drama a mysterious being called He-in-Gray. In his hand is a great wax candle. In the darkness we hear the cries of a woman in the pangs of giving birth to a child. Suddenly the candle is lighted by an unseen hand. Man is born. The flame of the candle is "the life of Man." From the scene of his birth we pass to scenes of his love and his poverty, of his marriage and his prosperity, of his misfortune and his death. The candle that has burnt brightly is running out. The wax is melting. The flame seems to be shivering and shielding itself from the cold. It flickers and goes out. "The life of Man" that has come from a dark beginning, goes to a dark end. Andreev's pessimism here is just the opposite of Satin's glorification of man in Gorki's *The Lower Depths.*

In 1907 Andreev wrote *King Hunger,* his great allegory of the Revolution of 1905. In the factory scene, the workers cry: "We are starving. We are crushed by the machines. We ourselves are part of the machines. We are forging our own chains." It is Hunger that persuades them to revolt. He calls on Time to ring the bell which is the signal for the Revolution. The cry goes abroad: "The starving, driven by Hunger, are marching on their masters." Machine-guns, however, crush the revolt. Children are raised to kiss the machine-guns. But from thousands of throats, there comes a great roar: "We shall yet come! Woe to the victorious! Those who have been killed shall arise. They died for an idea. They shall yet be masters of the world!" For a time it seemed that Andreev was the prophet of a second and more successful Russian revolution. In a wave of enthusiasm, 18,000 copies of *King Hunger* were sold in a single day. But Andreev's melancholy deepened. He never raised so revolutionary a cry again, but became more and more hostile to the masses, to all revolutionists.

In the next year, 1908, he wrote and had acted a play called *The Black Masks*. Taking, directly or indirectly, ideas from Edgar Allan Poe's *The Haunted Palace, The Mask of the Red Death,* and *William Wilson,* he represents Duke Lorenzo as giving a brilliantly lighted ball in his castle. When his guests appear they are wearing hideous, repulsive masks. He does not recognize them, but they explain that they are his secret thoughts, his hidden desires, his unuttered emotions. Among the guests appears his Alter Ego whom he challenges to a duel and stabs, only to find the wound appearing on his own breast. One by one those in the black masks quench all the lights in the castle—all the lights of the human soul. Andreev's wife tells us that in Lorenzo tortured by his own thoughts, Andreev had in mind the tragic personality of Nietzsche. In any case the philosophy of Nietzsche and the pessimism of Schopenhauer become more and more obvious as Andreev goes on. Practically the only exceptions are two rather more realistic plays dealing with student life as he had known it. One of these, also written in 1908, was called *The Days of Our Life* and had a continuous popularity throughout Russia even after the Russian Revolution. The other, written two years later, was called *Gaudeamus* (*Let Us Enjoy Life*), taking its name from the drinking song so characteristic of the bohemian student life Andreev had known.

Far more important than all of these was Andreev's impressive allegory, *Anathema,* which was acted in 1909 at the Moscow Art Theatre with Kachalov in the rôle of the Accursed One, Anathema. In the powerful prologue, Anathema appears defiant before the Closed Gates, There, corresponding to He-in-Gray of *The Life of Man,* stands He-Who-Guards-the Entrance. The Accursed One, Anathema, has no heart but has a powerful mind. He wants to know everything. He wants to know the name of Him who is beyond the Gates. Those who have called him "Love," or "Wisdom," or "God," have lied. He bids the Guardian: "Open the gates. For then I shall know and become as a god." But the Guardian answers: "Never!" Like Satan in the Book of Job attempting to try the patience of Job, Anathema makes a test-case out of a poor Jew named David Leizer. He brings him millions in money from America, which David spends among the needy, until the money is exhausted and the mob turns on him and stones him to death. In the Epilogue Anathema returns in triumph to the Gates. He is told that David Leizer has become immortal; but he goes away laughing sardonically, saying that in the name of David all men will become murderers.

This drama, which with its Prologue and Epilogue had something of the pretentiousness of Goethe's *Faust,* Andreev felt to be his masterpiece. After thirty-seven performances, however, it was suppressed by the Black Hundreds. It was said that this was because it had placed a Jew in too favorable a light.

Another play written in this same year was *Anfisa,* in which a brilliant man who, having one mistress, takes a second and is about to elope with a third, when his first mistress murders him. The Bishops attacked this play as containing advocacy of depravity which they said proved that Andreev must belong to some revolutionary organization. Yet the spirit of Anfisa was not that of revolution but a reflection of the eroticism which followed Artsibashev's *Sanin* in this period between the two revolutions.

In a tragedy called *The Ocean,* written in 1911, Andreev wrote one of his most powerful allegories. The Shore is the safe land where abide the Many-too-Many. The Ocean is the unknown expanse where a few bold spirits venture in quest of new horizons. One of these is Captain Haggart, a sort of Nietzschean Superman. He would take Mariette with him on his pirate vessel with its black sails, racing after the golden Sun, but she remains on shore, flinging her curse at him as he sets sail and prophesying that their little son will grow up to hang his father from the masthead.

The Pretty Sabine Women of 1912 is a curious political satire told in terms of Roman history. The Sabines are the Constitutional Democrats whose women—the liberties they thought they had achieved in 1905—have been abducted by the Roman soldiers who represent here the Czar's government. Andreev makes merciless fun of the Constitutional Democrats, or Sabines, who in trying to win back their wives—their liberties—reject the use of force as unworthy of their dignity and have as their only weapons documents proving the legality of their marriages. Their motto is "Two steps forward" (to prove their firmness of will) and "one step back" (to prove their opportunism).

In his *Letters on the Theatre,* published in 1912, Andreev announced his departure from symbolism to what he called "pan-psychism." He declared that a spectator at a Maeterlinck play was like "a perfectly sober person appearing at a party where everybody else is drunk." The symbolic form he now felt was not suitable for psychology. He wished to reform the theatre from one of external action to one of "soul" or of "pan-psyche." He would leave external action to the cinema. Instead of leading up to a climactic action in the ordinary theatrical fashion, Andreev now decided that his "new theatre" would begin the drama at the point where the external action ended and trace its effect on the psychology of the central character, who would no longer be a symbol but a real human being. This he exemplified in two plays written in that same year, 1912.

In *Professor Storitsyn* he depicted a refined intellectual, an esthete, whose wife, representing his ideal of pure beauty, has already been demoralized by the coarse and vulgar Savvich. This demoralization of his wife and indeed of his whole family has already taken place before the curtain goes up. Andreev is concerned only with its effect upon Professor Storitsyn; his inner struggle against the reign of vulgarity, ugliness, and the meanness of life.

Similarly in his *Katherina Ivanovna,* the demoralization of Katherina has already taken place. She was once a noble and beautiful soul, unjustly suspected by her husband, until she has become the very thing which he suspected her of being. Instead of giving us a play leading up to her husband's shooting her, the play begins with the pistol shot. As often in Russian plays, the pistol misses its mark. The husband does not succeed in killing his wife's body, but his shooting at her has, as she says, "killed her soul." Where her soul had been is now only an "abomination of desolation." It was a terrible picture of what had happened in this period to a certain stratum of high Russian society. As the scenic designer, Alexander Benois wrote: "In this play, as in a mirror, we see our own spiritual emptiness gazing out at us with dead eyes."

The play was acted at the Moscow Art Theatre with Germanova as Katherina and with Kachalov and Moskvin acting the chief male rôles. It caused a great sensation. As Nemirovich-Danchenko wrote: "It was a regular battle between applause and hisses." Throughout Russia mock trials were staged in which Katherina was accused or defended—usually accused by the men and defended by the women. Long afterwards, in 1929, the rôle of Katherina was powerfully interpreted by Nazimova at the Civic Repertory Theatre in New York.

In a play called *Thou Shalt Not Kill,* written in 1913, Andreev psychoanalyzed the character of a handsome youth named Yakov who is fundamentally good-natured, but on that very account is so eager to please the many women who love him that for their sakes he is led into murder and all sorts of horrible crimes.

Early in 1914, before the outbreak of the First World War, a play of Andreev's called *Thought,* developing an idea from an earlier short story of his with the same title, was acted by the Moscow Art Theatre. Here the central character, Dr. Kerzhentsev, powerfully acted by Leonidov, is a Russian intellectual who believes in the irresistible force of human thought. He uses it to trap his victim, the husband of a woman who has rejected him. But thought is a treacherous weapon and he himself becomes the victim of thought; his castle becomes a prison.

Another play of this year, called *The Waltz of the Dogs,* has as its subtitle "A Poem of Solitude." Under the stress of solitude, the central character, Henry Tille, betrayed by his betrothed, deteriorates much as Dr. Kerzhentsev had under the power of thought. Finally, playing on the piano Chopin's Opus 64, "The Waltz of the Dogs," he commits suicide. The implication of the title is that men are merely dancing dogs on leashes, trained by lumps of sugar to do tricks.

Still another play of this year, one called *Youth,* was enormously popular and continued to be acted for six years after the Russian Revolution, although it is usually said that the Bolsheviks rejected Andreev as completely as he rejected them.

Far more significant as drama is *Samson in Chains,* which some have considered Andreev's dramatic masterpiece. Here again the play begins when the action is almost over. Samson has already been betrayed, captured, blinded, and chained by the Philistines; but his real chains are his own carnal impulses, from which he tries in vain to break free.

With the beginning of the First World War in August 1914 and the invasion of Belgium, Andreev took up the cudgels on behalf of the invaded country in a play called *King, Law, Liberty,* but translated as *The Sorrows of Belgium.* Here he exalted not only the King of Belgium, but also a Belgian poet named Grelieu, who is spoken of as "the conscience of the people" and is clearly intended to be Maeterlinck. The Germans were not merely murderers of the body; they were murderers of the soul. Another war play, left unfinished, was called *A Conversation in the Night* and represented a midnight interview between the German Kaiser and a Belgian scholar who turns out to be a Russian revolutionist in disguise. Andreev accepted the war with enthusiasm, saying: "The war makes my heart rejoice." War was for him "a rejuvenating and regenerating force." Later he said: "The poisoning of my soul began with the war. While on the main floor Allied hymns were played pompously, down in the cellar something dark and terrible was going on. There madness and horror were hiding. I have captured a devil, swallowed him, and he stays inside me—alive."

During the war, in 1916, Andreev attempted to get away from this obsession in other plays. In *Dear Phantoms* the central character was young Dostoevski. This play was acted successfully at the Alexandrinski Theatre in Petrograd and at the end Andreev's admirers called for the playwright and presented him with laurel leaves. But Andreev in his black blouse, with sad face, wasted and exhausted, stood amidst these funereal wreaths like another "dear phantom."

The other play written in 1916 was *He Who Gets Slapped* which was acted by the Theatre Guild in New York and continued to hold the stage in the Soviet Union for some four years after the Revolution. It is in a way an epitome of Andreev's pessimism, fatalism, and even masochism. The central character again has no other name than "He." He has been a man of refined sensitiveness and great intelligence, who has been beaten down by life's disasters and forced to accept a position as a clown in a circus. Beneath his clown's costume, under the whitewash and the painted smile, his soul is suffering poignantly. The audience roars with laughter as he receives innumerable slaps from his fellow clowns. Yet even this is preferable to what he had suffered "out there," in the real world from which he has escaped into this world of the circus. With characteristic Russian love of suffering, he even welcomes these slaps.

In the following year, with the coming of the Russian Revolution in 1917

Andreev turned to a terrific denunciation of the Bolsheviks. "Never before has the world seen such a mob of traitors—tens of thousands of Judases—fiends let loose from Hell." In a final play called *A Requiem* he mourned the loss of the Russia that was no more. The Revolution was an insurrection of darkness against light, of stupidity against reason. He sent out his S.O.S.: "Save our souls! Come quickly! We are sinking! Help!" He turned and denounced Gorki who had helped him in his youth. He and all the other sympathizers of the Revolution were merely "blood-spattered jesters." They, he now discovered, were the black masks about which he had written, the uninvited guests, extinguishing one by one the lights of Russia. He wrote to Roerich: "My creative power is perishing along with perishing Russia. Russia is no more! I feel as if I were in a grave to my waist. I am thinking of suicide—or suicide is thinking of me."

He fled to Finland to seek the protection of the White Guards and there, within sound of the guns, he died of a hemorrhage of the brain, foaming at the mouth against the Bolsheviks. His end was more horrible than any that he had depicted in any of his plays.

In the period between the two revolutions, Andreev had enjoyed a great vogue in accord with the taste and temper of that time; but his plays have hardly outlived that unhappy period. To be sure, the Soviet Union, in spite of his denunciation, continued to act his plays, but gradually the enthusiasm for Andreev, not in Russia alone but everywhere, has died out. Andreev boasted that he had "invented a new shudder." To this Tolstoi gave his devastating reply: "Andreev wants to frighten me; but I am not frightened." The characters in his plays ask disquieting questions about the end of life, yet they seem only puppets behind which we hear the nervous bitter voice of the author. A photograph of Gorki and Andreev, sitting together, indicates the fundamental difference. Gorki, rugged and strong, the realist, stares straightforward at the spectator. Andreev with eyes averted, the symbolist, is playing on some strange old harp.

Alexander Alexandrovich Blok (1880-1921), if he had less vogue as a dramatist than Andreev, was a far greater poet. Like Andreev, Blok was disillusioned by the failure of the Revolution of 1905, but he took refuge not in despair and counter-revolution, but rather in a sort of symbolic irony and parody.

In 1906 his play called *The Puppet Show* was dedicated to Meyerhold and produced by him for Vera Kommissarzhevskaya. It was partly in Blok's alternating dual and triple rhymes and partly in prose. Columbine was supposed to be a symbol of the Constitution, which had been promised by the Czar's government but had never been realized. For Pierrot, the realist, she is simply the girl that he has been waiting for. For Harlequin, the symbolist, she is a symbol of death for which he has been waiting. He carries her off, but she proves to be only a stuffed doll. Heaven is only a piece of blue cloth through which he sticks his head.

The Unknown Woman, written in the same year and also staged by Meyerhold, was a somewhat similarly disconcerting allegory. A poet who has fallen in love with an unknown lady comes to a bridge where he sees an astrologer watching the stars. Suddenly a star falls to earth and becomes a woman in black who is picked up by a man in a derby hat and carried off to a night-club. Finally she returns to her heavenly place unrecognized by the poet as being the unknown woman for whom he was looking. Thereupon the poet, like Blok himself, abandons his vision.

In 1912 Blok wrote *The Rose and the Cross,* a lyrical drama dealing with the Middle Ages. Blok continued to live in a sort of dim mystic twilight. On the eve of the Russian Revolution he walked the streets in the snow, asking if others heard, as he did, the music in the air—the premonition of the dawn of a new day. He had a messianic feeling of a second coming, a kind of last judgment in which the mighty should be put down from their seats and the humble and meek should be exalted.

When the Russian Revolution came in November, 1917, Blok welcomed it as the answer to his dream and wrote his poem called *The Twelve,* in which he described twelve revolutionary workers as though they were the twelve Apostles following their leader.

In 1918, when the Germans invaded Finland in the north and the Ukraine in the south, Blok addressed to them a poem called *The Scythians.* The Germans, with their characteristic sense of their own racial superiority, had scorned the Russians as barbarians, descended from the ancient Scythians. Blok took up the challenge and said that if the Russians were Scythians, let the Germans beware what an invasion of Russia might mean. He had in mind the German interventionists of 1918, but it was curiously prophetic of the Nazi invasion of 1941.

With Fedor Sologub (1853-1926), whose real name was Fedor Kuzmich Teternikov, we find still another type of symbolism. If with Andreev symbolism was mixed with nihilism, and with Blok symbolism was mixed with irony, with Sologub, who was considerably older than either, symbolism was still mixed with old-fashioned estheticism—an estheticism which in turn was not unmixed with eroticism.

For Sologub, the poet was supreme in the theatre. The theatre should be a Temple of Religion. The poet should be the High Priest. Everything should be done to magnify the poet's importance and to minimize the physical medium. The curtain, the footlights, the picture-frame proscenium arch should be abolished. The ego of the audience should merge with the ego of the poet. The actors should be merely automatons, whose slow and beautiful movements and calm utterance should merely bring out the beauty of his poetry. The scenery should be so simplified as to suggest the right atmospheric background for his drama. As Sologub's plays were produced by Meyerhold for Vera Kommissarzhevskaya, the settings were to have "stylization" and "architecturalness"—an enormous staircase, with platforms and a vestibule above with suggestions of great columns beyond. On these various levels the actors were to stand "statuesquely."

The mission that Sologub undertook as a dramatic poet was "to impose the order of beauty upon the chaos of nature." In that struggle for beauty, the tragic hero or heroine is doomed, as in Greek tragedy, to destruction. Death is the only relief from the disillusion of life, the only abode of peace. His paganism is at times almost satanism. God is the creator of a world of evil. Satan is the ruler of the realm of peace—which is death.

For his subject-matter Sologub, then, naturally turns away from the realism of the modern world to the beauty of the classical or medieval world. This was his escape from the disillusions of the Revolution of 1905, and as in the case of Andreev and Blok and Artsybashev, his plays begin after that debacle. In 1907, his play called *The Gift of the Wise Bees* went back to Greek mythology and took up the story of Laodamia. The man she loves has left for Troy and is the first to fall in the Trojan War. But, according to Sologub, Aphrodite, the Goddess of Love, has pity on Laodamia and gets the Greek sculptor, Lysippus, to make a wax image of her lover—the wax is "the wise gift of the bees"—which she tenderly caresses. Her father, however, throws the statue into the fire; as it dissolves she sinks lifeless to the ground while the Greek Chorus chants: "Life melts like wax in the hot breath of Aphrodite."

Sologub's next play was *The Triumph of Death,* produced by Meyerhold for Kommissarzhevskaya in December, 1907, the last performance he did for her and the one that led to his break with her. Here Sologub turned from classical to medieval times. Algista is put to death by King Clovis, but her bleeding body comes to life and appears before him saying: "Take me, as thou wilt, alive or dead. Here I stand before thee, hardly living, hardly dead. My blood is upon the moist earth and my voice is in the magic moon. My eyes shine brighter than the diamonds of thy diadem. Here I am all life and all death!" So saying she turns him and all his court to stone, while the Chorus chants: "Love conquers by Death; for Love and Death are one!"

Two years later, in 1909, Sologub in his *Vanka the Butler and Jean the Page,* ingeniously contrasted the medieval and the modern world in a series of parallel scenes, showing on the one hand the more subtle and refined medieval France and on the other hand the more crude and impulsive Russia of his own day. In both cases it is substantially the same story. The difference is all in the tone. The French wife begs her husband to promote her page, Jean, who thereupon becomes her lover, till the husband returns and ruthlessly punishes both. Meanwhile the alternating scenes describe the same story in modern Moscow, where the lover is the butler, Vanka. Only now we see, in place of the grace of the medieval French, the coarseness of the modern version where the butler, for example, manages to substitute a beggar to get the punishment while he himself gets off free, and the husband, somewhat ignominiously decides to forgive his wife.

When we turn from Sologub to Michel Petrovich Artsybashev (1878-1927), we find the eroticism no longer clothed in classical or medieval beauty, but displayed with frank and brutal realism or naturalism. Like Sologub, he believed in the reality of only two things: sex and death. His method of treating them, however, is very different. His notorious novel, *Sanin,* although written in 1903, could not be published until 1907, two years after the Revolution, when it exerted an enormous influence on that inter-revolution period of disintegration. "It swept Russia as no book of our time has swept any country"—so said the sober London *Times.* "It was the Bible of every school boy and school girl in Russia"—so said Prince Mirski. It preached, so Artsybashev himself tells us, "the doctrine of anarchical individualism." In this Artsybashev was a disciple of Max Stirner, the mentor of Nietzsche. Vladimir Sanin, the hero of the novel, says: "Live as you want to live.... Enjoy absolute sexual liberty.... Enjoyment is the aim of human life.... Every one steals, and lies, and cheats, and commits adultery, as much as he can." At the end of the novel, Sanin was so disgusted with his fellow men, the crowd of peasants heaped like corpses in his railway train, that he hopped off the rear platform onto the open plain and "strode onward to meet the sun."

Artsybashev claimed to have derived his realism from Tolstoi, but this extreme individualism and self-indulgence and contempt for the many-too-many is obviously the complete antithesis and denial of Tolstoi's whole philosophy. The publication of *Sanin* created a tremendous sensation. It was hailed with wild enthusiasm and attacked with savage ferocity. As Artsybashev himself said: "Both the commendations and the condemnations were excessive." Imitations ran rife, including a "Female Sanin." Sanin clubs sprang up throughout Russia to carry on the cult of sexual self-indulgence. It tinged the whole philosophy—and drama—of this unhappy generation caught in this period of transition between the two revolutions.

Having launched this debauch in his novel, Artsybashev proceeded to study its effect in a series of very frank plays. Three of these, published in 1913 were, so his only son Boris, the artist, tells us, "produced in nearly every city in Russia." The first was called *Jealousy* and gave an appalling picture of the devastating effect of sexual jealousy. The central character was Elena or Helen who, like Helen of Troy, seemed to work havoc wherever she went. On the picnic in the Caucasus Mountains, at the villa in the country, in the apartment in the city, Elena is always the center of attraction for men. She is conscious of it. She enjoys it. Their attention, she says, is like "a concert of amorous tom-cats." The desires of various different men set her body aglow: her husband, a brilliant author; a Caucasian prince; a young student; a well-built servant boy. It is said, "she gives herself to them." Yet it is she herself who is constantly and consciously setting the trap for them and it might better be said, "she has caught them." From each love-affair she returns and "curls up to her husband like a kitten." He can stand it no longer. He turns to her and says: "Your mind is filled with men. The prostitute gives herself for need of money; but you give yourself from mere sensuality." He forces her to confess, but when at last she does admit that she has had lovers and begins to relate her affairs in detail, he cannot bear the agony of his jealousy and silences her by covering her mouth with his hand until he, hardly realizing what he is doing, has suffocated her to death.

In Artsybashev's next play, *The Law of the Savage,* the central character whose unbridled sex brings on the catastrophe is not a woman but a man, a prominent lawyer named Veresov. He still loves his wife; but he also falls in love with her younger sister, who now looks as his wife used to look; yes, and he loves, too, the wife of his best friend. He glories in sex. "Everything divine in man, his mental power, his creative genius, derives from the sex impulse. The soul feeds on love. When a man's sex urge dies, everything decays.... A man who loves only one woman is either a phenomenon or a cripple." Yet his is a "double standard." For himself he demands complete sex freedom, but when he finds his wife is receiving attentions from a lieutenant, he is furious. There is a duel. Just before the prearranged signal, he shoots and kills the lieutenant, and stalks away. The only law he knows is the law of the jungle, "the law of the savage."

The protest against these two plays was similiar to that against his novel. According to Artsybashev: "They called forth more vehement public comment than any other plays on the Russian stage called forth." The criticism against them he dubbed "social hypocrisy." He said: *"Jealousy* has been denounced by these critics as a 'calumny on woman' and *The Law of the Savage* as a 'calumny on man.'" To this Artsybashev answered: "Not all women are Elenas and not all men are Veresovs. But in nearly every woman there is a bit of Elena and in nearly every man a bit of Veresov. Not all family dramas resolve themselves so tragically as they do in my plays, but in every family there are the seeds of a tragic ending."

This leads up logically to the third play in Artsybashev's trilogy of 1913—the play called *Enemies,* which was acted in New York by Leo Bulgakov in 1927 under the title *Lovers and Enemies.* Here it is no longer a single demoralizing woman or a single demoralizing man, but the whole institution of marriage that is under fire. Artsybashev introduces an army physician who tells us: "Happy marriages are an impossibility." He argues that 90 per cent of marriages are outright failures; 10 per cent just bearable; and none happy. Marriage does not unite lovers. It separates them. Before marriage they have one common aim—to attract each other—which makes their relations easy and pleasant. After marriage, they take two divergent paths: that of the husband, and that of the wife. Sexual desire builds a narrow bridge between them. Across this bridge they walk toward each other, meet, and join—because they cannot pass. If they try to walk side by side they jostle and annoy each other. The bond between them becomes a chain. Artsybashev's *Enemies* is not to be confused with Gorki's play of the same name (there are at least five Russian plays by that title). In Gorki's play, characteristically enough, the "enemies" were Capital and Labor. In Artsybashev's play, again characteristically, the "enemies" are husband and wife. To illustrate his point he brings in three different types of marriages—that of the professor, that of his son, and that of his daughter—and shows in what way each marriage is unhappy. The old professor's wife is devoted enough but does not understand him and is constantly bothering him. He says: "My only interest is my work and my worst enemy is any one who interferes with that." He thus has come to look upon his wife as an enemy; but after her death, as he sits on the veranda in the autumn at the end of the play, he suffers the agony of not having appreciated her love while she was alive. His son is a dreamy musician, deficient in vitality, but married to a woman who requires it. Thinking him anæmic she turns to a more passionate lover. The professor's daughter, Valentina, is married to a man who also loves a young girl named Valeria. To him they are both Valya and he loves them both equally, intermittently, and indiscriminately. He argues that one can love two women equally, just as one can love both painting and music, both Pushkin and Lermontov, both the beauty of nature and the beauty of the human body. When the woman says, "I can't understand that," he replies "No woman can. But every man will understand me."

With the coming of the First World War in 1914 Artsybashev had an opportunity to study the effect of war upon marriage and sex. In his play called *War,* written in 1915 and acted shortly afterwards in America, he again takes up an elderly man—in this case a retired colonel—and his wife, and the love-affairs of their son and of their daughter. The opening scene is laid in a garden in a sunny day in spring and on the surface everything seems to be happy, although there are already latent the disruptive forces which break out in the second act with the coming of the war. The son is in love with a young girl but his rival, a consumptive, persuades him to volunteer; when he is killed in the war, the rival has the girl to himself. The old colonel's daughter is happily married and at first easily resists the blandishments of a neighboring prince. When, however, her husband returns from the war with both legs torn off, she can no longer resist the appeals of the prince. In the golden autumn of the final scene, which is again laid in the garden, one feels that Artsybashev has matured and his characters grow nobler, but they are still victims of the forces of war and of death and of sex, which are stronger than they.

With the coming of the Russian Revolution, Artsybashev's "anarchical individualism" seemed out of place in the Soviet Union. New editions of *Sanin* were not published there and he left in 1923 to live in Warsaw where he wrote articles against the Soviets until his death four years later.

Other lesser dramatists of the period of 1905-1917 carried Artsybashev's eroticism to still greater extremes. Some of them, unlike him, mixed their interest in sex with religious mysticism, much as D'Annunzio had in Italy.

In their plays, the odor of sanctity was curiously mingled with the odor of sensuality, the odor of incense with the odor of incest.

In that period of disillusion many intellectuals, or perhaps one should say rather many members of the intelligentsia, turned from the world of sordid reality in the life about them, to the world of the theatre as a sort of haven of refuge. In that world they could escape from ugly realities which they wished to forget. The theatre became almost more real to them than reality. They were fond of quoting, or rather misquoting, the words used by the great Russian critic Belinski, in the nineteenth century: "Let us live in the theatre! Let us die in the theatre!"

It is no wonder, then, that among the many tendencies that marked this inter-revolutionary period, was the tendency toward extreme theatricality, which was perhaps best represented by Evreinov.

With Nicholas Nikolaevich Evreinov (1879-   ) we come to what might be called the "theatre theatrical." From his earliest years Evreinov had a precocious interest in the theatre. At five he was taken to see a play; at seven he had written a play of his own; at thirteen he acted in a theatre and performed as an equilibrist in a circus. There was something of the equilibrist and of the circus in him ever afterwards. He had also studied music under Rimski-Korsakov, but was sent to the Imperial Law School at St. Petersburg. There, although he did well enough in law to graduate with the Silver Medal, he took still more interest in the Legal Dramatic Circle, for which he acted, wrote plays, and composed an opera. In 1902 he had written a play called *The Foundation of Happiness,* which consisted of an episode in the life of grave diggers—a lugubrious interest which constantly pursued him. His real dramatic output, however, like that of most of the other dramatists of his generation, did not begin until after the failure of the Revolution of 1905. It was in 1906, for example, that he wrote his first important play, *The Beautiful Despot,* which was acted successfully both in Russia and in England. It represents a tired liberal giving up the liberal ideas which he had held before 1905, and deciding, instead of being an ugly liberal, to become a "beautiful despot." His motto is: "Better beautiful and wrong than right and ugly." Accordingly he decides to live as an old-fashioned landed proprietor on his country estate, with his servants dressed in the more elegant costumes of a hundred years earlier and his lady companion playing to him on the harpsichord nothing more modern than Mozart.

In the following year, 1907, Evreinov decided to direct a series of plays from antiquity at what he called the Starinny Theatre or Ancient Theatre in St. Petersburg. In the following year he took Meyerhold's place as regisseur for Vera Kommissarzhevskaya at her theatre and directed a remarkable production there of Oscar Wilde's *Salomé.* In 1909 he started in St. Petersburg a theatre of his own called The Merry Theatre for Grown-Up Children. There he produced his own play *A Merry Death,* which was later popular both in England and America. This was a harlequinade following the vogue set by Lothar's *King Harlequin* of 1899, Rostand's *Laughing Pierrot and Weeping Pierrot* of 1901, and Alexander Blok's *Puppet Show* of 1906. In Evreinov's *Merry Death,* Harlequin is destined to die at midnight but decides to make his last hour a merry one. He invites Pierrot and his wife, Columbine, whose affection he has tried to steal, to dine and dance with him. Unlike Artsybashev, he makes light of love and light of jealousy. As in Andreev the lamp, representing his life, begins to flicker. Midnight begins to strike. Death enters, but instead of being an old skeleton, death proves to be a beautiful young girl. Harlequin rises to meet her gallantly, hands her the flickering lamp, and says: "Light the way, Death, there is still a tiny drop of oil in the lamp." Then the lamp goes out and in the moonlight Pierrot cries: "Let down the curtain—the farce is over."

In the same year and in the same theatre, Evreinov produced another of his own plays, *The Presentation of Love.* This was what he called a "monodrama," a drama in which one central character dominates everything and all the other characters are shown to us from that point of view alone. In connection with this play Evreinov published his *Introduction to Monodrama,* a treatise in which he explained this theory of intense subjectivism and artificiality in drama—a theory which in many ways anticipated the movement of Expressionism in drama in the 1920's.

In 1910 Evreinov started another theatre of his own in St. Petersburg called the Krivoe Zerkalo or Crooked Looking-Glass. Here were to be acted plays and parodies which gave an intentionally distorted and grotesque reflection of life. For example he brought together in one evening five different condensed versions of Gogol's famous play, the *Revizor* or *The Inspector-General.* The first was a classical production of the play. The second was an ultra-realistic version in the spirit of Stanislavski. The third was a grotesque performance in the manner of Max Reinhardt. The fourth was a mysterious conception of it in the style of Gordon Craig. Finally the fifth was a parody of what a film version of it might be as given in the motion pictures of that day. Similarly Evreinov gave parodies of Ostrovski, Chekhov, Andreev, and Bernard Shaw's *Candida.*

At this same Theatre of the Crooked Looking-Glass, Evreinov proceeded to give some new plays of his own. In 1911 he gave *The School of Stars,* in which he represented a theatre director and his interviews with a number of different types of actresses all hoping to become stars. In 1912, in *The Theatre of the Soul,* he carried his idea of monodrama almost to a *reductio ad absurdum.* Here the entire action is supposed to take place inside the soul of a professor in a period of half a second. Three different entities of the soul are represented. M_1, the Rational Soul, with a quiet sober manner and wearing spectacles, urges him to give up the café dancer and stick to his wife. M_2, the Emotional Soul, with an artist's blouse and a red tie, is bored with the wife, however, and wants to run after the dancer. We then see the two different concepts of the wife and the two different concepts of the dancer. There is a great heart whose throbs we can watch, and the strings of the nerves which, when they are touched, give out a jangled sound. In the conflict the Emotional Soul strangles the Rational Soul; the strings of the nerve snap; and the heart stops beating. Finally, M3, the Eternal Soul, in a black mask and traveling clothes, realizes that the body is dead and that the time has come for him to journey on.

Evreinov followed this with other plays for the same theatre: *The Happy Coffin-Maker* in 1912; *The Kitchen of Laughter* in 1914; and, in 1915, *The Fourth Wall,* in which he ridiculed the realists' conception of making the theatre a room with the fourth wall removed, and, to illustrate this, introduced a parody of *Faust.*

To explain his theories of drama, Evreinov wrote a number of theoretical books: *The Theatre as Such* in 1912; *Pro Scena Sua* in 1913; and *The Theatre in Life,* in three parts: the Theoretical, the Pragmatical, and the Practical, published in 1915, 1916, and 1917. In these treatises, Evreinov explains his theory that all men, whether they know it or not, have a will for the theatre. The child creates his world of make-believe—his theatre. In the childhood of the race, the primitive savages act out the scene of the hunt in front of a circle gathered around the camp fire. All the great men of history have been filled with the desire to act, to play a rôle before the audience of the world. Religion, revolution, crime: all have something theatrical in them. The theatre is the source of all transformation, and transformation is the basis of life. The divinity itself is the great transformer and all men, in spite of themselves, follow the example of the divinity. We all play at least one rôle in life and sometimes several rôles. The theatre implies the alteration of one's self. It surpasses life. It is greater than life. It heals the wounds that life inflicts.

With the coming of the Russian Revolution of 1917, Evreinov at first accepted the new order with wild enthusiasm, hoping that it might bring about a wonderful new theatre, in which he might have a unique opportunity to try out his latest and wildest theories of drama. If he did not turn against the Revolution as Andreev and Artsybashev had, it was perhaps because the theatre was more important to him than any political theory. He felt that the Revolution, instead of destroying the theatre, might force it to give birth to something marvelous. He said:

Burn, theatre, burn to ashes! I kiss your very ashes, because from them, phoenix-like, you will be reborn into more and more beautiful forms. It will soar from a boiling fountain in a rainbow comprising all the imaginary colors, in the hot spray of which is the cure for all dreamers who have grown cold.

On November 7, 1920, in celebration of the third anniversary of the Russian Revolution, he staged an enormous pageant called *The Storming of the Winter Palace.* This was enacted by some 8,000 persons on the very spot where that momentous historic event had actually taken place three years earlier. Many were reënacting what they had done on that occasion. But under the guidance of the all-too-imaginative Evreinov, the action became more symbolic than realistic. Two artificial stages were erected, a "White Stage" to the right and a "Red Stage" to the left. On the bridge between these two stages took place the symbolic struggle between Left and Right, between Reds and Whites. Out of the darkness thousands of voices were heard calling: "Lenin! Lenin!" The cruiser *Aurora* was again heard firing its cannon from the River Neva. Rockets shot up into the sky. A gigantic red flag was raised and the audience of 100,000 jumped to their feet singing the Internationale.

In the following year, 1921, Evreinov wrote another theoretic work, *What Is the Theatre?*, trying in vain to reconcile communist dialectic with his own theories of monodrama. Finally he became a voluntary émigré, living in Paris and visiting America, perpetually hoping in one place or another to be able to carry out his ideas and his ideals.

In that same year, 1921, he had written a play called *The Chief Thing*. In this he tells us that the chief thing, in life as well as in the theatre, is "illusion." Pushkin had said that an elevated lie is more precious than the darkness of a degrading truth, and Evreinov pushed this theory still further. Men instinctively prefer pleasant lies to unpleasant truths and Evreinov represents Mr. Paraclete, the Comforter, getting together a group of actors and "comforting" the miserable occupants of a drab boarding-house with the illusions that alone will make them happy—the very thing that Gorki's Luka had failed to do in *The Lower Depths*. The play was acted by the Pitoëffs in Paris, by the Harvard Dramatic Club in 1925 under the title *Quintessence,* and by the Theatre Guild in New York in 1926 under the title *The Chief Thing*.

In this play there was a play within the play and in *The Ship of Saints,* in 1924, Evreinov made confusion worse confounded by giving us a whole series of plays one within the other, like a series of oriental boxes inside each other. In 1926 came his *Radio Kiss,* and in 1928 his *Theatre of Eternal War;* but by this time, he seems to have pushed his extravaganzas and eccentricities to the utmost extreme with very little left beyond.

The tendency of the Russians has been to push each literary impulse farther than men in other countries had ventured to do. Just as Chekhov in his plays had raised psychological realism to its greatest heights and Gorki had deepened grim naturalism to its lowest depths; so, in the interrevolutionary period of 1905-1917, Andreev attempted in his plays to give us mystery with its most blood-curdling shudder; Alexander Blok to give symbolism its sharpest irony; Sologub to give estheticism its loveliest image; Artsybashev to give us eroticism in its most shocking form; and Evreinov to give theatricality its wildest extravagance.

Each tended to drive drama to its utmost limit in some one particular direction, thereby exhausting all the possible devices and leaving nothing more to be done. By the end of this period, then, Russian drama seemed to have reached an impasse in all directions. It seemed as worn out and bankrupt as Russia was itself in the First World War. Russian drama was ripe for a change and that change came with the Russian Revolution of 1917.

On November 7, 1917, when the forces of the Soviets stormed the Winter Palace in Petrograd and seized power, there was grave doubt as to what would be the effect of this Russian Revolution upon the Russian theatre. Would the Bolsheviks sweep away the theatre with all the other vestiges of the older Czarist régime? Or would the Revolution give the theatre a new impetus, a new lease of life?

Many persons, especially those living at a distance, felt that the Russian theatre would not survive the overthrow of the old order. With a will to believe evil of the Revolution, stronger than their sense of fact, they predicted that all the dramatic arts would perish. For a time this point of view prevailed everywhere outside the Soviet Union. Even in 1924, seven years after the Revolution, an American book on *The Contemporary Drama of Russia* stated that under the Bolsheviks the "theatres have fallen beneath contempt" and ended with the assertion: "All the theatres are soon to lose the support of the government. Thus the decadent dramatic art in Russia receives its coup de grâce."

Yet in the meanwhile, those who were actually connected with the theatres in Russia at the time of the Revolution, discovered, almost to their surprise, that the Russian Revolution, far from destroying or limiting the scope of drama, had served to open the doors of the theatres to a marvelous new audience—hundreds, thousands, literally millions of spectators who had never been to the theatre before. Stanislavski at the Moscow Art Theatre, as we have already seen, described how at the very moment of the Revolution these new spectators responded to Chekhov's *The Cherry Orchard*. His further experiences convinced him that the future of drama in Russia was in safe hands. He said:

> These new, unspoiled, trusting and unsophisticated spectators were spectators in the best sense of the word; they came into our theatre not through accident, but with trembling and the expectation of something important, something they had never experienced before. We began to understand that these people came to the theatre not in order to be amused, but in order to learn.

Night after night this marvelous new audience flooded the theatres. In the early months of the Revolution the theatres were often inadequately heated, but the crowds swarmed eagerly to the entrances of the theatre buildings well ahead of the opening hour. When the doors were opened, it was like the storming of the Bastille. The people rushed in to take possession of something that had become their own. Hungry as they were for food, they were still more hungry for the theatre. Sometimes they brought some food with them to eat and often were unable to dress up very much. In a play called *The List of Benefits,* Olesha represents Russian émigrés in Paris asking a visiting Soviet actress whether these new audiences in Moscow wore evening clothes, and when she answers, "No. They often come in their valenki or felt boots" they asked her, "Is that because they love their felt boots?" to which she answers, "No! It is because they love their theatres."

Since the Russian Revolution, then, the Russian theatre has strengthened its hold on the Russian people and to accommodate this ever-growing audience, every theatre building is needed. Fond as the new Russians are of films, they cannot afford to turn any of the theatre buildings into moving-picture houses, but have had to build new halls for that purpose; and for the legitimate drama have kept all the older theatre buildings and have had to construct an ever-increasing number of new theatres.

The theatre has expanded in still other ways. In addition to the regular professional theatres, there have grown up Peasant Theatres, Collective Farm Theatres, Factory Theatres, Club Theatres, Theatres of the Working Youth, School Theatres, Theatres of the Young Spectators, and Children's Theatres. These theatres for children, or as they are sometimes called, Theatres for the Young Spectators, are perhaps the most remarkable and so important are they considered that one of the largest theatres on the Theatre Square in the heart of Moscow is devoted to the Moscow Theatre for Children.

Rapidly as the theatres have grown among the Russian people, the theatres of the minor nationalities in the Soviet Union have grown even more rapidly. Many nationalities that before the Revolution had no theatres of their own now have a number of theatres where everything is done to encourage the development of the native languages, culture, and drama. "Soviet drama," then, has become something much wider and larger than mere "Russian drama."

In the Soviet Union one can no longer deny the growth of all the arts of the drama. Even those who are reluctant to admit any progress in Soviet painting or sculpture or architecture or any other form of art or culture, pay tribute to what the Russian Revolution has done for the theatre. Prince Mirski writes: "The Revolution, so destructive for every other branch of culture, was anything but destructive for the theatre. It had the time of its life during the worst years of famine, wholesale Communism, and civil war. Never was Russia more theatre-going than in the years 1918-1920."

What is the reason that the theatre should have flourished after the Revolution better than any of the other arts? One reason—apart from the native love of the Russians for the theatre and the excellence of the tradition which they inherited—is the fact that in the Soviet Union the art of the theatre is considered not as an individualist art, but as a collectivist art. The playwright is only one of the many component parts that combine to make up the composite art of the theatre. The dramatist, the regisseur, the actor, the costumer, the scenic designer, the electrician, the musician are all collaborators. The excellence of each one's achievement is only to be measured in its relation to the achievement of all the others. This collaboration, and indeed the whole art of ensemble acting, has been developed further in the Soviet Theatres than elsewhere and it is perhaps only natural that a collectivist art should flourish in a collectivist society.

Little by little, then, other countries have come to recognize, often rather reluctantly, what has been accomplished in the Soviet Theatres. One American dramatist, Martin Flavin, writes: "The Russians have the only real living theatre in the world today." The drama critic of *The New York Times,* Brooks Atkinson, when he visited Moscow in 1936, criticized some of the plays there rather severely, but when he returned to Western Europe, he headed his article significantly: "Back to Mediocrity."

During the Russian Revolution—the ten days that shook the world—and during the months that followed, the Revolution itself was, of course, the one great absorbing drama. It was naturally some time before the Soviet dramatists could produce new plays of their own.

Meanwhile, the theatres had to turn to older Russian plays or to foreign plays. Far from making a clean sweep of every vestige of Russian drama under the Czars, the Soviet Union was very glad to revive the earlier Russian plays. They even enlarged the scope of the former repertoire, by now including many plays of Tolstoi, Gorki, and others that had previously been precluded by the Czar's censor. They also were now able to restore to other earlier plays passages that had formerly been cut out. Indeed the Soviet theatres have given so many plays of Ostrovski and other nineteenth-century Russian dramatists, that it is doubtful whether any conservative country has conserved on the stage so many plays of the previous century as has revolutionary Russia.

In addition to these earlier Russian plays, the Soviet theatres were also glad to turn to plays from other countries. Here again it was possible now, after the Revolution, to widen the repertoire by including certain foreign plays, such as some of Schiller, Ibsen, Hauptmann, and Bernard Shaw, which had been banned under the Czars. The gates were now open wide to plays from various different countries and various different periods. The Soviet theatres came to offer a broader range of world drama than could be found elsewhere. Moscow, the home of the Third International, became the home of a sort of Theatre International.

Before long, however, this new Russian audience wished, in addition to older Russian plays and foreign plays, to have new plays written by Soviet dramatists. It was only gradually that Russian writers attained sufficient perspective to deal with the events of the Revolution in well-balanced plays. Immediately after the Revolution, it was the lyric poets—Symbolists such as Alexander Blok, Imagists such as Esenin, Futurists such as Mayakovski—who burst out in the first spontaneous expression of enthusiasm. Such plays as were written in this period were often written by the lyric poets, and dealt with other revolutions in other countries and other times and with imaginary world revolutions sweeping the whole earth and even out beyond to the planet Mars.

The Russian Revolution itself was still too near to be treated realistically. It was only after some years had passed that short-story writers and novelists could turn back to the experiences they had had in the Revolution and the Russian Civil War which followed it, and write about them with detached realism. Such plays as were written then were often dramatizations of the stories of these novelists—Bulgakov, Ivanov, Leonov, Kataev, Alexei Tolstoi —and the plays were often of more value as documents than as drama.

It was only still later, some ten years or more after the Revolution, that sufficient time had passed for Russian writers to get the perspective necessary to view those stirring events with enough objectivity to present the varying points of view of the characters fairly and so make the dialogue dramatically convincing. Then, at last, there emerged writers—Afinogenov, Kirshon, Pogodin, Korneichuk—who were primarily dramatists rather than lyric poets or novelists.

Let us, then, take up first the work of the poets, then the novelists, and then the dramatists.

First Futurism forged to the front. The Futurists saw at once in the Russian Revolution the chance they were waiting for—the opportunity to break with the past, to sweep out everything connected with the old Czarist Russia, and to plunge toward the future, toward every experiment in the political or artistic field.

Head and shoulders above all the other Futurists stood Vladimir Vladimirovich Mayakovski (1893-1930). With the coming of the Revolution, Mayakovski would lift his giant figure above the Red Square and stand with his brazen-throated voice roaring his verses to the marching workers. He would shout to them to burn all the bridges for retreat, to stop marching slowly, to leap into the future. "Our great god is speed! Our heart is a bellowing drum! ... We, the flood of a second deluge, shall wash the world like a bursting cloud!"

The "second deluge," this flood of revolution that would sweep the whole world, became the theme of an extraordinary drama which he wrote during the months immediately after the Bolshevik Revolution, a drama that proved to be the first important new play of the Soviet régime. It was called *Mystery Bouffe*. As in a medieval mystery play, the story of the Flood and Noah's Ark was to be reënacted, and the action was to pass freely from the earth to hell, to purgatory, or to paradise. But it was to be a mystery bouffe which, like opera bouffe, was to be a mock-heroic travesty. It was announced as "An Heroic, Epic, and Satiric Representation of Our Epoch." The poster that announced it had a globe marked "Old World" which was crossed out boldly by lines running through it—an emblem indicating that the old world was something that the Futurists were through with.

The verses were to be by the futurist poet Mayakovski; the settings were to be by the suprematist painter Malevich; the direction by the most daring of theatre revolutionists Meyerhold. This combination of the three mighty M's of revolutionary art promised something truly sensational. The performance was to take place on November 7, 1918, the first anniversary of the Russian Revolution. The Soviets were still struggling for their very existence there in Petrograd. Germany was still at war with the Allies, but was already in the throes of revolution and the armistice was only four days off. It seemed as if the flood of revolution might really sweep over the whole world and on that November night of the first performance the air of Petrograd was electric with excitement.

The production took place in the great hall of the old St. Petersburg Conservatory which had been converted into what was called The Communal Theatre of Musical Drama. The auditorium was packed with an enormous audience—including among others the great symbolist poet Alexander Blok —all waiting eagerly for the curtain to go up in the traditional way, but not knowing just what was going to happen.

The curtain was intentionally an elaborate velvet affair pasted over with tinsel emblems to indicate the old-fashioned theatre. But suddenly seven pairs of grimy workers—blacksmiths, miners, carpenters, bakers, farm-hands— were seen to emerge from the audience, to jump up on the stage, and to pull down the old-fashioned curtain, crying out:

Make way for us! The land, swollen with blood, has given birth to us! The earth has called upon us with a voice like the roar of cannon! We shall sweep everything before us! Above the dust of the old theatre, our slogan shines out in electric lights: "Everything Anew!"

This prologue to the original performance was the defiance of the Futurists to the old theatre. They were going to do away with the curtain which separated the actors from the audience. The action was to pass freely from the stage to the auditorium and from the auditorium to the stage, thereby increasing three-fold the field of action. From then on all of Mayakovski's plays, all of Meyerhold's productions, were to be given without benefit of curtain, footlights, or proscenium arch.

When the curtain was torn away, it revealed on the stage the north pole of our terrestrial sphere, covered with snow under the arctic glow of the aurora borealis. The world revolution, like a second Flood, was spreading to cover the whole surface of the earth and men were trying to escape on a new ark.

On board the ark the representatives of the "upper class"—the so-called Seven Clean Pairs—thrust the workers, whom they call the "unclean" into the hold, trying to keep them in subjection by putting first a Czar over them and then a provisional government, which is called a "Republic," but which the workers find is merely a "Czar with a hundred mouths." Finally the workers emerge from the hold and take control themselves of the Ship of

State. Suddenly they see walking toward them on the surface of the water "The Man of the Future," who bids them climb up on the shrouds, on ladders of sunbeams, along rainbows, to the sky.

The *Mystery Bouffe* then passes, like an old miracle play, to the other world. For the workers, however, who have already suffered on earth, hell has no horrors. The Song of the Workers resounds triumphantly as they march through the hollow halls of hell.

From hell they pass to heaven. But this paradise of prophets—of Methuselah with his long beard, of Rousseau with his Social Contract, of Tolstoi with his Non-Resistance—does not satisfy them and they want to pass "beyond paradise," to their own "promised land"—the commune.

This commune is not up in the clouds. It is on the solid ground of earth, but an earth that has been changed. The "sickle" and the "hammer," the emblems of the peasant and of the worker, come to welcome them with "bread" and "salt" at the gate of the City of the Future. Entering the city, they see a garden of stars surmounted by the shining crown of the sun. Thereupon they burst forth into their final "Hymn to the Sun," in which they shout:

Let the sun be warm and play and burn—our sun. The sleep of centuries is blasted. Now comes a sea full of mornings. Life is more intoxicating than barrels of wine. We are the builders of the world. Chains of iron have given place to chains of loving hands. All glory be to you! Shine forth, O Sunny Commune of Ours!

Such was the outburst of lyric enthusiasm with which the first Soviet play ended—the first fine careless rapture of the Revolution, which no later Soviet play seemed ever quite able to recapture. The failure of this second flood, the world Revolution, to spread spontaneously throughout the rest of the world, the hostility of enemies without and within, intervention and counter-revolution, all had a sobering and disillusioning effect. When *Mystery Bouffe* was revived on May Day, 1921, and acted at Meyerhold's new theatre in Moscow, Mayakovski's second variant of the text, which was printed and translated as the official text, introduced embittered references to the Treaty of Versailles, to Lloyd George, and to Clemenceau with his Cordon Sanitaire, and unfortunately omitted the tearing down of the curtain in the prologue and the Hymn to the Sun in the epilogue. Yet from then on Mayakovski, in the various plays he continued to write for Meyerhold, in his shorter skits for the Satire Theatres, in the scenarios he wrote for the cinema, and in the pageant he wrote for the circus, in his vain search for the Land of the Future in America, in his disappointments and his wounded pride, constantly expressed his boundless hope in the future.

In his *Bedbug,* produced by Meyerhold in 1929, Mayakovski satirized in the opening scenes the pernicious remnants of bourgeois society which were still lingering in Russia to his great disgust, even a dozen years after the

Revolution. The house where these objectionable elements are gathered together catches fire and most of them, soaked as they are in alcohol, are quickly burned up. The water which the firemen have poured on the building, however, freezes into a great lump of ice; and in that ice are accidentally preserved for the future some terrible specimens—a bedbug and a bourgeois gentleman in a tuxedo jacket, named Prisypkin, evidently considered as obnoxious as the bedbug. The last scenes of the play are laid fifty years in the future, in 1979, in a world that has become communist. The Soviets which now spread around the world from Shanghai to Chicago are all interested in these specimens of capitalist civilization which have been preserved in this cake of ice from the dark ages of 1929. Scientists approach these objectionable objects carefully protected by gas masks so as not to be contaminated by the vicious microbes. They finally decide to preserve the bedbug and his human counterpart in a museum as an awful warning of the sort of creatures that used to exist in the unenlightened days of the first half of the nineteenth century, before the whole world had become sanitary—and communist.

In *The Bath,* produced by Meyerhold in 1930, Mayakovski again "gives a hot bath," as the Russian phrase goes, to all the elements that are hindering the success of the revolution. The millinnium is now placed still further in the future, some hundred years later, in the year 2030. But the workers have invented a sort of time-machine which will enable them to receive into the present a "delegate from the year 2030." This proves to be a shining Phosphorescent Woman of the Future. She rejects all those who are impeding progress, but selects all those who are in league with the future, all those who are trying to increase the tempo of Soviet life, and as they embark with her on the time-machine and are projected into the future, they sing their vigorous "March of Time" with its refrain of "Forward, Time! Time, Forward!"

Mayakovski's final pageant, *Moscow is Burning,* was produced in the great Circus building in Moscow, just one week after Mayakovski's suicide. It was written in celebration of the twenty-fifth anniversary of the Revolution of 1905. As a symbol of the Czarist order that had prevailed in 1905, a huge "Pyramid of Classes" was constructed in the center of the Circus, with the Czar on top, then the Grand Dukes and the high potentates of the Church, and then the Generals and the bourgeois capitalists—the whole borne on the shoulders of the workers. As the pageant goes on and comes to the year 1917, the whole pyramid is reversed. At the end the herald announces that in the future "The whole world will rise up, as we did after 1905"; and the workers cry: "Forward! Forward!! Forward!!!"

These futurist poems and plays, with their insistence on going forward and not backward, gave the Revolution a much-needed impulse toward a brave new world. Yet if the insistence of these Futurists on sweeping away all traces of the old theatres, including the Moscow Art Theatre, had been taken literally, Soviet drama would have been so much the poorer. Fortunately their excesses in this negative direction were wisely counteracted by others. Lenin himself, although he was in sympathy with Mayakovski's enthusiasm for the future, did not share his contempt for the past—his desire to turn the cannon on Pushkin, to throw the old art out of the museum windows, to drive all nineteenth-century drama off "the ship of modern times." Lenin felt that the Moscow Art Theatre should be preserved at all costs, that the proletariat were the heirs of all the ages, and that they should be entitled to the best of the art and science of the past at the same time that they were reaching out toward the future.

The one man, however, who more than any other helped to keep the best of the earlier Russian art and drama alive was Anatol Vasilevich Lunacharski (1875-1933). As People's Commissar of Education during the first ten years of the Soviet Union, he had charge not merely of the schools and universities, but also of the museums and theatres. His long revolutionary record, longer and more consistent than that of Mayakovski, saved him in the eyes of the people from any charge of being counter-revolutionary. He was glad to encourage Mayakovski and Meyerhold in their futuristic experiments, but he insisted on the right of the older dramatists and older theatres also to be heard. In his famous letter to Meyerhold he wrote:

> The abolishing of the traditions of the older Russian drama would be an act for which the very proletarian itself would in the future censure us most severely. It is easier to wreck than to build. Let us build on the foundation of the older Russian theatres. By a process of evolution and natural selection, they have preserved the best art. To rob them of their continuity would mean the destruction of a valuable culture, without raising the general level. These theatres are not lifeless mummies, but capable of future development under the very revolutionary atmosphere in which we live and breathe.

The wisdom of these words has been amply borne out by the history of the Soviet theatre during the years since they were first uttered. To show that the future still had something to learn from the past, Lunacharski gave to the Soviet theatres as a slogan, "Back to Ostrovski." In the social dramas of that mid-nineteenth-century dramatist, the Soviet theatres have not merely found an almost inexhaustible storehouse of plays that have been more popular than those of any Soviet dramatist, but have also found an admirable Russian model upon which the new Soviet plays could be built.

Lunacharski felt that the Russian Revolution of 1917 had much to learn from earlier Russian revolutions. Accordingly he did much to encourage new plays by various dramatists dealing with earlier revolts, such as that under Stenka Razin in the seventeenth century, Emelian Pugachev in the eighteenth century, the Decembrists in the nineteenth century, and the Revolution of 1905 in the early twentieth century. A long series of plays, passing from the earlier individual revolutionary outlaws, through groups of revolutionary individuals, and emerging finally in mass revolutions of the workers, gave the people a chance to study in the theatre what might be called "the evolution of revolution."

With his wide knowledge of world history and philosophy and literature and drama, Lunacharski went beyond this. He encouraged plays dealing with earlier historical revolutions in various countries and various periods—in ancient Babylon and ancient Rome, in the England of Wat Tyler or Cromwell, in the France of the French Revolution or the Paris Commune. These served as prototypes of the Russian Revolution and offered to Soviet audiences not so much a justification of their own Revolution—that was not felt necessary—as a chance to see it in the light of the larger movement of the whole world's history.

Lunacharski's own plays were usually similarly based on some earlier legendary or historical figures, treated with some freedom as foreshadowing in one way or another the Russian Revolution. With his extraordinary modesty about his own writings, he realized that his plays were not very great as poetry or as drama; but they served to show how stories out of the past can be used to help inspire the present and the future.

For example Lunacharski turned back to the Faust legend and wrote a play called *Faust and the City,* which was acted on November 7, 1920, at the Alexandrinski Theatre in Petrograd, on the occasion of the celebration of the third anniversary of the Russian Revolution. Here Faust, who has acquired all human wisdom, dismisses Mephistopheles and abdicates all power to the people, who cry: "Faust is alive in all things! He lives in us! He lives forever!"

In the following year, on November 7, 1921, in celebration of the fourth anniversary of the Russian Revolution, Lunacharski's *Oliver Cromwell* was acted at the Maly Theatre in Moscow. Here the seizing of power by Cromwell and the Puritan Parliament, the execution of King Charles I and the establishment of the Commonwealth in England in the seventeenth century offered an interesting parallel to the Russian Revolution of 1917.

In 1921 another play of Lunacharski's was also acted, called *The Chancellor and the Locksmith,* in which an abortive revolution, which overthrows the Emperor but makes terms with the Chancellor, gives place to a genuine workers' revolution led by a locksmith.

A little later Lunacharski's play *The Emancipated Don Quixote* was acted at the Korsh Theatre in Moscow. Here Lunacharski depicts Don Quixote and Sancho Panza coming to free the revolutionists from prison. For this Don Quixote himself is thrown into prison. Later the revolutionists, remembering how he had freed them, came to free Don Quixote. Like Lunacharski himself, Don Quixote protests against their violences and their excesses, but they explain to him that they are paying the price without which he could not have been emancipated and could not now live in harmony and light.

At about the same time, another play of Lunacharski's called *Thomas Campanella*—in two parts, one called *The People* and one called *The Duke*

—was acted in Moscow. This dealt with the Italian philosopher Campanella who, in his famous book *The City of the Sun* in 1623, planned an ideal commonwealth. Because of his love of the people and his opposition to their oppressors he is thrown into prison by the Inquisition and kept there for twenty-eight years.

In 1924, another play of Lunacharski's, the *Bear's Marriage,* was acted at the Maly Theatre and turned into a moving picture. Based on Prosper Mérimée's story *Lokis,* it dealt with a cruel count, half man and half monster, who bites persons and sucks their blood, until at last the people rise in revolt against him.

Finally, in 1931, at the Second Moscow Art Theatre, Lunacharski in *Napoleon Intervenes,* adapted a play by Walter Hasenclever, making a wax image of Napoleon come to life and intrude once more, like a Mussolini or a Hitler, in international affairs.

In a long series of plays such as these, Lunacharski threw light on various aspects of the Russian Revolution by turning back to various legends of different periods and different countries. With his wealth of international culture it seemed natural to him to bring up these historical analogies. At least for himself, the time did not yet seem ripe to deal realistically with the Russian Revolution itself. That he left for others to do.

Oddly enough the first important Soviet play dealing realistically with the Russian Revolution itself was written by a Russian writer who at first was anything but sympathetic to the revolutionists. This was Michael Afanasevich Bulgakov (1891-1940). He had written in 1925 a two-volume novel called *The White Guard,* dealing with a family of Czarist officers, a family named Turbin, who were fighting with the "Whites" against the Revolution. In the following year, 1926, he condensed this long novel, in one case combining two characters into one, and turned it into a play called *Days of the Turbins.* This was beautifully acted by the Moscow Art Theatre with much of the charm of a Chekhov play. It was also acted in translation in England and America and is often considered the best written of all Soviet plays. It brings in all the confusing clashes that Bulgakov himself had experienced in his youth during the Revolution in the Ukrainian city of Kiev, which changed hands at least a dozen times. All the different conflicting forces fighting against each other there are brought in: the White Guard followers of the Czar, the native followers of the Ukrainian Hetman, the invading German armies, the outlaws under Petlyura. The Bolsheviks themselves never appear upon the stage; but at the end we hear them in the distance entering to take possession of the city, singing the Internationale. One of the younger members of the White Guard, half won over to the Revolution, cries: "That is the prologue to a great historical drama!" To this, an older White Captain replies: "For some it is a prologue—for others an epilogue!"

With this even-handed justice, Bulgakov seemed to hold the balances in which he was weighing the Whites against the Reds. Yet on the whole, his sympathies were so much with the White Guard that the discussions about the play became fast and furious. When some members of the audience, who were hostile to the Soviet, rose to their feet during the singing of the Czarist Hymn and tried to turn the play into a demonstration, it was decided after two years to withdraw the play temporarily. At Stalin's own insistence, however, it was restored to the repertoire and has continued to be played by the Moscow Art Theatre more than any other play dealing with the Russian Revolution. In spite of endeavors to prove the contrary, the continued existence of this play dealing so sympathetically with the White Guard shows how willing the Russians were to hear the other side presented in a play, provided it was beautifully done and not turned into a counter-revolutionary demonstration.

Meanwhile Bulgakov had written in the same year, 1926, a comedy called *Zoe's Apartment* which was acted at the Vakhtangov Theatre in Moscow. Here he made uproarious fun out of the difficulties of the housing problem and other features of the new Soviet life which lent themselves all too easily to ridicule.

Two years later, in 1928, while his play *Days of the Turbins* was temporarily banned from the stage, Bulgakov wrote a fantastic allegorical satire on Soviet censorship called *The Purple Island,* which was acted as the Kamerny Theatre in Moscow. He also attempted in 1929 a sequel to *Days of the Turbins,* to be called *Flight,* in which he represented the White Guard officers fleeing from Kiev toward the south to join the forces of Denikin and continue the fight against the Red Armies.

Since then he has held an important position as "dramaturg" at the Moscow Art Theatre, selecting and arranging their repertoire. For that theatre in 1932 he did a splendid dramatization of Gogol's great novel *Dead Souls.* In 1936 he wrote a play called *Molière* for the Moscow Art Theatre in which he dramatized the life of the great seventeenth-century French dramatist. In the same year he wrote a comedy of his own called *Ivan Vasilevich* in which he depicted the dilemma of a thief who cannot steal because money has been abolished. In 1940, for the Vakhtangov Theatre, he dramatized Cervantes' novel *Don Quixote;* and in 1943, three years after his death, his last play, *Pushkin,* dealing with the duel and death of the great Russian poet, was magnificently done by his favorite theatre, the Moscow Art Theatre.

If the Moscow Art Theatre did produce in 1926 a play showing sympathetically the White Guard, they followed that up by producing in the next year, as part of the celebration of the tenth anniversary of the Russian Revolution, a play showing the point of view of the Red Guard. This was *Armored Train 14-69* by Vsevolod Vyacheslavovich Ivanov (1895-   ). For a time they ran the two plays alternately: so that audiences might see one night the Russian Revolution from the angle of the Whites; and the next night from that on the Reds. Ivanov's play, like Bulgakov's, was based on a novel which he had written several years earlier. Ivanov had been born and brought up in Siberia and when the Revolution spread there in 1919, he had fought with the Red Guard, backed by peasant partisans and some Chinese, against the White Guard who, with the aid of the Japanese and an American expeditionary force in Vladivostok, were trying to crush the Soviets. These experiences he wrote up in two novels: one in 1921 called *Partisans* and one in 1922 called *Armored Train 14-69*. It is this second story, with some details from the first, that he dramatized five years later for the Moscow Art Theatre. An armored train numbered 14-69 is being sent by the Whites to overthrow the workers' republic. The leader of the peasants in that Far Eastern region, Vershinin, the part acted so powerfully by Kachalov, is at first very reluctant to join the revolutionists and take up arms against the Czarist generals. But when news is brought to him that the White Guard have burned his farm and killed his two sons, he gathers the other peasants about him and they are ready to lie down in a mass on the railroad tracks to prevent the passing of the armored train of the Whites. The train must be "held up by peasant flesh." Vershinin says: "If we don't protect the Russian soil, foreigners will come and take it away from us. The time has come to die!"

As it turns out, it is a young Chinese lad, whom they call Comrade China, who realizes that the fate of China at the hands of the Japanese is bound up with that of the Soviet Union; and, lying down in Vershinin's place on the rails, makes with his death the sacrifice necessary for the partisans to capture the armored train. The leader of the communists is treacherously killed by the Japanese, but the partisans and the Red Guard place his body in triumph at the head of the armored train and, raising the red flag above, advance boldly on the combined foes of the Soviet Union.

One episode in this play deserves special notice. The revolutionists and peasants are gathered beside the belfry on the roof of an old dilapidated church, when an American soldier is brought in as a captive. He has been ordered against his will to Vladivostok to fight against the Soviets. At first the muzhiks want to put him to death without mercy, but a young communist suggests that they ought to fill him up with propaganda first and then they can shoot him afterwards if they want to. Accordingly they begin shouting at him as one would at a deaf man, but "he doesn't understand Russian, the poor devil!" They then try showing him an old icon from the church representing Abraham about to put Isaac to death, explaining that this is capitalism suppressing the proletariat. He recognizes that word "proletariat" and the words "Lenin" and "revolution" and "republic" and cries "Republic, Hurrah!" Thereupon they declare he is beginning to understand Russian. The propaganda is working. "We can explain everything when we have hearts!" So they laugh with glee, gather around him, offer him their cigarettes and food—and forget all about killing him.

Armored Train 14-69 remained for years in the repertory of the Moscow Art Theatre and has been popular elsewhere. When it was acted at the Rustavelli Theatre in Tiflis, the action was shifted from the Siberian Taiga to the Caucasian mountains. A French translation by Vladimir Pozner was acted as the Théâtre d'Action Internationale at Paris. An English translation was acted in London and in New York, where a Yiddish translation was also acted. Unfortunately these translations took great liberties and in one case, to give "sex interest," the leader of the White Army was represented rather incongruously as marrying the sister of the leader of the Communists!

Ivanov followed up the success of this play of his at the Moscow Art Theatre by another play which was acted in the same theatre two years later, in 1929. This was called *The Blockade* and had to do with the temporary blockade by which the Russian revolutionists prevented the counter-revolutionary revolt on the Island of Kronstadt from spreading to the mainland. By the end of the play the Red Guards have crossed the ice to Kronstadt and, although their leader, Artem, is killed, the island is captured and the Revolution saved.

Some years later, in 1938, in a play called *Doves of Peace*, Ivanov continued the story of the Red Guards and Siberian Partisans who finally force the Japanese and their White Guard satellites out of Vladivostok and the whole Far Eastern Province. The play was acted at the Red Army Theatre and had a certain timeliness on account of the border fights that were beginning again with the Japanese by 1938; but none of these later plays of Ivanov ever recaptured the success of his initial *Armored Train 14-69*.

When *Armored Train 14-69* had first been produced at the Moscow Art Theatre and at the Leningrad Alexandrinski Theatre in November, 1927, in celebration of the tenth anniversary of the Russian Revolution, it was only one of the many plays dealing with the Revolution that were produced in honor of that occasion. Each theatre in Moscow, in Leningrad, and throughout the Soviet Union celebrated the anniversary by taking up some aspect of the heroic struggle of ten years before. Some of these gave a chronicle of the events of that most eventful year of 1917; others paid special attention to the storming of the Winter Palace or the sailors' taking over the armored cruiser *Aurora* and coming to the help of the revolutionists in Petrograd; others took up the struggle for power in the north against General Yudenich and the Finnish, Polish, and German interventionists; and still others dealt with the civil war against the White armies of General Denikin and Baron Wrangel in the south, against the French interventionists in Odessa or the English interventionists in Baku, or against Kolchak in the east.

Some of these plays—but not all—were rather crude and took sides rather too obviously: the Reds were always noble and always victorious; and the villains—the White Guard officers, the interventionist foreigners, the sly traitors—tended to be stereotyped stock characters. All the plays, however, contained vivid scenes that represented what the authors had actually experienced in the Revolution so that whatever may be their separate value as plays, they offer in their entirety an invaluable storehouse of documentation on the dramatic struggle for existence which the Soviets were carrying on upon so many fronts at once.

Parallel with these plays dealing with the struggle against the external enemies of the Soviet Union, there were other plays dealing with the enemies within: the counter-revolutionists, the spies, the "wreckers." The very subject-matter tended to make these plays melodramatic, and here too there was a temptation to paint the black sheep as very black indeed. There were many Soviet dramatists who tackled these themes, but perhaps the most remarkable and certainly the most sensational was Vladimir Mikailovich Kirshon (1902-   ). An actual murder that had taken place in the Soviet Union in 1925 inspired the subject of his first important play. A student named Korenkov, who had been a hero in the Civil War, later became degenerate and even committed murder. A violent discussion arose as to whether he should be executed for this or be pardoned on account of his past services and his possible future usefulness. Basing his play on this famous case, but changing the name of the central character, Kirshon called his play *Constantine Terekin* when it was finally acted at the Moscow Trade Union Theatre in 1927, and gave it the subtitle of *Rust*. The "rust" referred to the corruption which crept into the lives of some of the Soviet youths when they passed from the period of activity in the Civil War to the temporary stagnation and maladjustment of the period of the New Economic Policy, or NEP. It is, in the original play, from contact with these new capitalists, or Nepmen, that the "rust" came. The idea was a healthy bit of self-criticism, but the critics rightly objected to the melodramatic ending, when by a reading of Constantine's diary and a pretense that he has talked in his sleep, he is finally driven to confess that Nina did not commit suicide but was killed by him. A few years later, the play was acted in Paris and adapted to French taste by leaving out all the scenes with the Nepmen and all the social significance, and putting more emphasis on sex. It was unfortunately an adaptation of that adaptation, with a change of title to *Red Rust* and a changed content, which was acted here by the Theatre Guild Studio in 1929.

Kirshon's next play had the somewhat poetical title, *The Rails are Humming*, and was acted by the Trade Union Theatre in 1928. It dealt with the struggle to keep the railroad lines humming in the Soviet Union by repairing the ruined locomotives as quickly as possible. Here again there are "wreckers" who try to impede the progress of the work; but the triumph of the Soviet workers over all difficulties is symbolized when the engine they have been working on gives forth steam and begins to move along the rails.

In 1929 Kirshon produced a play called *The City of the Winds,* which took up the story of the oil city of Baku on its peninsula in the Caspian Sea and the twenty-six communists who had been put to death there by foreign interventionists. The play made so powerful an impression when it was acted at the Trade Union Theatre that it was turned into an opera with music by Knipper, and produced at the Musical Studio of Nemirovich-Danchenko, where the name was changed to *The North Wind,* implying the wind of revolution which was blowing so strongly from Moscow towards Baku.

With his next play, *Bread,* acted by the Moscow Art Theatre in 1931, Kirshon turned to the struggle for bread, for more wheat to prevent famine. Here again the element of melodrama was introduced by the greedy rich peasants or kulaks—the word means "fists"—who refuse to share their wheat but hold onto it with closed fists and even try to burn the public supplies.

The Trial, acted by the Second Art Theatre in 1933 just after Hitler had come into power, turned to Germany and depicted the struggle of the communists there against the growing menace of the Nazi régime.

In 1934 *The Miraculous Alloy* was acted by the Moscow Art Theatre and various other Russian theatres and by the Pitoëffs in Paris. It dealt with the struggle of a brigade of young communists to invent a new kind of alloy to be used in airplanes, and their final triumph over the pernicious elements that would try to prevent or steal their invention.

Finally *The Big Day* in 1937 already anticipated the day when the Nazis would launch their attack on the Soviet Union and represented the deeds of heroism of the Russian aviators, when that day should come.

It would be a mistake to suppose that all Soviet plays were so grimly serious in their dealing with the enemies without and within as the foregoing examples might indicate. There were other plays and other dramatists who found comedy and ridicule an even more effective weapon against these enemies than melodrama had been. The proportion of plays, or of parts of plays, using comic or satiric situations is far larger in Soviet drama, as it was in the older Russian drama, than is usually realized by foreigners who, unable to grasp Russian humor, insist that all Russian plays, old and new alike, are filled with nothing but what is grim, glum, and gloomy.

The writers of Soviet comedies found a great deal to be merry about. They could at first make merciless fun of the ridiculous "former people" and "useless people," remnants remaining over from the old régime, who were so out of place in the Soviet Union. Then, as things got better, they could even venture to poke fun at some of the excesses of Soviet regulations which needed to be rectified. Under the name of "self-criticism," a great deal of license was given to the comedians as it was to the clowns in the circus. With the successful conclusion of the first Five-Year Plan, a mood of optimism pervaded the theatre. Even a play dealing with a tragic death was called an *Optimistic Tragedy.* The plays were brimming with the love of life, and the word "life" kept recurring in titles such as *Life is Changing, Life is Calling, The Good Life, Personal Life,* and so forth. Stalin himself was able to say: "Life has become merrier!" Grim as Stalin used to seem, the late President Roosevelt was quite right in speaking of his "stalwart good-humor."

One of the earliest and most gifted of the Soviet writers of comedy was Valentine Petrovich Kataev (1897-   ). He was once more an example of a Russian novelist turned playwright. In 1928 he dramatized for the Moscow Art Theatre his own novel *The Embezzlers,* giving a hilarious picture of a humble bank clerk, delightfully acted by Moskvin, who embezzles money from the bank where he works and goes on a magnificent spree in the Soviet Union before he is finally arrested.

Even more successful, later in the same year and again at the Art Theatre, was his ingenious farce *The Squaring of the Circle.* Here in the midst of the housing shortage in Moscow, he represents two ill-assorted couples trying to occupy the same room with poor success. Finally the difficult problem of squaring the circle is solved and they change partners, the two more serious-minded deciding to live together, leaving the two more frivolous to make a match of it. The play was very popular as a much-needed Soviet comedy, and was acted around the world; although here again some of the translations took great liberties, leaving out some of the other characters and introducing new characters not in the original, and so altering the text as to turn it into a much more anti-Soviet play than it originally was.

This play was followed in 1929 by a satirical comedy in verse called *The Department Store,* and in 1930 by a comedy about the pioneering attempts on a collective farm, called *The Vanguard.* In 1931, taking his title from a famous line in Griboedov's *Woe from Wit,* he wrote a comedy called *A Million Torments* in which he satirized the unnecessary agonies of the self-torturing Intelligentsia. In 1932, taking his title this time from the slogan in Mayakovski's *The Bath,* he wrote a comedy called *Time, Forward!* giving an amusing picture of the hurried tempo of life in a Soviet factory. In 1934 he wrote a play which was acted at the Vakhtangov Theatre called *The Path of Flowers* or *The Primrose Path.* This made fun of the dilettante who flitted from flower to flower. It was later, rather inappropriately, acted by the Federal Theatre in New York. In that same year, 1934, as a novelty, Kataev collaborated with his brother who, to avoid confusion, had changed his name to Petrov (he was later killed after the fall of Sevastopol in 1941) and Petrov's fellow author, Ilf. This was a huge musical extravaganza acted in the Moscow Music Hall, dealing with the clowns and acrobats in a circus and called *Under the Circus Tent* or, if you prefer, *Under the Big Top.*

Occasionally Kataev turned to more serious subjects. In 1937, he dramatized his novel *A Lonely White Sail Gleams.* This title was taken from the opening line of Lermontov's well-known poem; but since this carried to every Russian the implication of the last line of the poem, "peace is where the tempest blows," we have perhaps been right to substitute that title in English, for it suggests the spirit of the hardy Russian welcoming the coming of the storm. In this case it is a hardy Russian sailor who, after the

Revolution of 1905, has escaped from the Armored Cruiser *Potemkin* and, with the help of two small boys, acts as a connecting link between that time and the successful Revolution of 1917.

Somewhat similarly, in 1938, taking his title this time from the opening phrase of the soldier's oath of allegiance in the Red Army, *I, Son of the Working People,* Kataev turned to the struggle against the German invaders of the Ukraine in 1918, but in a way that clearly foretold the danger of a similar German invasion of the Ukraine in the future.

With the coming of that invasion, Kataev again turned to comedy and, taking his title from a popular song *The Blue Kerchief,* wrote in 1943 a cheerful play about girls sending presents, including a blue kerchief, to soldiers at the front, and the soldiers returning to claim the girls. Like a good Russian, Kataev retained his good humor even in tragic times. Like a good Russian, he has his serious moments even in his comedies and puts touches of comedy even into his more serious plays.

In 1945 he wrote a play for children called *The Son of the Regiment* and after the victorious conclusion of the war in that same year a play called *The Parental Home* showing enthusiastic workers rebuilding their town that had been ruined by the invading Nazis.

As the Soviet Union passed from the period of revolution and civil war to that of reconstruction and industrialization, and every one became absorbed in the tremendous activities of the Five-Year Plans, it was natural that the playwrights should respond to that preoccupation of the people. Innumerable dramatists wrote innumerable plays about the dramatic struggle that was going on in factories, in mines, in the building of dams and railroads, ships and airplanes, and in the establishing of collective farms.

There is no one dramatist, however, who more fully embodies the spirit of enthusiasm in this gigantic and multiform undertaking than does Nicholas Fedorovich Pogodin (1900-   ). Born with the beginning of the new century, from a peasant family, he worked from childhood as a hired hand on a farm and later in blacksmith shops and bookbinderies. These experiences gave him the raw material for his newspaper sketches and stories and, later, plays. He was only a lad of seventeen at the time of the Revolution, but from 1930 on he continued to produce a successful play nearly every year. Indeed he may be called the most consistently successful playwright to be found in Soviet drama. Whereas earlier Soviet dramatists had been preoccupied with the bitter conflicts of the Revolution itself, Pogodin turned with optimism to the problems of reconstruction. For him, dramatic suspense depended not so much on personal tragedies or comedies as on the conquest by the masses of the means of production—the mastery of man over the machine. His plays are filled with the joy of struggle, rough humor, and friendly teasing among workers busy in a common cause. His themes were drawn from the everyday life of factory or farm. His hero is the common man. This new type of hero—a full-blooded, exuberant, good-natured worker, for whom there is no difference between his private interest and the larger social good—offers a striking contrast to the morbid, introspective heroes so common in Russian plays before the Revolution. It is these characteristics that help make Pogodin the dramatist who is perhaps the most peculiarly representative of Soviet drama.

His first successful play was *Tempo,* in 1930. As the title implied this took up the problem of transforming the slow tempo of the old-fashioned sluggish Slavic worker into the quicker "American tempo"—into "Bolshevik tempo." In this they are helped by an American engineer, Mr. Carter—said to have been modeled on Jack Calder of Detroit—who is sympathetic to the efforts of the Soviets in reconstruction. They are building the new tractor plant at Stalingrad and the climax of the play comes when, thanks to the help of the American engineer, they succeed in accomplishing this in record time. As acted at the Vakhtangov Theatre in Moscow, the great scaffolding in front of the building offered a vertical stage, so dear to the heart of the Russians, which succeeded in combining in the same set "constructivism" and "realism." It was also acted in America, but unfortunately with less effective settings.

In the following year, 1931, in a play called *The Poem of the Ax,* acted at the Theatre of the Revolution in Moscow, Pogodin turned to write with lyric enthusiasm about the workers in a metal factory who finally succeed in inventing a stainless steel with which axes can be made that will not rust, thereby achieving in Soviet construction not merely speed and quantity, but what is much harder—quality.

In *My Friend,* acted in the same theatre in Moscow and in the Big Dramatic Theatre in Leningrad in November, 1932, on the occasion of the fifteenth anniversary of the Russian Revolution, Pogodin presented in the central character a magnificent type of a Soviet chief of construction, upon whom, in spite of all difficulties, each Soviet worker can look as a friend.

In *Snow,* acted at the Moscow Trade Union Theatre in the same year, 1932, Pogodin showed a similar buoyant optimism in depicting the transformation of seemingly worthless characters, tempered under the stern ordeal of an expedition through the snow in the Caucasus Mountains.

Two years later, in *After the Ball,* acted at the Theatre of the Revolution, he turned his contagious good humor to describe the merry life of young workers on a new collective farm. In that same year, 1934, he expounded his theories of his new type of drama in a book called *About Dramaturgy.*

With *The Aristocrats* in 1935, Pogodin took up the question of the former thieves, bandits, degenerates, prostitutes, and murderers, who were being set to work by the O.G.P.U., helping build the canal from the White Sea to the Baltic, and showed how most of them were really intelligent, able, and even talented, though acting in the wrong direction, and how when given the correct development, their characters could be transformed into active participants of socialist construction. Whether acted realistically, as it was at the Vakhtangov Theatre, or in a more stylized way on platforms set in the midst of the audience, as it was when directed by Okhlopkov, the play proved enormously interesting and was translated into French and English and acted in Paris and London.

In *The Man with the Gun* in 1937, Pogodin turned back to the eve of the Russian Revolution and introduced a meeting between a peasant soldier coming from the front and a very human presentation of Lenin. As acted at the Vakhtangov Theatre by Shchukin shortly before his death, this was the first successful attempt to present the figure of Lenin on the stage. It was for this play that Pogodin was awarded the Stalin Prize of 100,000 rubles.

In the following year, 1938, Pogodin turned for the first time from plays of mass action to one of private life. This was called *Giaconda* and represented a man recuperating at a rest home and brought back to happiness by a woman whose smile reminds him of that in his favorite picture—Leonardo da Vinci's Mona Lisa.

With the beginning of 1939, in a play called *The Silver Ravine* acted at the Red Army Theatre, Pogodin took up the menace of Japanese invasion on the Manchurian border and the need of every Soviet citizen to be prepared to resist attack. In a comedy called *The Moth,* produced the same year, he pictured a Soviet aviator preparing for the defense of Moscow, in spite of the fact that his bourgeois wife, like a moth, seems to be secretly gnawing away at the fabric of his ideals.

In that same year, 1939, in honor of this long series of successful plays, Pogodin was awarded the Order of Lenin, and immediately set out to write what proved to be the most delightful of all his plays. This was called *The Kremlin Chimes* and was acted at innumerable Soviet Theatres from 1940 on. It was the first of his plays to be considered of sufficient literary merit to be included in the repertory of the Moscow Art Theatre. Here he went back to the early days after the Revolution, introduced once more a very charming characterization of Lenin and a curious half-humorous working man who mends the chimes in the tower of the Kremlin so that they may play the Internationale.

With the Nazi attack on the Soviet Union in 1941, Pogodin continued to put into his plays on national defense the same combination of stalwart determination and robust humor that he had earlier used in his plays about industrialization. In *Moscow Nights* he took up events of the heroic siege of Moscow from October, 1941, to January, 1942. In *The Boat Woman* in 1943, he turned to the siege of Stalingrad and depicted with characteristic gusto the heroic courage of a woman filled with the joy of service as she runs the ferry, transporting soldiers and food across the Volga River to the besieged city.

In 1945, after the war was over and the invaders were driven out, Pogodin wrote *A Sentimental Acquaintance* and *The Creation of the World.* In this last play he depicted a Russian town so wrecked by the Nazis that it looks like the ruins of Pompeii; and the new zeal with which the indefatigable Russian people turn to the reconstruction of the city as though it were the creation of a new world.

Diametrically different from Pogodin in almost every respect is Alexei Nikolaevich Tolstoi (1882-1945). If Pogodin represents the simple, almost naïve point of view of the Russian peasant and worker, Alexei Tolstoi may be said to represent the point of view of a Russian of aristocratic background —polished, sophisticated, widely traveled, widely read, a hospitable and generous host, the owner of a large library and beautiful pictures. At the time of the Revolution, he perhaps naturally found himself with the other Russian émigrés in Paris, but he was soon fed up by their attitude of hostility to the Soviet Union, and after several years of absence he returned to Russia in 1923. He is the most distinguished of the group of writers known as the "Changing Landmarks."

His earlier plays, like his earlier novels, covered a wide range of subjects. *Love is a Golden Book*, acted at the Second Moscow Art Theatre in 1923, was about the love between a princess and an officer at the time of Catherine the Great. *The Revolt of the Machines,* acted at the Big Dramatic Theatre in Leningrad in 1924, was a fantasy about mechanical workers or "robots," based on Capek's *R.U.R. Aelita* was a still wilder Wellsian—or should we say Wellesian—fantasy about the visit of a Soviet scientist and a Red Army soldier to the planet Mars, spreading revolution there. *The Plot of the Empress,* acted in Leningrad in 1925 and at Piscator's Theatre in Berlin in 1927, gave the dramatic story of the debauched monk Rasputin's intrigue with the Czarina and his assassination by Prince Usupov. *The Factory of Youth* was a farce about a machine which rejuvenates an elderly woman into a beautiful young movie star. This was acted in 1927 at the Korsh Theatre— the one remaining bourgeois private theatre in Moscow at that time—as were several of the other lighter plays of Alexei Tolstoi.

Far more important, however, than any of these were the serious historical novels and plays to which he now turned. As early as 1929 he began publishing his voluminous *Peter the Great,* upon which a number of plays and films have been built. This showed the great Russian Czar at the end of the seventeenth century as already a constructive force in Russia, a kind of forerunner of Lenin—the founder of the city which was first named after him and later after Lenin. If Peter "opens a window upon Europe," it was a window through which he looks with mingled admiration and admonition—admiration for all that is admirable in the civilization of the Germans, but admonition lest these same Germans may some day invade Russia. Accordingly he strongly fortifies St. Petersburg and founds the Russian navy. As the menace of Nazi invasion grew nearer, Alexei Tolstoi's *Peter the Great* became more and more popular; but it is well to note that plays such as this, reminding the Russian people of the danger of invasion and the need of national defense, antedate by many years the attack of June 22, 1941.

In 1939, in a play called *The Road to Victory,* Alexei Tolstoi dealt with the time of the Russian Civil War and the German interventionists of that period. He then turned to a more direct attack on Nazi Germany in *The Devil's Bridge,* done at the Kamerny Theatre in 1939, which satirized the nordic myth and the fascist theories of Aryan racial superiority and anti-semitism. Again in revising in 1942 a play called *The Evil Forces,* which he had originally written during the First World War, he makes his villain, a German named Wolf, a symbol of Nazi philosophy when he says: "Conscience is weakness. The strong man alone knows how to seize and conquer!"

Again Alexei Tolstoi returned to the history of one of the earlier Czars of Russia and wrote in 1943 his play in two parts called *Ivan the Terrible.* This was the same subject that an earlier Tolstoi, Alexei Constantinovich Tolstoi, had dramatized nearly eighty years before. This younger Alexei Tolstoi, however, had a very different approach to Ivan. Without mitigating all that was cruel and ruthless—all that was "terrible"—in him, he now showed that it was primarily to the enemies of Russia, the enemies without and the enemies within, that Ivan seemed terrible. It is they, because he would eliminate them, that call him a "blood-thirsty lion." It is the same boyars who hate the common people that also hate Ivan and plot his overthrow. It is the same foreign powers that would dismember Russia that denounce Ivan as the stumbling block in their way. If he insists on holding on to the Baltic provinces, it is not merely for the sake of a larger and more powerful Russia, but also because those ports will make a shorter and safer trip for ships and sailors, both Russian and foreign, than having to go around the North Cape to Archangel. If he seems to oppose the Poles, it is because, as he puts it: "Behind your Polish peace, I see the German sword!"

Paradoxical as it may seem at first, it is from this Soviet dramatist and not from the earlier Czarist dramatists, that the first apparent attempt at exoneration of Czar Ivan comes. Ivan would make Moscow a "Third Rome" and Alexei Tolstoi seems to make Ivan the Terrible an embodiment of the spirit of Moscow, much as he had made Peter the Great an embodiment of the spirit of Leningrad. In both cases he brings out all that is coarse, sensuous, merciless in them; but also all that is heroic, constructive, patriotic.

In these historical plays, then, Alexei Tolstoi did much to inspire in Soviet audiences a spirit of patriotism. The words of defiance toward foreign invaders which he puts into the mouths of these earlier defenders of Russia came thundering across the centuries to encourage those who were defending Moscow and Leningrad from Nazi invasion. He helped give to the Russian people a sense of unity and continuity with their own past which they had not had before. If this Count Alexei Tolstoi, who had formerly been an émigré with the other Russian aristocrats in Paris, now rallied more and more to the Soviet Union, it was because he felt it to be, after all, essentially the same Russia as that of the earlier Czars—and that of the earlier Count Tolstois.

Meanwhile, still other plays and other films exalted other earlier defenders of Russia and still further built up this spirit of national unity. Sergei Eisenstein, who made a film of Alexei Tolstoi's *Ivan the Terrible,* had still earlier made a film, with music by Prokoviev, on *Alexander Nevski,* who way back in 1242 had defeated the Teutonic Knights in the great "Battle on the Ice" at Lake Peipus. The words of defiance that he uttered to the Germans then—"Let them come against us with the sword and they shall perish with the sword!"—echoed across seven centuries to inspire those who were defending Russia from a later and still more terrible German invasion.

Similarly other plays and other films brought to the Russian people the words of Dmitri Donskoi, as he drove off the invaders of Russia in 1380: "Better an honorable death than an ignoble life!" Again drama brought back once more the words of those twin defenders of Moscow in 1612: the tradesman Minin, crying "There is so such force as can make us slaves!" and the nobleman Pozharski, crying "We are in the right: let us fight to the death!" So, too, the figure of the peasant Ivan Susanin, who in 1613 gave his life to defend Russia from the invader, inspired Soviet audiences to a similar spirit of sacrifice. The army leader, however, most loved by the common Russian soldier and the common Russian people was Suvorov. A play called *The Keys to Berlin* reminded Soviet audiences how Suvorov had actually entered Berlin in 1760. Another play called *Field-Marshal Suvorov,* acted in the Red Army Theatre in 1940, depicted him as leading his men across the Alps, telling them to conquer the mountains as though they were hills, and crying: "Where the deer cannot go, there a Russian soldier can go!" He said that the soldier who knows what he is fighting for is worth three soldiers who do not; and when on his death-bed he was made to say: "Suvorov is not dead; he lives in every Russian soldier!", the Red Army men in the theatre jumped to their feet with a shout to show that the spirit of Suvorov was still alive in them today.

These national heroes, made freshly familiar to the Russian people through plays and films, were reproduced on postage stamps and posters and their names were used, especially that of Suvorov, for honorary medals and for military orders. Well before the Nazi invasion of 1941, these patriotic plays had helped raise to the highest pitch the spirit of national defense.

The foreign invasion, however, that was clearest in the memory of Russian history was that of Napoleon in 1812. Leo Tolstoi's great historical novel, *War and Peace,* was dramatized most powerfully, and other plays and films brought home the lessons of that invasion. The character of the old fox Kutusov outwitting the lion Napoleon, his willingness to sacrifice that which is smaller for the sake of that which is larger, his strategy of absorbing the enemy like a sponge and then squeezing the sponge: all these had, through the power of drama, their influence upon the courage of the Russian people during the later German invasion.

In addition to the spirit of loyalty to these national heroes of Russia's past history, the theatre also evoked the spirit of loyalty to the heroes of the Russian Revolution who in more recent times had similarly defended Russia from interventionists. Plays and films on military leaders such as Chapaev and Shchors and Parkhomenko helped link Russia's heroic past with the present. A poster, widely distributed in the Soviet Union, brought together these figures, made familiar in the theatres, and bore the significant caption: "We are the grandchildren of Suvorov and the children of Chapaev!"

These patriotic plays, whether dealing with earlier invasions, such as that of Napoleon, or with the revolutionary struggles of the Russian Civil War, familiarized Soviet audiences with two methods of warfare. One was that of the scorched-earth policy, of burning the villages and farms before the advancing invaders so that they would not fall into their hands. The other was that of guerilla warfare, of partisans fighting in bands behind the enemy's lines. So accustomed had the Russian people become to these two methods that, when the German invasion came, it was almost instinctive with them to carry out in reality what they had so often seen enacted on the stage or screen.

In this way, well before the attack of 1941, the Russians were already filled with a strong feeling of national defense against foreign aggression and well prepared to offer effective resistance to such invasion.

This long series of patriotic plays had warned the Russian people of the danger of foreign invasion in general and, in many cases, of German invasion in particular.

Other plays were specifically directed against the Nazis. The moment the Nazis under Hitler came into power in 1933, such plays as Hermann's *Prelude* and Vishnevski's *Struggle in the West* emphasized the menace of this spread of fascism; and in the following year, 1934, other plays such as Shestakov's *Mik* and Brustein's *To Be Continued* repeated this warning. These and the other anti-Nazi plays that followed pointed out how in every essential respect—in the persecution of races, in the subjection of women, in the subordination of labor, in the suppression of culture—the Nazi régime was diametrically opposed to all that the Soviet Union stood for. Hitler had clearly indicated in *Mein Kamf* his hostility to the Soviet Union and his desire for the bread-basket of the Ukraine and the oil fields of the Caucasus; and Soviet plays never let their audiences forget the danger of German invasion.

Meanwhile Soviet dramatists had pointed out similar dangers from the forces of fascism and imperialism in other parts of the world. Already in 1931, when the Japanese occupied Manchuria and the League of Nations seemed reluctant to intervene, a Soviet theatre put on a version of Gilbert and Sullivan's *Mikado*, in which they satirized not merely the Japanese Emperor and Japanese imperialist ambitions, but also the Lord Lytton Commission, whom they introduced as Britishers bearing umbrellas—thus anticipating the Chamberlain appeasement at Munich seven years later. Such plays as Tretyakov's *Roar China!*, a ballet such as Glière's *Red Poppy*, or a children's play such as *China's Sword* aroused the sympathies of Russian audiences for the Chinese people. Similar plays took the side of the Ethiopians against the Italian aggression in 1935. Soviet dramatists and audiences instinctively took up cudgels against the foreign invaders and in defense of the oppressed races or classes everywhere.

Thus again, in 1936, when Italian Fascists and German Nazis sent troops to help Franco crush the Spanish Loyalists, such plays as Afinogenov's *Spain, We Salute You!*, Mdivani's *Alcazar*, or Ibragimov's *Madrid*, put before the Russian people clearly and eloquently the cause of the Spanish Loyalists. They repeated in no uncertain terms the words of La Passionaria: "Better to die standing on our feet, that to live crawling along on our knees!"

When the Nazis took over Czechoslovakia early in 1939, a Soviet play such as Brustein's *King Spider* showed how the Nazi spider was spreading out to catch other countries in its web; while another play of Brustein's, *The Day of the Living*, and Bek's *The Fatherland Lives*, showed the sympathy of the Russian people for the Czech people overrun by German aggression. Slobodski's *Schweik Against Hitler* depicted the half-humorous Czech hero of the last war, "good soldier Schweik," resisting all efforts of the Nazis to force him to fight in their armies. *The Snows of Finland* by Fibikh and Kuprianov showed up the efforts of the Nazis to use the airports of Finland as a convenient spring-board for their attack on Leningrad. Early in 1941, when the Nazi armies invaded Yugoslavia, such a play as Steinski's *Slavic Wind* championed the brave struggle of the Yugoslav partisans under Tito against the invaders.

For the ten years, then, from 1931 to 1941, Soviet dramatists had continued to point out to Russian audiences the ever-growing menace of fascist aggression which they knew would ultimately be turned in all its might against the Soviet Union itself. The necessity for every preparation to defend the motherland from the coming terrific onslaught was driven home in such films and plays as *If Tomorrow Brings War* and *The Struggle Between Two Worlds*. Afinogenov's *Distant Point* showed how important a rôle even a small out-of-the-way community may play in its contribution to national defense. Finally, in anticipation of the coming clash with Germany, a play by Vershinin and Ruderman called *Victory*, later adapted by Janet and Philip Stevenson and acted in New York as *Counter-Attack*, showed Russian and German soldiers trapped together in an underground cellar. Even during the illusive non-aggression pact with Germany, these anti-Nazi plays continued to be written and acted in the Soviet Union, to the great disgust of the Nazis. They did not like the way in which they were being attacked in these Soviet plays, but there was nothing they could do about it—nothing, that is, except hope to suppress them when they invaded Russia.

Meanwhile the Russian people were preparing themselves for the coming invasion. Plays such as *How the Steel Was Tempered* and *Restless Old Age* hardened Soviet audiences to a philosophy of stoicism. Schooled as they were by this long series of plays and films emphasizing national defense, the Russian people awaited the coming invasion with great calm and determination.

On June 21, 1941, on the very eve of the German attack, the Moscow theatres were filled with an atmosphere of beauty and culture. In the moonlit, sea-gull-haunted Moscow Art Theatre, they were acting Chekhov's *Three Sisters* much as they had when it was first produced during Chekhov's lifetime forty years earlier. In other theatres they were acting Lermontov's *Masquerade* and a dramatization of Tolstoi's *Anna Karenina*. Of foreign drama they were acting Lope de Vega and Benavente, Molière and Flaubert, Shakespeare and Sheridan. No less than five plays of Shakespeare on that night were saturating the Moscow theatres with their poetic beauty—among them, appropriately on that midsummer's night, Shakespeare's *Midsummer Night's Dream*. This was playing at the Red Army Theatre which bore over its portals the words of the Red Army leader, Voroshilov: "Every Red Army man must learn to know and love the culture he is fighting to defend!" Shakespeare was for them a part of that culture.

The next day, June 22, 1941, came the German attack. The calm, which had been like the calm before the storm, was rudely broken by bombs dropped by Nazi airplanes and the terrible mechanical rumble of advancing panzer divisions. Yet this attack found the Soviet theatres ready. On the very day after the invasion began, meetings of theatre people were held all over the Soviet Union. The theatres themselves were mobilizing for national defense. Between each theatre company and each company of soldiers at the front was organized a sort of mutual inter-relationship, called "patronage" or "shefstvo." Brigades of actors went from the theatres of drama to the theatres of war. Similar arrangements had already come into existence twenty years earlier at the time of the Russian Revolution and the ensuing intervention and civil war. For the people of the Soviet Union the theatres had become a sort of second home, and when these theatres came to the front it was like bringing this second home to them. It seemed to bring the front and the rear together and help unite the Russian people.

Hundreds of such troupes of actors were prepared to go to the front and act there on improvised stages, on platforms built on lorries, or the decks of battleships, the plays which the soldiers and sailors wished most to see. When these plays were interrupted by an enemy attack, there were groans of disgust with those uncultured Nazis who had tried to break up the drama. Once a Red Army Commander ordered his gunners to silence the enemy's batteries, adding with a smile: "Don't let those Nazis interrupt drama." Sometimes a performance had to be broken off "while the audience dealt with the enemy." A little later they would return and insist that the play be resumed.

Throughout the war, then, drama became a powerful weapon for strengthening both civilian and military morale. Olga Knipper Chekhova, the widow of Chekhov, wrote:

> We are hammering out the spiritual instruments of victory. We are mobilizing the spirit of resistance and steadfastness of our people. We are filled with a great calm for we know the unswerving and resolute spirit of the Russian people.

Another great actor from the Moscow Art Theatre, Kachalov wrote:

> We actors of Soviet Russia are heart and soul with the struggle that is being waged by our people. The hour is dark, but we know that it must end in victory. In the eternal words of our great poet Pushkin, we cry: "Let the darkness disappear! Long live the sun!"

Even in the midst of war, there had been no blackout of the arts in the Soviet Union. The Russians used to be fond of quoting the old proverb: "When the guns begin to speak, the Muses must be silent." Shostokovich, however, composing his Seventh Symphony in the midst of the terrific siege of Leningrad, said: "Let music be heard together with the guns." The same was true of drama. Drama was heard together with the guns. It proved to be a most stimulating and powerful force with which to mobilize the minds of men.

During the opening months of the German invasion of Russia, launched on June 22, 1941, the Nazis began taking their toll from the Russian arts of the theatre. In the following month, July, in one of their first air raids upon Moscow, they completely destroyed the Vakhtangov Theatre, the theatre nearest to their attack. During the following months they twice bombed the Bolshoi Theatre in the heart of Moscow. Finally on November 5, 1941, four and a half months after the beginning of the German invasion, another air-raid killed one of the most promising of all the Soviet playwrights, Alexander Nikolaevich Afinogenov (1904-1941).

Afinogenov, with a writer as his father and a school-teacher as his mother, had been encouraged to write at any early age. At fifteen he had started publishing his stories; at sixteen he had begun editing a newspaper; at nineteen his first play had been produced at the Proletcult Theatre in Moscow in 1923. This was called *Robert Tim* and dealt with the revolt of the weavers in England in the early nineteenth century. In 1926 came *South of the Slot*, a play based on Jack London's story of a workers' strike south of the cable line in San Francisco during the early years of the twentieth century. *At the Breaking Point,* also acted in 1926, had dramatized the unrest in Germany at the end of the First World War.

From these plays dealing with labor struggles in other countries and earlier periods, Afinogenov had then turned to the life he found around him in the Soviet Union. In 1927, *Look With Both Eyes* had emphasized the need for the young Communists to keep their eyes open to the snares laid by enemies of the Soviet Union. *Raspberry Jam* in the same year had shown the danger of a Red Army leader neglecting his duty and caring too much for the good things of life. *The Wolf's Trail,* also of 1927, had depicted an engineer of the old régime vainly trying to cover up his tracks in the new Russia.

More mature plays had followed and Afinogenov had turned from these external conflicts to deal, like Chekhov, with the inner drama of his characters; but instead of showing the disintegration of a decaying society he showed rather the birth-pangs of a new social order. He had the courage to discuss boldly the very problems in Soviet life which were most disturbing the minds of his audiences. In 1929, in a play called *The Eccentric,* he had ventured to show how a misunderstood but enthusiastic and hard-working non-Communist could play an important and useful part in a communist society. In 1931 in *Fear,* acted at the Alexandrinski Theatre in Leningrad and at the Moscow Art Theatre, throughout the Soviet Union and in many foreign countries, he had gone even further. He had boldly shown the director of a Soviet institute putting forward the theory that in the Soviet Union the majority of the people were living in a constant state of fear. It was only as the play went on that Afinogenov had shown how this scientist's conclusions had been influenced by enemies of the Soviet Union, some of them linked with hostile elements in Germany; how he had based his theory on insufficient evidence, taking into account only the disgruntled persons of his acquaintance and leaving out of account the fearlessness of the great mass of the people. As soon as the scientist himself became a friend of the people, he found in place of the stimulus of fear a new stimulus of enthusiasm.

In the same year, 1931, in which he first produced *Fear,* Afinogenov had also published a book called *The Creative Method of the Theatre,* in which he explained his theories of drama. These he later carried out in a number of other plays.

In 1940, in a play called *The Mother of her Children,* he seemed to be symbolizing Mother Russia and her devotion to her various children. Early in 1941 his play *Mashenka* was produced at the Moscow Soviet Theatre and was later done in America by the Harvard Dramatic Club, and in a much modified version in New York called *Listen Professor!* Here he depicts a fifteen-year-old girl awakening in her grandfather an interest in the new generation and the new Russia. Immediately after the invasion in June of that year he wrote a play called *On the Eve* depicting a Russian family on the eve of the invasion and their transformation into active service immediately afterwards. All their petty differences disappear. "It is as if a clean wind had scattered the husks of personal affairs and everything had become bigger and simpler." The father of the family cries: "We did not begin this war—but we will finish it!"

Afinogenov had scarcely finished this play and was about to turn to others which he had in mind, when suddenly on November 5, 1941, just two days before the celebrations of the anniversary of the Russian Revolution, while on duty for the Soviet Information Bureau and about to enter his building on the Ilyinka in the heart of Moscow, he was killed by a high-explosive bomb dropped from a Nazi bomber.

At that very time a play he had written in 1935, called *Distant Point,* was being acted in London. The English actor announced to the audience the news of the author's death and quoted as an epitaph on Afinogenov these lines from the play:

We all have a "distant point," a world in which men shall live together in freedom and happiness. We all dream of that, work for that, live for that up to the very last second of the last hour. And when death comes—why, we'll die alive!

Afinogenov himself died alive. He died full of life. He died full of ideas for new plays. Had he lived he might well have come to write still greater plays than any he had written. His plays, however, with all their imperfections, were none the less masterful dramatizations of problems that beset the new citizens of a new society. They had done much to awaken the Russian people to a consciousness of the importance of their lives and all the serious implications of the struggle to preserve the Soviet Union by an heroic national defense.

Alexander Evdokimovich Korneichuk (1905-   ), a year younger than Afinogenov, was born and brought up in the Ukraine, where the scenes of many of his plays are laid. His knowledge of the Soviet Union as a whole, however, and of international relations is so extensive that he was made Assistant People's Commissar for Foreign Affairs of the Soviet Union and later an independent People's Commissar for Foreign Affairs for his native Ukraine—a rather rare achievement for a young dramatist. His plays, those of a good fighting Ukrainian, express the heroic and stoical qualities that go to make up the Red Army and the Red Navy.

His first successful play, *The Sinking of the Squadron,* was acted in 1934 at the Theatre of the Revolution and later at the Red Army Theatre. It shows the brave sailors of the Red Navy who, at the time of the Revolution, go to their deaths as they scuttle their fleet rather than allow it to fall into the hands of the Whites who are attacking the Soviet Union. In the following year, 1935, his next play, *Platon Krechet,* acted both in the Red Army Theatre and the Moscow Art Theatre, turned to the life of a surgeon, but a surgeon who shows similar stoic qualities, undertaking, when under the strain of unjust suspicions, a serious operation on a high Soviet official. In 1936, in a play called *The Banker,* acted at the Alexandrinski,

Korneichuk turned to the life of a Soviet banker, who is a new type of financier, not running his bank for the sake of profit, but in the interests of the country. At the risk of alienating his daughter, he refuses to lend her husband money to cover up a mistake that the husband had made.

On November 7, 1937, in celebration of the twentieth anniversary of the Russian Revolution, a play by Korneichuk called *Truth* (*Pravda*) was acted at the Theatre of the Revolution. Here he turned back to the days just before the Bolshevik Revolution and represented a peasant, Taras, from his own native Ukraine going to seek Lenin in Petrograd in order to learn the "truth" from him. In 1938, Korneichuk turned back to a still earlier period in history and wrote *Bogdan Khmelnitski* about the leader of that name in the struggle of the Ukrainian people against the Polish nobles in the seventeenth century.

Early in 1941, Korneichuk was awarded the Stalin Prize of 100,000 rubles for drama, and went on to write for the Maly Theatre a play, once more about his native Ukraine, called *On the Ukrainian Steppes*. This gives a remarkably lovable picture of the Ukrainian peasants who are founding a collective farm to be called "The Quiet Life." Some of them have served under Budenny in his famous cavalry charges in the Ukraine during the civil war and now Budenny with his great black moustaches reappears to help them in their domestic problems. The various characters became so well loved by the audiences that Korneichuk was again awarded a Stalin Prize for this play; and a few months later, when the Ukraine was invaded by the German armies, he wrote a sequel bringing in the same characters and called *Partisans on the Ukrainian Steppes*. "The Quiet Life" farm has now become "The Active Life" under the stress of the terrific German onslaught. The peasants carry out the scorched-earth policy, resolved to leave nothing for the advancing Nazis. As they join the partisans fighting behind the German lines, two of their young women are killed. Saddened but determined, the peasants cry: "Forward for our honor, for our motherland, and for liberty!"

In the following year, in the midst of the German invasion, Korneichuk wrote a play called *The Front,* which was immediately acted throughout the Soviet Union and provoked so much discussion that it was published in full in the newspaper *Pravda* during the month of August, 1942. In the play an older Red Army commander, who has a splendid record from the Russian Civil War and has been four times decorated for courage, is content to rest on his past laurels and becomes narrow-minded, conservative, and unwilling to learn modern methods of warfare from younger men. In his obstinacy he is even responsible for a blunder in which a tank column is wiped out and his own son killed. Finally this older officer is removed to make place for a younger officer who better understands modern mechanical warfare and comes in closer touch with his soldiers. Naturally this play provoked angry rebukes from some of the old guard, but it met the overwhelming approval of the great majority and helped bring about necessary reforms in the Red Army. The very fact that a play, daring to criticise the high command of the army in the midst of war, was permitted and encouraged, shows a healthy state of self-criticism. Where there is a real clash of opinion like this, there is real drama. For the third time Korneichuk was awarded the Stalin Prize of 100,000 rubles—an honor no other dramatist has achieved so often. In 1944 he was married to the great Polish novelist Wanda Wasilewska, author of *The Rainbow,* a powerful novel about the German invasion which has also been dramatized and turned into a popular film.

In the same year, 1944, Korneichuk wrote an amusing skit called *Mr. Perkins' Mission to the Land of the Bolsheviks,* about an imaginary sausage king from Chicago who visits the Soviet Union and in spite of the endeavors of a hostile American newspaper man comes to have a real understanding of the fine qualities of the Russian people during the invasion. In 1945, since the end of the war and the beginning of the problems of reconstruction, Korneichuk has written a play called *Come to Zvonkovoe!,* in which he depicts a Red Army man returning to his home town in the Ukraine, which suffered more than any other part of Russia during the invasion. The soldier is looking forward to a well-earned rest after four years of terrific fighting, but finding his town completely demolished by the invading Nazis during his absence, realizes that he must now roll up his sleeves and work still harder rebuilding the town.

His fellow Ukrainians have been so much impressed with the deep understanding of human nature which Korneichuk has shown throughout this long series of plays that they were delighted to put him in charge of the art affairs of the whole of the Ukraine.

Next to the Red Army itself, it was the partisans—Russian peasants, men and women, carrying on a guerilla warfare in the rear of the advancing German armies—that won the admiration of the whole of Russia and indeed of the whole world. In their adventurous life, the constant danger of detection, the need of secrecy and disguises, the uncertainty and the suspense, there was something intrinsically dramatic. It is not surprising, then, that during the German invasion many plays were written about the partisans—more even than about the Red Army itself. Even in plays on other subjects, references were constantly made to these guerilla fighters and at every opportunity they were brought into the action. Among those who fought with the partisans behind the enemy lines were not merely the peasants but various workers of other types and some intellectuals— scientists, doctors, teachers. The dramas, then, dealing with the partisans offered a rich variety of types, ranging from old men and women to young boys and girls, and ranging through all sorts of professions.

No one has written of these partisans more understandingly than Leonid Maximovich Leonov (1899-   ). In celebrating the tenth anniversary of the

Russian Revolution he had written for the Vakhtangov Theatre in 1927 a play called *The Badgers,* based on his novel of the same name which had appeared two years earlier—a novel that was pronounced at the time to be "the greatest work of art yet produced by a Soviet writer." In both the novel and the play based on it he depicted the partisan fighters at the time of the Revolution, hiding in the forests of Siberia where they lived like badgers in holes in the ground under the trunks of fallen trees. But Leonov was not concerned with the external conflict alone. Under the influence of Dostoevski, he gives us a subtle psychological study of what is going on in the minds of the characters—a penetrating analysis of what makes the difference between two brothers, one of whom has sided with the Revolution and the other taken sides against it.

In *Untilovsk* in 1928, he turned to an imaginary town of that name in the tundra of Siberia to study the dying life of some of the backward people there in the period after the Revolution. It was a rather gloomy play, even when beautifully acted under Stanislavski's direction at the Moscow Art Theatre. Only at the very end of the play, when the songs of the young Communists are heard, does there seem to be a ray of hope. A similar gloom pervaded other rather unsuccessful plays of his written at this time. In *A Story of the Provinces* he depicted the head of a family who, to save himself from execution, has betrayed his friend and now lives in constant fear of detection. In *The Taming of Badadoshkin* he drew a ruthless picture of a rich vulgar Nepman at the time of the New Economic Policy. He was evidently trying, not too successfully, to apply Chekhov's psychological realism to the new conditions of Soviet life.

Far more successful, both as a novel and as a play, was *Skutarevski,* acted at the Maly Theatre in 1934. The old scientist of that name carries on important experiments for the Soviet Union in an electrical institute at the very time when his son and brother-in-law are plotting against the Soviets and stealing his notes. The character of Skutarevski, as he emerges from these domestic and national crises, offers the finest type of the older generation in the new Russia; and Leonov himself emerged as one of the most profound of the Soviet writers both as a novelist and a dramatist.

In 1938, in a play called *The Orchards of Polovchansk,* beautifully acted at the Moscow Art Theatre, Leonov seemed to recapture still more of the intimate charm of the Chekhov plays acted there. As in *The Cherry Orchard,* here too was a family gathering in an old house by an orchard, in this case an apple orchard rather than a cherry orchard, and there is much the same subtle psychological study of the different characters in the family circle with their arrivals and departures and their somewhat complicated relations to each other. The differences, however, are more important than the resemblances. The apple orchard, instead of being sold and cut down as the cherry orchard was in Chekhov's play, has been so developed as to yield a still larger and better crop each year for the benefit of all. Similarly, in place of the sense of futility, of frustration, of mental agony, the characters here are filled with a new joy in the communal life of which each is a willing part. One son is a doctor, one an engineer, one an athlete, one a submarine sailor, one a Red Army commander. They are like so many separate feathers on the wings of a great eagle that together enable it to soar higher. They are all "bearers of destiny." Over against them is set the miserable figure of Pilaev who has sold out to the Germans and is acting as a spy. Already Leonov foresaw the danger of a German invasion, but he felt confident in the sterling qualities of the new generation in Russia.

With the coming of the German invasion in 1941, he turned to write a play called *Invasion,* acted throughout the Soviet Union and summing up that whole heroic struggle in a drama that unites many of the characteristics of Leonov's earlier plays. Here a Soviet physician, Dr. Talanov, stays behind when the advancing German armies have captured his town. He tends the wounded partisans, concealing the fact from the Germans. With him is his devoted wife, who is called an "iron old lady," and their daughter, a school-teacher, who also is helping the partisans. Their son Theodore, however, is a weakling, socially useless, who wavers in his loyalty so that is mother is driven to say of him: "He is not one of us!" Little by little, however—and it is in these transitions of character that Leonov is so masterful—the son is stirred to admiration for the partisans. Their leader has been wounded and is being tended by the doctor, but the Germans are about to discover him and put him to death. It is then that the son, to save him, gives himself up as the leader and is hanged. It is only when her son has made this supreme sacrifice that the severe mother cries: "Now, at last, he has become one of us!"

In *Lenushka* in 1943, Leonov turned again to write of the partisans. Lenushka is a peasant girl living with her family in a hut in the Ukraine. When the Germans surround the village, there is at first some hesitation as to what to do. Like a ghost, however, an old peasant is brought in, broken and dazed. He had been found at the bottom of a well where the Germans had thrown him in with some dead bodies, and where he lived for four days. Now he cries pitifully: "Help us, Mother, Russian earth!" Without further hesitation, they all decide to continue fighting behind the German lines, though they become aware of the fact that one of them, they don't know which, is a traitor. Lenushka had been engaged to the traitor's son, but finds a Red Army lieutenant, who has been badly wounded and burned in a tank in which he was attacking the Germans, to be the man she really loves most. In the absence of any doctor she herself nurses him as best she can. When in spite of all her efforts he dies, she rushes off to join the other partisans in their attack on the Nazi aggressors.

Still later plays of Leonov's have been *The Capture of Velikoshumsk* and *An Ordinary Man.* In this last play he shows the splendid stamina which exists in the character of even an ordinary Soviet citizen when he comes face to face with the enemy. For his contributions to drama as well as to the novel, Leonov has been given the Order of the Red Banner of Labor, has been awarded a Stalin Prize of 100,000 rubles, and in 1945 was offered the Griboedov Prize for his dramatic work. Leonov, whose plays are literature as well as drama, has lived to justify the prophecy which Gorki made long ago: "Leonov will one day sing a song of his own making!"

If some of the Soviet dramatists were killed in the German invasion, as Afinogenov was, others have sprung up to take their place. The Russian proverb, which says that when one tree falls others grow up in its stead, has been fulfilled in this case too. Among these new Russian playwrights there is none whose rise to fame was more remarkable than that of Constantine Simonov (1915-   ).

Only two years old at the time of the Russian Revolution, it may be said that his whole intellectual life was under the Soviets. Indeed, since he says "our biography begins when we start earning our own bread," we may say that his life only really began in 1930, when at the age of fourteen he started to work as a mechanic in a factory. At that age, too, he began to read furiously and to write what he later called "wretched stories" and "awful poems." In 1934, when he was nineteen, he visited the canal which was being built by reformed thieves between the White Sea and the Baltic; like Pogodin, he was so much impressed by the transformations of character which he saw there that he wrote a poem about it called *Horizon*, which he later tried to turn into a play, in which those working on the canal recall their past lives and plan their various futures.

In 1939 he wrote a play called *Bearskin*, later called *The History of One Love*, in which his hero is a rough and taciturn Arctic explorer, nicknamed Bearskin, who suffers the anguish of finding that his friend is in love with his wife. This Simonov later attempted to turn into a war play. It was written for the Young Communists Theatre in two weeks and characteristically, when the first two acts were being read, the last act was still being typewritten. Nevertheless, when the time came he had everything ready, as he puts it, "punctually as a Yankee." It was performed in the fall of 1940, but was utterly condemned by the critics.

Meanwhile he had written another play which was produced at the same theatre only twenty-seven days later, and was praised to the skies by the same critics who had condemned his first play four weeks earlier. This was called *A Fellow from Our Town* and dealt with a seemingly unimportant school-teacher in a small town, rather undisciplined and given to boasting. To prepare for the threatening invasion he goes to a school for tankists, where he is reprimanded for his foolhardiness. When war comes, however, he develops into a splendid tank commander. His wife, formerly an actress, proves to be worthy of his mettle; and her brother, at first rather a pacifist, proves a heroic surgeon in wartime, though he is unfortunately killed by the enemy. After the beginning of the German invasion this play became more popular than ever, was acted by theatres throughout Russia, and was performed on improvised stages at the front. Early in 1942 it was awarded the Stalin Prize.

Simonov next wrote a play called *The Russian People,* in which he took up the same characters the audiences had come to love in *A Fellow From Our Town*—characters that he says were drawn from real life. Only now, instead of taking up merely one fellow from our town, he takes up the whole town, the whole of the Russian people. The main part of the town is in the hands of the Germans. Across the river, however, the Russians are holding out, waiting for the Red Army to come to their rescue. In this predicament, all sorts of persons volunteer their services. Sofonov, the former chauffeur of the tank commander in the earlier play, has now become the captain of the Russians at the river. Valya, the girl he has come to love, he now has to send as a scout across the river into the town. A poet, Panin, is made head of the Intelligence Department. An old Czarist soldier, Vasin, becomes Chief of Staff. A doctor, Globa, is sent on a desperate mission that will mean his death. They offer him vodka to give him courage, but he says: "Vodka is no good for courage. A song is good for courage!" And he goes singing to meet his death. Each one is ready to give up his life. As the captain says, each one is prepared "to die with a purpose." The fearlessness of these "Russian people" stems from their very love of life, of their motherland, of all they have created by their common labor. In the zero hour each has his image of what that motherland means. For Valya it means the two white birch trees that used to stand in front of her father's house. For others it has other meanings; but they all love it and are united in their willingness to die for it. As the captain says, there is something of the poet in each of them. The very menace of death intensifies their love of life. On the eve of their destruction, they dream of the future, appreciate the little jokes they share together, value each other's well-placed words and tenderly love each other.

Tragic as is their lot, it really seems happy in comparison with that of the miserable Nazi invaders across the river. They have put to death two old women, one merely because she was the mother of the Russian captain. But they live in a constant terror of the Russian people whom they have conquered. Even more miserable is the fate of the one Russian who has proved traitor, the mayor of the town, who has gone over to the Nazis as a Quisling; for in his moral fall he has ceased to be a man. In betraying his country he betrays his own family. The Germans torture him by forcing him to be glad that they have killed his son, a Red Army commander. Finally the Red Army enters the town singing, and the audiences familiar with *A Fellow from Our Town* got a thrill that other audiences did not get, in finding that the general at the head of that army was their old friend, the hero of the earlier play, the school-teacher who had turned tank commander.

The Russian People was acted by the Moscow Art Theatre and by a hundred different theatres throughout the Soviet Union, although it won only a Stalin Second Prize, rather than a First Prize, as *A Fellow from Our Town* had done. In America it was first performed by the Theatre Guild in Washington in the presence of Ambassador Litvinov and various members of the American Cabinet.

Simonov relates under what difficulties he had written the play, how in Moscow, on leave of absence from the front for a few days, he had dictated it at white heat to a stenographer. Indeed it has more of the scorching reality of something actually lived than the carefully premeditated and polished well-built play.

For Simonov was enormously busy, actively fighting in many capacities on many fronts and sending accounts of the fighting to the army paper, *The Red Star*. These despatches were later collected and published in book form under such titles as *From the Black Sea to the Berents Sea, Moscow, On the Petsamo Road, Stalingrad Fights On, No Quarter,* and so forth. The story of the siege of Stalingrad was also told in a powerful novel by Simonov in 1944, called *Days and Nights,* which has been translated into English and made into a Russian film.

Simonov also wrote a number of poems called *Front Line Ballads* and a series of letters in verse to his wife called *With You and Without You*. He found, so he says, that the war in Russia had somehow "made men's feelings keener, purer, stronger, more responsive to art and poetry." One of these poems of his became particularly popular, was printed in something like a million copies, and was set to music by at least eighteen different composers. This was called "Wait for Me" and expressed the belief that the very fact that there was some woman waiting for a soldier at home seemed to have the power of making him fight his way out of the very jaws of death. The popularity of this song led him in 1942 to write a play on the theme also called *Wait for Me*. Here the hero is an aviator whose plane has landed behind the German lines. At home all think he is dead and drink to his memory—all save his wife who still believes that he will return. Encouraged by his confidence that she, unlike some of the other wives, will still be waiting for him, he fights his way out of the trap and makes his way home, where he quietly unlocks the door with the house key he has always kept with him and finds his wife faithfully waiting.

In 1943 Simonov wrote with Dykhovichni a farcical play called *Friends Remain Friends* for the Theatre of Satire. In 1944 he wrote a play called *And So It Will Be*. In this he again takes a very simple theme—that of various people, some of whom have been bombed out of their own homes, all sharing a single apartment in Moscow during the war. Love springs up between a young girl and an older officer, but somehow even broader and more important than love seems to be the healing power of friendship among the Soviet people. Religion and science now understand each other and a woman surgeon tells a characteristic story of how, when no other building was left standing in a recaptured town, a priest allowed her to use the church as an operating room. One or two of the characters are engineers and architects and Simonov shows us how even in the midst of war their hearts are set on reconstruction and seeing to it that no future war shall destroy what they are building. This play was translated and acted as *The Whole World Over.*

Toward the end of the war, in 1945, Simonov was with the Red Army in Yugoslavia and Czechoslovakia helping free their fellow Slavs from Nazi occupation. It is upon the friendships that he found there that he based his play *Under the Chestnut Trees* of Prague.

Even in the midst of war, Simonov was constantly dwelling on the friendships that were being made which would outlast the war, and on the plans already being made for rebuilding after the war. That was a general and very striking characteristic of Russian war plays.

As soon as any Russian town was freed from the German invaders, in the wake of the Red Army entering the liberated town, came brigades of actors prepared to give a performance on the very next night even if it had to be in a partly ruined theatre. Gradually the destroyed theatres were rebuilt or newer and larger ones constructed in their place. As one Red Army general put it: "As soon as the war is over, we Red Army men will want to see large new theatres everywhere, with still better actors and still better plays. You must keep up and improve all the arts of the theatre." The Russian soldiers, like all the other Russian people, were eager not merely to see the standard of Soviet drama maintained, but to have it reach heights that it had never reached before.

VIII

Europe's Middle Zone

The Drama of the Baltic Regions

Despite many and deep-seated differences, both cultural and linguistic, the four national groups here designated, on the basis of geography, as Baltic, had one thing in common for more than three quarters of the period covered by our survey: all four belonged politically to the Russian Empire. Finland enjoyed the status of a Grand Duchy, with a separate constitution and a Diet. Estonians, Letts (Latvians), and Lithuanians had no such favorable standing within the Empire.

All four members of our Baltic group became independent as a result of the First World War and constituted themselves after 1918 and up to 1939 as sovereign and independent states.

Linguistically our Baltic group subdivides into two parts, the Finns and Estonians speaking two distinct variations of the Finno-Ugric branch of Indo-European, the Letts and Lithuanians two variations of the Baltic branch. The language of the Finns and Estonians is related to that of the Hungarians, while Lettish and Lithuanian have no linguistic cousins, but are themselves strikingly similar to the mother of all Indo-European tongues, Sanskrit.

The most powerful cultural influence in Finnish life has been that of Sweden, whereas the Lithuanians have come under Polish and German influence. German culture has left a deep mark also among the Letts and Estonians.

FINNISH DRAMA

JOHN B. OLLI

Up to about 1850, most writing in the country known to us as Finland and to the natives as Suomi was in Swedish. The early history of Finnish drama is to be found, therefore, in that of Swedish drama, already discussed.

The steps by which the Finnish language became a literary instrument can scarcely be given here in detail. Suffice it to say that they include first of all the pioneer agitation of the poet A. I. Arwidsson (1791-1858), famous as the popularizer of the slogan "We are not Swedes, we will not become Russians, and so we must be Finns," and the painstaking labors of Elias Lönnrot (1802-1884), who discovered and published the two great folklore collections *Kalevala* and *Kanteletar* from which so much of Finnish literature was subsequently to draw its inspiration. They embrace also the example of Johan Ludvig Runeberg (1804-1877), the national poet of Finland, and the services of J. V. Snellman (1806-1881) in the struggle for Finnish schools. Not to be forgotten also are the reforms, both political and economic, introduced by Alexander II at the time of the convening of the Finnish Diet in 1863.

The first condition of a Finnish literature, a Finnish-speaking educated class, began to be met in 1858, when the first Finnish secondary school was opened in Jyväskylä, in central Finland. More than two decades earlier, patriotic Finns had laid the groundwork for a native literature by founding in 1831 a Finnish Literary Society. This society, which is still in existence, aided promising young writers and published Finnish translations of the foreign classics.

The birth date of Finnish dramas is usually given as May 10, 1869, the date on which the miracle drama *Lea,* by Aleksis Stenvall (1834-1872), was first performed, in Helsinki.

Kivi, as Stenvall is known, was born at Palojoki, a village about a hundred miles northwest of Helsinki. His father was a tailor, somewhat given to strong drink, his mother a strong, deeply religious, and ambitious woman. It was thanks to her encouragement that Kivi entered the Swedish university in Helsinki. Here he read widely in foreign literatures and was powerfully influenced by The Bible, the *Kalevala, Don Quixote,* and by Shakespeare.

On completing his studies Kivi was given a living in the village of Suntio near Helsinki by the generous Mme Charlotte Lönnquist. Here he began to write, producing first the tragedy *Kullervo* (1864), based on a theme from the *Kalevala.* Kullervo, it will be recalled, was a kind of bungling Hercules, a creature of enormous strength but small wit, who spoils everything he touches and is finally driven in despair to suicide. In Kivi's drama the poor, misguided giant becomes the symbol of all humankind. *Kullervo* showed great promise, was enthusiastically hailed, and won for its author the title Father of Finnish Drama.[1]

Kivi made his greatest contribution to Finnish literature through his comedies, of which *The Village Shoemakers* (1864) is a masterpiece. A humorous drama of country life, this is still a favorite with Finnish audiences, as is also *The Betrothal* (1866), a homely and engaging one-act comedy strongly reminiscent of the plays of Lady Gregory.

A Finnish national theatre was established in 1872, thanks principally

[1] A statue of Kivi was unveiled in front of the National Theatre in Helsinki on October 10, 1939.

to the efforts of Kaarlo Juhan Bergbom (1843-1906), yet Finnish drama lagged in the seventies and it was only with the nineties, and the arrival on the scene of a generation reared in Finnish schools, that native drama began to stand on its own feet.

The outstanding figure of the new period was Minna Canth (1844-1897). Born Wilhelmina Johansson in the town of Tampere (Tammerfors), where her father was superintendent of a large cotton mill, Minna Canth decided at the age of nineteen that it was her mission to "teach the people." Accordingly she entered a normal school, only to leave after a year to marry. Thereafter, for eight years, during which time she bore seven children, Mme Canth effaced herself utterly, emerging at the end of that time as a crusading polemicist for the cause of prohibition. When her pen was silenced by various interests, she decided to give up writing, but the chance visit of a traveling theatrical troupe to the village in which she was living changed her mind. She began to write plays, training herself in the technique of the drama by wide reading in Swedish and Norwegian. The unexpected success of her first effort, a play entitled *Burglary* (1882) which deals with the plight of a girl unjustly accused of theft, spurred her on.

Whether she is dealing with country types and scenes, as in *Roinila Farm* (1893) and *The Parson's Family* (1891), or with urban problems, as in *The Workingman's Wife* (1896), Mme Canth is moved by a passionate desire to improve the lot of humankind, especially that of her own sex. If, on occasion, in the above-mentioned plays—as in *Anna Liisa* (1896), regarded by some as her masterpiece, and in *Sylvi* (1893)—she sometimes sacrificed art for the sermon, the sacrifice in no way detracted from the popularity of her plays with the audiences for which they were written and only served in the long run to enhance their author's reputation.

In strong contrast to Mme Canth's realism was the symbolism of Juhana Henrik Erkko (1849-1906) and Eino Leino (1878-1926), both of whom were primarily poets as Mme Canth was primarily a reformer. Erkko's principal dramas were the biblical *Prophet* (1887) and two lyrical pieces inspired by the *Kalevala, Aino* (1893), based on the tragedy of the maiden beloved of the bard Väinämöinen, and *Kullervo* (1890). Leino was the outstanding representative in Finnish of the neo-romanticism of the late nineteenth century. His best-known dramas were the historical trilogy *Bishop Maunu* (1909), *Simo Hurtta* (1904), and *Alkibiades* (1909).

Finnish drama was greatly retarded by the imperial program of Russification pursued in the years 1899-1905 and 1908-1914. It was only with the achievement of independence at the end of the First World War that Finland was in a position to develop freely in the field of drama.

The leading dramatist of the first generation of free Finland was Maria Jotuni (1880-1943), wife of the Finnish professor Viljo Tarkiainen. Although she had been reared in an atmosphere of symbolism and neo-romanticism, Jotuni repudiated these to achieve success in the slightly satirical, realistic comedy of provincial life. Most popular were her *Rib of Man* (1914), *The Golden Calf* (1918), and *The Henpecked Husband* (1924). The tragedy *I Am Guilty* (1929), a powerful drama on the biblical theme of Saul and David, was also well received.

French salon comedy had its Finnish representative in Erkki Kivijärvi (1882-   ), an artist of spirit and delicacy whose plays show strong traces of Maurice Pagnol. *His Son* (1923), *Eva* (1925), and *The Reckless One* are among his most popular.

The farce is represented in Finland in the works of the humorist Yrjö Soini (1896-   ), commonly known as Agapetus.

Of free Finland's more serious dramatists, in the Canth tradition, there is Hella Vuolijoki (pseudonym of Juhani Tervapää, 1888-   ), a radical who was early influenced by the works of the Russian dramatists whom she translated into her native tongue (Gorki, Andreev, and others). Her principal dramas are *The Women of Niskavuari* (1936), *Justina* (1937), *Juurako's Hulda* (1937), *Women and Masks* (1937), and *Green Gold* (1938). She is now director of the Finnish Radio.

Plays of rural life are not nearly so common in Finland as one might expect in view of the predominantly agricultural nature of the country and the high development of the coöperative movement among the Finnish peasantry. Two works of this type are to be noted: *The Last Struggle* (1884) by the well-known journalist Matti Kurikka [1] (1863-1915), reissued for the sixth time in 1924; and *Annie and Michael* (1932), a play about Karelian country life by the theatrical director Kersti Bergroth (1886-   ).

The outstanding figure in contemporary Finnish drama is Lauri Haarla (1890-1944). The heir artistically of Eino Leino and the German Expressionists, Haarla is the principal representative of the trend to neo-romanticism in post-war Finland. Although Haarla's early works suffer from the bombast inherent in expressionism, his later are pretty well free from this, and *The Son of Lemmi* (1922), *Sin* (1923), *Judas* (1927), and the 1938 prize play *The Diver,* to mention only a few of his many dramas, are moving and sincere.

ESTONIAN DRAMA

ELIZABETH JUDAS

Although the Estonian people achieved political independence only at the end of the First World War, they had long before this time experienced a great spiritual awakening and achieved nationhood in the cultural sense of the word. Long exposure to political, social and economic pressure by

---

[1] Kurikka came to the United States in the nineties and died here.

Germans and Scandinavians, Poles, and finally Russians, delayed the Estonians in their march forward, but with the emancipation of the serfs by Alexander I in 1816 and 1819 a basis was laid for cultural independence. Desire for this was further stimulated, and its realization made possible, by the reforms promulgated in 1861 by Alexander II. The first to unlock the rich treasures possessed by the Estonians in their native folk lore were the poets F. R. Faehlmann (1798-1850) and F. R. Kreutzwald (1803-1882). Then came Lydia Koidula (1843-1886), and with her the full expression of the native genius in modern literary form.

A remarkable person, with a many-faceted talent, and a great pioneer, Lydia Koidula was the daughter of J. W. Jannsen, a schoolmaster and writer and the founder of the influential nationalist newspaper *Pärnu Postimees*. Born in the harbor city of Pärnu on the Gulf of Riga, Koidula grew up in the most inspiring of family circles and it is not surprising that she herself became one of the great inspirational figures in Estonia's literary awakening.

It was a successful performance of Koidula's comedy *The Cousin from Saaremaa* in the university city of Tartu (Dorpat, Yuriev) in 1870 which gave the first impetus to the establishment of a regular dramatic repertory in the Estonian language. One of Koidula's most popular plays is the three-act comedy *Such a Mulk* (*mulk* means a native of the district of Viljandi in central Estonia) written in 1872. Romantic in feeling, yet true to the actual life of the Estonian people, the play deals with a conflict between adult and youthful notions of marriage.

Koidula had many followers, among these Juhan Kunder (1852-1888). At first Kunder wrote only comedies, of which *The Melancholy of Muru Miku, The Mulk's Wit and the Tartuan's Wisdom* (both 1881), and the satirical *Government Uncle* (1885) were the most popular, despite the fact that they were lampoons directed against native foibles. The success of *The Government Uncle* led Kunder to venture into a more serious type of drama. In *The Bride and the Fanatics* and *Kingu Laos* (written 1887, published 1890), which belong to this second period, he was so outspoken in his criticism of Russian officialdom that the first two scenes of both had to be rewritten "in Sunday garb," as Kunder put it, before the plays could pass the censor, and the author himself died before either was performed on the stage.

The past, both historic and legendary, was in Estonia, as in all countries, a fruitful source of inspiration for the drama. It was as a by-product of studies in native mythology, for example, that Peeter Jakobson (1854-1899) produced the fantasy *Dawn and Dusk* (1884) and later the more successful drama *The King of Udumäe* (1888). It was in native lore also that the founder of Estonian tragedy, Anton Jürgenstein (1861-1933) found the figures for his morality play *Juta* (1886). With Jakob Liiv (1859-1937), and his *Master of the Order* (1905), a tragedy of the thirteenth-century struggle with the Germans, we find actual historical events employed as dramatic material.

The form of play most popular in modern Estonia, after the first wave of interest in historical drama had somewhat subsided, was the comedy of everyday life. In this field must be mentioned *The Engagement Card* and *The Bear Hunter* (both 1890) by the above-mentioned Peeter Jakobson, and Jakob Liiv's *District Elder a Third Term* (1904), *The Nurse* (1904), *The Clouds* (1912), and *The Mortgage* (1914).

Under the expert hand of the versatile August Kitzberg (1856-1927), schoolmaster, journalist, and short-story writer in turn, Estonian drama, especially of rural life, reached a high level. Of Kitzberg's plays the most popular today are *In the Whirl of the Winds* (1906), a tragedy, and *The Were Wolf* (1912).

With Eduard Wilde (1865-1933), a widely traveled and cosmopolitan figure, we come to one of Estonia's most brilliant writers. A playwright as well as a novelist of great power, Wilde was a keen student of the native character and his dramas appeal to a wide public. His best plays are the delightful *Hobgoblin* (1913) and *The Uncomprehended Marvel* (1923).

In the second generation of Estonian playwrights we find Ernst Peterson (1868-   ), with two interesting dramas *The Fern Blossom* (1920) and *The New Minister* (1922); Hugo Raudsepp (1883-   ), and the outstanding humorist of modern Estonia, Oskar Luts (1887-   ). The two latter display remarkable skill in the handling of acute social problems. *Judge Simpson* (1924) is Raudsepp's most popular work, and Luts's best are the comedy *Paunvere* (a proper name), *The Businessmen, A Head of Cabbage, Heirs,* and *A Song of Happiness.*

Free Estonia, established February 24, 1918, produced a number of promising dramatists. Of these, Albert Kivikas (1898-   ) is notable for his patriotic play *The Names on the Marble Board* (1939), extolling those who fell in the Estonian War of Independence; August Jakobson (1899-   ), for his drama *Visions,* which was awarded the Presidential Prize in 1939 and presented at the opening of the new Vanemuine Theatre in Tartu. To Free Estonia belong also the historical drama *Judith* (1921) by Estonia's leading novelist Anton H. Tammsaare (1878-1940); *The General's Son* (1925) by Mait Metsanurk (1879-   ); *It Will Pass* (1923) by Arthur Adson (1889-   ); and the comedies of Henrik Visnapuu (1890-   ), *The Boys of Our Village* (1931) and *Madam Sohk and Sons* (1932).

LETTISH [LATVIAN] DRAMA

ALFRED SENN AND MARION MOORE COLEMAN

Up to the middle of the nineteenth century most writing in the country we know as Latvia was in German or Russian, for the region, consisting of the four districts of Kurzeme (Courland) and Zemgale, Vidzeme (Livonia) and Latgale, was from the middle of the thirteenth century under foreign rule. In the nineteenth century the four provinces were part of the Russian Empire.

Writing in Lettish began as the result of efforts undertaken by Protestant pastors to improve the intellectual condition of their parishioners as the agrarian reforms of 1817 and 1819 had improved their social and economic condition. Thus a journal in Lettish, *Latviešu Avizes* (*Lettish Gazette*) was founded in 1822 through the initiative of pastor Karl Friedrich Watson (1777-1826) and under similar encouragement a Lettish Literary Society sprang up in Riga in 1824.

The trend toward the vernacular thus started was encouraged by liberal Russian circles as a means of counterbalancing German influence among the Lettish people, and it was from this source that Christian Valdemars (1825-1891), father of the Lettish awakening, derived the support that enabled him, together with Christian Barons (1835-1923), to establish the second important journal in Lettish, *Peterburgas Avizes* (*Petersburg Gazette*), in 1862. Both Valdemars and Barons were University of Dorpat trained and the importance of this university—founded in 1632 by Gustavus Adolphus of Sweden and restored in 1802 by Alexander I—in the Lettish awakening can hardly be stressed too strongly.

Lettish writing began to stand on its own feet in the late sixties. Evidence of this is seen in the journal *Baltijas Vestnesis* (*Baltic Messenger*), founded in Riga in 1868, and, coming to our own field of interest, in the rise of a Lettish drama.

The father of Lettish drama was Adolf Alunans (1848-1912). Primarily a director, Alunans became a playwright from necessity, in order to supply a repertory in the native tongue for his own troupe, at first in the Riga Theatre, which was founded in 1868, later in the various provincial houses. Alunans' plays, of small literary value on the whole, were of two types, historical tragedies and comedies of local rustic life. Among the former must be noted *Our Forbears* (1905), *Who Were Those Who Sang* (1888), and *The Aldermen of Lielpils* (1888); among the latter *All My Relatives Weep* (1891).

Interest in literature languished in the seventies and early eighties, as the Lettish population, particularly in the key province of Livonia, taking advantage of the opportunities offered by the agrarian reforms of 1861, gave themselves up to strictly material pursuits, especially to land-buying. The result of this was to make property owners of about a fourth of the hitherto landless Letts, thus creating a Lettish middle class and, ultimately, the first *sine qua non* of a native drama, a Lettish intelligentsia.

The first important dramatist among the Letts was Rudolf Blaumanis (1862-1908), whose early works were the comedies *Thieves* (1891) and *The Evil Spirit* (1892), and the tragedy *The Prodigal Son* (1893). Blaumanis lived most of his life on his country estate Braki, and his plays took their style and themes alike from their author's own experience of rural life. Blaumanis' drama *The Indrans* (1904), a tragedy of family life, is one of the finest plays in the Lettish tongue. A later work, *In the Furnace* (1906), is also deserving of notice.

While Blaumanis was writing his dramatic works far removed from urban centers and literary battlegrounds, the new Lettish intelligentsia referred to above was beginning to make itself felt in the towns, especially in Jelgava (Mitau) and Riga. One of the great figures of this generation was Anna Brigadere (1861-1923), a gifted dramatist, a burning patriot, and the inspiration of modern Latvian womanhood. Mme Brigadere's plays fall into three classes: fantasies based on folk legend, among these the ever-popular *Tom Thumb* (1903) and *Princess Buttercup* (1912); children's plays, *Maija and Paija* (1922), said to be her masterpiece, and *Lolita's Wonderbird* (1926); and dramas of contemporary life dealing especially with the problems of woman, among these *At Dawn* (1907), *The Big Haul* (1925), and *The Divine Face* (1926). Brigadere was like Blaumanis, whom she admired and whose story *Raudup's Widow* she reworked as a play (1914), in that she represented no "trend" beyond the desire of the Lettish people to express themselves fully in their own tongue.

Currents and trends are seen, however, in the dramas of the talented Pliekšans pair, John, better known as Rainis (1865-1929) and Elsa (née Rosenberg, 1868-   ), generally known as Aspazija. These two dominated the Lettish literary scene up to the First World War and beyond.

Rainis and Aspazija appeared first in the early nineties, when a new movement known as "A New Direction," actually a literary brand of Marxism, began to launch an attack against romanticism and the cult of the past so dear to older Lettish writers. John Jansons (1871-1917) was the principal spokesman for the New Directionists and the principal object of his attack was J. Lautenbachs (Jūsminš, 1847-1928), a lector in the University of Dorpat[1] (later, 1922-1928, a professor in Riga), whose ambition was to create a national romantic drama much in the manner of the Polish Wyspiański.

Aspazija was a strong feminist and the very spearhead at first of the revolt against romanticism, as we see in her drama *Lost Rights* (1894), a realistic exposé of woman's debased position in bourgeois society. The play caused a great stir pro and con when it was produced in Riga in 1894. Realism is the dominant note also of Aspazija's symbolic *Silver Veil* (1904), a drama prophetic of the approaching revolution. In *The Vestal* (1894), however, a tragedy of the pagan Letts written for the jubilee of the Riga Literary Society, we see her in a romantic mood.

Rainis displays the same dualism as his wife, for, despite his partisanship of the realism advocated by the New Directionists, he too was a ro-

[1] Now Tartu.

mantic, even more than Aspazija. Love of the past and of frequently recondite symbolism is clearly seen in his use of the pagan theme of Lacplesis the Bear Killer, the national hero of the Letts, in the drama *Fire and Night* (1905), and of a heroic figure from Russian legend in *Ilya of Murom* (1922). Though his plays are always based on a personal experience or a public event, they have a symbolic meaning which transcends the bare facts or events. The fanciful *Golden Horse* (1910), *Induls and Arija* (1911), *Blow, Wind!* (1913), *Joseph and His Brethren* (1919), and *The Witch of Riga* (1928) are Rainis' most successful dramas.

Of the other pre-war figures, two continued popular in Free Latvia. These were Eduard Vulfs (1887-1919) and Andrew Upits (1877-   ), the former remembered chiefly for the play *Falsehoods* (1913), the latter for the comedy *Swimming Susanna* (1922). Vulfs' forte was the somewhat satirical comedy of middle-class life. So also was that of his contemporary Julius Pētersons (1880-   ), whose best-known plays are *Sensible People* (1924), *The Woman with Six Senses* (1927), and *People Who Run Away from Themselves* (1929).

After May 15, 1934, when a nationalistic authoritarian government came into power in Latvia, dramatic production was coördinated into the service of the new régime. Gigantic open-air performances employing hundreds of actors, both professional and amateur, were given, generally in connection with some peasant festival such as harvest or high summer. Tremendous patriotic fervor was whipped up by these performances, a typical one of which was the Festival of Fertility celebrated by the drama *Apjumibas,* glorifying Jumis, the Lettish god of fertility. Two writers whose services were used by the government in this cause were Ernest Brastinš, author of *Apjumibas,* and Alexander Grīns, who wrote *The Ring of Namejis,* in honor of a famous pagan ruler of the Letts.

LITHUANIAN DRAMA

ALFRED SENN AND MARION MOORE COLEMAN

The drama was slower in maturing among the Lithuanians than among their fellow Balts, the Letts and Estonians, because during the entire first period of the modern awakening (1864-1905) all Lithuanian writing of whatever nature was perforce expatriate, thanks to an imperial ukase of 1864 prohibiting all printing in Latin characters within the lands of the former Grand Duchy of Lithuania. Whatever writing was done in Lithuanian had to be published abroad. Most of it appeared in Tilsit on the Prussian side of the River Niemen.

The first Lithuanian play of literary significance was *America in the Bathhouse,* a comedy, in the Russian sense of the term, by Keturakis (pseudonym for Juozas Vilkutaitis, a farmer). The plot hinges about the troubles of a farmer who, on the verge of bankruptcy, tries to get a loan from a young man who is looking for a wife. The farmer's daughter is offered in exchange for the loan, which is negotiated by a young tailor. The latter, once he gets his hands on the money, runs off to America, leaving the farmer's daughter locked up in a bathhouse. The winner in the game is the Jewish money-lender Faibchik, who finds himself at the end with a firmer hold than ever on the farmer's property. The play was first published in Tilsit in 1895 and staged secretly. It was reissued in St. Petersburg in 1905 and later in Kaunas in 1921 and 1937. A comparison of the four editions yields an interesting picture of the rapid changes undergone by the Lithuanian language in its formative stages and during the two decades of Lithuanian independence.

The father of Lithuanian drama is the mystic Vydūnas (pseudonym for Vilius Storasta, 1868-   ), a native of Tilsit; a theosophist, vegetarian, and patriot. Vydūnas' first play was a comedy *Where Are Your Senses?* (Tilsit, 1907), but for the most part he has avoided the conventional forms of drama, to cultivate instead the dramatic mystery or legend drama, seeing in this the form best suited to convey the idea he wished to bring home to his people of Lithuania's cultural uniqueness. The basis of this uniqueness, as Vydūnas saw it, was the pagan culture which reached such a high state of development in the territory of the Lithuanians and which persisted there long after Lithuania's neighbors had embraced Christianity. Only the dramatic mystery, in Vydūnas' opinion, was adequate to convey all the pageantry and symbolism of Lithuania's rich paganism or to portray the heroic epoch of Great Lithuania (fourteenth century) in which paganism slowly gave way to militant Christianity bearing down from three sides at once upon the Lithuanian state.

Vydūnas' principal dramatic works were the trilogy *The Eternal Flame* (1912-1913) and *The World Conflagration* (1928). Although never staged in such a manner as to reach a wide public (this Vydūnas reached through his great singing societies), these had a deep and abiding influence on the dramas of two whose works did reach the masses, namely Vincas Krėvė Mickevičius (1882-   ) and Petras Viačiūnas (1890-   ).

In Krėvė's hands the dramatic mystery was developed into an almost religious spectacle dealing with the highest and most sacred problems of the nation. His *Šarūnas* (1911), based on a pagan theme, *Skirgaila* (1925), a drama of the heroic fourteenth century, and *The Death of Mindaugas* (1935), which has for its hero the first unifier of the Lithuanian domain, are typical, while the duo-drama *On the Paths of Destiny* (1926, 1929), a symbolic tragedy in prose and verse dealing with Lithuania's fateful geography, possesses poetic force never previously attained in Lithuanian literature.

In a contrasting style was Krėvė's comedy *The Son-in-Law,* a realistic piece with touches of good psychological observation. In this as in the first of all

Lithuanian plays the American theme appears. Here a young farmer escapes from the slavery imposed on him by his father-in-law only to meet a worse slavery in the coal mines of Pennsylvania and to return after this experience a chastened and more appreciative lad.

Petras Vaičiūnas, a second disciple of Vydūnas, was the leading playwright of free Lithuania. Though one of his best-known works is the dramatized fairy-tale *The Flower of Fortune* (1929), most of his plays were comedies dealing in a satirical manner with contemporary events. His political satire *The Patriots* (1927), based on the episode of a young doctor of German origin who becomes naturalized and engages in Lithuanian politics, enjoyed a particularly long run at the National Theatre in Kaunas. Vaičiūnas was in the habit of supplying this theatre with at least one play annually.

Other playwrights of free Lithuania were Vincas Mykolaitis-Putinas (1893-   ), with *The Sovereign* and *The Vestal,* of the dramatic mystery school; Kazys Binkis (1893-1942), at first an imitator of the Futurists, whose extravagances he later repudiated in the simple and unpretentious drama *Regrowth;* and Balys Sruoga (1896-   ), whose *Shadow of the Giant* is a historical drama of the epoch of Vytautas the Great (fourteenth century) and whose play *The Awful Night* depicts the revolutionary crisis of 1905. The lyric poet Maironis (pseudonym of Jonas Mačiulis-Mačiulevičius, 1862-1932) also wrote several historical dramas, notably *The Death of Keistut,* and two other dramas of the fourteenth century dealing with Vytautas.

The Drama of the Western Slavs

Until 1918 Poland, which from 965 to 1795 had been a powerful, independent kingdom, was in a state of partition, her lands being ruled by the three empires of Germany, Austria and Russia.

Far from being coterminal with statehood, Polish literary life flourished in the period of partition, especially in the Austrian part of the realm around Cracow. In the Kingdom of Poland, as in other parts of the Russian Empire, censorship was the rule, but, as a glance at Ferdinand Hoesick's charming *Memoirs of the Russian Censorship* (Warsaw, 1929) will attest, this was often to be circumvented by a well-placed bribe or by some skilful ruse. In Austrian Poland censorship, whether official or otherwise, was virtually nonexistent.

When we come to the two central branches of western Slavdom, we find the Slovaks under Hungarian rule and the Czechs under Austrian. Czechs and Slovaks speak two distinct but closely related tongues. Their union in the state of Czechoslovakia, following the First World War, came about as a result of this linguistic similarity and also because of the fact that the two parts complement each other, Slovakia being an agricultural country,

Bohemia to a large extent industrial. Slovak culture is intensely Roman Catholic, while the culture of Bohemia has since the time of John Hus been powerfully influenced by Protestantism.

POLISH DRAMA

MARION MOORE COLEMAN

Up to as late as the early 1860's Polish drama still labored under a dual bondage: on the one hand to French classical tragedy, from which its forms were derived, and on the other to romanticism's cult of sweet suffering, which dictated most of its themes. The two-fold servitude was long overdue to be thrown off when the process of accomplishing this was accelerated unexpectedly by the cyclonic tragedy of the ill-fated uprising of 1863 against Russia.

Though the portions of Poland most deeply involved in the uprising were the Russian-ruled Kingdom, centering around Warsaw, and the Lithuanian district around Wilno, the other two parts of the partitioned country, Austrian Galicia and the western provinces under Germany, were also affected almost as painfully as these by the fatal outcome of the uprising, so that for a long time after the collapse of the enterprise in 1864 artistic and intellectual activity were almost completely paralyzed throughout the entire Polish realm.

When the normal, healthy instincts of the nation began to reassert themselves, as they did about 1867, everything that reminded the country of the days before '63 was repudiated out of hand. In literature new forms were sought and new themes and the cult of reason was set up in place of the discredited cult of poetic dreaming. In the drama a whole new segment of society became available for use by the aspiring craftsman, as the nation's center of gravity shifted from the manor-house, where it had rested traditionally, to the great urban center, and from the landed gentry, now largely ruined or in exile, to the rising industrial class and the new bureaucracy. Under the impetus of the wave of national self-appraisal which swept over the country a new awareness now arose of the drama's potentiality as an instrument of the social and economic reform recognized by all as desperately needed.

Among the earliest plays to reflect the new emphasis was the comedy by Michał Bałucki (1837-1901) of the well-intentioned but incompetent city official, *The Counselors of Mr. Councilor,* presented for the first time in Cracow in 1867. Another was the primitive and immature but historically significant one-act comedy *Without a Dowry* by Kazimierz Zalewski (1849-1919), a youthful enthusiast of the drama still at his studies in Warsaw University. A satire on marriage-for-money, *Without a Dowry* was presented for the first time at a Sunday performance in the Warsaw Variety Theatre (Rozmaitości) on March 7, 1869.

The first one consciously to undertake the promotion of the new social drama in Poland was Józef Narzymski (1839-1872), a native of the Kingdom who, after a period of exile in France following the uprising, settled in Cracow and became a member of Modjeska's salon there. Narzymski was a disciple of Augier and a firm believer in the drama as an agency of reform. He first attracted notice in 1871, when a play of his entitled *Epidemic* won top ranking in a widely advertised prize contest. Strongly reminiscent of two plays of Augier, *La Contagion* and *Les Effrontés, Epidemic* was a sharp indictment of the gambling mania then at its height in Galicia. In a second play, *The Positivists,* performed for the first time on the eve of its author's death in 1872, Narzymski took a gibe at the militant young intellectuals of Warsaw who, under the leadership of Aleksander Swiętochowski, went about preaching the Comtian gospel of utilitarianism. The best character in the play is the Polish-Lithuanian squire of the old school Dowgiełło, whose parting words to the money-mad Alfred epitomize the play's principal theme. "In the name of all that's holy," Dowgiełło cries, "be off with you, to Vienna, Berlin, anywhere, so long as it's as far as possible away from us, so that you don't freeze the hearts out of us and bring a plague on the minds of our youth with your materialism!"

After the death of Narzymski the principal promoter of social comedy in Poland was Edward Lubowski (1837-1923), another Cracovian, whose drama *The Bats* (1875) won for its author the title of "second Polish Augier." An uncompromising portrayal of an attempted "smear campaign," the play is notable for the character of the major (created on the stage by the gifted character actor Rapacki) who, by his well-timed intervention, frustrates the designs of the various "bats," Babulewicz, Zerowicz, and others. Of Lubowski's other plays, one is a satire on sycophancy (*Speed Contests,* 1874), another (*Prejudices,* 1876) a timely exposé of class prejudice as between a new-poor aristocrat and a new-rich industrialist.

Another drama, often revived in Free Poland, on the same theme as that of *Prejudices* was *Wreckage* (1881), by Józef Bliziński (1827-1893). Like Becque's *Corbeaux,* which it antedated on the stage and somewhat resembled, *Wreckage* was a biting social drama. It was also capital comedy, thanks to the rôle of Dzieńdzierzyński, a shrewd but amiable fellow who, after making a fortune in trade, moves to the country and sets out to buy his way, through money and his daughter's hand, into the aristocracy. The hunting scene, in which his pretense is exposed through his failure to know even the rudiments of the huntsman's vocabulary and through his terror at sight of a harmless rabbit, is unforgettable.

Linked with the progress of social comedy in Poland is the name of the Warsaw journalist Aleksander Swiętochowski (1849-1938), already mentioned. A man of action himself, Swiętochowski liked the drama as a form of expression because, as he said, it eventuated in action, and he turned to it himself although he had no talent for it and no training. The best of his plays, none of which was more than partially successful, was the trilogy of contemporary life which he wrote under the pseudonym Władysław Okoński entitled *Immortal Souls* (1876).

If Swiętochowski's plays read better than they act, the opposite is true of those of Kazimierz Zalewski, author of the previously mentioned *Without a Dowry*. Written with no other purpose than to be seen on the stage and to hold the attention of an audience, Zalewski's plays were for season after season the very *pièce de résistance* of the Warsaw theatrical repertoire, especially at the popular new garden theatres. This was to have been expected of the works of one who gave his whole life to the theatre as Zalewski did. At first chief factotum of the Warsaw Grand Theatre (Wielki), later head of the official Actors' Training School, and finally director of the Mały (Little), Warsaw's first private indoor theatre, Zalewski was from first to last a man of the theatre and his plays show it.

Though Zalewski differed from many of his contemporaries in that he had no cause to promote, his plays, nevertheless, were always concerned with problems close to the human heart. One of his earlier works, popular all through the eighties, dealt with the theme of misdirected affection (*Evil Grain*, 1876). Several, including *Ours on Top* (1883), *Our Sons-in-Law* (1886), and *The Apfel Marriage* (1887), had to do with the complications arising from mixed marriages. Others—*Friebe* (1885) and the farcical *O Men, Men!* (1890)—concerned themselves with the demi-monde, still others with the ever-timely love triangle (*The Rights of the Heart*, 1892; *As You Think*, 1894; *The Vixen*, 1895; *The Son*, 1896, and so forth).

The satirical comedy reached its highest development in the perennially amusing plays of Michał Bałucki, author of *The Counselors of Mr. Councilor*, already mentioned. Unfortunately, Bałucki's best plays appeared at a time when popular taste, which since 1870 had favored the realistic and satirical, was beginning to reverse itself and to welcome only the more lyrical and imaginative type of drama it had previously shunned. Audiences in Cracow, where Bałucki spent most of his life and where his plays had their première, turned from his smile-provoking comedies, and in 1901 the unhappy author took his own life, unable to survive the chill reception accorded his *Impostors* (1900). Today, however, Bałucki is properly appreciated. His comedies were often revived in Free Poland, especially the immortal *Big Fish* (1881), a satire on the amours of two new-rich stuffed shirts, *Geese and Goslings* (1884), *Bachelors' Club* (1891), and *Open House* (1883). The last, it is interesting to note, was one of the mainstays of the Polish Theatre in Lwów during the Russian occupation of 1939-1941, and *Big Fish* was revived in the same period by Polish companies in Britain.

From 1870-1890 Poland was to a large degree isolated from western Europe thanks to the restrictions imposed by Russia, Prussia, and Austria in order to prevent a recurrence of 1863. Then in the late eighties came the inevitable reaction: a passion for escape and a determination, especially among intellectuals, to recement at whatever cost the old ties linking Poland with the west, particularly with France.

The first to give expression to the new mood in the drama was Jan August Kisielewski (1876-1918), a proud, stormy genius, scarred by a childhood barren of parental affection. In *Caricatures* and *Within the Net* (both 1899), both of which were born of their author's despair at having to slave away in Cracow when all his desire was to be in Vienna again worshipping at the feet of Schnitzler, Kisielewski evoked the epoch and its mood, depicting in the one a cross-section of Polish "rebel youth" at the time and in the other a distillation of that youth in the figure of "mad Julia." In the opinion of Przybyszewski, *Within the Net,* if pared down and coerced into strict dramatic form, would rank with *Ghosts* as a "great and universal symbol of the whole unhappy fin de siècle."

Many of the "mad Julias" of the century's end escaped from Poland and "lived," as Kisielewski's heroine yearned to do, and two of those who did performed, on returning home, immeasurable service to Polish drama. The two were Stanislaw Przybyszewski (1868-1927) and Gabryela Zapolska (1860-1921), the exponents, respectively, of "art for art's sake" and of naturalism in the drama of Poland.

Przybyszewski wrote a number of plays, always, as he confessed, with Duse in mind as their heroine. It was not alone through these somewhat misty and groping pieces—*For Happiness* (1900), *The Mother* (1902), *Snow* (1903), and so forth—however, that the "Przybyszewski influence" was wielded, but through the electricity, if one may call it that, of Przybyszewski's unique personality, communicating itself to a small circle of idolaters in the cafés of Cracow in the months between October 1898 and the end of 1900, during which time he served as editor of the influential and revolutionary journal *Życie* (*Life*). Przybyszewski was a veritable meteor in the staid, middle-class city of Cracow, and the effect of his sojourn there was to shock the dormant talents of the town into acute awareness of art's importance as an end in itself and to make them sensible to the mighty forces at work abroad, especially in the drama. To him more than to any other, world figures like Strindberg, whom he had known personally in Berlin, and Ibsen, Hauptmann, and Maeterlinck owed their acclimatization to the Polish scene. To him also Polish drama owed its final emancipation from positivism and materialism.

Gabryela Zapolska was a no less meteoric figure than Przybyszewski. Called by one critic "an exaggerated Sacha Guitry" and by Przybyszewski himself "a feminine Strindberg," Zapolska was, like Zalewski, theatre-born and theatre-bred. The daughter of a brilliant and beautiful opera singer, she had trouped her way through all the playhouses of Poland, from Lwów, near which she was born, to Poznań, and later acted for five seasons (1890-

1895) in Antoine's Théâtre Libre in Paris before she ever wrote a line of dramatic dialogue. Zapolska was also a woman who knew life: married when very young to a man she did not love, she had suffered later the shabbiest of treatment at the hands of the father of her child, to say nothing of the death of this child and years of racking illness, before enjoying the relative quiet of her writing years in Poland.

Zapolska's formula as a playwright was to "walk along the street" and there observe, through the frame of lace curtains surrounding the windows, the great, and often, as she said, "gigantic dramas" going on inside, then to write down, in a single frenzied sitting, the mingled tragedy and comedy she had witnessed. Her favorite characters were the middle-class folk of the city, though she did not neglect other elements, especially "submerged" types such as "the red-kneed housemaid" (*Kaśka Kariatyda,* 1899), the betrayed virgin (in *Madame Dulska's Moral Code,* 1907), and the poor Jewish shopkeeper (*Małka Szwarcenkopf,* 1897, and *Jojne Firułkes,* 1899).

The Zapolska dramas most often revived are *Life as a Jest* (1902), *The Highest Trump* (1909), *Miss Maliczewska* (1912), *Four of Them* (1912), and that masterpiece of tragi-farce, *Madame Dulska's Moral Code,* the leading character of which, Madame Dulska, with her elastic morals and steamroller tactics toward all who oppose her, is one of the true immortals of Polish comedy.

Another, besides Zapolska and Przybyszewski, to "escape" and then to return, was the keen and gifted Włodzimierz Perzyński (1878-1930), a veteran of the Paris stalls and a fin de sièclist without the usual neuroticism of the type. Perzyński was unique among Polish dramatists of his day in that he understood dramatic technique. He had, besides, a gift for dialogue and was an expert in the peculiar manners of the middle class, especially that of Warsaw where most of his plays are represented as taking place. Popular still are his *Prodigal Sister* (1904), a satire on the money morals of the middle class, and *The Luck of Poor Frank* (1909), the saga of an idealist whose supreme "luck" is having to marry a one-time sweetheart in order to save her from the fruits of a folly committed with his rival. A third comedy, *The Ashantee* (1906), employs an interesting variation of the Pygmalion theme.

One who did not escape from the bondage of eastern and central Europe at the turn of the century was Tadeusz Rittner (1873-1921). Born in eastern Poland but brought up in Vienna, where his father was a government official, Rittner lived a split life. Longing for the beauty and freedom of the Galician steppe of his childhood, he was doomed to live out his life in the slavery imposed by a post in the Austrian Ministry of Education, a circumstance which gives the peculiar "Rittner bias" to all his dramas.

Rittner's favorite device as a playwright was to isolate his characters, as Barrie did, in a pension by the sea (for example, *Summer,* 1913), or in a cottage (*In a Little House,* 1904), and then to invite the audience to watch the process by which the mean and trivial elements in the characters gradually triumphed over the noble and aspiring. Yet, despite his deep frustration and this persistent evidence of it, Rittner had a gift for the dramatic, and his plays are still popular, especially those in which the natural poetry of his nature triumphs over the acquired materialism and disillusion. The Rittner play most often revived is *Foolish James* (1910), a dramatic version of the theme treated by Somerset Maugham in *Of Human Bondage*. More significant than this historically, however, thanks to its Ibsenesque motif, is the above-mentioned *In a Little House,* in which a character whom Boy-Żeleński terms "a somewhat silly Nora" struggles for self-expression within the bonds of marriage.

The mania for escape which consumed Polish intellectuals in the nineties led those to whom physical exodus was denied to seek feverishly for release at home. Some found it in the study of history, others through delving into the picturesque but previously neglected lore of the native peasantry, especially of the Tatra mountaineers. It was at this time that the transformation of the hitherto provincial Cracow theatre into a great cosmopolitan institution friendly to native talent, under the inspired leadership of Tadeusz Pawlikowski (1894-1899), led many who might otherwise have expressed themselves through some other medium to do so through the drama.

Among those who turned to the drama were Jan Kasprowicz (1860-1926) and Lucjan Rydel (1870-1920), both of whom made use of themes from history and from folklore. Kasprowicz, a poet and one of the towering figures of the fin de siècle, produced, besides *Napierski's Revolt* (1899), a verse drama of a great folk uprising in the Tatras in the sixteenth century, a legend drama which he called *Marchołt* (1907), based on an old folk mystery. Rydel, the professor's son whose marriage to a peasant girl was immortalized by Wyspiański in *The Wedding* (1901), produced besides the ever-popular Christmas mystery *A Polish Bethlehem* (1905); a historical drama of Poland's Golden Age, *Zygmunt August* (1913); and also, most important of all, *The Enchanted Circle* (1899), in which folk magic is interwoven with a sinister drama of human disintegration. A bid on Rydel's part for the title of Polish Hauptmann, *The Enchanted Circle* created a sensation among populace and critics alike when it was presented for the first time in Warsaw in September, 1899.

As the century came to an end, all the currents discernible in the drama both inside Poland and without since the seventies met in the figure of Stanisław Wyspiański (1869-1907). One of the great currents, hitherto neglected but requiring notice now because of Wyspiański's indebtedness to it, was that of historical drama.

The great practitioner, in our period, of the art of historical drama was Józef Szujski (1835-1883). If only Szujski had possessed the magic touch he himself so readily admitted had been lacking in Polish historical drama up to this time, Poland would have had in this brilliant and patriotic scholar the Shakespeare he himself desired so earnestly to give her. One figure after another of Poland's great dead was exhumed and enshrined in a drama by this earnest and hardworking craftsman, from the appealing *Jadwiga* (1867) to the anarchical *Zborowski* (1869) and the adventurer *Jerzy Lubomirski* (1863). But Szujski's dramas lacked the breath of life and after him as before the same old curse, as one critic (Szyjkowski) puts it, lay over Polish historical drama. Nor were the historical plays of Szujski's principal disciple, Adam Bełcikowski (1839-1909), conspicuously more effective, though somewhat less tendentious, than Szujski's own.

It was the peculiarly influential position of the theatre in Polish life and the brilliance of the Cracow theatre in particular (referred to above) which were responsible for persuading Stanisław Wyspiański (1869-1907) to employ the drama rather than either painting or music, in both of which he excelled, as his principal medium of expression when it became clear in 1897 that he could not long survive the ravages of a vicious disease.

A many-sided genius, with the pale, elongated face of the saints in the primitive glass paintings of the Tatra mountaineers, Wyspiański made his début in 1898 with *The Maid of Warsaw*. Not so much a drama as a dramatic accompaniment to a song, "La Varsovienne"—sent by the French to Poland in 1831 in lieu of the army the Poles had expected—*The Maid of Warsaw* was a deliberate attempt on Wyspiański's part to arouse national fervor and as such was in strict accord with its author's declared purpose of "enclosing *the Polish idea* within the confines of a play" and of bringing it to living reality within the "twenty paces each way" of a stage.

Wyspiański's dramatic output was large, considering that he had only ten years left of life after he turned to the drama. It includes such a variety of works as *Liberation* (1903), *Bolesław the Bold* (1903), *November Night* (1904), and other classical tragedies on patriotic themes; village dramas such as *Anathema* (1899), a study of the consequences of indiscretion on the part of a priest, and *The Judges* (1900), a piece based, like Dreiser's *American Tragedy,* on a sensational news item; and, above all, the symbolic drama *The Wedding* (1901).

With audiences of his own day Wyspiański was enormously popular. Critics of the pre-war epoch were likewise extravagant in their praise of him, some going so far as to proclaim him not only Poland's but the world's greatest dramatist of all time! Later audiences, however, and many of the critics, received his plays more coldly, declaring his poetry turgid, his concepts fulsome, and his very language, even, not without flaws.

Whatever may be said of his other plays, one at least remains a unique achievement. This is *The Wedding (Wesele)*. Presented for the first time with stunning effect on the 16th of March, 1901, in Cracow, the play was a striking synthesis of all the "worthwhile elements in European drama from Æschylus to Maeterlinck," and at the same time an intensely Polish work. Clearly discernible were elements of classical tragedy, devices originating in the folk mystery, especially its Polish variant the picturesque Christmas *szopka,* and motifs characteristic of modern social comedy. The device used in it by Wyspiański was that of a country wedding, with the guests serving as the mouthpiece of the author and delivering for him a warning against national lethargy. Wholly apart, however, from its message and local implications, *The Wedding* is an arresting play as such, entitling Wyspiański to a high place among the world's dramatic artists.

The immediate heirs of Wyspiański and the principal representatives in Free Poland of the Cracow School which he founded were Karol Hubert Rostworowski (1877-1938) and Ludwik H. Morstin (1886-   ). Rostworowski's early dramas were of the lofty, monumental type, pageants rather than plays, in which mighty problems of human conduct and of man's relationship to the cosmos were worked out through historical figures, as in *Judas Iscariot* (1912) and *Caligula* (1916), or through allegory, as in the mystery *Charity* (1920). Later in the trilogy *The Surprise* (1929), *The Way Up* (1930), and *At the Goal* (1932), Rostworowski turned to less exalted forms, to trace, against a present-day background, the expiation of a crime through three generations of a family "on the way up." His plays were generally more popular with the critics than with the public.

The dramas of L. H. Morstin, while often staged, sometimes with polemical pros and cons in their wake, as in the case of his *Defense of Xantippe* (1939), were primarily "poets' plays," many of them improvisations on well-known classical or national themes.

The Cracow which produced Wyspiański produced also, in iconoclastic and self-willed Adolf Nowaczyński (1876-1944), the antidote to Wyspiański. Nowaczyński's historical dramas were as impudent and unorthodox as Wyspiański's were pious. His best were *Czar Dmitri* (1908), *The Great Frederick* (1910), and the much later *Cæsar and Man* (1937), in which a new twist is given the popular Copernicus theme as the name of the great astronomer is linked romantically with that of Lucretia Borgia! Nowaczyński's Aristophanean comedy *War for War* (1928) had some success, as did also his satirical treatment of events in Poland in 1848, *Spring of Nations* (1929).

It is well known that the dramatic form in which the Polish genius really excels is the comedy of manners. Before the First World War the Warsaw stage was famous all over Europe for this type of play. Among the leading exponents of the art at that time were Stefan Krzywoszewski (1866-   ) and Waclaw Grubiński (1883-   ), a protégé of Przybyszewski who, after shocking Warsaw with a daring first play *The Drunks* (1909), later held the town captive for a decade and more with his Wildean brilliance.

The Warsaw tradition of light comedy was carried on after the war by Stefan Kiedrzyński (1886-   )—a playwright of considerable "technical virtuosity but no warmth"—with *Light Love* (1922) and later *Luck Tomorrow* (1932). It was carried still further by the witty, but over-refined and excessively feminine Marja Pawlikowska-Jasnorzewska (1899-1945), whose many plays, all dealing with bloodless, artificial, and generally superfluous people, will probably be regarded, in the light of history, as peculiarly typical of the era between the wars.

The first decade of Free Poland (1920-1930) was marked by the rise of one new dramatist and the transformation into dramatists of two older writers already well known as novelists. The two latter were Stefan Zeromskil (1864-1925), who, after fumbling badly three times, finally achieved a taut and moving comedy of Polish life in the eighties with *My Little Quail Has Fled* (1924), and Ferdynand Goetel (1890-   ), whose spectacular and tendentious *Samuel Zborowski* (1929) marks the beginning of a revived interest in historical tragedy.

The new dramatist of Free Poland was Jerzy Szaniawski (1887-   ). Hailed at first as Poland's white hope in the field of drama, Szaniawski proved something of a disappointment. His dramas, from *The Bird* (1923) and *The Sailor* (1925) to *The Lawyer and the Roses* (1930), his best, and finally *The Girl from the Forest* (1939), all deal with the problem of an artist's adjustment to what he regards as "the mob." The problem is, of course both basic and universal and could be made the spring-board of great drama. In Szaniawski's hands it is not. He "pastellizes and be-glooms, removing all the brilliant dynamism from this mighty clash of elements," says one critic, so that only a kind of misty shadow-boxing results.

Poland's second decade of freedom (1930-1939) saw two other well-known novelists, Zofja Nalkowska (1885-   ) and Marja Dąbrowska (1892-   ), turn, as Zeromski and Goetel had previously done, to the drama. In *The Day of His Return* (1931) Nalkowska produced a successful play on the theme of secret guilt, while in *Orphan Genius* (1939) Dąbrowska achieved considerable success with a drama on the times of King Władysław IV (the seventeenth century) and the Polish struggle for a foothold on the Baltic coast.

The same period (1930-1939) witnessed also the rise of a new talent in Marja Morozowicz-Szczepkowska (1889-   ), whose *Dr. Monica* (1933) was seen in New York with Nazimova in the title rôle (1934). In *Silent Strength* (1933) and *Type A* (1934) Morozowicz performed variations on her favorite theme of woman's relationship to man in the modern world, the latter play tracing to its logical conclusion woman's emancipation. Later Morozowicz turned to a more local theme, to portray in *A Tottering Edifice* (1937) the decline of a once-proud family.

"Polish authors are running away from reality," wrote Antoni Słonimski, author of *The Tower of Babel* (1927), *The Warsaw Slave* (1928), *The Family* (1934), and other satires on contemporary life, in 1939:

Either they rework old farces, or write plays about Pushkin, Copernicus, Chopin, or Socrates. . . . Nor does their roaming about the maps of history result in their bringing back to us any answer to the desperate uneasiness of our times. Rather do they bury themselves in the attempted solution of problems entirely divorced from the various conflicts of present-day Europe.

Słonimski was right. The principal phenomena of the final years of Free Poland in the field of drama were, on the one hand, the sensational spy drama *Fräulein Doktor* (1933) by Jerzy Tepa (1908-   ) and the pseudo-scientific improvisations of Bruno Winawer (1883-   ) and Antoni Cwojdziński (1896-   ); and on the other, the escapist dramas of Jarosław Iwaszkiewicz (1894-   ), *A Summer in Nohant* (1936) and *Masquerade* (1939), which deal respectively with Chopin and Pushkin, and the widely discussed reworking by Jerzy Zawieyski of Żeromski's successful play *My Little Quail Has Fled,* under the title *Przełęcki's Return* (1937). According to one school of thought the reason for the dramatic doldrums was the censorship, unofficial and unspoken but real nevertheless, which prevailed not only in Poland but in all the states lying between Germany and Russia throughout the thirties; according to another, the universal petering out of talent for great dramatic creation.

LUSATIAN [WENDISH] DRAMA

CLARENCE A. MANNING

No form of literature played a more significant part in the upward movement of races which was one of the phenomena of nineteenth-century Europe than the drama, and among none of Europe's many submerged races did the drama wield a greater influence as a cultural leavener than among the Lusatians.

Occupying the portion of Germany which lies between the upper Elbe and Oder, south of Berlin and including the picturesque Spreewald, the Lusatians—known also as Sorbs and Wends—speak a Slavic dialect halfway between Czech and Polish. It is this Slavic speech that has kept the race from becoming German, though every pressure has been exerted to make its members German in spirit and sentiments as they are, of course, German by citizenship.

Up to the outbreak of the Second World War the Lusatians had no professional theatre. One would, however, undoubtedly have been established in Bautzen, the capital of Upper Lusatia, long before that time had it not been for the rise of the Nazis after 1933. The amateur theatre had by 1939 reached a high state of development in the Lusatian realm and traveling troupes played in all the principal centers. The drama also had made marked progress in Lusatia, as we see from a comparison of its state then with its condition a half century earlier, when there was hardly a single play in the Lusatian tongue beyond translations from Czech and German.

The history of Lusatian drama begins with the presentation on October 2, 1862, of a Lusatian versian of Václav Kliment Klicpera's farcical satire *Rohovin the Four-Horned* in Bautzen—either at the Shooting Club [1] or in the auditorium of the tavern At the Sign of the Golden Crown [2]—with the Lusatian leader Jan Arnošt Smoler̆ himself in the title rôle of the pompous mayor. The first original drama in the Lusatian tongue appeared eighteen years later. It was the historical tragedy *In the Castle* (1880) by the poet Jakob Bart, known generally as Ćišinski (1856-1909).

In the Castle, which Ćišinski wrote for the *skhadzovanky* (student get-togethers) which played so important a part in Lusatia's cultural awakening, was intended as the first of a dramatic trilogy to be known as *The Milecians*. Its scene was the ancient stronghold of Bautzen and its theme the epic duel between Paganism and Christianity waged in the ninth century in the Slav-German lands between the Elbe and Oder. The old faith is symbolized in the play by the Lusatian chief Miliduch, the new by Miliduch's son Wjelesław, and the conflict between the two is resolved in favor of the latter only by direct divine intervention, as the pagan High Priest and all his idols are struck down by lightning. As in most pioneer historical dramas the conflict is too gigantic for the author's prentice skill and it never quite becomes actual. For lack of more effective material, however, *In the Castle* was played over and over to enthusiastic audiences and was a milestone in Lusatian cultural history.

Ćišinski's principal successor in the field of drama was the priest Józef Nowak (1895-   ), a native of Ostro, the town in which Ćišinski himself was buried. Nowak undertook to complete *The Milecians,* and did so to the extent of producing a second part entitled *Wjelesław*. He then parted company with his master, however, to write a drama of Lusatia's *Last King* (1916), in imitation of Wildenradt's German epic *Der letzte Wendenkönig* (1882). *The Last King* proved so popular with the student societies and amateur circles for whose use Nowak had written it that he followed it with a second drama, *The Bride of Freedom* (1919), in which the spirit of Lusatia is extolled in the figure of Queen Wita, a kind of Slavic Lysistrata. Nowak's later *Elbe and Spree* (1928), although written for the stage, preferably for the amphitheatre, was like so many historical dramas of the nineteenth century a dramatic poem rather than a drama in the strict sense.

Lusatian dramatists tried hard after the First World War to free themselves from bondage to the past. In this they were not altogether successful, as we see in the somewhat anachronistic *Lord and Peasant* (1931) by Jurij Wjela (called Kupšćan, 1893-   ), Lusatia's most promising playwright to date. The work, which endeavors to show the superiority of the Lusatian peasant over his German master, deals with the peasant problem not as it is today but as it was in the days of serfdom. More timely and more realistic

[1] Goląbek (*see* Bibliography).
[2] Páta (*see* Bibliography).

was the play *From the Lives of the Lowly* (1930) by the Lower Lusatian dramatist Marjana Domaškojc (1872-   ).

Although historical themes continued to exert their somewhat unhealthy spell—as in *Napoleon,* by Jurij Słodeńk (1873-   ), a study of predestination—themes from folk legend also began to be used, thanks, of course, to the influence of Hauptmann. Of folk dramas the most important were *The Enchantress* (1925) by Marja Kubašec (1891-   ); Wjela's *Lost Bride;* the numerous plays for amateurs by Mikławš Hajna (1876-   ); and *The Lusatian Spinning Women,* a primitive but patriotic piece based on folk customs by the Lower Lusatian N. Nowy-Bórkojski (1871-   ).

Lusatian drama is rich in translations from English and French and German as well as from the more closely related tongues, Czech, Polish, and Russian. The above-mentioned Marja Kubašec, for example, began her career by translating Šubert's *Jan Výrava* (discussed in the section on Czech drama), and other playwrights got their start by translating such classics as Gogol's *The Inspector General,* Tolstoi's *First Distiller,* Shakespeare's *Julius Cæsar,* and Molière's *L'Avare.*

It is to be hoped that now the drama will resume its development among the Lusatians, serving again in its old rôle as a mighty cultural leaven.

CZECH [BOHEMIAN] DRAMA

MARION MOORE COLEMAN

A theatre of their own in which plays in Czech could be performed without let or hindrance had been the dream of patriotic Prague Czechs for more than three-quarters of a century, when in 1862 a partial realization of the dream was achieved in the so-called Temporary Theatre built in that year. Before this time, although plays had been performed in Czech on various stages of the capital ever since 1785, Czech drama had never had a home of its own. Czech companies had been pushed about at the whim of the all-powerful German companies and Czech drama, treated as a stepchild, had responded with a step-child's listlessness and remained almost slavishly dependent on translations, especially those from the popular German playwright August von Kotzebue.[1]

Only during the brief existence of the Kajetan Theatre (1834-1837), and then thanks to the work of the remarkable Tyl, who had once been a traveling player himself, did original plays in Czech have a chance on the Prague stage. When this venture was closed by order of the city council, translations again resumed their almost unchallenged reign.

But Tyl's enterprise had awakened an appetite for native drama that was not to be appeased by anything short of an independent Czech theatre. As

---

[1] See A. P. Coleman, "Kotzebue and the Czech Stage" (Schenectady, 1936, 58 pp.).

a result, committees began to be formed in 1845, funds were collected, and in 1862 the Temporary Theatre referred to above came into being. Its opening stimulated a demand for plays in the native tongue on native themes and Czech writers began to turn in increasing numbers to the drama.

The first original dramas of the new period were tragedies based on historical themes. This was natural, in view of Bohemia's tragic history and of the intense nationalism animating Czech life after 1848.

One of the earliest dramas of the period was *Záviš of Falkenstein* (1860) by Vitězslav Hálek (1835-1874), a tragedy based on the life of the great thirteenth-century Bohemian noble who defied the Hapsburgs. Other plays dealing with outstanding figures from Bohemian history by the same author were *King Rudolf II* (which was banned by the censor) again on the Czech versus Hapsburg theme, and the posthumously published *George of Poděbrad*, a dramatic treatment of Bohemia's famous "citizen king."

Historical dramas were written also by Gustav Pfleger-Moravský (1833-1875), who aspired to the title of Bohemian Shakespeare. Pfleger-Moravský's most ambitious work was *The Last of the Rosenbergs* (1862), significant chiefly because of its use of a theme developed earlier by Kolár in *Magelóna* (1852) and soon to be used again in *The Black Rose* (1867) by Karel Sabina (1813-1877), one of Smetana's librettists, and still later by František Šubert in the well-known *Petr Vok Rosenberg* (1880).

Still other historical dramas were produced at this time by Václav Vlček (1839-1908), whose most important work, *Přemysl Otakar* (1864), was intended by its author as the first of a series modeled on the Henry and Richard cycles of Shakespeare.

Modern Czech drama was given a powerful impulse forward by the opening of the long-dreamed-of National Theatre in 1881. The first figure to be noted in connection with the new theatre is František Šubert (1849-1915), its director from 1883, when the present building, erected to replace the original edifice which was destroyed by fire a few weeks after its gala dedication, began to function. As a playwright Šubert represents the successful harmonization of the two principal trends in Czech drama in the late nineteenth century: realism and fondness for the historical. His most popular dramas were *The Great Freeholder* (1891), a tragedy of the Czech gentry, torn between patriotism and the instinct of self-preservation; *The Drama of Four Bare Walls* (1893), a tendentious piece of stark realism based on an actual strike of Bohemian miners; and *Jan Výrava* (1886), a tragedy of the Czech middle class, cursed by a dual loyalty, to the aristocracy it serves and to the peasantry from which it is sprung.

In order to escape the eye of the censor even historical drama had to be largely allegorical and "to wear, as often as possible, a foreign mask." The device of a foreign setting was successfully employed by Emanuel Bozděch (1841-1889), the founder of modern Czech drama, in his *Baron Goertz* (1871), a tragedy of Sweden in the time of Charles XII. A powerful drama on the vanity of earthly glory, the play has a good plot, sharply drawn characters, and a poetic idiom. *A Statesman's Ordeal* (1874), in which Prince Kaunitz serves as the mouthpiece of the author's ideas for Bohemia, was no less successful than Goertz in eluding the censor, but *The Adventurer* (1879), in which Bozděch treated the epoch of Rudolf II, was not. The latter is important chiefly for its use of the theme, developed also by Šubert in *Petr Vok Rosenberg* and later by Dvořák, Dyk, and Vančura, of the dualism of Bohemian culture, compounded as that culture is of mutually hostile elements—Protestant and Catholic, local and universal, "northern" and "southern"—held together in a shifting and precarious equilibrium.

Like Šubert, Bozděch also represented, besides the prevailing trend toward the heroic and historical, the no less powerful counter-trend toward the realistic and contemporary. A disciple of Scribe, he popularized the Scribe formula in Bohemia with *Cotillion Time* (1872) and *A-Županned Gentleman of the World* (1876).

A native brand of realism had manifested itself earlier in Bohemia in the comedies offered in provincial and amateur theatres, especially in those of Josef Štolba (1846-1930) and Václav Štech (1859-   ). With *Our Swanky Peasants* (1887) by Ladislav Stroupežnický (1850-1892), this type of play achieved respectability. The work was indeed a milestone in the long struggle for recognition of native Czech elements. Based on the rivalry of a discharged soldier and a village tailor, *Our Swanky Peasants* has a good plot, lively situations, and vivid dialect in the native idiom. After its success Štech's comedy *The Wife* (1888) in similar vein and Štolba's *The Will* (1889) began to win serious notice.

Native realism also made its appearance in the comedies of Matěj Šimáček (1860-1913), *The World of Little People* (1890) and *Other Air* (1894), both of which deal with life in the new industrial towns of Bohemia. It appeared also in the famous drama of a Moravian village *Maryša* (1894) by Vilém (1863-1912) and Alois (1861-1925) Mrštik; in the realistic version of the romantic Janošik theme [1] in Jiří Mahen's *Janošik* (1906); and in the Slovak village dramas of Gabriela Preissová (1862-   ), especially *The Housewife Slave* (1889) and *Her Stepdaughter* (1890). Middle-class humor and sentiment were represented in the plays of František Svoboda (1860-   ), an active figure in Czech life up to our own time, as we see in his *Last Man* (1919) and *The Slain Dragon* (1922).

The influence of Hauptmann and Sudermann in Bohemia is seen in the works of Jaroslav Kvapil (1868-   ), Šubert's successor as director of the Prague National Theatre (1900-1918). A practical man of the theatre, often called the Reinhardt of the Czech stage, Kvapil wrote many of his plays specifically for his own wife, who was a popular actress. They are of two types: Prague salon comedies, as *At Twilight* (1895) and *Will o' the Wisp*

---

[1] See the discussion of Slovak drama, p. 513-15.

(1896); and fantasies on folk themes, as *Princess Dandelion* (1897) and *The Orphan* (1906).

The leading advocate of Ibsen in Bohemia was Jaroslav Hilbert (1871-1936). Hilbert's fame dates from the phenomenal success enjoyed by his earliest drama *Guilt* (1895) and from the subsequent controversy over his second play, *About God,* which was banned by the censor and only produced in free Czechoslovakia in a reworking entitled *The Fist* (1897).

Hilbert experimented for a time with symbolism (*The Outcasts,* 1900), but turned soon to historical themes, hard for the Czech to tear himself away from at this time owing to the searching self-appraisal then prevalent in all Czech circles and to the relative freedom from censorship permitted by historical drama.

Like Hálek before him, Hilbert took for the hero of his first effort in the new field Záviš of Falkenstein (*Falkenstein,* 1903) turning later to the nineteenth century in the one-act *Czech Comedy* (1908) which depicts the betrayal by Vienna of the Czech soldiers in the Austrian army in 1866. Many years later Hilbert combined this with *Homeward* (1923), which deals with the Czech anabasis of 1918, to form the duo-drama *Yesterday and Today* (1923).

After 1918 Hilbert devoted himself principally to the task of revealing by way of the drama the moral and ethical problems of the new state of Czechoslovakia, and in time he came to occupy the position of unofficial "playwright laureate." His outstanding achievement in the new period was *The Other Shore* (1924), a moving *Zeitstück* based on the assassination of Finance Minister Rašin. This was followed by a second almost religious drama, *The Standard of Humanity* (1925), also based on an actual event, and later by *Job* (1928), in which the place of God in modern life is debated through a father and son representing respectively Faith and Doubt. In these, as in the symbolical *Twin Spirits* (1930), a study of the mystical kinship linking two persons born at the same hour, and the earlier dramatic legend *Columbus* (1915), Hilbert is concerned throughout with the basic conflict in man of body versus spirit.

One of the great literary movements in Bohemia in the late nineteenth century was that led by the poets Vrchlický (Jaroslav, 1853-1912) and Zeyer (Julius, 1841-1901) which found expression through the journal *Lumir* (established in 1873). Both Vrchlický and Zeyer were thoroughgoing cosmopolites, both personally and artistically, and bitter foes of the local and nationalistic even when they wrote on local or national themes.

Vrchlický's motifs were culled from all lands and epochs, as we see from a casual sampling of his numerous and varied wares: *The Death of Odysseus* (1882); *The Brothers* (1889), based on the Czech tragedy of King Wenceslas and his brother Boleslaw; *The Vengeance of Catullus* (1887); *In the Ear of Dionysus* (1900), a drama of ancient Sicily; and *Night at*

Karlstein (1884), an admirable play of the times of Emperor Charles IV. Vrchlický's models were Hugo and Scribe and Augier.

Zeyer's favorite themes were those discovered in old legends—Biblical, Irish, Slavonic—as we see even in his, by implication, nationalistic drama of the Czechs and Slovaks, *Radúz and Mahalena* (1898).

The principal heirs of Vrchlický and Zeyer were Jaroslav Mayer (pseudonym, Maria, 1870-) and Viktor Dyk (1877-1931). The influence of Italy is strong in the plays of Mayer (*Tristan*, 1908, *Lucrezia Borgia*, 1917, and others), as it is in those of his master and also of his contemporary Jiří Karásek (1871-) (*Cæsar Borgia*, 1908), but even stronger in Mayer is the prevailing disillusion of the fin de siècle to which he belonged. This we see in his *Dramatic Sonata* (1904-1908), a trilogy of the decay of a family written in the crucial period of the Russian Revolution of 1905, an event which Mayer treated directly in *Vengeance Is Mine* (1908).

Although he was regarded as a progressive before the First World War and though he became an active political figure in post-war Czechoslovakia, Viktor Dyk remained distinctly pre-war in his thinking. His principal plays were the historical drama *The Messenger* (1907),[1] in which he attacked Slavonic passivity as exemplified in the creed of the Bohemian Brethren, attributing to it the collapse of Bohemia at White Mountain (1620); *The Coming to Wisdom of Don Quixote* (1913), a chart of the author's own progress in disillusionment; the charming satire *Andrew and the Dragon* (1920); and the ambitious study of the years 1908-1910 called *A Revolutionary Trilogy* (1921). Dyk's plays oscillate, as R. C. Bednar says, in an unstable borderland halfway between reality and abstraction, none more so, unfortunately, than the unsuccessful *Forgetful* with which Dyk closed his career in 1931.

Historical drama continued popular in Czechoslovakia as it had been in Bohemia, with its principal exponents a triumvirate consisting of Dvořák, Fischer, and Lom, all three of whom were well-known figures before the First World War.

Arnost Dvořák (1880-1931) began his career with a translation of the Polish playwright Przybyszewski's *For Happiness,* a typical drama of contemporary groping and frustration of the "art for art's sake" school, but he soon turned to strictly historical themes and personalities.

What caused Dvořák to change was a desire to account for the fierce anti-Czech feeling which he encountered as a student in Vienna. Soon this ceased to interest him, however, and he became absorbed in the problem of "the leader" in human affairs. A study of Nietzsche convinced him that the "strong man" who makes himself leader of the crowd is to be admired, and it was not long before he began to embody this figure, in one guise after another, in his plays.

We see the type first in *The Prince* (1908), with Bohemia's first king,

[1] Bohemia's dualism also figures in this.

Přemysl, in the rôle of strong man, and later in *Václav IV* (1910), Dvořák's most mature play, as well as in the sequel to this, *The Hussites* (1919), a work which, thanks to Karel Hilár's remarkable directing, enjoyed what was at the time a record run in Vinohrady's Municipal Theatre in Prague.

After *White Mountain* (1924), a tragedy of the Czech disaster of 1620, Dvořák seemed to lose his powers and his career came to an inglorious end with the bitterly polemical *Lioness* (1926), which was an attack on his critics, and the unsuccessful *Gunner Pidras,* produced just before his death in 1931. Dvořák did two ballad dramas that were, despite their crudities, excellent examples of this art: *Honest Matthew* and *The Ballad of the Bloodthirsty Wife* (both 1922).

Stanislav Lom (real name Mojžiš, 1883-) was, like Kvapil, a man of the theatre (for years he was manager of the Prague National Theatre), and, like Dvořák, a student of the problem of leadership as we see in his drama *Děvín* (1919).[1] In this, as in Dvořák's *Prince,* the leader is Přemysl. Here Lom creates in addition to the traditional figures of Přemysl and Libuša who figure in the legend a new character, Vlasta, who is a kind of Bohemian Ophelia and who stands as a symbol of the good Czech earth. In *Honza* (1913) Lom created a male counterpart to Vlasta in the honest, good-natured Czech peasant of the title rôle.

Lom's greatest drama was *Žižka* (1925), a study of the great Hussite commander of the fifteenth century and of the great leader in general. Of his post-war works, the most important are *Revolution* (1922), an attempt to phrase what its author regarded as Czechoslovakia's national mission of humanitarianism in a drama based on the uprising of 1918 against Austria; and *St. Wenceslas* (1929), which was probably the best of all the many plays written in 1929 to commemorate the good king's martyrdom. Both works suffer from oversimplification of their principal characters.

Otakar Fischer (1883-1938) was primarily a poet and critic rather than a dramatist and he came to the drama by way of translating Shakespeare. His best original play was *The Slaves* (1925), a study of the nature and origin of power, having its scene in ancient Rome at the time of the Spartacan uprising. The work had much in common with Lom's *Žižka,* being, like the latter, the fruit of gloomy reflection on the Russian Revolution, an event treated by Fischer directly in *The World's Timepiece* (1921). Fischer's life ended tragically in midstream, as he died from shock on learning of the Austro-German Anchluss of 1938.

The influence of the Russian Revolution was not confined to the works of Fischer and Lom but was seen everywhere in the drama of Czechoslovakia. Thus *The Return* (1920), by Frantisek Zavřel (1885-), is a tragedy based on the experiences of a Czech soldier in Russia, and *The Crowds,* by the distinguished critic František Šalda (1867-1937), an attempt to answer, in Christian terms, the question Bolshevism was then

---

[1] Děvín is the legendary site of the capital of Great Moravia.

answering in economic: What can be done to save the masses? The influence of the Revolution is seen also in the popular hit *Colonel Svec* (1928) by Rudolf Medek (1890-   ), written as the tenth birthday play of the Czechoslovak Republic. Received on the night of its première with wild acclaim, this play was later challenged by the clergy for its seeming approval of suicide as a means of retoring order among the Czech legionaries in Russia, but having survived this storm, it played all over the land to enthusiastic audiences. It was with a drama of the Russian Revolution that the legionary Josef Kopta (1894-   ) won his first notice (*Revolution,* 1925), and it was from his experiences as a physician with the Czech legions that František Langer (1888-   ) first took up play writing seriously (*Dawn*).

Although Langer's war play *Cavalry Patrol* (1930) is regarded as on a par with *Journey's End,* it is not for this work that its author is known abroad, but rather for the comedy of the Prague suburbs *The Camel Through the Needle's Eye* (1923), in which the biblical truism referred to in the title is disproved, and for *The Periphery* (1925), in which a man who has escaped punishment for a crime he had committed is forced to pay with his life for one of which he is innocent. Another of Langer's plays is *Ferdy Pištora's Conversion* (1929), in which we see some of the annoying consequences of an inadvertently kind act. Both Langer's humanitarianism and also his favorite technique are seen at their purest in *The Periphery* and *Angels in Our Midst* (1931), a legend drama reflecting the author's search for new spiritual values in modern life.

Comedy was provided for the post-war Czechslovak stage by Frána Šrámek (1877-   ), best known for his charming idyl *Moon over the River* (1922), which touches on the problem of vanishing youth; *The Weeping Satyr* (1923), a satire on the bigotry of age; *The Island of Great Love* (1926), a take-off on the amours of a stranded movie company; and finally the pacifistic parody of old Austria *Hagenbek* (1920). An interesting use of symbolism is seen in Šrámek's *The Bells* (1921).

Allegory was represented in Czech drama by the works of Vladislav Vančura (1891-1942), a physician, whose play *Teacher and Pupil* (1927) presents a poetic disputation between Rashness and Wisdom and whose *Sick Girl* (1928) brings to life in the figures of three doctors three different trends in contemporary medicine. Vančura's *Alchemist* (1932) is a slow-moving study of the Bohemian dualism previously referred to.

In Vančura's brother Antonín, better known as Jiří Mahen (1882-1902), are reflected all the misery and turmoil of post-war Central Europe. His *Heaven, Hell, Paradise* (1919), a brutally realistic drama of a blinded veteran's struggle for spiritual rehabilitation, is typical. To be noted also are *Progeny* (1921) and *The Deserter* (1924). A champion of the Czech theatre in the predominantly German city of Brno (Brünn), Vančura took his life when the Germans occupied Czechoslovakia after 1938.

A typical dramatist of the post-war epoch was Edmund Konrád (1889-) with his satirical comedies of everyday life, clever but heartless. Konrád began his career with a sensational failure (*The Yellow Rose,* 1907) and won success only after a long period of incubation with *The Return of Youth* (1923), a penetrating study of the older and younger generations of pre-war Czechoslovakia. After this came one hit after another including *The Chip Axe* (1923), *Comedy in a Cube* (1925), *Sitting on Thorns* (1929), and *The Clucking Hen* (1932), the whole crowned with an attack on mechanization called, from its central figure Thomas A. Edison, *The Wizard of Menlo* (1934).

Several new talents appeared over the horizon in the twenties, outstanding among these being Jan Bartoš (1893-), who held the post of Curator of the Theatrical Collection at the National Museum. Bartoš first captured the attention of the public with *The Ravens*, a comedy with usury for its theme which was produced at the Vinohrady Theatre in July, 1920. In this appeared for the first time the character Dlask (Grosbeak) whom Bartoš was to use over and over again, especially in *The Courtship* (1923). A type frequently recurring in Czech drama, Dlask is the fellow who, though he has a formula for correcting each and every one of the ills of the world, never actually does anything to set the world right. Bartoš enjoyed a brief popularity with his *Rebellion on the Stage* (1924), a philosophical piece that won him the title of Czech Pirandello, and *Heroes of Our Day* (1926), only to have his career come to an end abruptly in 1927 with *Jůra Dábel*, a play dealing with rural outlaws, which was so bad as to drive both critics and public from the theatre before the final curtain.

Another of the new talents to reach the capital in the twenties was Vilém Werner (1892-), who won a world-wide reputation with his comedy *The Right to Sin* (1931), which was eventually made into a film. The theme of this is the harmlessness of man's natural inclination to philander as contrasted with the harmfulness of society's disapproving attitude toward this propensity. In *Heart on a Halter* (1929) Werner offered a new version of the Pygmalion theme—here a poor girl saves the soul of a worn-out aristocrat—and in the powerful social drama *Men on an Ice-Floe* (1936) drew an arresting portrait of the effects of unemployment. Though his plays were generally more French than Czech in tone—"I hung up my coat in France because I couldn't find a hook for it at home," he told Bednar—Werner achieved in *Hermelin the Tight-Rope Walker* (1932) a genuine Czech comedy, somewhat in the Langer style.

The outstanding dramatist of free Czechslovakia was Karel Čapek (1890-1938). Čapek's plays, some of which were written with his brother Josef, a painter, did more to make the name of his country known and respected abroad than any other single thing, except perhaps the political creed of his friend and master, Thomas Masaryk. Whether the praise accorded Čapek's plays was due purely to the enduring, intrinsic worth of these, or rather to some fortuitous combination of their remarkable timeliness and brilliant theatricality with inspired press-agenting, time alone can tell. At any rate they were an expression, peculiarly and strikingly apt, of the era in which they were written and as such are of tremendous historical as well as artistic significance.

A typical son of the "end of the old world" era, uniting in his make-up the romanticism of the Slav with the realism peculiar to Slavdom's Czech branch and the perspective natural to the Central European, Čapek appeared on the scene at the close of the war which gave his country its independence, with a romantic comedy *The Robber* (begun 1911, completed 1920). In this a dashing brigand—Bartoš's Dlask—who represents Youth and the New Order is seen attacking Age and its prejudices by actually storming the citadel in which it is entrenched, this being conceived symbolically as a walled garden in which a young girl is kept sealed from the world by her professor father. The play was a curious, hybrid piece in which all sorts of trends, traditional and revolutionary, were represented. It was not particularly well received but it did attract notice.

Soon Čapek was ready with the work that was to prove his masterpiece. This was of course the novel *R.U.R. (Rossum's Universal Robots,* 1921). In this audiences saw projected in brilliantly theatrical manner the end Čapek believed to be in store for society once the soulless army of workers which was steadily being created took over the running of human affairs. The play enjoyed the most extravagant success on all the stages of the world, both professional and amateur.

After *R.U.R.* Čapek's powers continued strong. Before the twenties were over he had turned out, besides minor pieces, the spectacular *Insect Comedy* (1921, produced in English as *The World We Live In* and *And so ad infinitum*), an allegorical satire on the modern state and a warning against regimentation; *The Makropoulos Affair* (1923), an inquiry into the desirability of longevity; and *Adam the Creator* (1927), a search for some principle on which to rebuild society after its destruction has been accomplished by the robots of *R.U.R.*

The march of Europe toward the abyss which began with the rise of Hitler in the early 1930's was reflected in the plays of Čapek. Thus his *White Scourge* (1937) dramatized in striking fashion the effect of fear in a nation ruled by a dictator, and *The Mother* (1938) was an effort to ward off the war its author saw approaching by depicting war's horrible consequences. Čapek's own disillusion and despair were apparent in both plays and no one familiar with either can have been surprised to learn of their author's own death on the eve of that of his country, or have believed Čapek himself would have wished any other fate than to have perished along with the republic he did so much to advertise and adorn.

SLOVAK DRAMA

CYRIL J. POTOČEK

Up to the end of the First World War the drama lagged far behind the novel and poetry in Slovakia, yet, in spite of the fact that the Slovaks were a subject people in the Austro-Hungarian Empire and without a professional theatre of their own, the drama received considerable attention, especially after 1848. Many of the plays that were written, however, were never performed, and those that did reach the stage had to do so through amateur productions in makeshift theatres.

Ján Palárik (1822-1870) gave the Slovaks their first modern plays. A newspaper editor and patriot living in Budapest, Palárik made it his mission to arouse the Slovak nation to action, and although he realized he was not a great playwright—"I shall never be a Shakespeare or a Schiller or even a Slovak Kisfaludy," he said—he turned to the drama rather than to some other literary form because he saw in it the most effective medium for accomplishing this end. Turinský and Štěpánek, Klicpera and Tyl had used the drama as an instrument for arousing the Czechs to a sense of national consciousness: Palárik hoped to do the same among the Slovaks.

Palárik's first play was a four-act comedy *Incognito,* which appeared in 1858 under the pseudonym Beskydov. Its characters were the ardent patriots and virile peasants, on the one hand, the arrogant landowners and "fifth-column" renegades, on the other, well known to his countrymen from their daily life. Though lacking in literary merit, the play was a success, as any work would have been whose theme was the return to Slovak feeling of one who had been temporarily Magyarized.

Incognito was followed in 1860 by a three-act comedy *The Tinker,* based on the adventures of an itinerant Slovak handyman, a figure known everywhere in the Balkans and Central Europe. More French than Slovak in style, however, the play was not popular at home, but the Croatians relished it, as we know from their choice of it to head the opening bill of the 1863 season of the National Theatre in Zagreb.

Next Palárik attempted to dramatize some of the political slogans of the day in *Reconciliation* (1862), a drama which was not only weak intrinsically but, what was worse, no longer timely when it appeared, thanks to the somewhat liberalizing provisions of the October Diploma (1860). Later, in the five-act tragedy *Dimitrij Samozvanec* (1863), Palárik used the familiar episode from Russian history of the False Demetrius as a cloak for presenting his own views on Pan-Slavism, a doctrine he supported as an extension of another and dearer ideal, namely Slovak nationalism.

Historical drama was represented in Slovakia by Jonáš Záborský (1812-1876), who wrote more than a score of plays on themes not only from Slovak but also from Russian and Serbo-Croatian history. Of his plays dealing with the latter the best known are *Charles of Durazzo*,[1] *Croatian Helen*, and *Karageorge*, and of his strictly Slovak dramas, *The Rebellion of the Danubian Slovaks*, *The Sons of Arpad*, and *The Last Days of Great Moravia*. Zábroský's output is important as a pioneer effort to evoke the heroic past of Slovakia dramatically.

The most popular of all Slovak playwrights to date is Ferko Urbánek (1859-1934), for many years the secretary of St. Adalbert's Literary Society in Trnava. "Every Slovak has seen at least one of Urbánek's plays," says a leading authority on the Slovak theatre, and another reports that in the period of Slovak freedom (1918-1939), "out of 5000 amateur performances yearly in Slovakia, 800 are of plays by Urbánek." Slovakia's leading exponent of romanticism in the drama, Urbánek won his phenomenal popularity by employing themes close to the average heart and by representing virtue as ultimately triumphant and evil ultimately in retreat. His best known plays are *Rosemary*, *The Vagabond*, *O These Women*, *The Sinner*, *Truth Conquers*, *The Stone Walk*, and *Punishment of Wrong*.

In strong contrast to Urbánek is Pavel Sochań (1862-   ), a realist of versatile talents whose most important works are *Tobias Klepeto*, *Honorarium*, and *The Farmer's Wife*.

Two comedies by Jozef Hollý (1879-1912), *Kubo* and *Gelo Sebechlebský*, were well received, as were also Hollý's dramas of pre-war social and political conflict, *The Prodigal Son*, *The American*, and *The Village of Černova*.

One of the most popular themes in Slovak literature is that of Janošik, the Slovak Robin Hood, who plundered the caravans of rich Hungarian merchants as they crossed the Tatras, only to distribute his booty to the oppressed Slovak peasants, and who finally met his death on a Magyar gallows. Naturally the stage offered an excellent medium for the retelling of this patriotic tale. Of the many modern plays on the Janošik theme, the best were the five-act tragedy *Janošik* (1880) by Michal Vrba; another of the same title by F. Goldmanova; and *The Love of Janošik* (1929), a drama in five scenes by Adam Žiar.[2]

The establishment of the Czechoslovak Republic at the end of the First World War freed the Slovaks from Magyar rule and enabled them to have a professional theatre of their own, at first in Bratislava, later also in Košice in eastern Slovakia. Along with the rise of a professional theatre went, of course, continued expansion of the amateur stage.

The outstanding dramatist of the early post-war years was Jozef Gregor-Tajovský (1874-1940), a novelist of renown who, like Jirásek among the Czechs and his own fellow-Slovak Palárik, turned to the drama because it

---

[1] A theme used also by Markovič in Croatian.
[2] The Janošik theme was also treated by the Czech Jiří Mahen (pseudonym of Antonín Vančura).

offered the best medium for promoting national ideals. Tajovský's plays are characterized by vivid dialogue and realistic portraiture. His best-known works are *Sin* and *Darkness*, both of which are studies in secret guilt, and *The Law of Woman, Money Madness*, and *New Life*, three dramas of Slovak daily life. His historical drama *The Death of George Langsfeld* (1923), in which he attempted to admonish his countrymen for their excess of sentiment and lack of cool reason at the time of the Slovak uprising against the Magyars in 1848, was awarded second prize by the Slovak National Theatre in 1923, a year in which no play was found worthy of a first prize. It was revived under the title *Dawn over Slovakia* at the National Theatre in Prague in 1932.

Tajovský's closest competitor in the field of realistic comedy is Vladimir Hurban Vladimirov (1884-), whose most popular plays are *Homo Sapiens, SOS*, and the historical dramas *Restoration, Ludevít Štúr*, and *Matthew of Trenčin*.

The outstanding younger dramatist of post-war Slavakia is Ivan Stodola (1888-), best known for his satirical comedies exposing the pseudo-elegance and sham humanitarianism of the new official class. Worthy of note are *Tea at the Senator's, Joseph Pučik and His Career, The Shepherd's Wife, Gypsy Child, Our Mr. Minister*, and in another category the historical drama *King Svatopluk* (1931), in which the ruler of Czechoslovakia's earliest prototype, the Great Moravian Empire of the ninth century, is made the advocate of Czechslovak solidarity. *King Svatopluk* was presented in 1932 at a gala performance in the Prague National Theatre. A good technician, Stodola is at present Slovakia's best hope in the field of drama.

Other younger dramatists to be noted are K. F. Urbanovič and Ivan Barč. Urbanovič's two four-act plays *The Golden Morass* and *Shortcomings* (both 1926) were well received, and Barč's pioneer work, *3000 People* (1934), injected into Slovak drama a new, and to the predominantly rural population of Slovakia, unfamiliar note, by its portrayal of the poverty and ugliness that accompany industrialization.

Great progress was made by the drama in the two decades of full freedom but there may now be grave danger that what a Slovak writer in exile has said of all literary activity in the homeland is particularly true of the drama: "A vast impetus has been brought to a standstill," and a tree that was ready to burst into full bloom "has been lopped at its very roots."

HUNGARIAN DRAMA

EDMUND VASVARY AND MARION MOORE COLEMAN

Up to the second decade of the nineteenth century native drama in the Hungarian tongue was virtually non-existent. This was a result of the fact that from the time of the Counter Reformation (late sixteenth century) the literary language of the Magyars was not Hungarian but Latin, with the vernacular, which had previously been the language not only of the Scriptures but also of some excellent lyric poetry, a purely spoken tongue used only by the peasantry.

At the end of the eighteenth century Hungarian seemed headed for the oblivion that ultimately overtakes every non-literary language, when suddenly its downward course was halted and even reversed. Responsible for the reversal were Ferenc Kazinczy (1759-1831), the "restorer of the language," and other men of faith, among these the Transylvanian magnate Gedeon Ráday who, with Kazinczy, was instrumental in bringing into existence the first Magyar dramatic society in the Transylvanian capital of Kolozsvár (Rumanian Cluj).

The repertory of this society consisted at first exclusively of translations, most of them from the German, though it is interesting to note that both *Hamlet* and *Othello* were presented during the society's opening season in 1794. Efforts were made, however, to encourage the writing of original plays in the native language on national themes, especially on such themes as the conquest of Central Europe by the Magyars under Árpád in the ninth and tenth centuries.

The first drama of note in the Hungarian tongue was a "sport" that came out of no literary movement and had neither ancestors nor progeny. This was the tragedy *Bánk Bán* by Joseph Katona (1791-1830), a lawyer of Kecskemét, a provincial market-center far away from literary rendezvous, in the heart of the Danube-Tisza drift-plain which is the beginning of the "true Hungary." Katona wrote his drama at the age of twenty-three but it was not published until 1821. Even then it lay for more than a decade and a half unnoticed, winning the recognition it deserved only with the establishment of the National Theatre in 1837.

The theme of *Bánk Bán* is the old one of love versus duty, exemplified here in the career of a famous courtier of the thirteenth-century Hungarian King Andrew II. Of the many dramas that have been written about the great *bán* (palatine) who, after years of strict devotion to the House of Árpád, turns against it and to avenge his own wife's honor murders his sovereign's German Queen,[1] Katona's is the closest to Shakespearian in stature. After more than a century of time it is still regarded as the greatest of all tragedies in the Hungarian tongue.

Hungary in the early nineteenth century was a country centrifugal in the extreme. With its official capital far removed from the geographic center of the realm—at Pozsony (Pressburg, Bratislava) in what was then known as Upper Hungary—and most of its affairs managed high-handedly from

---

[1] Among these: *Andreas der ungarische König mit Bankbano* by Hans Sachs, 1562; *Elmerick, or Justice Triumphant* by George Lillo, 1740; *Ein treuer Diener seines Herrns* by Grillparzer, 1825; and *Benko Bot* (1872) by Marković (see the section on Croatian drama).

Vienna, it lacked almost every element of political cohesiveness. A land of enormous estates, of towering mountain ranges and limitless plains, it had as yet no focus. Especially was it lacking in the *sine qua non* of a successful literary awakening, an intellectual capital and marketplace of ideas. A very "poet's land" in its natural endowment, it was, nevertheless, a lonely land, rich in "soulless beauty," as the poet Kölcsey put it, but poor in opportunities for intellectual companionship and exchange.

Obviously the drama, which depends on human beings for its inspiration, could not flourish until this condition was changed. It began to be changed about 1820. At this time a new literary journal, called appropriately *Aurora*, was founded in Budapest and soon the city which from time immemorial the Magyar had dreamed of—the lonely herdsman of the steppe beholding its arresting silhouette in the weird *fata morgana* of the plains, the Transylvanian townsman longing for it in his mountain isolation—came to be the intellectual focus of all the Magyar realm. Aspiring writers from whatever province, from Burgenland to Transylvania and from Transdanubia to the Tatras, found themselves drawn as by a magnet to Budapest.

The leader of the awakening which crystallized around Budapest was Charles Kisfaludy (1788-1830), the brother of Alexander Kisfaludy, the poet. Kisfaludy was Hungary's pioneer dramatist. A scion of the dominant class in Hungary, the landed gentry, and a veteran of vagabond years in western Europe, Kisfaludy had all the romanticist's enthusiasm without his extravagant sentimentalism. His first dramatic works were historical tragedies, *The Tatar Horde in Hungary* (1811), *Clara Zách* (1812),[1] *Voivode Stibor* (1819), *Maria Szechy* (1820),[2] but it was only when he turned to comedy that he found his proper element. In *The Suitors* (1820), *Maidens' Guard* (1827), and *Disappointments* (1829), his principal works in this genre, Kisfaludy tapped the rich reservoir of Hungarian country life, using the numerically preponderant but inarticulate and hitherto neglected peasantry for the first time as dramatic material.

In 1825 an event of great moment for Hungary occurred when the national parliament met for the first time in thirteen years. The event had the effect not only of raising patriotic fervor to fever pitch but also of greatly stepping up the production of poetry, especially of epics and ballads. It had no correspondingly salutary effect on the drama, however, and for a decade and a half this branch of literature languished. Except for the dramatic poems of the popular idol Michael Vörösmarty (1800-1855)—the epic *Zalán's Rout* (1825), which extols the Magyar conquest of Pannonia under Arpád; the legend-drama *Csongor and Tünde* (1831); and the *Festspiel Árpád's*

---

[1] Clara Zách was the daughter of a Hungarian magnate. She suffered a tragic fate at the hands of the first Angevin sovereign of Hungary, Charles Robert I, about 1312.
[2] Maria Szechy, "The Venus of Murány," was the heroine of Murány Castle's defense against the Hapsburgs (1644).

Awakening, written for the opening performance of the National Theatre, August 22, 1837—the period was dramatically sterile.

With the forties, however, the drama revived and it was in this period that Hungary produced her first professional playwright. He was Edward Szigligeti (1814-1878), a native of Nagyvárad (Grosswardein, Oradea Mare) in Transylvania and a born man of the theatre. Like Kisfaludy, Szigligeti took his themes from the life of the people and he is commonly regarded as the founder of Hungarian popular drama. Of his more than a hundred pieces, crude and vaudevillian and redolent of the life of the *puszta* (steppe), the best known are *Liliomfi* (1849) the story of a shiftless, good-for-nothing youth; *The Deserter* (1843); *The Csikós* (1846) a mounted herdsman of the steppe; and *The Foundling* (1863).

Another popular playwright of the forties was Joseph Szigeti (1822-1902), a native of Transdanubia and for twenty years and more (1841-1865) a well-known character actor at the National Theatre. Szigeti's principal plays were the comedies *The Old Infantryman and His Hussar Son* (1856), *The Engagement Ring* (1856), and *The Fair Shepherdess* (1857), and the historical drama *Maria Szechy* (1863).

The forties witnessed the production of Count László Teleki's historical drama *The Favorite* (1841) and a short-lived spurt of popularity for the comedies of Sigmund Czakó (1820-1847), an actor, at first in provincial troupes, later at the National Theatre. Czakó's most popular plays were *The Merchant and the Sailor* (1845), *The Will* (1845), *Leona* (1846), and *The Frivolous One* (1847). Both Teleki (1811-1861) and Czakó died by their own hand, a fitting commentary on the mood of the period between 1845 and 1861 in which their works were played. Another commentary on the age is the gloomy *Tragedy of Man* (1861) by Imre Madách (1823-1864).

The Hungarian spirit, plunged in despair by the failure of the revolution of 1848-1849 and humiliated by the cultural and political restrictions dictated from Vienna after 1848, began to recover its balance with the consummation of the Ausgleich, or Compromise, of 1867. The first decade following the Ausgleich was a significant one for Hungarian drama, witnessing as it did the rise of two playwrights in the Szigligeti tradition and the establishment of a home for their plays in the fine People's Theatre opened in 1875.

The two playwrights were Ferenc Csepreghy (1842-1880) and Edward Tóth (1844-1876). The former became interested in the drama through his association in an artisan's capacity with a private theatrical society in Budapest. At least two of his numerous comedies, *The Yellow Colt* (1877) and *The Red Wallet* (1878) are still popular. Tóth, like Szigligeti, was for most of his life an actor in the various theatres of the provinces. His comedies are among the pearls of Hungarian popular drama, especially *The Organ-Grinder's Family* (1875), *The Village Loafer* (1875), and *The Vagabond* (1878).

In the eighties, as a result of the great changes which had taken place in

Hungarian life since 1848, a new spirit of realism, bordering on social criticism, was manifest in Hungarian literature. The principal exponent of the new trend in the drama was Gergely Csiky (1842-1891), often called the Hungarian Sardou. Csiky was born at Pankota in the county of Arad in the great south-Tisza steppe, and he began writing plays while serving on the staff of a Catholic seminary in Temesvár. After twice winning the annual Teleki Prize for Drama—in 1875 with *The Prophecy,* on a theme from antiquity, in 1878 with *The Irresistible*—Csiky left his studies and went to Budapest, to devote himself to writing and translation.

In Budapest Csiky underwent a complete change of mood, and this was speedily reflected in his dramas: as hitherto he had viewed life romantically, now he saw it realistically and was shocked by its crudity and shallowness. His first play in the new mood was *The Proletarians* (1880). In this and the many that followed—*Glittering Want* (1881), *A Match for Cecile* (1883), *The Stomfay Family* (1883), *Soap Bubbles* (1884), *The Grandmother* (1891), and so forth—Csiky found his characters and themes in the life of the Hungarian gentry which he saw all about him in Budapest seeking security in government jobs or in rich husbands for their daughters from the new industrial class.

Csiky had a great vogue in the eighties, but his popularity was rivaled by that of the epic dramas of Vörösmarty, which were now revived, and by that of such patriotic pieces as the tragedy *George Branković* (1856) by Charles Obernyik (1815-1855) and the dramatized novels of Maurus Jókai (1825-1904). Csiky had a rival also in the imaginative dramas of the new neo-romanticists, whose leading representative was the publicist Eugene Rákosi (1842-1929).

A native of Acsád in western Hungary, Rákosi was educated at Sopron, the commercial and cultural capital of northern Burgenland, and in Budapest, where he studied law. He was early attracted to the theatre and began his long association with it by translating Shakespeare and Æschylus. Appointed director of the People's Theatre in the year of its founding (1875), Rákosi left this about 1880 to become editor of the organ of the extreme nationalists, the *Budapesti Hirlap.*

Rákosi made his début as a playwright with the amusing fable-drama *Æsop* (1866). The favorable reception of this encouraged the young writer to produce more plays of the same imaginative variety. Most successful of all his many works were the historical dramas *Andrew and Joanna* (1885), based on the ill-starred romance of the Hungarian king and unscrupulous Joanna of Naples, and *Queen Tagma* (1902); and the light comedies *School of Love* (1873) and *The Quarrels of Queens* (1890). Rákosi's only attempt to depict life realistically, the peasant drama *Magdolna* (1889), was not a success.

In the same romantic vein as the plays of Rákosi were those of Louis Dóczi (1845-1919), author of one of the most famous of all Hungarian comedies, *The Kiss* (1871). A native of the Burgenland, Dóczi grew up in a German atmosphere and might never have used Hungarian as a literary instrument at all but for the influence of his school life at Sopron. As it was he used both German and Hungarian and became celebrated for his excellent translations both from and into both languages. Dóczi's best-known plays besides *The Kiss* were *The Last Love* (1879) and the historical drama *Maria Szechy* (1885).

An outstanding figure of the Rákosi era was the witty and polished Árpád Berczik (1842-1919), the Hungarian Labiche, whose comedies of Hungarian "high life" are masterpieces of smooth and elegant satire. A native of Temesvár in Transylvania, Berczik spent most of his life as a government official, writing plays only as an avocation. Of his almost numberless and perennially popular comedies, the following are typical: *The Hungarian Revolutionary in Paris* (1902), *The Quarter-Magnate* (1872), *Ministerial Crisis* (1905), and *The Artist's Wife* (1910).

The neo-romantic movement produced also the dramas of Louis Bartók (1851-1902), a poet and humorist whose historical plays—*Margit Kendi* (1884) and *Anna Thúran* (1888) in particular—had a great vogue at the National Theatre. To be noted in the same period also are Antal Váradi (1854-1923) and Alexander Somló (1859-   ), both of whom were at one time directors of the State Academy of Acting. Váradi is known especially for his symbolical tragedies on historical themes—*Iscariot* (1876), *Ferenc Rákóczy* (1893), *Atala* (1881), *King Stephen* (1885), and so forth—a number of which, including the two last mentioned, have been used as librettos for operas. Somló, like so many Hungarian dramatists an actor by profession, wrote not only tragedies, such as *Stephen IV* (1898), but also comedies —*First Love* (1884), *Ovid* (1885), *The Youth of Prince Zsolt* (1896), and so forth. Váradi, it might be added, spent much of his time in adapting the plays of others for the operatic stage. A famous adaptation was his reworking of Tóth's popular *Village Loafer* (1896).

The mention of Tóth's play reminds us that neo-romanticism had a powerful rival at the turn of the century in the so-called "folk drama." Audiences demanded more solid fare than the "Mendelssohn melodies" of Rákosi and Dóczi and their school.

Of the scores of ambitious young writers who sought to capitalize on the popularity of the folk play, three must be mentioned. Of these, two—Árpád Gabányi (1855-1915) and Stephen Geczy (1860-   )—were actors. A native of Eperjes in Upper Hungary (Slovakia), Gabányi was famous for his sparkling monologues. Of his comedies, *The House of Kókai* (1887), *The Fathers-in-Law* (1890), *The Pagan Magyars* (1891), *The Provincial Magnificos* (1895), and *The Mothers-in-Law* (1899) are to be noted. Géczy wrote a number of serious dramas—*Mother Earth* (1900), *The Apostle* (1904), and so forth—but he is remembered chiefly for his comedies *The Wild Rose of Gyimes* (1897) and *The Devil's Bride*.

The third and most important of the folk trio was Géza Gárdonyi (1863-1922), a school-teacher by profession who found his themes in the life of the farmers and herdsmen of the Upper Tisza near Eger (Erlau), where he spent much of his life. A deeply religious and intensely patriotic man, with an aversion to the city and a passionate love of the Hungarian land, Gárdonyi produced a number of pleasant and amusing, if somewhat idealized, comedies of country life, the most popular of which were *The Wine* and the fanciful *Christmas Dream* (both 1901).

The drama of the people, of which we have been speaking, found its greatest exponent in Sigmund Móricz (1879-1942), a novelist of peasant stock from the Trans-Tisza steppe associated, after 1906, with the revolutionary *Nyugat* (*The West*), a journal founded by Baron Louis Hatvany for the encouragement of Hungarian letters and the enrichment of Hungarian life through closer coöperation with the west.

Móricz made his début as a playwright in 1909 by winning the Academy of Science prize for that year with his comedy of country life, *Judge Sári*. This play, it should be noted, marks the culmination of the process begun by Charles Kisfaludy, the first to use the rich reservoir of Hungarian country life in the drama. Ever since Kisfaludy, the farmers and herdsmen who are the "true Hungarians" had been struggling to achieve full and proper representation on the stage. One after another had tried to portray them—Szigligeti, Szigeti, Csepreghy, Tóth, even Rákosi, and finally Gárdonyi and his contemporaries. All had succumbed in turn to the temptation either to caricature or idealize their subjects. Only Móricz painted them as they were, simply and naturally and with truth.

Judge Sári was followed in 1911 by a trilogy of short plays—*The Village* —and by a duo-drama *Love* (1913-1914). After the war Móricz continued not only to produce plays himself, and novels which were reworked as plays, but, what is more important, to inspire others to seek their themes among the Hungarian people. To his "school" belong Louis Bibó (1890-   ) with *The Inheritance* (1925), and Louis Zilahy (1891-   ), of whom more will be said later.

With Ferenc Herczeg (1863-   ), the next in order of Hungarian dramatists, begins a new chapter in Hungarian letters.

From 1820 and the beginning of the "trek toward Budapest," noted above, up to Herczeg's time, the various provinces of the culturally diverse and geographically isolated Hungarian realm had steadily poured their brightest treasures into the capital, enriching it greatly. Now, with the new century, the capital was to pour the treasures it received from the provinces into the wider community of the world, to the world's great enrichment. In no field was the phenomenon more strikingly evident than in that of the drama, where one playwright after another was to repeat the routine of first achieving renown at home and then duplicating, if not surpassing, that achievement abroad.

It is not surprising that Herczeg, like his forerunner Dóczi, should have made a name for himself on the German stage since he was by birth a German, being the son of the German Mayor of Versecz, a town in the southern Trans-Tisza steppe. Despite his German parentage and education, however, Herczeg was the outstanding interpreter in his generation of the Hungarian mind and soul. Two things operated to make him Hungarian: the soil on which he was reared, with its long tradition of being the one and only "true Hungary," and the Hungarian gentry with whom he was thrown during his service in the army and to whom he was drawn as by a magnet.

Herczeg began his literary career by writing feuilletons for a German newspaper, but in 1887 he abandoned German for Hungarian and about 1890 became a steady contributor to Rákosi's intensely national *Budapesti Hirlap*. About this time he began to write novels and eventually dramas.

Though his true genius lay in the comedy of manners,—we see it at its best in such plays as *The Daughter of the Nabob of Dolova* (1902), *The Gyurkovics Family* (1903), and so forth—Herczeg achieved no uncertain success also in the historical drama, especially in the three national tragedies *Brigadier Ocskai* (1901), which deals with the commander in Rakoczy's army who betrays his country's cause for love, *Orphan Ladislas,* a drama of the heroic fifteenth-century Hunyady epoch; and *The Bridge,* a study in contrasting personalities—Kossuth and Count Stephen Szechenyi—at the time of the 1848 uprising.

Herczeg found most of his material in the doings of the Hungarian gentry past and present, yet his most profound drama of all, *Byzantium* (1904), had a foreign theme and setting, being an allegorical tragedy, with present-day implications, of the fall of Constantinople.

Herczeg was fond of experimenting in dramatic technique, as we see in his one-act imitations of Pirandello and especially in the fable drama *The Witch Eve* (1912), which reminds us of Maeterlinck. Though he generally shied clear of controversial issues, one problem interested him so deeply as to invade and become the axis of more than one work (*The Pagans,* 1901; *The Gate of Life,* 1909). The problem was that of the conflicting forces of East versus West which he saw grappling with each other so disruptively in the Hungarian state as a whole and in each of its individual members, especially in himself. Herczeg is best known abroad for his sparkling society comedy *The Blue Fox* (1927).

The first decade of the twentieth century found most of the aspiring young intellectuals of Budapest involved in the journal *Nyugat,* mentioned above. Among those connected with it besides Móricz, already noted, were a number of other playwrights, including the spearhead of the realistic movement in modern Hungarian letters, Alexander Bródy (1863-1924). Popular alike on the German and Hungarian stages were Bródy's naturalistic dramas, *Royal Idyl* (1903), *Little Snow White* (1901), *The Nurse*

(1902), *The Teacher* (1909), *The Doctor* (1911), *Rembrandt* (1913), and others.

Also connected with *Nyugat* was the journalist, and friend of Alphonse Daudet, Desider Szomory (1873-1945), whose social comedies *Friday Evening* (1896), *The Parting* (1897), *The Doting Daughter of Bolzay, Dear Little Georgine,* and so forth, were well received. There was also Ernö Szep, and there was Eugene Heltai (1871-   ), popular on both the German and Hungarian stages for his amusing pieces *The Girls from Tünderlaki, The Little Pastry Shop, The Midinette,* and *The Silent Knight.*

The first decade of the twentieth century saw Budapest rival Vienna as the great drama manufactory of Europe. Plays became the principal article of export from Hungary, the outward flow of this commodity reaching flood proportions as the trio of Molnár, Lengyel, and Biró came on the scene.

The first of the trio, Ferenc Molnár, was born in Budapest in 1878 and educated there at the Royal College of Science and, as he says, in the cafés of Pest. Knowing from early youth exactly what he wanted to do, he began while still a student to write—short stories, novels, fantasies, skits, poems, plays—publishing some of these in the various journals of the capital, some in little magazines of his own that were born but to expire.

Molnár's first dramatic success was *The Devil* (1907), a work which won him not only an international reputation but, what was probably more difficult to achieve, a membership in the exclusive Petöfi Society. About this time he married but the venture, though entered into romantically, was not a success and its failure plunged Molnár into gloomy speculation on the nature of marriage and of love in general. The fruit of this speculation was the play that has become synonymous with its author's very name: *Liliom* (1909). A legend drama in which, through the figures of a Budapest good-for-nothing and his long-suffering wife, the biblical definition of love is illustrated, *Liliom* marked its author as a master of dramatic inventiveness and theatrical originality.

Liliom was quickly followed by *The Guardsman* (1911), a witty piece of sophisticated drollery on the theme of marital infidelity, and *The Wolf* (1912), a companion piece on the same theme. Next came *The Swan* (1914), in which royalty and the absurdities of court life were satirized. Later, while serving as a war correspondent during the First World War, Molnár found time to deride the business he himself was engaged in by way of the miracle play *The White Cloud* (1916), part of the action of which, as in *Liliom,* takes place in heaven.

In 1923 came *The Red Mill* (produced in New York as *Mima,* 1928) a kaleidoscopic piece of symbolism in which Life, conceived as a mill, grinds humanity into a tragic caricature of what it sets out to become. This was followed in 1924 by the fantasy *The Glass Slipper,* in which the Cinderella-heroine is a Budapest servant girl who has been nourished on too many romantic plays.

Next, in *The Play in the Castle* (1924), produced and published in the United States as *The Play's the Thing,* Molnár again proved his mastery of the art of capricious and sophisticated comedy, as in the later *Olympia* (1927) he was once more to demonstrate his skill as a satirist of royalty and high life in general. *The Good Fairy* (1931), in which a romantic usherette from a Budapest theatre gets involved in a series of adventures as a result of her desire to "do good" to everybody, while not adding to Molnár's stature, confirmed his reputation as a creator of amusing and theatrically effective situations.

Melchior Lengyel (1880-   ), whose career paralleled that of Molnár, began life as a journalist, scoring his first success in the theatre with *Grateful Posterity* (1907), his second play, which was awarded the coveted Academy Prize. *Village Idyl* and *The Maiden,* the latter written with the collaboration of Baron Louis Hatvany (1880-   ), followed in 1909, and in 1910 came *Typhoon,* a study in contrasting traditions and ideologies, French and Japanese, which made a great name for its author. *The Prophet* (1911), *The Czarina* (written with Biró, 1913), and numberless other witty and entertaining and thoroughly cosmopolitan plays followed, establishing Lengyel's reputation as a craftsman who could be relied upon. Drafted eventually by the film industry, Lengyel produced a number of screen successes, among these the delightful *Ninotchka.*

Lajos Biró (1880-   ) was the recognized leader of the young intellectuals of Budapest in the years following the founding of *Nyugat.* A journalist by profession, he got his start as a playwright during the First World War, when his duties took him to Berlin. There his trilogy *The Family Circle* (1909), a subtle and ironic exposé of family hypocrisy, had a favorable showing at the Freie Bühne and other liberal German theatres. His *Yellow Lily* (1910), a satire on the Hungarian aristocracy, brought Biró into the spotlight and was eventually suppressed. In 1928, like Lengyel, Biró began working for the film industry, at first as scenario editor for an American company in Berlin. He himself wrote a number of plays directly for the screen, among them the unforgettable *Last Command,* more recently the exciting *Five Graves to Cairo.*

During the Second World War Biró was in England, where, writing in English, he produced as his first two plays an amusing new version of the *Widowers' Houses* theme, *Patricia's Seven Houses*—about an English spinster who falls heir to seven brothels—and a drama of life in Nazi-occupied Poland, *School for Slavery* (both 1942).

Somewhat different from the Molnár-Lengyel-Biró triumvirate in his origins yet hardly less successful than they on the world stage is Ernö Vajda (1887-   ). Born at Papa, the capital of Hungarian Calvinism, and educated at the university there, the Hungarian Heidelberg, Vajda became thoroughly familiar, in his student days, with the steppeland which, as we have said before, is the "true Hungary." He was drawn to the theatre through becoming secretary of the Thalia Company, a Budapest imitation of Antoine's Parisian Théâtre Libre.

Among Vajda's early ventures in the drama was an ambitious historical work, *Ludas Matyi,* which a misguided director took for musical-comedy material, to the despair of its author but not to his discouragement, for he continued to write plays. His first successes were an extravaganza, *Mr. Bobby,* and *The Crown Prince,* based on the tragedy of Rudolf and Marie Vetsera. Vajda is best known abroad for his touching drama of first love and its disillusion, *Fata Morgana* (1915), in which the action takes place in a country house on the Hungarian steppe. He is known also for his successful film *The Great Garrick,* a reworking of an earlier drama *The Confession.*

To the latest generation of Hungarian playwrights to achieve success in the world market belong László Bús-Fekete and László Fodor (both born in 1896). The former is known here especially for his successes, *The Lady Has a Heart, Appointment for Love,* and *Twelve in a Box,* the last produced in 1938 as *Ladies and Gentlemen.* Fodor has more hits to his credit than can well be remembered, among these *A Church Mouse* (1928), *Good Morning, Bill* (1928, adapted by P. G. Wodehouse), *I Love an Actress* (1931), *Jewel Robbery* (1931), and other spirited and suave pieces. *Dr. Julia Szabo,* a drama of the "new woman" and her problems, had considerable success on the continental stage but has not been produced in America.

Not to be forgotten is Gábor Drégely (1883-), whose satirical comedy *The Tailor-Made Man* was a hit on the German stage (1908) and whose second play *The Divine Spark* (1913) was given with tremendous success at the National Theatre in Budapest.

The gifted short-story writer Sandor Hunyady (1893-1942) achieved success in the drama with his *Black Cherries,* which deals with life in the part of south Hungary lost by the treaty of Trianon. Others who were animated by irredentist sentiments in the post-war period were the two Transylvanians Joseph Nyirö (1889-) and Aron Tamási (1897-), poets of the Szekler land and spokesmen for the Szekler soul. Nyirö achieved his greatest success with *Bence Uz,* the story of a wily young Szekler mountaineer. His other plays, *The Woodcarver, Fair Julia,* and *The New Country,* also show marked talent. Primarily a novelist, Tamási has to his credit three successful symbolical fables in dramatic form: *The Singing Bird, Brave Soul,* and *Jeremy the Magnificent.*

In the folk tradition of Szigligeti and Móricz are the plays of Joseph Babay (1898-), *Village Comedy, Reel,* and *The Shepherd's Flute.*

The distinguished critic László Németh (1903-) tried his hand at the historical drama and met with success in *Pope Gregory VII,* as did also John Kodolányi (1899-) with *Earthquake.*

Bela Szenes (1895-1927) provided the lightest and most diverting kind of theatrical entertainment with his many comedies, including *The Stupid Man,*

The Sleeping Husband, The Rich Girl, The Rascal, The Italian Woman, and *I Won't Marry.*

The gifted novelist Zsolt Harsányi (1881-1945) employed his talents at one time in the adaptation of old novels to the stage. His best known adaption is *The Noszty Boy's Affair with Mary Tóth* of Kalman Mikszáth.

The outstanding figure of the Hungarian stage today is Lajos Zilahy. Born in 1891 at Nagyszalonta in westernmost Transylvania of an old and respected gentry family, Zilahy seemed destined to lead the quiet and uneventful life of a country squire, when the outbreak of the First World War catapulted him into a series of thrilling and perilous experiences.

Zilahy's first drama was a mirror of the tortured society of post-war Europe: *The Soul in Torment* (1922). It was followed by what is often regarded as his best dramatic work, *Bright Sunshine* (1924), a charming village idyl done with delicacy and taste. Next came *Musical Clowns* (1925), a satirical *commedia dell' arte* type of piece on the relationship of a poet to his public. *The White Stag* (1927) was next. A study of the struggle between the old and new generations in Hungary and of the efforts at resurrection of a nation condemned, through defeat on the field of battle, to slow extinction, the play is one of Zilahy's most ambitious. The symbolic title has reference to the miraculous white stag which is reputed to have guided the first Hungarians into their European homelands in the days of Árpád.

Problems arising out of the war, and its corollary the peace treaty, form the subject of most of Zilahy's plays—*The General* (1928), *Siberia* (1928), *Leona* (1930). In his highly successful *The Firebird* (1932) we have a polished comedy of manners dealing with the problem of equality between the sexes and the right of a young woman to lead her own life. In *The Twelfth Hour* (1933) Zilahy diagnoses the present epoch of human history, depicting its conflicts through the figures of a prophet, who preaches peace, and a bellicose statesman who whips up the nation for war. Though he does not provide a solution of the world chaos, he poses all of its problems, treating such issues as eugenics and technocracy and others on which he has much to say, also, in the Budapest daily press.

The turbulent political life of Hungary in the thirties, with the growing prejudice against non-Aryan dramatists, forced many of the leading figures, including Molnár, to remain permanently abroad. Others who remained were silenced and their plays laid on the shelf, with the result that the playwrights who happened to be of Aryan stock found themselves reaping inflated rewards.

In protest against this state of affairs, Zilahy offered his entire fortune of some three hundred thousand dollars in 1943 to a new literary foundation for the aid of Hungarian writers irrespective of race and religion. Zilahy's action is hailed as an important sign that Hungarian literary life is at last recovering its balance and former good will.

RUMANIAN DRAMA

MARION MOORE COLEMAN

Rumania is a country predominantly rural in its composition and economy, and its population, until the present neglected as dramatic material, has remained to date almost completely untouched by the drama as we know it. The only forms of dramatic presentation known to the average Rumanian, whether of Bessarabia or Transylvania or of the principalities of Moldavia and Wallachia which form the core of the Rumanian state, are the puppet play, in imitation of the Turkish *Karagöz,* and the religious pageant, a conspicuous example of which is the traditional Christmas spectacle *The Star of Bethlehem.* This play, of ancient origin, is known in one variant or another throughout the Rumanian realm.

Despite the slightness of the drama's influence on the great mass of the Rumanian folk, its influence on the cultural awakening of the Rumanian nation was, nevertheless, great.

The Rumanian awakening had its beginning in the late eighteenth century, in the very depths of the so-called Phanariote period when Greek influences pervaded and dominated Rumania's cultural life. It began in Rome, with a pair of Rumanian students from Blaj in Transylvania, the ancient Dacia, viewing the great triumphal Column of Trajan and being shocked by its sculptured rows of Dacian captives into awareness of their Latin heritage. The movement of which this experience was the fruit at first reached only the scholars and manifested itself only in the compilation of Daco-Rumanian grammars and grandiloquent histories of the Daco-Rumanian nation. In the 1820's, however, as a result of the Greek War of Independence, it spread beyond the scholar's study to the people; if not to its great folk mass, at least to its élite.

One of the first signs of the wider awakening was the establishment in 1827 of a society for the promotion of the national ideal. Soon this gave birth to another organization known as a Philharmonic Society. This had two branches, one in Bucharest, founded in 1833 by Ion Eliade (1802-1872), the other in Jassy, founded in 1836 by George Asachi (1788-1869). Out of these were to grow eventually the National Theatre of Rumania.

The first play, so far as we know, to be given in Rumanian was Gessner's popular pastoral *Myrtle and Chloe,* translated by the above-mentioned Asachi, the son of a Uniate priest from Polish Lwów, and presented at a private theatre in Jassy along with Voltaire's *Alzire* in French at a Christmas party in 1816.

The first generation to write plays for the Jassy and Bucharest theatres imitated French models almost exclusively. This was to have been expected, since the strongest cultural influence from outside, thanks to the French secretaries and tutors employed by the Phanariotes, was the French. The leading figure of this pioneer generation was Vasile Alecsandri (1819-1890), the son of a rich boyar, educated in Paris. Alecsandri was the first to see in the lore and legendary of his homeland material worthy of the drama. A poet and an amateur folklorist, he collected the native legends and songs and in one instance employed a native, if not a folk, theme in a successful drama. This was *The Despot Prince* (1880), a work still popular on the Rumanian stage. Most of Alecsandri's many plays were light comedies and vaudeville pieces in the French style.

To the same generation as Alecsandri belonged also the distinguished historian and linguist Bogdan P. Hasdeu (1836-1907), with his still-popular verse drama *Rasvan and Vidra* (1867), a romantic piece which deals with a colorful gypsy who is instigated by a designing woman, and *Domnita Rosanda* (1868), a tragedy based on the story of one of Rumania's most glamorous figures, the daughter of fabulous Basil Lupescu, hospodar of Moldavia in the times of the Cossack wars in the seventeenth century.

Rumanian drama reached a peak of excellence in the eighties which it was not destined to reach again for a long time. The one responsible for this was Ion Luca Caragiale (1853-1912), Rumania's first important playwright. The son and grandson of players, Caragiale made his début in the theatre as a prompter. Later he abandoned this, to earn his living for a time as the manager of a railroad buffet. Eventually, thanks to an unexpected legacy, he was able to travel and study abroad, especially in Germany. At the end of his life he achieved the post he had coveted from the beginning, the directorship of the National Theatre.

Caragiale was a master of the realistic, bourgeois comedy. In *The False Accusation* (1889) he tried to set forth the problems of the peasantry, but his true genius was displayed in the earlier comedies dealing with the new Rumanian middle class, in which he portrayed with keen wit the difficulties experienced by this class, with its oriental traditions and practices, in adjusting itself to the new occidental pattern of the capital. In *Leonida Faces the Reaction* (1879) and *The Lost Letter* (1884) we see various aspects of public and private corruption shown up humorously yet realistically, while in the admirable *A Stormy Night* (1879) we have a whole panorama, devastating but true, of the Rumanian bourgeoisie.

After Caragiale Rumanian drama suffered a lapse and for years adaptations and translations from the French were the principal dramatic fare of the capital. Then in 1900 came the powerful and controversial *Manasse* by Ronetti Roman (died 1908), a friend and admirer of Caragiale. A drama of the Moldavian village, with its conflicting mores, orthodox Jewish and orthodox Christian, at a time when old patterns are giving way and culture is fluid, *Manasse* is a unique achievement in the history of Rumanian drama.

With the appointment of Alexandru Davila as director of the National Theatre following the succes of his historical tragedy *Prince Vlaicu* (1902), the story of a fourteenth century Wallachian prince of the native Bassarao dynasty, the drama began to pick up. Its recovery was greatly accelerated and abetted by the famous Jorgan revolt of 1905, when the distinguished Professor Nicholas Jorga (1871-   ) headed a movement against foreign influences.

Historical tragedy was represented in the new period by *Domnita Roxandra* (1907)—on the same theme as an earlier work by Hasdeu already mentioned—from the pen of A. de Hertz (1887-   ), and by the trilogy of Barbu Delavrancea (1858-1918), *Sunset* (1909), *The Snowstorm* (1910), and *The Morning Star* (1910). Designed by its author as an antidote to the national lack of confidence which was so prevalent at the turn of the century in Rumania, the trilogy portrayed in a flattering yet on the whole realistic manner the figure of Moldavia's fifteenth-century warrior king Stephen the Great and was for a time a sensational success at the National Theatre in Bucharest.

Historical drama was not, however, the principal genre cultivated by the new generation, as we see from the example of de Hertz himself, who quickly abandoned it for the comedy of modern life in *The Mallow Flower* (1908), *The Conqueror* (1914), and other plays including the highly successful *The Spider* (1913).

An attempt to bring the imaginative fancies of the Rumanian folk into the drama was made by the poet Victor Eftimiu (1889-   ), in the poetic drama *Story Without End* (1911) and in the fantasy *The Black Cock* (1913). For years one of the main reliances of the Rumanian theatre, providing it annually with at least one piece, Eftimiu became the director of the National Theatre in Cluj, Transylvania, in 1932. His best-known plays besides the above mentioned are *Ave Maria* (1913), *Prometheus* (1919), and *Master Manole* (1925).

One of the most successful of the playwrights of the early twentieth century was Haralamb Lecca (1873-1920), a translator of Shakespeare and manager of a traveling stock company as well as a writer himself. His *Card Players* (1900), *Supreme Force* (1901), *The Dogs* (1902), *Cancer at Heart* (1907) are often reminiscent of Dumas fils.

Between the Jorgan revolt against foreign influences in 1905 and the First World War, nearly every Rumanian with any literary pretensions at all wrote at least one drama—diplomats (Zamfirescu and Florescu), professors (Kiritzescu and Pandelea), novelists (Rebreanu and Goga), poets (Blaga and Minulescu)—all striving to do their part toward the enrichment of what had by their time come to be recognized as one of the great instruments for the national welding together. The result is a bewildering welter of so-called dramatists, few of whom were more than amateurs and none of whom will probably be remembered in the long run for their contributions in this field.

Outstanding, however, among the pre-war generation was Mihail Sorbul

(1886-   ), whose *Chronicles* (1914) promised much in the realm of historical drama but who turned, in the altered atmosphere of the post-war period, to the social drama, to produce in this genre the realistic and often tragic *Red Passion* (1916), *Revenge* (1918), *The Deserter* (1919), *The Abyss* (1921), and other plays. In this period also must be noted the plays of George Diamandi (1867-1917)—*All Before* (1910), *The Beasts* (1910), *The Call of the Wood* (1913)—popular on the Rumanian stage even after the war, and the lyric dramas, notably *Red Roses* (1915), of Zaharia Barsan (1879-   ), the translator of Wilde's *Salomé* and at one time director of the Cluj Theatre. G. Ciprian's clever and lively grotesque *The Man with the Nag*, which achieved great popularity on the Berlin stage, and Octavian Goga's (1879-1938) *Village Notary* (1914) should also be noted. Goga, primarily a novelist and publicist, was the arch representative in post-war Rumania of the nationalist wing of Rumanian opinion. All his works, of whatever nature, are permeated with a kind of mysticism born of their author's passion for the soil of his native Transylvania and his desire to see that soil remain Rumanian.

There was no single school of drama in post-war Rumania, nor did the chaotic condition of the Rumanian state both economically and politically make such a school possible. Each dramatist wrote as he chose: on the whole, however, the tendency was toward a realistic treatment of human problems on the one hand, and a poetic exploration of the sources of the nation's strength on the other. The poet Lucian Blaga with his *Master Manole, Avram Iancu,* and *Children's Crusades,* is perhaps the best representative of the latter trend, along with Ion Marin Sadoveanu (1893-   ), who wrote *Metamorphosis* and *Anno Domini* (both 1927). The influence of Maeterlinck on Rumanian drama is seen in the plays of Ion Minulescu (1881-   ), whose post-war *The Cranes are Leaving* (1920) attracted notice. Probably the most interesting venture in the use of genuine folk characters dramatically was *Pacala* (1927), a verse drama by Horia Furtuna (1888-   ).

The Drama of the Southern Slavs

In 1918 the three westernmost branches of South Slavdom, the Croatians, Slovenians, and Serbians, united politically to form the state of Yugoslavia. This state endured with varying fortunes up to the German invasion of 1941.

Before 1918 vastly diverse cultural influences had made themselves felt in the three different branches and it is because of this divergent cultural orientation of the three that it seems wise to treat the three parts separately, despite the fact that they are closely related linguistically—especially the Serbians and Croatians—and despite their late, only partially successful, venture in political amalgamation.

Serbia was the only member of the Yugoslav triumvirate which enjoyed the status of a sovereign and independent state before 1918, both Croatia and Slovenia being provinces of the Austro-Hungarian Empire.

Serbia has been strongly influenced culturally by Islam, whereas Croatia and Slovenia have scarcely felt the impact of the Mohammedan civilization at all. The people of Croatia and Slovenia are prevailingly Roman Catholic, of Serbia for the most part Orthodox, though in Bosnia and Herzegovina there are many Moslem Serbians.

CROATIAN DRAMA

WAYNE S. VUCINICH

Modern Croatian drama had its origin in the cult of the past known as Illyrism, a movement inspired by Napoleon's short-lived Illyrian Republic (1810-1813) which crystallized in Zagreb about 1835 under the leadership of Ljudevit Gaj and which had for its object the rousing of national self-consciousness among the southern Slavs and the spiritual and political unification, ultimately, of Serbians, Croatians, and Slovenes.

Thus fathered, Croatian drama was from the beginning predominantly historical and has remained so throughout. A typical drama of the early period was the tragedy *Teuta* (1844) by Dimitrija Demeter (1811-1872), based on the legend of the Illyrian queen who disposed of a Roman embassy by having all its members murdered. A typical drama of our own times is Mirko Koroliya's (1893-   ) *Building of Skadra* (1921), written for the sixtieth anniversary of the Zagreb National Theatre and inspired by the old theme of the necessity for blood sacrifice in order to secure the foundations of the ancient Serbian stronghold. Between the two extremes, historical drama was with notable but rare exceptions the dominant type cultivated.

The reasons for Croatia's preference for the historical were, on the positive side, the steady preponderance of German and Austrian over French and Russian influence in Croatia—Schiller and Grillparzer were long the favorite masters—and on the negative, the certain knowledge of what the censor, under orders to delete everything anti-Hungarian and anti-Hapsburg, would do to a play which overstepped the line to treat realistically of contemporary events. The fate of Tomich's *New Order* was a case in point: written in 1881, it had to wait until 1918 for public presentation.

After 1861, when plays in Croatian were at last assured a home in the National Theatre in Zagreb, historical drama began to get rid of its more extravagantly romantic elements, as is evident from a comparison of the plays of Franjo Markovich (1845-1914) with those of Josip Tomich (1843-1906), the leading dramatists of the seventies and eighties respectively.

Markovich did not deviate from the well-tried formulas of the romanticists, either in his *Benko Bot* (1872), a highly nationalistic version of the theme used by Grillparzer in *Ein treuer Diener seines Herrns,* or in *Charles of Durazzo* (1872), a drama of the Croatio-Hungarian uprising against Rome at the time of the Great Schism,[1] or later in *Zvonimir, King of Croatia and Dalmatia,* which he wrote in 1876 for the eight hundredth anniversary of the coronation of Croatia's first king.

Tomich, on the other hand, managed to achieve a combination of the historical with the realistic, especially in the popular *Barun Franjo Trenk* (1880), a play depicting the patriarchal life of the Croatian countryside, though his *Veronika Deseniška* (1880) is dominated by the old romanticism. The latter play is based on the familiar tradition of the beautiful girl of the lower gentry who is murdered at the instigation of her lordly father-in-law because she stands in the way of a dynastic marriage for his son.[2] In *The Stepchild* (1892) Tomich broke completely with the historical to produce a realistic village drama in the spirit of the popular Austrian dramatist Anzengruber.

Preoccupation with the historical continued, however, throughout the nineties, despite strong currents of realism from nearby Serbia. Thus Eugeniy Kumičich (1850-1904), although known for his Zolaesque plays *The Sisters, The Deputies,* and *The Family Secret* (all 1891), was remembered for his conventional historical tragedy *Petar Zrinjski* (1901), based on the great Croatian tragedy of the fall of the houses of Zrinjski and Frangepan. The same theme, with its anti-Hapsburg implications, was used also by Ante Trešich-Pavičich (1867-   ) in *Katarina Zrinjska.* Other historical dramas of Trešich-Pavičich were *Herod* (1910), in the mood of Wilde's *Salomé; Cato of Utica* (1911); *Simeon the Great* (1897), based on an heroic Bulgarian theme; and *Louis Posavski* (1894), a drama of the Franko-Slavic struggle in the age of Charlemagne.

Historical plays would not have continued to be written in such numbers in Croatia if they had not been the most popular genre, as we know from the record of a practical man of the theatre, Stjepan Miletich (1868-1908), from 1894 until his death manager of the National Theatre in Zagreb. Miletich began by writing comedies in the French style—*The Dilettantes* (1887) and *Follow Your Nose* (1888). Next he sent up a trial balloon in the form of a social comedy, *Unmentionable Careers* (1890). It was not long, however, before he settled permanently on historical tragedy, to produce in this field *Boleslav* (1894), a Croatian *Hamlet* based on the life of a legendary Dalmatian prince; *Tomislav, First King of the Croatians* (1902); and the ambitious Macbethian *Sons of Kresimir* (1903), besides many other historical plays.

The one who offered the strongest resistance of all to the prevailing cult of the past in Croatia was Milan Begovich (1876-   ). A Dalmatian by birth, Begovich was educated in Vienna and later became a professor of lan-

---
[1] A theme used also by Záborský in Slovak.
[2] See Slovenian drama for further use of this theme: Jurčich, Župančič, Novačan, Kreft.

guages at Split. In 1908 he abandoned this to follow his friend and patron, the theatrical director Alfred von Berger, to the great Schauspielhaus in Hamburg. He remained here until 1912, then went to the Novi Sad Theatre and later to the Neue Bühne in Vienna. From 1920 he held a post in the Actors' School of the Zagreb Theatre.

Begovich began his career with a series of historical fantasies in the vein of Maeterlinck's *Monna Vanna*. His best work from this period was *Venus Victrix* (1905), which was followed by a variation à la Sardou of the Napoleon-Marie Walewska theme, *Madame Walewska* (also 1905). From this he proceeded, by way of an early social comedy *For Human Happiness* (1903), to the realistic drama of contemporary Dalmatian life *Stana Bjucicha* (1909). This was followed by a score of plays of various types and themes, culminating in *Man of God* (1924), *A Scoundrel at the Door* (1926), *An American Yacht in Split Harbor* (1930)—in which the American way of life is contrasted with the more conservative Dalmatian way—*Without a Third* (1931), and so forth.

A product of the "art for art's sake" school, Begovich was interested primarily in human motives and emotions and these he was able to present with subtle skill. What his dramas lack, however, is depth and the *sine qua non* of greatness in drama, human warmth, so that the most that may be said of him in final appraisal is that he played the rôle, historically crucial, of the one responsible for bringing all the varied world currents to bear at last upon Croatian drama.

The virtual impossibility of escaping from the grip of the historical in Croatian drama is nowhere more strikingly seen than in the case of Croatia's leading modern dramatist, Ivo Vojnovich (1857-1929).

Vojnovich commenced his career with a series of fantasies—*Psyche* (1889), *Vision of Gundulich* (1893)—following these with a dramatic profile of his native city of Dubrovnik (Ragusa) entitled *Equinox* (1893), inspired, as was also the above-mentioned *Vision of Gundulich,* by the unveiling of a monument to the great Ragusan poet of the sixteenth century, Ivan Gundulich. Next came what is generally regarded as Vojnovich's greatest work, *Dubrovnik Trilogy* (1901-1902), a cycle depicting with penetrating realism the history of Dubrovnik from the Illyrian Republic to the end of the nineteenth century.

From the friendship of his father with the great Bishop Strossmayer (1815-1905), Vojnovich became a loyal partisan of the Yugoslav Idea, successor to the defunct Illyrian idea of South Slav unity previously promoted by Gaj, and he desired earnestly to promote this idea by way of the dramn. To do this it was necessary to find some symbol valid for all three branches of the Southern Slavs and to center his dramas around this symbol.

What seemed to Vojnovich finally as the symbol with the greatest appeal for all three branches was that of The Sorrowing Mother, the mother of slain warriors who, despite her grief, never relaxes in her willingness to bear sons for her country. This symbol Vojnovich proceeded to clothe in historical drapery, first from the great Kossovo cycle of Serbian song, later from the actual history of the First Balkan War, producing in *The Death of the Jugovich Mother* (1906) and *The Resurrection of Lazarus* (1913) two moving dramas of the Yugoslav Idea. Vojnovich's endeavor to promote unity by means of the drama had its counterpart in Srgjan Tučich's excellent and timely play inspired by the First Balkan War, *The Liberators* (1913).

The old Croatian preoccupation with the historical is again seen in the plays of Milan Ogrizovich (1877-1923): *Hassan Aga's Wife* (1909), which is not to be confused with a Serbian play of the same title by the Bosnian Šantich (1911); *The Death of Czar Diocletian* (1913), based on a great event in the history of Split; and finally *The Zrinjski-Frangepan Tragedy* (1921), written to commemorate the two hundred and fiftieth anniversary of the tragic fall of those two houses, an event already referred to in connection with the plays of Kumičich and Trešich-Pavičich.

Russian literature, which played so decisive a rôle in Serbian drama, had almost no influence at all in Croatia until we come to the plays of Josip Kosor (1879-   ). A Dalmatian by birth, Kosor was associated in his early writing days with Zagreb and later with Munich and Vienna. During the First World War he was in Russia and later in England, where a number of his plays were translated. In all his dramas, from *Passion's Furnace* (1910), written under the influence of Bahr and Wyspiański, to those which won him the name of the Croatian Gorki, Kosor is occupied primarily with abstract problems of good and evil which he does not always succeed in making actual.

Closer to reality is Miroslav Krleža, Croatia's leading contemporary dramatist (1893-   ). Krleža, like so many others of his race, began by dealing with historical themes and personalities—*Kristofor Kolumbo* (1918), *Michelangelo Buonarroti* (1933), *Legend* (1933)—without, however, sacrificing actuality in his depiction of motive and conflict.

At first Krleža had the vision of a true revolutionist, which was what he seemed to be, but as pessimism gradually overtook him his idealism chilled and it was in a mood of gloom that he wrote his best dramas. These are the trilogy *In Agony* (1928), *The Glembays* (1929), and *Leda* (1930), in which Krleža traces the decline of Croatia's aristocracy and the decay of Croatian society in general.

To the category of revolutionists belongs, along with Krleža, August Cesarec (-   ), best known for his drama *Son of the Fatherland* (1940), based on the life of E. V. Kvaternik, a famous Croatian leader who, in emulation of Garibaldi, led a great uprising in the Rakovica district against the Empire in 1871. This play of Cesarec is in the direct tradition of one of Croatia's earliest dramatic works, the famous *Matija Gubec, Peasants' King* (1859) of Mirko Bogovich (1816-1893), the hero of which is the celebrated leader of the great Slovenian folk uprising in 1573.

To complete the picture of modern Croatian drama mention must be made of the trend to symbolism and expressionism which made some headway especially in the twenties. Traces of this trend are seen in the dramas of Tučich, especially his symbolical *Golgota* (1913), but most of all in the numerous works of Josip Kulundžich (1899-   ), of which the best known is the grotesque *Midnight* (1921). Kulundžich is sometimes dubbed "the anti-Pirandello."

SERBIAN DRAMA

WAYNE S. VUCINICH

Plays began to be produced in Serbia as early as in 1840, at Kragujevac the first capital of free Serbia, and were produced also, after 1861, at the Hungarian city of Novi Sad; yet Serbian drama had no fixed and worthy home on native soil until 1869, when the National Theatre in Belgrade was finally in full operation. This date marks the beginning of the modern period of Serbian drama.

Romanticism was still the prevailing cult in Serbian letters, as it had been in the time of Popovich (1806-1856), the father of Serbian drama. The principal playwrights of the first generation of the new period were direct heirs of Popovich, both of them—Djura Jakšich (1832-1878) and Laza Kostich (1841-1910)—having been nourished at the same source as he, namely the great folksong collections of Vuk Karadžich, *Srpske Narodne Pyesme* (*Serbian National Songs,* 1823-1833), from which all Serbian and much Croatian historical drama takes its origin.

Of the two playwrights, Jakšich is the more romantic and appealing figure. Like Popovich a native of the Banat, then a province of Austria, a talented painter trained in Munich and Vienna, a patriot of deeds as well as words—he enlisted in the Serbian army in 1849—Jakšich was handicapped all his life by poverty and ill health. His first drama was *The Serbian Migration* (1863), an epic of the Serbian settlement of the Balkans in the sixth century. It was followed by *Elizabeth, Princess of Montenegro* (1868), a verse drama inspired by the ballad *The Marriage of Maxim Crnojevich,* often called the Serbian Nibelungenlied, which recounts the collapse of the fifteenth-century Serbian kingdom of Zeta. In a third drama, *Stanoye Glavaš* (1878), Jakšich extolled the deeds of a famous Serbian revolutionary of the 1813-1818 epoch. Although suffering from the faults of lyricism, wordiness, and lack of dramatic conflict inherent in romantic drama itself, Jakšich's plays are important as pioneer efforts to erect, on the foundation established by Popovich, a native drama of native materials.

Jakšich's contemporary Kostich is called, because of his many translations, the Serbian Shakespeare. The son of a Serbian officer in the Austrian army, he was brought up in Novi Sad and there associated intimately with the

Serbian renaissance which took place in that city in the sixties. His first original play was the ballad drama *Maxim Crnojevich* (1866),[1] a better work artistically than Jakšich's treatment of the same theme because of its emphasis on character as well as event. With *Pera Segedinac* (1875), his most mature work, Kostich entered the field of contemporary politics, only to return in *Gordana* (1890) to the ballad drama so dear to the romanticist.

In the seventies a new spirit of realism arrived in Serbia from France and Russia and with its arrival romantic tragedy gave way to realistic comedy. The pioneer exponent of the new trend was Kosta Trifkovich (1843-1875), an official in the city government of Novi Sad. Trifkovich's *Love Letter* (1873) and *The Coquette* (1872), to mention the most popular of his many plays, won for their author the name of the Serbian Scribe.

Comedy gradually became less and less artificial in the eighties, as it drew into its orbit new types and situations, especially those connected with rural life. This is seen in the dramas of Milovan Glišich (1847-1908), a Positivist, an admirer of Gogol and Goncharov and, as a dramatist, an imitator of Ostrovski. Glišich's *Two Pennies* (1883) and *The Cheat* (1883), satirizing the usurious city creditor and the corrupt official, were the earliest comedies in Serbian to deal with the peasantry in any save an outrageously melodramatic or idyllic manner.

Except for the popular folk comedy *Djido* (1892) of Janko Veselinovich and Dragomir Brzak, drama languished in Serbia in the nineties, only to spring forth in full bloom with the new century. But this time Serbian literary activity had become decentralized, new centers having arisen in addition to Novi Sad and Belgrade. As a result new phases of Serbia's rich and varied life began to be reflected in the drama: for one thing, the patriarchal, half Slav, half Turkish life of Vranje, in the popular *Koštana* (1902) and other plays of Borisav Stankovich (1876-   ); for another, the curiously oriental life of the border province of Bosnia, in the dramas of Svetozar Chorovich (1875-1919)—*Adembeg* (1904), *The Rascal* (1910), and so forth —and Alexa Shantich (1868-   )—*Beneath the Mists* (1907)—leaders of the literary awakening in the Bosnian city of Mostar and founders of the literary journal *Dawn;* and finally the quaint habits of the Serbians of Lika in the many dramas of Petar Petrovich (1877-   )—*The Serbian Farmer* (1904), *The Forest* (1915), *The Torrent* (1918), *The Land* (1925), and others.

In connection with the rise of regionalism and especially apropos of the Bosnian awakening, note must be taken of a play by the Bosnian revolutionist Petar Kočich (1877-1916), *Before the Court of Justice* (1904). Its hero is David Strbac, a Bosnian peasant and the very spearhead of peasant resistance to Hapsburg aggression in the Balkans. The play had the effect not only of arousing sentiment for the Young Bosnia movement to which

---

[1] The single dramatic work produced in the Montenegrin portion of Serbia was based on this theme: *Elizabeth, Empress of the Balkans,* by King Nikola I Petrovich Njegoš, published at Cetinje, 1886.

its author belonged, but of encouraging the use of the vernacular in literary works, especially the drama. It was one of the most popular plays in all Serbian literature.

The outstanding figure in modern Serbian drama was Branislav Nušich (1864-1938). Born and educated in Belgrade in an atmosphere of intense realism, Nušich completed his studies in law and then, after serving a prison term for certain political articles he had written, secured a post as consul, first in Priština, later in Skoplje in Old Serbia. His connection with the theatre dates from 1899, when he became secretary of the National Theatre in Belgrade. Before this time he had written three plays: *Influence* (1889), *Representative of the People* (1896), and *The First Case* (1897), all of which were satires on unscrupulous officialdom.

After 1899 Nušich produced a steady and unbroken stream of dramas, beginning with the rather slight ballad drama of an early nineteenth-century folk hero *The Prince of Semberia* (1900) and two plays of character, *Schopenhauer* and *An Average Man* (both 1900).

A disciple of the Gogol-Ostrovski school which had such a decisive influence on modern Serbian letters, Nušich looked upon life as an ironic comedy, which he undertook to portray faithfully, somewhat satirically, yet without bitterness, and without partisanship in ideological controversies. Of his many plays, long popular with Serbian audiences, *A Trip around the World* (1910), an allegorical satire directed against the Serbians who ape the West, and *Madame Minister* (1927), a satire of pompous officialdom, are outstanding.

Nušich ended his career with a sober, almost pessimistic drama *Deceased*, based on the unsavory theme of denunciation of personal enemies for political reasons. The work clearly reflects the disillusion and neuroticism of the era leading up to the Second World War. Yet, despite his yielding to pessimism, Nušich did not give in, as did so many of his writing colleagues in the Balkans, to either brand of totalitarian ideology, whether fascist or communist. He remained to the end faithful to his lifelong conviction that there was another and better way out for humanity, and was recognized as a leader in the cause of democracy.

Social drama that was not afraid of ideological controversy or uncritical of modern society is seen in the work of Borivoye Jevtich (1893-   ) and Dushan Nikolajevich, the latter best known for his half frivolous, half serious "modern mystery" *Volga, Volga* (1927), in which Dostoevski and Lenin are represented as confronting each other "on the borders of Europe and Russia." Similar in spirit to *Volga, Volga* is Jevtich's *Czar's Cohorts* (1928). In *Revenge* (1938) Jevtich deals with the revolutionary movement known as Young Bosnia. Of the numerous attempts to depict dramatically the harsh but often inspiring realities of everyday peasant life in modern Yugoslavia, one of the most successful was *Water from the Mountain* (1938), by Rasha Plaovich and Milan Djokovich, based on an actual attempt by a group of Serbian peasants to bring water to their village from a mountain spring.

SLOVENIAN DRAMA

WAYNE S. VUCINICH

The first drama in Slovenian is believed to have been a work written in 1817 entitled *Ulrich, Count of Cilli* (Celje, in Slovenian). Whether this actually was the first Slovenian drama or not is of slight significance, but that the unknown dramatist should have chosen for his theme the meteoric fate of the last great representative of the Styrian house of Cilli was not only significant but prophetic. The theme proved to be the most popular of all with Slovenian dramatists, being used over and over again by them, with much heat generated for and against each time it was used, until eventually the very ideological foundations of Slovenian national identity were fought out over it in two dramas that presented in mutually hostile interpretations this pivotal tragedy of Slovenian's history.

The father of Slovenian drama was Josip Jurčich (1844-1881), author of *Tugomer* (1876), a romantic tragedy of the Schiller-Grillparzer school based on the betrayal of the Polabian Slavs [1] to the Germans by their own chieftain Tugomer in the tenth century. The theme was a popular one with Slav writers, Czech, Lusatian, and Polish as well as Slovenian, as it gave them an opportunity to express the traditional Slavic hatred of the Germans in a manner not readily offensive to the censor.

Besides *Tugomer,* Jurčich wrote part of one other drama which, after being completed by Ignace Borštnik, was presented under the title *Veronika Desiniška* at the opening performance of the Ljubljana Theatre on September 29, 1892 and again, at the thirtieth anniversary celebration of this important event, in 1922. The theme of the play was the above-mentioned tragedy of the House of Cilli, the heroine in this case the lowly born wife of one of the Counts of Cilli who is murdered by her father-in-law because she stands in the way of his dynastic ambitions for his son.[2] The play was more successful as propaganda for "the regathering together of the lands once constituting the Croatian realm" than as a work of art.

Other historical dramas of which the same might be said were those of the pastor-poet Anton Medved (1869-1919), among these the ambitious *Kacijanar* (1895), a would-be *Wallenstein; For Right and the Heart* (1896), a romanticized inprovisation on the theme of the peasant uprising of 1573 led by Matija Gubec;[3] not to mention the biblical *Saul* (1893).

Slovenia's bondage to romanticism in the field of drama was compara-

---
[1] See Lusatian drama.
[2] See Tomich, *Veronika Desenicka*, p. 541.
[3] See Bogovich, *Matija Gubec*, p. 534.

tively short-lived. This was due in part to the naturally realistic temper of the Slovenian people themselves, in part to the close contact of Slovenia with the Czechs, especially with the Czech theatre which for years supplied Ljubljana with most of its theatrical personnel.

Realism made its appearance in the drama of Slovenia with Josip Stritar (1836-1923), a disciple of Ibsen and Ibsen's advocate in Slovenian as early as 1880, as we see in his drama *Klara* of that year, in which a young governess who might almost be Nora herself is seen indoctrinating her wealthy pupil with the ideas commonly associated with Ibsen.

Other early Ibsenists were Josip Vošnjak (1834-1911), with *Doktor Dragan* (1894) a Slovenian *Enemy of the People* based on an actual episode; and Anton Funtek (1862-   ), with *Crystal Castle* (1897). In the early years of the twentieth century the trend set in motion by Ibsen had become so powerful as to divert the above-mentioned Medved from his interest in the historical to a new realism, which is seen in the dramas *On the Stage of Life* (1902), *Chums* (1905), *Wrong and Right,* and *Old and Young* (published 1921), the last a rustic piece in the style of the Ausrian Anzengruber.

Realistic comedy achieved world stature in Slovenia with the appearance of Ivan Cankar (1876-1918). The student years of this greatest of all Slovenian dramatists were spent in Schnitzler's Vienna, but when Cankar left Vienna to return to Slovenia it was to repudiate out of hand all that Schnitzler's Vienna, Schnitzler himself, and especially the then popular *Liebelei* represented. Cankar repudiated also whatever vestiges of Pan-Slavic romanticism were still to be found in Slovenia, to create a drama of the sharpest social criticism, rooted in the customs and soil and even in the folklore of his homeland. In this his masters were the Czech Hilbert (his *Jacob Ruda,* 1900, is strongly reminiscent of Hilbert's much-discussed *Guilt,* 1895), Hauptmann, and of course Ibsen.

Of Cankar's numerous dramas four should be noted. These are in chronological order: the controversial *For the Nation's Good* (1901), a denunciation of romantic pseudo-patriotism and political corruption notable for the figure of Mrmoljeva, whom Cankar creates as a symbol of Reason, which he longed to see set up in opposition to Pan Slavic sentimentalism; *The Scandal in St. Florian's Vale* (1908), a high-spirited farce, the best in Slovenian, satirizing the smallness and destructiveness of contemporary intellectuals; *Hired Men* (1910), a social drama rebuking the Slovenian intellectual for his escapism and general ineffectiveness; and finally *Fair Vida* (1912), a lyric drama inspired by a popular ballad of the Karst region near Trieste, the theme of which is the betrayal of a beautiful maiden by a lover from over the sea.

To the generation dominated by Cankar belonged Kristan Etbin (1867-   ), author of several social dramas, some of which were based on old Slavonic ballad themes—*Who is the Fool?* (1907), *Ljubislava* (1907), *The Factory* (1912),—and Lojz Kraigher (1877-   ), whose Freudian drama

The Shell (1911) had considerable influence on the dramas of the oncoming generation.

Thanks to the high level of Slovenian culture in general and to the Cankar tradition in particular, Slovenia contributed more dramatists to Free Yugoslavia in the two decades of that state's existence than might have been expected in view of her small size. Outstanding among these were Cvetko Golar (1879-   ), whose comedies of everyday life *The Widow Rošlinka* (1924), on the familiar theme of forced marriage, and *The Temptress* (1925) were among the stand-bys of the post-war stage in Ljubljana; and Frančišek Salezy Finžgar (1871-   ), whose dramas of rural life, reminding us of *Maryša* by the Czech Mrštiks, were well received, especially *The Chain* (1914) and *The Wreck of Life* (1921). To be noted also is Fran Govékar (1871-   ), for his problem play on the theme treated by Cankar in *Hired Men, The Knot in the Wood* (1910) and *The Mraks* (1921).

There was also Anton Aškerc (1856-1912), who, like his contemporary Cankar often used ballad material in a realistic drama of social criticism. Of his numerous works three are to be noted: the early *Golden Horn* (1904), *The Estranged Wife*—a Slovenian *Madame X,* and *The Gay Resort* (1927), a further development of the *Fair Vida* theme which was so popular with Slovenian writers.[1]

Social problems arising from the chaos that followed the First World War were treated in the dramas of Stanko Majcen (1888-   ), *Kasija* (1919), *Heirs of a Great Age* (1921), and *For a New Race* (1922); problems of rural life by Lojz Remec (1886-   ) in *Magda* (1924) and *Retired Landowners* (1923); unscrupulous manipulators of finance by the same dramatist in the comedy *Kirke* (1922). Sexual problems such as prostitution and adultery are highlighted in the plays of Angel Cerkvenik, *In the Vortex* (1925), *Sin* (1928), and *The Hand of Justice* (1928), all of which show strong traces of Strindberg and Wedekind, as do also the Freudian dramas of Slavko Grum, *The Perverse One* (1927) and *The Affair in the Town of Goga* (1928).

One of the most successful of Slovenia's contemporary playwrights was Pavel Golia (1887-   ), director of drama at the Ljubljana Theatre. Golia's most popular works were the children's plays *Peter's Last Dream* (1923), *Triglav Fable* (1927), and *Bethlehem Legend* (1928).

The leading Slovenian playwright of the thirties was Bratko Kreft, author of three dramas of social criticism; *Small-Town Folk,* a devastating portrait of Ljubljana at the beginning of the First World War; and the two historical dramas *Count Cilli* and *The Great Uprising.*

The theme of *Count Cilli,* as may be imagined from its title, was the one treated by the anonymous author of the first Slovenian play in 1817 and later by Jurčich in *Veronika Desiniška.* Its use by Kreft arose indirectly from the revival of Jurčich's drama at the Ljubljana Theatre in 1922, referred to

[1] Note, besides Cankar's drama on this theme, a novel by Jurčich.

above, and directly from the use to which the theme was put soon after this event by the great Slovenian translator of Shakespeare Oton Zupančich (1879-) and later by Anton Novačan (1887-).

Jurčich, in *Veronika Desiniška,* like Tomich in his Croatian version of the same theme, had presented the great feudal house of Cilli as a band of ruthless and self-willed tyrants who resorted willingly to murder in order to gain their ends. Zupančich and Novačan, however, the former in *Veronika Desiniška* (1924), the latter in *Herman of Cilli* (1928), rehabilitated the house to a degree and even represented its leading member, Count Herman, as the father of the Yugoslav Idea! Such an interpretation infuriated Kreft and to answer it he wrote his own dramatic version of the old theme, portraying in *Count Cilli* not the great lords but the native peasantry as the unifying element in South Slavdom and the guardian of freedom and justice. Thus the drama became the instrument of an ideological warfare, which was carried still further by Kreft in his third play, *The Great Uprising,* based on the theme of the peasant rebellion of 1573 under Matija Gubec which Anton Medved had used previously in *For Right and the Heart.*

To complete the picture of modern Slovenian drama we must note the comedies of Radoslav Murnik (1870-1936), especially *Napoleon's Samovar* (1897), a perennial favorite on both the professional and amateur stage, and the more recent works of two of the youngest of Yugoslavia's playwrights, *Lopeza* by Vladimir Bartol, as well as *Water* and *The Golden Calf* by Jože Vomberger.

BULGARIAN DRAMA

VICTOR SHARENKOFF

Before a native drama could come into being in Bulgaria a native stage had first to be possible. The beginnings of the latter are romantic in the extreme, being linked with the revolutionary movement of 1848-1849 which sent crowds of cultivated Polish and Hungarian refugees pouring over the Danube into northeastern Bulgaria, especially into the historic town of Shumen, and with the colorful schemes of the Polish adventurer Czajkowski, known as Sadyk Pasha, for stirring up a Pan-Slavic uprising in the Balkans. It was the refugees who aroused a taste for native drama in Shumen and a member of Czajkowski's embassy there, Josef Fric who, in association with the Czech Majzner, initiated the first theatrical performance in the Bulgarian tongue.

This performance took place on August 15, 1856, in a Turkish coffee house. The play presented was a translation from the Greek by the patriotic schoolmaster Sava Dobroplodni (1821-1894) entitled *Michael.* An amusing comedy in the Molière style, it delighted the audience and led to a demand for further plays in Bulgarian.

While this was going on in Shumen, a similar movement was taking place in the town of Lom, also on the Danubian frontier, where on December 12 a translation from the German called *Poor Genevieve* had its first public presentation. This was a sentimental piece which moved the audience to tears and it too, like *Michael,* created a demand for native drama.

The success of these early ventures led to the spread of interest in the drama and to the use of drama as a means of arousing the Bulgarian people to new efforts toward liberation. "There is no better school for a society than the theatre," declared Dobri Voinikov, the so-called father of the Bulgarian theater, and his view was shared by all sincere patriots.

The principal centers of encouragement for native drama were the reading rooms (*chitalista*) which played such an important part in the national liberation movement. Even during the turbulent epoch of the Russo-Turkish Wars (1877-1878) and the early years of national independence immediately following, when intellectual life was almost at a standstill in Bulgaria, the reading rooms continued to hold theatrical performances with a regularity that is nothing short of miraculous.

The first professional Bulgarian troupe was organized in 1866 by the above-mentioned Dobri P. Voinikov (1833-1878), a disciple of Dobroplodni, at Braila in Rumania. In order to supply his company with a working repertory Voinikov undertook to write plays in the vernacular himself. Among these were comedies of daily life (for example *The Doctor in Spite of Himself*) and historical dramas designed to awaken national fervor, as for example *The Christianization of the Court of Preslav* [1] (1868), *Voivoda Stojan* (1866), and *Velislava* (1870), a drama of the short-lived fourteenth-century Tarter dynasty of Trnovo. Although lacking in artistic worth, Voinikov's primitive efforts served their purpose, which was to awaken the Bulgarian people to a sense of national consciousness.

The first serious dramatic work in Bulgarian was *Ivanko* (1872), by Vasil Drumev (1841-1901), an historical tragedy of the times of the Bulgarian Emperor Asen I (1186-1196). Ivanko, a great commander, is torn between loyalty to his Emperor and lust for power. He succumbs to the latter and murders the Emperor, but is foiled at the moment when he is about to seat himself on the royal throne by the defection of the nobles, and is forced to flee to Constantinople. A drama of Macbethian theme and stature, *Ivanko* is still a favorite with Bulgarian audiences.

The second playwright of importance in Bulgaria was the distinguished poet and novelist Ivan Vazov (1850-1921). Vazov turned to the drama first as a matter of duty, in answer to a demand for dramatic works to be presented in the fledgling theatre of Plovdiv, when that city rose to prominence at the end of the Turkish wars as the capital of autonomous Eastern Rumelia. In 1907, when the Bulgarian National Theatre was opened in Sofia, Vazov

[1] The Bulgarian capital in the Golden Age of Czar Simeon.

was the one chosen to write the inaugural *Prologue,* and his works continued to be the main stand-by of the new theatre.

The list of Vazov's dramatic works is long. It includes on the one hand comedies ridiculing the new Bulgarian society and the institutions of the newly formed state—*Squire Michalaki* (1882), *The Office Seekers* (1903), *The Journalists* (1900), and others—and, on the other, historical dramas with strongly patriotic implications. Among the latter the best known outside Bulgaria is *Under the Yoke* (1911); the most popular in Bulgaria, however, are *Borislav* (1909), a work similar in theme to Drumev's *Ivanko,* and *Ivailo* (1913), in which the hero is a peasant who led a great uprising in the Middle Ages and actually became king for a few days.

An effort to break away from the historical and to create a drama of character based on contemporary life was made by Petko Todorov (1879-1916). Unfortunately, however, Todorov's use of symbolism, much of it from folk legend, caused his plays to read better than they act. *The Builders* (1902), in which he made use of the old Slavonic belief that a human being must be immured in the walls of a building in order to make that building secure,[1] is his outstanding dramatic work, with *Samodiva* (1904) and *The First* (1907) also deserving of notice.

The most prolific of all Bulgarian dramatists is Anton Strashimirov (1872-1937), a novelist, short-story writer, and essayist as well as a playwright. Besides his numerous symbolic (*Christmas Legend,* 1912, and so forth) and historical (*St. John of Rila,* 1911, and so forth) plays, he has produced several successful dramas of Bulgarian village life, the most popular of which are *The Mother-in-Law* (1907) and *The Vampire* (1902). Other plays of village life to be noted are *The Masters* (1927) by Racho Stojanov (1882-   ) and *Albena* (1928) by Yordan Yovkov (1887-1937).

Two plays of Bulgarian city life were written by the well-known poet Peyu Yavorov (pseudonym of Kracholov). These, however, *At the Foot of Vitosh* (1911) and *If Thunder Strikes* (1912), are of small permanent worth.

The best comedies of manners in Bulgarian are those by Stefan Kostov (1878-   ), a biting and fearless satirist of contemporary Bulgarian society. Outstanding are his *Gold Mine* (1926) and *Golemanov* (1928), the latter somewhat resembling Vazov's *Office Seekers.* Yovkov's *The Millionaire* (1930), a satire on provincial credulity and money-madness should also be noted in this connection.

Although the record of Bulgaria in the field of drama is not particularly distinguished, this does not mean that the Bulgarian theatre has had a correspondingly meagre history. On the contrary, the Bulgarian National Theatre, in the relatively short period of its existence, reached a high level of excellence both qualitatively and quantitatively. According to a survey of the two decades between 1907 and 1927, forty-one native Bulgarian plays were produced and eighty-five translations. Shakespeare is as well known

[1] See *The Building of Skadra* by Mirko Kolroliya in the section on Croatian drama.

to Bulgarian audiences as Ibsen and Chekhov, and Russian drama is very popular. The influence of the Bulgarian theatre was felt by wide areas of the population and that influence was always in the direction of democracy and progress. In view of this fact its present (1943) subservience to the totalitarian régime now in force in the unhappy country is the more to be regretted. The democratic Bulgarian people are confident, however, that the present situation of their theatre is but temporary.

Modern Greek Drama

EMANUEL S. ATHANAS

The achievement of modern Greece in the field of drama is, paradoxically, meagre and poor in direct proportion as that of her ancient prototype, ancient Hellas, was brilliant and prolific. One explanation of this is the almost incessant turmoil and strife both of party and actual arms which Greece had to endure from the time of her rebirth in 1821 to the Second World War; another, the poverty of the Greek realm throughout this period; and a third, more important explanation of the apparent reversal of the Greek tradition, the very magnificence of that tradition itself in the field of drama. The impossibility of living up to the Hellenic ideal was a deterrent to the potential dramatist. He felt dwarfed and frightened off by it and gave up without trying, or, if he did try, became, through emulating too lofty models, a poor Sophocles when he might have become a pretty fair Scribe.

A further cause of the lag dramatically in modern Greece was the linguistic schizophrenia prevailing in Greek letters throughout the nineteenth century. Every writer was confronted with a choice of two languages, the Hellenic (or *katharevousa*) and the vernacular (or *demotiki*). In order to maintain their own personal prestige most writers chose the *katharevousa,* thus greatly retarding the rise of a living, national drama.

It was not until just before the First World War that the *demotiki* won even lip-recognition as a literary language, the credit for whatever was accomplished in this direction belonging properly to the philologist John Psicharis (1854-1929) and the poet Kostes Palamas (1859-1943). Though Palamas himself wrote only one drama—*Trisevyene* (1902), a free translation with a Greek setting—he felt very keenly on the subject of language in the drama, holding neither Sophocles nor any other ancient to be the father of the "new dramatic art" of modern Greece, but rather "the old Cretan Hortatzis," who wrote the remarkable Cretan drama of the sixteenth century *Erophile.*

The language situation, it should be added, was more than once held up to ridicule by the dramatist, as we see in the *Korakistika* (*Learned Jargon,* 1913) by Jacob Rizos Nerulos (1778-1850), a gibe at the well-known "reforms" of Korais; in Byzantios' *Babylonia* (*The Tower of Babel*, 1836) and in Psicharis' comedy *Gouanakos* (1911).

The outstanding dramatist of the first generation after the rebirth was Joannes Zampelios (1787-1856), an Ionian islander of Leucas and a leader of the revolutionary society Philiké Hetairea which played such a large part in the erection of the modern Greek state. Like all pioneer dramatists of the nineteenth century, Zampelios took his themes at first from the reservoir of his nation's heroic past. His best play was the tragedy *Timoleon* (1939), based on the well-known theme from Greco-Carthaginian history previously used by Alfieri, who was Zampelios' great model. The presentation of *Timoleon* in Bucharest, a center of Greek nationalism, caused such a stir that it had to be banned.

Zambelios turned later for his themes to the Greek War of Independence (1821-1829), as we see in the dramas *Diakos, Rigos, Botzaris, Capodistrias, Andrutsos,* and so forth.

One reason for the poor quality of so much of early modern Greek drama was the lack of specialization of the various dramatists. Alexandre Rangabé (Greek Rangavis, 1810-1892) is a case in point.

The scion of a powerful Phanariot family of Constantinople, Rangabé was not only a playwright but an archæologist and a philologist as well— in the latter capacity the very spearhead of the Hellenists (*Katharevousists*). He was also a poet and historian, diplomat and translator. When he turned to writing dramas, Rangabé undertook to harmonize all the great writers he had read and translated, from Dante and Tasso to Shakespeare and Lessing and Schiller. It is not surprising that he achieved only a succession of "beautiful mosaics without warmth or passion" rather than living dramas.

Of these, four were tragedies in verse: *Phrosyne* (1837), based on a well-known theme from the Turkish conquest; *Dukas,* a drama of the Fourth Crusade (1204); *The Thirty Tyrants* (1866), in which the hero is Thrasybulus, defender of Athenian democracy in the fifth century; *The Vigil,* a drama of the War of Independence. Besides these there were the three comedies *Antroula's Affianced, A Visit from Jove,* and *The Marriage of Kutrulis* (1845), the last a political satire in the style of Aristophanes.

The outstanding dramatists of the late nineteenth century in Greece were Demetrios Vernadakis (1834-1907), a professor in the University of Athens, and Spyridion Vasiliadis (1845-1874). Both were purists, like Rangabé, and also strong partisans of Shakespearian drama as the model for the new Greek art.

Vernadakis' most popular work was the tragedy *Maria Doxapatri* (1858), a drama of a noble Greek girl who falls in love with one of the French Crusaders in 1204. After a favorable reception in Munich, where it was submitted in a prize contest, this became, with Vernadakis' *Merope* (1865), one of the two hits of the 1865-1866 theatrical season in Athens. *Merope,* based on the theme used so often in European drama (Torelli, Maffei,

Voltaire, Alfieri, Arnold), is a play of blood vengeance, as is also the author's *Kypselides* (1858). His *Phrosyne* (1870) makes use of the historical theme previously treated by Rangabé.

Although a purist linguistically, Vasiliadis was somewhat less slavishly so than Vernadakis, who only in the chorus of *Antiope* (1895) ventured to break away from the *katharevousa*. Vasiliadis realized the theatre's need of popular support, and he emphasized this principle in *Attic Nights*. He too, however, continued to find his themes in the past: that of *Galatea* (1873) in Hellas, of *Kalergis* (1868) and *Lukas Notaris* (1869) in Byzantium. Over his work, as over that of his predecessors, moreover, still hovered the twofold curse of the Greeks: the curse of uncertainty as to the worth of Byzantium in the Greek tradition, and of servility to Hellas linguistically.

With the rise of interest in Ibsen a new day began to dawn for Greek drama and its herald was Joannes Kambisis (1872-1902), a zealous partisan of the vernacular and a keen observer of contemporary life.

By Kambisis' time the cultural capital of Greece had removed from Paris to Athens, so that native drama had at last a native footing from which to spring. All Kambisis' own dramas deal with Athenian life. The most important are *The Farce of Life, The Mystery of Marriage, Miss Anna Cooksley,* a take-off on the Greek fondness for dead rather than living heroes, and *The Kurds,* an attack on the injustice and inequality of modern society. In *The Mother's Ring* we find Kambisis succumbing to the gloom commonly associated with the Scandinavians who were his masters.

The gloom of the North made itself felt also in the plays of Joannes Polemis (1862-1925), another Athenian, whose *Icon, The Dream, The Woman* (in verse), and *The King Condemned to Darkness* should be noted.

Most comedies reaching the Athenian stage in the nineteenth century were translations from the French or, as in the case of those of Nicholas Laskaris, imitations of the French. Indigenous comedy was represented by the plays of Charalambos Anninos (1852-   ), a Cephalonian, best known for his primitive but amusing comedy *Leonidas' Triumph,* in which a rich uncle returns from America and simulates poverty in order to test the sincerity of his relatives' affection.

The trend toward folk themes represented in the West by Hauptmann produced in Greece the plays of Demetrios Koromelas; the melodramatic verse-tragedy *Rhodope* based on an old folk-song by Nilcholas Poriotis; *The Priceless Treasure* from the theme of the famous folk ballad *The Bridge of Arta* by Panteles Horn; and a drama *For the Fatherland* in praise of the patriotic Suliotes of the mountainous Greco-Albanian frontier by Vassilis. Greek drama in this genre was not popular, probably because of the exclusive nature of the Athenian Theatre during the nineteenth century, due, of course, to the royal patronage under which it functioned.

The leading dramatists of the period between the First and Second World

Wars were Melas, Tangopoulos, and Xenopoulos, with the last by all odds the "ablest and most active" of the three.

A disciple of Ibsen and of Gorki and the other Russians of his own day, Spyros Melas (1880-   ) is known primarily as a novelist. His plays also must be taken into account, however, especially *One Night, One Life; The Ruined House,* a depressing picture of a group of Athenians who live by a girl's prostitution; *The Son of Shadow,* which deals with a youth suffering from delusions of grandeur; and *White and Black* (1914), a view of the middle-class life in which the sole ray of light is the artist son. Although Melas could, if he wished, write interesting dialogue and contrive clever plots, he generally refuses to do so, not wishing to discipline himself, with the result that his plays are foggy and verbose and beyond all reason gloomy.

Gregory Xenopoulos is popularly looked upon as the father of the contemporary Athenian Theatre. Born in 1867 on the Ionian Island of Zante, he has spent his entire artistic life in Athens. A keen analyst, especially of the modern woman, a champion of feminine freedom and of woman's right to self-expression, Xenopoulos possesses a good sense of form, a talent for dialogue, and a vigorous style. In his dramas he generally focuses the action on a single striking, central character.

Xenopoulos' most popular play is *Stella Violanti* (1909), a study in conflicting ideologies, which was made into a successful film (1931). Other well-known works are *The Temptation* (1910), a comedy of manners; *The Only Child* (1912), a psychological study; *The Couple* (1913), a pastoral comedy; *Love Triumphant* (1915), an historical comedy; *It Isn't I* (1915), a farce; *A Brother's Honor* (1916), a realistic comedy with sociological implications; *Intermezzo* (1911) and *Isabella's Destiny* (1921), two tragedies. Although he reflects all the various trends in the drama from Ibsen to Gorki, Xenopoulos may not be classed as dependent on any master outside himself save the Athenian society from which he derives his inspiration.

Demetrios Tangopoulos (1867-   ) is the author of a symbolical drama *The Quick and the Dead,* in which he asks the old question: Which are more important to the modern Greek state, the marble heroes of the Parthenon or the klephts who died for the Greek Idea in the War of Independence? Both types of hero are epitomized in Tangopoulos' drama, each in an individual who sues for the favor of a beautiful maiden who represents Modern Greece.

The question posed by Tangopoulos has not yet been answered satisfactorily. Greece is still bound to her past. Even the language has still not been completely stabilized in favor of the *demotiki*. Perhaps the present conflict will prove in the long run a blessing, by speeding the emancipation of Greece from "the archæologist and the Paris-loving snob," so that Greek drama may at last be free to press toward the goal aimed at by Rangabé and each of his successors in turn: that of equaling, at least, the classical drama of Hellas.

Albanian Drama

NELO DRIZARI

The Albanian drama is a product of the twentieth century. It was born under the most difficult conditions and its growth has been slow, due principally to the fact that the Ottoman Empire, which ruled Albania for four hundred years, forbade its Albanian subjects to read, write, or perform plays in the native tongue. This made the rise of dramatic literature virtually impossible until after the proclamation of Albanian independence in the year 1912.

Despite the ban on literary production within the country itself, plays in Albanian appeared before 1912 outside. These were smuggled in by secret couriers and read eagerly by peasants and townsfolk alike, but their existence had to be kept a secret from the ever-watchful Turkish constabulary.

The first play to win the approval of Albania's clandestine readers was *The Pledge of Honor* (1901) by Sami Bey Frasheri, a leader in the movement, begun in 1877, for the standardization of the Albanian language using the Latin alphabet. Written originally in Turkish, the play was quickly translated into the vernacular by Frasheri's friend Abdyl Ypi, a well-known Albanian patriot living abroad, and published by an Albanian printer in Sofia, Bulgaria. A skilfully wrought, highly dramatic social drama of the Albanian highlanders themselves, *The Pledge of Honor* is still a favorite with Albanian audiences everywhere. The author, a brother of Albania's most popular poet, Naim Bey Frasheri, is known also for his work on *Albania, Past, Present and Future*. Both the Frasheri brothers were members of the patriotic Bektashi sect.

Albania has enjoyed, historically, at least two generally recognized periods of flowering: the first was the period of Pyrrhus, King of Epirus (in the third century B.C.), when even Rome trembled before its might; the second was that dominated by the fabulous warrior Skënderbeg (fifteenth century).

The earlier of these two periods was made the scene of a patriotic drama, *The Death of Pyrrhus* (1906), printed by the same refugee press in Sofia as had published Frasheri's work. The leading characters of the drama are Pyrrhus and his wife Antigone, step-daughter of Emperor Ptolemy, who, when her husband is killed in a skirmish in Argos, dons the armor of a warrior and leads the Pyrrhic army to victory at the cost of her own life. The play, which is written in verse, has often been produced in the United States and was especially popular here just before the First World War during a visit of its author, Mihal Grameno to this country. Grameno is a native of Korcha (Koritsa) in southern Albania and a member of the Albanian Orthodox Church. He played an active rôle in the guerrilla warfare of the nineteenth century, an experience he describes in his *Albanian Revolt*.

A newspaper *Koha* (*The Times*), edited by Grameno, served for years as the organ of the Albanian underground.

The United States has long been an important center of Albanian publishing activity and it was here in 1907 that the drama *Israelites and Philistines* by Bishop F. S. Noli (1881-   ) was first published. Written in Athens in 1902, the play has its scene in Jerusalem, yet the flavor is Albanian, as are also the problems under discussion. It is a philosophical drama which brings home, by implication, the necessity for an independent Albania. Bishop Noli is the author of the *Story of Skënderbeg* (1921) and of many excellent translations, especially from Shakespeare and Ibsen. He is at present head of the Albanian Orthodox Church in the United States of America. In 1924 he served as Prime Minister of Albania, but is now an American citizen.

The first play in Albanian to be produced publicly on Albanian soil was the verse drama *St. Francis of Assissi* by Father Gjergj Fishta (1856-1941), written in 1909 to commemorate the founding of the Franciscan Order (1209) and staged openly in Scutari, the chief centre of Albanian Catholicism. The work owes its production to the position of special favor occupied by Albanian Franciscans thanks to the protection of Emperor Franz Joseph. The play stresses the human side of the saint. Another play by Father Fishta, never produced, bears the title *The Shepherds of Bethlehem*. It is a drama in verse dealing with the Nativity. In 1921 Father Fishta visited the United States in order to study social problems and their treatment here. At the time of the Axis invasion of Albania he was one of the outstanding figures to resist the new ideology.

An early drama of free Albania was Kristo Floqi's *Faith and Patriotism* (1914), a fast-moving melodrama in verse in which a young Albanian lord of the Moslem faith falls in love with and marries a Christian servant girl who is in the employ of his own aristocratic fiancée. According to its author, the play is "the first drama with a national theme, based on contemporary material and written in Albanian expressly for our own people." It has been produced a number of times in the United States. Floqi has written also several one-act plays as well as other literary works. He is a native of Korcha and a member of the Albanian Orthodox Church.

Two other contemporary Albanian playwrights are Foqion Postoli and Etëhem Haxhiademi. The former trained himself in the art of drama while working in a Massachusetts factory. His sentimental play, *The Mother's Duty*, was often produced in the United States in the twenties and thirties.

Haxhiademi is a classicist and all his dramas are patterned on the classical models of Hellas. All deal with lofty and patriotic themes. To be noted are *Ulysses* (1924), *Achilles* (1926), *Alexander the Great* (1926), *Pyrrhus* (1931), *Diomedes* (1931), and especially *Skënderbeg* (1935), a moving work with a truly Albanian theme and coloring. Haxhiademi is present-day Albania's most promising playwright.

IX

The Netherlands

JAN GRESHOFF

Insofar as it is fitting to generalize, it may be said that the Dutch national character moves between the lyric and the didactic. When, in the seventeenth century, this national character began to define itself clearly, these two tendencies outlined themselves immediately and distinctly. Along all lines and among all classes, life was completely dominated by Christian morality, which maintained a strongly built social culture. The clergy governed spiritual life and politics to a very considerable extent. Escape from this rigidly limited society was practicable as a rule only through the medium of lyric poetry.

The elements for a dramatic and emotional life were wanting. These elements—striking contrasts, almost unbearable tension, the sense of an all-dominating fate—were found in the Middle Ages, however; and so far as Dutch literature is concerned, a truly great dramatic art was in evidence only in that epoch. In every respect the Middle Ages constitute the most important period in Dutch literature. The drama that developed out of the clerical ritual clearly reflected the mixed and spontaneous life of a young world. The dramatic works of that period are almost innumerable. It saw the production of mystery and miracle plays, plays of moral tendency and plays of chivalry. One finds earthly life pictured in farces which, though they fail to satisfy our modern conceptions of good taste, are yet full of rich humanity and action. Systematic study of the Middle Ages began relatively late in Europe, including of course the Netherlands. In what is usually called the Golden Age (that is, the seventeenth century), people looked disdainfully upon all that was Gothic, as they phrased it. Both the architecture and the literature of the Middle Ages were regarded as uncivilized, unintelligible, and of little importance. There was an unbridgeable gap between the then contemporary Baroque and the Gothic, and even our greatest Baroque poet, Joost van den Vondel, who in many respects was still a man of the Middle Ages himself, lacked the "proper" (that is the modern) conception of the true value of Gothic art. It is the inestimable merit of romanticism in the early nineteenth century that it revealed the magnificence of the Middle Ages to humanity. From that moment the current of literature took a new turn also in the Netherlands and, as before stated, nowadays we consider the

Middle Ages to be the greatest art period which Western Europe has ever witnessed. This period is so rich and so varied that we are still unable to take complete stock of its values; and hence the drama of the period has not so far been thoroughly studied, evaluated, and appreciated. Between the era of the Middle Ages—the Gothic—and the Baroque, lies the short and remarkable period which may be characterized as that of the "Rhetorics." The drama was seriously practised, but at the same time it had lost its inner strength and meaning. The present chapter cannot, of course, outline in detail all phases of this development, but something should be said of the Golden Age. The separation of church and theatre had been completed and the drama became secular and worldly. The influence of the classics was still effective, however, and plays were more carefully and self-consciously written than ever before. In the Golden Age the contrast is clearly seen between the Dutch national character and Dutch life as set forth in the theatre. The greatest figure of the period, indeed one of the greatest figures in world literature, is Joost van den Vondel (1567-1679). Vondel's literary output, in which drama occupies an important place, was nevertheless predominantly lyric in character. His dramas are great lyric poems that happen to be suited to the stage. His richly variegated dramatic activities fully blossomed in the trilogy which comprises *Lucifer* (1654), *Adam in Exile* (1663), and *Noah* (1664). It is undeniable that these works possess dramatic qualities, yet in the main, the movement in them remains internal. The principal features are not externalized by physical actions, but by emotions and thoughts. In other words, the internal action dominates the external: they are most significant by reason of the lyric exaltation which runs through them. In Vondel's time a great deal was written for the stage, but none of Vondel's contemporaries equaled him. Pieter Cornelisz Hooft (1547-1626), also a distinguished lyric poet, wrote several historical plays of importance, but these were lacking in strong dramatic conflicts. At that time realistic drama was represented by Gerbrand Adriaansz Breero (1586-1618) and by Constantijn Huygens (1596-1687). The former wrote, among other things, *The Little Moor,* and an excellent character comedy, *The Spanish Brabanter.* Huygens wrote only one play, *Trijntje Cornelis' Daughter,* which featured at its best the life of the ordinary people of the time. He did this in a way which is occasionally extremely vulgar, but at the same time very naturally and with a pronounced gift for setting forth human relationships. This realistic picturing of simple life appeals primarily to Dutch writers. Up to our times the slice-of-life theory as applied to the drama, has from the earliest days remained typical of a great deal of Dutch dramatic writing. In the earlier part of the eighteenth century this type of naturalism was perfected by Pieter Langendijk (1683-1756). The influence of Molière is paramount in his works, yet both in the selection of his subject-matter and in the setting forth of his characters he was typically a product of his land and people. Langendijk, who was historian of the community of Haarlem, was not, it is true, a great artist, but he was fully capable of picturing in an inimitable way the comic peculiarities of the civil life of his time. Before the outbreak of World War II, his plays were still regularly performed in the Netherlands, both by professional and by amateur companies, and met with almost invariable success. Langendijk, though a man of his time, succeeded in making his subjects so universally human that they can still be appreciated by modern audiences. It is rather surprising that no one has yet modernized his plays: such plays as *Don Quixote, The Mutual Deceit of Marriage, The Mathematicians,* and *Quincampoix or the Jobbers,* could, with very few modifications, be transformed into effective pieces that would long remain in the popular repertory. His outstanding play is the farce *Crelis Louwen or Alexander the Great at the Poets' Feast* (1715). In recent times Jan Musch, one of Holand's most famous actors, has triumphed unnumbered times in the part of Crelis Louwen.

L. Simons, the well-known specialist on the Dutch theatre, gives in his manual *Drama and Stage in their Development* a correct description of Langendijk's position and importance in his day. He presents him as the central figure in a busy life which gave him a chance to get acquainted with many types of people. Langendijk, who lived the life of a more or less representative citizen in his world, offered in his plays a reflection of the world in which he played his part, but as a comic poet he ably unmasked the superficialities of his day and with a mixture of friendly mockery and bitter satire he created a world of characters both comic and true to life. Langendijk dominated the stage of the eighteenth century. Toward the end of that century, however, a Frisian nobleman, Onno Zwier Van Haren (1711-1779), published a play called *Agon, Sultan of Bantam* (1769). It is of no particular literary value, but is a work that is mentioned in all Dutch histories of literature because in it for the first time a Javanese motive was utilized for literary purposes. It was not until the middle of the nineteenth century that a play of outstanding importance was to make its appearance. The first play of Eduard Douwes Dekker (1820-1887), the writer who attained world fame under the name of Multatuli, was *The Bride Above*. That play was of little value and is now practically forgotten, but his later play, *School for Princes,* had more substance and remained a favorite in Holland until well into the twentieth century.

Since the literatures of Western Europe are so closely interrelated, it is noteworthy that Romanticism in the Netherlands failed to stimulate the writing of a stage play of any importance, whereas during the same period Romanticism in France reached its climax in the work of several playwrights. No trace can be found of either a direct or an indirect influence emanating from Victor Hugo in the dramatic work of the Netherlands. The Romanticism that is evident in the Netherlands showed itself exclusively in lyric works and reached its culmination there much later than elsewhere.

It is true that during the second half of the nineteenth century the Dutch public showed a lively interest in the theatre, but the writers themselves stood aloof. At all times the country had and still has actors of great talent and wide experience, but only exceptionally do these artists get a chance to display their very real ability in new and original work. The repertory for many decades before and after 1900 consisted mostly of translations of French melodramas, English comedies, and German farces. Louis Bouwmeester, the greatest actor in the history of the Netherlands theatre, and his no less talented sister Theo Mann-Bouwmeester, celebrated their greatest triumphs in foreign plays.

When between 1870 and 1900 a complete renewal of spiritual life made its appearance in the Netherlands, some of the younger writers began to pay attention to the theatre. This renewal was symbolized by two names. Reference is made here to the *New Guide* movement, since in the magazine of that name the authors of the time expressed their ideas and published their work. The same thing also is true of the Movement of Eighty, so named because that movement attained its peak in 1880. Three of the most important authors of the *New Guide* dedicated themselves to a great extent, and with obvious enthusiasm, to the stage. Albert Verwey dreamed of a rebirth of the verse drama and wrote two plays on themes taken from the history of his country, *Jacoba of Bavaria* (1902) and *Johan of Oldenbarnevelt* (1895). Much later he made one of his most important contributions to the stage, the Renaissance drama *Cola Rienzi* (1910). This last has become a classic of Dutch literature, and up to the present time it stands as one of the great monuments of Dutch dramatic writing. It is unfortunate that no effort has ever been made to produce it.

Verwey's brother-in-law, Frederick van Eeden (1860-1932), began his career as a playwright. He was an enthusiastic and devoted writer, and continued to contribute to the theatre as long as he lived. His first efforts were student farces, which revealed his sharp eye for stage effects and at the same time showed that the young author was capable of writing excellent dialogue. After publishing several collections of poems, studies, and novels, van Eeden published in 1894 his dramatic masterpiece, one of the outstanding works of Dutch literature, originally bearing the title of *The Brothers' Feud,* later rebaptized *The Brothers*. It is a lyric piece with marked social tendencies in which the author exposes his social philosophy. It is uncertain whether *The Brothers* has ever reached the stage; certainly if so, it was not through the professional theatre. Because of its want of technical skill, it would be difficult but by no means impossible to produce it on the stage. Frederick van Eeden was a medical doctor, a social reformer, and a novelist, yet he found time to write a number of stage plays of varying degrees of merit. *The Witch of Haarlem* (1915), a lively and moving historical play, engaging and human, should be mentioned together with a few others, particularly *Minstrel* (1907), *The Palace of Circe* (1910), *The Goat Ride or the Skeleton* (1917), *and Ijsbrand* (1908).

The third great figure in the Eighty Movement, a man who took particular interest in the stage, is Herman Heijermans. Though he wrote several novels and short stories, he was predominantly a playwright and the stage was his natural means of expression. An ardent supporter of the social-democratic movement, which at that time in the Netherlands was still young and ambitious, he put his great dramatic talents to the service and glorification of his social ideals. Van Eeden did this also, but by more indirect means, his exalted lyric and symbolic work not being clearly understood by the masses. But Heijermans mastered the art and craft of the theatre. Rarely have the Dutch people ever been so concerned over the development of a talent as they were over that of Heijermans. Practically all his plays roused considerable excitement and admiration, except for a small group "in the other camp" who were vehemently indignant. By means of his famous play, called in English *The Good Hope* (1901), he reached all the world— the first time such a thing had happened with the work of any Dutch playwright. It was translated into all European languages and has been also produced more than once in the United States. Thanks to this play, the wretched conditions which prevailed in the fishery trade were completely changed under the pressure of public wrath. Every one of Heijermans' plays has a clear social message, which occasionally is overaccentuated, but it must be said that because of his extraordinary talent Heijermans at least presents his problem in the clearest terms, in spite of whatever reverberations on the part of the public may be aroused. *The Good Hope* was followed by *The Armor, Ora et Labora, Blossoming Month,* and *Links.* In 1905 came *All Souls' Day,* a play that met with enormous success and precipitated equally strong protests. In some towns performances were even forbidden.

Every year in November or December the opening of a new Heijermans play was the big event in Dutch theatrical life, one for which all theatre-lovers had been eagerly waiting. *All Souls' Day* was followed by *Relief* (1907), *The Strange Hunt* (1907), *The Maid* (1907), *The Rising Sun* (1911), *Rusk with Candy* (1911), *Glueck Auf,* and *Eva Bonheur,* and in 1915 came *The Wise Tom-Cat,* one of Heijermans' wittiest and at the same time profoundest works.

The dominating influence of the period during which Heijermans was the most outstanding representative must be attributed to Ibsen and the young Hauptmann, the Hauptmann of *The Weavers.* Mention should be made of Marcellus Emants, a somewhat older contemporary of Heijermans. Compared with Heijermans, however, Emants was chiefly, by natural bent, a novelist. But he wrote several plays of some importance, of which *The Power of Stupidity* ranks first.

Apart from the Movement of Eighty and extending up to the present time, one may distinguish two clearly separated conceptions of artistic intent and idea, trends that were sharply opposed one to the other. The substance of this statement can be more clearly illustrated by offering two examples among the plays already cited: *All Souls' Day* and *The Brothers,* the first by Heijermans and the second by van Eeden. Lyric drama provides, at least in the Netherlands, a striking example of such a contrast because nearly all the examples that could be named are outstanding works, so far as the whole of Dutch literature is concerned. All the real "monuments" are lyric dramas: *The Rebels* by Henriette Roland Holst (1869-   ) is the first masterpiece arising from the young socialist movement in the Netherlands. In it the liberation of the laboring classes, which according to the author coincides with the liberation of mankind, is glorified. Generally speaking, *The Rebels* is the greatest work this woman poet has produced. Her importance in Dutch literature can hardly be overestimated. Both as poet and as author of literary studies, of philosophic-economic treatises, and of historical pictures, she is unparalleled in Dutch literature. She also played an important political rôle during the long middle period of her literary life. Besides *The Rebels* the dramatic output of Henriette Holst includes the drama *Thomas More.* The construction is firmer and more clearly outlined, and the play has more magnificent speeches than *The Rebels.* But taken as a whole, it lacks the lyric inspiration and movement of that earlier play. In later years Henriette Holst wrote several radio plays, mostly on behalf of religio-socialistic youth organizations. In these too one recognizes constantly the master's touch of Holland's greatest woman poet; yet as compared with the dramatic work of Dutch writers as a group, these last are of relatively minor importance.

Pandora (1919) is the only stage play of Arthur van Schendel (1874-   ), who is looked upon as Holland's greatest novelist, and *Astrid* is the only work of a younger author, Madeleine Bothlingk. Van Schendel's subject-matter is taken from the Italian Renaissance and Madeleine Bothlingk's stems from Norse mythology. It is not to the credit of the Dutch acting companies that none of the above-mentioned plays, which are of such supreme importance to Dutch spiritual life, has ever been staged. This statement also applies, so far as I am able to determine, to *Cola Rienzi, The Brothers,* and *The Rebels.* There is no doubt that the performance of such plays would involve producers in serious technical difficulties, yet it should be borne in mind that the difficulties mentioned are such as any competent stage director would be able to surmount. But the cause of the situation lies much deeper. Few Dutch acting companies are subsidized, and those that are receive insufficient grants; consequently they are forced to support themselves out of their box-office receipts. Hence they are unable to undertake big or expensive ventures. Since there is very little interest shown by the Dutch public for experiments of this sort, and since a performance of one of the above-mentioned masterpieces would require a very heavy investment, without any chance of breaking even, the situation is clear. Genuinely important dramatic work under present economic conditions is impossible in Holland without generous state, provincial, and community subsidies. The acting companies must be exempted from the bitter struggle for daily existence, a struggle which forces them very largely to select popular hits. As long as this deplorable situation exists, so long as good plays cost fortunes and bad plays produce fortunes, there is no room for a flourishing dramatic life without permanent and generous official support. If, as conditions are now, so large a number of plays important to Dutch spiritual life fail to reach the stage, it is evident that something is basically wrong with the Dutch theatre.

The realistic plays, plays of society and everyday life, have proved to be more in keeping with the desires and tastes of the average theatre-goer than the more ambitious literary works just mentioned. Among the popular products that have reached the stage during the past few decades may be mentioned the voluminous works of Josine Simone Mees. Her dramatic output consists exclusively of stage pieces. Two of her plays, *The Conqueror* (1906) and *Atie's Marriage* (1907), have been familiar to the Dutch stage for many years. Mme Mees seeks for more delicate psychological modulations and variations in her work than were possible to Heijermans, even if he had been interested in treating such matters in his plays. But she lacks Heijermans' masculine grasp of technical problems, his preponderant energy, and his love of life. Along with Mme Mees, one should mention Frans Mijnssen (1872-   ), another writer who has turned out only plays. He goes much further indeed in the direction of literary and psychological refinement. In his work he tries to dramatize states of mind, with the result that many of his plays, which are for the most part one-acters, hardly extend beyond the limits of subtle dialogue. The dramatic element, if any, is, as it were, almost completely internalized. No one ever denied Mijnssen qualities of intelligence, but one wonders whether it is possible to write for the stage with so little vitality. The value of Mijnssen's work is realized not on the stage but by reading what he writes.

During the period from 1905 to 1920 a number of writers, successful in other fields, made attempts at play writing. Well-known novelists like Top Naeff (1878-   ) and others wrote plays which received some notice and respect. However, the first "born" playwright on the scene was Jan Fabricius (1871-   ), who sought to escape from the ever-narrowing tradition of the ordinary play of everyday life by romanticizing it. At the outset of his career he found his themes and plots in the life of the people in the Netherlands and the Indies, but in his later products he introduced more popular elements by using contemporary types. However, at the same time he resorted also to the use of mythology. Fabricius was a fertile playwright, some of whose plays met with enormous popular success. Their literary value is a different matter: it is in many cases almost negligible. Yet he wrote one very touching play which throughout the years has not lost its appeal: *Lonely* (1907) pictures the mental and physical breakdown of a Dutchman on a desolate island in the Moluccas. It includes most of the characteristics of a "good" play. The psychology is deep and sound, and the work as a whole is plastically alive. Its thematic ideas are few but valid. The very peculiar atmosphere of tropical seclusion is matchlessly created. With all his weakness as an artist, Jan Fabricius proved nevertheless to be a marvelous expert of the stage and shows himself a robust personality who was able by his gifts to dominate Dutch dramatic art in his day, though this applies particularly to the beginning years of his career.

The desire for a romantic setting forth of life in the theatre was expressed in an exaggerated way through the work of A. W. G. van Riemsdkijk, who wrote a large number of inferior plays which, however, managed to fill the theatres to capacity. Some of his plays were performed hundreds of times in spite of the fact that critical opinion condemned them.

Comedy, which apparently does not appeal fundamentally to the Dutch national character, is rarely practised, but during the period just referred to C. P. van Rossum wrote several examples with considerable success. He wrote a large number of light comedies, of which *Pomarius* was the most successful. The title comes from the name of the chief character, a swindling solicitor, and is considered one of the best examples of comedy in Dutch literature.

It is hoped that the present brief résumé, which is merely an attempt to set forth a few of the highlights of Dutch dramatic art, will indicate the chief trends and prime categories. It will be seen that Holland's stage literature is not without importance, but that as compared with the works that grew out of the Romantic Movement, particularly the lyric works, its place is relatively humble. While a few incidental dramatic masterpieces and some well-conceived and well-written plays came out of the Dutch theatre, the nation as a whole has lacked an uninterrupted stage tradition.

X

Spain and Spanish America

MILDRED ADAMS

Five years before his death in 1916 José Echegaray received the Nobel Prize. In accord with the will of its donor it went to him for "the most distinguished work of idealist tendency" in the field of literature. He did not get the whole of it for 1909—half went to Frédéri Mistral of Provence. But even partial recognition by the Nobel Prize Committee so annoyed the then younger generation (which was the so-called generation of '98) that they made public protest against it. Thus he suffered the fate that awaited innovators then as it does now. Progress had moved faster than he had, and the man who broke the mold of nineteenth-century play writing and brought modern drama to Spain was in his turn frowned upon as old-fashioned by the generation that crowded at his heels.

Reading his plays at this distance it is hard to see how some of them could have caused a furor in the first place or why, in the second place, they were awarded even half the Nobel Prize. Yet the comments of his contemporaries cannot be disregarded. Benito Pérez Galdós, novelist and critic, who was himself writing plays about the same time, describes "the brilliant apparition of the genius of Echegaray on the Spanish scenes." He "broke up worn-out forms and imbued the actors' art with a new strength and new resources. He electrified the general public and threw among the critics a fearful whirlwind of fervent enthusiasms struggling with the lukewarm opinions of routine." And George Bernard Shaw, reviewing two of his plays in translation said, "I suspect the Spaniards will compel us to admit that they have produced a genius of a stamp that crosses frontiers, and that we shall get some of his work on our own stage." [1]

In view of such praise it is necessary to put aside the critical standards of 1943, and for a true picture of his place in play writing look at the theatre into which Echegaray's plays erupted like "a thundering, flashing hurricane which changed discreet emotions into violent passions."

It was a circumspect, not to say stodgy theatre, devoted to three-act plays in traditional verse forms, concerned (to quote Díez Canedo) "with legendary subjects in which the history was very freely treated and the legend turned out to be the pure invention of the author." Only certain set sub-

---

[1] G. B. Shaw, *Dramatic Opinions and Essays* (New York, Brentano's, 1906), p. 89.

jects could be treated, only certain kinds of people were thought worthy of a dramatist's attention. Stage stereotypes of romantic heroes, shadowed by cardboard servants, came and went and loved and died in attitudes and with sentiments dear to Sardou and Dumas fils. There had been a flare of colorful writing earlier in the century when *Don Alvaro* by the Duque de Rivas tore at the heartstrings of Madrid's best. But that (with the exception of Zorilla's *Don Juan Tenorio* which still lives) had withered away. The stage was reduced to the dimensions of a poor puppet show, without new plots, without new life, without excitement. Any upholstered matron of the upper class could go to the theatre as safely as she went to church, and with no more danger of being shocked or transported out of her traditional attitudes. She knew where to sigh "Ay de mi alma." And where to nod approval. Neither Ayala nor Tamayo y Baus offered any puzzle to her correct responses.

Echegaray changed all that. A famous mathematician and teacher of mathematics, a high-ranking politician, member of the cabinet of the short-lived first Spanish Republic, he was exiled to France when Alfonso de Borbón took the Spanish throne and became Alfonso XII. That year, 1874, Echegaray wrote his first play.

El libro talonario is just a one-act play, romantic, neo-romantic if you like. Were all of Echegaray no better he would not figure in books like this as the founder of modern Spanish drama. But something was there which won it a hearing, and that same year, before the public's enthusiasm could cool he wrote another, *La esposa del vengador,* which, though it was still poetic melodrama, had more feeling for reality, moved closer to the realism that was to be the new attitude.

In 1877 Ibsen, then hardly known outside his own Norway, wrote *Brand*. That same year in the southernmost country of Europe Echegaray wrote *O locura o santidad*. There is no proof that the Spaniard knew of the Norwegian at that time and every reason to suppose that he did not. The two plays are not much alike. But there is in both of them a social sense which is the unmistakable mark of the new drama. When *El Gran Galeoto* (1881) came along five years later, the theme of society as a force that could make or break the individual, that had power and should have a corresponding sense of responsibility, was fully formed. Society was the villain of the play, a villain against which the lonely hero and heroine, however pure of heart, struggled in vain.

Ibsen wrote *Ghosts* in 1881 and in 1892 Echegaray wrote *El hijo de don Juan*. Its last line bows to Ibsen with the famous "Give me the sun, Mother," and its hero is doomed to madness as the result of his father's wild indulgences. It was the beginning of an era when "social diseases," hitherto mentioned only in whispers by the previous generation, were to become the favorite material of novelists and playwrights alike, sure to shock each new generation of débutantes and their mothers for at least forty years. This play was translated into English and reviewed by Shaw in 1895. In spite of the use of the famous Ibsen line, he found that Echegaray's "treatment of the *Ghosts* theme is perfectly original: there is not a shadow of the peculiar moral attitude of Ibsen."

And when after having reviewed *Mariana,* which was translated at the same time, Shaw saw it on the London stage, he wrote the lines which have probably done more than anything else to perpetuate Echegaray's fame among English readers.[1] English women, he said, can never

...look at Mariana and say "But for the grace of God there go I" as they do at Ibsen's plays. But with this reservation the play is a masterly one. Not only have we in it an eminent degree of dramatic wit, imagination, sense of idiosyncracy, and power over words...but we have the drawing-room presented from the point of view of a man of the world in the largest sense.

Drawing-rooms were important in those days.

That was the good side of Echegaray. His fame rests on those plays, with perhaps the addition of *El loco Diós,* and *La desequilibrada* which is still a star's vehicle in South America. Every one who writes about him adds one or two other personal favorites.

The bad side lay in his lush use of melodrama, his neglect of character as such, his devotion to lurid effects and stage tricks. Though he started relatively late in life (he was forty-two when his first play was produced) he developed the same frightening fecundity which ever since Lope de Vega's day has been a continuing characteristic of Spanish playwrights. He has six or eight plays whose names are repeated by commentators, but he wrote some sixty-five in all. The general effect of them is perhaps conveyed by a sonnet of his describing his method, which S. G. Morley has translated into prose:[2]

I choose a passion, I take an idea, a problem, a character, and I bury it, like a mass of dynamite, in the depths of a personage whom my mind creates. The plot places about the protagonist a certain number of puppets who either wallow in the mire or are warmed by divine fire. I light the fuse. The fire spreads, the cartridge explodes, and the chief character is the one who suffers.

Echegaray had disciples while he lived. The Catalan Feliu y Codina who wrote in Castilian; Joaquín Dicenta whose *Juan José* put radical policies and working-men's lives on the scandalized Madrid stage; Eugenio Sellés who wrote in *El nudo gordiano* of that subject which is now taboo in Spain, divorce; Leopoldo Cano and José López Pinillos are in some measure to be considered his pupils. But for twenty years, from 1874 to 1894, it was Echegaray who ruled the Spanish stage. That year Jacinto Benavente's first play, *El nido ajeno,* appeared. But the old master continued to turn out

[1] *Ibid.,* p. 189.
[2] S. G. Morley, "José Echegaray," *University of California Chronicle,* Vol. 27, No. 4 (October, 1925).

plays for twenty years longer, holding his audience against both the disintegrating effect of *género chico* and the flooding competition of younger men.

His most formidable contemporary rival, Benito Pérez Galdós, was no real rival, because he preferred to be a novelist. The English scholar Aubrey Bell, says "the two most marked features in Spanish literature in the last third of the nineteenth century were the success of the novel and the rise of criticism," and Pérez Galdós is one of the reasons for that comment. But he found time while writing a hundred novels to turn out at least nineteen plays whose distinguishing characteristic was the skill and depth with which people in them were portrayed. He was not, as Echegaray was, a lover of stage tricks, of rhetoric in the grand manner, of shockers either verbal or visual. People and the motives that move them were what he dealt in, and therefore *El abuelo, La de San Quintín,* or *Doña Perfecta,* which was adapted from his novel of the same name, have far more life today than do the more spectacular plays of the first Spaniard to win half the Nobel Prize.

There are critics who think that if Pérez Galdós had written more plays, if his great talents had found the stage more congenial and the publishers less so, the *género chico* would not have broken the drama "into small pieces and divorced it from literature." But those who argue thus neglect the place which *género chico* has played in the whole long history of the Spanish stage. No less distinguished an English critic than Aubrey Bell says, "It was in the revolutionary year of 1868 that the Teatro de Recreo at Madrid began the vogue of one-hour pieces; the success obtained with this new departure caused the movement to spread rapidly." [1] But you will read his whole discussion without finding any mention of the fact that *zarzuelas, revistas líricas, sainetes* and their kind were forms of writing for the stage that were invented long before 1868.

Pedro Salinas, in his excellent study of twentieth-century Spanish literature, establishes the true genealogy of the *género chico*. It seems, he says,[2]

... to mark a very ancient trend in Spanish dramatic art. Coincidental with the most original and important products of our theatre there appear throughout the years works which are the farthest possible extreme from the cult of drama or the highly stylized. Their popularity is elemental, primary, simply organized. In Lope de Reuda it is the *paso* coming along at the same time as the Italianate comedy; in Cervantes, the *entremés* at the same time as *Numancia* or the *Rufián;* in the eighteenth century, the *sainete* of Ramón de la Cruz along with neo-classic experiments.

At times, as in the Cervantes *entremés* (a word which is still found on Spanish menus to designate olives, celery, hors-d'œuvres, or other small accompaniments to the main dishes) this lesser theatre took on literary

---
[1] Aubrey Bell, *Contemporary Spanish Literature* (New York, Alfred A. Knopf, 1925), p. 157.
[2] Pedro Salinas, *Literatura Española, Siglo XX* (Mexico City, Editorial Seneca, 1941).

dignity. At times, as in a prone moment of its cycle about 1910, "it descended into a competition in punning, abandoned the character sketch for topical allusions and ... ceased even to be a faithful mirror of life."

But Bell is wrong in assuming that its end was therefore at hand. The *género chico,* whether in the form of one-act topical comedies, song and dance acts, or operettas, is an integral part of Spanish theatrical life, whether in the homeland or in the South American countries that were once Spanish colonies. As long as the theatre endures it will keep reappearing. Sometimes it becomes so slight as to be truly *género ínfimo,* and seems about to disappear underground. Sometimes it takes to a wandering street-corner life as in the "teatro de carpa" of Mexico. And somehow in its lowest depths it gathers from the earthy people to whom it plays a strength and a vitality that makes its way up through the ranks and gives new vigor to the more self-conscious major theatre.

The best modern example of this phenomenon is Don Carlos Arniches, born in Alicante in 1866 and until his death in 1943 the unpredictable of the Spanish stage. He comes, as Salinas says, "not exactly from the realm of pure letters," but "from the zone of direct theatrical producers, from the purveyors of the first rank of repertory which the modern theatre demands with such voracity." His first play, *La casa editorial,* was produced when he was only twenty-two, and he has turned out every known variety of stage entertainment since. *Sainetes, zarzuelas, revistas líricas,* comedies, and stark and beautiful tragedies—he has run the gamut. As usual with these fantastically fertile writers no count can be sure to be accurate. He has made Madrid laugh, whistle, or weep for half a century, and even though his production slowed down in these latter years it would certainly average three or four plays a year, which would put him up around the two-hundred mark.

His first real success was *La leyenda del monje* in 1890. He followed that with *El Santo de la Isidra, Las estrellas, La Fiesta de San Antón, Sandías y Melones, San Juan de Luz, El puñao de rosas.* From then on his reputation as a writer of minor theatre was established, but the jump to major theatre, bidding for the serious attention of the critics, was thereby the more difficult. He made it in 1916 with *La Señorita de Trévelez,* a drama of the village old maid who is the butt of loafers' jokes. Ramón Pérez de Ayala, novelist and critic, was the first to render him the praise he sought. *Es mi hombre* appeared in 1921 to reinforce the growing body of what are now called grotesque tragedies, a form which can almost be said to be the invention of Arniches. The hero of *Es mi hombre* is a minor employee in a gambling house, kicked around by every one up to the point where the only thing he has left to be proud of, his daughter, is threatened by the hangers-on. At that point he rises above his own humility and becomes for the moment and the situation a hero.

This transfiguration of the less fortunate among human beings under the one stimulus which can raise them out of themselves is the stock theme of Arniches' grotesque tragedies. The gambling-house employee in *Es mi hombre,* the ribbon clerk who falls in love with a famous actress in *La Diosa ríe,* drudges and street cleaners and café waiters found in him an interpreter and a friend. Not that he wore rose-colored glasses in their presence. The working-men that Joaquín Dicenta put on the stage in 1895 in *Juan José* were there in the interests of social drama and carried a message. The proletariat of Carlos Arniches are what they are—men defeated by life, but having a human dignity that asks no quarter of a political doctrine. The differing values of the two approaches may be indicated by the fact that whereas the critics still make their bows to Dicenta, the working-men crowd to see themselves in any theatre in which Arniches is played.

Enrique Díez Canedo, poet and scholar, whose attitude toward this strange genius is one of even-handed praise and criticism, repeats the saying that the Madrid *chulo* (a word which is as untranslatable as the native to whom it applies) "learned to talk in Arniches' works. Not that there was any attempt to correct his slang, but that he found there terms of speech and phrase so perfectly adjusted to his mentality that he forthwith adopted them for his own." He credits Arniches with peculiar gifts of wit and observation, and an unusual ability to create types and even language. And Salinas tops the laurel wreath with this final judgment,[1]

Thus Arniches, popular writer and popularizer, emerging from a background that was wholly of the theatre, has entered today into that lofty eminence of literary esteem which formally was conceded only to those authors of a cultivated and lettered past. He now figures in the first rank of our contemporary dramatists.

We have described the work of Arniches at such length for three reasons —first because he is the outstanding playwright in an extremely popular sector of the Spanish theatre which is too often given less than its full value by foreign observers, a sector which is native to and characteristic of the Spanish stage; second because he made the difficult transition from minor to major theatre and has the unusual distinction of looming large in both fields; third, because in point of time and of type, he forms a kind of bridge between the great days of Echegaray and the greater days of Jacinto Benavente.

It must not, however, be thought that he was alone in his field. Perhaps his most famous rival was Don Pedro Muñoz Seca, who was born in 1881 in Puerto de Santa María, where so much sherry comes from. Parody was his dish—particularly parody of the more serious poetic theatre—and wisecracks his passion. Those who did not approve of his influence on the theatre included the more thoughtful critics who deplored the cynicism and flippancy of his farces which, they said, ridiculed theatrical values and perverted the public taste. *El verdugo de Sevilla, Los cuatro Robinsons, La barba de Carrillo* are samples of his title-making. He had a marked tendency

[1] Salinas, *op. cit.,*

to flout moral values with a wisecrack; he upheld the pudgy right arm of General Franco with much fervor.

Others famous in the field of *género chico* are Xavier de Burgos whose *Hoy, sale hoy*, written in 1884 in collaboration with Ricardo de la Vega (who wrote perhaps the most famous of the *zarzuelas, La Verbena de la Paloma*) is still played; the distinguished poet Carlos Fernandez Shaw, who wrote *La Revoltosa* in 1897 with José López Silva; Luceño Tomás who is sometimes described as the father of *género chico* because in 1870 he revived the *sainete* in such pieces as *Cuadros al fresco, El arte por las nubes*, and *El teatro moderno;* Vital Aza whose *El Señor Cura* is still a favorite among amateur groups in Mexico, though his *Tiquis Miquis* is perhaps better known in Spain; Miguel Ramos Carrión who collaborated with Aza in *Los lobos marinos* and whose most famous play was the liquid *Agua, azucarilios y aguardiente;* Felipe Pérez y González whose *La Gran Vía*, first played in 1886, is still famous, and its first night still one of those theatrical legends which old men recount with glowing eyes.

These men had a host of able musicians working with them—Manuel Fernández Caballero, Ruperto Chapí, Tomás Bretón (who wrote the music for *La Verbena de la Paloma*), Don Amadeo Vives, Federico Chueca. In their *zarbuelas* they produced a body of light opera that rivals Gilbert and Sullivan, Victor Herbert, and Harry B. Smith. That they have not been adapted in any volume for the American stage is one of the puzzles of international play exchange.

A less successful divergent from the main line of Spanish play writing, and one which has, for the moment at least, totally disappeared, is the Catalan theatre. Catalonians would, of course, claim that it was no divergent, but a stream of original theatre genius breaking out from under the suppression of an alien tongue. They talk that way in Catalonia.

The Catalan theatre began with Frederich Soler (1839-1895) who was the moving spirit in the organization called La Gata—a group whose purpose was to create a dramatic literature in Catalan for the people whose native tongue it was. The movement profited greatly from the coöperation of Angel Guímera, born in the Canary Islands but spending most of his life in Barcelona, and therefore speaking—and writing—Catalan. It also profited from the work of the painter Santiago Rusiñol, of José Feliu y Codina who was a friend of Echegaray, and of the director of Adria Gual.

The movement was partly artistic, and of high merit. The plays by these Catalans have a very real part in any account of the modern theatre. But the artistic impulse was fed and supported by political separatism. However much one may admire the courage of those small groups that sought to stimulate artistic productions of plays written in a minority language, the cold fact is that the Catalan dramatists owe their reputation largely to the generosity of men in other parts of Spain who translated their best works into Castilian (Echegaray translated Guimerá, Benavente translated Rusiñol) and thus made them available to a larger audience than the Catalonians could possibly have commanded by themselves.

How much life the Catalan literary movement had within itself, whether it could have gathered strength enough to flourish of and by itself, independent of politics, are questions that are now largely academic. It was already showing signs of weakness when Primo de Rivera, Spain's first dictator, stopped the separatist tide on which it fed. He took office in the 1920's and ordered Catalonia to join the rest of Spain in using Castilian. From 1931 to 1936, under the Republic, there was a recovery within the political movement. The Catalonians unlimbered their tongues again and enjoyed such spoken and written lingual autonomy that travelers complained. But five years of freedom was not long enough for the resurrection of the Catalan theatre. It remains today what it has been since its decline during World War I—an interesting flash of play-writing genius in a minority tongue, whose value now is largely historical.

In the sixteenth century that prodigy of nature Lope de Vega Carpio, who created the Spanish theatre, wrote in that process some 1800 plays, of which over four hundred survive. Ever since his day Spanish dramatists have been driven by his example into an attempt to rival that record. Fortunately for the modern critic, who would have to try to keep up with so stupendous a production, they have so far failed. Carlos Arniches and Jacinto Benavente, both of whom were born in 1866 and one of whom at the age of seventy-eight is still writing, have done their best. But glutton as the Spanish stage is for plays, it cannot absorb more than four or five a season from a single author. Arniches passed the fiftieth anniversary of his first play in 1938. Benavente comes to his in 1944. Both men are credited with somewhere around two hundreds plays apiece. So are the Alvarez Quinteros, who were born half a dozen years later. It was the number to which any dramatist had to aspire in the first four decades of the twentieth century if he wished to be considered a man of the theatre "en serio."

From the vantage point of 1944, with the world at war and Spain in the grip of a dictator who has turned the clock hands back, those first four decades (or three and a half of them, to be precise) look like a second golden age—Benavente for serious drama, Martínez Sierra and the Quinteros for charm, Linares Rivas, Carlos Arniches, Muñoz Seca, and a crowd of lesser competitors writing farces and musical comedies, Eduardo Marquina charged with the poetic tradition. And in the late 1929's and early 1930's a flood of promising new talent that was just beginning to offer sturdy challenge to the older men.

Part of it was what Manuel Altolaguirre calls "sleeping theatre," that is, the theatre of literary men whose work is more often seen lying between book covers than taking living form on the stage. The brothers Machado, fine poets and late comers to the theatre, belong in this list. *La Lola se va a los Puertos*, which with its rollicking title was done in 1929, was their most famous play. They followed it with a satire on political life, *La prima Fernanda* and a delightful bandit comedy, *La Duquesa de Benamejí*. Ramón Gómez de la Serna, who combined scholarship with surrealist clowning, and whose *Los Medios Seres* narrowly escaped being a *succès de scandale,* belongs in this group. So does the producer Cipriano Rivas Cherif (now serving life sentence as a political prisoner in one of Franco's jails) whose *El caracol* proved that he knew how to write plays as well as to put them on. And Eduardo Ugarte, who was Lorca's collaborator in the three seasons' journeyings (1931-1934) of La Barraca, and who is now in Mexico. And that most untheatrical of literary men Azorín, with his plays headed by mocking English titles *Old Spain* and *Brandy, mucho Brandy!* All of them were playwrights on the side, contributing greatly to the quality of the theatre, but not much to its quantity.

Then in 1936 the generals rose up and turned life into death on the stage as in the streets and the roads and the upland fields from Andalusia to the Basque country.

And because the Spanish theatre has always lived close to the heart of Spanish life, it died too. Died in spirit and in personages. Serafín Alvarez Quintero died in the spring of 1939, after the Republic had finally surrendered to the rebellious general and his Axis aides. Antonio Machado died in the moment of that defeat. The wife of Martínez Sierra died, she who had collaborated in all his writing and never signed a single play (some say she did much of the work, and indeed he has been silent since her death); Muñoz Seca with his meretricious wit died. Valle Inclán, whose plays emerged from the library to the stage all too infrequently, died in the first year of the war. Miguel de Unamuno, playwright as well as philosopher, died in 1936, a rebel to the last, though it finally meant rebelling against rebellion. And the youngest genius of them all, Federico García Lorca whose talents in the theatre were just beginning to unfold, died victim of the fascist scourge that was to plunge the whole world into war.

So the marvelous decades are ended now, and this is a good moment to survey them quite coolly.

From the point of view of the world theatre those decades gave Spain two Nobel Prize winners—Echegaray with his half prize in 1909, and Benavente with the whole prize in 1922. They brought it recognition from the outside world such as it had not had since the great days of Calderón. They tied it into a world current of good play writing that included such diverse figures as Pirandello and Andreyev, O'Neill and Bernard Shaw. Spain's plays were translated into French, Italian, German, English. Martínez Sierra, the Quinteros, Benavente were played with great acclaim in London and New York by the foremost stars of the two capitals. Nance O'Neil in Benavente's *Malquerida* (played here under the title *The Passion Flower*); Otis Skinner in the Quinteros' *Papa Juan* (called here *A Hundred Years Old*); and Ethel Barrymore in Martínez Sierra's *El Reino de Dios* (*The Kingdom of God*) and *Canción de cuna* (*Cradle Song*) gave them the best of Broadway playing in the late twenties and early thirties.

Thanks to this enthusiasm, and to the energy of their translators, the works of the internationally famous four can easily be studied by people who do not read Spanish. Benavente is represented by four volumes put into English by the indefatigable John Garrett Underhill, and half a dozen other plays of his have been separately translated. Martínez Sierra (and his wife) had the good fortune to attract Helen and Harley Granville-Barker whose English versions of the ten or more plays they translated flow with the same warm charm and gentle raillery as did the Spanish originals. They also did two volumes of the Quintero plays.

And what about the lasting values of this extraordinary spurt of modern theatre talent in terms of the history of the Spanish theatre? What do these playwrights look like, now that the marvelous decades are split off from the age in which we live by a war that has cracked the world apart?

The playwrights of that period fall automatically into groups. The first are the "serious" playwrights, men with literary standing who practised their vocation in the theatre. Don Jacinto Benavente was the acknowledged leader of these from 1922, his Nobel Prize year, on. Martínez Sierra belongs in this group, and the sunny Quinteros, of whom Enrique Díez Canedo wrote so discerningly, "When their fertile genius aids them the Quinteros accomplish marvels, when they weaken they fall into complete banality. Integrity of composition, however, palliates their worst defects."

So much has been written about Jacinto Benavente that until a definite study of all his plays is made after his death, there are only foot-notes to be added to the existing critical opinion. No other Spanish playwright of any other period has been so amply translated into English. John Garrett Underhill has published four volumes of translation, each containing four plays. And in addition to these sixteen there are other single plays done by Underhill and by others.

Translators' prefaces contain a mine of laudatory information. Walter Starkie has written a whole volume entitled *Jacinto Benavente* in which he classifies the playwright's work into periods and analyzes the characteristics of each period for the benefit of the inquiring student. Aubrey Bell writes at length concerning individual plays before 1925. Díez Canedo carries on the discussion further. George Freedley and John Adams Reeves have neatly summed up evidence for the praisers and the critics in their *History of the Theatre*.

The sum of it all seems to be that Benavente's work marks both the rise and fall of the well-made play in the twentieth-century Spanish theatre. Whether you like him or not he is there in the center of the stage from 1907, when he crowned his first period with *Los intereses creados* (the Theatre Guild's first offering in 1919 under the title *Bonds of Interest*) through *La Malquerida,* which was the most notable play of his second period up to 1931, when such a play as the popular *Cuando los hijos de Eva no son hijos de Adán* represented only the husk of what he might once have done. He is still in Madrid, still writing plays, and the aura of his reputation still hovers around them.

James Graham Luján, who with Richard O'Connell translated a volume of García Lorca's plays into English, insists that Benavente is to the Spanish Theatre what Edna Ferber is to the American novel—a rapid, able workman, possessed of a formula that has been highly successful, popular and witty, turning out a great deal of popular work, but not to be considered a great artist. The comparison is provocative. It does not, however, take account of Benavente's service in bringing to the Spanish stage all the currents that were blowing across the European stage in his half century of play writing. Pirandello, Giraudoux, Jean Cocteau, George Bernard Shaw, Synge, and Molnár are only a few of the playwrights whose ideas have been transmogrified in terms of the Spanish theatre by the versatile and indefatigable Don Jacinto. Anything that came his way was grist to his mill, whether it was an English novel like Margaret Kennedy's *Constant Nymph* which he put into Spanish stage terms as *Cuando los hijos de Eva no son hijos de Adán,* or the political misery of his own country. He wrote *Oración a Rusia* when Spain was supposed to be interested in Russia, and a cruel political satire called *Aves y páparos* when he regained his place in the sun under the dictatorship. (He had fled Madrid with the Republic, was captured in Valencia and taken back to Madrid by Franco forces, and kept under guard in his own house. Later he made his peace with Franco.)

He is a man of eighty now. A recent picture of him is contributed by Don Pedro Juan Navarro, Colombian diplomat and author, who saw him in Madrid in April of 1941. Thanks to the courtesy of a friendly diplomat, Señor Navarro saw

...two Madrid curiosities, Don Jacinto Benavente and the singers of *flamenco* songs. Don Jacinto is a dried up little old man, small and conspicuous. He talks of literature and politics, the war and the theatre, in a thin voice and with corrosive irony. He told us of his troubles during the Republic and his return to Franco's Madrid. He had no enthusiasm for Azaña, nor for Franco, nor for Hitler, nor for Churchill, nor for Domingo Ortega, nor for Roosevelt. His skepticism is lacerating, and so far as the theatre is concerned, he gave me the impression that for Don Jacinto Benavente there was only one great author in Spain—Jacinto Benavente. The Maestro is most "simpático," but his phrases cut like razor blades. He receives one with all the courtesy of an hidalgo and he is far from sparing of his opinions.... Referring to his famous library and to the Reds, he murmured "I shall always have to thank them for not carrying off my books." His smile is perfidious.[1]

In this country the fame of such men as the famous four, Benavente, Martínez Sierra, and the Quinteros tended to obscure the fact that in Spain the

---
[1] Pedro Juan Navarro, *Europa Barbara* (Bogota, Columbia, 1941).

tradition of the poetic theatre has never died. Don Eduardo Marquina, born in Barcelona in 1879, was the torch bearer who has carried that tradition into this century and fired the imagination of younger men as diverse in their talents as Villaespesa, Lorca, Pemán, to rise against the non-poetic theatre as represented by Benavente. Few of Marquina's plays have been translated. He wrote *Las hijas del Cid* in 1908, and brought into modern fame the ancient twelfth-century poem with all its mediaeval echoes. For the famous actress Maria Guerrero he wrote *Doña María la Brava* in 1909, *En Flandes se ha puesto el sol* in 1910, *El Rey Trovador* in 1912, and *El Gran Capitán* in 1916. These remain the best known of his dramas, though later ones like *El pobrecito carpintero, Era una vez en Bagdad* get praise from those who like them.

There is a marked religious strain in Marquina's plays which also influenced some of the younger men. José María Pemán, author of *El Divino Impaciente, Cisneros,* and *Cuando las Cortes de Cádiz* had the warm support of the Catholics in the period just before the war, when every aspect of Spanish life, including the theatre, was lining up for the great political struggle ahead. So did Eduardo L. de Palacio and Luis Martínez Kleiser who, in *Los Hermanos de Betania* put the story of Magdalene and Lazarus on the stage. That religious strain is even more marked now that Franco is Spain's dictator.

José María Pemán's *Cuando las Cortes de Cádiz* was a hit in 1934, the year that the abortive revolt in the northern provinces of Spain was put down with such severity. It is laid in the period of the Peninsular Wars, 1807-1814, and its plot concerns the heroic resistance of the Spaniards against the Napoleonic invaders. Its heroine is Lola la Piconera, a singer of the people, who makes her way through the enemy lines with a message to allies, is caught and executed, but keeps the message secret to the end. She and her lover Otero are real people, and well drawn, but most of the others are merely types set against conventional backgrounds, saying and doing the typical things expected of them. The verse form in which it is written is traditional, tightly packed, handled with ease. It has more charm than depth.

Pemán is a competent theatre craftsman, and (thanks to his pro-Franco sympathies) one of the few pre-war dramatists who survived the cataclysm of civil war; but in spite of his popularity he must so far be classed as a man of minor talent, however charming.

From a purely literary point of view neither Marquina nor Francisco Villaespesa can be compared with that bizarre and beloved pair of originals Don Ramón del Valle Inclán and Don Miguel de Unamuno. Enrique Díez Canedo, whose judgments are shrewd, says of them,

> Great writers not especially dedicated to the theatre have written for it works which contain the best hopes of a new life for the theatre. Thus the plays of

Don Miguel de Unamuno and of Don Ramón del Valle Inclán, whether or not they have ever appeared on the stage. When the history of the Spanish theatre in our day is finally written it is probable that the farces and the tragedies of both these authors will be recognized as marking its high point, though today the mentality of the producer sees in them only a novelist's whims or a philosopher's extravagances.

None of these plays—not Unamuno's melodramatic *Todo un hombre,* which had great success in both Spain and South America, nor *Fedra,* which was a modernization of Euripides, nor *Medea* (modernized from Seneca), which Margarita Xirgu played in 1933 and 1934 in the old Roman theatre in Mérida—has been put into English. Nor have Valle Inclán's farces, nor his rustic tragedy *Divinas palabras* which was played in Madrid in 1933. Nor *La cabeza del bautista, La Rosa de Papel, Farsa y licencia de la Reina Castiza,* which the young director Manuel Altolaguirre lists as the three he most wanted to put on when war intervened. They present great difficulties to a translator bent on doing them justice, but perhaps some day an American lover of the Spanish language who is also an adept in the theatre will stumble on this treasure trove and make at least a bit of it available for the delight of literate and imaginative audiences.

The only modern poet playwright of Spain who has made his way onto the American stage is Federico García Lorca. Born in 1899, killed in his own Granada by Franco sympathizers shortly after the outbreak of the war (August 1936), he achieved in his short life the distinction of being ranked without question as the leading poet of his generation. His lyric gift showed itself when he was very young and thanks to the Spanish tradition it moved without contradiction or conflict into an expression in terms of the theatre. It is more than chance that his first published work was an essay in tribute to Zorilla.

His first play was hardly more than an extension into theatrical terms of his way of writing verses about the smallest forms of life. *El maleficio de la mariposa* exists now only in memory, but the fact that it was put on in the Teatro Eslava under the direction of Martínez Sierra, that it was mounted by Salvador Dalí and acted by the company of Catalina Bárcena, argues that it must have had more than passing value. An insect comedy, it preceded Karel Capek's by two years. It was not a success, and no known copy now exists, but the début was made in honorable terms.

Not for seven years did another play of Lorca's appear in the professional theatre, though a puppet farce was played in Granada in 1923. Mostly he was writing lyrics and ballads that have since spread his fame far beyond Spain or the Spanish tongue. In October of 1927 *Mariana Pineda* appeared in the Teatro Fontalba of Madrid. It was a somewhat static drama founded on an incident in Granada's history and conceived more as a series of tragic tableaux evocative of an epoch and a mood than as a play moving of its own volition. Nevertheless it carried the germs of his later work in its combination of the folk theme, the classic tragedy, and the romantic treatment, as well as in the author's obvious intent to create an art theatre in which the dramatic, the lyric, the plastic, and the musical elements should be forged into a living unity. As first presented in the days of Primo de Rivera, *Mariana Pineda* was credited with raising the flag of revolt for freedom, and this note in a dictator's capital may have been partly responsible for its poor reception. It was revived later, under the Republic, and played to full houses. It was played in Buenos Aires in 1943 and won much applause.

La zapatera prodigiosa (according to its title "a violent farce in two acts") in the Teatro Español in 1930 had better luck. In 1933 appeared the highly stylized *Amor de Don Perlimplín, con Belisa en su jardín,* and in the same year the long-awaited *Bodas de sangre* (at the Teatro Beatriz). It was played unhappily in New York in 1935 under the title *Bitter Oleander.*

Not even now is the whole body of Lorca's work available for study and appraisal. Of the twelve plays he is known to have written, four are unpublished or unfinished: the insect comedy *El maleficio de la mariposa,* the puppet farce *La niña que riega la albahaca,* the surrealist tragedy *El Público,* and the great drama *La casa de Bernarda Alba,* which is the third of his trilogy. There is also a longer version of the puppet play, entitled simply *Los títeres de cachiporra.* There are no known copies of the first and second. The third exists in a few published scenes, and a manuscript of the whole is rumored to exist in one of the Latin American countries. The fourth, *La casa de Bernarda Alba,* is still in manuscript in New York City, and has been read to a favored few. To these four might be added a fifth, the charming *Los sueños de mi prima Aurelia* of which one act also exists in manuscript form.

That leaves eight plays, which is a very small body of work for a Spanish playwright to leave behind him when he dies at thirty-seven. Lorca was just getting into his dramatist's stride. He had taken time to become a major poet, polishing his poems until they satisfied his most exacting taste. He had spent years getting actual working experience in the theatre. From 1931 to 1934 he directed *La Barraca,* a jitney theatre under the patronage of the Minister of Education, whose players were college students and whose task it was to take Lope de Vega, the *autos* of Calderón, the newest bit of surrealist drama to the inn yards and bull rings of remote corners of the country, where Spanish peasants had never seen a play. He had staged Lope de Vega's famous *La dama boba* for Margarita Xirgu, first in Buenos Aires and then at the three hundredth anniversary in Madrid's Teatro Español. For it he designed the costumes, collected and set songs of the period, arranged the dances, managed the whole production with such skill that the old comedy became a twentieth-century hit.

The quality and character of his finished drama leaves no doubt as to his place in Spanish play writing. Yet what will the history of the Spanish stage say of a Spaniard who has only this handful to his credit?

So far, contemporary history says that all of Lorca's plays are major plays and that students know the full list better than they know a handful of Benavente's or of Lope's. So far history is admittedly prejudiced. The fame of the poet is still too dazzling, the horror of his death still too shocking. The young Shelley, dead in a Mediterranean storm and cremated on an Italian beach, was no more moving a figure for the English-speaking than is, for the Spanish-speaking, the young Lorca marched up the hill to the cemetery and shot by a Franco firing squad.

What of these eight published plays? One, *Retablillo de Don Cristóbal,* is a puppet play that was used during the Spanish war to amuse troops at the front. It belongs in the immemorial company of Punch and Judy at their most earthy and impolite. One, *Así que Pasen cinco Años,* is a piece of surrealist symbolism, obviously done under the influence of Jean Cocteau and Salvador Dalí, a strange and haunting piece of formal decadence which has not so far been played. It is available for study in translation under the title *If Five Years Pass.*

Of the remaining five, two are called farces—*La zapatera prodigiosa* and *Amor de Don Perlimplín y Belisa en su jardín.* Two, *Bodas de sangre* and *Yerma,* belong to the trilogy (of which the unpublished *Casa de Bernarda Alba* forms the third play), and the last, *Doña Rosita la soltera o el lenguaje de las flores,* stands alone as a sentimental tragicomedy. All of these (except *La casa de Bernarda Alba*) are available in translation.

The two farces have already proved themselves in the American tributary theatre. *La zapatera* has been played by college dramatic societies in Syracuse University, in Boston by the Harvard Dramatic Club, and at Johns Hopkins. *Don Perlimplín* has been given at Bennington and *Doña Rosita* by Harvard and Radcliffe together in Boston.

The first two of these are essentially ballet material, and it will be strange if they are not remade into the sister form by young American choreographers just as Alarcón's novel *The Three-Cornered Hat* was made into a ballet under the joint influence of Falla's music, Massine's choreography, and Picasso's décor.

But if the farces make their way in this country without difficulty, the tragedies may have to wait until the fashion in American theatre changes. *Bodas de sangre* was played in New York under the title *Bitter Oleander* in 1935 to celebrate the twentieth anniversary of the Neighborhood Playhouse. It was put on *con amore* by Irene Lewisohn, who had seen the play in Spain, and who gave a highly stylized, somewhat remote production which emphasized its folk values. The taut violence that pervades the play somehow failed to cross the footlights. The translated text must share responsibility for the play's failure here, for it was done more with affection than with sure knowledge of what constitutes good theatre language in the United States. The whole performance, into which had been poured skill, interest, and intelligence, was a prime example of the difficulty of playing Spanish tragedy in terms acceptable to American theatre-goers.

In both Madrid and Buenos Aires, on the other hand, the play made a sensation. In 1933 Margarita Xirgu and Lola Membrives played it to full houses in both cities, and it ran for an entire season. *Yerma*, the second play in this tragic trilogy, was equally successful in Spain, Mexico, and the South American countries.

These two, with the unpublished *La casa de Bernarda Alba,* show the power and sweep of Lorca's genius carried to its greatest height. The farces are gay, delightful, thoroughly competent play writing. But the tragedies, and particularly *Yerma,* are drama of a very high type. All three are plays of women who should have been fruitful and who are frustrated. In *Bodas de sangre* the spotlight touches three women: a mother whose eldest son was killed "by a knife just right for the hand" and whose youngest son is now to marry a girl once betrothed to a member of the killer's family; the bride; and the lover's unhappy wife. Perhaps this division of sympathy is responsible for a certain effect of confusion which the play gives, a weakness in spite of its strength.

The unpublished *Casa de Bernarda Alba* is the story of an immovable old woman with five daughters whom she keeps shut up as in a convent, and the passions that rage in that unholy house. Spanish in essence, in its stark violence it reminds an American of O'Neill at his New England best. It is to be hoped that this play will be put into printed form soon, so that both students and audiences may enjoy its fine and moving drama.

For many reviewers it is *Yerma* the barren whom Lorca pictures with the greatest power. Yerma, who was born "with the blood of a hundred sons," is married to a close and sullen peasant more interested in his land and his sheep than in his wife, whose Catholic faith and pride of family makes it impossible for her to break the virtuous code and still her longing with a child by another man. At last she goes on pilgrimage to pray the saint for a child, and her husband, following to order her home, is slain as he mocks her need, while she goes mad. The construction of *Yerma* is close, clear, inevitable as a Greek drama. Its translators into English call it "curiously pagan" and so it is, but with the paganism of Spain's elder gods that now and then stir beneath her altar cloths.

Time has a way of sifting its powdery sands into the cracks and hollows of a dramatist's reputation until only an empty plane is left, and a reviewer of the Spanish theatre who starts with Echegaray may well hesitate to predict undying fame for any modern playwright, however touched with genius he seems at the moment. If García Lorca's reputation rested only on the farces, on his wistful experiment into surrealism, his puppet plays, and his charming *Doña Rosita,* one could say that here was a fine poet whose theatrical experiments were promising. But the tragic trilogy is accomplishment of the most vigorous and enduring kind. Any playwright with these three to his credit need ask no shrift of fate.

Some day some one will write the story of the Spanish theatre during Spain's uncivil war and of the gallant work of *La Barraca* (its poet leader dead) and of Miguel Prieto's Guignol in reaching and entertaining the front-line soldiers. But this is not the place for it. All we can do here is to list the names of the new authors whose works were played under such incredible difficulties. They include Ramón J. Sender (better known as novelist than as playwright), Cesar Arconada, Pedro Garfias, Antonio Porras, Emilio Prados, Herrera Petere, Plá y Beltrán, Miguel Hernández.

And what of the Spanish theatre now that most of the great folk of its dazzling three dacades are dead? Wrapped in the rigid banner of Falange, muffled to the eyes against indiscretion of word or deed, it carries on a comatose and mediocre existence. T. J. Hamilton, reporter for *The New York Times* in Madrid in 1939-1941, found it "startling if nothing else, to go to the Spanish version of Clare Boothe's *The Women* and find that the comedy had been adapted, according to the principles of the new régime, into a sombre diatribe against divorce." He reports that both acting and production in the theatre were wretched. Don Pedro Navarro, there in 1941, wrote,[1]

In Madrid I did everything possible in the effort to see a really great work—and I did not succeed. I only managed to see Maruja Guerrero, beautiful and a fine artist, in a barbaric scene in which she cut her throat before the public with a jack-knife. My French companion was torn between horror and laughter. To her innate good taste, the whole thing was idiotic.

As for the plays that were done, Hamilton speaks of *Don Juan Tenorio* "revived as usual to cap off visits to the cemeteries on All Saints Day, and the Phalanx's gala performance of *Mocedades del Cid*." (This was written by Guillén de Castro—1569-1631—and was the inspiration of Corneille's more famous *Le Cid*) He also says, "some of the plays which had won Benavente a Nobel Prize were revived."

A gleaning of notes in the *Revista Hispánica Moderna,* published under the auspices of Columbia University, discloses the following plays described as put on in Madrid since Franco took control of the city in 1939. The list makes no pretence of being complete and its dates are far from certain, but at least it sheds some light into the kind of theatre preferred by Spanish Fascists—a subject hitherto completely obscure.

The first play noted is *La Santa Hermandad* by Eduardo Marquina, a play about the medieval religious brotherhoods which was put on in the Teatro Español in December 1939. *El Otro* by Unamuno was played in the spring of 1940. Benavente's *Aves y pájaros,* described as a sardonic play making fun of the late Republic, was forbidden production that spring, but was put on in the fall of 1940. So was his *Lo increíble*. In 1941-1942 he had

[1] Navarro, *op. cit.*

four new plays—*La última curva* and *La culpa es tuya,* written for the company of Irene López Heredia, *Zamarga* written for the company of Antonio Vico, and a fourth, title unknown, written for the Teatro Español. *La risa va por barrios* was one of the last in which the Quintero brothers collaborated; the last two comedies of Pedro Muñoz Seca—*La tonada del Rizo* and *Entre cuatro paredes; La florista de la Reina* by Fernández Ardavín; *Rosario Ortega* by Leandro Navarro were all put on. Also *La Cruzada y el Pilar,* a religious play by Arturo María Cayuela; *España bien maridada* by Augurio Salgado; *Mi niña* by Pérez and Fernández Quintero and *Cin-pin-sing* by Augustín Foxá (both these were *zarzuelas*); *Solera del Sacro-Monte* by Julian Sánchez; and *Gracia y Justicia* by Antonio Quintero.

As for the future, too much battle smoke obscures the crystal to be able to see clearly. The great ones of Spain's modern theatre are mostly dead, and those that survive are scattered to the four winds. Some, like Benavente, have made their peace with Franco, others find that the air of Latin America heals old wounds and saves them from new ones. Very few new Spanish plays appear. The war crushes lives, labor, inspiration itself. Rafael Alberti, the poet, wrote *El trébol florido* in South America; José Bergamín's *La Hija de Diós* was written in Mexico. He has also done ballets there, among them *La paloma azul.* As for the rest, the exiled critic Arturo Mori has the last word:

> The seed still lives and will come to bearing under the white wings of peace. The history of the Spanish theatre is too long and too ample to be destroyed by a few bombs. Where Attila's horse trod the earth no grass grew; but those were other times. Millions of modern Attilas are unable to destroy the seed that lies quiet and waiting under its cover of good Spanish earth.

Further news of the state of the theatre under Franco comes in an issue of the *Revista Nacional de Educación,*[1] devoted to The Theatre in Spain and issued under the direction of one Pedro Rocamora. An introductory editorial says,

> We are all acquainted with the indisputable advances made by the theatre in Spain these days. It must be declared by those who, for reasons more or less obscure, are persistent pessimists that it [the theatre] never had greater scope and higher quality than now. Two official theatres exist under the protection of the State—the veteran Teatro Español and the recently created Teatro Nacional —with economic means hitherto unknown for such purposes, whose directors and playing companies have achieved a tonic degree of social and esthetic purification such as has never been reached before, surpassing themselves each time with maximum determination and remarkable educative efficiency.

The Teatro Español, one learns further, belongs to the Falange, is under the Vice Secretary of Popular Education, will continue to play Spanish classics. The Teatro Nacional (formerly Teatro Real?) now closed and

[1] November, 1943, No. 35.

"awaiting the ultimate reform which will return it to its former splendor," and the Maria Guerrero (formerly Teatro de la Princesa) are both under the direction of Luis Escobar, Comisario de Teatros Nacionales. The latter theatre is devoted to modern plays.

The playwrights enlisted in this theatre effort for "social and esthetic purification" are divided into three groups; those "already consecrated, who continue their triumphal passage" such as Benavente, Tomás Borrás, Jardiel Poncela, Manuel Machado, Eduardo Marquina, José María Pemán, Mariano Tomás; the second groups "whose first dramatic productions have been rousing successes," include Emiliano Aguado, Ginés de Albarada, Joaquín Calvo Sotelo, Escohotado, Augustín de Foxá, José Vicente Puente, Torrente Ballester; the third group, of others still younger "whose works already known in published form await the favorable stage confirmation to which their magnificent gifts as dramatists entitle them," includes Ayesta, García Luengo, Ruiz Iriarte.

Of these, only the first group are known in the United States. None of the plays written under Falange domination is as yet available in translation. So these Falange encomiums must for the moment at least stand without confirmation from an objective source. Only time will tell whether or not they were merited.

THE DRAMA OF SPANISH AMERICA

If the modern theatre in Spain begins with Echegaray and a pervasive sense of social currents that were making themselves felt all over Europe, in South America it starts in a manner more picturesque and unexpected. Late in the nineteenth century a company of wandering circus clowns began to add gaucho legends to their circus stunts and to act them out. Their stage was, as in the long-gone days of Lope de Rueda in Spain or the *commedia dell' arte* in Italy, the tail of a cart. Their material of drama was the body of earthy, violent legends of the pampas sung by the *payadores,* those native, wandering minstrels who, gathering at night at campfires on the great estancias, earned food and lodging by the tales of gaucho life they told and the songs they sang. Wherever two of these rustic minstrels gathered, a song contest developed—spontaneous, improvised verses, sung to a traditional melody, which glorified the singer and insulted his competitor. It was a game possible only between men of fertile wit and great musical facility, a game the rules of which the audience knew and guarded with excited interest, for the audience was the judge and gave the prize. Out of these tough native artists rose Santos Vega, archetype of the *payador,* who was to make his way into plays far from the pampas.

In 1884 the company with which José J. Podestá performed (he had been a circus clown and now was about to branch out as an impresario), had one of these legends dramatized and played it. *Juan Moreira* proved so popular that Podestá's family formed themselves into a troupe and added others, *Santos Vega, Martín Fierro, Juan Cuello, Juan Soldao,* and *La Montaña de las Brujas.*

These were in essence melodramas of a very crude type in which the gaucho hero, a sort of hard-bitten Robin Hood, came galloping down the center aisle between rows of happily thunder-struck spectators who had gathered from the surrounding estancias. The race about the center court and up and down the aisles might have a number of excuses for being—the hero was, perhaps, fleeing from the unjust clutches of a tyrant, or he was pursuing the villainous and always unpopular rural police whose machinations he had exposed, or he was rescuing beauty in distress from the leering gallantries of the villain-buffoon, who was likely to be an Italian by birth or derivation, scheming and treacherous, but defeated in the end by the noble gaucho.

All the sympathy of the audience was with the gaucho. His trials were their trials, his triumphs their triumphs. They were some of them minor gauchos, some the children of gauchos, many had had brushes with the police or the soldiery, and sometimes they had come off not too well. Romantic, night-wandering, justice-loving, the hero of this new melodrama pictured them as they liked to think they were, and they rewarded him accordingly.

Along toward the end of the last century the gaucho drama reached Buenos Aires and began to put on literary airs. City audiences sitting in theatres found it as entrancing as had their country cousins gathered about estancia campfires. The South American theatre had found its authentic native inspiration.

There is a theory, better known to the natural sciences than to theatre history, which says that the living individual repeats in his development the history of his kind. In turning its back on the long pageantry of drama it had inherited from Spain and beginning its first native experiments with such earthy stuff as gaucho legends, the South American theatre was taking this theory over into cultural life.

The gaucho drama of South America represented a far sharper break with the past than did Ibsen in Norway or Echegaray in Spain. Those men were, after all, following in the great line of European theatre production. Revolutionary as their plays may have seemed at the time, they never came out from behind the gas footlights. In was content, not form, to which they gave new life. Social significance stiffened limp lines and made new heroes, but all within the skeleton of the three-act drama writen for a well-found stage.

But in South America the new drama owed little thanks to the great baroque theatres which the dictators built, to the grand tradition of Spanish theatrical literature, to the fashionable audiences, the well-made plays, the

European influences which ranked so high amid the cultured. Its inspiration came out of the plains, out of the wild struggles of men with beasts, and of men with men in the days of independence.

It represented a cutting of the silver cord. To understand its importance one must look at what it superseded, which means to look at the Latin American stage in its dependence on the mother-country Spain.

Four great influences, that are all part of one great influence, weave in and out of the theatre in South America and still play their part in shaping the complex of material that ferments there today. First there was the native rudimentary theatre—mostly ceremonious in nature. On the western coast of South America, before the Spaniards came, Indian poets recited long compositions to a background of monotonous music. They appeared at sacraments such as wedding feasts, where they recited "after the rape, and in the midst of the great drunkenness." This ceremonial theatre combined sacrifice, music, and dance.

At first this Indian drama seemed due to be swept away by the conquest, which imposed on the natives the best theatre in Europe, the mightiest organized religion in the world, and a new language. The three came hand in hand. The earliest recorded touring company visited Peru in 1599. In Chile in 1633 "on a stage one span and a half high, comedies were presented by captains, sergeants major, scribes, and nobles." Whose comedies were played on that eleventh day of September three hundred and ten years ago the historian neglects to say. It is, however, possible to guess. This happened two years before Lope de Vega's death, three years after the famous *Burlador de Sevilla* of Tirso de Molina was put into print, and at the height of Calderón's young popularity. It might have been a play of one of these, or a drama now forgotten, which appeared on that rude stage.

Whatever it was, the church quickly took hold of it. Religion is the second great influence that weaves in and out of the Spanish American theatre. The first *pasos, entremeses,* and *entradas a Jerusalén* were seen in monastery schools and convents established for the Indians. Soon those Indians were taking part in their own *nacimientos* and *pastorelas,* singing perhaps in the new Castillian they were learning, or speaking the dialogue in *quichua* or a Mexican dialect that came more easily to the tongue.

The mixture of the two cultures thus produced still plays an important part in popular entertainment. From the Río Grande down to Tierra del Fuego the famous struggle between Moors and Christians (a struggle which, in its original bloody terms, was hardly over when the first conquistadores touched the western hemisphere) still recurs in holiday fiestas. The villages in Mexico, each of which for centuries has had its own play handed down by oral tradition (there was a "House of Comedies" in Mexico City as early as 1597), still give those plays. Time has changed them, Indian songs and dances have entered into them. A *pastorela,* for example, may exist in the form of a prompt book in the possession of a village elder, preferably one with a good memory. The rôles of Gila, San Miguel, or Bartolo may be passed on for generations in the direct family line. The annual performances are given at Christmas or Easter, and the costumes are a gorgeous Indian interpretation of Spanish colonial dress, varied with local custom and resources. But the derivation is still clear.

Incidents show how deeply these Spanish-Indian celebrations colored daily living. Juan José Churión, writing of the theatre in Caracas, Venezuela, tells of a member of the Congress of 1811 who was always known as The Devil, not from any political chicanery, but because that was his customary rôle in a *nacimiento*. Thus the human was mixed with the divine, and the result was sometimes stuffed like a Christmas pudding with delicious incongruities. That same Caracas had a song which captures this essence:

> Se veía a San Miguel
> con el diablo platicando
> y a Don Cornelio bailando
> polka con Santa Isabel.

Which is to say that "one used to see Saint Michael gossiping with the Devil, and Don Cornelius [the hero] dancing a polka with Saint Elizabeth." As performances of the type to which this song belonged were frequently held in the church itself, there was no question of disrespect.

The third great influence is one which, in the United States at least, has usually been disregarded. This was the Spanish language—or in Brazil the Portuguese. We who have little sense of history, and who know even less about the history of South America than we know about our own, are prone to forget that Spanish and Portuguese were not the native tongues of that continent any more than English was of this one. But whereas we rendered the native Indian and his language negligible throughout most of North America, the Latins had a gentler policy in South America. They let him live, converted him to Christianity, and laid their own languages over his native tongue.

Unfortunately for the drama, this relative gentleness carried its own penalty. No greater handicap can be imposed on dramatic artists than the imposition of a new language. When that new language carried with it not only words and sentence structure, but a completely new body of thought and preferred form of artistic creation, the process of absorption, of digestion, of original creation within the new form takes much longer. So the intellectuals in the Spanish colonies had their long period of earnest imitation of the Spanish models. Quito, Ecuador, produced a new Luciano at the end of the eighteenth century. Mexico had its Ruiz de Alarcón, more Spanish than Mexican, and widely praised by Spanish critics who looked to the new Spain not for native expression but for something that met their own recognized and accepted standards.

But there was more serious danger here than that of mere imitation. The

Spanish syntax is simple and tough, not easily violated. The Spanish theatrical tradition is long, brilliant, enviable. So the actors in South America spoke stage Spanish, and the playwrights imitated the rolling octosyllabic lines dear to the Iberian peninsula. And because the priests sent over from Spain were the teachers, mestizo children learned only of part of their heritage—that the Spanish theatre was founded near the end of the twelfth century, that the *Auto de los Reyes Magos,* played in Toledo Cathedral, was one of its earliest manifestations, that it proceeded through Gil Vicente to the Golden Age of Lope de Vega, and that their own efforts were to be cast in that stately mold.

This had, of course, little to do with the speech of daily life or the ceremonies beloved of Indians. So the theatre and theatre speech became divorced from the people, took on an inevitable air of affectation, as of something artificial kept alive in a hothouse.

The colonial mentality (and this is the fourth of the great influences that have both made and hampered the Latin American stage) leaned on the prestige of Mother Spain, with its traditionally splendid culture, its complacence, its certainty of both achievement and destiny. The Spaniards were sure of themselves. The colonials were not. Spanish prestige was both fact and legend. Therefore why not make certain at least of reflected glory by importing Spanish plays, Spanish stars, Spanish standards? The great baroque theatres of the capital cities must have spectacles with an international prestige to satisfy the polyglot audiences that gathered in them. The province must prove itself cosmopolitan. So the wit of Benavente and the Quinteros, the fame of *zarzuelas,* the gayety of *género chico* spread over Spanish America. What was the cream of the jest in Madrid became the daily milk in the coffee of Buenos Aires. Famous companies crossed the sea to conquer American audiences. Famous actresses—María Guerrero and Eleanora Duse, Sarah Bernhardt and Margarita Xirgu—brought their plays and captivated society. Buenos Aires prided itself on being the Paris of the New World, and more truly cosmopolitan than was New York City.

This cultural dependence had both its good and its bad side. To quote James Graham Luján, translator of Lorca, himself a Mexican, and familiar with theatre life in South America,

> On the credit side must be counted the fact that nations which had just finished struggling for political independence and had not yet reached a self-defined culture of their own, had a splendid pattern brought to them ready-made. Madre España thus provided an early, if arbitrary and artificial, maturity for her children. Intellectually, theatrically, the American colonies, republics though they called themselves, became precocious little Spains.

But if that was the good side, the reverse of the medal was not so shining. A brilliant ready-made culture inspired imitation, but did not encourage original production. On the contrary, it offered a real handicap to native talent that sought not to imitate its grandeurs, but to find true norms of native theatrical expression.

Also it drew a sharp line between theatre (which is to say Spanish and European theatre) and what the people liked. No one could aim at fulfilling the exacting conditions of the motherland's dramatic tradition who did not have education enough to be aware of it. Education, culture, erudition are in the Latin Americas only belatedly democratic. Being in the first instance not a native but an imposed culture, this arbitrarily belonged to the intellectuals. Which is to say the upper classes.

Nor was class, in the sense understood in the United States, the only problem. Latin American countries have carried cross-breeding to the point where an infinite number of grades of blood mixtures exist, from the almost pure Indian to the pure Spaniard. At least two nations have in addition one or more social classes in which the Negro predominates. So the line between the upper-class theatre and the entertainment which the people liked had not only social but also racial implications, in that it marked a distant cleavage between the pure-blood classes and the mestizo masses.

In the light of this background it seems no longer a mere accident that the native theatre (which began in modern form when the Podestás put gaucho legends into dramatic form in 1884) had its first great successes in the realm below the demarcation line, the great field of what the people, as distinguished from the intellectuals, wanted.

At the close of the nineteenth century the Podestás (Juan, Pablo, Gerónimo, and Antonio) who were born in Uruguay took their gaucho plays to Buenos Aires, and the new fashion spread to dramatists with literary pretensions. Martínez Leguizamón wrote *Calandria*, a far cry from the first crude *Juan Moreira,* but based on the same theme. Martínez Coronado wrote *La piedra del escándalo,* crude but powerful. A Uruguyan, Crosmán Moratorio, wrote the famous *Juan Soldao,* no better as a play than any of the other blood, flood, and thunder melodramas that caught the bloodthirsty fancy of the time, but with the gauchos' gallopings far better timed. The characters were still the same, and the plot still alternated melodrama with songs and dances out of a particularly spicy folklore. But the craftsmanship was improving, and this play may be held up as the most expert of the *dramas criollos.*

Other writers found the material fruitful. Roberto Payró, also famous as a novelist, and a resourceful and interesting artist, wrote *Sobre los muros* and *Marcos Severi,* among other successful plays. Various critics have called him the "first real dramatist," and indeed the scope of his mind set him apart from those who preceded him. José de Maturana wrote charming comedies, *Canción de primavera, Canción de invierno, El campo alegre, La flor de trigo.* Martínez Cuitiño brought forth *El derrumbe, Rayito de sol, La fuerza ciega* in a more serious colloquial vein. The enthusiasm for the theatre was enormous, and variegated. Echoes of Ibsen began to appear, coming to South America by way of the plays of Echegaray. The novelist Otto Miguel Cione wrote his most successful play *El arlequín* on the theme of an inherited tendency to alcohol, and the better read in his audiences remembered Ibsen's *Ghosts*. This play, done by the omnificent Podestás, and many others from Cione's pen (*El Gringo, Partenza, Paja brava, Gallo ciego, La barca errante, Clavel del aire*) show a power of realism and observation that is marred by his carelessness as a craftsman, and his tendency to over-dramatize.

All this was prelude to the appearance on the scene of the man who made the period truly memorable, and who represents both the high point of the gaucho era and the beginning of native theatre worthy of the name. Florencio Sánchez is called "our greatest playwright" by both Argentina and Uruguay, thus underlining the fact that the cultural history of those two neighbor countries is inextricably mixed and must logically be studied together.

Sánchez was born in Montevideo, Uruguay, in 1875—the first of eleven children of a mother who was then only fifteen years old. For the first seven years of his life the family dwelt in a small town called Treinta y Tres, where a grandfather represented the only real stability which Florencio Sánchez was ever to know. His working life began in another small town, Minas, where at the age of fifteen a relative got him a job with the Junta Económico-Administrativa. This lasted long enough for him to use the glimpses he got of political life as material for lampoons in the local paper. He stepped from newspaper satire to the town theatre, where he doubled as actor and as author of sketches.

Then followed ten years of a roving and violent youth, devoted to newspaper work, political satire, and the writing of topical skits for any local theatre that would produce them. He learned about the theatre by working in it and for it, and about audiences by seeking their applause both for what he wrote and what he did. His fame in those years was purely local, but there is no doubt that he was gaining that sure theatrical touch which was afterward to show in all he did.

At last ambition took him to Buenos Aires, but there he had no fame at all, and the capital was no more hospitable than most capitals are to a young unknown. Hungry, jobless, he was seized with an idea for a play, and wrote the first act in a night. His friend Joaquín Vedía, dramatic critic for the newspaper *La Tribuna,* was not impressed. However Sánchez finished the play, copied it neatly on telegraph blanks (used at first because they cost nothing, and after he became famous because they were lucky) and entrusted it to the critic. When the latter got around to reading it he saw its possibilities and recommended it warmly to the director of the Teatro de la Comedia. Sánchez was offered ten pesos per act for each performance, but his shabby clothes almost kept him out of rehearsal. The play, *M'hijo el dotor,* opened August 13, 1903, and created an immediate sensation.

That same year it was translated and played in Italy, and later in Tokyo. Thereafter, every play that Sánchez wrote was successful.

Those plays seem dated now, but in their day they represented a peak of contemporary play writing that compares not unfavorably with what was being done in Europe. Not only were they the first important Latin American plays in terms of time, but they could hold up their heads as belonging in the first rank in terms of merit on any stage. They pictured social tragedy in terms of wide human appeal, set within an expertly fashioned dramatic frame. Their sense of drama was such as to make other plays of the time seem false and contrived. Their colloquial dialogue was almost phonographic in its fidelity, yet at the same time in key with the situation. The first of them, *M'hijo el dotor,* presented the problems that arise when two traditions clash. It was the story of the conflict between a young man whose parents have struggled to send him to the city to study, and his old gaucho grandfather who has no sympathy with such nonsense. That the young man was not worth the sacrifice made it harder. The audience knew that situation in their own families, and they rose to it with tears and cheers.

Dardo Cúneo, who has edited a volume of Sánchez' plays, classifies his work according to the social class in which the characters move. The first two, *Puertas adentro* and *La gente honesta,* he calls initial attempts. As first written, they have no importance in the serious body of the dramatist's work, but the second of them, which was stopped by the police before its opening because it contained a caricature of one Emilio Schiffner, a German newspaper editor with much political influence, was later rewritten and played under the title *Los Curdas.*

Cúneo classified *M'hijo el dotor, Cédulas de San Juan, La gringa,* and *Barranca abajo* as rural plays. Since in Argentina and Uruguay the plains and the cattle ranches roll right up to the capital city, these might better be called suburban plays. They derive their strength from the conflict between the standards of the pampas and those of the modern city. *Cédulas de San Juan* lacks the dramatic power which distinguishes some of the other plays, though as always its characters are truly drawn. *La Gringa,* written early, but not played until November, 1904, is a much more interesting work, dealing with the antagonism between the old gaucho settlers of the country and the Italian immigrants who were just being absorbed. *Barranca abajo,* following in 1905, is also a gaucho play, containing a sympathetic study of an old horseman whom progress was leaving behind. The gauchos' gallopings were slowing down.

The third group are dramas of city life. *Canillita, La pobre gente, Mano santa, Los muertos, El desalojo, La Tigra, Moneda falsa, Marta Gruni,* and *Un buen negocio* all dealt with the poorer classes. Most of them were short plays, based on themes of social protest. Of these, *Los muertos* was the most applauded, and deservedly.

And finally Sánchez wrote about the middle classes in *En familia, El pasado, Los curdas, Nuestros hijos,* and *Los derechos de la salud.* The last two were translated into Italian. In them the Ibsen influence is so strong that they become South American versions of the European problem drama which was transforming the theatre wherever western civilization flourished.

That there are lasting values in this body of drama is clear to the most hurried reader. They have power and humanity, fine characterization at times, a sense of social protest that was ahead of its era. The European influence is clear, but so is the native influence, and the two are fused into something which for the first time can be classed as first-rate drama springing from the soil of South America, in which the four conflicting influences that had hampered theatre production for four centuries were finally reconciled.

To a North American one of the most curious things about Sánchez' play writing is the fact that, with the exception of the first two attempts, it seems to have arrived fully formed, and to have made little progress thereafter. The first plays are, from the dramatic point of view, as good as the last. It is probable, to be sure, that Sánchez never could have attempted to portray a bourgeois family in his early days. Certainly his knowledge of character deepened and widened as he went on. But he was a mature man when his first plays were produced. His early skits, his lampoons and parodies, and all the proof of steps by which he arrived at his mastery of theatre form—these are scattered and not available to the curious student. The story is that his working habit was to concentrate furiously, producing a complete three-act play in as many days.

The span of his hard productive work and glowing fame was very short. In 1909 Sánchez persuaded the Uruguayan government to send him abroad, where he had plans for expanding his scope, his reputation, his country's name. His ambition was great, but luck turned her face away from him. Italy, which had given him his first foreign recognition, treated him badly, seeing in him only a foreigner who might be exploited. His health gave way and he was discovered to be in the last stages of tuberculosis. On November 7, 1910 he died. He had had six years of glory, and one—the last— of bitterest frustration. He was only thirty-five years old.

That year, as if by transmigration of genius, another young man whose life and talents closely paralleled Sánchez' had a first play, *El estanque,* produced. The critics hailed Ernesto Herrera as Florencio Sánchez' successor.

Herrera was born without benefit of wedlock into a rather prominent political and literary family, from whom he received no advantages. He lived, as best he could, working on newspapers, and moving among the lowest classes. Like Sánchez, he was influenced by the Russian realists, particularly Gorki. Ideas of social reform spurred on his talent. After his first play *El estanque,* came two short ones, *Mala laya,* and *El caballo del Comisario.* Then in 1911 came his second long play, *La moral de Misia Paca,* also a comment on the lives of the desperate rural poor, but technically a great improvement over his earlier plays. That same year in a feverish burst of creation he produced his masterpiece, *El león ciego*.

El león ciego is a study of the whole philosophy of a gaucho fighter, fully conceived and carried out, economical in its construction, sombre in its tone. As drama it is tremendously moving. Critics say of it that it could have been written by Sánchez at his best—which is meant to be highest praise.

This play brought Herrera prestige, success, and a small government pension which he used to go to Spain. There he wrote *El pan nuestro*. It is also known as *El pan amargo*, and the second title is more descriptive than the first. The play is laid in Madrid, and tells the tale of a woman who sacrifices everything, including honor, for her family, and wins only their hatred. It was considered too bitter and realistic for the Spanish stage. Taken back to America, it was played by a mediocre company, and did not have the success its author hoped.

Herrera died in 1917, still in his early thirties. Like the great dramatist he succeeded, he had gained theatrical skill of a high order, but proved himself unable to apply his craft sucessfully to non-American material. Both men dreamed of going to savor the greater cultural depth of Europe. Both men went, thanks to their success, and like more than one Yankee expatriate with similar ambitions, died early and defeated.

Meanwhile a man whose plays were at the furthest extreme from those of Sánchez and Herrera was showing Buenos Aires that the new current of native drama could be funny as well as tragic. Gregorio de Laferrére had no gaucho background, no thwarted land hunger, no conflict between city and country to bother him. He was a cosmopolitan of the early 1900's, a man who loved wit, satire and gayety, Italian operettas, and Spanish *zarzuelas*. His best plays are *Jettatore, Las de Barranco,* and *Locos de verano*. His were comedies of manners, portraying the metropolitan absurdities of Buenos Aires in those days, ironic, realistic if you like, at the same time deft and ingratiating. By a curious irony they have weathered our changing tastes better than have the far more substantial plays of Sánchez. Even now they might be good drawing-room comedy out of a New York season. And they give a truer commentary on the life of the city and its whims than the serious playwrights ever managed to achieve.

Theatrically, Buenos Aires was growing up. The gauchos still gallop today but mostly as ghosts, dear memories of things gone, and surrounded with the same nostalgia which we in the north have for cowboys, dwellers in sod houses, and travelers in covered wagons. Alberto Vacarezza, with the aid of two actors (Enrique Muiño and Elías Alippi) skilled in playing gaucho types, has given city audiences *Lo que pasó a Reynoso,* which ran for six hundred performances, and *El conventillo de la Paloma* which passed the thousand mark. But in spite of such reversions to a sentimental past, the most advanced and sophisticated theatre on the Southern continent is today to be found in Buenos Aires.

The leader among its dramatists is Samuel Eichelbaum, who also takes time to be the drama critic for the liberal newspaper *Argentina Libre*.[1] Over a decade ago such plays as *Un hogar, La cáscara de nuez, Señorita,* and *La mala se* brought him to the forefront of public popularity. More recently he has written such modern comedies as *Un tal Servando Gómez* and *Un guapo del 900*. His development has continued, and his technique as a dramatist is today considerably more advanced than was that of Sánchez, whose mantle he, like all southern playwrights of power, is said to have inherited. The inability of the older men to get away from purely regional themes seems not to bother him. At the same time he has taken the early *drama criollo* in his stride, picking it up where the older men left off, interpreting it in the modern manner, investing it with psychological nuance and a mordant power.

Buenos Aires has two play-writing teams that are famous throughout Latin America for the style and finish of their popular comedies. The first of these, Camilo Darthés and Carlos Damel, were awarded the Buenos Aires Municipal Prize in 1937 (a prize which has no counterpart in this country and is highly esteemed) for the comedy *Los chicos crecen*. Another, *No la quiero ni me importa* was written for the actor Luis Arata, and ran for 270 performances. *Mi felicidad y tus amigas,* played in 1942, was not so popular, but won high praise from the critics.

The other team consists of Pedro E. Pico and Rodolfo González Pacheco. In 1942 they wrote *Nace un pueblo,* with the famous actress Eva Franco playing the lead. Their most popular play bears the somewhat sinister title *Que la agarre quien quiera*. Pico himself has written many successful comedies alone. *Las rayas de una cruz* explored the theme of two lives which meet, like the lines of a cross, and are forever after separate.

With them should be mentioned the veteran playwright Edmundo Bianchi, a Uruguayan whose early plays include *La quiebra* and *Perdidos en la luz*. His much discussed *Los sobrevivientes* was recently performed in Buenos Aires at the Teatro Nacional de la Comedia by official invitation, but according to the critics it was too "literary" for the taste of the audience, and had no success. Another literary modern is the poet Enrique Larreta, whose *Santa María del Buen Aire* tells in symbolic form of the founding of Buenos Aires.

To move from the *rioplatense* theatre (as that of the Rio de la Plata basin, including both Argentina and Uruguay, is called) to other countries in South America is to move from the theatrical center to the periphery.

[1] *Argentina Libre* was closed by the military junta that seized control of Argentina in the summer of 1943. In December of that year the famous Teatro del Pueblo, headed by Leonidas Barletta and run as an art theatre presenting internationally famous plays, was taken over by the same government. Plays put on after government "intervention" were to be "inspired by Argentine themes or exalting national virtues."

The days when La Perricholi, mistress of the Viceroy Amata, made theatrical, if mostly unstaged, history in Peru are gone with the eighteenth century. There is still theatre there, but its place is modest. Felipe Sassone wrote *El miedo de los felices, ¡Calla, Corazón!; Lo que se lievan las horas; El intérprete de Hamlet; Campo Traviesa*. But to quote the all-too-telling commentary of one critic, they "seem to suffer from a dislocation of the Benavente." Manuel Bedoya, in the early years of this century, caused a tempest in Lima with his outspoken *La ronda de los muertos*. Julio Baudoin wrote an ambitious musical drama in 1916 called *El condor pasa*. Much more recently José Chiono wrote *La canción azul*. Isolated groups work hard at the task of forging a national theatre, but Peruvian talent seems to fall more naturally into novel and story form.

Chile is better off. Slow to start her own theatre, content to remain for a longer time under the influence of Spanish and French drama, it was not until the early decades of this century that she produced a playwright with real claims to originality. Antonio Acevedo y Hernández won his first fame with *Camino de flores* in 1910. Then he turned more and more to social drama, and in 1918 he produced *Almas perdidas* and *Irredentos*, which roused both dramatic critics and political liberals to excited applause. His most famous play is *Chañarcillo*, a drama concerned with conditions in the Chilean mines, and having a definite anti-imperialist (which in South America means anti-Yankee) point of view. The strong theme of social protest in this play has kept its fame alive for a quarter of a century, and was part of the reason why the dramatist was awarded one of Chile's famous Municipal Prizes in 1936.

Chile's other and more famous modern in the theatre is Armando Moock. His reputation is not confined to Chile, but is so widespread that he must be classed as one of the most able and interesting playwrights of the whole continent. Since 1914 he has been steadily piling up a play record which has won him fame on all the Spanish-speaking stages, even including those of Spain itself. He is the only Chilean whose work has progressed through the stages so familiar in the development of Latin American drama—from the romantic to the *sainete* and the burlesque commentary on national customs, then to vigorous social protest, then emerging out of propaganda to a pure use of the theatre medium for its own sake. He is a master of pleasant comedy, and the possessor of an original theatre intelligence. Among his better known plays are *Mundial, Pantomima, Isabel Sandoval, Modas, Pueblecito, La serpiente, Cuando venga el amor, Natacha, Señorita Charleston, Los hombres no lloran*. His experiment in drama for two players, *Del brazo y por la calle*, first produced in 1939, has a secure place in the repertoires of Mexican, Clilean, and Argentinean actors.

It is perhaps an augury for the future of the Chilean theatre that the greatest Spanish actress now makes her home in Chile. Margarita Xirgu, star of the short bright days between 1922 and 1936, went to Chile in 1937.

Her Spanish citizenship was taken away from her by Franco in 1941. She founded and now directs the Academia Dramática, which Chile has recognized by making it an integral part of the Teatro Nacional.

Of the theatre in other Spanish-speaking South American countries perhaps the safest comment is the old one about "least said, soonest mended." But even in lands where poetry has so completely absorbed literary attention that play writing is merely its neglected stepchild, there are occasional geniuses who persist in cultivating it. Thus Colombia has three dramatists, Antonio Alvarez Lleras, Alejandro Mesa Nicholls, and Luís Enrique Osorio, whose plays showed color and originality in a land too much given to imitating Spanish models. Alvarez Lleras, born in 1892, wrote among others *Los mercenarios, Fuego extraño,* and *Víboras sociales,* all of them mildly successful drama. His best known play, and perhaps the only one that will live, is *Como los muertos,* in which he has created a central character, Manuel, who seems as elemental a figure as Job. His contemporary and rival, Alejandro Mesa Nicholls (1896-1920) was only twenty-four when he died, but his *Golondrina errante, Juventud,* and *Lauro candente* had caught the attention of critics who promised a brilliant future for him. *Lauro candente* was awarded a national prize in 1919, and its fame traveled as far as Mexico, where Fernando Soler included it in his repertoire. Unfortunately it is one of the most bombastic of modern verse plays.

The third Colombian, Luís Enrique Osorio, born the same year as Mesa Nicholls, has had his plays produced in Mexico and France as well as in his own country. His works include *Flor tardía, Sed de justicia, El illuminado, Al amor de los escombros.*

Bolivia has one famous playwright, Mario Flores, popular and from the box-office point of view successful, if not approved by critics, but his career has been made in Buenos Aires. Paraguay enjoys the unexportable work of Julio Correa, a picturesque character who is not only playwright but also actor and director. He writes not in Spanish, but in that Indian dialect peculiar to Paraguay called Guaraní. Guaraní is seldom written, but is spoken "in the streets and the market places, in the children's games, among the groups of women gathered together, sometimes in the Congress, and nearly always at home.... A rich native tradition has been preserved in this language." Exploiting this spoken tongue, Correa organized the Elenco Teatral Guaraní in Asuncion. He plays there, and also in other Paraguayan towns where the success of his plays must in part be attributed to the popular speech in which they are written.

As for the other Latin American countries, aside from Brazil which is treated in a separate chapter there is not much of interest to report. Most of their modern adventures into playwrighting are the library type. No modern plays of importance have yet come out of Ecuador. Venezuela had an active popular theatre around the turn of the century, but has since enjoyed only touring companies and isolated attempts at an intellectual theatre which have died without issue. The five Central American countries —Guatemala, Honduras, Nicaragua, Costa Rica, Panamá—are no better off. They have a surplus of poets, and some of them write in drama form with a bow to the great tradition, but if an occasional play is produced it is as a student homage, and not as a commercial production which has possible influence on the theatre as a whole.

Mexico is in a very different position. If the logic of history had any reality, Mexico rather than Argentina should have developed the great Latin American theatre. Possessed of rich indigenous civilizations, first to feel the injection of European blood, possessing the first record of a theatrical performance in the European manner (1538), developing the famous playwrights Ruiz de Alarcón and Sor Juana Inés de la Cruz very early in her career, Mexico promised much and has performed little. An examination of the reasons for this failure lies outside the province of these pages. Experts in Mexican cultures like Anita Brenner claim that the native genius expresses itself in plastic, not verbal, forms. One is told that the native and the European cultures have never fused; that a truly Mexican culture has not come of age; or more crassly, that it is impossible to make a living writing for the Mexican stage because the professional companies have such bad taste.

Whatever the reason, with everything in its favor—artists, poets, and a national love for the medium—Mexico has never produced a great theatre. There have been innumerable cultured, educational, poetic, or merely propagandistic experiments, but never a continuing tradition.

The three facets of the stage in Mexico at present are the literary or art theatre in both play writing and producing, the professional stage, and the peoples' theatre. Obviously they touch edges, and there is a certain infiltration from one to the other. But the distance between these groups is greater than in the United States, and therefore it is not only possible but desirable to look at them individually and at what their contributions may be to the still embryonic Mexican theatre.

The experimental acting groups have in the main devoted their attention to good continental or American drama rather than to furthering the ambitions of Mexican playwrights. Teatro de Media Noche, Escolares del Teatro, El Teatro de Ahora and others represent a revolt against the commercialized theatre, just as the tributary theatre of the United States represents a revolt against too much Broadway. Their efforts have been heroic. They have developed a few actors and actresses, and given a first opportunity to a few new scenic artists, playwrights, directors, but there is little evidence that they have had much influence in creating a higher taste for drama or in leading the professional stage to change its policies. Even the most idealistic of them have shown a constant tendency to dissolve in financial failure or a clash of temperament.

The playwrights of note—which is to say of literary note—are such men as Xavier Villaurrutia, Rodolfo Usigli, Celestino Gorostiza, Juan Bustillo Oro, Carlos Díaz Dufoo, Alfonso Reyes, Mauricio Magdaleno.

Xavier Villaurrutia is one of Mexico's most brilliant young poets, and his plays have the same quality which distinguishes his poems—a kind of cerebral dramatic inquiry. They are exercises for the mind, and bear close kinship to the best European theatre of the avant-garde. *La hiedra* is a three-act drama written for María Teresa Montoya and recently played by her. *Parece mentira* (described as an "enigma in one act") and *¿En qué piensas?* were written for the experimental group called Orientación. Five of Villaurrutia's short plays were published this year under the title *Autos profanos*.

Rodolfo Usigli is not only a poet and a dramatist, but a teacher and a director of plays as well as a scholar learned in the history of the Mexican theatre. Among his plays are *Noche de estío, Estado de secreto, Medio tono, La mujer no hace milagros*.

Celestino Gorostiza was at one time director of María Teresa Montoya's company. In 1938 he was named director of the Departmento de Bellas Artes of Mexico, and in that position he has a hand in all the performances put on in the great Mexico City opera house. His plays are, unfortunately, a lesser manifestation of his skill in the theatre. *La escuela del amor, Ser o no ser,* and *Escombros del sueño* are merely pleasant comedies.

The professional companies devote themselves mostly to revivals of popular Spanish plays, or adaptations of plays popular in pre-war Europe or in the United States. This policy is, they claim, not so much their fault as their misfortune, for the output of native playwrights is too small and too far from the popular taste to satisfy the demand. All these companies work under a repertory system, which demands a great variety of plays to fill out a season. James Graham Luján reports,

As a result plays cannot be staged in the manner of the New York theatre. Paper sets and improvised costumes are the rule. Rôles are never fully learned, since each play must be rehearsed and put on in a few days' time, only to be replaced by another if it is not immediately successful. Actors play a great variety of rôles, keeping one ear cocked for the prompter who is as important here as he is in opera. For this reason, perhaps, the acting standard is not high. Success depends on an emotional tour de force in a single scene, which is supposed to compensate for pedestrian playing the rest of the evening.

But if both experimental and professional theatres in Mexico leave a lot to be desired by the searcher for vigorous talent, the peoples' theatre is quite another matter. Unhampered by literary ideals or foreign standards, under no need to pay rent, free to use their entertaining talents as they choose, the impresarios of the peoples' theatre flourish in good times and bad. Their sources of inspiration are all about them—the news, the circus, the movie, the radio, whatever happens or fails to happen in the life of nation, town, or family.

A few decades ago when literacy was scarcer than it is now, their entertainment was a combination of theatre and news broadcasting. "News vendors" would patrol the plazas and the market places reading lurid accounts of crimes of passion or of catastrophes. The nature of the news was not important. The suitably blood-curdling manner of reading was the true test of the star. Often a pious moral lesson was attached as a tag to make the heads of housewives wag. At the end, the reader took up a collection, or tried to sell a printed and highly colored version of his script. Some of these "news" stories passed into the repertoire of favorite actors and were good for years.

As in Argentina, the Mexican circus developed its own embryo theatre. At the end of the last century the Orrín circus had a marvelous spectacle called *La acuática*. It came under the heading of pantomime, but was definitely a production number. The name came from the fact that the ring was filled with water, into which comic or villainous characters were satisfyingly doused. The first *Acuática* was a play about a mother-in-law. Other circuses copied the act, and fashioned dramas of their own in which enough characters fell off bridges or trapezes so that the spectators could be splashed until they felt they had their money's worth.

This tent, or *carpa,* entertainment developed into *carpa* performances without benefit of water. At first the performers had their rôles mapped out for them. The characters were drawn from the lowest of folklore comedy types, the falls and dances were enriched with political allusions and combined with lechery to gladden the simple hearts of the audience. Finally the comedians grew so skilled that they depended only on scenarios of action, and improvised lines in true *commedia dell' arte* style.

The more famous of these comedians moved out of the *carpas* to stages where their gift for malice and innuendo might be enjoyed in a more sophisticated atmosphere. Cantinflas is the reigning dean of these geniuses, whose eminence depends on their skill in finding many roundabout ways to reach one point. Lesser stars are Palillo, Don Catarino, Chicote, La Flaca, El Panzón Soto.

Having lost their greatest and lewdest luminaries to a better-paying stage, the *carpas* are developing new performers and new acts. One ticket, costing around 35 centavos, usually entitles its holder to three *tandas,* or short reviews. The formula for these *tandas* usually includes a group of prettily made up guitar singers wearing *charro* costumes, one black-out act, a girl crooner clutching a dead microphone, a comedian, and a final big production number or *fin de fiesta* with the whole company on stage.

The inspiration for these acts comes from the movies, the radio, the Charleston of the twenties, or what have you. Joan Crawford and Greta Garbo are copied in make-up. There are *mestizo* versions of Shirley Temple. A few years ago audiences were sure to be convulsed with deprecatory remarks against the *gringos* whose idols the comedians were industriously imitating. Today, progress being what it is, the leading lady is apt to advertise chewing gum over the microphone while the audience take their seats. The *carpa* and its *tandas* are true popular theatre born of the dust and mud of Mexico, and using everything that comes as grist to their mill. The national talent for dramatic production finds its gayest and most unhampered expression here. What will come out of it, besides the droll and inexportable genius of a Cantinflas, remains to be seen, but such as it is it pleases multitudes and asks no quarter of superior dramatic traditions which also started in inn yards and at the tail of carts.

XI

Portugal and Brazil

MILDRED ADAMS

Compared with the richness of the post-Ibsen theatre in Spain, its neighbor Portugal has little of value to offer. The great days of Gil Vicente and Sá de Miranda are long gone. Worse, they seem to have left few traces of their genius outside the minds of scholars. The modern Portuguese play is deftly written, theatrically apt, frequently bombastic, about as deep and enduring as a soap bubble.

Before the war, Portuguese dramatists took their inspiration chiefly from French and Spanish models, and one of them—Júlio Dantas—learned his lesson so well that his plays have had the honor—unusual for a Portuguese dramatist—of being translated into both languages. Since 1940, when Lisbon became the febrile center where Axis, Allies, and refugees met but did not speak, the theatre has had as its prime problem the presentation of light plays which would lighten an aching heart without offending a suspicious mind. Under such circumstances it is not surprising that the production there of light bedroom farces has reached an all-time high. Even this relatively harmless common denominator in a world at war must proceed with care, for Dictator Salazar's code of morals is, like other fascist codes, high in the non-political fields.

Present conditions are in themselves enough to explain Portugal's present theatrical impotence. Countries which are neither the crossroads of a world at war nor the object of a dictator's jealous eye find themselves equally unable to do the moment justice. But in this instance one must also go behind present inadequacies and take a look at the tradition, or lack of it, which lies back of this preference for skits, monologues, farces, and other theatrical trifles. Is this a momentary deviation from a great past, which may end when the war ends and the world starts to rebuild? Or is there some deeper weakness in the Portuguese background which distinguishes the present plight of its drama from that of, say, the Spanish drama next door?

Looking down the long, thin line of Portuguese drama, from Gil Vicente at the dawn of the sixteenth century to the newest bright young playwright near the middle of the twentieth century, is unfortunately like looking down a long telescope and out at the small end. The record is not a strong and vital one, and, except for its brilliant beginning, not even a very interesting one. The Portuguese themselves are the first to recognize this. There are two theories as to its cause. Some think there is a quality in the dramatic form which is alien to Portuguese genius. Others argue that circumstances have been so severe that the theatre in Portugal has been withered every time it seemed to be gathering force enough to send out a new shoot.

There is evidence to support both theories. Those who believe that the drama is not the Portuguese way of expression point to the fact that even when the country seemed to be developing a really good dramatist he proved to have come under heavy foreign influence. Of her three greatest—Gil Vicente, Sá de Miranda, Antonio José da Silva—the first was half Spanish in his writing, the second spent most of his life outside of Portugal, the third was born in Brazil. Those who believe in environment point to the harsh disapproval exercised intermittently by both church and state for a period of three hundred years. Once in a while there was a king like João IV who loved Italian opera and fostered the theatre, or his successor who tried to be another "Roi Soleil." More often the record reads, "the king [or queen] was a religious fanatic who frowned on the theatre." These disapproving pressures are constants in the history of the Portuguese theatre, and their influence cannot be lightly disregarded.

On the positive side, the modern playwright in Portugal has five currents from which he can draw. There was the richly human and colloquial tradition set by Gil Vicente in the sixteenth century and reworked by Antonio José da Silva in the eighteenth. There are the classic models, stemming from Plautus and Terence, as interpreted by Sá de Miranda, Antonio Ferreiro, Luiz Vaz de Camões (usually spelled Camoens in English). To them should be added the romantic tradition best developed by Almeida Garrett, the realism moving in the arid footsteps of Scribe and Sardou, and always the pervasive habit of writing poetic drama.

Some day an American student of the theatre interested in exploring the ramifications of nineteenth-century Romanticism will delve into the lush history of Almeida Garrett, whose life spanned the first half of the nineteenth century and fortunately ended before Ibsen turned theatrical fashion away from him. He was a diplomat, a romantic liberal, a novelist and poet as well as a dramatist. It goes without saying that he admired Byron, and was exiled. Both were part of the romantic tradition. He is generally considered the best "modern" Portuguese playwright. His masterpiece was, as befitted his romantic temperament, a tragedy, *Frei Luiz de Sousa,* played first in 1844, and still ranking as one of the fine plays of the romantic period. His colorful personality and his success inspired many imitators. Cascais, Mendes Leal, César de Lacerda, Pinheiro Chagas, Rangel de Lima were among the best of his contemporaries; Gomes de Amorim followed him in the theatre.

But again the flame died, and the bitter currents of realism that then were building up found only embers to stir. From 1871 to 1900 there were no new plays of any note.

A Portuguese critic, Fidelino Figueiredo, in trying to acount for what he believes to have been the chilling effect of realism on Portuguese drama, contends that realism and the theatre are mutually incompatible. The theatre, he says, requires action that is neither banal nor like every-day life. The forms within which it flourishes are tragedy, high or satiric comedy, farce —all of them artificial. The theory fails to take account of Ibsen's success or the popularity of his realist followers in other countries. It does, however, shed an oblique light on the basic Portuguese attitude toward the theatre. Not since Gil Vicente wrote his famous trilogy on life and death (or as his titles put it, hell, heaven, and purgatory) has Portugal been willing to think seriously of the theatre as a place where daily problems are illumined, and even in those frank days the then modern problems were cast in symbolic terms.

There is unfortunately little material available in English for the student eager to study plays produced today on the Portuguese stage. Júlio Dantas may be read in French or in Spanish. He was born in 1876, has written historical plays in verse, and dramas of modern Lisbon. He knows how to put a play smoothly together, how to write expert dialogue, how to make characters walk and talk on the stage as they do on the street or in the drawing-room. *Rosas de todo o ano,* written with only two characters and appearing a tour de force for stars, is a fine example of his technical excellence. His *A ceia dos cardeais* was played successfully in France as *Le Souper des Cardineaux.* As Portugal is far more accustomed to seeing French plays in translation than to having its own plays put on in France, this added greatly to Dantas' repute.

A younger man, João da Câmara, covers a similar range—historical plays in verse, serious drama of Lisbon society, light comedy. His verse is too bombastic for American taste. *D. Afonso VI,* for instance, is written in heroic couplets that only a genius of the cloak-and-dagger school could handle. Of an opposite type is his *O pantano,* a study of madness and murder in modern Lisbon, whose characters are clearly and truly drawn, and whose chief theatrical fault is that the heroine, Luiza, talks too much. Also worthy of note is his *A toutinegra real,* slight in theme but excellent in dialogue. Senhor da Camara also did a free translation, in prose, of *The Merchant of Venice,* in which Portia, robbed of her creator's poetry, is merely sharp-tongued, long-winded, and unpleasantly contemporary.

To these two should be added the names of other men still writing and therefore still in a position to give the lie to the common belief that the modern Portuguese theatre has little to offer besides words that glitter in a vacuum. Abel Botelho and Fernando Caldeira, Augusto de Castro, José Maria de Sousa Monteiro, Antonio Enes, Augusto de Lacerda (who is also a critic of the theatre), Henrique Lopes de Mendonça, Marcelino Mesquita,

Bento Mantua, and Eduardo Schwalbach all enjoy a reputation in Lisbon. So do Vasco de Medonça Alves, Victoriano Graga, Alfredo Cortez, and the poet Jaime Cortesão. In their hands is the future of the Portuguese stage.

THE DRAMA OF BRAZIL

If the theatre of Lope de Vega and Calderon blossomed in strange and interesting ways on our side of the Atlantic, the sister theatre of Gil Vicente and Sá de Miranda has had a harder time. Not so well rooted at home, subjected to treatment that was even sterner, having only a single hotbed for the transplanting of its genius overseas, one cannot wonder that its Brazilian off-shoot has always suffered from a frail heredity. Nor have inclement surroundings and colonial timidity on this side of the ocean at all helped its growth.

Brazilian critics have been the first to deplore the results of this combination of circumstances. Machado de Assis, the country's most celebrated novelist and himself a playwright of some literary fame, said at the end of the nineteenth century, "As to our theatre, it can be summed up in two lines. There is no theatre in Brazil today." Múcio da Paixao, writing in 1936, carries on the same note, "Martins Penna died [in 1848] and nobody has since taken his place." Ronald de Carvalho, more analytical, says "In spite of its size in terms of number of plays written, theatrical literature [in Brazil] has never had the importance or the significance of poetry, the novel, or literary and historical criticism. "

In contrast to these gloomy condemnations it is cheering to find Alfredo Tomé, novelist and critic, saying that "1930 marks a decisive phase in the artistic and intellectual evolution of Brazil.... The Brazilian theatre is beginning to think."

It was in an attempt to overcome handidicaps and stimulate thinking that President Vargas in December 1943 approved appropriation of more than seven and a half million dollars for "an effective plan of cultural uplift for our national theatre." That plan includes eight steps—the formation of a Comedia Brasileira (perhaps on the general lines of the Comédie Française), a School of the Theatre for practical experience and training, a scheme for enlisting the enthusiastic support of audiences, an Experimental Theatre, an Opera Brasileira, a theatre magazine, and a Children's Theatre. This plan was the outcome of five years of experimenting carried on by the Servício Nacional do Teatro under the leadership of Abbadie de Faria Rosa. It is a part of the educational program which Vargas is having developed.

Not enough time has elapsed for the fruits of this plan to be visible, but one wishes it well. Obviously it cannot operate in a vacuum. The chances of its success or failure, the extent of its influence, become easier to estimate if one looks in more detail at the background against which the work must be done.

The colonial period in Brazil lasted, by strict definition, from the sixteenth century (when the Pope divided the then new world between Spain and Portugal) until 1821. In that year Pedro, son of King João VI of Portugal, revolted against his father and was proclaimed Emperor of Brazil. His son Pedro II, Emperor from 1831 to 1889, was a charming and conscientious ruler whose great desire was to raise the cultural level of his vast domain.

But if Brazil was no longer a colony under the two Pedros, its mental atmosphere continued to be what it had been before their advent. The attitude of its rulers was European, and the Pedro who loved learning and the arts loved them as had his ancestors a century or more before. The rule of the house of Braganza was not over until the revolt of 1889. Independent in political status though it may have been throughout the nineteenth century, Brazil was in every other regard still a colony. There are those who think she still suffers from the dampening effect of Portuguese overlordship, that she has not yet recovered from too-long subjection to the cultural influence of the mother country. Insofar as it affected drama, this influence was largely negative, first because Portugal herself had so little active theatre that was important, second because her oppressive religious and political strictures were even more harshly applied in the colony than at home.

In the case of her great eighteenth-century playwright António José da Silva this second factor worked very curiously. His mother was a Jewess, Lourença Coutinho, and as such the Inquisition sought her out in her native Brazil for questioning. His father, having little faith in the tender mercies of the Church militant, fled with his family to Lisbon where he could put them directly under the guardianship of the king. There they lived until 1739, when the Inquisition finally caught up with them.

In those thirty-six years of comparative freedom Antonio José da Silva had grown from a child of eight to a man writing plays that were compared with those of Molière in France and the sixteenth-century genius Gil Vicente in Portugal. He combined wit and malice with good humor, and an ability to please many tastes. His comedies satirized that false and precious period in which he lived, with Portugal dominated by a taste for Spanish comedy and Italian opera, meretricious to the last hair of its elegant wigs. His facility in caricaturing nobles and churchmen may have been a factor in his final end. Victim of an orgy of destruction with dramatic overtones, he was jailed, condemned to death, garrotted, and burned publicly in an *auto da fe*.

Thus the colony lost its greatest playwright to the mother country, and nowadays both Brazil and Portugal are proud to claim the Jew da Silva.

Perhaps it was in partial recompense that the mother country gave the colony its first theatre. In 1807 Napoleon invaded Portugal in his conquest of the Peninsula. The king Dom João VI fled with his nobles to the other side of the ocean and took refuge in his colony. Loving Italian opera, yearning in that new land for the European culture he had left behind, he built a sugar-candy playhouse in Rio and named it the Royal Theatre of St. John. For eleven years it housed drama imported from Europe by way of the Argentine. Then it burned down. Brazil's first Emperor, Dom Pedro I, rebuilt it and named it the Royal Theatre of St. Peter.

These European influences, loaded with the pomp and authority of power, weighed heavy on the new land. So pervasive were they throughout the nineteenth century that Brazil's "modern theatre," like Portugal's, flowered in the romantic era and withered when realism came into vogue. Only a handful of theatre names have survived, and all of them flourished before Ibsen brought fresh air and the problems of real life onto the world's stage.

Domingo José Gonçalves de Magalhães, Manuel de Araujo, Pôrto Alegre, Antonio Gonçalves Dias were poets first and dramatists second. Gonçalves de Magalhães (it is necessary to remember both names, for the Magalhães family was prolific in writers) is credited with having written in 1838 the first Brazilian play—*António José*. It dealt with the life of the famous playwright António José da Silva, but although the theme was Brazilian, the treatment was thoroughly European.

José Mariniano de Alencar was a famous novelist whose masterpiece *O Guaraní* has been made into a play. He also wrote plays on his own account, and one of them, *O demónio familiar,* was revived as recently as 1941 for the producer-comedian Procópio Ferreira in Rio. His *O Jesuita* may be read in English, one of the few Brazilian plays to be so translated.

Joaquim Manuel Macedo was another novelist who wrote plays more or less with the left hand, They were not very good plays, but good enough so that his name has survived. Another Joaquim, José da França Jr., was much more of a theatre draftsman. He wrote comedies designed for the stage rather than the library, and his satire *As Doutoras* ranks as one of the best of his period.

Brazil's pride among what are very loosely called "modern dramatists" is Luis Carlos Martins Penna. He was born in 1815, a romantic to the fingertips, and the whole of his short life was devoted to the theatre. Unlike so many of his contemporaries, his body of dramatic work is considerable. His plays are still produced, and for the best of all reasons—because they are good theatre and Brazilians like them. He lived only thirty-three years, but in that time he wrote thirty-seven plays. Nineteen of them are comedies, seventeen are serious plays, one is a tragicomic farce.

Martins Penna excelled in the comedy of manners. It is said of him that if all written chronicles of the first half of the nineteenth century in Brazil were destroyed—laws, history, literature—the life of the place and the period could be reconstructed from his plays. His most famous one, and the play usually regarded as Brazil's first national comedy, is *O Juiz de Paz na*

Roça. It was first played in 1838, the same year in which Gonçalves Magalhães' masterpiece was put on. Martins Penna regarded his surroundings with the merry eye which is still characteristic of Brazilians, and his wit, spontaneity, and grace have managed to survive for a hundred years.

With the second half of the nineteenth century came realism, and in Brazil, sterility. Whether Martins Penna would have been strong enough to stand out against the tide, or to make use of it for his own purposes, is anybody's guess. He died in 1848. With Martins Penna gone, the light and important virtues with which Brazilians meet life—wit, charm, gayety—were not strong enough to stand against the chilly currents sweeping down from Scandinavia. Neither Ibsen nor his imitators stimulated the Brazilians to try the realist way. Chilled by the fog, they withdrew into sterile imitations of the sunny past. Out of this whole latter half of the nineteenth century only two—Arthur Azevedo and the aging França Jr. are dramatists cited as writing anything that is now worth reading. Azevedo's *Amor por anexins* and *Uma víspera de Reis na Bahia* are typical.

As for the twentieth century, the history of Brazil's theatre in this present period remains to be written. Dr. Leo Kirschenbaum went to Brazil recently on a theatre research mission for the Office of the Coördinator of Inter-American Affairs, but the results of his study have not yet been published. Names there are in abundance, both of plays and playwrights, but no dramatist seems yet to have achieved any substantial body of work. It is what would be called here student theatre, improvised theatre, occasional theatre, rather than steady professional work. That is not to say that there are not professionals in the theatre world there—so able a man as the actor-producer Procópio Ferreira would by himself give the lie to any such charge. But the professionals are actors and their companies, producers and their stars. The playwrights are men to whom the theatre is only an avocation. They do their major work in other fields.

One must therefore be content with high-lighting a few names, and hoping that future research will provide the adequate criticism which is now missing.

In the 1920's, Cláudio de Souza held first place among dramatists. His sentimental play *Flores na sombra* had a long run. Joracy Camargo's satire on beggars and beggary, *Deus lhe pague,* celebrated as the first real social satire in Brazil, is still seen in revival. This play, and his *Anastácio* have been performed abroad.

R. Magalhães Jr. is the author of several comedies including the successful *Carlota Joaquina,* which played to full houses in 1939. Ernani Fornari, who bases his themes on folklore or on vaguely historical foundations, had long-run hits with *Yayá Boneca* and *Sinhá Mouca Chorou.* Viriato Correia, author of *Tiradentes* and other successes, adapted Martins Penna's *O Noviço* for Procópio Ferreira. Oduvaldo Vianna has seen his play *Amor...* played all over South America.

To these names may be added others which adorned the Brazilian theatre season of 1941—Mello Nobrega wrote *Nossa gente é assim,* J. Barroso wrote *Pensão de D. Stela.* Both of these were for the company of Jaime Costa and the latter, at least, was a great popular success. Gutta Pinho wrote *A casa branca da Serra;* Lirival Coutinho brought forth *Mulheres modernas;* Raul Pedrosa wrote *A comédia da vida*—all these for the Companhia Comédia Brasileira. That year also saw *Crescei e multiplicaivos* by Alcides Maciel and Silva Fontoura, and Amara Gurgel's *O pão duro.* Vicente Celestino had great popular success with *O ebrio.*

When the ambitious Vargas plan has been in operation long enough to begin to show results it may be possible to make a more just and complete appraisal. Until then, it is only fair to note that the evils which sap potential theatre strength in the rest of Latin America have also operated in Brazil. The theatre does not support its authors. Those who write plays must earn a living elsewhere—as government officials, as lawyers or doctors, even as writers in other fields. There are not plays enough tried out each season to inspire a movement or a school of drama. The companies must put on surefire audience material in order to survive, and this means translations of plays that have proved their worth elsewhere, or revivals of old favorites. Even so the skating is on thin ice, for the prices of admission bring few profits. The stars are more popular than the playwrights, and plays must be tailored to the particular talents of the popular male comedian or the popular female tragedian. Almost inevitably inspiration withers in the process. The educated theatre audience, interested in new ideas or in experimental forms, is very small, and limited as a rule to the colleges. The great mass audience is, in its power of understanding and enjoyment, far below the theatre-going level.

All these ills are known to Brazilians. Many of them are being attacked by the new Vargas program. Only time will tell whether intelligent state subsidy can cure them, or whether there is a basic weakness that lies deeper, and of which the well-known ills are only symptoms. There are those who allege that the Brazilian, for all his charm, is incurably frivolous, and incapable of achieving or appreciating important theatre. But this remains to be proved, and there is evidence against it. A public which stages and enjoys the great carnivals which are so important a feature of Brazilian life has in ample measure the love of make-believe, the depths of comic and tragic feeling, which are the root of all drama. Whether this genius can be fruitfully directed into the deep and narrow channel of the formal theatre is the real question still to be answered.

XII

Yiddish and Hebrew Drama

SAMUEL J. CITRON

The first language known to have been used by the Jews as a people was Hebrew, a Semitic language. The literature of the Jewish people, including the Old Testament, was, until the beginning of the third century A.D., written almost entirely in Hebrew and Hebrew has continued to be a language of Jewish creative writing until this very day. From the dawn of Jewish history until the Babylonian exile (586 B.C.) Hebrew was the language of everyday conversation as well as of literature. However, as the Jews in the course of history came in contact with peoples speaking other languages, and later, as the Jews spread over various other countries outside of Palestine, they created new languages and dialects which gained widespread acceptance and usage among them.

As far back as the sixth century B.C., Aramaic, a Semitic language closely akin to Hebrew, came into vogue among the Jews and quickly became the language of the people in Palestine and the surrounding countries. For some centuries the two languages were spoken side by side. But as time went on the circle of the Hebrew-speaking population grew smaller until Hebrew became exclusively the language of literature and prayer.

In many countries of their dispersion, Jews created new Jewish languages and dialects, based on the languages of the countries in which they were resident. Among the other languages which the Jews created one of the leading ones is Judesme or Ladino (Judeo-Spanish), in use now by *Sephardic* Jews (descendants of the Jews who were exiled from Spain and Portugal). But the most important of the diaspora languages now spoken by Jews is Yiddish. It was not until the revival of Hebrew which came as a result of the *Haskalah* (Enlightenment) movement in the nineteenth century and modern Zionism that Hebrew has again become a spoken, living language. At present, Hebrew is spoken by many Jews throughout the world and it is one of the three official languages of modern Palestine, where it is used almost exclusively by the approximate 600,000 Jews now living in that country.

Yiddish is the *Mame Loshon* (the mother-tongue) of all Eastern European Jewish communities as well as of many of the Jews throughout the world whose ancestors emigrated from those countries. In the 1940's there were about eleven million persons who spoke Yiddish. Although based on Middle German and sometimes mistakenly called a German dialect, the Yiddish language has had a development all its own. Like all modern languages, Yiddish shows strong influences of many other languages, in addition to German, particularly those of the countries in which the Yiddish-speaking Jews have lived. Strongly noticeable are Romanesque, Slavic, and of course Hebraic influences. Yiddish has been a spoken language, in one form or another, for about one thousand years. A vast folklore and important literature has been created in Yiddish. Not the least important branch of this literature is the Yiddish drama.

The acted drama is a comparatively recent development in Jewish life. The biblical injunction, "A man shall not put on a woman's garment" (Deuteronomy, XXII:5), as well as the fact that the early dramas were usually presented at festivals devoted to idol worship, were inimical to the development of the theatre among the Jews. With but minor exceptions, such as at Venice in the seventeenth century, there was simply no room for the theatre in the scheme of Jewish ghetto life. There are some Hebrew dramas in existence, which were written as early as the seventeenth century, among them the historical play *Yesod Olam (Foundation of the World)* by Moshe Zacuto (1630-1697) and *Asire Hatikvah (The Prisoners of Hope)* a morality play by Joseph Pensa de la Vega (1650-1703). The most noteworthy dramas of this period are the Biblical drama *Ma'ase Shimshon (The Story of Samson,* 1724) and the allegorical plays *Migdal Oz (The Mighty Tower,* 1727) and *La-Yesharim Tehillah* (1738) by the mystic, poet, and moralist Moses Hayim Luzzatto (1707-1746). There is no evidence, however, that these plays were ever produced or even intended for the stage.

Recently, new evidence has been discovered which leads to the conclusion that a comedy in Hebrew, intended for performance, was written as early as the middle of the sixteenth century. *Amon and Deborah* is attributed to the Jewish director of the Ducal Theatre of Mantua, Italy, Judah de Sumi. It is interesting to note that although the later plays of that period are historical or moralistic, *Amon and Deborah* deals with everyday problems.

Until the birth of the modern Yiddish theatre, Jewish dramatic activity seemed to be confined almost exclusively to presentations at weddings and on the occasion of the Festival of Purim. The "Fools" as the professional entertainers of the fifteenth, sixteenth, and seventeenth centuries were called, presented monologues and short sketches. Especially popular was the "Death Dance."

The theme of the Festival of Purim, the downfall of the arch anti-Semite Haman through the intercession of Queen Esther, is extensively used in the early Jewish drama. On this occasion, the rabbis condoned and often encouraged dramatic spectacles to add to the merriment of the festival. The Talmud speaks of early dramatic performances on Purim. At first these presentations were merely public hangings or burnings of an effigy of

Haman accompanied by quips and jokes. The better of these were handed down and repeated from year to year. In time the ceremonial acquired definite form so that as early as the fifth century A.D. we find in Italy a formal dialogue for the Purim celebrations.

An early dramatization of the story of Esther dates from the ninth or tenth century A.D. There are records of Jews participating in performances of the story of Haman's downfall from the fourteenth century A.D.

The *Purim Shpiels* (Purim plays) reached their greatest popularity during the seventeenth century and have continued to hold their own, in some places, to this very day. Some of these *Purim Shpiels* were presented in regular theatres, staged with scenery and costumes and accompanied by orchestras. Mainly, however, the *Purim Shpieler* (Purim player) was a strolling player presenting the plays in the homes of the important Jewish citizens of the town. The best known of these Purim plays and also the first to be printed is *A Beautiful, New Ahasuerus Play,* published anonymously in 1708. The cast of characters are Mordecai, Esther, Ahasuerus, Haman, Hatah, and a scribe. The piece was definitely composed for production, in a large place if available, otherwise in the homes of the townspeople. The play follows but loosely the plot of the Book of Esther. The chief emphasis seems to be on the comic dialogue, "gags," and rude jokes.

The appearance of this printed play aroused great opposition on the part of the Jews of Frankfort. Their opposition was not against Purim plays in general. It had by now become traditional to present plays on Purim for the merriment of the celebrants. They objected to the vulgarity of the piece, as witness the fact that when in 1710 Bermann of Limburg wrote and presented his *Purim Shpiel, Mechirat Yosef (The Selling of Joseph)*, a dramatization of the Biblical story of Joseph and his brothers, it was a huge success. Acted by Jewish students from Prague and Hamburg, presented with full stage effects, scenery, costumes, and orchestra it created such great excitement that two soldiers had to be detailed to handle the crowds.

The story of Esther and the sale of Joseph were the most popular themes for *Purim Shpiels*. The sacrifice of Isaac and the story of David and Goliath also served as subjects for *Purim Shpiels*. Until the latter half of the nineteenth century, the *Purim Shpiel* was practically the sole theatrical entertainment of the Jews.

The *Haskalah* (Enlightenment) movement among the Jews began in the second half of the eighteenth century under the influence of the German Jewish philosopher, Moses Mendelssohn. For centuries the Jew had been locked up in ghettos of Europe, from which he was just now beginning to emerge. Isolated from the life around him the Jew withdrew into himself, ignoring the new currents and devoting his entire time to the study and refinement of Rabbinic lore. Now that the ghetto walls were crumbling, Mendelssohn and his followers preached a rapprochement with other cultures. The *Maskilim* sought among other things to promote the study of sciences, foreign languages, a rational study of the Bible, and a revival of Hebrew literature. Among their other literary efforts, the *Maskilim* also took to writing dramas in Hebrew, not for performance but as a branch of the literary arts. The first dramatist in this new epoch was David Franks Mendez (1713-1792). He wrote two dramas which, though based on plays by Racine and Metastasio, nevertheless showed a good deal of originality. The first, *G'mul Athalia* (*Athalia's Reward*) is an adaptation of Racine's and Metastasio's dramas on the same theme. The second, *T'shuath Yisrael Bi'y'dei Yehudith* (*The Salvation of Israel Through the Hands of Judith*) is also an adaptation of Metastasio, and was written as a dramatic poem in two parts.

Other Hebrew dramas followed at fairly frequent intervals. Mendel Breslau wrote an allegorical drama *Yalduth U'Baharuth* (*Youth and Adolescence*, 1786). Samuel Humaneli was the author of the melodrama *Hakoloth Yehdalun* (*The Voices Shall Cease*, 1791). In the next four years there followed *Saul's Kingdom*, a biblical drama in six scenes by Joseph Trepolwitch; *War in Peace* by Hayim Abraham ben Aryeh; and *Esther* (after Racine) by Joseph Haltern.

The appearance of dramas in Hebrew became a common occurrence. Since these dramas were frankly not written for the stage, they did not have to take into consideration the tastes of the average theatre-goer. Consequently they were of high literary quality.

At about this time appeared the first two modern comedies in Yiddish. Isaac Eichel (1756-1804) was a disciple of Moses Mendelssohn and his biographer. A firm believer in *Haskalah*, he was exceedingly active in the movement to spread modern learning among the masses of the Jews. In 1793 or 1794 he wrote the first modern Yiddish comedy, *Reb Henoch*. The play is a satire of Jewish life of the time with its exaggerated fanaticism and parental despotism on the one hand and irresponsibility of the so-called "enlightened" elements on the other and is written in a thoroughly naturalistic style. There is a conscious attempt to copy the manners, style, and language of each character. The dialogue of the characters of the older generation is in Yiddish, that of the "enlightened" characters in German, and the Englishman and Frenchman that appear in the comedy use a mixture of German, English, and French. Although the play was not written for performance on the stage but was rather dedicated to the reading public it is of prime importance in the history of the development of Yiddish drama. With the exception of some early examples of Hebrew drama, this was the first time that a Jewish author took his theme not from classical literature or ancient history but from the everyday life of the Jewish people.

Ahron Halle (Wolfsohn) (1754-1835) was a rabid follower of Moses Mendelssohn. He was convinced that the *Haskalah* was the only means for combatting anti-Semitism. He waged bitter warfare against those Jews who stressed ritual observance to the exclusion of all worldly interests.

Editor, grammarian, translator, and Bible commentator he, like most other *Maskilim,* venerated Hebrew and held Yiddish, the "Diaspora language," in contempt. This attitude toward Yiddish did not prevent him from writing *Leichtsin und Fremmelai* in Yiddish. The play was published in Breslau in 1796 without the author's permission. An authorized version, with a foreword by the author, was published in Amsterdam in 1798. Unlike the Hebrew plays of the period, this play was definitely intended for the stage. In his foreword Halle states that he wrote the play with a threefold purpose: (1) to replace the Purim plays with modern drama which would deal with the living problem of the Jew; (2) to fight fanaticism in Jewish life; (3) to fight modern Jewish youth that has gone on the wrong path and under the guise of "enlightenment" has become totally irresponsible.

As may be seen from the author's own introduction, the play was definitely tendencious and typical of the *Haskalite* literature of the day. Reb Henoch, a pious Jew, is the father of Yettchen, who has had a smattering of modern learning. Believing herself to be a most progressive young lady, Yettchen dresses in the latest mode and scorns the company of Jewish young men, preferring the non-Jewish playboys. Her father decides to marry her off to a certain Yosefko, his son's teacher, who makes a pretense at being extremely pious but is in reality a charlatan of the worst sort. Yettchen's uncle Marcus, a modern, educated young man, is in love with her but he receives little encouragement from either Yettchen, who prefers her playboy friends, or from her father, who dislikes Marcus because of his modern education. When Yettchen learns of the proposed match she runs away from home seeking asylum with one of her friends, a certain Count. The Count, embarrassed at her presence in his house, sends her to the home of an acquaintance. This home proves to be a brothel. The hypocritical Yosefko comes to the brothel, where he has been a frequent visitor, and asks to be entertained by the "new girl." Yettchen's uncle and father, who have been frantically searching the town for her, come to the brothel. There they discover the perfidious teacher and also find the foolish girl who, overjoyed at her rescue from a life of shame, marries her rescuer, the noble Marcus.

Leichtsin und Fremmelai was the only Yiddish play which Halle wrote. It remained for the *Maskilim* in Russia to lay the foundations for the yet unborn Yiddish theatre. The battle for "enlightenment" was carried on very vigorously in that country. The majority of the Jews in Russia led an extremely pious existence. Many of them were *Hassidim.* The *Hassidim* were extremely pious, following to the letter every Jewish religious law. Formed at first as a protest movement against formalized learning, *Hassidism* developed an additional body of rituals all its own. In common with all other pious Jews of the time, they regarded their very dress as sacred. They believed in favorite saintly rabbis who, they felt, were God's messengers on earth and capable of performing miracles. A change in the traditional dress, the study of a foreign language, the reading of a secular book, were considered by them to be acts of heresy. Naturally, the *Maskilim* were anathe..... to the *Hassidim,* and the *Maskilim* in turn fought the fanaticism of the *Hassidim* with every weapon at their command. The pen was the *Maskil's* mightiest weapon and he wielded it with vigor. Most of the literature of the period was written in order to ridicule the *Hassidim,* to expose them as a sham and fraud—a dark force in Jewish life. Some of these accusations were undoubtedly justified; but many writers tended to exaggeration. Their work must therefore be considered with caution with the understanding that it was the result of bitterness engendered in an ideological war.

Despite the fact that the *Maskilim* were contemptuous of Yiddish, which they considered as being merely a jargon, they nevertheless wrote in that language when they wanted to reach the great mass of Jews, most of whom knew no other language. To this group of writers belong Solomon Ettinger, Israel Aksenfeld, and Abraham Ber Gottlober.

A pioneer of modern Yiddish drama, Dr. Solomon Ettinger (1800-1856) was born in Warsaw, Poland. Orphaned at an early age, he was brought up by his uncle, Mendel Ettinger, Rabbi of Lentshitz, who, despite his extreme piety and rabbinical position, displayed a tolerant attitude toward secular learning and was himself well versed in German. This greatly influenced Ettinger's later attitude—that one can be well educated in secular studies and still be a thoroughly observant Jew, an attitude which was most unusual at that time. Married at the age of eighteen, Ettinger tried business, at which he proved a failure. For a time he studied medicine in Lemberg and later in Warsaw. After a number of years as a practising physician, he organized an agricultural colony near Zamosc and settled there with his family. In this manner he was giving practical expressions to his creed that a Jewish back-to-nature movement would be the best antidote to anti-Semitism.

Ettinger wrote poetry, epigrams, and fables. He is best remembered, however, for his five-act play *Serkele.* This play, one of the first modern Yiddish dramas, played an important rôle in the development of later Yiddish playwrights and was directly responsible for the foundation of the modern Yiddish theatre through the influence which it exerted on Abraham Goldfaden.

Serkele was written in 1825 or 1826. For many years it remained in manuscript. In 1843 Ettinger attempted to have it published. The government censor, however, insisted on many changes which would have completely mutilated the play, and it was not until 1861 that the play was finally published in Johannesburg, Prussia. Nevertheless the play became popular. Copies of the manuscript passed from hand to hand and were read by many with a great deal of pleasure. Ettinger himself did no little to popularize it. He read it to friends and patients on the slightest provocation. Returning temporarily to the practice of medicine during a cholera epidemic, he would say to his patients, "Why worry about cholera? Just let me read for you my *Serkele* and you will get well immediately."

Though dealing with a well-worn situation, the treatment is refreshing. The characters are alive. They are real people and not types as was so often the case in the earlier Hebrew drama. Serkele's brother has gone on a journey and has been reported killed. Serkele forges his will and inherits his fortune. The brother's only daughter is brought up by Serkele, who mistreats her cruelly. Serkele's own daughter is betrothed to a merchant who turns out to be a swindler and a thief. To add to the retribution that is visited on Serkele, the report of her brother's death proves to be false. He returns home and Serkele has to give back all his property.

The play was never performed publicly during its author's lifetime. In 1862, six years after his death, the play was staged in the Government Rabbinical School of Zhitomir by Madame Slonimska, the wife of the school director Hayim Zelig Slonimsky. Students of the school acted in the performance, which created a furore among the intelligensia of Zhitomir. The main part of Serkele was acted by the Rabbinical student, Abraham Goldfaden, who later became the father of the modern Yiddish theatre. It is interesting to note that not only did *Serkele* influence the "father" of the Yiddish theatre but also the "reformer" of the Yiddish drama, Jacob Gordin. It will be noted later that *Serkele* was the prototype of Gordin's greatest character creation, Mirele Efros.

Israel Aksenfeld (born toward the end of the eighteenth century, died 1868) was a curiosity among the *Maskilim* in that to a degree greater than Ettinger, he wrote *only* in Yiddish, in order to reach the Jewish masses who knew no other language (although he himself was not limited in the use of languages). Though born of a *Hassidic* family, and receiving a traditional rabbinic education, through self-education he acquired a wide knowledge of law, literature, science, and languages. He spoke Russian, Polish, and German fluently, making his living as translator and notary.

Aksenfeld wrote most of his plays in the second decade of the nineteenth century. None of them was published however until nearly forty years after being written. Three of his works were published in 1862, six years before his death. Written on contemporary themes, they had lost a great deal of their value by the time they finally appeared in print, since the mode of life had changed completely. His most important play was *The First Jewish Recruits In Russia* (written around 1827, published 1862). The play deals with the terror among the Jews when the ukase of 1827 was promulgated by Czar Nicholas I, requiring that every Jewish community must contribute a number of recruits to the Imperial army. These recruits were required to serve in the army for a period of twenty-five years. To fill the quotas young children of twelve and even younger were impressed and exposed to the cruelest suffering. In the play, however, Aksenfeld develops the thesis that this ukase upon which the Jewish communities looked as on a calamity, was really a blessing in disguise. It would afford the Jewish recruits an opportunity to distinguish themselves in battle and thereby win from the Czar important concessions for their oppressed brothers. History has of course proven the falsity of his premise. However, though tendencious in the extreme, the author permits some of the characters in the play to express strongly different opinions from those held by him. Most of the characters are drawn true to life, employing the colloquial language spoken by the masses. His other published dramas are *Husband and Wife, Sister and Brother* (1862) a drama on the theme of mistaken identity, *The Treasure*, and *Rich Man, Poor Man* both published a few years later.

According to his own testimony, Abraham Ber Gottlober (1811-1899) turned to Yiddish play writing under the influence of Ettinger's *Serkele*. Gottlober was one of Dr. Ettinger's patients during the cholera epidemic in Zamosc and following his custom, Ettinger prescribed *Serkele* as a surefire cure for cholera. Gottlober says, "Ettinger read me his *Serkele* and I was cured...."

Despite the struggle which raged between the *Hassidim* and *Maskilim*, both Ettinger and Aksenfeld were on friendly terms with the opposing camps of *Hassidism* and *Haskalah*. Such was not the case with Gottlober. Because of his personal experiences he became a bitter enemy of the *Hassidim*. Married at an early age, he lived in Tshernichov with his father-in-law, who was a devout *Hassid*. The young Gottlober, under the influence of Joseph Perl, the well-known *Maskil* of Tarnopol, began to read secular books. When the Zhitomir *Hassidic* rabbi found out about the young man's *Haskalah* tendencies he prevailed upon his father-in-law to force him to divorce his young wife and leave her with his child, whom he loved very dearly. It was therefore natural for Gottlober to nurture a fierce hatred of *Hassidism* in general and *Hassidic* rabbis in particular. In his drama *The Marriage Veil* (written 1838, published anonymously 1876) Gottlober attacks the entire structure of *Hassidism*. He portrays the *Hassidim* as hypocrites and charlatans of the worst sort. The town rabbi is portrayed as a mere simpleton, while the *Hassidic* rabbi is depicted as an outright swindler, playing on the credulity and superstitions of his followers.

It is important to retell the story of *The Marriage Veil*, since it greatly influenced Goldfaden in his approach to the establishment of a practical theatre. Yossele, the hero, a devotee of *Haskalah* thought, is in love with Freudele. His father, however, has chosen for him a bride who, though blind, is a rabbi's daughter. Freudele's father has found for her a groom who is facially disfigured but stems from the "aristocracy of learning." Both weddings are to take place on the same night. Among the wedding guests is a *Hassidic* rabbi, a charlatan who impresses the wedding guests with tales of his own miracles. While the guests are at evening prayer, Yossele steals the rabbi's hat and pipe. Dressed in the rabbi's finery and covered with a shroud he meets the party that is bringing the noseless bridegroom to town. The bridegroom is wearing a veil so that his bride may not see his disfigured face until after the wedding ceremony. On seeing the shroud-covered apparition every one runs in fright, leaving the bridegroom behind. Yossele brings him to the blind bride's home where the noseless groom marries the blind bride. Yossele puts a veil on his own face and thus marries his true love.

The characters in *The Marriage Veil* are sharply drawn. Each uses his own characteristic language, the coach driver using coarse speech, the rabbi the language of Talmudic disputations, and so forth. The humor is broad and leans to the vulgar and the play is interspersed with amusing couplets. In short, it is the type of play which would appeal to the masses of the time, whose education was limited and whose esthetic sense was undeveloped. Although, by his own testimony, Gottlober did not write his play for theatrical performance but rather to be read aloud as parlor entertainment, he nevertheless exhibited an understanding of the kind of play that would be needed in the yet unborn Yiddish theatre in order to appeal to the ignorant masses who were to be the bulk of its audiences. There is no doubt that Goldfaden heeded well the lesson of *The Marriage Veil* when he wrote his early pieces for the new-born Yiddish theatre forty years later.

Another of the pre-Goldfaden playwrights, Ludwig Levinsohn (1842-1904) also directed his humor at the *Hassidim* in his comedy *The Women's Knots* (1874). It is interesting to note that in connection with this comedy there is quite a dispute as to who is its real author. The play appeared under the name of Israel Meir Wohlman (1821-1912). The preponderance of scholarly opinion is, however, that Levinsohn was the author of the play. He turned it over to Wohlman for publication and, while publishing it, Wohlman also put his name to it as author.

Whoever the author may have been, *The Women's Knots* is one of the best Yiddish comedies of the period. The title refers to the custom of the women who kept their savings tied in knots in the corners of their handkerchiefs. Yekel, a *Hassid* in need of money, tells his wife that the old noble to whom the town belonged has died and that his heir, the young noble, is demanding that the Jews pay up all the overdue taxes immediately. Unable to raise the needed funds, the townspeople have decided to abolish the prohibition against polygamy. Each man will marry a number of wives and every new bride will bring a dowry. The money thus realized will be used to pay the taxes. Yekel's wife spreads the word among the women of the town. Frightened, the women dig out their hidden hoards from their kerchief knots and turn the money over to their husbands. The men, surprised at the unexpected windfall, immediately spend their wives' life savings on a grand spree.

While the playwrights mentioned above were creating a repertory which was later to influence the founders of the Yiddish stage, the Broder Singers were creating an audience for the future theatre. Wandering troubadours, the Broder Singers appeared on the Jewish scene around 1850 and gave their primitive theatrical performance until the end of the 1870's. Their name was derived from Brod in Galicia, the city from which the first of these troubadours came. There were many troupes of Broder Singers and they gave their performances in the cafés, restaurants, and wine-cellars. They sang the popular Yiddish songs and ballads of the day. In time they added some dialogue as introduction to and connecting links between songs. They also used a certain amount of costuming and make-up. The dialogue and plot were incidental however to the songs. An example of the Broder Singers' type of repertory is the dramatization of the song "The Thief," a favorite written by Velvel Zbarzher (born the second decade of the nineteenth century, died 1883). The song is introduced by the following scene: a Jew is sitting on his bed reciting his bedtime prayer. The thief enters stealthily, packs up the Jew's belongings, and leaves. Suddenly noticing the theft, the Jew calls for help. A policeman apprehends the thief, who then proceeds to sing the song, "The Thief."

Primitive though these performances were, they were with the exception of the *Purim Shpieler* and the *Badhonim* (Wedding Jesters), the only theatrical entertainment available at the time to the Jewish masses. Consequently, they were very popular. Thus, the Broder Singers not only created the future audience of the Yiddish theatre but also formed its taste in theatrical entertainment, thereby pointing the road which was to be followed by Yiddish dramatists who were to write for the commercial Yiddish theatre. The influence of the Broder Singers is obvious to this very day in the repertory of that branch of the Yiddish stage.

With the exception of the Broder Singers and a few years of organized theatre production in Warsaw (1838-1839 and 1866-1870) no professional theatre was in existence in which plays might be performed. Nevertheless many writers of the period used the dramatic form in their literary work. In addition to the comedies already mentioned there were the social-problem play *Kohol in Shtetel* by Wolf Kamrash; the Biblical plays *Jacob and His Sons* (1868) and *Judith* (1870) by Gedaliah Belloi; *Reb Hayim'l the Tycoon* and *Rachel the Singer* by J. B. Falkowitch; and the comedies *The Three Cousins, The Kol Boi'nik,* and *Mondrish* by Isaiah Gutman.

A headstone in New York's Washington Cemetery proclaims that there lies "Abraham Goldfaden, poet, playwright, and founder of the Yiddish Theatre." Seldom is the historian able to point out with any degree of certainty that this person or the other was the father of any people's national theatre. There is no question, however, about the paternity of the Yiddish Theatre. Abraham Goldfaden (1840-1908) consciously and deliberately set out on the task of founding a professional Yiddish Theatre. It is true that even before Goldfaden there had been a number of professional theatre productions. They were, however, isolated ventures doomed to quick failure. It remained for this ex-rabbinical student to establish the theatre on a firm foundation and to give it its scope and direction.

Born in Old Constantine, Province of Volhynia, Russia, Goldfaden began writing poetry at a very early age. At the age of ten he had acquired a certain amount of local fame with a Hebrew poem which he had written. His father, an ardent follower of the *Haskalah,* gave him an education in the modern spirit which included the study of Russian, German, and Hebrew.

In the government school, where Goldfaden was enrolled at an early age, he became a favorite of Abraham Ber Gottlober, who was at that time a teacher in the school. Gottlober taught him Hebrew and fanned his poetic ambitions. From Gottlober too, Goldfaden acquired a love for the drama. When, upon completion of his studies at the Government School, Goldfaden was enrolled at the government Rabbinical college in Zhitomir, his reputation as a poet and composer of popular folk songs gained for him the favor of his teachers and fellow students. On more than one occasion this reputation helped him to pass certain subjects, such as mathematics, in which he was not very proficient. At the Rabbinical college, Goldfaden played the title rôle in that school's memorable production of *Serkele*. When he graduated in 1866 he had to his credit a published collection of his Hebrew poems (1865) and a group of Yiddish poems, published under the title of *Dos Yidele* (1866).

To earn a living he took a position as teacher in a government school in Simferopol. From there he transferred to a school in Odessa, in which city he also married. Dissatisfied with the low pay, he abandoned teaching and eventually opened a large ladies' hat shop. It seems that as a businessman Goldfaden was no better at figures than as a rabbinical student. His business failed and as a bankrupt he was forced to leave Russia.

He came to Munich with the intention of studying medicine, which idea he abandoned very quickly. By this time his name was already well known because of his songs which were sung in many Jewish homes. It was only natural for him to try and earn his living from journalism. In 1875 he published, together with Yoel Linetsky, the humorous weekly, *Yisrolik*. After a short time, the venture ended in failure. The following year in Bukovina, he published the *Bukovina Israelitishe Folks Blatt*. This newspaper too met with little success. After a few issues, it suspended publication. A subscriber, Isaac Lubrescu, urged him to move his newspaper to Yassy in Rumania. Goldfaden heeded Lebrescu's advice and came to Yassy. Although he never revived the paper, his arrival in Yassy marked a turning-point in his career as well as in the history of the Yiddish theatre and drama.

When Goldfaden arrived in Yassy, he already had to his credit two published Yiddish plays which he had written under the influence of Ettinger and Gottlober. *The Two Neighbors* and *Aunt Sosie* (both published in 1869) were written with the light, comic touch typical of Goldfaden. The first is only a satiric dialogue which demonstrates Goldfaden's ability to observe and record natural dialogue and human foibles. Two mothers are watching their children at play. In loving words they express their mutual devotion. Ecstatically they plan for the day when their children will marry each other. In the meantime a quarrel breaks out between the children, whereupon the love between the mothers changes to savage hate and the honeyed words become fierce curses.

Aunt Sosie is considered by many to be Goldfaden's masterpiece. Although it clearly shows the influence of Ettinger's *Serkele,* it contains some of Goldfaden's best work. It faithfully mirrors the Jewish life which its author knew so well. Sosie, like Serkerle, rules the household. She tries to marry off her sister to a "Lithuanian" who, although willing, is unable to go through with the match because his wife appears on the day of the wedding and "saves" him from committing bigamy. Sosie's hen-pecked husband, by enlisting the aid of a friend and a measure of deceit, proves to be a more successful matchmaker when he marries off his ill-treated niece to Sosie's own brother.

Goldfaden's fame as songwriter and playwright had preceded him to Yassy. At that time Israel Gradner, one of the most famous of the Broder Singers, was giving concerts in Yassy. Possessing a fine voice and excellent though undeveloped acting ability, Gradner was not satisfied with performing in private homes and wine-cellars. He played only the big cities. Wherever he came, he rented a large hall, built a platform, numbered seats, and advertised regular performances of dramatized songs. His repertory included a number of Goldfaden songs, and when Goldfaden came to Yassy, Gradner came to see him. In need of money, Goldfaden tried to sell some new songs to the singer. Gradner was willing to include them in his repertory but refused to pay any money, on the ground that the popularity which the author gained by having Gradner sing his songs should be sufficient payment. A joint concert, however, was arranged. Goldfaden appeared in a frock coat and recited some of his best poems, but was given a cold reception by the audience. Only the appearance of Gradner, with his outlandish costume and comic song and patter saved the day. The near-fiasco of this concert proved a valuable lesson to Goldfaden. The intellectuals preferred the more sophisticated gentile theatre. The great masses who were to be the future audiences for the Yiddish theatre preferred broad comedy—song and dance—to serious literature. Fired with the idea of founding a Yiddish theatre, Goldfaden realized that he would have to build from the bottom up. Determined consciously to write down to his audiences, he wrote a few songs, called in Gradner and the latter's assistant, Socher Goldstein, and outlined the action to them. Dialogue was left to chance. The play was in two acts and was presented for the first time in October, 1876, in Simon Mark's Wine-Cellar. Goldfaden thought so little of it that in later years he did not even remember its name. It was an experiment and a beginning, the first modern Yiddish play written for production—the first production of the modern Yiddish theatre.

From Yassy, Goldfaden went with his troupe to Batishani where he wrote his farce *The Recruits* (1877). This was just prior to the Russo-Turkish War and Rumania pressed into army service every available man. Goldfaden barely escaped by hiding in an attic. A play about recruits was a "natural."

As soon as the situation eased up somewhat, Goldfaden added to his two stars a number of boys, whom he hired off the streets to act as extras, and staged his *Recruits*. The action of the play is very simple and depends in large measure upon the songs. It deals with the recruits who are impressed against their will into the army. Unlike Aksenfeld's recruits in the latter's play of the same name, Goldfaden's recruits do not enter the army to prove the heroism of the Jew. The treatment which the Jews had received from their government left them little reason to want to fight for it. They proved themselves to be so useless that they were all soon released.

He soon moved his theatre to Bucharest where he remained until the end of the Russo-Turkish War (1878). Here Goldfaden added a number of talented actors to his troupe, most of whom were drawn from the ranks of synagogue choristers. Among them was the talented comedian Sigmund Mogulesco. Goldfaden now wrote and staged a number of slight pieces, such as *The Grandmother and the Granddaughter, The Intrigue,* and *Shmendrik* (1877). While in Bucharest the aversion to women on the stage was overcome when the first woman, Sophie Karp, joined Goldfaden's troupe. Up to this time all women's rôles were played by men. The story is told that Goldfaden induced Sophie Karp to appear in a play, but after her first performance, her mother forbade her to continue. She told her, "as long as you are in my home you will not disgrace me by appearing on the stage. After you are married, you can do as you wish." Taking Sophie's mother literally, Goldfaden induced Socher Goldstein, the only eligible man, to marry Sophie, and thus he acquired an actress for the troupe.

Shmendrik, which was based on a popular Rumanian theatre piece, was written for Mogulesco. This caused Gradner to leave the theatre and form his own troupe. Joseph Lateiner (1853-1935) became his staff playwright. Born in Yassy, Rumania, Lateiner received a traditional Jewish education. At the age of seventeen he came under the influence of the *Haskalah* and turned to general studies. The advent of Goldfaden awoke in him the desire to write for the theatre, and Gradner's need of plays for his new troupe gave Lateiner his first opportunity.

Lateiner's first plays, such as *Yente Die Pipernoterin* (1877), *The Two Shmuel Shmelkes* (1876), and *The Love of Jerusalem* (1877)—which was based in part on Mapu's novel of the same name and partly on Werbel's *The Weasel and the Well*—followed Goldfaden's style. Later, when Lateiner became one of the major staff authors of the Yiddish theatre in New York, he developed a style all his own.

About this time a new troupe was formed, for which "Professor" Moses Hurwitch (1844-1910) became the staff writer. Hurwitch was born in Stanislawow, Galicia. His education followed the line which has become almost classic for the time: a traditional Jewish education until the age of eighteen, then *Haskalah* and self-education in secular subjects. He emigrated to Rumania where he was in turn Hebrew teacher, newspaper editor, and director of a Jewish school. He began his writing career with *The Tyrannical Banker* (1877), an adaptation of a Rumanian theatre piece; *The Polish Boy* (1878), a dramatization of Linetzki's novel of the same name; and *The Island Wilderness* (1878), a translation of a Rumanian play.

Thus in the short space of two years from the time that the Yiddish theatre was founded, there were already numerous troupes playing, each with its own author, all of them giving the same type of plays, melodramas or farces which were mainly dependent on their songs and in which, in most cases, plot and dialogue were merely incidental. The "Dictatorship of Goldfaden," was felt very strongly in the Yiddish drama of that day. His models were followed by all dramatists. However, although plots and dialogue were highly exaggerated and the situations artificial and unnatural, nevertheless, each of the Goldfaden plays, even his earliest, had one or two real characters, sharply drawn. No matter how tailor-made the play, it had a healthy, realistic basis in everyday life.

The close of the Russo-Turkish War brought to an end the prosperity in Rumania and ushered in a hard time for the new-born Yiddish theatre. Goldfaden moved with his troupe to Odessa in 1879. Some of the others had preceded him. The rest soon followed and Russia now became the center of the Yiddish theatre. Though successful with the masses, the Jewish intelligentsia considered Goldfaden's plays poor literature and in bad taste. To counteract his influence they supported the theatre founded by J. J. Lerner (1847-1907) who believed that the function of the dramatist is not to write down to his audience but rather to lift the audience to the dramatist's intellectual level. Lacking adequate dramas in Yiddish, he translated plays from the non-Jewish repertory which dealt with Jewish heroes and themes. The most successful of these was his translation of Gutzkow's *Uriel Acosta* (1880). Nahum Meir Shaikewitch (1849-1905), the popular novelist of the time who wrote under the pen-name of Shomer, was induced to dramatize some of his novels, among them *The Jewish Noble, The Convict, The Penitent,* and *The Bloody Farewell.*

By way of answering his critics, Goldfaden turned to Jewish history for his subjects and wrote some of his best plays on historical themes. By far the best of these is *Shulamith* (1880, published 1886). The play is simple in theme and replete with tuneful songs, which have become a part of the folk music of the Jew. A tale of ancient Palestine, the play deals with the love of Shulamith and Absalom. They swear eternal love to one another, and they ask the weasel and the well to be witnesses to their eternal troth. Absalom, however, breaks his oath and marries another girl. The witnesses exact their vengeance—one of his children drowns in the well and the other is killed by the weasel. Penitent, Absalom divorces his wife and returns to his first love, Shulamith.

Shulamith marked the transition of Goldfaden from *Haskalah*—grotesqueries of Jewish life to *Hibbat Zion* (Romantic Zionism) as exemplified by his historical plays. To this later group also belong *Dr. Almosado* (1882), a musical drama of the Spanish Inquisition and *Bar Kochba* (1883), a musical drama of the last Judean revolt against the Romans. In addition such plays as the *Two Kuni Lemels* (1880), *Braindele Kozak* (1877), *The Tenth Commandment* (written 1882, produced 1887), and *The Witch* (1877) have remained to this day in the repetory of the Yiddish Theatre.

In the short period of seven years since its founding, the Yiddish theatre had made great strides forward. From the first skits of Goldfaden to his *Bar Kochba* there was tremendous growth. Now the intelligentsia, attracted to the Yiddish theatre, began to press for better dramas. Such outstanding writers as M. L. Lillienblum, Katzenelenbogen, and S. J. Abramowitch (Mendele Moher S'farim) the "grandfather" of Yiddish literature, tried their hands at the drama. It looked indeed as if the child so humbly begotten in Yassy would grow to healthy maturity in Russia. Then the whole movement collapsed. In September, 1883, the Russian Government issued an edict which forbade performances of Yiddish plays, an edict which sounded the death-knell of the nascent Yiddish drama in Russia.

Many efforts were made to have the edict rescinded. All to no avail, but permission was finally granted for performances in German. Now began an era of masquerading and subterfuge. The old repertory was staged but the actors no longer spoke their dialogue in Yiddish. Instead a mongrel German was heard in the Yiddish theatre. This was the era of the "broad *a*." To make their Yiddish sound like German, they spoke all words normally pronounced with an *o* as in *love* like *a* as in *father*. Thus purely Hebraic words like *L'vono* (moon) became *L'vana!* The Government soon became aware of the subterfuge and put a stop to this "German" theatre. Actors in need of a meal tried other ways out. For example, they would get permission to stage the Ukrainian operetta *Natalka Poltava*. The Jewish audiences on reading the announcements were aware of the ruse. Actually, the troupe gave one of the Goldfaden plays, such as *Shulamith*. Often, in the middle of a performance, the signal would be given that the chief of police was coming to check up. The actors would immediately leave the stage and return a few moments later with their ancient Hebrew costumes replaced by Ukrainian. The aged Manoah of *Shulamith* was now a peasant doing a Kamarinska and Shulamith appeared with two pails singing a Ukrainian folk song.

Needless to say, under such circumstances there could be no question of any new drama being created in Russia. The bulk of the actors and writers left that country. Many of them went to England, but eventually the majority came to the United States, which for many years became the center of the Yiddish theatre and drama.

There were theatres in several cities in the United States but it was New York, because of its heavy concentration of Jews which now shaped the destiny of the Yiddish drama.

As a result of the first pogroms against the Jews in Russia in the eighties of the last century, a stream of immigration to the United States began. Beginning with 1881, huge masses came annually from the Eastern European countries to the "Promised Land." These immigrants consisted of three types, the older orthodox Jews who found their spiritual satisfaction in the synagogues which they founded; the younger intellectuals, whose absorbing interests were the various political movements, such as socialism and the trade unions; and young workers who, for the most part, had very little education. The last group formed the great majority. They could not satisfy their spiritual needs by reading or attending lectures. It was only natural that the theatre should appeal to them very strongly. Many were acquainted with the Goldfaden repertory which they had seen in Europe. The songs from his plays were like a breath of home to them. At work they would sing these songs until each shop seemed like a miniature theatre, with workers singing the solos and duets from *The Witch* or *The Tenth Commandment*. Those who had not had the good fortune of witnessing a play in Europe, were regaled by their co-workers with wonder tales of the theatre. An audience was ready and waiting. Only an entrepreneur was needed to found a professional Yiddish theatre in the New World. One soon appeared in the person of Boris Thomashefsky (1886-1939), a young worker with theatrical ambitions. At his instigation, a certain Frank Wolf imported the Golubok brothers, professional actors, from London and, in the summer of 1882, they staged Goldfaden's *The Witch* in the Fourth Street Turner Hall in New York. Due to community opposition on the part of the older resident German Jews, as well as the sudden "illness" of the prima donna, this first venture ended in failure. Other attempts at staging Goldfaden repertory in the fall of 1882 fared no better. In the winter of that year a troupe took over the Old Bowery Garden, where they staged Goldfaden and Shomer plays. In need of new pieces, an actor by the name of Israel Barski (date of birth unknown, died approximately 1900), who later became an active union organizer, wrote for them *The Pogrom* and *The Insane* (1883). Although neither of these dramas was of any great consequence, they were far superior to the plays which were soon to become the mainstay of the repertory of the Jewish theatre. *The Insane* is the story of the daughter of a wealthy man, who loses her mind when her father refuses to grant permission for her marriage to a poor artist. The artist becomes famous and elopes with the girl, who is cured of her insanity. The father, in turn, loses his eyesight and his money, and turns to begging. By chance he comes to his daughter's home, asking for alms. Recognized, his daughter and her husband take him into their home and cure him of his blindness. Of no particular importance, *The Insane* nevertheless follows a clear-cut plot line, which cannot be said for most of the plays soon to be written by the "ruling authors" of the Yiddish Theatre.

In 1883 a theatrical company arrived from London with Joseph Lateiner as prompter. He soon became their staff author. They took over the Bowery Garden, which was renamed the Oriental Theatre. In 1884 Lateiner wrote and staged *Joseph and His Brethren* and *Esther and Haman*. It is interesting to note that although the Yiddish theatre in Russia had progressed to such plays as Gutzkow's *Uriel Acosta,* the theatre in New York reverted to the subjects of the *Purim Shpiels* in its new plays. Indeed, they were beginning all over again, as if all the progress made by the Yiddish theatre in Russia up to 1883 were a forgotten incident. In 1885 Lateiner wrote *The Immigration to America,* the first attempt to create a Yiddish drama dealing with the American scene. It seemed as if through a process of gradual development Lateiner might become a sincere craftsman if not a great dramatist. However, the competition which was soon to follow, forced him to vie for popular favor with a most artificial sort of writing. In 1886 Mogulesco arrived in New York with a troupe of actors. They took over the National Theatre, which they renamed the Rumanian Opera House and installed "Professor" Moses Hurwitch as staff author.

Hurwitch's first play in this new theatre was *Tissa Eslar* (1886) based on the famous Tissa Eslar trial, which at the time held the interest of every Jew. Hurwitch anticipated Eugene O'Neill in that his play required two successive nights to perform. The author acted the rôle of the defense attorney and nightly he would deliver a harangue which he freely improvised, and which lasted almost an hour. With his next play, *King Solomon* (1887), Hurwitch began his cycle of so-called historical plays.

Hurwitch was a theatrical architect. He would plan his plays as with a blueprint, indicating where laughter, tears, romance, mystery, and so forth were needed. He would then turn to his large library of dramatic literature, choose the needed scenes and, with only slight changes, add them to his plays. It was not unusual, for example, in a scene involving a shoemaker who is jealous of his wife, to recognize the dialogue of Desdemona and Othello. His historical plays often twisted facts for the sake of sensationalism. In all, Hurwitch built approximately ninety plays.

It was competition such as this which Lateiner had to meet. He did not have talent for characterization nor an eye for thoughtful observation. Neither did he have sufficient imagination to create sensational plays. At best he was a craftsman who knew the trick of building plays for the existing market. To meet the pressure of competition he turned to ready-made plays and adapted or translated them for production. He did not put the stamp of his individuality on any of his adaptations. In most instances the only thing Jewish about his plays were the names of his characters. Often, too, he would combine a number of novels to form the then necessary four acts, so that each act had hardly any connection with those that preceded it. The situations became so complex that the audience found it difficult to follow the involved plots. To this group belong such pieces as *The Lost Soul* (1895) and *The Seder Night* (1903). As long as the play contained the prescribed dose of tears, laughter, song, and mystery, it did not matter if one situation, or even speech, had no connection whatever with the other, or even with the play itself. In all he wrote over 150 plays of which only a few are even remembered at this time. Among the latter are *Hinke Pinke* (1907), *The Jewish Heart* (1908), and the two plays which he wrote for Molly Picon, *Plenty* (1928) and *The Comedienne* (1930).

Shaikewitch, who had also come to the United States and was active for a time during the Hurwitch-Lateiner period, did not depend so largely on borrowed material as did his contemporaries. Instead, he dramatized his own novels such as *The Convict, The Jewish Noble, The Penitent,* and *The Usurer*. Following the style set by Hurwitch and Lateiner, he too turned to the historical musical play. To this group belong *Titus* (1891), *Rabbi Judah Halevi* (1892), *Deborah the Prophetess* (1898), and many others. In the main, Shaikewitch used the novelist's technique in his writing, and his plays are composed of chapters rather than scenes.

Other playwrights of the same type, worthy of passing mention, are Moshe Seifert (1851-1922), Sigmund Fineman, Reuben Weissman, and David Apothekar (1855-1911).

As for Goldfaden, in 1887 he too came to the United States. He became the director of the Rumanian Opera House, but his troupe, recalling his dictatorial ways in Russia, wanted no further dealings with him. They left the theatre and declared a strike against the management. Goldfaden gathered another group of actors and staged his musical legend, *The Tenth Commandment* (1887), which he had written in Odessa in 1882. (The comedy is also known under the title of *Thou Shalt Not Covet*.) The production proved a failure financially, and Goldfaden was obliged to resign from his position. For a while he directed an amateur dramatic club and in 1889 he returned to Europe. After several attempts at professional production, Goldfaden came back to the United States, where he remained until his death. He now found himself completely excluded from the professional Yiddish theatre which he had founded. He spent his remaining years writing poetry and his autobiography. In 1904 he staged, with an amateur group composed of members of the Dr. Herzl Zion Club, his Hebrew one-act musical play *David in the War*. This was the first performance of a play in Hebrew in the United States. The aged dramatist was now suffering extreme poverty and only the occasional financial assistance which he received from some of his admirers kept him from starvation. His last play was the nationalist drama *Son of My People,* which was inspired by George Eliot's novel *Daniel Deronda*. In his autobiography Goldfaden states that he wrote this play in order to point out to the Jews the need for unity in their distress, to awaken the courage of the Jew, to bring him consolation and a message of hope for a better future. Goldfaden's last play was given its initial performance by Boris Thomashefsky at his People's Theatre. It seemed as if the play would be a complete box-office failure, but the death of Goldfaden two weeks later (January 9, 1908) awakened the public interest in *Son of My People* and the final work of the "father of the Yiddish Theatre" had a continuous run of fourteen weeks.

The undisputed rule of Hurwitch-Lateiner held sway until 1891, when Jacob Gordin (1853-1909) appeared on the scene with the avowed intention of reforming the Yiddish drama. His advent was in the nature of a revolt which, though it did not completely overthrow the ruling playwrights, nevertheless brought new life into the moribund Yiddish drama and left a lasting imprint on the Yiddish theatre.

Jacob Gordin was born in Mirgorod, Province of Poltava in the Ukraine. His father was a well-to-do merchant who, although a devout Jew and *Hassid,* was nevertheless inclined to the "modern" ideas of the *Haskalah.* Consequently, Jacob Gordin received an education which included the traditional Jewish as well as the modern studies.

At the age of seventeen he began to contribute articles to the provincial Russian dailies. In 1880 he published a series of stories and sketches of Jewish life in the Russian journal *Niediela*. He also wrote dramatic criticisms under the pen-name of Yan. While engaged in these activities he founded and promoted the work of *Dukhovnoye Bibleytskoye Bratstvo* (The Bible Brotherhood), a reform movement in Judaism. The Brotherhood preached an ethical deism and a return of the Jew to the soil and physical labor. The movement won but few adherents and was later disbanded. In 1891 he came to the United States with the hope of founding a colony based on communistic principles and the teachings of the Bible Brotherhood. Although he was not very fluent in Yiddish at this time, he began writing for the New York Socialist-Yiddish weekly, *Die Arbeiter Zeitung.* Having a large family Gordin found it necessary to seek additional income for their support. His friend the socialist author Philip Krantz, suggested to him that he should write plays for the Yiddish theatre and introduced him to the reigning stars of the Yiddish stage, Jacob P. Adler and Sigmund Mogulesco.

Gordin's first play, *Siberia* (1891), created a sensation. The intellectual, radical element, especially, received Gordin's drama with loud acclaim. Here was an author who approached the task of play writing with a spirit of holiness and dedication. There was none of the cynical play-tailoring of the Hurwitches and Lateiners but a conscious effort at rationality and literary truth.

In simple terms *Siberia* tells the story of a young man, Rubin Cohen, who has been deported to Siberia for a crime of which he was innocent. On the way to Siberia he escapes, rejoins his wife and children, changes his name to Rosenkrantz and settles in a city where he is completely unknown. He prospers in his new home. In his old age his competitor, Berl Taratutye, discovers his secret and informs on him to the Czarist police.

Even in this early piece, Gordin showed his superiority as a playwright.

Although his characterizations are weak, the play has continuity, simplicity, and an identification with real life.

In 1892 he produced his *Jewish King Lear*. Though taking his theme from Shakespeare, he did not, like his contemporaries, bodily appropriate the play. He created his own situations, which were indigenously Jewish. His characters, too, though not well rounded were identifiably Jewish.

It seems that the theme of King Lear held a peculiar fascination for Gordin. He returned to it in his *Mirele Efros* (1898) a feminine counterpart of King Lear. This play is one of the best which he has written. In his *Jewish King Lear,* Gordin shows his great dependence on the Shakespeare original, but in *Mirele Efros* he makes the theme his own and creates truly Jewish characters and environment. The dialogue and the very personality of the heroine are strongly reminiscent of Ettinger's *Serkele,* except that Serkele arouses the antipathy of the audience with her machinations and greed whereas Mirele Efros evokes our sympathy. Mirele Efros, a widow, has built up a fine business. When her children grow up, she turns the business over to them. Finding herself ignored by her children and treated disrespectfully, she leaves her home, of which she had been so proud, and takes lodgings in a furnished room. A reconciliation is finally effected between the proud matriarch and her ungrateful children when her grandson comes to her poor room, begging her to return home in order to celebrate with him his *Bar Mitzvah* (Confirmation). The matriarch, Mirele Efros, is the prototype of those fine Jewish women so well exemplified by Gluckel Von Hameln. There is more or less conscious effort at psychological development of the characters and situations. The action is real and true to life.

Gordin could not resist attempting to win "popular" acclaim by writing such plays as *Murder on Madison Avenue* (1893), *Mohamed and the Jews of Arabia* (1894), and *The Three Princes* (1895). However, in the field of cheap dramaturgy, Hurwitch and Lateiner were his masters.

Most of Gordin's plays were adaptations of themes from world literature. He has adapted or translated Goethe, Hebbel, Shakespeare, Ibsen, Hugo, Lessing, Schiller, Hauptmann, Gogol, Grillparzer, and Ostrovski. In many cases his work of adaptation consisted merely in utilizing non-Jewish themes for Jewish plots.

Perhaps the best play he wrote is *God, Man, and Devil* (1900), suggested by Goethe's *Faust*. Despite its inspiration, the play is thoroughly original, dealing as it does with living Jewish characters and a vital Jewish problem. Herschele, a poor and pious Jewish scribe, is suddenly enriched by the Devil, who appears to him in the guise of a shrewd business man. His sudden riches cause him to abandon his faithful wife for the love of a younger woman. He builds a prayer-shawl factory in which he exploits the labor of his former friends. An accident in the factory which kills the son of his boyhood friend reawakens in him his finer instincts. He suddenly realizes that his wealth has robbed him of his most precious possession—his joy in righteous living. Believing himself beyond redemption, Herschele commits suicide.

Also worthy of notice are Gordin's dramas *The Oath* (1900), *Kreutzer Sonata* (1902), *The Slaughter* (1899), and *Sapho* (1901).

Although Gordin has been criticized on the score that his plays are intrinsically foreign to the Jewish spirit, and also for his inability to create well-rounded characters and for his failure to bring the problems he poses to their logical dramatic conclusion, he nevertheless ranks high in the roster of Yiddish dramatists. In place of the falsities of life and character of the Hurwitch-Lateiner régime, he brought art, truth, and simplicity. His appearance on the Yiddish-theatre scene gave impetus to the latent ambitions of the highly skilled Jewish actors for better plays. Gordin's example also served as a powerful stimulant to other Yiddish writers in the creation of artistic literary Yiddish plays.

During this period Michael Sharkanski was writing historical operettas which were distinguished from the Hurwitch-Lateiner efforts in this medium by their continuity of action and simple dialogue. Among his plays are *Unsane Tokef* (1895), *Kol Nidrei* (1896), *Rachel* (1898), *The Trial* (1901), *Job,* and *The Rose of Sharon* (1904).

A number of writers now appeared on the scene who in their work bridged the gap between the imperfect, realistic plays of Gordin and the highly artistic plays of the later dramatists. One of this group of transition writers was Solomon Libin (1872-   ). Born in Mohilev, Russia, he went to London in 1891 and six months later he came to the United States. While earning his living in a sweatshop, Libin began writing short stories and sketches in which he realistically portrayed the life of the immigrant worker and the horrible conditions of the sweatshops. As a dramatist Libin made his debut in 1900 with his comedy *The Delayed Wedding.* His four-act drama *Broken Hearts* (1903) has been his most successful. In all Libin has written more than fifty plays, among which are *God's Punishment* (1909), *Crime and Love* (1918), and *Pauper, Where To?* (1922). Despite the high artistic merit of his short stories, Libin's dramas were a compromise between literature and the popular offerings of the period. His plays are usually about a family problem in which the tense moments are relieved by inconsequential comedy.

Like Libin, Leon Kobrin (1872-   ) was concerned with the life of the immigrant worker in New York. He has been spoken of as the "discoverer of the tenement." He has written both comedy and serious drama and his work has placed him in the forefront of Yiddish playwrights. Born in Vitebsk, Russia, Kobrin came to the United States in 1892, where for six years he was engaged in various occupations such as shirt-making, baking, and newspaper selling. In 1898 he made his literary debut with *Yankel Boile and Other Tales,* a book of stories which won him critical acclaim and caused Professor Wiener of Harvard to refer to him as the Yiddish

Gorki. The year 1899 saw the production of his first play, *Minna*, which he wrote in collaboration with Jacob Gordin. In all he has written some two dozen plays. His most successful drama was *Der Dorfsying* (1913) adapted from *Yankel Boile,* one of his early tales. The play presents a realistic picture of Jewish life in a Russian village. It is the story of the love of the village lad Yankel for a non-Jewish girl with whom he has grown up. It ends in the suicide of Yankel on the day he was to be married to another girl because of his superstitious belief in the oath he had given his father on his deathbed. Kobrin's best comedy is his satire, *Riverside Drive,* produced by Maurice Schwartz in 1927. Other plays worthy of note are *Israel's Hope* (1915), *Back To His People* (1917), and *Prince Lulu* (1922).

It would be misleading to give the impression that the advent of Gordin and the serious dramatists who followed him changed altogether the repertory of the Yiddish stage. In 1908 Lateiner's play *The Jewish Heart* was staged by David Kessler and had an unprecedented success. It was a definite reaction on the part of the mass of the theatre-going Jews against the better drama. In 1909 *Dos Pintele Yid* by M. Seiffert (1851-1922) ran for more than twenty weeks. The legacy of Hurwitch and Lateiner has remained with the commercial Yiddish theatre to this very day. Every season there is a plethora of cheap melodrama and musical comedy which caters directly to the "theatre benefit" trade. The melodramas and musical comedies of Isaac Zolotarefsky (1875-   ), Max Gebil (1877-   ), William Siegel (1893-   ), Abraham Bloom (1893-   ), Isadore Lillien (1882-   ), and I. Lesh (1887-   ), rule the boards of the commercial Yiddish stage.

In the course of the years, however, the Yiddish theatre had been maturing. The influence of Gordin and his successors gradually produced serious Yiddish drama of high artistic merit. An appreciative audience now demanded better dramatic fare. The new theatre was forthcoming both in producing troupes and literary playwrights. Side by side with the commercial playhouse, there developed a number of theatre ensembles who devoted themselves to the production of the literary drama. One of the earliest of these groups was the Kaminsky Troupe, which was active in Poland and Russia during the first decade of the twentieth century. This was a combination of unusually talented actors headed by the "Duse" of the Yiddish Theatre, Esther Rachel Kaminsky. The Hirschbein Troupe was founded in Russia in 1908. The Theatre Society was organized in 1911 under the leadership of Isaac Loeb Peretz in order to encourage the production of Yiddish drama of high literary quality. A. Veiter (pseudonym of Isaac Meir Devenishsky, 1878-1919) who wrote half-realistic half-symbolic dramas (*In Fire,* 1910, *The Dumb One,* 1912) was very active on behalf of the Society. Although it never succeeded as a producing unit, the Theatre Society nevertheless awakened the intelligentsia to the need of better Yiddish drama. The Vilna Troupe organized in Vilna during the First World War, gave its productions throughout Poland and Germany and later in the United States and was instrumental in introducing such writers as Veiter, Peretz, and Katzizne. Also noteworthy are Vikt (Warsaw Yiddish Art Theatre); Artef, a worker's theatre collective organized in New York in 1926; The Yiddish State Theatre in Soviet Russia, which has become famous for its provocative restaging of theatre classics of the nineteenth century; and the Yiddish Art Theatre of New York which was organized in 1919 by Maurice Schwartz and which has been instrumental in introducing many important Yiddish dramatists. Of the aforementioned the last two are still active. It is these ensembles that have nurtured the literary Yiddish drama and gave encouragement to a host of dramatists of high merit. Individual stars too, such as David Kessler, Jacob P. Adler, Keni Liptzen, Samuel Goldenburg, Jacob Ben-Ami, and others encouraged better drama from time to time.

David Pinski (1872-   ) ranks high among the better dramatists. Born in Mohilev on the Dnieper River, Pinski began writing while still an adolescent. Active as writer, editor, and leader in the workers' movement all his live, Pinski's early plays were devoted to pleading the cause of the economic underdog. His play *Isaac Sheftel* (1899) is a study of the inner conflicts and agonies of a young inventor whose employer's craftiness robs him of his invention. The sense of frustration and inadequacy engendered by his lack of technical training leads the inventor to suicide.

Yankel the Smith (1910) is a conflict in sexual attraction. Yankel is torn between his sexual attraction for a younger girl and his love for his sick wife. With *The Family Zevi* (written 1903-1904, produced 1906) Pinski turns from the problem of the individual to the problem of the Jewish people. In one household are represented three generations and five worlds. The old grandfather, Reb Moshe, is a symbol of the religious idealist of the older generation which has all but disappeared from Jewish life today. His son Yankel makes a pretense at piety in its outward form but his life is devoted to the accumulation of riches. Yankel's sons have within their souls the idealism of their grandfather. In one it finds expression in Zionism, the nationalistic revival of the Jewish people. The other grandson is a socialist, seeking the solution of the Jew's problem in the salvation of the entire world. The third grandson sees assimilation as the only hope for the Jew. The death of the old grandfather in a massacre is symbolic of the death of his entire generation. A new order is arising, to be ushered in by the idealists, his grandsons.

The Treasure (published 1911) was the first of Pinski's works to bring him to the attention of the non-Jewish world. First produced in German by Max Reinhardt in 1910, at the Deutsches Theatre, Berlin, the play was translated into English by Ludwig Lewisohn and produced by the Theatre Guild in New York. Combining realism with the supernatural, the play deals with the acquisitive instinct of man. In their anxiety to find the treasure which Yudke, the half-witted son of the grave digger, supposedly discovered, the people of the town desecrate the graves of their own ancestors.

In the mystical close of the play, in which the dead discuss their descendants' greediness for money, Pinski expounds the thesis that money in and of itself is not evil; it is the search for money that creates evil. When man learns to master his possessions, instead of being dominated by them, he will turn them into a powerful source for good.

Other outstanding plays by Pinski are *Gabri and The Women* (1916) and his Messianic plays, *The Dumb Messiah* (1912) and *The Eternal Jew* (1906). The latter was given a memorable production in Hebrew by the Habimah group in Russia 1918.

In his later years Pinski became more and more interested in the cause of Jewish nationalism, taking a very active part in the Labor Zionist movement. Under the nationalist influence he began turning more frequently than before to historical themes. The later plays which he wrote were a good deal more romantic, imaginative, and abstract than his earlier writings. To this category belong the aforementioned Messianic plays, to which he added *Solomon Molcho* (1932) a play dealing with the sixteenth-century Marrano and Messianic pretender, and *Sabbatai Zevi* (1936), a drama about the pseudo-Messiah of the seventeenth century. His poetic series of one-act plays, *King David and His Wives,* was written between 1913 and 1916. These five short plays center about David and his loves. They are not, however, a retelling of the Biblical incidents. Rather are they a reconstruction of the Biblical stories and characters. The character of David is symbolic of man, whose dreams and foibles are psychologically analyzed and revealed.

Pinski, now well over seventy, is still as active as he was in his youth. Although his plays have not been produced in recent years, due largely to the economic "statesmanship" in the Yiddish theatre, he has continued to write, mainly on historical themes.

Sholem Asch (1880-   ) is at present the most widely read of all contemporary Jewish authors. Although known to the non-Jewish world mainly through his novels, he has exerted a strong influence on the Yiddish theatre as a dramatist. Born in Kutno, Poland, of a middle-class family, Asch received a traditional Jewish education in his youth. Under Peretz's influence he began to write in Yiddish. Realistic in his portrayals of Jewish life, Asch is distinguished for his fine attention to detail, clear-cut character delineation, and poetic handling of scenes and situations. At times bordering on the sensational, he is nevertheless thoroughly honest in his handling of plot and character.

His best known play is *The God of Vengeance* (1907), which created a furore when it was first produced. Attacked as scandalous and sacrilegious when first given in Yiddish, the English production in New York was closed by the police, the cast placed under arrest and prosecuted in court.

The play deals with one Yekel Shapshowitch, who has accumulated a considerable fortune through the proceeds of a brothel which he operates in the basement of his house. Yekel hopes to find salvation for himself and his wife through Rifkele, his only daughter, whom he brings up as a virtuous girl, sheltered from the evil influences of the brothel. He consorts with holy men, gives large sums for charity, and donates a Holy Scroll to the synagogue. His efforts meet with tragic failure. Rifkele is fascinated by the life in the brothel, and is led astray by one of its inmates. Maddened by the frustration of his hopes, he drives out the holy men and thrusts his wife and daughter into the brothel.

Despite its sordid setting, the play has a certain grim beauty in the hopeless struggle of Yekel Shapshowitch. Though conditioned to look upon his occupation as an ordinary business, he nevertheless aspires to a finer life, and to be accepted by "respectable" people. Believing that love can be bought for money, he cannot understand why money will not also buy redemption. The fact that seeds planted in evil bring forth bitter fruit leaves him bewildered and with a feeling of having been victimized.

Asch draws his themes from all phases of Jewish life. In his dramas as well as in his novels and short stories he portrays the tremendous changes that have occurred during the past forty years. The adjustment of the East European Jewish immigrant to the American scene, the rise of the radical movement among the Jews of Russia, the First World War and the Russian Revolution with their cataclysmic effect upon Jewish life, and the new nationalist experiment in Palestine are all subjects for Asch's versatile pen. He is equally facile in exploiting the rich field of Jewish historical themes, as in *Sabbatai Zevi* (1908), which depicts the tragedy of the seventeenth-century false Messiah, and in *The Holy Maiden* (1916), as well as with the contemporary scene, as in *God of Vengeance*.

In addition to his dramas, a number of his novels have been dramatized, some by Asch himself, some by others, and were staged by such theatre ensembles as The Vilna Troupe and The Yiddish Art Theatre of New York. In this group are *Motke the Thief* (1917) which like *God of Vengeance* deals with the underworld in Poland; *Uncle Moses* (1926), a drama of the life of the early Jewish immigrants in America and their struggles for the unionization of the needle trades; *Kiddush Hashem* (1928), a historical drama dealing with Jewish heroism and martyrdom during the Chmelnicki uprising in the Ukraine in 1648; *Three Cities* (1938), a study of Jewish life in the decade 1910-1920; and *Salvation* (1939), a story of *Hassidic* life presented in its most beautiful and idealistic aspects.

Of the several dramatizations of Asch's novels, that of *Salvation* is, in this writer's opinion, the most felicitous. *Salvation* (known in Yiddish as *Tehilim Yid*) portrays *Hassidic* life three quarters of a century ago in the poetic manner so characteristic of Asch. The story revolves about the central character Yehiel, showing us the unfolding of his soul until it reaches the apex of spirituality. Unlike so many others who have voiced the age-old complaint, "Tzaddik v'ra lo, rasha v'tov lo?" ("How is it that the just live a life of suffering, while evil-doers prosper?"), Yehiel finds his answer. He concludes that suffering is only a means of ennobling the soul and an avenue of salvation for the individual as well as for all of Israel.

Isaac Loeb Peretz (1852-1915) and Sholom Aleichem (pseudonym of Solomon Rabinowitz 1859-1916) are neither of them primarily dramatists. The former is a master of style and mood in Yiddish literature, while Sholom Aleichem is the greatest of Yiddish humorists. They are considered the giants of Yiddish literature and their greatest contributions have been made in the field of the short story and poetry. However, they have also exerted a strong influence on the development of the Yiddish drama.

Peretz has written a number of one-act plays and full-length dramas. It was he who intrduced symbolism and mysticism to the Yiddish stage. Although his full-length plays such as *The Golden Chain,* a drama of Hassidic family life; *Chained in the Vestry* (1908), a dramatic poem; *Night on the Old Market Place* (published 1907), a symbolic-poetic drama; *What the Fiddle Contains* (published under the title *Musician* in 1907), a drama of the struggles of an artist against his environment have not been very successful on the stage, they have nevertheless exerted a very strong influence on the entire course of Yiddish drama. Both An-sky and Veiter are indebted for their inspiration to the plays of Peretz. Many able directors have been fascinated with his plays and have given them provocative productions. Their major fault as stage pieces is the fact that they are very fragmentary. The dialogue indicates but does not complete verbally the thoughts of the characters.

Peretz was very anxious for his plays to succeed on the stage and he continually revised them in the hope of arriving at a form that would express his ideas and would also be acceptable to theatre audiences. Consequently, many versions exist of each of his plays. The course of development of *The Golden Chain* is characteristic. It was originally written in Hebrew in prose under the title of *Destruction of the Tzaddik's House.* In 1906 Peretz revised the play and presented it in a Yiddish version in Warsaw under the title of *Der Nisoyon.* The play proved to be a failure and Peretz continued to rewrite it. In 1907 it was published in a poetic version in Yiddish under the title of *The Golden Chain.* In this version it was a drama of the doubts that assail a saintly rabbi in his own powers to help his followers. After publication, Peretz continued to revise and rewrite the play. In 1920, the play was produced at the Yiddish Art Theatre in New York in a version which was a synthesis of *The Golden Chain* and the earlier variant *Der Nisoyon.*

Peretz wrote many one-act plays and short sketches. These have proved particularly fascinating to Yiddish and Hebrew theatre directors. There is hardly an outstanding production ensemble that has not produced some of these short plays and unlike his full-length plays, Peretz's one-act sketches have been very successful on the stage. The very first program of the Hebrew theatre group Habimah in Moscow included one of these sketches. Outstanding have been *At the Window* (1902), *Of an Early Morning* (1907), *After the Funeral* (written 1901, published 1907), and *Champagne* (1907). *The Sisters* (1905, previously published in Hebrew 1904), a scene of Jewish life in Poland on the lowest economic level introduced for the first time the theme of pauperism to the Yiddish stage.

Many of his one-act plays have been translated into other languages and a representative group may be found in the English translations of Etta Block and Bessie F. White.

Sholom Aleichem has given to the Yiddish stage its outstanding comedy *Two Hundred Thousand,* also known as *Dos Groise Gevins* (1915). The play deals with the adventures of a poor tailor, who is notified that he is the winner of the 200,000 ruble first prize in the lottery. The towns-people, impressed with the tailor's newly acquired riches, fawn upon him. The tailor and his family suffer greatly in trying to live up to their new economic status and he harks back longingly to the days of his poor but comfortable existence. In the end, the notification proves to be an error. His newly found friends desert him immediately, but the tailor is delighted to return to his scissors and pressing iron. Written with a great deal of charm, *Two Hundred Thousand* is replete with folk humor, poking fun at social climbers, the newly rich as well as those who place an exaggerated importance on the "aristocracy of wealth." Because of its folk quality, the comedy has intrigued many theatre directors. It has been produced realistically, symbolically, as a fantasy, and in every other conceivable theatre medium. There is hardly a season that does not see a production of *Two Hundred Thousand* on the Yiddish or Hebrew stage.

Other plays of Sholom Aleichem are *Dispersed* (1903), dealing with the dispersion of Jewish life, *Samuel Posternack* (1907), and *The Treasure* (1908), one of the best comedies of the Yiddish theatre, which was later staged under the title of *The Gold Diggers. Hard to be a Jew* (published 1914, produced 1919) is another of his plays which has become a favorite of the Yiddish theatre-goer. The play deals with the difficulties of Jewish life under Czarist repressions and has become a standard item in the Yiddish repertory. Sholom Aleichem has also dramatized a number of his stories, among them *Der Oisvurf* (1906), *Stempeniu* (1905), and *Tevyeh, the Dairyman* (first produced 1919). In addition to his full-length plays, Sholom Aleichem also wrote one-act comedies which have become part of the repertory of the professional and amateur Yiddish theatre; notable among these are *Hands, the Doctor* (1887), *The Divorce* (1887), *Mazel Tov* (1889), and *Agents*.

In addition to his own dramatizations of his short stories, others have been dramatized, mainly by his son-in-law I. D. Berkowitz (1885-   ).

The great success of Sholom Aleichem in his dramatization as well as in his novels and short stories is due mainly to his mastery of observation and characterization and his sensitivity to genuine folk humor.

Of the younger dramatists, Peretz Hirschbein is perhaps the most gifted. Greatly influenced by the French symbolists and mystics, he later abandoned his early methods and began writing idyllic plays about simple Jewish people. Born in 1881 in Grodno, White Russia, his early youth was spent in the country, where his father owned a mill. He received a Talmudic education in the Yeshivoth of Brest-Litovsk and Vilna. His early literary efforts were in Hebrew. He wrote poetry which was published in various periodicals. His first play, *Miriam,* was written in Hebrew and printed in *HaZ'man* (1905). A Yiddish translation of the play appeared in *The Yiddisher Kemfer* (1906).

In 1908, when the edict against the Yiddish theatre was relaxed in Russia, he organized a company of amateurs in Odessa which later became known as *The Hirschbein Troupe.* This company was formed at the instigation of the Hebrew poet Hayim Nahman Bialik (1873-1934) and others of the Russian-Jewish intelligentsia, for the purpose of producing artistic Yiddish drama. The group staged plays by Asch, Peretz, and Gordin as well as Hirschbein's own symbolic plays. Of these the most important was *The Carcass* (first written in Hebrew and published in *HaZ'man,* 1905; later translated into Yiddish by the author, and staged in 1908). Others were *T'kiyas Kaf* (1908) and *Yoel* (1908, published 1911).

Although the troupe was disbanded in 1910, its work had exerted a strong influence in elevating the standards of the Yiddish drama. In 1911 Hirschbein came to New York. He now abandoned his earlier symbolism, which to a great extent made his plays seem pretentious, and began writing idyls of Jewish country life. Hirschbein, because of his early life in the country, was well acquainted with the simple type of Jew, who though unlettered and out of touch with the learned circles of the city tries to solve his problems in the light of his own simple philosophy. In 1911 he wrote *The Idle Inn* (first produced in 1913) which marked the beginning of his writing in the new genre. The play was produced in an English translation in New York in 1922. It was also produced in Hebrew in Palestine.

In 1913 he wrote his *In a Forsaken Nook.* The play deals with the petty rivalries of two country Jews. Their business antagonism is a stumbling block to the love of their children. But, unlike Romeo and Juliet, the play ends happily and the lovers are brought together through the intervention of the old grandfather. He who belongs to the older generation has known the animosities of middle age and the passionate unrestraint of youth, and can sympathize with both. With wisdom gained from experience, he brings about the victory of fiery youth over obstinate middle age.

In 1915 Hirschbein wrote his comedy *The Smith's Daughters,* which was published in 1916 and first staged in 1919 by the Yiddish Art Theatre. The play was also produced in a Hebrew translation in New York in 1921, and later in Palestine. It is another of his idyllic plays of Jewish country life dealing with the problem of a blacksmith who wants to follow the custom of marrying off his oldest daughter first, but does not want to hurt the chances of the younger to marry immediately.

Green Fields was written and published in 1916 and produced in 1919. A Hebrew translation was made by the author and published in 1922. A story of idyllic love of Jewish country folk, it is one of Hirschbein's best, and one of the finest plays in all Yiddish dramatic literature. A wandering, pious student of the Talmud comes to the quiet country place and unbeknown to himself disturbs the heart of two country girls. Their love brings about another of those country feuds so well treated by Hirschbein in his other plays. Of course only one girl can win the student and when she does, the families are reconciled.

Other Yiddish dramatists have written about the loves and problems of the simple Jew; but, whereas these dealt with sinful love, Hirschbein wrote of the pure, ideal love of the country Jews. His simple and honest treatment of his subjects have endeared to theatre audiences the country Jew, the simple man of the soil, a type which has been all too rare in Jewish life until the recent return to the land in Palestine.

Fishel Bimko (1890-   ) was born in Kielc, Poland. Bimko received a Talmudic education, but at the early age of fifteen he became an active worker in the Russian revolutionary movement. In 1905 he was arrested for his revolutionary activities and spent six months in prison.

His first play, *On the Shores of the Vistula* (1914), marked him as an important newcomer to the Yiddish Stage. His realistic drama *Thieves* (1919) was given a memorable production by the Vilna Troupe and later (1922) by the Yiddish Art Theatre in New York. Like Sholom Asch, Bimko is fascinated by the life and characters of the Warsaw underworld. In theme as well as locale, *Thieves* is very similar to Asch's *God of Vengeance*. The underworld character Shloyme, the leader of a gang of thieves, marries Gitel, a woman of the slums. As Yekel Shapshowitch felt about his daughter, so Shloyme feels about his wife. Through her he hopes to find redemption. Here too retribution strikes the evil-doer. His wife confesses to him that he is not the father of her child. The real father is Mazik, a member of the gang. Maddened, he sets fire to the house and strangles his faithless wife.

Thieves is almost photographic in its portrayal of underworld characters. The dialogue mirrors the language of the Warsaw underworld so faithfully that a glossary of underworld slang accompanies the published version of the play. It is interesting to note that, unlike *Thieves,* Bimko's other dramas are cast in the symbolic mystical mold. Some of his other produced plays are *Oaks* (1922, an adaptation of his *On the Shores of the Vistula*), *Sunken Worlds* (1922), and his comedies *Uncle, We Know You* and *America Bluff* (1922).

It is a curious fact that were it not for a single play, despite his many writings of a miscellaneous nature in Russian and in Yiddish, the name of

Sh. An-sky (pseudonym of Solomon Z. Rappaport, 1863-1920), would hardly be mentioned in the history of Yiddish literature, and certainly would have no place in any history of Yiddish drama. An-sky was born in Vitebsk, White Russia, of a prominent Jewish family. In conformity with the spirit of the time, he received a thorough Talmudic training. He was also well versed in modern Hebrew literature. He learned Russian and under the influence of the Russian radical literature he determined to learn a trade in order to earn his livelihood with his hands. He tried blacksmithing at first and later bookbinding. For a time he became immersed in studies of Russian folk life, about which he wrote. Through the influence of the Jewish emigrant colony in Bern, Switzerland, which he visited from time to time, he took an active interest in Jewish life and problems. After 1905 An-sky returned to Russia and under the patronage of the Russian Jew Baron Horace Ginzburg, he directed the first scientific expedition which conducted an investigation into Jewish folklore throughout the Provinces of Volyhnia and Podolia. The expedition collected numerous Jewish ceremonial objects and manuscripts. It also noted down several folk tales, legends, and folk songs.

In 1911, as a result of his research on Jewish folklore, An-sky conceived the idea of his drama *Between Two Worlds,* later known as *The Dybbuk.* The play was finally written in 1914. Although Stanislavsky seriously considered the drama for production by the Moscow Art Theatre and even suggested to An-sky the idea of the Messenger, which mystic character was later included in the play, *The Dybbuk* was not produced until December 9, 1920, at which time the Vilna Troupe staged it as a memorial to the author thirty days after his death.

The drama was an immediate sensation. Yiddish as well as non-Jewish theatres throughout the world staged the play and it created a furore wherever it was shown.

A realistic play, dealing with Jewish mysticism, *The Dybbuk* tells the story of the predestined and eternal love of Leah and Honon, which breaks through all barriers, both natural and supernatural. Even the death of Honon cannot extinguish their love, and his spirit enters the body of Leah as a "dybbuk," an additional soul, so that she becomes a spiritual composite of Leah-Honon. The Great Anathema pronounced upon the dybbuk-Honon finally forces him to leave the body of the maiden. But even anathemas cannot overcome the preordained love of the pair. Leah dies and her soul is fused with the soul of Honon in eternal love.

Basically a play of atmosphere, *The Dybbuk* owes its unprecedented success to its serious treatment of Jewish mysticism and superstitious beliefs. Unlike the *Haskalah* writers of the earlier period, An-sky had no need to mock at Jewish folk ways and *Hassidic* beliefs. The power of the fanatic *Hassidim* was gone and there was no longer any need to fight them with ridicule as in the days of Gottlober. Now these customs could be viewed in historical perspective and with the nostalgia of a bygone era. Like Peretz, An-sky saw inherent beauty in the folk legends, music, primitive beliefs, and customs, and he idealized them in his drama.

In addition to numerous productions in Yiddish throughout the world, *The Dybbuk* was given an outstanding production in Hebrew by the Hebrew theatre collective Habima in Moscow (1922). The translation was made by Hayim Nahman Bialik and the play was staged under the direction of the Armenian director Vakhtangov. In English, the play was given by the Neighborhood Playhouse in New York (1925) and has since become a standard item in the repertory of Anglo-Jewish dramatic groups. The last time *The Dybbuk* was seen in New York was in 1939, when it was staged by the Anglo-Jewish Theatre ensemble, Vilon. The play has also been produced in German, Polish, Ukrainian, Danish, Swedish, Bulgarian, Serbian, French, and Japanese.

Among An-sky's other dramatic works are his fragmentary *Day and Night,* which was produced by the Vilna Troupe in Warsaw (1921), adapted by An-sky's friend Katzizne, who added a complete third act. In 1924 the fragmentary play was given by the theatre ensemble Unser Theater in New York in an adaptation of David Pinsky, who did the first and third act, and Mendel Elkin who added a new second act. Also to be noted are *Father and Son* and *The Grandfather,* one-act comedies, and a two-act comedy, *In a Conspirative Home.*

H. Leivick (1888-   ) is considered by many as the greatest Yiddish literary figure in America today. His dramas are social in nature, with an undercurrent of Messianic striving.

Born in Igumen, Russia, Leivick (whose real name is Leivick Halpern) prepared himself for the Rabbinate in the Yeshivoth of Berezino and Minsk. At the age of sixteen he was expelled from the Yeshivah for reading modern Hebrew books. Thereafter he joined the Yiddish revolutionary movement and became active in the Bund (Jewish Socialist Party in Russia and Poland). In 1906 he was sentenced to four years' imprisonment for his revolutionary activities. While in prison he wrote for the *Zeitgeist,* a New York Yiddish periodical. In 1912 he was exiled to Siberia for life, but managed to escape and came to New York in 1913.

Leivick's outstanding play is *The Golem,* a dramatic poem in eight scenes. The play was published in 1921 and was first produced professionally in Hebrew by the Habima (1925). In 1928 the play was produced in Polish. The first professional production of the drama in the original Yiddish did not take place until 1929.

The Golem deals with the legend of Rabbi Judah Low (Maharal) of Prague (1513-1609) who fashioned a Golem, a human figure made of clay, breathed into it the spirit of life and used this Golem to act as a protector of the Jews against their oppressors. In this play Leivick deals with a number of problems which recur in his other works, among them the Messianic ideal, salvation through physical force and self-help as opposed to salvation through the spirit, and the relationship of the Creator to his creatures.

The Golem appeared in an English translation by J. C. Augenlicht in *Poet Lore* (1928). An oratorio version of the drama with music by Vladimir Heifetz was presented in Carnegie Hall in 1931.

Leivick's best-known plays, beside *The Golem*, are *Rags* (1921), *Shop* (1926)—also produced in Hebrew by Ohel in Palestine (1932)—*Hirsh Lekert* (1928), and *Chains* (1930)—also produced in Hebrew by the Habima in Palestine (1931). Leivick's most recent play, *The Miracle of the Warsaw Ghetto*, was produced in New York in 1945. It deals with the inner conflicts among the Jews just prior to the outbreak of their revolt against the Nazis in 1943. The heroic struggle against their common enemy unites them in the hope that their example will awaken the rest of the world to the fate of the "forgotten ally."

Another writer worthy of note is Ossip Dymov (1878-   ). Originally writing in Russian, he later turned to play writing in Yiddish. Dymov's blend of comedy and fantasy, symbolism and poetry, are universal in their appeal. Especially noteworthy are *Bronx Express* (1919) and *Human Dust* (1927). On the authority of Zalmen Zylbercwaig,[1] Dymov wrote all his plays in Russian and later translated them into Yiddish with the help of his friends.

Chone Gotesfeld (1890-   ) is another dramatist who was brought to the attention of theatre audiences through the pioneering efforts of Maurice Schwartz. Mainly a writer of domestic comedies, Gotesfeld's first produced play was *Married and Not Married* (1920). Others were *When Will He Die?* (1924), his most successful comedy, *Rich Paupers* (1922), *American Hassidim* (1928), *Sustenance* (1928), and *Angels On Earth*, a fantastic comedy (1929).

Harry Sackler (1883-   ) is equally at home in Yiddish, Hebrew, and English. Some of his plays he originally wrote in Yiddish and then translated into either Hebrew or English or both. Others were first written in either Hebrew or English. Born in Bohoredzany, Galicia, Sackler came to the United States in 1902. From 1906 to 1908 he studied law at the New York University Law School. Since the age of fourteen he had been writing Hebrew verse. In 1907 he made his debut with a published Yiddish story, *In Golden Chains*.

Sackler's first full-length drama, *Jose of Yokrath*, is built on a legend of an Amora in Palestine whose uncompromising piety caused him to curse his son and daughter with death because of their Hellenistic leanings. The play was written in Yiddish in 1915 and appeared in the author's own Hebrew translation in the *Hatoren* in 1921. In 1923 it was produced in Yiddish under the title *The Holy Tyrant*. *Yiskor*, a drama about a Jewish hero who is loved by a Polish princess and who chooses death rather than accede to

---

[1] *Yiddish Theatre Lexicon*, Vol. 1, Col. 560.

her carnal desires, was written in 1922 and staged in 1923. In 1924 he wrote *The Tsaddik's Journey* which was staged in 1926. This is a playful narrative of a *Hassidic* legend regarding a *Hassidic* rabbi's conquest of Satan and Lilith. Both plays were later produced in Hebrew by the Ohel Theatre of Palestine. Among his other plays are *Major Noah* (1928) and *Rahab,* a Hebrew play produced by Habima in Palestine (1932).

Sackler drew all his themes from Jewish history or legend. His specific contribution has been the imaginative recreation of historical setting and character.

Of the more recent dramatists worthy of note are Jacob Preger (1887-1943) who died a martyr's death in the Warsaw Ghetto, Alter Katzizne (1885-1943) also martyred in the Warsaw Ghetto, and Aaron Zeitlin (1889-   ).

Preger drew his themes from the Jewish folk tales which he treated in a highly imaginative manner. *The Trial* (1927) deals with a tale of a young Jewish boy who prefers to be buried alive rather than sin carnally with a Polish noblewoman who is in love with him. The play is based on the same theme as Sackler's *Yiskor*. *Simcha Plachte* (1935), a fantastic comedy, was staged in New York by the Yiddish Art Theatre under the title of *The Water Carrier* (1936). Other plays by Preger are *King Solomon* (1932), a dramatic poem, and the grotesque folk play *Melech Freylech* (1938).

Katzizne found his inspiration in Jewish history and legend. He is best known for his poetic dramas *Herod* and *The Duke,* which deals with the story of a Polish duke who embraced Judaism.

Aaron Zeitlin, like Preger and Katzizne, builds his plays on legendary themes. His fantastic comedy *Wise Men of Helm* (1933) is a dramatization of the Yiddish humorous folk tales of the city of Helm whose inhabitants are all extraordinary fools. *Estherke* (1938) is a romantic drama dealing with the love of the Polish King Kazimierz for a Jewish maiden.

Mention must also be made of Mark Arnstein (1878-1943, martyred in the Warsaw Ghetto) whose play *Der Vilner Balebesel* (first produced in Polish in 1902) is based on the legend of the Cantor of Vilna who abandoned his sacred calling because of his love for a Polish noblewoman and his operatic ambitions.

Since the October Revolution in Russia there has been a flourishing Yiddish theatre in that country. There are many fine theatre ensembles, the most noteworthy being the Jewish State Theatre in Moscow. Known mainly for its daring approach to the staging of the classical repertory of Goldfaden, Sholom Aleichem, and others, the Yiddish theatre in Russia has also nurtured a number of new and important Yiddish dramatists. Of those, the following deserve special mention:

David Bergelson (1884-   ), born in Kiev, Russia, left that country in 1921, finding himself out of sympathy with the political aims and methods of the Soviet Government. In 1933, when the Nazi régime in Germany began the execution of its anti-Jewish program, Bergelson returned to his native land. His plays *The Bread Mill* (1930), *Reubeni Prince of the Jews,* and *I Shall Live* (produced in Hebrew under the title of *Lo Omut Ki Echyeh*) show a genuine talent for observation, psychological insight, and skill in depicting the inner conflicts of the lonely and oppressed.

Peretz Markish (1895-   ) also left Russia after the Revolution only to return in 1926 because of his chagrin at the hopeless conditions of the Jews in Poland and the spread of anti-Semitism in that country. His plays have been performed on the Yiddish and Russian stages throughout the Soviet Union. Among them are *Nit Gedaiget* (1931), dealing with the yearning of the Jewish masses for life on the soil; *Fifth Horizon,* on the theme of the absorption of Jews in industry; *Who for Whom,* dealing with the movement among the Jews toward Socialistic reconstruction; and *An Eye for an Eye* (1944), epitomizing the undying spirit of heroism and defiance of the Jewish people in the face of the Nazi persecution in Poland.

Ezekiel Dobrushin (1883-   ) is best known for his modern adaptations of such Goldfaden classics as *The Witch* (1922), *The Tenth Commandment* (1926), and *Kabtzenson and Hungerman* (under the title of *The Bride Who Was Difficult to Please*). He has also dramatized the works of Abramowitch and Sholom Aleichem. Among his original plays are *Arum A Baidel* (1928), a play of life in the Jewish agricultural colonies, and *A Wonderful Story* (1944), dealing with Jewish partisans during the Nazi occupation.

Aaron Kushnirov (1898-   ) is best known for his dramatic poem *Hirsh Lekert* (1928). The play deals with the life of the revolutionary martyr, Hirsh Lekert, who killed the tyrannical governor of Vilna in May, 1902, because the latter had ordered the flogging of a group of May Day paraders. Other plays by Kushnirov are *Judgment Is in Sight,* a dramatic poem, and *Folk,* an adaptation of Lope de Vega's *Fuente Ovejuno* (published 1935).

In recent years there has been a tendency in the Yiddish theatre toward staging dramatizations of popular and classic novels of Yiddish literature. Mention has already been made of some of these dramatizations, notably of the work of Asch, Peretz, and Sholom Aleichem.

During the past few years some of the novels of I. J. Singer (1893-1944) have been dramatized and successfully staged by Maurice Schwartz. *Yoshe Kalb* (1932), a realistic drama of *Hassidic* life, ran for a year and a half and was later staged in Hebrew by Maurice Schwartz with the Ohel Theatre in Palestine. *Brothers Ashkenazi,* a panoramic study of the influence of industrialization on the life of the orthodox Jews of Poland, was dramatized and staged in 1937. Singer's novel *The Family Carnovsky,* dealing with the effects of the Nazis in Germany on the life of an assimilated German-Jewish family, was dramatized by Singer himself and staged in 1943.

It is difficult to generalize about trends in the Yiddish drama. Although basically a theatre of realism, the Yiddish theatre has also staged productions that were fantastic, mystical, naturalist, and impressionistic. There is hardly a style of drama or staging that has not been exploited by the Yiddish theatre.

The dramatists of the commercial Yiddish theatre have been turning more and more to themes of American Jewish life. In the field of melodrama, plays dealing with family problems of the American Jewish scene predominate. The musical comedy also holds an important place in the commercial Yiddish repertory and in that field the models of the American English-language stage are closely followed. The plays of the commercial Yiddish theatre have also been using, particularly in recent years, a great deal of English. The Yiddish dialogue of these plays is interspersed with many English expressions and sometimes complete speeches. This is undoubtedly done in order to make the plays more understandable to the English-speaking Jews who frequent these theatres. The result is sometimes a linguistic hodge-podge. In all the plays now staged by the commercial Yiddish theatre, the influences of Hurwitch and Laitner are strongly felt. It is true that a great deal more attention is paid to the continuity of plot and action, and in many of these plays there is clear-cut character delineation. However, very few of these plays are without incidental songs and couplets or comedy scenes to relieve the tension of the melodramatic moments, and in most instances the plots and situations are forced and to a great extent exaggerated.

The better dramatists whose plays have been produced by the various art theatres mentioned above have become more and more preoccupied with the problems of the Jewish people as a whole. Their themes concern themselves with such problems as Jewish nationalism, the rôle of the Jew in the class struggle, the question of the possible adjustment of the Jew in non-Jewish surroundings, the use of physical force versus spiritual perfection as a means of salvation for the Jewish people, and the problems engendered by assimilation. Others have been turning to historical and biographical plays, to bring to theatre audiences a realization of the heroic moments and figures in Jewish history in order to point out a promise of hope for the future. Most of the recent dramas are permeated with a strong undercurrent of Messianic striving.

At the present writing, with the extinction of Jewish community life in most of Europe as a result of the Nazi extermination policy against the Jews, the United States and Soviet Russia are the only countries in which Yiddish dramatic creativeness can now find expression. Pessimists are concerned over the future of the Yiddish drama. In America, they point out, the Yiddish language is being supplanted in the homes by English. A lack of understanding of Yiddish by the large mass of Jews is bound to affect adversely Yiddish creative expression. It would be foolhardy to prognosticate but it may be pointed out that a widespread net of Yiddish afternoon schools is bringing up a generation with a love for the Yiddish tongue and a conscious appreciation of its literary treasures. It may be that a crisis is impending. But pessimists have been foreseeing the death of Yiddish drama in this country since 1910. During the intervening period the best Yiddish dramas have been written and produced before appreciative audiences.

Hebrew drama has been referred to heretofore incidentally. It is a historic fact that long before Yiddish dramas were ever written there was an extensive dramatic literature in Hebrew. These plays were primarily intended for the reading public, since there was no Hebrew theatre in existence in which the Hebrew playwright might be able to see his plays produced.

In the beginning of the twentieth century many attempts were made to create a Hebrew theatre. A number of troupes were formed but they were purely amateur in personnel and approach, and were doomed to quick failure. In 1912 Nahum Zemach organized a troupe in Byalistock, Russia. This group, called Habima Halvrith toured in a number of cities and in 1913 staged in Vienna Osip Dymov's play *Hear O Israel* in a Hebrew translation. The advent of the First World War caused the disintegration of the group. Similar attempts in Palestine before and during the First World War also failed.

In 1917, during the Revolution in Russia, Nahum Zemach gathered a group of young people and organized a Hebrew Theatre studio in Moscow under the name of Habima. The director of the Moscow Art Theatre, K. A. Stanislavski, became interested in the studio and for a time was their teacher and artistic mentor. Later he suggested one of his students, Y. V. Vakhtangov, for the post of artistic director of the group. Vakhtangov was a director of unusual genius and under his guidance until the time of his death in 1922, the Habima established a reputation as one of the world's finest theatre collectives. The first production of Habima was called *An Evening of Beginnings* (1918). It consisted of four one-act plays, *The Sister* by Sholom Asch, *The Sun* by Yitzhak Katzenelenson, *Fire!* by J. L. Peretz, and *Nuisance* by I. D. Berkowitz.

Their second production in 1918 was Pinski's *The Eternal Jew*. That play established Habima as a theatre of the highest artistic merit. Approached with an uninhibited and completely fresh point of view, the play became in their hands the apotheosis of the Jew's age-old striving for Messianic redemption. The color and sounds of the ancient Orient served as a fitting backdrop for the tragic story of the destruction of the temple and the loss of Menahem, the predestined Messiah.

The collective spent three years working on their next production. The result was their breathtaking staging of An-sky's *Dybbuk*. It was both the Habima's and Vakhtangov's finest creation, and was hailed by the critics as the perfect play. There was complete harmony in every detail.

Then followed *The Golem* by Leivick, *Jacob's Dream* by the German-Jewish writer Richard Beer-Hoffman, and *The Flood* a comedy by H. Berger. After an extended tour throughout Europe and the United States, the Habima settled in Palestine where the collective has been active in presenting a repertory consisting mainly of translations of classic plays.

A few years before Habima settled in Palestine, Moshe Halevi, a former member of the Habima, founded in that country the workers' theatre collective Ohel. Originally Ohel planned to devote itself to the production of Biblical plays. This plan was soon abandoned for a repertory of classic Jewish and non-Jewish plays in Hebrew translation.

HaMatatey is a revue theatre in Palestine. Its programs are devoted to revue programs treating in a satirical vein the events and personalities in the news of the day. From time to time HaMatatey has also produced full-length plays.

In the United States a number of attempts have been made toward the establishment of a Hebrew theatre. Notable are Alil, active in 1939 and 1940, and Pargod which, after a number of years of experimentation along amateur lines, was finally reorganized on a professional basis and in the spring of 1945 gave its first professional production. The play was *King Solomon and Shalmai the Cobbler* by Semi Groniman, a comedy in a biblical setting reminiscent of Mark Twain's *The Prince and the Pauper*.

Whether it is due to accident or design, the fact remains that very few original Hebrew plays have been produced by these theatre collectives. In part it may be due to the fact that the Jewish population of Palestine uses Hebrew as its native tongue. Consequently, if they are to see plays of the world repertory, they must be presented to them in Hebrew. When the theatre collectives are given a choice between a mediocre original Hebrew play and an acknowledged classic of dramatic literature, they will choose the latter. Adaptations or translations of world and Yiddish classics have been made by such outstanding Hebrew writers as A. Shlonsky, Avigdor Hameiri, S. Tchernichovski, Hayim Nachman Bialik, Zalman Shneour, and many others. It may also be true that because of the fact that the modern Jewish settlement in Palestine is of comparatively recent origin, a native Hebrew drama could not yet become crystallized. In recent years, however, a number of original Hebrew works by Palestinian authors have been produced in that country. The historical play *Mihal, the Daughter of Saul*, by Aaron Ashman (1896-   ) was produced in 1941, and the following year saw the production of his play *This Soil*, which deals with the days of romantic pioneering in Palestine by the Halutzim (Jewish Pioneers) during the latter part of the nineteenth century. It glorifies their love for Palestine and their selfless devotion to the task of rebuilding the national homeland. In 1935 Habima produced Nathan Bistritski's (1896-   ) mystical drama *Belayilzeh* (*In This Night*) and the following year Ohel staged his *Shabbetai Zevi*. In 1941 his drama concerning Josephus, *Jerusalem and Rome* was produced by Habima.

These are isolated instances of productions of original Hebrew drama. For the bulk of its repertory, the Hebrew theatre is still very much dependent on translations and adaptations of plays which were written in other tongues. Despite the paucity of produced original Hebrew drama, a great many such plays are published in Palestine every year, and it seems a certainty that with time many of these will take their place in the repertory of the Palestinian Hebrew Theatre.

XIII

The United States

BARRETT H. CLARK

It is not possible to determine the exact point at which the modern American drama began unless one is ready to make the most arbitrary sort of definitions. Of course the same thing may be said of the modern drama in most other countries, though the line of demarcation between old and new is usually much clearer elsewhere than it is in the United States. In France the establishment of Antoine's Théâtre Libre in 1887 symbolized a new attitude toward life and the theatre on the part of a group of playwrights, actors, and directors, a clearcut break with certain dramatic traditions; and in Germany the establishment of Otto Brahm's Freie Buehne accomplished a similar service. It is true that neither in France nor in Germany was the process of development merely the result of the appearance of a theatre where exponents of the "new" drama might suddenly become "moderns": in both countries, as is shown elsewhere in this history, there had been literary and social and political forces operating for decades before the playwrights we now recognize as moderns were able to write their characteristic works and find audiences ready to accept them.

In France and Germany, then, and elsewhere in Europe, the break between the past and what was the present when the modern drama began, is relatively easy to describe, because it was usually associated with a man, a group of men, a theatre, a director, or a critic; and the process was usually recorded at the time by critics and historians. Sometimes the line of cleavage is so clear that disagreement on the essential facts is impossible, as in the case of the Soviet drama, which could not of course, have existed before the establishment of the U.S.S.R.; even though some of the writers who contributed to it after 1917 belonged chronologically to the Russian drama of Empire days.

In England it is a little more difficult to point to a single theatre or to one man who was responsible for what we term the modern drama, for in spite of the effective blows struck by Bernard Shaw in the nineties, he was not alone, nor was the Independent Theatre which produced his first play in 1891 the sole outstanding symbol of the beginning of the modern period in Great Britain. It is rather the translations of Ibsen's plays by William Archer, Edmund Gosse, and others, appearing as far back as the seventies, plus certain plays of Henry Arthur Jones and Arthur Wing Pinero, plus the philosophical, economic, and political writings of the pre-Fabians and others, including Annie Besant, in the seventies, eighties, and nineties, that culminated in the militant campaigns of Shaw against the technical and ideological absurdities of the English drama of his day, that made it possible for a new generation of English writers to band themselves into small groups which in the aggregate evolved what was to become the modern English drama.

The dramatic movement in Ireland is far easier to segregate and define than that in England, since this was definitely the work of a small group of writers in the early nineties, who established a theatre for Irish playwrights. Before the Irish Literary Theatre produced Yeats' *The Countess Cathleen* in 1892, no Irish drama existed.

What is true of the more or less clearcut lines of demarcation between old and new in Europe and the British Isles is true of most other countries except the United States. To begin with, this country was not, culturally, homogeneous; our theatrical activities were not confined to a single city but spread out over a continent; the drama we had was scarcely in any sense original, and was almost wholly dependent upon that of Europe and England, and such plays as were written for our theatre by native or naturalized Americans, or even by resident foreigners, were almost wholly imitative. There was in effect nothing that could be clearly identified as a body of native drama, and almost nothing that in form or idea could be recognized as distinctively American. The breach between American literature, as exemplified by such writers as Whitman, Howells, James, and Mark Twain, was complete, even when prominent literary men condescended, as they sometimes did, to write plays.

Now the line of demarcation, while distinct, between the typical nineteenth-century play of American authorship and the typical American play of the period 1920-1940, is a very broad line, and if it were graphically presented on paper, it would extend, in varying widths, between the late nineteenth century and the present day. Plays are even now being written which, except for a few externals of style, are as conventionally constructed and as remote from reality as we understand it, as any of the melodramas of J. J. McCloskey, whose popular successes of sixty years ago are remembered only by a few octogenarians and known, chiefly through their titles alone, to a few drama specialists. On the other hand, we are able to distinguish here and there in the work of Bronson Howard and James A. Herne, who flourished between 1870 and the beginning of the present century, occasional glimpses of the direction our dramatists were to take after 1900.

There can be no question that Eugene O'Neill's *Beyond the Horizon* is characteristically modern and American, and no question that the phenomenally successful play *Monte Cristo*, which his father adapted and played for decades, is not in the least modern, and only in a very limited sense American. Robert E. Sherwood's *The Road to Rome* is not only a typical modern American play, it has fulfilled a historical function in helping, in a small way, to create modern American drama. The Maxwell Anderson-Laurence Stallings war play *What Price Glory?* is something no one could mistake for a European play, nor could any one familiar with the products of American play writing of the past conceivably take it for a continuation of the tradition that gave us *Shenandoah* or *Held by the Enemy*.

These few examples of the old play writing and the new are mentioned to show that the extremes representing the two schools or traditions, are easily distinguished one from the other. But how to determine in what manner and at what time the new superseded the old, and why; and finally how to investigate the reasons for the change?

It will not do to assume that our modern writers are the result of some process of evolution either in ideas or craftsmanship, at least of any clear-cut process which can be observed and recorded. The theory of the evolution of literary forms, as set forth by Brunetière and certain other critics several years ago, presupposes "laws" and mystic compulsions which I cannot accept, and the adoption of any such theory has led some critics to clearly untenable conclusions. While no one can deny that influences of every imaginable kind do affect writers, it is uncritical to claim that any one can know precisely what these influences are and just how they operate. It has always struck me as absurd for a critic to maintain that a certain poet received from his great aunt the impetus to write simply because the lady at one period was alleged to have contributed verses to some magazine, or to repeat such nonsense as that Ibsen's concern with the sea was in any way attributable to the few drops of blood in his veins from some forebear who was a Scottish sea captain.

The fact is that Eugene O'Neill's father was a popular actor, and it is conceivable that the future playwright as a youngster *may* have got the notion from James O'Neill that he could write plays. The point to be made, however, is that it is impossible to know to what extent, if any, the older man influenced the younger to write plays.

A connected history of American drama has been attempted in recent times by only two men, the late Montrose J. Moses and Dr. Arthur Hobson Quinn, and it is significant that the wide divergence of critical opinion between these two, and the many playwrights and plays either not mentioned at all or only casually referred to by one or the other, is due not alone to personal preference or bias, but to the fact that materials on the subject are scarce, and in many cases not trustworthy. Very few American plays were ever published, and of those that once existed in manuscript form exceptionally few have survived. There are long stretches of our dramatic history that can be studied now only, if at all, in the files of old newspapers, and the general conclusions of modern historians can be formed, when they *are* formed, principally on second- or third-hand evidence or mere hearsay. A very large number of popular plays of the last century and a half are known to us now only as titles and only through the more or less occasional comments on them made by contemporaries. A good deal of our modern critical history consists largely of a repetition of such comments.

The problem of writing a history of nineteenth-century American drama is roughly comparable to that of writing on American non-dramatic literature of the same period if the historian were unable to discover anywhere a line of Poe, more than a half dozen stories of Hawthorne, a few scattered and poorly edited verses of Whitman, one novel of James, half of the total output of Mark Twain, only an occasional essay or poem of Lowell and Holmes; and were forced to depend on a more or less haphazard personal investigation of a few private and scattered collections of manuscripts and privately printed books and pamphlets; in other words, upon a fragmentary series of more or less unauthenticated texts from only a moderate number of writers.

It must always be remembered that our judgments on a large number of American plays of the past, especially on those that have not been published, are necessarily imperfect, and upon those of which the manuscripts are missing, entirely based on indirect and usually biased reports.

A record even of the past seventy-five or eighty years of American drama must be largely tentative. It would be simple to devise a pattern and elaborate it into a picture of progress from the earliest beginnings, tracing the evolution of our native drama from let us say *The Contrast* in 1787, to *Skylark* in 1939. There is something in the human mind that requires order in the presentation of material, that delights in the logical arrangement of data; and nothing is easier for the historian of any human activity than to create such a pattern, filling it with details that fit conveniently into it, whether the facts warrant such a procedure or not.

It is my belief that some confusion has been added to the records of our native play writing—as indeed to all literary history—by a too easy assumption that it follows some more or less logical course of evolution, or that such a course can be scientifically traced. It may be justly said that Royall Tyler wrote a rather inept comedy of manners in 1787, that Anna Cora Mowatt wrote another and perhaps a better one more than sixty years later, and that S. N. Behrman, eighty years after that, brought the form to a very high point of development (so far as the United States is concerned), in any one of his three best plays. But there is little if any evidence to show that each of these three writers forms a link in any evolutionary process. It is, indeed, improbable that Mrs. Mowatt ever saw, read, or heard of *The Contrast,* and very unlikely that Mr. Behrman was familiar with any play of either author except to the extent of seeing a late revival of *Fashion*.

In attempting to record the history of the modern drama in the United States, therefore, I am restricted by the lack of first-hand evidence on a number of important writers because the texts are lost or otherwise inaccessible; this is true to some extent even of many fairly recent playwrights. The collateral evidence in many instances is lacking, fragmentary or not reliable; and as I shall point out later, such influences as affected the writers under consideration, came from a variety of sources, most of them from abroad, and many of them not easy to trace.

To define exactly the words *modern drama* is impossible, but since this book is not primarily an analysis or criticism of the modern spirit in drama, but a record of the plays written and produced in modern times, an exact definition is not altogether necessary. The period included under the term is here used to cover the century between the time Ibsen began writing and the present day. It seems safe to say that before 1867, the year of Ibsen's *League of Youth,* the modern spirit in drama had not made itself clearly manifest anywhere, though it was indeed germinating. In spite of the manifestos and tentative experiments which even in the fifties and early sixties seemed to point forward to the creation of the dramatic "movements" in Europe that were later to bloom as Free Theatres and Independent Stage Societies; in spite of the plays of Ostrovski in Russia, the plays and novels of Zola and the Goncourts in France, there were few plays that exemplified any striking change of attitude toward life and art before the late sixties and early seventies.

In the United States, the modern drama as we now recognize it began at a considerably later time than in most other countries. Although I have just said that an exact definition of the term is impossible and unnecessary, some attempt should be made to characterize it. Now there can be no doubt that Mrs. Mowatt's *Fashion,* first produced in 1845, is the unmistakable product of an age and society not our own; that it is obvious, conventional, and designed to entertain the cash customers of a century ago; that its satire is broad, good natured, and unsubtle; and that it sets forth no original ideas. Conceivably one might mention the play in connection with a study of modern American play writing in order to illustrate the difference between the old and the new, which is precisely what I am doing when I mention Sidney Howard's *They Knew What They Wanted.* The Mowatt play does not belong in the category covered by this section, but the Howard play does. This is not alone because *Fashion* was produced in 1845 and *They Knew What They Wanted* in 1926. The earlier comedy, even making allowances for the respective differences in speech and technique that affected the dramatic products of the two epochs, strikes us as trivial and hollow, and even if we grant that the author never intended to write a profound work, it is only a very pale and unsatisfactory reflection of life; we feel that there is in it no basic truth to life. Edgar Allan Poe wrote of it, "There is not an event, a character, a jest, which is not a well-understood thing, a matter of course, a stage property time out of mind." To this criticism the author replied that at all events the actors seemed to have "infused themselves" into it, and "produced a very effective counterfeit of life." The expression "counterfeit of life" is a convenient one for the present purpose. It would probably never occur to a modern playwright to think of his work as being genuine or counterfeit, nor to defend it—except as a commercial property—by claiming that the actors breathed life into something that lacked it.

One difference, then, between the American drama of pre-modern days and the modern era lies in the author's intention. The best of our moderns aim, consciously or otherwise, at truth. From William Vaughan Moody to Lillian Hellman, by and large, the playwright seems intent upon persuading us to look upon his work as some kind of reflection of life as we know it, even when he writes historical chronicles or fantastic extravaganzas. He seems, even when he is least conscious of it, or most anxious merely to entertain or make money, to regard his problem as one involving the transfer to the theatre of something he feels or thinks about life. If his play fails to carry some conviction of truth, no matter how indirectly conveyed, he realizes that the audience will probably not respond.

While it may hardly be claimed that all modern playwrights look upon themselves as philosophers or psychologists, or that all playwrights of earlier days were interested only in contriving mechanical devices to serve as vehicles for actors, I think we can discover in the broad distinction between the two groups I have just named one marked difference between the old drama and the modern. Judging the drama of a century ago by those examples of it that survive, its best products succeeded in the theatre largely because they were acted in accordance with the tastes of the day, and were acquired by actors not because of their intrinsic qualities but because they were useful as a means to an end. That end was usually acting. The actor wanted something that would give him a chance to display his histrionic talents. Edwin Forrest played *Metamora* for about forty years. He thought it a very bad play but he went on using it. I cannot quite imagine Miss Cornell or Miss Hayes or the Lunts deliberately choosing what they thought bad plays solely in order to exploit their talents.

The plays of one generation become, of course, as dull to the next generation as old newspapers; but when we compare the American plays of the first three-quarters of the nineteenth century with those of certain other countries of the same period, there is probably not one that could be revived today and enjoyed by audiences except as curiosities.

If we accept the broad thesis that American plays of the nineteenth century before 1850 show no evidence of what we are going to use as a simple working definition of the modern spirit, let us see whether we can name some examples of that more or less conscious seeking after some sort of truth which can be recognized as characterizing our drama, something that may be properly designated as both modern and American.

Even from the remote days of the eighteenth century when native writers occasionally tried their hands at native themes and the treatment of native characters, we are able to find, usually in connection with the so-called Yankee types, something unmistakably American. Though the plays are derivative in technique and idea and in other respects seem little more than feeble imitations of French, German, or English originals, we do perceive in certain plays of William Dunlap, and of course in Tyler's *The Contrast,* clearly marked Yankee types; and these persisted, in play after play, throughout the entire period, and persist in more or less modified form up to the present time. A glance at Dr. Perley Isaac Reed's study, *The Realistic Presentation of American Characters in Native American Plays Prior to 1870,* shows how American playwrights, from 1751 throughout the period studied, consistently put into their work an amazing variety of native types. A few of the better-known plays of the past century, like Samuel Woodworth's *Forest Rose,* the various versions of *Rip Van Winkle* and *Uncle Tom's Cabin,* remained popular on the stage for decades, and it is likely that the reason for that popularity was to a great extent that the authors were able to present recognizable human types.

Yet we shall find no play until after the Civil War that can be properly regarded as foreshadowing the mature viewpoint of the best of our modern writers. The intellectual spirit that was spreading through Europe from 1850 onwards, that was even making itself felt in the United States by non-dramatic writers from the sixties to the end of the century, can scarcely be noted at all in any native play written (or at least produced) before 1900. I can recall no reference, for example, to Darwin or Huxley, no mention of Nietzsche, Marx, or Annie Besant, no shadow of a hint in any American play of the period that Ibsen ever existed, or Tolstoi, or Henry George, and no evidence that any *practising* native playwright had read a line of Emerson, Whitman, or Henry James.

Compare the most successful playwrights of the 1865-1900 period with the writers of fiction and poetry, and see how wide is the gap between theatre and literature. Where in the theatre is a single writer with the mental maturity of Whitman, Mark Twain, Lowell, or James? Where can we find a stage writer with the artistic gifts or integrity of an Emily Dickinson, a Sarah Orne Jewett, a Mary E. Wilkins? It seems, in reading the hundreds of surviving plays of the nineteenth century, that the best of them were the work of more or less ingenious children who lived in a world that had done no thinking since 1620.

Bronson Howard, whose career as playwright began before 1870 and ended about the turn of the century, was an intelligent man, a successful dramatist, an honest worker, a student of his subject, and certainly a better-educated person than most of his play-writing contemporaries. There is enough in his plays to warrant the hypothesis that while he himself in no sense inaugurated any movement in the theatre that developed into what we now recognize as our modern drama, there is in his output as a writer enough evidence to enable us to designate him as a symbol of what was, slowly and obscurely, happening to a few native playwrights.

Born in 1842, and receiving a certain amount of education, he took up newspaper work, but before the age of twenty-two he had tried his hand at play writing, and in 1864 his dramatization of an episode from *Les Misérables* was publicly produced. Coming to New York, he wrote what was to be his first successful play, *Saratoga*. This was produced in 1870. There is nothing very original about *Saratoga,* though in an epoch when most plays were laid against European backgrounds, it is not without meaning that the young playwright should have put his scene in an American town. It is also significant that the play was successful in London and Berlin as well as in the United States. *Moorcroft* (1874) was a drama on American slavery, based on a story by John Hay. The most interesting of the early works was *The Banker's Daughter* (1878), laid partly in New York and partly in Paris. The characters are American and French, and the big situation revolves round a duel. The dramatic contrast effected by setting the American characters against the Europeans is worth noting.

In 1882 came *Young Mrs. Winthrop,* a play about divorce, and it is noteworthy that this time the author had not concocted a situation in vacuo, without background or direct reference to the world about him. Dr. Quinn says, in his *History of the American Drama from the Civil War to the Present Day,* that Howard "placed on the stage for the first time in America a group of characters whose actions are determined by the power of social laws and the interruption of social distractions without making the prevailing note one of satire." He adds that the theme of "the growing complication of social and professional life in America, which interferes in the happiness of a man and a woman who really love each other, carried the play to success." Here, then, we have a pretty striking instance of an American theme, seriously treated, which because it was effectively worked out and bore some resemblance to the lives and thoughts of real persons, appealed to the public.

One of Our Girls, which came three years later, was also a decided success. Like *The Banker's Daughter* this was also a study in contrasted American and foreign types. The extremely conventional American girl who plays an important rôle, while far different from her European counterpart as developed in the plays of Ibsen (who was at the time getting into his stride as a social force in the theatre), was no doubt based largely upon fact.

The next significant Howard play was *The Henrietta,* produced in 1887. Here, perhaps for the first time, we have a relatively serious play about big business or rather, a play in which the author uses big business as a background. Yet, knowing what we now know about the Robber Barons of the time, and something of the politico-economic skulduggery of the financial wizards who controlled our destinies in the eighties, what Howard shows us bears the same relation to the facts as a Sunday School paper bears to the facts of the white-slave traffic. *The Henrietta* is largely a personal drama, worked out in terms of this man against that, with only the sketchiest background to suggest, or shall we say permit, the guess that mighty forces may have been at work. It is possible that Howard suspected a meaning behind his play, but at the end we are left to suppose that all would be well if only certain selfish and wicked men would allow themselves to have what used to be called a "change of heart." There is scarcely a hint here of anything but a personal problem. There are other plays of Howard's, never produced and existing only in manuscript, which show his interest in contemporary themes, economic, political, and social; four of these I have read, and in every one the conclusion is clear that he used his material largely or entirely as background. He seemed unable to weave a personal story into a pattern which would show how the personal problems he raised were part and parcel of problems of a much wider and more complicated nature than any that could be resolved by a mere change of heart on the part of the "villain."

Howard's Civil War play *Shenandoah,* whatever its good qualities, can scarcely be considered as announcing or reflecting the modern spirit, but *Aristocracy* (1892), like *The Banker's Daughter,* carries on the character contrasts which Howard had already found effective on the stage. Here the character drawing is somewhat more effective than in the earlier social satires. Again we find the wealthy unsophisticated American contrasted with members of social groups different from his own. The last of Howard's plays published during his lifetime was *Kate* (1906), another comedy of international contrasts. This was never produced. The year 1906 marks the approximate beginning of a period in which the ideas and technical methods of Howard began to be outmoded. It is not to be wondered at that in a country so largely subject to intellectual and political changes as the United States, the work of a man who began writing during the Civil War should have been outmoded eight years before the First World War.

In choosing Bronson Howard as a kind of symbol of the first stirrings of our modern American drama I do so with some hesitation, for it must be borne in mind that he was not a conscious forerunner, prophet, or would-be philosopher, but a conscientious craftsman trying to make money out of the show business; to say something (not too much, certainly, and not enough to puzzle or upset his customers) about the land he lived in, the men and women he knew; and to add some occasional comment on a few of life's perplexing problems.

Unless this section on American drama is to be extended to the length of a book, I shall not be able to trace in every writer from the Civil War to 1900 the same kind of evidence I have sought in the work of Howard. To make that sort of investigation would indeed serve only to suggest that there was more evidence than the facts will warrant.

But there is no lack of evidence to show that the plays of the last thirty years of the nineteenth century are rich in American character types, no matter how poor they may be in other respects. Even leaving out of account the thousands of texts that have disappeared, and considering only the perhaps 25 per cent of the grand total that can still be studied, it is possible to note that a considerable number of the successful dramatists made use of American backgrounds and characters even when the structure employed and ideas used were in no sense American. It is not surprising to find Mark Twain and Bret Harte, in their few and unsuccessful ventures in play writing, wholly occupied with native types and scenes. The same thing is true of Joaquin Miller.

Augustin Daly, whose writing career extended from the Civil War to the late nineties, was primarily concerned with adaptations from classic drama and the contemporary drama of France and Germany, though on occasion, particularly with *Horizon* and *Divorce,* he tried his hand at more or less original native plays. But like David Belasco, who will of course be mentioned later in these pages, he was more interested in providing his company with effective vehicles than in creating a new and original drama.

The writers of the post Civil War period, subject to the same influences that shaped the development of our writers of prose fiction and poetry, were somewhat more sensitive to the social changes in American life than their predecessors, though it was not until toward the end of the century that any play of American authorship showed distinct signs of being more than a framework for the presentation of native types, and occasionally for the introduction of local background. There was little until the nineties to show that any writer tried seriously to reproduce the spirit of his country or set forth more than the superficial details of its external aspects in this locality or that. The otherwise conventional popular successes *Davy Crockett, Across the Continent, Kit the Arkansas Traveler, The Old Homestead,* and *My Partner*—all great favorites of the second half of the nineteenth century—differ from European models chiefly in the scenic details and here and there in the dialogue.

Dr. Quinn has offered arguments to show that William Dean Howells, whom he calls "a master playwright," exercised considerable influence on the American drama, and to some extent foreshadowed the so-called realistic drama that was to come in later years. It is true that of the many plays written by Howells some were professionally produced, and a few were more or less successful; it is also true that they offered in their quiet and unemphatic way a pleasant contrast to the over-written and bombastic works of their time, and may have given an occasional hint to more than one playwright who sought to create his dramatic effects without going to extremes. On the other hand, the influence of Howells as novelist and critic, though difficult to trace, was without doubt far greater than his example as a practising playwright. It was his championship of Tolstoi and other revolutionary social and literary writers of Europe that brought to the

American literary world of his day a knowledge of forces and ways of treating them that gradually spread—particularly in the case of James A. Herne—to the drama.

Here and there we can trace specific instances of the leavening process fostered by Howells, as for example in Hamlin Garland's *Roadside Meetings,* where we read that the older novelist "was deeply moved by the social injustice of which we were all aware.... Sometimes ... he discussed Bellamy's *Looking Backward* and the growing contrasts between the rich and the poor, while I, in turn, dilated upon Henry George." [1] A still more striking instance is described at some length by Garland in the book just quoted from. Here is one of those fairly well-documented cases where a definite influence can be seen at work on a native playwright. It was in the middle eighties, and Garland had recently come to Boston from the west. "French Impressionism," he writes, "and Russian Veritism were still in the debate when the doctrine of dramatic realism swept upon us from the north, embodied in Henrik Ibsen's austere plays, and I, being already instructed in northland literature by Hurd of the Transcript, became its advocate." Garland had seen Beatrice Cameron play Nora in a special performance of *A Doll's House,* which was to him "a revelation of the power, naturalness, and truth of the great Norwegian's methods." Garland says he noted at that time that

> This performance marks an epoch in American dramatic art.... It moves me more deeply than Shakespeare. I left the theatre that afternoon converted to the new drama.... It became another "cause" for me.... Ibsen's method, alien as his material actually appeared.... pointed the way to a new and more authentic drama.

It should be remembered that these words were written nearly fifty years after the events described, and I point out that in the very next paragraph the American novelist speaks of having discussed the Independent Theatre of London and the Freie Buehne of Berlin, three or four years *before* either of them had come into existence. But the basic facts seem beyond dispute: the new literary movements, the artistic formulas from Norway, Germany, France, and Russia, had at least reached the knowledge of a few young American revolutionaries. "Instructed by Howells," says Garland, "we had read the novels of Valdes, Tolstoi, and Flaubert. Now, through William Archer, we studied the dramas of Ibsen and Björnson."

It was in Boston that Garland first saw James A. Herne, and learned to know and admire his art as actor and playwright. The date was 1888, and the play Herne's own *Drifting Apart.* A Boston critic had told Garland that Herne was "a local-color realist after your own heart. He's not an Ibsen, but he is trying to represent New England life."

There seems no doubt that James A. Herne was one of the influential

[1] This and the quotations immediately following are from Hamlin Garland, *Roadside Meetings* (New York, The Macmillan Co., 1930), reprinted by permission of the publishers.

forerunners of the native drama of modern times in the United States, not only because he was an honest, conscientious, and effective actor of the unemphatic, realistic type, but because he strove, in his later plays, to create true native characters; yet, except in a very few scenes in a very few of his plays, his work belongs to the conventional theatre of the seventies and eighties, the theatre in which he was trained.

Of special interest was the writing and production of *Margaret Fleming*. It expresses the author's attitude toward men and women as members of society, and is not simply a melodramatic pot-boiler or a vehicle for particular actors. Only six years after the production of this play Herne wrote words the like of which cannot be found in all the writings of all the native playwrights up to his day. In *The Critic* (1897) he says, "Art for truth's sake is serious. Its highest purpose has ever been to perpetuate the life of its time." Even more startling is the statement that follows: "If [the artist] has a truth to manifest and he can present it without giving offence and still retain its power, he should so present it, but if he must choose between giving offence and receding from his position, he should stand by his principle and state his truth fearlessly."

The importance of these words, uttered at a time when pleasing the public seemed the sole criterion with playwrights and managers alike, can hardly be overemphasized. The plain fact that he thought as he did, and publicly expressed himself, is remarkable. We shall, I think, find no more courageous or forthright declaration from any playwright until, in the nineteen twenties, we come to an interview in which Eugene O'Neill said,

> I intend to use whatever I can make my own, to write about anything under the sun that fits or can be made to fit the subject. . . . I want to do what gives me pleasure and worth in my own eyes, and don't care to do what doesn't. . . . It is just life that interests me as a thing in itself.

All the evidence we now have shows that Herne conscientiously tried to present the essential truth about his characters as he saw them, and that *Margaret Fleming* was a serious attempt in the direction of truth and away from the theatre that existed in order to exploit the personalities of actors. A serious domestic drama, devoid of the big scenes that were considered necessary in this type of play, *Margaret Fleming* strikes us today as a relatively unconventional piece, especially in the matter of dialogue. To realize the novelty introduced by Herne it is necessary only to read any other play produced at the same time. *Possibly* the text we now have is not precisely the text as first written: the original manuscript, of which no copy could be found, was reconstructed from memory by the author's widow, at least twenty years after its first production.

Hamlin Garland points out, in the work above mentioned, that *Margaret Fleming* was the first product of the first Little, or Experimental, Theatre in America. Tried out in Lynn, Massachusetts in 1890, it was brought to Boston at Herne's expense, and ran there for three weeks in May, 1891. It was played again at the same place some months later, then taken to New York, and during the next twenty-three years revived from time to time. Garland tells us that "it was the most naturalistic, the most colloquial, and the most truthful presentation of a domestic drama ever seen on the American stage up to that time."

Possibly in order to recoup his losses on *Margaret Fleming,* Herne next began work on the play that was to become his greatest success, *Shore Acres.* Even today some of its quietly amusing scenes will bear reading. There is genuine charm and veracity in them. It cannot perhaps be said that the elements of old-time melodrama with which the plot is carried to its lurid climax accounted for the play's extraordinary popularity, but the fact is that Herne was evidently not quite sure that what he deemed the play's essential truth was enough to hold it together as a show.

One of the last of the Herne plays was *The Reverend Griffith Davenport,* based on a Civil War story. The outline of the plot as we now have it suggests a character study of unusual dramatic effectiveness, but since the only first-hand evidence we possess is the bare text of the last act, there is little point in analyzing the play. Here again, as in *Margaret Fleming,* we have straightforward and relatively realistic dialogue.

If the historian is handicapped by the lack of textual evidence in determining the extent to which Herne has contributed ideas or technical skill to the sum total of American drama, he is almost completely at a loss to judge the work of several other writers who, to judge from criticism or the casual comments of contemporaries, wrote plays that might deserve serious consideration. The many immensely successful plays of Edward Harrigan, for example, have never been published, and the surviving manuscripts, jealously guarded by the Harrigan family, have been read by only a few persons. The critic of today, unless he has been lucky enough to see some of these manuscripts, is forced to rely upon hearsay. Dr. Quinn, who studied most of the Harrigan manuscripts several years ago, has written fully about them, and the late Montrose J. Moses has added his descriptive analysis. William Dean Howells compared Harrigan's work with that of Goldoni. I have read a rather extensive study of Harrigan that covers his entire career, but even this remains in manuscript. I have been unable to see more than two of the texts themselves,[1] and for that reason it is impossible for me to to do more than record my impression that Harrigan can hardly be regarded as a forerunner, except in the sense that he created a world of types—many of them from the streets of New York—treating them usually in farcical or sentimental fashion. A study of the synopses of the plays in the *Mulligan Guards* series, and of certain others, shows the author's affectionate concern with the immigrant Irish and Germans.

---

[1] The Theater Collection at the New York Public Library has just one manuscript, *Squatter Sovereignty.*

It should be noted here that my comments on Harrigan, indeed on all the writers who flourished before 1900, and on many who belong to the later years, are intended in no sense as anything more than brief summaries of one aspect of their importance: it is my aim only to indicate in what respects these writers pointed, or seemed to point, the way which our more mature contemporaries have taken.

The work of other writers of the last quarter of the nineteenth century shows, as I have pointed out, an occasional concern with character for its own sake and with certain ideas current at the time, but for the most part the playwright was apparently content to people his work with lightly sketched and conventional types. One wonders, in reading the political records of the eighties and nineties, to what extent Bartley Campbell, or Augustin Daly, or Charles Hoyt, believed that the theatre could or should reflect the drama of contemporary history. It is true, Harrigan did hint that municipal corruption was rampant; Howard perceived that Wall Street was not the exclusive province of wealthy but occasionally misguided philanthropists; and Hoyt seemed to take it for granted that Tammany Hall was not the platonic ideal of perfect government. In Hoyt's play *A Texas Steer,* and in Benjamin Woolf's *The Mighty Dollar* we have broadly farcical pictures of political scamps, but it was not until after the great muck-raking era of the early twentieth century that a student of our history, judging solely from the theatre, would be able to suspect that all was not substantially right with our government.

A consideration of the plays written, rewritten, adapted, arranged and produced by David Belasco, whose career covered most of the period between the 1870's and 1928, might lead one to believe that the work of this extraordinary man was more closely related to the development of modern American drama than it actually was, but it is impossible to determine the precise extent of his coöperation with other writers in all the plays to which his name is attached, either as sole author or collaborator; and even where his share as playwright is relatively clear, what he added as director and stage manager rather obscures his rôle as writer. He began in the early seventies and claims to have written at least twenty-five plays up to 1880, only five of which seem to have survived even in manuscript, and these are either adaptations from the French or are more or less "original" works written in collaboration. The only plays out of fifty listed up to 1895 that bear his name alone are the conventional and old-fashioned *May Blossom* (1882) and *The Heart of Maryland* (1895). Both are typical products of the nineteenth century. Even such picturesque and more or less "original" plays as *The Girl of the Golden West* (1905) and *The Return of Peter Grimm* (1911), among his most famous plays, are little more than local-color pastiches written largely to exhibit his own virtuosity as director and the special talents of his actors.

The value of the contribution of Belasco as manager and director to the development of the American theatre, and the importance of the man as a revolutionary of sorts in lighting and staging, I do not question, but it is doubtful whether the plays for which he was directly or indirectly responsible affected to any great extent the work of contemporary or later playwrights. This in spite of his having produced the picturesque and preëminently theatrical romantic plays of John Luther Long, especially *Madame Butterfly* (1900), *The Darling of the Gods* (1902), and *Adrea* (1904); and Eugene Walter's *The Easiest Way* (1908).

On the not too clearly marked pathway followed by those American playwrights whom I have considered as forerunners of the modern drama in this country, I shall next consider the work of the poet-playwright William Vaughan Moody, whose ideas on the theatre began germinating before 1900 and whose two produced plays belong to the decade after the turn of the century, but before I come to the next period in the development of our drama I shall try to explain certain assumptions on which this account is based.

This study is primarily a record, not a quest for artistic excellence; and it is not a discarding of all else and a welcoming of everything that may be looked upon as new, revolutionary, or esthetically commendable. The theatre as a whole has always been a form of popular entertainment. In many respects it is a crude thing, obvious, vulgar, and preëminently of the moment. The playwright commonly creates his effects by broad strokes. The drama, when compared with lyric poetry, or prose fiction, or philosophy, is unsubtle. By the very nature of its physical form and limitations a play must present its story in summary fashion. It is great art only once in a while, and often it seems, only by accident, as though its Shakespeares and its Molières happened to seize upon a medium in which they never were intended to excel. This statement of an obvious fact is made for the purpose not only of asking the reader to guard against the too common assumption of critics that because a play wins popular success it cannot be great art, but in order that I may not fall into the same error myself. It is easy to predicate one's judgment of acted drama on the theory that a play is good to the extent to which it approaches the excellence of the art of literature; and this, it seems to me, is as fallacious as to assume that an announcement by the ringmaster at a circus, if written in the best style of Robert Browning, improves the *artistic* quality of the circus. Each play, like each sonnet or short story, achieves its highest effects by means directly related to the end aimed at. A play *may* prove ultimately to contain passages that become part of our great heritage of literary art, and certain plays live through the ages because, like those of Sophocles and Shakespeare, they belong to literature rather than to the theatre; but when this happens it is not to be assumed that the incidental literary qualities of such plays are what made them good drama. A play which creates its immediate effect on the audience for which it was written, *at the time of writing,* and creates it to the greatest extent of which the material and ideas are susceptible—that is the most that can be reasonably expected of any play.

For example, *Charley's Aunt* is not only a better play, but a finer work of art—theatre art, of course—than *The King's Henchman,* that ambitious literary drama by the distinguished poet Edna St. Vincent Millay, because the English farce written by Brandon Thomas successfully achieved what its author aimed at, however trivial his goal may have been, whereas Miss Millay, however lofty her intentions, failed to make a really effective dramatic story of the material she chose to dramatize.

Nevertheless, crude as the theatre is in its means of expression, as compared with certain other arts, it is sometimes capable of achieving subtle effects, and even to use the language of the great poets. It does not follow that a play must always employ obvious means and create obvious effects. One of the most encouraging phenomena in our recent American drama is that, though our theatre continues to furnish popular entertainment, it at the same time holds its doors open to work which is neither obvious nor trite. The dramatic products of a fairly large number of playwrights since 1900 are exceptionally varied in subject-matter and treatment: poetic drama and farce, comedy and tragedy, "subversive" thesis drama, romance, satire; the work of conservatives and radicals, poets and newspaper men—there is place for every conceivable type of play in our playhouses. The period of the past forty-five years, particularly the second half of it, has revealed a wider variety of plays than can be found in any other country in the world. It may be, of course, that to future historians the product of this time will appear to be far more uniform in subject-matter and technique than it seems to us, but I do not think so. By and large the new century has witnessed a considerable extension of the field of dramatic material, and in this respect alone the drama had already become to some extent a true reflection of the life of the nation in most of its manifestations as a consciously growing people. Our theatre has for over a generation consistently satisfied to a greater extent than ever before the tastes and aspirations of a public that has become more and more fully conscious of what is going on in the world, and less willing therefore to regard the theatre as a means of expressing only a few limited and distorted aspects of that world. In other words, our dramatists have sought, more or less consciously, to grow up with the public, to partake more fully than ever before of its ideas, its aims and ideals. To too great an extent the American writers of the eighteenth and nineteenth centuries seemed to consider the theatre as something apart from the life of its time, to provide what we now call an escape from the ugliness and problems of life, and not to seek in that life a beauty and meaning even in those aspects of it that seemed to offer little or nothing either of beauty or meaning.

The figure of William Vaughan Moody, who began work on his plays before 1900 and saw them produced during the first decade of the new century, may be allowed to symbolize the emergence of a new spirit in

American drama, not so much because of what he actually achieved as by reason of his intentions. Because he approached the theatre as an artist and a craftsman knowing both its limitations and its possibilities, and not merely because he wrote two effective plays, he proved that it was possible to be an artist, a thinker, something of a philosopher, and at the same time appeal to the average play-goer in search of entertainment.

When all the documents and letters and all the personal testimony of friends and associates are made public it will be possible to know more exactly than we can now hope to know, to what extent Moody deliberately set out to write plays for the theatre of his time that should be more sincere and lifelike and beautiful than the kind of play ordinarily accepted before his day as merely effective theatre, and quite good enough for the not too discriminating public. That he was conscious of his position as a pioneer of sorts can hardly be questioned, and that he gave some thought to the state of the drama in his time is clearly proved by a study of his published letters.

He was not a reformer like Percy MacKaye, who by precept and example pointed the way to the establishment of a theatre and a drama that should be dedicated not to the making of profits but to humanity, and who succeeded in creating a viewpoint if not a physical playhouse of, by, and for the people. Moody was not a theorist or a closet dramatist. He was a college professor and a poet, a modern American who from the start of his career as a writer had been thinking about plays. When he was at work on the piece that was ultimately called *The Great Divide,* he intended that it should be acted, and he hoped that it would make money.

I am concerned here not so much with the intrinsic qualities of Moody's two stage plays as with the fact that they were written and produced when they were. I see in *The Great Divide* and *The Faith Healer* two signs of transition, mile-posts on the road between the make-believe and largely artificial drama of the nineteenth century, and the infinitely more genuine, grown-up American drama that began to develop about 1900, and flourished between 1920 and the present day.

In considering Moody as a pioneer it is well to remember that *The Great Divide* was produced in 1906, and *The Faith Healer* published in 1909, and that both are products of the nineteenth century. The latter had been in the author's mind at least fourteen years before he finished it, and it is likely that the germinal idea of the former had occurred to him before 1900. Neither play was commissioned by manager or actor, nor was the poet attempting to write for purely material rewards. Each is the result of an impulse that came to the writer to express himself in terms of modern dramatic form that should combine elements of beauty, with only the necessary elements of practical and technical expediency as he understood them.

The first reference to any play that I can find in his published letters dates from 1895; it is evident that Moody was in no hurry to master the tricks of the trade of successful play writing. He must have regarded his plays as he did his poems, as works he would not release until they satisfied him. Yet it is significant to note in a letter written from New York in 1898 the dual attitude of the man when he says,[1]

> I have already met a number of capital chaps here ... playwrights, not very big ones, I suspect, but full of enthusiasm and practical expedient. The great thing about them is that they get their things played, and that sort of thing, begad, begins to appeal to me. Do not believe me quite recreant to ideals. But the chaps here ... are splendidly American and contemporary. ...

And again he speaks of the same men, whose "allegiance to the sisters of the sacred well is tempered by their interest in the genie of the box-office till."

Moody, then, was no starry-eyed prophet who wrote "for antiquity," nor was he a recreant poet ready to betray his ideals in order to achieve popular success. He was ready to make use of a popular medium in order to convey to theatre-goers as much of his message as could be effectively fitted into an acted play.

"All through his life," writes Daniel Gregory Mason,[2] "the contrast between the fresh vitality of the West and the mellower civilization of the East exercised his imagination," and it was this contrast that Moody ultimately dramatized in his best-known play. In its first form and under the title *A Sabine Woman*, this drama was tried out in Chicago in the spring of 1906. It was revised and some months later, under the title of *The Great Divide*, it opened in New York, with Henry Miller and Margaret Anglin playing the leading parts.

A poet—a college professor, a mere outsider—had written a great dramatic hit. Not only was it popular with the public in New York and on the road but most of the reviewers and many eminent men of letters who were not regular theatre-goers, proclaimed it a serious work of art. That Moody was hailed occasionally as the Great American Dramatist is not remarkable: in those days it was hardly necessary to do much more than to write a fairly literate play with something of an idea in it, to be called that.

In spite of the much needed money that came to him from *The Great Divide* Moody was apparently never tempted to join the ranks of the purveyors of popular entertainment, and even a long time after the opening of *The Great Divide* he continued to insist, to the manager, that the spirit and mood of the play should be faithfully preserved. A year before his death in 1910 he was writing to Mason about a play that would evidently have been far from popular with the public. He says,[3]

> The thing I have most at heart just now is a poetic—I mean a *verse*—play. ... I am torn between the ideal aspect of a theme and the stage necessities—the old,

[1] Daniel Gregory Mason, editor, *Some Letters of William Vaughan Moody* (Boston, Houghton Mifflin Co., 1913).
[2] *Ibid.*
[3] *Ibid.*

old problem. Perhaps in the end I will let the stage go to ballyhoo, and write the thing as I see it, for that justly lighted and managed stage of the mind, where there can be no bad actors and where the peanut-eating public is reduced to a discreet minimum. But this—after all—is an uncourageous compromise.

There are echoes of such impatience with crude theatrical means in the more recent statements of Eugene O'Neill, Paul Green, and Maxwell Anderson, and usually the same determination to use these means and come to terms with them.

Moody, indeed, in spite of the many changes he made or allowed to be made in *The Great Divide,* was ready to come to terms with the theatre as it existed, but at the same time he tried to bend it to his own ends. Although he may have toyed with the idea of writing effective stage pieces he was at heart an artist who insisted that his work should be consistent with itself and with his knowledge of its requirements, and not with the captious demands of the public.

The Great Divide and *The Faith Healer,* read in the cold light of today, are of course exceptional plays, but both suffer from serious defects. Neither is free from a certain affectation in the writing, though in this respect *The Faith Healer* is better than the earlier work. Both plays likewise express a relatively superficial sort of optimism that seems peculiarly typical of the time, a philosophical aftermath of the nineteenth-century puritanical salvation-through-suffering dogma which was based on the comforting notion that because a "good" man has suffered therefore he shall be forgiven and all will be well.

I do not believe that Moody deliberately turned his potential tragedies into happy-ending plays because he thought that would make them successful with the public: he really thought that the human problems he treated could be solved in life the way he solved them in *The Great Divide* and *The Faith Healer.*

But what gives the Moody plays a meaning and importance beyond their intrinsic merits as stage pieces is the aim of the writer, the things he originally conceived as fitting material for presentation in the commercial theatre. Even if the finished products had been far more faulty than they are, they would still have made their effect on our later playwrights. When Moody began thinking of plays Percy MacKaye was a very young man; and except for James A. Herne and Bronson Howard, Edward Harrigan and Charles Hoyt (and then only to a limited extent) there was no one writing for the American stage—at any rate no native—who was giving the public anything more original and exciting than what it had long been used to. When Moody appeared on the scene with *A Sabine Woman* in 1906 the most important native playwrights were Clyde Fitch, Charles Klein, and Augustus Thomas.

The Faith Healer was first produced in 1909, revised and again produced in 1910. It was not a popular success. Moody's death the same year closed the career of a relatively young man who might have been able to find in the theatre of the next two decades a place where he would have had complete liberty to develop the powers that up to the time of his death had only begun to show themselves.

There can be small doubt that the phenomenon of Moody's appearance during the first decade of the new century and his concern over the expression of fresh ideas in dramatic form made it easier for his younger contemporaries to choose themes and adopt technical methods a little more original and "daring" than they would otherwise have been able to do. The young Eugene Walter and the younger Edward Sheldon could hardly have failed to see *The Great Divide* and to have been in some way affected by it.

The period 1900 to 1920, as we look back to it, marks a transition between two eras of which the first, with the few exceptions noted, is almost wholly devoid of anything approximating what I have called the modern spirit, and the second includes nearly all the writers who have made our modern drama a more or less complete and satisfactory reflection of the land and people which produced it.

Once more I point out that the dates marking the beginning and end of the period are somewhat arbitrarily chosen. A playwright may offer a striking instance of progress toward great freedom of expression one season and the next revert to an earlier style which, if we judged his work piecemeal, would place him among the dramatists of half a century before. The twenty-year period between 1900 and 1920, looked at as a whole, presents a picture of great variety, bewildering and abundant, but it is not a period in which it is easy to discover a single clearly distinguishable line of progress. Progress can indeed be noted, but evidence of it seems in most cases somewhat accidental. So again it is necessary to select more or less at random examples of work among many dramatic products that indicate an increasing skill in construction and writing, and a growing determination to treat a wider variety of subjects than had been treated in the past.

The dramatic career of Augustus Thomas (1859-1934) began in the middle seventies, and continued without interruption for half a century. As early as 1891, in *Alabama,* this prolific writer was interested in the externals of the American scene, and the titles of several of his later plays show a desire to exploit at least the "local color" backgrounds that had well before the turn of the century been skilfully used by novelists and short-story writers. *In Mizzoura, The Hoosier Doctor, Arizona, Colorado, The Member from Ozark,* and *Rio Grande* are in themselves titles that show Thomas' concern with background, but these are not, with one exception, his best or most characteristic plays. His most popular work was *Arizona* (1900), a skilful melodrama set against a southwestern backdrop, sufficiently well characterized for an adventure story. If Thomas had stopped writing after the production of this play he would have belonged wholly to the nineteenth-century tradition. But during the next quarter century he twice, in 1907 and 1911, proved that he understood how the theatre could be effectively used to dramatize ideas as well as physical clash—or rather that plays could be made to provoke thought without losing anything that made them popular as mere entertainment.

It is true that *The Witching Hour,* which was concerned with telepathy, sets forth no very profound idea, and that the validity of the thesis is more than questionable; but the fact that a popular playwright took it upon himself to add to his formula a relatively new element is not without meaning, and his doing it successfully, I believe, enabled later writers to enrich their work by doing the same thing, and occasionally doing it better. In the second of the two plays mentioned, *As a Man Thinks* (1911), Thomas made a more determined effort to dramatize ideas. It was not very satisfactory as a dramatic piece, but it showed courage for a popular playwright to risk possible failure in order to preach a sermon on what was then known as the double standard of sex morality and against the undemocratic attitude known as anti-Semitism. In stating that Thomas, even to a slight extent, helped blaze a trail by writing the two plays in question, I do not claim that thesis plays are necessarily signs of artistic or intellectual progress. The point is that this popular and successful writer did his small part by showing that a play may be made to do and say something in addition to telling a story in terms of physical action. Thomas' own statement, made after he had attempted to broaden the scope of his subject-matter, is worth quoting: "The theatre is a place for the visualizing of ideas."

The career of Clyde Fitch (1865-1909) offers at least a few parallels to that of Augustus Thomas, though his plays are in nearly all respects far different in mood, execution, and purpose.

Like Thomas, he was primarily a skilled craftsman, eager to write plays that would please the public; ready at all times to furnish a popular actor or actress with an effective "vehicle"; in no sense a philosopher, reformer, or revolutionary, but like his older contemporary, a man who occasionally wanted to express ideas or convey impressions about the world to his fellowmen, provided of course that in so doing he might remain popular and successful.

Fitch's writing career began in 1890, with the made-to-order character comedy *Beau Brummel,* and ended with the relatively "realistic" drama *The City,* in 1910. Fitch's most characteristic work, aside from his occasional ventures into pseudo-history, were social comedies and dramas, *The Climbers* (1901), *The Stubbornness of Geraldine* (1902), *The Girl With the Green Eyes* (1902), *Her Own Way* (1903), and *The Truth* (1906).

By the time Fitch began writing, it was possible for him to summarize to some extent the spirit of metropolitan society, and offer a more or less accurate if very limited picture of its people. Fitch was near enough to that society to know and understand it, and intelligent enough to realize something of what was wrong with it. But he obviously was not a dour critic of what he saw about him; he preferred to reflect the spirit of his day in terms of a not too bitter satire.

Like Thomas he too expressed his ideas on the function of the playwright, and again like Thomas his theory rarely squared with his practice. Yet the fact that he did occasionally think of such matters is in itself notable. He wrote,

I feel ... very strongly the particular value ... in a modern play, of reflecting absolutely and truthfully the life and environment about us; every class, every emotion, every motive, every occupation, every business, every idleness! Life was never so varied, so complex.... If you inculcate an idea into your play, so much the better for your play and for you and for your audience.... One should write what one sees, but observe under the surface.

Today even the best of the Fitch plays, like *The Climbers* and *The Truth,* seem conventional, overdrawn, superficial, but in attempting to reflect and in a way criticize the small world he chose to treat, and to do so with a critical eye, he made it clear to later playwrights of social satire that that was one of the directions they might follow.

Fitch's last play, produced shortly after his death in 1909, was *The City*. It is usually claimed, and I think justly, that in it Fitch attempted to adopt a new and forthright manner of treating a phenomenon of modern city life which in his day was coming to light, possibly through the reports of the muckrakers. *The City* is something more than a melodrama, it is a commentary on what a large city can do to corrupt a man, and it is possible to describe it as a dramatization of a social phenomenon rather than of an individual. In this respect alone the play has its historical importance.

It is impossible to write of the American drama of the past half century without taking into account the work of the poet-reformer-idealist-playwright Percy MacKaye, son of the actor-playwright-reformer H. Steele MacKaye.

It would be difficult in this place to trace the long and varied campaign waged by Percy MacKaye to arouse his fellow-men to a sense of their destiny as a modern nation, capable of using their history and folklore and the very processes of their democratic activities in dramatic form, to achieve what he has called Community Drama. Born in 1875, brought up in the finest traditions of literature and art, and from the first deeply influenced by the New England countryside in which he has spent the greater part of his life, he began writing in his early youth, his first finished play dating from 1901. From that year onward, for over thirty years, he wrote plays— full-length poetic dramas, comedies of modern life, fantasies, folk plays, short imaginative pieces, and community festival spectacles and masques. His earlier plays, several of them written in blank verse and in the tradition of literary drama, were based mostly on foreign material. Among these the most successful was *Jeanne D'Arc* (1906). But in 1908 he offered, in *Mater,* a modern prose play of American life. This was followed by what is still remembered and usually considered his best work, *The Scarecrow* (1908).

Anti-Matrimony (1909) was a rather mild but somewhat amusing comedy with a certain amount of social criticism, which had something to do with its (relatively) popular success. *Tomorrow* (1913), an idealistic and more didactic piece, failed to appeal to play-goers. *A Thousand Years Ago,* based on the old tale of Turandot, combined literary grace with theatric skill. In 1919 came the folk-historical ballad play *Washington, the Man Who Made Us,* a pageant-like chronicle history that seemed to prove once again that there was not sufficient material in the life of Washington to enable a writer to turn it into a successful stage piece. The last of the "regular" MacKaye plays to be produced was the Kentucky folk comedy, *This Fine-Pretty World* (1924).

The pageants and chronicles began in 1912 with *A Masque of Labor,* continued with the bird masque *Sanctuary* (1913) and *St. Louis* (1914), and reached their most ambitious height in 1916, with *Caliban.*

This bare catalogue of some of the products of the MacKaye pen can mean little until it is put into proper perspective: masque-making was only one of the many activities which, taken together, mean Percy MacKaye. For years the poet carried his gospel about the country, lecturing to poetry societies, college and school students, civic and drama clubs; and to this day in what must mathematically be his old age he seems not to have lost his youthful idealism, his belief in the high function of American drama to interpret and intensify the spirit of his native land to the American people. As early as 1909 he announced in the eloquent language of the poet-citizen an ambitious program in his book *The Playhouse and the Play,* and for the next eight years he elaborated and varied his theme in *The Civic Theater, A Substitute for War,* and *Community Drama.*

Any attempt to determine the extent of MacKaye's influence on the public, the playwright, the manager, or the actor of the past forty years must fail unless it is constantly borne in mind that the poet-playwright spread his gospel from a thousand pulpits, that the sum total of the influence exerted by him is important not because he wrote a few more or less "successful" plays for the professional stage, or brought together hundreds of thousands of people as participants in his masques, or wrote idealistic treatises which were read by small groups of persons, like himself, or that he was to some extent responsible for the teaching of modern drama in our colleges and universities. The simple fact of his presence among us during what I call the formative period of our national dramatic development; the fact that he was not ashamed to compete on Broadway with the despised "commercial managers" without trying to achieve popular success, and at the same time to cry aloud for beauty and inspiration; that on the contrary he followed a consistent policy of following his star in a day when to do so in the theatre marked him as a despised highbrow—this, I claim, is MacKaye's most valuable contribution. It is true that he often appeared to his generation as an impractical dreamer, but he who dared call the author of *Jeanne D'Arc* and *A Thousand Years Ago* a mere highbrow asking impossibilities, risked being called impractical himself, for there can be no doubt that MacKaye usually knew what he was about when he wrote for the professional stage.

It is common enough to see a closet-dramatist refuse to compromise with "public taste," and no credit is due the writer who sets forth an impossible ideal of perfection without the talent to achieve even some small part of it. MacKaye, like Eugene O'Neill and Maxwell Anderson in later years, was practical enough to achieve popular success in the theatre, and idealistic enough not to debase his ideals in order to succeed there. When in the early 1920's O'Neill said that he would "never be influenced by any consideration but one: 'Is it the truth as I know it—or better still, feel it?' " he was echoing that earlier call to arms of Percy MacKaye, and the fact that MacKaye uttered it enabled the younger man to say what he had to say more clearly and readily than if the older man had never existed. For it was MacKaye who proclaimed the dignity of the theatre and its function as a source of beauty and inspiration.

Yet it must be remembered, for this is a record of the drama as it was and is, that any history of the theatre must take into account the conventional plays as well as the unconventional, the plays that reflect the ideas and tastes of a season as well as those that attempt to create beauty and deal with permanently interesting themes. In spite of the Moodys and the MacKayes and the other exceptional writers to be considered in this section—or, rather existing in the same world of the theatre—were hundreds of playwrights who provided the public with the entertainment it wanted, who (in the words of an English critic) should be given their due simply because they kept the theatres open. There is no point in listing all their names, for in the aggregate they did little but reflect the current average taste in dramatic fare.

During the first few years of the century George Ade managed to carry over into the theatre a part of his talent as a writer of American slang, in a few musical comedies and three or four "straight" plays. *The County Chairman* (1903) and *The College Widow* (1904) won great success in their day, but they seem in the rereading conventional and superficial. The case of the actor-playwright William Gillette is different. For one thing, his writing career extended over a period of more than forty years, which in itself exemplifies one of the difficulties of attempting to record any chronological history of the "modern" American drama; and for another, no one who ever saw Gillette act in one of his better plays could quite separate in his mind the writer from the actor. It may be that Gillette as actor deserves particular credit for popularizing that peculiarly unemphatic playing he had made his own, but his plays, even the latest, which were seen in New

York in the 1920's, are scarcely more credible or less mechanical than the first. *Secret Service* and *Held by the Enemy,* entertaining and effective as they are, were no more than ingenious melodramas self-consciously put together, piece by piece, for the purpose of giving the actor a chance to show what he could do. The world might have suffered a dozen revolutions, the United States have become an imperial or communist state, yet the plays of Gillette would, we feel, have been written precisely as they were written. That most of these plays gave pleasure to more than one generation of theatre-goers is only another way of saying that Gillette was a playwright and actor who knew his business, even though he did nothing to change the form or content of the drama.

Virtually the same thing may be said of most playwrights who manage to serve the public. Yet, so far as the period 1900-1920 in our own theatre is concerned, it must be noted that occasionally a writer otherwise without distinction attempted to present an idea or utilized a technical device somewhat different from what the public expected. It was as though some leavening agency had been at work. We have many instances of playwrights brought up in the nineteenth-century tradition in one or more of whose plays we can detect some indication of what later writers would use and develop as a matter of course. The case of Owen Davis is significant. He began work in the nineties as a hack writer, turning popular sensational novels into popular and equally sensational melodramas. The titles of some of these are still famous, and Mr. Davis has done his best to forget them— hack work of the most obvious sort. He soon graduated into the more or less respectable profession of writing comedies and the less obvious type of mystery and melodrama during the first twenty years of the century, and then in 1921 and 1923 he gave us two plays, *The Detour* and *Icebound,* which if his name had not been signed to them might have been attributed to the pen of the then new and unquestionably dignified and highbrow O'Neill. There followed during the next decade a number of plays not characterized by anything but professional competence, but in 1932 he dramatized, in collaboration with his son Donald, *The Good Earth,* and four years later *Ethan Frome.* The man who signed the title-pages of *Nellie the Beautiful Cloak Model, Sinners, Icebound, The Good Earth,* and *Ethan Frome* is not one playwright but several playwrights. He belongs to the old Bowery days, to the current commercial theatre, and to the modern drama of the 1920-1945 period. He is, indeed, a symptom and a symbol. His work as a whole, including more than two hundred plays, reflects several of the varying currents in theatrical history of the past half century. That the author of *Beyond the Breakers* and *Tony the Bootblack* should be capable in later life of writing *The Detour* is of course to his credit as an adaptable writer: but it is also striking testimony to the fact that the American theatre had reached a point in its development where it could offer a man like Davis a chance to create something more genuine and beautiful than he could have created if he had been limited by the conventions that hemmed in the dramatic writer of the eighties and early nineties.

The case of Charles Klein is also worth considering. His first play dates from 1892, and his greatest success, *The Music Master,* from 1904. But the two plays of greatest interest to us are *The Lion and the Mouse* and *Maggie Pepper.* The first of these (1905) is obviously an attempt on the part of an able writer with a journalistic turn of mind to utilize the sensational findings of the muckrakers. The Klein play was in its time an exciting melodrama about a plucky young woman who beards the lion in his den—a wealthy malefactor who has unscrupulously used his power to oppress his fellowmen. For the first time, I believe, we saw on the stage this particular sort of social criticism. Klein's villain was not the old-time suave stage villain, but a more or less respected rich man, the kind who until the days of Lincoln Steffens and Ida M. Tarbell was pointed to as an ideal of successful American manhood.

Charles Klein was certainly no self-conscious trail-blazer, and his indictment was colored by no very deep-seated indignation. His was not the burning zeal that twenty-five years later actuated our John Howard Lawsons and Albert Maltzes, but the fact that there was a public for the sort of revelation he dramatized, and that he thought it worth while to treat such a subject at all in the theatre, and further that his play was popular and successful—these are matters of some historical importance.

Maggie Pepper (1911) was perhaps even more widely successful than *The Lion and the Mouse.* Here again the playwright took full advantage of a current trend in taste. It was O. Henry who was largely responsible for using the sympathetic figure of the working girl and bringing it before the public. The old-time working girl before his day was usually portrayed as the unsuspecting victim of some ruthless male, and her saga ended either in the gutter or in the arms of a handsome millionaire. Klein's Maggie is no routine figure of popular drama: she is drawn by a man who is not content simply to sketch the outlines and let the audience fill in the blank spaces. The play itself is a commonplace bit of carpentering, but the figure of its chief—practically its only—character is as clear to me today as when I first saw Rose Stahl interpret it. When only a couple of years later Bayard Veiller was ready to write his *Within the Law* he had in Maggie a prototype for his heroine, and from that day to this we have learned to expect and demand in the delineation of such characters far greater verisimilitude than any dramatist before Klein's day could apparently imagine or achieve.

Other examples of the playwright's dawning sense of mastery of characterization can be found in the period now under discussion, in the work of such men as George Broadhurst, Bayard Veiller, George M. Cohan, Charles Kenyon, Eugene Walter, and Edward Sheldon. It is probable that the "moderns" in fiction, many of them influenced by European novelists, showed how far it was possible to give the impression of reality by observing life much more carefully than earlier writers had done, and that the theatre need not necessarily hold itself aloof from the currents of modern life or art. As I have already said, it strikes us as anomalous that American plays written in the same land and produced at the same time when Whitman, James, and Melville were doing their best work should be so uniformly devoid of any of the truth or power or vision that informed the writings of such men.

But by the turn of the century it had become evident to more than one playwright that what Stephen Crane, for example, had done in the short story, might conceivably be done in the theatre. Theodore Dreiser, too, began writing more than forty years ago, and among the other "new generation" rebels were such men as Ambrose Bierce and David Graham Phillips. Some of our playwrights must have read the "revolutionary" works of the younger fiction writers. Frankness, brutality, and strong language were a long time coming to the theatre, and there was public prejudice and censorship in one form or other to prevent the playwright from saying what he wanted to say, on those rare occasions when he may have wanted to say it; but the tendency was there, and when a playwright appeared on the scene ready to adopt brutal means if need be, and with sufficient talent to make good use of his materials, he usually had his way without too much interference from the police or the public.

And so it came about that gradually between 1900 and 1920 a large number of playwrights, nearly all of them unconsciously and certainly without considering themselves reformers or martyrs but simply as craftsmen, sought occasionally to broaden the relatively rigid conventions of the theatre, daring to approach more closely than their predecessors what seemed the exciting realities of modern life. That Fitch should permit a character in his last play to utter the words "God damn" was a sign of revolution. It had begun to dawn upon some writers of the time that the public was no longer ready to accept the too-proper conventional moralities of the Victorian theatre, that the gap between life as revealed in fiction, in the newspapers and magazines as well as in the findings of science and psychology, was too apparent, and that if the plays they were writing were to appeal to the paying public they must present life more directly than it had been presented in the past. It must be emphasized that the urge to do this was as a rule not consciously felt, that few writers deliberately tried to exemplify this or that theory of life, or even to tell the truth as they saw it; it was a matter of gradual development, an increasing awareness that the theatre had not kept pace with most other means of interpreting the activities of the world of men.

What the German critics would call tendency plays are found sometimes among the works of popular and successful playwrights, and sometimes as the principal or only work of the occasional or as it were accidental playwright. Such works as *Rebellion* (1911) by Joseph Medill Patterson, a thesis play based on the problem of divorce, have meaning for us chiefly because they indicate a growing concern on the part of writers, and interest on the part of the public, in dramatic material that had hitherto been largely forbidden by custom or law, or had not been considered quite "proper" for exposition on the stage. True, a discussion of the problem of divorce was not, before 1911, precisely taboo, but Patterson's play *was* frankly based upon the difference in attitude toward the subject as held by Catholics and Protestants, and *that* was not usual. *Polygamy* (1914), by Harriet Ford and Harvey O'Higgins, for all its sensationalism, was another dramatization of a religious problem, the most extreme example of the problem play which its authors, who wrote a number of other plays in collaboration, ever attempted.

The work of Charles Rann Kennedy, a native of England but later an American citizen, does not perhaps belong exclusively to a record of the American drama, yet Kennedy's plays were almost without exception written and produced in the United States. Except for his first and most successful play, *The Servant in the House,* which opened in London in 1907, his eloquent pleas for the brotherhood of man hardly belong to the theatre at all, since their author has apparently been content to have most of them produced either by nonprofessional groups or publicly recited by himself and his wife Edith Wynne Matheson. Yet the effect produced on his contemporaries, not only by the phenomenally popular *Servant in the House* but by the less popular *Terrible Meek* and the *Army with Banners,* was not negligible, for Kennedy, like his contemporary Percy MacKaye, symbolized the militant idealism of a small number of men who were determined to make the theatre, so far as they could, a forum in which man should be able to proclaim that life is worth living. There was in Kennedy's work, as in the work of others of his kind, a good deal of naïve reasoning, and an evangelistic fervor that seems a little odd to us who think we have grown up; and too often his ambitious dramas fall short of theatric effectiveness by reason of an excess of argument and rhetoric. Yet the pioneering efforts of Kennedy made it just so much easier for later writers when they were ready to use the theatre for the exploitation of themes many of which had been made acceptable to the public by him. It cannot be proved, of course, but I am convinced that if Charles Rann Kennedy had not written *The Servant in the House* and *The Terrible Meek* and *The Idol Breaker,* we might not have had Philip Barry's *John* or Robert E. Sherwood's *There Shall Be No Night* or Maxwell Anderson's *Winterset;* at least that these last-named plays would have had to be offered as relatively experimental works rather than finished products.

What Kennedy accomplished without belonging in the ranks of the popular writers was to some extent carried on by Channing Pollock. For many years Pollock turned out routine dramas and comedies and librettos for musical shows, all of which were produced in the period of ferment before 1920. And then, in 1922, he became an evangelist. In every respect—except that his best and most popular successes were written from two to twelve years after the beginning of the period I have yet to discuss—he is a transition writer; which is further proof of my statement that historical facts are very hard to fit into a neat pattern. Yet the later work of Pollock had its effect on the theatre of its day, perhaps rather more on the audience than on other writers, for two out of his five latest plays were much more popular outside New York than on Broadway. *The Fool* (1923) carried to millions an obvious message of Christian faith, and *The Enemy* (1925) was hardly less popular, with a somewhat similar message. The first was simply a dramatic story of the birth of man's spiritual relationship with God, and the second man's no less necessary relationship with man. These two plays, together with *Mr. Moneypenny* (1928) and *The House Beautiful* (1931), were in effect dramatized sermons. But they differed from most of the Kennedy sermons because Pollock was primarily a showman, and rarely permitted his evangelistic enthusiasm to degenerate into mere arguments. Yet these plays were too naïve for Broadway. This gave Pollock a chance to carry his work to the country at large, to theatre-goers not alone in the recognized theatre centers, but into the churches (where his plays were often read by the clergy), to the women's clubs, and to the thousands of communities where schools, colleges, and civic groups were beginning to make their own theatre because the stock company and the road show were becoming rare phenomena. To this day there are schools and other local dramatic groups that still find excitement and spiritual satisfaction in *The Fool* and *The Enemy*. So Pollock, the evangelist-playwright who could not make a go of it on Broadway, built better than he knew, and for twenty years after our *most* modern American drama began its career, is still something of a force.

The case of George Middleton offers a parallel and a contrast. Like Pollock he began working in the early years of the century, but unlike him his most successful plays were his conventional comedies that had scarcely a spark of the reforming spirit which made his early dramas interesting. The most original contribution of this immensely enthusiastic writer was three volumes of one-act plays, *Embers, Tradition,* and *Possession* (1911, 1913, and 1915), and the full-length play *Nowadays* (1914). Very few of these were professionally produced, though several were among the standard so-called Little Theatre classics of the pre- and post-war era. They were rather widely read and discussed. Earnest, didactic, and controversial, they were especially popular with drama-study clubs. Practically all dramatized some more or less burning social or ethical question of the day—the Negro problem, the marriage problem, the economic problem. Some among them were particularly effective, but many were no more than sermons within a more or less sketchy dramatic framework.

Possibly for reasons of economic necessity, or perhaps because he wanted to prove to his fellow writers that he could turn out popular and paying plays if he set his mind to it, he wrote several successful shows (always in collaboration) which showed no trace of the reformer's concern with problems or ideas. Among the best of these were *Polly with a Past* (1917), written with Guy Bolton, *Adam and Eva* (1919), also written with Bolton, and *The Big Pond* (1928) written with A. E. Thomas. A late play is *Hiss! Boom!! Blah!!!* (1933) which, except that it shows that Middleton had benefitted by certain new technical methods popularized during the twenties, belongs in spirit to his pioneering days. Unfortunately this lively social and political satire has never been professionally produced.

It is natural that the newspaper man should have taken an important part in this reawakening, particularly the reporter who shortly after 1900 had been instrumental in investigating and publicizing the exciting news about the growing power of Big Business. Heretofore revelations of political and financial villainy had been used largely either in fiction or in the newspaper, and when on occasion they found their way into the theatre the social implications were either wholly by-passed or so attenuated as to make it seem that the playwright missed them entirely or chose to personalize them to such an extent that they were made to appear simply as moral mistakes of small moment; or else, as in the case of the plays of Hoyt, they were treated as political jokes. The plays of the 1900-1920 period, however, often show considerable understanding of the forces that were operating in our civic life. To put the matter another way, it may be said that the nineteenth-century playwright usually assumed that a robber baron would be "forgiven" for his malefactions if he repented or contributed generously to charity, whereas the twentieth-century playwright, when he thought of the matter at all, did not bother to turn his malefactor into a villain, but tried to show that the "system" and not the man was at fault.

The early plays of the newspaper man Eugene Walter, who began writing in 1901, showed few signs of any deep understanding of the underlying causes of political or economic problems, but the best of them showed a determination to deal frankly with certain economic and sexual problems which had not until his day been treated in the theatre. The two plays for which he is remembered are *Paid in Full* (1908) and *The Easiest Way* (1909).

Melodramatic and mechanical as the first of these plays is, it looked to the play-goers of thirty odd years ago like "strong meat." A courageous woman is ready to give herself to a hard man in order to save her weak husband from jail, but the hard man, recognizing in the woman the sort of power and courage he admires, refuses to accept her offer. *The Easiest Way* (1908) is a far better work. Here again we have melodrama, obviously written for stage effect, but under all its staginess is an honest attempt to show what happens when a woman has to choose between a life of expected poverty with the man she hopes to marry, and a life of luxury and sin when she has given up hope of marrying that man. In the end, and in spite of a gesture toward attempted suicide, Walter shows us his heroine cynically and without too much remorse making her choice by taking the "easiest way."

One more play of Walter's should be mentioned, the less successful but relatively important *Fine Feathers,* first produced in 1913. After that, though he wrote for the theatre more or less irregularly for another twenty years, he failed to live up to his earlier promise; other playwrights carried on what he had begun, and soon overshadowed him. *Fine Feathers,* like most of Walter's other work, is concerned with the struggle of average Americans to adapt their lives to the economic demands of their social position. The plot reminds us of Ibsen's *An Enemy of the People,* and the use to which the American has put the bursting of the dam, dishonestly constructed through the fault of a man who has become involved in a crooked deal, is similar. Here Walter has managed to use pure melodrama in order to drive home a problem in ethics.

A few years after Eugene Walter began writing for the theatre a younger man appeared on the scene, a boy wonder who was highly publicized and for a short time hailed as a White Hope. From his day onward critics have periodically proclaimed this writer or that as the Great American Playwright. In the early years of the century Walter and Edward Sheldon were for a season or two the twin messiahs, just as a generation later Odets and Saroyan were praised to the skies for their actual and imagined achievements. Now, what this meant was that in our eagerness to detect freshness and originality in the American theatre we were naturally ready to welcome any play at all that excited us or gave us hope that some new playwright might develop into an original genius. And it often happens that the messiah of the moment does in some way make a useful contribution, for American play writing is still relatively new, and we have not, as the English, the French, and the Germans have, a long and varied dramatic history.

Edward Sheldon had his first play produced when he was twenty-two, and it was a great success. *Salvation Nell* (1908) had, of course, the advantage of Minnie Maddern Fiske as leading actress, and Harrison Gray Fiske as director. In the light of our stage history since 1908 this play is not a striking achievement, but in its day it was properly recognized as a step forward in the presentation of a detailed, colorful, and decidedly "realistic" background. There is no particular virtue in creating on the stage a photographic picture of a saloon in the slums, especially if that background is not used to set forth a story of outstanding freshness; but I cannot help thinking that the young Sheldon was feeling his way in the direction of something that might later on provide him with material for a play that would show more of life than *Salvation Nell* had shown. At all events, the background of this play shows a writer intent on dramatic contrasts and local color.

His next play, *The Nigger* (1909), remains to this day one of his best works. It is characteristic of the man that he should dare to walk, as it were, straight into the heart of the Negro problem. Of course, the situation he contrived was pure theatre, but Sheldon faced it with courage and developed it with some skill. The mere fact of his dramatizing the tragedy of a prominent southerner who discovers he has Negro blood, puts Sheldon into the ranks of the men who contributed their part to the broadening of the scope of our contemporary drama.

The Sheldon plays of the next few years were to show that while the playwright rapidly acquired skill in the handling of his plots, and while *Romance* (1913) marked the high point in his career as a popular and successful writer, he was not again to take his place as a forerunner or contributor of anything very new or original. Sheldon's personal fortunes are of course no part of theatrical history, but we must bear in mind that for over twenty years he has suffered from a disease which would for almost any one else have ended every activity except breathing, but he has as collaborator and adviser managed through all that period to exercise a marked influence upon our theatre. The mere fact of his having written at least three plays (*Bewitched, Lulu Belle* and *Dishonored Lady*) with two of our younger writers is evidence of his importance in the 1920-1930 period.

Edward Sheldon was the first of the members of George Pierce Baker's play-writing class to call national attention to what was soon to be the famous English 47 group. During the early years of the century Professor Baker offered an informal course in practical play writing, which by the time of the First World War had attracted at least a dozen men and women who were later to make their mark in the American theatre. A partial list of these would show that what the Professor had to offer was not advice of any one brand, and that, as we know to have been the case, he was concerned first and last with helping and encouraging the beginner to learn the business of making the best use of his individual talents to express what he had to say in play form. Aside from Sheldon the following were students of Baker's either at Harvard or Radcliffe (up to 1924 when he left Harvard), or since that time at Yale:

Eugene O'Neill, S. N. Behrman, Sidney Howard, Edward Knoblock, George Abbott, Lewis Beach, Fred Ballard, Philip Barry, Maurine Watkins, Paul Osborn, Hubert Osborne, E. P. Conkle, Talbot Jennings, George Sklar, Albert Maltz, and George Haight.

One of the best short statements of the value of the Baker course is O'Neill's comment made in 1935: [1]

It is difficult in these days, when the native playwright can function in comparative freedom, to realize that in that benighted period a play of any imagination, originality or integrity by an American was almost automatically barred from a hearing in our theatre.... In the face of this blank wall, the bitterest need of the young playwright was for intelligent encouragement...of the rare few

---

[1] From *George Pierce Baker, A Memorial* (New York, Dramatists Play Service, 1939).

who had the unselfish faith and vision and love of the theatre to devote their life to this encouragement, Professor Baker's work stands preëminent.... He helped us to hope—and for that we owe him all the finest we have in memory of gratitude and friendship.

The precise effect of Baker's courses on the men and women who studied under him cannot be accurately measured, but there seems no doubt that the plain fact that he offered sane practical advice to student-playwrights, and a chance to see their apprentice work on a stage, was one of the many evidences that a new spirit of inquiry was in the air, a new determination on the part of certain persons that the theatre should be studied as a living means of expression and a medium for the interpretation of modern life. That Baker, a scholar and an instructor at Harvard, and later at Yale, should look upon the theatre as a contemporary phenomenon deserving of academic consideration, was likewise a kind of proclamation that the American theatre was beginning to grow up.

At this point it is necessary to remind ourselves once more that we are dealing with an infinite number of scattered phenomena—experimental theatres, literary and artistic "movements," with hundreds of playwrights, with lecturers, critics, laymen, to whom, in varying ways, there seemed to exist a definite if ill-defined urge to set forth the ideas and ideals of our country in ways hitherto hardly dreamed of. A mere enumeration of a few characteristic experiments that were more or less successful during the fifteen years before 1920 will indicate some of the multifarious ideas that were beginning to circulate here and there throughout the country. The Robertson Players in Chicago, the Little Theatre of the same city somewhat later, the Drama League of America, the New Theatre of New York, the Toy Theatre of Boston; the growth of interest among students in the more or less recent dramatic works of Europe, both on the stage and in book form; the popularity of drama-study clubs; the production by professional companies of the plays of Ibsen and Shaw; the visits paid to our larger cities by the Russian Players, the Irish Players, the Manchester Players; the establishment of courses in the colleges and universities for the study of dramatic technique—these activities were in the aggregate a sort of fumbling and self-conscious prelude to the era when, shortly after 1920, an unusually large number of playwrights began to write the kind of play that made the 1920-1930 period the most brilliant, fruitful, and interesting in our theatre history.

In the years between 1905 or 1906 and the beginning of the First World War great emphasis was laid on the dramatic products of Europe, first because there were few American plays of sufficient substance to warrant the sort of study and discussion that even the most superficial study groups, as they were called, were ready to devote to them, and second, because the drama of Europe was stimulating and so far as the ideas were concerned, aroused discussion of human problems in terms of personal ethics and society at large. True, the extent to which the "problem plays" of Europe were studied, discussed, lectured upon and written about in books and articles and produced both by professionals and amateurs, caused in later years a reaction among the more sophisticated critics: to this day there exists a patronizing attitude on the part of many of them toward the over-earnest Drama League ladies who thirty-five years ago raised the torch of Culture and carried the message of Ibsen and the rest to the country at large. The same people who read and studied Ibsen and Björnson, Brieux and Hauptmann, who attended the lectures of Dr. W. N. Guthrie, Richard Burton, Louis K. Anspocher, George P. Baker and so many others who were preaching the gospel of the New Order, flocked to the cities where on occasion they could see competent professionals act these same plays. Mme Nazimova in the Ibsen plays, Mrs. Patrick Campbell in Sudermann and Pinero, Arnold Daly in Shaw—it was such productions that added stimulus to the study of social problems in every state of the Union, in small sewing circles and in large universities. And gradually, because the mere study of printed play texts was not always exciting enough, small groups here and there would establish their theatres and drama workshops, and take a hand in making their own productions. Inept as many of these productions were bound to be, and hazy and ineffective as many of the plays were, there is little doubt that the torch bearers who brought Maeterlinck to the provinces and read strange meanings into the verse fantasies of Yeats, were doing their important part in preparing the way for an American theatre *and* an American drama.

Long before 1920 a number of writers had already attempted to record and sum up the enthusiastic activities of the first few years of the present century, and some of these saw, or hoped they saw, emerge from the various "movements" of the time the promise of a native American drama. Such pioneer works as Richard Burton's *New American Drama* (1913), Montrose J. Moses' *The American Dramatist* (1910), Thomas H. Dickinson's *The Case of American Drama* (1915) and *The Insurgent Theatre* (1917), Constance D'Arcy Mackay's *Little Theatre in the United States* (1917), and the collected periodical reviews of Clayton Hamilton and Walter Prichard Eaton did a good deal to spread the gospel of the New Drama and the New Stagecraft, and stimulated the determination of local organizers to establish their own producing groups.

Until a few years after 1914 the plays studied by the women's clubs and college groups and the plays produced by the professional and nonprofessional local theatres were mainly foreign. Ibsen and Maeterlinck, Sudermann, Hauptmann, Echegaray, and Björnson, were among the most popular playwrights, though on occasion a choice was made from the classic repertory, Euripides, Goldoni, Molière. As a high-school youngster in Chicago between 1906 and 1908 I attended productions of the Donald Robertson Players of the works of Ibsen, Björnson, Echegaray, Voltaire, Goldoni,

Milton (John Milton!), Pailleron, Giacosa, Gogol, Hauptmann, and Goethe.

Yet even in the days before 1914 an effort had been made to use plays of American authorship, not only in connection with study courses but for production. It is significant that in the matter of production the native plays were not those of the current theatre, but tentative and usually feeble attempts to imitate the Europeans—symbolic poetic dramas (usually in the one-act form) or crude problem plays on sex, drink, or politics. A welter of one-act plays, some of which were to become minor classics in the Little Theatre repertory of post-war days, came a few years later.

It is not without meaning that the *Drama Quarterly,* the official organ of the Drama League of America, while publishing translations of a number of foreign plays, was consistently on the lookout for new plays of American authorship. It is also to the credit of the editors of the Drama League series of plays [1] that out of twenty-five titles issued between 1914 and 1918, ten were by American writers.

The record I have just sketched is no more than a short summary of a period of wide and varied activity; it leaves out of account a great deal of material which would serve further to prove how deep was the desire on the part of the more or less educated and economically well-off "cultured masses" of this country to learn as much as they could about the theatre of Europe, and to bring examples of that drama to America, and at the same time to stimulate young authors to write seriously and freshly about the American scene. It was becoming evident here and there that the commercial theatre, centered large in New York City, could not or would not furnish the rest of the country with what it wanted, and that with the decline of the road and the resident stock company almost the entire country would shortly be deprived of a considerable part of its "legitimate" dramatic fare. The spread of the motion picture was at one time thought to be a threat to the legitimate theatre, and it was feared that the public would have to accept film drama as a substitute for the other. It has, however, become clear that the celluloid theatre will not displace the flesh-and-blood theatre, and today we see that although every town has its well-patronized picture house, it has also its more or less well-patronized group of amateur players.

The outbreak of the World War in 1914 marked a pretty clearly defined close of the period I have just tried to sketch.

If the period between 1900 and 1914 may be roughly described as one of ferment and enthusiasm, of awakening to the "new" European drama and of expectation and hope for the emergence of a genuine American drama, the years 1914 to 1920 mark the beginning of a period of conscious and directed activity. The leaders of the movement, if I may call leaders the outstanding critics, scene designers, actors, playwrights, and directors who not too self-consciously played their respective rôles, were far better

---

[1] Published in New York by Doubleday, Page & Co.

trained and more fully informed on the European theatre than their predecessors had ever been. They were not wholly dependent on books and articles for their knowledge of what was going on abroad; they were men who had in some cases studied with Gordon Craig, worked under Max Reinhardt, who had investigated on the spot the Moscow Art Theatre and talked with Konstantin Stanislavski himself. The torch bearers of 1914 to 1920 were no longer to be found among groups of well-intentioned ladies whose knowledge of the theatre was gained at the public library or in the lecture hall; they were more commonly far better equipped; but the spirit that actuated them was the same eagerness to create a native theatre and drama that should be exciting and alive and beautiful. Hiram Kelly Motherwell had just come back from Europe after the outbreak of the war with his *Theater of Today,* a storehouse of information on Craig and Reinhardt, on Fortuny lighting, on the strange new revolutionary movements in Germany and Russia, and what he wrote popularized such relatively new devices as the cyclorama. Shelden Cheney's *New Movement in the Theater,* more philosophical and not quite so expository, was no less influential. The names of the other men and women of the time are still familiar to those of us who remember the exciting era I am writing of, and in mentioning a few of them I am not forgetting the others. Sam Hume was in the forefront, he who had actually known the legendary Craig and was able to stimulate his associates with a desire to make our "New Theatre" a place where music and lighting and simple unrealistic sets should heighten the illusion and not destroy it. Hume's exhibition of stage sets, illuminated by his own ingenious mechanical devices, was carried from city to city, and seen by directors, playwrights, and public alike. Sidney Howard has told in later years how deeply he was affected by the enthusiastic Hume when the two knew each other at Harvard. And there were others: Irving Pichel, Samuel A. Eliot Jr., and Mrs. Edith Isaacs, who was to carry on the work begun by Cheney after he established his magazine, *Theatre Arts,* in 1916.

And now, before we come to the year 1920 I must mention certain playwrights whose work does not conveniently fall into any of the more or less arbitrary categories which for convenience' sake I have adopted up to this point. Again the reader is asked to bear in mind that the American theatre is a complex of many varied activities, that progress and retrogression are not phenomena to be readily distinguished and explained; that at the same moment we can perceive in one playwright clear signs of genius and a determination to write honestly, and an equally strong determination to give the public what the manager says it wants; that, in a single season in one city there is evidence that the public will accept and pay for grim tragedy and inconsequential farce. It must be borne in mind that *Getting Gertie's Garter* and *Beyond the Horizon,* the flea circus, *Hamlet,* Avery Hopwood, *Theatre Arts Monthly,* the *Police Gazette,* Rudolph Valentino,

Percy MacKaye, all functioned and found their respective followers in the same city at the same time.

Take, for example, the long career of Rachel Crothers, and consider it carefully. Miss Crothers is today no back number. She is respected as a conscientious and talented writer. It was only a few years ago that her *Susan and God* had a long and successful run, and no one would be surprised if she turned out this year or five years hence another play equally brilliant and entertaining. Yet she began writing as long ago, probably, as the Spanish-American War. A one-act play of hers, according to the records, was performed at the Madison Square Theatre in 1902. A full-length play, *The Three of Us,* belongs to the year 1906, a sincere but conventional play, showing plainly its author's concern for characterization. Her first markedly original play, *A Man's World,* came three years later. Thirty-five years ago Miss Crothers established her claim to be regarded as an independent writer of thoughtful plays; she was able to make her point because she could argue convincingly, and did so in a play that was intrinsically effective drama. She was not a woman with a grievance who expected the public to condone poor play writing because her cause was just, but a skilled dramatist who knew that the best cause in the world could not be effectively pleaded unless the means of presenting it were acceptable to play-goers. Throughout her career the author of *The Three of Us,* even when she had little to say or said it badly, has consistently borne in mind that though the theatre can be used to persuade and reform, its function is not primarily hortatory.

Rachel Crothers is not today, of course, the pseudo-revolutionary feminist she was considered a generation ago, and her notions on the rights of women have been accepted long ago. She has never, so far as I know, allied herself to any one school of thought, nor departed from her conviction that a play is intended to interest and entertain. From decade to decade, as Miss Crothers' work has come to our stage, it has seemed that she was sometimes a little ahead of her public, and at other times out of the main current, but a consideration of her entire output will show it to have been consistently intelligent and to have reflected accurately many of the social and ethical problems of the well-to-do in metropolitan centers. Miss Crothers has nearly always been attracted by the moral implications of the common variety of maladjustments in modern marriage, particularly from the woman's viewpoint, though from time to time she has essayed satire. Having said her say on marriage, sex, and modern youth, having proved herself capable (in *Old Lady 31,* 1916) of turning out a popular sentimental potboiler, she turned (in *Expressing Willie,* 1924) to straight satire, and succeeded in writing a light comedy that showed up the everlasting faddist under the influence of the latest ideas on art and psychology.

It cannot be claimed, I think, that Miss Crothers to any great extent influenced the writers of her day or that she was herself influenced by her predecessors; she has followed her own devices and developed her skills, refusing to be swept off her feet by social or esthetic dogmas; she contributed plays the best of which have served not only to entertain but to express the tolerant mature common sense of the average well-bred American adult.

If this section on the American drama were a record of the work of all native dramatic writers since 1900, the twenty-year period now under consideration would require another twenty or more pages for a mere enumeration of the playwrights who helped keep the theatres open. But we are concerned here with an era of ferment, of not too conscious experimentation, of changing ideas and ideals, and my intention is only to point out a few striking examples of the change in mental attitudes that was to some extent altering the character of our dramatic writing.

George M. Cohan served the theatre for more than a generation as actor, director, manager, and playwright. We are concerned here only with his nonmusical work. His first produced play dates from 1897, and his last was seen in 1937. Cohan was practically born in the theatre. He was the child of actors and made his début on the stage at the age of ten—in 1888. The first of his plays to show his characteristic talent was *Get Rich Quick Wallingford* (1910), based on the work of another writer. Yet, even in this play that peculiar and characteristic mixture of impudence, observation, breeziness, sentiment, and optimism, which remains the sign-manual of Cohan's dramatic output, was in full evidence. *Broadway Jones* (1912) was another popular and wholly typical product. Here again the playwright had sketched contemporary types that were recognized by the public as unmistakably native. That the self-satisfied young men and women who skipped through these comedies were hardly more than sketched in was not considered a defect; that was precisely what made the Cohan comedies so strikingly genuine. For these characters were drawn very much as they presented themselves in life, smart ("wise" is the word they used), sentimental, self-satisfied, not over-honest, sophisticated in their own small way, yet pleasant enough. The Cohan hero often wore a dress suit and was not ashamed to do so, yet he was ready enough to proclaim his homespun Americanism in blatant fashion.

What George Ade expressed in his *Fables in Slang,* but could not (or did not) express in his plays, George M. Cohan expressed in many of his comedies. Whereas Ade invented a part of his vernacular vocabulary, Cohan recorded and perfected what he heard on his beloved Broadway. But with a certain marked difference, for it is not so much the words in Cohan's work as the manner of using them. Seldom if ever had any American playwright before reproduced the vernacular as skilfully as Cohan. In *Get Rich Quick Wallingford* and *Broadway Jones* there is not a trace of the old rhetoric which was one of the annoying mannerisms of most of the comedies of the nineteenth century, British as well as American. The speech is supple, unaffected, full of the rhythms that seem to spring naturally from the mouths of those Americans who don't know much about the science of language and care less.

Cohan combined his gift for natural and amusing dialogue with a philosophy of life exemplified by the success stories that for years were the chief literary diet of a large part of the American reading public. Life as exemplified in the Cohan comedies was apparently a fairy-tale, and to succeed one's heart had to be in the right place, and provided one were smart, and not too crooked, and of course happened to meet the "right girl," everything usually came out all right in the end. The Cohan formula was not, as we understand now, so far from the truth as it was sometimes thought to be, for there was a fairy-tale atmosphere in the epoch that followed the Mauve Decade; men became millionaires overnight, office boys did occasionally rise in a few years to be heads of great corporations, wealth seemed plentiful, the good old U.S.A. was forever secure against war and disaster, and few had ever even heard of the income tax, even as a crack-brained theory. Even when the World War intruded itself for a short time on the American scene the result of its impact on the ever-youthful Cohan was simply a rousing song, *Over There*. Meantime the Cohan plays, written alone or in collaboration, but always with the unmistakable Cohan touch, came and went—through the post-war boom and up to the black years that followed 1929.

But Cohan's contribution to the American theatre had already been made, and his effect on other dramatists established long before the early twenties. It was he who showed his fellow-craftsmen how to create light and entertaining comedies that reflected the pleasanter and less complicated aspects of modern life. It is not hard to trace the influence of Cohan on a long succession of plays which in the aggregate reveal truthfully at least a small part of the metropolitan American scene. James Montgomery's *Ready Money,* Megrue and Hackett's *It Pays to Advertise,* Smith's and Ongley's *Brewster's Millions,* are among the many early examples, but the tradition has lasted to this day, as any one can see who remembers the Spewacks' entertaining farce, *Boy Meets Girl,* or the Murray-Boretz farce, *Room Service.*

Cohan's plays, from *The Song-and-Dance Man* (1923) to *Fulton of Oak Falls* (1937) show, with few exceptions, clear evidence of a new note and more than a touch of bitterness; it is as though the happy youth who wrote *Broadway Jones* and thought that nothing could happen to what seemed a pretty good old world suddenly awoke at the age of forty-five to discover that good intentions do not necessarily create good works. Whether Cohan realized that life was not so simple as he once thought it, or whether the new generation of writers—the O'Neills and Andersons and Rices—had opened his eyes, I do not know. But in half a dozen plays during the twenties and thirties, there is more than an occasional hint of disillusion. In *The Home Towners* (1926) one can feel the mood of a writer who no longer believes that man is the noblest of God's creatures; in *The Baby Cyclone* (1927) is an undercurrent of savagery; in *Friendship* (1931) we are conscious—the use of the title proves it—that the author can use irony with telling effect; and in *Dear Old Darling* (1936) we have what comes nearest of all the Cohan works to being an "unpleasant" play.

At the time of his death, in 1942, Cohan must have felt that the world of his youth had crumbled. He had tried, possibly without realizing it, to adapt the old Cohan formula to a changing society, and the result was not right.

What remains to be said of the plays of the pre-1920 period applies largely to several works by many different writers. There are few playwrights whose careers covered any long period, who consistently or successfully made conspicuous progress either as craftsmen or as seekers after new ideas.

Some plays have won a sort of classic status, and are remembered to this day as landmarks from an era in which a certain part of the public was always looking for what was then called The Great American Play. When any play appeared that was relatively new in style or treatment, or even seemed more or less reminiscent of the sort of thing the Europeans were doing, it was likely to be hailed in some quarters as a masterpiece. It was not unusual for the critics to see in a play like *Salvation Nell* a "trend" in the direction of realism; or, noting the public reaction to Josephine Preston Peabody's *The Piper,* hail it as the beginning of a renaissance of poetic drama. Trends do not, of course, make themselves felt in a single season, and what was actually happening was that a number of able writers were turning away from routine comedies and melodramas and writing freely about what appealed to them.

In another connection I have already mentioned the exceptional plays of Moody, MacKaye, and others, and I have just referred to *The Piper*. The author of that charming blank-verse romance tried her hand, without much success, at other verse plays, and even a modern play in prose, but never succeeded in mastering the trick of writing well or easily for the stage. It remained for two men, George C. Hazleton Jr. and J. Harry Benrimo, to contrive a poetic romance that was outstanding as good writing and good drama: *The Yellow Jacket* (1912) a play in the Chinese manner, while not successful on Broadway, was revived more than once and then taken on tour by Mr. and Mrs. Charles Coburn who for several years carried it triumphantly to audiences all over the country. The fact that the Coburns believed in the play and knew that a vast provincial audience was ready to accept it, is proof that the old Drama League had done its propaganda job thoroughly.

To what extent *The Yellow Jacket* should be regarded as an expression of the American spirit I am not sure, but the fact in itself that the American public was ready to accept its strange beauty means that playwrights, actors, and public alike have proved that our theatre need not restrict its products to any one type of fare.

Another "unusual" play that is still remembered is Eleanor Gates' fantasy *The Poor Little Rich Girl* (1913). It has its place in the history of our drama because, as George Jean Nathan writes in the preface to the printed text, it presents "to the native audience a playful, meadow-larking imagination such as it probably never till then—and has certainly not since then—felt in and from an American pen." Mr. Nathan wrote this in 1916, several years before Philip Barry was to give us *White Wings,* but it is not unlikely that Miss Gates had pointed and prepared the way for the latter, a much richer and subtler dramatic fairy-tale.

If one were to list all the more or less successful fantasies and romantic plays produced between 1900 and 1920 it might be possible to make it seem that during any season a marked tendency existed to "bring romance back to the theatre." The fact is that the so-called escape play, the imaginative drama that for the most part had little or nothing to do with contemporary life, is always with us, and that in this country, at least, it has been able to thrive side by side with plays of many other different kinds. It would be hard to support the claim that the public wants only this or that type of play: one of the encouraging phenomena of the period now under consideration is that the public patronized any kind of play that offered those undefined qualities that will make an effective work in the theatre.

It is not without meaning that the author of *Salvation Nell* and *The Boss* was also the author of *Romance* and *The Garden of Paradise;* that Edwin Milton Royle, who could write popular melodrama, made a play of *Lancelot and Elaine;* that Booth Tarkington, who wrote *Clarence,* began his dramatic career with *Monsieur Beaucaire.*

In attempting to outline the dramatic work of the first twenty years of the present century, to point out at least the general direction taken by some of the more important playwrights and to describe the ferment which was in a way to stimulate new writers to use new themes and evolve new means of treating them, it has been necessary to omit mention of several writers who kept the theatres open, and a small number even of those who were consciously or otherwise doing their part to bring the theatre closer to contemporary life and thought than it had yet come. There remains, before we reach the crucial year 1920, only to point out how certain writers, while remaining in the broad current of the traditional theatre, yet managed to contribute an occasional play which, either by reason of its material or its technical treatment, caused playgoers to be just a little more exacting than before. Even the routine purveyors of theatrical fare—the Avery Hopwoods and Winchell Smiths, the Paul Armstrongs, Bayard Veillers, and the unnumbered and less conspicuous show writers of the period, had felt the necessity of doing away with certain outworn technical traditions, and in their most successful work they showed themselves far and away better stage carpenters than most of their predecessors. They had also begun to realize that it was no longer necessary to apologize for introducing into their work certain contemporary themes, and that what the best Europeans had done to express the color and complexity of life, to propound and even to attempt to solve contemporary social and ethical problems, they too could do. More and more native plays were produced, and succeeded; and gradually it became clear that our drama, based as it was upon European prototypes, had become unashamedly American. Sometimes the effort to create American characters, speech and background resulted in nothing more than a pale imitation of Ibsen or Pinero, either because the writer was unable to do any better or, as was often the case, because he knew more about Europe than he did about his own country. But on the other hand, among the young writers, and particularly among those who knew more about life and less about show business, there came occasionally somewhat tentative or experimental efforts to present native themes and characters that struck an authentic note of sincerity. This note is found in the work of MacKaye and Moody as well as in the more conventional work of Walter and Sheldon, Fitch, Thomas, and Klein.

Our record of the period of ferment would be incomplete without some mention of certain writers who helped, in one way or another, to establish what we can now see was in many respects a considerable body of dramatic work which in spirit, tendency, and execution was definitely recognizable as American. As long ago as 1906 James Forbes wrote *The Chorus Lady*, and during the next sixteen years a series of entertaining comedies which are as native in flavor and tendency as anything seen in their time. The very titles of *The Traveling Salesman* (1908) and *The Commuters* (1910) connote and proclaim something of the American spirit. Though Forbes wrote two more characteristic plays—*The Show Shop* (1914) and *The Famous Mrs. Fair* (1919)—before 1920, what he contributed to the theatre for the next ten years was negligible.

Thompson Buchanan, whose writing career began in 1909 and ended in 1930, was another competent workman, who in *A Woman's Way* (1909) skilfully followed in the Fitch tradition, proved that one could be an American and yet write a good comedy of manners. The same thing is true of A. E. Thomas whose *Her Husband's Wife* (1910) is another expert example of the native social comedy.

Louis Kaufman Anspacher is one of those men who refuse to classify easily. Beginning in 1906 with the thoroughly conventional *Embarrassment of Riches*, continuing with the sentimental and equally conventional *Our Children* (1915), the next year he produced a bitter character study, *The Unchastened Woman*, a work that could hardly have been expected either from the author of *Our Children* or indeed from any American of the time. There was very little, if anything, in its structure that differed from the best European models, but for the first time in the American theatre a writer had had the courage to offer his audience the spectacle of an unscrupulous woman neither conventionally immoral nor forgivably weak. The production of this play proved not only that a native writer could adapt an "advanced" European method of dramaturgy to the exploitation of American characters, but that he was able at the same time to make his audience accept a realistic and unsentimental attitude toward them.

The work of two playwrights, Clare Kummer and Jesse Lynch Williams, will show the extent to which American comedy had developed between the first part of the new century and the close of the period now under discussion. Miss Kummer's comedy *Good Gracious, Annabelle* (1916), devoid of "meaning" in the obvious sense, was probably the first of our sophisticated comedies to rely almost wholly on wit and lightness of touch; in a word to assimilate some of the qualities that made certain European comedies seem almost unattainably remote. When Philip Barry, S. N. Behrman, Arthur Richman, and Vincent Lawrence began to write, they all owed something to the pioneering of Miss Kummer. A *Successful Calamity* (1917) and *Be Calm, Camilla* (1918) both belong to the pre-1920 period, and *Rollo's Wild Oat* (1920) preceded O'Neill's first long play by only a few weeks, and for another thirteen years their author continued to furnish the theatre with agreeable and more or less successful plays. Yet she remains precisely where she started, a precursor.

Her contemporary Jesse Lynch Williams, better known as a journalist and fiction writer, wrote one play which was to make its mark and contribute its ideas to play-goers who were ready to accept its particular brand of philosophy. Originally published in 1914 as *And So They Were Married*, revised and professionally produced in 1917 as *Why Marry?*, this play was a genuinely American comedy of discussion in the Shavian manner. Mild as this play may now seem to us as a social document, it was in its day regarded as an unusual if not a daring piece. To begin with, it was based on the assumption that marriage is a very imperfect institution, and the author analyzed his problem in a frank and matter-of-fact manner, but his conclusion was no more daring than Shaw's "To get married is a great mistake—not to get married is a worse." Nevertheless, Williams' importance as a playwright lies in his having adapted the ideas and to some extent the technique of Shaw, at a time when few others were able or willing to do so.

The era of ferment and occasional experiment, the score of years between the beginning of the century and the production of O'Neill's first long play, came to a close in no definite sense except in the arbitrary sense of reaching the year 1920. As I have already shown, there were a number of writers who, mostly unconscious of what was happening, were once in a while able to adopt certain ideas, evolve new means of expression, and in a way break the bonds of theatrical convention—in a word, to use the theatre to a greater extent than other writers had previously used it in this country, to reflect the life and thought of the people of their day. Some of these transition playwrights began their work even before 1900; some continued to flourish after 1920, some consistently fought to broaden the functional powers of the theatre, some helped to accomplish the same end only on rare occasions and as though accidentally.

The playwrights who were to become best-known during the next decade, 1920-1930, and some among them who continued through the thirties and are writing today, were to receive their first impressions of life and the theatre long before they grew up and began to offer their first work to the managers.

Eugene O'Neill's first full-length play to be professionally acted was *Beyond the Horizon,* produced by John D. Williams in New York on February 2, 1920. Considering that O'Neill was not the product of himself alone, that he had already written several plays and had many of them produced, and that he, like every playwright, is the result of an infinite combination of diverse influences, I nevertheless feel that the first long play of our most important dramatic writer is a landmark in the history of our native drama.

It is not necessary to claim that *Beyond the Horizon* was the finest play written by an American up to that time; I am not concerned so much with its actual merits as with the plain fact that it announced the opening of the career of the most original and gifted dramatic writer born and brought up in the United States. The young writer's attitude toward life and the theatre, his determination to write as directly and as sincerely as he possibly could, without compromising what he understood to be the truth, and his complete disregard of the so-called demands of the public—some of these things were realized by those who saw or read the play in 1920. This must not be taken to mean that no other playwright had tried to express his honest convictions before, or had disregarded monetary considerations in writing for the theatre: O'Neill had not only a fierce determination to present life as he saw it, he was to continue from 1920 onward to persist in that determination. Yet honesty, sincerity, and determination alone would scarcely entitle O'Neill to the position of historical importance he now holds and will continue to hold in the history of the development of our drama, no matter what the final judgment of posterity may be on the intrinsic merits of his work. He was able from the first to implement his ideas and articulate his themes through plays which, even the poorest of them, belong in the main current of the dramatic traditions of the world, and are essentially of the theatre: his plays are dramatic shows peopled by human beings, provided with moving plots, and worked out with skill. Whatever else he may be, or wish to become, O'Neill is above all a practical writer for the theatre. The relative novelty of ideas that has often attracted critical attention, and the apparent novelty of means adopted to throw an idea or a theme into relief, are hardly novelties at all, they are simply the result of the writer's effort to discover in the workshop of the theatre of the past some striking means of setting forth themes and characters.

O'Neill has told us more than once of the writers who have most directly influenced him, and it is curious to observe that though Nietzsche, Wedekind, and Strindberg were all foreigners, the sum total of his work is distinctly American. I have already spoken of European influences on our native playwrights, but it seems that many of those who were more susceptible to European influences than to American have best succeeded in creating a genuine American drama.

O'Neill, like Rice and Howard and Kelly (to mention only a few), *had* lived his life in America and he and they had been molded to a far greater extent than they perhaps realized by native life and plays and books. The most original playwrights of the 1920-1930 period were coming to realize that American audiences were readier than ever before to see and study American types, to hear American themes and ideas discussed—in a word, to become conscious of and excited about their Americanness. The same impulse that lay behind Henry Ford's mania for collecting American furniture, books, and glass, that spread through the country in the craze for the acquisition of American rather than English or French antiques and precipitated floods of historical novels and biographies, that brought foreigners to our shores to tell us about our own land and our future destiny, drove our playwrights—and continues to drive them—to compress into dramatic form the colors and shapes of American life. It would be hard to think of one geographical part of the land that has not been used as dramatic background, and it is not without meaning, I think, that certain playwrights, as though in despair at finding no background or human type yet untreated, have occasionally turned to fantasy and by abstract means restated their convictions on the soul and destiny of man. A late indication of this trend is Thornton Wilder's *The Skin of Our Teeth,* a fitting continuation of his militantly and locally American *Our Town.*

It was not O'Neill who caused or began the "movement" to exploit American life in the theatre, but it was he who consistently sought to reveal those aspects of the truth as he saw them in terms of American drama—even when, on occasion, he laid his scenes in Medieval China or Italy, or the ancient Near East.

The writing career of O'Neill actually began some years before 1920. Of his earliest plays six one-acters were printed in the volume *Thirst,* published in 1914. In the fall of that year the young author became a member of Professor Baker's English 47 play-writing class at Harvard, where he turned out a fair amount of prentice work. He was given his first chance to write for a theatre when the Provincetown Players produced *Bound East for Cardiff* in the summer of 1916. When the Players decided to establish a playhouse of their own in New York they created, with the Playwrights'

Theatre in Macdougal Street, one of the most important experimental theatres of modern times. Influenced chiefly by the idealism of its director, George Cram Cook, and coöperating with a number of devoted and talented directors and playwrights, O'Neill was enabled during the next few years to write precisely the kind of plays he wanted to write.

After the reading of *Bound East for Cardiff* in Provincetown, Susan Glaspell, one of the original group, tells us that "then we knew what we were for."

By 1920 O'Neill was ready to compete with other playwrights by offering a full-length play to the "regular" theatre-going public. By this time, with the help and encouragement of George Jean Nathan, who directed John D. Williams' attention to the manuscript, O'Neill was able to interest a Broadway manager in *Beyond the Horizon,* which opened at the Morosco Theatre on February 2. While the play had only a short run it was well received by the critics. No one, apparently, was ready to berate it as unduly pessimistic or arty, and those who looked upon the theatre as the abode of sweetness and light were not too upset in finding that it gave the lie to the age-old dictum that a play should leave the audience in a happy mood.

Beyond the Horizon made it clear that provided a play rang true and its story was dramatically effective, it did not much matter if it were also pessimistic in tone and reversed another ancient rule of the native theatre that good must triumph over evil. Broadly speaking, *Beyond the Horizon,* if we reduce it to its simplest elements, shows that what we superficially accept as evil does not invariably bring punishment, and that good intentions by no means bring a reward.

The reception of *Beyond the Horizon* in a way symbolized the beginning of an era in which the playwright was able to present problems and ideas and even draw conclusions which in the past had been generally unacceptable to the public. From 1920 onward, in spite of periodic interference from the police, the vice societies, and the church, playwrights were able to treat almost any subject that appealed to them, without compromise and with almost complete frankness. The theatre had at last become a place where a self-respecting, thoughtful and courageous writer could compete freely with the most conventional amusement purveyors and succeed, provided of course he knew his business as a craftsman. And it is due partly to O'Neill that this is so.

Not content with writing one play that happened to achieve at least critical approval, O'Neill had several other plays ready. In fact, the year 1920 saw the production of four other O'Neill plays, the one-acter *Exorcism, The Emperor Jones,* and *Diff'rent,* all Provincetown Players' productions, and *Chris Christopherson,* a full-length play tried out in Atlantic City under George C. Tyler, but not seen in New York until after its revision under the title *Anna Christie.*

The first of these (never published) is an unimportant work, but the other three provided striking evidence of the young writer's versatility and his constant quest for new ways of setting forth his stories and revealing the basic truth, as he saw it, that underlay the thoughts and actions of his men and women. *The Emperor Jones* was in its day recognized as a highly original and imaginative treatment of those hidden forces that determine the fate of man, forces which we are too apt to dismiss as primitive or barbaric, but which, after all, are latent even in so-called civilized man. *The Emperor Jones* was the first of the O'Neill plays to attract attention in the theatrical world outside America; it was eventually produced in nearly every country of the world.

Diff'rent was a two-act character study, bitter, drab, relentless. After its opening in Macdougal Street it was taken uptown to one of the commercial theatres. It is curious to reflect that about the time its author received the Pulitzer Prize for *Beyond the Horizon* the police were trying to stop *Diff'rent* as an indecent play. It is also curious to learn that O'Neill wrote to George Jean Nathan, commenting on the poor press the play received, saying "Well, it is rather reassuring. I had begun to think I was too popular to be honest."

Meantime the young playwright, his head full of ideas and his notebook crammed with synopses of plays to be written, was constantly at work. His next great success, *Anna Christie,* produced by Arthur Hopkins in 1921, proved that the author of *Beyond the Horizon* and *The Emperor Jones* was not just another promising young man. *Anna Christie* resembled, so far as background and characterization went, the early sea plays which in book form and on the stage of the Provincetown Players' theatre were beginning to become well known; but covering as it did a larger canvas, it was far more ambitious. To this day there persists some disagreement as to the precise implications of the story, but this evidently has not obscured its pure theatricality from creating the intended effect. Unlike most of the later O'Neill plays, this one stands firmly on its own merits as a good story set against a romantic background, with Anna and her father preëminently satisfying the play-goer simply as human beings skilfully set forth in a moving story.

Less successful, both as business ventures and as works of dramatic art, were *Gold,* which preceded *Anna Christie* by a few months; *The Straw,* produced at about the same time; and *The First Man* (1922). Interesting as these are to the student of O'Neill's work, they are limited in appeal, and rather overburdened with undramatic passages.

Though O'Neill had two years before gone to the professional managers with certain of his manuscripts, he had not severed his connection with the Provincetown Players, who in 1922 produced *The Hairy Ape,* one of his most original experiments. This play, like *The Emperor Jones,* soon became known to the managers abroad and to this day remains one of the best-known O'Neill works. It was the result of a deliberate effort to express in terms of drama something fundamental about the problem of man in a perplexing world. "The subject here," wrote the author at the time, "is the same ancient one that always was and always will be the one subject for drama, that is man and his struggle with his own fate." *The Hairy Ape,* he declared, "was a symbol of man, who has lost his old harmony with nature."

The nonrealistic form of *The Hairy Ape* reminds us of certain products of the so-called Expressionist theatre of Germany and Russia, and O'Neill was, at the time—at least so far as *The Hairy Ape* and to some extent *The Emperor Jones* were concerned—called an Expressionist. He himself told me in 1926 that

...the first expressionistic play that I ever saw was Kaiser's *From Morn to Midnight* in 1922, after I'd written *The Emperor Jones* and *The Hairy Ape.* I had read *From Morn to Midnight* before *The Hairy Ape* was written but not before the idea for it was planned. The point is that *The Hairy Ape* is a direct descendant of *Jones,* written long before I had ever heard of Expressionism.[1]

I believe, however, that the American playwright had indirectly, through reading the plays of Strindberg and Wedekind, with whose work he had for some time been familiar, adapted to some extent some of the technical devices used by these precursors of Expressionism. The point to be stressed is that O'Neill, like other American playwrights of his day, was striving to express certain aspects of life by means of techniques other than those of pure, or photographic, realism.

Welded (1924), a failure, and *The Ancient Mariner* (1924), the latter a Provincetown Playhouse production, are relatively unimportant, though the former shows an increasing skill in compression, and a desire to set forth a viewpoint on modern marriage that the author was not again to treat as a problem in itself. In his effort to get at the heart of the tragedy inherent in the subject he made his characters so abstract as almost to strip them of their humanity.

In *All God's Chillun Got Wings* (1924), another Provincetown Playhouse production, O'Neill based his tragedy on that same Negro problem that had so often provided playwrights and novelists with provocative themes and plots. His play is the chronicle history of an educated Negro who marries a white woman, and ultimately pays a heavy price for daring to question the social law laid down by the white man in a white man's land.

A few months later (1924) the Provincetown Playhouse company produced *Desire Under the Elms,* a tragic drama of New England folk which to this day remains one of the high points in O'Neill's writing career. A short time after it opened (at the Greenwich Village Theatre) it was taken uptown to a larger playhouse and subsequently toured the country. Like *All God's Chillun* and *Diff'rent,* it encountered censor trouble. Here again

---

[1] This and other quotations from O'Neill are reprinted from B. H. Clark, *Eugene O'Neill, The Man and His Plays,* Rev. ed. (New York, 1936).

the playwright has sought to reveal the fundamental passions of men and women burning themselves out in accordance with the writer's own conception of the laws that govern human life. In essence *Desire Under the Elms* is a demonstration of the effect of the passion of sex love on a young man and a young woman (his father's wife) contrasted with the passion of the older man who is at the same time jealous of his wife and the victim of a fanatic desire for power. In no sense a thesis play, *Desire Under the Elms* was, with one exception, the last of its author's plays that can be called realistic. From 1924 onward he was to seek other means of expressing the truth and beauty of life. Two years before *Desire Under the Elms* was finished he wrote, in answer to those who had charged him with pessimism and a tendency to treat the more somber aspects of life, "I don't love life because it's pretty. Prettiness is only clothes deep. I am a truer lover than that. I love it naked. There is beauty to me even in its ugliness."

The Fountain (1925), though produced after *Desire Under the Elms,* was written long before—as a matter of fact, in 1921. It was a failure, and it remains one of the least popular of his plays. Following the pattern of the conventional romantic drama, it lacks to a great extent the magic of exalted poetic expression. Yet it shows an aspect of the playwright's consistent attitude toward life, and foreshadows the much finer and subtler *Lazarus Laughed.* Based on the Ponce de León story and the Spaniard's quest for eternal youth, it is a dramatic hymn to man's never-ending aspirations toward love and beauty.

The Ancient Mariner, already mentioned, which was a "dramatic arrangement of Coleridge's poem," is of interest mainly because it was the first play in which the author made use of masks. James Light, one of the directors of the Provincetown Playhouse, wrote in the program, "We are using masks [because] we wish to project certain dramatic motifs through that spiritual atmosphere which the mask peculiarly gives."

O'Neill was to make elaborate use of masks in his next play, *The Great God Brown* (1926) and in at least two other works, not because he was trying to revive an ancient and picturesque custom, but for the same reason that led him to employ other non-realistic conventions; in effect, he felt that what he had to express could not be so effectively conveyed in terms either of romance or of realism. He held that mere surfaces, mere prose, mere photography, were inadequate.

The Great God Brown is the most abstract and obscure play O'Neill ever wrote. When it opened in New York, and for a long time afterward, it caused a good deal of discussion, to which the author himself added a letter of explanation, in which he confessed that there was a "mystical pattern which manifests itself as an overtone ... dimly behind and beyond the words and actions of the characters." He intended, he says, that the "background pattern of conflicting tides in the soul of man should ever overshadow ... the living drama of the recognizable human beings." The essence of the play, however, remains "the mystery any man or woman can feel but not understand as the meaning of any event... in any life on earth."

Marco Millions, though begun several years earlier, was produced in January, 1928, by the Theatre Guild. Far simpler in its outlines and a good deal less subtle in its ideas than *The Great God Brown,* it offers another example of O'Neill's intention to try by various means to express within the limits of the theatre some part of his passionate eagerness to set forth what had to be uttered about the strange mind and soul of man. Not that this entertaining romantic extravaganza probes very deep into the hidden by-paths of the human psyche; but it does show the hand of a playwright who has always sought by every means at hand to throw into relief what he feels and thinks about the world. *Marco Millions* is basically a satire on Occidental hardheadedness set against a colorful background. Marco Polo is the eternal go-getter whose desire for material success blinds him to the beauty of the world about him.

A few weeks after *Marco Millions* opened on Broadway the Theatre Guild produced another O'Neill play, *Strange Interlude.* On this grandiose work he had been making notes for a long time. Its inordinate length, for one thing, seemed to prove that he was much more concerned over the problem of self-expression than of getting the work produced in a theatre. O'Neill was sceptical, when he thought of the matter at all, as to whether *Strange Interlude* would have a "run" or not, and presumably the Guild was just as sceptical. A play in nine acts that began at five-thirty in the afternoon, and with an intermission of only a little over an hour lasted until eleven, was surely something that could not have appealed to play-goers on the grounds of novelty alone. But it was an enormous success in New York and on the road, and in several countries abroad. What was it that held theatre-goers by the tens of thousands?

It is not the story, which could easily have been condensed into three acts; it is not the strangeness of the asides and monologues (that novelty wears off in five minutes); it is no more nor less than the triumph of O'Neill's art, his amazing gift for understanding and laying bare some of the complexities of the human mind and heart. He was clearly unwilling to make use of the conventional dramatic form which, in its latest manifestations, does not admit the aside and the soliloquy, and refuses to allow the dramatist much more than two or two and a half hours' time.[1]

Both *The Great God Brown* and *Strange Interlude* show signs of a growing concern on the dramatist's part to philosophize upon the rôle of man in a hard and perplexing world. Even in the earliest O'Neill plays the writer expressed strong convictions, but generally the spectator was left to draw his own conclusions. In 1922 the Austrian poet-playwright Hugo von Hofmannsthal, basing his estimate of O'Neill upon only three plays, wrote that it was

[1] B. H. Clark, *op. cit.*

...a little disappointing to a European with his complex background to see the arrow strike the target toward which he has watched it speeding all the while.... The reason for this general weakness is, I think, that the dramatist, unable to make his dialogue a complete expression of human motives, is forced at the end to squeeze it out like a wet sponge.

This criticism was valid so far as some of the early plays are concerned, and I believe that O'Neill felt this weakness; *The Great God Brown* and *Strange Interlude* represented reactions on his part against the surface realism of the plays that preceded them.

At all events his later works, with one exception, are far richer in philosophical content, even when the subject-matter and technical means are unwisely chosen or scantily worked out. It has always seemed to me that popular success or artistic triumph, when they were achieved, meant nothing to him but another chance to probe deeper into the hearts and minds of his characters without reference to the limitations of the playhouse or the tastes of the play-goer.

Lazarus Laughed, begun in 1926, was publicly produced only once, and then by a nonprofessional company, at the Pasadena Playhouse under the direction of Gilmor Brown in April, 1928. In spite of a lavish use of masks and an unduly large amount of philosophical commentary in the text, *Lazarus Laughed* is at bottom a very simple play. This work "for an imaginative theatre," as the author described it, is the exposition of a philosophy, expressed and reëxpressed throughout its great length:

> Laugh! Laugh!
> There is only life!
> There is only laughter!
> Fear is no more!
> Death is dead!

Lazarus, risen from the grave and fortified by this belief, tests its validity by setting himself against those who fear life because they fear death. And at the end the great affirmer Lazarus, the embodiment of the will to live, proclaims his faith: "Believe! What if you are a man and men are despicable? Men are always unimportant! Men pass! Like rain into the sea! The sea remains!... For Man death is not! Man, Son of God's laughter, *is!*"

The element of pageantry, so lavishly used in this play; the use (or suggested use) of music, of masked crowds; the simple straightforward story; above all, the exultant and assertive optimism of its theme, should have made *Lazarus Laughed* one of the most popular of its author's plays.

Dynamo, a Theatre Guild production, opened in New York in 1929, and had only a short run. The author stated that it was a

...symbolical and factual biography of what is happening in a large section of the American (and not only American) soul right now. It is really the first play of a trilogy that will dig at the roots of the sickness of today as I feel it—the death of an old God and the failure of science and materialism to give any satisfying new one for the surviving primitive religious instinct to find a meaning for life in.... The two other plays will be *Without Ending of Days* and *It Cannot Be Mad*.

Dynamo, being only a part of what O'Neill intended as a unified whole, should not be judged as an independent work, yet the fact that the author decided not to write the other two plays seems to prove either that he was no longer interested in the theme, or that another idea came to him and appealed to him more strongly. At all events *Dynamo*, for all its nervous tensity, seemed strangely vague and was apparently too abstract to hold an audience. Fortunately, I think, O'Neill set to work on another trilogy, which appeared in 1931 under the title *Mourning Becomes Electra*. Basing his story on the broad outlines of the tragic tale of Agamemnon, Clytemnestra, Electra, and Orestes as treated in the *Oresteia* of Æschylus, the modern poet has rewritten and reinterpreted the Greek tragedy in terms of modern life. Instead of following the ancient conception of fate as an instrument in the hands of captious gods, O'Neill has substituted the to us more reasonable motives by which we know that man is driven in his efforts to realize his destiny. The O'Neill trilogy tells the story of a New Englander who has transgressed the moral code of his time and people; the son of his victim turns upon the living representatives of his family and takes revenge upon them. In spite of all the technical devices which the dramatist has used to set forth the multitudinous details of his plot, *Mourning Becomes Electra* stands forth clearly as a moving tragedy, written out of that "deep curiosity," in the author's words, "about the underlying motives that actuate human interrelationships in the family."

The writing of *Ah, Wilderness!*, produced in 1933, is said to have been very easy. It came, according to Burns Mantle,[1] when O'Neill "awoke one morning," after the completion of the second draft of *Days Without End*, "with the full plot and all the characters clamoring to be put on paper." This play is an unpretentious bit of nostalgic writing about a sensitive youth on the verge of manhood. It is chiefly interesting to the student of O'Neill's work as showing a reaction in the playwright's mind, possibly unconscious, against a tendency in the direction of what he once playfully admitted was "foggily mystical" in his work. He was aiming, he said, to be "clearly psychological and mystically clear, too." *Ah, Wilderness!* should be considered as a serene interlude in the writing life of a man who is usually too much concerned with the depths of life to think of its lighter aspects.

Days Without End, though offered to the public after *Ah, Wilderness!*, was written before it. It was first produced in January, 1934 and is the latest of its author's plays to reach the stage. In mood it belongs with the fragmentary *Dynamo*, and dramatizes another aspect of man's tortuous quest for faith in a modern world where spiritual values are constantly changing. John

---

[1] *Contemporary American Playwrights*.

Loving symbolizes the dual nature of man, loses the old simple religion of his fathers, turns atheist, and through suffering accepts again the formal faith he had once abjured. The play failed in the theatre not, I think, because of its theme, but because it was too patently the dramatization of a series of intellectual processes; it lacked warmth and human appeal.

The play-writing activities of O'Neill during the past dozen years scarcely belong to any history of the American drama, since none of the many plays he has been working on has been acted or published. Reports have been current for years on this or that play or series of plays in preparation or actually finished. Even before 1930 he told me that a great many of the most dramatic experiences of his life

... have so far been left out of my plays.... I've hardly begun to work up all this material, but I'm saving up a lot of it for ... a cycle of plays I hope to do some day. There'll be nine separate plays, to be acted on nine successive nights; together they will form a sort of dramatic autobiography.

This cycle, or something like it, has been O'Neill's principal concern since the early 1930's. In 1937 he wrote me that the cycle involved working out a "continuity of family lives over a space of 150 years." In 1940 he wrote of having finished "two plays outside the cycle"; no immediate plans, he added, for their production; and a final ominous note on the "changing times," together with outlines completed of three more "outside" plays.

There is no predicting when the cycle will be finished or produced, and as these pages go to press, there is no definite word on any of the other "outside" plays. So far as the theatre is concerned, O'Neill's career ended early in 1934. But the far-reaching effects of that career have been so noticeable and important, as I have already pointed out, that if no other play of his should ever be produced, O'Neill's position as our most distinguished and influential playwright could not be questioned.

Shortly after *Beyond the Horizon* first came to Broadway early in 1920, it began to dawn upon us that we were already in the midst of what could be properly termed a movement of some kind. Within the next two years several writers who were to become well known and successful during the twenties and thirties, had had plays produced in the professional theatre; among them Sidney Howard, Elmer Rice, George S. Kaufman, Marc Connelly, Philip Barry, Maxwell Anderson, and George Kelly.

Broadly speaking, these writers—together with O'Neill—were to become the new "regulars" of the 1920-1930 period, the men who every season or two produced a new play. There were others, beginning earlier, who were occasionally represented in the theatre, and still others, toward the end of the decade—like Robert E. Sherwood, John Howard Lawson, and Paul Green—whose most characteristic work was not to appear until somewhat later.

Elmer Rice, a careful and intelligent craftsman whose first play, *On Trial* dates from 1914, has for thirty years exemplified the American playwright's concern with contemporary life and social problems. His plays, as well as his ventures into production and his public services to the Federal Theatre and other socio-artistic institutions, show him to be a man of practical commonsense with a leaning toward political idealism. Though his first play won critical praise and wide public approval, it was clearly a product of the old commercial theatre. Between 1914 and 1923 Rice had one play, *The Iron Cross,* produced by a small experimental group, and two by regular managers. These last were the pot-boiler *For the Defence* (1919), and *Wake up, Jonathan!* (1921), a pleasant character comedy written in collaboration with Hatcher Hughes. Then, in 1923, came *The Adding Machine,* one of the first really original American plays accepted by the Theatre Guild. This was one of the earliest successful adaptations of the so-called German Expressionistic drama ever seen in the United States, but it is worth noting that O'Neill's *Emperor Jones* was produced in 1920, and that Lawson's *Roger Bloomer* preceded it on the stage by three weeks. The play's importance lies not so much in its form as in its social implications. The common man, its "hero," is not a hero at all, but a cipher, his name being Mr. Zero; he is not sentimentalized by the author, and he is not offered as an object of pity: he is ruthlessly exhibited as a victim of our particular brand of social and economic regimentation, a system which kills the individual. *The Adding Machine* is shot through with tragic irony, a rare quality conspicuously absent from most earlier examples of native play writing.

A good deal of what we now see was a kind of groundwork had been done to prepare the way for the flourishing of a "serious" native drama in the 1920-1930 decade. The nationwide interest in drama stimulated by playwrights, critics, directors, and scene designers, and by lecturers and club members as well, had years before encouraged the establishment of special producing groups that brought new plays, native and foreign, to the attention of at least a part of the public. Some of the pioneer groups, like the Little Theatre of Chicago, the Provincetown Players of Provincetown and New York, and the Toy Theatre of Boston, have already been mentioned. The Provincetown Players managed to survive until the late twenties, but most of the others had ceased to function long before 1920. One group, however, the Washington Square Players, founded in 1915, marks an important connecting link between the innumerable small groups of amateur experimenters and the "new" professional theatre of the modern era. It is not without meaning that in its first manifesto the Players made reference to the Drama League. The new group had "one policy in regard to the new plays which we will produce—they must have artistic merit." Preference would be given to "American plays, but we will also include in our repertory the works of well-known European authors which have been ignored by the commercial managers." Opening at the Band Box Theatre early in

1915, they produced several bills of one-acters, mostly American, and two or three full-length European works. In 1917 the group rented the Comedy Theatre, continued to produce long plays and short, and in May, 1918, because of economic difficulties resulting from the war, they disbanded. A few months later some of the founders decided to continue the project so hopefully begun in 1915, and in the spring of 1919 the new organization, called the Theatre Guild, made its first production, Benavente's *The Bonds of Interest,* at the Garrick Theatre. Although the Guild for the first four or five years was apparently more interested in foreign than in native plays, it was later to produce a number of important works by Americans. During the next ten years the Guild was to be the most important producing group in the country, combining what was best in the so-called Art Theatre of Europe, and a certain amount of experimentation in new dramatic forms, both native and imported. It rarely went out of its way to encourage the very young or very radical writer, leaving that sort of trail-blazing to the self-proclaimed experimental theatres, but occasionally it opened its doors to some unknown or to one who had not yet achieved popular success. It welcomed some of the early work of Elmer Rice, Sidney Howard, S. N. Behrman, and consistently produced O'Neill after his earlier plays had been done elsewhere. It also from time to time sandwiched in between its major productions an occasional play of "social significance," and on even rarer occasions an original and outstanding work like Lynn Riggs' *Green Grow the Lilacs.* To its credit must also be set down the direct and indirect influence it wielded as a training ground for actors, directors, and stage designers. The Group Theatre, which was later to win distinction as an independent producing unit, was organized within the walls and among the employees of the Guild itself.

Elmer Rice's work was not again, after *The Adding Machine,* to appear under Guild auspices. His next play, written with Dorothy Parker, was *Close Harmony* (1924), later called *The Lady Next Door,* a slight work, but of some consequence as one of the first dramatic commentaries on the "little man" in modern American life. *Cock Robin* (1928), in which Rice collaborated with Philip Barry, was just another mystery play, a "whodunit" without the usual noise and bustle. Then came *The Subway* (1929), an artistic relative of *The Adding Machine,* and a good example of the "significant" left-wing drama which came into prominence here during the 1920's. The same year saw also the production of what remains Rice's best-known and most successful play, *Street Scene.* Realistic in setting and detail, this is a successful evocation of a mood, a recreation of city sounds and city rhythms. In spite of its somewhat lurid story of jealousy and murder, it creates a mood as a painter would create it, or a composer.

Rice's next play, *See Naples and Die* (1929), is a light fantastic comedy laid against a European background; it is almost wholly devoid of social tendency. It is entertaining and wittily written, and to some students of

Rice's work it seemed as though the author had intended to prove that he was not merely a social reformer. Another play with a European background is *The Left Bank* (1931), a comedy of character laid in Paris, about American expatriates. It reveals the point of view, somewhat indirectly, of many of our intellectuals of the time who had been seeking in Europe an answer to those questions that had plagued many writers who wanted to "belong" in their native land and send down their roots there, but were irked by the materialism and barrenness that was apparently all they were able to see in America. Rice's conclusion, in *The Left Bank,* was that real Americans belong at home.

Counsellor-at-law (1931) is a full-length portrait of a self-made Jewish lawyer, a brilliant though over-theatricalized story contrived with undoubted reportorial skill. An entertaining comedy, *Black Sheep* (1932), which was a failure but deserved a good run, belonged in mood and treatment to Rice's apprentice years. It was followed (1933) by *We the People,* a typical "purpose" play. This many-scened angry indictment of capitalist society reflected more directly than most of his other plays the author's concern with the cruelty and intolerance of the money classes toward those who threatened their complacent existence. *Judgment Day* (1934) fell short of popular success in the United States probably because Rice foresaw in it more clearly than most the ominous threat of Nazidom to the entire world, and in dramatizing the Reichstag trial, he was preaching to a public that was not to be aroused to action against rearmed Germany until some years later.

Between Two Worlds (1934), another failure so far as the public was concerned, was a commentary on what was going on under the surface of modern politics; but *Not for Children* (never produced professionally but tried out at the Pasadena Playhouse in 1936) belonged in the category of comic satire so ably exemplified in *See Naples and Die*. It makes delightful reading and should, I believe, be resurrected and brought to the stage.

American Landscape (1938) again showed Rice's concern over the fate of his native country in a changing world. It dramatized the threat of fascism to American institutions. Technically, the play was somewhat overloaded with discussion and symbolism.

Two on an Island (1940) is a sort of sentimental pilgrimage—a dramatization of the eternal quest of youth for success and happiness. Like *Street Scene,* it was another attempt to recapture the spirit of metropolitan New York where Rice was born and brought up. Devoid of preaching, and with more than a hint that he has outgrown his earlier attitude toward bourgeois society as the *sole* villain in the tragedy of modern life, it shows tenderness and a mature and tolerant concern for life not as something to be challenged or criticized or even radically altered, but as a subject for contemplation and enjoyment.

Rice's latest play, *A New Life* (1943), is one of his few relatively negligible pieces. "Purposeful" only to a limited extent (it preaches the right of a woman to bring up her son as she sees fit), it is good theatre largely by reason of its incidental details.

The first of the plays of Maxwell Anderson to reach the stage was *White Desert* (1923); it ran for only a short time and attracted little attention. Though it was followed by several plays far different in mood and background, it pointed the direction Anderson was to take in later years. The play dramatizes the plight of a farm woman driven to distraction by the loneliness to which she is condemned by circumstances. What is worth noting is that though the play is fundamentally stark realism, a good deal of it is written in verse, a somewhat looser blank verse than the author was to use afterward in some of his best work.

The next Anderson play was written in collaboration with Lawrence Stallings. *What Price Glory?* (1924) is a vigorous and mature war play. The authors claimed that it showed "war as it is, not as it has been presented theatrically for thousands of years. The soldiers talk and act much as soldiers do the world over." They added that the play "may seem bold." It did, to some extent, but its value lay not so much in its relatively realistic picture of war as in the power of its dialogue and characterization. *What Price Glory?* was followed by two other plays also written with Stallings, *First Flight* (1925) and *The Buccaneer* (1925), each of them well-enough written, but both somewhat "literary" and conventional, and both failures on the stage. The same year saw also the production of *Outside Looking In,* based on Jim Tully's *Beggars of Life.* There is little form to the varied scenes that make up the play, but to compensate for this there is an abundance of rugged humor.

In 1927 *Saturday's Children,* a great popular success, was to prove that Anderson was not only a dramatist in his own right, but a playwright of versatility. This tender serious comedy of youth, though conventional in form, was clear proof that Anderson was not the kind of writer who was content to repeat himself. *Gods of the Lightning* (1928), written with Harold Hickerson, strengthened that impression and proved that the young playwright was not only a man of the theatre but a sensitive and indignant citizen. The play is an impressive dramatization of the Sacco-Vanzetti case.

Gypsy (1929) seems to some of those who remember it like an experimental interlude between the first period of trial and error and the second period during which the dramatic poet realized more fully his power and his limitations. He was never again to try to write tragedy out of the commonplaces of modern life without heightening his effects by language suitable to the theme. The decade beginning in 1930 was to give us one of his finest works, *Elizabeth the Queen* (1930). This was the most mature play he had yet written. It marks a return to the problem attacked in his first play: to find, or adapt, a poetic medium of expression that should provide the emotional impact of conventional English blank verse and at the same time prove speakable without seeming too remote or archaic to the ears of modern play-goers, for as he once said in an interview: "If we are to have a great theatre in this country somebody has got to write verse, even if it is written badly. It is at least a beginning." *Elizabeth the Queen*, though adding little if anything to what is already known of the Elizabeth-Essex story, is none the less an impressive tragedy. But in the next play, *Night Over Taos* (1932), Anderson seemed to answer a scarcely uttered criticism that an American background is more fitting material for an American playwright than a foreign and all too familiar one. *Night Over Taos*, which had a short run under the auspices of the recently organized Group Theatre, tells the tale of the last stand of an old Mexican chieftain who, though realizing that the old order is giving way before a growing sentiment for democracy, makes a heroic stand against the forces of the new day, represented by the American pioneers of the southwest. He says,

> "Our race is done,
> The Spanish blood runs thin. Spain has gone down....
> ... The north will win.
> Taos is dead ...
> It's right
> Because what wins is right. It won't win forever.
> The kings will come back, and they'll be right again
> When they win again. Not now. The gods are weary
> Of men who give orders, playing at God."

Seawife belongs to the middle twenties, but it was never produced in the professional theatre, and it has not been published. Somewhat more obscure in theme than the other Anderson plays, this work indicates an ever-increasing determination on the author's part to express life and ideas in poetic form. Some years later a similar theme was treated more effectively in *The Wingless Victory*.

In 1933 came *Both Your Houses,* a modern realistic play that belongs with *Gods of the Lightning* in the category of thesis drama. It seems as though the playwright had determined to act the part of the good citizen occasionally and to counter-balance his poetic plays with dramatized social and political documents, alternating *White Desert* with *What Price Glory?, Elizabeth the Queen* with *Gods of the Lightning,* and *Night Over Taos* with *Both Your Houses.* Later on he was to combine to some extent poetic expression with satire or social commentary, as in *High Tor, Knickerbocker Holiday,* and *Key Largo.*

Both Your Houses was, I believe, the first play of any moment written by an American that dealt exclusively or largely with political crookedness in the federal government.

The central figure is not a person at all, but an appropriations bill in committee; a young idealistic congressman tries to make it relatively honest, but finding himself up against an age-old system, turns round and puts into it everything that any one seems to want, hoping to kill it through its patent absurdity. He learns, however, that this is exactly what every one wants, and wakes up to find himself proclaimed a political genius.[1]

The Anderson gift for trenchant dialogue was never put to better use, and the characterization, especially of the hard-boiled congressman, is true and convincing.

In the pursuit of new themes and methods of treatment Anderson was to return often again to the past. But neither in *Mary of Scotland* (1933) nor in *The Masque of Kings* (1937) was he to rest content, as in *Elizabeth the Queen,* with a mere exposition of the facts of history. The old stories he chose for his plots were used to express a personal attitude toward the world of today. *The Masque of Kings* in particular, remote as the tragedy of the Crown Prince of Austria now seems to us, is Anderson's vision of an old world contrasted with a new and presumably better one. Rudolph's last words, "We are all ghosts...walking the halls of Europe in a dream," point vaguely to a new dream of human dignity. Anderson rarely wrote more effective drama nor better dramatic verse than in *The Masque of Kings.*

During the first ten or twelve years of his play-writing career Anderson published little or nothing of his ideas as a writer, but during the past decade he has ventured on many occasions to formulate certain notions and theories, several of which he published in a small volume, *The Essence of Tragedy* (1939). The booklet is preëminently quotable, and should be studied by all who are curious about the workings of an artist's mind. One line only is here quoted; it best expresses Anderson's quest for beauty and some meaning in life. "A play," he says, "is almost always, probably, an attempt to recapture a vision for the stage."

High Tor (1936) is, I feel, the best example among its author's works of a play that is both vision and commentary. There is in it the nostalgia of the poet for fair things past and dead, and the anger of the citizen who sees greed personified in the unimaginative human hogs who would despoil beauty for financial gain. There is vision (and some commentary) in *Valley Forge* (1934) as well, the vision of a splendid new world seen through the eyes of George Washington; and there is vision even in *Knickerbocker Holiday* (1938), a riotous satirical fantasy in which the background is ostensibly New Amsterdam, but actually New York City, or Washington.

The Wingless Victory (1936) marks a return to the historical past, to that New England of the early 1800's when the power of the puritanical ideal was still vigorous enough to provide the basis of a tragedy of social ostracism. This simple tale of the Malay princess who marries a sea captain and suffers for daring to love a man whose traditions and prejudices forbid

---

[1] B. H. Clark, in pamphlet, *Maxwell Anderson, the Man and His Plays.*

intermarriage between white-skinned and dark-skinned races, exemplifies the dramatist's statement that a "glimpse of the godlike in man occasionally vouchsafed in a work of art or prophecy is the vital spark in a world that would otherwise stand stock still."

The Star Wagon (1937) is, on the other hand, less genuinely inspired than the other Anderson plays of the 1930 decade. It is a somewhat mechanical fantasy.

The Spanish Civil War was the direct inspiration of *Key Largo* (1939), a not too successful attempt to dramatize, in Lord Jim fashion, the workings of the conscience of a young American who in his moment of trial made a fateful decision, and in the end somehow realized that in the face of death it is enough "to win, dying."

One of the late Anderson plays seen in the theatre is *The Eve of St. Mark* (1942), a work set against two backgrounds, an American farm, and the Bataan Peninsula in the Philippines—a war play on the surface, but fundamentally a quest play in which a young soldier, seeking, like the author, an answer to the riddle that lies at the heart of most of Anderson's work, makes his decision to die that he may realize some part of that inner longing for realization that made life to him something more than mere existence.

Though not his latest play, nor in many respects the most successful as a work of art, *Winterset* may ultimately be considered the most characteristic. The play is not entirely clear in outline, and in places the poet seems to have sacrificed legitimate theatric effectiveness for the sake of expressing an idea that was a mere corollary and not an integral part of his story. Nevertheless *Winterset* was one of the very few modern American plays written in verse with an American theme and characters that won conspicuous artistic and commercial success. Says the author in his preface to the printed text:

Winterset is largely in verse, and treats a contemporary tragic theme, which makes it more of an experiment than I could wish, for the great masters themselves never tried to make tragic poetry out of the stuff of their own times. To do so is to attempt to establish a new convention, one that may prove impossible of acceptance, but to which I was driven by the lively historical sense of our day.... Whether or not I have solved the problem in *Winterset* is probably of little moment. But it must be solved if we are to have a great theatre in America. Our theatre has not yet produced anything worthy to endure—and endurance, thought it may be a fallible test, is the only test of excellence.

The latest of the Anderson plays is *Storm Operation* (1944), a heavily documented play about the invasion of Africa by the American army. It is not up to the standard set by the author in his other war plays, and lasted only a short time in the theatre.

Sidney Howard was a follower of no school or movement, though it may justly be said that he was not an experimenter or a trail-blazer. He cannot properly be classified in any one group of writers who flourished during the two decades of his activity in the theatre. Influenced by what was most admirable in the pre-1920 decade of experiment, by the European drama, and by the technical advice given him by Professor Baker, he began his work in the theatre by writing verse dramas. The first of these to reach the stage was *Swords* (1921), a clever pastiche melodrama in blank verse with an Italian Renaissance background. Though his next produced play was not to reach Broadway until three years later, he wrote several comedies, collaborated with other writers, translated and adapted three plays that attracted some notice in the theatre, and collaborated with Edward Sheldon on the partly successful fantasy, *Bewitched* (1924).

They Knew What They Wanted (1924) was the first of the Howard plays that satisfactorily expressed the man who with remarkable accuracy was to typify the eagerness of several of our writers to carry over into the theatre some feeling for or reflection of the multiplicity, color, and vigor of American life. Too intelligent to be sidetracked by political panaceas, though always an independent and sometimes a radical thinker, too mature to believe that a play can ever do much more than reflect or reveal something about life and let it go at that, and too fine an artist to add anything much by way of commentary to the situations he set forth on the stage, Howard was usually content to let his plays stand on their own feet. Life as he saw and felt it was enough for him.

Lucky Sam McCarver (1925), not quite so brilliant or incisive as *They Knew What They Wanted,* was another of his successful portraits of a vigorous full-grown set of characters such as filled the framework of the earlier play; while *Ned McCobb's Daughter* (1926) glowed with his immense enthusiasm for character as he had seen it manifested in the rural districts of Maine. *The Silver Cord* (1926), although closely approaching the thesis play, was in reality the result of a dual impulse, to register a protest against the old conventional attitude toward mother-love and (to a far greater extent) to throw upon the stage a number of living people who stood out independently as glowing and breathing human beings.

Salvation (1928), written with Charles MacArthur—and not a commercial success—was still another portrait, but only partly realized, of a woman religious revivalist. This was followed the next year by *Half Gods,* a quick failure. But here again the portrayer of living people added something incisive to the collection of human types whose characteristics never failed to capture his imagination. Howard, the impatient analyst (for the time being) of modern society, perceived what he thought to be a serious defect in the modern woman's attitude toward marriage and motherhood, and proceeded to remind her that her principal function, whether she liked it or not, was to bear and rear children.

Between *Half Gods* and the appearance of his next original play, came two adaptations from the French, *Marseilles* (1930) and *The Late Chris-*

topher Bean (1932), the first based on an original by Marcel Pagnol and the second derived from René Fauchois.

Alien Corn (1933), which had a relatively successful run with Katharine Cornell in the leading rôle, fails, for all its theatrical trappings and two effective scenes, to convince either as a portrait or as the expression of the essential truth about the relation between the artist and the world he must live in. The play does not ring true; it lacks the feeling for life and truth that is usually the outstanding characteristic of the best of the Howard plays, and the thesis which stems from it is neither important nor very skilfully set forth.

Dodsworth (1934) was another of Howard's adaptations, and one of the best. It was based, of course, on the Sinclair Lewis novel.

Yellow Jack (1934), in spite of the generous "credit line" naming Paul De Kruif as collaborator, is to all intents and purposes Howard's own play. It is one of the ablest technical feats ever seen in the American theatre. It sets forth in sufficient detail and with the utmost clarity the essential episodes in the discovery of the means by which yellow fever is carried and stamped out. Step by step the playwright has dramatized the patient search and heroic struggle in Cuba and elsewhere. This is no melodrama depending on a few pseudo-scientific incidents, but a theatrically sound and factually accurate history. The play was not a financial success in the professional theatre, but ever since it first appeared on Broadway it has been pretty constantly seen on the stages of university and community (non-professional) theatres.

Three more adaptations followed *Yellow Jack*: *Gather Ye Rosebuds* (1934), written with Robert Littell, *Ode to Liberty* (1935), and *Paths of Glory* (1935), this last a moving but commercially unsuccessful stage version of Cobb's story.

Paths of Glory deserved a better fate at the hands of the public. In no other Howard play are the author's powers of dramatic irony more clearly shown. The play sets forth an episode of the First World War which struck Howard, himself an air ace who saw active service, as admirably adapted to dramatic treatment.

The Ghost of Yankee Doodle (1937), although laid against a background of international tension that soon breaks out into war, is fundamentally a play of character. It typifies the irrepressible gusto with which Howard always approached his job of creation in the theatre. There seemed to him little reason to go beyond the limits of what he once called enthusiastic reporting, but to him reporting ordinarily meant pinning down on paper, for immediate transfer to the stage, a character or characters that would come alive in the theatre. There is in *The Ghost of Yankee Doodle* a thesis as well, but one feels that the play was written not so much to show how a certain American family reacts to the threat of war, but rather how Sara Garrison reacts to life and to James Clevenger. The play of ideas, as written by Howard and typified by *The Silver Cord* and *The Ghost of Yankee Doodle*, is usually a work dedicated to the essential humanity of its people and not to the exposition of this or that philosophy.

The Ghost of Yankee Doodle was the last play of Howard's to reach Broadway, but shortly before his death in 1939 he had practically finished a philosophical fantasy, *Madam Will You Walk*. Though put into rehearsal by the Playwrights' Company, of which he was one of the founders, this delightful work has never been seen in New York. It closed after a first showing in Baltimore—a matter of "casting difficulties."

George Kelly is one of the few important playwrights of the twenties whose career was limited almost entirely to that decade. An experienced actor and director, a man wise in the ways of the theatre, Kelly began his professional life as playwright with a finished text. *The Torchbearers* (1922), a light farce comedy ridiculing the faddists who used to organize "amateur theatricals" for the purpose of self-exploitation, is fairly entertaining and bright, but in view of the later development of the kind of groups which Kelly satirized, it now seems rather pointless.

This play was followed in 1924 by *The Show-Off*, Kelly's best play. It is my belief that this dramatized full-length portrait of an eccentric, or should we say concentric, egotist is one of the outstanding plays of the modern theatre. It stems from Molière and Dickens; it carries with it few didactic implications and conceals no "hidden" meanings. It boldly, truly, and amusingly creates a character as genuinely conceived, as complete and satisfying, as Mr. Micawber or George F. Babbitt.

Craig's Wife (1925) is patently the work of the same writer, an incisive full-length portrait, carefully drawn and skilfully revealed. The woman here is one whose epic selfishness is symbolized by her home, from which she finally drives her husband and all her friends. But *Craig's Wife* suffers by comparison with *The Show-Off* in that Kelly's predilection for moralizing shows too clearly through the otherwise realistic and credible fabric of the work. In some of the later Kelly plays, particularly in *Behold, the Bridegroom* (1929) and *Philip Goes Forth* (1931), the writer's eagerness to point a moral nearly destroys our pleasure in the presentment.

Two relatively minor plays, however, offer admirable examples of Kelly's extraordinary skill as a playwright and portraitist of the American woman. These are *Daisy Mayme* (1926) and *Maggie the Magnificent* (1929). Each reveals the hand of a man who, though familiar with the tricks of his trade, provides a minimum of plot in order that the carefully motivated and admirably articulate people may stand fully developed on their own feet as human beings.

In *Behold, the Bridegroom,* however, Kelly's determination to preach a sermon deprives us of the pleasure of watching wholly credible people, and the result is a dramatized jeremiad.

The same thing is substantially true also of the comedy *Philip Goes Forth,* which is in part an amusing play about a young would-be playwright, and partly a diatribe—very effective in itself—against incompetence in art.

No other Kelly play was produced until 1936, when *Reflected Glory* appeared on Broadway for a few months' run. A competent work, but by no means comparable with the best of the early plays. Since 1936 Kelly has not been heard from, except for *The Deep Mrs. Sykes* (1945), a deft if not very convincing character study.

Philip Barry is probably best known as a writer of suave entertaining comedies about the well-bred, the well-to-do, the sophisticated. Several of his most popular plays are indeed high comedies peopled by members of the leisure class, but no estimate of his position as an American playwright would be just if we neglected those more or less experimental works that are in many ways more important and interesting than such conventional pieces as *The Animal Kingdom* and *The Philadelphia Story*. The first of the Barry plays to reach Broadway was *You and I* (1925), an agreeable comedy about a man who retires from business to do what he has always wanted to do, paint—a theme which was to be more adroitly managed in *Holiday* (1929). *The Youngest* (1925) was another light comedy that offered no particular grounds to suppose that the author was going to do anything spectacular or unusual in the theatre. Then came *In a Garden* (1926), a remarkably subtle analysis of the psychology of the artist-intellectual, witty, sophisticated, setting forth ideas that few American audiences up to that time had been required to think about in a theatre. The same year Barry gave us *White Wings,* an original contribution to the theatrical literature of fantasy, an imaginative, tender, and lovely bit of folklore, which dramatized the era between the introduction of the horseless buggy and the day horses were superseded by automobiles. There is no telling why this beautiful play failed to attract audiences. It should be revived.

Barry's next play marked an even greater departure from the sort of smart comedy with which he had so successfully begun his career: *John* (1929) is a free fantasia on the story of John the Baptist and his relation to Jesus. The character of John, in particular, is successfully realized and depicted, and the story—partly based on the Bible narrative—holds our interest. But the play, as a result perhaps of the casting, was a failure in the theatre.

Paris Bound (1929) is in a way a comedy of manners, amusingly and brightly written and full of shrewd observation, but essentially it is the plea of a modern man (and incidentally a Catholic) against the notion that sexual infidelity is sufficient grounds for divorce, inasmuch as the institution of marriage is more important than the personal feelings of those who have accepted the sacrament.

Between *Paris Bound* and *Hotel Universe* came the pot-boiler mystery play *Cock Robin* (1928, written with Elmer Rice), and *Holiday* (1929), which have already been mentioned.

Hotel Universe (1930) was an ambitious attempt to put into drama form certain theories of the psychoanalysts. As such it commands a certain respect, but aside from the question of his success or failure as an expositor of a mass of rather questionable scientific data, is is worth while to note that Barry has managed to probe brilliantly and with considerable intuition certain obscure corners of the mind of the human animal.

With *Tomorrow and Tomorrow* (1931) he again forsook the drawing-rooms of the socially prominent to write an occasionally moving drama inspired by the passage in Kings II telling of Elisha and the Shunemite woman. Basically the play is a love story, but with overtones that seem to bear out the impression that Barry was trying to convey a message which somehow never becomes quite clear.

The Animal Kingdom (1932), a light and agreeable comedy, should be compared with the earlier attempts of American writers of social comedy if one wishes to see how far dramatic writing had developed since Bronson Howard and Clyde Fitch were considered our best exponents of the form. It deals, again, with the well-to-do, and in its moment of revelation preaches unobtrusively that a mistress may be more of a wife than a woman who wears a wedding ring.

The Joyous Season (1934) and *Bright Star* (1935) are relatively minor efforts; so likewise was *Spring Dance* (1936); but *Here Come the Clowns* (1939) marks a return to the more earnest and experimental tone of *Hotel Universe*. *Here Come the Clowns* is a parable, in which the characters are a strange collection of show folks. Not content with contriving a mere spectacle, Barry has here shown us a man in search of the meaning of life, a man who is looking for God. Dan Clancy finds it in the free will of man. For all its oddness, and its slightly perverse use of symbols, this play is an absorbing theatre piece. Much more so than *The Philadelphia Story* (1939) and *Without Love* (1942). The latest of the Barry plays to reach the stage were *Liberty Jones* (1941), an idealistic fantasy that failed to "jell," and *Foolish Notion* (1944), a suave bit of light comedy.

S. N. Behrman, like Philip Barry, has consistently brought to his work a certain distinction in the writing and a point of view that may be described as adult. Both men have looked upon the writing of plays as a means of expressing a mature and sophisticated attitude toward contemporary life, and have scrupulously tried to write dialogue that should be something more than a means of translating action into "theatre."

Behrman's first play, aside from a slight comedy written in collaboration with Kenyon Nicholson and produced in 1927, was *The Second Man* (1927), a suave and witty comedy of manners. *Meteor* (1929) was a character piece about a temperamental play producer, and *Serena Blandish* (1929) a fantastic piece adapted from a novel. This last was a wholly delightful exercise in imaginative creation.

Brief Moment (1931) marked the beginning of a series of plays that showed a mature and complicated outlook on life. To some extent nearly all the later Behrman plays presented some problem of the leisured and sophisticated in a modern world where they felt they did not belong. *Biography* (1932), for all its wit and fun, was in effect a social commentary on the radical as contrasted with the conservative viewpoint; *Rain from Heaven* (1934), one of Behrman's finest plays, dramatized the impact of pre-war Europe on a young German intellectual; *End of Summer* (1936) the passing of an earlier generation and all it symbolized, and the emergence of a new way of looking at things, and a new energy; *Wine of Choice* (1938) again contrasted two opposing philosophies; *No Time for Comedy* (1939) and *The Talley Method* (1941) were directly based upon issues raised by the Second World War.

Contrasting the work of Behrman with that of his predecessors in the United States, it may be noted that he, like so many of his contemporaries, seems somewhat uncertain whether to write what might be termed "straight" comedies laid in a world apart from the world he knows, or to try to interpret what he sees about him and seek a possible solution for the problems he knows exist. At times his evident passion for preaching gets the better of him, as in *The Talley Method,* but even when this happens he is usually able to make theatrically effective the discussions that he believes essential in the unfolding of his stories. Like Sidney Howard, he is extraordinarily skilful in making an argument part and parcel of a dramatic play. This was particularly true of *Rain from Heaven*. But even aside from his skill in revealing people in situations that set forth certain philosophical dilemmas which face the present-day intellectual, he remains a playwright who has brought the social satiric comedy in the American theatre to a high point of development.

The 1920-1930 period during which O'Neill, Rice, Anderson, Kelly, Barry, Howard, and Behrman all began writing, also saw the first plays of Robert Emmet Sherwood. His first produced play was *The Road to Rome* (1927), a high-spirited comedy about Hannibal in Italy, written in the style of the Bernard Shaw who gave us *Cæsar and Cleopatra*. It is difficult to see in this early play any sign of the mature and earnest man who was to write *Abe Lincoln in Illinois* and *There Shall Be No Night*. *The Love Nest* (1927), based on a Ring Lardner story, and *The Queen's Husband* (1928), showed technical facility and an unmistakable talent for play writing. But it was not until *Waterloo Bridge* (1930) that Sherwood could be taken seriously as a playwright who had very much to say. The play was a tender love story laid in London during the First World War. *This Is New York* (1930) was not a success: it was neither very skilful play writing nor in any serious sense a play of ideas. But in *Reunion in Vienna* (1931) acted by the Lunts with enormous success, we have one of the best of the Sherwood plays, a happy combination of character comedy and idea. Precisely as with S. N. Behrman, Sherwood concerned himself here with a decaying

European society contrasted with new forces and new ideas, yet never did the writer forget that an idea in a play has no validity unless it is made part and parcel of the characters and inexorably woven into the texture of the plot.

The Petrified Forest (1935), likewise a popular success, shows a writer rather more concerned with ideas and the desire to comment on life than he had yet shown himself in any earlier play. But this otherwise amusing and dramatic comedy leaves us a bit confused, expecting something to emerge that never quite comes to the surface. The young man who dominates the play is one of the lost generation of the twenties who sees no future in civilization and passes out of the picture with a sentimental gesture.

Sherwood was growing up with his generation. It is plain that to him a playwright's business was not alone to write entertaining stage pieces; his later works for the theatre show an increasing concern over what was happening to man in an increasingly mad world. Like Maxwell Anderson, he believes that the theatre should be a revelation. In *Idiot's Delight* (1936) the prophet and commentator in Sherwood struggle with the writer to produce a play that is heavy with implications of the imminence of world conflict, yet immensely entertaining in those parts that concern two American show people caught in the whirlpool of European politics and intrigue. Here once again, as in *The Petrified Forest,* Sherwood seems to have been unable to balance theatre with commentary.

As though to prove that he *could* function merely as a playwright, he adapted a play of Jacques Deval under the title *Tovarich* (1936), a serene and satisfactory stage piece.

In 1938 came *Abe Lincoln in Illinois*. In a way this nobly conceived drama is a declaration of faith in the democratic idea, an answer to Sherwood's own question as to how to restore the world to sanity. A simple chronicle play in many scenes, covering the years between 1830 and Lincoln's election to the presidency, there is no extraneous comment in the text, simply the implication that in the figure of Lincoln we have an imperishable example of faith and courage.

There Shall Be No Night (1940) belongs to the period of World War II. The scene is laid in Finland in 1943 (for the London production, the characters and background were changed and the scene was made modern Greece) and the chief figure is a patriotic and courageous scientist who by the same power that sustained Lincoln was able to stand up and face the legions of evil. *There Shall Be No Night* is in one sense a modern version of the Lincoln story, quietly and simply pointed in the last scene: "I have always believed in the mystic truth of the resurrection. The great leaders of the mind and the spirit—Socrates, Christ, Lincoln—were all done to death that the full measure of their contribution to human experience might never be lost."

For the past few years Sherwood has been actively engaged in war work, and presumably he has done little or no play writing. (For the record, it should be mentioned that Sherwood wrote one play, *The Acropolis,* that was publicly produced only in England, for a short run, and by a non-professional group in New York. It has not been published.)

There is clear evidence during the decade now under discussion of an ever-widening interest in science, politics, philosophy, and the arts on the part of many of those writers who managed to get their plays produced in the professional theatre. A quick glance through a few of the many *Best Plays* volumes which Burns Mantle has been publishing for a quarter of a century will show such a variety of subject-matter and treatment as to lead one to conclude that the American playwright, beginning soon after 1920, had deliberately set out to describe and interpret his country and people in as many different ways as he could possibly conceive. It is plain that any attempt to classify types of play movements and tendencies would serve only to confuse the picture. But one marked tendency can be observed, one that became manifest about 1923 or 1924, a tendency shared by several writers to use the theatre as a forum for the discussion of current problems—mostly social and political—and often with the avowed aim of pleading a cause. The desire to prove that war is wasteful, that the Negro is oppressed, that the workingman should join a union, that the bourgeoisie is selfish and useless, that the government is corrupt, that communism is preferable to democracy—all find expression in many plays of the past twenty years. It was not alone in the work of the professional radicals that such themes were treated; the theatre, in a word, reflected some of the thinking of the period.

We find in the so-called radical or left-wing drama of the 1923-1940 period a mixture of artistic methods and themes and problems not always of a wholly controversial nature. Often the radical playwright will be more interested in a new form than in a political idea, or perhaps in one play he will show himself an esthetic rebel and a political conservative; the point is that a large number of playwrights felt impelled to try new methods of presenting life, as well as new ideas.

Probably the most consistent exponent of the left-wing drama is John Howard Lawson, whose first play, *Roger Bloomer* (1923), stems esthetically from the Expressionist theatre of Germany. The play was definitely experimental, in parts odd and confused, yet strangely affecting. *Processional* (1925) was a more mature and stageworthy work, and though not completely realized, it did manage to express excitingly a part of the American scene—its tempo, its color and vigor—that had not yet been brought into the theatre. *Nirvana* (1926), *Loudspeaker* (1927), and *The International* (1928), were further proof of Lawson's eagerness to utilize new forms in drama, but it seems that the young rebel of 1923 had realized after ten years' trial that a play need not necessarily be odd or obscure in order to be effective, either as entertainment or propaganda, for in *Success Story* (1932), one of his best plays, he was apparently satisfied with character set within the framework of a conventionally well-made play. In *Gentlewoman* and *The Pure in Heart* (both of 1934) he moved still further away from the field of experiment and, like S. N. Behrman, presented the dilemma of the radical in a world not yet ready to welcome The Revolution. But his latest play, *Marching Song* (1937), marks a return to the earlier type of left-wing propaganda. In 1937 that play seemed out of date. The type of "strike, strike!" drama which it exemplified had almost disappeared from the theatre.

Concerned somewhat less with politics and rather more with character and mood was the late Emjo Basshe, whose first play, *Adam Solitaire,* was produced at the Provincetown Playhouse in 1925. Often confused and obscure, this play, like most of the others he wrote, had lyric qualities and occasional flashes of depth and beauty. *Earth* (1927) in particular, was somewhat less tortured and subjective than *Adam Solitaire,* and to this day remains one of the best of several plays about Negroes that have for over twenty years been an almost annual event in our theatre.

The novelist John Dos Passos wrote three plays in the middle twenties, of which two were produced, *The Moon Is a Gong* (later called *The Garbage Man,* 1926), and *Airways Inc.* (1929). Each is a mixture of fantasy, poetry, and political argument. The last named is especially typical of the effort made by the radicals to compress into their work the feeling for the "common man," usually the obscure laborer, and to explain the environment in which he passes his life.

Occasionally the experimenters went to extremes and produced work that was plainly beyond ordinary comprehension. Such was E. E. Cummings' *him* (sic) (1928). Charles Webster's *The Man Who Never Died* (1925), while not wholly incomprehensible, was one of the most extreme instances of experiment during the mid twenties.

Somewhat more theatrical in the conventional sense, and considerably more successful in conveying by new methods a sense of the multiplicity of modern metropolitan life were J. P. McEvoy's *God Loves Us* (1926) and Francis Edwards Faragoh's *Pinwheel* (1927).

Michael Gold's *Hoboken Blues* (1928) and *Fiesta* (1929) are, considering the author's known political convictions, strangely devoid of direct propaganda. Both are in the Dos Passos tradition, dramatic poems rather than thesis plays.

Paul Sifton's *The Belt* (1927) is less the work of an experimenter than that of a hard-headed radical determined to portray the little man caught in a trap, the trap of modern dehumanized industry. *Midnight* (1930) was not so successful either as plea or play, but *1931*—(written with his wife Claire Sifton), managed to combine with considerable skill a picture of the post-1929 depression among industrial workers and a plea for social justice.

Upton Sinclair's *Singing Jailbirds* (1928), Irving Stone's *The Dark Mirror* (1928), and Sophie Treadwell's *Machinal* (1928) were, each in its way, evidence of experimentation both within and outside the ranks of the regular left-wing theatres, of which one—the New Playwrights—existed long enough to encourage several new playwrights. With the opening of the third decade of the century the young insurgents were continuing to organize into groups, to issue manifestos, and to write plays, good and bad, following pretty closely the models that had proved most successful in Germany and Russia, as well as—more recently—in the United States.

I. J. Golden wrote an effective dramatization of the Tom Mooney case in *Precedent* (1931), and on a broader scale and with considerably more imaginative force John Wexley dramatized the Scottsboro case in *They Shall Not Die* (1934). This was the John Wexley who, as a very young man, had made his start in the theatre with the moving prison drama, *The Last Mile*, in 1930.

Stevedore (1934), by Paul Peters and George Sklar, was one of the best of the plays to come out of the Theatre Union, a left-wing group that was to operate for some time at the Fourteenth Street Theatre, which was still operating under the name of the Civic Repertory Theatre. *Stevedore* combines stirring drama, a plea for justice to the Negro, and a call for unionization as solutions for the wrongs of the southern Negro.

In 1932 Albert Maltz and George Sklar came very near proving that the political rottenness they exhibited in *Merry-Go-Round* (1932) was factually true when the municipal authorities in New York, evidently uneasy about something, caused a great deal of trouble to the management, and curtailed the run of the play. The same authors, in *Peace on Earth* (1933), again combined to good effect in dramatizing the close and vicious relationship between big industry and war.

Albert Maltz, this time alone, wrote *Black Pit* (1935), a play about coal miners which failed to attract audiences, and since that time he has practically abandoned play writing.

Albert Bein, a poet by instinct and a radical by conviction, began his sporadic career in the theatre with a tender and understanding play of adolescence, *Little Ol' Boy* (1933); followed it with *Let Freedom Ring* (1935), a violent and rather effective thesis play about North Carolina mill workers; and followed that in turn with the highly imaginative hobo fantasy, *The Heavenly Express* (1940), which makes one devoutly wish that he would leave propaganda to the prosaic-minded and devote himself wholly to poetic drama. His latest play, *Land of Fame* (1943), written in collaboration with Mary Bein, is a juvenile attempt to dramatize Greece's struggle in the world conflict.

The figure of Frederick Schlick may stand here for a fairly large number of experimental writers who for the past twenty years have been unwilling or possibly unable to learn the essential business of play construction, but who have sometimes given evidence of considerable talent and imagination. Only a single play of Schlick's has been seen on Broadway, one of at least forty on which he has worked. *Bloodstream* (1932) had a very short run, but its grim power gave promise of something which up to now the author has not fulfilled.

The man who calls himself Michael Swift gave us *Hot Pan* (1928), but he wrote another play, *The King of the Mountains,* which has often been announced but never produced. Here is another case of great talent going hand in hand with insufficient discipline.

George O'Neil, lyric poet and story writer, had just one play produced professionally (if we except *Mother Lode,* written in collaboration with Dan Totheroh), and that is *American Dream* (1933). This play, a kind of fable on the degeneration of the democratic dogma, is one of the most powerful satires yet seen on our stage, and a work of extraordinary eloquence. O'Neil had completed two other plays at the time of his death a few years ago, but he had evidently given up hope of ever having them produced. He spent the last five disillusioned years of his life in Hollywood.

A few more words here on another of the experimenters, a man of whose many plays only two have been seen on Broadway. The first of the Virgil Geddes plays offered in New York was *The Earth Between* (1929), done at the Provincetown Theatre, and the other a cycle called *Native Ground,* produced by the Federal Theatre in 1937. Geddes probably regards the theatre as an institution that is basically hostile to his intensely subjective rural tragedies, yet it is to be hoped that some of the many examples of his work that have been published may one day find the sort of director and actors who can give them sympathetic treatment.

The Negro drama, using Negro characters and dealing with themes and problems affecting the American Negro, has always been with us. Except for Boucicault's *The Octoroon* (1859), in earlier days, the Negro fared badly in the theatre, where he was used almost entirely for comic or sentimental relief. Edward Sheldon, as already stated here, attacked the most controversial aspect of the Negro problem in *The Nigger,* but there was in his play no attempt to show the Negro at home, as he really is, nor to understand his problems.

Among the first intelligent and effective treatments of Negroes on the American stage was Ernest Howard Culbertson's *Goat Alley* (1921). Another Negro play of merit was Nan Bagby Stephens' *Roseanne* (1923). (O'Neill's *All God's Chillun Got Wings* has already been mentioned and Paul Green's *In Abraham's Bosom* will be mentioned later.) Aside from Basshe's *Earth,* Frank Wilson's *Meek Mose* (1928) and Frank Dazey and Jim Tully's *Black Boy* (1926), the most glamorous Negro plays of the period were Dorothy and DuBose Heyward's *Porgy* (1927) and Marc Connelly's *The Green Pastures* (1930), which are among the finest dramatic achievements of the American theatre.

The life of the city Negro in New York was effectively set forth in the somewhat melodramatic *Harlem* (1929) of William Jourdan Rapp and Wallace Thurman.

The more tragic implications of the Negro's existence side by side with the white man are found in DuBose Heyward's *Brass Ankle* (1931), Richard Maibaum's *The Tree* (1932), and Samson Raphaelson's *White Man* (1936). Mention should also be made of such other typical works on Negro themes as Frank Wilson's *Walk Together Chillun* (1936), Hall Johnson's *Run Little Chillun* (1933), Rudolph Fisher's *Conjur Man Dies* (1936), and Langston Hughes' *Mulatto* (1935).

Paul Green, philosopher, teacher, poet, novelist, first became known in the professional theatre through his Negro folk tragedy, *In Abraham's Bosom* (1926), a Provincetown Playhouse production and Pulitzer Prize winner. In chronicle fashion this deeply stirring play was only incidentally a plea for justice to the black man; it was clearly the work of a dramatic poet inspired by the spectacle of human beings (who happened to have black skins) struggling to attain some small share in the high destiny of man in a white man's world which was determined not to allow it.

Green was a product, in part, of the inspiring work undertaken and for many years pursued at the University of North Carolina by the late Professor Frederick H. Koch, whose Playmakers' Theatre had offered chances to a large number of young writers to see their plays produced on the stage. (To Koch may be attributed to a great extent the impulse that ultimately gave our theatre some of its best folk plays.)

Green's *The Field God* (1927), revised and produced in North Carolina several years later, had a moderate run in New York. A folk tragedy about a white North Carolina farmer, this play, for all its passion and in spite of a few scenes of compelling power and beauty, lacked direction and form and, probably because the idea on which it was based never became wholly articulated, it must be set down as a tentative and relatively unsuccessful effort on the author's part.

The House of Connelly, which the new Group Theatre chose in 1931 for its first production, was much more effective. While the author used certain poetic folk material as background, the play is fundamentally a dramatic revelation of the dry-rot that is undermining the old South. Few American plays have offered so vivid a picture of human beings at odds with the life about them.

In *Roll, Sweet Chariot* (1934), a Negro play with music, we come to one of the most beautiful and original plays ever seen in our theatre. It ran in New York for only a few days. A rewritten version of the earlier (unproduced) play *Potter's Field, Roll Sweet Chariot* combined many of those elements which Green has always considered most effective in a stage play —music, pantomime, and poetry. Few plays of the modern theatre have so completely fused these elements into homogeneous form; yet in the process the dramatic poet was not quite able to render the finished work clear enough to allow the audience to understand precisely what was happening or why.

Except for an intensely dramatic short play, *Hymn to the Rising Sun* (produced by the Theatre Union in 1936), the next Green play to be professionally acted was *Johnny Johnson* (1936), another Group Theatre offering. Here again Green used music—not too effectively—but he was able to achieve great clarity in the writing. *Johnny Johnson* is an imaginative work about a soldier who seeks to reconcile the insanity of war with what he considers the sanity of man. Brooks Atkinson characterized the hero as a "natural man in a sick world."

The latest of Green's plays produced in New York was his dramatization of Richard Wright's Negro novel, *Native Son*. But because this was based on a novel, and subjected to rather drastic revision during production, it can scarcely be considered as an integral part of Green's work. Green is far too subjective a writer to be able to do his best with material other than of his own choosing and shaping.

Green's achievements cannot be properly appraised unless some account is taken of his activities in the theatre outside Broadway. He is actually much more interested in the community theatre than in any other. In one sense he fulfils the early hopes and aims of Percy MacKaye. A few of the more experimental folk dramas and poetic fantasies, too fantastic and "impractical" for Broadway, or too remote in subject-matter, have been produced by some of the country's more courageous community theatres and university groups. *Shroud My Body Down* (described by the author as "as experiment in mood and atmosphere") was tried out by the Carolina Playmakers; *Tread the Green Grass* by the University of Iowa; *The Lost Colony,* acted for several summer seasons on Roanoke Island; *The Highland Call* produced by non-professionals in Fayetteville, North Carolina; and *The Enchanted Maze,* a satire on college life, by students at the University of North Carolina.

Paul Green's position in the American theatre is in a way more important than the sum total of his plays that have been seen on Broadway. He has refused to cater to popular taste, and is content to write the kind of plays that seem most completely to express his abundant impressions of life, regardless of their appeal to any one type of play-goer. Yet when he ventures to compete with work of a more conventional character he is usually recognized by metropolitan audiences as a writer of exceptional power.

Another writer whose aims as an artist to some extent resemble those of the North Carolinian is Lynn Riggs, a child of the Oklahoma frontier, a poet who has created in his best plays the flavor of the countryside from which he got his earliest impressions. His work is lyrical, full of mood, predominantly poetic. *Big Lake,* produced at the American Laboratory Theatre in 1927, was a sensitive fantastic tragedy of youth, written in a style as distinctly imaginative as any ever used by an American playwright. The next of his plays to be done on Broadway remains his best known, *Green Grow the Lilacs* (1931), which was eight years later to reappear in the theatre as the musical play *Oklahoma*. *Green Grow the Lilacs* was a poetic fantasy combining drama, tragedy, comedy, and music, and a feeling for native speech that was at the same time highly dramatic. Riggs recaptured, without affectation or self-consciousness, the clear-skied romance and joy of the southwestern pioneer.

Shortly before the Theatre Guild production of *Green Grow the Lilacs,* Arthur Hopkins had brought out *Roadside* (1930), a hilarious folk comedy which, probably because of unwise casting or simply because the public were not ready to accept a play so naïvely charming and devoid of theatrical trickery, failed to win popular success. But there was something in this joyous piece which neither the reviewers nor any large part of the public could see; Arthur Hopkins wrote that the author had caught in it "our fading glory and left it for posterity." Hopkins' belief has in a way been justified, for during the years since its "failure" in New York it was seen over a hundred times on the stage of Jasper Deeter's Hedgerow Theatre, and in little, community and university theatres all over our land.

Russet Mantle (1936) is distinguished by graceful dialogue and a sense of high comedy, and is likewise a kind of poetic evocation of a southwest background, but it is the work of a man who has, rather regrettably, put his mind to the problems of youth in a twisted world. In a word, Lynn Riggs has in this play ceased to evoke, except incidentally, and begun to argue. Although *Russet Mantle* won a certain amount of public approval and success, it was not Riggs at his best. *The Cherokee Night* (produced in 1936 by the Federal Theatre for a limited engagement), though written some years before, was not produced in New York until 1936. It met with only limited success in a small theatre. In many respects this moody and thrilling evocation of the passing of the Cherokees (Riggs is himself partly Cherokee) is the most ambitious work he has ever undertaken. But, like Paul Green's *Tread the Green Grass* and *Shroud My Body Down,* it is probably too poetic, too subjective, and not sufficiently articulate to be effective in a theatre which must appeal to large numbers of cash patrons.

Rather more in the direction of the theatre, though again a failure so far as popular approval went, was *The Cream in the Well* (1942), a tragic, introspective study in human relationships.

Riggs wrote several other plays that never reached Broadway; some have been published, and many produced at the Hedgerow Theatre and elsewhere by nonprofessional groups. Among the most interesting and best written of these are *Sump'n Like Wings* and *A Lantern To See By. Sump'n Like Wings,* it is curious to note, was produced in a Flemish translation in Belgium, and was well received by the public.

During the 1920's a growing interest in the American scene, its physical shape and moods, its people and its dialects, its beliefs and dreams, is shown in the relatively large number of playwrights who tried to carry over certain aspects of it to the stage. Many such efforts were immature and inept, but occasionally some playwright was able to transmute his material into works that caught the popular imagination. *In Abraham's Bosom* did precisely that, and so did *Green Grow the Lilacs, Porgy, The Green Pastures,* and *The Emperor Jones.* Dan Totheroh's *Wild Birds* (1925) is another such work, one that twenty years after its brief run at an out-of-the-way New York theatre is still remembered. Hatcher Hughes, though he conducted play-writing courses at Columbia University, was able himself to write one of the most popular and distinguished folk plays of its time in *Hell Bent fer Heaven* (1924), though *Ruint* (1925), not a success, seems to be more carefully observed in the matter of characterization and not quite so conventionally melodramatic. Lulu Vollmer, in *Sun-Up* (1923), and not so successfully in *Dunce Boy* (1925) and *Trigger* (1927), also proved that it was possible to write competently for Broadway and at the same time keep something of the sincerity and charm of the primitive folk who are the basis and reason for being of such plays.

Many of the younger men and women of the twenties were ready to express with more or less honesty and skill what was familiar to them; they were determined to write out of their own lives rather than what they might "imagine" or restate from what they had read.

It is impossible to follow in any detail the varieties of subject-matter used in the typical plays of the period now under discussion, but it can be pointed out that in certain loosely defined categories were a number of playwrights who turned out work some of which is still not yet forgotten.

The 1920's were a period of discovery, discovery of an America which in some respects had long been known to poets and novelists, but sparingly used in the theatre. The small-town folk and the inhabitants of the provinces (meaning to Broadwayites any part of the country outside New York) not treated as they had been often treated in the past as stock figures for purposes of ridicule, found sympathetic interpreters in the plays of Zona Gale (*Miss Lulu Bett*, 1920, and *Mr. Pitt*, 1924); Lewis Beach (*A Square Peg*, 1923, *Ann Vroome*, and *The Goose Hangs High*, 1924); Barry Connors (*Applesauce*, 1925, and *The Patsy*, 1925); Frank Craven (*The First Year*, 1920, *New Brooms*, 1924, and *That's Gratitude*, 1930); J. P. McEvoy (*The Potters*, 1923); Lynn Starling (*Meet the Wife*, 1923); Tom Barry (*Courage*, 1928); Caroline Francke (*Exceeding Small*, 1928); Marie Baumer (*Town Boy*, 1929, and *Penny Arcade*, 1930); Elliott and J. C. Nugent (*The Poor Nut*, 1925), Dorrance Davis (*Apron-Strings*, 1930); Hugh Stange (*Veneer*, 1929); Louis Weitzenkorn (*First Mortgage*, 1929); Kenneth Webb (*One of the Family*, 1925); and Don Mullally (*Conscience*, 1924).

This list is necessarily a short one, and includes only a few characteristic names and titles. The writers were neither poets, nor prophets, nor experimenters; they were for the most part the relatively young writers who wanted not only to say something about the people they knew, and say it more or less honestly, but write plays that should be well received by the public and earn money.

A consideration of the "regulars"—the professional purveyors of theatrical fare—will show that a number of them, while turning out conventional plays to satisfy an expanding market, every so often managed to contribute some play that employed means or treated subjects which in earlier days were unfamiliar or quite unknown to play-goers. Such for instance is the case with the otherwise undistinguished William J. Hurlbut, who wrote *Bride of the Lamb* (1926) on a tragic theme that might have appealed to O'Neill. The case of Owen Davis and *The Detour* and *Icebound* has already been mentioned. And even when these regulars made no attempt to follow any particular trend of the day or to explore new fields, it was usually necessary for them to write somewhat more sincerely, and to respect the material they treated, than had been the case twenty years earlier. As I have said, the 1920-1930 period was one of expansion and experiment so far as many of the younger writers went, but a large number of regulars, young and old, experienced and inexperienced, continued to offer their wares, most of them pretty conventional samples of play writing. While Rachel Crothers and George M. Cohan, Edward Childs Carpenter and Mark Swan, Edgar Selwyn and Bayard Veiller, Booth Tarkington and Harry Leon Wilson and fifty others could be counted upon to turn out acceptable and occasionally superior plays, the newer writers (among the regulars) began to fill in the gaps left by the older generation. Among the newer figures that were to continue the traditional forms were Harriet Ford and Harvey J. O'Higgins, Paul Dickey and Charles W. Goddard, Aaron Hoffman and Jules Eckert Goodman, Samuel Shipman and George V. Hobart, Max Marcin and Frederic and Fanny Hatton.

On occasion the traditional theatre would offer some outstanding "hit," with no trace of originality or imagination, yet a play which by its very popularity must be regarded as a typical reflection of what the public recognized as essentially right. Indeed it is probable that in many cases such popularity is itself a sound criterion not alone of popular taste but of fundamental merit in the playwright's work. Here it should be noted that since Anne Nichols' *Abie's Irish Rose* (1922) appealed for years to hundreds of thousands of play-goers, it should not be dismissed as popular trash. After all, popularity in the theatre, since the theatre is a popular amusement, is *one* of the proofs of quality. It is a sign of health in the American theatre that what critics consider the "good" plays are usually just as successful as the less "good" plays: side by side with *Abie's Irish Rose* were such outstanding works as *The Green Pastures, Porgy,* and *Strange Interlude,* all "popular hits" and big moneymakers.

It was the traditional or conventional theatre that gave us Avery Hopwood and Wilson Collison's *Getting Gertie's Garter* (1921); John Colton and Clemence Randolph's *Rain* (1922); Mae West's *Diamond Lil* (1928);

Russell Medcraft and Norma Mitchell's *Cradle Snatchers* (1925); and Edward Childs Carpenter's *Bachelor Father* (1925).

Though it can be justly claimed that most writers of the 1920-1930 period were interested largely in modern themes and backgrounds, the tradition of romance and the use of historical materials persisted. Philip Moeller, one of the founders of the Theatre Guild, devoted himself entirely to the conventional historical-biographical romance, contributing three well-written comedies: *Madame Sand* (1917), *Molière* (1919), and *Sophie* (1919). Though these antedated 1920, they belong in spirit to the decade now under discussion. Except for a few adaptations of foreign plays, Moeller has done no more play writing.

Porter Emerson Browne's *The Bad Man* (1920) combined a Mexican background with satire, and incidentally offered a delightfully amusing comedy.

Arthur Goodrich, who for nearly twenty years was an occasional contributor to the theatre of comedies and adaptations, wrote one pleasant fantastic satire, *So This Is London* (1922), and one distinguished romantic drama in the grand manner, a verse drama based on Browning's *Ring and the Book, Caponsacchi* (1926), in collaboration with Rose A. Palmer.

Tom Cushing, another competent craftsman, wrote a fantasy-satire in *The Devil in the Cheese* (1926). Austin Strong, author of several fantasies and modern plays, combined romance and local color in *Seventh Heaven* (1922). David Carb and Walter Prichard Eaton wrote a chronicle play, *Queen Victoria* (1923) that was scarcely less effective than the English *Victoria Regina,* which some years later was to prove much more successful with the public. Margaret Ayer Barnes' stage version of Edith Wharton's *The Age of Innocence* (1928), an agreeable period piece, enjoyed considerable success.

Of a more experimental nature were Stark Young's *The Saint* (1924), and Don Marquis' *Out of the Sea* (1927), both more subtle and poetic than the common run of such plays, and neither a commercial success.

Edwin Justus Mayer's *The Firebrand* (1924) proved popular, but his ambitious *Children of Darkness* (1930), a far more "literary" work, did not. Mayer has striven, with partial success, to write dialogue which should be readable as good writing, but to judge from his latest play (published but as yet unacted professionally), *Sunrise in My Pocket,* he appears more interested in writing than in contriving a story to be acted on the stage.

More decidedly original in mood and technique than most plays of its kind was Kate Parsons' *The Commodore Marries* (1929), a robust comedy based on a novel of Smollett's. John L. Balderston's eighteenth-century fantasy *Berkeley Square* (1929) can scarcely be regarded as American since it was based on a novel by the Anglo-American Henry James, and had a London background; but it should be mentioned as a charming work of its kind.

In the realm of modern fantastic satire two other plays deserve mention. Both were failures, but each showed a tendency of the time. F. Scott Fitzgerald came very near creating a minor masterpiece in *The Vegetable* (1929, published 1923), and there is cause for regret that the author was not able to express himself more skilfully in the dramatic form. Channing Pollock's *Mr. Moneypenny* (1928) essayed to tell a modern parable in terms already a trifle commonplace; if this play had been produced ten years earlier it would probably have been hailed as an Expressionistic success. The same thing is true of his *House Beautiful* (1929).

One of the most satisfying plays of the time was *Alison's House* (1930), the work of the pioneer Provincetown playwright and novelist Susan Glaspell. It was one of the few genuinely American plays used by the Civic Repertory Theatre under the courageous and intelligent Eva Le Gallienne. Based on the life of Emily Dickinson, it evoked a sense of the past and re-created a mood such as few dramatists up to the time had attempted to suggest in the theatre.

Mention has already been made of the considerable advances made in the field of high comedy. The work of Philip Barry and S. N. Behrman proves that good writing and satire such as had been considered the distinguishing marks of European authors could also be found in native comedies. A few further examples are worth noting. Arthur Richman, an irregular contributor to our theatre, is noted for his early play *Ambush* (1921), though *Heavy Traffic* (1928) is a better sample of social satire. Harry Wagstaff Gribble, who has done a number of writing jobs in various capacities, wrote one engaging comedy—*March Hares* (1921)—that is still remembered. Gilbert Seldes' *The Wisecrackers* (1925) is important as a commentary, and is a good example of neat writing. Edwin Burke's *This Thing Called Love* (1928) is a kind of Shavian comedy adapted for American consumption, and Donald Ogden Stewart's *Rebound* (1929) a more or less successful adaptation of American sophistication to an American theme.

The political play, the drama satirizing big business or war, the melodrama that reflects some aspect of social upheaval—there is no one word or phrase to describe the type, and probably there is no type that any description will fit; at all events, the play that reflects the author's excitement or indignation over the state of the world is one of the relatively new things that came into our theatre between 1920 and 1930. Mention has already been made of certain plays of this type among the works of O'Neill, Howard, Rice, Anderson, and others.

Bartlett Cormack's *The Racket* (1927) was not only a first-rate gangster drama, it was a forthright exposure of racketeering. Heretofore the playwright had generally been content to hint darkly at the political higherups who were responsible for gangsterism and let it go at that: Cormack was a well-informed and courageous reporter and wrote his play with all the fervor of a muckraker. The rest of Cormack's short life was spent for the most part in Hollywood.

Another play that was partly inspired by indignation was Maurine Watkins' *Chicago* (1926), a romping melodramatic satire on the courts. Louis Weitzenkorn's *Five Star Final* (1930), one of the first dramatic satires on the press, showed a convincing picture of a sensational trial as exploited by a yellow journal. *Spread Eagle* (1927) by George S. Brooks and Walter B. Lister, was a brilliant scathing satire on war and revolution, the scenes of which were set mostly in Mexico.

Laid against European backgrounds and showing an increasing awareness of political and social trends behind the news of the day were William Bolitho's *Overture 1920* (1930) and Laurence Stallings' dramatization of Hemingway's *A Farewell to Arms* (1930).

Nearly all the plays just mentioned are characterized by a note of more or less deliberate cynicism resembling the mood created by the "hard-boiled" novelists who tried to conceal under an air of pessimism and despair a kind of pity, or even a certain amount of sentimentality. The newspaper man, a common type in most of these plays, became a counterpart of the raisonneur of the nineteenth-century European play; time and again it was through him that the American playwright directly expressed his own viewpoint. One of the best of these plays is *The Front Page* (1928) by Ben Hecht and Charles MacArthur: hard-boiled on the surface, more or less realistic in detail, full of colorful incident and highly picturesque in language, this play is basically a plea for decency and humanity. But its importance lies not so much in the idea as in the extraordinary vitality and reality of the characters.

Rather more a picture than a commentary was another newspaper play, *Gentlemen of the Press* (1928), by Ward Morehouse and several collaborators; yet here again the element of criticism was present. The law, medicine, politics, religion, each was in turn to be examined, in part, by the playwright, and each was to be more or less severely criticized.

The mystery play, with the usual mixture of comedy and melodrama, and often with at least a tinge of "purpose" or commentary, has always been with us, and the best examples during the twenties showed clear signs of skill both in dialogue and plot structure. Some of the outstanding mysteries of the period were Bayard Veiller's *The Trial of Mary Dugan* (1927), John Willard's *The Cat and the Canary* (1922), and Fulton Oursler and Lowell Brentano's *The Spider* (1927). Every season saw at least half a dozen plays of this type, and such dependable writers as Samuel Shipman, Willard Mack, Max Marcin, and John B. Hymer consistently kept alive the public's interest.

The era of Prohibition and the spectacular feats of racketeering that grew out of it stimulated the writing of a hundred plays on the subject, of which the best was probably Philip Dunning and George Abbott's *Broadway* (1926). Closely related to this in mood and subject-matter was Philip Dunning's *Night Hostess* (1928), a skilful melodrama and a picture of a small and exciting phase of metropolitan life.

The "little man" and his concerns, both the city dweller and the small-town citizen, were made the subject of many middle-class dramas and comedies, the best of which showed an increasing preoccupation with backgrounds which had hitherto been used either for purposes of broad comedy or sordid melodrama. The struggle of the "unimportant" low-salaried American, his worries over money or the attainment of prestige, precipitated the writing of several plays which deserve mention here. One early example was Frank Craven's *The First Year* (1920). Another is Maxwell Anderson's *Saturday's Children,* already mentioned. Others are Edith Ellis's *White Collars* (1925), Harry Delf's *The Family Upstairs* (1925), Daniel Rubin's *Women Go On Forever* (1927), Patrick Kearney's *A Man's Man* (1925).

Three playwrights are here mentioned who functioned for the most part during the 1920's, but did not carry on into the next decade. The most characteristic work of Zoë Akins appeared at the beginning of the period and ended in 1930. *Déclassée* (1919), conventionally English in inspiration, was a considerable success with the public. This was followed by *Daddy's Gone A Hunting* (1921) and *The Texas Nightingale* (1922), both of which were likewise conceived in the well-bred tradition, but *The Varying Shore* (1921) indicated a desire to experiment in a more original way. *The Greeks Had a Word For It* (1930) was the best play she had so far written—suave, competent, and characteristically American in form and atmosphere. It was, among other things, a satirical commentary on the kind of young woman who was once known as a gold digger. One more venture into the theatre, and a successful one, was Miss Akins' dramatization of Edith Wharton's story *The Old Maid* (1935).

Martin Flavin was one of the most successful playwrights of the period. His output was varied and he seemed to have started out knowing his business, since his first play, *Children of the Moon* (1923) was the work of a mature craftsman. Primarily a play of mood, it revealed soberly and effectively a personal drama of insanity. The romantic fantasy *Lady of the Rose* followed it in 1925; then came the fast-moving conventional routine farce, *Service for Two* (1926). Wholly different, but even more dramatically effective, was the successful drama *The Criminal Code* (1929). The same year saw also the production of the unpretentious "little-man" comedy, *Broken Dishes,* and a serious study of youth, *Crossroads*. During the thirties the versatile author of *Children of the Moon* and *The Criminal Code* made two (financially) unsuccessful attempts at symbolic fantasy, *Achilles Had a Heel* (1935) and *Tapestry in Gray* (1935). Each was an effort to use technical devices popularized by the Expressionists, and each deserved respect as an honest effort to express moods and ideas which were somewhat uncommon in the commercial theatre. Flavin wrote several other plays during the 1930's, most of them experimental in form, which never reached the professional stage. Of these the most interesting were *Amaco,* a parable of modern business and industry in a hostile world, and *Spindrift,* a deft Chekhovian social comedy of manners. The latest Flavin play to be seen on Broadway was *Around the Corner* (1936), a dramatized sermon on the economic depression. Flavin has of late years turned, with conspicuous success, to the writing of novels.

The name of Vincent Lawrence is all but forgotten today, yet twenty years ago he was considered one of the most gifted of our young writers. His forte was comedy and satire. *Two Fellows and a Girl* (1923) and *Two Married Men* (1925) were followed the next year by *Sour Grapes,* a hard-hitting domestic satire. *Among the Married* (1929) continued to arouse hope that Lawrence would ultimately write the sort of well-balanced and revealing comedy which all his earlier work had indicated he could write. But *Washington Heights* (1931) was disappointing, and from that time to this Lawrence has not been heard from, except for *The Overtons* (1945), which had a long run; but it would have been better for the author's reputation if it had never been offered to the public.

Kenyon Nicholson began his career in earnest with *The Barker* (1927), a somewhat original treatment of carnival folk in a small-town setting. This character study announced a writer of genuine gifts with an eye to the more picturesque varieties of the American vernacular as spoken by the show folk and small-time odds and ends of the human race. While several of his plays (chiefly *Eva the 5th,* written in collaboration with John Golden and produced in 1928, and *Torch Song,* 1930) are concerned with show business, Nicholson's interest seems to center upon humble people wherever they may be, to whom their own environment and concerns seem to constitute the entire world. In fact, Nicholson has been able to create what look like self-containing oases of American life, sympathetically observed and painstakingly set forth in most of his comedies and dramas. No matter what may be thought of his less successful ventures into play writing, his entire product remains a colorful contribution to the American scene. Fortunately, he is still writing, and during the 1930's, he gave us one of the most delightfully boisterous comedies of the decade in *Sailor, Beware!* (1935), written in collaboration with Charles Robinson. Two other plays, also written with Mr. Robinson, continued the line of amusing characterizations begun with *Sailor, Beware!: Swing Your Lady* (1936) and *The Flying Gerardos* (1940). Though neither was financially successful, they do indeed, together with *The Barker* and *Sailor, Beware!,* indicate an original strain in our contemporary drama and lead one to hope that the authors will explore further in the rich field they have begun to exploit.

The outline of American dramatic activity during the 1920-1930 period would not be complete without reference to a few other plays which made their mark at the time, plays that in some way indicated an advance either in workmanship or viewpoint. But it cannot be too strongly emphasized that no mere outline can do more than hint at the large number of plays written, nor more than touch upon the variety of themes treated. Playwrights appeared on the scene, wrote a play or two, and were never heard of again; some wrote one distinguished play and a dozen others not worth mentioning. Two comedies should be mentioned here: *Mrs. Partridge Presents* and *Strictly Dishonorable*. The first was the joint work of Ruth Hawthorne and Mary Kennedy and appeared in 1925. It showed great promise and an understanding of character and comedy values. Nothing else of note has come from either author. Preston Sturges' one successful play was *Strictly Dishonorable* (1929), a suave comedy which shows to what an extent the public's views on sex morality had changed since the days when *The Second Mrs. Tanqueray* and *Mrs. Dane's Defence* were looked upon as strong meat.

Gilbert Emery wrote the satirical play *The Hero* (1921), and the affecting family drama *Tarnish* (1923). Very little of moment has come from him since. James Gleason the actor should be remembered for at least two character comedies, *Is Zat So?* (1925), written with Richard Taber, and *The Shannons of Broadway* (1927). Another play which, aside from its merits as solid entertainment, should be noted as an indication of the public's altered attitude toward sex is the Floyd Dell-Thomas Mitchell comedy, *Little Accident* (1928). The late John V. A. Weaver brought to the theatre a sample of the American vernacular in *Love 'Em and Leave 'Em* (1928), which he wrote in collaboration with George Abbott.

The drawing of a rather arbitrary line of demarcation between the 1920-1930 period and the period from 1930 to the present day is not too drastic a sacrifice to one's desire for classification, since the theatre, after the stock-market crash in 1929, tended more and more to reflect the attitude of the public on most matters of common concern—economic, political, and moral. It is also true that during the past fifteen years the American drama entered a period of economic stress which reduced the number of theatres and made for a time more difficult than ever the problem of raising money to finance productions. The increasing power of all the unions and associations involved in the writing, production, acting, and exploitation of plays had, through necessity or mere greed, or a mixture of both, discouraged to some extent both writing and production. As George Freedley has recently written in an article summing up the situation,[1] the "theater has swallowed a tapeworm," the tapeworm being organized labor.

The threat, and later the actual fact, of world war also had its depressing effect, and while it inspired the production of a few first-rate plays, it also in some measure discouraged certain writers from writing at all. The problem of making a living out of the theatre (unless one happened to be a member of one of the stronger and less enlightened trade unions) drove

[1] In the *Saturday Review of Literature*.

several dramatists either to Hollywood or into other fields of writing. It was no longer possible to try out plays as they had been tried out in earlier years, simply by investing a small sum and offering two or three matinees as a kind of preview to critics and public, nor was it possible for the small experimental groups to get along on a modest budget. Ten, fifteen, or twenty years before 1940 many playwrights had been given their first chance in the theatre by groups like the Provincetown Players, the Washington Square Players, the Actors' Theatre, the Neighborhood Playhouse, and many an experimental production cost as little as $500 to $1000. Such experimentation today is impossible, with the result that the young playwright, unless he is content to write routine plays, and write them well, gets almost no encouragement. The wonder is that there are still enough of them to fill the ranks as the older men pass on. Just now (1945) there are not.

It has already been shown how the most important "regular" playwrights of the 1920 decade continued to turn out work after 1930. Nearly all of them are still alive and active, though O'Neill, for reasons which to him are entirely sufficient, has refused to release any of the several plays he has been writing during the past twelve years. Maxwell Anderson is still, after more than twenty years' activity, a regular contributor to the theatre and one of the most important contemporary writers. Until recently (when he devoted himself entirely to war work with the government) Robert E. Sherwood could be counted on for a play every season or two. S. N. Behrman, Elmer Rice, and Philip Barry have given us no reason to suppose that they are written-out or tired. Sidney Howard was in the midst of his most active period at the time of his death in 1939. And there are newcomers, some who have developed after an apprenticeship undertaken in the twenties, and others who were children when *Beyond the Horizon* was first shown in 1920. No drama can be said to have declined or even to be in eclipse which counts among its practitioners such writers as Lillian Hellman, John Steinbeck, William Saroyan, Thornton Wilder, Robert Ardrey, Paul Osborn, Howard Lindsay, Russel Crouse, Clifford Odets, Paul Green, Lynn Riggs, George S. Kaufman, Irwin Shaw, and Moss Hart—to mention only some of the men and women who are now writing.

The 1930-1945 period brings fewer new distinguished "regulars" into the ranks, though the less inspired writers, those content to furnish thrills and entertainment, are able to find audiences at all times ready to patronize their wares. The same type of farce and melodrama, mystery and domestic comedy, could be seen at any time on Broadway, and often on the road. The Avery Hopwoods and Roi Cooper Megrues and Paul Armstrongs of an earlier day were succeeded by others of their kind.

We now come to a consideration of the new writers, some of whom began work in the 1920's and some not until after 1930.

Samson Raphaelson started with a popular sentimental play of Jewish domestic life, *The Jazz Singer* (1927). His next, *Young Love* (1928), a fair success with the public, showed an unusual talent for witty dialogue and an understanding of human psychology. *Young Love* remains one of the most intelligent comedies of the American theatre. *The Wooden Slipper* (1934), a sentimental comedy set against a European background, was a commercial failure, but it proved once again the author's ability to write dialogue. In 1936 came *Accent on Youth,* a gracious, amusing high comedy about a playwright who seeks to act the rôle of a young man in love. The same year (1936) a far different play (a failure on Broadway) was seen and rejected by playgoers. *White Man,* based on a complication similar to that in Sheldon's *The Nigger,* demonstrated that the man who is today best known as a writer of high comedy was capable of writing distinguished and moving tragic drama. *Skylark,* written first as a novel and then turned into a play for Gertrude Lawrence, neatly balances pure entertainment with a timely theme. It was first seen in 1939. A later play was *Jason* (1942), suavely written, amusing, but also a revealing study of character. This play, in common with the best high comedies of Barry and Behrman, combines entertainment with social criticism of a sort. It is a revealing study of the attitude assumed by a sophisticated critic toward a creative genius whom he personally dislikes, but whose talent he is forced to recognize. *The Perfect Marriage* (1945) is Raphaelson's latest play—a failure on Broadway, it showed very little that had not been more brilliantly stated in the author's other mature work.

Dan Totheroh, still remembered for his *Wild Birds* (1923), has not been able to win popular success; the nearest he has come was with his biographical play on the Brontës, *Moor Born* (1934), the least characteristic of all his works. *Distant Drums* (1932) was a moving drama of the '49 migration; it just fell short of what it might and should have been. Another play of pioneer days, written with George O'Neil, was *Mother Lode* (1934), which ran only a few days and was quickly forgotten. *Searching for the Sun* (1936) marked a return to the mood of poetry and compassion that characterized *Wild Birds,* but it failed to attract audiences. It set forth the plight of a group of young people, "lost children," in a western hobo camp. The author, as in his first play, created in lyric mood a tender drama of youth.

Marc Connelly, whose work in collaboration with George S. Kaufman will be considered later, created in *The Green Pastures* one of the noblest poetic dramatic works of our theatre. He has not consistently contributed to the professional theatre as playwright, and only three times during the past fourteen years has his name appeared on plays as writer, and then only as a collaborator. The picturesque *Low Bridge* of Frank B. Elser, dramatized from Walter D. Edmonds' novel *Rome Haul* under the title *The Farmer Takes a Wife* (1934) brought to the theatre a delightful picture of life on the old Erie Canal in its heyday. *Everywhere I Roam* (1938), written originally by Arnold Sundgaard, and later rewritten as a work of collaboration, was a more deliberate attempt to recreate the background of American rural life, and at the same time to quicken our sense of unity as a nation. The play was laden, possibly to too great an extent, with implications of our national destiny. *The Flowers of Virtue* (1942), a sort of political "morality," lasted less than a week, but it showed evidence of considerable merit as a play of ideas.

Ben Hecht, who began as collaborator with Charles MacArthur what promised to be a brilliant career in *The Front Page,* has done little since that time, with one exception. Once he collaborated with Gene Fowler—*The Great Magoo* (1932), a sort of dramatic cartoon—and twice again with MacArthur—in *Twentieth Century* (1932), founded on an earlier play by Charles B. Millholland, and *Ladies and Gentleman* (1939), the first a high-spirited character comedy, the latter a not too inspired adaptation of a foreign original. But with *To Quito and Back* (1937) Hecht proved that without a collaborator, and using original material, he was capable of writing one of the most satisfactory plays of the modern American theatre. Though it failed to win popular success, *To Quito and Back* was a well-built, well-written study of a modern member of the lost generation who, after associating with the leader of a hopeless cause in a South American revolution, discovers what used to be called his social conscience, and realizes that in sacrificing himself to an ideal he has found some meaning in life. The same theme, doubtless inspired by the political upheaval and the Civil War in Spain, was to be used with striking effect in Anderson's *Key Largo,* Robert Ardrey's *Thunder Rock,* and Ernest Hemingway's *The Fifth Column.*

Bella (Cohen) and Samuel Spewack began with a most unpretentious comedy, *The Solitaire Man* (1926), which never reached Broadway. In 1928 came *Poppa,* and in collaboration with George Jessel, *The War Song* (1928). Their first really mature comedy was *Clear All Wires* (1932), a high-spirited and fast-moving character comedy verging on farce, and a somewhat romantic character study of an old-time American reporter in modern Russia. An ambitious study of Jewish family life, *Spring Song* (1934), revealed depths of feeling not suspected in the earlier plays. The most popularly successful of all the Spewacks' plays was another comedy, *Boy Meets Girl* (1935), a satire on the writing and making of pictures in Hollywood. The latest of the Spewack plays was *Miss Swan Expects* (1939), a mild but amusing comedy satirizing certain aspects of the publishing business. It failed on Broadway. (It was published later as *Trousers to Match.*)

Paul Osborn is a slow worker. During the past eighteen years nine plays of his, four of them adaptations of the work of others, have been seen on Broadway. His first, *Hot Bed* (1928), not a popular success, was an earnest and incisive satire set in a college background. *A Ledge* (1929) came next, and was likewise a failure in the theatre. But with *The Vinegar Tree*

(1930) came popular success. This was a gay and witty high comedy written with warmth and understanding. Somewhat more brittle and superficially clever was *Oliver Oliver* (1934). But the best and most mature of all his plays to date was *On Borrowed Time* (1938), based on the story by L. E. Watkin. The play is far more than a mere dramatization: it manages to integrate into dramatic form the quintessence of the story's magic. It treats with imagination the coming of death to an old man and his young grandson. A more original work was *Morning's at Seven* (1939), a strange and bitter satire on human futility, written apparently under the influence of Chekhov, with occasional overtones from Strindberg. A late play was *The Innocent Voyage* (1943), dramatized from Richard Hughes' novel of the same name. It failed to win popular approval, and added little or nothing to the book on which it was based. The latest Osborn play is *A Bell For Adano* (1945), a dramatization of John Hersey's novel. This was a sensitively written and reverent adaptation of a timely and moving story.

Another slow worker is Sidney Kingsley. His first play, *Men in White* (1933) was one of the most successful productions of the Group Theatre. Like all of Kingsley's other work, this drama was a serious and carefully written play of contemporary American life, effective according to the best standards of the day, and at the same time a revelation of the young author's concern over the problem of the conscientious citizen in a world of changing ethical standards. *Dead End* (1935) was even more striking evidence of his desire to exhibit social trends: aside from its striking dramatic effects, it illuminates the dark corners of metropolitan slum life which breed juvenile delinquency and encourage crime. *Ten Million Ghosts* (1936), more imaginative and ambitious in scope, was evidently inspired by recent newspaper revelations of the double-dealing of the great international munitions manufacturers. The result is somewhat confused. The play lasted only for a short time in the theatre. *The World We Make* (1939) was a dramatization of a novel by Millen Brand, and shows far less social purposefulness than any of his other plays; it is primarily a study of character. *The Patriots* (1943) is a historical play based on the life of Thomas Jefferson during the most critical decade of his life.

Rose Franken, short-story writer and novelist, made her first appearance as a playwright with *Another Language* (1932), a pleasant but not particularly brilliant or novel family comedy in the well-worn tradition, and it was another ten years before she was to write again for the stage. Her second play was *Claudia* (1941), a mature, "ingoing" and brilliant study of the sex life of a young married woman. It would be hard to name another American comedy of its time that so clearly shows the extent to which the play-going public has now become accustomed to accept a frank and sincere analysis of the social and ethical implications of sex in modern life. Mrs. Franken's interest in the more scientific aspects of sex abnormality, already evident in at least one of her serious novels, is also shown in her far less successful and somewhat confused play, *Outrageous Fortune* (1943). Another play, *Doctors Disagree* (1943) was seen the same season. It is her weakest, a conventional and generally unconvincing comedy. *Soldier's Wife* (1944), a popular success, was entertaining and competently written.

If Leopold Atlas had persisted in developing the talent he showed in the two early plays that have been professionally produced, he might have taken an honored place among the major figures of our theatre. *Wednesday's Child* (1934) was a promising work—a tender and moving study of an adolescent boy deprived of his home when his parents go their separate ways. In *But for the Grace of God* (1937) the social intent, strong as it is and obviously as it is pointed, is not so obvious as to obscure the basic human warmth of the story. Both plays, however, remain rather as evidence of promise than anything else.

It is interesting to note that the exemplars of "purpose" drama during the 1930-1940 decade have not to any great extent been very closely associated, or for very long, with any of the organized class-conscious theatre groups. This was first because the larger and more influential organizations had by the middle of the decade ceased to exist, and the others were for the most part sporadic groups often formed by one person and for the purpose of producing a single play, which almost always failed to attract a public. Besides, the newer writers interested in treating themes of political and sociological significance were too independent-minded—in a word, too conscientious as artists—to ally themselves for long with any one "movement."

The outstanding playwright in what would a few years before have been called the left-wing movement, was Clifford Odets. Influenced to a great extent by the Group Theatre, with which he had acted, and encouraged by its sympathetic members, he created considerable stir when early in 1935, within a month's time, three of his plays were produced. The somewhat extravagant praise of one New York critic—"Mr. Odets' talent for dramatic writing is the most exciting to appear in the American theatre since the flaming emergence of Eugene O'Neill"—was echoed throughout the critical world, and the young playwright was for two or three years the white-haired boy of the American drama. The three plays in question were *Awake and Sing!*, full-length, and *Waiting for Lefty* and *Till the Day I Die*, both of them relatively short. Odets was clearly a talent, and he knew the fundamentals of his business. The long play was an honest and on the whole convincing study of a middle-class metropolitan Jewish family. Of the other two, *Waiting for Lefty* was an exciting if rather confused episode inspired by a recent taxi-drivers' strike, and *Till the Day I Die* the first (I think) of the plays in our theatre to dramatize the underground anti-Nazi movement in Germany, which—as it now appears—was probably nonexistent.

Paradise Lost (1935), which followed the three earlier plays by only a few months, was a more mature attempt to interpret the phenomena of what one critic called "the decay of the middle class." It was, as a matter of fact, another picture—like *Awake and Sing!*—of one localized phenomenon of American life, strictly limited by the author's own background, and having little to do with American life as a whole. However, it would be unfair to accept as a statement of the author's own intention the interpretations of his critics or well-wishers. *Paradise Lost* is essentially a pretty effective character study, an exposition of humanity rather than a commentary or a criticism. Nearly two years later came *Golden Boy* (1937), further evidence that in spite of his social conscience Odets was primarily an artist seeking to reveal what he saw of the life about him. The play is clearer in outline than *Paradise Lost,* and rather less concerned with what is said to have been the writer's intention in the first play ("a modern allegory"). It is ostensibly the struggle of an artist who becomes a prize-fighter in order to gain material rewards, and who meets his death because he is unable to avoid compromise. As in the earlier plays, Odets shows once more his grasp of character and his ability to write supple and rhythmical dialogue.

With *Rocket to the Moon* (1938) Odets showed himself so little concerned with social criticism that when he published the text he evidently considered that a preface was unnecessary: it is the only one of his early printed plays that has been allowed to stand on its own feet in this respect. Read into it as they may such symbolism or significance as they will, the Odets idolaters have found it a little hard to see in this fine and human play much beyond its simple story of a woman in search of a man who can give her the love and sympathy she is so ready to return. *Rocket to the Moon,* not so successful or so highly praised as the earlier plays, is in most respects the clearest and most dramatically effective.

With *Night Music* (1940), however, Odets enters what seems to be a kind of middle period of his development, and it is not, I think, without meaning that here again he permits an explanatory preface to introduce the printed text. Harold Clurman's introduction, nevertheless, does clarify (officially, we assume, since it was he who played a large part in producing the Odets plays) what the author's intentions were. Mr. Clurman says that *Night Music* stems from "the basic sentiment that people nowadays are affected by a sense of insecurity," and that they are homeless. True, in a limited way, and especially true of certain present-day city dwellers who are apt to generalize from restricted evidence. In this sense *Night Music* does clearly dramatize a sense of homelessness, especially the homelessness of the man who is looking for evidence from which to deduce certain social "laws"; but in a broader sense *Night Music* is the result of very special, local, phenomena; it seems somewhat remote, and the sense of tragedy far from impressive. It has not the (relatively) broad appeal of

Awake and Sing! which, although it deals specifically with Jews in one locality, touches a responsive chord even among those who are not familiar with the people treated. In a word, *Night Music* leaves one with a sense of the author's skill in setting forth a human predicament, but also a sense of Odets' own frustration, which is neither universal nor sufficiently typical.

The latest Odets play (aside from a foreign play which he adapted with S. N. Behrman in 1943), is *Clash by Night* (1941), which offers a curious parallel to *Rocket to the Moon*. It lacks the relative clarity and serenity of the earlier work. Its social implications are neither obvious nor particularly important; there is in it a seemingly deliberate attempt to create a somber mood not unlike the atmosphere of some of the old plays produced by the Berlin Freie Bühne. Though *Clash by Night* is the latest of its author's plays to be produced, aside from the adaptation above mentioned, it seems to mark the beginning of a new departure. In the preface to a volume of his first six plays Odets says that much of his "concern during the past years has been with fashioning a play immediately and dynamically useful as well as psychologically profound," and that we are living in a time "when new art works should shoot bullets." He implies that the period of shooting bullets may be past and that possibly his future work may not be as "dynamically useful" as were the earlier plays. A talent for revelation lies buried somewhere in Odets, revelation which need not, should not, be devoted to marksmanship. The author of *Waiting for Lefty* has begun to grow up.

A contemporary of Odets, less active but equally gifted, eager to dramatize his youthful and passionate feelings about man and society, is Irwin Shaw. His first play, *Bury the Dead* (1936) is a deeply felt dramatic fantasy, emotionally moving and eloquent, about the "war that is to begin tomorrow." It shows six dead soldiers who refuse to be buried until they have aroused the living to a sense of the horror and waste of war.

Siege followed in 1937, dramatizing an incident of the Spanish Civil War. Conceived as a heroic tribute to a band of Loyalists, the play somehow fails to ring true, possibly because the young author, like Odets, was over-eager to persuade his audience to take immediate action on a current issue. If Shaw had written nothing more for the theatre than the two plays just mentioned he would have been forgotten among the dozens of others who shot their little bullets after enjoying a short spell of popularity. But Shaw, like certain others of his day, has matured. He realized that shooting bullets was all very well on occasion, but he perceived that the targets were constantly changing.

The Gentle People (1939) was produced with considerable popular success by the Group Theatre. Shaw calls it "a Brooklyn fable," and in a note in the printed book he says, "This play is a fairy tale with a moral. In it justice triumphs and the meek prove victorious over arrogant and violent men. The author does not pretend that this is the case in real life."

The note throws a curious light not only on Shaw but on many of the "tendency" writers of his day: it seems to suggest shooting, but with the implication that probably the "bullets will not prove effective." A fable *The Gentle People* is, and there is an unmistakable moral, but the interesting point is that the play can stand free of any implication, as an independent and imaginative presentment of life. You may, if you like, interpret it as a clarion call to the downtrodden peoples of the earth to arise and rebel, but this is no more necessary to its understanding than it would be to add to *Hamlet* an exhortation to know one's mind and exert one's will. The fact is that *The Gentle People* is a heartwarming story of two elderly men who are driven to turn upon and destroy a racketeer who almost succeeds in destroying them. The artist in Shaw has definitely superseded the preacher.

Retreat to Pleasure (1940) is a curious interlude between plays of far greater moment, though it shows the writer's evident intention to widen the field of his interests. Confused and obscure as parts of this satirical comedy are, it is none the less, like *The Gentle People,* a step in the direction of drama as revelation, and away from drama as an instrument of social reform.

Sons and Soldiers (1943) is further proof of this, though it is not nearly so good a play as *The Gentle People*. It ran in New York for less than a month. Though the technical means used are those of fantasy, the play is at bottom simply the setting forth of the optimistic "constructive" theme that life is worth living in spite of everything. An expectant mother learns that if she bears the child that is stirring within her she will probably die. In a series of visions she lives through twenty-five years of her future life, sees what her sons will (or may) become, and even though they turn out, in her vision, to be far from what she had hoped, she chooses without hesitation to take the risk.

Shaw's latest play, *The Assassin* (1945), was first seen in London.

Lillian Hellman, whose first play, *The Children's Hour,* was produced in 1934, cannot be said to belong to any group, although all her later plays reveal purposeful qualities. *The Children's Hour* is an effective study in evil, pure and simple, largely unrelated to the life of our time; for this reason it breathes an almost classic coldness. It is pure theatre. To what extent the author may have practised the art of play writing before 1934 is not known, but *The Children's Hour* is in some respects a mature work.

It was followed by *Days to Come* (1936), a failure with the public. Here the writer comes close to the radical formula, using as she does a strike as the motivating force of a strong and occasionally effective drama. Though the moral is pointed and the meaning of the social struggle clearly shown, the author maintains throughout an attitude of partial aloofness, as though she were undecided whether to preach or simply to reveal.

The Little Foxes (1939) is in most respects the most completely satisfying of Miss Hellman's five produced plays. Its sociological implications are there for those who are looking for them, and they are clearly marked, but they need not, indeed cannot, be reduced to a formula. The play is an incisive and brilliant picture of the savage greed of a Southern family, intent upon seizing power from any one weak enough to yield in to them. Devoid of ethical scruples or social conscience, both the strong and weak in this play are in turn victims and aggressors in a struggle which marks the final stages in their degeneracy. At the very end the author seems to relinquish her hold and momentarily to step into the picture with an upraised finger of warning.

Miss Hellman's technical proficiency has often been noted, but it should be added that her skill in dialogue, her flair for suggesting the inner compulsions of her people without indulging in the "fine manner," is extraordinary.

Watch on the Rhine (1941), ostensibly the story of a liberal German and his struggle with a Nazi agent-informer, is much more than an exposé of Nazi villainy. Using a more or less ready-made dramatic situation, she has turned it into a hero play with almost romantic overtones. Yet behind or beyond the hero-worship to which the character of Kurt so easily lends itself, is the author's clear and ever-present desire to say something. As Miss Hellman declares in the preface to *Four Plays*,[1] "I am a moral writer, often too moral a writer, and I cannot avoid, it seems, that last summing up. I think that is only a mistake when it fails to achieve its purpose, and I would rather make the attempt, and fail, than fail to make the attempt."

And yet Miss Hellman seems to be learning that to sum up, literally to point her moral, is a sign of weakness. Even in her latest play, *The Searching Wind* (1944), which is a pronouncement on the futility of political appeasement, the play itself, despite a good deal of preaching, seems to convey nearly all that is necessary, and the implications remain properly implied. The less the author feels called upon to point (provided the play itself is articulate according to its own logic) the more effective will the basic idea, the preachment if you will, become. Despite her moral bias, and her decidedly Communist sympathies, Miss Hellman promises to write plays that may be even more effective and moving than any she has yet given us, because among other things she is learning that social criticism is useful largely to the extent to which it is not added to, but inherent in, the works which attempt to drive it home.

Another writer whose career so far coincides with Lillian Hellman's is Robert Ardrey. If he had begun a few years earlier (his first play, *Star-Spangled*, was seen in 1936), he might have belonged to one of the many doctrinaire groups, but like Miss Hellman, he preferred to develop his talent as an independent. And this in spite of the fact that two of his four plays were brought out by the Group Theatre. The first of his plays,

[1] Lillian Hellman, *Four Plays* (New York, The Modern Library, 1942).

mentioned above, showed very little aside from amusing characterization. Then, within a very short period, two of his plays were brought out by the Group Theatre: *Casey Jones* (1938), and *Thunder Rock* (1939). *How to Get Tough About It* (1938) was produced under another management. All three failed in New York, though the last-named, in somewhat revised form, opened in London in 1940, where it had a long and successful run. In further revised form, a short time after, it was published and released to nonprofessionals in the United States and has since then been widely used by the community and university theatres.

There are few playwrights so widely known and highly regarded who have had so little popular success as Mr. Ardrey. *How to Get Tough About It* and *Casey Jones* showed ingenuity and a decided sense of character values, but somehow failed to stand squarely on their own feet, but *Thunder Rock,* even in its earlier form, was marked by unusual skill. It was clearly the work of a "moral writer," a play which was deliberately shaped (in the words of Galsworthy) into a "spire of meaning." A fantastic and imaginative fable about a young man who, facing the prospect of world disaster and having become disillusioned over the futility of a struggle to prevent it, *Thunder Rock* shows its "hero" retiring from the world, only to emerge once again with renewed faith in the power of man to rise from the wreck of his own disillusions. The precipitating motive in this play is a belief that man can somehow shape his own destiny. But instead of arguing and exhorting, the dramatist adopts a subtler method, sending his chief character back into the history of man's earlier struggles, and from the midst of an imagined experience of nearly a century ago his hero learns what can be done and how he is to do it.

In the summer of 1935 the Federal Theatre Project was established by the government under the Works Progress Administration, with Hallie Flanagan in charge. As Mrs. Flanagan pointed out in the introduction to a collection of *Federal Theatre Plays,* the theatre project came into being because the "government... took the position that the talents of these professional theatre workers, together with the skills of painters, musicians, and writers, made up a part of the national wealth which America could not afford to lose." The importance of the Project, so far as playwrights were concerned, lay in the opportunity that was given for trying out plays that had hitherto been considered too experimental, and the encouragement given writers to turn out work that would use actors, scene designers, and musicians who had to be employed in order to comply with government regulations. In other words, the Project was from an official viewpoint a social and economic necessity, and it was up to the theatre people to make the best use of what was given them. It was up to the directors to use a national crisis for the purpose of doing something interesting and useful for the theatre: whatever came out of the experiment aside from relief was all to the good. In spite of regulations and political interference, of problems different from and in many cases more trying than any commercial manager had ever had to face, the Federal Theatre was a success. Much of what it acomplished lies outside the scope of the present volume, and it may be that what was done to stimulate directing, acting, scene designing, and above all to attract vast audiences which had before been kept away from the legitimate theatre, was more valuable than what the playwrights achieved, but the playwrights did indeed have many chances to try out new forms and means of production that could not otherwise have been possible. By the very terms of the federal grant it was not possible to exclude from the theatre much that was shoddy and incompetent, but it cannot be denied that during the four years when the Federal Theatre functioned an immense number of playwrights, some of them established and some new, had a chance to express themselves freely and in an infinite variety of forms. The folk playwrights and the propagandists, some of them without dramatic talent and some with, the soap-box orators who had never had a chance to preach from the stage, could call in large crowds of players, a full orchestra and loud-speakers to spread their gospels; the eager young men and women, many of whom had not learned the tools of their trade, were often able to see what was wrong with their scripts. The project was alive, and in spite of everything that gets in the way of such wholesale efforts to handle large numbers of people, real progress was made. Without distinguishing between those plays that came into existence because of the Project and those that had already been written but remained unproduced, it is worthwhile to remind ourselves that to the Federal Theatre we owe productions of E. P. Conkle's *Prologue to Glory* (1938); the Sinclair Lewis-J. C. Moffett *It Can't Happen Here* (1936); Theodore Pratt's *Big Blow* (1938); the Mike Gold-Michael Blankfort *Battle Hymn* (1936); Lynn Riggs' *The Cherokee Night* (1936); Frank Wilson's *Brother Mose* (1936); Harold A. Clarke and Maxwell Nurmberg's *Chalk Dust* (1936); Orrie Lashin and Milo Hastings' *Class of '29* (1936); and Virgil Geddes' *Native Ground* (1937). But the best-publicized play-writing product of the Federal Theatre, which grew out of the ideas galvanized by those who ran it, was the so-called Living Newspaper. As Mrs. Flanagan tells us, a Living Newspaper was simply the dramatization of the "news with living actors, light, music, movement." The same thing had been done before both in Germany and in Russia, sometimes effectively and sometimes not so. The Federal Theatre productions in this country were occasionally exciting, and came to us as novelties; certainly the enthusiasm of the writers and actors, some of it stimulated rather by the subject-matter than the means of treatment, helped put over certain productions that would not otherwise have attracted the general public.... *One-third of a Nation* ... (1938), by Arthur Arent; *Triple-A Plowed Under* (1936), by an editorial staff under the same author; and *Power* (1937), also by Mr. Arent, were the most successful Living Newspapers. These were timely works, brilliantly produced and occasionally dramatic; the same thing is true of Arnold Sundgaard's *Spirochete* (1938), called "A History," but in reality a sort of Living Newspaper. Each of these products was really a bit of special pleading set forth in many scenes and usually with a commentator to supply action which in an ordinary play would have been woven into the plot by what a conservative would call "dramatic technique." When all is said, indeed, it seems fair to hold that the Living Newspaper lives generally just as a newspaper lives, so long as the immediacy of the news has any appeal to the reader. The technique employed is too often, but of course not always, a frank confession that the writer cannot turn out a play that will stand solidly on its own feet.

In midsummer of 1939 the Project was brought to an end by act of Congress. There were political reasons for this, all of which were not entirely based on the fear of "radicalism" so often charged against the directors, but whatever the motives that drove Congress to withhold further funds, most of us feel that this was a mistake. However, the solid accomplishments, social as well as artistic, of the Federal Theatre Project are known and their effects were widespread and beneficial.

Not to be classified under any of the clearly marked categories is the novelist Thornton Wilder. Better known for some years as the author of *The Bridge of San Luis Rey* and other works of distinguished and delicate fiction, Wilder had none the less tried his hand at plays—adaptations, one-acters, and the like—before he offered his best-known and most successful original play, *Our Town,* in 1938. In the middle twenties his *The Trumpet Shall Sound,* a play with a Civil War background, had been put on by students in a metropolitan dramatic school; in 1932 he adapted Obey's *Lucrèce* for Katharine Cornell, and in 1937 made another adaptation, *A Doll's House,* for Ruth Gordon. In 1938 a more or less original comedy, *The Merchant of Yonkers* (though inspired by a nineteenth-century Austrian original), had a short run.

Our Town, remote from current politics and controversy, serene with the serenity we commonly associate with certain ancient classics, looked like a deliberate attempt to create a sense of all that was abiding and safe in American life; even though it proved to be, at bottom, a mournful and pessimistic setting forth of the doctrine that life cannot be wholly savored by the living. The play tells the story of a woman who dies and comes back to the scene of her girlhood where she learns, too late, that the happiness of life had not been prized as highly as she should have prized it. She returns to the grave. "We don't have," in life, she remarks, "time to look at one another...I didn't realize." The folks on earth, while they are living, "don't understand much, do they?"

The Skin of Our Teeth (1942) is a far more ambitious play, and perhaps for that reason it lacked the wide appeal of *Our Town.* Yet at bottom this fantastic fable is as simple and devoid of controversy as the earlier play. It dramatizes, stylistically, the everlasting aspiration of man over the short period during which he has been able to learn something of his history. In the words of John Anderson, "humanity is as indestructible as his hopes ... from the glacial age up to right now, man is forever improving himself and eternally falling in ruins, forever building and tearing down, but ... somehow ... he manages to survive."

This idea is dramatized not only with considerable skill but in a spirit of high comedy and boyish glee which remind us of the lusty theatrical pronouncements of William Saroyan.

For over a quarter of a century George S. Kaufman has been in the public eye as a practicing playwright, and in every case but one as collaborator. He has had a hand in over a score of plays, musical comedies, and revues; he has functioned as director, producer, credited and uncredited play doctor, and on occasion even as actor. To segregate and appraise precisely or even approximately what he has in each case contributed to each venture he was connected with would be impossible: two of his collaborators, Marc Connelly and Moss Hart, have won success either alone or with other collaborators, while two others, Alexander Woollcott and Edna Ferber, have done no play writing of their own with any degree of success. Kaufman's sole venture alone, *The Butter and Egg Man,* was not particularly brilliant.

His first produced play, *Some One in the House,* was a work of collaboration which appeared in 1918. But it was not until 1921 that he really arrived as a successful writer. *Dulcy,* written with Marc Connelly, was a light comedy of character, marked by considerable theatric skill and signs of that wit which was later on to be the hallmark of Kaufman's best work. *To the Ladies* (1922), and *Merton of the Movies* (1922), both also the joint work of Kaufman and Connelly, were neatly contrived light comedies. But with *Beggar on Horseback* (1924), also written with Connelly, something new and fresh came into our theatre. Based though it was on a contemporary German play, *Beggar on Horseback* was the first genuinely native satire of its kind that, without heat or apparent moral indignation, attempted to expose the barren machine-age efficiency that had to some extent become a religion to Homo Americanus. Using just a hint from the recently popular technical experiments of Expressionism, the authors contrived a highly entertaining fable showing, through a dream, how a young composer sold himself to a rich wife and almost lost his artistic integrity. The dream technique was not particularly original (the same device had been used in *The Poor Little Rich Girl*), but the satiric intent of the piece, with its impish insistence upon the serio-comic ritual of big business, assuredly was. Even as late as 1924 the theatre was apparently not considered a proper place to question the sacred aims and procedures of Big Business.

But it should be noticed that the playwrights attacked their problem not as reformers but as artists—or shall we say as tolerant and intelligent gentlemen who could smile at fatuity and "kid" the theology of Success.

Beggar on Horseback was, unfortunately, the last play on which Kaufman and Connelly collaborated. But the following year, 1925, Kaufman tried his hand alone, with *The Butter and Egg Man,* a pretty amusing comedy on show business, based largely on the old Cohan formula.

Meantime (1924) Kaufman and Edna Ferber made a play, under the title of *Minick,* from Miss Ferber's story of *Old Man Minick:* a competent job, a big theatrical success, and a pleasant bit of characterization.

Following *The Butter and Egg Man* came *The Good Fellow* (1926), written with Herman J. Mankiewicz, a quick failure.

And again, in 1928, another collaboration with Miss Ferber, *The Royal Family,* a glamorous and successful character comedy about the Barrymores.

June Moon (1929), the work of Kaufman and Ring Lardner, was a familiar type of routine comedy about singers. It had a long and successful run.

The Channel Road (1929), based on Maupassant's *Boule de Suif,* and *The Dark Tower* (1933), both written with Alexander Woollcott, were fairly adept jobs in construction, the latter being an amusing variation on a plot already treated by Molnár in *The Guardsman.*

Dinner at Eight (1932), another play written with Miss Ferber, presented a basically serious theme in terms of drama. Using many scenes after the manner of the Expressionists, the authors attempted, with considerable success, to make their commentary on the idle rich and socially ambitious something more than routine drama.

First Lady (1935), written with Katharine Dayton, is a satirical comedy in the best Kaufman manner. Using contemporary Washington society as background, the authors dramatized certain personal aspects of Capitol politics by using the quarrel of two women over a cook to show how trivialities may closely affect the nomination of a presidential candidate.

Stage Door (1936), which Kaufman wrote with Miss Ferber, is a comedy of character with a serious and somewhat idealistic strain running through it. It shows a group of young women in a theatrical boarding house all intent on becoming actresses. The story centers round one young woman who determines to stick to the legitimate stage rather than give in to an easier and more profitable career to be found in motion pictures. There is a good deal of genuine observation in this play, and in its idealistic treatment of youthful courage it resembles to some extent the other plays of theatre life (*The Fabulous Invalid, Merrily We Roll Along,* and *The Royal Family*) with which Kaufman has been associated.

The best of the later Kaufman plays are those written pretty regularly between 1930 and the present time with the considerably younger Moss Hart. The first of these was the high-spirited satire *Once in a Lifetime* (1930), a masterpiece of its kind and one of the most entertaining commentaries ever devised on the ridiculous excesses which, it seems, are a necessary part of the motion-picture industry. It is curious—and probably a healthy sign—that this play, like *Stage Door,* was bought by a picture company, and turned into a film.

In 1934 Kaufman and Hart produced *Merrily We Roll Along,* in intention at least the most serious play which either of them had been associated with as writers. It was this play more than any other that caused some critics to complain that the talents of these writers, so considerable in light comedy, had not been devoted to work of greater significance and depth. *Merrily We Roll Along* exhibits the career of a gifted young playwright who is spoiled by material success and popular acclaim. In intent the play is a plea for the integrity of the artist in a society which seems almost deliberately to try to deflect him from his highest aims.

In some ways the light and unpretentious comedy *You Can't Take It with You* (1936) is the most successful work of Kaufman and Hart. This immensely popular piece, devoid though it is of any directly stated philosophy, happens to sum up something of that American spirit of tolerance and happiness that seems to set the American middle class apart from all other peoples of the earth and give impulse and direction to what we loosely term the benefits of democracy.

In the *Fabulous Invalid* (1938) the writers constructed—the word is deliberately chosen—an elaborate spectacle which dramatized the life cycle of a playhouse and demonstrated that drama, like life itself, manages to persist and perpetuate itself in spite of everything that seems to conspire to kill it. The play failed (ironically enough) to attract the paying public.

The next of the Kaufman-Hart plays was another spectacle, *The American Way* (1939), a panoramic presentment of the epic tale of the European immigrant who comes to the United States with his family in pursuit of liberty, political and economic, and remains to contribute his generous share toward creating a land which is still, in spite of everything, a haven of refuge for the oppressed.

The Man Who Came to Dinner (1939), one of the most brilliant of the Kaufman-Hart successes, is one of the outstanding character comedies of our native stage. Based on the half-legendary figure of the late Alexander Woollcott, this outrageously grotesque play offers the spectacle of an almost medieval individualist at odds with a conventional middle-class family. An impishness, born of high spirits, pervades the work, taking it out of the realm of the immediately real.

George Washington Slept Here (1940) is far less elaborate and sophisticated, and in spite of the authors' inborn metropolitanism, it treats somewhat sympathetically, and with a wealth of comic incident, the universally human desire of the average man to possess a "place of his own" in the country. This is the latest of the Kaufman-Hart plays.

Mr. Hart has done well on his own, with *Lady in the Dark* (1941), an elaborate spectacle with music, and with *Winged Victory* (1943), the latter a carefully documented chronicle play showing the evolution of an aviator in training and combat. Neither play, however, though each has qualities and merits not present in the joint work of Hart and Kaufman, is characterized by the extraordinary wit and peculiarly individualized humor that made *Once in a Lifetime* and *You Can't Take It with You* the minor classics they are.

The latest play with which Kaufman's name is associated is *The Land Is Bright* (1941), which he wrote with Edna Ferber. This ambitious drama somehow failed to win popular success on Broadway, though it has been frequently produced by the larger community theatres of the country. A sort of chronicle history of the rise and progress of a wealthy American robber baron and his family during three generations, it is an effective drama and an interesting bit of social history.

No consideration of the work of either Kaufman or Hart would be complete without at least passing mention of several musical comedies, revues, and satires with music. The most important of these are the musicals in which Kaufman has had a hand, though one of them, *I'd Rather Be Right* (1937), is the joint work of Kaufman and Hart. This contemporary satire on the New Deal marked a successful attempt to focus attention on the political scene, and remains (with one exception) the most successful play of its kind in the American theatre. The exception is *Of Thee I Sing* (1931), which Kaufman wrote with Morrie Ryskind. This was probably the first and surely the best musical satire ever written on American politics.

The work of Kaufman as play doctor, uncredited collaborator, and even producer can only be mentioned here. There are at least half a dozen popular successes, unsigned by him, on which he received (and deserved) an author's share of the royalties.

Among the playwrights who were in some way influenced by, or at least who wrote in the vein of Kaufman, both as creators of wit and purveyors of social satire, must be mentioned Clare Boothe who, after an unsuccessful start with *Abide With Me* (1935), won remarkable success with *The Women* (1936), an incisive satire on the well-to-do idle rich. *Kiss the Boys Goodbye* (1938) satirized again the sophisticates, and was characterized by a metropolitan brand of smartness. Her latest produced play was *Margin for Error* (1939), a combination of satire on the Nazi official mind, and comedy-mystery melodrama. Clare Boothe, as Mrs. Henry R. Luce, has evidently given up the theatre to pursue a political career, but it is hoped that she will resume work as a playwright, and develop those limited if genuine talents she has already shown in her three successful plays.

More consistently successful as practical purveyors of comedy and satire are Joseph Fields and Jerome Chodorov. Their first play, a serious study of young people, was *Schoolhouse on the Lot* (1938), which had only a short run. Far different in conception and finish was *My Sister Eileen* (1940), a slight but continuously entertaining character comedy based on the Ruth McKinney stories. Here, as in some of the Kaufman-Hart plays and in two of the Clare Boothe comedies, the peculiar metropolitan type of wit already mentioned is at its heyday. *Junior Miss* (1941), based on the Sally Benson stories, depended rather more on character observation, and gives reason to hope that Fields and Chodorov will again try their hand at interpreting life through people rather than comic situations.

The *Doughgirls* (1942) was signed by Fields alone. This fast-moving farce satire is a clever and wholly metropolitan bit of high-spirited fooling laid in wartime Washington.

Approaching the end of our chronicle it becomes more difficult to classify playwrights and even to touch upon technical or psychological tendencies; and again, as already noted, playwrights refuse to write and produce their plays in proper chronological sequence. Though it is not possible or advisable to catalogue all the dramatists of any one era, there are certain recent writers who, either apart from or well within, some current of dramatic writing, must be mentioned.

The two plays of the novelist John Steinbeck are far too important to be noted incidentally. In the past eight years Steinbeck has offered to the theatre only *Of Mice and Men* (1937) and *The Moon Is Down* (1942), both of them dramatic versions of his own stories. Each is marked by extraordinary theatric skill, neither showing any evidence of having been dramatized in the usual way. In fact, it has been said that both were first written as plays.

Of Mice and Men is a somber and most impressive character drama about an itinerant farm worker whose deep affection for his friend causes him to protect the other man from punishment when the latter (unconsciously and a prey to homicidal mania) commits a murder, and ultimately to kill him with his own hands. *Of Mice and Men* has been criticized as meaningless and gratuitously melodramatic. It lacks meaning only, I believe, to those who demand that every revelation of the strange heart of man should carry with it a direct message of some kind.

No such criticism could be possibly made of *The Moon Is Down*. The scene is laid in a small town of occupied Europe during World War II, and the action shows a courageous and patriotic mayor and a few of his companions who refuse to "collaborate" with the Master Race, and at last pay the supreme penalty.

Steinbeck is reported to have said that he was dissatisfied with the theatre as a means of expression. It can only be hoped that some means will be found to encourage him to try again.

The case of Howard Lindsay (and so far as his latest and most successful work is concerned, of his collaborator Russel Crouse) offers an object lesson to the critics who claim that progress in the drama is marked rather by the introduction of new ideas than by "mere" dramatic talent. Lindsay's contribution to the theatre, sometimes made alone but usually with other writers, includes not only the recent plays in which he acted, or wrote, or directed, but several musical and non-musical shows. He has for over twenty years consistently labored as play doctor, adviser, author, actor, and manager. In a word he has gone through the mill, and apparently everything that he has so carefully noted and learned by observation and participation has been stored up for later use.

The first straight play that bears his name was *Tommy* (1927), an agreeable and conventional comedy written in collaboration with Bertrand Robinson. With the same writer he also turned out *Your Uncle Dudley* (1929) and *Oh Promise Me* (1930), acceptable, competent, but by no means distinguished popular comedies. In 1935 came *She Loves Me Not,* dramatized from a novel, a far better play than any of the earlier comedies. Unpretentious, and intended simply as a quick-moving comedy of situation, it was among the best of its kind.

Far more original was *A Slight Case of Murder* (1935), in which Damon Runyon was named as co-author. The play was a failure on Broadway, for reasons which are still not clear. This was a character study, with a great deal of incidental local color and grotesque comedy, about a group of former beer racketeers trying to go respectable. Lindsay's knowledge of the ways of the theatre was here put to excellent service: he was evidently a man who understood that to reveal something of the inner workings of man was a harder and finer object than simply to show him involved in plot complications.

In 1939, with Russel Crouse as collaborator, Lindsay gave the theatre one of the few plays that may be thought of as an American theatre classic, *Life With Father*. This character comedy, in its seventh year on Broadway at the present writing—exhibits no articulate philosophy of life; it is as barren of significance as *The School for Scandal,* and as well constructed and written. Based though it is on the Clarence Day book, it is as "original" as any play can be that derives its central character from a book; as original, that is, as many of the accepted classics of the world. The authors have been satisfied to present a full-length portrait with all the skill of the most adept showmen, and have done so with restraint and a lack of exaggeration which set their play apart from most works of its kind.

Their share as authors in Joseph Kesselring's *Arsenic and Old Lace* (1941) has not been publicly announced, but it is known that it was they who made this entertaining extravaganza the tremendous success it became.

The latest Lindsay-Crouse play, *Strip For Action* (1942) failed to win popular success, possibly because it was too elaborate as a production. Less concerned with character than *Life With Father,* and emphasizing the purely farcical incidents, this amusing play about burlesque actors in an army camp deserved better success and more intelligent critical notices than it got.

It is of course too early to read into such plays as *Life With Father* a distinct tendency in present-day American dramatic work, but it may be noted that the playwrights, practical men of the theatre, yet not detached as so many of their forerunners were from the world about them, are content to use the theatre as a framework for the exhibition of man without feeling that it is their job to utter "significant" generalizations about the society which produced them or to point the way to social reform. The same thing is equally true of such other expert craftsmen as Kaufman and Hart.

In approaching the end of our outline history of the America drama the temptation should be resisted to sum up tendencies or predict the future, but before discussing the work of the latest of a long line of "promising youngsters," William Saroyan, and bringing this narrative to a close, it may be remarked that at the present moment (late 1945), the problem of the young playwright is more serious than it has ever been within the past quarter of a century. It would be hard to name half a dozen new people who can be expected to offer work that can be properly described as promising. Edward Chodorov, not as young as some others who are still hovering just outside Broadway, has recently shown more than ordinary talent with *All Those Endearing Young Charms* (1943), *Decision* (1944), and *Common Ground* (1945). Tennessee Williams and Arnold Sundgaard are, I think, to be counted on to make worthwhile contributions; Mr. Williams having already shown (in *The Glass Menagerie,* 1944) skill and understanding in the treatment of character, and ability to hold an audience without utilizing too many conventional tricks. Likewise Horton Foote (whose *Only the Heart* had a short run in New York in the spring of 1944); Betty Smith, Arthur Miller, Arthur Laurents, Stanley Young, Ruth Gordon, Garson Kanin, Elsa Shelley—who else? The prospects are slim. And the reasons? Chiefly, I believe, economic. The day when it was possible to get together a few actors and a small sum of money and try out a play in New York are gone; the costs of production have so mounted that managers and backers can no longer afford, as a rule, to test new plays unless they look like sure things; the more or less permanent stock company has disappeared and the young playwright has nowhere to go in the professional theatre to watch the workings of a competent theatrical troupe from week to week; he finds it more and more difficult to get experienced companies to experiment with his scripts; and what is the result? The youngster cannot afford to take the time to learn his trade, and he goes into radio, or moving pictures, or into business.

It is sometimes possible for the young playwright to get a little help from the nonprofessional theatre, and there are a few cases where a community or so-called Little Theatre, or a university theatre, can give a writer a chance to see one of his plays tried out. But the nonprofessional theatre (valuable as it is in carrying the contemporary drama to every community in the country) has its own problems, largely economic, and to survive it must almost entirely confine its productions to the well-known true and tried products of Broadway.

William Saroyan, a popular and successful writer of short stories, brought to the theatre in 1939 his first play, *My Heart's in the Highlands,* a fresh and invigorating fantasy. It was plain to a good many play-goers and critics that here was something apart from routine play writing, something that had its roots in a kind of ecstasy of living. In the first of a long series of prefaces, notes, and interviews which Saroyan has given the public in order to persuade it and himself what a great writer he was, he said that "A classic is simply a first work, the beginning of a tradition, and an entry into a fresh realm of human experience, understanding and expression. I believe *My Heart's in the Highlands* is a classic." Well, in a way that may be true, but what is more to the point, the author brought to the theatre an attitude of mind, a kind of exultation and love of people, a sort of lyric expression which have created classics in the past. The people in this first play, as in all his plays, are indeed suffused with an unreflecting joy in the mere act of being alive; and the creation of a world of such people, being utterly themselves, is what marks the characteristic Saroyan play.

The Time of Your Life (1939) was a little less lyric in tone and a trifle more realistic in detail, but remained essentially another ebullient hymn to the joy of life; indeed all the Saroyan plays, despite a considerable difference in background, are hardly more than variations on a single theme. *Love's Old Sweet Song* (1940) and *The Beautiful People* (1941) added little that was new to the themes already announced and used in the first plays, and several other works—some of them one-acters, some produced professionally and some by amateurs only, and others circulated only in printed or manuscript form—showed in some cases a tendency on the writer's part to repeat himself. Others (*Jim Dandy* in particular) showed a more or less successful effort to dramatize metaphysical problems of personality, just as Pirandello had done some years before.

The enthusiasm which Saroyan has brought to our theatre, the lyric note which runs through all his plays, the spirit of affirmation one feels permeating everything he writes, are not enough to warrant the hope that this new writer will revolutionize the American theatre, but his writings have already shown that that theatre is ready to welcome and assimilate whatever is fresh.

Reading Lists

The references that follow are intended primarily to supplement the material in the various sections of the present volume and to provide a certain amount of background for further reading and study. No claim is made to completeness, first because the available material is very extensive, and second because this book is intended not for specialists or scholars, but for the layman and the student who has not yet found it necessary to go to original sources in all cases.

It is to be noted that reference works that have not been translated into English are as a rule mentioned only when works in English, covering the same material, are not available. Because of incomplete data on sources, due often to the interruption of communications caused by war, it has in some cases been impossible to furnish all details usually supplied on the names of publishers, their addresses, and other similar information.

THE SCANDINAVIAN COUNTRIES

The first three entries below are standard histories of the Scandinavian literatures; they have not been translated. The next four cover various aspects of the Scandinavian literatures, none of them being entirely satisfactory.

ANDERSEN, Vilhelm, "Det nittende Aarhundredes anden Halvdel." (Vol. 4 of Petersen og Andersen, *Illustreret dansk litteratur-historie*.) Gyldendal, Copenhagen, 1925.

BULL, Francis, "Norges litteratur fra februarrevolutionen til verdenskrigen, 1-2." (Vol. 4, 1-2 of Bull, Paasche, og Winsnes, *Norsk litteratur historie*.) Aschehoug, Christiania, 1937.

CASTRÉN, Gunnar, "Den nya tiden, 1870-1914." (Vol. 7 of Schück och Warburg. *Illustrerad svensk litteraturhistoria*. Tredje, fullständigt omarbetade upplagan, 1926 ff.) Hugo Geber, Stockholm, 1932.

GOSSE, Edmund, *Northern Studies*. Walter Scott, London, 1890.

GRÖNDAHL, Illit, and RAKNES, Ola, *Chapters in Norwegian Literature*. London, 1923.

JORGENSON, Theodore, *History of Norwegian Literature*. The Macmillan Co., New York, 1933.

TOPSÖE-JENSEN, H. G., *Scandinavian Literature from Brandes to Our Day*. Trans. by Isaac Anderson. The American Scandinavian Foundation, 1929.

The following nine entries are English and American books on modern drama which include a certain amount of material on Scandinavian drama.

CHANDLER, Frank W., *Aspects of Modern Drama*. The Macmillan Co., New York, 1922.

———, *Modern Continental Playwrights*. Harper & Bros., New York, 1931.

CLARK, Barrett H., *A Study of the Modern Drama*. Rev. ed., D. Appleton-Century Co. New York, 1938.

Dukes, Ashley, *Modern Dramatists*. Charles H. Sergel, Chicago, 1911.
Freedley, George, and Reeves, John A., *A History of the Theatre*. Crown Publishers, New York, 1941.
Henderson, Archibald, *Modern Dramatists*. Stewart Kidd Co., Cincinnati, O., 1918.
Huneker, James, *Iconoclasts*. Charles Scribner's Sons, New York, 1905.
Jameson, Storm, *Modern Drama in Europe*. Harcourt, Brace & Co., New York, 1920.
Lewisohn, Ludwig, *The Modern Drama*. B. W. Huebsch, New York, 1915.

Note: The *American-Scandinavian Review*, published by The American-Scandinavian Foundation, New York, 1913 ff., includes fairly frequent news items on the Scandinavian theatre, and on playwrights and others connected with the theatre and the drama. See particularly Brunius, August, "The Modern Drama in Sweden" IX, pp. 25-28, 1921; Schmidt, Robert, "A Workers' Theatre," XXII, pp. 53-58, 1934; Skavlan, Einar, "Drama with a Purpose," XXIII, pp. 242-247, 1935 and "The Norwegian Stage: New Forces," XXVII, pp. 240-245, 1939.

The August, 1940, issue of *Theatre Arts Monthly* is devoted almost entirely to the contemporary Swedish theatre, its playwrights, actors, producers, and so forth.

On Henrik Ibsen:

The standard edition, edited by Francis Bull, Halvdan Koht, and Didrik Arup Seip, is the *Samlede verker: hundrearsutgave*, 20 vols., Gyldendal, Oslo, 1928 ff. Has valuable introductions. The standard edition in English, with introductions by William Archer and C. H. Herford, is *The Collected Works of Henrik Ibsen*, 11 vols., Charles Scribner's Sons, New York, 1908 ff.

Brandes, Georg, "Henrik Ibsen," in *Creative Spirits of the Nineteenth Century*. Thomas Y. Crowell Co., New York, 1923.
Firkins, Ida ten Eyck, *Henrik Ibsen: A Bibliography of Criticism and Biography*. H. W. Wilson Co., New York, 1921.
Gosse, Edmund, *Henrik Ibsen*. Charles Scribner's Sons, New York, 1908.
Heller, Otto, *Henrik Ibsen: Plays and Problems*. Houghton Mifflin Co., Boston, Mass., 1912.
[Ibsen, Henrik], *Letters of Henrik Ibsen*. Trans. by J. N. Laurvik and Mary Morrison. Fox, Duffield & Co., New York, 1905.
———, *Speeches and New Letters*. Trans. by Arne Kildahl. Richard G. Badger, Boston, Mass., 1910.
Jaeger, Henrik, *Henrik Ibsen: A Critical Biography*. Trans. by William Morton Payne. A. C. McClurg, Chicago, Ill., 1901.
Koht, Halvdan, *The Life of Ibsen*. Trans. from the Norwegian. 2 vols. W. W. Norton & Co., New York, 1931. (The Standard "life.")
Weigand, H. J., *The Modern Ibsen: a reconsideration*. Henry Holt, New York, 1925.
Zucker, A. E., *Ibsen the Master Builder*. Henry Holt, New York, 1929.

On August Strindberg:

The standard edition, edited by John Landquist, is *Samlade Skrifter*, 55 vols. Bonniers, Stockholm, 1912 ff. (with valuable notes, bibliographical and textual, in the appendices).

The three chief collections of English translations of Strindberg's plays contain informative introductory material. These are by Edwin Björkman, 4 vols., Charles Scribner's Sons, New York, 1912-16; by E. and W. Oland, 3 vols., John W. Luce Co., Boston, Mass., 1912-14; and that appearing under the editorial supervision of the Anglo-Swedish Literary Foundation, 4 vols., London and New York 1929 ff.

Björkman, Edwin, "August Strindberg," in *Voices of Tomorrow*. Mitchell Kennerley, New York, 1913.
Bulman, Joan, *Strindberg and Shakespeare*. Jonathan Cape, London, 1933.
Hedén, Eric, *Strindberg: en ledtråd vid studiet av hans verk*. Bokförlaget Nutiden,

Stockholm. Rev. ed., 1926. (First really significant extended biographical work.)
JOLIVET, J., *Le théâtre de Strindberg.* Boivin & Cie., Paris, 1931.
LAMM, Martin, *Strindbergs dramer.* 2 vols. Bonniers, Stockholm, 1924, 1926.
———, *August Strindberg.* 2 vols. Bonniers, Stockholm, 1940, 1942.
Professor Lamm's works are the first definitive investigations of Strindberg's total literary production.
McGILL, V. J., *August Strindberg the Bedevilled Viking.* Brentano, New York, 1930.
MORTENSEN, Johan, "Strindberg's Personality." *American-Scandinavian Review,* X, pp. 289-95, New York, 1922.

On the contemporary Scandinavian drama:
GUSTAFSON, Alrik, Introductions to *Scandinavian Plays of the Twentieth Century:* First and Second Series. The American-Scandinavian Foundation, New York, 1944.

GERMANY

ARNOLD, Robert F., Ed., *Das deutsche Drama,* C. H. Beck, Munich, 1925.
BAB, Julius, *Die Chronik des deutschen Dramas,* 5 vols. Oesterheld, Berlin, 1922 ff.
BERTAUX, Felix, *Panorama of German Literature from 1871 to 1931.* Trans. with Bibliographies by J. J. Trounstine. Whittlesey House, New York, 1935.
BITHELL, Jethro, *Modern German Literature, 1880-1938.* Methuen & Co., London, 1939.
CLARK, Barrett H., *A Study of the Modern Drama.* Rev. ed., D. Appleton-Century Co., New York, 1938.
ELOESSER, Arthur, *Modern German Literature.* Trans. by Catherine A. Phillips. Alfred A. Knopf, New York, 1933.
FEISE, Ernst, *Fifty Years of German Drama. A Bibliography of Modern German Drama, 1880-1930.* Johns Hopkins University Press, Baltimore, Md., 1941. (Dates of first editions and performances.)
FREEDLEY, George, and REEVES, John A., *A History of the Theatre.* Crown Publishers, New York, 1941.
KNEVELS, Wilhelm, *Das moderne Drama. Gesicht unserer Zeit, Darstellung, Deutung, Wertung.* H. Wollermann, Brunswick, Germany, 1930.
MORGAN, Bayard Quincy, *A Critical Bibliography of German Literature in English Translation. 1481-1927.* 2nd ed., with Supplement embracing the years 1928-1935. Completely revised and greatly augmented. Leland Stanford University Press, Stanford University, Calif., 1939.
SOERGEL, Albert, *Dichtung und Dichter der Zeit: eine Schilderung der deutschen Literatur der letzten Jahrzehnte.* R. Voigtländer, Leipzig, 1928.

AUSTRIA

There is no history of Austrian literature available in English. However, Austrian writers are discussed in all histories of German literature. In this section books are mentioned which contain material on the Austrian as distinguished from the German drama.

BIANQUIS, Geneviève, *La Poésie autrichienne de Hofmannsthal à Rilke.* Les Presses universitaires de France, Paris, 1926. (Contains excellent discussion of "Young Vienna" group and its background.)
BITHELL, Jethro, *Modern German Literature, 1880-1938.* Methuen & Co., London, 1939. (Most up-to-date survey of German literature in English. Discusses several Austrian playwrights.)
CHANDLER, Frank W., *Modern Continental Playwrights.* Harper & Bros., New York, 1931. (With chapter on "The Austrian Contribution" and bibliographies.)

CLARK, Barrett H., *A Study of the Modern Drama*. Rev. ed., D. Appleton-Century Co., New York, 1938.
GOLDBERG, Isaac, *The Drama of Transition*. Stewart Kidd Co., Cincinnati, O., 1922.
HENDERSON, Archibald, *European Dramatists*. D. Appleton-Century Co., New York, 1926. (Contains an appreciation of Schnitzler's work.)
LIPTZIN, Solomon, *Richard Beer-Hofmann*. Bloch Publishing Co., New York, 1936.
———, *Arthur Schnitzler*. Prentice-Hall, New York, 1932. (The only long study of Schnitzler available in English.)
———, *Germany's Stepchildren*. Jewish Publications Society of America, Philadelphia, Pa., 1944. (Chapters on Beer-Hofmann, Herzl, Schnitzler, Zweig, and Werfel.)
NADLER, Josef, *Literaturgeschichte der deutschen Staemme und Landschaften*. 4 vols., Regensburg, 1932 ff. (Contains a basic discussion of the cultural traditions of Austria. Vol. 4 has sections on modern Austrian literature.)
NAEF, Karl J., *Hugo von Hofmannsthals Wesen und Werk*. Max Niehans Verlag, Zurich, 1938. (The most comprehensive study of Hofmannsthal's work.)
NAGL, J. W., and ZEIDLER, J., ed. by Eduard Castle. *Deutsch-Oesterreichische Literaturgeschichte*. 4 vols., Carl Fromme, Vienna, 1899 ff. (Written by several hands, this monumental work is a vast and invaluable storehouse of factual information. Vol. 4 deals with the period from 1890 to 1937.)

ENGLAND

AGATE, James, *A Short View of the English Stage, 1900-1926*. H. Jenkins Ltd., London, 1926.
———, *Immoment Toys, A Survey of Light Entertainment on the London Stage, 1920-1943*. Jonathan Cape, London, 1945.
———, *The English Dramatic Critics, 1660-1932*. Arthur Barker, London, 1932.
ARCHER, William, *English Dramatists of Today*. S. Low, Marston, Searle and Rivington, London, 1882.
BORSA, Mario, *The English Stage of Today*. Trans. by Selwyn Brinton. John Lane, London, 1908.
CLARK, Barrett H., *A Study of the Modern Drama*. Rev. ed., D. Appleton-Century Co., New York, 1938.
CORDELL, Richard A., *Henry Arthur Jones and the Modern Drama*. Long & Smith, New York, 1932.
COWARD, Noel, *Present Indicative*. William Heineman, London, 1937.
CRAIG, Edward Gordon, *Ellen Terry and Her Secret Self*. S. Low, Marston & Co., London, 1931.
CUNLIFFE, J. W., *Modern English Playwrights: A Short History of the English Drama from 1825*. Harper & Bros., New York, 1927.
DICKINSON, Thomas H., *The Contemporary Drama of England*. Little, Brown & Co., Boston, Mass., 1931.
DUNKEL, Wilbur Dwight, *Sir Arthur Pinero*. University of Chicago Press, Chicago, 1941.
EATON, Walter Prichard, *The Drama in English*. Charles Scribner's Sons, New York, 1930.
ELLEHAUGE, Martin, *Striking Figures Among Modern English Dramatists*. Levin & Munksgaard, Copenhagen, 1931.
ELLREDGE, H. J., *The Stage Cyclopedia*. The Stage, London, 1909.
FREEDLEY, George, and REEVES, John A., *A History of the Theatre*. Crown Publishers New York, 1941.
GASSNER, John, *Masters of the Drama*. Random House, New York, 1940.

GREIN, J. T., *Dramatic Criticism*. 4 vols. J. Long, London, 1899-1905.
GRUNDY, Sydney, *The Play of the Future, by a Playwright of the Past*. Samuel French Ltd., London, 1914.
HARRIS, Frank, *Bernard Shaw*. Simon & Schuster, New York, 1931.
HARVEY, Sir Paul, *The Oxford Companion to English Literature*. Clarendon Press, Oxford, 1932.
HENDERSON, Archibald, *Bernard Shaw, Playboy and Prophet*. D. Appleton-Century Co., New York, 1932.
HOWE, P. P., *Dramatic Portraits*. Martin Secker, London, 1913.
JONES, Henry Arthur, *The Foundations of a National Drama*. George H. Doran, New York, 1912.
———, *The Renaissance of the English Drama*. The Macmillan Co., New York, 1895.
MACCARTHY, Desmond, *The Court Theatre, 1904-1907*. A. H. Bullen, London, 1907.
MILLER, Anna Irene, *The Independent Theatre in Europe*. Long and Smith, New York, 1927.
MORGAN, A. S., *Tendencies of Modern English Drama*. Charles Scribner's Sons, New York, 1934.
NICOLL, Allardyce, *British Drama: An Historical Survey from the Beginning to the Present Time*. George G. Harrap & Co., Ltd., London, 1932.
NORWOOD, Gilbert, *Euripides and Shaw, With Other Essays*. Methuen & Co., London, 1921.
O'CASEY, Sean, *The Flying Wasp*. Macmillan & Co., London, 1937.
PALMER, John, *The Future of the Theatre*. G. Bell & Sons, London, 1913.
PARKER, John, compiler and editor. *Who's Who in the Theatre. A Biographical Record of the Contemporary Stage*. 9 editions, 9 vols., Pitman Publishing Corp., New York, 1939.
PEARSON, Hesketh, *G.B.S., A Full Length Portrait*. Harper & Bros., New York, 1942.
———, *Oscar Wilde, His Life and Wit*. Harper & Bros., New York, 1946.
PELLIZZI, Camillo, *English Drama: The Last Great Phase*. Trans. by Rowan Williams. Macmillan & Co., London, 1935.
SCOTT, Clement, *The Drama of Yesterday and Today*. 2 vols. Macmillan & Co., London, 1899.
SHAW, George Bernard, *Dramatic Opinions and Essays*. 2 vols., Brentano's, New York, 1906.
SHORT, Ernest, and COMPTON-RICKETT, Arthur, *Ring Up the Curtain*. Herbert Jenkins, London, 1938.
Stage Year-Book, The. The Stage, London, 1907-1928.
THOULESS, Priscilla, *Modern Poetic Drama*. Basil Blackwell, Oxford, 1934.

IRELAND

BOYD, Ernest A., *The Contemporary Drama of Ireland*. Little, Brown & Co., Boston, Mass., 1926.
———, *Ireland's Literary Renaissance*. John Lane, New York, 1916.
BYRNE, Dawson, *The Story of Ireland's National Theatre*. Talbot Press, Dublin, 1929.
CORKERY, Dawson, *Synge and Anglo-Irish Literature*. Longmans Green & Co., New York, 1931.
FAY, W. G., and CASWELL, Catherine, *The Fays and the Abbey Theatre*. Harcourt, Brace and Co., New York, 1935.
GREGORY, Lady Augusta, *Our Irish Theatre*. G. P. Putnam's Sons, New York, 1913.
MALONE, Andrew E., *The Irish Drama*. Charles Scribner's Sons, New York, 1929.
ROBINSON, Lennox, *The Irish Theatre*. Macmillan & Co., London, 1939.

WEYGANDT, Cornelius, *Irish Plays and Playwrights.* Houghton Mifflin Co., Boston, Mass., 1913.

YEATS, William Butler, *Autobiography of William Butler Yeats.* The Macmillan Co., New York, 1938.

FRANCE

BISSEL, Clifford H., *Les Conventions du théâtre bourgeois en France, 1887-1914.* Presses universitaires de France, Paris, 1930. (Comprehensive analysis of subjects and conventions in drama of the period.)

BLOCH, Jean-Richard. *Destin du théâtre.* Librairie Gallimard, Paris, 1930. (Penetrating essay on modern French theatre.)

BLOCK, Anita, *The Changing World in Plays and Theatre.* Little, Brown & Co., Boston, Mass., 1939. (Excellent study on modern drama with material on French playwrights.)

BROWN, John Mason, *The Modern Theatre in Revolt.* W. W. Norton & Co., New York, 1929. (A good account of naturalism and Free Theatre movement.)

CHANDLER, Frank W., *The Contemporary Drama of France.* Little, Brown & Co., Boston, Mass., 1925. (Authoritative survey of period between Free Theatre and First World War.)

――――, *Modern Continental Playwrights.* Harper & Bros., New York, 1931. (Contains valuable chapters and bibliographies on French playwrights.)

CLARK, Barrett H., *Four Plays of the Free Theater.* Trans. with Introduction. Stewart Kidd Co., Cincinnati, O., 1914. (Contains condensed and valuable account of the Free Theatre.)

――――, *Contemporary French Dramatists.* Stewart Kidd Co., Cincinnati, O., 1915. (Judicious essays on pre-war dramatists: Free Theatre, Curel, Brieux, Porto-Riche, Hervieu, Lavedan, Donnay, Rostand, Lemaître, Capus, Bernstein, Bataille, and Flers and Caillavet.)

――――, *European Theories of the Drama. An Anthology of Dramatic Theory and Criticism.* Rev. ed., D. Appleton-Century Co., New York, 1929. (Useful text for the student of drama.)

――――, *A Study of the Modern Drama.* Rev. ed., D. Appleton-Century Co., New York, 1938. (Authoritative manual for the student.)

COINDREAU, Maurice Edgar, *La Farce est jouée. Vingt-cinq ans de théâtre français, 1900-1925.* Editions de la Maison Française, New York, 1942. (A study of considerable interest.)

CRÉMIEUX, Benjamin, "Les Tendances actuelles du théâtre." In *Encyclopédie Française,* Vol. XVII. Librairie Larousse, Paris, 1936. (Discusses contemporary trends authoritatively.)

DICKINSON, Thomas H., Ed., *The Theatre in a Changing Europe.* Henry Holt & Co., New York, 1937. (Contains an authoritative survey of French drama by Edmond Sée.)

DELPIT, Louisa, *Paris-Théâtre contemporain.* Part I; *Rôle Prépondérant des scènes d'avant-garde depuis trente ans.* Part II: *Tableau du mouvement dramatique en France de 1925 à 1938.* Smith College *Studies in Modern Languages,* Northampton, Mass., Part I, 1925; Part II, 1938. (Highly valuable for the study of the contemporary French theatre.)

DUBECH, Lucien, *Les Chefs de file de la jeune génération.* Librairie Plon, Paris, 1925. (Penetrating views on the contemporary French drama.)

――――, *La Crise du théâtre.* Librairie de France, Paris, 1928. (Fine analysis of contemporary French drama.)

FRANK, Waldo, *The Art of the Vieux-Colombier. A Contribution of France to the Contemporary Stage.* Librairie Gallimard, New York, 1918. (Excellent analysis of Copeau's work.)

FREEDLEY, George, and REEVES, John A., *A History of the Theatre.* Crown Publishers, New York, 1941. (Contains significant pages on modern French theatre.)

KNOWLES, Dorothy, *La Réaction idéaliste au théâtre depuis 1890.* Librairie E. Droz, Paris, 1934. (Scholarly study of the idealistic movement in the modern French theatre.)

LEMAÎTRE, Jules. *Theatrical Impressions.* Trans. from *Impressions de théâtre,* by Frederic Whyte. H. Jenkins Ltd., London, 1924.

MARSAN, Jules, *Théâtre d'hier et d'aujourd'hui.* Editions des Cahiers Libres, Paris, 1926. (Discerning lectures on modern French drama.)

MATTHEWS, Brander, *French Dramatists of the Nineteenth Century.* Charles Scribner's Sons, New York, 1905. (Early standard work still interesting for the period covered.)

MILLER, Anna Irene, *The Independent Theatre in Europe, 1887 to the Present.* Ray Long & Richard R. Smith, Inc., New York, 1931. (Good survey of the advance-guard theatres.)

MORNET, Daniel, *Introduction à l'étude des écrivains français d'aujourd'hui.* Boivin et Cie., Paris, 1939. (Contains penetrating observations on contemporary dramatists.)

PALMER, John L., *Studies in the Contemporary Theatre.* Little, Brown & Co., Boston, Mass., 1927. (Sound and valuable study of post-World War I dramatists.)

RHODES, S. A., *The Contemporary French Theatre.* F. S. Crofts & Co., New York, 1942. (Contains representative plays edited with survey and notes.)

ROLLAND, Romain, *The People's Theatre.* Trans. by Barrett H. Clark. Henry Holt & Co., New York, 1918. (Tells the story of the people's theatre movement.)

SÉCHÉ, Alphonse, and BERTAUT, Jules, *L'Evolution du théâtre contemporain.* Société du Mercure de France, Paris, 1908. (Fine analysis of the pre-war drama.)

SÉE, Edmond. *Le Théâtre français contemporain.* Armand Colin, Paris, 1928. (Excellent history of modern French drama.)

SMITH, Hugh Allison, *Main Currents of Modern French Drama.* Henry Holt & Co., New York, 1925. (A good text on pre-war drama.)

THALASSO, Adolphe, *Le Théâtre libre. Essai critique, historique et documentaire* ... Mercure de France, Paris, 1909. (Authoritative history of the Free Theatre.)

WAXMAN, Samuel M., *Antoine and the Théâtre libre.* Harvard University Press, Cambridge, Mass., 1926. (Highly valuable history of the Free Theatre.)

BELGIUM

BITHELL, Jethro, *Contemporary Belgian Literature.* Frederick A. Stokes Co., New York, 1915. (Devotes some pages to dramatic authors.)

CHANDLER, Frank W., *Modern Continental Playwrights.* Harper & Bros., New York, 1931. (Studies some of the Belgian dramatists.)

CLARK, Barrett H., *A Study of the Modern Drama.* Rev. ed., D. Appleton-Century Co., New York, 1938. (Has interesting section on Belgian drama.)

Commission à l'Exposition Internationale de New York, 1939-1940. Contemporary Literature in Belgium. Commissariat Général of the Belgian Government, New York World's Fair, New York, 1939. (Contains interesting references to Belgian dramatists by Camille Poupeye.)

DOUTREMONT, Georges, *Histoire Illustrée de la Littérature Française en Belgique.* Marcel Didier, Brussels, 1939. (Has comprehensive chapter on Belgian-French drama.)

GAUCHEZ, Maurice (pseud. of M. Gilles), *Histoire de Lettres Françaises de Belgique des Origines à nos Jours.* Edition de la Renaissance d'Occident. Brussels, 1922. (Has brief but interesting chapter on the drama.)

GORIS, Jan-Albert, *Belgian Letters.* Belgian Government Information Center, New York, 1946. (Has succinct section on the drama.)

HEUMANN, Albert, *Le Mouvement Littéraire Belge d'expression française depuis 1880.* Mercure de France, Paris, 1913. (Has a concise chapter on the drama.)

SOLVAY, Lucien, *L'Evolution théâtrale.* Librairie nationale d'Art et d'Histoire, Brussels, 1922. (Contains a good chapter on Belgian drama.)

ITALY

ANTONINI, G., *Il teatro contemporaneo in Italia.* Corbaccio, Milan, 1927. (Informative study on contemporary drama.)

CHANDLER, Frank W., *Aspects of Modern Drama.* The Macmillan Co., New York, 1915.

COSTETTI, G., *Il teatro italiano nel 1800.* Rome, 1901. (Informative study by a contemporary on the drama of the late nineteenth century.)

CROCE, B., *La letteratura della nuova Italia.* 6 vols., Bari, 1921-40. (A notable contribution to the criticism of Italian literature from the middle of the nineteenth century to World War I. Contains essays on Ferrari, Giacometti, Torelli, Butti, Giacosa, D'Annunzio, and Pirandello.)

D'AMICO, S., Ed., *Il teatro del Novecento.* Treves, Milano, 1932. (Excellent work on modern period. Shows typical hostility toward nineteenth century.)

EVOLA, N. D., *Bibliografia degli studi sulla letteratura italiana.* Milan, 1938. (Lists critical works written between 1920 and 1934.)

FREEDLEY, George, and REEVES, John A., *A History of the Theatre.* Crown Publishers, New York, 1941. (With material on modern Italian theatre and drama.)

LEMMI, C., "The Italian Stage of Today." In *The Drama,* Charles H. Sergel, Chicago, 1916.

MACCLINTOCK, Lander, *The Contemporary Drama of Italy.* Little, Brown & Co., Boston, Mass., 1920. (A good presentation of the modern Italian theatre and drama, with bibliography.)

MACLEOD, Addison, *Plays and Players in Modern Italy.* Charles H. Sergel, Chicago, 1912.

PREZZOLINI, G., *Repertorio bibliografico della storia e della critica della letteratura italiana dal 1902 al 1932.* 2 vols. Edizioni Roma, Rome, 1937-39. (An indispensable work for bibliography of modern period.)

PRAGA, M., *Cronache teatrali.* 9 vols., Fratelli Treves, Milan, 1919-29.

SANESI, I., *La commedia.* 2nd vol. Milan, 1935. (Deals with most significant figures down to Pirandello. Good critical work, with bibliography.)

TONELLI, L., *Il teatro italiano dalle origini ai giorni nostri.* Modernissima, Milan, 1924. (Authoritative presentation of development of the Italian theatre.)

———, *L'evoluzione del teatro contemporaneo in Italia.* Milan, 1913-36. (New edition, 1936, deals with the more recent aspects of Italian drama.)

Note: Two Italian journals, *Comoedia,* published in Milan, and *Il Dramma,* published in Turin, offer considerable material on the modern Italian drama and theatre.

RUSSIA

BAKSHY, Alexander, *The Path of the Modern Russian Stage and Other Essays.* Palmer, London, 1916. (Covers Moscow and Leningrad theatres on the eve of the Russian Revolution. Illustrated.)

READING LISTS 749

———, *Soviet Scene: Six Plays of Russian Life*. Yale University Press, New Haven, 1946. (Introductory Chapter: "The Soviet Drama.")

BATES, Alfred, Ed., *The Russian Drama*. Smart & Stanley, London, 1906. (In Vol. 18 of larger work, *The Drama*. Gives extracts from plays.)

BLOCK, Anita, *The Changing World in Plays and Theatre*. Little, Brown & Co., Boston, Mass., 1939. (Ch. 8 gives account of some new Soviet plays.)

BROWN, Ben W., *Theatre at the Left*. The Booke Shop, Providence, R. I., 1938. (Impressions made by Soviet theatres on a professor of economics.)

BROWN, John Mason, *The Modern Theatre in Revolt*. W. W. Norton & Co., New York, 1929. (Ch. 6: "Russia's Theatre of Social Revolt.")

CARTER, Huntly, *The New Theatre and Cinema of Soviet Russia*. Chapman & Hall, London, 1924. (An account of the Left, Center, and Right groups of theatres in Moscow. Fully illustrated.)

———, *The New Spirit in the Russian Theatre, 1917-28*. Brentano's, Inc., New York, 1929. (The planning, building, and completing of the Soviet theatres, etc. Illustrated.)

CHANDLER, Frank W., *Modern Continental Playwrights*. Harper & Bros., New York, 1931. (Ch. 4-8 on Russian drama, with lists of plays, translations, and reference works.)

CLARK, Barrett H., *A Study of the Modern Drama*. Rev. ed., D. Appleton-Century Co., New York, 1938. (Section on Russian drama, with appreciations, play lists, and bibliographies.)

DANA, H. W. L., *Handbook on Soviet Drama*. American Russian Institute, New York, 1938. (See this work for more complete lists of books and articles than present list. Gives accounts of theatres, plays, operas, ballets, and films. Full bibliographies.)

———, *Drama in Wartime Russia*. National Council of American-Soviet Friendship. New York, 1943. (Pamphlet on Soviet war plays, theatres, and actors during the Nazi invasion. Illustrated.)

———, *Seven Soviet Plays*. The Macmillan Company, New York, 1946. (With a general introduction and biographical sketch of each dramatist.)

DICKINSON, Thomas H., Ed., *The Theatre in a Changing Europe*. Henry Holt & Co., New York, 1937. (See Joseph Gregor's chapter, "The Theatre of Soviet Russia," and H. W. L. Dana's chapter, "The Development of Soviet Drama." Lists theatres, dramatists, and plays. Illustrated.)

FLANAGAN, Hallie. *Shifting Scenes of the Modern European Theatre*. Coward-McCann Inc., New York, 1928. (Six chapters on impressions of Soviet theatres and plays. Illustrated.)

FREEDLEY, George, and REEVES, John A., *A History of the Theatre*. Crown Publishers, New York, 1941. (Includes accounts of the chief Russian dramatists. Illustrated.)

FREEMAN, Joseph, KUNITZ, Joshua, and LOZOWICK, Louis, *Voices of October: Art and Literature in Soviet Russia*. Vanguard Press, New York, 1930. (Ch. 3 on the Soviet theatre. Illustrated.)

FULOP-MILLER, René, and GREGOR, Joseph, *The Russian Theatre: Its Character and History*. Trans. by Paul England. J. B. Lippincott Co., Philadelphia, Pa., 1930. (Brief text with 405 superb illustrations.)

GASSNER, John, *Masters of the Drama*. Random House, New York, 1940. (Two chapters on Russian dramatists. Bibliography.)

GORELIK, Mordecai, *New Theatres for Old*. Samuel French, Inc., New York, 1940. (Constant references to Soviet theatres, and especially to Soviet scenic design. Illustrated.)

GRIFFITH, Hubert, Ed., *Playtime in Russia*. Methuen & Co., London, 1935. (See A. E.

Wilson, "Some Russian Plays," and Geoffrey Whitworth, "Amateur Theatre Movement in U.S.S.R." Illustrated.)

Gsell, Paul, *Le Théâtre soviétique*. Editions Sociales internationales, Paris, 1937. (Impressions on a French critic of plays seen in Soviet Russia.)

Houghton, Norris, *Moscow Rehearsals*. Harcourt, Brace & Co., New York, 1936. (An account of methods of production seen in the Soviet theatres. Illustrated.)

Komisarjevsky, Theodore, *Myself and the Theatre*. E. P. Dutton & Co., New York, 1930. (Autobiography of the Russian theatre director. Illustrated.)

Leyda, Jay, Ed., "The Soviet Theatre Speaks for Itself." In *Theatre Arts Monthly*, New York, Sept. 1936. (Articles by Russian theatre directors, actors, playwrights, etc. Illustrated. Bibliography.)

Lo Gatto, Ettore, *Il teatro Russo*. Fratelli Treves, Milan, 1937. (Italian treatment of twentieth-century Russian drama. Lists of dramatists and plays. Bibliography.)

London, Kurt, *The Seven Soviet Arts*. Faber & Faber, London, 1937. (With section on the theatre. Illustrated.)

Lunacharski, Anatoli Vasilevich, *The Theatre and the Revolution* [*Teatr i Revolyutsiya*], Moscow, 1924. (A series of articles by the first People's Commissar of Education.)

———, *The Theatre of Today* [*Teatr Sevodnya*.] Moscow, 1928. (Further articles by the same.)

Lyons, Eugene, *Six Soviet Plays*. Houghton Mifflin Company, Boston, 1934. (With a Preface by Elmer Rice and Introductions to each play.)

Macleod, Joseph, *The New Soviet Theatre*. George Allen & Unwin, London, 1943. (Reflections on theatres throughout the Soviet Union. Illustrated.)

———, *Actors Cross the Volga*. George Allen & Unwin, Ltd., London, 1946. (A Study of the 19th Century Russian Theatre and the Soviet Theatres in War.)

Markov, P. A., *The Soviet Theatre*. Victor Gollancz, Ltd., London, 1934. (By the former director of the literary department of the Moscow Art Theatre. Illustrated.)

Mogilevski, A. I., Filippov, V., and Rodionov, A. M., *The Theatres of Moscow* [*Teatry Moskvy*], Moscow, 1928. (Contains statistics for the first ten years of Soviet drama, with tables of plays, numbers of performances, etc.)

Moskvin, I., *The Soviet Theatre*. Moscow, 1939. (By the successor of Stanislavski and Nemirovich-Danchenko as director of the Moscow Art Theatre. Illustrated.)

Nemirovitch-Danchenko, Vladimir, *My Life in the Russian Theatre*. Little, Brown & Co., Boston, Mass., 1936. (An account of the Moscow Art Theatre by one of its two co-directors. Illustrated.)

Noyes, George Rapall, *Masterpieces of the Russian Drama*. D. Appleton and Company, New York, 1933. (With an Introduction, Biographical Notes, and Reading List.)

Oruzheynikov, N., and others, *The Theatre in the USSR*. Soviet Union Society for Cultural Relations, Vol. VI, 1934. (A collection of articles summing up the progress of the theatre in the Soviet Union.)

Rafilovich, V. E., Chief Editor, *History of the Soviet Theatre* [*Istoriya Sovetskogo Teatra*]. Leningrad, 1933. (First volume of a detailed history. Covers period 1917-21. Illustrated.)

Sayler, Oliver M., *The Russian Theatre Under the Revolution*. Little, Brown & Co., Boston, Mass., 1920. (The first adequate account in English after the Revolution. Illustrated.)

———, *The Russian Theatre*. Brentano's, New York, 1922. (Same as above with four additional chapters.)

———, *Inside the Moscow Art Theatre*. Brentano's, New York, 1925. (Covers the various branches of the Art Theatre, especially the Musical Studio. Illustrated.)

SIMMONS, Ernest J., "The New Russian Theatre." Reprinted from *Harvard Graduates Magazine*, Boston, March 1931. (Reflections on Soviet drama based on a visit to Russia. Illustrated.)

STANISLAVSKI, Constantin, *My Life in Art*. Trans. by J. J. Robbins. Little, Brown & Co., Boston, Mass., 1924. (An account of the founding of the Moscow Art Theatre, and an explanation of the philosophy of its director. Illustrated.)

——, *An Actor Prepares*. Trans. by Elizabeth Reynolds Hapgood. Theatre Arts Inc., New York, 1936. (An account of the actor's work to perfect his art.)

STRUVE, Gleb, *Soviet Russian Literature*. George Routledge & Sons, London, 1935. (Ch. XI on drama. Bibliography.)

VAN GYSEGHEM, André, *Theatre in Soviet Russia*. Faber & Faber, London, 1943. (An account of the different theatres in Moscow and their styles of acting. Illustrated.)

VARNEKE, B., *History of the Russian Theatre* [*Istoriya Russkogo Teatra*]. Moscow, 1939. (A history of the theatre in Russia from the seventeenth century through the nineteenth century. Bibliography. Illustrated.)

VSEVOLODSKI, V. (Gerngross), *History of the Russian Theatre*. Leningrad-Moscow, 1929, 2 vols. (A social interpretation of the development from the beginnings to 1925, with bibliography and charts. Illustrated.)

WIENER, Leo, *The Contemporary Drama of Russia*. Little, Brown & Co., Boston, Mass., 1924. (Survey of nineteenth and twentieth century, with lists of dramatists and plays. Bibliography.)

EUROPE'S MIDDLE ZONE

Finland

GODENHIELM, B. F., *Handbook of the History of Finnish Literature*. F. H. Butler, London, 1896.

Estonia

KAMPAA, Mikhel, *Eesti Kirjandusloo Peajooned* [*Principal Facts of Estonian Literature*]. Tartu, 1938.

Latvia [Lettish Drama]

KRODERS, Roberts, *Le Théâtre des fêtes lettones*. Edition Pagalms, Riga, 1937. (Description of Lettish drama after 1934.)

MATTHEWS, William K., *The Tricolour Sun*. W. Heffer & Sons, Cambridge, England, 1936. (Contains excellent introduction on Lettish literary trends.)

VIRZA, ed., *La littérature lettone depuis l'époque du réveil national*. Section de la Presse du Ministère des affairs étrangères, Riga, 1925.

WIHGRABS, Georg, *Das lettische Schrifftum*. Riga, 1924. (Not very good as a whole, but indispensable because of a few details not available elsewhere.)

ZEIFERTS, T., "Die lettische nationale Literatur." In P. Smidts, *Die Letten*. Walters & Rapa, Riga, 1930. (Excellent.)

——, *Latviešu Rakstniecibas Vesture*, III. A Gulbis, Riga, 1930. (History of Lettish literature.)

Lithuania

COLEMAN, Arthur Prudden, "Survey of Lithuanian Literature." In *Books Abroad*, VIII, pp. 391-93, Norman, Okla., 1934.

MAUCLÈRE, J., *Panorama de la littérature lithuanienne contemporaine*. Editions du Sagittaire. Paris, 1938.

VAIČIULAITIS, A., *Outline History of Lithuanian Literature.* Lithuanian Cultural Institute Publications. Sec. I: Lithuanian Language and Literature, No. 1. Chicago, 1938.

Poland

CHMIELOWSKI, Piotr, *Nasza literatura dramatyczna* [*Our Dramatic Literature*]. K. Grendyszynski, St. Petersburg, 1898.
LORENTOWICZ, Jan, *Teatr Polski w Warszawie, 1913-38* [*The Polish Theatre in Warsaw*]. Biblioteka polska, Warsaw, 1938.
ORLICZ, Michal, *Polski teatr współczesny* [*The Contemporary Polish Theatre*]. Warsaw, 1932.
SZYJKOWSKI, Marjan, *Dzieje komedji polskiej* [*History of Polish Comedy*]. Krakowska Spolka Wydawnicza, Kraków, 1921.
———, *Dzieje nowożytnej tragedji polskiej* [*History of Modern Polish Tragedy*]. Krakowska Spółka Wydawnicza, Kraków, 1923.
WIERZYŃSKI, Kazimierz, *W garderobie duchów.* Warsaw, 1938. (Theatrical reviews reprinted from the daily press.)
ZELEŃSKI, Tadeusz, *Romanse cieniów.* Towarzystwo wydawnicze "Rój." (Reprints of theatrical reviews.)
———, *Murzyn zrobił....* Warsaw, 1939. (Reprints of theatrical reviews.)

Note: Theatrical reviews appear in *Wiadomości literackie,* the leading Warsaw literary journal; and in *Skamander,* a literary monthly published in Warsaw.

Lusatian [Wendish] Drama

GOLABEK, Jozef, *Literatura serbsko-luzycka* [*Serbo-Lusatian Literature*]. Instytut staski. Katowice, Poland, 1938. (With excellent résumé in French.)
———, "Sorb-Lusatian Literature." In *Slavonic and East European Review,* Vol. XIX, pp. 226-90. Menasha, Wis., 1940.
PATA, Josef, *Introduction à l'étude de la littérature serbe.* Prague, 1925.

Czech Drama

BEDNAR, Rudolf C., "Chief Post-War Czechoslovak Dramatists (1918-32)." Prague, 1933. (Typescript in New York Public Library.)
KONRÁD, Edmond, "Contemporary Drama in Czechoslovakia." In *Books Abroad,* XI, pp. 399-403, Autumn 1937, Norman, Okla., 1937.
MÁCHAL., Jan, *Dějiny českého dramata* [*History of Czech Drama*]. Prague, 1929.
WELLEK, René, "Karel Čapek." In *Slavonic and East European Review.* Vol. XV, Menasha, Wis., 1936.

Slovak Drama

BEDNAR, Rudolf G., "Chief Post-War Czechoslovak Dramatists (1918-32)." Prague, 1933. (Typescript in New York Public Library.)
BUJNÁK, P., *Sbórnik Jozefa Gregora Tajovského.* Bratislava, 1925.
UHLAR, R., "Nova slovenska drama a divadlo." In *Kultura,* Sept., 1934. Trnava, Czechoslovakia.

Hungary

HANKISS, J., and JUHÁSZ, G., *Panorama de la littérature hongroise contemporaine.* Editions Kra, Paris, 1930.
REICH, Emil, *Hungarian Literature.* Jarrold & Sons, London, 1898.

READING LISTS

RIEDL, Frederick, *A History of Hungarian Literature*. D. Appleton & Co., New York, 1906.
SCHÖPFLIN, Aladár, *A Magyar irodalom története a XX században* [History of Hungarian Literature in the Twentieth Century]. Budapest, 1937.

Rumania

ADAMESCU, George, *Contribution to Rumanian Literary Bibliography*. (Published in Rumanian: *Cartea românească*, Fasc. Ia.) Bucharest, 1928. (Excellent for dates and exact titles.)
HANES, P. V., *Histoire de la littérature roumane*. E. Leroux, Paris, 1934.
ILCUS, Peter, *Die moderne rumänische Literatur*. Leipzig, 1933.

Croatian and Serbian Drama

LUCERNA, Camilla, *Das Balladendrama der Südslaven*. Leipzig, 1923.
WOLLMAN, Frank, *Srbochorvatské Drama*. Universita Komenského, Bratislava, 1924. (Full account, complete in every detail, covering the period up to 1914.)
———, "Desetiletí srbochorvatské dramatiky." In *Slovanský Přehled*, pp. 351-63, 1925. (Full account covering the years 1914-24.)
———, *Dramatika slovanského jihu*. Prague, 1930. (Same, from 1924 on.)

Slovenian Drama

WOLLMAN, Frank, *Slovinské Drama*. Universita Komenského, Bratislava, 1925.
———, *Dramatika slovanskehojihu*. Nákladem Slovanského ustavu, Prague, 1930.

Bulgaria

HATEAU, Georges, *Panorama de la littérature bulgare contemporaine*. Editions du Sagittaire, Paris, 1937. (Excellent for verification of titles and dates.)
WOLLMAN, Frank, *Bulharské drama*. Vydala filosofická fakulta university komenského za podpory ministerstva školstvi a národní osvéty. Bratislava, 1928. (With résumé in French, pp. 157-66.)
———, *Dramatika Slovanského jihu*. Nákladem Slovanského ustavu, Prague, 1930.

Modern Greek Drama

ANNINOS, Ch., "The New Phase of the Modern Greek Theatre." [In Greek.] Philological Hestia, Athens, 1890.
HESSELING, D. C., "Histoire de la littérature grècque moderne." In *Les Belles Lettres*, Institut néo-hellénique, Paris, 1924.
VOUTIERIDES, E., *Modern Greek Literature*. [In Greek.] Athens, 1934.

Albania

KLANCAR, A. J., "Modern Albanian Literature." In *Books Abroad*, Winter, 1942, pp. 40-43, Norman, Okla.

THE NETHERLANDS

BLES, Dop, "Het tooneel enzijn toekomst." In *Groot, Nederland*, 15th year, IV, pp. 521-64, Amsterdam, 1917.
ROSSING, J. H., "Het tooneel." Nederland in den sanvanj der twintigste eeuw, pp. 425-52, A. W. Sijthoff, Leyden, 1910.

WORP, J. A., *Geschiedenis van het drama en van het tooneel in Nederland*. 2 vols. J. B. Wolters, Groningen, 1904-8.

SPAIN

ALTOLAGUIRRE, Manuel, "Nuestro teatro." In *Hora de España*, Sept., 1937. (Moving account of the young Spanish theatre written during the Civil War.)

BELL, Aubrey, *Contemporary Spanish Literature*. Alfred A. Knopf, New York, 1925. (Good section on Spanish drama, including seldom treated género chico.)

BUENO, Manuel, *Teatro español contemporáneo*. Biblioteca Renacimiento, Madrid, 1909. (With an account of the revolt against Echegaray.)

CHANDLER, Frank W., *Modern Continental Playwrights*. Harper & Bros., New York, 1931. (Covers period between Echegaray and Martinez-Sierra.)

CLARK, Barrett H., *A Study of the Modern Drama*. Rev. ed., D. Appleton-Century Co., New York, 1938.

———, Ed., *Masterpieces of Modern Spanish Drama*. New ed., Stewart Kidd Co., Cincinnati, O., 1922. (Contains translations of three plays, prefaces, and biographical sketches of authors.)

DICKINSON, Thomas H., Ed., *The Theatre in a Changing Europe*. Henry Holt & Co., New York, 1937. (Contains valuable chapter by Enrique Diez Canedo, famous Madrid critic, on the theatre of the 1930's. Also chapter by J. G. Underhill covering period 1914 to 1936.)

FITZMAURICE-KELLY, James, *A New History of Spanish Literature*. Oxford University Press, Oxford, 1926. (Has superseded Ticknor as authoritative history. Special attention paid to drama as part of the whole literary stream.)

FREEDLEY, George, and REEVES, John A., *A History of the Theatre*. Crown Publishers, New York, 1941. (Contains excellent chapter on the Spanish theatre from the beginning. Bird's-eye view of everything, with amazing amount of detail. See account of the Catalan Theatre.)

GOLDBERG, Isaac, *The Drama of Transition*. Stewart Kidd Co., Cincinnati, O., 1922.

GRAHAM, James, and O'CONNELL, Richard, "Introductions" to *From Lorca's Theatre*. Charles Scribner's Sons, New York, 1941.

HAMILTON, Thomas J., *Appeasement's Child*. Alfred A. Knopf, New York, 1943. (Journalistic account of life in early Franco régime. Contains first-hand picture of Spanish theatre of the time.)

MORLEY, S. Griswold, "José Echegaray." In *University of California Chronicle*, Berkeley, Calif., Oct., 1925, Vol. 27, No. 4, pp. 368-79. (Critical study of this first modern Spanish dramatist.)

NAVARRO, Pedro Juan, *Europa bábara*. Bogtá, Colombia, 1941. (Most recent picture of Benavente in this diplomat's account of Europe after the fall of France.)

SALINAS, Pedro, *Literatura española, Siglo XX*. Editorial Seneca, Mexico City, 1941. (Especially good for Unamuno, Valle Inclán and Arniches, poetic drama and género chico.)

SHAW, George Bernard, *Dramatic Opinions and Essays*, 2 vols., Brentano's, New York, 1906.

STARKIE, Walter, "Gregorio Martinez-Sierra and the Modern Spanish Drama." In *Contemporary Review*, Vol. 125, pp. 198-205, London, 1924.

———, *Jacinto Benavente*. Oxford University Press, Oxford, 1924. (Good critical study of the earlier years and plays of this prolific playwright.)

VALBUENA, Angel, *Literatura dramatica española*. Editorial Labor, 1930. (Competent handbook. Ends with Galdos and the realists.)

Spanish American Drama

Amunategui Solar, Domingo, *Las letras chilenas*. Editorial Nacimiento, Santiago de Chile, 1934. (Critical but incomplete account of Chilean theatre, with some discussion of origins.)

Bierstadt, Edward Hale, Ed., *Three Plays of the Argentine*. Duffield & Co., New York, 1920. (Contains translations of three plays. See Introduction.)

Brady, Cyrus T., Jr., "Lively Theatre in Buenos Aires." In *Theatre Arts Monthly*, Vol. XXIII, No. 5, New York, May, 1930.

Cerretani, Arturo, "El teatro de Samuel Eichelbaum." In *Síntesis*, Año 3, No. 30, Buenos Aires, May, 1930.

Churión, Juan José, *El teatro en Caracas*. Tipografía Vargas, Caracas, 1924. (Chatty journalistic account of the beginnings of the Venezuelan theatre and its early twentieth-century manifestations.)

Covarrubias, Miguel, "Slapstick and Venom." In *Theatre Arts Monthly*, Vol. XXII, No. 8, New York, Aug., 1938. (Interpretation of Mexican "carpa" theatre and its artists, with estimate of its values. Entertaining and intelligent.)

Crow, John A., "El drama revolucionario mexicano." In *Revista Hispánica Moderna*, Año V, No. 1, Jan., 1939. (Account of six anti-Yankee plays, by Juan Bustillo Oro and Mauricio Magdaleno.)

Cúneo, Dardo, *Teatro completo de Florencio Sánchez*. Editorial Claridad, Buenos Aires, 1941. (Plays, plus biographical sketches from different points of view, with contemporary newspaper critiques.)

de la Guardia, Alfredo, "The Argentine Modern Theatre." In *Tomorrow*, Vol. II, No. 7, March, 1943. (Condensed account of the trends which produced today's theatre in the Argentine.)

de María y Campos, Armando, *Breve historia del teatro en Chile y su vida taurómaca*. Cia. de Ediciones Populares. Mexico City, 1940. (Short history of the theatre and the bullfight, from a modern point of view.)

Erskine, John, "The People's Theatre." In *Tomorrow*, Vol. II, No. 7, March, 1943. (Describes an experimental theatre, self-supporting and popular, in Buenos Aires.)

Finot, Enrique, *Historia de la literatura boliviana*. Librería de Porrua Hnos. & Cia., Mexico City, 1943. (Exhaustive study of Bolivian literature, with sidelights on the theatre.)

Flores, Angel, "Florencio Sánchez, Uruguayan Playwright." In *Panorama*, No. 23, Washington, D. C., 1944. (Crisp biography with ample detail. Bibliography and list of plays.)

Gonzales, Manuel E., *Lecciones de literatura castellana*. Herrera Hnos., Mexico City, 1940. (Contains some accounts of the early colonial theatre, and bibliographies, and a short anthology of excerpts. Prepared for Mexican high-school students.)

Graham-Lujan, James, "Refugee Theatre in Buenos Aires." In *Theatre Arts Monthly*, Vol. XXVI, No. 6, New York, June, 1942. (Account of the attempts of Spanish refugees to continue their theatre work in Buenos Aires.)

Herrera, Ernesto, *Obras completas*. Editorial Renacimiento, Montevideo, 1917. (Complete plays, with highly laudatory biography.)

Jones, Willis Knapp, "Latin-American Drama—A Reading List." In *Books Abroad*, Vol. XVII, No. 1, Norman, Okla., Winter, 1943.

Magaña Esquival, Antonio. *Imagen del teatro*. Ediciones Letras de México. Mexico City, 1940. (Full account of the experimental theatre in Mexico--plays, actors, and directors.)

Novo, Salvador, "Spellbound Stages." In *Theatre Arts Monthly*, Vol. XXII, No. 8, New York, Aug., 1938. (Analysis of reasons for the backwardness of the commercial theatre in Mexico.)

OTERO MUNOZ, Gustavo, *Resumen de historia de la literatura colombiana.* 3rd ed., Editorial el Escolar, Bogotá, Colombia, 1940. (With short paragraphs on Colombian dramatists; written as a text.)

SÁNCHEZ, Luis Alberto, *Historia de la literatura americana.* Ediciones Ercilla, Santiago de Chile, 1937. (Most complete, and fulsome, account of Latin American literature and its makers. Should be watched for errors of detail.)

USIGLI, Rodolfo, *México en el teatro.* Imprenta Nacional, Mexico City, 1932. (Very scholarly research into Mexico's theatrical history.)

ZUM FELDE, Alberto, *Proceso intelectual del Uruguay.* Editorial Claridad, Montevideo, 1941. (Contains critical studies of Uruguayan dramatists. Very solid work.)

Note: Panorama, mimeographed magazine issued by the Department of Intellectual Coöperation, Pan-American Union, Washington, D.C., contains occasional material of interest on Latin American drama.

PORTUGAL

BELL, Aubrey F., *Studies in Portuguese Literature.* Aubrey Blackwell, Oxford, 1914.
———, *Portuguese Literature.* Clarendon Press, Oxford, 1922.
FIGUEIRIDO, Fidelino, *Historia da literatura realista 1870-1900.* Livraria Classica, Lisbon, 1914.
LACERDA, A. de, *Teatro futuro.* Imprenta da Universidad. Coimbra, Portugal, 1924.

BRAZIL

BANDEIRA, Manuel, *Noções de história das literaturas.* Companhia Editora Nacional, Rio de Janeiro, 1940. (A historical survey.)

CARVALHO, Ronald de, *Pequena História da literatura brasileira.* 6th rev. ed., Rio de Janeiro, 1937.

GOLDBERG, Isaac, *Brazilian Literature.* Alfred A. Knopf, New York, 1922. (General survey, with material on the theatre from the literary point of view.)

JONES, Willis Knapp, "Dramatic Brazil." In *The High-School Thespian,* Vol. 13, Cincinnati, O., April, 1942.

MAGALHÃES, Raymundo, "Brazil's Twenty-five Cent Theatre." In *Theatre Arts Monthly,* Vol. XXVII, No. 4, New York, April, 1943.

MOTTA, Arthur, *História da literatura brasileira.* Sec. VIII. Co. Editora Nacional, São Paulo, Brazil, 1930. (Because regional feeling runs high, and regional authors are not always recognized elsewhere, this work is valuable.)

PAIXÃO, Múcio de, *O teatro no Brazil.* Editora Nacional, Rio de Janeiro, 1936. (This work deals entirely with the theatre, and is very critical.)

SILVA, Lafayette, *Coleção brasileira de teatro.* Serie D., Estudo sobre o teatro. Ministerio da Educação, Rio de Janeiro, 1938. (Material on the theatre, being collected by the Ministry of Education, has been included in this book. The Ministry's *História do teatro brasileiro,* also issued at Rio de Janeiro, is good source material.)

TOMÉ, Alfredo, *Leopoldo Frois e o teatro brasileiro.* Rio de Janeiro, 1942. (A laudatory biography of a producer important in the declamatory theatre, who died in 1922. Contains interesting observations on the theatre.)

YIDDISH AND HEBREW DRAMAS

BEN-ARI, R., *Habima.* [In Yiddish.] L. M. Publication, Chicago, 1937.
GOLDBERG, Isaac, *The Drama of Transition.* Stewart Kidd Co., Cincinnati, O., 1922.

GORIN, B., *The History of the Jewish Theatre*. [In Yiddish.] 2nd ed., 2 vols. Max N. Maisel, New York, 1923.
MOKDONI, A., "Moderner Yiddisher Theater." [In Yiddish.] In *Algemeine Encyclopedia, Yiden*, 2nd ed., Part II, pp. 415-66. General Yiddish Culture Council, New York, 1940.
ROBACK, A. A., *The Story of Yiddish Literature*. Yiddish Scientific Institute, New York, 1940.
SHATZKY, Dr. Jacob, Ed., *Archiv Far Der Geshichte fun Yidishn Teater Un Drame*. [In Yiddish.] Vol. I, Yiddish Scientific Institute, Vilna, 1930.
WAXMAN, Meyer, *A History of Jewish Literature*. (See Vol. 6.) Bloch Publishing Co., New York, 1941.
ZYLBERCWAIG, Zalmen, *Lexicon of the Yiddish Theatre*. [In Yiddish.] Vol. 1, Elisheva Verlag, New York, 1931. Vol. 2, Elisheva Verlag, Warsaw, 1934.

Note: See also *Bamah*, a bimonthly Hebrew Theatre magazine, published at Tel Aviv, Palestine, between 1935 and 1945.

THE UNITED STATES

ANDERSON, John, *The American Theatre*. Dial Press, New York, 1938. (A sketch.)
———, *Box Office*. Jonathan Cape & Harrison Smith, New York, 1929.
BLOCK, Anita, *The Changing World in Plays and Theatre*. Little, Brown & Co., Boston, Mass., 1939. (Stimulating on the new playwrights and tendencies.)
BRICKER, Herschel L., Ed., *Our Theater Today*. Samuel French, Inc., New York, 1936. (A collection of essays. Valuable material.)
BROWN, John Mason, *Upstage*. W. W. Norton & Co., New York, 1930. (Reprints of reviews, stimulating and provocative. Very readable.)
———, *Broadway in Review*. W. W. Norton & Co., New York, 1940. (Reviews, challenging viewpoints set forth.)
BURTON, Richard, *The New American Drama*. The Macmillan Co., New York, 1913. (Very early book, with a good deal of valuable source material.)
CLARK, Barrett H., *A Study of the Modern Drama*. Rev. ed., D. Appleton-Century Co., New York, 1938. (Play lists and bibliographies on American dramatists.)
———, *An Hour of American Drama*. J. B. Lippincott Co., Philadelphia, Pa., 1930. (Short, with a good deal of new source material.)
DEUTSCH, Helen, and HANAU, Stella, *The Provincetown: A Story of the Theatre*. Farrar & Rinehart, New York, 1931. (Very readable account, with a great deal of material on individual playwrights.)
DICKINSON, Thomas H., *The Case of American Drama*. Houghton Mifflin Co., Boston, Mass., 1915. (A general consideration, with philosophical implications. Excellent early work.)
———, *The Insurgent Theatre*. B. W. Huebsch, New York, 1917. (One of the very first works on the new community theatre movement.)
———, *Playwrights of the New American Theatre*. The Macmillan Co., New York, 1925.
EATON, Walter Prichard, *The American Stage of Today*. Moffat, Yard & Co., Boston, Mass., 1908. (Reprints of reviews; excellent material on theatre of early twentieth century.)
———, *At the New Theatre and Others*. Moffat, Yard & Co., Boston, Mass., 1910. (Reprints of reviews. Valuable material.)
———, *Plays and Players*. Stewart Kidd Co., Cincinnati, O., 1916. (Reprints of reviews. Same comment as above.)

———, *The Drama in English*. Charles Scribner's Sons, New York, 1930. (Good compact survey of the subject.)
———, *The Theatre Guild: the First Ten Years*. Brentano's, New York, 1929.
FLANAGAN, Hallie, *Arena*. Duell, Sloan & Pearce, New York, 1940. (Full account of the Federal Theatre Project.)
FREEDLEY, George, and REEVES, John A., *A History of the Theatre*. Crown Publishers, New York, 1941. (Excellent outline, with material on American drama. Lists and bibliographies.)
GASSNER, John, *Masters of the Drama*. Random House, New York, 1940. (Contains some material on American drama. Stimulating and informative.)
GLASPELL, Susan, *The Road to the Temple*. Frederick A. Stokes, New York, 1927. (Has some material on Provincetown Players, especially on Cook and O'Neill.)
GOLDBERG, Isaac, *The Drama of Transition*. Stewart Kidd Co., Cincinnati, O., 1922.
GORELIK, Mordecai, *New Theatres for Old*. Samuel French Inc., New York, 1940. (A good deal of material on American drama. Philosophical in outlook.)
HALLINE, Allan Gates, *American Plays*. American Book Co., New York, 1935. (An anthology, but introductory material, reading lists and bibliographies particularly full and useful.)
HAMILTON, Clayton, *Studies in Stagecraft*. Henry Holt & Co., New York, 1914. (Reprints of reviews. Much valuable material on American drama.)
———, *Problems of the Playwright*. Henry Holt & Co., New York, 1917. (Reprints of reviews. Good deal of material not available elsewhere.)
———, *Seen on the Stage*. Henry Holt & Co., New York, 1920. (Reprints of reviews.)
———, *Conversations on Contemporary Drama*. The Macmillan Co., New York, 1924. (A series of interesting lectures.)
HAPGOOD, Norman, *The Stage in America. 1897-1900*. The Century Co., New York, 1901. (Reviews. Especially valuable in view of their early date.)
HORNBLOW, Arthur, *A History of the American Theatre*. 2 vols. J. B. Lippincott Co., Philadelphia, Pa., 1919. (A standard work on the theatre, but contains some material on drama.)
HUGHES, Glenn, *The Story of the Theatre*. Samuel French Inc., New York, 1928. (Excellent outline, with some material on American drama.)
KRUTCH, Joseph Wood, *The American Drama Since 1918*. Random House, New York, 1939. (Compact and readable, with philosophical viewpoint.)
LAWSON, John Howard, *Theory and Technique of Playwriting*. G. P. Putnam's Sons, New York, 1936. (A careful and intelligent analysis of the subject, with special emphasis in many sections on contemporary American playwrights.)
LEWISOHN, Ludwig, *The Drama and the Stage*. Harcourt Brace & Co., New York, 1922. (Reprints of reviews; sound criticism.)
MACKAYE, Percy, *The Playhouse and the Play*. Mitchell Kennerley, New York, 1909. (Early propaganda. Interesting for its tendencies.)
———, *The Civic Theatre*. Mitchell Kennerley, New York, 1912. (Supplements the above title.)
MANTLE, Burns, *The Best Plays of 1919-1920*. Dodd, Mead & Co., New York, 1920. (The first of a series of annual books, each summarizing the theatrical season, with programs, notes, excerpts from the best plays, etc. The books have been issued annually to date, same author and publisher.)
———, *Contemporary American Playwrights*. Dodd, Mead & Co., New York, 1938. (Sketchy but with much valuable information on playwrights.)
———, and SHERWOOD, Garrison P., *The Best Plays of 1899-1909*. Dodd, Mead & Co., New York, 1944. (An extension, in abbreviated form, backward in time, of the Mantle *Best Plays* books. Very valuable for lists and dates.)

———, and SHERWOOD, Garrison P., *The Best Plays of 1909-1919*. Dodd, Mead & Co., New York, 1933. (As above. The record of performances, and programs, is now complete, in the Mantle and the Mantle-Sherwood volumes from 1899 to date.)
MATTHEWS, Brander, *Playwrights on Playmaking*. Charles Scribner's Sons, New York, 1919. (With valuable references to American drama.)
———, *Rip Van Winkle Goes to the Play*. Charles Scribner's Sons, New York, 1926. (Comments of a veteran critic on later American plays.)
MAYORGA, Margaret, *A Short History of the American Drama: Commentaries on Plays Prior to 1920*. Dodd, Mead & Co., New York, 1932. (Large number of excerpts from plays, with lists and commentaries.)
MERSAND, Joseph, *The American Drama 1930-1940*. Modern Chapbooks, New York, 1941. (Essays on recent American playwrights.)
MOSES, Montrose J., *The American Dramatist*. Rev. ed., Little, Brown, & Co., Boston, Mass., 1925. (One of the first books to bring together source and other material on the American drama. An invaluable reference work.)
NATHAN, George Jean, *Another Book on the Theatre*. B. W. Huebsch, New York, 1915. (Reprints of the author's reviews. A good deal of new and original material; somewhat unconventional attitude toward theatre and drama, especially revolutionary in its impact in the earlier years of the century. Beginning in 1917, the author has issued an average of one new book a year, reprinted, with revisions, from his critical reviews. Among the best and most useful of these are *Comedians All, The World in Falseface, Art of the Night, The Popular Theatre*. All are published by Alfred A. Knopf, New York.)
ODELL, George C. D., *Annals of the New York Stage*. Columbia University Press, New York, 1927 ff. (Over a dozen volumes of this monumental work have already appeared, but the author has not yet reached the twentieth century. An encyclopedic work.)
O'HARA, Frank H., *Today in American Drama*. University of Chicago Press, Chicago, 1939. (A very useful handbook.)
QUINN, Arthur Hobson, *A History of the American Drama from the Civil War to the Present Day*. Rev. ed., F. S. Crofts & Co., New York, 1936. (The standard history of the American drama. The first attempt to collect source material and other data into a single unit. The outstanding work on the subject. Play lists and bibliographies.)
RUHL, Arthur, *Second Nights*. Charles Scribner's Sons, New York, 1914. (Reprints of reviews, very useful for early period.)
SAYLER, Oliver M., *Our American Theatre*. Brentano's, New York, 1923. (A stimulating work on the early days of the "adult" drama.)
SIMONSON, Lee, *The Stage Is Set*. Harcourt, Brace & Co., New York, 1932. (Outstanding essays, informative and philosophical.)
SOBEL, Bernard, *The Theatre Handbook and Digest of Plays*. Crown Publishers, New York, 1940. (An encyclopedic reference work, with much valuable data on American drama, theatre, and playwrights.)
THOMAS, Augustus, *The Print of My Remembrance*. Charles Scribner's Sons, New York, 1922. (An autobiography, with much material on early American theatre.)
TRENT, W. P., ERSKINE, John, SHERMAN, Stuart P., and VAN DOREN, Carl, editors. *The Cambridge History of American Literature*, 4 vols. G. P. Putnam's Sons, New York, 1917-21. (See Vol. 3, article on modern American drama by Montrose J. Moses.)
WOOLLCOTT, Alexander, *Enchanted Aisles*. G. P. Putnam's Sons, New York, 1924. (Entertaining personal papers on theatre and drama.)
YOUNG, Stark, *The Flower in Drama*. Charles Scribner's Sons, New York, 1923. (Philosophical essays.)

Index

ELIZABETH P. BARRETT

A. E. *pseud.*, 221
A Damme en Flandre, 313
A la recherche des coeurs, 285
A l'auberge des apparences, 312
A l'ombre du mal, 287
A souffert sous Ponce Pilate, 288
Abbey Players, 185, 218, 219, 220, 221, 222, 223, 224, 226, 227, 228, 229, 230
Abbott, George, 670, 717, 720
Abe Lincoln in Illinois, 704, 705
Abel, Gustave, 316
Abell, Kjeld, 65
Abenteurer und die Saengerin, Der, 129
Abercrombie, Lascelles, 190, 214
Abide with Me, 736
Abie's Irish Rose, 714
Abigail und Nabal, 109
About Dramaturgy, 463
About God, 507
Abraham ben Aryeh, Hayim, 604
Abraham Lincoln, 189
Abramowitch, S. J., 615, 634
Abtruennige Zar, Der, 94-95
Abu Casem's Slippers, 44
Abuelo, El, 561
Abyss, The, 530
Academia Dramatica, 588
Academy of Science Prize, 521, 524
Accent on Youth, 722
Acevedo y Hernandez, Antonio, 587
Achard, Marcel, 277-8, 304, 308, 311
Acheteuse, L', 282
Achilles, 549
Achilles Had a Heel, 718
Acidalia, 342
Ackerley, Joe Randolph, 298
Ackland, Rodney, 210
Acropolis, The, 706
Across the Continent, 648
Acta Sanctorum, 255
Actors' Theatre, The, 721
Acuática, La, 591
Adam, Paul, 274
Adam and Eva, 668
Adam in Exile, 551
Adam Solitaire, 707
Adam the Creator, 512

Adam's Opera, 203-04
Adami, Giuseppe, 340
Adamus, Franz, *pseud.*, 140, 151
Adder, The, 190
Adding Machine, The, 692, 693
Addinsell, Richard, 203
Ade, George, 662, 676
Adelchi, 319
Adler, Jacob P., 619, 623
Admet, 115
Admirable Crichton, The, 179
Adored One, The, a Legend of the Old Bailey, 180
Adrea, 653
Adrienne Lecouvreur, 237
Adson, Arthur, 487
Advent, 35
Adventurer, The, 506
Aegyptische Helena, Die, 132
Aelita, 465
Aeon; dramatische Trilogie, 95
Ärzte im Kampf, 119
Aeschylus, 120, 252, 306, 499, 519, 690
Aesop, 519
Affair, The, 391, 392
Affair in the Town of Goga, The, 540
Affaire Dreyfus, Die, 113
Affaires sont les affaires, Les, 165, 261-2
Affranchie, L', 266
Affranchis, Les, 264
Afinogenov, Alexander N., 208, 449, 469, 471, 472, 478
After All, 197
After October, 210
After the Ball, 463
After the Fire, 43
After the Funeral, 627
Afternoon Theatre Company, The, 250
Agapetus, 485
Age de fer, L', 284
Age de Juliette, L', 294
Age of Innocence, The, 715
Agents, 627
Aglavaine et Sélysette, 250
Agnes Jordan, 88
Agon, Sultan of Banatam, 552
Agua, Azucarilios y Aguardiente, 564

Aguado, Emiliano, 576
Ah, Wilderness! 690
Aiglas Herabkunft, 95
Aiglon, L' (Dane), 204
Aiglon, L' (Rostand), 251, 305
Aimer, 281
Aînée, L', 267
Aino, 484
Air du Temps, L', 286
Airways, Inc., 707
Ajax, 113
Akins, Zoë, 283, 297, 298, 718
Aksenfeld, Israel, 606, 607, 613
Al amor de los escombros, 588
Alabama, 658
Alarcón, Ruiz de, 572, 579
Alarm Clock, The, 271
Albania, Past, Present, and Future, 548
Albanian Revolt, 548
Albarada, Ginés de, 576
Albena, 543
Albergo sul porto, Un, 358
Albertí, Rafael, 575
Alcazar, 469
Alcestis, 130
Alchemist, The, 510
Aldermen of Lielpils, The, 488
Alecsandri, Vasile, 528
Alegre, Porto, 598
Aleichem, Sholom, *pseud.*, 626, 627, 633, 634
Alencar, José Martiniano de, 598
Alexander Nevski, 467
Alexander the Great, 549
Alpieri, Count V. A., 319, 545, 546
Ali, 352
Alibi, 213
Alice Sit-by-the-Fire, 180
Alien Corn, 700
Alison's House, 716
Alkibiades, 484
All Before, 530
All God's Chillun Got Wings, 686, 709
All My Relatives Weep, 488
All Souls' Day, 554, 555
All Those Endearing Young Charms, 739
Alleluja, 328
Alles um Liebe, 93
Almas perdidas, 587
Along Came Ruth, 316
Alsberg, Max, 118
Altolaguirre, Manuel, 565, 570
Altra Nanetta, L', 357
Alunans, Adolf, 488
Alvarez Lleras, Antonio, 588
Alvarez Quintero, Joaquin, 565-7-8, 575, 580
Alvarez Quintero, Serafín, 565, 566, 567, 568, 575, 580

Alzire, 527
Am Glockenturm, 109
Amaco, 719
Amante du Christ, L', 258
Amants, Les, 266-7
Amants de Sazy, Les, 271
Amazed Evangelist, The, 199
Amazing Dr. Clitterhouse, The, 209
Ambidextre journaliste, 313
Ambush, 716
Ame en folie, L', 263
Ame en peine, L', 285
America Bluff, 629
America in the Bathhouse, 490
American, The, 514
American Dramatist, The, 672
American Dream, 709
American Hassidim, 632
American Laboratory Theatre, 284, 302, 711
American Landscape, 144, 694
American Repertory Theatre, The, 173, 180
American Tragedy, An, 499
American Way, The, 735
American Yacht in Split Harbor, An, 533
Ames ennemies, Les, 264
Amiel, Denys, 278, 284, 306
Amitié, 299
Amon and Deborah, 602
Among the Married, 719
Amor, 599
Amor de Don Perlimplín con Belisa en su Jardin, 571, 572
Amor por Anexins, 599
Amore dei tre Re, L', 351
Amoroso tragedia, L', 352-53
Amour médecin, L', 275
Amour veille, L', 272
Amoureuse, 265, 267
Amphitryon 38, 282, 307
Amys et Amyle, 256
Anarchie in Sillian, 152
Anastacio, 599
Anathema (Andreev), 432
Anathema (Wyspiański), 499
Anatol, 134, 184
Anatols Groessenwahn, 134
Anatomist, The, 199, 200
Ancey, Georges, 257, 258
Ancient Mariner, The, 686
And so ad infinitum: The Life of the Insects, 512
And So It Will Be, 480
And So They Were Married, 681
And So To Bed, 196
And Then There Were None, 213
Andere, Die, 127
Andersen, Hans Christian, 26, 35, 46, 91

Anderson, John, 733
Anderson, Maxwell, 641, 657, 662, 666, 677, 691, 695, 696, 697, 698, 704, 705, 716, 718, 721, 723
Andre Hofer, 141
Andreas der ungarische König mit Bankbano, 516
Andreas Hollmann, 116
Andreas und die Koenigin, 98
Andreev, Leonid, 249, 423, 430, 431, 438, 443-5, 485, 566
Andreu and Joanna, 519
Andrew and the Dragon, 508
Androcles and the Lion, 173
Andrutsos, 545
Ane de Buridan, L', 272
Anfisa, 432
Ange gardien, L', 274
Angel Street, 209
Angels in Our Midst, 510
Angels On Earth, 632
Animal Kingdom, The, 702, 703
Anja und Esther, 119
Ann Vroome, 713
Anna Christie, 684, 685
Anna Karenina, 387, 470
Anna Liisa, 484
Anna Thúran, 520
Anna Walewska, 93
Anne of England, 207
Annie and Michael, 485
Anninos, Charalambos, 546
Anniversary, The, 410
Anno Domini, 530
Annonce faite à Marie, L', 247, 253, 254
Another Language, 724
Another Love, 294
Another Love Story, 196
Anouilh, Jean, 289, 296-97
Ansel, Franz, pseud., 312
An-sky, 626, 630, 631, 636
Anspacher, Louis Kaufman, 672, 680
Anthony, C. L., pseud., see Smith, Dodie
Anthony and Anna, 224
Antigone (Cocteau), 302
Antigone (Hasenclever), 105
Antigone (Poizat), 253
Anti-Matrimony, 661
Antiope, 546
Antoine, André, 31, 78, 243, 244, 245, 246, 247, 257, 258, 263, 265, 274, 278, 290, 306, 325, 398, 497, 525, 639
Antoine, André-Paul, 306
Antona-Traversi, Camillo, 326, 328
Antona-Traversi, Giannino, 326, 328, 329, 330, 343
Antonelli, Luigi, 344, 345
Antonia, 250
Antonio José, 598

Antony, 236
Antropov, 393
Antroula's Affianced, 545
Anzengruber, Ludwig, 94, 125, 140, 159, 532, 539
Apfel Marriage, The, 495
Aphrodite, 271
Apjumibas, 490
Apollinaire, Guillaume, 302
Apostel, Der, 127
Apostelspiel, Das, 144
Apostle, The, 520
Apothekar, David, 618
Apôtre, L', 264
Appia, Adolphe, 275, 279
Apple Cart, The, 176
Applesauce, 713
Appointment for Love, 525
Après l'amour, 295
Apron-Strings, 713
Arabella, 132
Araignée de cristal, L', 247
Araujo, Manuel de, 598
Arbeider-Foreningernes Blad, 3
Arbeiter, Bauern, Soldaten, 111
Archer, William, 10, 164, 167, 168, 169, 639, 649
Arciduca, L', 355
Arconada, Cesar, 574
Ardavín, Fernández, 575
Ardrey, Robert, 721, 723, 729, 730
Arène, Emmanuel, 272
Arent, Arthur, 731
Aren't We All? 195
Aretino, Pietro, 318
Argentina Libre, 586
Ariadne, 96
Ariadne auf Naxos, 131
Ariel, 264
Aristocracy, 647
Aristocrats, The, 463
Aristophanes, 120, 139, 266, 276, 308, 500, 545
Aristotle, 376
Aristotelian Theatre, 121
Arizona, 658
Arlen, Michael, 212
Arlequín, El, 582
Arlésienne, L', 241
Arliss, George, 208
Arliss, Mrs. George, 208
Arme Heinrich, Der, 81
Arme Konrad, Der, 117
Arme Vetter, Der, 106
Armendoktor, Der, 143
Armor, The, 554
Armored Train 14-69, 456, 457, 458
Arms and the Man, 169, 217
Armseligen Besenbinder, Die, 94

Armstrong, Anthony, 209, 213
Armstrong, Paul, 679, 721
Armut, 150
Army With Banners, The, 666
Arne, 45
Arniches, Don Carlos, 562-63, 565
Arnold, 546
Arnstein, Mark, 633
Around the Corner, 719
Arséne Lupin, 298
Arsenic and Old Lace, 738
Art and Mrs. Bottle, 202
Art moderne, L', 310
Arte por las nubes, El, 564
Artef, 623
Arthuis, Gaston, 283
Arthur, 189
Article 330, L', 272
Artist's Wife, The, 520
Artists, 52
Artsybashev, Michel Petrovich, 430, 433, 438, 439, 440-41, 443-45
Arum A Baidel, 634
Arwidsson, A. I., 482
Arzigogolo, L', 353
As a Man Thinks, 659
As Doutoras, 598
As You Desire Me, 363, 366
As You Think, 495
Asachi, George, 527
Ascent of F. 6, The, 215
Asch, Sholem, 624-25, 628-29, 634, 636
Asche, Oscar, 189
Aschenbroedel, 161
Ashantee, The, 497
Ashman, Aaron, 637
Ashton, Winifred, *see* Dane, Clemence, pseud.
Asi que pasen cinco anos, 572
Aškerc, Anton, 540
Asmodée, 283
Aspazija, pseud., 489, 490
Assassin, The, 728
Assaut, L', 270
Assemblée des femmes, L', 266
Assommoir, L', 242, 255
Assumption of Hannele Mattern, The, 244
Assunta Spina, 326, 350
Astonished Heart, The, 195
Astrid, 555
At Dawn, 489
At Mrs. Beam's, 193
At Rindal Camp, 64
At Storhove, 50
At the Breaking Point, 471
At the Foot of Vitosha, 543
At the Gates of the Kingdom, 410
At the Goal, 500
At the Jolly Spot, 385

At the Window, 627
At Twilight, 506
Atala, 520
Atelier, L', 276, 304
Athalia's Reward, 604
Atie's Marriage; or, Continuation of the Conqueror, 556
Atkinson, Brooks, 448, 711
Atlantic, The, 71
Atlas, Leopold, 725
Atlas-Hôtel, 302-03
Attack, The, 270
Attic Nights, 546
Attila, 189
Au rat mort, cabinet No. 6, 259
Aubes, Les, 311
Auden, W(ystan) H(ugh), 214-16
Aue, Hartmann von der, 81
Auernheimer, Raoul, 138
Aufruhr des Goldes, Der, 112
Aufstieg und Fall der Stadt Mahagonny, 121, 122
Auge um Auge, 108
Augenlicht, J. C., 632
Augier, Emile, 162, 164, 168, 177, 185, 234, 237, 239, 240, 244, 245, 261, 267, 274, 281, 324, 494, 508
Augustus in Search of a Father, 185
Aumône, L', 314
Aunt of England, The, 208
Aunt Sosie, 611, 612
Aurora, 517
Aus dem buergerlichen Heldenleben, 101
Ausgang der Moderne, Der, 96
Auszug aus Ägypten, Der, 96-97
Auto de los Reyes Magos, 580
Autos profanos, 590
Autos sacramentales, 132, 233, 561
Autre Messie, L', 315
Autumn Crocus, 201
Autumn Fire, 225
Avare, L', 380, 504
Avaricious Knight, The, 380
Avariés, Les, 260
Ave Maria, 529
Aventures de Gilles ou le saint malgré lui, Les, 255
Aventurière, L', 162
Averkiev, 393
Avermaete, Roger, 316
Aves y Pajaros, 568, 574
Aveugles, Les, 247, 249
Avram Iancu, 530
Avuentura terrestre, L', 360
Awake and Sing, 725-27
Awful Night, The, 492
Axël, 246
Ayesta, 576
Aza, Vital, 564

INDEX

A-zeupanned Gentleman of the World, 506
Azevedo, Arthur, 599
Azorín, J. M. R., 566

Baba-Yaga, 372
Babay, Joseph, 525
Baby Cyclone, 678
Babylone, 252
Baccarat, 269
Bacchusfest, Das, 136
Bachelor Born, 202
Bachelor Father, 715
Bachelors' Club, 495
Back to His People, 622
Back to Methuselah, 175
Bacmeister, Ernst, 98
Bad Man, The, 715
Badgers, The, 476
Bagnes d'enfants, Les, 259
Bahr, Hermann, 126-28, 132, 534
Baker, Elizabeth, 185
Baker, George Pierce, 221, 671, 672; see also George Pierce Baker's English 47 Workshop
Balcony, The, 53-54, 72
Balderston, John, 715
Baldus et Josina, 313
Ballad of the Bloodthirsty Wife, The, 509
Ballade von der Stadt, 149
Ballard, Fred, 670
Ballester, Torrente, 576
Balloon, 225-26
Bałucki, Michał, 493, 495
Balzac, Honoré de, 91, 195, 234, 237, 241, 262, 395
Bambi, 138
Banco, 292
Bancroft, Squire, 160-62
Bandello, 332
Bánk Bán, 516
Banker, The, 473
Banker's Daughter, The, 646, **647**
Bankrupt, The, 384
Bankruptcy, A, 45, 47, **48**
Banque Némo, La, 297
Baptême, Le, 292
Bar Kochba, 615
Barabbas, 71
Baraonda, La, 330
Barba de Carrillo, La, **563**
Barbara's Wedding, 181
Barbarians, 426
Barbarò, I, 330
Barbusse, Henri, 428
Barč, Ivan, 515
Barca errante, La, **582**
Barker, The, 719

Barlach, Ernst, 106
Barnes, Margaret Ayer, 715
Baron Goertz, 505
Barons, Christian, 488
Baroque theatre, 124-25, 131-32, 550-51, 577, 580
Barraca, La, 566, 571, 574
Barranco abajo, 583
Barretts of Wimpole Street, The, 206
Barricade, La, 262
Barrie, Sir James Matthew, 177-82, 184, 190, 191, 200, 497
Barroso, J., 600
Barry, Philip, 666, 670, 679, 680, 691, 693, 702, 703, 704, 716, 721, 722
Barry, Tom, 713
Barson, Zaharia, 530
Barski, Israel, 616
Bart, Jakub, see Ćišinski
Bartel Turaser, 140
Bartlett, Basil, 283
Bartók, Louis, 520
Bartol, Vladimir, 541
Bartoš, Jan, 511
Barun Franjo Trenk, 532
Barzini, Luigi, 344
Basset, Serge, 273
Basshe, Emjo, 707, 709
Bataille, Henry, 269, 281, 284
Bataille de la Marne, La, 306
Bataille des dames, 237
Bath, The, 452, 461
Bats, The, 494
Battle Hymn, 731
Baty, Gaston, 202, 276-79
Bauche, Henri, 259
Baudelaire, Charles, 285, 312
Baudoin, Julio, 587
Bauer Baetz, 117
Bauer unterm Hammer, 118
Bauern, 106
Bauernfeld, Edward, 125, 138
Baumer, Marie, 713
Bax, Clifford, 207
Be Calm, Camilla, 681
Beach, Lewis, 670, 713
Bear, The, 487
Bear Hunter, The, 487
Bear's Marriage, The, 455
Bearskin, 478
Beasts, The, 530
Beau Brummell, 659
Beaubourg, Maurice de, 247
Beaumarchais, Pierre, 234, 291
Beautiful Despot, The, 442
Beautiful, New Ahasuerus Play, A, 603
Beautiful People, The, 740
Because She Loved Him So, 273
Becher, Johannes R., 111

Becker, Julius Maria, 108
Becque, Henri, 234, 242-43, 261-62, 267, 291, 325, 494
Bedbug, 451
Bedmates, 231
Bednar, R. C., 508
Bedoya, Manuel, 587
Beerbohm, Sir Max, 204
Beer-Hoffman, Richard, 137, 636
Bees on the Boatdeck, 204
Beethoven, 294
Beffardo, Il, 354
Beggar on Horseback, 733, 734
Beggar's Opera, The, 121
Beggars of Life, 695
Begovich, Milan, 532, 533
Behold, the Bridegroom, 701
Behrman, S. N., 307, 642, 670, 680, 693, 703, 704, 707, 716, 721, 722, 727
Bein, Albert, 708
Bein, Mary, 708
Bek, 469
Belasco, David, 270, 357, 648, 652
Bełcikowski, Adam, 499
Belfagor, 356
Belfagor arcidiavolo, 356
Belinda, 192
Belinde, 93
Belinski, 442
Bell, Aubrey, 561, 562, 567
Bell for Adano, A, 724
Bella addormentata, La, 360
Bella Donna, 196
Bellamy, Edward, 649
Bell' Apollo, Il, 327
Belle Madame Héber, La, 268
Belloi, Gedaliah, 610
Bells, The, 510
Belt, The, 707
Belval, Maurice, see Maubel, Henri, pseud.
Ben-Ami, Jacob, 623
Benatzky, Ralph, 144
Benavente, Jacinto, 470, 560, 563, 565, 566, 567, 568, 569, 572, 574, 575, 576, 580, 587, 693
Bence Uz, 525
Bending of the Bough, The, 187
Benedetti, Aldo de, 341
Benedix, Roderick, 161
Benelli, Sem, 339, 347, 350-53
Benjamin, René, 296
Benko Bot, 516, 531
Bennett, Arnold, 187, 392
Bennett, Charles, 213
Benois, Alexander, 434
Benrimo, J. Harry, 678
Benson, Sally, 737
Berczik, Árpád, 520

Bérénice, 286
Bergamín, José, 575
Bergbom, K. J., 484
Bergelson, David, 633
Berger, Alfred von, 532
Berger, H., 636
Bergerat, Emile, 243
Bergère au pays de loups, La, 255
Bergman, Hjalmar, 65, 66
Bergroth, Kersty, 485
Bergson, Henry, 246
Bergström, Hjalmar, 57, 58
Bergwerk, Das, 149
Bergwerk zu Fahn, Das, 129
Berkeley, Reginald Cheyne, 208
Berkeley Square, 715
Berkowitz, I. D., 627, 636
Bermann of Limburg, 603
Bernard, Jean-Jacques, 248, 266, 279, 281, 284-85, 286, 308
Bernard, Tristan, 272, 284, 297
Bernardo l'Eremita, 345
Bernhard von Weimar, 109
Bernhardt, Sarah, 86, 163, 239, 240, 297, 332, 580
Bernstein, Henry, 269, 270, 339, 341
Berr, Georges, 274, 297
Berretto a sonagli, Il, 362, 364
Berrini, Nino, 354
Bertolazzi, Carlo, 326
Besant, Annie, 640, 645
Besetztes Gebiet, 150
Besier, Rudolf, 206
Beskydov, 513
Besnard, Lucien, 252, 283
Besserer Herr, Ein, 105
Best Sellers, 291
Bethlehem Legend, 540
Betrothal, The (Kivi), 483
Betrothal, The (Maeterlinck), 250
Betti, Ugo, 357-58
Bettler, Der, 104
Bettler von Syrakus, Der, 87
Betty's Guardian, 51
Between Sunset and Dawn, 212
Between the Battles, 45
Between Two Worlds (An-sky), 630
Between Two Worlds (Rice), 694
Bevilacqua, Giuseppe, 340
Bewitched, 670, 699
Beyond, 105
Beyond Human Power I, 47-49, 50, 52
Beyond Human Power II, 50
Beyond the Breakers, 663
Beyond the Horizon, 640, 674, 682, 684, 685, 691, 721
Bialik, Hayim Nahman, 628, 631, 637
Bianca Capello, 57
Bianchi, Edmundo, 586

INDEX 767

Biberpelz, Der, 80, 81
Bibesco, Antoine, 299
Bibi, Jugend, 1928, 101
Bibó, Louis, 521
Biedermann, Felix, *see* Doermann, Felix, pseud.
Bierce, Ambrose, 665
Bifur, 301
Big Blow, The, 731
Big Day, The, 460
Big Fish, 495
Big Haul, The, 489
Big House, The, 224
Big Lake, 711
Big Pond, The, 668
Big We, The, 67
Bildschnitzer, Die, 141
Bill of Divorcement, A, 203
Billeted, 200
Billinger, Richard, 156-58
Bimko, Fishel, 629
Binet, Alfred, 259
Bing Boys Are Here, The, 214
Binkis, Kazys, 492
Binyon, Laurence, 189, 214
Biography, 704
Birabeau, André, 266, 297
Bird, The, 501
Bird in Hand, 189
Birds, The, 139
Biró, Lajos, 523, 524
Birthright, 225
Bishop, G. W., 255
Bishop Maunu, 484
Bismarck, 100
Bisson, Alexandre, 273
Bistritski, Nathan, 637
Bit o' Love, A, 183
Bitter Fate, 384, 390
Bitter Oleander, 571, 572
Bitter Sweet, 194
Bizet, Georges, 241
Björnson, Björnstjerne, 1, 2, 8, 9, 22, 44-55, 75, 649, 672
Black Boy, 709
Black Cherries, 525
Black Cock, The, 529
Black Eye, The, 200
Black Glove, The, 44
Black Masks, The, 432
Black Pit, 708
Black Rose, The, 505
Black Sheep, 694
Black Virgin, The, 212
Blackmail, 213
Blaga, Lucian, 529, 530
Blanchette, 244, 260
Blankfort, Michael, 731
Blaue Boll, Der, 107

Blaumanis, Rudolf, 488, 489
Bleus d'amour, Les, 271
Blind Man's Buff, 231
Blinde Göttin, Die, 110, 231
Blithe Spirit, 195
Bliziński, Józef, 494
Bloch, Jean-Richard, 236, 245, 254, 306
Block, Etta, 627
Blockade, The (Ivanov), 458
Blockade (Schoenherr), 143
Blok, Alexander, 430, 436, 437, 438, 443, 445, 448, 450
Bloodstream, 798-99
Bloody Farewell, The, 614
Bloom, Abraham, 622
Blossoming Month, 554
Blow, Sydney, 196
Blow, Wind! 490
Blue Bird, The, 250
Blue Fox, The, 522
Blue Kerchief, The, 462
Bluebeard's Eighth Wife, 292
Blume, Bernard, 114-15
Blumenthal, Oskar, 144
Boadicea, 189
Boat Woman, The, 464
Bocksgesang, 146
Bodas de Sangre, 571-73
Bodson, Felix, 312
Bogdan Khmelnitski, 474
Bogen des Odysseus, Der, 83, 85
Bogovich, Mirko, 534, 538
Bohême, La, 333
Bois sacré, Le, 272
Boleslav, 532
Bolesław the Bold, 499
Bolitho, William, 717
Bolton, Guy, 668
Bon petit diable, Un, 305
Bon roi Dagobert, Le, 252
Bonaparte (Blume), 114
Bonaparte (Unruh), 106
Bonds of Interest, 567, 693
Bondwomen, The, 387
Bonmariage, Sylvain, 316-17
Bonnet Over the Windmill, 201
Bontempelli, Massimo, 367, 368
Boom Boom, 297
Boothe, Clare, 564, 736, 737
Borberg, Svend, 65, 66
Borden, Ethel, 207
Boretz, Allen, 677
Borga Estate, 56
Borgen, Johan, 65
Borgese, Giuseppe Antonio, 355
Boris Godunov, 379, 380, 394, 408
Borislav, 543
Bork, 118
Borras, Tomás, 576

Borštnik, Ignace, 538
Boss, The, 679
Bosse, Harriet, 36, 40
Botelho, Abel, 595
Both Your Houses, 696
Bothlingk, Madeleine, 555
Bottomley, Gordon, 190, 214
Botzaris, 545
Boubouroche, 244, 271, 272
Boucicault, Dion, 709
Bouffons, Les, 252
Bouhélier, Saint-Georges de, 255, 256
Boule de suif, 734
Bound East for Cardiff, 683, 684
Bourdet, Édouard, 273, 289, 290-91
Bourgeois aux champs, Le, 260
Bourgeois drama, 234, 235, 240, 245, 257, 260, 325, 528, 718
Bourgeois, Gentilhomme, Le, 131
Bourget, Paul, 245, 262, 264
Bourgmestre de Stilemonde, Le, 249, 250
Boussac de Saint-Marc, André, 287-88
Bovis, Giovanni, 337
Boy David, The, 182
Boy Meets Girl, 677, 723
Boyd, Ernest, 285
Boyle, William, 226
Boys of Our Village, The, 487
Boy-Zaleński, 498
Bozděch, Emanuel, 505, 506
Braaten, Oskar, 65, 67
Braccialetto, Il, 330
Bracco, Roberto, 324, 325, 326, 333, 334, 335, 340, 347, 366
Bräute von Bamberg, Die, 97
Brahm, Otto, 78
Braindele Kozak, 615
Brand, Millen, 724
Brand, 7, 8, 9, 15, 23, 54, 559
Brand im Opernhaus, Der, 103
Brandes, Edvard, 51
Brandes, Georg, 2, 49, 64, 74
Brandy, mucho brandy! 566
Brass Ankle, 710
Brastiņš, Ernest, 490
Brave Soul, The, 525
Bread, 460
Bread Mill, The, 634
Breakfast in Bed, 273
Breaking a Butterfly, 166
Break-Up, 72, 73
Brebis, La, 271
Brecht, Berthold, 120-22
Breero, Gerbrand Adriaansz, 551
Brennende Dornbusch, Der, 149
Brennende Erde, 109
Brenner, Anita, 589
Brent, Romney, 190
Brentano, Lowell, 717

Breslau, Mendel, 604
Brest-Litowsk, 113
Bretón, Tomás, 564
Breughel, 316
Brewster's Millions, 677
Bridal Crown, The, 39, 41
Bride Above, The, 552
Bride and the Fanatics, The, 486
Bride for the Unicorn, A, 231
Bride of Freedom, The, 503
Bride of the Lamb, 714
Bride Who Was Difficult to Please, The, 634
Bridge, The, 522
Bridge of Arta, The, 546
Bridge of San Luis Rey, The, 732
Bridie, James, *pseud.,* 196, 199-200
Brief Moment, 703
Brieux, Eugène, 244, 257-60, 268, 289, 314, 672
Brigadere, Anna, 489
Brigadier General, The, 375
Brigadier Ocskay, 522
Brighouse, Harold, 186
Bright Star, 703
Bright Sunshine, 526
Brighter Side, The, 268
Brigette, 94
Brignolle et sa Fille, 268
Broadhurst, George, 664
Broadway, 717
Broadway Jones, 676, 677
Broder Singers, The, 609, 610, 612
Bródy, Alexander, 522
Broken Dishes, 718
Broken Hearts, 621
Broken Soil, 225
Brokenbrow, 110
Bromfield, Louis, 291
Bronnen, Arnolt, *pseud.,* 151-52
Bronner, *see* Bronnen, Arnolt, *pseud.*
Bronner, Ferdinand, *see* Adamus, Franz, *pseud.*
Brontës, The, 208
Bronx Express, 632
Brooks, George S., 717
Brother and Sister, 61
Brother Jacques, 269
Brother Mose, 731
Brother's Honor, A, 547
Brothers, The (Van Eeden), 553, 555
Brothers, The (Vrchlický), 507
Brothers Ashkenazi, 634
Brothers Karamazov, The, 274, 276, 396
Brothers' Feud, The, see Brothers, The (Van Eeden)
Browne, E. Martin, 214
Browne, Maurice, 207
Browne, Porter Emerson, 715

Browning, Robert, 160, 206, 653, 715
Bruckner, Ferdinand, *pseud.*, 152, 311
Bruecke, Die, 145
Brückengeist, Der, 107
Brües, Otto, 109
Bruges-la-morte, 312, 313
Brulador de Sevilla, 578
Brunetière, F., 641
Brunhilde, 96
Brust, Alfred, 107
Brustein, 468, 469
Bruyez, René, 288
Bryant, Arthur, 207
Buccaneer, The, 695
Buchanan, I. Thompson, 680
Büchner, Georg, 99, 114, 115, 150
Büchse der Pandora, Die, 99, 100
Buckle, Henry T., 24
Buen negocio, Un, 583
Buenos Aires Municipal Prize, 586
Buerger Napoleon, 94
Bürger Schippel, 101
Bürger von Calais, Die, 102
Büxel, 85
Bufere, 337
Builders, The, 543
Building Fund, The, 226
Building of Skadra, 531, 543
Bulgakov, Michael, 380, 449, 455, 456, 457
Bull, Francis, 19
Bull, Ole, 4
Bulwer-Lytton, Edward George, 160
Bunch of Violets, A, 165
Bunin, I. A., 413
Bunty Pulls the Strings, 187
Buona figliuola, La, 336
Buona novella, La, 343
Burckhardt, Jakob, 130
Burglary, 484
Burgos, Xavier de, 564
Burgraves, Les, 236
Burke, Edwin, 716
Burlador de Sevilla, 578
Burlesques, 116, 161, 178, 180, 293, 301, 315, 587
Burte, Hermann, 112
Burton, Richard, 672
Bury the Dead, 727
Bús Fekete, László, 525
Business Is Business, 165, 262
Businessmen, The, 487
Busman's Honeymoon, 216
Busnach, William, 242
Bustillo Oro, Juan, 590
But for the Grace of God, 725
But Tomorrow, 71
Butors et la Finette, Les, 304
Butter and Egg Man, The, 733, 734
Butterfly on the Wheel, A, 196

Butti, Enrico Annibale, 337, 338
By the Open Sea, 32
Byrne, M. St. Clare, 216
Byron, George Gordon, Lord, 381, 406, 594
Byron, H. J., 161
Byzantios, 545
Byzantium, 522

Caballo del comissario, El, 584
Cabeza del Bautista, La, 570
Caccia al lupo, La, 325
Cadet Roussel, 252
Caducée, Le, 290
Caesar and Cleopatra, 170, 171, 704
Caesar and Man, 500
Caesar Borgia, 508
Café de danse, 271
Cage, La, 261
Calandria, 581
Caldeira, Fernando, 595
Calderon, George, 185
Calderón de la Barca, Pedro, 132, 233, 253, 254, 276, 370, 566, 578, 596
Caliban, 661
Caligula, 500
Call It a Day, 201
Call of the Wood, The, 530
Calla, corazón! 587
Calvo Sotelo, Joaquín, 576
Calzini, Raffaele, 354
Calzolais di Messina, Il, 340
Camara, Joãs da, 595
Camargo, Joracy, 599
Camel Through the Needle's Eye, The, 510
Camille, 239
Camino de flores, 587
Cammino sulle acque, Il, 369
Campbell, Bartley, 652
Campbell, Joseph, 226
Campden Wonder, The, 188
Campo alegre, El, 581
Campo Travieso, 587
Canard Sauvage, Le, 278
Canaries Sometimes Sing, 195
Cancer at Heart, 529
Canción azul, La, 587
Canción de Cuna, 567
Canción de invierno, 581
Canción de primavera, 581
Candida, 169, 170, 172, 443
Candidat, Le, 241
Candle-Light, 154
Canfield, Mary Casa, 207
Canicola, 360
Canillita, 583
Cankar, Ivan, 539, 540

Cano, Leopoldo, 560
Canossa, 96
Cant, 74
Cantab, A, 161
Canth, Minna, 484, 485
Cantinflas, 592
Çap des tempêtes, Le, 270
Čapek, Josef, 511
Capek, Karel, 465, 511, 512, 570
Capelli bianchi, I, 341
Capodistrias, 545
Caponsacchi, 715
Caprice, 154
Captain Brassbound's Conversion, 171
Captive, The, 290
Capture of Velikoshumsk, The, 477
Capuana, Luigi, 325, 365
Capus, Alfred, 268, 289, 308
Caracol, El, 566
Caragiale, Ion Luca, 528
Carb, David, 715
Carcass, The, 628
Card Players, 529
Caricatures, 496
Caritá mondana, La, 330
Carlota Joaquima, 599
Carnaval des enfants, Le, 256
Carolina Playmakers, The, 710, 711
Carpas, 592
Carpenter, Edward Childs, 714, 715
Carr, Philip, 307
Carroll, Paul Vincent, 229
Carrots, 186, 272
Cartel des Quatre, 279
Carvalho, Ronald de, 596
Casa a due piani, La, 341
Casa branca da serra, A, 600
Casa de Bernarda Alba, La, 571, 572, 573
Casa del sonna, La, 326
Casa Editorial, La, 562
Casa segreta, La, 342
Casalis, Jeanne de, 206
Casanova in Wien, 138
Cascais, 594
Cáscara de Nuez, La, 586
Case of American Drama, The, 672
Case of the Frightened Lady, The, 209
Casella, Alberto, 358
Casey Jones, 730
Cassandra, 93
Cassilis Engagement, The, 184
Caste, 161
Castello del sogno, Il, 337
Castro, Augusto de, 595
Castro, Guillén de, 574
Cat and the Canary, The, 717
Catalan Theatre, 564, 565
Cataline, 3, 4
Caterina Sforza, 352

Catherine the Great, 372, 373, 374, 375, 376, 377, 383
Cathleen Listens In, 227
Cathleen ni Houlihan, 217
Cato of Utica, 532
Cattle Driver, The, 64
Catto, Max, 209
Cattura di Sansone, La, 355
Cause ed effetti, 322, 323
Cause of it All, The, 398
Cavacchioli, Enrico, 344, 346, 347, 361
Cavalcade, 193, 194
Cavaliere (Goetz), 114
Cavalière, La (Richepin), 252
Cavaliere d'industria, Il, 320
Cavalière Elsa, La, 315
Cavalleria rusticana, 325
Cavalotti, Felice, 337
Cavalry Patrol, 510
Cavicchioli, Giovanni, 355
Cayuela, Arturo María, 575
Ce n'était qu'un rêve, 312
Céard, Henri, 258
Cecchi, Alberto, 318, 358
Cédulas de San Juan, 583
Ceia dos Cardeais, A, 595
Celestin, Jack, 213
Celestina, La, 118
Celestino, Vicente, 600
Cena delle beffe, La, 351
Cenci, The, 118, 247
Cercle des Escholiers, 278-79
Cercle Gaulois, Le, 243
Cerkvenik, Angel, 540
Cervantes, Miguel de, 456
Ces messieurs, 257
Cesare Borgia, 353
Cesarec, August, 534
Cézan, Claude, 280
Chaev, 393-94
Chain, The, 540
Chaine, Pierre, 259, 296
Chaine, Une, 165
Chained in the Vestry, 626
Chains (Baker), 185
Chains (Leivick), 632
Chalk Dust, 731
Chamber Plays, 35, 43, 44, 58
Chambers, C(harles) Haddon, 185
Chambre blanche, La, 269
Champagne, 627
Chañarcillo, 587
Chance de Françoise, La, 244, 265
Chancellor and the Locksmith, The, 454
Chandelier, Le, 237, 304
Channel Road, The, 734
Chantecler, 251
Chapeau de paille d'Italie, Le, 240
Chapelle ardente, La, 264

INDEX 771

Chapí, Ruperto, 564
Chapin, Harold, 185
Chapons, Les, 261
Charity, 500
Charles and Mary, 208
Charles XI, 57
Charles of Durazzo, 514, 532
Charley's Aunt, 163, 214, 654
Charlot Revues, 214
Charlotte Corday, 237
Charnay, Robert, 274
Chartreuse de comédiens, 275
Chase, Ilka, 298
Châtelaine, La, 268
Chatterton, 236
Chaussée, Nivelle de la, 234
Cheapside, 208
Chekhov, Anton Pavlovich, 163, 174, 183, 197, 210, 218, 227, 278, 339, 393, 394, 395, 400-421, 423, 425, 430, 443, 445, 446, 455, 470, 472, 476, 544, 719, 724
Chekhov, Michael, 392
Chekhova, Olga Knipper, 411, 414, 415, 423, 427, 471
Chelkash, 429
Chemineau, La, 252
Cheney, Sheldon, 674
Chénier, Marie Joseph, 234
Cherokee Night, The, 712, 731
Cherry Orchard, The, 183, 415, 416, 417, 418, 419, 420, 446, 476
Chiarelli, Luigi, 339, 344-45
Chicago, 717
Chicanery, 377
Chicos Crecen, Los, 586
Chief Thing, The, 445
Children, The, 427
Children of Darkness, 715
Children of the Ghetto, 186
Children of the Moon, 718
Children of the Sun, The, 425, 430
Children's Crusades, 530
Children's Hour, The, 728
Chimere, 345
China's Sword, 469
Chiono, José, 587
Chip-Axe, The, 511
Chlumberg, Hans, *pseud.*, 155
Chodorov, Jerome, 736, 737, 739
Chorus Lady, The, 680
Chris Christopherson, 684
Christ's Comet, 216
Christa, die Tante, 108
Christian, 299
Christianization of the Court of Preslav, The, 542
Christiansen, Einar, 63
Christiansen, Sigurd, 65, 67
Christie, Agatha, 213

Christine, 282
Christmas Books, The, 35
Christmas Dream, 521
Christmas Eve, 212
Christmas Legend, 543
Christophe Colomb, 315
Chronicles, 530
Chu-Chin-Chow, 189
Chueca, Federico, 564
Chums, 539
Church Mouse, A, 525
Churchill, 207
Churión, Juan José, 579
Ciascuna a suo modo, 365
Cid, Le, 574
Cinematic devices, use of, 70, 110
Cin-pin-sing, 575
Cione, Otto Miguel, 582
Ciprian, G., 530
Circle, The, 191
Circle of Chalk, The, 109
Čišinski, 503
Cisneros, 569
Citta di Roma, La, 330
Citta morta, La, 347, 348
City, The, 659, 660
City of the Plague, The, 380
City of the Sun, The, 455
City of the Winds, The, 459
Civetta, La, 330
Civic Repertory Theatre, 285, 434, 708, 716
Civic Theatre, The, a Substitute for War, 661
Clairière, La, 261, 266
Clancy Name, The, 224
Clara Záchs, 517
Clarence, 679
Clark, Barrett H., 167, 221, 279, 686, 687, 688
Clarke, Harold A., 731
Clash By Night, 727
Class of '29, 731
Classical drama, 235, 276, 279, 280, 282-84, 285, 302, 309, 319, 373, 493, 499, 648, 672
Claudel, Paul, 233, 244, 247, 248, 253, 254, 278, 279, 309
Claudia, 724
Claudius, 103
Clavel del aire, 582
Clean-Shaven Secretary with a Pistol, A, 404
Clear All Wires, 723
Clerc, Henri, 296
Climbers, The, 659, 660
Clive of India, 207
Cloak, 382
Cloister, The, 311

Cloître, Le, 311
Close Harmony, 693
Closson, Herman, 315-16
Clouds, The, 487
Clucking Hen, The, 511
Clurman, Harold, 726
Coburn, Mr. and Mrs. Charles, 678
Cochran, Gifford, 121
Cock Robin, 693, 702
Cocteau, Jean, 119, 276, 302, 568, 572
Cocu magnifique, Le, 293, 294
Codicillo dello zio Venanzio, Il, 321
Coeur partagé, Le, 283
Coffret, Le, 312
Coggerers, The, 230
Cohan, George M., 664, 676, 677, 678, 714, 734
Cola Rienzi, 553, 555
Colbourne, Maurice, 168
Coleman, A. P., 504
Coleridge, Samuel T., 687
College Widow, The, 662
Collinge, Patricia, 298
Collison, Wilson, 714
Colonel Svec, 510
Colonel Witherspoon, 200
Colorado, 658
Colpo di vento, Un, 354
Colton, John, 714
Colum, Padraic, 225, 226
Columbus, 507
Come le foglie, 333
Come mi vuoi, 363, 366
Come of Age, 203, 204
Come prima, meglio di prima, 363
Come to Zvonkovoe! 475
Comedia Brasileira, 596, 600
Comedia da vida, A, 600
Comédie due génie, La, 262
Comédie Française, 389
Comédie rosse, 245, 257, 270
Comedienne, The (Lateiner), 618
Comedienne (Novello), 201
Comedy in a Cube, 511
Comedy of manners, 321, 500, 526, 543, 547, 702, 703, 719
Coming to Wisdom of Don Quixote, The, 508
Commedia dell'arte, 96, 131, 293, 306-07, 318, 526, 576
Commodore Marries, The, 715
Common Ground, 739
Communal Theatre of Musical Drama, The, 450
Community Drama, 660, 661; *see also* Little Theatre
Commuters, The, 680
Como los muertos, 588
Compagne de mes jours, 314

Compagnie Art et Action, 279
Compagnons de Notre-Dame, Les, 255
Compères du Roi Louis, Les, 305
Comrades, 28, 39
Comte, Auguste, 245
Conditionnel passé, Le, 288
Condor pasa, El, 587
Condottieri, I, 340
Confession, The, 525
Confession of a Fool, The, 27, 28
Congreve, William, 191
Conjur Man Dies, 710
Conkle, E. P., 670, 731
Connaître, 283
Connelly, Marc, 691, 709, 722, 733, 734
Conners, Barry, 713
Conquering Hero, The, 187
Conqueror, The (Hertz), 529
Conqueror, The (Mees), 556
Conrad, Michael Georg, 78
Conrardy, Charles, 315
Conscience, 713
Constant Nymph, The, 202, 568
Constant Wife, The, 191
Constantine Terekin, 459
Contagion, La, 494
Conte di Carmagnola, Il, 319
Conte Rosso, Il, 331
Contemporary American Playwrights, 690
Contemporary Drama of Russia, The, 446
Contemporary Spanish Literature, 561
Contes drôlatiques, 91
Contessa di Challant, La, 332
Contrast, The, 642, 645
Contrôleur des wagons-lits, Le, 273
Conventillo de la Paloma, El, 585
Conversation in the Night, A, 435
Conversation Piece, 194
Convict, The, 614, 618
Cook, George Cram, 684
Coolus, Romain, *pseud.*, 270
Copeau, Jacques, 251, 260, 274, 275, 276, 277-79, 304, 309, 311, 396
Copiaux, Les, 276, 278
Coq rouge, Le, 310
Corbeaux, Les, 242, 243, 265, 267, 494
Corinne ou la jeune fille folle de son âme, 293
Cormack, Bartlett, 716, 717
Corn Is Green, The, 211
Corneille, Pierre, 23, 241, 253, 287, 288, 309, 574
Cornelius, 204
Coronation at Mrs. Beam's, The, 193
Corradini, Enrico, 339
Corrazini, Sergio, 356-57
Correa, Julio, 588
Correia, Viriato, 599

INDEX

Corriere della Sera, 326, **340**
Corrinth, Curt, 117
Corsa al piacere, La, 337
Corsaire, Le, 304
Cortesão, Jaime, 596
Cortez, Alfredo, 596
Cortile, Un, 357
Cosa di carne, Una, 360
Così è (se vi pare), 364
Cossa, Pietro, 337
Cossack Poet, The, 378
Cotillion Time, 506
Council of the People, The, 55
Counsellor-at-Law, 694
Counselors of Mr. Councilor, The, 493, 495
Count Cilli, 540, 541
Count Peasant and His House, 64
Counterattack, 469
Countess Cathleen, The, 217, 640
Countess Julie, 410
Country Dressmaker, The, 226
County Chairman, The, 662
Coup de fusil, Un, 259
Coup du deux décembre, Le, 296
Couple, The, 547
Cour du roi Petaud, La, 312
Courage, 713
Course du flambeau, La, 260
Courteline, Georges, 244, 259, 271, 297
Courtship, The, 511
Cousin Billy, 240
Cousin from Saaremaa, The, 486
Cousin Kate, 186
Coutinho, Lurival, 600
Couturière de Lunéville, La, 292
Coward, Noel, 191, 193, 206, 293, 298
Crabbed Youth and Age, 224
Cradle Snatchers, 715
Cradle Song, The, 567
Craig, Gordon, 275, 279, 443, 674
Craig's Wife, 701
Crainquebille, 261
Crane, Stephen, 665
Cranes Are Leaving, The, 530
Craven, Frank, 713, 718
Cream in the Well, The, 712
Creation of the World, The, 464
Creative Method of the Theatre, The, 472
Credé, Karl, 119
Creditors, The, 29, 31, 39
Crelis Louwen, or Alexander the Great at the Poets' Feast, 552
Cremers, Paul Joseph, 119
Cremieux, Benjamin, 366
Crepuscolari, 356
Crescei e multiplicaivos, 600
Crier by Night, The, 190
Crime and Love, 621

Crime and Punishment, 396
Crime on the Hill, 213
Criminal at Large, 209
Criminal Code, The, 718
Criminals, 51
Crisi, La, 328
Cristinas Heimreise, 130
Critic, The, 650
Critics, The, 223
Croatian Helen, 514
Croce, Benedetto, 324, 335, 338, 339
Croisset, Francis de, 298, 311, 315
Cromedyre-le-vieil, 289
Crommelynck, Fernand, 278, 293-94, 311, 315
Cromwell, 235
Cronache teatrali, 326
Cross Roads, The (Robinson), 224
Crossroads (Flavin), 718
Crothers, Rachel, 675, 714
Croué, Jean, 274
Crouse, Russel, 721, 737, 738
Crowds, The, 509
Crown Prince, The, 525
Cruz, Sor Juana Inés de la, 589
Cruzada y el Pilar, La, 575
Crystal Castle, 509
Csepreghy, Ferencz, 518, 521
Csikós, The, 518
Csiky, Gergely, 519
Csokor, Franz Theodor, 149-50
Csongor and Tünde, 517
Cuadros al fresco, 564
Cuando las Cortes de Cadiz, 569
Cuando los hijos de Eva no son los hijos de Adán, 568
Cuando venga el amor, 587
Cuatro Robinsons, Los, 563
Cuirs de boeuf, Les, 271
Cuivre, Le, 274
Culbertson, Ernest H., 709
Culpa es Tuya, La, 575
Cummings, E. E., 707
Cúneo, Dardo, 283
Cuore in due, Il, 368
Cupid and the Don, 290
Curdas, Los, 583, 584
Curel, François de, 244, 257, 258, 261, 262, 263, 264, 265, 278, 313
Curnieu, Georges de, *see* Ancey, Georges
Cushing, Tom, 715
Cwojdziński, Antoni, 502
Cyankali—Paragraph 218, 117, 119
Cycle des douze génies, 313
Cyclone, Le, 301
Cynara (Galsworthy), 183
Cynara (Harwood and Gore-Browne), 200
Cyrano de Bergerac, 250, 251, 303
Czakó, Zsigmond, 518

774 INDEX

Czar Boris, 394
Czar Dmitri, 500
Czar Fedor Ivanovich, 394, 400, 411
Czar's Bride, The, 393
Czarina, The, 524
Czech Comedy, A, 507

D. Afonso VI, 595
Dabrowska, Marja, 501
Daddy's Gone A-Hunting, 718
Dämmerung, 89
Daily Telegraph, The, 167
Daisy Mayme, 701
Dal tuo al mio, 325
Dalí, Salvador, 570, 572
Dalilah, 315
Daly, Augustin, 648, 652
Dama Boba, La, 571
Dama duende, La, 132
Damaged Goods, 260
Damask Cheek, The, 199
D'Ambra, Lucio, 340, 366
Dame aux Camélias, La, 238, 299
Dame aux gants verts, La, 294
Dame de bronze et le monsieur de crystal, La, 295
Dame de chez Maxim, La, 273
Dame Kobold, 132
Dame Nature, 297
Damel, Carlos, 586
D'Amico, Silvio, 325, 358
Dance of Death, The (Auden), 215
Dance of Death, The (Strindberg), 19, 39, 40
Dancing Mice, The, 58
Dandy Dolls, The, 226
Dane, Clemence, pseud., 202-04
Dangerous Corner, 204
Daniel Deronda, 618
D'Annunzio, Gabriele, 255, 339, 347-50, 353, 430, 441
Dans sa candeur naïve, 294
Danseurs de gigue, Les, 315
Dantas, Julio, 593, 595
Dante Alighieri, 253, 350, 354, 421, 545
Danton, 257
Dantons Tod, 99, 114
Danza del ventre, La, 346
Danza su un piede, La, 360
Dard, Le, 265
Dardamelle ou le cocu, 293
Darien, Georges, 261
Dark Forest, The, 402
Dark Lady of the Sonnets, The, 174
Dark Mirror, The, 707
Dark Tower, The, 734
Darkness, 515
Darling of the Gods, The, 653

Darthés, Camilo, 586
Darwin, Charles, 77, 645
Darzens, Rudolphe, 258
Das bist Du, 117
Daudet, Alphonse, 241, 523
Daughter of the Nabob of Dolova, The, 522
Dauthendey, Maximilian, 95
David, 208, 485
David Garrick, 161
David in the War, 618
David and Goliath, 102
Davies, Hubert Henry, 185
Davignon, Henri, 316
Daviot, Gordon, pseud., 207
Davis, Donald, 663
Davis, Dorrance, 713
Davis, Owen, 663, 714
Davy Crockett, 648
Dawn, 510
Dawn and Dusk, 486
Dawn over Slovakia, 515
Day, Clarence, 738
Day, Holman, 316
Day and Night, 631
Day of His Return, The, 501
Day of the Living, The, 469
Dayland, 50
Days and Nights, 480
Days of Our Life, The, 432
Days of the Turbins, 455, 456
Days to Come, 728
Days Without End, 690
Dayton, Katharine, 734
Dazey, Frank, 709
Dea Gallia, 313
Dead City, The, 347, 348
Dead End, 724
Dead Souls, 456
Dean, Basil, 202
Dean Bomander, 61
Dear Brutus, 181
Dear Father, 212
Dear Little Georgine, 523
Dear Octopus, 201
Dear Old Darling, 678
Dear Phantoms, 435
Dearden, Harold, 209
Death Dance, The, 602
Death of Czar Diocletian, The, 534
Death of George Langsfeld, The, 515
Death of Ivan the Terrible, The, 394
Death of Keistut, The, 492
Death of Mindaugas, The, 491
Death of Odysseus, The, 507
Death of Pazuhkin, The, 392
Death of Pushkin, The, 380
Death of Pyrrhus, The, 548
Death of the Jugovich Mother, The, 534

Death's Harlequin, 65
Death takes a Holiday, 358
Deauville, Max, *pseud.*, 314
Deborah, 190
Deborah the Prophetess, 618
Deburau, 299
Debussy, Claude, 250, 255
Décadence, 267
Decision, The, 739
Déclassée, 718
Declercq, Aimé, 311
Decorating Clementine, 272
Dédale, Le, 261
Deep Mrs. Sykes, The, 702
Deeter, Jasper, 712
Deevey, Teresa, 229
Defeat, The, 71
Defense of Xantippe, 500
Deirdre (A. E.), 221
Deirdre (Yeats), 218
Deirdre of the Sorrows, 221
Déjeuner de soleil, 297
Dekker, Eduard Douwes, 552
De Kruif, Paul, 700
Del brazo y por la calle, 587
Delacour, 165
Delard, Eugene, 271
Delaurancea, Barbu, 529
Delayed Wedding, The, 621
Delf, Harry, 718
Delirio dell'oste Bassa, Il, 360
Delius, 189
Dell, Floyd, 720
Dell, Jeffrey, 210
De Marney, Terence, 213
Demasy, Paul, 255, 315
Demeter, Dimitrija, 531
Démetrios (Ernst), 96
Demetrius (Lernet-Holenia), 154
Demoiselle de magasin, La, 316
Demónio familiar, O, 598
Denby, Edwin, 240
Denham, Reginald, 210, 213
d'Ennery, A. E. P., 237
Department Store, The, 461
Député Leveau, Le, 267
Deputies, The, 532
Derechos de la salud, Los, 584
Dernier Empereur, Le, 306
Dernière Dulcinee, La, 313
Dernière nuit de Don Juan, La, 251
Derrumbe, El, 581
Desalojo, El, 583
Desbonnets, Charles, 317
Descaves, Lucien, 261, 266
Desequilibrada, La, 560
Desert Highway, 205
Deserter, The (Mahen), 510
Deserter, The (Sorbul), 530

Deserter, The (Szigligeti), 518
Design for Living, 194
Désir, Le, 271
Desire Under the Elms, 225, 686, 687
Despot Prince, The, 528
Destin du théâtre, 254
Destruction of the Tzaddik's House, 626
Detour, The, 663, 714
Deus lhe pague, 599
Deutsche Heinrich, Der, 154
Deutsches Bekenntnis, 146
Deux écoles, Les, 268
Deux visages, Les, 271
Deval, Jacques, 289, 294-95, 705
Devenishsky, Isaac Meir, *see* Veiter, A., *pseud.*
Devil, The (Levy), 202
Devil, The (Molnár), 523
Devil and Mr. Bolfry, The, 200
Devil in the Cheese, The, 715
Devil Passes, The, 202
Devil to Pay, The, 216
Devil's Bride, The, 520
Devil's Bridge, The, 466
Devil's Disciple, The, 170
Devil's Dyke, 216
Děvín, 509
Dewez, M., *see* Deauville, Max, *pseud.*
Di notte, 336
Diable marchand de goutte, Le, 256
Diakos, 545
Diamandi, George, 530
Diamond Lil, 714
Diarmuid and Grania, 217
Diaz Dufoo, Carlos, 590
Dicenta, Joaquín, 560, 563
Dickens, Charles, 26, 35, 701
Dickey, Paul, 714
Dickinson, Emily, 645
Dickinson, Thomas H., 186, 672
Dictateur, Le, 289
Dictator, 67
Diderot, Denis, 101, 234, 235, 375
Didring, Ernst, 63
Dies Irae, 151
Diez Canedo, Enrique, 558, 563, 567, 569
Diff'rent, 684, 685, 686
Dilettantes, The, 532
Dimitrij Samozvanec, 513
Dinner at Eight, 734
Diomedes, 549
Diosa Rie, La, 563
Diritti dell' anima, I, 332
Disappointments, 517
Dishonored Lady, 670
Disonesti, I, 331
Dispersed, 627
Disraeli, 187, 208
Distaff Side, The, 198

776 INDEX

Distant Drums, 722
Distant Point, 208, 469, 473
District Elder a Third Term, 487
Diver, The, 485
Diversion, 197
Divin Aretin, Le, 253
Divinas Palabras, 570
Divine Face, The, 489
Divine Spark, The, 525
Divino Impaciente, El, 569
Divorce, The (Aleichem), 627
Divorce (Daly), 648
Divorce, Un, 262
Divorçons, 239
Divorzio, Il, 328
Djokovich, Milan, 537
Dmitrevskoi, Ivan, 374
Dmitri Donskoi, 377
Dobroplodni, Sava, 541
Dobrushin, Ezekiel, 634
Doctor, The, 623
Dr. *Almosado*, 615
Dr. *Faustus*, 247
Doctor in Spite of Himself, The, 542
Dr. *Julia Szabo*, 525
Doctor Knock, 184, 290
Dr. *Mamlocks Ausweg*, 117
Doctor Monica, 501
Dr. *Rung*, 62
Doctor's Dilemma, The, 172
Doctors Disagree, 725
Dóczi, Louis, 519, 520, 522
Dodsworth, 700
Döblin, Alfred, 119
Doermann, Felix, *pseud.*, 138
Dog Beneath the Skin, The, 215
Dogs, The, 529
Doktor Dragan, 539
Doll's House, A, 9, 10, 11, 12, 16, 26, 46, 60, 78, 166, 167, 178, 241, 649, 732
Domaškojc, Marjana, 504
Domino, 304
Dommita Rosanda, 528, 529
Dompteur ou l'Anglais tel qu'on le mange, Le, 292
Don, 206
Don Alvaro, 559
Don Juan (Flecker), 189
Don Juan (Molière), 380
Don Juan (Sternheim), 101
Don Juan Tenorio, 559, 574
Don Quixote (Bulgakov-Cervantes), 456, 483
Don Quixote (Laugendijk), 552
Doña Maria la Brava, 569
Doña Perfecta, 560
Doña Rosita la soltera, O el Lenguaje de las flores, 572, 573
Donna di nessuno, La, 343

Donna di quarant' anni, Una, 320
Donnay, Maurice, 261, 266, 289
Donne, John, 204
Donne moderne, 335
Donogoo, 290
Dorfsying, Der, 622
Dorothea Angermann, 83
Dos Passos, John, 707
Dostigaev and Others, 428
Dostoevski, Fedor, 78, 339, 394, 395, 396, 399, 435, 476
Doting Daughter of Bolczay, The, 523
Doughgirls, The, 737
Doumic, René, 260
Doutoras, As, 598
Dover Road, The, 192
Doves of Peace, 458
Dowerless Girl, The, 386
Doyle, Sir Arthur Conan, 178
Drama and Stage in their Development, 552
Drama at Inish, 224
Drama Behind the Scenes, A, 403
Drama criollo, 581, 586
Drama League of America, 671, 672, 673, 678, 692
Drama of Four Bare Walls, The, 505
Drama Quarterly, 673
Drama subjects:
  Alexander the Great, 152, 378
  Anne, Queen of England, 207
  Anti-semitism, 466, 604, 659
  Arthurian legends, 92
  Bánk Bán, 516
  Bernhardt, Sarah, 269
  British Broadcasting Corporation, 205
  Brontës, The, 203, 722
  Brown, John, 212
  Browning, Elizabeth and Robert, 206
  Caesar, Julius, 170, 173
  Capitalism, 77, 103, 117
  Casanova, 129, 131
  Catherine I of Russia, 95
  Catherine the Great, 359, 465
  Catholicism, 125, 128, 145, 146, 156, 157, 254, 255, 262, 292
  Cenci, The, 85
  Charles II, 177
  Charles VI, 305
  Chopin, Frederic, 501, 502
  Christianity, 550, 578, 667, 702, 705
  Civil War (U. S.), 732
  Cleopatra, 171
  Columbus, 156, 534
  Communism, 104, 117, 147, 227, 228, 265, 266, 296, 706, 629
  Copernicus, 500, 501
  David, King, 137, 313, 624
  Deirdre legend, 218, 221

INDEX 777

Drama Subjects (cont'd):
Dickinson, Emily, 716
Don Juan, 143, 287, 303, 404
Don Quixote, 308, 313, 454, 456, 508
Edison, Thomas A., 511
Elizabeth, Queen, 153, 695, 696
Esther, Queen, 603
Fascism, 67, 117, 215, 468, 469, 694
Francesca da Rimini, 350
Frederick the Great, 98, 112
French Revolution, The, 100-01, 135, 256, 354, 454
Galileo Galilei, 143
Gaugin, Paul, 108, 111
Goethe, J. W. von, 112
Goldoni, Carlo, 321
Gregory VII, Pope, 96, 97, 146
Gwynn, Nell, 177
Hassidism, 608
Helen of Troy, 312
Henri III, 291
Henry IV, 365, 366
Henry VIII, 74, 207
Herod, 74, 86
Hitler, Adolf, 117, 122, 147, 153, 176, 455, 460
Italian Renaissance, 135, 354, 555, 699
Ivan the Terrible, 393, 466, 497
Jack the Ripper, 99
Janošik, 506, 514
Jefferson, Thomas, 724
Joan of Arc, 103, 176, 208, 304
Joanna of Naples, 98, 519
Joseph, 603
Judaism, 137
Judas Iscariot, 143, 289, 500
Judith, 95, 102
Lamb, Charles and Mary, 208
Lazarus, 355, 534, 569, 687, 689
Lenin, Nikolai, 464, 474
Lincoln, Abraham, 189, 705
Lesbianism, 197
Louis XVII, 211
Louis XIII, 313
Lucrece, 306
Lucretia Borgia, 500
Luther, Martin, 111
Machiavelli, Niccolo, 64
Mary Stuart of Scotland, 207, 697
Maximilian, 147
Medici, Lorenzino de', 351, 354
Melba, Dame Nellie, 212
Montez, Lola, 90, 114
Montezuma, 83
Mozart, W. A., 200
Mussolini, Benito, 74, 176, 455
Napoleon Bonaparte, 94, 98, 100-01, 106, 114, 126, 141, 145, 169, 170, 206, 235,
251, 288, 294, 377, 378, 397, 455, 467, 468, 504, 533, 569
Napoleon IV, 251, 305
Nationalism, 339
Nazism, 67, 70, 73, 74, 96, 110, 111, 112, 117, 123, 140, 146, 147, 150, 152, 153, 155, 156, 460, 462, 464, 466, 468, 469, 479, 512, 524, 634, 694, 725, 729, 736, 737
Negroes, 667, 670, 686, 706-711
Nero, 337
Nibelungs, The, 5, 96, 112, 535
Nightingale, Florence, 208
Ninon de l'Enclos, 92
Noah, 306
Oedipus, 144, 287
Orpheus and Eurydice, 307
Pacifism, 105, 268
Penelope, 354
Pepys, Samuel, 196, 207
Peter the Great, 465, 466
Politics, 652, 668, 673, 696, 705, 706, 708, 716, 717, 736
Pushkin, A. S., 501, 502
Rasputin, 465
Renaissance, 57, 64
Richard II, 207
Richelieu, Cardinal, 313
Rudolph of Austria, 355, 525, 697
Russian Revolution, The, 110, 115, 315, 425, 428, 431, 444-45, 449-60, 464, 468, 473, 474, 476, 508, 509, 510
Sacco-Vanzetti case, 695
St. Francis of Assisi, 549
Samson, 100, 112, 355, 435
Savonarola, 303, 312
Shakespeare, William, 316
Shelley, Percy Bysshe, 190
Slavery, 646
Social-democratic proletariat, 77, 116, 148, 245, 257, 289, 339, 431
Socialism, 103, 116, 264
Socrates, 501, 705
Spanish Civil War, 122, 469, 698, 723, 727
Sutter, John, 113
Swift, Dean, 232
Tolstoi, Leo, 64
Tristan and Isolde, 92, 102, 285
Ulysses, 83, 354
Van Gogh, Vincent, 111, 294
Washington, George, 697
Wilde, Oscar, 162, 208, 305
Wilhelm II, 127
World War I, 66, 71, 87, 94, 117, 141, 142, 143, 145, 155, 194, 198, 205, 207-08, 224, 291, 293, 296, 303, 306, 311, 342, 360, 441, 471, 526, 540, 695, 700, 704

Drama Subjects (cont'd):
  World War II, 307, 464, 465, 468, 469, 472, 473, 477, 698, 704, 705, 708, 737
  Yankees, 645, 686, 690, 697, 699
  Zola, Emile, 113
Dramatic Opinions and Essays, 164, 558
Dramatic Scenes, 380
Dramatic Sonata, 508
Drame sous Philippe II, Un, 265
Drames philosophiques, 307
Dream, The, 546
Dream Play, The, 35, 39, 41-44, 104, 231
Dreamers, The, 224
Drégely, Gábor, 525
Drei Reiherfedern, Die, 87
Dreigroschenoper, Die, 121
Dreiser, Theodore, 499, 665
Dreyer, Max, 87, 89, 102
Drifting Apart, 649
Drink, 242
Drinkwater, John, 188
Dritter November 1918, 150
Drowning Man, The, 409
Druid's Rest, The, 211
Drumev, Vasil, 542, 543
Drunks, The, 500
Dublin Gate Theatre, 231-32
DuBois, Albert, 313
Dubrovnik Trilogy, 533
Due dame, 322
Duel, Le, 268
Duel, The, 409
Duell am Lido, 113
Duello, Il, 322, 323
Duet in Floodlight, 204
Duhamel, Georges, 246, 291-92
Dujardin, Edouard, 250
Dukas, 545
Duke, The (Katzizne), 633
Duke, The (Lunacharski), 454
Duke in Darkness, The, 209
Dukes, Ashley, 196, 200, 214, 215, 299
Dulcy, 733
Dullin, Charles, 276, 279, 302, 304
Dumas, Alexandre, 235, 236, 324
Dumas, Alexandre, fils, 77, 234, 237, 238, 240, 241, 243, 244, 245, 259, 260, 261, 263, 274, 281, 299, 307, 529, 559
Du Maurier, Guy, 185
Dumb Messiah, The, 624
Dumb One, The, 622
Dunce Boy, The, 713
Dunlap, William, 645
Dunning, Philip, 717, 718
Dunsany, Lord, 189, 222
Duquesa de Benamejí, La, 566
Duran, Michel, 299
Duschinsky, Richard, 153
Duse, Eleonora, 275, 496, 580
Duterme, Marguerite, 314
Duvernois, Henri, 259, 295
Dvořák, Arnošt, 506, 509
Dybbuk, The, 630, 631, 636
Dybeck, Mikael, 60
Dyk, Viktor, 506, 508
Dykhovichni, 480
Dymov, Ossip, 632, 636
Dynamo, 689, 690
Dynasts, The, 184
Dynasty Peterberg, The, 61

Earth, 707, 709
Earth Between, The, 709
Earthquake, 525
Easiest Way, The, 653, 668, 669
East of Suez, 191
Easter, 35, 39, 40, 41
Easy Virtue, 194
Eaton, Walter Prichard, 174, 672, 715
Eau de vie, L', 255
Ebers, Georg, 78
Ebrio, O, 600
Eccentric, The, 472
Échange, L', 253
Echegaray, José, 558, 559, 560, 561, 563, 564, 566, 573, 577, 582, 672
Echten Sedemunds, Die, 106
Eckermann, 112
École de Werther, L', 312
École des amants, L', 312
École des voeufs, L', 257
École intimiste, L', 283-84
Écolière, L', 258
Eden End, 204
Edgar, Marriott, 213
Editor, The, 47, 48, 51
Edmonds, Walter D., 722
Edmund Jahr, 67
Eduard II, 120
Education of Mr. Surrage, The, 187
Eekhoud, Georges, 310, 312
Effrontés, Les, 494
Eftimiu, Victor, 529
Egan, Michael, 196
Egge, Peter, 63
Egoista, L', 326
Egor Bulychev and Others, 428
Ehe, 113, 119
Ehen werden im Himmel geschlossen, 105
Ehre, Die, 85-86, 89
Eichel, Isaac, 604
Eichelbaum, Samuel, 586
Eighty Movement, The, 554
Einarson, Indridi, 61
Einsame, Der, 111
Einsame Menschen, 79-80, 82
Einsame Tat, Die, 115

Einsame Weg, Der, 135
Eisenstein, Sergei, 386, 467
Eisler, Hans, 121
Elbe and the Spree, The, 503
Eldest Son, The, 182
Eleanora Duse, 110
Electra (Hofmannsthal), 130, 131
Electre (Giraudoux), 307
Electre (Poizat), 253
Elefante, L', 353
Elën, 247
Elévation, L', 270
Elga, 81
Eliade, Ion, 527
Eliot, George, 618
Eliot, Samuel, Jr., 674
Eliot, T. S., 214, 216
Elisabeth, Kaiserin von Oesterreich, 154
Elisabeth von England, 152
Elizabeth of England, 200
Elizabeth, Princess of Montenegro, 535
Elizabeth the Queen, 695, 696
Elkin, Mendel, 631
Ellis, Edith, 718
Ellis, Walter W., 196
Elmerick, or Justice Triumphant, 516
Eloquent Dempsey, The, 226
Elser, Frank B., 722
Emancipated Don Quixote, The, 454
Emants, Marcellus, 554
Embarrassment of Riches, 680
Embers (Duvernois and Wolff), 295
Embers (Middleton), 667
Embezzlers, The, 461
Emerson, Ralph Waldo, 248, 645
Emery, Gilbert, 720
Emperor and Galilean, The, 9
Emperor Jones, The, 277, 684, 685, 692, 713
Emperor's New Clothes, The, 91
Empire de Darius, L', 314
Empreinte, L', 268
Empress of Rome, The, 188
En familia, 583
En famille, 243, 258
En que piensas? 590
Enchanted Circle, The, 498
Enchanted Maze, The, 711
Enchanted Sea, An, 218
Enchantress, The, 504
End of Summer, 704
End of the Beginning, The, 228
Endlose Strasse, Die, 119
Enemies (Artsybashev), 440
Enemies (Gorki), 426
Enemy, The, 667
Enemy of the People, An, 6, 9, 12, 13, 14, 47, 539, 669
Enes, Antonio, 595

Enfant de l'amour, L', 269
Enfants terribles, Les, 119, 302
Engaged, 162
Engagement Card, The, 487
Engagement Ring, The, 518
Engel, Lehman, 228
Engelbrekt, 37
England, Paul, 131
Englishman's House, An, 185
Ennemie, L', 306
Enough Stupidity in Every Wise Man, 385
Enquête sur l'évoulution littéraire, 245
Enthoven, Gabrielle, 200
Entkleidung des Antonio Carossa, Die, 108
Entre cuatro paredes, 575
Entre trois feus, 316
Entremés, 561
Entscheidung der Lissa Hart, Die, 87, 119
Envers d'une sainte, L', 244, 263
Envers vaut l'endroit, L', 311
Epervier, L', 298
Ephraims Breite, 94
Epic Theatre, 121
Epidemic, 494
Epidémie, L', 256
Equinox, 533
Era una vez en Bagdad, 569
Erde, 141
Erdgeist, 99
Erik XIV, 37, 39
Erkko, Juhana Henrik, 483
Ernst, Otto, *pseud.*, 87, 90, 97, 102
Ernst, Paul, 95-96, 112
Erophile, 544
Eroticism, 429, 430, 433, 437, 439, 440, 441, 449
Erotikon, 57
Erste, Der, 105
Ervine, St. John, 174, 222-24
Erziehung durch Kolibri, Die, 113
Es, 142
Es brennt an der Grenze, 116
Es mi hombre, 562, 563
Escape, 183
Escape Me Never, 202
Escapism, 190, 301, 302, 303, 306, 308, 429, 498, 502, 679
Escohotado, 576
Escolares del Teatro, 589
Escombros del sueño, 590
Escuela del amor, La, 590
Esenin, 448
Esodo, L', 339, 340
España bien Maridada, 575
Espiau, Marcel, 296
Esposa del vengador, La, 559

Essai de rénovation dramatique, Un: Le Théâtre du Vieux-Colombier, 275
Essence of Tragedy, The, 697
Essig, Hermann, 100
Estado de secreto, 590
Estanque, El, 584
Esther, 372
Esther (Haltern-Racine), 604
Esther and Haman, 617
Esther Waters, 187
Estherke, 633
Estranged Wife, The, 540
Estrellas, Las, 562
Etapes, Les, 314
Etbin, Kristan, 539
Eté, L', 295
Eternal Flame, The, 491
Eternal Jew, The, 624, 636
Ethan Frome, 663
Etienne, 294
Ettinger, Dr. Solomon, 606, 608, 612, 620
Etudiants russes, Les, 312
Eugene Bazarov, 395
Eugene Onegin, 380
Eugene O'Neill, The Man and His Plays, 686
Eulenberg, Herbert, 92-93
Euripides, 115, 130, 146, 189, 570, 672
Europa, 102
Europa Barbara, 568
Eva, 485
Eva Bonheur, 554
Eva the 5th, 719
Evasion, L', 260
Eve of St. Mark, The, 698
Eve toute nue, 296
Evening of Beginnings, An, 636
Evensong, 212
Everyman, 431
Everyman Theatre, 276
Everywhere I Roam, 722
Evil Forces, The, 466
Evil Grain, 495
Evil Spirit, The, 488
Evreinov, 430, 442-45
Ewige Mensch, Der, 107
Ewige Traum, Der, 148
Exaltation, L', 264
Exceeding Small, 713
Exchange, The, 253
Exiled, 183
Exodus, 207
Exorcism, 684
Experimental Theatre, 643, 650, 671, 684, 692, 693, 707, 708, 721
Expressing Willie, 675
Expressionism, 37, 42, 43, 67, 88, 94, 99, 100, 102, 104-13, 115, 117, 119, 120, 122, 145, 147-51, 231, 389, 443, 485, 535, 686, 692, 706, 716, 718, 733, 734
Exzesse, Die, 152
Eye for an Eye, An, 634
Eyton, Frank, 213
Eyvind of the Hills, 62

Fables in Slang, 676
Fabre, Emile, 262, 316
Fabricius, Jan, 556, 557
Fabulous Invalid, The, 734, 735
Fackel, Die, 139
Factory, The, 539
Factory of Youth, The, 465
Faehmann, F. R., 486
Faesi, Robert, 112
Fagan, James Bernard, 196
Faguet, Emile, 284
Fahnen, 110
Fahnenweihe, Die, 90
Fahrt nach der Südsee, 114
Fahrt nach Orphid, Die, 94
Faible femme, Une, 294
Failures, The, 287
Fair Julia, 525
Fair Sheperdess, The, 518
Fair Vida, 539, 540
Fairy Gold, see *Mad Money*
Fairy-tale plays, 124, 125, 131, 143, 679
Faisons un rêve, 299
Faith and Patriotism, 549
Faith Healer, The, 655, 657
Faithful, The, 188
Falck, August, 36, 43
Falena, Ugo, 368
Falkenstein, 507
Falkowitch, J. B., 610
Fall des Schülers Uegesack, Der, 102
Fallen Angels, 193
False Accusation, The, 528
False Coin, The, 427
False Demetrius, The, 394
Falsehoods, 490
Familie Selicke, Die, 79, 85, 88
Familie Wawroch, 140
Famille Benoîton, La, 239
Family, The, 501
Family Album, 195
Family Carnovsky, The, 634
Family Circle, The, 524
Family Failing, 226
Family Reunion, The, 215
Family Secret, The, 532
Family Upstairs, The, 718
Family Zevi, The, 623
Famous Mrs. Fair, The, 680
Fanatics, The, 196
Fangen, Ronald, 65, 67

Fanny, 291
Fanny's First Play, 173
Fantaisie amoureuse, 295
Fantasmi, I, 334
Fantasy, 298, 299, 300, 303, 304, 307, 309, 312, 315, 316, 345, 358, 465, 486, 489, 492, 523, 529, 533, 597, 632, 634, 660, 672, 679, 697-703, 707, 708, 711, 712, 715, 716, 718, 726, 728, 740
Faragoh, Francis E., 707
Farce de la Mort qui faillit trépasser, La, 315
Farce of Life, The, 546
Faria Rosa, Abbadie de, 596
Farigoule, Louis, *see* Romains, Jules
Farjeon, Frank and Eleanor, 213
Farjeon, Joseph Jefferson, 196
Farm of Three Echoes, 196
Farmer Takes a Wife, The, 722
Farmer's Wife, The, 189, 514
Far-off Hills, The, 224
Farsa y dicencia de la Reina Castiza, 570
Fascinating Mr. Vanderveld, The, 186
Fashion, 642, 643
Fata Morgana, 525
Fatal Dowry, The, 137
Father, The, 19, 28, 29, 31, 39
Father and Son, 631
Fatherland Lives, The, 469
Fatherless, 404-07, 412, 413, 415, 417
Fathers and Sons, 395, 631
Fathers-in-Law, The, 520
Fatica, 337
Fauchois, René, 211, 294, 305, 700
Fauré-Frémiet, Philippe, 288
Faust, 62, 100, 130, 432, 444, 454, 620
Faust and the City, 454
Faux Ménages, Les, 324
Favorite, The, 518
Fay, Frank and William, 221
Fear, 472
Feast at Solhaug, The, 5
Feast during the Plague, The, 380
Federal Theatre Proect, 110, 173, 214, 461, 692, 709, 712, 730-32
Fédora, 240
Fedotov, Alexander, 401
Fedra, 349, 570
Féerie dramatique, 315
Felicita Colombo, 341
Feliu y Codina, José, 560, 564
Fellow from Our Town, A, 478, 479, 480
Femina—Vie Heureuse Prize, 190
Femme de César, La, 296
Femme de Claude, La, 239
Femme en fleur, La, 284
Femme et son ombre, La, 254
Femme masquée, La, 271
Femme nue, La, 269

Femme qui à le coeur trop petit, Une, 293
Femme seule, La, 268
Femme X, La, 273
Ferber, Edna, 568, 734, 736
Ferdinand, Roger, 299
Ferdy Pistora's Conversion, 510
Ferenc Rakoczy, 520
Fern Blossom, The, 487
Fernandez Caballero, Manuel, 564
Ferni-Ost, 118
Ferrari, Paolo, 171, 318, 321-25, 336
Ferreira, Antonio, 594, 599
Festspiel Arpad's Awakening, 517-18
Festspiel in deutschen Reimen, 83
Feu de la Saint-Jean, Le, 316
Feu qui reprend mal, Le, 284
Feuchtwanger, Lion, 120
Feuer aus den Kesseln, 110
Feuerbach, Ludwig, 77
Feuillet, Octave, 165
Feurige Ofen, Der, 114
Feydeau, Georges, 273, 297
Fiaba dei tre maghi, La, 345
Fiaccola sotto il moggio, La, 350
Fiamme nell'ombra, 338
Fiançailles, Les, 250
Fibikh, 469
Fiddler's House, The, 225
Field, Nathaniel, 137
Field God, The, 710
Field-Marshal Suvorov, 467
Fields, Joseph A., 736, 737
Fiesta, 707
Fiesta de San Antón, La, 562
Fifth Column, The, 723
Fifth Horizon, 634
Figlia di Iorio, La, 350
Figueiredo, Fidelino, 595
Fil à la patte, Un, 273
Fille d'Artaban, La, 253
Fille sauvage, La, 263
Fils de Giboyer, Le, 238
Findling, Der, 107
Fine del protagonista, 341
Fine Feathers, 669
Fineman, Sigmund, 618
Fink und Fliederbusch, 136
Finne, Gabriel, 51
Finnish National Theatre, 483
Finžgar, František S., 540
Fiore sotto gli occhi, Il, 357
Fiorentino, Anonimo, pseud., *see* Martini, Vincenzo
Fiorenza, 352
Fire! 636
Fire and Night, 490
Firebird, The, 526
Firebrand, The, 715
Fires of St. John, The, 87

First, The, 543
First Distiller, The, 398, 504
First Flight, 695
First Jewish Recruits in Russia, The, 607
First Lady, 734
First Love (Akins-Verneuil), 297
First Love (Somló), 520
First Man, The, 685
First Mrs. Fraser, The, 223-24
First Mortgage, 713
First Year, The, 713, 718
Fischer, Leck, 65
Fischer, Otakar, 508, 509
Fisher, Rudolph, 710
Fishta, Gjorgj, 549
Fiske, Harrison G., 669
Fist, The, 507
Fiston, 298
Fitch, Clyde, 238, 240, 269, 657, 659, 660, 665, 680, 703
Fitzgerald, F. Scott, 716
Fitzmaurice, George, 226
Five Graves to Cairo, 524
Flachsmann als Erzieher, 90, 102
Flaireurs, Les, 247, 248, 312
Flambée, La, 271
Flamme, 143
Flanagan, Hallie, 730, 731
Flandes se la puesto el sol, En, 569
Flare Path, 211
Flashing Stream, The, 197
Flaubert, Gustave, 241, 242, 470, 649
Flavin, Martin, 448, 718, 719
Flecker, James Elroy, 189, 214, 222
Fleg, Edmond, 292
Flers, Robert de, 272, 298
Fleur des pois, La, 290
Flight, 456
Flood, The, 636
Floodlight, 212
Floqi, Kristo, 549
Flor de trigo, La, 581
Flor tardiá, 588
Flores, Mario, 588
Flores na sombra, 599
Florescu, 529
Florian Geyer, 81
Floridsdorf, 117
Florista de la Reina, La, 575
Flotta degli emigranti, La, 339, 340
Flower of Fortune, The, 492
Flowers of the Forest, 198
Flowers of Virtue, The, 723
Flying Gerardos, The, 719
Fodor, László, 212, 525
Foire aux sentiments, La, 299
Fokine, 189
Foleys, The, 225
Folie, Franz, *see* Ansel, Franz, *pseud.*

Folies Calvin, Les, 276
Folk, 634
Folk comedy, Viennese, 124, 125
Folk plays, 124, 134, 140, 141, 143, 380, 387, 409, 504, 507, 520, 521, 525, 529, 543, 572, 599, 627, 628, 629, 631, 633, 660, 661, 710-13
Follies of a Day, The, 234
Follow Your Nose, 532
Followers, 186
Foma Gordeev, 421, 429
Fonson, Jean-François, 316
Fontaines lumineuses, Les, 297
Fontoura, Silva, 600
Fonvizin, 375, 376, 377, 381
Fool, The (Egge), 63
Fool, The (Pollock), 667
Foolish James, 498
Foolish Notion, 703
Foote, Horton, 739
For a New Race, 540
For Happiness, 496, 508
For Human Happiness, 533
For Right and the Heart, 541
For Services Rendered, 191
For the Defence, 692
For the Fatherland, 546
For the Nation's Good, 539
Forbes, James, 297, 680
Forbes, Kathryn, 199
Ford, Harriet, 666, 714
Foreigners, The, 195
Forest, The (Galsworthy), 183
Forest, The (Ostrovski), 387
Forest Rose, 645
Forgetful, 508
Fornari, Ernani, 599
Fort, Paul, 247, 305
Fortnightly Review, The, 162
Forzano, Giovacchino, 354
Foscolo, Ugo, 319
Fossil, Das, 101
Fossiles, Les, 244, 263
Foundation of Happiness, The, 442
Foundation of the World, 602
Foundations, The, 183
Foundling, The, 518
Fountain, The, 687
Four of Them, The, 497
Four Poetic Plays, 189
Fourchambault, Les, 324
Fourth Wall, The, 444
Fowler, Gene, 723
Fox, Paul Hervey, 202
Foxa, Augustin de, 575, 576
Foyer, Le, 262
Fraccaroli, Arnoldo, 344
Fräulein Doktor, 502
Frana allo scalo nord, 358

França, Jr., 599
France, Anatole, 261
Francerie, La, 288
Francesca da Rimini, 350
Francillon, 243
Francke, Caroline, 713
Frank, Bruno, 112-13, 202
Frank, Hans, 97-98
Frank, Leonhard, 118, 120
Franken, Rose, 201, 724
Franziska, 100
Franzl, Der, 127
Frasheri, Naim Bey, 548
Frasheri, Sami Bey, 548
Frau Gittas Suehne, 138
Frau im Fenster, Die, 129
Frau ins Haus, 113
Frau mit dem Dolche, Die, 135
Frau mit den hundert Masken, Die, 89
Frau ohne Schatten, Die, 131
Frau Suitner, 142
Frauenarzt, Der, 119
Frauenopfer, 103
Frauenschuh, 114
Freedley, George, 567, 720
Freethinker, The, 22
Frei Luiz de Sousa, 594
Freie Buehne, 78, 79, 246, 398, 524, 639, 649, 727
Freie Knechte, 98
Freiligrath, Ferdinand, 77, 80
Freitag, Gustav, 78
Freiwild, 134
French Without Tears, 211
Frénésie, 283
Frère Jacques, 269
Frères Karamazov, Les, 274
Fresh Fields, 201
Freud, Sigmund, 130, 133, 151, 286, 539, 540
Friday Evening, 523
Friebe, 495
Friedensfest, Ein, 79, 85
Friedrich und Anna, 103
Friends Remain Friends, 480
Friendship, 678
Frisky Mrs. Johnson, The, 274
Frith, John Leslie, 285
Fritzchen, 86, 89
Frivolous One, The, 518
Fröding, Gustaf, 56
Fröhliche Stadt, Die, 111
Fröhliche Weinberg, Der, 115
From Ibsen's Workshop, 10
From Morn till Midnight, 103, 200, 686
From the Black Sea to the Berents Sea, 480
From the Lives of the Lowly, 504
Frondaie, Pierre, 271
Front, The, 474

Front Line Ballads, 480
Front Page, The, 717, 723
Froufrou, 240
Frou-Frou, 240
Frühlings Erwachen, 90, 98-99, 100, 102
Fruit vert, Le, 298
Fruits of Culture, The, 398
Fuego extraño, 588
Fuente ovejuno, 634
Fuerza ciega, La, 581
Fugitive, The, 182
Fuhrmann Henschel, 81
Fulda, Ludwig, 87, 91
Fulton of Oak Falls, 677
Fumed Oak, 195
Funtek, Anton, 539
Fuochi d'artificio, 345
Furber, Douglas, 213
Furcht und Elend des Dritten Reichs, 122
Furtuna, Horia, 530
Futurism, 448-53, 492

G. B. S.: A Full Length Portrait, 172
Gabányi, Árpád, 520
Gabri and the Women, 624
Gabriel Schillings Flucht, 82
Gabrielle, 238
Gageure, La, 312
Gaités de l'escadron, Les, 272
Galantière, Lewis, 284
Galatea, 546
Gale, Zona, 713
Gallo ciego, 582
Gallows Glorious, 212
Gallows Man, The, 60
Galsworthy, John, 182-83, 184, 190, 730
Gamblers, The, 383
Game of Love and Death, The, 257
Gandillot, León, 272
Gang zum Weiher, Der, 137
Gantillon, Simon, 277, 301, 308
Gaol Gate, The, 219, 279
Garbage Man, The, 707
García Lorca, Federico, 566, 568-73, 580
García Luengo, 576
Garden of Paradise, The, 679
Gárdonyi, Géza, 521
Garfías, Pedro, 574
Garland, Hamlin, 649-51
Garrett, Almeida, 594
Garrick, David, 374
Garten der Jugend, Der, 143
Gartenlaube, Die, 148
Gas I, 103
Gas II, 103
Gaslight, 209
Gastineau, Octave, 242
Gastliche Haus, Das, 10

Gata, La, 564
Gate of Life, The, 522
Gates, Eleanor, 679
Gather Ye Rosebuds, 700
Gats, 104
Gaucho drama, 577, 581, 585
Gaudeamus, 432
Gaukler, Tod und Juwelier, 94
Gauntlet, A, 47, 49
Gavault, Paul, 273, 274, 297
Gawân, 92
Gay, John, 121
Gay Lord Quex, The, 165
Gay Resort, The, 540
Gebil, Max, 622
Geburt der Jugend, Die, 151
Géczy, Stephen, 520
Geddes, Virgil, 709, 731
Geese and Goslings, 495
Gefaehrtin, Die, 135
Geibel, Emanuel, 78
Geijerstam, Gustaf af, 34, 35, 51
Gelbe Nachtigall, Die, 127
Gelo Sebechlebský, 514
Gemeine, Der, 138
Gémier, Firmin, 278
Gendre de M. Poirier, Le, 238, 267
General, The, 526
General Levy, 378
General und das Gold, Der, 113
General's Son, The, 487
Género chico, 561, 562, 564, 580
Geneva, 176
Gente honesta, La, 583
Gentle People, The, 727, 728
Gentleman, The, 393
Gentlemen of the Press, 717
Gentlewoman, 707
George, Grace, 282, 294, 297, 304
George, Henry, 645, 649
George and Margaret, 202
George Branković, 519
George of Podĕbrad, 505
George Pierce Baker, A Memorial, 670
George Pierce Baker's English 47 Workshop, 276, 670, 683, 699
George Washington Slept Here, 735
Géraldy, Paul, 281, 282
Gérard, Mme. Rosamonde, 305
Gerettete Alkibiades, Der, 103
Gerettete Venedig, Das, 130
Gert's Garden, 52, 72
Gertie Maude, 198
Gertrud, 64
Geschichten aus dem Wiener Wald, 156
Geschlagen! 98
Geschlagene, Der, 94
Geschlecht, Ein, 106
Geschwister, Die, 119

Gesellschaft, Die, 78
Gesellschaft der Menschenrechte, 150
Gesellschaft des Abbé Chateauneuf, Die, 92
Gesetz in dir, Das, 146
Gessner, 527
Gestern, 129
Get-Rich-Quick Wallingford, 676
Getting Gertie's Garter, 674, 714
Getting Married, 173
Gewehre der Frau Carrar, Die, 122
Gewesene Menschen, 150
Geyer, Siegfried, 154
Ghelderode, Michel de, 315
Ghéon, Henri, 255
Ghetto, The, 266
Ghost For Sale, 213
Ghost of Yankee Doodle, The, 700, 701
Ghost Train, The, 209
Ghosts, 9-12, 18, 27, 78, 167, 178, 244, 258, 260, 496, 559, 560, 582
Giacometti, Paolo, 320, 321
Giacomo, Salvatore di, 326, 350
Giaconda, 464
Giacosa, Giuseppe, 324-26, 331-33, 340, 347, 366, 673
Gianni Schicchi, 354
Gibbs, Anthony, 208
Gide, André, 254, 275, 278, 339
Gielgud, John, 210
Gierow, Karl Ragnar, 67
Gift of the Wise Bees, The, 438
Giftgas über Berlin, 116
Gigant, Der, 158
Gignoux, Régis, 298
Gilbert, Sir William Schwenk, 162, 468-69, 564
Gilkin, Ivan, 310, 312
Gille, Valère, 312
Gilles und Jeanne, 103
Gillette, William, 662, 663
Ginevra degli Almieri, 354
Ginsbury, Norman, 207
Gioconda, 347, 348
Giordano Bruno, 145
Giorni più lieti, I, 330
Giraudoux, Jean, 277, 280, 281, 282, 306-08, 568
Girl Behind the Gun, The, 273
Girl from Maxim's, The, 273
Girl from Montmartre, The, 273
Girl from Rector's, The, 273
Girl from the Forest, The, 501
Girl of the Golden West, The, 652
Girl Who Did Not Want to Go to Kuala Lumpur, The, 199
Girl With the Green Eyes, 659
Girls from Tünderlaki, The, 523
Guida, 353, 354

Gläserne Frau, Die, 97
Glaspell, Susan, 684, 716
Glass Menagerie, The, 739
Glass Slipper, The, 523
Glatigny, 252
Glaube und Heimat, 142
Glauco, 356
Gleason, James, 720
Glembays, The, 534
Glière, Reinhold, 469
Glittering Gate, The, 222
Glittering Want, 519
Gloire, La, 305
Gloria, La, 348-49
Glorious Morning, 210
Glorious Uncertainty, The, 230
Glover, Halcott, 207
Glück, 95
Glück Auf! 554
Glück im Winkel, Das, 86
Glückskuh, Die, 100
Gneisenau, 114
Goat Alley, 709
Goat Ride or the Skeleton, The, 553
Gobseck, 105
God Loves Us, 707
God, Man, and Devil, 620
God of Vengeance, The, 624, 625, 629
God's Orchid, 65, 66
God's Punishment, 621
Godam (Mensch aus Erde gemacht), 116
Goddard, Charles W., 714
Godefroi de Bouillon, 315
Godfermaux, André, 273
Godiva, 98
Gods of the Lightning, 695, 696
Gods of the Mountain, The, 222
Goering, Reinhard, 105
Goetel, Ferdynand, 501
Goethe, Johann W. von, 23, 76, 84, 87, 125, 130, 170, 277, 370, 432, 620, 673
Goetz, Wolfgang, 114
Goetz von Berlichingen, 23
Goga, Octavian, 529, 530
Gogol, N. V., 102, 114, 377, 381, 382, 383, 386, 401, 443, 456, 504, 620, 673
Golar, Cvetko, 540
Gold, Michael, 707, 731
Gold, 685
Gold and Green Forests, 56
Gold Diggers, The, see also *Treasure, The* (Aleichem)
Gold Mine, The, 543
Golden, I. J., 708
Golden, John, 719
Golden Boy, 726
Golden Calf, The (Jotuni), 485
Golden Calf, The (Vomberger), 541
Golden Chain, The, 626

Golden Cuckoo, The, 231
Golden Horn, 540
Golden Horse, 490
Golden Morass, The, 515
Goldenburg, Samuel, 623
Goldene Harfe, Die, 84
Goldenen Strassen, Die, 94
Goldenen Waffen, Die, 113
Goldfaden, Abraham, 606, 607-16, 618, 633, 634
Goldmanova, F., 514
Goldoni, Carlo, 401, 672
Goldoni, e le sue sedici commedie nuove, 321
Goldsmith, Oliver, 376
Golem, The, 631, 632, 636
Golemanov, 543
Golgota, 535
Golia, Pavel, 540
Golondrina errante, 588
Gomes de Amorim, 594
Gomez de la Serna, Ramon, 566
Gonçalves de Magalhães, Domingos Jose, 598, 599
Gonçalves Dias, Antonio, 598
Goncourt, Edmond de, 240
Goncourt, Jules de, 240
González Pacheco, Rodolfo, 586
Good Companions, The, 204
Good Earth, The, 663
Good Fairy, The, 524
Good Fellow, The, 734
Good Friday, 188
Good Gracious, Annabelle! 681
Good Hope, The, 554
Good Life, The, 460
Good Little Devil, A, 305
Good Losers, 212
Good Morning, Bill, 525
Goodman, Jules Eckert, 714
Goodness, How Sad, 196
Good-Night, Children, 205
Goodrich, Arthur, 715
Goose Hangs High, The, 713
Gooseberry Fool, 203
Gordin, Jacob, 607, 619-22, 628
Gordon, Leon, 209
Gordon, Ruth, 739
Gore-Browne, R., 200
Gorgona, La, 352
Gorki, Maxim, 121, 221, 396, 413, 414, 416, 419-31, 436, 440, 441, 445, 448, 478, 485, 493, 499, 534, 547, 584, 622
Gorostiza, Celestino, 590
Gorsse, Henri de, 273
Gosse, Sir Edmund, 162, 164, 167, 639
Gotesfeld, Hune, 632
Gottlober, Abraham Ber, 606, 608, 609, 611, 630

Gouanakos, 545
Goulding, Edmund, 198
Govékar, Frau, 540
Government Uncle, The, 486
Gow, Ronald, 212
Gozzano, Guido, 356-57
Gracia y Justicia, 575
Graf Essex, 77
Graf von Charolais, Der, 137
Graf von Gleichen, Der, 93
Graff, Sigmund, 115, 119, 120
Graga, Victoriano, 596
Graham, Harry, 213
Gral, Der, 92
Grameno, Mihal, 548
Gran Capitán, El, 569
Gran Galeoto, El, 559
Gran teatro del mundo, El, 132
Gran Via, La, 564
Grand, Sarah, 164
Grand Cham's Diamond, The, 187
Grand duc, Le, 299
Grand Duchess and the Waiter, The, 292
Grand Guignol, 258, 259, 296, 574
Grand Prize, The, 55
Grande Duchesse et le garçon d'étage, La, 292
Grandfather, The, 631
Grandmother, The, 519
Grandmother and the Granddaughter, The, 613
Grands, Les, 273
Grangecolman, 218
Grania, 219
Granite, 203
Grant, Neil, 196
Granville-Barker, Harley, 134, 172-74, 182-84, 206, 290, 299, 420, 567
Granville-Barker, Helen, 184, 567
Grateful Posterity, 524
Grattan, Harry, 213
Great Adventure, The, 187, 392
Great Divide, The, 655-58
Great Frederick, The, 500
Great Freeholder, The, 505
Great Garrick, The, 525
Great God Brown, The, 687-89
Great Highway, The, 44
Great Magoo, The, 723
Great Rôle, The, 60
Great Uprising, The, 540, 541
Great We, The, 72
Greek drama, 28, 29, 85, 96, 105, 113, 115, 130, 132, 149, 215, 221, 233, 234, 253, 276, 277, 313, 371, 390, 397, 438, 544, 547, 549, 573, 690
Greeks Had a Word for It, The, 718
Green, Paul, 657, 691, 709-12, 721
Green Bay Tree, The, 210

Green Fields, 629
Green Goddess, The, 208
Green Gold, 485
Green Grow the Lilacs, 693, 711-13
Green Hat, The, 212
Green Knight, The, 92
Green Pastures, The, 709, 713, 714, 722
Green Waters, 209
Greenbank, Percy, 213
Greenwood, Walter, 212
Gregor und Heinrich, 146
Gregory, Lady Augusta, 173, 217, 218, 219, 222, 225, 226, 279, 483
Gregson, James R., 208
Grein, Jacob T., 167, 168, 246
Greluchon delicat, Le, 295
Gresac, Fred de, 298
Grevenius, Herbert, 65, 67
Grey, Clifford, 213
Gribble, Harry Wagstaff, 716
Griboedov, A. S., 377, 378, 379, 380, 381, 408, 461
Griboedov Prize, 403, 425, 478
Griechischer Frühling, 85
Grief Goes Over, 212
Grieg, Nordahl, 65, 66, 70, 71, 72, 75
Griese, Friedrich, 116
Griffith, Hubert, 202, 208
Grillparzer, Franz, 81, 124, 159, 516, 531, 532, 538, 620
Grimpette, La, 297
Gringa, La, 583
Gringo, El, 582
Grīns, Alexander, 490
Griselda, 82
Grobe Hemd, Das, 140
Groise Gevins, Dos, 627
Groniman, Semi, 637
Grossbürger Möller, 102
Grosse Leidenschaft, Die, 138
Grosse Salzburger Welttheater, Das, 132
Grosse Szene, 136
Grossmith, George, 214, 417
Grotesque Theatre, 338, 339, 343, 344, 346, 358, 366-68, 443, 562-63
Group Theatre, The, 693, 696, 710, 724, 725, 727, 729, 730
Gruach, 190
Grubiński, Wacław, 500
Gruene Kakadu, Der, 135
Grum, Slavko, 540
Grundy, Sydney, 162, 165
Guapo del 900, Un, 586
Guarani, 588
Guarani, O, 598
Guardez à la peinture, 211
Guardia alla luna, La, 368
Guardsman, The, 523, 734
Gubec, Matija, 538

INDEX

Gudrun, 92
Guerre de Troie n'aura pas lieu, La, 307
Guerrini, Olindo, 324
Guillemaud, Marcel, 297
Guilt, 507, 539
Guilty Without Guilt, 588
Guimera, Angel, 564
Guinon, Albert, 267
Guitry, Sacha, 299, 305, 496
Gundulich, Ivan, 533
Gunner Pidras, 508, 509
Gunther und Brunhild, 96
Guntwar, die Schule eines Propheten, 104
Gurgel, Amara, 600
Gurney, Claude, 200
Gustaf III, 37, 57
Gustaf Vasa, 37, 39
Gustaf (II) Adolf, 37
Gute Zeit, Die, 107
Guthrie, W. N., 672
Gutman, Isaiah, 610
Gutzkow, Karl, 76, 617
Gyges und sein Ring, 95
Gypsy, 695
Gypsy Child, 515
Gyurkovics Family, The, 522

Haarla, Lauri, 485
Habima, 400, 624, 626, 631, 632, 636, 637
Habima Ha Ivrith, 636
Habit vert, L', 272
Habsburgerlegende, 153
Hackett, Albert, 677
Hackett, Walter, 212
Hadda Padda, 63
Hagenbeck, 510
Hahn, Reynaldo, 299
Hahnenkampf, Der, 100
Haight, George, 670
Hairy Ape, The, 685, 686
Hajna, Mikławš, 504
Halbe, Max, 87, 88
Hale, Lionel, 208
Hálek, Vitězslav, 505, 507
Halevi, Moshe, 637
Halévy, Ludovic, 165, 240, 272, 316
Half an Hour, 181
Half Gods, 699
Halle, Ahron, 604, 605
Hallo, Ernest, pseud., 316
Hallström, Per, 56, 57
Halpern, Leivick, see Leivick, H.
Haltern, Joseph, 604
Halvorsen, Finn, 65, 67
Ha Matatey, 637
Hameiri, Avigdor, 637
Hamilton, Cicely, 196
Hamilton, Clayton, 672

Hamilton, Cosmo, 208
Hamilton, Patrick, 208, 213
Hamilton, T. J., 574
Hamilton, 208
Hamlet (Shakespeare), 38, 83, 84, 130, 373, 378, 380, 404, 406, 408, 516, 532, 674, 728
Hamlet (Sumarokov), 373
Hamlet in Wittenberg, 84
Hamlet ou le triomphe de la vertu, 315
Hammer und Amboss, 77
Hamsun, Knut, 56, 410
Hand of Justice, The, 540
Hands Across the Sea, 195
Hands, the Doctor, 627
Hangman, The, 67-71
Hankin, St. John, 184, 187
Hanna Jagert, 89
Hannele, 80, 81, 91
Hanneles Himmelfahrt, 80
Hannequin, Maurice, 271, 273
Hannibal, 96
Hans im Schnakenloch, 109
Hansson, Ola, 32
Happy Boy, A, 45
Happy Coffin-Maker, The, 444
Happy Days, The, 298
Happy Ending, A, 409
Happy Hyprocrite, The, 204
Harald Svan's Mother, 55
Haraucourt, Edmond, 255
Hard Earned Bread, 386
Hard to be a Jew, 627
Hardt, Ernst, 92, 93, 109
Hardy, Thomas, 184
Harlan, Walter, 97
Harlem, 709
Harrigan, Edward, 651, 652, 657
Harsányi, Zsolt, 526
Hart, Heinrich and Julius, 78
Hart, Moss, 721, 733-37
Harte, Bret, 648
Hartleben, Otto Erich, 87, 89
Hartmann, Eduard von, 97
Harvard Dramatic Club, 445, 472, 572
Harvest, 224
Harvester, The, 252
Harwood, H. M., 196, 200
Hasdeu, Bogdan P., 528, 529
Hasenclever, Walter, 104-05, 151, 455
Hassall, Christopher, 214-16
Hassan, 189
Hassan Aga's Wife, 534
Hastings, B. MacDonald, 196
Hastings, Milo, 731
Hatoren, The, 632
Hatton, Fanny and Frederic, 714
Hatvany, Louis, 521, 524
Haubenlerche, Die, 90

Haunted Palace, The, 432
Hauptmann, Carl, 94
Hauptmann, Gerhart, 78-85, 87, 88, 89, 91, 94, 104, 110, 117, 122, 140, 244-47, 339, 354, 401, 448, 496, 498, 504, 506, 539, 546, 554, 620, 672, 673
Hauptmann Toboggan, 119
Hauptmann von Köpenick, Der, 115
Haus am Meer, Das, 144
Hawk, The, 298
Hawthorne, Nathaniel, 642
Hawthorne, Ruth, 720
Haxhiademi, Etëhem, 549
Hay, Ian, 196, 202
Hay, John, 646
Hay Fever, 194
Hazelton, George C., 678
HaZ'man, 628
He Sits by the Melting-Pot, 74
He Was Born Gay, 211
He Who Gets Slapped, 435
He Who Lived His Life Over Again, 69
Head of Cabbage, A, 487
Hear O Israel, 636
Heart of a City, 211
Heart of Maryland, The, 652
Heart on a Halter, 511
Heart Was Not Burned, The, 190
Heartbreak House, 174, 175, 183, 398
Heather Field, The, 218
Heaven, Hell, Paradise, 510
Heavenly Express, The, 708
Heavy Traffic, 716
Hebbel, Friedrich, 2, 95, 96, 99, 154, 204, 620
Hecht, Ben, 717, 723
Hedberg, Tor, 56, 57
Hedda Gabler, 17, 61, 178
Hedgerow Theatre, 712
Hegel, G. W. F., 392
Heiberg, Gunnar, 49, 51-55, 72, 75
Heidenstam, Verner von, 56
Heifetz, Vladimir, 632
Heijermans, Herman, 266, 554-56
Heilandsflur, 109
Heilige Crispin, Der, 96
Heilige Johanna der Schlachthöfe, Die, 122
Heimat, 86
Heimkehr des Matthias Bruck, Die, 120
Heine, Heinrich, 3, 76, 77, 80
Heinrich von Andernach, 106
Heirs, 487
Heirs of a Great Age, 540
Held by the Enemy, 641, 663
Hélène de Sparte, 312
Hell Bent fer Heaven, 713
Hellenists, The, 545
Hellman, Lillian, 644, 721, 728, 729
Hellseherei, 104
Heltai, Eugene, 523
Hemingway, Ernest, 723
Hemmerde, E. E., 196
Henderson, Archibald, 168
Hennique, Léon, 243, 258
Henpecked Husband, The, 485
Henri III et sa coeur, 235
Henrietta, The, 646, 647
Henriette Maréchal, 240
Henry, Charles, 213
Henry, O., 664
Henry IV, 366
Henschke, Alfred, *see* Klabund
Her Cardboard Lover, 294
Her Husband's Wife, 680
H. M. S. Pinafore; or, the Lass That Loved a Sailor, 162
Her Own Way, 659
Her Stepdaughter, 506
Herakles, 100
Herbert, Sir Alan, 214
Herbert, Eleanor, 196
Herbert, Victor, 298, 564
Herczeg, Ferenc, 521, 522
Here Come the Clowns, 703
Herman, Henry, 166, 167
Herman of Cilli, 541
Hermanos de Betania, Los, 569
Hermann, 468
Hermant, Abel, 268
Hermelin the Tight-Rope Walker, 511
Hermione, 22
Hernandez, Miguel, 574
Hernani, 235, 242
Herne, James A., 417, 640, 649-51, 657
Hero, The, 720
Herod, a Tragedy, 188
Herod (Katzizne), 633
Herod (Tresich-Pavičich), 532
Herod and Mariamne, 204
Herodes und Mariamne, 95
Hérodienne, L', 313
Heroes of Our Day, 511
Heroische Leidenschaften, 145
Hérold, A.-Ferdinand, 253
Herr Arne's Hoard, 83
Herr Bengt's Wife, 26
Herr Doktor, haben Sie zu essen? 142
Herrera, Ernesto, 584
Hertz, A. de, 529
Hervieu, Paul, 260, 261, 289, 314
Herzl, Theodor, 140
Herzog, Wilhelm, 113, 116
Herzog Heinrichs Heimkehr, 98
Herzog Utz, 112
Herzog von Reichstadt, Der, 98
Hesse, Otto Ernst, 118
Hetairea, Philiké, 545

Hettner, Hermann, 1, 5
Heure H., L', 296
Heux, Gaston, 317
Hexe von Passau, Die, 158
Hexenritt, 84
Heynicke, Kurt, 113
Heyse, Paul, 78
Heyward, Dorothy, 709
Heyward, Du Bose, 709, 710
Heywood, Thomas, 275
Hichens, Robert, 196
Hickerson, Harold, 695
Hicks, Seymour, 213
Hidalla, 99
Hiedra, La, 590
Hieram und Salomo, 97
High Road, The, 195
High Stakes, 63-64
High Tor, 696-97
Highest Trump, The, 497
Highland Call, The, 711
Hija de Dios, La, 575
Hijas del Cid, Las, 569
Hijo de Don Juan, El, 559
Hilbert, Jaroslav, 507, 539
Hilfe! Ein Kind ist vom Himmel gefallen, 94
Hillarys, The, 186
him, 707
Himmel und Hoelle, 148
Himmlische Handelsmann, Der, 93
Hindle Wakes, 60, 184, 185
Hinke Pinke, 618
Hinkemann, 110
Hinrichs, August, 118
Hintze, Ernst, 119
Hiob, 149
Hired Men, 539-40
Hirschbein, Peretz, 628-29
Hirschbein Troupe, The, 628
Hirschfeld, Georg, 87-89
Hirsh Lekert, 632, 634
His Grace's Last Testament, 66
His Son, 485
Hiss! Boom!! Blah!!! 668
Histoire du jeune Bernard de Menthon, L', 255
Historical drama, 1, 5, 23, 34, 36-39, 44, 46, 57, 74, 81, 83, 86, 91, 94-96, 108-10, 112-13, 119, 141, 153-54, 171, 188-89, 205-08, 212, 224, 232, 234-35, 237, 240, 256, 258, 263, 304, 307, 312, 315, 321-22, 331-32, 337, 340, 347, 350, 352-55, 359, 369, 373-75, 387, 390, 393-94, 409, 433, 454-55, 465-74, 484, 486-88, 492, 498-99, 500-01, 503, 505, 507-08, 513, 515, 517-20, 522, 525, 528-31, 534-35, 540, 542-43, 547, 551, 595, 599, 614-15, 617-18, 621, 625, 633, 635, 644. 660-61, 697, 715

Historie vom Koenig David, Die, 137
History of Civilization in England, 24
History of One Love, The, 478
History of the American Drama from the Civil War to the Present Day, 646
History of the Theatre, 567
Hitler, Adolf, 468
Hobart, George V., 714
Hobgoblin, The, 487
Hoboken Blues, 707
Hobson's Choice, 186
Hochzeit der Sobeide, Die, 129
Hockewanzel, 116
Hodge, Merton, 196, 212
Hoesick, Ferdinand, 492
Hoffman, Aaron, 714
Hofmannsthal, Hugo von, 91, 92, 93, 128-137, 138, 159, 430, 688-89
Hogar, Un, 586
Holberg, (Baron) Ludwig, 3, 81
Holcroft, Thomas, 234
Holiday, 702
Hollandische Kaufmann, Der, 120
Hölle, Weg und Erde, 103
Hollý, Jozef, 514
Hollywood Holiday, 198, 202
Holmes, O. W., 642
Holst, Henriette Roland, 555
Holy Maiden, The, 625
Holy Tyrant, The, 632
Holz, Arno, 79, 85, 102
Hombres no lloran, Los, 587
Home, 161
Home Chat, 194
Home Towners, The, 677
Homère, 313
Homeward, 507
Homicide, L', 283
Homme à l'Hispano, L', 271
Homme et ses fântomes, L', 281, 287
Homme et son désir, L', 254
Homme mystérieux, L', 259
Hommes, Les, 296
Homo Sapiens, 515
Honegger, Arthur, 302
Honest Matthew, 509
Honor of the Family, The, 262
Honorarium, 514
Honza, 509
Hooft, Pieter Cornelisz, 551
Hoosier Doctor, The, 658
Hopkins, Arthur, 425, 685, 712
Hoppla! 110
Hoppla, wir leben! 110
Hopwood, Avery, 674, 679, 714, 721
Horizon (Daly), 648
Horizon (Simonov), 478
Horn, Panteles, 546
Horniman, A. E. F., 184, 185, 222

Horse Eats Hat, 240
Horst, Louis, 306
Hortatzis, 544
Horvath, Oedoen von, 155-56
Hose, Die, 101
Hot Bed, 723
Hot Pan, 709
Hotel Universe, 702, 703
Houghton, Stanley, 60, 175, 184, 186
Hour-Glass, The, 218
House Beautiful, The, 667, 716
House of Borgia, The, 207
House of Connelly, The, 710
House of Dance, 271
House of Danger, The, 213
House of Kokai, The, 520
House of the Dead, The, 396
House of the Jarl, The, 67, 72
House That Went to Sea, The, 190
Houseman, John, 284
Housemaster, 202
Housewife Slave, The, 506
Housman, Laurence, 183, 206
How He Lied to Her Husband, 172
How the Steel Was Tempered, 470
How to Get Tough About It, 730
Howard, Bronson, 640, 645, 647, 657, 683, 703
Howard, Leslie, 196
Howard, Sidney, 251, 283, 285, 286, 291, 294, 643, 646, 670, 674, 691, 693, 698-701, 704, 716, 721
Howells, W. D., 640, 648, 651, 679
Hoy, Sale Hoy, 564
Hoyt, Charles, 652, 657, 668
Hraun Farm, The, 62
Hughes, Hatcher, 692, 713
Hughes, Langston, 710
Hughes, Richard, 724
Hugo, Victor, 235, 256, 508, 552, 620
Huitième femme de Barbe-Bleue, La, 292
Hulbert, Jack, 213
Hulla, Der, 95
Human Dust, 632
Humaneli, Samuel, 604
Humble, The, 396
Hume, Sam, 674
Humperdinck, Engelbrecht, 89
Hundred Years Old, A, 566
Hungarian Revolutionary in Paris, The, 520
Hunger Blockade, 143
Hunyady, Sándor, 525
Huret, Jules, 245
Hurlbut, William J., 714
Hurwitch, Moses, 613, 617-20, 622, 635
Husband and Wife, Sister, and Brother, 608
Hussites, The, 509

Huygens, Constantijn, 551
Hyacinth Halvey, 219
Hymer, John B., 717
Hymn to the Rising Sun, 711

I Am Guilty, 485
I Have Been Here Before, 204
I Knock at the Door, 227
I Love an Actress, 525
I Remember Mama, 199
I Shall Live, 634
I, Son of the Working People, 462
I Was Waiting for You, 295
I Will Defend My Country, 55
I Won't Marry, 526
Ibraginov, 469
Ibsen, Henrik, 1-20, 22-23, 26-27, 36, 43, 45-49, 51-52, 54, 56-57, 59-65, 68, 75, 78-80, 86, 89, 91-92, 95, 102, 113, 162-68, 177-78, 185, 218, 225, 241, 244-45, 247, 258, 260, 262-63, 278, 311, 314, 316, 325, 335, 339, 366, 410, 448, 496, 498, 507, 539, 544, 546-47, 549, 554, 559-60, 577, 581-82, 584, 593-95, 599, 620, 639, 641, 643, 645-46, 649, 669, 671-72, 680
Ibsen's Ghost; or, Toole Up to Date, 178
Icebound, 663, 714
Icon, 546
I'd Rather Be Right, 736
Ideal Husband, An, 163
Idealism, 246-48, 250-53, 255, 257, 274, 276, 279, 304-06, 319, 321, 333, 352, 661-62, 666, 684, 692, 703
Idealist, An, 73, 74
Idées de Mme. Aubray, Les, 239
Idiot, The, 396
Idiot's Delight, 705
Idle Inn, The, 628
Idol Breaker, The, 666
Idyl, The, 63
If, 222
If Five Years Pass, 572
If I Were You, 202
If Thunder Strikes, 543
If Tomorrow Brings War, 469
Ignorabimus, 85
Ihr stilles Glück, 100
Ijsbrand, 553
Il faut que chacun soit à sa place, 296
Ilf, 461
Illica, Luigi, 333
Illusione dei giorni e delle notti, L', 367
Illusioniste, L', 299
Illyrism, 531, 533
Iluminado, El, 588
Ilya of Murom, 490
I'm a Stranger Here, 204, 205
Im Chambre Séparée, 95

Im Dickicht der Städte, 120
Im Namen des Volkes, 115
Im Spiel der Sommerluefte, 137
Im weissen Roessl, 144
Im Westen Nichts Neues, 119
Image, L', (Beaubourg), 247
Image, The (Gregory), 219
Immagine, L', 368
Immigration to America, The, 617
Immortal Souls, 495
Imperatrice si diverte, L', 359
Importance of Being Earnest, The, 163
Imposteur Magnanime, L', 312
Imposters, 495
Impressionism, 247, 306, 308, 634, 649
Impromptu de Paris, L', 307
In a Conspirative Home, 631
In a Forsaken Nook, 628
In a Garden, 702
In a Little House, 497, 498
In Abraham's Bosom, 709, 710, 713
In Agony, 534
In einer Nacht, 147
In Ewigkeit Amen! 150
In Fire, 622
In Golden Chains, 632
In Good King Charles's Golden Days, 176
In Mizzoura, 658
In Reih und Glied, 77
In Rome, 22
In the Autumn, 405
In the Breakers, 73, 74
In the Castle, 503
In the Ear of Dionysus, 507
In the Furnace, 489
In the Vortex, 540
In the Whirl of the Winds, 487
In the World, 429
In This Night, 637
In Tyrannos, 123
In Which We Serve, 193, 195
Incognito, 513
Inconstant George, 272
Increible, Lo, 574
Independent Theatre, The, 167, 168, 246, 639, 649
Index Expurgatorius, 249
Indifférents ou on s'amuse comme on peut, Les, 315
Indipohdi, 83
Indiscreet Copyist, The, 300
Indiscret, L', 271
Indrans, The, 489
Induls and Arija, 490
Industrie, 93
Infernal Machine, The, 302
Inferno, The, 33-35, 44, 350, 354
Infinite Shoeblack, The, 210

Inheritance, The, 521
Innocent Voyage, The, 724
Insane, The, 616
Insect Comedy, The, 512
Insel, Die, 93
Inspector General, The, 102, 115, 381, 382, 384, 386, 443, 504
Insulted and Injured, The, 396
Insurance Money, 231
Insurgent Theatre, The, 672
Intelligence Comes to Grief, see *Woe from Wit*
Intereses creados, Los, 567
Interferences, 209
Intérieur, 249
Interior, 250
Intermezzo, 547
International, The, 706
Interprete de Hamlet, El, 587
Intimacy, 300
Intimate Theatre, The, 36, 43
Intrigue, The, 613
Introduction to Monodrama, 443
Intruse, L', 247, 249
Invasion, 477
Invitation au voyage, L', 285
Iolanthe, 162
Iphigénie, 253
Iphigénie in Delphi, 84
Irene Wycherly, 196
Iris, 165
Irish Literary Theatre, The, 172, 217, 220, 222, 225, 640
Irish Players, 671
Iron Cross, The, 692
Irredentos, 587
Irresistible One, The, 519
Is Life Worth Living? 224
Is Zat So? 720
Isaac Sheftel, 623
Isaacs, Edith R., 674
Isabeau, 305
Isabel Sandoval, 587
Isabella von Spanien, 156
Isabella's Destiny, 547
Iscariot, 520
Isherwood, Christopher, 214-16
Island of Great Love, The, 510
Island Wilderness, The, 614
Isola delle Scimmie, L', 346
Israël, 270
Israel's Hope, 622
Israelites and Philistines, 549
Isrealita, L', 335
It Cannot Be Mad, 690
It Can't Happen Here, 731
It Isn't I, 547
It Pays to Advertise, 677
It Will Pass, 487

It's a Family Affair—We'll Settle It Ourselves, 384
It's the Poor That 'Elps the Poor, 185
Italian Society of Playwrights, 336
Italian Woman, The, 526
Italienische Nacht, 155
Ivailo, 543
Ivan the Terrible, 466, 467
Ivan Vasilevich, 456
Ivanko, 542, 543
Ivanov, V. V., 449, 456-58
Ivanov, 405-08, 411-13, 416, 419
Ivory Door, The, 192
Ivresse du sage, L', 263
Iwaszkiewicz, Jarosław, 502

Jaakobs Traum, 137
Jackson, Sir Barry Vincent, 255
Jacob and Christopher, 63
Jacob and His Sons, 610
Jacob Ruda, 539
Jacob's Dream, 636
Jacoba of Bavaria, 553
Jacobines, Les, 268
Jacobs, William Wymark, 187
Jacques Damour, 243, 258
Jadwiga, 499
Jagt ihn—ein Mensch! 146
Jahnn, Hans Henny, 107
Jahrmarkt zu Pulsnitz, Der, 97
Jailbird, The, 231
Jakobson, August, 487
Jakobson, Peeter, 486, 487
Jakšich, Djura, 535
Jalouse, 273
James, Henry C., 167, 208, 640, 642, 645, 665, 715
Jan Výrava, 504, 505
Jane Annie; or the Good Conduct Prize, 178
Jane Clegg, 223
Jane Shore, 207
Jannsen, J. W., 486
Janošik (Goldmanova), 514
Janoshik (Mahen), 506
Janošik (Vrba), 514
Jansons, John, 489
Jarl of Bjälbo, The, 37
Jarry, Alfred, 247, 301
Jasager, Der, 121
Jason, 722
Jazz, 291
Jazz Singer, The, 722
Je suis trop grand pour moi, 303
Je t'attendais, 295
Je vivrai un grand amour, 283
Jealous God, The, 202
Jealousy, 439, 440

Jean de la lune, 304
Jeanne, 295
Jeanne d'Arc, 661, 662
Jeanne d'Arc, la pucelle de France, 256
Jeans, Ronald, 196, 213
Jeanson, Henri, 283
Jedermann (Hofmannsthal), 131
Jedermann (Loeser-Hofmannsthal), 131
Jennings, Gertrude, 196
Jennings, Talbot, 670
Jenseits, 105
Jeppe paa Bjerget, 81
Jeremias, 145
Jeremy the Magnificent, 525
Jerome, Helen, 196
Jerrold, Douglas, 160
Jerschke, Oskar, 85, 102
Jerusalem and Rome, 637
Jerzy Lubomirski, 499
Jesse, F(ryniwyd) Tennyson, 196, 200
Jessel, George, 723
Jest, The, 353
Jesters, The, 252
Jesuita, O, 598
Jésus de Nazareth, 255, 315
Jettatore, 585
Jeu de l'amour et de la mort, Le, 257
Jeune Belgique, La, 310, 312, 313
Jewel Robbery, 525
Jewett, Sarah Orne, 645
Jewish Heart, The, 618, 622
Jewish King Lear, 620
Jewish Noble, The, 614, 618
Jewish State Theatre, 633
Jim Dandy, 740
Jitta's Atonement, 138
Joaquim, José da Franca, Jr., 598
Job (Hilbert), 507
Job (Sharkanski), 621
Jochumsson, Matthías, 61
Johan Wvstjerna, 56, 57
Johau van Oldenbarnevelt, 553
Johannes, 86
Johannesfeuer, 87
Johansson, Wilhelmina, see Canth, Minna
John, Graham, 213
John, 666, 702
John Bull's Other Island, 167, 172
John Ferguson, 223
John Gabriel Borkman, 14, 16, 17, 18
John Glayde's Honour, 186
John the Baptist, 86
Johnny Johnson, 711
Johnson, Hall, 710
Johnson, Philip, 196
Johnson over Jordan, 205
Johnston, (William) Denis, 231
Johst, Hans, 111, 113
Jojne Firulkes, 497

INDEX 793

Jókai, Maurus, 519
Jonah and the Whale, 199
Jones, Henry Arthur, 162, 165, 174, 640
Jonson, Ben, 145
Jorga, Nicholas, 529
Jörgenson, Johannes, 56
Jose of Yokrath, see Holy Tyrant, The
Joseph and His Brethren (Lateiner), 617
Joseph and His Brethren (Rainis), 490
Joseph d' Arimathée, 255
Joseph Pučik and His Career, 515
Josephine, 126
Josephson, Ragnar, 65
Jotuni, Maria, 484, 485
Journalists, The, 543
Journey's End, 119, 206, 510
Jours heureux, Les, 298
Jouvet, Louis, 277, 279
Joy, 182
Joyce, James, 366
Joyous Season, The, 703
Juan Cuello, 577
Juan José, 560, 563
Juan Moreira, 577, 581
Juan Soldao, 577, 581
Juana, 103
Juarez und Maximilian, 147
Judas, 485
Judas Iscariot, 500
Judas von Tirol, Der, 143
Jude von Konstanz, Der, 97
Judge, The, 428
Judge Sári, 521
Judge Simpson, 487
Judgment Day, 694
Judgment Is in Sight, 634
Judges, The, 499
Judith (Belloi), 610
Judith (Chekhov), 409
Judith (Hebbel), 95, 99
Judith (Tammsaare), 487
Jüdische Witwe, Die, 102
Jugend, 87
Jugend von Heute, 90
Jugendfreunde, 91
Juiz de paz da Roça, O, 598-99
Juliette et Roméo, 252
Julius Caesar, 23, 504
Jullien, Jean, 257, 258
June Moon, 734
Junge Baron Neuhaus, Der, 154
Junge David, Der, 137
Junge Deutschland, Das, see Young Germany
Junge Medardus, Der, 136
Junge Mensch, Der, 111
Junge Welt, Die, 98
Jungen von Mons, Die, 117
Jungfern von Bischofsberg, Die, 82

Jungfrau, 106
Jungfrau von Orleans, 122
Junior Miss, 737
Juno and the Paycock, 227
Jůra Dábel, 511
Jurčich, Josip, 532, 538, 540, 541
Jürgenstein, Anton, 486
Jusminš, 489
Justice, 182
Justina, 485
Justizkrise, 119
Juta, 486
Juurako's Hulda, 485
Juventud, 588

Kaatje, 313
Kabale und Liebe, 76, 112
Kabtzenson and Hungerman, see Bride Who Was Difficult to Please, The
Kacijanar, 538
Kadelburg, Gustav, 144
Kaergel, Hans Christoph, 116, 118
Kain, 151
Kain and Artem, 429
Kaiser, Georg, 42, 102-04, 686
Kaiser Franz Joseph I von Oesterreich, 153
Kaiser Karls Geisel, 82
Kaiser Napoleon, 94
Kaiser und die Hexe, Der, 129
Kaiser und Kanzler, 96
Kalergis, 546
Kalevala, 483, 484
Kalidasa, The, 189
Kalkutta, 4. Mai, 120
Kaltneker, Hans, 149
Kamare, Cokorac von, see Kamare, Stephan, pseud.
Kamare, Stephan, pseud., 154
Kamban, Gudmundur, 61-63
Kambisis, Joannes, 546
Kaminsky Troupe, 622
Kammersänger, Der, 99
Kampf, Der, 142
Kampf um Kitsch, 117
Kampf ums Rosenrote, Der, 92
Kamrash, Wolf, 610
Kanin, Garson, 639
Kanteletar, 483
Kanzler und König, 98
Kanzler von Tirol, Der, 154
Kanzlist Krehler, 103
Kapnist, V. V., 377
Karadžich, Vuk, 535
Karageorge, 514
Karásek, Jiří, 508
Karen Bornemann, 59, 60
Karl Hetmann, der Zwerg-Riese, 99

Karl und Anna, 120
Karl XII, 37
Karlfeldt, Erik Axel, 56
Karlweis, C., pseud., 140
Karolinger, Die, 90
Karrnerleut', 141
Kasack, Herman, 111
Kasija, 540
Kaśka Kariatyda, 497
Kasprowicz, Jan, 498
Kassette, Die, 101
Kataev, 449, 461, 462
Katalaunische Schlacht, 152
Katarina Zrinjska, 532
Katbenelenson, Yitzhak, 636
Kate, 647
Katharina Graefin von Armagnac und ihre beiden Liebhaber, 91
Katharina Knie, 115
Katherina Ivanovno, 434
Katie Roche, 229
Katona, József, 516
Katte, 112
Katzenelenbogen, 615
Katzizne, Alter, 623, 631, 633
Kaufman, George S., 691, 721, 722, 733-37
Kaufmann Christleit, 107
Kazinczy, Ferenc, 516
Kearney, Patrick, 718
Keller, Gottfried, 91
Kelly, George, 683, 691, 701, 702, 704
Kennedy, Charles Rann, 666, 667
Kennedy, Margaret, 196, 202, 568
Kennedy, Mary, 720
Kenyon, Charles, 664
Kesselring, Joseph, 738
Kesser, Hermann, 118
Kessler, David, 623
Kesten, Hermann, 115
Kestner, Rene, pseud., 113; see also Rehfisch, Hans Jose
Keturakis, pseud., see Vilkutaitis, J.
Key Largo, 696, 698, 723
Keys of the Kingdom, The, 32
Keys to Berlin, The, 467
Khorev, 373
Kiddush Hashem, 625
Kiedrzynski, Stefan, 500
Kielland, Alexander, 51
Kiki, 274
Kilian, oder die gelbe Rose, 148
Kinck, Hans E., 64
Kind, Das, 95
Kinder, Die, 127
Kinder der Freude, 138
Kindertragoedie, 142
Kindred, 230
King, The (Björnson), 47, 48, 51
King, The (Flers-Caillavet-Arène), 272

King, The (Lagerkvist), 69
King and Mistress Shore, The, 20,
King Condemned to Darkness, The, 546
King David and His Wives, 624
King Harlequin, 443
King Henry IV, 505
King Hunger, 431, 432
King, Law, Liberty, see Sorrows of Belgium, The
King Lear, 29, 83, 140, 408, 620
King Lear's Wife, 190
King Midas, 52
King of Nowhere, The, 200
King of the Mountains, The, 709
King of Udumäe, The, 486
King, Queen, Knave, 200
King Richard II, 505
King Rudolf II, 505
King Solomon, 617, 633
King Solomon and Shalmai the Cobbler, 637
King Spider, 469
King Stephen, 520
King Svatopluk, 515
King Sverre, 45
King's Daughter, A, 188
King's Henchman, The, 654
King's Threshold, The, 218
Kingdom of Youth, The, 225
King-Hall, Stephen, 202
Kingsley, Sidney, 724
Kingu Laos, 486
Kipps, 206
Kiritzescu, 529
Kirk, Laurence, 200
Kirke, 540
Kirschenbaum, Dr. Leo, 599
Kirshon, V. M., 449, 459, 460
Kisfaludy, Alexander, 517
Kisfaludy, Charles, 513, 517, 518, 521
Kisielewski, Jan August, 496
Kismet, 189
Kiss, The, 520
Kiss for Cinderella, A, 181
Kiss in a Taxi, A, 273
Kiss the Boys Goodbye, 736
Kistemaeckers, Henri, 271, 311, 315
Kit the Arkansas Traveler, 648
Kitchen of Laughter, The, 444
Kitzberg, August, 487
Kivi, pseud., 483
Kivijärvi, Erkko, 485
Kivikas, Albert, 487
Klabund, 109
Klara, 539
Klaus Michel, 98
Klein, Charles, 657, 664, 680
Kleine Heim, Das, 143
Kleine Komoedie, 154

Kleine Mann, Der, 140
Kleine Welttheater, Das, 129
Kleist, Heinrich von, 153, 154
Kleist, 98
Klicpera, Vaclav Kliment, 503, 515
Kloster bei Sendomir, Das, 81
Knickerbocker Holiday, 696, 697
Knight-errant, The, 60
Knipper, Olga, *see* Chekhova, Olga Knipper
Knoblauch, Edward, *see* Knoblock, Edward
Knoblock, Edward, 187, 189, 204, 212, 670
Knock, ou le triomphe de la médecine, 276, 290
Knot in the Wood, The, 540
Knyazhnin, Jacob Borisovitch, 377
Kobrin, Leon, 621, 622
Koch, Frederick H., 710
Kodolányi, János, 525
König, Der, 111
König David, 104
König Hahrei, 102
Köenig Harlekin, 139
König Oedipus, 131
Könige, 143
Königskinder, 89
Königsleutnant, Der, 76
Königsmaske, 114
Koha, 549
Kohol in Shtetel, 610
Koidula, Lydia, 486
Kokoschka, Oskar, 149
Kol Boi'nik, The, 610
Kol Nidrei, 621
Kolár, 505
Kolbenheyer, Erwin Guido, 145-46
Kölcsey, 517
Kollege Crampton, 80
Kolonne Hund, 117
Kolportage, 103
Kommandantur, Le, 316
Kommissarzhevskaya, Vera, 411, 416, 425, 426, 431, 436, 437, 438, 442
Kommissarzhevski, Theodore, 401
Kommt ein Vogel geflogen, 105
Komoediant, Der, 142
Komodie am Klavier, 111
Komoedie der Verfuehrung, 137
Komoedie der Worte, 136
Komtesse Mitzi, 136
Konflikt, 118
Konrad, Edmund, 511
Konzert, Das, 127, 128
Kopta, Josef, 510
Koralle, Die, 103, 104
Korneichuk, E., 449, 473-75
Kornfeld, Paul, 148

Koroliya, Mirko, 531, 543
Koromelas, Demetrios, 546
Kosor, Josip, 534
Kostich, Laza, 535
Kostov, Stefan Lazarov, 543
Kotzebue, August von, 91, 504
Kotzebue and the Czech Stage, 504
Krach um Jolanthe, 118
Kracholov, *see* Yavorov, Peyu, *pseud.*
Kräfte, 106
Kraigher, Lojz, 539
Kranewitter, Franz, 140-41
Krankheit der Jugend, 152, 311
Kraus, Karl, 139, 159
Kreatur, Die, 153
Krechinski's Wedding, 391, 392
Kreft, Bratho, 532, 540, 541
Kreidekreis, Der, 109
Kremlin Chimes, The, 464
Kreutzer Sonata, 621
Kreutzwald, F. R., 486
Kreuzweg, Der, 115
Krēvē, Vincas, 491
Krieg, 94
Kriegsgefangenen, Die, 120
Krimsky, Jerrold, 121
Krisis, 109
Krist vor Gericht, 112
Kristina, 37
Kristofor Kolumbo, 534
Kritische Waffengaege, 78
Krleza, Miroslav, 534
Krönung König Richards III, Die, 107
Krog, Helge, 65, 66, 67, 72, 73, 75
Krylov, 379
Kryukovski, Michael, 378
Krzywoszewski, Stefan, 500
Kubašec, Marja, 504
Kubo, 514
Kuckuck und sein Kind, Der, 93
Kuckuckseier, 114
Kullervo (Erkko), 484
Kullervo (Kivi), 483
Kulundzich, Josip, 535
Kumičich, Eugeniy, 532, 534
Kummer, Clare, 681
Kunder, Juhan, 486
Kunst, ihr Wesen und ihre Gesetze, Die, 79
Kuprianov, 469
Kuprin, 413
Kupšćan, J., *see* Wjela, Jury
Kurds, The, 546
Kurfürst, Der, 108
Kurikka, Matti, 485
Kushnirov, Aaron, 634
Kvapil, Jaroslav, 506, 509
Kypselides, 546
Kyser, Hans, 116

La de San Quintýn, 561
Labiche, Eugène, 165, 240, 271, 297, 520
Laboremus, 50
Laburnum Grove, 204
Labyrinth, The, 261
Lacerda, Cesar de, 594, 595
Ladies All, 299
Ladies and Gentlemen (Bus-Fekete), 525
Ladies and Gentlemen (Hecht & MacArthur), 723
Ladies in Retirement, 210
Ladies' Tea, 59
Lady Frederick, 191
Lady from Lobster Square, The, 273
Lady from the Provinces, The, 394
Lady from the Sea, The, 16, 86, 218, 544
Lady Has a Heart, The, 525
Lady in the Dark, 735
Lady Inger of Östraat, 4
Lady Macbeth of the Mtsensk District, A, 392
Lady Next Door, The, 693
Lady of Belmont, The, 223
Lady of Dreams, The, 250
Lady of Pskov, The, 393
Lady of the Orchids, The, 295
Lady of the Rose, 718
Lady Patricia, 206
Lady Windermere's Fan, 163
Lady with a Lamp, The, 208
Laferrére, Gregorio de, 585
La Fontaine, Jean de, 379
Lagerkvist, Pär, 65-72, 75
Lagerlöf, Selma, 56, 83
Laitner, 635
Lake, The, 197
Lame Hulda, 45
Lamm, (Prof.) Martin, 38, 43
Lamm des Armen, Das, 145
Lampel, Peter Martin, 116
Lancelot, 92
Lancelot and Elaine, 679
Land, The, 225
Land for the People, The, 230
Land is Bright, The, 736
Land of Fame, 708
Land of Heart's Desire, The, 217
Landgraefin von Thueringen, Die, 154
Landi, Stefano, *pseud.*, 341
Lang, André, 278, 279, 295
Lange Jule, Die, 94
Langendijk, Pieter, 551, 552
Langer, František, 510, 511
Langley, Noel, 196
Langmann, Philipp, 140
Lantern To See By, A, 712
Lanval, 92
Laquelle? 299
Lardner, Ring, 704, 734

Larreta, Enrique, 586
Las de barranco, 585
Lasca, 318
Lashin, Orrie, 731
Laskaris, Nicholas, 546
Last Command, 524
Last Days of Great Moravia, The, 514
Last Guest, The, 64
Last King, The, 503
Last Knight, The, 37
Last Love, The, 520
Last Man, The (Lagerkvist), 68
Last Man, The (Svoboda), 506
Last Mile, The, 708
Last Night of Don Juan, The, 251
Last of Mrs. Cheyney, The, 195, 196
Last of the De Mullins, The, 184
Last of the Rosenbergs, The, 505
Last Ones, The, 427
Last Sacrifice, The, 386
Last Struggle, The, 485
Last Trump, The, 200
Late Christopher Bean, The, 294, 699-700
Lateiner, Joseph, 613, 616-22
Laube, Heinrich, 76-77
Lauchner, Rolf, 108-09
Laugh, Clown, Laugh, 357
Laughing Lady, The, 186
Laughing Pierrot and Weeping Pierrot, 443
Laurents, Arthur, 739
Lauro candente, 588
Laus im Pelze, Die, 116
Lautenbachs, J., *see* Jūsminš
Lautensack, Heinrich, 100
Lavedan, Henri, 267, 268
Laver, James, 190
Law of the Savage, The, 440
Law of Woman, The, 515
Lawrence, D. H., 208
Lawrence, Vincent, 681, 719
Lawson, John Howard, 664, 691, 692, 706
Lawyer and the Roses, The, 501
La-Yesharim Tehillah, 602
Lazarus Laughed, 687, 689
Lazzarina fra i coltelli, 360
Lazzaro (Borgese), 355
Lazzaro (Pirandello), 364
Lea, 483
League of Youth, The, 2, 8, 9, 643
Leal, Mendes, 594
Learned Jargon, 544
Leave Her to Heaven, 198
Lebendige Stunden, 135
Leblanc, Maurice, 298
Lecca, Haralamb, 529
Leclerq, Adolphe, 273
Leda, 534

INDEX

Lederköpfe, Die, 104
Ledge, A, 723
Ledige Leute, 138
Lee, Auriol, 198
Lee, Bert, 213
Leerlauf, 112
Left Bank, The, 694
Left-wing drama, 706-08, 725, 728
Le Gallienne, Eva, 716
Legend, 534
Legend of Leonora, The, 181
Legende eines Lebens, 145
Legouvé, Ernest, 237
Leguizámon, Martínez, 581
Leidenschaft, 93
Leigh, Rowland, 213
Leihtsin und Fremmelai, 605
Leinen aus Irland, 154
Leino, Eino, 484, 485
Leivick, H., 631, 632, 636
Lemaître, Jules, 267
Lemercier, N., 234
Lemonnier, Camille, 310
Lenéru, Marie, 264
Lengyel, Melchior, 423, 524
Lenin, Nikolai, 400, 427, 452
Lenormand, Henri-René, 249, 259, 277, 278, 281, 286-87, 288, 308
Lenushka, 477
Leon, Jack de, 213
León ciego, El, 585
Leona (Czakó), 518
Leona (Zilahy), 526
Leonarda, 47, 48
Leonida Faces the Reaction, 528
Leonidas' Triumph, 546
Leonov, L. M., 449, 475-78
Lermontov, M. Y., 378, 380, 381, 383, 441, 461, 470
Lerner, J. J., 614
Lernet-Holenia, Alexander Maria, 154-55
Leroux, Gaston, 270
Lesage, Alain-René, 234
Lesh, I., 622
Leskov, N. S., 392
Lessing, G. E., 545, 620
Let Freedom Ring, 708
Let Them Say, 200
Letter, The, 191
Letter of the Law, The, 260
Letters on the Theatre, 433
Lettish Literary Society, 488
Letzte Gericht, Das, 107
Letzte Nacht, Die, 139
Letzte Wendenkönig, Der, 503
Letzte Zeuge, Der, 112
Letzten Masken, Die, 135
Letzten Tage der Menschheit, Die, 139
Levinsohn, Ludwig, 609

Levy, Benn W., 196, 198, 202, 208
Lewis, Cecil, 288
Lewis, Sinclair, 262, 700, 731
Lewisohn, Ludwig, 623
Leyenda del Monje, La, 562
Liar, The, 62
Liars, The, 166
Liberation, 499
Liberators, The, 534
Liberté, 256
Liberty Jones, 703
Libin, Solomon, 621
Libro talonario, El, 559
Lie, Jonas, 51
Liebe, 151
Liebelei, 134
Liebrecht, Henri, 312
Liens, Les, 314
Life as a Jest, 497
Life Is Calling, 460
Life Is Changing, 460
Life of Man, The, 431, 432
Life With Father, 738
Light, James, 687
Light Love, 500
Light of Heart, The, 211
Light Shineth in Darkness, The, 399
Ligne de coeur, La, 298
Liiv, Jakob, 486, 487
Lilies of the Field, The, 197
Liliom, 523
Liliomfi, 518
Lillien, Isadore, 622
Lillienblum, M. L., 615
Lillo, George, 516
Lily, The, 270
Linares Rivas, Manuel, 565
Lindau, Paul, 77, 85
Lindsay, Howard, 721, 737, 738
Linetzki, 614
Link, The, 32
Links, 554
Liolà, 360
Lion and the Mouse, The, 664
Lion Tamer, The, 292-93
Lioness, The, 509
Lippl, Alois, 116
Lipscomb, William Percy, 207
Liptzen, Keni, 623
Lissauer, Ernst, 112
List of Benefits, The, 447
Listen Professor! 472
Lister, Walter B., 717
Lit nuptial, Le, 271
Literatur (Kraus), 139
Literatur (Schnitzler), 135
Literatura Española, Siglo XX, 561
Litigation, 383
Littell, Robert, 700

Littérature brutale, 269
Little Accident, 720
Little Café, The, 273
Little Dark Horse, 298
Little Dream, The, 182
Little Eyolf, 17, 19
Little Foxes, The, 728
Little Man, The, 183
Little Minister, The, 178, 179
Little Moor, The, 551
Little Ol' Boy, 708
Little Pastry Shop, The, 523
Little Plays of St. Francis, 206
Little Snow White, 522
Little Theatre in the United States, 672, 739
Little Theatre of Chicago, 671, 692
Living Corpse, The, 392, 399
Living Newspaper, 731, 732
Lizard, The, 61
Ljubislava, 539
Lo que Pasó a Reynoso, 585
Lo que se llevan las Loras, 587
Lob des Landes, 158
Lobgesänge des Claudian, Die, 87
Lobos marinos, Los, 564
Loco dios, El, 560
Locos de verano, 585
Loeser, Franz, 131
Lohengrin, 341
Loi de l'homme, La, 261
Lokalbahn, Die, 90
Lokis, 455
Lola se va a los puertos, La, 565
Lolita's Wonderbird, 489
Lom, Stanislav, *pseud.*, 508, 509
London, Jack, 471
London Theatre Studio, 278
London Wall, 197
Lonely, 556
Lonely White Sail Gleams, A, 461
Lonesome-like, 186
Long, John Luther, 653
Long Mirror, The, 205
Longford, Earl and Countess of, 231-32
Lönnrot, Elias, 483
Lonsdale, Frederick, 195, 213
Look at the Heffernans, 230
Look With Both Eyes, 472
Looking Backward, 649
Lope de Reuda, 561, 576
Lope de Vega Carpio, 370, 470, 560, 565, 571, 572, 578, 580, 596, 634
Lopes de Mendonça, Henrique, 595
Lopez, Sabatino, 326, 336, 337, 340
López Silva, Jose, 564
Lopeza, 541
Lorbeer, 142
Lord and Peasant, 503
Lord Byron, 313
Lorde, André de, 258, 259
Lorenzino, 354
Lost Bride, The, 504
Lost Colony, The, 711
Lost Leader, The, 224
Lost Letter, The, 528
Lost Rights, 489
Lost Soul, The, 617
Lothar, Rudolf, *pseud.*, 139, 443
Loudspeaker, 706
Louis Ferdinand, Prinz von Preussen, 106
Louis Jouvet et le Théâtre d'aujourd'hui, 280
Louis Posavski, 532
Loup de Gubbio, Le, 288
Loups, Les, 257
Loute, 273
Louÿs, Pierre, 271
Love, 521
Love and Friendship, 63
Love and Geography, 50
Love Child, The, 269
Love 'Em and Leave 'Em, 720
Love from a Stranger, 213
Love, Honor and Betray, 306
Love Is a Golden Book, 465
Love Nest, The, 704
Love of Janošik, The, 514
Love of Jerusalem, The, 613
Love of the Three Kings, The, 352
Love of Women, 197
Love on the Dole, 212
Love Triumphant, 547
Love Watches, 272
Love Your Neighbor, 55
Love's Comedy, 2, 6, 7, 12
Love's Old Sweet Song, 740
Lovely Lady, 297
Lover's Luck, 265
Lovers and Enemies, 440
Lovers and Friends, 201
Low Bridge, 722
Lowell, J. R., 642, 645
Lower Depths, The, 420-25, 431, 445
Loyalties, 183
Loyson, Paul-Hyacinthe, 264
Lublinski, Samuel, 96
Lubowski, Edward, 494
Luce, 337
Luciano, 579
Lucifer, 551
Luck of Poor Frank, The, 497
Luck Tomorrow, 500
Lucky One, The, 192
Lucky Pehr, 26
Lucky Sam McCarver, 699
Lucrèce (Ponsard), 236
Lucrece (Wilder-Obey), 306, 732

Lucrezia, 355
Lucrezia Borgia, 508
Ludas Matyi, 525
Ludevit Štur, 515
Ludovici, Cesare Vico, 339, 341, 343
Ludwig II, 108
Lueger, 154
Lugné-Poe, 163, 247, 250, 253, 254, 278, 279
Lui, 258
Luise von Koburg, 138
Luján, James Graham, 568, 580, 590
Lukas Notaris, 546
Lulu Belle, 670
Lumpenbagasch, 95
Lunacharski, A. V., 453, 454, 455
Lupa, La, 325, 350
Lusatian Spinning Women, The, 504
Lusk, Milton, 228
Luther und Thomas Münzer, 142
Luts, Oskar, 487
Luzzatto, Moses Hayim, 602
Lyndon, Barré, 209
Lynggaard & Co., 59
Lyrische Dramen, 128
Lys, Le, 270
Lysistrata, 266

M. P., 162
Ma soeur et moi, 297
MacArthur, Charles, 699, 717, 723
Macbeth, 310, 393, 532, 542
MacDermot, Robert, 213
Macedo, Joaquim Manoellde, 598
Machado, Manuel and Antonio, 565-67
Machado de Assis, 596
Machiavelli, Niccolo di Bernardo, 318, 356
Machinal, 707
Machine infernale, La, 302
Machine Wreckers, The, 200
Maciel, Alciades, 600
Mačiules, Jonas, *see* Maironis, *pseud.*
Mack, Willard, 717
Mackay, Constance D'Arcy, 672
MacKaye, Percy, 655, 657, 660-62, 666, 675, 678, 680, 711
MacKaye, Steele, 660
Mackenzie, Ronald, 197, 210
Mackintosh, Elizabeth, *see* Daviot, Gordon, *pseud.*
MacNamara, Brinsley, 230
Macowan, Norman, 210
Macrae, Arthur, 213
Mad Money, 386
Madách, Imre, 518
Madam Sohk and Sons, 487
Madam Will You Walk, 701
Madame Béhard, 286

Madame Bovary, 202, 277
Madame Butterfly, 333, 653
Madame Dulska's Moral Code, 497
Madame et son Filleul, 273
Madame Flirt, 274
Madame Legros, 100
Madame Marie, 315
Madame Sand, 715
Madame Sans-Gêne, 240
Madame Walewska, 533
Madame X, 273, 540
Madcap, The, 299
Mademoiselle, 294
Mademoiselle Fifi, 259
Mademoiselle Josette, ma femme, 274
Mademoiselle ma mère, 297
Mademoiselle Pascal, 283
Madras House, The, 184
Madre, La, 330
Madrid, 469
Maerchen, Das, 134
Maestro, Il, 346
Maeterlinck, Maurice, 14, 40, 65, 91, 92, 102, 244, 247, 248, 249, 255, 279, 283, 286, 293, 310, 311, 312, 315, 317, 339, 430, 433, 435, 496, 499, 522, 530, 533, 672
Maeve, 218
Maffei, 545
Magalhães, Raymundo (Jr.), 599
Magda (Remec), 540
Magda (Sudermann), 17, 60, 86, 89, 388
Magdaleno, Mauricio, 590
Magdolna, 519
Magelóna, 505
Mages sans étoile, Les, 264
Maggie Pepper, 664
Maggie the Magnificent, 701
Magic Flute, The, 124
Magic Glasses, The, 226
Magistrate, The, 164
Magnanimous Lover, The, 223
Maheli wider Moses, 98
Mahen, Jiří, 506, 510, 514
Maibaum, Richard, 710
Maid, The, 554
Maid of France, 186
Maid of Warsaw, The, 499
Maiden, The, 524
Maidens' Guard, The, 517
Maija and Paija, 489
Main Currents in 19th Century European Literature, 2
Maironis, *pseud.*, 492
Maison de danses, La, 271
Maison des chimères, La, 314
Maison du Peuple, 256
Maison natale, La, 276
Maison recommandée, 316

Maitlands, The, 197, 210
Maître, Le, 258
Maître de son coeur, Le, 288
Majcen, Stanko, 540
Major Barbara, 172
Major Noah, 633
Makropoulos Secret, The, 512
Mal de jeunesse, Le, 311
Mala laya, 584
Mala se, La, 586
Malefactor, The, 419
Maleficio de la Mariposa, El, 570-71
Malka Schwarzenkopf, 497
Malleson, Miles, 196
Mallow Flower, The, 529
Malquerida, La, 566, 567
Maltby, Henry Francis, 196
Maltz, Albert, 664, 670, 708
Malva, 429
Malvern Festival, 176, 255
Maly Theatre, 388, 389, 393, 407, 412, 418, 428, 454, 455, 474, 476
Mama's Bank Account, 199
Maman Colibri, 269
Mamelles de Tiresias, Les, 302
Mammon, 165
Man and Superman, 171, 183
Man and the Masses, 110
Man From Cairo, The, 299
Man in Half-Moon Street, The, 209
Man in Possession, The, 200
Man of Aran, 231
Man of Destiny, The, 169, 172
Man of God, 533
Man of Honour, A, 191
Man Went Down from Jerusalem, A, 64
Man Who Ate the Popomack, The, 197
Man Who Came to Dinner, The, 735
Man Who Married a Dumb Wife, The, 200
Man Who Never Died, The, 707
Man With a Load of Mischief, The, 200
Man With Red Hair, The, 202
Man With the Gun, The, 464
Man with the Nag, The, 530
Man Without a Soul, The, 69, 70
Man's House, A, 189
Man's Judgment Is Not God's, 390
Man's Man, A, 718
Man's World, A, 675
Manasse, 528
Manchester Players, 671
Manchester School of Playwrights, 185, 186
Manichäer, Die, 97
Mankiewicz, Herman, 734
Mann, Heinrich, 100-01
Mann, Klaus, 119
Mann ist Mann, 121

Mann Nummer Soundsoviel, 108
Mano santa, 583
Manon Lescaut, 102
Mantellacio, Il, 352
Mantle, Burns, 690, 706
Mantle of Nessus, The, 57
Mantua, Bento, 596
Manzoni, Alessandro, 235, 318, 319
Marâtre, La, 395
Marble, 63
Marcel, Gabriel, 264
March Hares, 716
Marchand, Léopold, 298
Marchand de Paris, Le, 292
Marchand d'estampes, Le, 265
Marchands de gloire, Les, 291, 296
Marche nuptiale, La, 269
Marching Song, 707
Marcholt, 498
Marcin, Max, 714, 717
Marco Millions, 688
Marcos Severi, 581
Margaret Fleming, 650, 651
Margaret Gillan, 230
Margin for Error, 736
Margit Kendi, 520
Margot, 290
Maria, Jaroslav, pseud., 508
Maria Doxapatri, 545
Maria Magdalena, 95
Maria Szechy (Doczi), 520
Maria Szechy (Kisfaludy), 517
Maria Szechy (Szigeti), 518
Mariae Heimsuchung, 100
Mariage de Figaro, Le, 234
Mariage de Mlle Beulemans, Le, 316
Mariage de maman, Le, 297
Mariage d'Hamlet, Le, 303
Mariage d'Olympe, Le, 238
Mariana, 560
Mariana Pineda, 570, 571
Marianne, 94
Marie-Magdaleine, 255
Mariners, 203
Marion Delorme, 236, 239
Marionette, che passione! 359-61
Marionette Plays, 65
Marionetten, 135
Marionettes, 83, 315, 346, 368, 371, 401, 527, 571-73
Marionnettes, Les, 270
Mariti, I, 335, 336
Marito amante della moglie, Il, 331
Marito e l'amante, Il, 320
Marius, 197, 291
Marivaux, P. C., 234, 236, 288
Marjolaine, 187
Markish, Peretz, 634
Markovic, Franjo, 514, 516, 531

INDEX 801

Markurells i Wadköping, 65
Marlowe, Christopher, 120, 247, 312
Marneschlacht, Die, 119
Marguina, Don Eduardo, 565, 569, 574, 576
Marquis, Don, 715
Marquis de Priola, Le, 268
Marquis von Keith, Der, 99
Marquise, The, 194
Marquise von Arcis, Die, 102
Marquise von O., Die, 153
Marriage, 383
Marriage Game, The, 238
Marriage Is No Joke, 200
Marriage of Kitty, The, 298
Marriage of Kutrulis, The, 545
Marriage of Maxim Crnojevich, The, 535
Marriage Veil, The, 608, 609
Married, 27, 29
Married and Not Married, 632
Marrying of Ann Leete, The, 183, 184
Marseilles, 291, 699
Marta Gruní, 583
Marthe et Marie, 250
Martin, Eduard, 240
Martin du Gard, Roger, 283
Martín Fierro, 577
Martin-Harvey, Sir John, 189
Martine, 276, 281, 284
Martínez, Coronado, 581
Martínez Cuitino, Vicente, 581
Martínez Kleiser, Luis, 569
Martínez Leguizamón, 581
Martínez Sierra, Gregorio, 184, 565, 567, 568, 570
Martínez Sierra, Señora, 566, 567
Martini, Fausto Maria, 356-57
Martini, Vincenzo, 320-22
Martino Penna, Luiz Carlos, 596, 598, 599
Martiri del lavoro, I, 330
Martyn, Edward, 217, 218
Martyre de Saint Sebastien, Le, 255, 349
Maruf, der tolle Lügner, 94
Marvelous History of St. Bernard, The, 255
Marx, Henry, 264
Marx, Karl, 645
Mary Baker Eddy, 115
Mary, Mary, Quite Contrary, 223
Mary, Mother of Jesus, 65
Mary of Scotland, 697
Mary Read, 200
Mary Rose, 181
Mary Stuart, 189
Mary Stuart of Scotland, 46
Mary und Lisa, 119
Maryša (Mrštis), 540
Maryša (Vilém), 506
Maschera di Bruto, La, 351

Maschera e il volto, La, 344-45
Maschinenstürmer, Die, 110
Maschwitz, Eric, 213
Masefield, John, 188-89
Mashenka, 472
Mask of the Red Death, The, 432
Masked Woman, The, 271
Masks, 687, 689
Mason, Daniel Gregory, 656
Masque of Kings, The, 697
Masque of Labor, A, 661
Masquerade (Iwaszkiewicz), 502
Masquerade, The (Lermontov), 380, 381, 470
Masqueraders, The, 166
Masques, 660-61
Masse Mensch, 110
Massière, La, 267
Massinger, Philip, 137
Massingham, Dorothy, 197
Massnahme, Die, 121
Master, The, 230
Master Builder, The, 17-19
Master Manole (Blaga), 530
Master Manole (Eftimiu), 529
Master of the Order, 486
Master Olof, 1, 22, 23, 25, 37
Masters, The, 543
Mastersingers, The, 253
Mata Hari, 108
Match for Cecile, A, 519
Mater, 661
Maternità, 334
Mathematicians, The, 552
Matija Gubec, Peasant's King, 534, 538
Matriarch, The, 197
Matrimony, Pfd, 297
Matrosen von Cattaro, Die, 117
Matthew of Trenčin, 515
Matumbo, 108
Maturama, José de, 581
Maubel, Henri, pseud., 310, 314
Mauclair, Camille, 247
Maugham, William Somerset, 191, 498
Maupassant, Guy de, 259, 734
Maurey, Max, 259
Mauriac, François, 283
Maurice Harte, 225
Mauvais bergers, Les, 261, 262
Mavor, Osborne Henry, see Bridie, James, pseud.
Maxim the Bitter, see Gorki, Maxim
Maxwell Anderson, the Man and his Plays, 697
May Blossom, 652
Maya, 277, 301
Mayakovski, V. V., 448-53, 461
Mayer, Edwin Justus, 715
Mayer, Jaroslav, see Maria, Jaroslav, pseud.

Mayne, Rutherford, 226
Mazaud, Émile, 278, 293
Mazel Tov, 627
McCloskey, J. J., 640
McCracken, Esther, 202
McDonagh, Thomas, 226
McEvoy, J. P., 707, 713
McKinney, Ruth, 737
Mdivani, 469
Measure for Measure, 122
Mécanique du théâtre, La, 311
Medcraft, Russell, 715
Medea (Jahnn), 107
Medea (Unamuno-Seneca), 570
Medek, Rudolf, 510
Medicina di una ragazza malata, La, 321
Medio tono, 590
Medios seres, Los, 566
Medved, Anton, 538, 539, 541
Meek Mose, 709
Meer, Das, 113
Mees, Josine Simone, 556
Meet My Sister, 297
Meet the Wife, 713
Meeting, The, 427
Megrue, Roi Cooper, 677, 721
Mei, Leo, 393
Meilhac, Henri, 165, 240, 272, 316
Mein Kampf, 468
Meiningen Players, 244, 401
Meister, Der, 127
Meister Balzer, 91
Meister Ölze, 85
Melancholy of Muru Miku, The, 486
Melas, Spyros, 547
Melech Freylech, 633
Melford, Austin, 213
Mell, Max, 144
Mello Nobrega, 600
Melloney Holtspur, 188
Mélo, 270
Melodrama, 112, 148, 160-61, 166, 170, 222, 227, 235-36, 239, 252, 259-60, 271-73, 292, 302, 460, 549, 553, 559-60, 577, 581, 622, 635, 640, 651, 663-64, 669, 679, 699, 716-18, 721
Melting Pot, The, 186
Melville, Thomas, 665
Member from Ozark, The, 658
Memoirs of a Trans-Moskva Denizen, 384
Memoirs of the Russian Censorship, 492
Men in White, 724
Men on an Ice-Floe, 511
Mendelssohn, Moses, 604
Mendès, Catulle, 252
Mendez, David Franks, 604
Mendonça Alves, Vasco de, 506
Mensch mit uns, 112
Menschen, Die, 105

Menzel, Gerhard, 118, 119
Menzies, Archie, 213, 214
Mercadet, 237
Mercenarios, Los, 588
Merchant and the Sailor, The, 518
Merchant of Venice, The, 223, 595
Merchant of Yonkers, The, 732
Merchants of Glory, 291
Méré, Charles, 259, 271, 281
Meredith, George, 164
Merely Mary Ann, 186
Merget, Robert, 317
Mérimée, Prosper, 455
Meroë, 97
Merope, 545
Merrily We Roll Along, 734, 735
Merry Death, A, 442, 443
Merry-Go-Round, 708
Merton of the Movies, 733
Mesa Nicholls, Alejandro, 588
Mesmer, 212
Mesquita, Marcelino de, 595
Messenger, The, 508
Messenger from Mars, The, 424
Metamora, 644
Metamorfosi politiche, Le, 321
Metamorphosis, 530
Metanoïte, 104
Metastasio, 604
Meténier, Oscar, 243, 258, 259
Meteor, 703
Metsanurk, Mait, 487
Meyerhold, V. E., 279, 379, 388, 392, 400, 412, 431, 436, 437, 438, 442, 450, 451, 452, 453
M'hijo el dotor, 582, 583
Mi felicidad y tus amigas, 586
Mi Niña, 575
Michael, 541, 542
Michael and His Lost Angel, 166
Michael and Mary, 192
Michael Kramer, 81, 104
Michel Auclair, 285
Michel Gaissmayr, 141
Michel Pauper, 242
Michelangelo Buonarroti, 534
Mickevičius, Vincas Krėvė, 491
Midchannel, 165
Middle Watch, The, 202
Middleman, The, 166
Middleton, George, 667, 668
Midinette, The, 523
Midnight (Kulundžich), 535
Midnight (Sifton), 707
Midsummer Night's Dream, 470
Miedo de los felices, El, 587
Miettes, Les, 271
Mieze und Maria, 89
Mighty Dollar, The, 652

INDEX 803

Mighty Tower, The, 602
Mihal, the Daughter of Saul, 637
Mijnssen, Frans, 556
Mik, 468
Mikado, The, 162, 469
Mikszath, Kálmán, 526
Milecians, The, 503
Milestones, 187
Miletich, Stjepan, 532
Milhaud, Darius, 254, 302
Mill, John Stuart, 77
Millar, Robins, 210
Millay, Edna St. Vincent, 654
Miller, Arthur, 739
Miller, Joaquin, 648
Million, Le, 297
Million Torments, A, 461
Millionaire, The, 543
Millionairess, The, 176
Milne, Alan Alexander, 191-92, 206
Milton, John, 673
Minaret, Le, 252
Minawer, Bruno, 502
Mineral Workers, The, 226
Minick, 734
Ministerial Crisis, A, 520
Minna, 622
Minney, R. J., 207
Minnie, la candida, 368
Minor, The, 375, 376, 381, 384
Minstrel, 553
Minulescu, Ion, 529, 530
Miracle, The, 92
Miracle of Saint Anthony, A, 250
Miracle of the Warsaw Ghetto, The, 632
Miracle plays, 144, 156, 188, 233, 255, 371, 451, 523, 550
Miraculous Alloy, The, 460
Mirage, Le, 312
Mirakel, Das, 91
Mirande, Yves, 252
Mirbeau, Octave, 165, 249, 256, 259, 261, 291
Mirele Efros, 620
Miriam, 628
Miroir qui fait rire, Le, 296
Mirski, Prince, 370, 439, 447
Misalliance, 173
Misanthrope, Le, 379
Misérables, Les, 646
Misfortune of Being Clever, The, see *Woe from Wit*
Miss Anna Cooksley, 546
Miss Julia, 28-31
Miss Lulu Bett, 713
Miss Maliczewska, 497
Miss Swan Expects, 723
Mississippi, 104
Mr. Bobby, 525

Mr. Gladstone, 208
Mr. Moneypenny, 667, 716
Mr. Pepys, 207
Mr. Perkins' Mission to the Land of the Bolsheviks, 475
Mr. Pim Passes By, 192
Mr. Pitt, 713
Mr. Samuel, 292
Mr. Sleeman Is Coming, 65
Mrs. Dane's Defense, 166, 720
Mrs. Gorringe's Necklace, 186
Mrs. Moonlight, 202
Mrs. Partridge Presents, 720
Mrs. Siddons, 208
Mrs. Warren's Profession, 169
Mit der Liebe spielen, 154
Mitchell, Norma, 715
Mitchell, Thomas, 720
Mixed Marriage, 223
Mob, The, 182
Moberg, Vilhelm, 65, 67
Mocedadas del Cid, 574
Modas, 587
Moderne Drama, Das, 1, 5
Modjeska, Helena, 494
Möller, Eberhard Wolfgang, 116
Moeller, Philip, 715
Mörder für uns, 118
Moerder, Hoffnung der Frauen, 149
Moffat, Graham, 187
Moffett, J. C., 731
Moglie, La, 335
Moglie del dottore, La, 326
Moglie ideale, La, 328
Mogu, The Wanderer, 225
Mogulesco, Sigmund, 619
Mohamed and the Jews of Arabia, 620
Mojžiš, Stanislav, see Lom, Stanislav, pseud.
Molière, J.-B. P., 91, 131, 233, 234, 241, 274, 275, 293, 294, 295, 299, 309, 311, 370, 372, 379, 380, 386, 389, 401, 470, 504, 541, 551, 597, 653, 672, 701
Molière (Bulgakov), 456
Molière (Moeller), 715
Molina, Tirso de, 97, 578
Mollusc, The, 186
Molnár, Ferenc, 311, 523, 524, 526, 568, 734
Moloch, 288
Mombert, Alfred, 95
Mommsen, Theodor, 170
Mon ami Teddy, 252, 283
Mon héritier, 299
Monde où l'on s'ennuie, Le, 240
Monde renversé, Le, 298
Mondrish, 610
Moneda Falsa, 583
Money Madness, 515

Monicelli, Tomaso, 339, 340
Monkey Talks, The, 294
Monkey's Paw, The, 187
Monkhouse, Allan, 186
Monna Vanna, 247, 249, 533
Monodrama, 443, 445
Monologues, 520, 688
Monsieur Beaucaire, 679
Monsieur de cinq heures, Le, 273
Monsieur de Courpière, 268
M. Le Trouhadec saisi par la débauche, 290
Monsieur Vernet, 272
Montaña de las brujas, La, 577
Monte Cristo, 640
Montemezzi, Italo, 352
Montgomery, James, 677
Month in the Country, A, 395
Monti, Vincenzo, 319
Montjoye; In Honour Bound, 165
Montmartre, 271
Montoya, María Teresa, 590
Moock, Armando, 587
Moody, William Vaughn, 644, 653-58, 662, 678, 680
Moon in the Yellow River, The, 231
Moon is a Gong, The, 707
Moon is Down, The, 737
Moon over the River, 510
Moonlight Is Silver, 203
Moonlighter, The, 226
Moor Born, 722
Moorcroft, 646
Moore, George, 187, 217
Moral, 90
Moral de Misia Paca, La, 584
Morale che corre, La, 336
Morale della favola, La, 328
Morality plays, 131, 431, 602
Moratorio, Crosmán, 581
Mord, 105
Moreas, Jean, 253
Morehouse, Ward, 717
Morello, Vincenzo, 339, 340
Moretti, Marino, 356
Morgan, Charles Langbridge, 197
Morgan, Diana, 213
Morgenröte, Die, 90
Mori, Arturo, 575
Móricz, Sigmund, 521, 522, 525
Morisseaux, F. Ch., 317
Morituri, 86
Morley, Robert, 196
Morley, S. G., 560
Mörne, Arvid, 60
Morning Star, The, 211, 529
Morning's at Seven, 724
Morozowicz-Szczephowska, Marja, 501
Morris, Lloyd, 199
Morselli, Ercole Luigi, 339, 356

Morstin, Ludwik H., 500
Mort du Duc d'Enghien, La, 258
Morte civile, La, 321
Morte degli amanti, La, 345
Morte in vacanze, La, 358
Mortgage, The, 487
Mortier, Alfred, 253
Morton, Michael, 213
Moschino, Ettore, 353
Moscow, 480
Moscow Art Theatre, 385, 386, 388, 390, 392, 394-406, 411-32, 434, 446, 452, 453, 456-58, 460, 461, 464, 470-72, 476, 480, 630, 636, 674
Moscow Art Theatre, Second, 392, 396, 400, 455, 460, 465
Moscow Is Burning, 452
Moscow Nights, 464
Moscow Philharmonic Society, 402
Moses, Montrose J., 641, 651, 672
Moss, Carlton, 306
Most of the Game, 198
Moth, The, 464
Mother, The (Capek), 512
Mother (Gorki), 428
Mother, The (Przybyszewski), 496
Mother Earth, 520
Mother Lode, 709, 722
Mother Mews, 90
Mother Nature, 314
Mother of Her Children, The, 472
Mother's Duty, The, 549
Mother's Ring, The, 546
Mother-in-Law, The, 543
Mothers-in-Law, The, 520
Motherwell, Hiram Kelly, 674
Motifs, 67
Motion pictures, 524, 547, 673, 735
Motke the Thief, 625
Mountain, The; or The Story of Captain Yevan, 193
Mourning Becomes Electra, 690
Mowatt, Anna Cora, 642, 643
Mozart, W. A., 124
Mozart (Dukes), 200
Mozart (Guitry), 299
Mozart and Salieri, 380
Mraks, The, 540
Mrštik, Alois, 506, 540
Mucio da Paixao, 596
Mudder Mews, 90
Müller, Georg Wilhelm, 119
Mueller, Hans, 143-44
Müller-Schlosser, Hans, 116
Muertos, Los, 583
Mütter, Die, 88
Mulatto, 710
Mulberry Bush, The, 196
Mulheres modernas, 600

INDEX 805

Mulk's Wit and the Tartuan's Wisdom, The, 486
Mullally, Don, 713
Muller, Charles, 271
Mulligan Guards, 651
Multatuli, pseud., *see* Dekker, Eduard Douwes
Mundial, 587
Munk, Kau, 65-67, 73-75
Muñoz Seca, Don Pedro, 563, 565, 566, 575
Munro, C. K., 191-93, 206
Muntere Seifensieder, Der, 128
Murder Has Been Arranged, A, 211
Murder in the Cathedral, 214, 215
Murder on Madison Avenue, 620
Murnik, Radoslav, 541
Murray, John, 677
Murray, T. C., 225
Murray, William B., 298
Musch, Jan, 552
Music at Night, 205
Music Master, 664
Musical Chairs, 197, 210
Musical Clowns, 526
Musical comedy, 105, 213
Musical drama, 614-16, 618, 621-22, 635, 662, 666, 736, 738
Musical Studio of Nemirovich-Danchenko, 400, 460
Musician, see What the Fiddle Contains
Musik (C. Hauptmann), 94
Musik (Wedekind), 100
Musorgski, M. P., 380
Musset, Alfred de, 234, 236, 237, 280, 288, 293, 298, 304, 309
Mutter, Die (Bahr), 126
Mutter (Brecht-Gorki), 121
Mutter Erde, 88
Mutter Landstrasse, 94
Mutual Deceit of Marriage, The, 552
My Friends, 463
My Friend Teddy, 252, 283
My Heart's in the Highlands, 740
My Life in Art, 402
My Life in the Theatre, 402
My Little Quail Has Fled, 501, 502
My Partner, 648
My Sister Eileen, 736
My Wife, 274
Mykolaitis-Putinas, Vincas, 492
Myrrha, 92
Myrtle and Chloe, 527
Mystery Bouffe, 449-51
Mystery drama, 233, 255, 258, 308, 315, 371-72, 449, 491-92, 500, 550
Mystery of Marriage, The, 546
Mystical drama, 34-35, 39-44, 104, 128-29, 254, 288, 437, 624, 687

Mysticism, 165, 166, 309, 429, 430, 441, 530, 626, 628, 630, 634

Naboth's Vineyard, 203
Nace un pueblo, 586
Nachfolge Christi Spiel, Das, 144
Nacht, 106
Nacht der Könige, Die, 108
Nacht in Florenz, Eine, 95
Nacht vor dem Beil, Die, 119
Nachtasyl, 424
Nachthorn, Das, 107
Nachtwandler, Die, 109
Naderer, Hans, 154
Naeff, Top, 556
Najac, Émile de, 239
Nałkowska, Zofja, 501
Names on the Marble Board, The, 487
Nannie's Night Out, 227
Nansen, Peter, 51
Napierski's Revolt, 498
Napoleon (Bruckner), 153
Napoleon (Sangster), 208
Napoleon (Stodeńk), 504
Napoleon at Elba, 409
Napoleon greift ein, 105
Napoleon Intervenes, 455
Napoleon III and Empress Eugénie, 409
Napoléon IV, 305
Napoléon unique, 288
Napoleon's Samovar, 541
Narrenspiel des Lebens, 142
Narzymski, Józef, 494
Natacha, 587
Natalka Poltava, 615
Natanson, Jacques, 248, 289, 295
Nathan, George Jean, 227, 228, 679, 684, 685
National Bulgarian Theatre, 542, 543
National Czech Theatre, 505, 506, 509, 515, 516, 518, 520
National Theatre (Belgrade), 535
National Theatre (Budapest), 525
National Theatre (Norwegian), 4
National Theatre (Rumania), 527, 528, 529
National Theatre (Zagreb), 531, 532
Native Ground, 709, 731
Native Son, 711
Natürliche Vater, Der, 93
Naturalism, 2, 27-32, 34-35, 37, 63, 79-83, 85, 87-91, 95-96, 98, 100, 104, 106, 109, 111, 113, 117, 122, 126, 138, 140, 240-48, 250-51, 255, 257, 259, 274, 280, 282-83, 286, 310, 325-26, 350, 365, 397, 400, 419, 429, 439, 445, 522, 551, 634
Naturalisme au théâtre, Le, 241
Naturisme, 255

Navarro, Leandro, 575
Navarro, (Don) Pedro Juan, 568, 574
Nave, La, 349
Navire aveugle, Le, 259
Nazimova, 501
Neal Maquade, 231
Nebeneinander, 103
Ned Kean of Old Drury, 208
Ned McCobb's Daughter, 699
Neighborhood Playhouse, 175, 286, 572, 631, 721
Neilson, Francis, 196
Neinsager, Der, 121
Nellie the Beautiful Cloak Model, 663
Nellina, 334
Németh, László, 525
Nemica, La, 342
Nemirovich-Danchenko, V. I., 394, 400-03, 412, 434
Neo-classicism, 95-98, 122, 233, 250, 256
Nero, 188
Nerone, 337
Nerulos, Jacob Rizos, 544
Nesbitt, Robert, 213
Nest, The, 282
Nestroy, Johann, 124, 139
Neue Ghetto, Das, 940
Neuen Kerle, Die, 109
Neuen Menschen, Die, 126
Neumann, Alfred, 114
1918, 120
1913, 101
1914, 119
Neurode, 113
New American Drama, 672
New Brooms, 713
New Country, The, 525
New Gossoon, The, 231
New Life, A (Rice), 694-95
New Life, A (Tajovský), 515
New Minister, The, 487
New Morality, The, 185
New Movement in the Theatre, 674
New Order, 531
New Secretary, The, 298
New System, The, 47
New Theatre of New York, 671
New Word, The, 181
New York Drama Critics' Circle, 229
Newly-Weds, The, 2, 46, 47
Newman, Greatex, 213
Nibelungen, Die, 95
Nic, 226
Niccodemi, Dario, 339, 341-43
Nicholas Stravrogin, 386
Nichols, Ann, 714
Nichols, Beverly, 212, 213
Nichols, Robert, 207
Nicholson, Kenyon, 703, 719

Nido ajeno, El, 560
Niels Ebbesen, 73, 74
Nietzsche, Friedrich, 82, 90, 104, 130, 348, 432, 433, 439, 508, 645, 683
Nie wieder Friede! 110
Nigger, The, 669, 709, 722
Night at an Inn, A, 222
Night at Karlstein, 507-08
Night before the Trial, The, 405
Night Boat, The, 273
Night Hostess, 718
Night Music, 726, 727
Night Must Fall, 211
Night on the Old Market Place, 626
Night Over Taos, 696
Night Scenes, 52
Night's Adventure, A, 161
Nightingale of Wittenberg, The, 37
Nina, 113
Niña que riega la albahaca y el principe pregunton, La, 571
Nine til Six, 197
1931, 707
Ninetta, 336
Ninety-Sail, 207
Ninon de l'Enclos, 96
Ninotchka, 524
Nirvana, 706
Nisoyon, Der, 626
Nit Gedaiget, 634
Nivoix, Paul, 291, 296
Njal's Saga, 62
No la quiero ni me importa, 586
No more peace! 110
No One, 66
Nō plays of Japan, 218, 254
No Quarter, 480
No Time for Comedy, 704
Noah (Moss-Obey), 306
Noah (Vondel), 551
Noah (Wilmurt-Obey), 306
Nobel Prize, The, 66, 558, 561, 566, 567, 574
Nobility, Clergy, Citizen, and Peasant, 58
Noces d'argent, Les, 282
Noche de estío, 590
Noé, Yvan, 299
Noé, 306
Noli, Fan S., 549
Noli me tangere, 103
Non-Commissioned Officer Prischbeev, 419
Nonna Felicità, 341
Nora, 78
North, Christopher, 380
North Wind, The, 460
Nos auteurs dramatiques, 241
Nossa gente e assim, 600
Nostra Dea, 367
Nostra pelle, La, 336

Noszty Boy's Affair with Mary Toth, The, 526
Not a Kopek and Suddenly a Ruble, 386
Not for Children, 694
Not for Nothing Did the Hen Cluck, 404
Nothelfer, Der, 143
Notorious Mrs. Ebbsmith, The, 165
Notre Déesse, 313
Nounouche, 259
Nous ne sommes pas si forts, 296
Nous ne sommes plus ses enfants, 298
Nouveau jeu, Le, 267
Nouveau Testament, Le, 299
Nouvelle idole, La, 263
Nouvelle Revue Française, 275, 301
Nova polemica, 324
Novačan, Anton, 532
Novalis, 248
Novecento, 367
Novello, Ivor, 196, 200-01, 213
November Night, 499
Noviço, O, 599
Nowaczyński, Adolf, 500
Now-a-Days, 667
Nowak, Jozef, 503
Nowy-Bórkojski, N., 504
Nozière, Fernand, 271, 292
Nozze dei centauri, Le, 352
Nudo gordiano, El, 560
Nürnbergisch Ei, Das, 97
Nuestros hijos, 584
Nugent, Elliott, 713
Nugent, J. C., 713
Nuisance, 636
Nuit au bouge, Une, 259
Nuit bergamasque, La, 243
Nuit de Shakespeare, Une, 316
Nuits rouges de la Tchéka, Les, 259
Nuovo colonia, La, 364
Nurnberg, Maxwell, 731
Nurse, The (Bródy), 522-23
Nurse, The (Liiv), 487
Nyirö, Joseph, 525
Nymph Errant, 190
Nyugat, 521, 522, 523, 524

O locura o Santidad, 559
O Men, Men! 495
'O mese mariano, 326
O Tempora! 375
O These Women! 514
'O voto, 326
Oaks, 629
Oasi, L' (Cavacchioli), 346
Oasis, L' (Jullien), 258
Oath, The, 621
Obernyik, Charles, 519
Obey, André, 284, 306, 732

Objectivity, 121
O'Brien, Seumas, 226
Obstfelder, Sigbjörn, 56
O'Casey, Séan, 217, 221, 225-29, 230
Occupe-toi d'Amélie, 273
Ocean, The, 433
O'Connell, Richard, 568
Octoroon, The, 709
O'Cuddy, The, 196
Odd People, 427
Ode to Liberty, 700
Odets, Clifford, 669, 721, 725-27
Odysseus und Nausikaa, 112
Oedipe, 305
Oedipus Rex (Sophocles), 130
Oedipus Rex (Yeats-Sophocles), 218
Oedipus und die Sphinx, 130
Oehlenschläger, 1
Oesterreichische Komoedie, 155
Oeuvre des athlètes, L', 291
Of an Early Morning, 627
Of Human Bondage, 498
Of Mice and Men, 737
Of Thee I Sing, 736
Offenbach, 139
Offenen Türen, Die, 112
Office Seekers, The, 543
Official, The, 390
Official's Morning, An, 383
Offiziere, 105
Ogrizovich, Milan, 534
Oh Mama, 297
Oh! Oh! Delphine, 297
Oh, Promise Me, 738
Ohel Theatre in Palestine, 633, 634, 637
O'Higgins, Harvey, 666, 714
Oiseau blessé, L', 268
Oiseau bleu, L', 249
Oiseaux de passage, 261, 266
Oisvurf, Der, 627
O'Kelly, Seumas, 226
Oklahoma, 712
Okonski, Władysław, pseud., 494, 495
Oktobertag, 104
Olaf Liljekrans, 5
Old Acquaintance, 198
Old and Young, 539
Old English, 183, 208
Old Foolishness, The, 230
Old Friends, 180
Old Homestead, The, 417, 648
Old Infantryman and His Hussar Son, The, 518
Old Ladies, The, 210
Old Lady Says 'No'!, The, 231
Old Lady Shows Her Medals, The, 181
Old Lady 31, 675
Old Maid, The, 283, 718
Old Man, The, 428

Old Man Minick, 734
Old Spain, 566
Old Times of Kashira, 393
Old Vic Theatre Company, 218
Oleg, 375
Oliver Cromwell (Drinkwater), 189
Oliver Cromwell (Lunacharski), 454
Oliver Oliver, 724
Ollapotrida, 155
Olympia, 524
Ombra, L', 342
On and Off, 273
On Approval, 195
On Baile's Strand, 218
On Borrowed Time, 724
On Erkre Estate, 64
On the Eve, 472
'On the Fells,' 19
On the Frontier, 215
On the Harmfulness of Tobacco, 405
On the High Road, 405
On the Paths of Destiny, 491
On the Petsamo Road, 480
On the Rocks, 176
On the Shores of the Vistula, 629
On the Spot, 209
On the Stage of Life, 539
On the Steppes, 403
On the Sunny Side, 72
On the Ukrainian Steppes, 474
On the Way, 72
On Trial, 691-92
Once in a Lifetime, 734, 736
Once Is Enough, 195
Ondine, 307
One Night, One Life, 547
One of Our Girls, 646
One of the Family, 713
One Third of a Nation, 731
O'Neil, George, 709, 722
O'Neill, Eugene, 42, 43, 225, 227, 277, 278, 286, 308, 566, 573, 617, 640, 641, 650, 657, 662, 663, 670, 677, 681-93, 704, 709, 714, 716, 721, 725
O'Neill, James, 641
Ongley, Byron, 677
Onkel Toni, 140
Only Child, The, 547
Only the Heart, 739
Open House, 495
Open-air Theatres, 256
Opera, 124, 131, 380, 393, 520
Opera Studio, The, 400
Operette, 195
Opfer, Das, 83
Opferspiel, 112
Opferung, Die, 149
Optimistic Tragedy, 460
Ora et labora, 554

Oración a Rusia, 568
Orange Blossoms, 298
Orchard Walls, The, 212
Orchards of Polovchansk, The, 476
Order of St. Vladimir, 3rd class, The, 382
Ordinary Man, An, 477
Organ Grinder's Family, The, 518
Oriana, 336
Orientación, 590
Orione, 356
O'Riordan, Conal O'C., 221, 227
Orlov Couple, The, 429
Orphan, The, 507
Orphan Genius, 501
Orphan Ladislas, 522
Orphée, 302
Orpheus and Eurydice, 372
Orpheus und Eurydike, 149
Ortner, Hermann Heinz, 156
Osborn, Paul, 721, 723, 724
Osborne, Hubert, 670
Oscar Wilde (Sternheim), 102
Oscar Wilde (Stokes), 196
Oserov, V. A., 377
Osorio, Luis Enrique, 588
Ostpolzug, 152
Ostrovsky, A. N., 383-90, 392, 393, 401, 409, 418, 443, 448, 453, 620, 643
Otage, L', 254, 264
Othello, 28, 380, 516, 617
Other Air, 506
Other Shore, The, 507
Otro, El, 574
Otway, Thomas, 130
Ould, Herman, 212
Our Betters, 191
Our Children, 680
Our Forbears, 488
Our Heritage, 60
Our Honor and Our Power, 66, 71
Our Mr. Minister, 515
Our Sons-in-Law, 495
Our Swanky Peasants, 506
Our Town, 683, 732
Ours, 161
Ours on Top, 495
Oursler, Fulton, 717
Ouspensky, 204
Out of the Past, see *My Life in the Theatre*
Out of the Sea, 715
Outcast, 186
Outcasts, The, 507
Outlaw, The, 22, 23
Outrageous Fortune, 725
Outside Looking In, 695
Outward Bound, 210
Overruled, 174
Overtons, The, 719

Overture—1920, 717
Ovid, 520
Owl, The, 51

Paar nach der Mode, Das, 138
Pacala, 530
Pacifism, 510
Padre ci vuole, Un, 341
Padrona del mondo, La, 340
Pagan Magyars, The, 420
Pagans, The, 522
Pageants, 500, 527, 661, 689
Pagnol, Marcel, 197, 291, 296, 700
Pagnol, Maurice, 485
Paid in Full, 668
Paid on Both Sides, 215
Pailleron, Edouard, 240, 324, 673
Pain, Le, 255
Pain dur, Le, 254
Pair of Spectacles, A, 165
Pair of White Gloves, A, 259
Paix chez soi, La, 272
Paja brava, 582
Palace of Circe, The, 553
Palacio, Eduardo L. de, 569
Palamas, Kostes, 544
Palárik, Ján, *see* Beskydov, *pseud.*
Palme, oder der Gekraenkte, 148
Palmer, John Leslie, 309
Palmer, Rose A., 715
Paloma Azul, La, 575
Pamplemousse, 298
Pan, 312
Pan amargo, El, see Pan nuestro, El
Pan nuestro, El, 585
Panama, 116
Panamaskandal, 116
Pandelea, 529
Pandora, 555
Pankraz und die Hinterwäldler, 115
Pantalon und seine Söhne, 96
Pantaloon, 180
Pantano, O, 595
Pantomima, 587
Pantomimes, 106, 160, 302, 315
Pão duro, O, 600
Paolo and Francesca, 188
Papa Eccellenza, 331
Papa Hamlet, 79
Papa Juan; o El centenario, 566
Papa Wrangel, 109
Paquebot Tenacity, Le, 285
Paquet, Alfons Hermann, 110, 113
Parade Bed, The, 55
Paradise Lost, 726
Paragraph 218, 119
Parassiti, I, 329
Parazelsus, 135

Pardon, Le, 267
Parece mentira, 590
Parental Home, The, 462
Pariah, 31
Parini e la satira, 322
Paris and Oenone, 189
Paris Bound, 702
Parisienne, La, 242
Parker, Dorothy, 693
Parker, Louis Napoleon, 187
Parrish, James, 208
Parson's Family, The, 484
Parsons, Kate, 715
Partage de midi, Le, 254
Partenza, 582
Parting, The, 523
Partisans, 457
Partisans on the Ukrainian Steppes, 474
Partita a scacchi, Una, 331
Pasadena Playhouse, 689, 694
Pasado, El, 583-84
Pascal, André, *pseud.*, 290
Pascal, Gabriel, 174
Passé, Le, 265
Passerelle, La, 298
Passeur, Stève, 249, 276, 277, 278, 282-83, 311
Passing of the Third Floor Back, The, 424
Passion, La, 255
Passion de la révolte, La, 264
Passion Flower, The, 566
Passion's Furnace, 534
Passion plays, 108, 143, 255, 315
Passionspiel, 143
Pasteur, 299
Pastor Ephraim Magnus, 107
Pastor Hall, 110
Path of Flowers, The; or The Primrose Path, 461
Paths of Glory, 700
Patience; or Bunthorne's Bride, 162
Patissière du village, La, 293
Patricia's Seven Houses, 524
Patriot, Der, 114
Patriot, The, 200
Patriots, The (Kingsley), 724
Patriots (Robinson), 224
Patriots, The (Vaičiunas), 492
Patsy, The, 713
Patterson, Joseph Medill, 665, 666
Pattes de mouche, Les, 239
Paul Bunyan, 215
Paul Lange and Tora Parsberg, 50, 51
Paul Twyning, 231
Paulus unter den Juden, 147
Paunvere, 487
Pauper, Where To? 621
Pauvre Homme, Le, 295

Pauvre sous l'escalier, Le, 255
Pavlova, Tatiana, 358-59
Pawlikowska-Jasnorzewska, Marja, 501
Payment Deferred, 210
Payró, Roberto J., 581
Peabody, Josephine Preston, 678
Peace, The, 120
Peace Is Where The Tempest Blows, see *Lonely White Sail Gleams, A*
Peace on Earth, 708
Pearson, Hesketh, 168, 172, 173
Pêcheur d'ombres, Le, 303
Pedrosa, Raul, 600
Peer Gynt, 7-10, 13, 14, 19, 64, 65, 247
Péladan, Joséphin, 252, 256
Pelican, The, 200
Pelléas et Melisande, 249
Pellerin, Jean-Victor, 300, 308
Pellizzi, 325
Pemán, José María, 569, 576
Penitent, The, 614, 618
Penny Arcade, 713
Pensa de la Vega, Joseph, 602
Pensao de D. Stela, 600
Penthésilée, 253
Penzold, Ernst, 115
People, The, 454
People at Sea, 205
People Who Run Away from Themselves, 490
People's Theatre, 518, 519
Per vanità, 330
Perchtenspiel, Das, 157
Percy, Edward, 210, 213
Perdidos en la luz, 586
Père de famille, Le, 234
Père humilié, Le, 254
Père prodigue, Un, 239
Peretz, Isaac Loeb, 622, 623, 626, 631, 634, 636
Pérez de Ayala, Ramón, 562
Pérez Galdós, Benito, 558, 561
Pérez y González, Felipe, 564
Perfect Alibi, The, 192
Perfect Marriage, The, 722
Périer, Odilon-Jean, 315
Periphery, The, 510
Perleberg, 101
Perlenkomödie, 112
Perplexed Husband, The, 186
Persians, The (Aeschylus), 306
Persians, The (Feuchtwanger), 120
Personal Life, 460
Pertwee, Roland, 209
Perverse One, The, 540
Perzyński, Włodzimierz, 497
Peshkov, A. M., see Gorki, Maxim
Pest—und Pessionsgelübde von anno 1633 zu Oberammergau, Das, 108

Petar Zrinjski, 532
Peter Brauer, 83
Peter Pan, 179
Peter the Great, 372, 373, 383, 465
Peter von Russland, 96
Peter's Last Dream, 540
Petere, Herrera, 574
Peters, Paul, 708
Peterson, Ernst, 487
Petersons, Julius, 490
Petit café, Le, 273
Petite chocolatière, La, 274
Petite fonctionnaire, La, 268
Petite Marquise, La, 240
Petits oiseaux, Les, 165
Petofi Society, 523
Petr Vok Rosenberg, 505, 506
Petrified Forest, The, 705
Petroleuminseln, Die, 120
Petrov, 461
Petty Bourgeois, The, 421
Peyret-Chappuis, Charles, 283
Pfarrerstochter von Strehladorf, Die, 89
Pfarrhauskomödie, Die, 100
Pfingstorgel, Die, 116
Pfleger-Moravský, Gustav, 505
Phaea, 106
Phantom, Das, 128
Philadelphia Story, The, 702, 703
Philanderer, The, 168
Philharmonic Society, 527
Philip Goes Forth, 701
Philip the King, 188
Philippe II, 312
Phillips, David Graham, 665
Phillips, Stephen, 188-89, 214
Phillpotts, Adelaide, 189
Phillpotts, Eden, 189
Phoenix (Abercrombie), 190
Phoenix (Brust), 107
Phrosyne (Rangabé), 545
Phrosyne (Vernadakis), 546
Piacere dell' onestà, Il, 304, 362
Picard, André, 274
Picard, Edmond, 310, 313
Picasso, Pablo, 302
Piccola fonte, La, 334
Piccolo santo, Il, 334
Pichel, Irving, 674
Pico, Pedro E., 586
Picture of Dorian Gray, The, 305
Pictures in the Hallway, 227
Pièce muflle, 245, 253
Piéchaud, Martial, 283
Pie-Dish, The, 226
Piedra del escándalo, La, 581
Pierre et Jack? 298
Pietro Caruso, 333
Pigeon, The, 182

INDEX

Pile ou face, 297
Pillars of Society, 9-11, 13, 78
Pinero, Sir Arthur Wing, 162, 164-66, 226, 640, 672, 680
Pinheiro Chagas, Manuel, 594
Pinho, Gutta, 600
Pinillos, José López, 560
Pink Lady, The, 297
Pinski, David, 623, 624, 631, 636
Pintele Yid, Dos, 622
Pinto, 234
Pinwheel, 707
Piper, The (O'Riordan), 221, 227
Piper, The (Peabody), 678
Pirandello, Luigi, 249, 276, 277, 278, 286, 296, 300-04, 306, 318, 338-40, 344, 359-67, 368, 369, 511, 522, 535, 566, 568, 740
Pirandello, Stefano, *see* Landi, Stefano, *pseud.*
Pirates of Penzance, The, 162
Piscator, Erwin, 279, 428, 465
Pisemski, A. F., 384, 390, 401
Pitoëff, Georges and Ludmilla, 278, 279, 300, 445, 460
Più che l'amore, 349
Più forte, Il, 333
Pixerécourt, Guilbert de, 235
Plá y Beltrán, 574
Plaovich, Rasha, 537
Plato, 103
Platon Ketchet, 473
Platz, 106
Plautus, 594
Play, 161
Play in the Castle, The, 523, 524
Play Room Club, The, 302
Play's the Thing, The, 524
Playboy of the Western World, The, 220, 226, 227
Playhouse and the Play, The, 661
Playwrights' Company, The, 701
Pleasure of Honesty, The, 362, 366
Pledge of Honor, The, 548
Plenty, 18
Pliekšans, Elsa Rosenberg, *see* Aspazija, *pseud.*
Pliekšans, John, *see* Rainis, *pseud.*
Plot of the Empress, The, 465
Plough and the Stars, The, 227
Plus beaux yeux du monde, Les, 303
Plus bel homme de France, Le, 301
Plutarch, 170
Pobre gente, La, 583
Pobrecito carpintero, El, 569
Podestás (Juan, Pablo, Gerónimo and Antonio), 581
Poe, Edgar Allan, 31, 432, 642, 643
Poem of the Ax, The, 463
Poet Lore, 632

Poeta e la ballerina, Il, 321
Poetic drama, 83, 85-87, 91-94, 108-109, 113, 125, 216-32, 236, 243, 247-52, 255-56, 275, 285, 287, 289, 294, 301, 303-06, 308-09, 311, 313, 347, 352-53, 356-57, 359, 362, 379, 388, 390, 393, 419, 436-37, 448-50, 452, 500, 510, 529-30, 535, 548, 563, 565, 569, 571, 588, 594, 598, 604, 626, 632-33, 654, 656, 660, 673, 678, 695-99, 707-08, 710-12, 715, 722
Pogodin, N. F., 449, 462, 463, 464, 465, 478
Pogrom, The, 616
Poil de carotte, 272
Point Valaine, 195
Poizat, Alfred, 253, 256
Polemis, Joannes, 546
Police Gazette, 674
Polish Bethlehem, A, 498
Polish Boy, The, 614
Pollock, Channing, 666, 667, 716
Polly With a Past, 668
Polotski, Simeon, 372
Polti, Georges, 271
Polyeucte, 253
Polygamy, 666
Polyphème, 253
Pomander Walk, 187
Pomarius, 557
Pompey the Great, 188
Ponanski, Alfred, *see* Savoir, Alfred
Poncela, Jardial, 576
Ponsard, François, 236, 237
Pont de l'Europe, Le, 302
Poor Bride, The, 384
Poor Folk, 396
Poor Genevieve, 542
Poor Girl, The, 134
Poor Little Rich Girl, The, 679, 733
Poor Little Thing, 267
Poor Nut, The, 713
Pope Gregory VII, 525
Popovich, 535
Poppa, 723
Porché, François, 304
Porges-Bernstein, Elsa, *see* Rosmer, Ernst, *pseud.*
Porgy, 709, 713, 714
Poriotis, Nicholas, 546
Porras, Antonio, 574
Porta chiusa, La, 328
Portefeuille, Le, 261
Portineria, Il, 325
Porto, Luigi da, 252
Porto-Riche, Georges de, 244, 257, 265, 267, 269, 281, 282
Portugalesische Schlacht, Die, 115
Positivists, The, 494
Possédés, Les, 288

Possessed, The, 396
Possession, 667
Postoli, Foqion, 549
Pot of Broth, The, 217
Potekhin, A. A., 390
Potter's Field, 710
Pottercher, Maurice, 256
Potters, The, 713
Pour l'amour de la Sulamite, 313
Pour vivre heureux, 252
Poverty Is No Crime, 384
Power, 731
Power of Darkness, The, 244, 390, 397, 398, 399
Power of Hypnotism, The, 404
Power of Stupidity, The, 554
Pozharski, 378
Pozner, Vladimir, 458
Prados, Emilio, 574
Praga, Emilio, 326
Praga, Marco, 324-29, 343
Pratt, Theodore, 731
Precedent, 708
Predigt in Litauen, 108
Preger, Jacob, 633
Preissová, Gabriela, 506
Prejudices, 494
Prelude, 468
Přemysl Otakar, 505
Prenez garde à la peinture, 294
Present Laughter, 195
Presentation of Love, The, 443
Press Cuttings, 173
Prete Nero, 342
Pretenders, The, 5-7, 46
Pretty Sabine Women, The, 433
Preussengeist, 96
Prévost, Abbé, 102
Priceless Treasure, The, 546
Pride and Prejudice, 196
Prière pour les vivants, 295
Priestley, J. B., 204-05, 214
Prieto, Miguel, 574
Prima Fernanda, La, 566
Prima volta, La, 330
Prince, The, 508-09
Prince and the Pauper, The, 637
Prince d'Aurec, Le, 267
Prince Lulu, 622
Prince Vlaicu, 528
Princess Buttercup, 489
Princess Dandelion, 507
Princesse Lointaine, La, 250
Princesse Maleine, La, 248-49
Prinzip, Das, 127
Prisoners of Hope, The, 602
Prisoners of War, 208
Prisonnière, La, 290
Private Account, A. 272

Private Life of the Master Race, The, 122
Private Lives, 194
Pro scena sua, 444
Probekandidat, Der, 89, 102
Problem plays, *see* Social problem plays
Procès d'Oscar Wilde, Le, 305
Processional, 706
Prochaine, La, 306
Prodigal Sister, 497
Prodigal Son, The (Blaumanis), 488
Prodigal Son, The (Hollý), 514
Professor Bernhardi, 136
Professor Mamlock, 117
Professor Storitsyn, 433
Professor Tim, 231
Profitable Position, A, 384
Profligate, The, 165
Progeny, 510
Progress, 314
Progress, Its Law and Cause, 77
Prokopovich, Theophan, 373
Prokoviev, Sergei, 467
Proletarians, The, 519
Prologue, 543
Prologue to Glory, 731
Promessi Sposi, I, 319
Prométhée (Gilkin), 312
Prométhée (Herold and Lorrain), 253
Prométhéide, La, 252
Prometheus (Burte), 112
Prometheus (Eftiniu), 529
Property of Another, The, 390
Prophecy, The, 519
Prophet, The (Erkko), 484
Prophet, The (Langyel), 524
Prophet von Lochau, Der, 109
Propheten, Die, 111
Proposal, The, 408
Prose, La, 258
Protagonist, Der, 104
Protégée of the Mistress, The, see Ward, The
Provincetown Players, 42, 105, 286, 683-87, 692, 707, 709, 710, 716, 721
Provincia, 341
Provincial Magnificos, The, 520
Prunella, 183
Przetecki's Return, 502
Przybyszewski, Stanisław, 496, 497, 500, 508
Pseudo-classic drama, 234-37, 252-53, 256, 320
Psicharis, John, 544, 545
Psyche, 533
Psychological drama, 20, 28, 31, 72-73, 92, 94, 97, 100, 125, 130, 133, 187-88, 190, 197-98, 204, 209, 213, 236, 265, 267-70, 278, 281, 283-86, 288-90, 292, 296, 300, 326, 334, 340, 351, 357, 359, 361, 365-67, 395-96, 399, 433-34, 476, 547, 556

Público, El, 571
Puccini, Giacomo, 333
Puccini, Mario, 347
Pueblecito, 587
Puente, José Vicente, 576
Puertas adentro, 583
Pujet, Claude-André, 298
Pulitzer Prize, The, 685, 710
Puñao de rosas, El, 562
Punishment of Wrong, 514
Puppenspieler, Der, 135
Puppet Show, The, 436, 443
Purcell, Lewis, 226
Pure in Heart, The, 707
Purim Shpiels, 603, 605, 610, 617
Purple Dust, 228
Purple Island, The, 456
Pushkin, A. S., 379, 380, 381, 383, 387, 394, 401, 408, 441, 445, 453, 471
Pushkin, 456
Putsch, 116
Pygmalion, 174, 511
Pygmalion and Galatea, 162
Pyrrhus, 549

Quality Street, 178
Quando si è qualcuno, 361
Quarrels of Queens, The, 519
Quarter-Magnate, The, 520
Que la agarre quien la quiere, 586
Queen of Scots, 207
Queen Tagma, 519
Queen Victoria, 715
Queen Was in the Parlour, The, 194
Queen's Enemies, The, 222
Queen's Husband, The, 704
Quella che t'assomiglia, 346
Quello che non t'aspetti, 344
Querelle, 316
Querulant, Der, 128
Quick and the Dead, The, 547
Quiebra, La, 586
Quiet Wedding, 202
Quiet Weekend, 202
Quin's Secret, 231
Quincampox or the Jobbers, 552
Quinn, Arthur Hobson, 641, 646, 648, 651
Quintero, Pérez and Fernández, 575
Quinteros, The, *see* Alvarez Quintero, Joaquín *and* Alvarez Quintero, Serafín
Quintessence, 445
Quintessence of Ibsenism, The, 168
Quitzows, Die, 90

R. U. R., 465, 512
Rabagas, 239
Rabbi Judah Halevi, 618

Rabble, The, 66
Rabensteinerin, Die, 91
Rabinowitz, Solomon, *see* Aleichem, Sholom, *pseud.*
Rabouilleuse, La, 262
Race Errante, La, 304
Rachel, 621
Rachel the Singer, 610
Rachilde, Mme. Marg. Eymery, 247
Racine, Jean, 233, 234, 236, 265, 266, 270, 280, 282, 286, 287, 309, 370, 374, 375, 401, 604
Racines, Les, 314
Racket, The, 716
Ráday, Gedeon, 516
Radio Kiss, 445
Raduz and Mahalena, 508
Raeuber, Die, 76
Rafale, La, 269
Raggio di luna, Il, 368
Ragno, Il, 353
Rags, 632
Rahab, 633
Rails Are Humming, The, 459
Raimund, Ferdinand, 124
Rain, 714
Rain From Heaven, 704
Rainbow, The, 475
Rainis, *pseud.*, 489, 490
Rakhmaninov, Serge V., 413
Rákosi, Eugene, 519, 521, 522
Raleigh, Cecil, 213
Ramón de la Cruz, 561
Ramos Carrión, Miguel, 564
Randolph, Clemence, 714
Rangabé, Alexandre, 545-47
Rangel de Lima, Francisco, 594
Rape of Lucrece, The, 306
Raphaelson, Samson, 710, 721, 722
Rapp, William Jourdan, 709
Rappaport, Solomon Z., *see* Sh. An-sky, *pseud.*
Rascal, The, 526
Raspberry Jam, 472
Rassen, Die, 153
Rasvan and Vidra, 528
Ratés, Les, 287
Ratten, Die, 82
Ratti, Federico Valerio, 353
Rattigan, Terence, 196, 202, 211
Raudsepp, Hugo, 487
Raudup's Widow, 489
Rauhnacht, 157
Ravens, The, 511
Ravine, The, 409
Rayas de una cruz, Las, 586
Rayito de sol, 581
Raynal, Paul, 248, 280, 288-89, 309
Re pensieroso, 357

Reade, Charles, 242
Ready Money, 677
Realism, 77, 81, 85, 87, 99, 105, 110-11, 116, 119, 122, 141, 147, 160, 184, 191, 208, 218, 225, 229, 237-38, 240, 244-48, 251, 255, 257, 262, 265, 272, 276, 285, 300, 302-03, 306, 308, 318-19, 324-26, 335, 337, 350, 361, 364, 381, 385-87, 390, 393, 400-03, 420, 429-30, 439, 443, 445, 463, 476, 484-85, 498, 505-06, 510, 519, 522, 528, 530, 532, 539, 547, 551, 556, 559, 582, 584-85, 595, 599, 621-23, 630, 634, 648-49, 659, 665, 678, 687, 689, 693, 695-96, 717
Realistic Presentation of American Characters in Native American Plays Prior to 1870, The, 645
Realistic Theatre, The, 400, 428
Realtà, La, 331
Reb Hayim'l, the Tycoon, 610
Reb Henoch, 604
Rebellion (Drinkwater), 189
Rebellion (Patterson), 665
Rebellion in Balleycullen, The, 230
Rebellion of the Danubian Slovaks, The, 514
Rebellion on the Stage, 511
Rebels, The, 555
Rebound, 716
Rebreanu, 529
Reckless One, The, 485
Reconciliation, 513
Recruits, The, 612, 613
Red André, The, 61
Red Mill, The, 523
Red Passion, 530
Red Peppers, 195
Red Poppy, 469
Red Room, The, 25
Red Roses, 530
Red Roses for Me, 228, **229**
Red Rust, 459
Red Sunday, 208
Red Wallet, The, 518
Redemption, 399
Reed, P. I., 645
Reel, 525
Reeves, John Adam, 567
Reflected Glory, 702
Regent, The, 37
Regrowth, 492
Rehfisch, Hans José, 113, 119
Reich Gottes in Boehmen, Das, 147
Reigen, 134
Reinhardt, Max, 92, 105, 130, 131, 339, 424, 427, 443, 506, 623, 674
Reino de dios, El, 566
Reise gegen Gott, Die, 108
Reiter der Apokalypse, Die, 108

Rektor Kleist, 102
Relief, 554
Religious drama, 124, 233, 253, 254, 257, 258, 315, 371, 372, 409, 624, 637
Remarque, Erich Maria, 119
Rembrandt, 523
Remec, Lojz, 540
Remembrance of Things Past, 210
Renan, Ernest, 307
Renard, Jules, 272
Renascence of the English Drama, The, 166
Rency, Georges, 317
Rendl, Georg, 154
Reparationen, 152
Repas du lion, Le, 261-63
Requiem, A, 436
Résignés, Les, 258
Restless Old Age, 470
Restoration, 515
Résurrection (Bataille-Tolstoy), 269
Resurrection (Morton-Tolstoi), 213
Resurrection (Tolstoi), 397
Resurrection of Lazarus, The, 534
Retablillo de Don Cristobal, 572
Retired Landowners, 540
Retour de Jerusalem, Le, 266
Retour eternal, Le, 250
Retreat to Pleasure, 728
Retter, Die (Goering), 105
Retter, Der (Hasenclever), 105
Return, The, 509
Return from Jerusalem, The, 266
Return of Peter Grimm, The, 652
Return of the Soldier, The, 197
Return of Youth, The, 511
Reubeni Prince of the Jews, 634
Reunion in Vienna, 704
Revenge, 530
Reverend Griffith Davenport, The, 651
Revista Hispánica moderna, 574
Revista nacional de educacion, 575
Revistas líricas, 561, 562
Revolt, The, 241
Revolt of the Machines, The, 465
Révolte, La, 241
Revolte im Erziehungshaus, 116-17
Revoltosa, La, 564
Revolution (Kopta), 510
Revolution (Lom), 509
Revolutionary Trilogy, A, 508
Rey Trovador, El, 569
Reyde-Smith, Naomi, 208
Reyes, Alfonso, 590
Rheinische Rebellen, 152
Rhodope, 546
Rib of Man, 485
Rice, Elmer, 144, 677, 683, **691-94**, 702, 704, 716, 721

INDEX

Rich Brides, 386
Rich Girl, The, 526
Rich Man, Poor Man, 608
Rich Paupers, 632
Richard of Bordeaux, 207
Richard Savage, 177
Richard Strauss' Briefwechsel mit Hugo von Hofmannsthal, 131
Richard III, 374
Richepin, Jacques, 252
Richepin, Jean, 252
Richest Girl, The, 274
Richman, Arthur, 681, 716
Riders to the Sea, 219, 220, 221
Ridi, pagliaccio! 357
Ridicolo, Il, 322, 323
Ridley, Arnold, 209, 213
Riehl, Heinrich, 78
Riemsdijk, Adriaan Willem Gerrit van, 557
Rien qu'un homme, 314
Rift, The, 63
Rifugio, Il, 341
Riga Literary Society, 489
Rigby, Arthur, 213
Riggs, Lynn, 693, 711, 712, 721, 731
Right to Sin, The, 511
Right You Are, If You Think You Are, 364
Rights of the Heart, The, 495
Rigos, 545
Rimbaud, Arthur, 111
Rimsky-Korsakov, N. A., 393, 442
Ring and the Book, The, 715
Ring of Namejis, The, 490
Ringelspiel, 127
Rio Grande, 658
Rip Van Winkle, 645
Risa va por Barrios, La, 575
Rising of the Moon, The, 219
Rising Sun, The, 554
Ritter Blaubart, 93
Ritter Lanval, 95
Rittner, Thaddaeus, 143, 497, 498
Ritualmord in Ungarn, 109
Rivale, La, 271
Rivale de l'homme, La, 314
Rivals, The, 163
Rivas Cherif, Cipriano, 566
Riverside Drive, 622
Rivoire, André, 252, 283
Rivoli, 294
Road to Rome, The, 641, 704
Road to Victory, The, 466
Roadside, 712
Roadside Meetings, 649
Roar China! 118, 469
Robber, The, 512
Robbers, 387

Robe rouge, La, 260
Robert Blum, 118
Robert E. Lee, 189
Robert Emmet, 114
Robert et Marianne, 282
Robert Owen, 208
Robert Tim, 471
Robert's Wife, 224
Roberto Pregalli, 322
Robertson, Thomas William, 160, 161, 162, 216, 226
Robertson, W. Graham, 213
Robertson Players, 671, 672
Robinson, Bertrand, 738
Robinson, Charles, 719
Robinson, Lennox, 224-25
Robinson, Percy, 213
Roccia e i monumenti, La, 360
Roche, Mazo de la, 196
Rock, The, 214
Rocket to the Moon, 726, 727
Rode, Helge, 64
Rodenbach, Georges, 312, 313
Roger Bloomer, 692, 706
Rohmer, Sax, 213
Rohovin the Four-Horned, 503
Roi, Le, 272
Roi Candaule, Le, 254
Roimila Farm, 484
Roll, Sweet Chariot, 710
Rolland, Romain, 256, 257, 279
Rollo's Wild Oat, 681
Romains, Jules, 184, 246, 276, 277, 278, 289-90, 305, 311
Roman, Ronetti, 528
Roman expérimental, 78
Romance, 670, 679
Romanesques, Les, 250
Romantic Age, The, 192
Romanticism, 41, 81-82, 87, 94, 95, 97, 101, 104, 109, 112-13, 235-38, 244, 250-52, 266, 280, 282-83, 303, 305, 308, 320, 380, 417, 419-20, 484-85, 493, 514, 531, 535, 538, 550, 552, 557, 559, 587, 594, 624, 653-54, 678, 687-88, 715, 718
Romanticism, Norwegian National, 1, 4, 45, 47
Romanticismo, 331
Rome Haul, 722
Romeo and Juliet, 41, 250
Ronda de los muertos, La, 587
Roof, The, 183
Room Service, 677
Rope, 208
Rope's End, 208
Rosa de Papel, La, 570
Rosalind, 180
Rosario Ortega, 575
Rosas de todo o ano, 595

Rose and the Cross, The, 437
Rose Bernd, 82
Rose of Sharon, The, 621
Rose Without a Thorn, The, 207
Roseanne, 709
Rosemary, 514
Rosenkavalier, Der, 131
Rosenmontag, 89
Rosmer, Ernst, *pseud.,* 87, 89
Rosmersholm, 14-17, 50, 51, 61, 79, 218, 247
Rosmunda, 352
Rosse, 158
Rosso, Pier Maria, *see* San Secondo, Rosso di
Rossum, C. P. van, 557
Rostand, Edmond, 91, 250-51, 252, 303, 443
Rostand, Maurice, 305, 339
Rostworowski, Karol Hubert, 500
Rosy Rapture, the Pride of the Beauty Chorus, 181
Rotation, 118
Rote Hahn, Der, 81
Rote Strasse, Die, 149
Rothschild, Henri de, *see* Pascal, André, *pseud.*
Rouge, 295
Rouleau, Raymond, 311
Round Heads, Peak Heads, 122
Roundabout, The, 204
Roussalka, La, 253
Rousseau, Jean-Jacques, 26, 451
Rovetta, Gerolamo, 326, 330, 331
Rowe, Nicholas, 207
Royal Academy of Dramatic Art, 182
Royal Family, The, 734
Royal Idyl, 522
Royal Wrestling, The, 63
Royle, Edwin Milton, 679
Rozeno, Le, 329
Rubens, Paul A., 213
Rubenstein, H. F., 207
Rubicon, Le, 290
Rubin, Daniel, 718
Ruderman, M. I., 469
Ruederer, Josef, 90
Ruf des Lebens, Der, 136
Ruge Hoff, De, 90
Rugged Path, The, 231
Ruint, 713
Ruiz de Alarcón, 589
Ruiz Iriarte, 576
Rumour, The, 193
Run Little Chillun, 710
Runa Society, The, 22
Rundköpfe und die Spitzköpfe, Die, 122
Runeberg, J. L., 483
Runyon, Damon, 738

Ruota, La, 343
Rusalka, 380
Rusiñol, Santiago, 564
Rusk with Candy, 554
Russell, George W., *see* A. E., *pseud.*
Russet Mantle, 712
Russian Imperial Academy, The, 422
Russian People, The, 479, 480
Russian Players, 671
Rust, 459
Ruth, Léon, 283
Rutherford and Son, 187
Ruysbroeck the Admirable, 248
Rydel, Lucjan, 498
Ryskind, Morrie, 736

S O S, 515
Sa de Miranda, Francisco de, 593, 594, 596
Sabatini, Rafael, 197
Sabbatai Zevi, 624, 625
Sabina, Karel, 505
Sabine Woman, A, 656, 657
Sachs, Hans, 516
Sackler, Harry, 632, 633
Sacred Flame, The, 191
Sadoveanu, Ion Marin, 530
Saga of the Folkungs, The, 37-39
Sailor, The, 501
Sailor, Beware! 719
Sailors of Cattaro, The, 117
Sainetes, 561, 562, 564, 587
Saint, The, 715
St. Adalbert's Literary Society, 514
St.-Denis, Michel, 278
St. Francis of Assisi, 549
St. Helena, 206
Saint Joan, 176
St. John of Rila, 543
Saint Louis, 661
Saint-Marc, André Boussac de, 287, 288
St. Simon, Count Claude Henry de, 76
St. Wenceslas, 509
Saints and Sinners, 166
Sakichi, Kineya, 254
Sakuntala, 189
Salacrou, Armand, 302, 308
Salandri, Gaston, 258
Salda, František, 509
Salgado, Augurio, 575
Salias, Pedro, 561-63
Salomé, 163, 442, 530, 532
Salten, Felix, *pseud.,* 138
Saltykov-Shchedrin, M. E., 392, 420
Salvation (Asch), 625
Salvation (Howard and MacArthur), 699
Salvation Nell, 669, 678, 679
Salvation of Israel Through the Hands of Judith, The, 604

Salzburg Festivals, 131
Salzmann, Siegmund, *see* **Salten,** Felix, *pseud.*
Sam Abramowitch, 304
Samain, Albert, 253
Samaritaine, La, 250
Samodiva, 543
Samson, 270
Samson in Chains, 435
Samuel Posternack, 627
Samuel Zborowski, 501
San Juan de Luz, 562
San Secondo, Rosso di, 359-61, 367
Sánchez, Florencio, 582-86
Sánchez, Julian, 575
Sanctuary, 661
Sand, 115
Sandías y melones, 562
Sangster, Alfred, 208
Sanin, 433, 439, 441
Sanna, 127
Santa Hermandad, La, 574
Santa María del Buen Aire, 586
Santa primavera, La, 352
Šantich, 534
Santo de la Isidro, El, 562
Santos Vega, 576, 577
Sanvic, Romain, 317
Sapho, 621
Saratoga, 646
Sardou, Victorien, 77, 85, 164, 239, 244, 271, 519, 533, 559, 594
Sarment, Jean, 234, 277, 278, 303, 308
Saroyan, William, 669, 721, 733, 739, 740
Sarunas, 491
Sassmann, Hans, 153
Sassone, Felipe, 587
Satire, 7-8, 12, 25, 52, 54-58, 61, 71, 90, 101-02, 103, 105, 113, 115, 124-25, 127, 135-36, 139-40, 155, 162, 172, 190, 192-94, 199, 205, 215, 220, 223-24, 229, 230-31, 233, 239-40, 242, 250, 255, 260-62, 267-69, 272-73, 282, 286, 289-93, 295-96, 298, 312, 316, 328, 342, 344-45, 356-57, 375-77, 379, 398, 429, 433, 451, 456, 461, 466, 492, 494, 495, 497, 500-01, 503, 508, 510-11, 515, 520, 523-24, 527, 539, 543, 545, 552, 566, 568, 599, 637, 654, 660, 668, 675, 688, 694, 696-97, 701, 704, 709, 711, 715-20, 723, 733-34, 736-37
Saturday Review of Literature, The, 720
Saturday's Children, 695, 718
Satyr Plays, 58
Satyre, Le, 297
Saül (Gide), 305
Saul (Medved), 538
Saul's Kingdom, 604
Sauterelles, Les, 262
Sauvage, Le, 273

Saviours, The, 204
Savoir, Alfred, 259, 292-93
Savonarole, 312
Savory, Gerald, 196, 202
Savva, 430, 431
Saxon Shillin', The, 225
Sayers, Dorothy L., 216
Saynètes, 266
Scala di seta, La, 345
Scampolo, 342
Scandal in St. Florian's Vale, The, 539
Scandinavian Plays of the Twentieth Century, 75
Scapa Flow, 105
Scarecrow, The, 661
Scarron, 252
Schächer zur Linken, Der, 107
Schäfer, Walter Erich, 119
Schäferfdick, Willi, 118
Schafschur, Die, 116
Schatten fiel über den Tisch, Ein, 95
Schauspieler, Die, 94
Schauspielerin, 100
Scheffel, Victor von, 78
Schelm von Bergen, Der, 116
Schendel, Arthur van, 555
Schickele, René, 109
Schicksal um Yorck, 116
Schiff Bruchig, 191
Schildt, Runar, 60
Schiller, J. C. F. von, 46, 76, 87, 112, 122, 123, 125, 154, 235, 370, 387, 401, 448, 513, 531, 538, 545, 620
Schillers deutscher Traum, 116
Schinderhannes, 115
Schirin und Gertraude, 92, 109
Schlaf, Johannes, 79, 85
Schlaflied fuer Mirjam, 137
Schlageter, 111
Schleier der Beatrice, Der, 135
Schlick, Frederick, 708
Schloss Wetterstein, 100
Schloss Zeitvorbei, 88
Schluck und Jau, 81
Schmelz, der Nibelunge, 140
Schmetterlingsschlacht, Die, 86
Schmidt, Otto Ernst, *see* Ernst, Otto, *pseud.*
Schmidtbonn, Wilhelm August, 93-94
Schmoff, 107
Schneider, Edouard, 264
Schneider Wibbel, 116
Schneider Wibbels Auferstehung, 116
Schnitzler, Arthur, 112, 128, 132-37, 141, 159, 184, 227, 496, 539
Schoene Weserin, Die, 154
Schoenherr, Karl, 141-43, 156
Schoepfer, Der, 143
Scholz, Wilhelm von, 97

School, 161
School for Princes, 552
School for Scandal, The, 738
School for Slavery, 524
School Mistress, The, 164
School of Common Sense, 236, 237, 238
School of Love, 519
School of Stars, The, 443
Schoolhouse on the Lot, 736
Schopenhauer, Arthur, 77, 432
Schreiner, Olive, 212
Schreyer, Lothar, 106
Schreyvogl, Friedrich, 153
Schroeder-Devrient, Wilhelmine, 253
Schule des Lustspiels, 97
Schule von Uznach, Die, 102
Schuré, Edouard, 253
Schuster Anton Hitt, 156
Schutzengelspiel, Das, 144
Schwallbach, Eduardo, 596
Schwartz, Maurice, 622, 623, 632, 634
Schwarze Maske, Die, 84
Schwarzmann und die Magd, 119
Schweiger, 147
Schweigsame Frau, Die, 145
Schweik Against Hitler, 469
Schwester, Die, 149
Schwestern, Die, oder Casanova in Spa, 137
Schwierige, Der, 131
Scott, Clement, 167
Scoundrel at the Door, A, 533
Scrap of Paper, A, 239
Scribe, Eugène, 6, 11, 77, 164, 165, 235, 240, 243, 258, 263, 391, 506, 508, 544, 594
Scrollina, 335
Sculpteur de masques, Le, 293
Scuola degli artisti, La, 335
Scythe Struck a Stone, The, 403-04
Scythians, The, 437
Sea Fever, 198
Sea-Gull, The, 403, 410-12, 416
Searching for the Sun, 722
Searching Wind, The, 729
Seawife, 696
Sebastianlegende, 156
Sechste Heinrich, Der, 154
Second Man, The, 703
Second Mrs. Tanqueray, The, 164, 194, 720
Secret, Le, 270
Secret de Polichinelle, Le, 270
Secret of Heaven, The, 68
Secret of the Guild, The, 26
Secret Service, 663
Secrets, 206
Sed de justicia, 588
Seder Night, The, 617

Sée, Edmond, 271
See Naples and Die, 693, 694
Seeschlacht, 105
Sei personaggi in cerca d'autore, 338, 363, 365, 366, 369
Seiffert, Moshe, 618, 622
Sektion Rahnstaetten, 117
Seldes, Gilbert, 716
Sellés, Eugenio, 560
Selling of Joseph, The, 603
Selwyn, Edgar, 714
Sender, Ramón J., 574
Sendung Semaels, Die, 109
Seneca, 570
Señor Cura, El, 564
Señorita, 586
Señorita Charleston, 587
Señorita de Trevelez, La, 562
Sensible People, 490
Sentimental Acquaintance, A, 464
Ser o no ser, 590
Sera del trenta, La, 357
Serbian Migration, The, 535
Serbian National Songs, 535
Serena Blandish, 703
Serenade, La, 257-58
Serkele, 606-08, 611, 612, 620
Serpiente, La, 587
Servant in the House, The, 424, 666
Servants' Ball, The, 383
Service (Lavedan), 268
Service (Smith), 201
Service for Two, 718
Servicio Nacional de Teatro, 596
Servir, 268
Seventeenth-Century Comedian, The, 388
Seventh Heaven, 715
Séverac, Déodat de, 312
Sex Fable, The, 291
Sexe Faible, Le, 273, 291
Sexe Fort, Le, 273
Sh. An-sky, pseud., 630-31
Shabbetai Zervi, 637
Shadow, A, 65
Shadow and Substance, 229
Shadow of a Gunman, The, 227
Shadow of the Giant, The, 492
Shadow of the Glen, The, 220
Shadow Play, 195
Shadowy Waters, The, 217
Shaikewitch, Nahum Meir, 614, 616, 618
Shairp, Alexander Mordaunt, 210
Shakespeare, William, 23, 28-29, 37-38, 46, 57, 81-84, 93, 114, 122, 130, 140, 153, 167, 170-71, 217, 227, 233, 235-36, 254, 276-78, 305-06, 309, 316, 370, 373-75, 378-80, 383, 401, 408, 420, 470, 483, 499, 504-05, 509, 513, 516, 519, 529, 535, 541, 543, 545, 549, 620, 649, 653

Shakespeare, 207
Shakhovski, Prince A. A., 378
Shall We Join the Ladies? 181
Shannons of Broadway, The, 720
Sharkanski, Michael, 621
Shaw, Carlos Fernandez, 564
Shaw, George Bernard, 138-39, 162, 164-77, 182, 184, 189-90, 193, 217, 219, 246, 262, 277-78, 307, 311, 398-99, 420, 429, 443, 448, 558, 560, 566, 568, 639-40, 671-72, 681, 704, 716
Shaw, Irwin, 721, 727, 728
She Had to Know, 282
She Loves Me Not, 738
She Passed Through Lorraine, 208
She Stoops to Conquer, 376
She, Too, Was Young, 197
Sheldon, Edward, 658, 664, 669, 670, 680, 699, 709, 722
Shell, The, 540
Shelley, Elsa, 739
Shelley, Percy Bysshe, 118, 247
Shenandoah, 641, 647
Shephard, Firth, 214
Shepherd's Flute, The, 525
Shepherd's Wife, The, 515
Shepherds of Bethlehem, The, 549
Sheridan, Richard Brinsley, 163, 191, 217, 234, 376, 470
Sherriff, Robert Cedric, 119, 206, 207
Sherwood, Robert E., 294, 298, 641, 666, 691, 704, 706, 721
Shestakov, 468
Shewing up of Blanco Posnet, The, 173
Shiels, George, 231
Shining Hour, The, 211
Ship, The, 223
Ship of Saints, The, 445
Shipman, Samuel, 714, 717
Shirley, Arthur, 208
Shlonsky, A., 637
Shmendrik, 613
Shneour, Zalman, 637
Shomer, *pseud., see* Shaikewitch, Nahum Meir
Shop, 632
Shore Acres, 417, 651
Short Story, 196
Shortcomings, 515
Shostakovich, D. D., 392, 471
Show Shop, The, 680
Show-off, The, 701
Shroud My Body Down, 711, 712
Shudraka, 120
Shuiler's Child, The, 226
Shulamith, 614, 615
Si je voulais, 282
Siberia, 526
Sick Girl, 510

Sieben gegen Theben, Die, 144
Sieben Legenden, 91
Sieben Todsuenden, Die, 141
Siebzehnjährigen, Die, 90
Siege, 727
Siegel, William, 622
Siegfried, 307, 308
Siepe a nordovest, 367
Sifton, Claire, 707
Sifton, Paul, 707
Sign of the Leopard, The, 209
Signora Morli, una e due, La, 363, 368
Sigurd, the Bastard, 45, 46
Sigurjónsson, Jóhann, 61, 62
Silberer, Geza, *see* Sil-Vara, *pseud.*
Silbersee, Der, 104
Silent Knight, The, 523
Silent Strength, 501
Silent Witness, The, 213
Silva Antonio, José da, 594, 597, 598
Sil-Vara, *pseud.,* 154
Silver Box, The, 182
Silver Cord, The, 283, 699, 701
Silver King, The, 166
Silver Ravine, The, 464
Silver Tassie, The, 228
Silver Veil, The, 489
Šimáček, Matěj, 506
Simcha Plachte, 633
Simeon the Great, 532
Simo Hurtta, 484
Simoni, Renato, 340
Simonov, Constantine, 478-81
Simons, L., 552
Simoon, 31
Simoun, Le, 286
Simpleton of the Unexpected Isles, The, 176
Simpson, Harold, 213
Simpson, Helen, 203
Simson (Burte), 112
Simson (Eulenberg), 93
Simson (Wedekind), 100
Sin (Cerkvenik), 540
Sin (Haarla), 485
Sin (Tajovský), 515
Sin and Sorrow Are Common to All, 385
Sin of David, The, 188
Sinclair, Upton, 707
Singe qui parle, Le, 294
Singende Fisch, Der, 107
Singer, I. J., 634
Singing Bird, The, 525
Singing Jailbirds, 707
Sinhâ Mouça Chorou, 599
Sinking of the Squadron, The, 473
Sinner, The, 514
Sinners, 663
Sir Lanfal, 92

Sire, 268
Sirocco, 194
Sister, The, 636
Sisters, The (Kumičich), 532
Sisters, The (Peretz), 627
Sitting on Thorns, 511
Siwertz, Sigfrid, 65
Six Characters in Search of an Author, 300, 338, 363, 366
Six of Calais, The, 176
Skënderbeg, 549
Skin Game, The, 183
Skin of Our Teeth, The, 250, 683, 732
Skirgaila, 491
Sklar, George, 670, 708
Sklavin, Die, 91
Skutarevski, 476
Skylark, 642, 722
Slain Dragon, The, 506
Slaughter, The, 621
Slaves, The, 509
Slavic Wind, 469
Sleeping Clergyman, A, 199
Sleeping Husband, The, 526
Sleeping Partners, 299
Slice of Life, A, 180
Slight Case of Murder, A, 738
Slobodski, 469
Słodeńk, Jurij, 504
Słonimski, Antoni, 501, 502
Slovotekov the Workman, 428
Small-Town Folk, 540
Smetana, Fredrich, 505
Smith, Betty, 739
Smith, Dodie, 196, 201
Smith, Dorothy Gladys, *see* Smith, Dodie
Smith, Harry Bache, 564
Smith, Paul Gerard, 213
Smith, Winchell, 212, 677, 679
Smith's Daughters, The, 628
Smoleŕ, Jan Arnošt, 503
Smollett, Tobias, 715
Smug Citizen, The, 421, 422, 423, 430
Snegurochka, 409
Snellman, J. V., 483
Snob, Der, 101
Snow (Pogodin), 463
Snow (Przybyszewski), 496
Snow Maiden, The, 387
Snows of Finland, The, 469
Snowstorm, The, 529
So ist das Leben (Koenig Nicolo), 100
So This is London, 715
Soap Bubbles, 519
Sobre los Muros, 581
Sobrevivientes, Los, 586
Socháň, Pavel, 514
Social drama, 319-22, 325, 333, 390, 399, 453, 494, 511, 530, 539, 563, 587, 634, 659-61, 664, 680, 694, 703, 706
Social problem plays, 9-10, 20, 47, 52, 54, 59, 63, 72, 104, 146, 149, 166, 178, 236-38, 257, 262, 265, 313, 339, 487, 540, 584, 666-68, 672-73, 692
Société Coopérative des Auteurs Dramatiques, 278
Society, 161
Society of Art and Literature, 401
Society of Dramatic Authors and Operatic Composers, 388
Society of Playwrights, 326
Socrates, 103
Söderberg, Hjalmar, 63-64
Sodoms Ende, 86
Soeur Béatrice, 91
Sohn, Der, 104, 151
Soini, Yrjö, *see* Agapetus
Soir au front, Un, 271
Solco quadrato, Il, 353
Soldier's Wife, 725
Soler, Fernando, 588
Soler, Frederich, 564
Solera del Sacro-Monte, 575
Solitaire, 198
Solitaire Man, The, 723
Solitudine, 367
Sologub, Fedor, 437, 438, 439, 445
Sologub, Count Vladimir Alexandrovich, 390, 430
Solomon, 409
Solomon Molcho, 624
Some Letters of William Vaughn Moody, 656
Some One in the House, 733
Somebody Knows, 198
Somló, Alexander, 520
Sommer, 143
Somnambulist Nights in Broad Daylight, 26
Somov and Others, 428
Son, The, 495
Son of a Servant, The, 21, 27
Son of Lemmi, The, 485
Son of My People, 618, 619
Son of Shadow, The, 547
Son of the Fatherland, 534
Son of the Regiment, The, 462
Song and Dance Man, The, 677
Song of Happiness, A, 487
Song of Songs, The, 313
Son-in-Law, The, 491
Sonnenfinsternis, 85
Sonnette d'alarme, La, 271
Sonnwendtag, 141
Sons and Soldiers, 728
Sons of Arpad, The, 514
Sons of Kresimir, 532
Sophie, 715

INDEX

Sophocles, 96, 105, 113, 130, 131, 218, 544, 653
Sorbul, Mihail, 529
Sorge, Reinhard, 104, 111
Sorina, Die, 102
Sorrows of Belgium, The, 435
Sorrows of the Spirit, The, see *Woe from Wit*
Souffle du désordre, Le, 288
Soul in Torment, The, 526
Soulier de satin, Le, 254
Soumagne, Henri, 315
Souper des Cardineaux, Le, 595
Sour Grapes, 719
Souriante Mme. Beudet, La, 276, 284, 306
Sousa Monteiro, José Maria de, 595
South of the Slot, 471
Souveraine, La, 314
Souza, Claudio de, 599
Sovereign, The, 492
Soviet drama, 377, 379, 393, 429, 447-55, 459-62
Soviet theatres, 445-481
Sowerby, Greta, 187
Spaak, Claude, 312
Spaak, Paul, 313
Spain, We Salute You! 469
Spaini, Alberto, 355
Spanish Brabanter, The, 551
Speed Contests, 494
Spencer, Herbert, 77
Spender, Stephen, 216
Sperduti nel buio, 334
Spewack, Bella and Samuel, 677, 723
Spider, The, 529, 717
Spiegelmensch, 146
Spiel vom Blute Luzifers, Das, 108
Spiel von den deutschen Ahnen, Das, 144
Spielereien einer Kaiserin, Die, 95
Spielhagen, Friedrich, 77
Spindrift, 719
Spirochete, 732
Spitzer, Robert, 282
Spitzer, Rudolf, *see* Lothar, Rudolf, *pseud.*
Spook Sonata, The, 42-44
Spread Eagle, 717
Spreading the News, 219
Spring Dance, 703
Spring of Nations, 500
Spring 1600, 211
Spring Song, 723
Springtime for Henry, 202
Spuk, 84
Spurius, Der, 142
Spy, The, 271
Square Peg, A, 713
Squaring of the Circle, The, 461
Squatter Sovereignty, 651
Squeaker, The, 209
Squire Michalaki, 543
Šrámek, Fraňa, 510
Sruoga, Balys, 492
Stadt der Besessenen, Die, 94
Stage Door, 734, 735
Stage Society, The, 169-72
Stalin, Joseph, 456, 460
Stalin Prize, 474, 475, 478, 479, 480
Stalingrad Fights On, 480
Stallings, Laurence, 641, 695, 717
Stana Bjucica, 533
Standard of Humanity, The, 507
Stange, Hugh, 713
Stanislavski, Constantine Sergeev, 275, 394, 395, 398, 400-03, 409, 412-14, 417, 419, 421-24, 443, 446, 476, 630, 636, 674
Stanoye Glavaš, 535
Star, Der, 127
Star of Bethlehem, The, 527
Star Spangled, 729
Star Wagon, The, 698
Starkie, Walter, 567
Starlight, 269
Starling, Lynn, 713
Stars Turn Red, The, 228
Statesman's Ordeal, A, 506
Stavenhagen, Fritz, 90
S. S. Tenacity, 285
Štech, Václav, 506
Stefani, Alessandro de, 340
Steffen, Albert, 96
Steffens, Lincoln, 664
Steinbeck, John, 721
Steinski, 469
Stella Violanti, 547
Stemmle, Robert L., 117
Stempeniu, 627
Stenvall, Aleksis, *see* Kivi, *pseud.*
Štěpánek, 513
Stepchild, The, 532
Stephen IV, 520
Stephens, Nan Bagby, 709
Stern, G. B., 197
Sterne, Die, 143
Sternheim, Carl, 101-02, 104, 113
Steuerfaust, Die, 118
Stevedore, 708
Stevens, Eugène, *see* Hallo, Ernest, *pseud.*
Stevenson, Janet and Philip, 469
Steward Vanka, The, 393
Stewart, Donald Ogden, 716
Stifter, Adalbert, 159
Still Life, 195
Stille Gaeste, 158
Stimme, Die, 128
Stinchen von der Krone, 110
Stirner, Max, 439
Stodola, Ivan, 515
Stojanov, Racho, 543

Stokes, Leslie, 208
Stokes, Sewell, 208
Štolba, Josef, 506
Stomfay Family, The, 519
Stone, Irving, 707
Stone Guest, The, 380
Stone Walk, The, 514
Stor, Jean, 306
Storasta, Vilius, 491, 492
Storm, Lesley, 211
Storm, 193
Storm Operation, 698
Storm over Patsy, 113
Storm Song, 231
Storming of the Winter Palace, The, 444
Stormy Night, A, 528
Story of an African Farm, The, 212
Story of Samson, The, 602
Story of Skënderbeg, The, 549
Story of the Provinces, A, 476
Story Without End, 529
Stramm, August, 105-06
Strandkinder, 87
Strange Hunt, The, 554
Strange Interlude, 688, 689, 714
Strange Orchestra, 210
Strashimirov, Anton, 543
Straus, Oscar, 138
Strauss, Richard, 131, 132, 145, 156
Straw, The, 685
Street Scene, 693, 694
Streit um den Sergeanten Grischa, Der, 109
Streltsi, The, 373
Strictly Dishonorable, 720
Strife, 182
Strike at Arlingford, The, 187
Strindberg, August, 1, 2, 8, 14, 17, 19-45, 48, 51, 52, 55, 56, 57, 58, 61, 63, 65, 67, 68, 75, 104, 107, 111, 163, 231, 243, 410, 496, 540, 683, 686, 724
Strings, My Lord, Are False, The, 230
Strip for Action, 738
Stritar, Josip, 539
Stroh, 111
Strom, Der, 88
Strong, Austin, 715
Stronger, The, 31
Stroupežnický, Ladislav, 506
Strube, H., *see* Burte, Hermann
Struensee, 77
Struggle Between Two Worlds, The, 469
Struggle in the West, 468
Stuart, Aimée, 197
Stuart, Philip, 197
Stubbornness of Geraldine, The, 659
Stucken, Eduard, 92
Studies in the Contemporary Theatre, 309
Stürme, 106

Stunde des Erkennens, 136
Stunde des Sterbenden, Die, 111
Stupid Man, The, 525
Sturges, Preston, 720
Sturm im Wasserglas, 113
Sturm und Drang, 76, 78, 99
Sturmflut, 110
Sturz des Apostels Paulus, Der, 108
Šubert, František, 504-06
Substitute for War, A, 661
Subway, The, 693
Success Story, 706-07
Successful Calamity, A, 681
Such a Mulk, 496
Sudermann, Hermann, 17, 60, 85-90, 108, 119, 388, 506, 672
Südpolarexpedition des Kapitäns Scott, Die, 105
Sündflut, Die, 107
Sueños de mi prima Aurelia, Los, 571
Suicidio, Il, 322, 323
Suitors, The, see Marriage
Suitors, The (Kisfaludy), 517
Sukhovo-Kobylin, A. V., 390-92
Sulky Fire, The, 284
Sullivan, Sir Arthur, 162, 468-69, 564
Sumarokov, A. P., 373, 374, 377
Sumbatov, Prince Alexander Ivanovich, 393, 403
Sumi, Judah de, 602
Summer, 497
Summer Folk, 425
Summer in Nohant, A, 502
Summit, The, 231
Sump'n Like Wings, 712
Sun, The, 636
Sundgaard, Arnold, 722, 732, 739
Suñer, Luigi, 320
Sunken Bell, The, 80, 247
Sunken Worlds, 629
Sunlight Sonata, The, 199
Sunny Days, 273
Sunrise in My Pocket, 715
Sunset (Delavrancea), 529
Sunset (Sumbatov), 393
Sun-Up, 713
Supreme Force, 529
Surgery, 419
Surprise, The, 500
Surrealism, 572-73
Susan and God, 675
Susannah and the Elders, 200
Suspect, 210
Sustenance, 632
Sutro, Alfred, 186
Sutton, Maurice, *see* Tumerelle, Maurice, pseud.
Sutton-Vane, Sutton, 210
Suvorin, A. S., 393, 407-09

Suzanne, 316
Svoboda, František, 506
Swan, Mark, 714
Swan, The, 523
Swan-Song, A, 408
Swanwhite, 40
Swedenborg, Emanuel, 33
Sweeney Agonistes, 215
Sweet Lavender, 164
Swietochowski, Aleksander, *see* Okonski, Władysław, *pseud*.
Swift, Jonathan, 44
Swift, Michael, 709
Swimming Susanna, 490
Swinburne, Algernon Charles, 160
Swing Your Lady, 719
Switchback, The, 199
Swords, 699
Sylvaine, Vernon, 214
Sylvi, 484
Symbolism, 12, 14, 16, 40, 69, 71, 82, 91, 102, 104, 106-08, 117, 122, 126, 131, 146, 149-50, 253-55, 258, 262, 292-93, 301, 305-06, 310, 312-13, 318, 339, 352-53, 356, 381, 410, 429, 430, 433, 437, 445, 448, 484, 489-91, 499, 507, 510, 523, 525, 535, 543, 547, 554, 572, 586, 595, 622, 626, 628, 632, 673, 694, 703, 718
Symphony in Two Flats, A, 201
Synge, John Millington, 217-222, 225, 226, 227, 568
Synnöve Solbakken, 45
System of Logic, 77
Szaniawski, Jerzy, 501
Szenes, Bela, 525
Szep, Ernö, 523
Szigeti, Joseph, 518, 521
Szigligeti, Edward, 518, 521, 525
Szomory, Desider, 523
Szujski, Jozef, 498, 499

Taber, Richard, 720
Tabula rasa, 101
Taciturne, Un, 283
Taenzchen, Das, 127
Tag, Der, 119
Tag, Der; or The Tragic Man, 181
Tagger, Theodor, *see* Bruckner, Ferdinand, *pseud*.
Tai Yang erwacht, 117
Tailor-Made Man, The, 525
Taine, Hippolyte Adolphe, 77, 245, 300
Tajovský, Jozef Gregor, 515
Tal Servando Gomez, Un, 586
Talbot, A. J., 207
Talents and Their Admirers, 388
Talisman, Der, 91
Talley Method, The, 704

Tamási, Aron, 525
Tamerlan, 314
Taming of Badadoshkin, The, 476
Taming of the Shrew, The, 81, 140, 335
Tammsaare, Anton, 487
Tandas, 592
Tangopoulos, Demetrios, 547
Tannhäuser, 247
Tantalizing Tommy, 274
Tante, 185
Tante Ulrikke, 52
Tantris der Narr, 92
Tapestry in Gray, 718
Tapfere Cassian, Der, 136
Tarbell, Ida M., 664
Tarelkin's Death, 392
Tarkington, Booth, 679, 714
Tarnish, 720
Tartuffe, 386
Tasso, Torquato, 545
Tatar Horde in Hungary, The, 517
Tatyana Tepina, 393, 407-08
Taylor, Deems, 306
Tchernikovski, S., 637
Tea at the Senator's, 515
Teacher, The, 523
Teacher and Pupil, 510
Teatro breve, 357
Teatro d'Arte del Convegno, Il, 276
Teatro de Ahora, El, 589
Teatro de carpa, 562
Teatro de Media Noche, 589
Teatro moderno, El, 564
Teatro Nacional, 588
Tedious Story, A, 408
Tela di Penelope, La, 354
Teleki, László, 518
Teleki Prize for Drama, 519
Temperamental Journey, The, 252
Tempest, The, 83
Temple, Joan, 208
Tempo, 463
Temporary Theatre, 504-05
Temps difficiles, Les, 291
Temps est un songe, Le, 278, 286
Temptation, The, 547
Temptress, The, 540
Ten Little Indians, 213
Ten Little Niggers, 213
Ten Million Ghosts, 724
Tenailles, Les, 261
Tendresse, La, 269
Ten-Minute Alibi, 209
Tennyson, Alfred, Lord, 160
Tenth Commandment, The, 615, 616, 618, 634
Tepa, Jerzy, 502
Terence, 594
Terra promessa, La, 339, 350

Terre est ronde, La, 303
Terrible Meek, 666
Terrible Tsar Ivan Vasilevich, The, 394
Tersites, 144
Tervapaä, Juhani, *see* Vuolijoki, Hella
Tête d'or, 254
Teternikov, Fedor Kuzmich, *see* Sologub, Fedor
Têtes de rechange, 300
Tetralogy, 246
Teufelspakt, Der, 109
Teuta, 531
Tevyeh, The Dairyman, 627
Texas Nightingale, The, 718
Texas Steer, A, 652
Thal des Lebens, Das, 89
Thalasso, Adolph, 244
Thalia Company, The, 525
Thank You, Mr. Pepys, 207
That Worthless Fellow Platonov, 404
That's Gratitude, 713
Theater der Dichtung, 139
Theatre, 68
Theatre Arts Monthly, 200, 674
Theatre as Such, The, 444
Théâtre Civique, 256
Théâtre d'Amour, 265, 266, 269, 281
Théâtre d'Art, 247, 277, 305
Théâtre de la Coöpération des Idées, Le, 256
Théâtre de l'Oeuvre, 247, 253, 278
Théâtre des Jeunes Auteurs, 278
Théâtre du Marais, Le, 276, 311
Théâtre du Vieux-Colombier, Le, 253, 274-78, 285, 304, 306, 311
Theatre Guild, 102, 120, 174-76, 223, 276, 287, 291, 311, 395, 396, 435, 445, 459, 480, 567, 623, 688, 689, 692, 693, 712, 715
Theatre Guild: The First Ten Years, 174
Theatre in Life, The, 444
Théâtre Libre, 30, 31, 78, 243, 244, 245, 246, 247, 248, 253, 257, 258, 259, 261, 263, 265, 270, 271, 274, 277, 279, 280, 306, 325, 398, 497, 525, 639
Theatre of Eternal War, 445
Theatre of the Crooked Looking-Glass, The, 443
Theatre of the Soul, The, 253, 443
Theatre of Today, 674
Theatre Union, 117, 708, 711
There Are Crimes and Crimes, 35, 43
There Shall Be No Night, 666, 704, 705
There's Always Juliet, 198
There's Many a Slip, 237
Thérèse Raquin, 52, 241
Thersites, 162
Théry, Jacques, 298
These Charming People, 212

Thesis plays, 239-40, 242-43, 259, 262-63, 267, 274, 321, 328, 654, 665, 696, 699-700, 708
They Came to a City, 205
They Knew What They Wanted, 643, 699
They Shall Not Die, 708
They Walk Alone, 209
Thibaut, Armand, 314
Thief, The, 270
Thieves, 488, 629
Things That are Caesar's, 229
Thinker, The, 409
Thirst, 683
Thirty Tyrants, The, 545
This and That, 27
This Fine—Pretty World, 661
This Happy Breed, 195
This is New York, 704
This Soil, 637
This Thing Called Love, 716
This Was a Man, 194
This Woman Business, 202
This Year of Grace, 194
Thoma, Ludwig, 90
Thomas, Augustus, 657-60, 668, 680
Thomas, Brandon, 163, 214, 654
Thomas Campanella, 454-55
Thomas More, 555
Thomas Muskerry, 225
Thomas Paine, 111
Thomas Wendt, 120
Thomashefsky, Boris, 616, 618
Thompson, Denman, 417
Thompson, Fred, 213
Thou Shalt Not Covet, see Tenth Commandment, The
Thou Shalt Not Kill, 434
Thousand Years Ago, A, 661, 662
Thought, 434
Thousand and One Nights, The, 94
Three and One, 284
Three Cities, 625
Three Couples, 51
Three Cousins, The, 610
Three Men, 429
Three of Us, The, 675
Three Princes, The, 620
Three Sisters, The, 394, 414-16, 470
Three Thimbles, The, 230
3000 People, 515
Three-Cornered Hat, The, 572
Three-Penny Opera, The, 121
Thunder in the Air, 210
Thunder Rock, 723, 730
Thunderstorm, The, 385, 387
Thurman, Wallace, 709
Tignola, 350-51
Tigra, La, 583
Till the Day I Die, 725

Time and the Conways, 204
Time Forward! 461
Time is a Dream, 286
Time of Your Life, The, 740
Times Have Changed, 291
Timon, 153
Tinker, The, 513
Tinker's Wedding, The, 221
Tiquis Miquis, 564
Tiradentes, 599
Tissa Eslar, 617
Titano, Il, 342
Titus, 618
T'Kiyas Kaf, 628
To Be Continued, 468
To Damascus, 34-36, 38, 42-44, 104
To Love, 282
To Quito and Back, 723
To the Ladies, 733
To the Stars, 430
To Understand Is to Suffer, see *Woe from Wit*
Too Thoughtful to be Happy, see *Woe from Wit*
To What Red Hell, 213
Tobias and the Angel, 199
Tobias Buntschuh, 94
Tobias Klepeto, 514
Tobias Wunderlich, 156
Tochter der Kathedrale, Die, 84
Tod, Der, 95
Tod des Tizian, Der, 129
Tod und Teufel, 100
Toddles, 273
Todo un hombre, 570
Todorov, Petko Yurdanaov, 543
Toi et moi, 282
Toi que j'ai tant aimé, 283
Tolkening, 107
Toller, Ernst, 42, 109-10, 115, 120, 231
Tolstoi, A. C., 394, 466
Tolstoi, Alexei N., 449, 465, 466, 467
Tolstoi, Leo, 78, 164, 213, 244, 245, 256, 278, 339, 390, 392, 394, 397, 398, 399, 401, 436, 439, 448, 451, 467, 470, 504, 645, 648, 649
Tom, Dick and Harry, 304
Tom Thumb, 489
Tomás, Luceño, 564
Tomás, Mariano, 576
Tombeau sous l'Arc de Triomphe, Le, 288
Tomé, Alfredo, 596
Tomich, Josip, 531, 532, 538, 541
Tomislav, First King of the Croatians, 532
Tommy, 738
Tomorrow, 661
Tomorrow and Tomorrow, 703
Tonada del Rizo, La, 575

Tonelli, Luigi, 325
Tonight at 8:30, 195
Tony the Bootblack, 663
Too Thoughtful to be Happy, 378
Too True to be Good, 176
Topaze, 291
Topelius, 21
Tor und der Tod, Der, 129
Torch Song, 719
Torchbearers, The, 701
Torelli, Archille, 326, 335, 336, 545
Torrent, Le, 266
Tosca, 333
Tote Tag, Der, 106
Tote Zeit, 92
Totentanz, 100, 108
Tóth, Edward, 518, 520, 521
Totheroh, Dan, 709, 713, 722
Tottering Edifice, A, 501
Touch and Go, 208
Touchwood, 201
Toulet, Jean, 269
Tour à terre, 302
Toutinegra Real, A, 595
Tovarich, 705
Tovaritch, 294
Toward Carnival Time, 64
Tower of Babel, The, 501, 545
Town Boy, 713
Toy Theatre of Boston, 671, 692
Tra vestiti che ballano, 360
Tradition, 667
Tragédia dell'anima, 334
Tragédie de Tristan et Yseult, La, 256
Tragédies de la Foi, 257
Tragédies de la Révolution, 257
Tragedy of Love, The, 53, 72
Tragedy of Man, The, 518
Tragedy of Nan, The, 188
Tragic Muse, The, 208
Translations and Tomfooleries, 139
Trarieux, Gabriel, 255, 264
Traumgesichte des Adam Thor, Die, 88
Traumstueck, 139
Traumtheater, 139
Traumulus, 85, 102
Traveling Salesman, The, 680
Travers, Ben, 214
Tread the Green Grass, 711, 712
Treadwell, Sophie, 707
Treasure, The (Aksenfeld), 608
Treasure, The (Aleichem), 627
Treasure, The (Pinski), 623
Trebitsch, Siegfried, 138
Trébol florido, El, 575
Tree, The, 710
Treibjagd, 114-15
Trelawney of the Wells, 165
Trenkwalder, Die, 141

Trente-six situations dramatiques, Les, 271
Trepolwitch, Joseph, 604
Tresich-Pavičich, Ante, 532, 534
Trésor des humbles, Le, 249
Tretyakov, S. M., 118, 121, 122, 469
Treuer Diener seines Herrns, Ein, 516, 532
Trial, The (Kirshon), 460
Trial, The (Preger), 633
Trial, The (Sharkanski), 621
Trial of a Judge, 216
Trial of Jesus, The, 188
Trial of Mary Dugan, The, 717
Tribun, Le, 262, 264
Trigger, 713
Triglav Fable, 540
Trijuntje Cornelis' Daughter, 551
Trilogia di Dorina, La, 330-31
Tripes d'or, 293
Triple-A Plowed Under, 731
Triplepatte, 273
Trisevyene, 544
Tristan, 508
Tristan and Isolde, 253
Tristan and Isolt, 188
Triste realtà, 336
Tristi amori, 332
Triumph of Death, The, 438
Triumph of Minerva, The, 374
Troerinnen, Die, 146
Trois acteurs et un drame, 315
Trois et une, 284
Trojaner, Die, 117
Trommeln in der Nacht, 120
Trotski, Lev, 113
Trousers to Match, see *Miss Swan Expects*
Trovarsi, 364
Trumpet Shall Sound, The, 732
Trunkene Schiff, Das, 111
Truth, The (Fitch), 659, 660
Truth (Korneichuk), 474
Truth About Blayds, The, 192
Truth Conquers, 514
Truth Game, The, 201
Tsaddik's Journey, The, 633
Tucich, Srgan, 534, 535
Tuda, 364
Tugomer, 538
Tully, Jim, 695, 709
Tumerelle, Maurice, *pseud.*, 314
Tumiati, Domenico, 353
Tunnel Trench, 208
Turandot, 661
Turcaret, 234
Turgenev, I. S., 339, 394, 395, 397, 401, 406
Turinský, 513
Turm, Der, 132

Turner, John Hastings, 197
Turner, W. J., 197
Tutto per bene, 365
Twain, Mark, 637, 640, 642, 645, 648
12th Hour, The, 526
Twelve, The, 437
Twelve in a Box, 525
Twelve-Pound Look, The, 180
Twentieth Century, 723
Two Fellows and a Girl, 719
Two Hundred Thousand, 627
Two Kuni Lemels, The, 615
Two Married Men, 719
Two Mr. Weatherbys, The, 184
Two Mrs. Carrolls, The, 209
Two Neighbors, The, 611
Two on an Island, 694
Two Schools, The, 268
Two Shmelkes, The, 613
$2 \times 2 = 5$, 58
Tyl, Josef K., 504, 513
Tyler, Royall, 642, 645
Type A, 501
Typhoon, 524
Tyrannical Banker, The, 614
Tyranny of Love, The, 265
Tyranny of Tears, The, 185
Tyrant, The, 197

Ubu Roi, 247, 301
Uccello del paradiso, L', 346
Ueber die Bruecke, 142
Ueber die Oper, 121
Ueberteufel, Der, 100
Ugarte, Eduardo, 566
Uhl, Frieda, 33
Ulrich, Count of Cilli, 538
Ulrich, Fürst von Waldeck, 93
Ulrich und Brigitte, 101
Ultima curva, La, 575
Ultimo convegno, L', 335
Ultimo romanzo, L', 337
Ulysses (Haxhiademi), 549
Ulysses (Phillips), 188
Uma Véspera de Reis na Bahia, 599
Umkehr des Abtruennigen, Die, 109
Umorismo, 366
Unamuno, Miguel de, 566, 569, 570
Unanimism, 289
Unaussprechliche Hirt, Der, 107
Unbedingte, Der, 117
Unchastened Woman, The, 680
Uncle Moses, 625
Uncle Tom's Cabin, 645
Uncle Vanya, 410-13, 416, 417
Uncle, We Know You, 629
Uncle's Dream, The, 395
Uncomprehended Marvel, The, 487

INDEX

Und Pippa tanzt, 82
Under the Big Top, see *Under the Circus Tent*
Under the Chestnut Trees, 481
Under the Circus Tent, 461
Under the Yoke, 543
Underhill, John Garrett, 567
Ungar, Hermann, 148
Unicorn from the Stars, The, 218
Unities, dramatic, 233, 234, 236
Unknown Warrior, The, 288
Unknown Woman, The, 437
Unmentionable Careers, 532
Unquiet Spirit, The, 285
Unruh, Fritz von, 105
Unsane Tokef, 621
Unternehmen Michael, 119
Unterwegs, 143
Untilovsk, 476
Unueberwindlichen, Die, 139
Unwilling Martyr, An, 408
Uomini seri, 322, 323
Uomo dhe incontrò se stesso, L', 345
Upits, Andrew, 490
Urbánek, Ferko, 514
Urbanovič, K. F., 515
Uriel Acosta, 76, 614, 617
Ursache, Die, 118
Usigli, Rodolfo, 590
Usurer, The, 618
Utopias in Reality, 27

Vacarezza, Alberto, 585
Václav IV, 508
Vadim of Novgorod, 377
Vae Victis, 314
Vagabond, The (Toth), 518
Vagabond, The (Urbánek), 514
Vaičiunas, Petras, 491, 492
Vainqueurs, Les, 316
Vajda, Ernö, 524, 525
Vakhtangov, Y. V., 631, 636
Vakhtangov Theatre, 400, 428, 456, 461, 463, 464, 471, 476
Valdemars, Christian, 488
Valentine, Rudolph, 674
Valérie, 243
Vale, Martin, 209
Valle Inclán, Ramon, 566, 569, 570
Vallette, Mme. Alfred, see Rachilde, Mme. M. E.
Valley Forge, 697
Value of Life, The, 403
Vampire, The, 543
Van Druten, John, 191, 196, 197-99, 202
Van Eeden, Frederick, 553-55
Van Haren, Onno Zwier, 552
Van Lerberghe, Charles, 247, 248, 310, 312

Van Offel, Horace, 316
Vančura, Antonín, see Mahen, Jiří, pseud.
Vančura, Vladislav, 506, 510
Vanguard, The, 461
Vanka the Butler and Jean the Page, 438
Vanzype, Gustave, 313-14
Váradi, Antal, 520
Vargas plan, 600
Varlomont, M., see Waller, Max, pseud.
Värnlund, Rudolf, 65, 67
Varying Shore, The, 718
Vasantasena, 120
Vasiliadis, Spyridion, 545, 546
Vassa Zheleznova, 427
Vatermord, 151
Vaudeville, 240, 271, 273, 291-92, 294, 297, 403-04, 408, 528
Vaughan, Hilda, 197
Vaz de Camoes, Luiz, 594
Vaz de Camoens, Luiz, see Vaz de Camoes, Luiz
Vazov, Ivan Minchev, 542, 543
Veau gras, Le, 296
Véber, Pierre, 273
Vedía, Joaquin, 582
Vedova, La, 340
Vega, Ricardo de la, 564
Vegetable, The, 716
Veiller, Bayard, 664, 679, 714, 717
Veiller, Mrs. Bayard, see Vale, Martin
Veine, La, 268
Veiter, A., pseud., 622, 623, 626
Veland, 83
Velislava, 542
Vena d'oro, La, 368
Veneer, 713
Venetian, The, 207
Venetian Comedy, A, 57
Vengeance is Mine, 508
Vengeance of Catullus, The, 507
Ventres dorés, Les, 262
Venus Victrix, 533
Verbena de la Paloma, La, 564
Verbrecher, Die, 152
Verbündeten Mächte, Die, 138
Verdugo de Sevilla, El, 563
Verfuehrung, Die, 148
Verga, Giovanni, 325, 326, 340, 365
Vergani, Orio, 369
Vergini, Le, 327, 329
Verhaeren, Emile, 310-12, 317
Verloebnis, Das, 158
Vermaechtnis, Das, 135
Vernadakis, Demetrios, 545, 546
Verneuil, Louis, 297
Veronika, 143
Veronika Deseniška (Tomich), 532
Veronika Desiniška (Jurčic-Borštnik), 538, 540, 541

Veronika Desiniška (Zupancic), 541
Vershinin, Ilya, 469
Versuchung, Die, 102
Versunkene Glocke, Die, 80, 81, 89, 91
Vertauschte Seelen, 97
Verwandelte Komoediant, Der, 144
Verwey, Albert, 553
Vestal, The, 489, 492
Vestire gli ignudi, 365
Via Basento, Lanterna Rossa, 340
Vialer, Paul, 296
Viandante, Il, 340
Vianna, Oduvaldo, 599
Viboras sociales, 588
Vicente, Gil, 580, 593, 594, 596, 597
Viceroy Sarah, 207
Victoire, La, 316
Victoria Regina, 206, 715
Victory, The (Munk), 67, 74
Victory (Vershinin and Ruderman), 469
Victory in the Dark, 69, 70
Vida es sueño, La, 132
Vie dell' oceano, Le, 339
Vie muette, La, 247
Vie publique, La, 262
Vie secrète, Une, 288
Vieil homme, Le, 265, 267
Vient de paraître, 291
Vierge au grand coeur, La, 304
Viergetier, Das, 97
Vierset, Auguste, 312
Vierte Gebot, Das, 125
Vigil, The, 545
Vigliacco, Un, 369
Vigny, Alfred de, 236
Vikings at Helgeland, The, 4-6, 22
Vikt, 623
Vildrac, Charles, 227, 285, 286
Vilkutaitis, Juozas, 590
Villaespesa, Francisco, 569
Village, The, 521
Village Comedy, A, 525
Village Idyl, 524
Village Loafer, The, 518, 520
Village Notary, 530
Village of Cernova, The, 514
Village of Stepanchikovo, The, 395
Village Shoemakers, The, 483
Village Wooing, 176
Villaurrutia, Xavier, 590
Villiers de l'Isle-Adam, 241, 246-48
Vilna Troupe, The, 622, 625, 629-31
Vilner Balebesel, Der, 633
Viluppo, Il, 337
Vincent, 111
Vinegar Tree, The, 723
Vintage Wine, 200
Viol de Lucrèce, Le, 306

Viola, Cesare Giulio, 341, 368
Vishnevski, Vsevolod, 468
Vision of Gundulich, 533
Visions, 487
Visit from Jove, A, 545
Viskovatoy, S. I., 378
Visnapuu, Henrik, 487
Vivat Academia, 142
Vives, Don Amadeo, 564
Vixen, The, 495
Vladimir, 373
Vladimirov, V. H., 515
Vlček, Václav, 505
Voce, La, 338
Voevoda, The, or *A Dream on the Volga,* 387
Voice of the Turtle, The, 199
Voices Shall Cease, The, 604
Voile, Le, 312
Voinikov, Dobri P., 542
Voivoda Stojan, 542
Voivode Stibor, 517
Vojnovich, Ivo, 533, 534
Volata, La, 342
Voleur, Le, 270
Volk in Not, 142
Volk ohne Heimat, 116
Volkov, Theodore, 374
Volksbuene, 256
Vollmer, Lulu, 713
Vollmöller, Karl Gustav, 91
Vollo, Giuseppe, 320
Volonté de l'homme, La, 273
Volpone, 145
Voltaire, J. F. M., 25, 233, 373, 374, 527, 546, 672
Vom andern Ufer, 138
Vomberger, Jože, 541
Von Morgens bis Mitternacht, 102
Von Moser, Gustav von, 165
Vondel, Joost van den, 550, 551
Vor der Eintscheidung, 106
Vor Sonnenaufgang, 78, 79
Vor Sonnenuntergang, 84
Vörösmarty, Mihály, 517, 519
Vortex, The, 193
Vortice, 337
Voruntersuchung, 118
Vosnjak, Josip, 539
Vosper, Frank, 213
Voulez-vous jouer avec moâ, 304
Voyage de M. Perrichon, Le, 240
Voyageur sans bagage, Le, 296
Voysey Inheritance, The, 183
Vrba, Michal, 514
Vrchlický, Jaroslav, 507, 508
Vuillard, Edouard, 247
Vulfs, Eduard, 490
Vulpius, Paul, 208

INDEX 829

Vuolijoki, Hella, *pseud.*, 485
Vydunas, *pseud.*, see Storasta, V.

W. P. A. Negro Theatre Unit, 306
Wächter am Galgen, Der, 108
Wagner, Richard, 246, 252, 253, 276
Wahnschaffe, 108
Wait for Me, 480
Waiting for Lefty, 725, 727
Wake Up, Jonathan, 692
Wakefield, Gilbert Edward, 196
Waldleute, 94
Walk Together Chillun, 710
Walker, London, 178
Wall, Harry, 196
Wallace, Edgar, 209, 213
Wallenstein: For Right and the Heart, 538
Waller, Max, *pseud.*, 310
Walls of Jericho, The, 186
Walpole, Sir Hugh, 202, 210
Walrus and the Carpenter, The, 196
Walter, Eugene, 653, 658, 664, 668, 669, 680
Waltz of the Dogs, The, 434
Walzertraum, Ein, 138
Wandlung, Die, 120
Wandlung, das Ringen eines Menschen, 110
Wanted for Murder, 213
War, 441
War and Peace, 397, 467
War for War, 500
War God, The, 186
War in Peace, 604
War of Souls, The, 264
War Song, The, 723
Ward, The, 384, 390
Warm Heart, A, 386
Warrior's Barrow, The, 423
Warsaw Slave, The, 501
Washington Heights, 719
Washington Square Players, The, 250, 692, 721
Washington the Man Who Made Us, 661
Wasilewska, Wanda, 475
Waste, 184
Watch on the Rhine, 729
Watched Pot, The, 229
Water, 541
Water Carrier, The, 633
Waterloo Bridge, 704
Watkin, L. E., 724
Watkins, Maurine, 670, 717
Watson, H. B. Marriott, 177
Watson, Karl Friedrich, 488
Watts, Richard Jr., 229
Wawroch Family, The, 151

Way Things Happen, The, 203
Way Up, The, 500
Ways and Means, 195
We Are No Longer Children, 298
We Moderns, 186
We Murderers, 63
We the People, 694
We Were Dancing, 195
Weak Woman, A, 294
Weaker Sex, The, 58
Wealth, 166
Weasel and the Well, The, 613
Weaver, J. V. A., 720
Weavers, The, 80, 140, 244, 554
Webb, Kenneth, 713
Weber, Die, 80, 110, 117
Webster, Charles, 707
Webster, John, 312
Webster, Margaret, 420
Wechsler und Händler, 111
Wedding, The (Chekhov), 408
Wedding, The (Wyspianski), 498, 499
Wedding Guest, The, 178
Wedding Jesters, 610
Wedding March, The, 240
Wedekind, Frank, 42, 43, 52, 90, 98-102, 104, 111, 114, 540, 683, 686
Wednesday's Child, 725
Weeping Satyr, The, 510
Weg der Verheissung, Der, 147
Weg zur Form, Der, 95
Weg zur Macht, Der, 100
Weib auf dem Tiere, Das, 112
Weib des Jephta, Das, 112
Weiber von Weinsbert, Die, 100
Weibsteufel, Der, 142
Weill, Kurt, 104, 121
Weill, René, see Coolus, Romain, *pseud.*
Weismantel, Leo, 108
Weiss, Karl, see Karlweis, C., *pseud.*
Weisse Faecher, Der, 129
Weisse Heiland, Der, 83
Weissman, Reuben, 618
Weite Land, Das, 136
Weitzenkorn, Louis, 713
Welded, 686
Well of the Saints, The, 220
Well Remembered Voice, A, 181
Welles, Orson, 240
Well-made play, The, 10, 185-86, 237, 239-40, 242, 245, 274, 391, 577, 707
Wells, H. G., 206
Wenn die Blätter fallen, 95
Wenter, Joseph, 154
Wer gewinnt Lisette? 113
Wer weint um Juckenach? 113
Wer will unter die Soldaten? 156
Werbel, 613
Werewolf, The (Gierow), 67

Were Wolf, The (Kitzberg), 487
Werfel, Franz, 42, 146-47, 159
Werner, Vilém, 511
West, Con, 214
West, Mae, 714
West, Rebecca, 197
Weston, Jessie, 92
Weston, Robert P., 214
Wettlauf mit dem Schatten, Der, 97
Wexley, John, 708
Wharton, Anthony P., 196
Wharton, Edith, 283, 715, 718
What Every Woman Knows, 180
What Is the Theatre? 445
What Price Glory? 641, 695, 696
What the Fiddle Contains, 626
Wheel of Fortune, The, 225
When the Vineyards Are in Blossom, 50
When We Are Married, 205
When We Dead Awaken, 17, 19, 20, 263
When Will He Die? 632
Where Are Your Senses? 491
Where Poppies Bloom, 271
Where There is Nothing, 218
Where There's a Will, 299
While the Sun Shines, 211
Whirlwind, The, 269
Whispering Gallery, 213
White, Bessie F., 627
White and Black, 547
White Cargo, 210
White Cloud, The, 523
White Collars, 718
White Desert, 695, 696
White Guard, The, 455
White Horse Inn, The, 144
White Horses, see *Rosmersholm*
White Man, 710, 722
White Mountain, 509
White Scourge, 512
White Stag, The, 526
White Steed, The, 229
White Wings, 679, 702
Whiteheaded Boy, The, 224
Whiteoaks, 196
Whitman, Walt, 110, 112, 311, 640, 642, 645, 665
Who for Whom, 634
Who is the Fool? 539
Who Were Those Who Sang, 488
Why Marry? 681
Wicheler, Fernand, 316
Widow Rošlinka, The, 540
Widowers' Houses, 168, 524
Widowing of Mrs. Holroyd, The, 208
Wie die Träumenden, 87
Wied, Gustaf, 57, 58
Wiener, Frantz, see Croisset, Francis de
Wiener Kripperl von 1919, Das, 144

Wienerinnen, 127
Wiers-Jensen, H., 188
Wife, The (Moberg), 67
Wife, The (Štech), 506
Wife with a Smile, The, 284
Wild Birds, 713, 722
Wild Decembers, 203
Wild Duck, The, 8, 9, 13-16, 18, 51, 244, 410
Wild Rose, The, 402
Wild Rose of Gyimes, The, 520
Wilde, Eduard, 487
Wilde, Oscar, 162-64, 177, 191, 442, 500, 530, 532
Wildenbruch, Ernst von, 87, 90-91
Wildenradt, 503
Wilder, Thornton, 250, 306, 683, 721, 732
Wildgans, Anton, 150
Wilhelmina's Bureau, 63
Wilkins, Mary E., 645
Will, The (Barrie), 180
Will, The (Czakó), 518
Will, The (Štolba), 506
Will o' the Wisp, 506
Will Shakespeare, 203
Willard, John, 717
William ou la comédie de l'aventure, 315
William Penn, 110
William Wilson, 432
Williams, Emlyn, 210-11, 213
Williams, Jesse Lynch, 681
Williams, John D., 684
Williams, Tennessee, 739
Williamson, Hugh Ross, 208
Wilmurt, Arthur, 306
Wilson, Frank, 709, 710, 731
Wilson, Harry Leon, 714
Wiltfeber, der ewige Deutsche, 112
Wilton, Marie, 160-62
Wimperis, Arthur, 214
Wind and the Rain, 212
Windows, 183
Wine, The, 521
Wine of Choice, 704
Winged Victory, 735
Wingless Victory, The, 696-98
Wings over Europe, 207
Winter, Keith, 211
Winter's Tale, The, 140
Winterballade, 83
Winterschlaf, 89
Winterset, 666, 698
Wir sind Kameraden, 117
Wise Men of Helm, 633
Wise Tom-Cat, The, 554
Wisecrackers, The, 716
Wish, The, 62
Wissen und Gewissen, 111
Wit Works Woe, see *Woe from Wit*

Witch, The (Chekhov), 409
Witch, The (Goldfaden), 615, 616, 634
Witch, The (Masefield), 188
Witch Eve, The, 522
Witch of Haarlem, The, 553
Witch of Riga, The, 490
Witching Hour, The, 659
With You and Without You, 480
Within the Gates, 228
Within the Law, 664
Within the Net, 496
Without a Dowry, 493, 495
Without a Third, 533
Without Ending of Days, 690
Without Love, 703
Wizard of Menlo, The, 511
Wjela, Jury, 503, 504
Wjelestaw, 503
Wodehouse, P(elham), G(ranville), 214, 525
Woe from Wit, 378, 380, 381, 384, 408, 461
Wölfe, Die, 107
Woelfe in der Nacht, 143
Wohlman, Israel Meir, 609
Wolf, Friedrich, 117-18, 119
Wolf, The, 523
Wolf's Trail, The, 472
Wolfenstein, Alfred, 118
Wolff, Pierre, 270, 295
Wolfsohn, Ahron, see Halle, Ahron
Wolkenkuckuksheim, 139
Wolves, The, 257
Wolves and Sheep, 386
Woman, The, 546
Woman Killed with Kindness, A, 275
Woman of Bronze, The, 271
Woman of No Importance, A, 163
Woman with Six Senses, The, 490
Woman's Way, A, 680
Women, The, 574, 736
Women and Masks, 485
Women Go On Forever, 718
Women of Niskauuari, The, 485
Women's Knots, The, 609
Wonderful Story, A, 634
Woodcarver, The, 525
Wood-Demon, The, 409, 410, 411, 412
Wooden Slipper, The, 722
Woodworth, Samuel, 645
Woolcott, Alexander, 733, 734, 735
Woolf, Benjamin, 652
Word, The, 74, 75
Word Art and Graphic Art, 67
Workhouse Ward, The, 219
Workingman's Wife, The, 484
World Conflagration, The, 491
World of Little People, The, 506
World We Live In, The, 512

World We Make, The, 724
World's Timepiece, The, 509
Worse Things Happen at Sea, 212
Woyzeck, 99
Wreck of Life, The, 540
Wreckage, 494
Wright, Hugh E., 214
Wright, Richard, 711
Wrong and Right, 539
Würmer, Die, 107
Wunder in Amerika, 115
Wunder um Verdun, 155
Wurzel-Flummery, 192
Wycherley, William, 191
Wylie, Lauri, 214
Wyspiański, Stanisław, 489, 498-500, 534

X = O; A Night of the Trojan War, 189
Xenopoulos, Gregory, 547
Xirgu, Margarita, 587-88

Yahoo, 232
Yan, pseud., see Gordin, Jacob
Yankel Boile and Other Tales, 621, 622
Yankel the Smith, 623
Y'avait un prisonnier, 296
Yavorov, Peyu Krachelov, 543
YaYá Boneca, 599
Yeats, William Butler, 172, 217, 219, 222, 430, 640, 672
Yellow Colt, The, 518
Yellow Jack, 700
Yellow Jacket, The, 678
Yellow Lily, 524
Yellow Rose, The, 511
Yellow Sands, 189
Yente Die Pipernoterin, 613
Yerma, 572, 573
Yesterday and Today, 507
Yesterday's Magic, 211
Yiddish Art Theatre, The, 623, 625, 626, 628, 629, 633
Yiddish State Theatre, The, 623
Yiddish Theatre Lexicon, 632
Yiddisher Kemfer, The, 628
Yidele, Dos, 611
Yiskor, 632, 633
Yoel, 628
Yoshe Kalb, 634
You and I, 702
You Can't Take it With You, 735, 736
You Never Can Tell, 170
Young, Stanley, 739
Young, Stark, 715
Young Germany, 76-78, 99
Young Hopeful, The, see *Minor, The*
Young Love, 722

Young Madame Conti, 202, 208
Young Man's Love, A, 71
Young Mrs. Winthrop, 646
Young Vienna, 126, 128, 137, 138, 139, 143, 145
Young Woodley, 197
Youngest, The, 702
Your Uncle Dudley, 738
Youth, 434
Youth and Adolescence, 604
Youth at the Helm, 208
Youth of Prince Zsolt, The, 520
Youkov, Yordan, 543
Ypi, Abdyl, 548

Zaborsky, Jonáš, 513, 514, 532
Zacuto, Mosche, 602
Zalan's Rout, 517
Zalewski, Kazimierz, 493, 495
Zamacois, Miguel, 252
Zamarga, 575
Zambaldi, Silvio, 326
Zamfirescu, 529
Zampelios, Joannes, 545
Zangwill, Israel, 186
Zapatera prodigiosa, La, 571, 572
Zapolska, Gabryela, 496, 497
Zar lässt sich photographieren, Der, 104
Zarzuelas, 561, 562, 564, 575, 580, 585
Zaviš of Falkenstein, 505
Zavřel, František, 509
Zawieyski, Jerzy, 502
Zborowski, 499
Zeal of Thy House, The, 216
Zech, Paul, 111
Zeitlin, Aaron, 633
Zensur, Die, 100

Zentaur, Der, 102
Zerbrochene Krug, Der, 154
Zero, 106
Zeromski, Stefan, 501
Zeyer, Julius, 507, 508
Zia Lu, La, 337
Ziar, Adam, 514
Ziese, Maxim, 119
Zilahy, Lajos, 521, 526
Zimmer, Bernard, 296
Zimmerherren, 138
Žižka, 509
Zoe's Apartment, 456
Zola, Emile, 2, 27-29, 52, 78, 237, 241-45, 252, 255, 397, 532
Zolotarefsky, Isaac, 622
Zoo, The, 212
Zorilla, 559
Zorn des Achilles, Der, 94
Zorzi, Guglielmo, 368
Zouaves, Les, 296
Zrinjski-Frangepan Tragedy, The, 534
Zu Hause, 88
Zuckmayer, Carl, 115-16
Zum Grossen Wurstel, 136
Zupančic, Oton, 532, 541
Zvonimir, King of Croatia and Dalmatia, 532
Zwehl, Fritz von, 119
Zwei Krawatten, 103
Zweig, Arnold, 109
Zweig, Stefan, 144-45
Zweite, Der, 105
Zwischenspiel, 135
Zwölftausend, 112
Zygmunt August, 498
Zykovs, The, 427
Zylbercwaig, Zalmen, 632